lonely planet

W9-BRT-289

East Africa

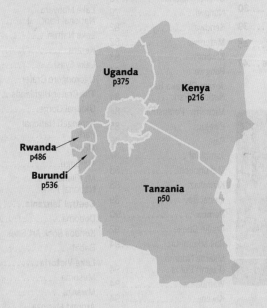

Uganda
p375

Kenya
p216

Rwanda
p486

Burundi
p536

Tanzania
p50

THIS EDITION WRITTEN AND RESEARCHED BY

Anthony Ham,
Stuart Butler, Mary Fitzpatrick, Trent Holden

Contents

ERIC LAFFORGUE / LONELY PLANET ©

RWANDA P486

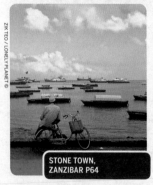

ZIK TEO / LONELY PLANET ©

STONE TOWN, ZANZIBAR P64

Contents

LAMU, KENYA P332

ERIC LAFFORGUE / LONELY PLANET ©

LAMU, KENYA P332

ERIC LAFFORGUE / LONELY PLANET ©

Contents

Welcome to East Africa

East Africa is the Africa of childhood imaginings, a wild realm of extraordinary landscapes, peoples and wildlife in one of our planet's most beautiful corners.

Wild Animals

Welcome to the true home of the African safari. This is untamed Africa, where wildebeest, shadowed by zebras, stampede in their millions across the earth, where lions, leopards and cheetahs, hyenas and wild dogs roam free in search of their next meal. Chimpanzees and the powerful yet silent silverback male gorillas and their families withdraw into remote islands of forests. Such stirring scenes of life and death, such overwhelming images of abundance coexist with evidence of surprising fragility. To draw near to this wildness is to experience something so profound that it will live forever in your memory.

Enthralling Landscapes

This is the land of the Masai Mara and the Serengeti, of an immense red sun setting behind a flat-topped acacia. Here on the African savannah, the world remains unspoiled by human presence. Nearby, rising from the Rift Valley floor are Mt Kilimanjaro, the Ngorongoro Crater, the Crater Highlands, Mt Meru, Mt Kenya and the Rwenzoris. By climbing these peaks on foot and scaling the Rift, you add your own footprints to Africa's marvellous human story and explore in ways unimaginable to those who never leave their vehicles.

Captivating Cultures

Wherever you go, don't miss the chance to get to know East Africa's people. Whether you're exploring Maasai land accompanied by the aloof, dignified red-shawled Maasai warriors, or standing in solidarity with victims of genocide at the sobering Kigali Memorial Centre, or hunting with the ancient Hadzabe people of Lake Eyasi, there are countless opportunities to immerse yourself in the everyday beauty, realities and vibrancy of East African life. It is, after all, East Africans themselves, with their warmth, hospitality and unique way of looking at life, who are at the heart of the region's legendary allure.

Beaches & Islands

In few places do fascinating human cultures come together quite so agreeably as they do along East Africa's Indian Ocean coastline. Travel back in time to the days when this part of the world was at the centre of a far-flung trading network whose influences – African, Asian, Middle Eastern – continue to dance their way through modern Swahili culture. From Lamu to Zanzibar and just about everywhere in between, you can relax on white-sand beaches, dive amid colourful marine life or sail on a dhow (ancient Arabic sailing vessel). Some might call it paradise.

Why I Love East Africa

By Anthony Ham, Author

East Africa is where my love affair with Africa took hold and promised never to let go. Wildlife (big cats especially) and wilderness rank among the grand passions of my life and it was here that I saw my first lion on the march, my first cheetah on the hunt, my first leopard on a kill, where I came so close to elephants and black rhinos that I could have reached out and touched them. And this is the home of Maasai friends who give me hope that the old ways can survive.

For more about our authors, see page 664

Above: Maasai warrior, Lewa Wildlife Conservancy (p283), Kenya

East Africa

Volcanoes NP
East Africa's best gorilla encounters (p501)

Rwenzori Mountains
Fabled Mountains of the Moon (p427)

Kibale NP
Chimp families in the forest (p423)

The Nile
Raft the river's strength and beauty (p401)

Lake Turkana
Remote beauty and rich tribal cultures (p346)

Laikipia Plateau
Kenyan conservation's true home (p273)

Masai Mara
The world's greatest wildlife spectacular (p251)

LEGEND

CA   Conservation Area
GR   Game Reserve
NP   National Park
NR   National Reserve

0 ____ 150 km
0 ____ 90 miles

SOUTH SUDAN

ETHIOPIA

SOMALIA

KENYA

UGANDA

RWANDA

Ilemi Triangle (Area of Dispute)

Addis Ababa

Mandera

El Wak

Takaba

Buna

Wajir

Moyale

Woyamdero Plain

Mado Gashi

Garissa

Hola

Tana River Primate NR

Arawale NR

Boni NR

Paté Island

Lamu

Lokichoggio

Kidepo Valley NP

Bokora-Mathenika WR

Kitgum

Moroto

Gulu

Lira

Soroti

Mt Elgon NP (4321m)

Mt Elgon

Mbale

Tororo

Lodwar

Sibiloi NP

North Horr

South Horr

Loyangalani

Central Island NP

South Island NP

Lake Turkana

Laisamis

Marsabit

Marsabit NR

Losai NR

South Turkana NR

Samburu NR

Maralal

Shaba NR

Bisanadi NR

Meru NP

Rahole NR

North Kitui NR

Meru

Isiolo

Nanyuki

Mt Kenya (5199m)

Thika

El Wak

Rift Valley

Eldoret

Kakamega FR

Kisumu

Kisii

Sirari

Nyahururu

Nakuru

Lake Baringo

Lake Bogoria

Lake Nakuru

Naivasha

NAIROBI

Kajiado

Namanga

Amboseli NP

Mt Kilimanjaro

Tsavo West NP

Tsavo East NP

Athi River

Masai Mara NR

Masai

Musoma

Nyahanga

Maswa

LAKE VICTORIA

Mara River

Serengeti NP

Ngorongoro Crater

Lake Natron

Lake Eyasi

Mwanza

Bukoba

Kyaka

Ukerewe

Rubondo Island NP

Entebbe

KAMPALA

Kasubi Tombs

Jinja

Lake Kyoga

Victoria Nile

Nile

Luwero

Mubende

Masaka

Ssese Islands

Kibale NP

Fort Portal

Rwenzori Mountains NP

Kasese

Mt Stanley (5109m)

Bunia

Budongo FR

Murchison Falls NP

Murchison Falls

Masindi

Pakwach

Nimule

Albert Nile

Lake Albert

Rutshuru

Parc National des Virungas

Goma

Gisenyi

Lake Kivu

Cyangugu

Bukavu

Mt Stanley (5109m)

Volcanoes National Park

Musanze (Ruhengeri)

KIGALI

Huye (Butare)

Nyungwe Forest NP

Kimisi

Lusahunga

25°S

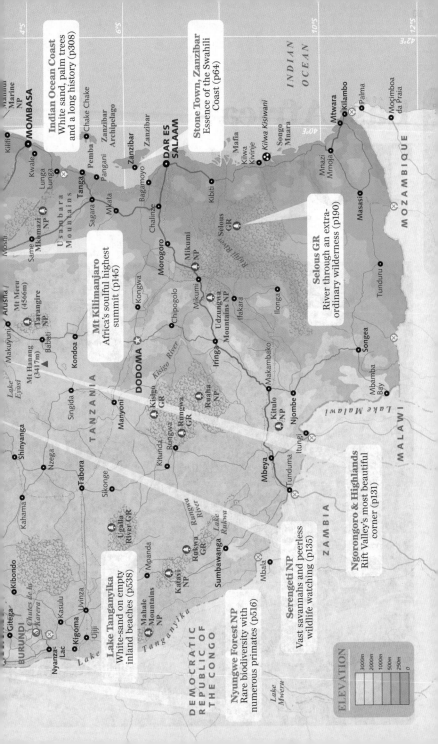

Indian Ocean Coast
White sand, palm trees and a long history (p308)

Stone Town, Zanzibar
Essence of the Swahili Coast (p64)

Mt Kilimanjaro
Africa's soulful highest summit (p145)

Selous GR
River through an extraordinary wilderness (p190)

Lake Tanganyika
White-sand on empty inland beaches (p538)

Nyungwe Forest NP
Rare biodiversity with numerous primates (p516)

Serengeti NP
Vast savannahs and peerless wildlife watching (p135)

Ngorongoro & Highlands
Rift Valley's most beautiful corner (p131)

INDIAN OCEAN

MOMBASA
Kilifi
Kwale
Lunga Lunga
Pemba
Chake Chake
Zanzibar Archipelago
Zanzibar
Zanzibar
Mafia
Kilwa Kivinje
Kilwa Kisiwani
Songo Mnara

DAR ES SALAAM

Tanga
Pangani
Bagamoyo
Mkata
Sagara
Same
Moshi
Usambara Mountains
Mkomazi NP

Chalinze
Kibiti
Mnazi Mmoja
Mtwara
Kilambo
Palma
Moçimboa da Praia

MOZAMBIQUE

Masasi
Tunduru
Songea
Mbamba Bay

Morogoro
Mikumi NP
Mikumi
Selous GR
Rufiji River
Ilonga
Ifakara
Udzungwa Mountains NP
Makambako

Kongwa
Chipogolo
Iringa
Kitulo NP
Njombe
Itungi

DODOMA

Babati
Kondoa
Mt Hanang (3417m)
Manyoni
Singida

Makuyuni
Mt Meru (4566m)
Arusha
Tarangire NP

Lake Eyasi

TANZANIA

Shinyanga
Nzega
Kahama
Tabora
Sikonge
Kisigo GR
Rungwa GR
Ruaha NP
Rungwa River
Kitunda
Rungwa

Mbeya
Tunduma

ZAMBIA

Mbala
Sumbawanga
Rukwa GR
Lake Rukwa
Katavi NP
Mpanda
Ugalla River GR

Mahale Mountains NP
Ujiji
Kigoma
Kasulu
Uvinza
Nyanza-Lac

DEMOCRATIC REPUBLIC OF THE CONGO

BURUNDI
Gitega
Kibondo
Kibondo
Chutes de la Karera

Lake Tanganyika

Lake Mweru

MALAWI

Lake Malawi

ELEVATION
3000m
2000m
1000m
500m
250m
0

East Africa's
Top 16

Wildebeest Migration (Kenya & Tanzania)

1 Welcome to one of the greatest shows on earth (p35). The pounding hooves draw closer, and then, suddenly, thousands of wildebeest stampede by, sweeping across the plains of the Serengeti National Park in Tanzania (from October to July) and the Masai Mara in Kenya (from July to October). Wherever you catch up with them, you'll find up to a million of these ungainly animals along with herds of zebras, elephants and giraffes. With predators never far away, this is natural drama on an epic scale.

Gorilla Tracking, Volcanoes National Park (Rwanda)

2 Nothing can really prepare you for that first moment when you find yourself in the midst of a family of mountain gorillas. It's an utterly humbling experience, sharing the forest with the silverback, whose sheer size and presence will leave you in awe, or with adorable fuzzy babies clowning about and tumbling from trees. The term 'once in a lifetime' is bandied about a lot, but gorilla tracking in Volcanoes National Park (p501) is one experience for which it just happens to be true.

500PX.COM / ANTHILL TIGER / GETTY IMAGES ©

DANITA DELIMONT / GETTY IMAGES ©

Mt Kilimanjaro (Tanzania)

3 It's difficult to resist the allure of climbing Africa's highest peak (p145), one of the Holy Grails of East African travel, with its snow-capped summit, views over the surrounding plains and otherworldly gravitas. If you can't make the summit, there are other rewarding ways to experience the mountain. Day-hike on the lush lower slopes, spend time learning about local Chagga culture or sip a sundowner from a nearby vantage point with the mountain as a backdrop.

Masai Big Cats, Masai Mara (Kenya)

4 Studded with flat-top acacia trees, the rolling savannahs of the Masai Mara National Reserve (p251) support some of the highest concentrations of wildlife on the planet. The great herds of wildebeest may bring sound and movement to the plains, but it's the big cats – the Marsh Pride of lions, lords of their domain, the leopards lurking in riverine thickets and the cheetahs surveying the world from a termite mound before exploding into a chase – who are the Mara's most soulful inhabitants.

ADAM JONES / GETTY IMAGES ©

PANORAMIC IMAGES / GETTY IMAGES ©

Stone Town, Zanzibar (Tanzania)

5 Zanzibar's Stone Town (p64) never loses its atmosphere of exoticism. First you'll see the skyline, with the spires of St Joseph's Cathedral and the Old Fort. Then, wander through narrow alleyways that reveal surprises at every turn. Linger at shops scented with cloves, watch men wearing *kanzu* (white robe-like outer garment) play *bao* (game), and admire intricate henna designs on the hands of women in their *bui-bui* (black cover-all). Island rhythms quickly take over as mainland life slips away.

Serengeti National Park (Tanzania)

6 In this most superlative of East African parks (p135), time often seems to stand still. The Seronera River and its hinterland could just be the easiest place on earth to encounter wildlife at any time of the year. But this is a vast park, one that rewards those who linger with the southern kopjes standing sentinel out over the eternal plains, the fine rock-and-river prospects of the Grumeti River in the west, and the endless plains and Mara River in the north.

Chimp Tracking, Kibale National Park (Uganda)

7 Traversing muddy paths, stumbling over twisted roots and making your way through dense vegetation – chimpanzee tracking can be hard work. But oh my, is it worth it. The struggle and sweat is all but forgotten as chimpanzees become visible in a clearing ahead and then draw near in curiosity – you could almost reach out and touch them. Of the four places to see habituated chimps in East Africa, Kibale National Park (p423) is the best all-round experience.

BEN CRANKE / GETTY IMAGES ©

Ngorongoro & Crater Highlands (Tanzania)

8 On clear days, the magic of Ngorongoro (p131) begins while you're still up on the rim, with sublime views. Down in the crater itself, amid hues of blue and green, an unparalleled concentration of iconic African wildlife calls to mind the unspoilt Africa of our imaginations. Nearby, Ol Doinyo Lengai and Lake Natron are the pick of the fabulous Crater Highlands.

Laikipia (Kenya)

9 In the shadow of Mt Kenya, Kenya's Laikipia plateau (p273) hosts a network of conservancies and private wildlife reserves – it's both beautiful and one of the most exciting stories in African conservation. At the forefront of efforts to save endangered species such as lions, African wild dogs, Grevy's zebras and black rhinos, the plateau's ranches offer an enticing combination of high-end lodge accommodation, big horizons and charismatic megafauna. Best of all, you'll scarcely see another vehicle in sight. Above right: African wild dog

Rwenzori Mountains (Uganda)

10 Known in ancient times as the Mountains of the Moon, the Unesco World Heritage–listed Rwenzoris (p427) today retain a powerful sense of being a world apart. Here in tropical Africa, along the continent's highest range of mountains, ice-bound summits swirl into view then disappear, among them Mt Stanley (5109m), Africa's third-highest peak. Rainforest and an extraordinary array of plants, animals and birds make for some of East Africa's most challenging yet most rewarding trekking trails.

Lake Turkana (Kenya)

11 Amid the deserts and horizonless tracts that characterise so much of Kenya's north, Lake Turkana (p346) glitters like a jade and turquoise mirage. Rising from its waters is Teleki, one of the world's most perfectly shaped volcanic cones, while the shores are dotted with dusty and utterly intriguing villages that are home to the beguiling mix of traditional peoples – Turkana, Samburu, Gabbra, El Molo – who call this isolated corner of Africa home. And there are crocodiles here. Lots of them.
Right: Teleki Volcano

NIGEL PAVITT / GETTY IMAGES ©

ARIADNE VAN ZANDBERGEN / GETTY IMAGES ©

Nyungwe Forest National Park (Rwanda)

12 With no fewer than 13 species of primate, a rich tapestry of birdlife and a degree of biodiversity seldom found elsewhere, Nyungwe Forest National Park (p516) is one of Africa's most important conservation areas. The vast forest is home to plenty of primates, including habituated chimpanzees and a huge troop of colobus monkeys. Whether hiking through this equatorial rainforest in search of our evolutionary kin or just in search of a waterfall, Nyungwe is guaranteed to nurture your inner Tarzan.

Above: Black-and-white colobus

Boat Safari, Selous Game Reserve (Tanzania)

13 Vast Selous (p190), with its tropical climate, profusion of greenery and massive Rufiji River, is completely different to Tanzania's northern parks. Take a boat safari, and as you glide past borassus palms, slumbering hippos and cavorting elephants enjoy the many attractions large and small along the riverbanks. These include birdlife of astonishing richness, vast elephant herds and the largest population of lions on the planet. They're all part of the daily natural symphony in this, one of Africa's largest wildlife reserves.

White-Water Rafting on the Nile (Uganda)

14 With rapids that go by names like A Bad Place or Dead Dutchman, the idea of being flung head-on into surging torrents of water sounds like a nightmare. But for those who've experienced it, it's one of the most exciting things they've done in Africa. Things start off as a leisurely paddle along the source of the Nile River (p401) close to Jinja. Next thing you know you're looking up at a towering wave that mercilessly smashes upon you. It's breathtaking stuff and a ridiculous amount of fun.

Indian Ocean Coast (Kenya & Tanzania)

15 East Africa's Indian Ocean coast is one of Africa's prettiest shores. Long stretches of white sand, translucent waters and coves sheltered by palm trees would be sufficient reason for many to visit. But trade winds through the centuries have brought an intriguing mix of African and Arab cultures, resulting in a coastline with attitude: at once laid-back in the finest spirit of *hakuna matata,* yet bristling with ruins and the evocative signposts of Swahili culture. Below: Bagamoyo (p96), Tanzania

Lake Tanganyika Beaches (Burundi)

16 As unlikely as it sounds, some of the region's best inland beaches are found on the shores of Lake Tanganyika (p538) in Burundi, and unlike others in East Africa, you can safely swim here without fear of crocs. After years of internal conflict, peace is slowly taking hold in the country, though infrastructure is limited and the situation remains precarious. But intrepid travellers are once again setting down their towels on the sandy shores first made famous by the explorers Stanley and Livingstone.

PLAN YOUR TRIP EAST AFRICA'S TOP 16

Need to Know

For more information, see Survival Guide (p617)

Currency

Kenyan shilling (KSh),
Tanzanian shilling (Tsh),
Ugandan shilling (USh),
Rwandan franc (RFr),
Burundi franc (BFr)

Visas

Available on arrival in
Kenya and Uganda, at
Burundi's international
airport, and at major
airports and borders in
Tanzania; Rwanda visas
must be obtained in
advance.

Money

ATMs widespread and
credit cards widely
accepted in Kenya,
Tanzania and Uganda,
less so in Rwanda (Visa
only) and Burundi.

Mobile Phones

Local SIM cards widely
available and can be
used in most interna-
tional mobile phones.

Time

Kenya, Tanzania and
Uganda are on East
Africa Time (GMT/
UTC plus three hours);
Rwanda and Burundi
one hour behind.

When to Go

Kampala
GO Jun–Mar

Nairobi
GO Jun–Feb

Kigali
GO Jun–Mar

Arusha
GO Jun–Feb

Bujumbura
GO May–Feb

Mombasa
GO Jun–Mar

Dar es Salaam
GO Jun–Feb

Tropical climate, rain year round
Tropical climate, wet & dry seasons
Warm to hot summers, mild winters
Desert, dry climate

High Season
(Jun–Aug)

➡ Much of the region
is cool and dry.

➡ Hotels in popular
areas are full, many
with high-season
prices.

➡ Animal-spotting is
easiest, as foliage is
sparse and animals
congregate around
water sources.

Shoulder
(Sep–Feb)

➡ An ideal travel
time, with greener
landscapes and
fewer crowds.

➡ Peak-season
prices from mid-
December to mid-
January.

➡ Short rains
in October and
November rarely
interrupt travel.

Low Season
(Mar–May)

➡ Heavy rains in
much of the region
make secondary
roads muddy, some
areas inaccessible
and landscapes
green.

➡ Some hotels close;
others offer low-
season discounts.

Useful Websites

Lonely Planet
(www.lonelyplanet.com/africa)
Destination information, hotel bookings and traveller forum.

Kenya Wildlife Service
(www.kws.org) Conservation news and information on national parks and reserves.

Tanzania National Parks
(www.tanzaniaparks.com) The lowdown on Tanzania's fabulous protected areas.

Uganda Wildlife Authority
(www.ugandawildlife.org) Detailed coverage of Uganda's national parks.

Rwanda Tourism
(www.rwandatourism.com) Rwanda's tourist information portal.

Safari Bookings
(www.safaribookings.com) Invaluable resource for choosing safari operators and destinations.

Important Numbers

Kenya country code	☎254
Tanzania country code	☎255
Uganda country code	☎256
Rwanda country code	☎250
Burundi country code	☎257

Exchange Rates

For exchange rates, see p51 (Tanzania), p217 (Kenya), p378 (Uganda), p488 (Rwanda) and p538 (Burundi)

Daily Costs

Budget:
Less than US$50

➡ Room in basic budget guesthouse: US$10–US$20

➡ Local-style meal: US$5

➡ Nairobi–Arusha bus journey: from US$13

Midrange:
US$50–US$200

➡ Double room in midrange hotel: US$50–US$200

➡ Meal in Western-style restaurant: US$10–US$20

➡ Nairobi–Arusha shuttle bus: US$25–US$35

Top End:
More than US$200

➡ Upmarket hotel room: from US$200

➡ All-inclusive safari package: from US$300 per person per day

Opening Hours

The following applies, with some local variations.

Banks 9am to 3pm Monday to Friday; 9am to 11am Saturday

Restaurants 11am to 2pm and 5pm to 9pm

Shops 8.30am or 9am to 3pm Monday to Friday; 9am to 11am Saturday

Supermarkets 8.30am to 8.30pm Monday to Saturday; 10am to 8pm Saturday.

Arriving in East Africa

Jomo Kenyatta International Airport, Nairobi (p369) Taxis to city centre cost KSh1500 to KSh2000.

Julius Nyerere International Airport, Dar es Salaam (p207) Taxis to city centre cost Tsh30,000 to Tsh35,000.

Kilimanjaro International Airport (p207) Taxis to Arusha or Moshi cost US$50.

Entebbe Airport Taxis to Kampala cost USh60,000 to USh80,000. Shuttle bus to Kampala city centre costs Ush2500.

Overland Cross-border buses link Tanzania, Uganda and Kenya, and Rwanda with Burundi.

Getting Around

East Africa is relatively easy to get around by African standards, with road and air the most comfortable and reliable options.

Air Flying between Kenya, Tanzania, Uganda, Rwanda and Burundi is a relatively simple proposition – Kenya Airways has the largest regional network.

Car Driving is on the left in Tanzania, Kenya and Uganda; on the right in Rwanda and Burundi. 4WD required in some areas and recommended in some parks. Consider renting a car with a local driver for a little extra.

Bus Buses are the most useful type of public transport but they're sometimes overcrowded and far from luxurious. They're usually faster than trains or trucks, and safer and more comfortable than minibuses and prices are inexpensive for the distance travelled.

If You Like...

Primates

Tanzania, Uganda and Rwanda have no peers when it comes to watching primates. Encounters with mountain gorillas and chimpanzees are the major draws, but there's also golden monkeys and charismatic colobus.

Bwindi Impenetrable National Park Almost-guaranteed sightings of eastern mountain gorillas. (p437)

Volcanoes National Park Eastern mountain gorillas and golden monkeys. (p501)

Kibale National Park Thirteen species, including red colobus and L'Hoest's monkey. (p423)

Semuliki National Park Nine species, including De Brazza's monkey. (p425)

Queen Elizabeth National Park Chimpanzees in beautiful Kyambura Gorge. (p431)

Nyungwe Forest National Park Chimpanzees and Angolan colobus. (p516)

Gombe Stream National Park Chimps where Jane Goodall made them famous. (p167)

Mahale Mountains National Park Up-close chimpanzees in a stunning setting. (p169)

Kakamega Forest Kenya's best primate reserve. (p265)

Big Cats

Lions sleeping under (or up!) a tree, a lone leopard draped along a branch, a cheetah accelerating across the savannah – these are some of East Africa's most unforgettable experiences.

Masai Mara National Reserve Arguably the best place to spot all three cats, especially from July to October. (p251)

Serengeti National Park The Seronera River is big-cat central. (p135)

Ngorongoro Conservation Area The continent's highest lion density. (p131)

Tsavo East National Park A good spot for relatively easy sightings of all three cats. (p307)

Ol Pejeta Conservancy Go lion-tracking with the experts. (p282)

Queen Elizabeth National Park Leopards and tree-climbing lions in Uganda. (p431)

Murchison Falls National Park Lions and leopards in north-western Uganda. (p459)

Rhinos & Elephants

The African elephant and the rhinoceros are enduring icons of the continent, whether as a symbol for the gravitas of its wildlife or the natural world's remarkable resilience.

Amboseli National Park As close as you'll ever get to a big-tusked elephant, with Mt Kilimanjaro in the background. (p298)

Samburu National Reserve Elephants set against one of Kenya's most beautiful regions. (p339)

Ruaha National Park Some of East Africa's largest herds, with 12,000 elephants in total. (p179)

Tsavo East National Park Kenya's largest elephant population with over 11,000. (p307)

Tarangire National Park Large dry-season elephant herds in one of Tanzania's most underrated parks. (p124)

Ol Pejeta Conservancy East Africa's largest population of black rhinos in Kenya's Laikipia. (p282)

Lewa Wildlife Conservancy Both black and white rhinos in central Kenya. (p283)

Nairobi National Park The world's densest concentration of black rhinos. (p221)

Meru National Park Both black and white rhinos without the crowds. (p296)

Ngorongoro Conservation Area Best chance to see black rhinos in Tanzania. (p131)

Top: Kizimkazi Dimbani (p88), Zanzibar, Tanzania
Bottom: Rhinos, Amboseli National Park (p298), Kenya

Hiking & Trekking

Soaring Rift Valley mountains with accessible summits, snaking forest trails and flatland savannah – East Africa has a range of trekking experiences to suit most time frames and fitness levels.

Mt Kilimanjaro Trek to the roof of Africa. (p145)

Mt Kenya Africa's second-highest mountain with arguably better views. (p286)

Rwenzori Mountains National Park Fabulous high-altitude trekking in mist-soaked forests. (p427)

Mt Elgon A vast volcano with quieter hiking trails. (p270)

Usambara Mountains Trails wind through pretty villages and even prettier landscapes. (p104)

Crater Highlands Enjoy rugged beauty and Rift Valley vistas with a Maasai guide. (p134)

Islands

The islands of East Africa's Indian Ocean coastline capture the essence of the region's appeal. For an utterly different experience, Lake Turkana and Lake Rubondo are remote and rarely visited.

Zanzibar A magical name for a magical place, from Stone Town to perfect beaches. (p63)

Pemba Hidden white-sand coves and an intriguing culture. (p90)

Mafia Island Indian Ocean paradise with a marine park and few visitors. (p187)

Lamu Archipelago Manda, Manda Toto and Paté Islands are simply superb. (p332)

Wasini Island One of Kenya's little-known jewels and a real step back in time. (p324)

Central Island National Park Otherworldly volcano rising above the extraordinary Lake Turkana. (p352)

Rubondo Island Beautiful Lake Victoria island with birdwatching, elephants and chimps. (p160)

History & Ruins

East Africa's Swahili coast lies at the confluence of empires and trade routes with some stunning landmarks still in place. The powerful kingdoms of ancient Uganda also left their mark.

Gede Ruins Ancient and exceptional Swahili trading post in Kenya. (p328)

Kilwa Kisiwani Imposing and predominantly 15th-century Arab ruins in Tanzania. (p194)

Mnarani Medieval Swahili port with fine mosques and massive baobab trees. (p326)

Kasubi Tombs Ancient royal tombs of the Buganda kings with other sites nearby. (p378)

Zanzibar Palaces Crumbling reminders of Zanzibar's past grandeur. (p63)

Kondoa Rock-Art Sites Beguiling ruins of a very different (and more ancient) kind. (p152)

Kigali Memorial Centre Sobering monument to Rwanda's tragic recent history. (p489)

Beaches

East Africa's coastline is utterly gorgeous and there are some near-perfect beaches, including some with stunning, remote stretches of sand that have yet to be discovered.

Kilifi Fishing village, empty sand and Indian Ocean perfection. (p325)

Zanzibar's East Coast White sand and offshore reefs. (p63)

Watamu Seven kilometres of unspoiled beach with a lovely fishing village nearby. (p327)

Pemba Lovely white-sand coves with plenty of space to spread your towel. (p90)

Tiwi Beach The alter ego to nearby Diani Beach resorts and its equal in beauty. (p320)

Diving & Snorkelling

Reefs proliferate all along East Africa's coastline and the diving and snorkelling here ranks among the best in Africa, with abundant marine life and an exceptional array of coral.

Pemba Divers in the know rave about Pemba's reefs. (p90)

Manda Toto Island Outstanding snorkelling in Kenya's Lamu archipelago. (p339)

Zanzibar Archipelago Coral reefs and shipwrecks offshore from Stone Town. (p63)

Kisite Marine National Park Snorkel with dolphins; diving is also possible. (p325)

Watamu Marine National Park Fabulous reefs, fish and sea turtles. (p327)

Diani Beach Professional dive schools and even a purpose-sunk shipwreck. (p320)

Creature Comforts

East Africa does luxury extremely well. There's nothing quite like returning from a day's safari to plush accommodation and impeccable standards of personal service out in the African bush.

Ol Donyo Utterly extraordinary place close to Amboseli. (p301)

Segera Retreat *Out of Africa* experience in Kenya's Laikipia. (p283)

Serengeti Bushtops Camp Extraordinary lodge in an extraordinary place. (p139)

Giraffe Manor Top-end luxury with a Rothschild's giraffe looking in your window. (p230)

Cottar's 1920s Camp Safari luxury and nostalgia in over-drive. (p258)

Serengeti Migration Camp Watch the migration from a privileged vantage point. (p139)

Mara Plains Palatial tents with details no-one else has thought of. (p258)

Sabyinyo Silverback Lodge Exclusive base for visiting Rwanda's gorillas. (p507)

Month by Month

January

January is one of the most popular months for visiting East Africa, with animals congregating around waterholes and the bird migration well and truly underway. Days are usually warm and dry and it's a great time to be in the southern Serengeti.

February

High season continues; days are hot and dry. The same principles apply as in January, with excellent wildlife watching around waterholes and countless bird species on show.

☆ Zanzibar Song & Dance

Zanzibar gets even more rhythm than usual with the three-day Sauti za Busara (www.busaramusic.org). Swahili songs from every era fill the night, and dance troupes take over the stages of Stone Town and elsewhere on the island. (p72)

◉ Wildebeest Births

The annual wildebeest migration mid-year may grab the headlines, but the species' great calving, a similarly epic yet also heart-warming sight, occurs in February in Tanzania's Serengeti National Park. Approximately 500,000 births occur in a three-week period.

March

March is traditionally when the area's big annual rains begin, flooding many areas and making wildlife watching difficult. Prices are low and safaris can be excellent if the rains are late.

April

Unless the rains have failed entirely, this is one month to avoid. The inundation that should have begun in March continues to batter the region into submission. Getting around is difficult, and at times impossible.

May

The rains usually continue well into May. By late May, the rains may have subsided; when they stop and you can see the horizon, the country is wonderfully green, although wildlife can still be tough to spot.

June

East Africa emerges from the rains somewhat sodden but ready to make up for lost time. The annual migration of wildebeest and zebra in their millions is usually well underway.

🐾 Kwita Izina

Rwanda stages the Kwita Izina (p503; www.kwitizina.org), aka the Gorilla Naming Ceremony, a countrywide event that honours the country's newborn gorillas with community events and gala balls. Watch out for the odd celebrity conservationist in Kigali (Rwanda).

✨ Lake Turkana Cultural Festival

One of Kenya's biggest cultural events, this fascinating festival focuses on the numerous tribal groups that inhabit Northern Kenya, among them the El Molo, Samburu, Pokot and Turkana.

✨ Run with Lions

In late June or early July, Kenya's Lewa Wildlife Conservancy hosts Lewa Safaricom Marathon (www.safaricom.co.ke/safaricommarathon). One of the world's more unusual marathons, it's a winning combination of wildlife watching and serious fundraising.

July

The wildebeest migration is in full swing, and so, too, is the annual migration of two-legged visitors who converge on Kenya's Masai Mara and Tanzania's Serengeti. Weather is fine and warm, with steaming conditions on the coast.

◉ Wildlife Spectacular

Wildebeest cross the Mara River en masse, passing from Tanzania's Serengeti National Park to Kenya's Masai Mara National Reserve, with predators following in their wake. It's one cliché that just happens to be true: this is the greatest wildlife show on earth.

✨ Festival of the Dhow Countries

Arguably East Africa's premier cultural festival, this Zanzibar extravaganza in early July runs over two weeks with live performances, literary events with an East African focus, and the Zanzibar International Film Festival. (p72)

August

The high season continues with the Serengeti and Mara the focus, although other parks are also rewarding. Europeans on holiday flock to the region, so prices go up and room availability goes down.

☆ Kenya Music Festival

Kenya's longest-running music festival, and one of East Africa's most prestigious, is held over 10 days in Nairobi, drawing some worthy African and international acts.

🏃 Camel Derby

Maralal's International Camel Derby (p348) in Kenya is both serious camel racing and a chance to join the fun. It's a huge event.

September

The weather remains fine and tourist numbers drop off slightly, even though the Serengeti, the Mara and Rwanda's Volcanoes National Park are still filled to bursting with wildlife. Prices remain high.

◉ Royal Ascot Goat Racing

Kampala's expats dress in their finest and funniest for the Royal Ascot Goat Races. It all happens on the shores of Lake Victoria and is the biggest event on the *muzungu* (white person) social calendar. (p381)

October

The short rains begin but rarely disrupt travel plans. Wildebeest are still in the Mara until mid-October, it's the best season for diving and snorkelling, and visitor numbers start to fall.

November

The short rains occur almost daily, but disruptions are minimal. Migratory birds arrive in their millions; it's an aerial version of the Serengeti and Mara wildebeest migration and, for some, every bit as spectacular.

🏃 East African Safari Rally

This classic car rally (www.eastafricansafarirally.com) held in late November is more than 50 years old, and there's more than a whiff of colonial atmosphere about it. The rally traverses Kenya, Tanzania and Uganda and is open only to pre-1971 vehicles.

December

A reasonable month in which to visit, with lower prices and fine weather. Plenty of migratory birds in residence, and much of the region is swathed in green.

✨ Maulid Festival

This annual celebration of the Prophet Mohammed's birthday rouses the Swahili coast from its slumber as Muslims from up and down the coast converge on Lamu, Zanzibar and other Swahili ports.

Itineraries

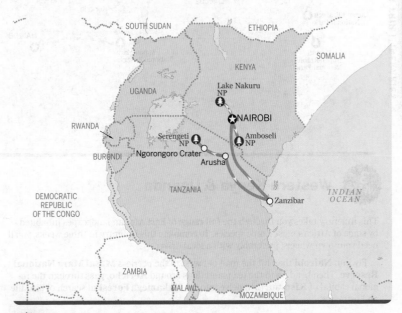

 Classic East Africa

This itinerary samples the best that East Africa has to offer, combining some of Africa's best wildlife watching with beaches and the Swahili coast. To manage this itinerary in two weeks, you'll need to travel some parts of the journey by air.

After arriving at Tanzania's Kilimanjaro International Airport, and then **Arusha**, head to **Ngorongoro Crater** and **Serengeti National Park**. Then head back to Arusha to catch a flight to the **Zanzibar Archipelago** for diving, snorkelling and relaxing. While you're there, take in the charm and historical attractions of Zanzibar's old Stone Town.

Fly from Zanzibar to **Nairobi**, then head straight out on safari again, driving north to **Lake Nakuru National Park** for some more wildlife watching. After returning to Nairobi, again by road, take another short flight, this time to **Amboseli National Park** for peerless Mt Kilimanjaro views and some of Africa's best elephant viewing.

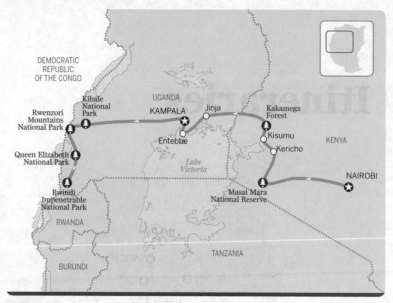

3 WEEKS Western Kenya & Uganda

This itinerary takes you through the full range of East African landscapes inhabited by some of Africa's most iconic species. To complete this itinerary in three weeks, you'll need your own wheels, preferably with a local driver.

Fly into **Nairobi** then hit the road out west to the peerless **Masai Mara National Reserve**. Then head on to the tea plantations around **Kericho**, pass through the regional capital of **Kisumu**, then delve into the **Kakamega Forest** in search of bird life and primates.

After crossing into Uganda, set aside a few days to make the most of **Jinja**, East Africa's adrenaline-sports capital and home to the Source du Nil (source of the Nile). From here, it's a short hop to **Entebbe**, with its Lake Victoria beaches, and on to **Kampala**. Tracking west, explore the rainforests of **Kibale National Park**, with 13 primate species and some of East Africa's best chimpanzee tracking. From here, it's a short hop to the mist-shrouded **Rwenzori Mountains National Park**. Away to the south, **Queen Elizabeth National Park** has extraordinarily rich bird life and tree-climbing lions, and **Bwindi Impenetrable National Park** is one of the best places in the world to see mountain gorillas.

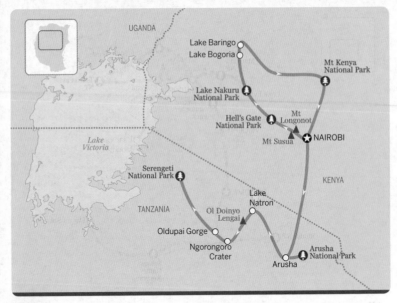

3 WEEKS Best of the Rift

The dramatic uplands of the Great Rift Valley have a gravitas all their own – this itinerary is all about some of the region's most spectacular scenery. This trip could be accomplished with public transport, supplemented with day or longer tours, and could take a week more or less, depending on how many mountains you climb and how far you plan on walking.

Begin in **Nairobi**, and track northwest to **Mt Longonot**, a shapely volcano and one of few Rift Valley crater rims that can be reached and returned from in a day. If you've the time and a desire for have-it-all-to-yourself experiences, detour to **Mt Susua**, a Maasai heartland and fabulous Rift Valley formation. **Hell's Gate National Park**, too, is good for day treks, while **Lake Nakuru National Park** is a fine example of a Rift Valley lake that can draw flamingos, not to mention lions, leopards and rhinos. You could detour north from here to **Lake Bogoria** and **Lake Baringo** – the latter is one of Kenya's most prolific birdwatching locations – but your main goal lies to the east, where **Mt Kenya National Park**, Africa's second-highest peak, is a week-long undertaking if you plan on trekking to one of its summits.

A day-long road trip south via Nairobi takes you into Tanzania via the border crossing at Namanga and then on to **Arusha**, gateway to **Arusha National Park** and its picturesque Rift Valley volcano of Mt Meru; this is another of East Africa's premier high-altitude trek-climbs. Arusha is also the place to organise a trip out into the Crater Highlands, the place where the Rift's fractures and otherworldly landscapes come alive like nowhere else in Africa. Flamingo-rich and deliciously remote, **Lake Natron** is utterly unforgettable, as is **Ol Doinyo Lengai**, surely one of the most perfectly formed mountains on the planet; set aside a day to climb it, and double that to rest in its shadow admiring the view. Southwest of here is the simply magnificent **Ngorongoro Crater**, the epitome of Rift Valley beauty. Out to the west, **Oldupai Gorge** is one of the cradles of humankind, while the **Serengeti National Park**, the alter ego to all those volcanoes, is an extraordinary place to end your journey.

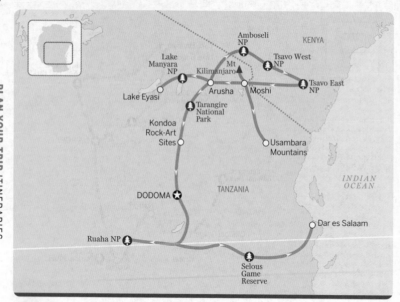

Mountains & Savannah

3 WEEKS

This predominantly Tanzanian odyssey could link up with all manner of other itineraries. Three weeks is doable at a leisurely pace in your own vehicle, or in a rush on public transport. Add an extra week if you plan on climbing Mt Kilimanjaro.

Fly into Kilimanjaro International Airport and spend a day or two getting your bearings in **Arusha**. Head north out of town and into Kenya. If you've got your own wheels, take the dusty trails that lead into **Amboseli National Park** from the Namanga–Nairobi highway. After a minimum two days with the elephants in Kili's shadow, and an extra possible day to explore Amboseli's Maasai hinterland, go east into **Tsavo West National Park** for red soils, man-eating lions, black rhinos and utterly beguiling views. Go east again, and you'll find yourself in the sweeping savannahs of **Tsavo East National Park**.

From Voi, take the road through the Taita Hills to Tanzania and spend a night or two in **Moshi**. As much as we like this agreeable town, its claim to fame is obvious whenever the clouds part – this is the gateway to **Mt Kilimanjaro**. Plan on at least a week as you climb all the way to Africa's highest point. If you have the mountain-climbing bug and aren't utterly exhausted, detour southeast for some green-hills trekking in the **Usambara Mountains**.

Back to the north (via Moshi and Arusha), **Lake Manyara National Park** is famous for its tree-climbing lions, while **Lake Eyasi** is a remote side trip that takes you among the Hadzabe, one of East Africa's most ancient peoples. Back on the main roads, **Tarangire National Park** is a wonderful park, rich in elephants and baobabs. Continuing south, the Unesco World Heritage–listed **Kondoa Rock-Art Sites** are a fascinating insight into the wisdom of the ancients, while **Dodoma** is a capital in name only but a good place to break the journey.

Ruaha National Park is at once the cultural heartland of the Barabaig and a wildly beautiful park known for its elephants and lions. Away to the east, **Selous Game Reserve** is one of our favourite protected areas in Africa, not to mention one of the largest; it's also home to the biggest lion populations on the planet. From Selous, you could either head for the coast or make for **Dar es Salaam** for the journey home.

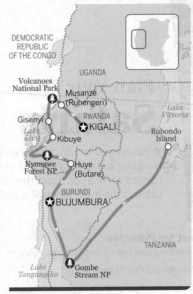

3 WEEKS — The Swahili Coast

Warning: this itinerary could take far longer if you find your own slice of paradise and never want to leave.

From **Dar es Salaam**, travel south to the ruins at **Kilwa Kisiwani**, and further south still to pretty, palm-fringed **Lindi**, and tiny **Mikindani**, a charming Swahili village. Returning north, **Mafia Island** is like Zanzibar without the crowds. And yet, there's nowhere on earth quite like **Zanzibar**, the essence of East Africa's Indian Ocean coast. **Pemba**, its northern neighbour, is an adventurous detour. Your last Tanzanian port of call is **Pangani**, while just across the Kenyan border, **Kisite Marine National Park** is home to crocs along the banks of mangrove-lined rivers, dolphins crashing through the surf and humpback whales from August to October. Just before you arrive in the roiling Swahili port city of **Mombasa**, pause in **Tiwi Beach**, a tranquil white-sand paradise away from the resorts. Continuing north, stop in the charming town of **Kilifi** and at the **Gede Ruins**, an ancient Swahili city. But **Lamu**, a Swahili heritage gem, is the main event; a dhow (ancient Arabic sailing vessel) trip out into the wonderful Lamu archipelago is a must while here.

2 WEEKS — Gorillas & Chimps Out West

Although this itinerary focuses on Rwanda, Burundi and Tanzania's far west, it can link up seamlessly with the national parks of southwestern Uganda or the other wildlife-rich protected areas of Tanzania's far west.

Rwanda's capital **Kigali** has a lush, mountainous setting and lively nightlife, with the sobering counterpoint of a genocide memorial. From Kigali, it's a short hop to **Musanze (Ruhengeri)** and the mountain gorillas of **Volcanoes National Park**. Next, head south along the shores of Lake Kivu and the scenic inland beaches around **Gisenyi** and **Kibuye** to **Nyungwe Forest National Park**, with its chimpanzees and other primates. Travel west to **Huye (Butare)**, pass through Burundi (security situation permitting) and its capital **Bujumbura**, before continuing south into Tanzania and **Gombe Stream National Park**, former home park of legendary conservationist Jane Goodall and one of the best places on earth to view chimpanzees. A loop back up around to the northeast takes you to the shores of lovely Lake Victoria; **Rubondo Island**, with its unlikely populations of chimpanzees and elephants is a wonderful place to end your journey.

Safaris

Whether you're watching the eternal dance of predator and prey, mingling with a mighty herd of elephants or sleeping under luxury canvas while a lion roars the savannah's unrest, an East African safari is the experience of a lifetime.

Best for Primates

Mahale Mountains National Park (Tanzania; p168)

Kibale National Park (Uganda; p423)

Volcanoes National Park (Rwanda; p501)

Bwindi Impenetrable National Park (Uganda; p437)

Best for Elephants

Tarangire National Park (Tanzania; p124)

Amboseli National Park (Kenya; p298)

Samburu National Reserve (Kenya; p342)

Best for Rhinos

Lake Nakuru National Park (Kenya; p246)

Nairobi National Park (Kenya; p221)

Ngorongoro Crater (Tanzania; p131)

Best for Birdwatching

Kakamega Forest Reserve (Kenya; p266)

Rubondo Island National Park (Tanzania; p160)

Selous Game Reserve (Tanzania; p190)

Murchison Falls National Park (Uganda; p459)

Best Times to Go

Dry season (July to September) for spotting the Big Five

Rainy season (March to May) for birdwatching

Dry and shoulder seasons (June to January) for chimpanzee tracking

Planning Your Safari

You can't spend too much time planning your safari. Partly this involves deciding where to go – which landscapes appeal? Which species are on your must-see list? But another big part of your planning is choosing *how* to travel. Self-drive or an organised safari package? Overland truck or no-expenses-spared luxury? The choice is yours and we'll give you the tools to help you make the all-important decisions.

Choosing an Operator

A good operator is the single most important variable for your safari, and it's worth spending time thoroughly researching those you're considering. Competition among safari companies is fierce and standards of professionalism vary greatly. Some companies use glorified matatu (minibus) or dalla-dalla (minibus or pick-up truck) drivers as guides, offer sub-standard food and poorly maintained vehicles, or underpay and poorly treat their staff, while others are high-quality companies with excellent track records. Following are some things to keep in mind when looking for an operator:

➡ Do some legwork before coming to East Africa. Check out traveller forums and the 'User Reviews' section of the Safari Bookings website (www.safaribookings.com). Get personal recommendations, and once in the region, talk with as many people as you can who have recently returned from a safari or trek with the company you're considering.

KATO & TATO

The **Kenyan Association of Tour Operators** (KATO; www.katokenya.org) and the **Tanzanian Association of Tour Operators** (TATO; ☏027-250 4188; www.tatotz.org) serve as local regulatory bodies. Reputable safari companies in Kenya and Tanzania will be registered members. While they're not always the most powerful of entities, going on safari with one of their members (both have member lists on their websites) will at least give you some recourse to appeal in case of conflict or problems. They're also good sources of information on whether a company is reputable or not, and it's well worth checking in with them before finalising your plans.

Uganda's equivalent, the **Association of Uganda Tour Operators** (AUTO; www.auto.or.ug), has no policing power, but does screen prospective new members to confirm they are at least competent. Other good sources of information on tour operators include:

Safari Bookings (www.safaribookings.com)

Tanzania Tourist Board Tourist Information Centre (☏027-250 3842; www.tanzania touristboard.com)

Uganda Tourist Board (www.visituganda.com)

Kenya Professional Safari Guides Association (www.safariguides.org)

Ecotourism Society of Kenya (ESOK; ☏0726366080, 020-2574059; www.ecotourism kenya.org)

Rwanda Tourism (www.rwandatourism.com)

➡ Be sceptical of price quotes that sound too good to be true, and don't rush into any deals, no matter how good they sound.

➡ Don't fall for it if a tout tries to convince you that a safari or trek is leaving 'tomorrow' and that you can be the final person in the group. Take the time to shop around at reliable outfits to get a feel for what's on offer. If others have supposedly registered, ask to speak with them.

➡ Don't give money to anyone who doesn't work out of an office, and don't arrange any safari deals at the bus stand or with touts who follow you to your hotel room. Also be wary of sham operators trading under the same names as companies listed in guidebooks. Don't let business cards fool you either; they're easy to print up and are no proof of legitimacy.

➡ Go with a company that has its own vehicles and equipment. If you have any doubts, don't pay a deposit until you've seen the vehicle (and tyres) that you'll be using. Also be aware that it's not unknown for an operator to show you one vehicle, but then on the actual departure day, arrive in an inferior one.

➡ Especially at the budget level, there's often client swapping between companies whose vehicles are full and those that aren't. You could easily find yourself on safari with a company that isn't the one you booked with; reputable companies will inform you if they're going to do this. Although getting swapped into another company's safari isn't necessarily a bad thing, be sure that the safari you booked and paid for is what you get.

➡ Unless you speak the local language, be sure your driver and/or guide can speak your language.

➡ Go through the itinerary in detail, confirming in writing what's expected and planned for each stage of the trip. Be sure that the number of wildlife drives per day and all other specifics appear in the written contract, as well as the starting and ending dates and approximate times.

➡ Normally, major problems such as complete vehicle breakdown are compensated for by adding additional time onto your safari. If this isn't possible, reliable operators may compensate you for a portion of time lost. However, don't expect a refund for 'minor' problems such as punctured tyres or lesser breakdowns. Park fees are non-refundable.

Safari Style

While price can be a major determining factor in safari planning, there are other considerations that are just as important:

Ambience Will you be staying in or near the park? (If you stay well outside the park, you'll miss the good early morning and evening wildlife-viewing hours.) Are the surroundings atmospheric? Will you be in a large lodge or an intimate private camp?

WHAT TO BRING

→ Binoculars

→ Good-quality sleeping bag (for camping safaris)

→ Mosquito repellent

→ Mosquito net (many lodges and tented camps have nets, but you may need one for budget guesthouses)

→ Rain gear and waterproofs for high-altitude trekking and/or wet-season camping safaris

→ Sunglasses

→ Camera and extra batteries, memory and zoom capacity

→ Extra contact lens solution and your prescription glasses (the dust can be irritating)

→ Toilet paper, snacks and extra water for budget safaris

→ For walking safaris, bring lightweight, long-sleeved shirts and trousers in subdued colours, a head covering, and sturdy, comfortable shoes

Equipment Mediocre vehicles and equipment can significantly detract from the overall experience. In remote areas, lack of quality equipment or vehicles and appropriate back-up arrangements can be a safety risk.

Access & activities If you don't relish the idea of spending hours on bumpy roads, consider parks and lodges where you can fly in. To get out of the vehicle and into the bush, target areas offering walking and boat safaris.

Guides A good driver/guide can make or break your safari. With operators trying to cut corners, chances are that staff are unfairly paid, and are not likely to be knowledgeable or motivated.

Community commitment Look for operators that do more than just give lip-service to ecotourism principles, and that have a genuine, long-standing commitment to the communities where they work. In addition to being more culturally responsible, they'll also be able to give you a more authentic and enjoyable experience.

Setting the agenda Some drivers feel that they have to whisk you from one good 'sighting' to the next. If you prefer to stay in one strategic place for a while to experience the environment and see what comes by, discuss this with your driver.

Going off in wild, hurried pursuit of the 'Big Five' means you'll miss the more subtle aspects of your surroundings.

Extracurriculars In some areas, it's common for drivers to stop at souvenir shops en route; most shops pay drivers commissions to bring clients, which means you may find yourself spending more time souvenir shopping than you'd bargained for. If you're not interested, discuss this with your driver at the outset, ideally while still at the operator's office.

Less is more If you'll be teaming up with others to make a group, find out how many people will be in your vehicle, and try to meet your travelling companions before setting off.

Special interests If birdwatching or other special interests are important, arrange a private safari with a specialised operator.

Booking

Booking (and paying for) a safari before arriving in East Africa is strongly recommended if you'll be travelling in popular areas during peak season or if your schedule is tight or inflexible. Only prebook with operators that you have thoroughly checked out, and take particular care if prebooking at the budget end of the spectrum. Confirm that the operator you're considering is registered with the relevant national regulatory body and get as much feedback as possible from other travellers.

If cutting costs and maintaining flexibility are priorities, then it can work out better to book your safari once you are in East Africa. Allow at least a day to shop around, don't rush into any deals, and steer clear of any attempts at intimidation by touts or dodgy operators to get you to pay immediately or risk losing your place in a departing vehicle.

Costs

→ Camping safaris cater to shoestring travellers and those who are prepared to put up with a little discomfort and who don't mind helping to pitch the tents and set up camp. Safaris based in lodges or tented camps cost more, with the price usually directly proportional to the quality of the accommodation and staff.

→ Most safari quotes include park entrance fees, accommodation and transport costs to/from the park and within the park, but confirm before paying. Drinks (alcoholic or not) are

Above: Cheetahs, Masai Mara National Reserve (p251), Kenya

Right: Giraffe spotting, Serengeti National Park (p135), Tanzania

MICHAL VENERA / GETTY IMAGES ©

generally excluded, although many operators provide one bottle of water daily. Budget camping safari prices usually exclude sleeping bag rental (US$5 per day to US$20 per trip). For group safaris, find out how many people will be sharing the vehicle with you (the prices we quote are based on a group size of four), and how many people per tent or room.

➡ If accommodation-only prices apply, you'll need to pay extra to actually go out looking for wildlife, either on wildlife drives, boat safaris or walks. There is usually the opportunity for two of these 'activities' per day (each around two to three hours). Costs range from about US$25 per person for a walk, up to US$200 or more per day per vehicle for wildlife drives.

➡ There isn't necessarily a relationship between the price paid and the likelihood of the local community benefiting from your visit. Find out as much as you can about an operators' social and cultural commitment before booking.

Budget

At the budget end, reliability is a major factor, as there's often only a fine line between operators running no-frills but good-value safaris, and those that are either dishonest or have cut things so close that problems are bound to arise.

Most budget safaris are camping safaris. To minimise costs, you'll camp or stay in basic guesthouses, travel in relatively large groups and have no-frills meals. In some areas the camping grounds may be outside park boundaries to save on park entry fees and high park camping fees; however, this means you'll lose time during prime morning and evening wildlife viewing hours shuttling to and from the park. Most budget safaris also place daily kilometre limits on the vehicles, meaning your driver may be unwilling or unable to follow certain lengthier routes.

In Tanzania, expect to pay US$150 to US$200 per person per day for a budget safari with a registered operator. The cost in Kenya will be slightly lower. Genuine budget camping safaris are few and far between in Uganda, although a few companies offer reasonably priced three-day trips to Murchison Falls and Queen Elizabeth National Parks for about US$70 to US$100 per person per day, camping or sleeping in dorms.

To save money, bring drinks with you, especially bottled water, as it's expensive to buy in and near the parks. Snacks, extra food and toilet paper are other worthwhile items. During the low season, it's often possible to find lodge safaris for close to the price of a camping safari.

Midrange

Most midrange safaris use lodges, where you can expect to have a comfortable room and to eat in a restaurant. In general, you can expect reliability and reasonably good value in this category. A disadvantage is that the safaris may have a packaged-tour atmosphere, although this can be minimised by carefully selecting a safari company and accommodation, and giving attention to who and how many other people you travel with. Expect to pay from about US$200 to US$300 per person per day in Kenya and Tanzania for a midrange

---

TIPPING

Assuming service has been satisfactory, tipping is an important part of the East African safari experience (especially to the drivers, guides, cooks and others whose livelihoods depend on tips), and it will always be in addition to the overall safari price quoted by the operator. Many operators have tipping guidelines. Depending on where you are, for camping safaris this averages from about US$10 to US$15 per day per group for the driver/guide/cook, more for upscale safaris, large groups or an especially good job.

Another way to calculate things is to give an additional day's wage for every five days worked, with a similar proportion for a shorter trip, and a higher than average tip for exceptional service. Wages in East Africa are low, and it's never a mistake to err on the side of generosity when tipping those who have worked to make your safari experience memorable. Whenever possible, give your tips directly to the staff you want to thank, although many safari camps and lodges keep a box for tips that are later shared among all staff.

lodge safari. During low season, always ask about special deals. In Uganda, plan on anywhere from US$100 to US$150 per person per day.

Top End

Private lodges, luxury tented camps and sometimes private fly camps are used in top-end safaris, all with the aim of providing guests with as authentic and personal a bush experience as possible while not foregoing comfort. For the price you pay (from US$250 or US$300 up to US$800 or more per person per day), expect a full range of amenities, as well as top-quality guiding, a high level of personalised attention and an intimate atmosphere.

In Kenya, private or community-run conservancies are increasingly a part of the mix. Most of these conservancies restrict entry onto the conservancy to those who stay in what is usually a luxury lodge, ensuring a more intimate safari experience. Accommodation prices sometimes (but don't always) include a fee that goes towards the conservancy's conservation and community projects. Most of the conservancies are concentrated in Laikipia, northern Kenya and around the Masai Mara, with just two in Tanzania (close to Lake Manyara and in West Kilimanjaro).

When to Go

Climate Considerations

Getting around is easier in the dry season (July to October), and in many parks, reserves and conservancies this is when animals are easier to find around waterholes and rivers. Foliage is also less dense, making wildlife easier to spot. However, as the dry season corresponds in part with the high-travel season, lodges and camps in some areas get crowded and accommodation prices are at a premium.

June is also good (and sometimes considered to be high season), while the short rains in late October and November rarely interrupt travel plans. Unless these rains have been particularly heavy, the recommended safari season extends into February.

As a general rule (unless you're a birdwatcher) avoid March to May, when the region's long rains bucket down, wildlife disperses and many tracks become impassable.

FIELD GUIDES

➡ *The Kingdon Field Guide to African Mammals* by Jonathan Kingdon

➡ *A Field Guide to the Carnivores of the World* by Luke Hunter

➡ *The Behaviour Guide to African Mammals* by Richard Despard Estes

➡ *Field Guide to the Birds of East Africa* by Terry Stevenson and John Fanshawe

➡ *Birds of Kenya and Northern Tanzania* by Dale Zimmerman, Donald Turner and David Pearson

➡ *Lonely Planet's Watching Wildlife East Africa* Not a field guide, but full of tips on spotting wildlife, maps of East Africa's parks and background information on animal behaviour and ecology.

Wildebeest Migration

When it comes to visiting Kenya's Masai Mara or Tanzania's Serengeti to see the wildebeest migration, deciding when to go and where always involves some element of risk. What follows is a general overview of what usually happens, but it's a guide only and exceptions are common.

January to March During the rains, the wildebeest are widely scattered over the southern and southwestern section of the Serengeti and the western side of Ngorongoro Conservation Area.

April Most streams dry out quickly when the rains cease, nudging the wildebeest to concentrate on the few remaining green areas, and to form thousands-strong herds that begin to migrate northwest in search of food.

May to early July In early May, the herds cross northwest towards the Western Corridor. The crossing of the crocodile-filled Grumeti River usually takes place between late May and early July, and lasts only about a week.

Mid-July to August By the second half of July, the herds are moving north and northwest into the northern Serengeti and Kenya's Masai Mara. As part of this northwards push, they make an even more incredible river crossing of the Mara River.

September to October In early September, the last stragglers leave the Serengeti and most will remain in the Masai Mara throughout October.

November to December The herds usually begin moving south again in November in anticipation of the rains, crossing down through the heart of the Serengeti and to the south in December.

Safari Itineraries

Wherever you plan to take your safari, don't be tempted to try to fit too much into the itinerary. Distances in East Africa are long, and moving too quickly from park to park is likely to leave you tired and unsatisfied.

Tanzania

Northern Circuit

Half-Week

➤ Any of the northern parks alone

➤ Ngorongoro Crater together with Lake Manyara or Tarangire National Parks

One Week to 10 Days

➤ Lake Manyara or Tarangire National Parks plus Ngorongoro Crater and the Serengeti

➤ Serengeti National Park, Ngorongoro Crater and Lake Natron

➤ Serengeti and Rubondo Island National Parks

➤ One or two of the northern parks plus cultural tourism programs around Arusha or hiking in the Usambara Mountains

Southern Circuit

Half-Week

➤ Any one of the following: Mikumi, Saadani or Ruaha National Parks or Selous Game Reserve

One Week

➤ Selous Game Reserve and Ruaha National Park

➤ Ruaha and Katavi National Parks

➤ Selous Game Reserve and Mafia or Zanzibar Island

➤ Mahale Mountains National Park plus Lake Tanganyika

➤ Katavi National Park and Lake Tanganyika

10 Days

➤ Ruaha, Katavi and Mahale Mountains National Parks

➤ Kaavi and Mahale Mountains National Parks plus Lake Tanganyika

Western Parks

Half-Week

➤ Katavi National Park

➤ Gombe Stream National Park

➤ Rubondo Island National Park

One Week

➤ Mahale Mountains and Katavi National Parks

Kenya

Half-Week

➤ Masai Mara National Reserve

➤ Lake Nakuru National Park

➤ Amboseli National Park

➤ Tsavo West or Tsavo East National Parks

One Week

➤ Masai Mara National Reserve and Amboseli National Park or Lakes Nakuru and Baringo

➤ Laikipia Conservancies and Samburu National Reserve

➤ Samburu and Buffalo Springs National Reserves

10 Days

➤ Masai Mara, Amboseli and Tsavo

➤ Laikipia and Masai Mara, Amboseli or Tsavo

➤ Rift Valley lakes plus Samburu and Buffalo Springs National Reserves

➤ Samburu and Buffalo Springs National Reserves plus Marsabit National Park and Lake Turkana

➤ Meru National Park or Shaba National Reserve plus Marsabit and Lake Turkana

Uganda

Most safaris in Uganda last one week to 10 days and focus on the southwest, usually combining a gorilla visit in Uganda or neighbouring Rwanda with wildlife watching in Queen Elizabeth and Murchison Falls National Parks and chimp visits in Kibale National Park.

Rwanda

It's easy to visit the highlight parks – Volcanoes National Park, Nyungwe Forest National Park and Akagera National Park – within one week to 10 days. Most organised safari packages are short (less than a week), and concentrate on trips to Volcanoes National Park.

Types of Safari

Organised Vehicle Safaris

Four to six days on an organised vehicle safari is often ideal. At least one full day will normally be taken up with travel, and after six days you may well feel like a rest. If you pack too much distance or too many parks into a short period, you'll likely feel as if you've spent your whole time in transit. If you can, build in rest days spent at camp or on walking safaris and other non-vehicle-based activities.

Minivans are the most common safari transport throughout Kenya and northern Tanzania, but if you have a choice, go for a good 4WD instead – preferably one with a pop-up style roof (versus a simple hatch that flips open or comes off), as it affords some shade. Minivans accommodate too many people for a good experience, the rooftop opening is usually only large enough for a few passengers to use at once, and at least some passengers will get stuck in middle seats with poor views.

Whatever the vehicle, avoid crowding. Most price quotes are based on groups of three to four passengers, which is about the maximum number of people most vehicles can hold comfortably.

Other Safaris

Walking, Hiking & Cycling Safaris

At many national parks (and at almost all of the private and community-run

---

TRACKING CHIMPANZEES

After hanging out with the mountain gorillas (see p39) many people carry on up the evolutionary tree to spend a day tracking our even closer relatives, chimpanzees. There are four main national parks in which to see chimps and, as with the gorillas, the experience in each is different.

Mahale Mountains National Park (Tanzania)

With steep forested mountains falling sharply down to beaches of feather-soft white sands and the turquoise waters of Lake Tanganyika, Mahale Mountains is the park with the most spectacular setting. Lots of chimps here are very used to humans; many will happily walk right up to you. As such, many rate Mahale as the best park to see chimps. However, getting to Mahale can be time consuming and expensive. You're also limited to one hour a day with the chimps and for the rest of the day there's actually not much else to do. Face masks must be worn when with the chimps.

Gombe Stream National Park (Tanzania)

Located on the shores of Lake Tanganyika, access to Gombe Stream is relatively easy and the park is good value. The chimps here have been studied for decades (this is where Jane Goodall worked) and couldn't be more used to people. Chimp encounters are limited to an hour a day and there's not much else to do once your time with the chimps is up. Face masks must be worn.

Nyungwe Forest National Park (Rwanda)

One of the most important forest systems in East Africa, Nyungwe is home to a large number of chimps, but of all the big chimpanzee parks, the apes here are the least habituated and most skittish around people. Access to the park is cheap and easy and there are lots of other things to do when your hour with the chimps is up.

Kibale National Park (Uganda)

Access to this important forest is cheap and easy and there's an array of brilliant value accommodation for all budgets. The chimps here are very well habituated and up-close encounters are pretty much guaranteed. The one-hour chimp permit here is more expensive than any of the other parks but you can pay a little extra and join a full day 'chimp experience'. When not with the chimps there are lots of other wildlife and cultural activities available. Face masks not required.

conservancies), you can arrange walks of two to three hours in the early morning or late afternoon, with the focus on watching animals rather than covering distance. Following the walk, you'll return to the main camp or lodge, or to a fly camp.

Multi-day or point-to-point walks are available in some areas, as are combination walking-hiking-cycling itineraries with side trips by vehicle into the parks to see wildlife. Popular areas in Kenya include Mt Kenya National Park and Mt Elgon National Park for trekking and hiking and Hell's Gate National Park for cycling. Walking (and sometimes horse-riding) safaris are staples of the Laikipia, northern Kenya and Mara conservancies. Lion-tracking is also possible in Ol Pejeta Conservancy.

In Tanzania, places where you can walk in big game areas include Selous Game Reserve and Ruaha, Mikumi, Katavi, Tarangire, Lake Manyara, Serengeti and Arusha National Parks. There are also several parks – including Kilimanjaro, Mahale Mountains and Gombe Stream National Parks – that can only be explored on foot. Short walks are easily arranged in Rubondo Island National Park. Multi-day walks are possible in the Crater Highlands, Serengeti National Park and Selous Game Reserve, and cycling is possible in the area around Lake Manyara National Park.

In Uganda, opportunities include everything from tracking gorillas and chimpanzees to birdwatching walks in Bwindi Impenetrable and Kibale National Parks, to wildlife walks in Queen Elizabeth, Kidepo Valley and Lake Mburo National Parks, to climbing Mt Elgon or trekking in the Rwenzoris.

Boat & Canoe Safaris

Boat safaris are an excellent way to experience the East African wilderness and offer a welcome break from dusty, bumpy roads. Good destinations include:

➡ Along the Rufiji River in Tanzania's Selous Game Reserve (p190), with two- to three-hour boat safaris.

➡ Uganda's Queen Elizabeth National Park (p431).

➡ Launch trip up the Victoria Nile (p459) to the base of Murchison Falls.

Camel Safaris

Most camel safaris take place in northern Kenya's Samburu and Turkana tribal areas, with Maralal a logical base. Although you may see wildlife along the way, the main attractions are the journey itself, and the chance to immerse yourself in nomadic life and mingle with the indigenous people. You can either ride the camels or walk alongside them. Most travelling is done in the cooler parts of the day. Most operators provide camping equipment or offer it for rental. There are also camel safaris in Maasai areas near Arusha National Park.

Balloon Safaris

The places for balloon safaris are Kenya's Masai Mara National Reserve and Tanzania's Serengeti National Park. Everything depends on wind and weather conditions; spotting animals can't be guaranteed and flight time is generally limited to a maximum of one hour. But the captains try to stay between 500m and 1000m above ground, which means that if animals are there you'll be able to see them. Most balloon safaris are followed by a champagne breakfast in the bush.

Do-It-Yourself Safaris

It's possible to visit most of East Africa's parks with your own vehicle, without going through a safari operator. Some travellers rave about the experience and the freedom it gives you. For others, unless you're experienced at bush driving, the modest cost savings may be offset by having someone else handle the logistics; if you're renting, hiring a local driver rarely costs a whole lot more.

For most areas, you'll need a 4WD. In addition to park admission fees, there are daily vehicle fees and, in some areas, a mandatory guide fee. You may need to carry extra petrol, as it's not available in all parks, as well as spare tires. Carrying a tent is also recommended.

Plan Your Trip
Gorilla Tracking

Nothing quite prepares you for the moment when you come upon a gorilla family in the wild; the first glimpse of black as a juvenile jumps off a nearby branch, a toddler clings to its mother's back and a giant silverback rises to size you up. No bars, no windows – you're a humble guest in their domain. Coming face to face with mountain gorillas is one of life's great experiences. And we'll help you make it happen.

Planning Your Trip
When to Go?

Any time you can. The experience will be incredible no matter when you go, but there are advantages to going at different times of the year.

It's generally easier to track gorillas in the rainy seasons (March to May and September to November) because they hang out at lower altitudes. You may also get better photos in the rainy season, assuming it isn't raining at the time you're with the gorillas, because they love to sunbathe after getting wet. Then again, you'll need to be wearing some serious wet-weather gear.

The busiest times on the mountains are December to February and July to August. Scoring permits takes more effort during these months, but that won't matter if a tour company is handling things for you.

Booking Ahead

Permits are required to visit the gorillas and booking ahead is always a good idea, particularly if you're planning to visit Uganda's Bwindi Impenetrable National Park and Rwanda's Volcanoes National Park from December to February or July to August. If you aren't travelling in these months and you only have a very small window of opportunity, you should still make a reservation as far in advance as possible to be safe.

At a Glance

Best for Seeing Gorillas
Bwindi Impenetrable National Park (Uganda; p437)

Volcanoes National Park (Rwanda; p501)

Best for Independent Travellers
Mgahinga Gorilla National Park (Uganda; p448)

Dry Season
When December to February, June to August

Advantages Generally dry weather

Disadvantages Permits more difficult to obtain

Wet Season
When March to May, September to November

Advantages Fewer visitors so permits easier to obtain; permits cheaper at Bwindi Impenetrable National Park; generally easier to track gorillas

Disadvantages Can be extremely wet

Cheapest Permits
Bwindi Impenetrable National Park (Uganda): US$350 in April, May, October and November

To make a phone booking for Rwanda, you need to pay a deposit by bank transfer, while in Uganda you'll need to provide all the money up front. If you can't get a permit on your own, you'll need to go through a tour operator, which is often a good idea anyway.

Required Fitness Levels

With the combination of mud, steep hills and altitude, gorilla tracking is hard work. Although gorillas sometimes wander near the visitor centres and might be found quickly, you're far more likely to be hiking for two to four hours, and some trackers have wandered across the mountains for an entire day.

What to Bring

For the most part, you don't need anything special beyond the usual outdoor essentials such as sunscreen, insect repellent, and food and water (enough for the whole day, just in case). Good boots are important. Some people like rubber boots because they keep the mud and fire ants at bay, but they have no ankle support. Plan for rain no matter what month you're tracking (you'll be in a rainforest after all). It's also often chilly in the morning, so you might want a warm top.

You may have to trudge through thorns and stinging nettle, so trousers and long-sleeve shirts with some degree of heft may save you some irritation. For the same reason, garden gloves can come in handy.

Finally, bring your passport with you on tracking day; you'll need it for registration.

Costs

For most of the year, demand for gorilla-tracking permits far outstrips supply: permits cost the following:

➡ Rwanda US$750

➡ Uganda US$600

The price includes park entry, guides and armed escorts, while porters are available for a little extra. These people are paid very little, and work hard, so they will expect a small tip.

Understanding Gorillas

Gorillas are the largest of the great apes and share 97% of their biological make-up with humans. Gorillas used to inhabit a swathe of land that cut right across central Africa, but the last remaining eastern mountain gorillas number just over 700, divided between two 300-plus populations in the forests of Uganda's Bwindi Impenetrable National Park and on the slopes of the Virunga volcanoes, encompassing Uganda's Mgahinga Gorilla National Park and Rwanda's Volcanoes National Park. For more on the conservation status of mountain gorillas, see p574.

RULES FOR GORILLA TRACKING

➡ Anyone with an illness cannot track the gorillas. In Rwanda you'll get a full refund if you cancel because of illness and produce a doctor's note, while in Uganda, you'll get back half.

➡ Eating and smoking near the gorillas is prohibited.

➡ If you have to cough or sneeze, cover your mouth and turn your head.

➡ Flash photography is banned; turn off the autoflash.

➡ Speak quietly and don't point at the gorillas or make sudden movements; they may see these as threats.

➡ Leave nothing in the park; you shouldn't even spit.

➡ Keep a few metres back from the gorillas and promptly follow your guide's directions about where to walk.

➡ When faced with 200kg of charging silverback, never, ever run away...crouch down until he cools off.

➡ Children under 15 years of age aren't allowed to visit the gorillas.

Above: Bwindi Impenetrable National Park (p437), Uganda

Right: Volcanoes National Park (p501), Rwanda

DANITA DELIMONT / GETTY IMAGES ©

PARC NATIONAL DES VIRUNGAS (THE DRC)

Established in 1925 by the Belgian colonial government as Albert National Park, **Parc National des Virungas** (☎+243 99 1715401; www.visitvirunga.org; Boulevard Kanya Mulanga, Goma) is Africa's oldest and largest protected area. To put things in perspective, Virungas is contiguous with five different national parks in Uganda, and protects an incredible range of endangered animals, from forest elephants to chimpanzees and mountain gorillas.

The park lies at the centre of a war-torn region, and has been threatened by poaching, land invasions, charcoal producers and rebel factions. The park was forced to close in 2012, but parts of it re-opened to tourism in 2014. Assuming that the security situation is safe, the DRC receives far fewer visitors than Uganda's Bwindi Impenetrable National Park or Rwanda's Volcanoes National Park. Given that permits are also easier to come by here (and they are cheaper), this is probably the easiest place for independent travellers to see the gorillas. And the setting is stunning.

The habituated mountain gorillas of the Parc National des Virungas can be seen on a gorilla tracking trip (US$465). The other drawcard is the chance to climb, and sleep on the rim of, the Nyiragongo Volcano (US$255), whose crater contains the world's largest permanent lava lake.

Bookings for all park activities should be made through the impressively organised Virunga Visitors Centre in Goma or through their website. While tourist visas for the Congo are extremely difficult to obtain, the park can help arrange what is known as a Virunga Visa which is valid for the park itself, Goma, Bukavu and the Parc National Kahuzi-Biega, (kahuzibiega.wordpress.com), which is home to habituated groups of Eastern Lowland gorillas (permits US$400). Visas take around a week to issue and cost US$105.

The security situation in this part of the world changes fast and often. Be sure to double check the latest before venturing here.

Daily Life

Gorillas spend 30% of their day feeding, 30% moving and foraging, and the remainder resting. They spend most of their time on the ground, moving around on all fours but standing up to reach for food. Gorillas are vegetarians and their diet consists mainly of bamboo shoots, giant thistles and wild celery, all of which contain water and allow the gorillas to survive without drinking for long periods of time. A silverback can eat his way through more than 30kg of bamboo a day.

A group's dominant silverback dictates movements for the day, and at night each gorilla makes its own nest. Gorillas usually travel about 1km a day, unless they have met another group, in which case they may move further.

Families

Gorillas generally live in family groups of varying sizes, usually including one to two older silverback males, younger blackback males, females and infants. Most groups contain between 10 and 15 gorillas, but they can exceed 40. The largest habituated group in Uganda's Bwindi Impenetrable National Park has 26 members, and in Rwanda's Volcanoes National Park the largest group has 28.

There are strong bonds between individuals and status is usually linked to age. Silverbacks are at the top of the hierarchy, then females with infants or ties to the silverbacks, then blackbacks and other females. Most gorillas leave the group when they reach maturity, which helps prevent inbreeding among such a small population.

Conflict

Gorillas are relatively placid primates and serious confrontations are rare, although violence can flare up if there's a challenge for supremacy between silverbacks. Conflicts are mostly kept to shows of strength and vocal disputes.

Conflict between groups is also uncommon, as gorillas aren't territorial; if two groups meet, there's usually lots of display and bravado on the part of silverbacks, including mock charges. Often the whole group joins in and it's at this point that young adult females may choose to switch allegiance.

If gorillas do fight, injuries can be very serious as these animals have long canine teeth and silverbacks pack a punch estimated to be eight times stronger than that of a heavyweight boxer. If a dominant male is driven from a group by another silverback, it's likely the new leader will kill all the infants to establish his mating rights.

Communication

Gorillas communicate in a variety of ways, including facial expressions, gestures and around two dozen vocalisations. Adult males use barks and roars during confrontations or to coordinate the movement of their groups to a different area. Postures and gestures form an important element of intimidation and it's possible for a clash to be diffused by a display of teeth-baring, stiff-legging and charging.

Friendly communication is an important part of group bonding and includes grunts of pleasure. Upon finding food, gorillas will grunt or bark to alert other members of the group.

Biology

Gorillas are the largest primates in the world and mountain gorillas are the largest of the three gorilla species; adult male mountain gorillas weigh as much as 200kg (440lb). Females are about half this size.

Males reach maturity between eight and 15 years old, their backs turning silver as they enter their teens, while females enter adulthood at the earlier age of eight. Conception is possible for about three days each month, and once a female has conceived for the first time, she spends most of her life pregnant or nursing.

The duration of a gorilla pregnancy is about 8½ months. Newborn infants are highly dependent on adults, and a young infant will rarely leave its mother's arms during its first six months. In its second year, a young gorilla begins to interact with other members of the group and starts to feed itself. Infant gorillas and silverbacks often form a bond, and it's not uncommon for a silverback to adopt an infant if its mother dies. This distinguishes gorillas from other primates, where child-rearing duties are left to females. From about three years, young gorillas become quite independent and build their own nests.

Mountain gorillas are distinguished from their more widespread lowland relatives by longer hair, broader chests and wider jaws. The most obvious thing that sets the gorillas in Bwindi apart from those of the Virungas is that they are less shaggy, most likely due to the lower altitude.

Where to Track Gorillas
Bwindi Impenetrable National Park (Uganda)

Home to around half of the world's eastern mountain gorilla population, Bwindi Impenetrable National Park remains one of the top spots to track mountain gorillas. The evocatively named park lives up to its name, with stunning scenery comprising dense, steep virgin rainforest. And yes, it means tracking can occasionally be hard work, but with the aid of a good walking stick (or a porter to lend a hand), you'll get there without too much difficulty. And while visibility often isn't as good as it is in the open spaces where the Virunga gorillas hang out, in Bwindi you'll get just as close to them and they're more likely to be seen swinging from the trees.

GORILLA LOCATIONS

COUNTRY	LOCATION	DAILY PERMITS AVAILABLE	COST (US$)	HABITUATED GORILLA GROUPS
Uganda	Bwindi Impenetrable NP	96	600 (350 Apr, May, Oct & Nov)	12
Uganda	Mgahinga Gorilla NP	8	600	1
Rwanda	Volcanoes NP	80	750	10

Arranging Permits

Even though the number of tracking permits has increased to around 96 per day, it can still be difficult to get them. There are 12 mountain gorilla groups spread across four areas of the park.

Permits, which cost US$600, must be booked at the Uganda Wildlife Authority (p474) headquarters in Kampala or through a Ugandan tour operator. It's theoretically possible to arrange permits online via a bank transfer, but the UWA is notoriously tricky to get in touch with via email.

Discount permits are available for US$350 for the low season months of April, May, October and November; whether this remains an ongoing fixture is yet to be determined.

Mgahinga Gorilla National Park (Uganda)

Mgahinga Gorilla National Park encompasses Uganda's share of the Virunga volcanoes, which sit squarely on the tri-nation border. This park is popular with independent travellers because reservations aren't possible more than two weeks in advance, due to the only habituated gorilla group's tendency to duck over the border into Rwanda or the DRC. Of course, the down side of this is that it means they can't always be tracked. It often takes longer to find the gorillas here than in Bwindi, but the walking is usually (but not always) much easier.

Arranging Permits

Reservations for the eight places available daily are only taken at the Mgahinga Gorilla National Park Office (p448) in Kisoro. The US$600 fee is paid at the park headquarters on the morning of your tracking.

Volcanoes National Park (Rwanda)

Rwanda's Volcanoes National Park ranks up there with Uganda's Bwindi Impenetrable National Park as one of the best places in East Africa to see gorillas. Part of its appeal is that this is where Dian Fossey was based and where the film about her work was made. Also, the towering volcanoes form a breathtaking backdrop. Tracking here is usually easier than in Bwindi because the mountains offer a more gradual climb, and the visibility is often better too; remember, however, that the trekking here is extremely strenuous. One other thing to remember is that visitors here, unlike in Bwindi, are assigned gorilla groups on tracking day, not when reservations are made, so those who aren't in such good shape will get one of the groups requiring the least amount of walking.

Arranging Permits

There are 10 habituated gorilla groups. Eighty tracking permits (US$750 per person) are available each day.

You can book a permit with the RDB Tourist Office (p496) in Kigali or through a tour operator.

Plan Your Trip

Travel with Children

East Africa is a wonderful destination in which to travel as a family. Yes, there are vaccinations to worry about, distances can be large and there are some regions you'll want to avoid (such as the far north of Kenya and Uganda, and western and southern Tanzania; all areas in which facilities are often very limited). But by casting your worries aside you'll most likely have the family holiday of a lifetime.

East Africa for Kids

Health & Safe Travel

Africa's list of potential health hazards is formidable, although a little preparation can ameliorate most risks – talk with your doctor before departure, take special care with hygiene once you're on the road and make sure your children always sleep under a mosquito net.

Safaris & Cultures

The safari could have been custom-built for older children, but younger kids may not have the patience to sit for long periods in a car. Driving up to within touching distance of elephants and watching lion cubs gambolling across the plains are experiences your kids won't quickly forget. A number of very top end lodges, particularly in Kenya, operate 'Warrior for a Week' programmes where in between safaris the kids get taught how to make fire without matches, track buffalo, shoot their little sister with a bow and arrow and other such things you don't really want a five-year-old child learning! If such top end lodges are out of your budget then you'll be pleased to hear that throughout the region there are numerous other 'cultural experience' programmes that are often both easier

Best Regions for Kids

Tanzania

Tanzania combines fabulous safari destinations – the Ngorongoro Conservation Area, a true place of the imagination, and the Serengeti National Park in particular – with a lengthy Indian Ocean coastline; safari lodges and beach resorts (especially in Zanzibar) are often family-friendly.

Kenya

Like Tanzania, Kenya combines stirring safaris with fabulous coastline. The Masai Mara National Reserve during the wildebeest migration (July to October) is an extraordinary spectacle; other national parks such as Nairobi and Lake Nakuru are more manageable in size. Anywhere along the coast can be good for families, although Diani Beach and (security-depending) Lamu are our pick.

Uganda

With wildlife-rich national parks and a slew of water-based activities at Entebbe and Jinja, Uganda can be a great destination. Queen Elizabeth, with its boat rides and good roads, is ideal for a family safari. Remember minimum age requirements (usually 12 or 15 years old) apply for chimp and gorilla tracking.

on the wallet than a safari and, more importantly, most of these are likely to leave a stronger imprint in your child's mind than any number of animal encounters.

Beach Holidays

Beach holidays are a sure-fire way to keep the kids happy, and factoring in some beach time to go with the safari can be a good idea. Kenya's and Tanzania's beaches alone should be sufficient, but some of the watersports on offer and other pursuits such as snorkelling may be suitable for children, depending on their age. And packing a picnic lunch and sailing out to sea on a dhow (ancient Arabic sailing vessel) is fun family time.

Children's Highlights

National Parks & Reserves

➡ **Masai Mara National Reserve** (p251) Africa's charismatic megafauna in abundance.

➡ **Serengeti National Park** (p135) Arguably the best national park in East Africa.

➡ **Nairobi National Park** (p221) Good roads, easy access and loads of animals.

➡ **Lake Nakuru National Park** (p246) Flamingos, leopards and monkeys.

➡ **Saadani National Park** (p98) Perfect combination of beach and bush.

Beaches

➡ **Zanzibar** (p63) Intriguing island culture and glorious beaches.

➡ **Lamu** (p332) Indian Ocean port.

➡ **Pangani & around** (p100) Terrific beaches on Tanzania's north coast.

➡ **Entebbe** (p395) White-sand beaches on Lake Victoria's shore.

Activities

➡ **Swimming with dolphins** Take the plunge at Kisite Marine National Park or Zanzibar.

➡ **Snorkelling** Snorkel at Manda Toto Island or Pemba.

➡ **Sailing** Take a dhow trip at Zanzibar or Lamu.

➡ **White-water rafting** Enjoy white-water rafting for teens at Jinja.

Planning

What to Bring

Canned baby foods, powdered milk, disposable nappies and the like are available in most large supermarkets, but they are expensive. Bring as much as possible from home, along with child-friendly insect repellent (this can't be bought in East Africa). Child seats for hire cars and safari vehicles are generally not available unless arranged in advance.

For protection against malaria, bring mosquito nets for your children and ensure that they sleep under them.

Accommodation

Although some wildlife lodges have restrictions on children aged under 12 years, most lodges can handle the practicalities with aplomb, whether it's the extra bed or cot, or serving buffet meals for fussy eaters; some lodges even have children's playgrounds and almost all have swimming pools.

Budget hotels are probably best avoided for hygiene reasons. Most midrange accommodation should be acceptable, though it's usually only top-end places that cater specifically for families. Camping can be exciting, but make sure little ones don't wander off unsupervised.

Children under two years can stay for free in most hotels; you'll also get a cot thrown in. Children between two and 12 years are usually charged 50% of the adult rate. Large family rooms are sometimes available, and some places also have adjoining rooms with connecting doors.

Transport

Safari vehicles are usually child-friendly, but travelling between towns on public transport is rarely easy. Functional seatbelts are rare even in taxis and accidents are common. A child seat brought from home is a good idea if you're hiring a car or going on safari.

Countries at a Glance

East Africa is a vast region of astonishing diversity.

Kenya and Tanzania rank among the premier wildlife-watching destinations on the planet. Their savannah parks and conservancies shelter just about every African species of charismatic megafauna, from elephants, rhinos and millions-strong herds of wildebeest to the predators that pursue them. If it's primates you're after, Uganda and Rwanda are the places to go for gorillas, while western Tanzania is one of the best places anywhere for observing chimpanzees in the wild.

Fascinating traditional cultures (including in Burundi) are another East African speciality, while the landscapes – from the continent's highest mountains to deep volcanic craters, from lush rainforest and palm-fringed coastlines to epic deserts – could just be the most varied of any African region.

Tanzania

Wildlife
Beaches
Culture

Serengeti to Selous

Whether you're watching wildebeest on the Serengeti Plains, communing with lions in Ngorongoro Crater or floating past hippos and crocs in Selous Game Reserve, the variety of wildlife in Tanzania is unsurpassed.

Beaches & Islands

Let yourself be seduced by miles of Indian Ocean coastline, magical archipelagos, swaying palms, and fine diving and snorkelling. You may never want to leave.

Tribal Groups

Tanzania has a rich array of tribal traditions and long Swahili roots. To get to know the cultural melange, travel off the beaten track. Cultural tourism programs offer an accessible introduction.

p50

Kenya

Wildlife
Beaches
Culture

Predators & Elephants

From the predator-filled plains of Masai Mara National Reserve to the elephant-rich landscapes of Amboseli National Park, Kenya offers superb wildlife watching against stunning natural backdrops.

Lamu to Mombasa

Kenya's coast is enchanting, whether you're relaxing on the beaches around Mombasa or wandering sleepy lanes on Lamu island. Come for a week, but wind up staying much longer.

Culture

The beaded Turkana and the red-robed Maasai are just a sampling of Kenya's vibrant tribal mix. Getting to know the different peoples and rich traditions is a highlight, no matter which part of the country you visit.

p216

Uganda

Gorillas & Lions
Landscapes
Adventure Sports

Gorillas & Lions

Uganda's Bwindi Impenetrable National Park is home to almost half of the world's surviving mountain gorillas, and a visit here is a highlight. Elsewhere, lions and other predators are plentiful in many parks.

Mountains & Waterfalls

Lovely Murchison Falls National Park, wild Kidepo Valley National Park and the peerless Rwenzoris are just three of the many attractions in this country that's painted in every shade of green.

White-Water Rafting

Uganda's upper Nile stretch, with its Class IV and Class V rapids, is a challenging white-water rafting destination. Or, take a family float trip for a gentler introduction.

p375

Rwanda

Gorillas
Landscapes
Culture

Gorillas

The bamboo- and rainforest-covered slopes of the Virunga volcanoes are home to some of the last remaining sanctuaries of the endangered eastern mountain gorilla. A hike here in search of silverbacks is an unforgettable experience.

Mountains & Forests

The 'Land of a Thousand Hills' has endless mountains and stunning scenery. Lake Kivu offers lovely inland beaches, while Nyungwe Forest National Park protects extensive tracts of montane rainforest.

Post-Genocide Recovery

Rwanda has moved impressively far from its troubled history, and getting to know its vibrant cultural backdrop is a highlight of travelling here.

p486

Burundi

Beaches
City Life
Culture

Inland Beaches

Burundi's fine beaches, with their powdery white sands and gentle waves, are some of the best to be found in inland Africa. Saga Beach (Plage des Cocotiers) just outside Bujumbura is a good place to start your relaxing.

Bujumbura

Burundi's steamy capital – with its wide boulevards, imposing public buildings and busy Lake Tanganyika port – is the focal point for most visitors to the country.

Drums & Dancing

Burundi's famous dance troupe, Les Tambourinaires, and the irrepressible *joie de vivre*, which you'll sense on the streets of Bujumbura, are merely at the starting point when getting to know the country's vibrant culture and traditions.

p536

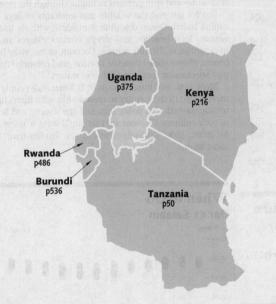

On the Road

Tanzania

Why Go?

Tanzania is *the* land of safaris, with wildebeest stampeding across the plains, hippos jostling for space in rivers, massive elephant herds kicking up the dust on their seasonal migration routes and chimpanzees swinging through the treetops.

But it's not just the wildlife that enchants visitors. Tanzania's Indian Ocean coastline is magical, with its tranquil islands, long beaches and sleepy coastal villages steeped in centuries of Swahili culture. Coconut palms sway in the breeze, dhows glide by on the horizon, and colourful fish flit past spectacular corals in turquoise waters.

More than anything, though, it is Tanzania's people who make a visit to the country so memorable, with their characteristic warmth and politeness, and the dignity and beauty of their cultures. Chances are that you'll want to come back for more: most Tanzanians would say '*karibu tena*' (welcome again).

Best for Nature

➡ Serengeti National
Park (p135)

➡ Ngorongoro Crater (p131)

➡ Selous Game
Reserve (p190)

Best for Culture

➡ Usambara Mountains
(p104)

➡ Cultural Tourism
Programs (p114)

➡ Zanzibar Archipelago
(p63)

When to Go
Dar es Salaam

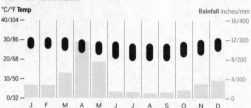

Mar–May Heavy rains bring green landscapes, lower prices, top-notch birdwatching and muddy roads.

Jun–Aug Cool, dry weather, with wildlife watching at its prime.

Sep–Oct Weather remains dry, and wildlife watching is good, without the crowds.

DAR ES SALAAM

With a population of more than four million and East Africa's second-largest port, Dar es Salaam is Tanzania's commercial and cultural hub. Yet beneath the thriving urban bustle, the city retains its down-to-earth vibe, with a picturesque seaport, a mixture of African, Arabic and Indian influences, close ties to its Swahili roots and excellent craft markets and restaurants.

⊙ Sights & Activities

National Museum & House of Culture
MUSEUM

(Map p58; ☑ 022-211 7508; www.houseof culture.or.tz; Shaaban Robert St; adult/student Tsh6500/2600; ☺ 9.30am-6pm) The National Museum houses the famous fossil discoveries of *zinjanthropus* (nutcracker man) from Oldupai Gorge (although only a copy), along with other archaeological finds. Wander through the History Room and ethnographic collection for insights into Tanzania's past and its mosaic of cultures, including the Shirazi civilisation of Kilwa, the Zanzibar slave trade, and the German and British colonial periods. But despite recent renovations the museum still has much work to do on appropriate displays and the curation of a coherent narrative.

Village Museum
MUSEUM

(☑ 022-270 0437; cnr New Bagamoyo Rd & Makaburi St; adult/student Tsh6500/2600; ☺ 9.30am-6pm) The centrepiece of this open-air museum is a collection of authentically constructed dwellings illustrating traditional life in various parts of Tanzania. Each house is furnished with typical items and surrounded by small plots of crops, while 'villagers' demonstrate traditional skills such as weaving, pottery and carving. The idea behind the project is to demonstrate some of the nation's architectural and social traditions, although these days some of the houses are sorely in need of some maintenance. For many, the highlight of the museum is the hour-long tribal dances (adult/child Tsh2000/1000) held in the afternoon.

The museum is 9km north of the city centre; the Mwenge dalla-dalla runs there from New Posta transport stand (Tsh400, 45 minutes).

TANZANIA AT A GLANCE

Area 943,000 sq km

Capital Dodoma (legislative), Dar es Salaam (economic)

Country code ☑ 255

Population 45 million

Currency Tanzanian Shilling (Tsh)

Languages Swahili, English

Money ATMs in major towns; credit cards accepted by some upmarket hotels and tour operators, often with a 5% to 10% commission.

Mobile Phones Local SIM cards widely available; mobile coverage extensive, but patchy in remote areas.

Visas Usually available on arrival at major airports and land borders; valid for three months.

Exchange Rates

Australia	A$1	Tsh1426
Canada	C$1	Tsh1465
Euro Zone	€1	Tsh2071
Japan	¥100	Tsh1541
New Zealand	NZ$1	Tsh1353
UK	UK£1	Tsh2782
USA	US$1	Tsh1828

For current exchange rates see www.xe.com

Tanzania Highlights

1 Marvel at nature's rhythms on the Serengeti Plains and elsewhere in Tanzania's **northern circuit** (p107).

2 Scale **Mt Meru** (p122) and **Mt Kilimanjaro** (p145), or hike their lower slopes.

3 Watch an Indian Ocean moonrise, lose yourself in Zanzibar's Stone Town and explore Pemba's hidden corners on the **Zanzibar Archipelago** (p63).

4 Discover colourful markets, hike through rolling hills and see elephants in Ruaha park in Tanzania's **Southern Highlands** (p172).

5 Visit **Lake Victoria** (p153) for fine birdwatching and tranquil Rubondo Island National Park.

6 Hike in the Usambaras or relax on the coast in **northeastern Tanzania** (p96).

7 Discover Swahili culture, boat past grunting hippos, and dive and snorkel in **southeastern Tanzania** (p187).

8 See chimpanzees up close, watch wildlife in Katavi and explore Lake Tanganyika's shoreline in **western Tanzania** (p162).

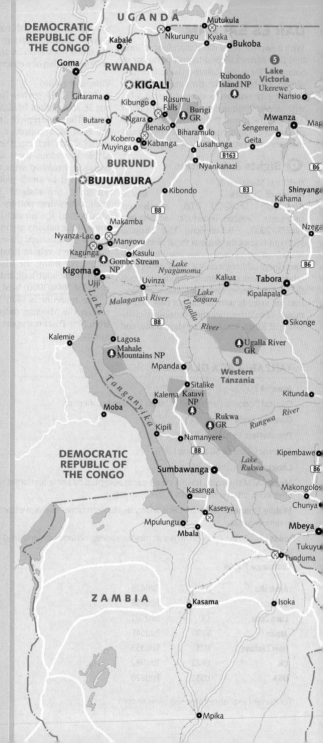

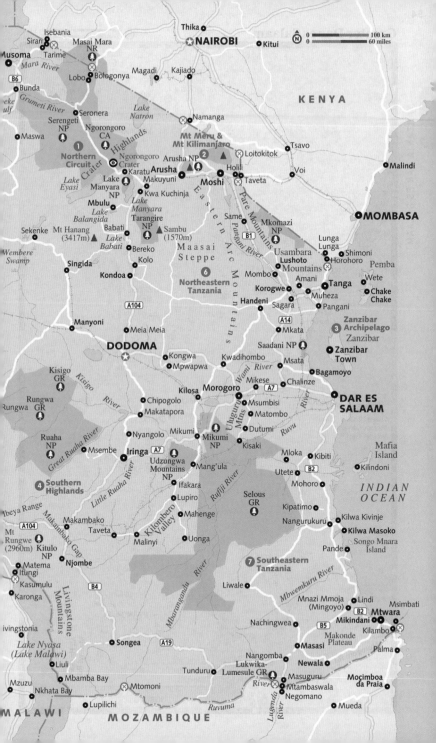

Greater Dar es Salaam

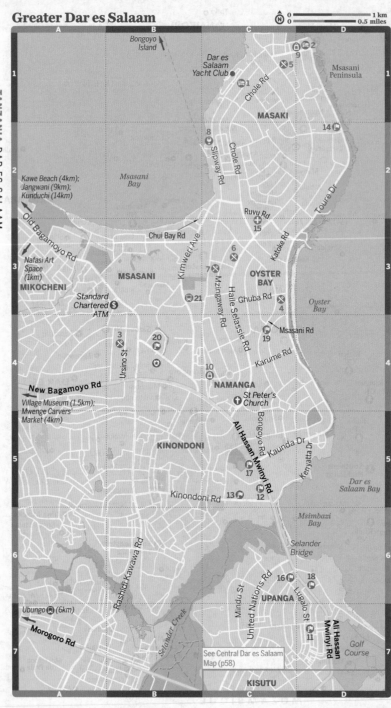

N
0   1 km
0   0.5 miles

Bongoyo
Island

Dar es
Salaam
Yacht Club

Msasani
Peninsula

MASAKI

Chole Rd

Slipway Rd

Chole Rd

Toure Dr

Kawe Beach (4km);
Jangwani (9km);
Kunduchi (14km)

Old Bagamoyo Rd

Msasani
Bay

Chui Bay Rd

Kimweri Ave

Ruvu Rd

Nafasi Art
Space
(1km)

MIKOCHENI

MSASANI

Standard
Chartered
ATM

Mzingaway Rd

Haile Selassie Rd

Katoke Rd

OYSTER
BAY

Ghuba Rd

Oyster
Bay

Msasani Rd

Ursino St

Karume Rd

NAMANGA

New Bagamoyo Rd

Village Museum (1.5km);
Mwenge Carvers
Market (4km)

St Peter's
Church

KINONDONI

Ali Hassan Mwinyi Rd

Bongoyo Rd

Kaunda Dr

Kenyatta Dr

Dar es
Salaam Bay

Kinondoni Rd

Msimbazi
Bay

Selander
Bridge

Rashidi Kawawa Rd

Ubungo (6km)

Morogoro Rd

Selander Creek

Mindu St

United Nations Rd

UPANGA

Lugalo St

Ali Hassan Mwinyi Rd

Golf
Course

See Central Dar es Salaam
Map (p58)

KISUTU

Greater Dar es Salaam

Bongoyo Boat Trips   SNORKELLING
(Map p54; ☑0713 328126; the Slipway, Msasani; adult/child return Tsh36,000/28,000; ☺departures 9.30am, 11.30am, 1.30pm & 3.30pm) If you don't have a car, the quickest and easiest way to enjoy some off-shore island fun is to hop on the ferry to Bongoyo at the Slipway. Once there you can snorkel, hike and enjoy simple meals of grilled fish at a shack on the beach. The last boat returns at 5pm and the marine fee is included in the price.

🛏 Sleeping

🏙 City Centre

Safari Inn   HOTEL $
(Map p58; ☑0754 485013, 022-213 8101; www.safariinn.co.tz; Band St; s/d with fan Tsh28,000/35,000, with air-con Tsh35,000/45,000; ✳@) A popular travellers' haunt in Kisutu with English-speaking staff. The Safari Inn has 42 rooms, 10 of which are air-conditioned. All rooms have mosquito nets and a simple continental breakfast is provided.

Econolodge   HOTEL $
(Map p58; ☑022-211 6048, 022-211 6049; econolodge@raha.com; Band St; s/d with fan Tsh25,000/35,000, with air-con Tsh35,000/45,000; ✳) Clean, bland but good-value rooms hidden away in an aesthetically unappealing high-rise. There are no mosquito nets, but rooms have fans for circulation. Payment is in cash only.

YWCA   HOSTEL $
(Map p58; ☑0713 622707; Maktaba St; dm/s without bathroom Tsh10,000/15,000, d Tsh30,000) Located on a small side street between the post office and the Anglican church. Very basic rooms with concrete floors have fans, sinks and clean shared bathrooms. Rooms around the inner courtyard are quieter. Men and women are accepted, and the restaurant serves inexpensive local-style meals.

YMCA   HOSTEL $
(Map p58; ☑0755 066643, 022-213 5457; Upanga Rd; dm/s/d Tsh12,000/25,000/28,000) No-frills rooms in a small compound around the corner from the YWCA, and marginally quieter (though the step up in price from the YWCA isn't justified). There's a canteen with inexpensive meals. Men and women are accepted.

Holiday Inn   HOTEL $$
(Map p58; ☑0684 885250, 022-213 9250; www.holidayinn.co.tz; India & Maktaba Sts; r excl breakfast US$189-229, ste excl breakfast US$269; P✳@) Undoubtedly the most popular downtown hotel, the Holiday Inn offers spotless modern rooms, courteous service, a handsome buffet breakfast (US$13.50) and a rooftop restaurant. Add to all that a free daily shuttle service to/from Jangwani Sea Breeze Lodge for guests wanting a swim and helpful travel advice booking charter flights to Zanzibar and Pemba, and even helicopter pick-ups to the airport for the hard-pressed business traveller.

DON'T MISS

CULTURAL TOURISM IN DAR ES SALAAM

Afriroots (p204) runs a Sunday morning history walk ($50 per person) around the city centre and a 'behind-the-scenes' cycle tour ($40 per person) where you'll get to meet locals and hear their stories.

Investours (☑0684 504212; www.investours.org; adult/student US$75/50) ⌀ offers tours to Mwenge Woodcarvers' Market that give visitors the chance to meet locals, get a glimpse into their lives and invest in their business ideas.

Kigamboni Community Centre (☑0788 482684; www.kccdar.com; Kigamboni; ☉Mon-Sat) offers reasonably priced walking and cycling tours (Tsh36,000) plus a 'day-in-the-village' experience (Tsh70,000). Take the ferry to Kigamboni and get a *bajaji* (tuk-tuk) to the centre; it's opposite Kigamboni police station next to Kakala bar.

Southern Sun HOTEL $$$
(Map p58; ☑022-213 7575; www.tsogosunhotels.com; Garden Ave; r from US$211; P❄❂☎☀) With its Afro-Islamic decor, popular restaurant and professional service, the Southern Sun punches way above its weight. Rooms are furnished with plush, comfortable beds and all mod-cons, while the enormous buffet breakfast can be enjoyed on a terrace overlooking the Botanical Gardens. Come evening, the bar and Bazara restaurant fill up with businessmen, expats and locals who come to enjoy first-rate food and the pretty garden terrace.

Dar es Salaam Serena Hotel HOTEL $$$
(Mapp58;☑0732123333,022-2112416;www.serenahotels.com/serenadaressalaam; Ohio St; r from US$240; P❄❂☎☀) Although overshadowed in the luxury stakes by the Hyatt, the Serena has an unbeatable location in enormous gardens overlooking the golf course of the Gymkana Club. This makes the champagne Sunday brunch on the terrace a local ritual, and although rooms are a touch dated they offer all the bells and whistles you'd expect from a five-star hotel.

🛏 Msasani & Mikocheni

If you don't mind paying for taxis, or travelling the distance from the airport (about 20km), the hotels on Msasani Peninsula offer a break from the urban bustle. Mikocheni, which is off the peninsula en route to Bagamoyo, has a good hostel.

CEFA Hostel HOSTEL $
(☑022-278 0425, 022-278 0685; cefahostel@gmail.com; off Old Bagamoyo Rd, Mikocheni B; s/d/tr/q Tsh40,000/60,000/80,000/100,000; P@☎) Simple, clean, quiet rooms in a private guesthouse, with good meals available

(Tsh10,000). It's popular with volunteers, and often full. It's one block in from Old Bagamoyo Rd (the turn-off is three blocks north of Bima Rd, and about 2km north of Mikocheni B cemetery), and signposted.

★**Alexander's Hotel** BOUTIQUE HOTEL $$
(Map p54; ☑0754 343834; www.alexanders-tz.com; Mary Knoll Lane; r $185; ❄☎☀) With its Corbusier-style modernist lines, large rooftop terrace and shady setting, family-run Alexander's is a true boutique hotel. Instead of business blandness there are 17 stylish room with comfortable beds, plump pillows and bright *kikoi* throws and cushions, all of which front the curvaceous, kidney-shaped pool. Breakfast is served in the art- and book-filled dining room, while sundowners and lobster dinners are best taken on the roof terrace.

Sea Cliff Hotel HOTEL $$$
(Map p54; ☑022-552 9900, 0764 700600; www.hotelseacliff.com; Toure Dr; r in village US$180-240, in main bldg US$320-470; P❄@☎☀) Sea Cliff has an excellent setting overlooking the ocean at the northern tip of Msasani Peninsula. The hotel is a rather sprawling affair with 93 rooms spread between the main building and the less-appealing and viewless 'village' next door. There are extensive facilities including a fitness centre, a beauty salon, a casino and restaurants; however, the best feature is the large cliff-top garden and pool.

🛏 Ubungo

For travellers passing through the Ubungo bus station there's a handful of cheap accommodation (around Tsh25,000 to Tsh35,000) located just west of the bus station or in Ubungo village to the south. Taxis, located just outside the bus station, should cost no more than Tsh5000.

Rombo Green View Hotel · HOTEL $

(022-461042; www.rombogreenviewhotel.com; Shekilango Rd; r without bathroom US$20, s US$25, d US$30-40;) This big, boxy hotel offers well-priced rooms close to the bus station. Rooms are simply furnished with tiled floors, pine beds and rumpled pillows, but the linen is clean, the water hot and the restaurant and bar decent and lively. It's about 500m east of the bus station just off Morogoro Rd.

Eating

City Centre

Most restaurants in the city centre are closed on Sunday.

★ Chapan Bhog · INDIAN $

(Map p58; 0685 401417; Kisutu St; meals Tsh2000-10,000; 7am-10pm;) Chapan's Gujurati *dhoklas* (savory steamed chickpea cakes), south Indian dosas (fermented crepes) and thalis are a vegetarian nirvana in a sea of *nyama choma* (roasted meat). The all-vegetarian menu is extensive and the restaurant has a prime position on temple-lined Kisutu St.

Chef's Pride · TANZANIAN $

(Map p58; Chagga St; meals Tsh1500-6000; lunch & dinner, closed during Ramadan) This long-standing and popular local eatery serves roasted chicken, biriyani and coconut-crusted fish. In addition, the large menu features fast-food favourites such as pizza, Indian and vegetarian dishes, popular with hungry office workers.

Patel Brotherhood · INDIAN $

(Map p58; Patel Samaj, off Maktaba St; meals Tsh5000-7000; lunch & dinner;) This large compound is a favourite evening spot for local Indian families, with good-value Indian veg and non-veg meals (thali, chicken biryani and more). Service can be slow, but there's plenty of local atmosphere to soak up while you're waiting. It's a social club so an additional Tsh2000 per person entry fee is charged to non-members.

Al Basha · LEBANESE $$

(Map p58; 022-212 6888; Bridge St; meals Tsh8000-9500; breakfast, lunch & dinner) Dar es Salaam's best Lebanese restaurant serves a good selection of hot and cold meze dishes, shish kebabs and salads. No alcohol is served but there's a wide selection of fresh juices.

★ Oriental · PAN-ASIAN $$$

(Map p58; 0764 701234; Hyatt Regency, Kivukoni Front; meals US$30-50; lunch & dinner;) From the high sheen of the marble-tiled floors to the elegant Asian-inspired furnishings, gloved waiters and immaculate sushi bar, the Hyatt's gourmet Asian restaurant aims to seduce and impress. Fortunately with a Thai chef behind the counter, the expertly prepared sushi, bright papaya salads and intensely spiced curries and seafood live up to the opulent surroundings. Book in advance.

Msasani Peninsula

Village Supermarket · SUPERMARKET $

(Map p54; Seacliff Village, Toure Dr) Pricey but wide selection of Western foods and imported products.

SOMETHING DIFFERENT: FRIENDLY GECKO GUESTHOUSE

If you want to stay in Dar a couple of days and connect with an interesting project and people, consider checking into the **Friendly Gecko Guesthouse** (0759 941848; www.friendlygecko.com; Africana area; dm US$20, s/d US$45/60;), 20km north of the city centre off the New Bagamoyo Road.

The guesthouse has a mix of simple rooms in a large, private house with a garden and kitchen but it's the affiliated NGO help2kids (p207) that makes this a special place to stay. Firstly, because the house is always full of interesting volunteers and secondly because 100% of the profits go to support the help2kids orphanage and educational outreach programs in local nursery and primary schools.

It's possible to arrange volunteering opportunities plus a host of activities like market visits, PADI diving courses and day trips to Bagamoyo.

Central Dar es Salaam

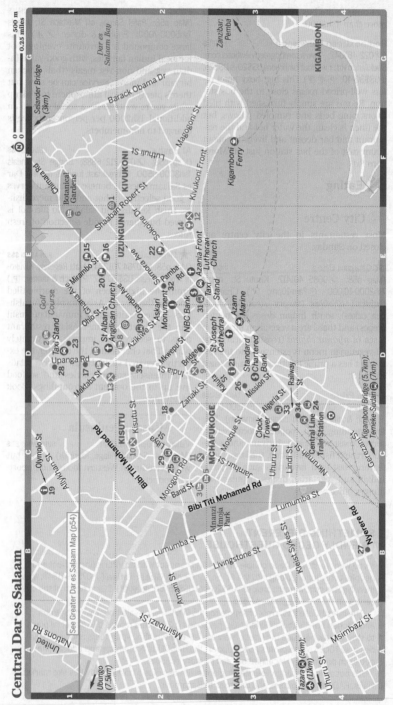

500 m
0.25 miles

See Greater Dar es Salaam Map (p54)

Central Dar es Salaam

Black Tomato   DELI **$**
(Map p54; ☑0787 866286; Oyster Bay Shopping Center, Toure Dr; ⊗8am-6pm; 🅿🖉) Located in the courtyard of the Oyster Bay Shopping Centre, this trendy deli serves salads, sandwiches, smoothies, burgers and brunches. You can count on freshness as the farmers market is also held here. For weekend brunches arrive early or you'll miss out on the sweet corn fritters with crispy bacon. Check out its Facebook page for live music and art exhibits.

Jackie's   TANZANIAN **$**
(Map p54; Haile Selassie Rd; snacks from Tsh1500; ⊗lunch & dinner) *Mishkaki* (marinated, grilled kebabs), plus *chipsi mayai* (omelette mixed with French fries) and other local staples, and a good mix of local and expat clientele in the evenings, when everyone stops by after work.

★ Addis in Dar   ETHIOPIAN **$$**
(Map p54; ☑0713 266299; www.addisindar.com; 35 Ursino St; meals Tsh10,000-20,000; ⊗dinner Mon-Sat; 🖉) Addis is decked out with embroidered umbrella lampshades, handcarved seats and woven tables where food is served communally. Go for one of the combination meals to sample a range of flavours. Everything is served on a large platter covered with *injera* (a sourdough flatbread made of fermented teff flour), which you tear off in pieces and use to scoop up the spicy curries.

Épi d'Or   CAFE **$$**
(Map p54; ☑0786 669889, 022-260 1663; cnr Chole & Haile Selassie Rds; meals Tsh8,000-12,000; ⊗8am-7pm Mon-Sat) This French-run bakery-cafe has a good selection of freshly baked breads, pastries, light lunches, paninis, banana crêpes and Middle Eastern dishes, plus good coffee.

Zuane Trattoria & Pizzeria   ITALIAN **$$**
(Map p54; ☑0766 679600, 022-260 0118; www.zuanetrattoriapizzeria.com; Mzingaway Rd; meals Tsh20,000-50,000; ⊗lunch & dinner Mon-Sat; 🅿♿) With its luxuriant garden setting, this Italian trattoria housed in an old colonial villa is one of Dar's most atmospheric dining options. The menu features classics such as wood-fired pizzas, *melanzana parmigiana* (an aubergine and parmesan layered bake), pastas, seafood and the ever-popular grilled fillet steak. There's also a children's playground in the garden. Book ahead; it's very popular.

DON'T MISS

DAR BY NIGHT
....

Dar has a richly textured music scene that remains largely off-limits to travellers due to a dearth of information on popular bands and current hot venues. Bypass the problem on one of Afriroots (p204) new Dar by Night tours ($50 per person) for an energising insight into some of the city's best foot-thumping, butt-shaking clubs, community centres and bars. The fee includes pick-up and drop-off at your hotel, entrance to clubs and an authentic barbecue dinner.

Drinking & Nightlife

Level 8 Bar   BAR
(Map p58; ☑0764 701234; 8th fl, Hyatt Regency, Kivukoni Front; ⊙5-11pm Sun-Thu, 5pm-1am Fri & Sat) The Hyatt's sexy rooftop bar has the best views over the harbour, lounge seating and live music some evenings.

Waterfront   BAR
(Map p54; ☑0762 883321; the Slipway, Msasani; ⊙noon-midnight) Sundowners with prime sunset views.

Shopping

Wonder Workshop   ARTS & CRAFTS
(Map p54; ☑0754 051417; www.wonderwelders. org; 1372 Karume Rd, Msasani; ⊙8am-6pm Mon-Fri, 10am-6pm Sat) ✐ At this excellent workshop, disabled artists create world-class jewellery, sculptures, candles, stationery and other crafts from old glass, metal, car parts and other recycled materials. There's a small shop on the grounds. Crafts can also be commissioned (and sent abroad), and you can watch the artists at work.

Mwenge Carvers' Market   ARTS & CRAFTS
(Sam Nujoma Rd; ⊙8am-6pm) This market, opposite the Village Museum, is packed with vendors, and you can watch carvers at work. Take the Mwenge dalla-dalla from New Posta transport stand to the end of the route, from where it's five minutes on foot down the small street to the left. The best way to visit Mwenge is with Investours (p56).

Slipway   ARTS & CRAFTS
(Map p54; www.slipway.net; Yacht Club Rd, Msasani; ⊙9.30am-6pm; 🛱) This waterfront shopping centre features upmarket boutiques such as **One Way** leisurewear and **Sandstorm** safa-

ri gear, as well as a traditional **craft market**, an ice-cream parlour and children's play area. A great place for unusual souvenirs is the **Green Room** (Map p54; www.thegreenroomtz.com), where high-quality giftware, home furnishings and artworks are all made from upcycled materials. Coastal Travels (p61) has a branch office here.

ℹ Information

DANGERS & ANNOYANCES

Dar es Salaam is safer than many other cities in the region, notably Nairobi, though it has its share of muggings and thefts, and the usual precautions must be taken. Watch out for pickpocketing, particularly at crowded markets and bus and train stations, and for bag snatching through vehicle windows. Stay aware of your surroundings, minimise carrying conspicuous bags or cameras and leave your valuables in a reliable hotel safe. At night, always take a taxi rather than taking a dalla-dalla or walking, and avoid walking alone along the path paralleling Barack Obama Drive (previously Ocean Rd), on Coco Beach (which is only safe on weekends, when it's packed with people), and at night along Chole Rd. With taxis, use only those from reliable hotels or established taxi stands. Avoid hailing taxis cruising the streets, and never get in a taxi that has a 'friend' of the driver or anyone else already in it.

IMMIGRATION OFFICE

Ministry of Home Affairs (☑022-285 0575/6; www.moha.go.tz; Uhamiaji House, Loliondo St; ⊙visa applications 8am-noon Mon-Fri, visa collections until 2pm) Just off Kilwa Rd, about 3.5km from the city centre.

INTERNET ACCESS

Post Office Internet Café (Map p58; Maktaba St; per hr Tsh1500; ⊙8am-7pm Mon-Fri, 9am-3pm Sat) Terminals inside the post office.

MEDICAL SERVICES

IST Clinic (Map p54; ☑022-260 1308, 022-260 1307, 24hr emergency 0754 783393; www. istclinic.com; Ruvu Rd, Msasani; ⊙8am-6pm Mon-Thu, 8am-5pm Fri, 9am-noon Sat) A fully equipped Western-run clinic, with a doctor on call 24 hours.

MONEY

Forex bureaus give faster service and marginally better exchange rates than the banks. There are many scattered around the city centre, particularly on or near Samora Ave where you can easily compare rates. All are open standard business hours.

There are ATMs all over the city, and in major shopping centres.

TOURIST INFORMATION

Tanzania Tourist Board Information Centre (Map p58; ☑ 022-212 8472; www.tanzaniatouristboard.com; Samora Ave; ☺ 8am-4pm Mon-Fri, 8.30am-12.30pm Sat) Free tourist maps and brochures, and limited city information.

TRAVEL AGENCIES

Coastal Travels (Map p58; ☑ 022-211 7959, 022-211 7960; www.coastal.co.tz; 107 Upanga Rd) Especially good for travel to Zanzibar, and for flights linking northern and southern safari circuit destinations (it has its own airline). Also offers reasonably priced city tours, day trips to Zanzibar and Mikumi National Park excursions. It has a branch at Slipway.

Kearsley Travel (Map p58; ☑ 022-213 7713, 022-213 7718; www.kearsleys.com; 16 Zanaki St) One of the oldest travel agencies in Dar. As well as the usual flight, car and hotel bookings it offers well-priced southern circuit safaris. Offices are at Southern Sun (p56) and Sea Cliff Village (Map p54; Toure Dr; ☺ 9.30am-5.30pm).

ⓘ Getting There & Away

AIR

Julius Nyerere International Airport has two terminals, with a third under construction. Most regularly scheduled domestic flights and all international flights depart from Terminal Two, while charters and light aircraft depart from Terminal One, about 700m further southwest. Useful local and regional airlines include the following:

Coastal Aviation (Map p58; ☑ reservations 022-284 2700; www.coastal.co.tz; Upanga Rd)

Fastjet (Map p58; ☑ 022-286 6130, 0767-007903, 0685-680533; www.fastjet.com; Samora Ave)

Kenya Airways (p208)

Precision Air (Map p58; ☑ 0787 888417, 022-216 8000; www.precisionairtz.com; cnr Samora Ave & Pamba Rd)

Tropical Air (☑ 0687 527511, call centre 024-223 2511; www.tropicalair.co.tz; Terminal One)

ZanAir (Map p58; ☑ 022-33768, 024-223 3670; www.zanair.com; Haidery Plaza, Kisutu St)

BOAT
Zanzibar

The only place at the port to buy legitimate tickets is the tall blue-glass building at the southern end of the ferry terminal on Kivukoni Front. The building is marked 'Azam Marine – Coastal Fast Ferries', and has ticket offices and a large waiting area inside. Avoid the smaller offices just to the north of this building.

Don't fall for touts at the harbour trying to collect extra fees for 'doctors' certificates', departure taxes and the like. The only fee is the ticket price (which includes the US$5 port tax). Also, avoid touts who want to take you into town to buy 'cheaper' ferry tickets, or who offer to purchase ferry tickets for you at resident rates.

Depending on season, the ferry crossing can be choppy, and most lines pass out sea sickness bags at the start of each trip. If you're travelling on the night ferry, it may be worth paying extra for the VIP section, although the fresh air is arguably better than the air-con of VIP.

In addition to Azam's catamarans there are several slow ferries, notably *Flying Horse*, which departs daily at 12.30pm (one way US$25) and takes almost four hours.

Azam Marine (Map p58; ☑ 022-212 3324; www.azammarine.com; Kivukoni Front; standard/VIP $35/40; ☺ departures 7am, 9.30am, 12.30pm, 3.45pm) Azam operates four fast catamarans daily between Dar and Zanzibar. All take about two hours, with a luggage allowance of 25kg per person. VIP tickets get you a seat in the air-con hold, but arrive early if you want to sit together.

On Wednesday and Saturday, the two morning services continue to Pemba (standard/VIP $70/80) after a 30 minute transit in Zanzibar.

BUS

Except as noted, all buses currently depart from and arrive at the main bus station at **Ubungo**, 8km west of the city centre on Morogoro Rd. However, with the planned imminent implementation of the new DART bus network, all upcountry transport will be switched to Mbezi (past Ubungo on the Morogoro Rd) and a new bus station will be built at Ubungo.

Keep an eye on your luggage and your wallet and try to avoid arriving at night. Ask your taxi driver to take you directly to the ticket office window for the line you want to travel with. Avoid dealing with touts.

Dalla-dallas to Ubungo (Tsh500) leave from New Posta and Old Posta transport stands. Taxis from the city centre cost from Tsh30,000. If you're coming into Dar es Salaam on **Dar Express** (Map p58; ☑ 0754 049395; Libya St, Kisutu; ☺ 6am-6pm) or **Kilimanjaro Express** (Map p58; ☑ 0755 233077; Libya St, Kisutu; ☺ 4.30am-7pm), you can usually stay on the bus to the town offices on Libya St. Outward bound buses, however, usually depart from Ubungo. Tickets are purchased at Ubungo, and, for Dar Express and Kilimanjaro, at their offices on Libya St. Only buy tickets inside the bus offices.

Following are some sample prices from Dar es Salaam. All routes are serviced at least once daily.

DESTINATION	PRICE (TSH)	DURATION (HR)
Arusha	30,000-35,000	9
Dodoma	25,000	7
Iringa	20,000-25,000	8
Kampala	90,000	24-29
Mbeya	40,000	12
Mwanza	45,000	15
Nairobi	65,000-70,000	14-18
Songea	40,000	12

Buses to Kilwa Masoko and Lindi depart from Mbagala Rangi Tatu and buses to Mtwara depart from Temeke (Sudan Market area); both are south of the city.

TRAIN

Tazara (p214) train station is 6km southwest of the city centre (Tsh10,000 to Tsh12,000 in a taxi). Dalla-dallas to the station leave from either New or Old Posta transport stands, and are marked Vigunguti, U/Ndege or Buguruni.

Tanzanian Railways Corporation (Map p58; ☑ 022-211 7833; cnr Railway & St Sokoine Dr) train station is just southwest of the ferry terminal.

❶ Getting Around

TO/FROM THE AIRPORT

Julius Nyerere International Airport is 12km from the city centre (taxi fares are Tsh30,000 to Tsh35,000, one to two hours in rush hour; Tsh35,000 to Tsh40,000 to Msasani Peninsula).

CAR & MOTORCYCLE

Most rental agencies offer self-drive options in town; none offer unlimited kilometres. Try **Avis** (Map p58; ☑ 0754 451111, 022-211 5381; www.avistanzania.com; Amani Place, Ohio St) or **Green Car Rentals** (Map p58; ☑ 0713 227788, 022-218 3718; www.greencarstz.com; Nyerere Rd).

PUBLIC TRANSPORT

Dalla-dallas (minibuses) currently go almost everywhere in the city for Tsh300 to Tsh600. They are invariably packed to overflowing, and are difficult to board with luggage. First and last stops are shown in the front window, but routes vary, so confirm that the driver is going to your destination.

Once the first phase of DART is completed, 2000 dalla-dallas will be assigned new routes as the hybrid buses take over. Other than the terminals at Ubungo and Kivukoni, new city-centre bus stops will be at Nyerere Sq, Kisutu and Jangwani. Prices are expected to be in the same range as dalla-dallas.

Current city-centre terminals include **New Posta** (Map p58; Maktaba St), **Old Posta** (Map p58; Sokoine Dr) and **Stesheni** (Map p58; Algeria St).

TAXI

Taxis don't have meters. Short rides within the city centre cost from Tsh4000. Fares from the city centre to Msasani Peninsula start at Tsh12,000.

Taxi stands include those opposite the Dar es Salaam Serena Hotel, at the corner of Azikiwe St and Sokoine Dr, and on Msasani Peninsula, at the corner of Msasani and Haile Selassie Rds.

For a reliable taxi driver for travels in and outside of Dar es Salaam and for airport pick-ups, contact the highly recommended **Jumanne Mastoka** (☑ 0784 339735; mjumanne@yahoo.com).

Never get into a taxi that has others in it, and always use taxis affiliated with hotels, or operating from a fixed stand and known by the other drivers at the stand.

AROUND DAR ES SALAAM

Northern Beaches

The jetty-studded beaches, resorts and water parks 25km north of Dar es Salaam are popular weekend getaways for families. Leave Dar early to avoid heavy traffic.

🕴 Activities

Kunduchi Wet 'n' Wild   WATERPARK
(☑ 0688 058365, 022-265 0050; www.wetnwild.co.tz; Kunduchi; weekday/weekend adult Tsh12,000/14,000, child 2-8yr Tsh10,000/12,000; ☻9am-6pm) This large complex next to the Kunduchi Beach Hotel has multiple pools, 30 waterslides, video arcades, a Jungle Gym and an adjoining go-kart track.

🛏 Sleeping & Eating

All hotels charge an entry fee for day visitors on weekends and holidays, averaging Tsh3000 to Tsh5000 per person.

Kunduchi Beach Hotel & Resort   HOTEL $$$
(☑ 0688 915345, 022-265 0050; www.kunduchi.com; Kunduchi Beach; s/d from US$165/190; ℙ❋🐕☲) This former government hotel is set on the best stretch of beach – a large expanse of clean white sand, with no jetties to mar the view – with a long row of attractive

beach-facing rooms and expansive land-scaped grounds. All the rooms have floor to ceiling windows with balconies, while the restaurant serves a popular Sunday buffet (adult/child Tsh25,000/18,000).

White Sands Hotel RESORT $$$
(☏ 0784 467150, 022-264 7620; www.hotelwhite sands.com; Jangwani Beach; s/d US$165/180, 1-/2-bedroom apt US$225/335; P✳@🛜🏊) A large 88-room resort with rooms in two-storey rondavels lined up along the water-front. All have TVs, minifridges and sea views. In addition, there are 28 self-catering apartments – some directly overlooking the beach, others just behind overlooking a well-tended lawn. There's also a gym and a business centre, and the restaurant does weekend buffets (per person Tsh25,000).

❶ Getting There & Away

White Sands Hotel is reached via a signposted turn-off from New Bagamoyo Rd. About 3km further north along New Bagamoyo Rd is the signposted turn-off for Kunduchi Beach.

Via public transport, take a dalla-dalla from New Posta transport stand in Dar es Salaam to Mwenge (Tsh400). Once at Mwenge, take a 'Tegeta' dalla-dalla to Africana Junction (Tsh200), and from there a *bajaji* (tuk-tuk; Tsh2000) or taxi (Tsh3000 to Tsh4000) the remaining couple of kilometres to the hotels. It's also possible to get a direct dalla-dalla from Kariakoo to Tegeta. For Kunduchi Beach, once at Mwenge, take a 'Bahari Beach' dalla-dalla to 'Njia Panda ya Silver Sands'. From here, it's Tsh500 on a motorcycle or *bajaji* the remaining distance. Don't walk, as there have been muggings along this stretch of road.

Taxis from Dar es Salaam cost about Tsh60,000 one way. All hotels arrange airport pick-ups.

Driving, the fastest route is along Old Bagamoyo Rd via Kawe.

Southern Beaches

The long, white stretch of sand south of Kigamboni (South Beach), around Mjimwema village, is the closest spot to Dar es Salaam for camping and chilling.

🏃 Activities

Dekeza Dhows SNORKELLING, KAYAKING
(☏ 0787 217040, 0754 276178; www.dekezadhows. com; Kipepeo Beach) Dekeza's daily dhow trips ($35 per person) depart from Kipepeo Beach to Sinda Island. Boats set off at 10am, trace the edge of nearby coral reefs for an hour or so of snorkelling before setting up lunch on a deserted beach. Fishing trips aboard the dhows are also possible ($220 for four people), as are sunset cruises ($18 per person).

🛏 Sleeping & Eating

Mikadi Beach BACKPACKERS $
(☏ 0758 782330; www.mikadibeach.com; camp-site per person US$8, d with/without bathroom US$46/30; P@🏊) This chilled place has a backpacker-friendly vibe, a convivial bar with a pool table and 16 thatched beach *bandas* on stilts. Two of them are ensuite (with fresh water provided in a drum), the rest share four showers and toilets. It gets busy with overland companies between mid-July and September.

Kipepeo Beach Village LODGE $$
(☏ 0754 276178; www.kipepeovillage.com; Kipepeo Village; campsite per person US$9.50, s/d/tr chalet US$65/85/115; P) Laid-back Kipepeo, located 8km south of the ferry dock, has 20 raised chalets with balconies situated just back from the beach. Closer to the water, but enclosed behind a fence and a bit of a walk to the nearest bathroom, are 15 thatched beach huts without windows, and a camping area. It's a sand-in-the-toes kind of place and has a very popular beachside restaurant-bar. Dekeza (p63) dhow tours depart from here.

❶ Getting There & Away

Take the **Kigamboni ferry** (Map p58; per person/vehicle Tsh200/2000) from Kivukoni Front. Once on the other side, catch a dalla-dalla heading south and ask the driver to drop you off at Mjimwema village (Tsh400), from where it's a 1km walk to Kipepeo. For Mikadi Beach, you can be dropped directly at the entrance. *Bajajis* from Kigamboni charge about Tsh4000 to Kipepeo, less to Mikadi Beach.

ZANZIBAR

Zanzibar's allure is legendary. One of East Africa's great trading centres, it has for centuries been a crossroads of culture where Africa, India and Arabia meet. It's a complete change of pace from the mainland, a place where life's rhythms are set by monsoon winds and the cycles of the moon.

Zanzibar's attractions are exotic Stone Town and the spectacular sea, edged by fine, white-sand beaches. The island offers a wide choice of hotels and restaurants and many places to explore: from Stone Town,

Zanzibar Archipelago

with its balconied merchants' houses and grand Beit el-Ajaib (House of Wonders), to dense, moist Jozani Forest and tiny Chumbe island, with its pristine coral garden. Rural villages snake up the coastline, including community-minded Jambiani; the surf-and-party hub of Paje; and traditional Matemwe, with its seaweed harvesters. At Zanzibar's northern tip are the tourist hubs of Nungwi and Kendwa, with their beaches, bars and dance-til-dawn full moon parties. Here, you'll want to choose your spot carefully, as increasing development threatens to mar the area's ineluctable magic and overwhelm fragile community resources.

Stone Town & Ng'ambo (Zanzibar Town)

POP 594,000

Zanzibar Town on the western side of the island, is the heart of the archipelago, and the first stop for most travellers. Its best-known section by far is the old Stone Town (Mji Mkongwe), surrounded on three sides by the sea and bordered to the east by Creek Rd. Here, narrow alleyways wind past Arabic-style houses with their recessed inner courtyards and Indian-influenced buildings boasting ornate balconies and latticework. Bustling oriental bazaars alternate with lively street-side vending stalls. And, each twist and turn of the streets brings something new, be it a school full of children chanting verses from the Koran, a beautiful old mansion with overhanging verandas, a coffee vendor with his long-spouted pot fastened over coals, clacking cups to attract custom, or a group of women in *bui-bui* (black coverall worn by some Islamic women outside the home) sharing a joke and local gossip.

◉ Sights

It's easy to spend days wandering around and getting lost in Stone Town's jumble of alleyways although you can't get lost for long because, sooner or later, you'll end up on either the seafront or Creek Rd.

While the best part of Stone Town is simply letting it unfold before you, it's worth putting in an effort to see some of its major features.

Beit el-Ajaib (House of Wonders) MUSEUM
(Map p68; Mizingani Rd; adult/child US$4/1; ⊙9am-6pm) Built for ceremonial chutzpah by Sultan Barghash in 1883, the 'House of Wonders' rises in im   pressive tiers of slender steel pillars and balconies overlooking the Forodhani Gardens. It is the grandest structure in Zanzibar and in its heyday it sported fine marble floors, panelled walls and never-before-seen running water and

electricity. Now it houses the **National Museum of History & Culture** with exhibits on the dhow culture of the Indian Ocean and Swahili civilisation.

Beit el-Sahel   MUSEUM
(Palace Museum; Map p68; Mizingani Rd; adult/child US$4/1; ⊙9am-6pm) Occupying several blocks along the waterfront, the imposing Palace Museum is a reconstruction of the Sultan Seyyid Said's 19th-century palace home, which was destroyed by the British bombardment of 1896. It was renamed the People's Palace in 1964 when the last sultan, Jamshid, was overthrown. Remarkably, much of the royal paraphernalia – banqueting tables, portraits, thrones and water closets – have survived and now provide the human interest story in this museum dedicated to the Sultanate from 1828 to 1896.

Old Fort   HISTORIC BUILDING
(Map p68; ⊙9am-10pm) FREE The defining features of the waterfront are the ragstone ramparts of *Ngome Kongwe,* the Old Fort. It was the first defensive structure built by the Busaidi Omani Arabs when they seized the island from the Portuguese in 1698, and it did duty as a prison and place of execution until the British transformed it into a ladies tennis club in 1949. Nowadays, the open-air amphitheatre provides a dramatic screening venue for the International Film Festival, while restored rooms house offices for the Zanzibar Cultural Centre.

Forodhani Gardens   GARDENS
(Jamituri Gardens; Map p68) One of the best ways to ease into life on the island is to stop by these formal gardens, originally laid out in 1936 to commemorate the Silver Jubilee of Sultan Khalifa (r 1911–60). In the center of the grassy plaza is a domed podium where a brass band would play while the marooned ceremonial arch near the waterfront was built to welcome Princess Margaret on a state visit in 1956. Renovated in 2010 by the Aga Khan Trust for Culture, the gardens are now a social hub, with three waterfront cafes, shady benches and an evening food market.

St Joseph's Cathedral   CHURCH
(Map p68; Cathedral St) One of the first sights travellers see when arriving by ferry are the spires of the Roman Catholic cathedral, designed by French architect Berange, who built the cathedral in Marseilles. It was built by local French missionaries between 1893 and 1897 and still serves the local Catholic community of Zanzibaris, Goans and Europeans. It's only open for mass on Sunday.

Anglican Cathedral   CHURCH
(Map p68; off New Mkunazini Rd; admission incl slave chambers Tsh6000; ⊙8am-6pm Mon-Sat, noon-6pm Sun) Constructed in the 1870s by the Universities' Mission to Central Africa (UMCA), this was the first Anglican cathedral in East Africa. It was built on the site of the old **slave market**, the altar reputedly marking the spot of the whipping tree where slaves were lashed with a stinging branch. It's a moving sight, remembered by a white marble circle surrounded by red to symbolise the blood of the slaves.

ℹ️ PAPASI: STREET TOUTS

In Zanzibar Town you will undoubtedly come into contact with street touts. In Swahili they're known as *papasi* (street touts; literally ticks). They are not registered as guides with the Zanzibar Tourist Corporation (ZTC), although they may carry (false) identification cards, and while a few can be helpful, others can be aggressive and irritating.

If you decide to use the services of an unlicensed tout, tell them where you want to go or what you are looking for, and your price range. You shouldn't have to pay anything additional, as many hotels pay commission. If they tell you your hotel of choice no longer exists or is full, take it with a grain of salt, as it could well be that they just want to take you somewhere where they know they'll get a better commission.

Another strategy is to make your way out of the port arrivals area and head straight for a taxi. This will cost you more, and taxi drivers look for hotel commissions as well, but most are legitimate and once you are 'spoken for', hassles from touts usually diminish.

Most *papasi* are hoping that your stay on the island will mean ongoing work for them as your guide. If you're not interested in this, explain (politely) once you've arrived at your hotel. If you want a guide to show you around Stone Town, it's better to arrange one with your hotel or a travel agency.

TANZANIA STONE TOWN & NG'AMBO (ZANZIBAR TOWN)

Zanzibar

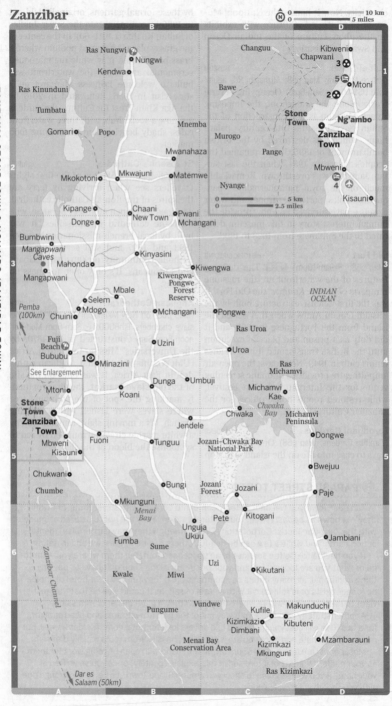

Zanzibar

◎ Sights
1 Kidichi Persian Baths A4
2 Maruhubi Palace D1
3 Mtoni Palace D1

⌂ Sleeping
4 Mbweni Ruins Hotel D2
5 Mtoni Marine Centre D1

⊗ Eating
Mtoni Marine ....(see 5)

Slave Chambers   HISTORIC SITE
(Map p68; off New Mkunazini Rd; admission incl Anglican cathedral Tsh6000; ☺8am-6pm Mon-Sat, noon-6pm Sun) Although nothing of the old slave market remains, some 15 holding cells are located beneath the Anglican Cathedral and St Monica's Hostel. Two of them, beneath St Monica's, are open to the public and offer a sobering glimpse of the appalling realities of the trade. Dank, dark and cramped, each chamber housed up to 65 slaves awaiting sale. Tiny windows cast weak shafts of sunlight into the gloom and it's hard to breathe even when they're empty.

Old Dispensary   HISTORIC BUILDING
(Map p68; Mizingani Rd) With its peppermint-green latticework balconies and sculpted clock tower, the most attractive landmark on the waterfront is this late-19th-century charitable dispensary. It was built by Tharia Topan, a prominent Ismaili Indian merchant who also acted as financial adviser to the sultan and banker to Tippu Tip, Zanzibar's most notorious slave trader. You're free to wander through the interior, which now accommodates offices.

Darajani Market   MARKET
(Map p68; Creek Rd; ☺predawn–mid-afternoon) One of the most compelling sights is the main market. Here mountains of spices, sneakers and sandals, meat, fish, live chickens and mobile phones are for sale in a series of covered halls and twisting alleys. The main hall, **Estella market**, reeks of caged birds, while Kanga St billows with vegetal prints, and wood and fish are auctioned in loud voices in their respective areas. It's hot, heaving and entertaining.

Come in the morning before the heat and the crowds, and dress appropriately. Tourists wandering around in skimpy clothes while locals try to shop is considered the height of rudeness.

Hamamni Persian Baths   HISTORIC BUILDING
(Map p68; Hamamni St; admission Tsh1500) Built by Sultan Barghash in the late 19th century, these were the first public baths on Zanzibar. Although there's no longer water inside, it doesn't take much imagination to envision them in bygone days. Ask the caretaker across the alley to unlock the gate.

Maruhubi Palace   RUINS
(Map p66) This once-imposing palace, 4km north of Zanzibar Town, was built by Sultan Barghash in 1882 to house his large harem. In 1899 it was almost totally destroyed by fire, although the remaining ruins (primarily columns that once supported an upper terrace, an overhead aqueduct and small reservoirs covered with water lilies) hint at its previous scale. The ruins are just west of the Bububu road and are signposted.

Mtoni Palace   RUINS
(Map p66) Built for Sultan Seyyid Said in 1828, Mtoni is the oldest palace on Zanzibar. It was home to sultan's only legitimate wife, many secondary wives and hundreds of children. Located overlooking the sea, the palace was a beautiful building with a balconied exterior, a large garden courtyard complete with peacocks and gazelles, an observation turret and a mosque. Now only an artful ruin remains with grand, roofless halls and arabesque arches framing glimpses of tropical foliage and an azure sea.

Kidichi Persian Baths   HISTORIC SITE
(Map p66) These baths, 11km northeast of Zanzibar Town, are another construction of Sultan Seyyid Said, built in 1850 for his Persian wife, Scheherezade. It's located among the island's spice plantations, and the royal pair would come here after hunting to refresh themselves in the stylised stucco interiors, which sport typical Persian motifs of birds and flowers. Although poorly maintained you can still make out much of the carving and see the bathing pool and massage tables.

🏃 Activities

One Ocean   DIVING

(Map p68; ✆024-223 8374; www.zanzibaroneocean.com; off Shangani St) This five-star PADI centre has more than a decade of experience on Zanzibar. In addition to its main office in Stone Town, it has branches at a number of locations along the east coast. It organises dives all around the island, for divers of all levels.

Stone Town

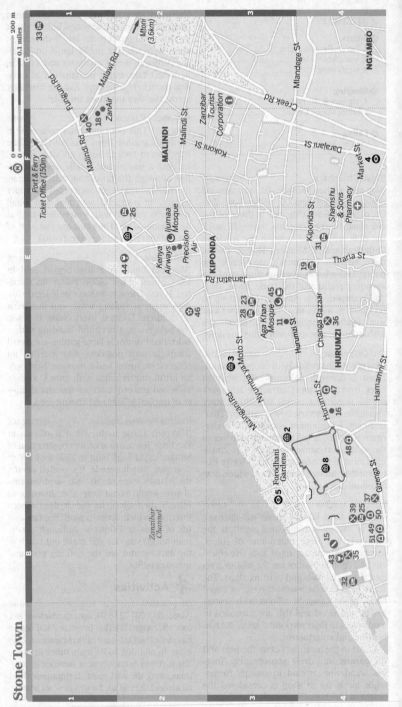

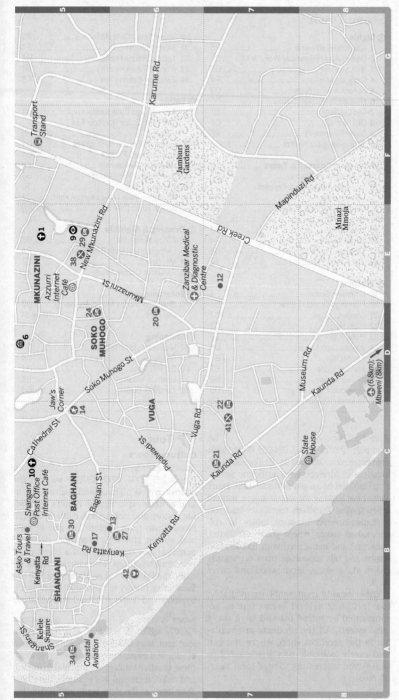

Stone Town

Mrembo Spa   SPA

(Map p68; ☏0777 430117, 024-223 0004; www.
mrembospa.com; Cathedral St; ⊙10am-6pm) 🌸
Imaginative Mrembo is an authentic Swahili
spa housed in an old antique shop. Don't
come here looking for sterile suites, instead
softly spoken Zanzibari therapists lead you
to kanga-covered massage tables in colourwashed
rooms where you're exfoliated,
massaged and manicured with handcrafted
scrubs and oils concocted from organically
grown ylang ylang, sandalwood and sweet
basil.

Other beauty treatments are available,
too, including natural henna tattoos accompanied
by spiced tea and *kachata* (a
local sweet). All the products are available
in the excellent shop, where you can
find rarely available handmade *udi* (incense)
and interesting CDs of local *taarab*
music.

☞ Tours

Cultural Tours

Zanzibar Different   CULTURAL TOUR

(☏024-223 0004, 0777 430117; www.zanzibar
different.com; ♿) Thoughtful, culturally engaging
tours exploring the island's fascinating
history and rich artisan culture. Unique
Stone Town tours explore the role of men
and women, children's education, rituals of
marriage and mourning and a plethora of
handcraft traditions. Tours further afield include
the Princess Salme Tour, retracing the
fascinating history of this Zanzibari princess
by dhow and flower-fringed donkey chariot.

Kawa Tours   CULTURAL TOUR

(☏0777 488311, 0779 065511; www.zanzibarkawa
tours.com; tours US$15-60; ♿) Aimed at benefiting
and engaging Stone Town residents,
these creative tours cover unusual historical
and cultural ground. For example, the Ghost
Tour looks at the slave trade and revolution

through houses and locations believed to be haunted; the Kids Tour engages children in research and allows them to interact with local games; and the Cooking Workshop takes you shopping in the market and into the kitchen of a home cook for a lesson in regional dishes and local spices.

Eco + Culture Tours CULTURAL TOUR
(Map p68; ☑024-223 3731, 0755 873066; www.ecoculture-zanzibar.org; Hurumzi St) 🏐 Excursions to Unguja Ukuu, Jambiani village and Stone Town, plus spice tours, all with a focus on environmental and cultural conservation. Guides speak English, French, Spanish, Italian and German. The Unguja Ukuu boat trip (US$80 per person for two people, US$45 per person for five people) is one of the best on offer. Focusing on small groups it heads out of this unspoilt village

in a traditional dhow to the uninhabited islands of Miwi, Nianembe or Kwale.

Mr Mitu's Office CULTURAL TOUR
(☑024-223 4636; off Malawi Rd; US$12 per person) The cheapest spice tours on offer are these half-day group tours of 15 people. They depart at 9.30am and return by about 2.30pm. Book a day in advance in high season. The office is signposted just in from Ciné Afrique.

Guided Tours
Zanzibar's tour operators can help with island excursions, as well as plane and ferry tickets. Only make bookings and payments inside the offices, and not with anyone outside claiming to be staff.

Gallery Tours & Safaris TOUR
(☑024-223 2088; www.gallerytours.net) Top-of-the-line tours and excursions; it can also

DIVING

Tanzania's waters offers an array of hard and soft corals and a diverse collection of sea creatures, including manta rays, hawksbill and green turtles, barracudas and sharks. Other draws include the possibility for wall dives, especially off Pemba and the opportunity to combine wildlife safaris with underwater exploration. On the down side, visibility isn't reliable, and prices are considerably higher than in places such as the Red Sea or Thailand. Also be aware that you'll need to travel, often for up to an hour, to many of the dive sites.

Planning

Diving is possible year-round, although conditions vary dramatically. Late March until mid-June is generally the least favourable time because of erratic weather patterns and frequent storms. July or August to February or March tends to be the best time overall.

Water temperatures range from lows of about 22°C in July and August to highs of about 29°C in February and March, with the average about 26°C. Throughout, 3mm wetsuits are standard; 4mm suits are recommended for some areas during the July to September winter months, and 2mm are fine from around December to March or April.

Costs & Courses

Costs are fairly uniform, with Pemba and Mafia island slightly pricier than elsewhere along the coast. Expect to pay up to US$500 for a four-day PADI open water course and from US$55 to US$85 for a single dive (with better prices available for multi-dive packages). Discounts average about 10% if you have your own equipment, and for groups.

Where to Dive

Zanzibar is known for the corals and shipwrecks offshore from Stone Town, and for fairly reliable visibility, high fish diversity, and the chance to see pelagics to the north and northeast. There are many easily accessed sites for beginning and mid-level divers.

Unlike Zanzibar, which is a continental island, Pemba is an oceanic island located in a deep channel with a steeply dropping shelf. Diving here tends to be more challenging, with an emphasis on wall and drift dives, though there are some sheltered areas for beginners, especially around Misali island. Most dives are to the west around Misali, and to the north around the Njao Gap.

Mafia offers divers fine corals, good fish variety, including pelagics, and uncrowded diving, often done from motorised dhows.

arrange Zanzibar weddings, honeymoon itineraries and dhow cruises.

Grassroots Traveller CULTURAL TOUR

(✆0772 821725; www.grassroots-traveller.com) ✆Working closely with community-based projects, NGOs and organisations striving for sustainable development, this forward-thinking company helps travellers craft interesting itineraries blending adventure with community engagement to discover that there's more to Zanzibar than sun, sand and sea. It also helps volunteers hook-up successful short- and long-term projects.

Madeira Tours & Safaris TOUR

(Map p68; ✆024-223 0406, 0777 415997; www.zanzibarmadeira.com; Baghani St) A large outfit offering tours, cruises, car hire and deep-sea fishing in all price ranges.

Sama Tours TOUR

(Map p68; ✆024-223 3543; www.samatours.com; Hurumzi St) Reliable and reasonably priced boat trips and spice tours. Multilingual staff are extremely helpful.

Tropical Tours TOUR

(Map p68; ✆0777 413454; Kenyatta Rd) Reliable, budget tour operator. You'll find up-to-the-minute deals on its Facebook page.

Zan Tours TOUR

(Map p68; ✆024-223 3042, 024-223 3116; www.zantours.com; Migombani St) The largest tour operator in Zanzibar, this professional outfit offers upmarket tours to Zanzibar, Pemba and beyond. It's affiliated with ZanAir, which facilitates easy transfers.

✮✮ Festivals & Events

Eid al-Fitr, marking the end of Ramadan, is a particularly fascinating time to be in Stone Town, with lanterns lighting the narrow passageways, families dressed in their best and a generally festive atmosphere. Many restaurants close during Ramadan.

The festival of **Mwaka Kogwa**, celebrating the Shirazi New Year (usually in July), is at its best in Makunduchi.

Sauti za Busara CULTURAL

(Voices of Wisdom; www.busaramusic.com; festival pass nonresident US$80-120; ⊘ Feb) Showcasing some of the hottest musical talent in Africa, this three-day festival fills the Old Fort and venues across the island with the best *taarab*, jazz, Afro-pop and Bongo Flava.

Zanzibar International Film Festival CULTURAL

(Festival of the Dhow Countries; www.ziff.or.tz; ⊘Jul) Zanzibar's film festival celebrates and nurtures arts from Indian Ocean countries as diverse as India, Iran, Madagascar and the Horn of Africa. For 16 days in July venues around Stone Town host screenings, performing-arts groups, media-related workshops and musical masterclasses.

🛏 Sleeping

🛏 Stone Town

★ Jambo Guest House GUESTHOUSE $

(Map p68; ✆024-223 3779; info@jamboguest.com; off Mkunazini St; s/d/tr without bathroom US$25/40/60; ❄@) Probably the best budget accommodation in town and extremely popular with backpackers, Jambo runs as smooth as clockwork. Nine spick-and-span rooms with Zanzibari beds share four bathrooms, there's complimentary tea and coffee, and the atmospheric Green Garden Restaurant provides for an easy dinner opposite.

Garden Lodge GUESTHOUSE $

(Map p68; ✆024-223 3298; gardenlodge@zanlink.com; Kaunda Rd, Vuga; s/d/tr US$40/60/70) This efficient, friendly, family-run place offers 18 rooms (two with air-con) in a characterful Swahili house fringed with balconies and decorated with stained-glass windows. Rooms are good value, especially the upstairs ones, which are bright and spacious, and all have hot water, ceiling fans and Zanzibari beds. There's a rooftop breakfast terrace, but otherwise no food.

Hotel Kiponda HOTEL $

(Map p68; ✆024-223 3052; www.kiponda.com; Nyumba ya Moto St, Kiponda; s/d/tr from US$30/50/65; 🛜) A popular, quiet budget place with the feel of the seaside in its whitewashed rooms with blue trim. Ensuite rooms are spread out over several floors, with the more newly renovated ones on upper levels. The breakfast terrace with its open arches and through breeze is a great place to chill out and use the wi-fi. The hotel has close links with Sama Tours, which offers a good range of excursions.

St Monica's Hostel HOSTEL $

(Map p68; ✆024-223 0773; www.stmonicahostelzanzibar.s5.com; New Mkunazini Rd; s/d US$40/50, s/d/tr without bathroom US$25/35/50)

Built in the late 19th century to accommodate nuns and teachers for UMCA mission, this rambling place next to the Anglican Cathedral has small rooms crowded with beds and friendly staff. All rooms have fans and nets. The restaurant is run by the parish Mother's Union and serves Swahili cuisine (no alcohol).

Flamingo Guest House   GUESTHOUSE $
(Map p68; ✆024-223 2850; http://flamingoguesthouseznz.com; Mkunazini St; s/d US$17/34, without bathroom US$14/28) The total lack of decor and stark concrete atrium may put some people off, but the Flamingo offers fine, no-frills accommodation at rock-bottom prices. All rooms have fans and mosquito nets and there's a rooftop sitting/breakfast area.

Karibu Inn   HOTEL $
(Map p68; ✆0777 417392, 024-223 3058; karibuinnhotel@yahoo.com; Shangani; dm US$20, s/d/tr US$35/50/75; ✳) The Karibu's complete lack of atmosphere and aggressive 'rules' signposted everywhere are compensated for by a very convenient location in the heart of Shangani. Accommodation is in dorms of five to eight beds or basic rooms with soft beds and private bathroom (rooms upstairs are brighter and better ventilated). Towels, linen and hot water all have to be requested at reception. Breakfast is minimal and served in a gloomy hall downstairs.

★ **Hiliki House**   GUESTHOUSE $$
(Map p68; ✆0777 410131; www.hikikihouse-zanzibar.com; Victoria St, Vuga; d with/without bathroom US$80/60; ✳ 🐾) Shhh, don't tell anyone but the six rooms at Hiliki are probably the best-value accommodation in town. From the minute you step inside to be greeted by gentle Aboud to the quiet, elegant rooms furnished with authentic Zanzibari pieces and the wonderful breakfast spread of fruit, pancakes, eggs and honey, you'll feel comfortable and cared for. Also at your disposal are the expansive 1st-floor lounge with views over Victoria Gardens, books and an honesty bar.

Kholle House   BOUTIQUE HOTEL $$
(Map p68; ✆0772 161033; www.khollehouse.com; off Malindi Rd; s US$105-150, d US$130-170; ✳ 🐾 ⊠) This mini palace was built in 1860 to showcase the finest collectibles of Princess Kholle, society tastemaker and favoured daughter of Sultan Said. Now after three years of meticulous renovation it offers 10 rooms with bright tumeric-stained walls,

gleaming nutmeg-coloured floors and a mix of Zanzibari and art deco furniture. The small garden with its delightful plunge pool is a rare luxury in Stone Town and there are views over the port from the rooftop gazebo.

Swahili House   HOTEL $$
(Map p68; ✆0777 510209; www.moivaro.com; Mchambawima St, Kiponda; s/d US$141/156; ✳ @) This grand Indian merchant's home is over a century old and once accommodated members of the Sultan's family. Restored to its original state it offers 22 vast rooms (some with open bathrooms) furnished Swahili-style with handcrafted furniture, Zanzibari beds and colourful cushions and throws. The 5th-floor terrace, one of the highest in Stone Town, offers stunning views, a jacuzzi plunge pool and an excellent bar and restaurant.

Tembo House Hotel   HOTEL $$
(Map p68; ✆0779 413348, 024-223 3005; www.tembohotel.com; Shangani St; s/d/tr from US$110/130/170; ✳ @ 🐾 ⊠) This attractively restored building has a prime waterfront location, including a small patch of beach (but no swimming) and 44 comfortable, excellent-value rooms – some with sea views – in new and old wings. There's a small pool, a restaurant (no alcohol) and a great buffet breakfast on the seaside terrace. Unsurprisingly, it's enormously popular, especially with families.

Stone Town Café B&B   B&B $$
(Map p68; ✆0778 373737; www.stonetowncafe.com; Kenyatta Rd, Shangani; s US$70, d US$80-90; ✳ @) Simple, unpretentious and uncluttered the Stone Town Café has five rooms with Zanzibari beds dressed in pristine white linens. Black-and-white photos, decorative chests and rugs lend atmosphere, while breakfast smoothies, coffee and avocado toast are served downstairs on the palm-shaded patio.

Warere Town House   HOTEL $$
(Map p68; ✆0782 234564; www.warere.com; off Funguni Rd, Malindi; s US$35-55, d US$55-70; ✳ 🐾) A well-run budget hotel with front-room balconies overlooking a flowering garden. Ten rooms come with Zanzibari beds dressed with kanga-lined mosquito nets, blue stucco trim and palm-woven furniture. Laundry and good wi-fi are available and the reception will organise taxis to the beach and local excursions. It's just a few minutes' walk from the port (staff will meet you there).

FORODHANI GARDENS FOOD FEAST

Every evening, starting at about 5pm, Forodhani Gardens is transformed into a large outdoor dining room. Vendors set up food stalls beneath the banyan trees and locals come out to enjoy the sunset and nibble on island delicacies, including skewers of *mishkaki* (marinated, grilled kebabs), Zanzibari pizzas and roti stuffed with minced meat. Locals advise against eating the seafood (freshness is questionable especially in the dim lighting). While most prices are reasonable, with some vendors you'll need to bargain.

★ **Kisiwa House**   BOUTIQUE HOTEL $$$
(Map p68; ☑024-223 5654; www.kisiwahouse.com; 572 Baghani St, Baghani; r US$180-240; ❉ 🛜) The lovely Kisiwa House has nine spacious rooms and an excellent rooftop restaurant with sea views. Reached via a grand, steep staircase, all rooms have king-size Zanzibari beds, Persian rugs and dark beamed ceilings. A mix of minimalist ethnic and European decor and grand proportions gives the house an understated glamour, making it popular as a honeymoon destination. It's just off Kenyatta Rd.

★ **Emerson Spice**   BOUTIQUE HOTEL $$$
(Map p68; ☑0775 046395, 024-223 2776; www.emersonspice.com; Tharia St; r $175-250; ❉ 🛜) With its stained-glass windows, wooden latticework balustrades, tinkling fountains and romantic, soft-hued colour scheme, Emerson Spice is the most atmospheric hotel in Stone Town. Its intimate collection of 11 rooms are carved creatively out of a 19th-century palace and filled with antiques, rich textiles and deep baths. It's hosted celebrities and made the 2012 Conde Nast hotlist, and the set-course dinner on its lattice-framed terrace is deeply memorable.

Zanzibar Serena Inn   HOTEL $$$
(Map p68; ☑024-223 2306, 024-223 3587; www.serenahotels.com; Kelele Sq, Shangani; r US$380-500; ❉ @ 🛜 ≋) Stone Town's most upmarket hotel, with a beautiful setting on the water, plush rooms with all the amenities, and a business centre. It's an undeniably wonderful spot, with a waterfront pool, an English bar and white-suited waiters serving afternoon tea. Still, with the massive, new Park

Hyatt nearly next door it remains to be seen whether it can keep up.

Seyyidda Hotel & Spa   BOUTIQUE HOTEL $$$
(Map p68; ☑024-223 8352; www.theseyyida-zanzibar.com; off Nyumba Ya Moto St; r US$170-290; ❉ @ 🛜) Lighter, brighter and different in style to many Stone Town hotels, the Seyyida is arranged around a verdant courtyard hung with island art. Rooms are modern and styled in neutral tones, and all have satellite TV, and some have sea views and balconies. There's also a rooftop terrace restaurant and a spa.

Outside Stone Town

Mtoni Marine Centre   LODGE $$
(Map p66; ☑024-225 0140, 0774 486214; www.mtoni.com; Bububu Rd; s US$70-135, d US$85-180, apt $175-240; P ❉ @ 🛜 ≋) This long-standing family-friendly establishment offers spacious, well-appointed 'club rooms', family apartments and more luxurious 'palm court' sea-view rooms with private balconies. There's a small beach, large gardens, a fantastic 25m infinity pool and a popular waterside bar and restaurant. A branch of Mrembo Spa (p70) is located here, and the lodge arranges a host of activities. One of the best events is the candlelit Swahili dinner held in the ruins of Mtoni Palace (p67) every Tuesday and Friday evening.

★ **Mbweni Ruins Hotel**   LODGE $$
(Map p66; ☑024-223 5478; www.proteahotels.com/mbweniruins; Mbweni; s/d US$125/180, ste US$180-250; P ❉ @ 🛜 ≋) Originally the site of the UMCA mission school for the children of freed slaves, Mbweni Ruins is a tranquil establishment set in lovely, expansive botanical gardens. In addition to well-appointed rooms and a private beach, it has a very good restaurant and a bar with an unimpeded view over stands of mangroves – ideal for bird-spotting.

✖ Eating

During the low season and Ramadan, many restaurants close or operate reduced hours.

Stone Town

★ **Luukman Restaurant**   ZANZIBARI $
(Map p68; New Mkunazini Rd; meals Tsh1500-5000; ⊙7am-9pm) Probably the best local restaurant for quality Zanzibari food. There's no menu, just make your way inside to the 1950s counter and see what's on

offer. Servings are enormous and include various biryanis, fried fish, coconut curries and freshly made naan. Occasionally it also serves Zanzibari sweets like *maandazi* (a deep-fried, golden-brown doughnut slightly sweetened and spiced with cardamom).

Luis Yoghurt Parlour INDIAN $
(Map p68; ☑ 0765 759579; 156 Gizenga St; meals Tsh10,000-12,000; ⊙ 10am-3pm & 6-9pm Mon-Sat; 🖋) Reserve ahead for a platter of tasty curried pulses with chickpeas or coconut crab curry. Madam Blanche Luis cooks all the Goan specialties herself, offering them up with freshly made naan and creamy lassies (yoghurt drink), fruit smoothies or spiced tea. The restaurant is opposite the Friday mosque.

Passing Show ZANZIBARI $
(Map p68; Malawi Rd; meals Tsh2500-5000; ⊙ 7am-9pm) Mingle with the locals and enjoy inexpensive pilaus, goat and fish biryani, stewed vegetables and an assortment of deep-fried snacks. To accompany it order a glass of fresh, sweet tamarind juice. If you want to nab a spot on the small shaded patio, come early or late to miss the lunch crowd.

New Radha Food House VEGETARIAN $
(Map p68; ☑ 024-223 4808; thalis Tsh10,000; ⊙ 8am-9.30pm; 🖋) This great little place is tucked away on the small side street just before the Shangani tunnel. The strictly vegetarian menu features thalis, lassis, homemade yoghurt and other dishes from the subcontinent.

Stone Town Café CAFE $
(Map p68; Kenyatta Rd; meals Tsh8000-15,000; ⊙ 8am-6pm Mon-Sat) All-day breakfasts, milkshakes, freshly baked cakes, veggie wraps and good coffee.

Archipelago Café-Restaurant CAFE $$
(Map p68; ☑ 024-223 5668; Shangani St; meals Tsh12,000-18,000; ⊙ 8am-10pm; 🖋) An excellent local restaurant with a fine location on a terrace overlooking the sea and a dhow repair yard below. The well-priced menu features coconut curries, orange and ginger snapper, and chicken pilau, topped off by an array of homemade cakes and sweets. There's no bar, but the smoothies are good and you can bring your own alcohol.

House of Spices Restaurant ITALIAN $$
(Map p68; ☑ 024-223 1264; www.houseofspices zanzibar.com; Hurumzi St; meals Tsh12,000-15,000; ⊙ lunch & dinner Mon-Sat) Laid out on a lantern-lit terrace, this Mediterranean restaurant is known for its well-executed seafood dishes and wood-fired pizzas. The seafood platter of grilled lobster, prawns and calamari comes with a choice of five spiced sauces, and there's a good wine list for pairings.

Sambusa Two Tables Restaurant ZANZIBARI $$
(Map p68; ☑ 024-223 1979; meals US$15; ⊙ by advance arrangement) For sampling authentic Zanzibari dishes, it's hard to beat this restaurant in a family house just off Kaunda Rd, where the proprietors bring out course after course of delicious local delicacies. Advance reservations (preferably the day before) are required; 15 guests can be accommodated.

★**Emerson Spice Rooftop Tea House** FUSION $$$
(Map p68; ☑ 024-223 2776; www.emersonspice. com; Tharia St; prix fixe dinner menu US$30; ⊙ 7-11pm Fri-Wed) Perched on top of a Swahili mansion in an intricately carved wooden gazebo, Emerson's Tea House screams 'date night'. Enjoy expertly made cocktails with 360-degree views over Stone Town. Mojitos are followed by multicourse dinners with an emphasis on seafood, spices and island fruit. Try the delicate passionfruit ceviche or the prawns with grilled mango, and refreshing sorbets of custard apple and a hint of saffron.

🍴 Outside Stone Town

Mtoni Marine EUROPEAN $$$
(Map p66; ☑ 024-225 0117; meals Tsh15,000-38,000; ⊙ lunch & dinner) Mtoni Marine's waterfront restaurant has a range of seafood and meat grills, and waterside barbecues several times weekly, sometimes with a backdrop of traditional music.

🍷 Drinking & Nightlife

Zanzibar Coffee House CAFE
(Map p68; ☑ 024-223 9319; snacks Tsh5000-12,000) East African coffee is some of the finest in the world, and the top spot in Zanzibar for a serious cup is this charming cafe. It's affiliated with Utengule Coffee Estate in Mbeya, from where much of the coffee is sourced, and coffee beans are available for sale. Besides coffee (and a range of smoothies and milkshakes), you can nibble on sweet and savory crepes, salads, sandwiches and toasted bruschetta topped with prawns, vegetables and seafood.

Livingstone Beach Restaurant BAR
(Map p68; ☑ 0779 701472; off Shangani St; meals Tsh17,000-32,000; ☺10am-2am) This worn but popular place in the old British Consulate building has seating directly on the beach – perfect for sundowners and lovely in the evening, with candlelight. While the restaurant chaotically serves some mediocre food, it's a wonderful place for a drink and hosts regular live music.

Mercury's PUB
(Map p68; ☑ 024-223 3076; Mizingani Rd; ☺9.30am-midnight) A very popular place for waterside sundowners watching local football matches on the beach. International football is also screened here and there's live music on Saturday evenings until 1am. Food is served and consists of crowd-pleasers such as pizza, pasta and seafood grills. During Ramadan opening hours are 6pm to midnight.

Africa House Hotel BAR
(Map p68; www.theafricahouse-zanzibar.com; Shangani St) With a front-row view of the sunset, the terrace bar of the Africa House Hotel – once the British Club – is a perennially popular place for sundowners.

☆ Entertainment

Dhow Countries Music Academy TAARAB
(Map p68; ☑ 0777 416529; www.zanzibarmusic. org; Old Customs House, Mizingani Rd; concerts Tsh10,000; ☺9am-6pm) Zanzibar's celebrated music genre, called *taarab*, is a form of mellifluously sung poetry. The tradition is kept alive by this dynamic academy, which trains next-generation masters and hosts weekly *taarab* concerts as well as a lively program of Afro-jazz and fusion bands. If you like what you hear you can always take a lesson. Concerts start at 7pm and CDs are on sale.

Old Fort DANCE
(Map p68; admission Tsh6000) On Tuesday, Thursday and Saturday evenings from 7pm to 10pm there are traditional *ngoma* (dance and drumming) performances at the Old Fort.

🔒 Shopping

Items to watch for include finely crafted Zanzibari chests, kanga (cotton wraps worn by women all over Tanzania), *kikoi* (the thicker striped or plaid equivalent worn by men on Zanzibar and in other coastal areas), spices and handcrafted silver jewellery.

A good place to start is Gizenga St, which is lined with small shops and craft dealers.

Upendo Means Love CLOTHING
(Map p68; ☑ 0772 744086; www.upendomeanslove. com; off Kenyatta Rd) This unique interfaith women's project aims to build bridges between Zanzibar's minority Christians and the largely Muslim population, through its multifaith sewing school and fashionable boutique. The result: stylish, pared-down ladies' and children's summerwear in funky kanga and *kikoi* fabrics, and cross-cultural friendships and economic independence. Resident Danish fashion students help keep the line fresh and full of on-trend ideas.

Sasik HANDICRAFTS
(Map p68; ☑ 0773 132100; Gizenga St) The bold appliqué cushions, coverlets and throws in Sasik are the work of self-taught Saada Abdullah Suleiman and a team of over 45 Zanzibari women. Their intricate vegetal designs in bright primary colours are influenced by typical Swahili and Arabian patterns, many of them originating in the carved doors around Stone Town. Buy off the shelf or order bespoke designs and colour schemes.

Surti & Sons ACCESSORIES
(Map p68; ☑ 0777 472742; http://surtiandsons. wordpress.com; Gizenga St) For over 30 years, Parvin Surti and his family have been shoeing Zanzibaris in beautiful, durable leather sandals (US$25 to US$35) in a range of understated styles in soft, natural colours. All the sandals are handstitched and made from good-quality leather, and great attention is shown to comfort and customer satisfaction. Belts and bags are also available.

Moto Handicrafts HANDICRAFTS
(Map p68; www.motozanzibar.worldpress.com; Hurumzi St) 🖉 This island-wide handicraft co-operative aims to support the island's rural economy by providing a platform for the sale of handcrafted *ukili* bags, sun hats, baskets, mats and other woven products. The cooperative itself is based in Pete, where it also has a small shop selling bright batik wraps in vegetable dyes.

Zanzibar Gallery SOUVENIRS
(Map p68; ☑ 024-223 2721; http://zanzibargallery. net; cnr Kenyatta Rd & Gizenga St; ☺9am-6.30pm Mon-Sat, to 1pm Sun) This long-standing gallery has a fine collection of souvenirs, textiles, woodcarvings, antiques and more.

ℹ Information

DANGERS & ANNOYANCES

While Zanzibar remains a relatively safe place, robberies, muggings and the like occur with some frequency, especially in Zanzibar Town and along the beaches.

Follow the normal precautions: avoid isolated areas, especially isolated stretches of beach, and keep your valuables hidden. At night in Zanzibar Town, take a taxi or walk in a group. Also avoid walking alone in Stone Town during predawn hours. As a rule, it's best to leave valuables in your hotel safe, preferably sealed or locked.

If you've rented a bicycle or motorcycle, be prepared for stops at checkpoints, where traffic police may demand a bribe. Assuming your papers are in order, the best tactic is respectful friendliness.

INTERNET ACCESS

Azzurri Internet Café (Map p68; New Mkunazini Rd; per hr Tsh1000; ⊙8.30am-8.30pm) Around the corner from the Anglican cathedral.

Shangani Post Office Internet Café (Map p68; Kenyatta Rd; per hr Tsh1000; ⊙8am-4.30pm Mon-Fri, 8am-12.30pm Sat) Also international telephone calls.

MEDICAL SERVICES

If you experience any serious ailments, accidents or emergencies, you should go straight to Dar es Salaam or Nairobi (Kenya) for treatment.

Shamshu & Sons Pharmacy (Map p68; ☑0715 411480, 024-223 2199; Market St; ⊙9am-8.30pm Mon-Thu & Sat, 9am-noon & 4-8.30pm Fri, 9am-1.30pm Sun) Convenient, reasonably well stocked pharmacy behind the Darajani Market.

Zanzibar Medical & Diagnostic Centre (Map p68; ☑0777 750040, 024-223 1071; off Vuga Rd; ⊙24hr emergency) The best private clinic on the island.

MONEY

There are several ATMs in Stone Town (though none elsewhere) mostly located on Kenyatta Rd, New Mkunazini Rd and Shangani St; all accept Visa and MasterCard. There are also numerous forex bureaus (most open until 8pm) where you can change cash. Rates for US dollars are better than those for British pounds and euros. Officially, accommodation on Zanzibar must be paid for in US dollars, and prices are quoted in dollars, but especially at the budget places it's rarely a problem to pay the equivalent in Tanzanian shillings.

TOURIST INFORMATION

Zanzibar Tourist Corporation (ZTC; Map p68; Creek Rd; ⊙8am-5pm) About 200m north of Darajani Market on the same side of the road, with tourist information and standard tours.

ℹ Getting There & Away

AIR

Coastal Aviation and ZanAir have daily flights connecting Zanzibar with Dar es Salaam (US$70), Arusha (US$265), Pemba (US$95), Selous Game Reserve and the northern parks. Coastal Aviation goes daily to/from Tanga via Pemba (US$120), and has good-value day excursion packages from Dar es Salaam to Stone Town. Tropical Air flies daily between Zanzibar and Dar es Salaam, and Precision Air has connections to Nairobi (Kenya).

Coastal Aviation (Map p68; ☑024-223 3489, airport 024-223 3112; www.coastal.cc) At the airport, with a booking agent next to Zanzibar Serena Inn.

Kenya Airways (Map p68; ☑024-223 4520/1; www.kenya-airways.com; Bububu Rd, Mlandege) Just north of town in the Muzamil Centre.

Precision Air (Map p68; ☑0786 300418, 024-223 5126; www.precisionairtz.com; Bububu Rd, Mlandege) Located in the Muzamil Centre, north of Zanzibar Town

ZanAir (Map p68; ☑024-223 3678, 024-223 3670; www.zanair.com; Migombani St) Located with affiliated ZanTours.

BOAT

You can get tickets at the port (the ticket office is just to the right when entering the main port gate), or through any of the listed travel agents. The departure and arrivals areas for the ferry are a few hundred metres down from the port gate along Mizingani Rd. If you leave Zanzibar on the night ferry, take care with your valuables, especially when the boat docks in Dar es Salaam.

Dhows link Zanzibar with Dar es Salaam, Tanga, Bagamoyo and Mombasa (Kenya), although foreigners are not permitted on dhows between Dar es Salaam and Zanzibar.

Azam Marine (☑Dar es Salaam 022-212 3324, Zanzibar 024-223 1655; www.azammarine.com) Operates the most reliable scheduled service between Dar es Salaam, Zanzibar and Pemba aboard a fleet of fast, modern catamarans. There are four daily services from Dar to Zanzibar (VIP/adult/child US$40/35/25) and two weekly services from Zanzibar to Pemba (VIP/adult/child US$40/35/25).

ℹ Getting Around

TO/FROM THE AIRPORT

The airport is about 7km southeast of Zanzibar Town. A taxi to/from the airport costs Tsh15,000. Dalla-dalla 505 also does this route (Tsh500, 30 minutes), departing from the corner opposite Mnazi Mmoja hospital. Many Stone Town hotels offer free airport pick-ups for confirmed bookings, though some charge. For hotels elsewhere on the island, transfers usually cost about US$25 to US$50, depending on the location.

CAR & MOTORCYCLE

It's easy to arrange car, moped or motorcycle rental and prices are reasonable, although breakdowns are fairly common, as are moped accidents. Considering how small the island is, it's often not that much more expensive to work out a good deal with a taxi driver.

You'll need either an International Driving Permit (IDP; together with your home driving licence), a licence from Kenya (Nairobi), Uganda or South Africa, or a Zanzibar driving permit; there are police checkpoints along the roads where you'll be asked to show one or the other. Zanzibar permits can be obtained on the spot from the **traffic police** (cnr Malawi & Creek Rds). If you rent through a tour company, they'll sort out the paperwork.

Daily rental rates average from about US$25 for a moped or motorcycle, and US$40 to US$55 for a Suzuki 4WD, excluding petrol. Full payment is required at the time of delivery, but don't pay any advance deposits.

Asko Tours & Travel (Map p68; ✆ 024-223 4715, 0777 411854; www.askotours.com; Kenyatta Rd) Offers reasonable rates for car hire.

DALLA-DALLAS

Open-sided dalla-dallas piled with people link all major towns on the island. For most destinations, including the beaches, there are several vehicles daily, with the last ones back to Stone Town departing by about 3pm or 4pm. None of the routes cost more than Tsh2000, and all take plenty of time (eg about one to 1½ hours from Zanzibar Town to Jambiani). All have destination signboards and numbers. Commonly used routes include the following:

ROUTE NO	DESTINATION
116	Nungwi
117	Kiwengwa
118	Matemwe
206	Chwaka
214	Uroa
308	Unguja Ukuu
309	Jambiani
310	Makunduchi
324	Bwejuu
326	Kizimkazi
501	Amani
502	Bububu
505	Airport ('U/Ndege')

PRIVATE MINIBUS

Private tourist minibuses run daily to the north- and east-coast beaches and are cheaper than hotel transfers and taxis, which routinely cost US$50. Book through any travel agency the day before you want to leave, and the minibus will pick you up at your hotel in Stone Town at 8am. Travel takes from one to 1½ hours to most destinations, and costs Tsh10,000 per person. Return buses depart Nungwi at 9.30am and Paje, Bwejuu and Jambiani at 10am.

TAXI

Taxis don't have meters, so you'll need to agree on a price with the driver before getting into the car. Town trips cost from Tsh3000, more at night.

Offshore Islands

Day trips and snorkelling excursions are possible to most of the offshore islands within view of Stone Town (approximately US$25 to US$30 for a half-day excursion with a licensed tour operator, including lunch). Boats depart every morning (weather permitting) from the beach by the Big Tree on Mizingani Rd and outside the Tembo House Hotel. If you choose to visit the islands with unlicensed operators who tout for business along the waterfront, bear in mind that safety equipment is likely to be inadequate and boats may be overloaded.

All the islands within reach of Stone Town also have lodges, although if you base yourself here, keep in mind that it's not possible to travel between Stone Town and the islands after dark, and factor in the costs of transport to/from Stone Town.

Islands further afield, such as Chumbe and Mnemba, are reached from Mbweni and Matemwe, respectively.

Changuu

Also known as Prison Island, Changuu lies about 5km and an easy boat ride northwest of Zanzibar Town. It was originally used to detain 'recalcitrant' slaves and later as a quarantine station. Changuu is also known for its large family of **giant tortoises**, who were brought here from Aldabra in the Seychelles around the turn of the 20th century. There's a small beach and a nearby reef with **snorkelling**, as well as the former house of the British governor, General Lloyd Matthews. There's accommodation at **Changuu Private Island Paradise** (✆ 0773 333241; www.privateislands-zanzibar.com; Changuu Island;

CHUMBE ISLAND CORAL PARK

The uninhabited island of Chumbe, about 12km south of Zanzibar Town, has an exceptional shallow-water coral reef along its western shore that abounds with fish life. Since 1994, when the reef was gazetted as Zanzibar's first marine sanctuary, the island has gained widespread acclaim, including from the UN, as the site of an impressive ecotourism initiative centred on an ecolodge and local environmental education programs. It's now run as **Chumbe Island Coral Park** (www.chumbeisland.com), a private, nonprofit nature reserve.

Chumbe can be visited as a day trip, although staying overnight in one of the eco-bungalows is recommended. Each bungalow has its own rainwater collection system and solar power, and a loft sleeping area that opens to the stars. Advance bookings are essential. Day visits (also by advance arrangement only) cost US$90 per person. Boats depart from Mbweni Ruins Hotel (p74) at 10am.

full board per person US$350; ☎). Day trips to visit the tortoises cost about US$30 per person including lunch and island entry fee, but excluding boat transfer costs from Stone Town (usually US$60 to US$70 per boat).

Bawi

Tiny Bawi, about 7km west of Zanzibar Town and several kilometres southwest of Changuu, offers a beach and **snorkelling**. For years marketed as a day out from Stone Town, it's now privately owned, and while snorkelling in the surrounding waters is possible, the island itself can only be visited by guests of **Bawe Tropical Island Lodge** (☏ 0773 333241; www.privateislands-zanzibar.com; Bawe Island; full board per person US$400; ☎).

Mnemba

Tiny Mnemba, just northeast of Matemwe, is the ultimate tropical paradise for those who have the money to enjoy it, complete with white sands, palm trees and turquoise waters. While the island itself is privately owned, with access restricted to guests of **Mnemba Island Lodge** (☏ 027-252 4199; www.andbeyond.com/mnemba-island/; Mnemba Island; full board per person US$1200-1600; ☺ mid-May–Mar), the surrounding coral reef can be visited by anyone. It's one of Zanzibar's prime **diving** and **snorkelling** sites.

Other Islets

Just offshore from Zanzibar Town are several tiny islets, many of which are ringed by coral reefs. These include **Nyange**, **Pange** and **Murogo**, which are sandbanks that partially disappear at high tide, and which offer snorkelling and diving (arranged through Stone Town dive operators).

Nungwi

This large village, nestled among the palm groves at Zanzibar's northernmost tip, is a dhow-building centre and one of the island's major tourist destinations.

Nungwi is also where traditional and modern knock against each other with full force. Fishers sit in the shade repairing their nets while the morning's catch dries on neat wooden racks nearby, and rough-hewn planks slowly take on new life as skilled boat builders ply their centuries-old trade. Yet you only need to take a few steps back from the waterfront to enter into another world, with blaring music, an internet cafe, a rather motley collection of guesthouses packed in against each other, interspersed with the occasional five-star hotel, and a definite party vibe. For some travellers it's the only place to be on the island (and it's one of the few places you can swim without needing to wait for the tides to come in); others will probably want to give it a wide miss. Most hotels and the centre of all the action are just north and west of Nungwi village, where it gets quite crowded. If partying isn't your scene, there are some lovely, quiet patches of sand on Nungwi's eastern side (where swimming is more tidal).

⊙ Sights & Activities

Mnarani Aquarium   AQUARIUM
(☏ 0777 496569; admission US$5; ☺ 9am-6pm) Traditionally Zanzibar's turtles have been hunted for their meat but in 1993, with the encouragement of conservationists, the

villagers of Nungwi opened this sanctuary in a natural tidal pool near the lighthouse. Now fishermen who end up with a turtle in their net are paid a small fee to bring them here, while nests on Nungwi beaches are monitored and protected. A logbook is kept and every year hatchlings are released into the sea in February.

ZanziYoga YOGA
(☏ 0776 310227; www.yogazanzibar.com; per person US$20) Centre yourself with morning (at 8am) and evening (at 5.15pm) yoga practice with Marisa van Vuuren at Flame Tree Cottages. The Hatha Yoga practice is suitable for all levels and focuses on breathing techniques, posture and reiki. Recently Marisa has joined forces with **Divine Diving** (www.scubazanzibar.com) at Amaan Bungalows, combining the efficient breathing practice of yoga with diving.

Spanish Dancer Dive Centre DIVING
(☏ 0777 417717; www.spanishdancerdivers.com; 2/6 dives US$132/320) Based in a breezy rondaval at the southern end of the beach, Spanish Divers is a big, friendly five-star PADI outfit with five instructors teaching courses in a dedicated classroom in seven languages. Fast boats whisk divers to Mnemba, Tumbatu and, weather permitting, to waters just south of Pemba. There's also a live-aboard diving option in *Julia*, a gorgeous 50ft catamaran (six to eight people maximum).

East Africa Diving & Water Sport Centre DIVING
(☏ 0777 420588; www.diving-zanzibar.com; 2/4 dives US$110/190) Nungwi's oldest diving outfit is located on the beach in front of Jambo Brothers Bungalows. It's five-star PADI ac-

credited, and has two fast, inflatable boats carrying a maximum of 14 divers with two instructors. Mnemba, Tumbatu and Hunga are all frequent dive sites. Tanks are smaller here, which may suit female divers better.

Zanzibar Watersports DIVING
(☏ 0773 235030; www.zanzibarwatersports.com; 2/6 dives US$100/295) This long-term Nungwi PADI outlet is located at Paradise Beach Bungalows. Dive sites are predominantly on the western side of the island and boats accommodate up to 20 divers. Snorkelling, kayaks, dhow cruises and wakeboarding are also offered.

Kiteboarding Zanzibar KITEBOARDING
(☏ 0779 720259; www.kiteboardingzanzibar.com) Nungwi's only kitesurfing centre is IKO certified and equipped with Cabrinha, Dakine and NPX kit. It also has a kite mobile to transfer surfers to Matemwe. The best wind conditions are between January and February, and June and July. Proof of certification is required.

👉 Tours

Cultural Village Tour CULTURAL TOUR
(per person US$15) Adjacent to the aquarium you can sign up for village tours, which last two hours and are a great way to see the village, its dhow-builders and thriving fish market. Best of all, the volunteer who accompanies you offers interesting insights into local life and allows you to ask questions about the skills and techniques used in the dhow-building. Note: most dhow-builders don't like their picture being taken so always ask permission first.

Nungwi Cycling Adventures CULTURAL TOUR
(☏ 0778 677662; www.zanzibarcyclingadventures.com; per person US$25-40) Get away from the beach with these off-road tours to rural villages, Portuguese ruins and coral caves filled with stalactites. One tour visits the blacksmiths in Kilimani while another traverses rice plantations to lunch on beaches known only to locals. A minimum of three people is required.

🛏 Sleeping & Eating

🛏 West Nungwi

Safina Bungalows GUESTHOUSE $
(☏ 0777 415726; www.newsafina.com; s/d/tr from US$30/50/70) Safina is a decent budget choice,

with no-frills bungalows around a small garden, just in from the beach in the centre of Nungwi, and meals in a double-storey pavilion. Seven of the 25 rooms have air-con.

Baraka Beach Bungalows　　BUNGALOW $
(☑ 0777 422910, 0777 415569; http://baraka bungalow.atspace.com; s/d US$35/50) Small and friendly, Baraka has nine no-frills stone-and-thatch cottages with ensuite bathrooms around a tiny well-kept garden. There's also a restaurant, serving pizza and curries, where you can bury your toes in the sand.

Nungwi Guest House　　GUESTHOUSE $
(☑ 0772 263322; http://nungwiguesthouse.tripod. com; Nungwi village; d/tr US$35/40) A good budget option in the village centre, with simple, clean ensuite rooms around a small garden courtyard, all with fans. There's no food. Spot it by the walls painted with light-blue fish.

Union Beach Bungalows　　BUNGALOW $
(☑ 0776 583412; http://unionbungalow.atspace. com; s/d from US$40/50; ✳🛜) Very simple no-frills bungalows plus rooms in a two-storey block, some with air-con and fridge. Meals are available at the Blue Wimbi restaurant.

Langi-Langi Beach Bungalows　　HOTEL $$
(☑ 0733 911000, 024-224 0470; www.langilangi zanzibar.com; s US$90 d US$100-180; ✳@🛜) A flashpackers place with 32 comfortably furnished rooms in a neat multistorey complex overlooking the beach. There's a small pool in a flowering courtyard, a massage deck, an internet cafe and a well-regarded restaurant serving Swahili dishes and excellent curries. If you like what you eat, you can even take a cookery course.

Flame Tree Cottages　　B&B $$
(☑ 0777 479429, 024-224 0100; www.flametree cottages.com; s/d US$120/170; ✳🛜) The cosy Flame Tree offers simply but thoughtfully furnished cottages in a flowering garden with a small pool. It's a perfect secluded spot for families or romancing couples in a quieter spot on the northeastern edge of Nungwi. Breakfast is served on your veranda; dinner can be arranged with advance order. In the evenings ZanziYoga (p80) takes place on one of the flat roofs overlooking the beach.

Amaan Bungalows　　HOTEL $$
(☑ 0775 044719, 024-550 1152; www.amaan bungalows.com; s US$70-150, d US$80-160; ✳@) This large, efficient place is at the centre of the action. There are 86 rooms of varying size, ranging from small garden-view with fan to nicer, spacious sea-view rooms with air-con and small balconies. All have hot water. Also in the crowded complex is a waterside restaurant-bar, internet access, moped rental, diving and fishing outfits and a travel agency.

East Nungwi

Mnarani Beach Cottages　　LODGE $$
(☑ 0777 415551, 024-224 0494; www.light houseanzibar.com; east Nungwi; half board s US$80-107, d US$130-200; ✳@🛜) The Mnarani is the first place you come to on the eastern side of Nungwi, just after the lighthouse (the name means 'at the lighthouse' in Swahili). It's set on a small rise overlooking the sea, with easy access to the narrow beach below. Accommodation is in pleasant cottages, larger family rooms or the two-storey Zanzibar House. It is well suited to couples and families, and has a surprising feeling of space despite the fact that it is often fully booked.

Sazani Beach Hotel　　BUNGALOW $$
(☑ 0776 668681, 0774 271033; www.sazanibeach. com; s/d/tr US$80/130/160; @🛜) Sazani is a quiet, quirky place with 10 agreeably rustic cottages on a somewhat overgrown hillside overlooking the sea. It's on the eastern side of Nungwi, past Mnarani Beach cottages. The area immediately in front is popular for kitesurfing.

Ras Nungwi Beach Hotel　　HOTEL $$$
(☑ 024-223 3767; www.rasnungwi.com; east Nungwi; garden r US$125-210, sea-view r US$175-305; ☺ Jun-Mar; ✳@) This beautifully situated, upmarket place has long been a standout in Nungwi, with a low-key ambience, luxurious sea-view chalets in mature tropical gardens, and less-expensive rooms in the main lodge. The hotel can organise fishing and watersports, and there's a dive centre and a spa. It's the last (for now) hotel down on Nungwi's eastern side, and has managed to retain an atmosphere of quiet charm.

ℹ Information

There's an internet cafe and forex bureau at Amaan Bungalows.

ℹ Getting There & Away

Bus 116 runs daily between Nungwi and Zanzibar Town (Tsh2000) along a sealed road.

Kendwa

About 3km southwest of Nungwi is Kendwa. It's a long, wonderfully wide stretch of sand, although the once-quiet ambience is now gone, thanks to a rash of resort development and an almost nonstop party vibe. That said, there is more space than at Nungwi, and amenable tidal patterns mean that there is swimming at all hours. For diving, there's the longstanding, eco-friendly and recommended **Scuba Do** (☑ 0777 417157; www.scuba-do-zanzibar.com; 2/6 dives US$120/330), with a full range of PADI courses.

🛏 Sleeping & Eating

Kendwa Rocks BUNGALOW $$
(☑ 0777 415475; www.kendwarocks.com; dm US$17, bandas without bathroom s US$30-40, d US$40-70, bungalows s US$55-70 d US$65-115; ☀) A Kendwa classic, although it has considerably expanded from its humble beginnings. Accommodation is in no-frills beach *bandas* sharing toilets, nicer self-contained bungalows on the sand, cool stone garden cottages, and suites and rooms up on the cliff top. Full-moon parties are an institution.

Sunset Kendwa BUNGALOW $$
(☑ 0777 414647; www.sunsetkendwa.com; s US$65-85, d US$85-98; ☀) This long-standing place has a mix of rooms on the beach and on the cliff top, some with air-con and all with bathrooms with hot water, plus some cliff-top rooms in two-storey blocks. There's a resident dive operator and a popular beachside restaurant-bar with evening bonfires on the beach.

Les Toits du Palme BUNGALOW $$
(☑ 0777 851474; www.lestoitsdepalme.com; d US$50-80, with air-con & hot water US$100) Three basic wooden beach bungalows on the sand, and six more rooms up on a small cliff. Everything's no-frills, but it's one of the few backpackers' chill spots left at Kendwa, although for how much longer is unknown as the owners are in discussions to sell.

La Gemma del'Est RESORT $$$
(☑ 024-224 0087; www.diamonds-resorts.com; full board per person from US$265; ☐☀@☎☀) Kendwa's quietest, most family-friendly resort, with large grounds, a good beach, several restaurant-bars (including one on a jetty over the water), a gym, a spa and a huge pool.

ⓘ Getting There & Away

You can walk to Kendwa from Nungwi at low tide in about 25 to 30 minutes, but take care as there have been some muggings. Alternatively, you can arrange boats with hotels in both Nungwi and Kendwa for the short jaunt. Via public transport from Stone Town, have dalla-dalla 116 drop you at the Kendwa turn-off, from where it's about a 2km walk to the beach.

Matemwe

The long, idyllic beach at Matemwe has some of the finest sand on Zanzibar. It's also the best base for diving and snorkelling around Mnemba, which lies just offshore. In the nearby village, life moves at its own pace, with women making their way across the shallows at low tide to harvest seaweed, strings of fish drying in the sun and chickens wandering across the road.

🏃 Activities

One Ocean DIVING
(www.zanzibaroneocean.com; Matemwe Beach Village; 2/6 dives US$120/325; ☺ Jun–mid-Apr) This experienced five-star PADI dive outfit is located at Matemwe Beach Village. Aside from a range of courses, it offers excellent dive trips to Mnemba with a maximum of nine divers or 16 divers and snorkellers per group. Snorkelling trips cost US$45 per person.

DADA COOKERY
(☑ 0777 466304; http://dadazanzibar.wordpress.com; per person in group of 2/4 US$25/15) Bestir yourself from the sunbed and head into the village for a cooking masterclass with Matemwe's *dadas*. Learn to make the perfect tomato sauce balanced with coconut and cassava leaves, or mould and mix perfect date balls and baobab jam. Classes run from 10am to 1pm, for a maximum of four people.

🛏 Sleeping & Eating

Key's Bungalows BUNGALOW $
(☑ 0777 411797; www.allykeys.com; s/d US$40/50) This quirky backpackers' place on the beach at the north end of Matemwe village has a chilled beach bar arranged around a dhow bar and a darts board. Nine simple rooms are located in a two-storey block. Meals are also available.

Mohammed's Restaurant & Bungalows BUNGALOW $
(☑ 0777 431881; http://mohammedsbungalows.wordpress.com; s/d/tr US$35/50/60) This establish-

ment has four very basic ensuite bungalows, each with two large beds, in Mohammed's small garden just back from the beach. Grilled fish and other local meals can be arranged.

Matemwe Beach Village   LODGE $$
(☑ 0777 437200, 0777 417250; www.matemwe beach.net; half-board per person r US$90-110, ste US$130-150; P ❄ @ ᗆ ▨) This recommended beachfront place has a low-key ambience and good-value bungalows with small verandas. Most are on the beach, with a few more set back about 100m on a low rise. There's also a private beachfront honeymoon suite with its own plunge pool and a huge open lounge area padded with colourful pillows.

Panga Chumvi   LODGE $$
(☑ 0777 862899; www.pangachumvi.com; garden/sea view s US$110/140, d US$150/180; ☺ Jun-Apr; @) ⚐ Lovely Panga Chumvi was the family home of Rebecca, Abdulla and Othman for many years before they converted it into this unpretentious beach haven set on a large seafront plot shaded by tall palms. Fifteen rooms are spread about the property in separate *makuti*-thatch bungalows with nutmeg-coloured concrete floors and elegant coconut wood furnishings. For two months of the year an artist in residence works with villagers and guests on inspiring creative projects.

Sele's Bungalows   BUNGALOW $$
(☑ 0776 931690; http://selesbungalows.wix.com/zanzibar; d with/without bathroom from US$70/45, f US$120; ☺ May-Feb) This friendly, no-frills place has seven simple cottage-style rooms in a dhow-themed garden on the beach. The two family rooms (each with two double beds) are upstairs, open on one side and sharing a toilet. The others (all doubles) have private bathroom, and all have fans. There's also a small restaurant and a bar.

Green & Blue   BOUTIQUE HOTEL $$$
(☑ 0774 411025; www.greenandblue-zanzibar.com; d garden US$300-306, sea view US$490-600; ☺ Jun-Apr; @ ᗆ ▨) A gorgeously designed lodge nestled in luxuriant green gardens on a rocky bluff facing off with Mnemba. Fourteen independent cottages are styled in a turquoise-and-yellow colour scheme and come with indoor and outdoor showers, and private verandas with hammocks and plunge pools. The communal areas are just as photogenic, with a two-storey bar, restaurant and pool area projecting over the beach, and dining here is as refined as the surroundings would suggest.

Sunshine Hotel   HOTEL $$$
(☑ 0774 388662; www.sunshinezanzibar.com; s US$130-150, d US$170-230; @ ᗆ ▨) This immaculate place on curve of white sand has 12 rooms in two-storey blocks, all with louvered doors, sunshine-yellow soft furnishings and cleverly concealed moulded bathrooms. All look over the lush garden and tempting infinity pool towards the beach. There are also two suites, a garden apartment and an excellent restaurant.

❶ Getting There & Away

Matemwe village is located about 25km southeast of Nungwi and is reached via a sealed road branching east off the main road by Mkwajuni. Dalla-dallas travel here daily from Stone Town (Tsh1500). Early in the day, they continue as far as the fish market at the northern end of the beach (and this is where you can catch them as well). Otherwise, the start/terminus of the route is at the main junction near Matemwe Beach Village hotel.

Kiwengwa

Kiwengwa, with its fine, wide beach, is the focus of Zanzibar's package tourism industry, although there are some quieter stretches to the north and south.

🏃 Activities

★ Maisha Mazuri
Horse Riding Club   HORSE RIDING
(per hour US$45) This well-maintained stables with 13 sleek-looking horses offers a truly unique chance to get out and experience the natural tranquility and beauty of the interior of the island. Five-hour hacks through waving rice fields, dank coral caves and tropical scrub cost US$200. Shorter rides along the beach at Kiwengwa are also possible.

🛏 Sleeping & Eating

Shooting Star Lodge   BOUTIQUE HOTEL $$$
(☑ 0777 414166; www.shootingstarlodge.com; s/d garden view US$130/200, sea-view cottages US$170/300; ❄ @ ▨) This intimate small lodge is recommended both for its location on a low cliff overlooking a beautiful, quiet beach, and for its service and cuisine. The closely spaced, impeccably decorated rooms range from three garden-view 'lodge rooms' to 11 spacious sea-view cottages and two honeymoon suites. There's also a salt-water infinity pool, and a raised beachside bar.

Bluebay Beach Resort RESORT $$$
(☑ 024-224 0240/1; www.bluebayzanzibar.com; s/d with half-board from US$190/300; P ❋ @ ❂ ☎ ☒) Quieter than many of its neighbours, enormous Bluebay has a large range of rooms and an expansive freshwater swimming pool. The grounds are expansive, green and serene and there are a host of activities on offer from sailing and tennis to windsurfing. There's also a spa and a fitness centre and One Ocean Dive Centre has a base here.

❶ Getting There & Away

Dalla-dalla 117 runs daily between Kiwengwa village and Stone Town along the sealed road.

Pongwe

Pongwe's quiet arc of beach is dotted with palm trees and backed by dense vegetation, and is about as close to the quintessential tropical paradise as you can get. Thanks to its position in a semi-sheltered cove, it also has the advantage of having less seaweed than other parts of the east coast. To the southeast, around the headland of Ras Uroa, is the small fishing village of Uroa and a stretch of Italian-owned resorts. Most are aimed at the package-holiday market and don't permit public access without prior booking.

⛱ Sleeping & Eating

Seasons Lodge LODGE $$
(☑ 0776 107225; www.seasonszanzibar.com; r US$165-195; @ ☒) Eschewing palm and thatch for bungalows of coral rag and *chokaa* limestone, Seasons offers a level of comfort above many beachside hotels. Each of the seven bungalows is lined with windows, with a deck over the beach and sparkling, modern bathrooms with claw-foot tubs. Thoughtful touches include torches, *kikoi,* mosquito spray and free mountain bikes and kayaks, and meals include vegetables and fruit from the garden.

★ **Pongwe Beach Hotel** HOTEL $$$
(☑ 0784 336181, 0773 000556; www.pongwe. com; r US$176-250, ste US$230-300; ☉ Jun-Apr; P @ ❂ ☒) The intimate and unassuming Pongwe Beach Hotel has 20 bungalows among the palms on a wonderful, deep arc of bleached white beach. Most rooms are seafacing, spacious and breezy, the restaurant is excellent, and when you tire of the turquoise panoramas at your doorstep, there's an infinity pool, fishing and excursions to Stone Town. It's justifiably popular and often fully booked.

❶ Getting There & Away

Dalla-dallas to Pongwe depart from Zanzibar Town's Mwembeladu junction; take dalla-dalla 501 from Darajani towards Amani stadium and ask to be dropped at Mwembeladu (Tsh300, 10 minutes), from where you can get dalla-dalla 233 to Pongwe-Pwani (Tsh1500, one hour), and then walk the last stretch. Dalla-dalla 214 runs between Mwembeladu and Uroa several times daily. A taxi or hotel transfer costs US$50.

Jozani-Chwaka Bay National Park

This cool and shady patch of green is the largest area of mature forest left on Zanzibar. Living among Jozani's tangle of vines and branches are populations of the rare red colobus monkey, as well as Sykes monkeys, bushbabies, Ader's duikers (although you won't see many of these), hyraxes, more than 50 species of butterflies, about 40 species of birds and several other animals. There's a nature trail in the forest, which takes about 45 minutes to walk.

Jozani Forest (☑ 0777 488350; adult/child with guide US$10/5; ☉ 7.30am-5pm) is 35km southeast of Zanzibar Town off the road to Paje, and best reached via bus 309 or 310, by chartered taxi, or with an organised tour from Zanzibar Town. The best times to see red colobus monkeys are in the early morning and late evening.

When observing the monkeys, take care not to get too close (park staff recommend no closer than 3m) both for your safety and the safety of the animals. In addition to the risk of being bitten by the monkeys, there's considerable concern that if the monkeys were to catch a human illness it could spread and rapidly wipe out the already threatened population.

Michamvi Peninsula

Curling around Chwaka Bay, the 10km stretch of beach along the eastern side of the Michamvi Peninsula offers fine, white, coral sand offset against a sea of extraordinary colours. So far, hotels are spaciously strung out along the peninsula with dense vegetation in between, but development has started to gather pace here, too. Luxury options can be found just north of Bwejuu while up at the tip of the headland you'll find some spectacular midrange places.

🛏 Sleeping & Eating

Sagando Hostel HOSTEL $
(☎0773 193236; http://sagandohostel.com; s/d/tr US$25/45/60) Just back from the beach, this is an amenable budget option, with a handful of single- and two-storey bungalows on the sand in a small, enclosed garden and meals on order.

Hotel Ras Michamvi HOTEL $$
(☎0777 413434; www.rasmichamvi.com; s US$105-145, d US$130-180; P@⛱) Occupying one of the most scenic locations on the island at the tip of the peninsula, Ras Michamvi sits on a bluff with expansive views. Idyllic, deserted beaches flank both sides and can be accessed via steep staircases although the views from the infinity pool are mesmerising enough. After a candlelit dinner of roast guinea fowl or grilled fish, retire to one of the thatched bungalows and dream of impossibly blue seas and coral gardens.

Kae Funk BUNGALOW $$
(☎0777 222346, 0777 439059; www.kaefunk.com; s US$50-100, d US$70-120; @) This chilled place has a large reggae bar decorated in lots of beach flotsam, loft swings and eight double rooms perched up on the cliff. They're nicely decorated with simple furniture and African print fabrics and just manage a peak at the sea over the high wall that a developer has built in front of the plot. In season, the bar is a cool place to hang out, with all-day music, sundowners and spicy curry lunches (pre-booking required).

Breezes Beach Club & Spa RESORT $$$
(☎0774 440883; www.breezes-zanzibar.com; half-board per person US$130-228; ❄@⛱) This long-standing place on the east side of the peninsula near Bwejuu receives consistently good reviews. Accommodation is in well-appointed rooms and suites in lovely gardens. There's diving, a gym and other activities. Advance bookings only – you won't get by the tight gate security without one.

❶ Getting There & Away

Dalla-dallas travel regularly from Stone Town (Tsh2000). There's also at least one dalla-dalla between Michamvi village and Makunduchi (Tsh1500). Local boats cross between Michamvi village (on the northwestern side of the peninsula) to Chwaka. Hiring one will cost from about Tsh30,000/50,000 for sail/motorboat.

Bwejuu

The large, dusty village of Bwejuu sits back from the beach 4km north of the main junction to Zanzibar Town. It's quieter than the party hub of Paje and the beach is nicely shaded by palms, with women going about their seaweed-gathering on the white-sand beach.

🛏 Sleeping & Eating

Mustapha's Place BUNGALOW $
(☎0776 718808, 024-224 0069; www.mustaphasplace.com; dm US$15, r per person US$20-25) Rasta-run Mustapha's has a variety of creatively decorated rooms, some with their own bathroom and all with their own theme. Meals are taken family style, and staff can assist with bike rental, drumming lessons and other diversions. It's south of Bwejuu village, and just across the road from the beach.

★ Bellevue Bungalows BUNGALOW $$
(☎0777 209576; www.bellevuezanzibar.com; s US$50-90, d US$60-100; @🕾) Lovely Bellevue is deservedly popular not only for its creatively decorated rooms, terrific sunrise terraces and bountiful breakfasts of spiced juices, local honey and pancakes, but also for its laid-back atmosphere and engaging hosts Melanie and Dim. Dim runs Kite Centre Zanzibar (p86) in Paje (free transfers and 10% discounts apply if you stay at Bellevue) while Melanie is the driving force behind **Jenga** (http://jengazanzibar.com), a social enterprise enabling artisans and producers to sell their work.

Upepo Boutique Beach Bungalows BUNGALOW $$
(☎0784 619579; www.zanzibarhotelbeach.com; s/d/tr US$45/70/90) This neat, friendly place is owned by a Zanzibari-Canadian couple who work hard to maintain the homey feel of the place. Two simple bungalows house spacious rooms with comfortable beds, beamed ceilings and lazy ceiling fans. All have small terraces and views over the garden to the glorious beach. The thatched restaurant-bar is the most popular on the beach, serving pasta, curries and fish with jugs of sangria.

Robinson's Place GUESTHOUSE $$
(☎0777 413479; www.robinsonsplace.net; s US$30, d US$60-80) An extension to the family home of Ann and Ahmed, this *Robinson*

Crusoe-style getaway has a small collection of brightly styled, quirky rooms directly on the beach. The two-storey Robinson House has an upstairs tree-house double, open to the sea and the palms. Some rooms have their own bathroom, and the shared *makuti*-thatch bathroom is spotless.

Twisted Palms Lodge
BUNGALOW $$

(☑0776 130275; www.twistedpalms.zanzibarone. com; d on hill US$35-55, on beach US$60-70) Twisted Palms offers five, clean, bright cottages up on a hill just behind the road, each with one double and one twin bed. Directly on the beach are five more beachside cottages (two quads, two triples, one double). There's a dhow for excursions and seafood meals are served in its restaurant up on stilts over the water.

ℹ Getting There & Away

Bus 324 goes daily between Stone Town and Bwejuu, and will drop you along the main road, from where it's about 500m down to the beach.

Paje

Paje has a wide, white beach at the junction where the coastal road north to Bwejuu and south to Jambiani joins with the road from Zanzibar Town. It's more built-up, with a cluster of small-scale places on the beach, and a party atmosphere. Paje is also Zanzibar's main kitesurfing centre; on fine days in season, the sea is filled with kitesurfers, often so much so that it can be difficult to find a quiet spot to swim.

🏃 Activities

Kite Centre Zanzibar
KITESURFING

(www.kitecentrezanzibar.com; board & kite rental per day/week US$100/370; ☺mid-Dec–mid-Mar & mid-Jun–mid-Oct) Affiliated with Bellevue Bungalows, this IKO-accredited outfit offers branded kites, experienced instructors and excellent courses catering to all abilities.

Airborne Kite Centre
KITESURFING

(☑0715 548464; www.airbornekitecentre.com; board & kite rental per day US$115) IKO-accredited courses and private tuition for beginners up to would-be instructors. Full-moon trips and kite-surfing at Mnemba are also possible.

Buccaneer Diving
DIVING, SNORKELLING

(www.buccaneerdiving.com; s dive US$50) This large five-star PADI dive center, based in the Arabian Nights hotel, offers well-structured courses in a classroom and pool. Three experienced instructors and a dive master speak six languages between them. Snorkelling at Mnemba Island is also offered (US$90).

☞ Tours

★ Seaweed Center
CULTURAL TOUR

(☑0777 107248; www.seaweedcenter.com; tour Tsh20,000) ✐ This social enterprise enables the women of Paje to not only harvest their seaweed – which is the island's second-biggest export – but also make a healthy living out of transforming it into desirable organic soaps, scrubs and essential oils. Head to the centre in the village for a fascinating tour of their farms and the processing centre where they dry and make the soaps. You can also have a go at making soap, while recharging with a surprisingly sweet-tasting seaweed smoothie.

🛏 Sleeping & Eating

Demani Lodge
LODGE $

(☑0777 460079, 0772 263115; www.demanilodge. com; dm/s/d/tr US$17/20/39/67; @) Calling backpackers and beach-lovers of all stripes, Demani Lodge is setting new standards for budget accommodation in Paje with a mix of neatly constructed *bandas* and cabins lined with *makuti*. Three of the 17 rooms are ensuite while the rest share a spotless shower block tiled in fashionable mosaic (towels require a US$10 deposit). White dressed beds, kanga curtains, a small pool and a sociable bar with a cool soundtrack make for instant success.

The only drawback: Demani is not on the beach. To get there take the road south to Jambiani and you'll see it signposted to the right of the main road.

Jambo Beach Bungalows
BUNGALOWS $

(☑0774 529960, 0772 271401; jambo.booking@ hotmail.com; dm/s/d/tr US$20/25/45/65) Run by the friendly Saidi Simba, Jambo is located on the beach just north of the village. Eight thatched bungalows and two dorm rooms (sleeping eight people) have a mix of sand and concrete floors, rustic wooden furniture, fans and mosquito nets. There's also a beach bar and simple restaurant. Even better, Jambo is located in front of Dhow Inn so when the going gets tough you can pop over and use its laundry (open to the public), and have a top-notch meal and a swim.

Kilimani Kidogo GUESTHOUSE **$$**

(📞 0777 201088; www.kilimakidogo.com; s/d/f US$70/180/$270; ✳🛜🗙) This fully staffed villa can either be rented in its entirety or rooms can be booked individually. Either way the friendly house-party atmosphere is a highlight, as are the well-equipped communal rooms (games, jigsaws, books, pool table), colourful ensuite bedrooms and pretty flower-filled garden and pool. The house is slightly south of Paje, on the road to Jambiani.

Kitete Beach Bungalows HOTEL **$$**

(📞 0772 361010; www.kitetebeach.com; s/d/tr US$60/90/110) This good-value place on the beach has 17 spacious, whitewashed rooms in double-storey bungalows on a small plot, all with ceiling fans and ocean views. It's aimed mainly at the kitesurf crowd, with equipment lockers, a pool table and a terrace restaurant overlooking the beach. Diving, snorkelling, sailing and deep-sea fishing can also be arranged.

Paje by Night LODGE **$$**

(📞 0777 880925; www.pajebynight.net; s/d from US$70/85; ⊘ Jun–mid-Apr; ✳@🛜🗙) Located in the thick of things in the centre of Paje, this noisy place is known for its party atmosphere and has a crowded mix of no-frills standard and more spacious rooms, plus several four-person rustic 'jungle bungalows'. Air-con is available only in the larger rooms and jungle bungalows. There's a restaurant with a pizza oven and an on-site kitesurf centre, **Paje by Kite**.

Dhow Inn BOUTIQUE HOTEL **$$$**

(📞 0777 525828; www.dhowinn.com; d US$150–250; 🅿✳🛜🗙) With its 28 architect-designed bungalows clustered around three pools and set amid sculptural gardens of bright-red canna flowers and palms, Dhow Inn is a vision of style amid Paje's rough-and-ready hotel scene. Beige-on-white interiors soothe heat-weary travellers, while the main clubhouse offer a games room, a laundry (Tsh10,000 per load), a spa, a TV room and an excellent boutique stocked with local crafts and own-brand clothes.

❶ Getting There & Away

Bus 324 runs several times daily between Paje and Stone Town en route to/from Bwejuu, with the last departure from Paje at about 4pm. The Makunduchi–Michamvi dalla-dalla also stops at Bwejuu.

Jambiani

Jambiani is a long village on a stunning stretch of coastline. The village itself, a sun-baked and somnolent collection of thatch and coral-rag houses, is stretched out over more than a kilometre. The sea is an ethereal shade of turquoise and is usually dotted with *ngalawa* (outrigger canoes) moored just offshore. It's quieter than Paje and Nungwi, and with a good sense of community spirit. Eco + Culture (p71) has a branch here, and offers village tours.

🛏 Sleeping & Eating

⭐ **Mango Beach House** GUESTHOUSE **$**

(📞 0773 498949, 0784 405391; www.mango-beachhouse.com; s US$25-45, d US$35-60, house US$60-100; ✳) With only three bedrooms and a shared dining table in Kiddo's Café, Mango Beach House is a sociable place. Rooms are simple with king-size beds, artful decor and colourful fabrics collected from Lisa's peregrinations around the island. The real action happens in the open-plan living area, which is like a lounge on the beach with day beds and furniture made out of driftwood.

Self-catering applies to whole house rental. And you'll need to book for lunch and dinner at Kiddo's Cafe.

Garden Bungalows BUNGALOW **$**

(📞 0773 551613; www.gardenbungalows-zanzibar. com; dm US$20, s/d $35/45) These beautifully constructed bungalows with terraces and *makuti*-thatch roofs are a steal at this price. They're also located right on the beach in a tranquil spot and presided over by the creative owner, Dula. The popular bar serves pina coladas as well as *dafu* (young coconuts), fresh juices and shakes; and there's some wonderful Swahili cuisine on offer from coconut crusted fish to *pili pili* prawns (spicy prawns). Bike hire can be arranged (US$10 per day).

⭐ **Red Monkey Lodge** BUNGALOW **$$**

(📞 0777 713366; www.redmonkeylodge.com; s/d US$72/104; 🛜) 🌿 An inspiring place run by the charming Angelo, Red Monkey has nine minimal-chic rooms overlooking the beach at the southern end of the village. It has an ethical, environmentally friendly outlook with furniture made from recycled dhows, soaps supplied by the Seaweed Centre in Paje and a free water dispenser in the restaurant. It's surrounded by protected forest and, if you're lucky, you'll see the monkeys commute along the beach while you breakfast.

Coral Rock
HOTEL $$

(☑ 024-224 0154; www.coralrockzanzibar.com; r US$110-160; ✴ @ 🛜 🌊) The aptly named Coral Rock is on a large coral rock jutting out into the sea at the southern end of Jambiani. Thatched bungalows have smart ethnic furnishings and air-con, while the meandering beachfront is dotted with terraces and chill-out zones as well as a gorgeous infinity pool. There are free kayaks, paddle skis and windsurf boards, and kite-surfing can be arranged with Red Monkey next door.

Blue Oyster Hotel
HOTEL $$

(☑ 0787 233610, 024-224 0163; www.blueoyster hotel.com; s US$60-110, d US$70-120; P 🛜) Personable and professional, Blue Oyster continues to offer good-value accommodation in Jambiani with locally furnished rooms in two-storey villas overlooking the sea. Loungers dot the beach in front and there's an open-air terrace restaurant serving plates of coconut curry and mango kingfish. You can also arrange diving excursions and tours onsite with affiliated operators.

Casa del Mar Hotel
HOTEL $$

(☑ 024-224 0400; www.casa-delmar-zanzibar.com; d downstairs/upstairs US$96/118; ✴) Colourful Casa del Mar brings a dash of design to Jambiani with 14 rooms in two double-storey houses set amid tropical gardens full of papaya, guava and fragrant frangipani. All the furniture and artworks were made in Jambiani and many of the staff come from the village. Good food and conversation are to be had in the beachside restaurant where you'll find detailed information on local activities.

❶ Getting There & Away

Dalla-dalla 309 runs several times daily to Jambiani from Darajani market in Stone Town. The Makunduchi–Michamvi dalla-dalla also stops at Jambiani.

Makunduchi

The main reason to come to Makunduchi is for the **Mwaka Kogwa festival**, when this small town is bursting at its seams with revellers.

The only accommodation is at a large gated resort that was undergoing renovation at the time of research. Otherwise, during the festival, it shouldn't be too hard to arrange accommodation with locals as it's considered an unfavourable omen if you don't have at least one guest.

Bus 310 runs to Makunduchi on no set schedule, with plenty of additional transport from both Zanzibar Town and Kizimkazi during Mwaka Kogwa. A sealed road connects Makunduchi with Jambiani and Paje, but there's no regular public transport.

Kizimkazi

This small village consists of two adjoining settlements: Kizimkazi Dimbani to the north and Kizimkazi Mkunguni to the south. It has a small, breezy and in parts attractive beach broken by coral rock outcrops. However, the main reason people visit is to see the **dolphins** that favour the nearby waters, or to relax at one of the handful of resorts.

Kizimkazi is also the site of a Shirazi **mosque** dating from the early 12th century. Inside, however, in the mihrab are inscribed

---

WATCHING THE DOLPHINS

If you want to watch the dolphins, heed the advice posted on the wall of the Worldwide Fund for Nature (WWF) office in Zanzibar Town:

➡ As with other animals, viewing dolphins in their natural environs requires time and patience.

➡ Shouting and waving your arms around will not encourage dolphins to approach your boat.

➡ Be satisfied with simply seeing the dolphins; don't force the boat operator to chase the dolphins, cross their path or get too close, especially when they are resting.

➡ If you decide to get in the water with the dolphins, do so quietly and calmly and avoid splashing.

➡ No one can guarantee that you will see dolphins on an outing, and swimming with them is a rare and precious occurrence.

verses from the Koran dating to 1107 and considered to be among the oldest known examples of Swahili writing. You'll need to take off your shoes, and you should cover up bare shoulders or legs. The mosque is in Kizimkazi Dimbani, just north of the main beach area.

🏃 Activities

Most Kizimkazi hotels organise tours to view the dolphins, as does Cabs Restaurant in Kizimkazi Dimbani (US$50 per boat including snorkelling equipment). You can also arrange trips through tour operators in Stone Town, with Safari Blue in Fumba or with some of the hotels at Paje and Jambiani from Tsh20,000 per person.

While the dolphins are beautiful, the tours, especially those organised from Stone Town, can be quite unpleasant, due to the hunt-and-chase tactics used by some operators, and they can't be recommended. If you do go out, the best time is early morning when the water is calmer and the sun not as hot. Late afternoon is also good, although winds may be stronger.

🛏 Sleeping & Eating

Karamba   LODGE $$
(☎ 0777 418452, 0773 166406; www.karamba resort.com; Kizimkazi Dimbani; s US$60-95, d US$70-120; @ ☯) Karamba, on the northern end of the beach in Kizimkazi Dimbani, has a string of 23 rooms in whitewashed cottages lined up along a small cliff overlooking the sea. They're simple and in need of a bit of maintenance. There's a restaurant, and a beachside chill-out bar with throw pillows, and a small pool.

Swahili Beach Resort   LODGE $$
(☎ 0777 416614, 0777 844442; www.swahili beachresort.com; Kizimkazi Mkunguni; s/d/tr from US$100/120/140; ⊙ Jun-Mar; 🅿 @ ☯) This place, with stone cottages set around manicured grounds, is lacking in shade and atmosphere, but the accommodation is comfortable and good value, and it works with a dive centre in Paje.

★ Unguja Lodge   LODGE $$$
(☎ 0774 477477; www.ungujalodge.com; Kizimkazi Mkunguni; half-board per person US$210-262; 🅿 @ 🛜 ☯) 🌿 This secluded, low-key lodge has 12 organically designed two-storey villas shaded by thick indigenous forest. They're impeccably decorated by owner Elies, with gorgeous coconut wood furniture, found-art objects and woven rugs, and all have either

sea views or private plunge pools. A stretch of private beach, an infinity pool, an on-site dive centre (the only one in the area) and an excellent restaurant mean it is regularly booked out.

❶ Getting There & Away

To reach Kizimkazi from Stone Town take bus 326 (Kizimkazi) direct (Tsh2000), or take bus 310 (Makunduchi) as far as Kufile junction, where you'll need to get out and wait for another vehicle heading towards Kizimkazi, or walk (about 5km). The last vehicle back to Stone Town leaves Kizimkazi about 4pm. As you approach from Stone Town go right at Kufile junction (ie towards Kizimkazi) and then right again at the next fork to Kizimkazi Dimbani. Kizimkazi Mkunguni is to the left at this last fork.

Menai Bay

Menai Bay, fringed by the sleepy villages of **Fumba** to the west and **Unguja Ukuu** to the east, is home to an impressive assortment of corals, fish and mangrove forests, some idyllic sandbanks and deserted islets, and a sea-turtle breeding area. Since 1997 it's been protected as part of the **Menai Bay Conservation Area**. Unguja Ukuu is notable as the site of what is believed to be the earliest settlement on Zanzibar, dating to at least the 8th century, although there is little remaining today from this era.

🏃 Activities

★ Safari Blue   CRUISE
(☎ 0777 423162; www.safariblue.net; Fumba; adult/child 6-14yr $65/35) Safari Blue organises group-based (maximum 20 people) day excursions on well-equipped dhows around Menai Bay. The excursions, which leave from Fumba at 9.30am, include a seafood lunch, plus snorkelling equipment and time to relax on a sandbank. Before booking, check weather conditions, as some months, notably April/May and July/August, can get quite windy or rainy.

🛏 Sleeping & Eating

Menai Beach Bungalows   COTTAGES $$
(☎ 0777 772660, 0777 4068009; www.visit zanzibar.se; Unguja Ukuu; s/d/f $40/60/75; 🅿) Marooned on a broad sandy beach beneath the palms and mangroves that make up the shoreline of Unguja Ukuu, these five independent bungalows offer a unique opportunity to see a corner of the island so far

unaffected by tourism. Comfortable, white-washed rooms open onto an empty beach, hammocks rock in the breeze and each evening fish bought from the local fishermen makes its way to the barbecue.

Fumba Beach Lodge LODGE $$$
(☏0777 860504; www.fumbabeachlodge.com; Fumba; s/d half-board from US$217/366; P�🛜) Set on a secluded peninsula on Menai Bay, Fumba Beach has 26 spacious cottages set in expansive grounds. The feel is more safari camp than beach hotel, with rooms spread out amid the vegetation with decks overlooking the water. There's also a small pool and

a resident dive operator. Although the beach at Fumba isn't picture-perfect and has a considerable amount of coral rock, the setting is beautiful and uncrowded. It's 18km south of Zanzibar Town next to Fumba village.

PEMBA

POP 407,000

For much of its history, Pemba has been overshadowed by Zanzibar, its larger, more visible and more politically powerful neighbour to the south. Although the islands are separated by only 50km, very few

Pemba

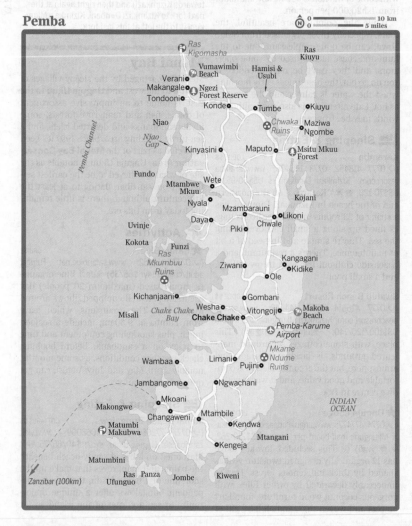

0 — 10 km
0 — 5 miles

ℹ PEMBA PECULIARITIES

Tourism in Pemba is different from anywhere else in the country; even Zanzibar. Keep the following in mind.

➡ Despite the scarcity of tourists, prices are as high as (and sometimes higher than) those in Zanzibar.

➡ Most businesses operate from 8am to 3pm and many reopen from 7pm to 9pm. Outside Chake Chake few stores open on Sunday. Many also shut down for a few minutes at 1pm so the men can pop over to the mosque for prayers.

➡ Other than local brews (the most common of which is *nazi*, a fermented coconut wine), there's little alcohol available on the island once away from the expensive resorts.

➡ Unmarried couples are not allowed to share a room in most hotels in towns (no problems at the resorts) and you may be asked to produce a marriage certificate as proof.

---

tourists cross the channel. Those who do, however, are seldom disappointed because Pemba offers an authentic experience that's largely disappeared in the archipelago's other half.

Unlike flat, sandy Zanzibar, Pemba's terrain is hilly, fertile and lushly vegetated. In the days of the Arab traders it was even referred to as 'Jazirat al Khuthera' (the Green Island). Throughout much of the period when the sultans of Zanzibar held sway over the East African coast, it was Pemba, with its extensive clove plantations and agricultural base, that provided the economic foundation for the archipelago's dominance.

Much of Pemba's coast is lined with mangroves and lagoons; however, there are stretches of sand and some idyllic uninhabited isles where you can play castaway for a day. The healthy coral reefs, the steeply dropping walls of the Pemba Channel and an abundance of fish provide world-class diving.

Unlike Zanzibar, where tourist infrastructure is well developed, Pemba is very much a backwater. Other than a few multistar resorts, facilities range from fairly basic to nonexistent. Pemba remains largely 'undiscovered' and you'll still have most things (even the lovely beaches) more or less to yourself, which is a big part of the island's appeal.

ℹ Getting There & Away

AIR

Pemba-Karume Airport (HTPE; Chake Chake) is 6km east of Chake Chake. ZanAir and Coastal Aviation both offer daily flights from Dar es Salaam to Pemba via Zanzibar (about US$95 from Pemba to Zanzibar, and US$140 to Dar es Salaam). Flightlink also does this routing more

cheaply, and both Coastal and Auric fly between Pemba and Tanga (US$65 to US$100).

BOAT

Ferries to/from Zanzibar and Dar es Salaam dock in Mkoani.

Azam Marine (p77) offers the most reliable service twice a week from Dar es Salaam (VIP/adult/child US$80/70/50), departing at 7am on Wednesday and Saturday and transiting through Zanzibar (around 10am) to arrive in Pemba around 1pm. Zanzibar–Pemba tickets cost US$40/35/25.

Otherwise, the *Royal* also runs twice weekly from Dar es Salaam via Zanzibar (US$75 from Dar to Pemba, US$40 from Zanzibar to Pemba), returning on Thursday and Sunday morning at 7.30am. Other ferries, such as the *Maendeleo* and *Serengeti*, also run, but their seaworthiness and safety record are questionable. Dhows run from Wete to Tanga and to Mombasa (Kenya), but foreigners are prohibited from sailing on them.

Tickets for all companies can be booked commission-free at various businesses in Chake Chake, Wete and Mkoani. Buying in advance ensures a seat.

An immigration officer usually checks passports on arrival. If you don't see them at the port and you aren't coming from Zanzibar, you're required to go the immigration office and sign in.

ℹ Getting Around

Crowded dalla-dallas plod down the main roads, most of which are sealed, but for many places you'll have to get off at the nearest junction and walk, wait for a lift or try to negotiate an additional fee with the bus driver to deliver you. There are few taxis.

Cycling is another good alternative; distances are short and roads are lightly travelled.

TANZANIA CHAKE CHAKE

Chake Chake

Lively Chake Chake, set on a ridge overlooking mangrove-filled Chake Chake Bay, is Pemba's main town and the best base for visiting the island's southern half, including Misali.

◉ Sights & Activities

Pemba Museum MUSEUM
(adult/student US$5/3; ☺8.30am-4.30pm Mon-Fri, 9am-4pm Sat & Sun) Filling what's left of an 18th-century Omani-era **fort**, which was probably built on the remains a 16th-century Portuguese garrison, this is a small but well-executed museum with displays on island history and Swahili culture. You'll enjoy your visit to Ras Mkumbuu, Mkame Ndume and Chwaka ruins much more if you stop here first.

Pemba Essential Oil Distillery TOUR
(tour Tsh3000; ☺8am-3.30pm Mon-Fri) Visitors to this out-of-town factory can see the tanks where clove stems, cinnamon leaves, eucalyptus leaves, lemongrass and sweet basil are turned into essential oils. Check in at the office and someone will show you around. From July through February locals deliver their clove stems here. The tour may be a little lackadaisical, but the process is fascinating and many of the essential oils are for sale. To reach it head 10 minutes northeast out of town towards Machomani or take dalla-dalla 316.

☞ Tours

Coral Tours TOUR
(☎0777 437397; tours_travelpemba@yahoo.com; Main Rd; ☺8am-5pm) Headed up by the charming and energetic Nassor Haji, Coral Tours can fix you up with knowledgeable guides for island tours (to Misali, Ngezi, Kidike and the spice plantations) at backpacker-friendly prices. A half-/full-day tour with a driver typically costs US$70/120, while a car alone costs US$50/70. The office also sells ferry and plane tickets and can help you with bike hire and small tourism maps.

🛏 Sleeping

Le Tavern HOTEL $
(☎0777 429057; Main Rd; s/d US$20/30) The cheapest rooms in town are simple and clean, if a little dusty, and they could all do with a lick of paint. Still, they have mosquito nets and fans and there are cold-water showers.

Pemba Island Hotel HOTEL $
(☎0777 490041; pembaislandhotel@yahoo.com; Wesha Rd; s/d/tw US$40/60/80; ▣☏) Clean rooms with cable TV, air-con, nets and hot water, plus a rooftop restaurant serving good homecooked meals such as *samaki na uali* (fish and rice) with spicy kachumbari (tomato and onion) salad. Nothing special, nothing wrong.

Hifadhi Hotel HOTEL $$
(☎0777 245777, 024-2542775; http://hifadhi-hotel.com; Tibirinzi St; s/d/ste US$90/110/150; ▣@☏▣) This glass-fronted hotel brings a shock of modernity to Chake Chake with

---

DON'T MISS

MISALI

A little patch of paradise surrounded by crystal waters and some of the most stunning coral reefs in the archipelago, a trip to Misali never disappoints. There are underwater and terrestrial nature trails, and you can arrange guides at the visitor centre. On the northeast of the island is **Mbuyuni beach**, with fine, white sand and a small visitor centre.

The island is part of the **Pemba Channel Conservation Area** (PECCA; adult/student US$5/3), which covers Pemba's entire west coast. All divers, snorkellers and beach-goers to Misali or any other place here must pay the admission fee.

To get to Misali on your own, head to Wesha (taxi Tsh10,000). Once in Wesha, you can negotiate with local boat owners to take you to Misali. If you can bargain well, you might find a boat for about US$70 return. It's easier, and not much more expensive, to arrange excursions through hotels. Coral Tours in Chake Chake, Ocean Panorama Hotel in Mkoani and Sharook Guest House in Wete all arrange tours (under US$110 for two people including lunch and entry fees). There's no food or drink on the island, so bring everything with you. Camping is not permitted.

Chake Chake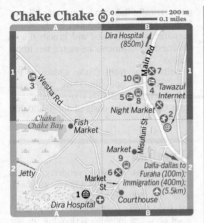

14 turquoise rooms with swagged curtains, Zanzibari beds, mini-fridges and bathroom toiletries. It also has the only pool in town and two Swahili restaurants.

Pemba Misali Sunset Beach RESORT $$
(☎0775 044713; www.pembamisalibeach.com; Wesha Rd; s/d US$90/120; ❋@❀) ✎ Out amid the mangroves just before Wesha, 7km from Chake Chake, this resort is quite reasonably priced for Pemba. Its most expensive bungalows sit on the white-sand beach, and diving, snorkelling and canoe trips through the mangroves are available. The restaurant sits on a deck looking out towards the sunset.

✖ Eating

There's a small town-centre night market where you can get grilled *pweza* (octopus) and *maandazi* (doughnuts) and experience a slice of Pemban life.

Samail Modern Hotel & Restaurant ZANZIBARI $
(☎0776 627619; meals Tsh4000-6000) A welcome addition to Chake Chake's restaurant scene, Samail serves marinated chicken with rice, as well as grilled fish and biriyani. Ice cream, cakes and fresh fruit juice are a bonus.

Balloon Brothers SNACKS $
(Market St; snacks from Tsh100; ⊙lunch) This is a local haunt which offers snacks such as samosas, sugar-coated *ubuyu* (baobab fruit) and bungo juice, the latter being very popular on Pemba. For something more substantial the *mishkaki* (marinated meat skewers) are good.

Ahaabna TANZANIAN $
(Le Tavern, Main Rd; meals Tsh5000-6000; ⊙dinner) Located on the top floor of Le Tavern, this restaurant offers just one meal a day, either pilau or biryani with a choice of green bananas, chicken or fish.

ⓘ Information

Since the closure of Barclays Bank there are no ATM facilities on Pemba. A few local banks and forex bureaus will change money (preferably US dollars), although all have unfavourable rates. To be safe, be sure to bring enough cash with you.

Dira Hospital (☎0777 424418; Wete Rd, Machomane; ⊙7am-9pm) A private clinic with pharmacy.

Tawazul Internet (Main Rd; per hr Tsh1000; ⊙8am-9pm) Conveniently located with the most reliable service.

ⓘ Getting There & Away

Most buses depart from points along Main Rd rather than the bus stand. Mkoani (Tsh1500, 1½ hours) dalla-dallas park near Coral Tours. Wete (Tsh1400, 1½ hours), Konde (Ths2000, two hours) and Vitongoji (Tsh500, 30 to 45 minutes) dalla-dallas park near PBZ bank, while much less frequent ones for Wesha (Tsh500, 30 minutes) are around the corner on Wesha Rd. Pujini (Tsh1000, one hour) is the only notable destination that uses the bus stand.

PEMBA FLYING FOX

Pemba's only endemic mammal is a large and critically endangered bat (*Pteropus voeltzkowi*) called *popo* in Swahili. They spend their days in trees rather than caves and the island's biggest roosting site, home to some 4000 bats, is in a burial forest at **Kidike Sanctuary** (✆0777 472941; adult/student/child US$5/3/1; ☺9am-6pm) about 10km northeast of Chake Chake. If you arrange things in advance, there are cooking classes, fishing and even bullfights. Kidike is 3.5km off the Chake–Wete road. Some people at the junction will hire their bicycles or you can wait for a lift.

❶ Getting Around

TO/FROM THE AIRPORT

Dalla-dallas from Chake Chake to Furaha will drop you off at the airport (Tsh500, 20 minutes), but they don't come there to pick people up. They're quite infrequent, so leave early. A taxi to town costs Tsh15,000 to Tsh20,000.

CAR & MOTORCYCLE

There are a few taxis around Chake Chake, and cars and motorbikes can be hired through travel agencies. Prices are fairly standard: US$40 to Mkoani and US$70 to Ras Kigomasha.

Ras Mkumbuu

Ras Mkumbuu is the long, thin strip of land jutting into the sea northwest of Chake Chake. At its tip are the ruins (adult/student US$5/4) of a settlement believed to be Qanbalu, the oldest known Muslim town in Africa.

During the rainy season you're likely to be able to drive no further than Kichanjaani (Depu), leaving about a 3.5km walk. You could also go by boat from Wesha.

Mkame Ndume (Pujini) Ruins

About 10km southeast of Chake Chake, near Pujini, are the atmospheric ruins (late 15th century to early 16th century) of what was either a fort or a palace of the infamous Mohammed bin Abdul Rahman, who ruled Pemba prior to the arrival of the Portu-guese. Locally, Rahman is known as Mkame Ndume (Milker of Men) and for Pembans, his name is synonymous with cruelty due to the harsh punishments he meted out to his people.

Dalla-dallas from Chake Chake to Pujini (Tsh1000, one hour) are infrequent and the ruins are poorly signposted. A taxi from Chake Chake costs about Tsh30,000 return.

Wambaa

Pemba's most exclusive property, **Fundu Lagoon Resort** (✆0774 438668; www.fundu lagoon.com; r full board hillside US$750-880, beachside US$830-980; ☺mid-Jun–mid-Apr; @✉) is set on a low hillside overlooking the sea near little Wambaa town. The luxurious tents, some with their own private plunge pools, are tucked away amid the vegetation. Particularly notable is its bar, set over the water on a long jetty. Children under 12 are not allowed.

Kiweni

Tranquil Kiweni, marked as Shamiani on some maps, is just off Pemba's southeastern coast. It's a remote backwater island with undisturbed stretches of sand, quiet waterways and a nesting ground for sea-turtle colonies. Offshore is some good **snorkelling**.

Until recently, tourism was unknown on the island, where villagers get by on fishing and farming. Now, **Pemba Lodge** (✆0777 415551; www.pembalodge.com; per person full board US$165) ✐, the only accommodation in these parts, brings adventurous souls for a truly off-the-beaten track experience.

Mkoani & Around

Although it's Pemba's major port, Mkoani has managed to fight off all attempts at development and remains a small and rather boring town. There's one good guesthouse. Dining options are limited to street stands by the port.

Immigration is 500m up the main road from the port in the town proper

Buses run regularly to Chake Chake (Tsh1500, 1½ hours), Wete (Tsh3000, two hours) and Konde (Tsh3500, 2½ hours) from in front of the port.

🛏 Sleeping

Zanzibar Ocean Panorama HOTEL $
(☑0773 545418, 024-245 6166; www.zanzibar oceanpanorama.com; Mkoani; dm/s/tw US$20/35/50; ❄ @) The welcoming Ocean Panorama is set up on a hill overlooking the sea and has bright, clean rooms with decks and Zanzibari beds. Manager Ali has lots of information on Pemba and arranges good-value trips, including dhow cruises and snorkelling at Misali or the old wreck (between about October and March) at Ras Ufunguo. Head left when exiting the port and walk 700m up the hill.

Wete

The run-down town of Wete, Pemba's second-largest port, is a good base for exploring northern Pemba. It's also the easiest place to see Pemba flying foxes, with a large colony hanging from some trees just uphill from the port.

🛏 Sleeping & Eating

Pemba Crown Hotel HOTEL $
(☑0777 493667; www.pembacrown.com; Bomani Ave; s/d US$30/40; ❄) This large, whitewashed and balconied hotel is Wete's best accommodation option, with 15 rooms sporting firm beds, air-con and simple furnishings. There's no restaurant, but a simple breakfast is provided.

Sharook Guest House GUESTHOUSE $
(☑0777 431012; www.pembaliving.com; Wete; s/d US$35/50) Run by the Sharook brothers, this four-bedroom guesthouse is the homiest option in town. The friendly English-speaking owners know much about travel on the island, and can recommend good-value excursions to the off-shore Mtambwe Mkuu ruins (US$5 per person), Fundo Island (US$30 for the boat) and the Ngezi Forest (US$35 per person), as well as organise car, bike and motorcycle rental. There's no restaurant, but pre-ordered dinners can be served in the TV room.

Sharook Riviera Grand Lodge GUESTHOUSE $
(☑0777 431012; www.pembaliving.com; dm US$20, s/d US$30/50; ❄) Bigger and better than the original, but less cosy, this so-called 'grand lodge' has eight simple, ensuite rooms with Zanzibari beds, nets and air-con. There's a nice narrow view of the bay from the rooftop restaurant.

ℹ Information

Barky Bureau de Change (Bomani Ave; ⏲8.30am-3.45pm Mon-Sat, 8.45am-12.30pm Sun) Best place in town to change money.

Royal Tours & Travel (☑0777 429244; royal tours@live.com; Bomani Ave; ⏲8am-3pm Mon-Sat, 8am-noon Sun) Books plane and ferry tickets, hires vehicles and leads tours.

ℹ Getting There & Away

There are two dalla-dalla routes (both use 606) between Wete and Chake Chake (Tsh1400, 1½ hours). Most vehicles use the faster eastern 'new' road (these are labelled in green) while some (red) travel via Ziwani along the 'old' road, which features more forest and some ocean vistas. There are also frequent dalla-dallas to Konde (Tsh1500, one hour).

A shuttle bus from Wete to Mkoani (Tsh3000) is timed to connect with most ferry departures and arrivals. It picks up passengers at various points around town and leaves Wete three hours before the boat departure.

Tumbe

The large village of Tumbe lies on a sandy cove fringed at each end by dense stands of mangroves. The beach north of the village is the site of Pemba's largest **fish market**, and if you're in the area it's well worth a stop to watch the bidding. There's no accommodation in Tumbe or nearby Konde. Dalla-dallas from Chake Chake to Konde pass Chwaka and Tumbe (Tsh2000, two hours). From Wete, you'll have to change vehicles in Konde for the final leg.

Ngezi Vumawimbi Forest Reserve

The dense and wonderfully lush forest at **Ngezi** (admission/transit fee US$5/2; ⏲7.30am-3.30pm) is one of the last remaining patches of the forest that once covered western Pemba. There are two nature trails tunnelling beneath the shady forest canopy, and off-trail walks are allowed. All visits must be done with a naturalist guide, some of whom speak English.

The visitor centre is 4km west of Konde on the road to Kigomasha Peninsula. A taxi from Konde costs Tsh5000. Kervan Saray Beach Lodge will deliver its guests here for free.

Kigomasha Peninsula

With good resorts on the peninsula's west shore and the beautiful palm-fringed **Vumawimbi beach** stretching along the east, Kigomasha Peninsula (Ras Kigomasha), in Pemba's northwestern corner, has become the centre of Pemba's small tourist industry. **Verani beach** on the western side of the peninsula suffers unfairly by comparison, but is hardly less beautiful.

Vumawimbi beach itself is an isolated place; don't bring anything valuable and women shouldn't come alone.

◉ Sights & Activities

Ras Kigomasha Lighthouse   LIGHTHOUSE
(admission US$5) Located at the northern tip of Pemba, the Ras Kigomasha lighthouse was built by the British in 1900 and is still actively maintained by its keeper. Scale the tiny staircase (95 steps) for wonderful views back across the island.

Swahili Divers   DIVING
(www.swahilidivers.com) This five-star PADI Dive Centre is located at Kervan Saray and has been operating on the island since 1999. It offers good-value dive packages; for example, its seven-night package includes accommodation, meals, transfers, dive gear and 10 dives, plus a kayak and walking excursion, for US$1865 per person.

⌷ Sleeping & Eating

Matango Beach Resort   RESORT $$
(☑ 0777 009315, 0777 481629; www.matango beachresort.com; Makangale; d/f US$100/160; ❄ ☒) A welcome addition to Verani beach is this well-priced new resort with neatly constructed beach chalets with thatched roofs, small decks and private barbecues. Rooms are huge, air-conditioned and situated just back from the beach so you can watch the sun go down from your deck.

Kervan Saray Beach Lodge   LODGE $$
(☑ 0773 176737; www.kervansaraybeach.com; dm full board US$55, s/d US$160/250; ℗ @ ☎ ☒) The almost luxurious Kervan Saray is a lovely, relaxing lodge on the shore (there's a beach only half the year) near Makangale village. Accommodation is in a vaguely Arabian-themed high-roof bungalow or a six-bunk dorm, and the restaurant serves a daily set menu (nonguests US$15). Swahili Divers is based here and diving, naturally, is the main activity, but snorkelling and kayaking are also offered, as is camping on deserted isles.

Manta Resort   RESORT $$$
(☑ 0776 718853, 0776 718852; www.themanta resort.com; full board d garden US$495-595, seafront US$745; ❄ @ ☎ ☒) Superbly situated on Verani beach, the Manta Resort rests on a breezy escarpment with perfect ocean views. Accommodation is in a mix of seafront and garden cottages with private terraces, polished concrete floors and comfy king-sized beds. Pride of place goes to its new wacky, but wonderful, floating suite (US$1500 per night) with a sun- and star-gazing roof deck, a dining deck and an underwater bedroom, with surreal views of cruising manta rays, dancing octopus and tropical fish.

❶ Getting There & Away

The only dalla-dallas on this road leave Makangale for Konde (Tsh1000, one hour) at 7am and return at 1pm. Sometimes a second truck follows a short time later.

NORTHEASTERN TANZANIA

Northeastern Tanzania's highlights are its coastline, its mountains and its cultures. These, combined with the area's long history, easy access and lack of crowds, make it an appealing focal point for a Tanzania sojourn.

Step back to the days of Livingstone in Bagamoyo, relax on palm-fringed beaches around Pangani, or explore Saadani, a seaside national park. Inland, hike forested footpaths in the Usambaras while following the cycle of local market days.

Bagamoyo

In the mid-19th century Bagamoyo was one of the most important settlements along the East African coast and the terminus of the trade caravan route linking Lake Tanganyika with the sea. In 1868 French missionaries established Freedom Village at Bagamoyo as a shelter for ransomed slaves.

From 1887 to 1891 Bagamoyo was the capital of German East Africa, and in 1888 it was at the centre of the Abushiri revolt, the first major uprising against the colonial government. In 1891 the capital was transferred to Dar es Salaam, sending Bagamoyo into a slow decline from which it has yet to recover.

Northeastern Tanzania

0 — 50 km
0 — 30 miles

Arusha
(80km)

Moshi
Himo
Taveta
Voi
Tsavo East
NP

Nyumba
ya Mungu
Reservoir

Mwanga
Usangi
Mt Kindoroko
(2113m)

Kisangara
Chini

Tsavo West
NP

KENYA

Same
Kisiwani
Mwembe
Mbaga
Shengena Peak
(2462m)

Mkomazi
NP

Mombasa
(5km)

Shimba Hills
NR

Mtae
Shagayu Peak
(2220m)
Sunga

Mlalo

Usambara Mountains

Lunga
Lunga

Funzi

Horohoro
Shimoni

Buiko

Lushoto
Migambo
Irente Viewpoint
Soni
Bumbuli
Mombo
Mazumbai
FR

Mkulumuzi River

Galanos
Sulphur Springs

TANZANIA

Kwamkoro
Amani NR
Amani
Ngomeni
Amboni
Tanga

Korogwe
Zigi
Muheza

Pemba Channel

Hale
Segera
Pangani Falls
Pangani River
Pangani
Kigombe

Korodigo
Handeni

Bweni
Mwera
Maziwe Island
Marine Reserve
Ushongo

Mkoani

Kimamba

Mkata
Saadani
NP
Mkwaja

Tumbatu
Mkokotoni

Manga

Mligaji
Zanzibar

Miono
Mvave
Saadani

Lukigura River

Mandera
Zaraninge
FR

Kinyonga

Zanzibar
Town

Kwadihombo
Mvomero
Kibaoni

Msata
Wami River

Zanzibar Channel

Uzi

Bagamoyo
Kaole
Ruins

Chalinze
Ruvu
Bridge
Ruvu River

Mbudya
Bongoyo

Morogoro
Mlandizi
Kibaha

Dar es
Salaam

Today almost every worthwhile sight now has an admission price, making a Bagamoyo visit a rather expensive endeavour. Both the Catholic Museum and the **Caravan Serai Museum** (⊙9am-6pm) offer tourist information and guides.

◎ Sights

Bagamoyo Town   HISTORIC SITE
(adult/child Tsh20,000/10,000) With its cob-webbed portals and crumbling German-era colonial buildings, **central Bagamoyo**, or *Mji Mkongwe* (Stone Town) as it's known locally, is well worth exploration. The most interesting area is along Ocean Rd. Here you'll find the old **German boma** (a fortified living compound; in colonial times, an administrative office), built in 1897, **Liku House**, which served as the German administrative headquarters. There is also a school, which dates to the late 19th century and was the first multiracial school in what is now Tanzania.

Catholic Museum   MUSEUM
(☑023-244 0010; admission Tsh10,000; ⊙10am-5pm) About 2km north of town and reached via a long, mango-shaded avenue is the Catholic mission and museum, one of Bagamoyo's highlights. In the same compound is the chapel where Livingstone's body was laid before being taken to Zanzibar Town en route to Westminster Abbey. The mission dates from the 1868 establishment of Freedom Village and is the oldest in Tanzania.

🛏 Sleeping & Eating

Funky Squids B&B   B&B $
(☑0755 047802, 0778 227276; the.funky.squids@gmail.com; s/d Tsh50,000/65,000; P🛜) This newish place has seven clean, modest rooms and a large beachfront bar-restaurant. It's at the southern end of town, next door to (and immediately south of) the Bagamoyo College of Arts (Chuo cha Sanaa).

Travellers Lodge   LODGE $$
(☑0754 855485, 023-244 0077; www.travellers-lodge.com; camping US$12, s/d cottages from US$60/80; ✻) With its relaxed atmosphere and reasonable prices, this is among the best value of the beach places. Accommodation is in clean, pleasant cottages scattered around expansive grounds, some with two large beds. There's a restaurant and a children's play area. It's just south of the entrance to the Catholic mission.

New Bagamoyo Beach Resort   LODGE $$
(☑0783 261655; www.facebook.com/new bagamoyobeachresort; camping US$9, bandas per person without bathroom US$20, s/d US$75/88; P✻🛜) This seaside place is fine, friendly and very relaxed, with adequate rooms in two blocks (ask for the one closer to the water). It also has a few no-frills budget *bandas* on the beach that have just a bed. The cuisine is French-influenced and tasty. It also has a boat for excursions.

ℹ Information

CRDB At the town entrance; ATM.

ℹ Getting There & Away

Bagamoyo is about 70km north of Dar es Salaam and an easy drive along a good sealed road. The best routing for drivers is via Old Bagamoyo Rd through Mikocheni and Kawe.

Via public transport, there are dalla-dallas throughout the day from 'Makumbusho' (north of Dar es Salaam along the New Bagamoyo road, and accessed via dalla-dalla from New Posta) to Bagamoyo (Tsh2200, two hours). There is also a daily dalla-dalla to Saadani village via Msata on the main Arusha highway (Tsh10,000, three hours).

Nonmotorised dhows to Zanzibar cost about Tsh5000 (from Tsh10,000 for motorised boats). You'll need to register first with the immigration officer in the old customs building.

Saadani National Park

About 70km north of Bagamoyo along a lovely stretch of coastline, and directly opposite Zanzibar, is tiny **Saadani**, (www.saadanipark.org; adult/child US$30/10) a 1000-sq-km patch of coastal wilderness.

While terrestrial wildlife watching can't compare with that in the better-known national parks, animal numbers are slowly but surely increasing. In addition to hippos and crocs, it's quite likely that you'll see giraffes, and elephant spottings are increasingly common. With luck, you may see Lichtenstein's hartebeests and even lions, although these are more difficult to spot.

🛏 Sleeping & Eating

**Saadani Park
Resthouse & Bandas**   BANDA $$
(☑0689 062346, 0785 555135; saadani@tanzaniaparks.com; banda/resthouse per person US$40/50) Saadani's nice, new park *bandas* and resthouse are just back from the beach near Saadani village, in an area that elephants

ℹ️ SAADANI NATIONAL PARK

Why Go To enjoy the long, mostly deserted coastline plus some wildlife; ease of access from Dar es Salaam for those without much time.

When to Go June to February.

Practicalities Drive, bus or fly in from Dar es Salaam; bus from Bagamoyo; drive from Pangani. Entry points are Mvave gate (at the end of the Mandera road, for visitors from Dar es Salaam); Madete gate (for those coming from Pangani along the coastal road); and Wami gate (for those coming from Bagamoyo). Entry fees are valid for 24 hours, single entry only. Entry, camping, guide, walking and boat safari fees can be paid with Visa, MasterCard or cash at Mvave gate, and with cash only at Madete and Wami gates. All entry gates are open from 6am to 6pm; exiting the park is permitted up to 7pm. **Saadani Tourist Information** (📞 0689 062346, 0785 555135; infosaadani@tanzania parks.com), near Saadani village, can help with park accommodation bookings and guides.

Budget Tips There's no vehicle rental at the park. Best budget bet: get together a group and arrange a day safari with one of the lodges outside Saadani.

seem to like. The resthouse has three singles and a suite; the *bandas* have spacious double- and single-bedded rooms. Both have cold-water showers and self-catering kitchens. Bottled water is available in Saadani village; otherwise, bring all food and drink.

Kisampa   TENTED CAMP **$$**
(📞 0769 204159; www.afrikaafrikasafaris.com; per person full board US$180) 🌿 For genuine bush adventure, it's difficult to beat this unique, family-friendly camp. Set off on its own about a two-hour drive from Saadani in a private nature reserve, Kisampa is integrated with the surrounding community, and offers many ways for guests to get involved. Accommodation is in rustic bungalows. Saadani safaris, bush walks, beach camping and other activities fill the days.

Tent With a View Safari Lodge   LODGE **$$$**
(📞 0713 323318, 022-211 0507; www.saadani. com; s/d full board US$355/550, s/d all inclusive US$655/750; 🅿️) 🌿 This hideaway has raised tree-house-style *bandas* on a lovely stretch of deserted, driftwood-strewn beach, just north of the Saadani park boundary. All have verandas and hammocks. Excursions include safaris in the park and boat trips on the Wami River. The same management runs a lodge in Selous Game Reserve, and combination itineraries can be arranged.

ℹ️ Getting There & Away

AIR
Flights from Dar es Salaam (one way US$140) and Zanzibar (one way US$75) can be booked with Coastal Aviation (p61).

BOAT
Boat charters can be arranged with Saadani lodges, or through lodges near Pangani.

CAR
From Dar es Salaam, the main route is via Chalinze on the Morogoro road, and then north to Mandera village (about 50km north of Chalinze on the Arusha highway). At Mandera bear east along a good gravel road and continue about 60km to Saadani. It's also possible to reach Saadani from Dar es Salaam via Bagamoyo: from Bagamoyo town, head north for 44km along a mostly rough road to the Wami entry gate and the Wami River, which is now bridged, except during the heavy rains; check with park headquarters or the camps about the bridge's status before venturing up. Once at the bridge, it's 21km further to Saadani village.

Coming from Pangani, take the ferry across the Pangani River, then continue south along a reasonably good, scenic road past stands of cashew, sisal and teak to the reserve's northern Madete gate. (At the large signboard for Mkwaja, continue straight, then take the right fork at the next 'Y' junction.) Transfers can be arranged with Saadani or Pangani (Ushongo) lodges from about US$150 per vehicle each way (1½ to two hours).

Although Saadani officially stays open year-round, roads within the park get very muddy and difficult to pass during the rains, and you'll probably be limited to the area around the beach and the camps. When driving away from the main park routes during the rains, be watchful to avoid getting your vehicle stuck in the area's treacherous black cotton soil.

Pangani

About 55km south of Tanga is the small and dilapidated Swahili outpost of Pangani. It makes an intriguing step back into history, especially in the area within about three blocks of the river, where you'll see some carved doorways, buildings from the German colonial era and old houses of Indian traders. More of a draw for many travellers are the beaches running north and south of town.

Pangani's centre, with the market and bus stand, is on the corner of land where the Pangani River meets the sea. About 2km north is the main junction where the road from Muheza joins the coastal road, and where you should get off the bus if you're arriving from Muheza and staying at the beaches north of town.

◉ Sights & Activities

Staff at the **Pangani Cultural Tourism Program Office** (☉8am-5pm) in the yellow building at the bus stand (not to be confused with the similarly named cultural tourism office diagonally opposite the ferry dock), organise town tours (per person US$10), river cruises (US$70 for up to three people) and other excursions. All of the hotels south of Pangani also offer excursions, often more reliably and at more economical rates than the cultural tourism program office.

🛏 Sleeping & Eating

🛏 Town Centre

Seaside Community Centre Hostel   GUESTHOUSE **$$**
(☑0755 276422; s/d/tr US$20/30/60, with aircon US$30/50/75; 🅿🛜) This church-run place has spotless, pleasant rooms with fans and verandas, and meals on order. Its motto: 'Lovely and tenderly service is our joy and mission'. It's about 1km from the bus stand (Tsh2000 in a taxi).

🛏 North of Pangani

Mkoma Bay   LODGE **$$**
(☑0786 434001, 0784 283565; www.mkomabay.com; s/d luxury tents from US$90/155, 4-8-person house from US$320; 🅿@🛜🏊) The highlights at this stylish lodge are the magnificent views over Mkoma Bay and the subdued, comfortable ambience. Accommodation is in seven raised, well-appointed tents of the sort you find in upmarket safari camps, set around expansive grounds on a low cliff overlooking the beach. There is also a four-bedroom self-catering house and a good restaurant. This is excellent value.

Capricorn Beach Cottages   BOUTIQUE HOTEL **$$**
(☑0784 632529; www.capricornbeachcottages.com; s/d US$82/120; 🅿@🛜) This classy place on the beach 19km north of Pangani has three lovely, spacious self-catering cottages set in large grounds dotted with baobab trees. Each cottage has a hammock and a veranda. There's a clothing boutique, pizza oven, a deli selling homemade bread and other gourmet essentials, and the possibility of catered dinners under the stars. Wonderfully relaxing.

Peponi Holiday Resort   CAMPGROUND, BANDAS **$$**
(☑0784 202962; www.peponiresort.com; camping US$6.50, s/d half board US$75/98; 🅿@🛜🏊) Relaxing Peponi is set in expansive palm-studded grounds on the beach 20km north of Pangani. There's a shady beachfront campsite, simple, breezy double and family bungalows, a restaurant and bar, a small pool and a handcrafted dhow for snorkelling excursions. It's an ideal spot for families and campers. Buses running along the Pangani–Tanga road will drop you at the gate.

🛏 Ushongo Beach

The beaches get more beautiful the further south you go. Ushongo is about 15km south of the Pangani River.

Beach Crab Resort   CAMPGROUND, COTTAGES **$**
(☑0784 543700, 0767 543700; www.thebeachcrab.com; camping US$6, s/d/tr beach huts US$23/36/54, s/d/tr bungalows US$70/100/120; 🅿🛜) 🍴 This backpacker- and family-friendly place is at the southern end of Ushongo beach. It has beachside camping, spotless, good-value backpacker huts sharing clean ablution blocks with the campsite, plus simple, comfortable and airy double and family bungalows. It also has a large, beachside bar-restaurant. It has windsurfing, kayaks, beach volleyball, snorkelling excursions and a raised tree-house lounge.

Tides   LODGE **$$$**
(☑0784 225812; www.thetideslodge.com; s/d half board from US$245/340; 🅿@🏊) The beautiful Tides has a prime seaside location on a wonderful stretch of beach, delightful, spacious,

upmarket cottages directly on the sand and excellent cuisine. The cottages have huge beds surrounded by billowing mosquito nets, large bathrooms and stylish decor. There are also several family cottages and a private honeymooners' luxury suite, plus a beachside bar and restaurant.

Sange Beach

Lovely Sange is about midway between Pangani town and the northern border of Saadani National Park.

★ **Tembo Kijani** LODGE $$
(☑ 0687 027454, 0785 117098; www.pangani -ecolodge.com; d tree house/cottage full board US$160/215; Ⓟ) ❂ This small ecolodge on a wonderful stretch of beach has four completely open-sided tree-house *bandas* nestled into the bush just back from the sea, two comfortable ground-level beach cottages and delicious, healthy cuisine. The owners have made great efforts to minimise the lodge's footprint and maximise sustainability. The overall results are impressive, with the lodge running on solar and wind power.

❶ Information

The closest banks and ATMs are in Tanga.

❶ Getting There & Away

BOAT

The fast MV *Ali Choba* sails three times weekly between Ushongo (south of Pangani), Pangani and Zanzibar. The trip takes about 90 minutes, and costs US$290 per boat for up to five passengers, or US$55 per person for five or more passengers between Ushongo and Zanzibar (US$310 per boat or US$60 per person between Pangani and Zanzibar). Book through your hotel or **Emayani Beach Lodge** (☑ 0782 457668, 027-264 0755; www.emayanilodge.com).

The reliable **Mr Wahidi** (☑ 0784 489193) offers motorised dhow transfers between Pangani town and either Nungwi or Kendwa on Zanzibar for US$150 per boat for up to four people, plus US$35 per additional person. Allow about four hours for the trip.

ROAD

The best connections between Pangani and Tanga are via the rehabilitated coastal road, with about five buses daily (Tsh2500, 1½ hours). The first departure from Pangani is at about 6.30am, so you can connect with a Tanga–Arusha bus. There's also at least one daily direct bus between Pangani and Dar es Salaam (Tsh13,000).

For Ushongo and the beaches south of Pangani, all the Ushongo hotels do pick-ups from both Bweni (the village just across the river from Pangani town) and Tanga. There's also a daily bus between Tanga and Mkwaja (at the northern edge of Saadani National Park) that passes Mwera village (6km from Ushongo) daily at about 7am going north and 3.30pm going south. It's then usually possible to hire a motorcycle to take you from Mwera to Ushongo.

The vehicle ferry over the Pangani River from Pangani to Bweni village runs regularly between about 6am and 10pm daily (per person/vehicle Tsh200/5000). From Bweni, you can arrange a taxi in advance with the Ushongo hotels (about Tsh30,000 per taxi for up to three passengers). Otherwise, motorcycles charge about Tsh10,000 to the Ushongo hotels.

Tanga

POP 273,300

Tanga, a major industrial centre until the collapse of the sisal market, is Tanzania's second-largest seaport and its third-largest town behind Dar es Salaam and Mwanza. Despite its size, it's a pleasant-enough place with a sleepy, semicolonial atmosphere, wide streets filled with bicyclists and motorcycles, and faded charm.

◉ Sights & Activities

The most interesting areas for a stroll are around Jamhuri Park overlooking the harbour, near which you'll find the old German-built **Clock Tower**, and the park and cemetery surrounding the **Askari monument** at the end of Market St.

Urithi Tanga Museum MUSEUM
(☑ 0784 440068; Independence Ave; ⊙ 9am-5pm Mon-Sat, 10am-2pm Sun) **FREE** Tanga's old *boma* (fortified living compound) has been rehabilitated, and now houses this small but worthwhile museum, with historical photos and artefacts from the area.

Toten Island HISTORIC SITE
Directly offshore from Tanga is this small, mangrove-ringed island ('Island of the Dead') with the overgrown ruins of a mosque dating at least to the 17th century and some 18th- and 19th-century gravestones. Pottery fragments from the 15th century have also been found, indicating that the island may have been settled during the Shirazi era. Toten Island's apparently long history ended in the late 19th century, when its inhabitants moved to the mainland.

Tanga

Tanga Bay

Tanga Yacht Club SWIMMING
(☎ 027-264 4246; www.tangayachtclub.com; Hospital Rd, Ras Kazone; day admission Tsh3000) This place has a small, clean beach, showers and a restaurant-bar area overlooking the water. It's a pleasant place to relax and, especially on weekend afternoons, it's a good spot to meet resident expats and get the lowdown on what's happening in town.

🛏 Sleeping

🛏 Central Tanga

Regal Naivera Hotel HOTEL **$**
(☎ 0765 641464, 027-264 5669; regalnaiverahotel@yahoo.com; r Tsh45,000-100,000; P ❊ 🕾) This large, pink edifice is in a quiet location two blocks in from Hospital Rd and behind Katani House. It has clean, modern rooms in varying sizes, all with a double bed, fan, air-con and minifridge. It also has a restaurant.

Central City Hotel HOTEL **$**
(☎ 0718 282272, 027-264 4476; centralcityhotel ltd@yahoo.com; Street No 8, Ngamiani; r Tsh45,000-60,000; P ❊) This bland but reliable budget choice is the closest hotel to the bus stand that we can recommend. Rooms have fans,

hot water, a minifridge and a double bed. There is also a restaurant. From the bus stand, go right onto Taifa Rd ('Double Rd') to the roundabout. At the roundabout, go right onto Street No 8; Central City is 600m down on your left.

Mkonge Hotel HOTEL **$$**
(☎ 027-264 3440; mkongehotel@kaributanga. com; Hospital Rd; s/d US$80/90, with sea view US$90/100; P ❊ 🕾 ☒) The imposing Mkonge Hotel, in a lovely setting on a vast, grassy lawn overlooking the sea, has reasonably comfortable rooms (worth the extra money for a sea view), lackadaisical service, a restaurant and wonderful views. The pool costs Tsh5000 for nonguests.

🛏 Outside Tanga

Fish Eagle Point LODGE **$$**
(☎ 0784 346006; www.fisheaglepoint.com; per person full board US$90-144; P ☒) ✿ Fish Eagle Point, on a mangrove-fringed cove, has spacious beachfront cottages in varying sizes, a dhow, snorkelling, sea kayaking, fishing and birdwatching. It's ideal for families. Follow the Horohoro road north from Tanga for 38km to the signposted right-hand turn-off, from where it's 10km further.

Tanga

⊚ **Sights**
1 Urithi Tanga Museum A3

🛏 **Sleeping**
2 Mkonge Hotel E1
3 Regal Naivera Hotel D3

🍴 **Eating**
4 SD Supermarket F2

ℹ **Information**
5 Tatona Tourist Information
    Centre...B3

ℹ **Transport**
6 Coastal Aviation C3

✗ Eating

SD Supermarket   SUPERMARKET **$**
(Bank St; ⊙ 9am-1.30pm & 3-6pm Mon-Fri, 9am-2pm Sat) A good stop for self-caterers; it's behind the market.

Tanga Yacht Club   EUROPEAN **$$**
(⌕ 027-264 4246; www.tangayachtclub.com; Hospital Rd, Ras Kazone; admission Tsh3000, meals from Tsh9000; ⊙ lunch & dinner Wed-Mon) Seafood and mixed grill dishes, overlooking the water.

ℹ Information

Barclays (Independence Ave) ATM.
Click On-Line (Custom St; per hour Tsh2000; ⊙ 8.30am-6pm Mon-Sat) Internet cafe.
Exim (Independence Ave) Next to Barclays; ATM.
NBC (cnr Bank & Market Sts) Just west of the market. Changes cash; ATM.
Tatona Tourist Information Centre (www.tangatourism.com; ⊙ 8am-4.30pm Mon-Fri, to 1pm Sat) The helpful staff at Tatona can provide information on nearby attractions, and advice for accommodation and transport options. They will also link you up with Tatona-approved (ie reliable) tour agencies and guides for excursions. Stop in here first, before visiting any of the other 'tourism offices' in town.

Its office is diagonally opposite the post office in the small white gazebo.

ℹ Getting There & Away

AIR

There are daily flights on **Coastal Aviation** (⌕ 0778-242966, 0658-777762; pembaaviationtanga@gmail.com; Independence Ave) between Tanga, Dar es Salaam, Zanzibar and Pemba (one way between Tanga and Pemba/Zanzibar/Dar es Salaam US$70/100/130). Its booking agent is near Exim Bank, and at the airport. The airstrip is about 3km west of town along the Korogwe road (Tsh4000 in a taxi).

BOAT

At the time of research, the ferry service between Tanga and Wete on Pemba was suspended, but it is likely to soon resume.

BUS

Buses for Dar es Salaam, Simba, Raha Leo and other lines depart daily every few hours from 6.30am to 2pm in each direction (Tsh12,000 to Tsh15,000, five hours).

To Arusha, there are at least three departures daily between about 6am and 11am (Tsh13,000 to Tsh14,000, seven hours). To Lushoto (Tsh5000 to Tsh6000, three to four hours), there's a direct bus departing by 7am, or you can take any Arusha bus and transfer at Mombo.

To Pangani (Tsh2000, 1½ hours), there are small buses throughout the day along the coastal road.

ℹ Getting Around

There are taxi ranks at the bus station, and at the junction of Usambara and India Sts. If you're keen on cycling, the tourist information office can help with bicycle rental. There are occasional dalla-dallas that run along Ocean Rd between the town centre and Ras Kazone.

Muheza

Muheza is a scrappy junction town where the roads to Amani Nature Reserve and to Pangani branch off the main Tanga highway.

🛏 Sleeping

GK Lodge GUESTHOUSE
(r Tsh13,000) This local guesthouse has clean, basic rooms and no food. It's 1.2km from the bus stand: follow signs to Amani Nature Reserve; after crossing the railroad tracks, continue along the Amani road for 500m to the signposted right-hand turn-off.

❶ Getting There & Away

Transport to Amani leaves from the bus stand just off the Tanga road. There are two buses daily to and from Amani, departing Muheza about 2pm (Tsh3500, two hours), and Amani at 6am. There are connections to Tanga (Tsh2000, 45 minutes) throughout the day, and direct daily buses in the morning to Lushoto (Tsh4000, three hours).

Usambara Mountains

With their wide vistas, cool climate, winding paths and picturesque villages, the Usambaras are one of northeastern Tanzania's delights. Rural life revolves around a cycle of bustling, colourful market days that rotate from one village to the next, and is largely untouched by the booming safari scene and influx of 4WDs in nearby Arusha. It's easily possible to spend at least a week trekking from village to village or exploring with day walks.

The Usambaras, which are part of the ancient Eastern Arc chain, are divided into two ranges separated by a 4km-wide valley. The western Usambaras, around Lushoto, are the most accessible, with a better road network, and are quite heavily touristed these days, while the eastern Usambaras, around Amani, are less developed.

Paths get too muddy for trekking during the rainy season. The best time to visit is from July to October, after the rains and when the air is clearest.

Amani Nature Reserve

This often-overlooked reserve (adult/child US$10/5 per visit, not per day) is located west of Tanga in the heart of the eastern Usambaras. It's a peaceful, lushly vegetated patch of montane forest humming with the sounds of rushing water, chirping insects and singing birds, and is exceptionally rich in unique plant and bird species – a highly worthwhile detour for those ornithologically or botanically inclined. For getting around, there's a network of short walks along shaded forest paths that can be done with or without a guide. The reserve gate – where you pay your entry fees – is at Zigi, about 12km below Amani.

🛏 Sleeping & Eating

Amani Conservation Centre Rest House CAMPGROUND, GUESTHOUSE **$**
(📱027-264 0313, 0784 587805; www.amani nature.org; camping US$30; s/d Tsh15,000/30,000; breakfast/lunch/dinner Tsh3000/6000/6000; 🅿) The setting and rustic atmosphere here are better than at Zigi Rest House, but rooms aren't as comfortable and they can be less peaceful. There is also a small area to pitch a tent, a supply of hot water and simple meals available. Continue straight past the main fork in Amani to the reserve office. The guesthouse is next to the office.

Zigi Rest House CAMPGROUND, GUESTHOUSE **$**
(📱027-264 0313, 0784 587805; www.amani nature.org; camping US$30; s/d Tsh15,000/30,000; breakfast/lunch/dinner Tsh3000/6000/6000) Rooms here have bathrooms, three twin beds and are quieter and marginally more comfortable than those at Amani Conservation Centre Resthouse. There is hot water for bathing and meals are available, though it's a good idea to bring fruit or snacks as supplements. Camping is possible; bring all supplies. It is located at the main reserve gate.

Amani Forest Camp CAMPGROUND, COTTAGES **$**
(Emau Hill; 📱0782 656526; www.amaniforest camp.com; camping US$7, s/d/tr tented bandas US$74/98/132, s/d/tr cottage US$94/128/177; ☺mid-Jun–Mar; 🅿) 🌱 This rustic place has good camping, comfortable permanent tents sharing amenities and the four-person Turaco cottage with bathroom. All are in a wooded setting with fine birdwatching and walking trails. Continue 1.5km past Amani on the Kwamkoro road to the signposted turn-off, from where it's 3km further along a narrow bush track. Half- and full-board options are also available.

❶ Information

There's an **information centre** (☺8am-5pm) at the old Station Master's House at Zigi with details about the area's history, animals and medicinal plants.

The **reserve office** (☎ 027-264 0313, 0784-242045; www.amaninature.org; adult/child per visit (not per day) US$10/5, Tanzania-registered/foreign vehicle per visit Tsh10,000/US$50) is at Amani. Fees for entry and guides (per person per day US$15) can be paid here or at Zigi.

❶ Getting There & Away

Amani is 32km northwest of Muheza along a dirt road that is in fair condition the entire way, except for the last 7km, where the road is rocky and in bad shape (4WD only). There's at least one truck daily between Muheza and Amani (Tsh3000, two hours), continuing on to Kwamkoro, 9km beyond Amani. Departures from Muheza are between about 1pm and 2pm. Going in the other direction, transport passes Amani (stopping near the Amani reserve office as well as at the Zigi entry gate) from about 6am.

Lushoto

This leafy highland town is nestled in a fertile valley at about 1200m, surrounded by pines and eucalyptus mixed with banana plants and other tropical foliage. It's the centre of the western Usambaras and makes an ideal base for hikes into the surrounding hills.

🏃 Activities

The western Usambaras around Lushoto offer wonderful walking. Routes follow well-worn footpaths that weave among villages, cornfields and banana plantations, and range from a few hours to several days. It's easy to hike on your own, though you'll need to master basic Swahili phrases, carry a GPS, get a map of the area and plan your route to go via the handful of villages where local guesthouses are available. This said, a spate of robberies of solo hikers, mostly en route to Irente Viewpoint, means that for all routes, hiking with a guide is recommended.

All of the tourist information centres also organise hikes. Don't go with freelancers who aren't associated with an office or a reliable hotel. Rates vary depending on the hike and have gotten very costly. Expect to pay Tsh30,000 per person for a half-day hike to Irente Viewpoint, up to about Tsh75,000 per person per day on multiday hikes, including camping or accommodation in very basic guesthouses, guide fees, forest fees for any hikes that enter forest reserves (which includes most hikes from Lushoto) and

Lushoto

food. Note that if you're fit and keen on covering some distance, most of the set stages for the popular hikes are quite short and it's easy to do two or even three stages in a day. However, most guides will then want to charge you the full price for the additional days, so you'll need to negotiate an amicable solution. A basic selection of vegetables and fruits is available along most routes and bottled water is sold in several of the larger villages, though if you're hiking on your own, you should carry a filter.

Lushoto can get chilly and wet at any time of year, so bring a waterproof jacket.

🛏 Sleeping & Eating

IN & NEAR TOWN

Tumaini Hostel   HOSTEL $

(☎ 027-264 0094; tumaini@elct-ned.org; Main Rd; d/ste/f Tsh30,000/40,000/50,000, s without bathroom Tsh17,000; P) This good-value place run by the Lutheran church offers clean, twin-bedded rooms and hot-water showers in a two-storey compound overlooking tiny gardens. A restaurant is attached. It's directly in the town centre, near the Telecom building. Profits support church-run community projects in the area.

HIKES FROM LUSHOTO

An easy walk to get started is to **Irente Viewpoint** (6km, allow two to three hours return), which begins on the road running southwest from the Anglican church and leads gradually uphill to the viewpoint, with wide views on clear days. It's impressive to see how abruptly the Usambaras rise up from the plains below. En route is **Irente Farm** (Irente Farm; ☑0784 502935, 0788 503002; www.irentebiodiversityreserve.org; camping Tsh8000, s/d/tr from Tsh30,000/50,000/95,000, 4-/6-person house Tsh200,000/175,000; P) ✎, where you can buy fresh cheese, yoghurt and granola, and get accommodation.

There's also a lovely three- to four-day hike that you can do from Lushoto to **Mtae** through stands of pine and past cornfields, villages and patches of wild asters, a six-day walk to Amani Nature Reserve, plus many other possibilities. The tourist information centres have wall maps detailing some of the routes.

St Eugene's Lodge
GUESTHOUSE $

(☑0784 523710, 027-264 0055; www.usambara-st-eugene.com; s/tw/tr/ste US$25/45/54/60) Run by an order of sisters, the unpretentious St Eugene's has pleasant rooms with balconies and views over the surrounding gardens. Tasty meals are served, and homemade cheese and jam are for sale. St Eugene's is along the main road, about 3.5km before Lushoto, on the left coming from Soni. Ask to get dropped at the Montessori Centre.

Rosminian Hostel
GUESTHOUSE $

(☑0785 776348, 0684 116688; d Tsh30,000; P) This small church-run place has straightforward double-bedded rooms overlooking a tiny compound. All have hot-water showers, mosquito nets and TVs; meals are available with advance order. It's 1.8km before town, and about 300m off the main road to the left when coming from Soni. Ask the bus driver to drop you at the turn-off.

St Benedict's Hostel
GUESTHOUSE $

(☑0712 369174; camping Tsh7000, s/d/tr Tsh20,000/30,000/45,000) St Benedict's offers one larger double plus several smaller rooms. The rooms are no-frills, and rather dark and gloomy, but the location is convenient. Meals are available with advance order. It's next door to and run by the Catholic church.

Lawn's Hotel
LODGE $$

(☑0784 420252, 0754 464526; www.lawnshotel.com; camping US$12, s/d/tr US$45/55/70; P🛜) This Lushoto institution is faded but full of charm, with vine-covered buildings and extensive gardens. It has spacious, slightly dilapidated wooden-floored rooms with fireplaces, plus newer doubles and twin-bedded bungalows, a bar and a restaurant. Go left at the traffic circle at the town entrance, following the unpaved road up and around to the right through the pine trees to the hotel.

OUTSIDE TOWN

Swiss Farm Cottage
LODGE $$

(☑0714 970271, 0784 700813; www.swiss-farm-cottage.co.tz; per person half board in standard/luxury bungalow US$50/65; P) This tranquil spot, complete with cows grazing on the hillsides, does a good job of mixing Tanzania with Switzerland. There are standard family rooms, and a bungalow with two doubles sharing a sitting area with a fireplace. The rooms are comfortable and there's hiking at your doorstep.

Mullers Mountain Lodge
LODGE $$

(☑0784 500999, 0782 315666; www.mullersmountainlodge.co.tz; camping US$10, s/d US$45/60, q without bathroom US$90, cottage US$120; P) This old family homestead is set in sprawling grounds, with rooms in the main house or, for more privacy, in nearby cottages (with two rooms sharing a sitting room). There are also a few less appealing cement huts with shared bathroom, a camping area and a restaurant. It's about 17km from Lushoto past Migambo village, and signposted.

ℹ️ Information

Bosnia Internet Café (Main Rd; per hour Tsh2000; ⏱8.30am-6pm Mon-Fri, 9am-2pm Sat) At the southern end of town.

CRDB (Main Rd) ATM; at the Western Union building, diagonally opposite the prison.

Friends of Usambara Society (www.usambaratravels.com) Just down the small road running next to NMB bank, with hikes and cycling tours (bring your own bicycle).

National Microfinance Bank (Main Rd; ⊘8am-3pm Mon-Fri) Changes cash only.

SED Tours (☑0784 689848; www.sed adventures.com; Main Rd) Reliable hikes and cultural tours; on the main road opposite the park.

❶ Getting There & Away

Dalla-dallas go throughout the day between Lushoto and Mombo (Tsh2000, one hour), the junction town on the main highway.

Daily direct buses travel from Lushoto to Tanga (Tsh6000, four hours), Dar es Salaam (Tsh12,000, six to seven hours) and Arusha (Tsh12,000 to Tsh13,000, six hours), with most departures from 7am. To get to the lodges near Migambo, take the road heading uphill and northeast of town to Magamba, turn right at the signposted junction and continue for 7km to Migambo junction, from where the lodges are signposted. Via public transport, there's a daily bus between Tanga and Kwamakame that goes to within around 2km of Mullers, departing Tanga at about 9am or 10am and reaching the Migambo area at around 2pm.

Mtae

Tiny Mtae is perched on a cliff about 55km northwest of Lushoto, with fantastic 270-degree views over the Tsavo Plains and down to Mkomazi National Park. Just to the southeast is **Shagayu Peak** (2220m), one of the highest in the Usambara Mountains.

About 3km before Mtae is the excellent **Mambo Viewpoint Eco Lodge & Mambo Cliff Inn** (☑0785 272150, 0769 522420; www.mamboviewpoint.org; camping US$8-10, s/d in Cliff Inn US$20/35, s/d in Viewpoint from US$60/85; ℗🛜) 🅿, with stunning views, comfortable permanent tents and cottages. The owners offer a wealth of information on the area, and can sort out hikes, village stays and more.

❶ Getting There & Away

If travelling by public transport you'll need to spend at least one night in Mtae as buses from Lushoto (Tsh7000, four hours) travel only in the afternoons, departing Lushoto by about 1pm. The return buses from Mtae to Lushoto depart between 4am and 5am en route to Dar es Salaam. For Mambo, negotiate with the driver to take you all the way, or get dropped at the Mtae–Mambo junction, from where it is just a short walk.

Soni

Tiny Soni lacks Lushoto's infrastructure, but makes a good change of pace if you'll be staying longer in the Usambaras. It's also the starting point for several wonderful walks, including a two- to three-day hike to the Mazumbai Forest Reserve and Bumbuli town.

Sleepy **Maweni Farm** (☑0784 279371, 0784 307841; www.maweni.com/lodge; d US$60-80, without bathroom US$50; ℗🛜) is an atmospheric old farmhouse set in lush, rambling grounds, with Kwa Mungu mountain rising up behind. The rooms (some in the main house and some in a separate block) are spacious and comfortable. There are also safari-style tents with private bathrooms, plus meals and guides for walks. Maweni is 2.9km from the main Soni junction along a dirt road, and signposted.

❶ Getting There & Away

Soni is 12km south of Lushoto along the Mombo road, and easy to reach via dalla-dalla from either destination (Tsh1000 from Lushoto, Tsh1000 from Mombo).

Mombo

Mombo is the scruffy junction town at the foot of the Usambara Mountains where the road to Lushoto branches off the main Dar es Salaam–Arusha highway. As most buses from either Arusha or Dar es Salaam pass at a reasonable hour, you should have no trouble getting a dalla-dalla up to Soni or Lushoto to sleep.

NORTHERN TANZANIA

For many visitors to Tanzania, it's all about the north. With snow-capped Mt Kilimanjaro, wildlife-packed Ngorongoro Crater, red-cloaked Maasai warriors and the vast plains of the Serengeti, northern Tanzania embodies what is for many the quintessential Africa. But there's much more to this majestic and mythical place and it would draw scores of visitors even if it didn't host these African icons.

Crater-capped Mt Meru is a climb that rivals its taller neighbour, dry-season wildlife watching in Tarangire National Park is as good as any other park in Africa, and the desolate Rift Valley landscapes between Lakes Manyara and Natron will mesmerise

Northern Tanzania

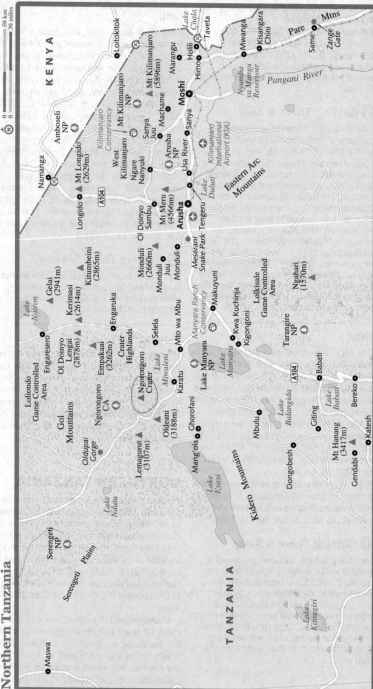

50 km
30 miles

KENYA

Loitokitok

Amboseli NP

Namanga

Mt Longido (2629m)

Longido

Ol Doinyo Sambu

Lake Natron

Gelai (2941m)

Kerimasi (2614m)

Engaruka

Engaresero

Engangesero

Loliondo Game Controlled Area

Ol Doinyo Lengai (2878m)

Empakaai (3262m)

Crater Highlands

Gol Mountains

Ngorongoro CA

Ngorongoro Crater

Oldupai Gorge

Lemagurut (3107m)

Oldeani (3188m)

Mang'ola

Ghorofani

Lake Ndutu

Lake Eyasi

Kidero Mountains

Serengeti NP

Serengeti Plains

Maswa

Lake Kitangiri

Kitumbeini (2865m)

Monduli (2660m)

Monduli Juu

Monduli

Meserani Snake Park

Selela

Mto wa Mbu

Lake Miwaleni

Karatu

Lake Manyara NP

Mbulu

Dongobesh

Gendabi

Lake Balangida

Lake Babati

Citing

Mt Hanang (3417m)

Katesh

Bereko

Babati

West Kilimanjaro

Ngare Nanyuki

Arusha NP

Mt Meru (4566m)

Arusha

Usa River

Ol Doinyo Sambu

Tengeru

Lake Duluti

Kilimanjaro Conservancy

Mt Kilimanjaro NP

Sanya Juu

Machame

Moshi

Sanya

Kilimanjaro International Airport (KIA)

Eastern Arc Mountains

Mt Kilimanjaro (5896m)

Marangu

Holili

Himo

Taveta

Lake Chala

Mwanga

Kisangara Chini

Pare Mtns

Same

Zange Gate

Nyumba ya Mungu Reservoir

Pangani River

Makuyuni

Manyara Ranch Conservancy

Kwa Kuchinja

Kigongoni

Lolkisale Game Controlled Area

Ngahari (1570m)

Tarangire NP

A104

TANZANIA

you. Sleep in a coffee plantation, hunt with modern-day nomads, ride camels, canoe with hippos...well, you get the point.

You couldn't possibly do it all in one trip, but you'll make a lifetime of memories no matter how much time you have.

Arusha

POP 416,440

Cool, lush and green, Arusha is one of Tanzania's most developed and fastest-growing towns and the seat of the East African Community, a revived attempt at regional collaboration. It sprawls near the foot of Mt Meru at about 1300m altitude and enjoys a temperate climate throughout the year. Arusha's location is convenient for all Northern Circuit parks, and as such, it's the safari capital of Tanzania and a major tourism centre: with all the good and bad that brings.

Prices are high and the chorus of *hi how are you?, hey my friend, what are you looking for? want something special? good price* and *remember me?* lead many tourists to fits of exasperation. On the other hand, Arusha's food and facilities are excellent. For travellers making an extended trip across Tanzania it can be a nice break from the rigours of the road. For first-timers to Africa, it provides a gentle introduction.

Sights

Natural History Museum MUSEUM
(☏027-250 7540; Boma Rd; adult/student US$5/2; ⏰9am-5.30pm Mon-Fri, 9.30am-5.30pm Sat & Sun) This museum inside the old German *boma*, completed in 1900, has three parts. The best is the wing dedicated to the evolution of humans, since much of what we know about the topic came from fossils unearthed in Tanzania. There are also displays on insects, the history of Arusha during the German colonial era, and many wildlife photos and mounts.

Arusha Declaration Museum MUSEUM
(☏027-250 7800; Makongoro Rd; adult/child Tsh8000/4000; ⏰9.30am-5pm) Despite the promising subject matter, you'd have to be pretty bored to come to this unfocused little museum. Half the space is filled with photos of government officials. It improves slightly after that, with some photos from the colonial era and a handful of ethnographic artefacts.

Tours

★**Via Via Cultural Tours** CULTURAL TOUR
(☏0754 038981; www.viaviacafe.com/en/arusha; Boma Rd; 1hr/1 day drum lesson US$20/50, city/market tour US$20/40, cooking class US$30; ⏰9am-4pm) Run out of the Via Via Cafe just off the back of the Natural History Museum, this place offers drum lessons (including an all-day version in which you learn to make your own drum), two-hour city tours, three-hour 'Maasai Market Tours', and cooking classes.

Sleeping

The best budget area in Arusha is the Kaloleni neighbourhood, north of Stadium St and east of Colonel Middleton Rd (a 10-minute walk from the bus stand), followed by the busy central market area south of the stadium. Things are slightly quieter around the Clock Tower. For midrange and top-end options, head to leafy eastern Arusha.

City Centre & Clock Tower

Kitundu Guesthouse GUESTHOUSE $
(☏027-250 9065; Levolosi Rd; s/d Tsh25,000/30,000, with shared bathroom Tsh15,000/20,000) A decent, reliable choice. It's worth paying extra for a room with attached bathroom. Also, avoid the claustrophobic ground-floor rooms and go for the far better, light-filled rooms up on the first or second floors where there are Mt Meru views from the shared landing. All rooms have mosquito nets.

Raha Leo GUESTHOUSE $
(☏0753 600002; Stadium St; s/d Tsh25,000/30,000, with shared bathroom Tsh20,000/25,000) Undistinguished although adequate double and twin rooms, some along the corridor, others around an open-air lounge. With hot water and cable TV it's one of the best value options in town, and the location is central but quieter than most.

Arusha Centre Tourist Inn HOTEL $
(☏0764 294384, 027-250 0421; atihotel@habari.co.tz; Livingstone Rd; s/d US$25/30; @☎) Unremarkable but clean and fairly spacious rooms are on offer here – they're just about fine for the price (ask for a discount anyway), but be prepared for an early morning wake-up call from the neighbouring mosque. The three storeys ring a courtyard, and there's a

Arusha

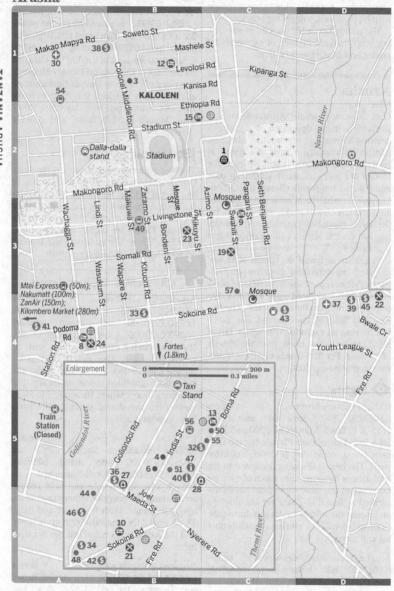

restaurant at the front with okay food and plenty of Maasai men staring at the TV.

Arusha Backpackers BACKPACKERS **$**
(☎0773 377795; www.arushabackpackers. co.tz; Sokoine Rd; dm/s/d with shared bathroom

US$10/12/20; @) There's a buzz about this place in more ways than one – it's popular for those looking to hook up with other travellers, but the absence of mosquito nets may deter some. Shared bathrooms have somewhat of an institutional feel. Un-

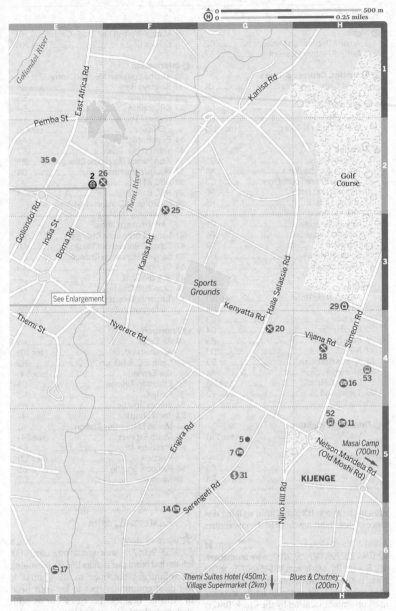

less you're looking for travel buddies, you might want to look elsewhere.

New Safari Hotel HOTEL **$$**
(☏0787 326122, 027-254 5940; www.thenewsafari hotel.com; Boma Rd; s/d/tr US$100/125/180; ❄@)

Once the favourite of white hunters and their tall tales from the African bush, the New Safari was reborn in 2004 and is the pick of the city-centre midrange options. Rooms are generally large, have tiled floors and a touch of

Arusha

class in the decor. It's also within walking distance of just about anything in the city centre.

Arusha Naaz Hotel   HOTEL **$$**
(☏ 0744 282799, 027-257 2087; www.arushanaaz.
net; Sokoine Rd; s/d/tr from US$45/60/75; ⊛ 🕾)
Naaz is short on atmosphere, but otherwise
okay value, with comfortable 1st-floor rooms
in a convenient location by the Clock Tower;
the main reason to stay here (as opposed to
Eastern Arusha) is to be within walking distance of the city centre. Rooms are not all
the same, so check out a few first; we think
those around the triangular courtyard are
best.

🛏 **Eastern Arusha**

★**Ujamaa Hostel**   HOSTEL **$**
(☏ 0753 960570; www.ujamaahostel.com; Fire
Rd; dm half board plus laundry US$18) Focussing
on volunteers, but open to all, Ujamaa is
the most communal spot to lay your head
in Arusha. Besides the clean dorms with
shelves, lockable draws and hot-water baths,
there's a TV lounge, book exchange, plenty
of travel advice and a quiet backyard. It can
also hook you up with a variety of volunteer
opportunities (minimum two-week commitment) in Arusha.

★ **Blues & Chutney** B&B **$$**
(☑0658 127380, 0732 971668; www.bluesand
chutney.com; House No 2 Olorien, Lower Kijenge;
s/d US$120/160; ☎) An intimate and sophisti-
cated boutique B&B on a quiet street south-
east of the centre, Blues & Chutney has the
feel of a tranquil enclave for people in the
know. The decor is white-wood and classy,
the atmosphere refined, and four out of the
six light-and-airy rooms have large private
balconies. The restaurant serves home-style
cooking and there's a small bar.

Themi Suites Hotel APARTMENT **$$**
(☑0732 979621, 0732 979617; www.themi
suiteshotel.com; Njiro Hill Rd; 2-/3-bedroom apt
US$150/180; ✱☎) This excellent place is ide-
al for families or for those who want their
own spacious serviced apartments with
kitchen, dining and lounge area. They come
with attractive wrought-iron furnishings,
as well as flat-screen TVs, microwaves and
washing machines. The two-bedroom apartments fit four, the three-bedroom ones can
accommodate six. There's also a good on-site
restaurant.

Outpost Lodge LODGE **$$**
(☑0754 318523; www.outposttanzania.net;
Serengeti Rd; s/d/tr US$62/81/94; @☎☀)
The rooms here are nothing special, but
come with attractive stone floors, and the
lush grounds and communal poolside res-
taurant-lounge with couches, board games
and fresh-squeezed juices make for a decent
overall package. It's in a quiet residential
area off Nyerere Rd.

Spices & Herbs GUESTHOUSE **$$**
(axum_spices@hotmail.com; Simeon Rd; s/d
US$40/50; @☎) The 19 rooms behind this
popular Ethiopian restaurant are simple but
warm, with woven grass mats and wooden
wardrobes adding character not often found
at this price level. There's an internal patio
and it's cheaper than most in eastern Arusha – excellent value.

Impala Hotel HOTEL **$$**
(☑0774 878679, 027-254 3082; www.impalahotel.
com; Simeon Rd; s/d/tr US$100/130/175; ℗✱@
☎☀) Filling a gap between the small family-
run guesthouses and the big luxury hotels,
the nothing-special Impala offers adequate
rooms (be sure you get one of the newer ones
with parquetry floors and safari-themed fur-
nishings) and abundant services like a forex
bureau and 24-hour restaurant. It's always
worth asking for discounts or an upgrade to
a better room.

★ **African Tulip** BOUTIQUE HOTEL **$$$**
(☑0783 714104, 027-254 3004; www.theafrican
tulip.com; Serengeti Rd; s/d/tr US$190/230/300,
ste US$310-500; ℗✱@☎☀) ⚑ Marketing
itself as a luxury boutique hotel, the deservedly popular African Tulip inhabits a green,
quiet side street and successfully combines
an African safari theme with a genteel ambience. The large rooms are supremely comfortable havens from Arusha's noise. There's
a whimsical baobab tree in the restaurant,
carved wood around the common areas and
a small garden around the swimming pool
at the back.

Outside Arusha

Meserani Snake Park CAMPGROUND **$**
(☑027-253 8282; www.meseranisnakepark.com;
camping incl snake park admission US$10; ℗)
This overlander-oriented place has good

ARUSHA TREKKING OPERATORS

If you're organising a Kilimanjaro trek in Arusha, look for operators that organise treks
themselves rather than subcontracting to a Moshi- or Marangu-based operator. Many
safari operators also organise treks. In addition, try the following:

Dorobo Safaris (www.dorobosafaris.com; midrange) Community-oriented treks in and
around the Ngorongoro Conservation Area and wilderness treks in Tarangire Park border
areas and in the Serengeti.

Kiliwarrior Expeditions (www.kiliwarriorexpeditions.com; top end) Upmarket Kilimanjaro
climbs, treks in the Ngorongoro Conservation Area and safaris.

Summits Africa (p204) Upmarket adventure safaris, including treks in the Ngorongoro Conservation Area and to Lake Natron with the option to climb Ol Doinyo Lengai,
West Kilimanjaro walking safaris, multiday fully equipped bike safaris and combination
bike-safari trips.

CULTURAL TOURISM PROGRAMS

Numerous villages outside Arusha (and elsewhere in the country) run 'Cultural Tourism Programs' that offer an alternative to the safari scene. Most centre on light hikes and village activities.

Although the line is sometimes blurred between community empowerment and empowering the enterprising individuals who run the community, they nevertheless provide employment for locals and offer an excellent chance to experience Tanzanian life and culture. Most have various 'modules' available, from half a day to several nights. Overnight tours are either camping or homestays; though expect conditions to be basic. Payments should be made on-site; always ask for a receipt.

All tours in the Arusha area can be booked through the Tanzania Tourist Board (TTB) Tourist Information Centre (p118). The office can also outline the best transport options. Most tours should be booked a day in advance; but some guides wait at the TTB office on standby each morning. If you have further questions, the **Cultural Tourism Program office** (☑ 0786 703010, 027-205 0025; www.tanzaniaculturaltourism.com; Natural History Museum, Boma Rd) in the back of the Natural History Museum in Arusha may (or may not) be able to assist. You can also contact many of the places directly to make the necessary arrangements.

Ilkurot (☑ 0784 459296, 0713 332005; kinyorilomon@yahoo.com) A good choice for those interested in Maasai culture. Stops on their village and trekking (using donkeys or camels, if you wish) tours include a *boma,* herbal doctor, midwife and other community members. Overnighters have the choice of camping or sleeping in a guesthouse or *boma.* The village is 25km north of Arusha off the Nairobi Rd.

Mkuru (☑ 0784 724498, 0784 472475; www.mkurucamelsafari.com) The Maasai village of Mkuru, 14km off the Nairobi road north of Mt Meru and 60km from Arusha, hosts the region's pioneering camel camp. You can take a short camel ride around the village or multiday safari as far away as Mt Kilimanjaro and Lake Natron. There's a simple tented camp in the village or pitch your own tent.

Mulala (☑ 0784 747433, 0784 499044; agapetourism@yahoo.com) Set on the southern slope of Mt Meru about 30km northeast of Arusha, this program is completely run by women. Tours focus on farming and daily life and include visits to a women's cooperative and cheese makers. Camping is possible if you have camping gear, though with an early start, you could do this tour as a day trip from Arusha.

Ng'iresi (☑ 0754 320966, 0754 476079; lotisareyo@yahoo.com) One of the most popular programs, the primary tours at Ng'iresi village (about 7km northeast of Arusha on the slopes of Mt Meru) include visits to Wa-arusha farms, houses and a school. There is also a traditional medicine tour, along with several waterfalls and a hike up a small volcano. There's no public transport here; arrange transport as part of your booking.

Peace Matunda (☑ 0787 482966; www.peacematunda.org) Near Kimundo, around 15km northeast of Arusha, this place offers half- to three-day hiking, camping and mountain-biking tours, visits to local families and to coffee and banana plantations, as well as volunteer programs with a focus on underprivileged kids.

facilities, including hot showers, a bar-restaurant with cheap meals and a vehicle repair shop. It's 25km west of Arusha along the Dodoma road.

⭐**Karama Lodge**　LODGE $$
(☑ 0754 475188; www.karamalodge.com; s/d/tr US$104/138/199; P@🕸🏊) Truly something different, on a forested hillside in the Suye Hill area just southeast of town, Karama offers 22 rustic and rather lovely stilt bun-

galows, each with a veranda and views to both Kilimanjaro and Meru on clear days. It's signposted north of Old Moshi Rd.

⭐**Onsea House**　B&B $$$
(☑ 0787 112498; www.onseahouse.com; s/d US$250/300; P🕸🏊) Run by a Belgian chef whose keen eye for the little things is what really makes this lovely bed and breakfast such a great place. The rooms each have their own themes, plus there's the Machweo Wellness

Retreat and Fine Dining, a fabulous spa and yoga centre with a top-notch restaurant. Very tranquil and very classy. It's about 1km off the Moshi road on the edge of town.

Kigongoni LODGE $$$
([✆]0732 978876; www.kigongoni.net; s/d/tr incl guided walks from US$170/198/315; [P][@][🛜][♨]) [✈] Kigongoni's tranquil hilltop perch about 5km past Arusha gives it an almost wilderness feel. Spacious cottages, all with porches, fireplaces and wide views, are scattered around the forest, some quite a hilly walk from the cosy common areas. It's about 5km beyond Arusha towards Moshi.

Eating

City Centre & Clock Tower

★**Khan's Barbecue** BARBECUE $
(Mosque St; mixed grill from Tsh7500; [⏱]from 6.30pm Mon-Fri, from 4.30pm Sat & Sun) This Arusha institution is an auto-spares store by day and the best known of many earthy roadside barbecues around the market area by night. It lays out a heaping spread of grilled, skewered meat and salad. If you want to feel like a local, this is a fine place to begin.

Big Bite INDIAN $
(Swahili St; mains Tsh5000-12,000; [⏱]noon-2.30pm & 6-9.30pm Wed-Mon; [✐]) One of the oldest and most reliable Indian restaurants in Arusha. Don't let the modest premises or fast-food-esque name fool you.

Shanghai CHINESE $
([✆]0756 659247; Sokoine Rd; meals Tsh4000-14,000; [⏱]noon-3pm & 6-10.30pm; [✐]) Very good Chinese-owned restaurant with fast service and 'Far East meets the Wild West' decor – let's face it, when did a Chinese restaurant in Africa ever win a style award? It's hidden behind the post office.

Arusha Naaz Hotel TANZANIAN $
([✆]027-257 2087; Sokoine Rd; buffet Tsh10,000; [⏱]buffet noon-6pm) This place has an all-you-can-eat lunch buffet and large snack counter.

Café Barrista CAFE $
([✆]0754 288771; www.cafebarrista.com; Sokoine Rd; meals Tsh4000-10,000; [⏱]7.30am-6.30pm Mon-Sat, 8am-5pm Sun; [🛜][✐]) A recent move a little upmarket has done nothing to diminish the appeal of this friendly place. Try their chocolate croissant, or fill up with

sandwiches, salads and wraps, as well as great coffee. There's also an internet cafe and wi-fi (free with meal purchases).

★**Fifi's** INTERNATIONAL, BAKERY $$
([✆]0786 487727, 027-254 4021; Themi St; breakfast Tsh3000-17,000, mains Tsh14,000-18,000; [⏱]7.30am-10pm Mon-Fri, 8.30am-10pm Sat & Sun) As good for breakfast or a quiet afternoon coffee as for a more substantial meal, this sophisticated bakery has free wi-fi and serves up exciting dishes such as beef fillet with blue cheese sauce. A very cool place.

Via Via CAFE $$
([✆]0782 434845; www.viaviacafe.com/en/arusha; Boma Rd; mains Tsh10,000-16,000; [⏱]9am-10pm Mon-Sat) Cultured and laid-back with the best soundtrack of any restaurant in Arusha, this place along the river behind the Natural History Museum is a popular meeting spot. They serve coffee, salads and sandwiches plus more substantial meals like pastas and grilled fish. There's a decent bar and live music.

Eastern Arusha

★**Blue Heron** INTERNATIONAL $$
([✆]0785 555127; www.blue-heron-tanzania.com; Haile Selassie Rd; mains Tsh13,000-23,000; [⏱]9am-4pm Mon-Thu, to 10pm Fri, 10am-10pm Sat) Our pick of the garden restaurants that are a recurring theme out in Arusha's east, the Blue Heron gets the tricky combination of lounge bar and family restaurant just right. Sit under the leafy veranda or out on the lawn tables to enjoy a menu that ranges from paninis and soups up to beef tenderloin and creative specials like rice-and-broccoli fried balls with curry ratatouille.

Spices & Herbs ETHIOPIAN, EUROPEAN $$
([✆]0685 313162, 0754 313162; Simeon Rd; mains Tsh8000-18,000; [⏱]10.30am-10.30pm; [🛜][✐]) Unpretentious al fresco spot serving two menus: Ethiopian and Continental – ignore the latter and order *injera* (Ethiopian bread) soaked in beef, chicken or lamb sauce, or *yegbeg tibs* (fried lamb with Ethiopian butter, onion, green peppers and rosemary). The service is good and there's plenty of art on the walls.

TapaSafari SPANISH, INTERNATIONAL $$
([✆]0757 009037; www.tapasafari.co.tz; Kanisa Rd; small/large tapas from Tsh3000/5000, mains Tsh10,000-35,000; [⏱]11am-10pm; [🛜][✐]) With a semi-outdoor setting, this restaurant and

wine bar ticks many boxes. There are snacks, grills, pizza and pasta, but the real stars are the Spanish tapas and extensive list of South African wines to choose from. Sundays are especially popular with a four-course set menu (Tsh22,000).

★ **Bay Leaf** EUROPEAN $$$
(☏027-254 3055; www.bayleaftz.com; Vijana Rd; mains Tsh11,000-37,000; ☺8am-11pm; 🛜) Arusha's poshest menu features dishes such as figs primavera (parma-wrapped brie and stuffed figs with sticky balsamic toffee), slow-cooked West Kili lamb shanks, and Wellington of game birds (wrapped in 'ethereal' filo pastry). It also offers a great wine list (by the glass and bottle), as well as separate lunch, dinner and Indian menus. Book ahead.

Outside Arusha

★ **River House** INTERNATIONAL $$
(☏0689 759067; www.shanga.org; Dodoma Rd; 4-course lunch US$18; ☺9.30am-4.30pm) 🌿 An offshoot of the inspiring Shanga project, diners at River House are greeted with champagne and then served a huge and delicious four-course lunch in gorgeous gardens – it's part buffet, although soup and the dessert are served to your table. It's an event as much as a meal. It's on the Burka Coffee Estate, 3km west of the Nakumatt supermarket; reservations are required.

Self-Catering

Village Supermarket SUPERMARKET $
(Njiro Hill Rd; ☺9am-9pm) Part of the Njiro Hill Shopping Complex southeast of the centre, this place is Arusha's best-stocked supermarket. There's a decent open-air food court outside the door and a cinema complex in the same building.

Nakumatt SUPERMARKET $
(Dodoma Rd; ☺8.30am-10pm Mon-Sat, 10am-9pm Sun) On the edge of the city centre, this is the largest supermarket in central Arusha.

🍷 Drinking & Nightlife

Via Via CAFE
(Boma Rd; ☺9am-4am Mon-Sat) This cafe is a good spot for a drink and one of the best places to find out about upcoming cultural events, many of which are held here. On Thursday nights there's karaoke and a live band. Things get started at 9pm and admission is a steep Tsh7000.

Masai Camp CLUB
(Old Moshi Rd; admission Tsh5000; ☺9pm-dawn Fri & Sat) Arusha's loudest and brashest club is an institution on the Arusha party scene. The music is a mix of African and Western.

🔒 Shopping

★ **Shanga** HANDICRAFTS
(☏0689 759067; www.shanga.org; Dodoma Rd; ☺9am-4.30pm) 🌿 What started out as a small enterprise making beaded necklaces has branched into furniture, paper, clothing and many other products, mostly using recycled materials and made by disabled workers. Their products are sold around the world, and a visit to their workshop and store just out of town (3km west of Nakumatt) is quite inspiring.

★ **Schwari** HANDICRAFTS, HOMEWARES
(Haile Selassie Rd; ☺9am-5pm Mon-Thu & Sat, to 8pm Fri) Fabulous handicrafts and classy homewares, children's toys and national parks maps – Schwari has picked the best of local crafts to produce one of the loveliest collections on offer in Arusha. Better still, it's attached to the equally lovely Blue Heron (p115).

Maasai Women Fair Trade Centre HANDICRAFTS
(☏0784 210839, 027-254 4290; www.maasai womentanzania.org; Simeon Rd; ☺9am-4pm Mon-Sat) 🌿 A project of Maasai Women Development Organisation (MWEDO), this small shop raises money for education and other projects. It has expensive, but high-quality beadwork (and a few other crafts), including some items seldom sold elsewhere, like Christmas ornaments. There's an on-site coffee shop.

Kase BOOKS
(☏027-250 2640; Boma Rd; ☺9am-5.30pm Mon-Fri, to 2pm Sat) Best bet for national park books and maps. If the Boma Rd shop doesn't have what you want, try the other branch (☏027-250 2441; Joel Maeda St; ☺9am-2pm & 5-8pm Mon-Fri, 9am-2pm Sat) around the corner.

ℹ Information

DANGERS & ANNOYANCES

After Zanzibar, Arusha is the worst place in Tanzania for street touts. Their main haunts are the bus stations and Boma Rd, but they'll find you just about anywhere.

NORTHERN CIRCUIT SAFARI OPERATORS

Access2Tanzania (www.access2tanzania.com; budget to midrange) Customised, community-focused itineraries.

Africa Travel Resource (ATR; www.africatravelresource.com; midrange to top end) A web-based safari broker that matches your safari ideas with an operator and offers excellent background information on its website.

African Scenic Safaris (www.africanscenicsafaris.com; midrange) Small, family-run operator focusing on customised northern circuit safaris and Kilimanjaro treks.

Base Camp Tanzania (www.basecamptanzania.com; midrange) Northern circuit safaris and treks.

Hoopoe Safaris (www.hoopoe.com; India St; upper midrange) Community-integrated luxury camping and lodge safaris in the northern circuit; also has its own tented camps at Lake Manyara and mobile camps in the Serengeti.

IntoAfrica (www.intoafrica.co.uk; midrange) Fair-traded cultural safaris and treks in northern Tanzania, including a seven-day wildlife-cultural safari in Maasai areas.

Lake Tanganyika Adventure Safaris (www.safaritourtanzania.com; midrange) Adventure safaris focusing on Katavi and Mahale Mountains National Parks and Lake Tanganyika.

Maasai Wanderings (www.maasaiwanderings.com; midrange) Northern Tanzania safaris and treks.

Peace Matunda Tours (www.peacematunda.org; budget) Cultural walks and tours around Arusha plus northern circuit wildlife safaris.

Roy Safaris (www.roysafaris.com; Serengeti Rd; upper midrange) Budget and semiluxury camping safaris in the northern circuit, as well as competitively priced luxury lodge safaris and Kilimanjaro and Meru treks; known especially for their high-quality safari vehicles.

Safari Bookings (www.safaribookings.com; all budgets) A web-based safari planning resource with a large database of operators and a wealth of information on Tanzania's national parks.

Safari Makers (www.safarimakers.com; budget) No-frills northern circuit camping and lodge safaris and treks.

Summit Expeditions & Nomadic Experience (www.nomadicexperience.com; upper midrange) Expertly guided Kilimanjaro treks, plus cycling, walks and cultural excursions on the mountain's lower slopes and customised northern circuit wildlife safaris.

Tanzania Journeys (www.tanzaniajourneys.com; midrange) Northern circuit, community-focused vehicle, active and cultural safaris, including Kilimanjaro treks, day hikes and cultural tours in the Moshi area.

Wayo Africa (www.wayoafrica.com; top end) Northern circuit active and vehicle safaris, including Serengeti walking safaris plus visits to Hadzabe areas.

At night, take a taxi if you go out. It's not safe to walk after dusk except around the market area. Even during the daytime, try to avoid carrying a bag or anything that could tempt a thief.

IMMIGRATION

Immigration Office (East Africa Rd; ⊙7.30am-3.30pm Mon-Fri) Near the Makongoro Rd junction.

INTERNET ACCESS

Café Barrista (Sokoine Rd; per hour Tsh1000; ⊙7.30am-6.30pm Mon-Sat, 8am-5pm Sun)

Has computers and wi-fi (the latter is free if you buy a meal).
New Safari Hotel (Boma Rd; per hour Tsh1000; ⊙24hr) In the hotel lobby.

MEDICAL SERVICES

Arusha Lutheran Medical Centre (☑027-254 8030; www.selianlh.habari.co.tz; Makao Mapya Rd; ⊙24hr) The best medical facility in the region, but for anything truly serious, get yourself to Nairobi.

Moona's Pharmacy (☎ 0754 309052; Sokoine Rd; ☺ 8.45am-5.30pm Mon-Fri, to 2pm Sat) Well-stocked pharmacy, west of NBC bank.

MONEY

Forex bureaus are clustered along Joel Maeda and India Sts, and Sokoine Rd near the Clock Tower. Sanya Bureau de Change, with several locations along Sokoine Rd, is open until 8pm Sundays and public holidays.

TOURIST INFORMATION

Ngorongoro Conservation Area Authority (NCAA) Information Office (☎ 027-254 4625; www.ngorongorocrater.org; Boma Rd; ☺ 9am-5pm Mon-Fri, to 1pm Sat) Has free Ngorongoro booklets and a cool relief map of the conservation area.

Tanzania National Parks Headquarters (Tanapa; ☎ 027-250 3471; www.tanzaniaparks.com; Dodoma Rd; ☺ 9am-5pm Mon-Fri, to 1pm Sat) Just west of town, this office has info on Tanzania's national parks.

Tanzania Tourist Board Tourist Information Centre (TTB; ☎ 027-250 3842, 027-250 3843; www.tanzaniatouristboard.com; Boma Rd; ☺ 8am-4pm Mon-Fri, 8.30am-1pm Sat) Knowledgeable and helpful staff have information on Arusha, Northern Circuit parks and other area attractions. They can book Cultural Tourism Program tours and provide a good free map of Arusha and Moshi. The office also keeps a 'blacklist' of tour operators and a list of registered tour companies.

TRAVEL AGENCIES

Skylink (☎ 0755 351111, 027-250 9108; www.skylinktanzania.com; Goliondoi Rd) Domestic and international flight bookings.

❶ Getting There & Away

AIR

There are daily flights to Dar es Salaam and Zanzibar (Coastal Aviation, Precision Air, Regional Air, Safari Plus, ZanAir), Nairobi (Kenya; Fly540, Precision Air), Seronera and other airstrips in Serengeti National Park (Air Excel, Coastal Aviation, Regional Air, Safari Plus), Mwanza (Precision Air), Lake Manyara National Park (Air Excel, Coastal Aviation, Regional Air) and Tarangire National Park (Coastal). Kigali (RwandAir) is served four times a week. Some sample one-way prices: Arusha–Dar es Salaam (Tsh239,000), Arusha–Mwanza (Tsh235,000) and Arusha–Seronera (US$175).

Most flights use Kilimanjaro International Airport (KIA), about halfway between Moshi and Arusha, while small planes, mostly to the national parks, leave from Arusha airport, 8km west of town along the Dodoma Rd. Verify the departure point when buying your ticket.

Air Excel (☎ 027-254 8429; www.airexcel online.com; 2nd fl, Subzali (Exim Bank) Bldg, Goliondoi Rd) Flights from Arusha to various Serengeti airstrips and Lake Manyara National Park.

Coastal Aviation (☎ 0752 059650, 027-250 0343; www.coastal.co.tz; Arusha Airport) Arusha to Lake Manyara, Serengeti and Ruaha National Parks, as well as West Kilimanjaro and Zanzibar.

Ethiopian Airlines (☎ 027-250 4231; www. ethiopianairlines.com; Boma Rd; ☺ 8.30am-12.30pm & 2-5pm Mon-Fri, 8.30am-1pm Sat) International services to Kilimanjaro International Airport from Addis Ababa.

Fastjet (☎ 0783 540540; www.fastjet.com/tz; 2nd fl, Blue Plaza, India St; ☺ 8am-6pm Mon-Sat) Good for low-cost domestic and other African destinations, with direct Kilimanjaro International Airport to Dar es Salaam flights and onward connections.

Precision Air (☎ 0756 979490; www.precision airtz.com; Boma Rd) Flies to Dar, Mwanza and Zanzibar from both Kili International and Arusha Airports. Also handles Kenya Airways bookings.

Regional Air (☎ 0784 285753; www.regional tanzania.com; Great North Rd) Connects Arusha Airport with Serengeti and Lake Manyara airstrips, as well as Zanzibar.

RwandAir (☎ 0732 978558; www.rwandair. com; Swahili St) Twice weekly Kigali to Kili International service.

ZanAir (☎ 027-254 8877; www.zanair.com; Summit Centre, Dodoma Rd) Connects Arusha with Dar es Salaam, Pemba and Zanzibar.

BUS

Arusha has two bus stations. The **central bus station** near the market is the biggest while the **Makao Mapya bus station** (Wachagga St) (aka Dar Express bus stand) a little to the northwest handles most of the luxury buses to Dar es Salaam. The central bus station is intimidatingly chaotic in the morning and both are popular haunts for flycatchers and touts. If you get overwhelmed head straight for a taxi, or, if arriving at the central bus station, duck into the lobbies of one of the hotels across the street to get your bearings. If you want to avoid the bus stations altogether, most buses make a stop on the edge of town before going to the bus stations. Taxis will be waiting.

When leaving Arusha, the best thing to do is book your ticket the day before, so that in the morning when you arrive with your luggage you can get straight on your bus. For predawn buses, take a taxi to the bus station and ask the driver to drop you directly at your bus.

Despite what you may hear, there are no luggage fees (unless you have an extraordinarily large pack).

Dar es Salaam

The best companies to/from Dar es Salaam (eight to 10 hours) include the following. If you take an early departure, with luck you *might* be able to catch the last ferry to Zanzibar. Super luxury means there's a toilet on board.

The last departure of the day to Dar es Salaam is the non-air-conditioned Akamba bus (Tsh25,000) that arrives from Nairobi (Kenya) around noon at its own office north of the city centre.

Dar Express (✆ 0784 946155, 0754 525361; Wachagga St; luxury/full luxury Tsh25,000/30,000) Generally the best company, Dar Express has luxury and full-luxury buses departing Makao Mapya bus station from 5.50am to 8am.

Metro Express (Wachagga St; luxury/full luxury Tsh33,000/36,000) Metro Express has two early morning services to Dar from Makao Mapya bus station.

Moshi

Buses and minibuses (about Tsh3000, 1½ hours) run up to 8pm from the central bus station. It's pricier (US$10) but more comfortable to take one of the Arusha–Nairobi (Kenya) shuttles.

Lushoto

Buses (Tsh12,000 to Tsh13,000, six hours) depart daily at 6am and 6.45am from the central bus station. It's often more comfortable (although more expensive) to take an express bus towards Dar es Salaam as far as Mombo, and then get local transport from there to Lushoto.

Tanga

Buses depart from the central bus station between 6am and noon (Tsh16,000, seven hours).

Babati, Kolo & Kondoa

Mtei Express (✆ 0742 941707; Wachagga St) buses depart from the central bus station, but also stop at their own office on Kilombero Rd, 300m north of Nakumatt, where you won't have to deal with touts. Buses leave hourly to Babati (Tsh6000, three hours) between 6am and 4pm. Their 6am bus continues on to Kondoa (Tsh15,000, seven hours) via Kolo (Tsh14,000, 6½ hours).

Dodoma

Early morning buses (Tsh25,000, 11 hours) via Singida from the central bus station, including Mtei Express.

Musoma

Various companies have buses (Tsh33,000, 11 to 12 hours) leaving at 6am from the central bus station, passing through Serengeti National Park and Ngorongoro Conservation Area. Foreigners must pay the park entry fees (US$100) to ride this route.

Mwanza

Most buses to Mwanza (Tsh33,000 to Tsh38,000, 12 hours) leave the central bus station (some use Makao Mapya), between 6am and 7.30am; all travel via Singida.

ⓘ Getting Around

TO/FROM KILIMANJARO INTERNATIONAL AIRPORT

The starting price for taxis from town to KIA is US$50, though some drivers will go for less. Others will only go for more.

TO/FROM ARUSHA AIRPORT

Taxis from town charge from Tsh17,000. Any dalla-dalla heading out along the Dodoma Rd can drop you at the junction, from where you'll have to walk almost 1.5km.

CAR

A standard 4WD typically costs from US$150 per day with limited kilometres. A smaller RAV4-style 4WD, which isn't ideal for wildlife viewing but can get to just about all attractions in and around the area's national parks (albeit at a slower pace) in the dry season, can be had for US$600 per week and about 100km free per day. Drivers are included in the price. Book as early as possible because demand is high.

Arusha Naaz (✆ 0786 239771, 027-250 2087; www.arushanaaz.net; Sokoine Rd; ◷ 9am-5pm)

Fortes (✆ 027-250-6094; www.fortescarhire. com; off Factory Rd) Excellent and experienced operator that also allows self-drive.

Rainbow (✆ 0765 046006; www.rainbowcar hire.com; New Safari Hotel, Boma Rd)

LOCAL TRANSPORT

Dalla-dallas (Tsh400) run along major roads from early until late. There are taxi stands all around the city centre and some park in front of most hotels, even many budget ones. A ride across town, from the Clock Tower to Makao Mapya bus station, for example, shouldn't cost more than Tsh3500. Motorcycle taxi drivers will almost always tell you Tsh2000 for a ride in the city centre, but will go for Tsh1500 if you insist.

Arusha National Park

Arusha National Park (✆ 0767 536136, 0689 062363; www.tanzaniaparks.com/arusha. html; adult/child US$45/15; ◷ 6.30am-6.30pm) is one Tanzania's smallest (322 sq km) but most beautiful and topographically varied

Arusha National Park

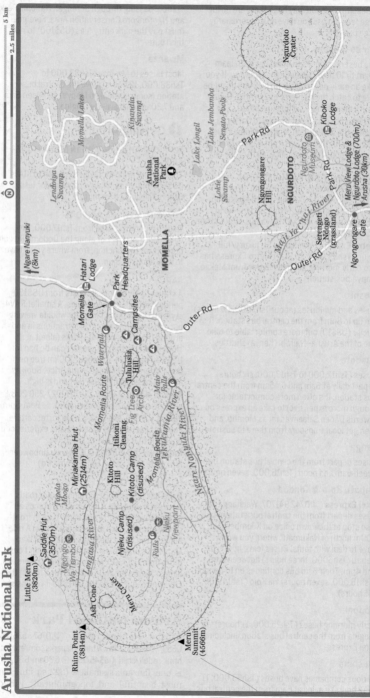

northern circuit parks. It's dominated by **Mt Meru**, an almost perfect cone with a spectacular crater. Also notable is **Ngurdoto Crater** (often dubbed Little Ngorongoro) with its swamp-filled floor.

Wildlife is nowhere near as abundant as in the other northern circuit parks and the dense vegetation reduces visibility; nevertheless you can be fairly certain of sighting zebras, giraffes, waterbucks, bushbucks, klipspringers, dik-diks, buffaloes and hippos. There are no lions or rhinos due to poaching.

🏃 Activities

Besides climbing Mt Meru (p122) on the Momella Route, **walking safaris** (US$25 per person per half-day) are popular. Several trails pass below Mt Meru and another follows the **Ngurdoto Crater rim trail** (it's not permitted to descend into the crater). Wayo Africa (p117) offers half-day Momella Lake **canoe safaris** (per person US$65 plus canoeing fee paid at the park gate US$20).

🛏 Sleeping & Eating

The park has three **public campsites** (camping US$30) in the vicinity of Momella Gate (including one with a shower).

Momella Route

There are two blocks of four-bed bunkhouses ('huts') spaced for a four-day trek. Especially during the July–August and December–January high seasons, they're often full, so it's a good idea to carry a tent (though if you camp, you'll still need to pay hut fees). It's currently not possible for independent trekkers to book beds in the bunkhouses, which operate on a first-come, first-served basis. Each bunkhouse has a cooking and eating area; bring your own stove and fuel. There's a separate dorm for guides and porters.

🛏 Outside the Park

Kiboko Lodge   LODGE $$
(☑0784 652260; www.wfkibokolodge.com; s/d half board from US$75/130) 🌿 Most employees at this nonprofit, charity-run lodge are former street kids who received training at the Watoto Foundation's vocational training school. But, it's not just a feel-good project, it's a great place to stay. The spacious and attractive stone cottages have fireplaces, hot water and safes, and the thatched-roof lounge is

almost homey. It's 5km down a 4WD-only road east of Ngongongare gate.

Meru View Lodge   LODGE $$
(☑0784 419232; www.meru-view-lodge.de; s/d US$100/140; @ 🛜 ➔) This unassuming place has a mix of large and small (all priced the same) cottages set in quiet grounds just 1km south of Ngongongare gate. They also run the nearby **Ngurdoto Lodge**, which has the same prices and similar facilities.

Hatari Lodge   LODGE $$$
(☑0752 553456, 027-255 3456/7; www.hatari lodge.com; s/d full board US$480/640) The most atmospheric and upmarket of the park lodges – the property was originally owned by Hardy Kruger, of *Hatari!* film fame – with 'modern retro' room decor, a prime location on large lawns frequented by giraffes, and views of Meru and Kilimanjaro on clear days. It's on the edge of the park, about 2km north of Momela Gate.

Rivertrees Country Inn   LODGE $$$
(☑0732 971667, 027-255 3894; www.rivertrees. com; s/d/tr from US$180/220/290, 2-room River House US$1000; 🅿 @ 🛜 ➔) With a genteel old-world ambience and excellent cuisine served family-style around a large wooden dining table, Rivertrees is a perfect post-national park stop. A variety of rooms and cottages, some wheelchair accessible, are spread throughout vast natural gardens with huge trees along the Usa River. It's east of Usa River Village, set back off the Moshi Hwy.

---

❶ ARUSHA NATIONAL PARK

Why Go Climbing Mt Meru; canoe and walking safaris; fine birdwatching; easy day trip from Arusha.

When to Go Year-round

Practicalities Drive in from Arusha or Moshi. The main entrance is at the southern Ngongongare gate. Momella gate is 12km further north near park headquarters, which is the main contact for making campsite or resthouse reservations. Both gates are open 6.30am to 6.30pm.

Budget Tips Join a pre-arranged safari or charter a dalla-dalla for the day with other travellers in Arusha: if not climbing Mt Meru, visit on a day trip to avoid camping fees.

TREKKING MT MERU

At 4566m, Mt Meru is Tanzania's second-highest mountain. Although completely overshadowed by Kilimanjaro in the eyes of trekkers, it's a spectacular volcanic cone with one of East Africa's most scenic and rewarding climbs, since it involves a dramatic and exhilarating walk along the knife edge of the crater rim.

Costs

Trekking companies in both Arusha and Moshi organise treks on Mt Meru. Most charge from US$450 to US$700 for four days. That said, you can do things quite easily on your own: park entrance, hut, rescue and guide fees total US$380 for a four-day trek. You'll also need to add in the costs of food (which you should get in Arusha, as there's nowhere to stock up near the park), and of transport to and from the park.

Tipping

Park rangers receive a fixed monthly salary for their work, and get no additional payment from the park for guiding; the fee of US$15 per day is paid to the national park rather than to the guides themselves, which means that tips are much appreciated. Generally the rangers and porters on Mt Meru are hard-working and reliable, but as the popularity of Meru has increased, so has their expectation of the big tips demanded by their counterparts on Kilimanjaro. Although rare, it's not unheard of for some poorly motivated rangers to ask you what their tip will be and if they're not satisfied, they won't continue up the mountain. If this happens, work out an arrangement to keep going, and then report them to headquarters when you get down the mountain.

As a guideline, for a good guide who has completed the full trek with you, plan on a tip of about US$50 per group. Cook and porter tips should be around US$30 and US$20 respectively. Tip more with top-end companies.

Guides & Porters

A ranger-guide is mandatory and can be arranged at Momella gate. Unlike on Kilimanjaro, guides on Meru are regular park rangers whose purpose is to assist (and protect) you in case you meet some of the park's buffaloes or elephants, rather than to show you the way (which is why the park refers to 'ranger services' rather than guiding), although they do know the route. There has been a shortage of rangers, resulting in the need to trek in large groups (10 trekkers is normal and it could be as high as 20) sometimes. More staff have been promised.

Optional porters are also available at Momella gate. The charge is US$10 per porter per day and this is paid directly to them at the end of the trek. They come from one of the nearby villages and are not park employees so you'll also need to pay their park entrance (Tsh1500 per day) and hut (Tsh800 per night) fees at Momella gate before starting to trek. Porters will carry rucksacks weighing up to 20kg (excluding their own food and clothing).

Maps

The best map is the Maco *Arusha National Park* map.

Momella Route

The Momella Route is the only route up Mt Meru. It starts at Momella gate on the eastern side of the mountain and goes to the summit along the northern arm of the horseshoe crater. The route can be done comfortably in four days (three nights). Some trekkers do it in three days by combining Stages 3 and 4 of the trek, but the park authorities now actively discourage this and even if you're in good shape, it's so rushed it's hard to enjoy your last day on the mountain. Trekkers aren't allowed to begin after 3pm, which means that if you travel to the park by bus you'll almost certainly have to camp and wait until the next day to start climbing.

While Meru is small compared with Kilimanjaro, don't underestimate it: because of the steepness, many have found that Meru is almost as difficult a climb. And it's still high enough to make the effects of altitude felt, so don't try to rush up if you're not properly acclimatised.

Stage 1: Momella Gate to Miriakamba Hut

(10km, 4-5hr, 1000m ascent)

There are two routes, one long and one short, at the start of the climb. Most people prefer taking the mostly forested long route up and the short route down so that's how the trek is described here. However, since the long route mostly follows a road, some people prefer the shorter route's wilderness feel for both ascent and descent. Either way, don't stray far from the ranger, there are many buffalo in this area.

From Momella gate, the road winds uphill for an hour to **Fig Tree Arch**, a parasitic wild fig that originally grew around two other trees, eventually strangling them. Now only the fig tree remains, with its distinctive arch large enough to drive a car through. After another hour the track crosses a large stream, just above Maio Falls and one hour further you'll reach Kitoto Camp, with excellent views over the Momella Lakes and out to Kilimanjaro in the distance. It's then one final hour to Miriakamba Hut (2514m). From Miriakamba you can walk to the **Meru Crater floor** (a two- to three-hour return trip) either in the afternoon of Stage 1, before Stage 2, or during Stage 4, but you need to let your guide know you want to do this before starting the climb. The path across the floor leads to Njeku Viewpoint on a high cliff overlooking a waterfall, with excellent views of the Ash Cone and the entire extent of the crater.

Stage 2: Miriakamba Hut to Saddle Hut

(4km, 3-5hr, 1250m ascent)

From Miriakamba the path climbs steeply up through pleasant glades between the trees to reach **Topela Mbogo** (Buffalo Swamp) after 45 minutes and **Mgongo Wa Tembo** (Elephant Ridge) after another 30 minutes. From the top of Mgongo Wa Tembo there are great views down into the crater and up to the main cliffs below the summit. Continue through some open grassy clearings and over several stream beds (usually dry) to **Saddle Hut** (3570m).

From Saddle Hut a side trip to the summit of **Little Meru** (3820m) takes about an hour and gives impressive views of Meru's summit, the horseshoe crater, the top of the Ash Cone and the sheer cliffs of the crater's inner wall. As the sun sets behind Meru, casting huge jagged shadows across the clouds, the snows on Kili turn orange and then pink as the light fades.

Stage 3: Saddle Hut to Meru Summit & Return

(5km, 4-5hr, 816m ascent, plus 5km, 2-3hr, 816m descent)

This stage, along a very narrow ridge between the outer slopes of the mountain and the sheer cliffs of the inner crater, is one of the most dramatic and exhilarating sections of trekking anywhere in East Africa. During the rainy season, ice and snow can occur on this section of the route, so take care. If there's no mist, the views from the summit are spectacular. You can see the volcanoes of Kitumbeini and Lengai along the Rift Valley Escarpment and also far across the plains of the Maasai Steppe beyond Arusha.

If you're looking forward to watching the sunrise behind Kilimanjaro, but you're not keen on attempting this section in the dark, the views at dawn are just as impressive from **Rhino Point** (3814m), about an hour from Saddle Hut, as they are from the summit. Perhaps even more so because you'll also see the main cliffs of the crater's inner wall being illuminated by the rising sun.

Stage 4: Saddle Hut to Momella Gate

(5km, 3-5hr, 2250m descent)

From Saddle Hut, retrace the Stage 2 route to Miriakamba (1½ to 2½ hours). From Miriakamba, the short path descends gradually down the ridge directly to Momella gate (1½ to 2½ hours). It goes through forest some of the way, then open grassland, where giraffes and zebras are often seen. Most companies will finish the day with a wildlife drive through the park.

❶ Getting There & Away

Arusha National Park is 25km outside Arusha, and Ngongongare gate is 6.5km north of the Arusha–Moshi road. From the northern entrance, by Momella gate, it's possible to continue via a rough track that joins the main Nairobi highway near Lariboro.

Via public transport, there are four daily buses between Arusha and Ngare Nanyuki village (6km north of Momella gate) that depart Arusha from 1.30pm to 4pm and Ngare Nanyuki between 7am and 8am. The park has asked the drivers to wait at Ngongongare gate (Tsh3500, 1½ hours) while climbers pay all their fees, but if they don't (which is common) you may have to catch the next bus or perhaps one of the irregular dalla-dallas heading to Ngare Nanyuki from Usa River. Another option is to take any bus between Arusha and Moshi, get off at Usa River village and take a taxi to Momella gate for about Tsh30,000. A taxi direct from Arusha should cost about Tsh45,000.

If you're driving your own vehicle, officially the park prohibits parking during the climb, but unofficially it can be arranged with staff at headquarters: for a fee, of course.

Tarangire National Park

Beautiful baobab-studded **Tarangire National Park** (☑0767 536139, 0689 062248, 025-31280/81; www.tanzaniaparks.com/tarangire.html; adult/child US$45/15; ☉6am-6pm) stretches along its namesake river, covering 2850 sq km, plus adjacent preserves that form part of an extended ecosystem. It's usually assigned only a day-visit as part of a larger northern circuit safari, but is worth much more, at least in the dry season when it has the second-highest (after Serengeti) concentration of wildlife of any Tanzanian national park. Large herds of elephants, zebras, wildebeest, hartebeests, elands, oryx, waterbucks, lesser kudus, giraffes and buffaloes gather along the Tarangire River and several large permanent swamps until the short wet season allows them to disperse across the Maasai Steppe, over an area 10 times larger than the park. Lion, leopard and cheetah are also on offer, but these predators are harder to spot here than in Serengeti. With more than 450 species, including many rare ones, Tarangire is also an excellent birdwatching destination.

⊙ Sights & Activities

The northern triangle area, bordered by the park boundaries to northeast and west and

by the Tarangire River and Tarangiri Safari Lodge in the south, offers some of the most accessible and rewarding **wildlife watching**, with elephants, zebras and wildebeest in abundance, and lions also a possibility. Further south, wildlife draws near to the water all along the Tarangire River valley that cuts the park in two. Gurusi Swamp, in the park's southwestern bulge, is another rich wildlife area.

Three-hour **walking safaris** (US$20 per person plus US$20 per group) can be organised from the park gate (though the armed rangers are simply security and haven't had much training about wildlife). Walking and night drives are also available from most of the camps and lodges outside the park boundaries.

🛏 Sleeping

Staying in the park gets you right into the heart of the action from the moment you wake up. Outside, the closer you are to the gate the better if you don't want to miss that crucial first hour or two inside the park.

A further option is the Tarangire Conservation Area (TCA), a remote region outside the park to the northeast with animals aplenty from November to March, many fewer in other months.

🛏 Inside the Park

Public Campsite CAMPGROUND **$**
(camping US$30) A public campsite is a short drive into the park near the northwestern tip. It has a good bush location but simple cold-water facilities. Bring supplies from Arusha.

Tarangire Safari Lodge LODGE, TENTED CAMP $$$
(☑ 0784 202777, 027-254 4752; www.tarangiresafari
lodge.com; s/d full board US$250/400; ⊞ 🖷 🏊)
A fabulous location overlooking the Ta-
rangire River, excellent service, good food
and well-priced accommodation make this
lodge our pick of the in-park options. The
sweeping vistas are such that there's no need
to go elsewhere for a sundowner, while the
accommodation includes stone bungalows
or standard en-suite safari tents; the latter
have good views from their doorsteps. It's
10km inside the park gate.

🛏 Outside the Park Gate

Zion Campsite CAMPGROUND $
(☑ 0754 460539; camping US$10; ⊞) A bare
and unkempt compound 6km before the
park gate it may be, but it's cheaper than
camping inside the park, and the showers
are warm. Bring your own food.

Maramboi Tented Lodge TENTED CAMP $$$
(☑ 0784 207727; www.tanganyikawilderness
camps.com; s/d/tr full board US$250/375/510;
⊞ @ 🖷 🏊) Unlike any other lodge around
Tarangire, Maramboi sits amid palms and
savannah on Lake Manyara's southeastern
shore, 17km from Tarangire's entrance. The
20 large, airy tents with wooden floors all
have decks looking out towards the lake,
Rift Valley Escarpment and sunset. Staff are
friendly. The turn-off to the lodge is 6km
south of Kigongoni.

**Roika Tarangire
Tented Lodge** TENTED CAMP $$$
(☑ 0754 001444, 027-250 9994; www.tarangire
roikatentedlodge.com; camping US$30, s/d
US$225/350; ⊞ @ 🖷 🏊) Though it's set
off from the park, 5km southwest of the
gate, Roika sits in the bush and is visited
by lots of wildlife, especially elephants.
The 21 widely spaced tents sit on elevated
platforms under thatched roofs and have
bizarre concrete animal-shaped bathtubs.
Maasai village visits and night drives are
available. The campsite has hot showers
and a kitchen is planned.

🛏 In the Tarangire
Conservation Area

Lodges in this remote region outside the
park to the northeast, with access through
the Boundary Hill gate, can all do night
drives and walking safaris. There are an-
imals aplenty from November to March,
many fewer in other months. The main
downside is that it's a long way from the
wildlife viewing circuit inside the park.

Boundary Hill Lodge LODGE $$$
(☑ 0787 293727; www.tarangireconservation.com;
per person full board US$550; ⊞ @ 🖷 🏊) 🍴 Widely
praised for its commitment to the environment and the Maasai community (it owns
a 50% stake), Boundary Hill has eight large
individually designed hilltop rooms with
balconies peering out over Silale Swamp in
the park.

ℹ Getting There & Away

Tarangire is 130km from Arusha via Makuyuni
(the last place for petrol and supplies). At Kigongoni village there's a signposted turn-off to the
main park gate, which is 7km further down a
good dirt access road. The only other entrance
is Boundary Hill gate along the northeast border
which provides access to some lodges located in
the area. The park doesn't rent vehicles.

Coastal Aviation (p212) and Air Excel
(p212) stop at Tarangire's Kuro Airstrip (one
way US$120) on request on their flights between
Arusha and Lake Manyara.

Mto wa Mbu

Mto wa Mbu is the busy gateway to Enga-
ruku, Ol Doinyo Lengai, Lake Natron and
Lake Manyara. The latter is fed by the town's
eponymous 'River of Mosquitoes'. Over the
years, it has evolved into something of a
travellers centre, with plenty of lodges,
campsites, hole-in-the-wall eateries, petrol
stations, moneychangers, souvenir stalls
and more. The busy Cultural Tourism Program (☑ 0784 606654, 027-253 9303; http://
mtoculturalprogramme.tripod.com; day trip from
US$30; ☺ 8am-6.30pm) 🍴, along the main
road, offers tours to surrounding villages.

🛏 Sleeping & Eating

Maryland Resort GUESTHOUSE $
(☑ 0754 299320; camping Tsh10,000, s/d from
Tsh35,000/45,000, d with shared bathroom
Tsh25,000; ⊞) Signposted off the main road
just before Lake Manyara National Park
gate, this bright peach building is metic-
ulously maintained by the friendly owner
who lives on-site. Most of the nine rooms
are on the small side, but with hot water
and cable TV they're priced right. Meals are
available by request and there's a kitchen.

ENGARUKA

Halfway to Lake Natron, on the eastern edge of the Ngorongoro Conservation Area, are 300- to 500-year-old **ruins** (adult/child Tsh10,000/5000) of a farming town that developed a complex irrigation system with terraced stone housing sites. Archaeologists are unsure of their origin, though some speculate the town was built by ancestors of the Iraqw (Mbulu) people, who once populated the area and now live around Lake Eyasi, while others propose it was the Sonjo, a Bantu-speaking people.

Though important among researchers, casual visitors will likely be more impressed with the up-close views of the escarpment than the vaguely house-shaped piles of rocks. Knowledgeable English-speaking guides (no set prices) can be found at Engaruka Ruins Campsite, or arranged in advance through the Tanzania Tourist Board (TTB) Tourist Information Centre (p118) in Arusha. Admission is payable at the government office in Engaruka Juu.

Engaruka Ruins Campsite (camping US$10; P) in Engaruka Juu is dusty but shady with acceptable amenities. You can use its tents for free and meals are available on request.

The ruins are unsigned above the village of Engaruka Juu. Turn west at Engaruka Chini, a smaller village along the Lake Natron road, and follow the rough track 4.5km until you reach Engaruka Juu Primary Boarding School. There's a daily bus to Arusha (Tsh8000, four to five hours) via Mto wa Mbu (Tsh4500, 1½ hours) leaving Engaruka at 6am and turning right around for the return trip shortly after arrival.

Njake Jambo Lodge & Campsite CAMPGROUND $$
(☑027-250 5553; www.njake.com; Arusha–Karatu Rd; camping US$10, s/d US$90/120; ☒) A base for both independent travellers and large overland trucks, there's a shaded and well-maintained grassy camping area, plus 16 good rooms in double-storey chalet blocks.

Twiga Campsite & Lodge BACKPACKERS $$
(☑0713 334287; www.twigacampsitelodge.com; Arusha–Karatu Rd; camping US$10, r US$40-140; P@☒) This popular place is a real travellers' hub with simple but well-kept standard rooms, bungalows and a decent campsite. It's a good place to hook up with other safari-goers, and bike hire is available.

❶ Getting There & Away

BUS
Buses and dalla-dallas run all day from Arusha (Tsh5500 to Tsh6500, two hours) and Karatu (Tsh2500, one hour) to Mto wa Mbu. You can also come from Arusha on the minibuses that run to Karatu. All vehicles stop along the main road in the town centre.

CAR
Car hire (US$150 including fuel and driver) for trips to the park is available in Mto wa Mbu through the Cultural Tourism Program office and Twiga and Njake Jambo campsites.

Lake Manyara National Park

Lake Manyara National Park (☑0767 536137, 0689 062294, 025-39112; www.tanzaniaparks.com/manyara.html; adult/child US$45/15; ◷6am-6pm) is one of Tanzania's smallest and most underrated parks. The dramatic western escarpment of the Rift Valley forms the park's western border, while to the east is the alkaline Lake Manyara, which covers one-third of the park's 648 sq kms but shrinks considerably in the dry season. During the rains the lake hosts millions of flamingos (best seen outside the park on the lake's east shore) and a diversity of other birdlife.

While Manyara lacks the raw drama and many of the particular animals of other northern circuit destinations, its vegetation is diverse and it supports one of the high biomass densities of large mammals in the world. Elephants, hippos, zebras, giraffes, buffaloes, wildebeest, waterbucks, klipspringers and dik-diks are often spotted. Leopards, hyenas and the famous tree-climbing lions are here, but seldom seen.

❷ Sights & Activities

Wonderfully rewarding wildlife watching begins just inside the park's main gate, where the woodland is dense, green and overrun by baboon troops. Sightings of blue monkey are also possible. There's also a **hippo pool** at the lake's northernmost tip. Between the water's edge and the steep Rift Valley walls, the **floodplains** host wildebeest, buffaloes, zebras and Lake Manyara's much-studied elephants, while the thin **acacia belt** that shadows the lake shore is where you're most likely to see arboreal lions.

Night drives are offered by Wayo Africa (p117) for US$55 to US$77 per person plus park fees with advance booking. Two- to three-hour **walking safaris** (US$20 per person and US$20 per group up to eight people) are possible with an armed ranger, though the park has no vehicles to take hikers to the trailheads. Wayo Africa also leads walks down the escarpment from the Serena lodge.

🛏 Sleeping & Eating

There are only a handful of options inside the park but they come with the advantage that you can be out among the wildlife from dawn, unlike those who have to drive into the park from elsewhere. Staying atop the escarpment does, however, generally mean sweeping views. Mta wa Mbu is another good base for visiting the park, especially for budget travellers.

🛏 In the Park

Public Campsite No. 1 CAMPGROUND $
(📞 025-39112; camping US$30) One of two public campsites in the park, Campsite 1 is close to park headquarters and the park gate, with toilet and shower.

Lake Manyara Tree Lodge LODGE $$$
(📞 028-262 1267; www.andbeyond.com; per person all inclusive US$1205; ⊗ closed Apr; 🅿 🛜 ⊠) This lovely, luxurious place is one of the most exclusive lodges in all of Tanzania, and the only permanent camp inside the park. The 10 gorgeous stilted treehouse suites with private decks and views from the bathtubs and outdoor showers are set in a mahogany forest at the remote southern end of the park. The food is excellent and the rooms have butler service.

🛏 Atop the Escarpment

⭐ **Panorama**
Safari Campsite CAMPGROUND $
(📞 0784 118514; camping Tsh10,000; 🅿) The first accommodation you reach going up the hill is hot and dusty with run-down warm-water amenities, but the price is great and the views are as wonderful as any of the luxury lodges up here. Dalla-dallas from Mto wa Mbu heading to Karatu pass the entrance (Tsh750).

Lake Manyara Serena
Safari Lodge LODGE $$$
(📞 027-254 5555; www.serenahotels.com; s/d full board US$308/519; 🅿 @ 🛜 ⊠) A large complex with shady grounds, the 67 well-appointed rooms are in appealing two-storey conical thatched bungalows. Nature walks and village visits are available, as is massage; fine views come at no extra cost. It lacks the intimacy and naturalness of other properties up here on the escarpment, but is nevertheless a justifiably popular choice.

🛏 Below the Escarpment

This area is east of Mto wa Mbu.

Migunga Tented Camp TENTED CAMP $$$
(📞 0754 324193; www.moivaro.com; camping US$10, s/d/tr full board US$247/348/450; 🅿 @) The main attraction of this place (still often known by its previous name, Lake Manyara Tented Camp) is its setting in a grove of enormous fever trees (*migunga* in Swahili) that echoes with bird calls. The 21 tents ringing large, grassy grounds are small but quite adequate and fairly priced. There's also a great rustic dining room. It's 2km south of the main road.

Ol Mesera Tented Camp TENTED CAMP $$$
(📞 0784 428332; www.ol-mesera.com; s/d full board US$135/245; 🅿 @) Run by a spritely

---

ℹ LAKE MANYARA NATIONAL PARK

Why Go Excellent birdwatching; tree-climbing lions; dramatic Rift Valley Escarpment scenery.

When to Go Year-round. June to October is best for large mammals, November to June best for birds.

Practicalities Stay in Mta wa Mbu, atop the escarpment or inside the park; bring binoculars to optimise wildlife watching over the lake. The entry gate is open from 6am to 6pm.

Budget Tips Stay in Mta wa Mbu to avoid camping fees; charter a dalla-dalla for the day.

Slovenian pensioner, this personalised place, in a bush setting amid baobab and euphorbia trees, has four straightforward safari tents and is an ideal spot to do cultural walks, cooking classes or just relax for a few days. It's 14km up the Lake Natron road.

ℹ️ Information

There's an ATM and a couple of slow internet cafes in Mto wa Mbu.

ℹ️ Getting There & Away

Public transport can only get you as close as Mto wa Mbu. Car hire for the park is available there. Air Excel (p212), Coastal Aviation (p212) and Regional Air (p212) offer daily flights between Arusha and Lake Manyara.

Lake Natron

Shimmering amid the sun-scorched Kenyan border northeast of Ngorongoro Conservation Area, this 58km-long but just 50cm-deep alkaline lake should be on every adventurer's itinerary. The drive from Mto wa Mbu is remote, with a desolate, otherworldly beauty and an incomparable feeling of space and ancientness. After the drive, the lake itself is secondary; except during the June to November breeding season when upwards of three million flamingos gather here.

The base for visits is the small oasis of **Engaresero** (also spelled Ngare Sero) on the southwestern shore. The **Engaresero Cultural Tourism Program** (☎ 027-205 0025; www.tanzaniaculturaltourism.go.tz/engaresero) offers guided walks, climbs of Ol Doinyo Lengai, 25km to the south, and other activities.

🛏️ Sleeping & Eating

World View Campsite   CAMPGROUND $
(☎ 0786 566133; www.worldviewcampsite.com; camping US$10, full board in own tent US$25; P) A few kilometres south of town along the escarpment and amid several Maasai *bomas*, there are unbeatable views of Ol Doinyo Lengai, and good ones of the lake, too. It's a grassy area with a little shade, a lot of wind, and clean bathroom facilities with sit-down toilets. A luxury lodge is planned, but the owner says budget camping will remain.

Lake Natron
Tented Camp   CAMPGROUND, TENTED CAMP $$
(☎ 0754 324193; www.moivaro.com; camping US$10, s half board US$157-242, d US$203-343;

P ⛱) Near the village with a view of the lake. The tents, some with both indoor and outdoor showers, and pleasant grass-roofed cottages (called 'Maasai rooms' and 20% cheaper) are in shady grounds near the river. There's a large and sometimes busy campground with good facilities next door, and campers can use all lodge amenities, including the restaurant and swimming pool.

ℹ️ Getting There & Away

The road from Mto wa Mbu is part sandy, part rocky, all bad: 4WD is necessary. During the rainy season you may have to wait a few hours at some of the seasonal rivers before you can cross. District fees (ie tourist taxes) must be paid at three points along the way: Engaruka Chini (US$10); 7km before Engaresero (US$10); and Engaresero (US$15).

The road past the lake to Loliondo and into the Serengeti is in better shape than the road from Mto wa Mbu because it's used far less. Those continuing this way should carry extra supplies of petrol since the last proper station is in Mto wa Mbu.

A rickety, crowded bus runs between Arusha and Loliondo, stopping in Engaresero (Tsh23,000, nine hours from Arusha). It departs Arusha 6.30am Sunday and passes back through Engaresero on Thursday around 10am. Trucks run between Mto wa Mbu and Engaresero pretty much daily (including sometimes 4WDs operating as public transport) but it's not unheard of to have to wait two days to find a ride, especially in the rainy season.

Karatu

This charmless town 14km southeast of Lodoare gate makes a convenient base for visiting Ngorongoro if you want to economise on entry fees. There are ATMs plus a few internet cafes. There are also several mini-supermarkets, but it's better to stock up in Arusha. The **Ganako-Karatu Cultural Tourism Program** (☎ 0767 612980, 0787451162; www.kcecho.org) offers walks and bike excursions.

🛏️ Sleeping & Eating

🛏️ In Karatu

Vera Inn   GUESTHOUSE $
(☎ 0754 578145; Milano Rd, Bwani, Karatu; s/d Tsh30,000/40,000) One of the best guesthouses in Karatu, rooms are small but sparkling

OL DOINYO LENGAI

The northernmost mountain in the Crater Highlands, Ol Doinyo Lengai (2878m), 'Mountain of God' in the Maasai language, is an almost perfect volcanic cone with steep sides rising to a small flat-topped peak. It's still active, with the last eruptions in 2008. At the peak, you can see hot steam vents and growing ash cones in the north crater. With a midnight start, a trek from the base village of Engaresero at Lake Natron is possible in one long day. Although the number of climbers scaling Ol Doinyo Lengai has grown in recent years, the loose ash along most of the path makes it a difficult climb and an even tougher, often painful, descent. And don't overlook the significant danger the bubbling lava in the north crater poses to trekkers who approach too closely. Some local guides no longer climb out of fear of another eruption. For a detailed overview of the mountain see www.oldoinyolengai.pbworks.com.

The most direct way to reach Engaresero base village to start a climb is with hired or private vehicle via the partly sandy, partly rocky road from Mto wa Mbu. During the rainy season you may have to wait a few hours at some of the seasonal rivers before you're able to cross. The road past the lake to Loliondo and into the Serengeti is in better shape because it's used far less. Travellers heading this way after climbing Ol Doinyo Lengai should carry extra supplies of petrol since the last proper station is in Mto wa Mbu, though some people sell expensive petrol from their homes. There's also a bus that runs between Arusha and Loliondo, which stops in Engaresero (Tsh23,000, nine hours from Arusha). It departs Arusha 6.30am Sunday and passes back through Engaresero on Thursday around 10am. For those driving from Ngorongoro: you'll need to set out early and count on an entire day to reach Lake Natron; ask at NCA headquarters and Nainokanoka ranger post about track conditions before setting off.

---

clean and have hot-water showers and cable TV.

★ **Eileen's Trees Inn**   LODGE **$$**
(✆0754 834725, 0783 379526; www.eileenstrees.com; s/d full board US$100/150; P@🕸🎏) This place gets consistently good reports from travellers and it's easy to see why – the rooms are large and come with wooden four-poster beds (with mosquito nets) and wrought-iron furnishings in some bathrooms. But the food and friendly service are what really elevate this place above others in its price range in Karatu.

Octagon Safari Lodge & Irish Bar   LODGE **$$**
(✆027-253 4525; www.octagonlodge.com; camping with own/hired tent US$15/30, s/d half board US$85/150; @🕸) The unexpectedly lush and lovely grounds at this Irish-Tanzanian-owned lodge mean you'll soon feel far away from Karatu. The cottages are small but comfortable, and by Karatu standards the rates are excellent. The restaurant and Irish bar round out the relaxing vibe. It's 1km south of the main road on the west side of town.

Bump's Café   TANZANIAN, EUROPEAN **$**
(✆0783 116694; Arusha Rd; meals Tsh4500-8500; ⊙7am-7pm; 🕸) A simple (but fancy by Karatu standards) American-Maasai-owned restaurant on the west end of town with a mix of local and Western meals, this is a good spot to order lunch boxes. The menu is limited after lunchtime. There's also an internet cafe costing Tsh1000 per hour.

🏠 **Around Karatu**

★ **Gibb's Farm**   LODGE **$$$**
(✆027-253 4397; www.gibbsfarm.net; s/d/tr half board US$562/850/1175; P@🕸) The long-standing Gibb's Farm, filling a 1920s farmstead, has a rustic highland ambience, a wonderful setting with views over the nearby coffee plantations, a spa, and beautiful cottages (a few standard rooms, too) set around the gardens. The lodge gets consistently good reviews, as does the cuisine, which is made with home-grown organic produce. It's about 5km north of the main road.

★ **Plantation Lodge**   LODGE **$$$**
(✆0784 260799, 027-253 4405; www.plantation -lodge.com; s/d half board US$275/400, ste from US$600; P@🕸🎏) A place that makes you feel special, this relaxing lodge fills a renovated colonial farmstead and the decor is gorgeous down to every last detail. The

uniquely decorated rooms spaced around the gardens have large verandas and crackling fireplaces to enhance the highland ambience. Excellent home-grown food, too. It's west of Karatu and about 2.5km north of the highway.

Rhotia Valley
Tented Lodge
TENTED CAMP $$$

(☑0784 446579; www.rhotiavalley.com; s half board US$155-280, d US$250-390; P@🕏🕱)
🍃 Right up against the Ngorongoro Conservation Area, this refreshingly unpretentious hilltop lodge has 15 large tents (two are family sized) with either forest or valley views, the latter offering a peek at Lake Manyara and even Mt Meru and Mt Kilimanjaro on a clear day. Good meals are served under the big thatch roof. It's 10km northeast of Karatu, well signposted off the highway.

Ngorongoro Farm House
LODGE $$$

(☑0736 502471, 0784 207727; www.tanganyika wildernesscamps.com; s/d/tr full board US$250/375/510; P@🕏🕱) This atmospheric place, 4km from Lodoare gate, is set in the grounds of a 500-acre working farm that provides coffee, wheat and vegetables for this and the company's other lodges. The 50 well-appointed rooms, some a long walk from the restaurant and other public areas, are huge. Farm tours and coffee demonstration are available, as is massage.

❶ Getting There & Away

There are several morning buses between Karatu and Arusha (Tsh6000, three hours); some continuing to Moshi (Tsh9000, 4½ hours). There are also more comfortable nine-seater minivans to/from Arusha (Tsh8000, three hours) that depart throughout the day. Transport departs from several spots along the main road.

Lake Eyasi

Uniquely beautiful Lake Eyasi lies at 1030m elevation between the Eyasi Escarpment in the north and the Kidero Mountains in the south. Like Lake Natron way to the northeast, Eyasi makes a rewarding detour on a Ngorongoro trip for anyone looking for something remote and different. It's a hot, dry area, around which live the Hadzabe (also known as Hadzapi or Tindiga) people who are believed to

have lived here for nearly 10,000 years. Several hundred still follow ancient nomadic hunting and gathering traditions. Also in the area are the Iraqw (Mbulu), a people of Cushitic origin who arrived about 2000 years ago, and Datoga, noted metal smiths whose dress and culture is quite similar to the Maasai.

At the **Lake Eyasi Cultural Tourism Program** (☑0764 295280; rangergotz@yahoo. co.uk; ⊗8am-6pm) office, at the entrance to Ghorofani, you can hire guides to visit nearby Hadzabe and Datoga communities or the lake. All foreigners must also pay a US$10 village tax here.

🛏 Sleeping & Eating

Basic supplies are sold in Ghorofani, but it's better to stock up in Karatu.

Eyasi-Nyika Campsite
CAMPGROUND $

(☑0762 766040; camping US$10; P) One of Eyasi's best campgrounds, Eyasi-Nyika has seven widely spaced grassy sites, each under an acacia tree and you can cook for yourself. It's in the bush, 3km outside Ghorofani, signposted only at the main road: after that, just stick to the most travelled roads and you'll get there.

Kisima Ngeda
TENTED CAMP $$$

(☑027-254 8715; www.anasasafari.com/kisima ngeda; camping US$10, s/d half board US$335/445; P🕱) Kisima Ngeda roughly translates as 'spring surrounded by trees', and there's a natural spring at the heart of this lakeside property creating an unexpectedly green and lush oasis of fever trees and doum palms. The seven tents are plenty comfortable and the cuisine (much of it locally produced, including dairy from their own cows) is excellent. It's signposted 7.5km from Ghorofani.

❶ Getting There & Away

Two daily buses connect Arusha to Barazani passing Ghorofani (Tsh11,500, 4½ to five hours) on the way. They leave Arusha about 5am and head back about 2pm, and you can also catch them in Karatu (Tsh4500, 1½ hours to Ghorofani).

There are also several passenger-carrying 4WDs to Karatu (Tsh5500; they park at Mbulu junction) departing Ghorofani and other lake towns during the morning and returning throughout the afternoon.

Ngorongoro Crater

Pick a superlative: amazing, incredible, breathtaking...they all apply to the stunning ethereal blue-green vistas of the **Ngorongoro Crater** (crater services fee per vehicle per entry per 24hr US$200). At 19km wide and with a surface of 264 sq km, it is one of the largest unbroken calderas in the world that isn't a lake. Its steep, unbroken walls soar 400m to 610m and provide the setting for an incredible natural drama as lions, elephants, buffaloes, ostriches and plains herbivores such as wildebeest, elands, buffaloes, zebras and reedbucks graze and stalk their way around the grasslands, swamps and acacia woodland on the crater floor. Chances are good that you'll also see the critically endangered black rhino, and for many people this is one of the crater's main draws. There are plenty of hippos around **Ngoitoktok Springs** picnic site and **Lake Magadi** attracts flocks of flamingos to its shallows in the rainy season. Put simply, this is one of Africa's premier attractions and this world-renowned natural wonder is deservedly a Unesco World Heritage site.

Early morning is the best wildlife-watching time and if you depart at first light, you'll have some time in the crater before the masses arrive. Afternoons are less busy than mornings. The gates open at 6am and close for descent at 4pm; all vehicles must be out of the crater before 6pm.

Entering the crater costs US$200 per vehicle per entry and you're only allowed to stay for six hours (although this is often not enforced). Only 4WDs are allowed into the crater. The roads down are in good shape, though steep and thus somewhat difficult when wet. The main route in is the Seneto descent road, which enters the crater on its western side. To come out, use the Lerai ascent road, which starts south of Lake Magadi and leads to the rim near NCA headquarters. The Lemala road is on the northeastern side of the crater near Ngorongoro Sopa Lodge and used for both ascent and descent. Self-drivers are supposed to hire a park ranger (US$20 per vehicle) for the crater, but are sometimes let in without one.

🛏 Sleeping & Eating

There are three special campsites around the crater rim: **Simba B** (camping US$50), just up the road from Simba A; and **Tembo A** (camping US$50) and **Tembo B** (camping US$50) north of Ngorongoro Sopa Lodge. None of them have facilities and all should be reserved as far in advance as possible.

Simba A Public Campsite　　CAMPGROUND $
(camping US$30) The only public campsite is Simba A, up on the crater rim not far from headquarters. It has basic facilities and can get very crowded, so hot water sometimes runs out. Even so, it's a fine location and far and away the cheapest place to stay up on the rim.

Kitoi Guesthouse　　GUESTHOUSE $
(📱0754 334834; r without bathroom Tsh8000; P) This unsigned place is the best of four guesthouses in Kimba village, near the crater. The ablution block is out the back, and so

---

NGORONGORO CONSERVATION AREA IN A NUTSHELL

Lying within the boundaries of the 8292 sq km **Ngorongoro Conservation Area** (NCA; 📱027-253 7006; www.ngorongorocrater.org; adult/child (5-16 years old) US$50/10; ⊙6am-6pm) are the Ngorongoro Crater, Oldupai Gorge and much of the Crater Highlands (although not Ol Doinyo Lengai and Lake Natron).

The main NCA gates are **Lodoare** (the main park entrance if you're coming from Arusha) and **Naabi Hill** (well outside the NCA boundaries and shares premises with the Naabi Hill entrance to Serengeti National Park).

Other important things to note:

➜ If you're transiting through Ngorongoro en route to the Serengeti, you still have to pay the NCA entrance fee.

➜ Entry fees apply for a 24-hour period. If you enter the NCA at, for example, 10am and you're staying overnight, then you must leave before 10am the next morning to avoid incurring an additional day's fee.

➜ In theory all entry, camping and crater fees should be paid in advance at a bank, but in practice you can pay at the gate. Although credit cards are accepted, cash is preferred.

Ngorongoro Conservation Area

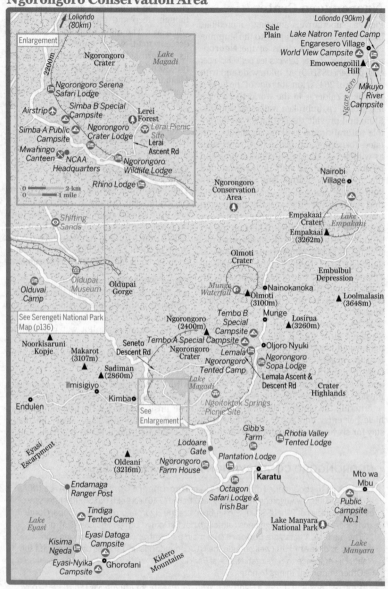

are awesome views of Oldeani. On request someone will cook food or heat water for bucket showers. Officials at the park gate may insist you pay the camping fee upon entering the park, even if you plan to sleep in this village.

Rhino Lodge LODGE $$$
(☎ 0768 578856, 0762 359055; www.ngorongoro.cc; s/d with full board US$150/270; ☎) This small, friendly lodge, run by Italians in conjunction with the Maasai community, is the cheapest place in the NCA. The rooms

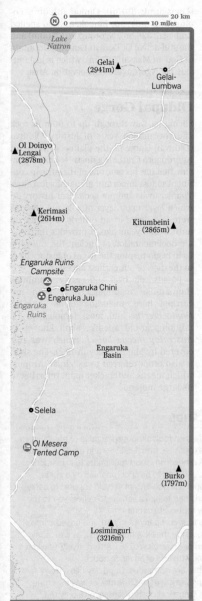

Ndutu Safari Lodge   LODGE $$$

(☎ 027-253 7015; www.ndutu.com; s/d full board US$297/493) This good-value place has a lovely setting in the far western part of NCA, just outside the Serengeti. It's well located for observing the enormous herds of wildebeest during the rainy season and watch for genets who lounge in dining room rafters. The 34 Lake Ndutu–facing cottages lack character, but the lounge is attractive and the atmosphere relaxed and rustic.

Ngorongoro Serena Safari Lodge   LODGE $$$

(☎ 027-254 5555; www.serenahotels.com; s/d full board US$625/805; [P] [@] [🕿]) The popular Serena sits unobtrusively in a fine location on the southwestern crater rim near the main descent route. It's comfortable and attractive (though the cave motif in the rooms is kind of kitschy) with good service and outstanding views (from the upper-floor rooms), though it's also big and busy.

Ngorongoro Wildlife Lodge   LODGE $$$

(☎ 027-254 4595; www.hotelsandlodges-tanzania. com; r per person full board US$220/440; [P] [@] [🕿]) The rooms here are tired and in desperate need of an overhaul, the service can be dysfunctional and wi-fi costs a ridiculous US$10 per hour. But (and it's a big but), the crater views here (from the rooms, from the bar...) are the best on the rim. In fact, the views are

are simple and tidy, and the balconies have fine forest views, often with bushbucks or elephants wandering past. It's arguably the best-value place up here, as long as you don't need a crater view.

ℹ NGORONGORO CRATER

Why Go Extraordinary scenery and fabulous wildlife watching.

When to Go Year-round

Practicalities Usually visited en route to Serengeti from Arusha via Karatu. It can get *very* cold on the crater rim, so come prepared. All fees, including those for the crater and walks, are paid at Lodoare gate, just south of Ngorongoro Crater on the road from Arusha, or Naabi Hill gate on the border with Serengeti National Park.

Budget Tips Stay outside the conservation area to avoid camping fees: visit as part of a larger group to reduce your portion of the Crater Services Fee. Even though the fee is per vehicle, guards check the number of passengers against the permit so it's not possible to join up with people you meet at your campsite or lodge.

so good that they may just outweigh all of the lodge's shortcomings.

ⓘ Information

The crater falls within the Ngorongoro Conservation Area Authority (NCAA), which has its **headquarters** (☑ 027-253 7006; www. ngorongorocrater.org; ⓧ 8am-4pm) at Park Village at Ngorongoro Crater and an information centre (p118) in Arusha. Ignore the signs for a tourist information office at the park headquarters – even they couldn't explain to us what their purpose was.

ⓘ Getting There & Around

If you aren't travelling on an organised safari and don't have your own vehicle, the easiest thing to do is hire a vehicle in Karatu, where most lodges charge about US$160 per day – including fuel – for a 4WD with a pop-up top.

Driving is not allowed before 6am or (officially, anyway) after 7pm. Petrol is sold at headquarters, but it's cheaper in Karatu.

The Crater Highlands

The ruggedly beautiful Crater Highlands consist of an elevated range of volcanoes and calderas rising up along the Great Rift Valley on the NCA's eastern side. There are many rewarding treks. The peaks and craters include Oldeani (3216m), Makarot (Lemagurut; 3107m), Olmoti (3100m), Loolmalasin (3648m), Empakaai (also spelled Embagai; 3262m), Ngorongoro (2200m) and the still-active Ol Doinyo Lengai ('Mountain of God' in Maasai; 2878m), which is just outside the Ngorongoro Conservation Area.

Oldupai Gorge

Slicing its way through up to 90m of rock and two million years of history, Oldupai (Olduvai) Gorge on the plains northwest of Ngorongoro Crater is a dusty, 48km-long ravine that has become one of the African continent's most important archaeological sites. Thanks to its unique geological history, in which layer upon layer of volcanic deposits were laid down in an orderly sequence up until 15,000 years ago, it provides remarkable documentation of ancient life, allowing us to begin turning the pages of history back to the days of our earliest ancestors.

Fossils of over 60 early hominids (human-like mammals) have been unearthed here, including *Homo habilis*, *Homo erectus* and most famously a 1.8 million-year-old ape-like skull known as *Australopithecus boisei*, which was discovered by Mary Leakey in 1959. The skull is also often referred to as 'zinjanthropus', which means 'nutcracker man', referring to its large molars.

TREKKING IN THE CRATER HIGHLANDS

The best way to explore the Crater Highlands is on foot, although because of the logistics and multiple fees involved, trekking here is expensive; from US$350 and up (less if you have a large group) for overnight trips. Treks range from short day jaunts to excursions of up to two weeks or more. For all routes, you'll need to be accompanied by a guide, and for anything except day hikes, most people use donkeys or vehicle support to carry water and supplies. For most hikes you'll also need to hire a vehicle to deliver you to the starting point and collect you at the end; few routes are circuits.

Nearly all visitors arrange treks through a tour company. Many Arusha-based companies can take you up Ol Doinyo Lengai (just outside the NCA boundaries), as can many of the accommodation places in Lake Natron or Engaruka (p126). Alternatively, you can contact the NCA directly to arrange your trek, with lots of advance notice.

There are no set routes, and the possibilities are numerous. Good day hikes from Ngorongoro Crater or Karatu include climbing **Makarot** or **Oldeani**, or walking along **Empakaai or Olmoti Craters**. Apart from transport costs, these involve only the US$50 NCA entry fee and US$20 per group guide fee. If you're trying to do things on your own through the NCA, rather than through a tour operator, the least complicated option is Oldeani, since the climb starts at headquarters. From Oldeani, it's possible to camp and continue on down to Lake Eyasi where there's public transport.

Good two-day trips include the **Ngorongoro Crater rim**, **Olmoti to Empakaai Crater** and **Empakaai Crater to Lake Natron**. These three can be strung together into an excellent four-day trip: start at Nainokanoka to make it three days or extend it one day to climb **Ol Doinyo Lengai**.

The turn-off to Oldupai museum (the focal point for visits to the gorge) is 27km north-west of Ngorongoro Crater's Seneto descent road. From this turn-off, it's then a further 5.5km along a rutted track to the museum.

◎ Sights

Oldupai Museum　　　　　　　MUSEUM
(adult/child Tsh 27,000/13,000; ⊙ 7.30am-4.30pm)
The small Oldupai Museum on the rim of Oldupai Gorge stands on one of the most significant archaeological sites on earth. It was here in 1959 that Mary Leakey discovered a 1.8-million-year-old ape-like skull from an early hominid (human-like) now known as *Australopithecus boisei*. This discovery, along with fossils of over 60 early hominids (including *Homo habilis* and *Homo erectus*) forever changed the way we understand the dawn of human history.

Laetoli　　　　　　　　RUINS, MUSEUM
(adult/child Tsh10,000/5000; ⊙ 7.30am-4.30pm)
About 45km south of Oldupai Gorge at remote Laetoli is a 27m-long trail of 3.7-million-year-old hominid footprints, probably made by *Australopithecus afarensis*. Discovered by Mary Leakey's team in 1976 and excavated two years later, it's an extraordinarily evocative and remote site. A long-planned (and still under construction) EU-funded museum is slated, but there's a small temporary museum on the site. There are cast copies of the prints are in Oldupai Museum.

Serengeti National Park

In the vast plains of the **Serengeti National Park** (✆ 0689 062243, 0767 536125, 028-262 1515; www.tanzaniaparks.com/serengeti.html; adult/child US$60/20; ⊙ 6am-6pm), nature's mystery, power and beauty surround you. It's here that one of earth's most impressive natural cycles has played out for eons as hundreds of thousands of hoofed animals, driven by primeval rhythms of survival, move constantly in search of fresh grasslands. The most famous, and numerous, are the wildebeest (of which there are some 1.5 million) and their annual migration is the Serengeti's calling card. During the rainy months of January to March, the wildebeest are scattered over the southern section of the Serengeti and the western side of Ngorongoro Conservation Area. Most streams dry out quickly when the rains cease, nudging the wilde-

ℹ️ SERENGETI NATIONAL PARK

Why Go Wildebeest migration; excellent chance of seeing predators; overall high wildlife density; fine birdwatching; stunning savannah scenery.

When to Go Year-round; July to August for wildebeest migration across Mara River; February for wildebeest calving; February to May for birdwatching.

Practicalities Drive in from Arusha or Mwanza, or fly in. To avoid congestion, spend some time outside the central Serengeti/Seronera area.

Budget Tips Catch the Arusha–Musoma bus and hope to see something along the way; stay in the public campsites; book a budget safari from Arusha

beest to concentrate on the few remaining green areas, and to form thousands-strong herds that by April begin to migrate northwest in search of food. The crossing of the crocodile-filled Grumeti River, which runs through the park's Western Corridor, usually takes place between late May and early July, and lasts only about a week. Usually in August they make an even more incredible river crossing while leaving the Serengeti to find water in the Masai Mara (just over the Kenyan border) before roaming back south in November in anticipation of the rains. Besides the migrating wildebeest, there are also resident populations in the park and you'll see these smaller but still impressive herds year-round. In February more than 8000 wildebeest calves are born per day, although about 40% of these die before reaching four months old.

The 14,763-km-Serengeti National Park is also renowned for its predators, especially its lions. Hunting alongside the lions are cheetahs, leopards, hyenas, jackals and more. These feast on zebras (about 200,000), giraffes, buffaloes, Thomson's and Grant's gazelles, topis, elands, hartebeest, impalas, klipspringers, duikers and so many more.

◎ Sights & Activities

Wayo Africa (p117) leads multiday **walking safaris** in the Moro Kopjes and Kogatende regions. A few lodges, mostly in the north, are allowed to lead short (under two-hour)

Serengeti National Park

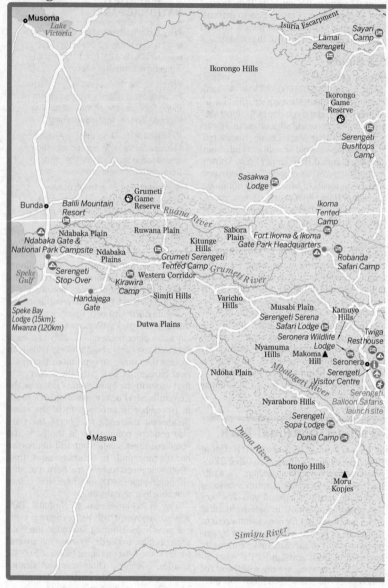

walks. **Balloon safaris** – including an hour floating over the plains at dawn, followed by breakfast in the bush – are run by **Serengeti Balloon Safaris** (☎ 0784 308494, 027-254 8077; www.balloonsafaris.com; per person US$539).

The **Serengeti Visitor Centre** (☎ 0732 985761; serengeti_tourism@yahoo.com; ⊙ 8am-5pm) at Seronera has an excellent **self-guided walk** through the Serengeti's history and ecosystems that is well worth doing before exploring the park.

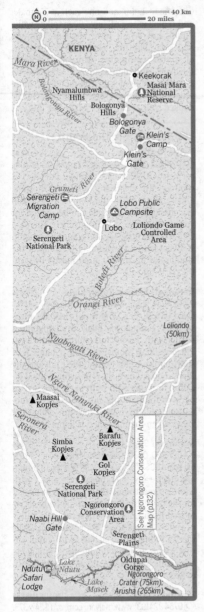

and the Western Corridor, the Central Plains and the Northern Serengeti – requires careful planning and an understanding of what each has to offer and at which time of the year will determine how you experience this wonderful place.

Seronera & the South

Seronera, at the heart of the park and readily accessed from both Arusha and Mwanza, offers almost guaranteed sightings of lions, leopards and cheetahs. However, this abundance comes at a price: you may find yourself observing lions with a pack of 20 vehicles jostling to look at a lion. Southeast of Seronera is a prime base for wildlife watching during the December–April wet season, when it's full of wildebeest. This corner of the Serengeti also has year-round water and a good mix of habitats. Most Seronera safaris concentrate along the **Seronera River**, as the trees along the riverbank are home to one of the world's densest concentration of leopards, while lion sightings are common. Lion sightings are also plentiful around the **Maasai Kopjes**, **Simba Kopjes**, **Moru Kopjes**, **Gol Kopjes**, **Barafu Kopjes** and around **Makoma Hill**. The vast plains south of the Seronera River, often known simply as the **Serengeti Plains**, are particularly good for cheetahs.

Grumeti & Western Corridor

The wildebeest migration usually passes through Serengeti's Western Corridor, and the contiguous Grumeti Game Reserve, sometime between late May and early July. While the crossing of the Grumeti River may not rival that of the Mara River further north, it's still one of the migration's great spectacles.

During the rest of the year, lions and leopards are prevalent along the forest-fringed **Grumeti River**, which also has hippos and giant crocodiles. North of the river, try the **Kitunge Hills**, **Ruaha Plain** and just about anywhere in the **Grumeti Game Reserve**, while south of the river concentrate on the **Ndabaka Plain**, **Simiti Hills**, **Dutwa Plain**, **Varicho Hills** and down to the **Mbalageti River**.

Western Serengeti is best accessed from Mwanza. From the Ndabaka gate, count on at least half a day to reach Seronera.

A **wildlife drive** in the Serengeti – either self-drive, as part of an organised safari or as operated by your Serengeti lodge – is one of the most enjoyable things you can do in Africa. Exploring the Serengeti's four major areas – Seronera and the South, Grumeti

Central Plains

Except when the migration passes through (usually in November and December), this is not the Serengeti's most prolific corner when it comes to wildlife. Its mix of light woodland, acacia thorn and open plains can also be dispiriting during the heat of the day, which, given the lack of lodges in the area, is when most people pass through as they travel between the north and south of the Serengeti. This is also one area of the park experiencing a growing problem with local communities encroaching into the park, with a concomitant effect on wildlife numbers. In other words, you're more likely to visit here on your way elsewhere, rather than for its own sake.

Even so, there are some fine vistas along this north–south route through the park, plus a remote, untrammelled feel. If nothing else, the park's central area is worth passing through to gain a deeper appreciation of just how vast the Serengeti ecosystem really is.

Northern Serengeti

Compared with Seronera and the south, the Serengeti's north receives relatively few visitors. It begins with acacia woodlands, where elephants congregate in the dry season, but north of Lobo is vast open plains. The migration usually passes through the western side during August and September and comes down the eastern flank in November.

Where the park narrows and the **Grumeti River** crosses the park from east to west, as well as the areas immediately to the north and south of the river, are excellent wildlife regions. Further north, the **Bologonga Hills**, **Bologonga River**, **Nyamalumbwa Hills** and **Mara River** are all outstanding.

Outside the park, the little-visited **Ikorongo Game Reserve**, which shadows the northwestern boundary of the park, is wild and worth visiting. The **Loliondo Game Controlled Area**, just outside the Serengeti's northeastern boundary, offers the chance for Maasai cultural activities, walking safaris, night drives and off-road drives. A loop east across Loliondo and then down through the Crater Highlands or Ngorongoro is a wonderfully remote alternative to driving back down through the park.

Sleeping

There are nine **public campsites** (camping US$30) in the Serengeti: six around Seronera, one at Lobo, and one each at Ndabaka and Ikoma gates. All have flush toilets while Pimbi and Nyani have kitchens, showers and solar lighting. There are also dozens of **special campsites** (camping US$50) in the park, although many are occupied on a semipermanent basis by mobile or more sedentary camps. The others should be booked well in advance (☑ 028-262 1515).

Seronera & the South

Twiga Resthouse GUESTHOUSE **$$**
(☑ 028-262 1510; serengeti@tanzaniaparks.com; per person US$30; **P**) Simple but decent rooms with electricity and hot showers, and satellite TV in the lounge. Guests can use the kitchen or meals can be cooked for you if you order way in advance. There's a well-stocked little bar and a bonfire at night. If Twiga is full, there might be room at the similar Taj Resthouse, used mostly by visiting park officials.

Serengeti Serena Safari Lodge LODGE **$$$**
(☑ 027-254 5555; www.serenahotels.com; s/d full board US$391/651; **P @ 🛜 🏊**) Serena's Maasai-style bungalows boast well-appointed rooms with lovely furnishings and views. The top-floor rooms are best. Guides lead short nature walks around their hill and the Maasai do a dance show at night. A good location for those who want to explore several parts of the park but not switch accommodation, and the hilltop location offers fine views when the migration is happening.

Serengeti Sopa Lodge LODGE **$$$**
(☑ 027-250 0630; www.sopalodges.com; s/d/tr full board US$370/650/829; **P @ 🛜 🏊**) Though architecturally unappealing and with less-inspired rooms than you might expect for the price, the Serengeti Sopa Lodge is removed from the Seronera scrum in a valley of yellow acacia trees. As is the Sopa style, the 73 rooms are spacious, with small sitting rooms and two double beds, and some even come with views. It's 45 minutes south of Seronera.

Robanda Safari Camp TENTED CAMP **$$$**
(☑ 0754 324193; www.moivaro.com; s/d $247/373; **P**) A refreshingly small budget (by Serengeti standards) camp on the plains near Robanda village just outside Ikoma gate with seven no-frills tents covered by a thatched roof. You can do guided walks and night drives here, if you have your own vehicle.

Ikoma Tented Camp   TENTED CAMP **$$$**
(☏0754 324193, 027-250 6315; www.moivaro.com; s/d full board US$287/433; P) Just outside the Ikoma Gate and handy for just about anywhere in the park, this relatively simple tented camp combines a closeness to the local community with excellent prices and high levels of comfort.

Grumeti & Western Corridor

Serengeti Stop-Over   CAMPGROUND **$**
(☏028-262 2273; www.serengetistopover.com; campsite/banda per person US$10/35; P) Just 1km from Ndabaka gate along the Mwanza–Musoma road, this sociable place has camping with hot showers and a cooking area, plus 14 simple rondavels, and a restaurant-bar. Safari vehicle rental is available and Serengeti day trips are feasible. It also offers trips on Lake Victoria with local fishermen, visits to a traditional healer, and other Sukuma cultural excursions.

Balili Mountain Resort   TENTED LODGE **$$**
(☏0754 710113, 0764 824814; www.bmr.co.tz; camping with own/hired tent US$15/20, s/d/tr US$50/70/90, day entry US$5; P) Neither a mountain nor a resort, but 'no-frills tented lodge on a big rocky hill' just doesn't have the same ring to it. It's perfectly comfortable, but its main draws are the views of Lake Victoria and the Serengeti. It's up above Bunda, north of Ndabaka gate, reached by a rollercoaster of a road.

★Grumeti Serengeti Tented Camp   TENTED LODGE **$$$**
(☏028-262 1267; www.andbeyond.com; per person all-inclusive US$595-1245; ⊙closed Apr; P🛜📶) Instead of taking to the hills for panoramic views, Grumeti gets down into the thick of the action along the Kanyanja River; a prime spot during the migration when you can watch crocs catch wildebeest as you lounge in the swimming pool. It mixes its wild location with chic pan-Africa decor and the 10 tents are superluxe; only three have unobstructed river views.

Northern Serengeti

★Serengeti Bushtops Camp   LODGE, TENTED CAMP **$$$**
(www.bushtopscamps.com; s/d all-inclusive US$1300/1980; P@🛜📶) In a remote corner of the northern Serengeti, close to the boundary with the Ikorongo Game Reserve, this remarkable camp has large permanent tents with expansive wood floors and decks with a spa bath, perfectly placed sofas and fabulous views. Many Serengeti lodges are luxurious, but this place is simply magnificent. The food is similarly excellent.

Serengeti Migration Camp   TENTED CAMP **$$$**
(☏027-250 0630; www.elewanacollection.com; s/d full board US$1118/1490; P🛜📶) One of the most highly regarded places in the Serengeti with 20 large, stunning tents with decks, and a plush lounge, around a kopje by the Grumeti River. The blend between a tent's immersion in the surrounds and the luxury of permanence is perfectly executed here. Great views and front-row seats during the few weeks the migration passes through. Walks are also possible.

Sayari Camp   TENTED CAMP **$$$**
(http://sayaricamp.asiliaafrica.com; s/d all-inclusive US$1260/1990; ⊙Jun-Mar; P🛜📶) Deep in the far north, near the Mara River, this wonderfully remote camp has an understated elegance and genuine style. The 15 tents have wooden floors and decks, are large yet cosy, and the pool is built into the boulders. Short bush walks and spa treatments are both available, and if you're lucky with the timing it's the perfect place for the wildebeest river crossing.

Mobile Camps

Mobile camps are a great idea, but something of a misnomer. They do move (though never when guests are in camp), following the wildebeest migration so as to try to always be in good wildlife-watching territory. But with all the fancy amenities people expect on a luxury safari, relocating is a huge chore and most only move two or three times a year. They're perfect for some and too rustic (or, at least too rustic for the typically high prices) for others.

Wayo Green Camp   TENTED CAMP **$$$**
(☏0784 203000; www.wayoafrica.com; per person all-inclusive from US$300) These 'private mobile camps' combine the best aspects of both tented camps and budget camping safaris and are the best way possible to get a deep bush experience in the Serengeti. They use 3m x 3m dome tents and actual mattresses (off the ground) and move from site to site every couple of days. Wayo also runs excellent walking safaris.

ℹ️ Getting There & Around

AIR

Air Excel (p212), Coastal Aviation (p212) and Regional Air (p212) have daily flights from Arusha to the park's seven airstrips.

BUS

Although not ideal, budget travellers can do their wildlife watching through the window of the Arusha–Musoma buses that cross the park, but you'll need to pay US$110 in entrance fees for Serengeti and Ngorongoro. The buses stop at the staff village at Seronera, but you're not allowed to walk or hitchhike to the campsites or resthouses and the park has no vehicles for hire, so unless you've made some sort of prior arrangement for transport it's nearly pointless to get off here.

CAR

Access from Arusha is via the heavily used **Naabi Hill gate** (☺6am-6pm), 45km from Seronera. The Western Corridor's **Ndabaka gate** (☺6am-6pm), a 1½-hour drive from Mwanza, is 145km from Seronera. **Klein's gate** (☺6am-6pm) in the far northeast allows a loop trip combining Serengeti, Ngorongoro and Lake Natron, the latter just two to three hours from the park. The last entry at these gates is 4pm. Bologonya gate would be on the route to/from Kenya's Masai Mara National Reserve, but the border is closed and unlikely to open any time soon. Driving is not permitted in the park after 7pm, except in the visitor centre area where the cut-off is 9pm. Petrol is sold at Seronera.

Moshi

The noticeably clean capital of the densely populated Kilimanjaro region sits at the foot of Mt Kilimanjaro and makes a good introduction to the splendours of the north. It's a low-key place with an appealing blend of African and Asian influences and a self-sufficient, prosperous feel, due in large part to it being the centre of one of Tanzania's major coffee-growing regions. It's also less expensive than nearby Arusha. Virtually all visitors are here to climb Mt Kilimanjaro.

👁 Sights & Activities

Even inside the city, **Mt Kilimanjaro** is the main attraction and you'll probably be continually gazing north trying to catch a glimpse. Most of the time it will be hidden behind a wall of clouds, but nearly every evening around sunset it emerges from the mist to whet your appetite for altitude. From December through June it's usually visible during the mornings, too, and during these months it's extra beautiful because it's topped by much more snow.

Trekking agencies and many hotels lead easy, scenic **walks** along the footpaths linking various villages on Kilimanjaro's lower slopes.

🛏 Sleeping

🛏 Central Moshi

Most of central Moshi's accommodation options are an easy walk from the bus station.

AA Hill Street Accommodation   GUESTHOUSE $
(📞0784 461469, 0754 461469; azim_omar@hotmail.com; Kilima St; s/d/tr Tsh20,000/30,000/40,000) Walk past the seamstresses plying their trade just off Kilima St, and climb the stairs to this quiet, friendly place that's ideal for those looking for an alternative to the busy backpacker scene. Don't be put off by the list of restrictions (no alcohol, no shared rooms for nonmarried couples) – if those things matter, go elsewhere.

Haria Hotel   HOTEL $
(📞0752 328042; Mawenzi Rd; d US$27, dm/d with shared bathroom US$12/24; 🕿) This laid-back, switched-on place has a devoted following and it's not hard to see why. The rooms are nothing special, but they're large and come with a friendly overall feel, thanks to the predominantly female staff. It's worlds better than other, better-known and more expensive places nearby and the restaurant serves a limited menu of local meals at fair prices. Breakfast costs Tsh3000.

Kindoroko Hotel   HOTEL $
(📞0757 369628; www.kindorokohotels.com; Mawenzi Rd; s/d/f US$25/35/50; @🕿) Rooms here are small and sit somewhere between basic and simple, but they come with cable TV and hot water. The main reason to stay is the guests-only, rooftop bar, an excellent meeting place with fine Kilimanjaro views. As their promotional material says, the hotel 'leaves you in no doubt that you are in Africa' – make of that what you will.

Buffalo Hotel   HOTEL $
(📞0756 508501; New St; s/d/tr/ste US$30/35/45/50; ❄) The long-popular Buffalo Hotel has straightforward rooms and they've recently given the place an overhaul so all have private bathrooms. Avoid the

ground-floor rooms and head up the stairs; there's no elevator. The lack of wi-fi lets it down a little, but there's an internet cafe next door and it's generally a good deal.

Lutheran Umoja Hostel
GUESTHOUSE $

(☎027-275 0902; Market St; s/d Tsh30,000/40,000, with shared bathroom Tsh15,000/25,000; ᴾ@) The cheapest place in the city centre has clean, no-frills rooms around a small (mostly) quiet courtyard. It's popular with volunteers.

Bristol Cottages
HOTEL $$

(☎027-275 5083; www.bristolcottages.com; 98 Rindi Lane; s/d US$60/70, s/d/tr cottage US$70/80/100, s/d/tr ste US$80/100/120; ᴾ❄🛜) This place exudes a sense of peace upon entering – the leafy compound is an attractive counterpoint to busy Moshi streets – and the rooms are well-presented; the suites are particularly spacious. For all this talk of peace, however, early morning noise can be a problem. Even so, it's probably our mid-range pick in the downtown.

🛏 Outside the City Centre

★Hibiscus
B&B $

(☎0768 146589, 0766-312516; www.thehibiscusmoshi.com; off Taifa Rd; s/tw US$25/40; 🛜) This cosy B&B has six spotless, impeccably decorated rooms, all with fan and most with private bathroom, plus a delightful garden and meals on request. Highly recommended. It's in a quiet residential area just northwest of the town centre.

Honey Badger
GUESTHOUSE $

(☎0767 551190, 0787 730235; www.honeybadgerlodge.com; dm from US$15, s/d from US$50/70; ᴾ@🛜❄) A large family-run place with shady gardens and a variety of rooms. Dorm dwellers must pay US$3 to use the large pool. It offers a variety of tours and lessons (drumming, cooking etc) and volunteer opportunities can be arranged. The restaurant serves gourmet pizzas from its stone oven from Thursday to Sunday. It's 7km from town off the Marangu road.

★AMEG Lodge
LODGE $$

(☎0754 058268, 027-275 0175; www.ameglodge.com; off Lema Rd; s/d from US$70/94, s/d ste US$127/149) This friendly place wins plaudits from travellers for its lovely setting in 4.5 acres of manicured gardens with palm trees and frangipanis, 4km northwest of the town centre. Attractive rooms with broad verandas and plenty of space lie dotted around the compound, service is friendly, and the overall feel is that of a rural oasis on the fringe of the city.

★Kaliwa Lodge
LODGE $$

(☎0762 620707; www.kaliwalodge.com; s/d US$80/160; ᴾ) At an altitude of 1300m and close to Machame gate, this new German-run place opened in 2012 and has a refreshingly contemporary Bauhaus architectural style with soothing grey cube-like structures. Rooms have abundant glass, the colour scheme is muted but very modern, and the setting amid palm trees and lush gardens is as lovely as the rest of the place.

MOSHI TREKKING OPERATORS

The following Moshi-based companies focus on Kilimanjaro treks, although most can also organise day hikes on the mountain's lower slopes.

Just Kilimanjaro (www.just-kilimanjaro.com; midrange) A small, highly regarded operator offering expertly guided Kilimanjaro treks.

Kessy Brothers Tours & Travel (www.kessybrotherstours.com; budget to midrange) Kilimanjaro treks.

Moshi Expeditions & Mountaineering (MEM Tours; www.memtours.com; budget to midrange) Kilimanjaro treks.

Shah Tours (www.kilimanjaro-shah.com; midrange) Reasonably priced Kilimanjaro and Meru treks, plus treks in the Ngorongoro highlands and on Ol Doinyo Lengai.

Summit Expeditions & Nomadic Experience (p117) Expertly guided Kilimanjaro treks, plus cycling, walks and cultural excursions on the mountain's lower slopes and customised northern circuit wildlife safaris.

Tanzania Journeys (p117) Northern circuit, community-focused vehicle, active and cultural safaris, including Kilimanjaro treks, day hikes and cultural tours in the Moshi area.

Moshi

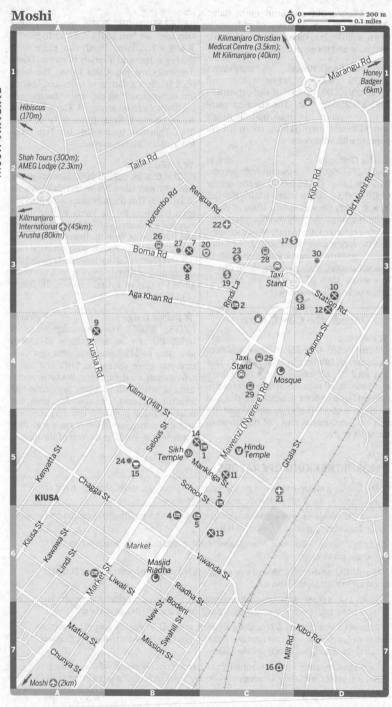

0 — 200 m
0 — 0.1 miles

Kilimanjaro Christian
Medical Centre (3.5km);
Mt Kilimanjaro (40km)

Marangu Rd

Honey
Badger
(6km)

Hibiscus
(170m)

Shah Tours (300m);
AMEG Lodge (2.3km)

Taifa Rd

Kibo Rd

Old Moshi Rd

Kilimanjaro
International (45km);
Arusha (80km)

Horombo Rd

Rengua Rd

22

Boma Rd

26   27 7 20
              23   17
        8   28   30
       19
              Taxi
              Stand   10

Aga Khan Rd

Rindi La   Station Rd
        2   18   12

Arusha Rd

9

Kilima (Hill) St

Taxi
Stand   25

        Mosque
        29

Selous St

Kenyatta St

Chagga St

KIUSA

24   14
15   1   Mawenzi (Nyerere) Rd

Sikh
Temple   Mankinga St   Hindu
              Temple

Kiusa St

Kawawa St

Lind St

School St   3
              21

4
5

Market

13

Market St

Liwali St

6   Masjid
      Riadha   Viwanda St

Ghala St

Riadha St

Boderni St

Mafuta St

New St

Swahili St

Mission St

Kibo Rd

Mill Rd

Chunya St

Moshi (2km)

16

Moshi

Eating & Drinking

★ Kaliwa
THAI **$**

(☑ 0762 620707; Arusha Rd; mains Tsh7000-9000; ⊙ 11am-11pm; 🛜) This welcome addition to Moshi's rather limited eating scene sits at the southwestern end of Uhuru Park, offering a stylish outdoor eating area and fragrant Thai dishes like basil beef. Wines, good coffee and a sophisticated vibe have attracted a well-to-do local crowd from the beginning and its popularity shows no sign of waning.

Milan's
INDIAN **$**

(Mankinga St; meals Tsh5000-6500; ⊙ 11am-9.30pm; 🚗) This colourful all-vegetarian spot is our favourite Indian restaurant, and not only because the prices are so low: it's really delicious.

The Coffee Shop
CAFE **$**

(☑ 027-275 2707; Kilima St; mains Tsh6500-9000; ⊙ 7.30am-9.30pm Mon-Sat; 🛜) 🍽 Garden seating, good coffee and homemade breads, cakes, yoghurt, breakfast, soups and low-priced light meals. Of the latter, the local dishes (choose a sauce with ugali or chapati) are generally preferable to the Chinese-inspired selections. Proceeds go to a church project.

Pamoja Cafe
TANZANIAN, INTERNATIONAL **$**

(New St; mains Tsh3500-8000; ⊙ 8am-10pm Mon-Sat, 10am-9pm Sun; 🛜) Following a time-honoured tradition of budget-traveller hangouts the world over, Pamoja Cafe is basic but gives the punters what they want with free wi-fi, a funky musical soundtrack, Western snacks (burgers and sandwiches) and cheap local cuisine, such as *nyami mchuzi* (beef stew with rice, ugali or chapati). There's also a nightly barbecue from 5.30pm.

★ Kilimanjaro Coffee Lounge
CAFE **$$**

(☑ 0754 610892; Station Rd; meals Tsh7000-13,000; ⊙ 8am-9pm Mon-Sat, 10am-8pm Sun; 🛜) A recent move opposite the Nakumatt Supermarket has done this place the world of good. The semi-garden setting is set back from the road, bringing a semblance of peace, and the food ranges from pizza and Mexican dishes to salads, sandwiches, burgers and steaks, alongside excellent milkshakes and juices. Throw in free wi-fi and you've all the makings of a travellers' classic.

KAHAWA SHAMBA COFFEE TOURS

The most popular coffee tour in town is offered by **Kahawa Shamba** (☑ 0784 324121, 0754 461376; www.kilimancultural-tourism.com; per person Tsh30,000, transport from Moshi Tsh50,000) 🍽, a laudable community-run venture that not only shows you how beans are grown, picked and roasted, but offers insight into the lives of the Chagga coffee farmers who live on Kilimanjaro's lower slopes. Meals with local families can be arranged, as can additional village and waterfall walks. It's easiest to book at Union Café (p144).

★ **Union Café**   CAFE
(☑ 0784 590184, 027-275 2785; Arusha Rd;
⏰ 7.30am-8.30pm; ☎) ✎ The Kilimanjaro
Native Cooperative Union, which represents
tens of thousands of small-holding coffee
farmers, runs this stylish shop. Although it
also serves good pizzas, pastas and burgers
(meals Tsh7000 to Tsh15,000), it's all about
the coffee – the cooperative's own beans are
roasted on-site. It also has a generator, reliable wi-fi and an atmosphere that's at once
trendy and carries echoes of colonial Africa.

Self-Catering

Abbas Ali's Hot Bread Shop   BAKERY $
(Boma Rd; ⏰ 9am-6pm Mon-Fri, to 5pm Sat)
Moshi's best bakery.

Aleem's   SUPERMARKET $
(Boma Rd; ⏰ 8.45am-1pm & 2-5pm Mon-Fri,
8.45am-1pm & 2-4pm Sat) Small, reasonably
well-stocked grocery store.

Nakumatt   SUPERMARKET $
(Station Rd; ⏰ 8.30am-10pm Mon-Sat, 10am-9pm
Sun) Moshi's largest supermarket.

🛍 Shopping

Shah Industries   LEATHER
(☑ 0754 260348; www.kiliweb.com/shah; Mill Rd;
⏰ 9am-5pm Mon-Fri, to 2pm Sat) ✎ Lots of interesting leatherwork, some of it made by
people with disabilities.

ℹ Information

Immigration Office (Boma Rd; ⏰ 7.30am-
3.30pm Mon-Fri)

Jaffery Charitable Medical Services (☑ 027-
275 1843; Ghala St; ⏰ 8.30am-5pm Mon-Fri, to
1pm Sat) Moshi's most reliable laboratory.

Kemi Pharmacy (☑ 027-275 1560; Rengua Rd;
⏰ 7am-7pm Mon-Sat) One of numerous pharmacies dotted around the city centre.

Kilimanjaro Christian Medical Centre (☑ 027-
275 4377/80; www.kcmc.ac.tz; Sokoine Rd;
⏰ 24hr) Around 4.5km north of the centre.

ℹ Getting There & Away

AIR

Kilimanjaro International Airport (KIA) is 50km
west of town, halfway to Arusha. There's also
the small Moshi airport just southwest of town,
along the extension of Market St, which handles
small planes and charters.

Coastal Aviation (☑ 0785 500445, 0785
500729; www.coastal.co.tz; Arusha Rd) Flies
daily from Moshi airport (if there are enough

passengers) on their Arusha–coast circuit, and
possibly also to the northern national parks.

Fastjet (☑ 0685 680533; www.fastjet.com)
Flights between KIA and Dar es Salaam with
onward connections across Tanzania and East
Africa.

Precision Air (☑ 0787 800820, 027-275 3495;
www.precisionairtz.com; Old Moshi Rd; ⏰ 8am-
5pm Mon-Fri, 9am-1pm Sat & Sun) Flies from
KIA to Dar, Zanzibar and Mwanza.

BUS

Buses and minibuses run throughout the day
to Arusha (Tsh3000, 1½ hours) and Marangu
(Tsh2000, 1½ hours).

The chaotic bus station is conveniently located
in the middle of the city. There are many touts
and arrivals can be quite annoying if you're new
to this sort of thing. This is one good reason to
travel with the companies that have their own
offices. It's best to buy tickets the day before you
plan to travel.

The following buses use their own offices
rather than the bus station. Ordinary buses
(Tsh20,000) and a few less-reliable luxury companies use the bus station.

Dar Express (☑ 0759 942550; Boma Rd) Eight
daily departures to Dar (Tsh36,000, seven
to eight hours) from 7am to noon aboard full
luxury buses (with air-con and toilets). Their
7am bus sometimes arrives early enough for
you to catch the afternoon ferry to Zanzibar,
but don't count on it.

Kilimanjaro Express (☑ 0715 213231; Rengua
Rd) Four morning departures to Dar aboard
luxury buses (Tsh33,000).

ℹ Getting Around

TO/FROM THE AIRPORT

Precision Air has a shuttle (Tsh10,000) to/from
KIA for its flights (except Nairobi, Kenya), departing from its offices a few hours before flight
time. Taxi drivers are tough negotiators; try for
US$30, but expect to pay more.

TAXI & DALLA-DALLA

There are taxi stands near the Clock Tower and
at the bus station, plus you can find taxis by most
hotels. From the bus station to a city-centre
hotel should cost Tsh2500, and it's Tsh3500
to Shantytown. Motorcycle taxi drivers expect
Tsh1000, even for a very short ride. Dalla-dallas
run down main roads from next to the bus
station.

Marangu

Nestled on the lower slopes of Mt Kilimanjaro, 40km northeast of Moshi, amid dense
stands of banana and coffee plants, is the

lively, leafy market town of Marangu. It has an agreeable highland ambience, cool climate and a good selection of hotels, all of which organise treks. While you'll generally get slightly better budget deals in Moshi, Marangu makes a convenient base for Kili climbs using the Marangu or Rongai routes, and it's an enjoyable stop in its own right.

Marangu is also the heartland of the Chagga people, and there are many possibilities for walks and cultural activities. Marangu means 'place of water' and the surrounding area is laced with small streams and waterfalls (most with a small entry charge) to visit.

◉ Sights & Activities

Most hotels can arrange **walks and cultural activities** in the area. At Kilimanjaro Mountain Resort, there's also the **Chagga Live Museum** (adult/child US$3/2; ⊙10am-5pm), a small outdoor museum illustrating traditional Chagga life.

It's possible to do a **day hike** in Mt Kilimanjaro National Park from Marangu gate as far as Mandara Hut (about three hours up, 1½ hours down; US$70 per person for park fees, plus about US$10 per guide, arranged at the park gate).

🛏 Sleeping & Eating

Coffee Tree Campsite CAMPGROUND $
(☑0754 691433; www.coffeetreecampsite.com; campsite per person US$10, rondavel/chalet per person US$15/18; @) 🍴 This place has expansive, trim grounds, hot-water showers, tents for hire, double rondavels and four- to five-person chalets. It's 700m east of the main road, signposted near Nakara Hotel. There's no food, but there are several eateries nearby. The owner is committed to slowing the environmental destruction of Kilimanjaro, and is a good source of information on local conservation efforts.

Bismarck Hut Lodge GUESTHOUSE $
(☑0754 318338; camping US$5, r per person without bathroom US$10-15; P) Along the road to the park gate and shortly before the turn-off to Capricorn Hotel, the no-frills Bismarck has a few clean, basic rooms, a small camping area, two large, old resident tortoises and meals on order.

Babylon Lodge LODGE $$
(☑027-275 6355; www.babylonlodge.com; s/d/tr US$40/60/80; P@🛜) Friendly Babylon has simple and clean twin- and double-bedded

MARANGU TREKKING OPERATORS

Most Marangu hotels organise Kilimanjaro treks. Also worth inquiring about is Marangu Hotel's 'hard way' option that's one of the cheaper deals available for a reliable trek. For a variable yet reasonable fee (amount depends on group size and number of porters required) the hotel will take care of hut reservations and provide a guide with porter(s), while you provide all food and equipment. Marangu Hotel also offers 'hard way' deals on the other Kilimanjaro routes.

rooms clustered around small, attractive gardens. It's often somewhat more flexible than other properties on negotiating Kili trek packages. It's 700m east of the main junction.

Marangu Hotel LODGE $$$
(☑0754 886092, 027-275 6594; www.maranguhotel.com; campsite per person US$6.50, s/d/tr half board US$105/160/215; @🛜🏊) This long-standing hotel is the first place you reach coming from Moshi. It has an appealingly faded British ambience, pleasant rooms in expansive grounds, lovely gardens and a campground with hot-water showers. Low season rates (double US$110) apply if you join one of the hotel's fully equipped climbs.

❶ Getting There & Away

Minibuses run throughout the day between Marangu's main junction (Marangu Mtoni) and Moshi (Tsh2000, 1½ hours). Once in Marangu, there are sporadic pick-ups from the main junction to the park gate (Tsh1500), 5km further. For the Holili border, change at Himo junction.

Mt Kilimanjaro National Park

Since its official opening in 1977, **Mt Kilimanjaro National Park** (☑0767 536134, 0689 062309, 027-56605; www.tanzaniaparks.com/kili.html; adult/child US$70/20; ⊙6.30am-6.30pm) has become one of Tanzania's most visited parks. Unlike the other northern parks, this isn't for the wildlife, although it's there. Rather, it's to gaze in awe at a mountain on the equator capped with snow, and to climb to the top of Africa.

Kilimanjaro Area

Map labels:

Namanga (85km)

KENYA

Rongai
Loitokitok

Londorosi Gate
Mt Kilimanjaro National Park
Londorosi
Shira Plateau
Mt Kilimanjaro
Shira Plateau Route
Rongai Route
Shira
Johnsell Point (3962m)
Western Breach
Site of Arrow Glacier Hut (4800m)
Mawenzi
The Saddle
Ndarakwai Camp
Shira Hut (3840m)
Kibo
Hans Meyer Peak (5149m)
Uhuru Peak (5896m)
Machame Route
Barranco Hut (3950m)
Maundi Crater
Marangu Route
Sanya Juu
Umbwe Route
Barranco Wall
Mweka Route
Mandara Hut (2700m)
Machame Gate
Kilimanjaro National Park Headquarters & Marangu Gate (1980m)
Machame
Kyalia
Umbwe
Mweka
Marangu
Boma Ng'ombe
Mamba
Sanya
Ngangu Hill
Moshi
Usa River (15km);
Arusha (35km)
Himo
Kilimanjaro International Airport (KIA)

0 / 10 km
0 / 5 miles

At the heart of the park is the 5896m Mt Kilimanjaro, Africa's highest mountain and one of the continent's magnificent sights. It's also one of the highest volcanoes and among the highest freestanding mountains in the world, rising from cultivated farmlands on the lower levels, through lush rainforest to alpine meadows, and finally across a barren lunar landscape to the twin summits of Kibo and Mawenzi. The lower rainforest is home to many animals, including buffaloes, elephants, leopards and monkeys, and elands are occasionally seen in the saddle area between Kibo and Mawenzi.

A trek up Kili lures around 25,000 trekkers each year, in part because it's possible to walk to the summit without ropes or technical climbing experience. Yet, nontechnical does not mean easy. The climb is a serious (and expensive) undertaking, and only worth doing with the right preparation.

Trekking Mt Kilimanjaro

Mt Kilimanjaro can be climbed at any time of year. Though weather patterns are notoriously erratic and difficult to predict, during November and March/April, it's more likely that paths through the forest will be slippery, and that routes up to the summit, especially the Western Breach, will be covered by snow. That said, you can also have a streak of beautiful, sunny days during these times. Overall, the best time for climbing the mountain is in the dry season, from late June to October, and from late December to February or early March, just after the short rains and before the long rains.

What to Bring

Don't underestimate the weather on Kilimanjaro. Conditions on the mountain are frequently very cold and wet, and you'll need a full range of waterproof cold-weather clothing and gear, including a good-quality sleeping bag. It's also worth carrying some additional sturdy water bottles. No matter what the time of year, waterproof everything, especially your sleeping bag, as things rarely dry on the mountain. It's often possible to rent sleeping bags and gear from trekking operators. For the Marangu Route, you can also rent gear from the Kilimanjaro Guides Cooperative Society stand just inside Marangu gate, or from a small no-name shop just before the gate. However, especially at the budget level, quality and availability can't be counted on, and it's best to bring your own.

Apart from a small shop at Marangu gate selling a limited range of chocolate bars and tinned items, there are no shops inside the park. You can buy beer and soft drinks at high prices at huts on the Marangu Route.

Costs

Kilimanjaro can only be climbed with a licensed guide. Unless you're a Tanzanian resident and well-versed in the logistics of Kili climbs, the only realistic way to organise things is through a tour company. No-frills five-day/four-night treks up the Marangu Route start at about US$1100, including park fees, and no-frills six-day budget treks on the Machame Route start at around US$1400. Better-quality six-day trips on the Marangu and Machame routes start at about US$1500. The Umbwe Route is often sold by budget operators for about the same price as Marangu, and billed as a quick and comparatively inexpensive way to reach the top. Don't fall for this; the route should only be done by experienced trekkers and should have an extra acclimatisation day built in. Prices start at about US$1200 on the Rongai Route, and about US$1600 for a seven-day trek on the Shira Plateau Route. As the starting points for these latter routes are further from Moshi than those for the other routes, transport costs can be significant, so clarify whether they're included in the price.

Whatever you pay for your trek, remember that at least US$525 of this goes to park fees for a five-day Marangu Route climb, and more for longer treks (US$745 for a seven-day Machame Route climb). The rest of the money covers food, tents (if required), guides, porters, and transport to and from the start of the trek. Most of the better companies

---

TAKE YOUR KILI CLIMB SERIOUSLY

Whatever route you choose, remember that ascending Kilimanjaro is a serious undertaking. While many thousands of trekkers reach Uhuru Peak without major difficulty, many more don't make it because they suffer altitude sickness or simply aren't in good enough shape. And, every year some trekkers and porters die on the mountain. Come prepared with appropriate footwear and clothing, and most importantly, allow yourself enough time. If you're interested in reaching the top, seriously consider adding at least one extra day onto the 'standard' climb itineraries. Although the extra US$150 to US$250 may seem a lot when you're planning your trip, it will seem insignificant later on if you've gone to the expense and effort to start a trek and then can't reach the top. Don't feel badly about insisting on an extra day with the trekking companies: standard medical advice is to increase sleeping altitude by only 300m per day once above 3000m, which is about one-third of the daily altitude gains above 3000m on the standard Kili climb routes offered by most operators.

It's also worth remembering that it's not essential to reach Uhuru Peak, and you haven't 'failed' if you don't. If time (or money) is limited, choose other treks and you can experience several different mountain areas for the price of a single Kili climb. Consider trekking up to an area such as the Saddle, the top of the Barranco Wall or the Shira Plateau to appreciate the splendour and magnificence of the mountain without the gruel of summiting.

ⓘ MT KILIMANJARO NATIONAL PARK

Why Go The chance to climb Africa's tallest mountain.

When to Go Year-round, but best late June to October and late December to February.

Practicalities Park entry gates include Machame, Marangu (the site of park headquarters), Londorosi and several other points; trekkers using the Rongai Route should pay their fees at Marangu gate. There are six routes to the summit: Machame, Marangu, Umbwe, Rongai, Shira Plateau and Mweka. Requirements have recently changed and you must pay at least six days worth of park fees for all routes except Marangu (five-day minimum).

Budget Tips Climb the Marangu Route, but don't try and skimp on supplies and other essential elements that may compromise your safety.

provide dining tents, decent to good cuisine and various other extras to both make the experience more enjoyable and maximise your chances of getting to the top. If you choose a really cheap trip you risk having inadequate meals, mediocre guides, few comforts, and problems with hut bookings and park fees. Also remember that an environmentally responsible trek usually costs more.

Park entry fees (calculated per day, and not per 24-hour period) are US$70 per adult. Huts (Marangu Route) cost US$60 per person per night, and there's a US$20 rescue fee per person per trip for treks on the mountain. Camping costs US$50 per person per night on all routes. Park fees are generally included in price quotes, and paid on your behalf by the trekking operator, but you'll need to confirm this before making any bookings. Guide and porter fees (but not tips) are handled directly by the trekking companies. For anyone paying directly at the gate, all entry, hut, camping and other park fees must be paid with either Visa or MasterCard.

Most guides and porters receive only minimal wages from the trekking companies and depend on tips as their major source of income. As a guideline, plan on tipping about 10% of the total amount you've paid for the trek, to be divided up among the guides and porters. Common tips for satisfactory service are from about US$10 to US$15 per group per day for the guide, US$8 to US$10 per group per day for the cook, and US$5 to US$10 per group per day for each porter.

Guides & Porters

Guides, and at least one porter (for the guide), are obligatory and are provided by your trekking company. You can carry your own gear on the Marangu Route, although porters are generally used, but one or two porters per trekker are essential on all other routes.

All guides must be registered with the national park authorities. If in doubt, check that your guide's permit is up to date. On Kili, the guide's job is to show you the way and that's it. Only the best guides, working for reputable companies, will be able to tell you about wildlife, flowers or other features on the mountain.

Porters will carry bags weighing up to 15kg (not including their own food and clothing, which they strap to the outside of your bag), and your bags will be weighed before you set off.

While most guides, including those working for the budget companies, are dedicated, professional, properly trained and genuinely concerned with making your trip safe and successful, there are exceptions. If you're a hardy traveller you might not worry about basic meals and substandard tents, but you should be concerned about incompetent guides and dishonest porters. Although it doesn't happen often, some guides leave the last hut deliberately late on the summit day to avoid going all the way to the top. Going with a reputable company, preferably one who hires full-time guides (most don't), is one way to prevent bad experiences. Also, insist on meeting the guide before signing up for a trip, familiarise yourself with all aspects of the route, and when on the mountain have morning and evening briefings so you know what to expect each day. The night before summiting talk to other climbers to be sure your departure time seems realistic (though note that not everyone leaves at the same time) and if not, get an explanation from your guide. Should problems arise, be polite but firm.

Maps

Topographical maps include *Map & Guide to Kilimanjaro* by Andrew Wielochowski and *Kilimanjaro Map & Guide* by Mark Savage.

Trekking Routes

There are six main trekking routes to the summit. Trekkers on all but the Marangu Route must use tents.

Officially a limit of 60 climbers per route per day is in effect on Kilimanjaro. It's currently not being enforced, except on the Marangu Route, which is self-limiting because of maximum hut capacities. If and when this limit is enforced, expect the advance time necessary for booking a climb to increase, with less flexibility for last-minute arrangements.

Marangu Route A trek on this route is typically sold as a five-day, four-night return package, although at least one extra night is highly recommended to help acclimatisation, especially if you've just flown in to Tanzania or arrived from the lowlands.

Machame Route This increasingly popular route has a gradual ascent, including a spectacular day contouring the southern slopes before approaching the summit via the top section of the Mweka Route.

Umbwe Route Very steep, with a more direct way to the summit: enjoyable, if you can resist the temptation to gain altitude too quickly. Although the route is direct, the top, steep section up the Western Breach is often covered in ice or snow, which makes it impassable or extremely dangerous. Many trekkers who attempt it without proper acclimatisation are forced to turn back. An indication of its seriousness is that until fairly recently, the Western Breach was considered a technical mountaineering route. Only consider this route if you're experienced and properly equipped, and travelling with a reputable operator. Reliable operators will suggest an extra night for acclimatisation.

Rongai Route Growing in popularity, this route starts near the Kenyan border and goes up the northern side of the mountain.

Shira Plateau Route Also called the Londorosi Route, this attractive route is somewhat longer than the others, but good for acclimatisation if you start trekking from Londorosi gate (rather than driving all the way to the Shira Track trailhead), or if you take an extra day at Shira Hut.

Mweka Route For descent only, and often used as part of the Machame, Umbwe and (sometimes) Marangu routes.

ℹ Information

Kilimanjaro National Park Headquarters (☏ 027-275 6602/5; info@tanzaniaparks.com; ☺ 8am-6pm) is located at the Marangu entry gate.

CENTRAL TANZANIA

Although well off most tourist itineraries, central Tanzania has several attractions. Prime among these are the enigmatic Kondoa Rock-Art Sites scattered across remote hills along the Rift Valley Escarpment. Dodoma, Tanzania's legislative capital, hosts interesting architecture and the region's best facilities.

CULTURAL TOURISM IN CENTRAL TANZANIA

Babati and Kondoa districts are home to a colourful array of tribes, many of whom have changed their lifestyle little over the past century. Many villages welcome visitors, but, unlike those around Arusha, none are geared towards tourism. The most famous (and most visited) tribe is the Barabaig, who still follow a traditional semi-nomadic lifestyle and are recognisable by the goatskin garments still worn daily by many women. Unrelated to the tribes around them, the Sandawe are one of the oldest peoples of Tanzania and they may have been the ones who painted the early rock art around Kondoa and Kolo. They speak a 'click' language and still hunt with bow and arrow.

Kahembe's Culture & Wildlife Safaris (☏ 0784 397477; www.kahembeculturalsafaris. com; Sokoine Rd) In Babati, this reliable and knowledgeable outfit have been offering cultural tours in the region since 1992. Besides village visits, it's the main operator organising Mt Hanang climbs.

Kondoa Irangi Cultural Tourism Program (☏ 0784 948858; www.tanzaniacultural tours.com) The Kondoa Rock-Art Sites are the bread and butter of this company in Kondoa town, but director Moshi Changai also leads Barabaig, Sandawe and Irangi village visits by bicycle or car. Overnights in local homes are possible.

Central Tanzania

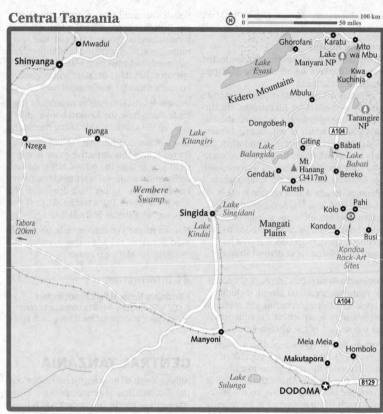

Dodoma

POP 410,960

Arid Dodoma sits in not-so-splendid isolation in the geographic centre of the country, at a height of about 1100m. Although the town was located along the old caravan route connecting Lake Tanganyika and Central Africa with the sea, and the Central Line railway arrived just after the turn of the 20th century, Dodoma was of little consequence until 1973 when it was named Tanzania's official capital and headquarters of the ruling Chama Cha Mapinduzi (CCM) party. Although the legislature meets here (hence the periodic profusion of 4WDs), Dar es Salaam remains Tanzania's unrivalled economic and political centre.

◉ Sights

The most interesting sights in Dodoma are its grand houses of worship. The Bunge (parliament) is an African-influenced round building. It's only open to visitors during sessions (bring your passport) but well worth a gander from the outside at other times. Photography is strictly prohibited.

🛏 Sleeping

Kilondoma Inn GUESTHOUSE $
(☎ 0745 477399; www.kilondoma.blogspot.com; off Ndovu Rd; d Tsh20,000; 🅿 ❋ 🛜) We're not sure how this new place can offer so much (rooms have air-conditioning, cable TV, fans and hot water) for so little. Even if the price rises a bit it would still be one of the best-value properties in Dodoma. Double beds are just barely big enough for two.

Kidia Vision Hotel HOTEL $
(☎ 0784 210766; Ninth St; d Tsh30,000-45,000, ste Tsh70,000-80,000; 🅿 🛜) Well-managed and, unlike most other hotels in its class, well maintained, this is a very solid choice at this

level. Rooms are comfy and clean, though you don't get much extra as the price rises.

New Dodoma Hotel
HOTEL **$$**

(☑ 026-232 1641; www.newdodomahotel.com; Railway Rd; s/d with fan US$50/70, with air-con from US$70/95; P ❈ @ ☎ ☎) The former Railway Hotel's flower-filled courtyard is a lovely oasis and the rooms have some style. The suites face the main street and are noisier than the standard rooms. There's a gym, good dining and a not-so-clean swimming pool.

✗ Eating

Aladdin's Cave
SWEETS, EUROPEAN **$**

(CDA St; snacks from Tsh350, meals Tsh2500-8000; ⏰ 9.30am-1pm daily & 3.30-5.30pm Tue-Sat; 🖉) Dodoma's version of an old-fashioned candy store and soda fountain. It also serves veggie burgers and pizzas.

Leone l'Africano
ITALIAN **$$**

(☑ 0754 073573, 0788 629797; Mlimwa Rd; meals Tsh8500-14,000; ⏰ 5-10pm Tue-Fri, noon-3pm & 5-10pm Sat & Sun) Tasty Italian food, including one of Tanzania's better pizzas, served in the shadow of Lion Rock. You can try local wines or play it safe with a European vintage. There's a playground and a 12-hole minigolf course.

New Dodoma Hotel
INTERNATIONAL **$$**

(Railway Rd; meals Tsh5000-16,000; ⏰ 7am-10pm) The menu here goes global with choices such as pizza, fish and chips, *dhal tadka* and fajitas. The Indian and local dishes are

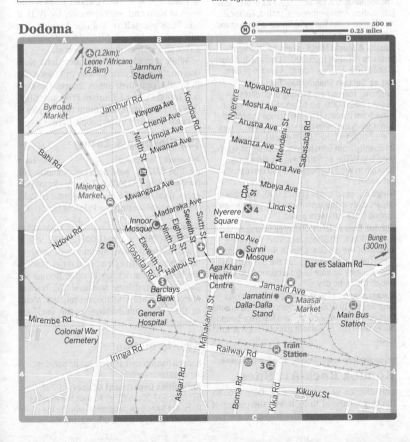

the most reliable and the outdoor Barbeque Village grills up all kinds of meat at dinnertime. The Chinese-owned restaurant within the hotel is a lucky dip, since dishes can be both good and awful.

❶ Information

Aga Khan Health Centre (☏ 026-232 1789; Sixth St; ◷ 8am-8pm Mon-Sat) First destination for illnesses. Has a good pharmacy.

❶ Getting There & Away

AIR
The airport is just north of the city centre (Tsh4000 in a taxi).

Flightlink (☏ 0787 845200, 0754 972173; www.flightlinkaircharters.com) Flightlink has a daily service between Dodoma and Dar es Salaam with onward connections to Pemba, Zanzibar and Arusha.

BUS
The following bus services leave from the main bus station unless otherwise stated. For local destinations, use the Jamatini dalla-dalla stand west of the bus stand.

Arusha & Moshi Mtei Express has the best buses to Arusha (Ts25,000, 11 hours) and Moshi (Tsh28,000, 12 to 14 hours). All leave at 6am.

Dar es Salaam Shabiby has 'full luxury' (meaning four-across seating and toilets) buses (Tsh24,000, six to seven hours), which leave from its own terminal across the roundabout from the main bus station. Other buses (Tsh12,000 to Tsh20,000) depart Dodoma frequently from 6am to 1pm. Buses that started their trip to Dar es Salaam in Mwanza pass through in the afternoon and you can usually get a seat.

Iringa Buses to Iringa (Tsh12,000, four hours) depart daily in the mornings. The route is now around three-quarters paved.

Kondoa Buses (Tsh7000, three hours) depart 6am, 6.30am, 10.30am and noon: they use a section of the old Great North Rd connecting Cape Town and Cairo. If you take the morning bus, you may be able to get a connection to Babati the same day.

Mwanza Buses (Tsh36,000, eight hours) via Singida (Tsh16,000, three hours) leave Dodoma between 6am and 7.30am, and Mwanza-bound buses from Dar es Salaam pass through around noon.

Kondoa Rock-Art Sites

The district of Kondoa, especially around the tiny village of Kolo, lies at the centre of one of the most impressive collections of an-

cient rock art on the African continent, and it is one of the most overlooked attractions in Tanzania. If you can tolerate a bit of rugged travel, this is an intriguing and worthwhile detour.

Some experts maintain that the oldest paintings date back around 6000 years and were made by the Sandawe, who are distantly related linguistically to South Africa's San, a group also renowned for its rock art. Others are definitely more recent and were done from 800 up until probably 200 years ago by Bantu-speaking peoples who migrated into this area.

There are 186 known sites (and surely many more), of which only a portion have been properly documented. The most visited, though not the best, the **Kolo sites** (B1, B2 and B3), are 9km east of Kolo village and 4WD is required. You'll need to climb a steep hill at the end of the road to see them. The most varied, and thus best overall collection of paintings, is at Thawi, about 15km northwest of Kolo and reachable only by 4WD. If you base yourself in Kolo or Kondoa, you can comfortably see three of these places in a day, and all four if you really rush.

While very few safari operators use Kondoa on their itineraries, some will tack a day in Kondoa onto their longer safaris. The Kondoa Irangi Cultural Tourism Program (p149) (US$60 per person, minimum two people) in Kondoa regularly bring people here.

🛏 Sleeping & Eating

Amarula Campsite   CAMPGROUND $
(☏ 0754 672256; www.racctz.org; camping with own/hired tent US$10/20) This work in progress, 6km east of Kolo on the road to Pahi, has beautiful scenery and simple facilities.

New Planet   GUESTHOUSE $
(☏ 0787 907915; s/d Tsh18,000/23,000; ℗) In Kondoa, about a five-minute walk north of the bus stand, this clean and quiet place is the best the district has to offer. Rooms are fairly large and have fans and TV; buckets of hot water are available on request. Meals at the restaurant hidden in the back are reasonable.

❶ Information

Kondoa has internet access, but no banking services for travellers.

Antiquities Department Office (☏ 0752 575096; ◷ 7.30am-6pm) To visit the Kondoa Rock-Art Sites independently, stop by the Antiquities Department office along Kolo's main road to arrange a permit (adult/child Tsh27,000/13,000) and mandatory guide (free, but tips expected), some of whom speak English. There's a good little museum here covering not only archaeology, but also the culture of the Irangi people.

ⓘ Getting There & Away

Kolo is 80km south of Babati and 25km north of Kondoa. Buses to Kolo (Tsh7500, 3½ hours) depart Babati at 7am and 8.30am. From Arusha, Mtei Express buses to Kondoa, leaving at 6am, pass Kolo (Tsh11,500, 6½ hours). The last bus north from Kondoa leaves at 9am. There are only buses to Dodoma (Tsh8500, three hours) from Kondoa, not Kolo. They leave at 6am, 10am and 12.30pm. Catching a bus in Kondoa means you'll get a seat; wait for it to pass Kolo and you'll need to stand.

It could be possible to visit as a day trip from Babati (or as a stop en route to Dodoma) using public transport if you're willing to hitchhike after visiting the Kolo sites; there are *usually* some trucks travelling this road in the afternoon.

It is possible to hire motorcycles in Kolo and these can reach all the main rock art sites, but you'll have to get off and walk up some hills. Hiring motorcycles is very expensive if done through the Antiquities Department (Tsh25,000 just to the Kolo sites, for example) but you can try to get a better price with locals or hire a vehicle in Kondoa, the nearest proper town to the rock art.

Babati

The dusty market town of Babati, about 175km southwest of Arusha in a fertile spot along the edge of the Rift Valley Escarpment, is notable as a jumping-off point for climbs of Mt Hanang, 75km southwest.

🛏 Sleeping & Eating

Kahembe's Modern Guest House　　　　　　　GUESTHOUSE $
(📱0784 397477; www.kahembeculturalsafaris. com; Sokoine Rd; s/d Tsh25,000/30,000; 🛜) Home of Kahembe's Culture & Wildlife Safaris, this friendly place just northwest of the bus stand has decent twin- and double-bedded rooms with TVs and reliable hot-water showers. Their full breakfast complete with sausages, cornflakes, fruit, toast and eggs is included in the price, not to mention a great way to start the day.

White Rose Lodge　　　　　　　　GUESTHOUSE $
(📱0784 392577; www.manyarawhiterose.blogspot. com; Ziwani Rd; d Tsh25,000; 🅿🛜) A good-value spot set somewhat inconveniently (unless you're driving) off the Singida Rd south of town. Rooms are similar in standard to other Babati cheapies, only much newer.

Ango Bar & Restaurant　　　　　TANZANIAN $
(Arusha–Dodoma Rd; buffet breakfast Tsh6000, lunch or dinner Tsh8500; ⏰7am-9.30pm; 🖉) Behind a petrol station near the bus stand, this unexpectedly colourful place offers local fare, always including a few veggie dishes.

ⓘ Information

NBC (Arusha–Dodoma Rd) bank changes cash and has an ATM.

ⓘ Getting There & Away

The Babati–Dodoma road is still rough in parts but quite passable. For the final section before Dodoma you need to go in a security convoy if travelling after 4pm.

Bus connections from Babati include the following:

Arusha (Tsh9000, four to five hours) The first departs in both directions at 5.30am and the last leaves at 4pm, though dalla-dallas go until 6pm.

Dodoma (Tsh17,000) Though you'll be sold a single ticket to Dodoma, there's no direct bus. You'll be shifted to another bus at Kondoa.

Kondoa (Tsh8500, 3½ hours)

Mto wa Mbu Catch an Arusha bus and change in Makuyuni.

Mwanza (Tsh29,000 to Tsh35,000, 10 hours).

Singida (Tsh8500, four hours) Last bus leaves Babati around 10am.

LAKE VICTORIA

Tanzania's half of Africa's largest lake sees few visitors, but the region holds many attractions for those with a bent for the offbeat and a desire to immerse themselves in the rhythms of local life beyond the tourist trail. The towns of Musoma and Bukoba have a quiet waterside charm while most villagers on Ukerewe Island follow a subsistence lifestyle with little connection to the world beyond the shore.

Mwanza, Tanzania's second-largest city, is appealing in its own way and it's the perfect launch pad for a Serengeti–Lake Natron–Ngorongoro loop. Adding idyllic Rubondo Island National Park, deep in the lake's southwesternmost reaches, gives you a well-rounded safari experience.

Lake Victoria

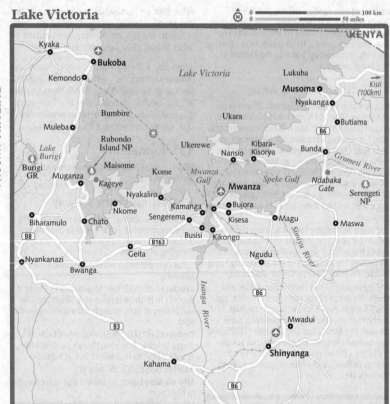

Musoma

Little Musoma, capital of the Mara region, sits serenely on a Lake Victoria peninsula with both sunrise and sunset views over the water.

There are banks and internet cafes along and just off of Mukendo Rd.

Tiny Butiama, about 45km southeast of Musoma, is the site of the **Mwalimu Julius K Nyerere Museum** (Butiama; admission Tsh8000; ⏰9am-5pm), and a worthwhile excursion for anyone interested in the renowned statesman's life.

🛏 Sleeping

⭐ **Tembo Beach Club**   CAMPGROUND, GUESTHOUSE **$**
(☏028-262 2887; camping Tsh15,000, r Tsh45,000; 🅿🛜) It has a sociable bar-restaurant (mains Tsh3000 to Tsh5000) and a reasonable camping area that's often busy with the clients of overland truck tours. Best of all, it

has some recently tarted-up rooms with African art on the walls. They are far enough from the bar that you can be lulled to sleep by waves rather than kept awake by music.

Mlima Mukendo Hotel   HOTEL **$**
(☏0768 065003; Mukendo Rd; s/d Tsh20,000/30,000) A bright green tower of a hotel on the main road (take a room at the back). It offers the best town-centre accommodation with smart, well-cared for rooms with wardrobes, desks and big bathrooms.

Matvilla Beach & Lodge   CAMPGROUND, BUNGALOW **$$**
(http://matvillabeach.co.tz; Matvilla Beach; camping Tsh10,000, bungalows s/d US$40/50; 🅿🛜) Out at the tip of the peninsula, 1.5km from the centre, this is a gorgeous multipurpose spot amid the rocks. There are hot showers for campers and new stone bungalows that are calm, quiet and blend into giant, granite boulders.

✖ Eating

Matvilla Beach & Lodge   TANZANIAN **$**
(meals Tsh5000-7000) With its lakeside setting, Matvilla Beach is everyone's favourite place for fried fish or chicken and a beer. Staff will arrange taxis to take you back to town. There are no set opening hours – according to staff it's open all the time.

Mara Dishes   BUFFET **$**
(Kivukani St; buffet Tsh5000; ⊙ 9am-10pm) Mara Dishes, east of CRDB bank, has a relatively large buffet and masses of locals piling in for a good feed.

❶ Getting There & Away

The bus terminal is 6km out of town at Bweri (Tsh4000 and 20 minutes via dalla-dalla, Tsh10,000 in a taxi), although booking offices remain in the town centre.
Arusha (Tsh35,000, 11 to 12 hours) Coast Line, Kimotco and Manko leave at 6am daily, passing through Serengeti National Park (using Ikoma Gate) and Ngorongoro Conservation Area, but you'll need to pay US$110 in park fees to ride this route.
Butiama (Tsh3000, one hour) Dalla-dallas go throughout the day.
Mwanza (Tsh8000, four hours) Mohammed Trans departs from its ticket office east of CRDB bank at 5am and 1pm.
Ukerewe Island (Tsh3000, one hour) Dalla-dallas go to Bunda between 5.30am and 4pm, from where you can get boat transport to the island.

Mwanza

POP 706,500

Mwanza is Tanzania's second-largest city, and the lake region's economic heart. The surrounding area – marked by hills strewn with enormous boulders – is home to the Sukuma, the country's largest tribe. In addition to being a jumping-off point for Rubondo Island National Park, Mwanza is a great starting or finishing point for safaris through Ngorongoro and the Serengeti.

◉ Sights

Central Mwanza along Temple St and west to Station Rd has an oriental feel due to its many **temples** (both Hindu and Sikh) and **mosques**, as well as Indian trading houses lining the streets. The street-side market and ambience continue west through the **Makoroboi** area where the namesake scrap-metal workshop is hidden away in the rocks.

Kerosene lamps (*makoroboi* in Swahili), ladles and other household goods are fashioned from old cans and other trash. East of Temple St, the huge and confusing **central market** is fun to explore. Visiting **Saa Nane National Park** (☑ 028-254 1819; office on Capri Point; adult/child US$30/15; ⊙ 6.30am-6.30pm, last entry 5pm) may help to while away a slow morning.

🖝 Tours

Tour operators hire 4WDs and can organise safaris to Serengeti and Rubondo Island National Parks. None of Mwanza's operators are as on the ball as the best agencies in Arusha, but we're also unaware of any in town that will blatantly rip you off. It's not easy to meet other travellers in Mwanza, but you can ask the agencies whether they have other clients interested in combining groups to save money or try posting a notice at Kuleana Pizzeria.

Fortes Africa   SAFARIS
(☑ 028-250 0561; www.fortes-africa.com; Station Rd) The most upmarket, reliable and professional company. There's also a branch inside Ryan's Bay hotel (p157).

Fourways   SAFARIS
(☑ 028-254 0653; www.fourwaystravel.net; Kenyatta Rd) Also books plane tickets.

Kiroyera Tours   SAFARIS
(☑ 0784 568276; www.kiroyeratours.com) Can generally beat others for car-rental rates (and the vehicles and drivers they use are recommended). There's no walk-in office.

Masumin Tours & Safaris   SAFARIS
(☑ 028-250 0192; www.masuminsafaris.com; Kenyatta Rd) Also books plane tickets.

Serengeti Expedition   SAFARIS
(☑ 028-254 2222; www.serengetiexpedition.com; Nkrumah Rd) One of the cheaper operators in Mwanza. Also books plane tickets.

Serengeti Passage   SAFARIS
(☑ 028-250 0061; www.serengeti-passage.com; Uhuru St) Low-cost safari specialist.

🛏 Sleeping

Midland Hotel   HOTEL **$**
(☑ 0718 431255; www.midlandhotel.com.tz; Rwagasore Rd; s Tsh50,000-60,000, d Tsh60,000-90,000; ❋ 🛜) This eye-catching blue tower is solid all-round with well-equipped rooms (free wi-fi reaches most), good service, a

Mwanza

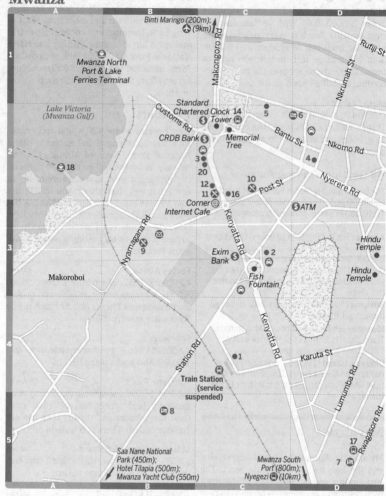

rooftop bar and a proper breakfast buffet. Best of all, it will sometimes discount. There are no mosquito nets, but the rooms are sprayed daily.

Isamo Hotel HOTEL $
(☑028-254 1616; Rwagasore St; r Tsh25,000-50,000; ❋☎) There's a lot of street noise seeping into the rooms here, but grab a pair of ear plugs and enjoy one of the cheapest and best deals in town. The well-kept rooms are a good size and some have little balconies overlooking the chaos.

Kishamapanda Guesthouse GUESTHOUSE $
(☑0755 083218; Kishamapanda St; d with/without bathroom Tsh15,000/13,000, tw Tsh20,000) This tidy little place is down a tiny alley behind the less-appealing New Geita Lodge. It's one of the best budget places in Mwanza. The shared bathrooms have ceiling fans and Western toilets.

Mwanza Yacht Club CAMPGROUND $
(☑0762 891280; Capri Point; camping Tsh10,000) This is where the big, overland tourist trucks stop. It has a great lakeside location, hot showers and security.

which are dated but decent and look out at the lake. It also has rooms on a historic boat. Though they are smaller and a little off-kilter, their special character makes them fun.

✕ Eating

Sizzlers Restaurant INDIAN $
(Kenyatta Rd; mains Tsh8000-12,000; ⊙noon-3pm & 6-11pm) Quiet during the day, this cheap Indian joint transforms into a hive of buzzing activity in the evenings. This is when people grab a streetside table and tuck into the chicken tikka which sizzles on the hot coals of the outdoor barbecue. It also does a range of other Indian meals.

DVN Restaurant TANZANIAN $
(Nyamagana Rd; meals Tsh3000-4000; ⊙7am-5pm) Excellent local fare served fast and cheap in this church-run place with a cute, old-fashioned cafe look and feel. It's behind the post office and quite hidden with just a small sign above a tucked-away door. You might need to ask for someone to point it out.

Kuleana Pizzeria INTERNATIONAL $$
(028-256 0566; Post St; pizzas Tsh10,000-12,000; ⊙7am-9pm; 🍴) 🍴 Don't expect

Ryan's Bay RESORT $$
(028-254 1702; www.ryansbay.com; Capri Point; s/d from US$110/140; 🅿✳🛜🏊) The flashest place in Mwanza has lake views and large, well-appointed rooms with acacia-tree murals on the walls. It's a bit resort-like but there's a great pool complex (guests only) and one of the best Indian restaurants in town (mains Tsh10,000 to Tsh17,000).

Hotel Tilapia HOTEL $$
(0784 700500, 028-250 0517; www.hoteltilapia. com; Capri Point; s/d/ste US$100/120/150; ✳🛜🏊) The ever-popular Tilapia, on the city side of Capri Point, has a variety of rooms, most of

> ### ℹ CROSSING THE MWANZA GULF
>
> Travelling west from Mwanza along the southern part of Lake Victoria entails crossing the Mwanza Gulf. There are two ferries, each with advantages.
>
> The Kamanga ferry (per person/vehicle Tsh1000/7200) docks right in town. It departs Mwanza hourly between 7am and 6.30pm, except Sunday when departures are every two hours from 8am to 6pm. If you're travelling to Bukoba or anywhere along that highway, ask which ferry the bus will use; you may be able to save a trip to the bus station by boarding the bus here.
>
> The government-run Busisi (aka Kigongo) ferry (per person/vehicle Tsh400/8000), 30km south of Mwanza, has the advantage of the road west being paved and it sails more often: every 30 minutes from 7am to 10pm. But, there are often delays since many trucks use this boat and also government officials sometimes call and tell the pilots to wait for them.

Italian-class food, but this is a relaxed and popular place for pizzas and snack-style food (omelettes, sandwiches and breads) with a good mix of locals and expats. The friendly owner feeds many street children.

Binti Maringo INTERNATIONAL **$**
(Balewa Rd; meals Tsh7500, pizzas Tsh12,000; ⊗8am-8pm) Sandwiches, pizzas and the classic meat stew get dished up in this simple open-air spot. Profits support the Kuleana Center for Children's Rights, which houses and educates street children. To get there go out of town a hundred metres. Take the first right after the dirty stream and it's 30 metres down on your right.

Hotel Tilapia INTERNATIONAL **$$**
(Capri Point; meals Tsh12,000-19,000; ⊗7am-midnight; 🐟) The hub of Mwanza's expat population and a magnet to passing tourists, the restaurant of the Hotel Tilapia has an attractive terrace overlooking the lake. You can choose everything from Japanese tepanyaki to Indian to continental.

ℹ Information

INTERNET ACCESS
Corner Internet Cafe (Kenyatta Rd; per hour Tsh1500; ⊗8am-7pm Mon-Sat, 10am-4pm Sun) Central internet cafe.

MEDICAL SERVICES
Aga Khan Health Centre (☎028-250 2474; www.agakhanhospitals.org; Miti Mrefu St; ⊗24hr) For minor illnesses.

Bugando Hospital (☎028-250 0513; www.bugandomedicalcentre.go.tz; Wurzburg Rd) The government hospital has a 24-hour casualty department.

MONEY
All the major banks have branches in Mwanza with ATMs. Most also change cash.

ℹ Getting There & Away

AIR
Air Tanzania (☎0782 737730; www.airtanzania.co.tz; Kenyatta Rd) flies to Dar es Salaam five days a week. **Fastjet** (☎0756 7540543; www.fastjet.com; Kenyatta Rd) also flies to Dar.

Coastal Aviation (☎0752 627825; www.coastal.cc; airport) has a daily flight to Arusha airport stopping at various Serengeti National Park airfields. It also flies to Dar es Salaam, Zanzibar and, internationally, to Kigali (Rwanda).

Precision Air (☎028-250 0819; www.precisionairtz.com; Kenyatta Rd) flies to Dar es Salaam, Kilimanjaro, Bukoba and, internationally, to Nairobi (Kenya). Auric Air (p212) also has a Bukoba flight as well as to Kigoma and Mpanda.

BOAT
The **MV Victoria** (1st class/2nd-class sleeping/2nd-class sitting/3rd class Tsh36,000/27,600/24,000 /17,500) connects Mwanza with Bukoba. There are also ferries to Ukerewe Island.

BUS
Nyegezi bus station, about 10km south of town, handles buses to all points east, south and west, including Dar es Salaam.

Arusha (from about Tsh30,000, 12 hours) Jordan departs its city centre office at 5am and the bus station at 6am, travelling via Singida.

Bukoba (Tsh20,000, six to seven hours) Buses depart regularly between 6am and 1pm, mostly using the Busisi ferry.

Dar es Salaam (Tsh45,000, 15 hours) Mohammed Trans departs at 6am from its city-centre ticket office before heading to the bus stations.

Kigoma (Tsh31,000, 10 hours) Adventure is the best of four companies departing daily at 5.30am.

Musoma (Tsh8000 to Tsh10,000, three to four hours, last bus 4pm) Departures are from Buzuruga bus station in Nyakato, 4km east of the city centre.

Tabora (Tsh15,000, six hours) Try NBS, with buses daily in the mornings.

There's no need to travel to the bus stations to buy tickets since numerous ticket agencies are stationed at the old city-centre bus station (now a car park). They don't charge an official commission, but they will overcharge you if they can get away with it.

TRAIN

Mwanza is the terminus of a branch of the Central Line and trains run to Tabora (Tsh26,900/22,700/11,800 in 1st/2nd/3rd class) on Thursday and Sunday at 4pm.

ⓘ Getting Around

TO/FROM THE AIRPORT

Mwanza's airport is 10km north of town (Tsh10,000 in a taxi). Dalla-dallas to the airport (Tsh400) follow Kenyatta and Makongoro Rds.

BUS & TAXI

Dalla-dallas (labelled Buhongwa) to Nyegezi bus station run south down Kenyatta and Pamba Rds. The most convenient place to find a dalla-dalla (labelled Igoma) to Buzuruga bus station is just northeast of the Clock Tower, where they park before running down Uhuru St.

There are taxi stands all around the city centre, with town trips about Tsh5000. Taxis to Buzuruga/Nyegezi bus stations cost Tsh7000/12,000. Motorcycle taxis are everywhere (Tsh1000 within the city centre).

Around Mwanza

Sukuma Museum

The **Sukuma Museum** (🌐0765 667661; admission Tsh15,000, video Tsh200,000; ⊗9am-6pm Mon-Sat, 10am-6pm Sun) in Bujora village is an open-air museum where, among other things, you'll see traditional Sukuma dwellings and the grass house of a traditional healer. Also on the grounds is the **royal drum pavilion**, built in the shape of a king's stool, holding a collection of royal drums that are still played at special events, and a **round church** with many traditional Sukuma stylings that was built in 1958 by David

Fumbuka Clement, the Québecois missionary priest who founded the museum.

🛏 Sleeping & Eating

The centre has no-frills **bandas** (per person with meals Tsh30,000) in the style of Sukuma traditional houses and a **campground** (camping Tsh15,000). There's a little bar and you can use the kitchen.

ⓘ Getting There & Away

Bujora is 18km east of Mwanza off the Musoma road. Take a dalla-dalla (Tsh500, 30 minutes) to Kisesa from Uhuru Rd north of the market in Mwanza. From Kisesa, motorcycle taxis cost Tsh1000. Or, walk a short way along the main road and turn left at the sign, following the small dirt road for 1.7km. A taxi from Mwanza, with waiting time, will cost Tsh45,000 to Tsh50,000.

Ukerewe

With its simple lifestyle and rocky terrain broken by lake vistas and tiny patches of forest, Ukerewe Island, 50km north of Mwanza, makes an intriguing, offbeat diversion. Nansio, the main town, has no internationally linked ATMs. Shared taxis and dalla-dallas connect Ukerewe's few sizeable villages.

🛏 Sleeping & Eating

La Bima Hotel   GUESTHOUSE $
(☑0732 515044; s/tw Tsh20,000/25,000; P) Despite cramped rooms (some with hot water) and peeling paint, this OK place is Nansio's best lodging. It has the top restaurant, too.

ⓘ Getting There & Away

The passenger ferry MV *Clarius* sails daily from Mwanza North Port to Nansio (Tsh5000, three to four hours) at 9am weekdays (10am weekends), returning at 2pm. Two other similarly priced ferries dock at Kirumba, north of Mwanza's centre near the giant Balimi ad: the MV *Nyehunge* departs Mwanza at 9am and Nansio at 2pm, while the MV *Samar III* departs Mwanza at 2pm and Nansio at 8am.

It's also possible to reach Nansio from Bunda, on the Mwanza–Musoma road, which means that you can go from Mwanza to Ukerewe and then on towards Musoma or the Serengeti without backtracking. Via public transport, take any Mwanza–Musoma bus and disembark at Bunda. Here buses and sometimes dalla-dallas head to Nansio (Tsh6000, five to to six hours) daily at 10am and 1pm using the Kisorya ferry (per person/vehicle Tsh300/5000, 40 minutes), which crosses four times daily in each direction.

In the reverse, vehicles to Bunda leave Nansio at 8am and 10am. After these buses depart there are no vehicles direct to Nansio, but you can take a dalla-dalla to Kisorya and catch another on the island. The last ferry to Ukerewe sails at 6.30pm. The last ferry leaving Ukerewe is at 5pm, but don't use it unless you have your own vehicle or are willing to try hitching part of the way to Bunda.

Rubondo Island National Park

Rubondo Island National Park (adult/child US$30/10), alluring for its tranquillity and sublime lakeshore scenery, is one of Tanzania's best-kept secrets. **Birdwatching** brings the most visitors, but **walking safaris** (half-day walks per person US$25) and **boat rides** (per person US$25) can also be rewarding. Elephants, giraffes, black and white colobus, and chimpanzees were long ago introduced alongside the island's native hippo, bushbuck and sitatunga. Rubondo's chimps are not yet habituated and are currently seldom seen. Though Rubondo's beaches look inviting, there are enough crocodiles that swimming is prohibited.

🛏 Sleeping & Eating

Rubondo Park Bandas & Resthouse   CAMPGROUND, BANDA **$**
(camping US$30, r per person US$30) The *bandas* facing the beach at Kageye on Rubondo's eastern shore are some of the better national park–run *bandas* in Tanzania. Each

---

ⓘ RUBONDO ISLAND NATIONAL PARK

....

Why Go Tranquil setting and lovely lakeshore scenery; fine birdwatching; chance to see sitatungas.

When to Go June through to early November.

Practicalities Start from Bukoba or Mwanza, travel to the nearest port and continue by park boat. Alternatively, arrive by charter flight.

Budget Tips Travel by bus to the nearest lakeshore town, where you can arrange an expensive boat ride to the island. However, once on Rubondo, the park *bandas* offer excellent cheap accommodation and self-catering. Safaris are taken on foot.

---

has a comfortable double and single bed, hot-water bathroom, and privacy afforded by surrounding jungle trees. There's also a resthouse in the same location with similar quality rooms, but with TVs.

⭐**Rubondo Island Camp**   TENTED CAMP **$$$**
(☑0736 500515; http://rubondo.asiliaafrica.com; s/d all-inclusive US$1090/1650; ⊘closed Apr–May; ☎✉) ✐ Recently taken over by the very upmarket Asilia group, this is a wonderful lakeside perch with stunning safari tents. Well, we say tents, but these 'tents' have three solid walls, fine furnishings, bathrooms to splash in and deliciously comfortable beds. There's a fabulous wooden bar and restaurant area hanging onto a low cliff with lake views.

ⓘ Information

Book accommodation and transport through **park headquarters** (☑028-252 0720). If the phones are down, staff at the Saa Nane/Tanapa office on Capri Point in Mwanza can help.

ⓘ Getting There & Away

AIR

Auric Air (☑0783 233334; www.auricair.com) will make a Rubondo (return US$325) diversion on its Mwanza–Bukoba flights. This requires a two-night stay if flying return out of Mwanza, since arrival is in the late afternoon and departure in the early morning. **Coastal Aviation** (☑0752 627825; www.coastal.co.tz) also flies to the park from Mwanza on a request basis. A charter flight with Auric Air costs around US$3000.

BOAT

There are two ways to reach Rubondo by park boat (up to seven passengers); both should be arranged in advance. Local fishermen are prohibited from carrying tourists to the island.

The first option, and the one recommended by the park, is via Kasenda, a small port about 5km from Muganza (Tsh1500 on a motorcycle taxi and Tsh5000 in a taxi), from where it's 20 to 30 minutes by boat (US$100 return) to Rubondo Island and another 15 minutes by park vehicle to drive across the island to Kageye. Muganza is just off the main Mwanza–Bukoba road and public transport is frequent, but buses normally drop you at the Muganza turn-off junction on the main road. Motorbikes are available to whizz you into the town or Kasenda. All buses between Bukoba (Tsh12,000, two hours) and Mwanza (Tsh12,000, four hours) pass through, as do Bukoba–Dar es Salaam buses. Dalla-dallas run to nearby destinations such as Biharamulo (Tsh5000, two hours).

The second option is via Nkome, at the end of a rough road north of Geita, where the boat costs US$100 to Kageye and takes about two hours. Expect choppy water on this crossing. The warden's office, where you get the boat, is located outside Nkome, which is a short motorcycle (Tsh500) or taxi (Tsh2000) ride from where the final dalla-dalla stops. Two buses go direct from Mwanza to Nkome (Tsh12,000, four to five hours), leaving Mwanza at 10am; you can also meet them at the Kamanga ferry. Alternatively, it is possible to take a bus to Geita, from where dalla-dallas to Nkome (Tsh5000, two hours) are fairly frequent.

Bukoba

Bukoba is a bustling town with an attractive waterside setting and amenable small-town feel. The surrounding Kagera region is home of the Haya people, known for their powerful kingdoms. **Musira Island** and **Kagera Museum** (admission Tsh2000; ⏱9.30am-6pm) are worthwhile excursions.

🛏 Sleeping & Eating

⭐ **Balamaga Bed & Breakfast** B&B $
(☑0789 757289; www.balamagabb.com; s/d Tsh55,000/85,000, s/d without bathroom Tsh50,000/70,000; 🅿) High up in the hills overlooking the lake, this great-value homey place has four spacious, comfortable rooms (two self-contained and two sharing a bathroom) decorated in artistic photos. The garden is so gorgeous and full of birds you'll forget you're in Bukoba. It's a world away from most cheap Tanzanian hotels.

ELCT Bukoba Hotel HOTEL $
(☑0754 022682; www.elctbukobahotel.com; Aerodrome Rd; s/tw/ste US$40/45/60; 🅿@) This Lutheran conference centre between the lake and the city centre is a very good choice. The rooms in this rambling complex have a slight sanatorium feel but it's impeccably maintained and well-run. The gardens, which include a tree of roosting pelicans, are

Bukoba

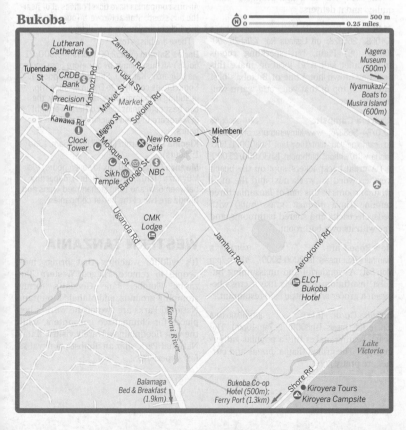

KIROYERA TOURS

Kiroyera Tours (☎028-222 0203; www.kiroyeratours.com; Shore Rd) is a clued-up agency leading cultural tours in Bukoba and the Kagera region, and an essential stop for travellers in Bukoba. In addition to making local culture readily accessible to visitors, Kiroyera has established several community projects and has won awards for promoting community development through tourism. Destinations and activities for its half- and full-day tours include visiting ancient rock paintings and walking in nearby Rubale Forest. Kiroyera also runs half-day bike tours (US$15), sells bus, boat and plane tickets, and organises visits to national parks in Tanzania and gorilla tracking in Uganda.

a real treat. The hotel sign promises 'Tranquility' and it delivers.

CMK Lodge   HOTEL **$**
(☎0682 265028; off Uganda Rd; r Tsh25,000-35,000; **P**) Plain, but sparkling rooms and a quiet side-road location make this near-downtown hotel one of Bukoba's best values. On top of that you get a warm welcome for free.

Kiroyera Campsite   CAMPGROUND **$**
(☎0784 568276; www.kiroyeratours.com; Shore Rd; camping your tent/their tent Tsh8000/11,500, banda with/without bathroom Tsh30,000/25,000; **P**) A great backpackers' spot on the beach (very crowded on weekends) and the most original rooms in this half of Tanzania: three genuine Haya *msonge* (grass huts) with beds, electricity and shared bathrooms, and one with its own bathroom.

New Rose Café   TANZANIAN **$**
(Jamhuri Rd; meals Tsh2000-5000; ⊙8am-7pm Mon-Sat) A wonderful and unassuming Bukoba institution that feels like a cross between a grocer and a little cafe-restaurant.

Bukoba Co-op Hotel   INTERNATIONAL **$**
(Shore Rd; meals Tsh8000; ⊙7am-10pm) The beach seating makes this a popular gathering spot. The grilled tilapia, pizzas and curries are pretty good.

❶ Information

NBC (Jamhuri Rd) Changes cash. The ATM works with Visa and MasterCard.

❶ Getting There & Away

AIR

There are daily flights between Bukoba and Mwanza on **Auric Air** (www.auricair.com), and between Bukoba and Dar es Salaam via Mwanza with **Precision Air** (☎0782 351136; www.precisionairtz.com; Kawawa Rd). Auric also continues onwards to Kampala (Uganda).

BOAT

There's passenger-ferry service between Bukoba and Mwanza on the historic MV *Victoria* (p158). Tickets for all classes are sold at the port at the window labelled 'Booking Office 3rd Class'. Kiroyera Tours can often find tickets even when the booking office says they're sold out and if not, can arrange for you to sleep in the assistant captain's cabin.

BUS

All bus companies have ticket offices at or near the bus stand. Staff at Kiroyera Tours can also buy tickets for you, for a small fee.

There are buses to:

Dar es Salaam (Tsh52,000 to Tsh60,000, 21 hours) All buses leave by or before 6am and go via Muganza, Kahama, Singida and Dodoma. Some buses continue to Dar in a single trip, including Mohammed Trans and Sumry, the two best companies, while others overnight in Morogoro to avoid reaching Dar in the wee hours.

Kigoma With Visram (Tsh27,000, 6am, 13 to 15 hours).

Mwanza (Tsh20,000, six to seven hours) Via Muganza (Tsh12,000, two hours), departing between 6am and 1pm; Mohammed Trans and Bunda are two of the better companies.

WESTERN TANZANIA

It's wildlife watching that brings most people to remote, rugged Western Tanzania: Gombe, Jane Goodall's former stomping grounds, and Mahale Mountains National Parks are two of the world's best places for chimpanzee encounters, while the vast floodplains of rarely visited Katavi National Park offer an almost primeval safari experience.

Western Tanzania

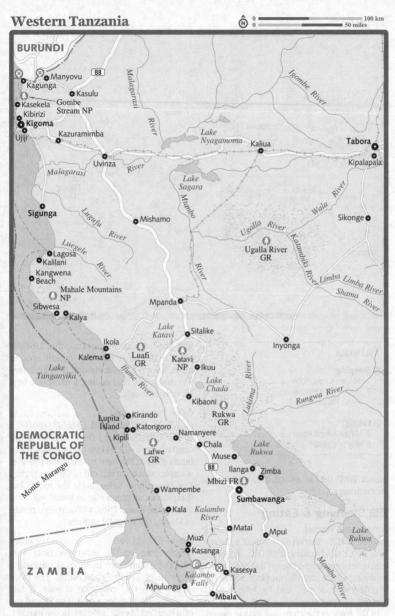

0 100 km
0 50 miles

BURUNDI

Manyovu
Kagunga
Kasulu
Kasekela
Gombe
Stream NP
Kibirizi
Kigoma
Ujiji
Kazuramimba
Malagarasi River
Lake Nyaganoma
Kaliua
Tabora
Kipalapala
Uvinza
Igombe River
Lake Sagara
Wala River
Sikonge
Sigunga
Lugufu River
Mishamo
Mramba River
Ugalla River
Katambiki River
Ugalla River GR
Luegele River
Lagosa
Kalilani
Kangwena Beach
Mahale Mountains NP
Sibwesa
Kalya
Mpanda
River
Limba River
Shama River
Lake Katavi
Sitalike
Inyonga
Ikola
Luafi GR
Katavi NP
Ikuu
Ifume River
Kalema
Lake Tanganyika
Lake Chada
Lukima River
Rungwa River
Kibaoni
Rukwa GR
Kirando
Lupita Island
Katongoro
Kipili
Namanyere
Chala
Lake Rukwa
DEMOCRATIC REPUBLIC OF THE CONGO
Lafwe GR
Muse
Monts Marangu
Ilanga
Zimba
Mbizi FR
Wampembe
Sumbawanga
Kala
Kalambo River
Muzi
Matai
Mpui
Lake Rukwa
Kasanga
Z A M B I A
Kalambo Falls
Kasesya
Momba River
Mpulungu
Mbala

Tabora

Leafy Tabora was once the most important trading centre along the old caravan route connecting Lake Tanganyika with Bagamoyo and the sea. Today it's primarily of interest to history buffs and rail fans, who will have to wait here if taking a branch line to Mpanda or Mwanza. **Livingstone's Tembe** (admission Tsh10,000; ⊙8am-4pm) – the one-time residence of the great explorer – is 8km south of town in Kwihara village

Tabora

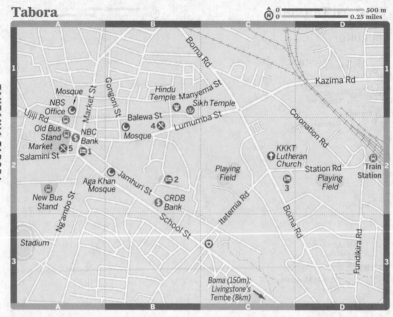

Tabora

🛏 **Sleeping**
1 Golden Eagle Hotel	A2
2 John Paul II Hostel	B2
3 Orion Tabora Hotel	C2

🍽 **Eating**
4 Mayor's Fast Food	B2
5 Mayor's Hotel	A2

(about Tsh15,000 in a taxi), and well worth an excursion.

🛏 Sleeping & Eating

John Paul II Hostel — GUESTHOUSE **$**
(☏ 0755 344128; Jamhuri St; r without bathroom Tsh10,000; r with breakfast Tsh20,000; 🅿) Spotless, quiet, secure and cheap. You can't really go wrong at this church-run place where the foundation stone was laid by John Paul II himself. The entrance to the quiet compound is in the back. If the cathedral gate is closed, you'll have to walk around to the east; it's at the back of the big yellow building.

Golden Eagle Hotel — GUESTHOUSE **$**
(☏ 026-260 4623; Market St; tw without bathroom Tsh15,000, tw Tsh20,000-25,000; 🅿) Thanks to the friendly owner (plus the central location

and good, cheap restaurant), this 1st-floor place is the most traveller-friendly spot in town. Rooms are old, though tidy, and have TVs, hot water and ceiling fans. It can be a bit noisy, though.

Orion Tabora Hotel — HISTORIC HOTEL **$$**
(☏ 026-260 4369; Station Rd; s Tsh65,000-90,000, d Tsh85,000-105,000; 🅿🛜) The old railway hotel, originally built in 1914 by a German baron as a hunting lodge, has been restored and provides unexpected class in this out-of-the-way region. The atmosphere fades inside the rooms but it outshines anything else in town. Ask for a room in the Kaiser Wing, with screened porches looking out onto the gardens.

Mayor's Fast Food — TANZANIAN **$**
(snacks from Tsh300, buffet per plate from Tsh2500; ⊙7am-11pm) It offers samosas and other snacks, plus a good buffet. The price depends on the meat you choose. It has two branches: one on Lumumba St and the other, called **Mayor's Hotel**, in the market.

ℹ Getting There & Away

AIR

Air Tanzania (☏ 026-260 4401; www.airtanzania.co.tz) flies twice weekly to both Kigoma and Dar es Salaam.

BUS

NBS, mostly offering four-across seating, is the top company operating out of Tabora. Some of its buses depart from its office at the 'old' bus stand. All other buses use the nearby 'new' bus stand. Several buses depart daily between 6am and 10am to Mwanza (Tsh15,000, six hours). Buses also go to the following destinations:

Arusha (Tsh30,000, 10 to 11 hours) Plus an early departure via Singida (Tsh20,000, four hours) and Babati (Tsh25,000, six hours)

Dodoma (Tsh40,000, eight hours)

Kigoma (Tsh25,000, eight hours)

Mpanda (Tsh20,000, eight hours)

TRAIN

Tabora is an important train junction, with connections to the following:

Dar es Salaam (Tsh54,900/40,600/20,400 in 1st/2nd/economy class, Monday and Friday at 7am)

Kigoma (Tsh31,700/24,900/12,500 in 1st/2nd/economy class, Wednesday and Saturday at 9pm)

Mpanda (Tsh27,500/21,200/11,100 in 1st/2nd/economy class, Monday, Wednesday and Saturday at 9pm)

Mwanza (Tsh29,600/22,700/11,800 in 1st/2nd/economy class, Wednesday and Saturday at 10pm)

Kigoma

The regional capital and only large Tanzanian port on Lake Tanganyika is a scrappy but agreeable town. It's also the end of the line of the Central Line train and a starting point for the MV *Liemba* and visits to Gombe National Park. About 8km south of Kigoma is tiny Ujiji, one of Africa's oldest market villages. A terminus of the old caravan route to the coast, Ujiji has earned a place in travel lore as the spot where explorer-journalist Henry Morton Stanley uttered his famously casual 'Dr Livingstone, I presume?' – now immortalised at the site of the **Livingstone Memorial Museum** (admission Tsh20,000; ⊘8am-6pm).

👉 Tours

Mbali Mbali   SAFARIS
(☑ 028-280 4437; www.mbalimbali.com) Western Tanzania–focused safari operator based at Kigoma Hilltop Hotel. It does boat and air charters.

🛏 Sleeping & Eating

Jakobsen's Guesthouse   GUESTHOUSE $
(☑ 0753 768434; www.kigomabeach.com; camping with own/hired tent Tsh15,000/20,000, r per person 40,000, cottage Tsh240,000; P) This comfortable guesthouse has a lovely clifftop perch above Jakobsen's Beach, while the two shady campsites with bathrooms, lanterns and grills are down near the lake. It's good value and a wonderful spot for a respite, but there is no food available so you'll need to self-cater. You can rent kayaks (per day Tsh25,000), sailboats (Tsh50,000) and snorkelling gear (Tsh10,000). Water and soft drinks are available.

Gombe Executive Lodge   GUESTHOUSE $
(☑ 0758 891740; r Tsh10,000-30,000; P❄) This is the standout cheapie in town. It's on a quiet and dusty side road and has a real homely feel to it, with spotless rooms, attached hot-water bathrooms and air-con. Breakfast is Tsh3000 extra.

New Mapinduzi Guest House   GUESTHOUSE $
(☑ 0753 771680; Lumumba St; s/d Tsh12,000/14,000, s/d without bathroom Tsh6000/8000) This guesthouse down a tiny alley is a good choice if you want to be right in the centre of town. The basic, self-contained rooms have TVs and fans. There is no food available.

Kigoma Hilltop Hotel   HOTEL $$
(☑ 028-280 4437; www.mbalimbali.com; s/d/ste US$90/140/225; ❄🛜🏊) This hotel is atop an escarpment overlooking the lake. The double and twin cottages are within a large walled compound roamed by zebras. Rooms have all the mod-cons and are easily the best in town. The pool (nonguests Tsh10,000) is large, but not as clean as it could be.

Sun City   TANZANIAN $
(Lumumba St; meals Tsh3000-5000; ⊘7am-8pm) A clean and almost artistic spot for *wali maharagwe* (rice and beans) and other local meals. There's also chicken *biryani* on Sunday.

ℹ Information

CONSULATES

The **Burundian consulate** (☑ 0739 22849; Bangwe Rd; ⊘9am-3pm Mon-Fri) will issue two-week tourist visas for most Western nationalities while you wait. The **Democratic Republic of Congo consulate** (☑ 0765 947249; Bangwe Rd; ⊘9am-4pm Mon-Fri) may

Kigoma

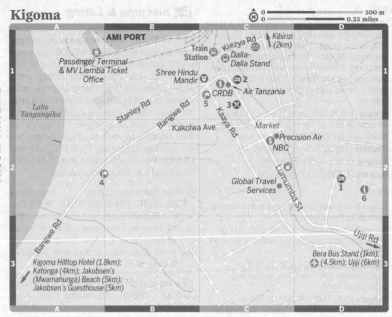

Kigoma

🛏 Sleeping
1 Gombe Executive Lodge	D2
2 New Mapinduzi Guest House	C1

🍴 Eating
3 Sun City	C1

ℹ Information
Baby Come & Call	(see 2)
4 Burundian Consulate	A2
5 Democratic Republic of Congo Consulate	C1
6 Gombe/Mahale Visitors Information Centre	D2

grant you a visa. However, Congolese visas are only valid if issued through the Congolese embassy in your home country. If you're just planning on visiting Virunga National Park and Goma then so-called Virunga Visas are once again being issued easily via the Visit Virunga website (www.visitvirunga.org).

IMMIGRATION

Formalities for those riding the MV *Liemba* are handled by an officer who boards the boat in Kasanga. If you're headed to Burundi or DRC, there are immigration offices at Ami Port and Kibirizi.

INTERNET ACCESS

Baby Come & Call (Lumumba St; per hour Tsh1500; ⊙8am-8pm Mon-Sat) Internet access just up from the train station.

MONEY

CRDB bank (Lumumba St) Changes US dollars, Euros and British pounds. The ATM accepts MasterCard and Visa.

NBC bank (Lumumba St) ATM. Accepts MasterCard and Visa.

TOURIST INFORMATION

Gombe/Mahale Visitors Information Centre (☑028-280 4009; gonapachimps@yahoo.com; ⊙9am-4pm) It's signposted off Ujiji Rd near the top of the hill; turn left at the T-junction. The staff know plenty about Gombe, but seem quite misinformed about Mahale.

ℹ Getting There & Away

AIR

Precision Air (☑028-280 4720; www.precision airtz.com) flies daily to Dar es Salaam via Mwanza, while **Air Tanzania** (☑0782 7377321; www.airtanzania.go.tz) flies twice weekly to Tabora and five times weekly to Dar es Salaam. Air travel to Kigoma is in a constant state of flux, so seek information on site.

Global Travel Services (☑0759 896711; Lumumba St) sells tickets for most airlines in Kigoma and elsewhere.

BOAT
Ferry

The sporadic MV *Liemba* (p211) is scheduled to cruise on alternate weeks between Kigoma and Mpulungu (Zambia) via Lagosa (for Mahale Mountains National Park) and other lakeshore towns, departing from the Passenger Terminal, north of the Lake Tanganyika Hotel.

Cargo ships to Burundi and the DRC, which also take passengers, depart from Ami Port near the train station.

Lake Taxi

Lake taxis are small, wooden motorised boats, piled high with people and produce that connect villages along the entire Tanzanian lakeshore. They're inexpensive, but offer no toilets or other creature comforts, little if any shade, and can be dangerous when the lake gets rough. Nights are very cold. Lake taxis going north depart from Kibirizi village, 2km north of Kigoma; you can walk here following the railway tracks or the road around the bay. Boats to the south leave from Ujiji.

BUS

All buses depart from the dusty streets behind the unsigned Bero petrol station. (Coming from Kigoma, look for the large, white petrol station with an NBC ATM.) The bus station is unusually organised with all the bus companies having little ticket offices with destinations clearly signed in a long row. Other bus ticket offices are scattered around the Mwanga area just to the west.

Buses go to the following destinations:

Bukoba (Tsh27,000, 12 hours) Via Biharamulo (Tsh25,000, eight hours). Service operated by Ya-Alli and Takbir.

Mpanda (Tsh20,000, eight hours) Operated by Adventure.

Mwanza (Ts31,000, 10 to 12 hours) Via Nyankanazi (Tsh20,000, seven hours). The best services are provided by Adventure and NSL Express.

Tabora (Tsh23,000, eight hours) Best service provided by NBS and Sasebosa.

Uvinza (Tsh5000, four hours) Any bus to Tabora or Mpanda will work.

Dalla-dallas to Ujiji (Tsh400, 20 minutes) run throughout the day.

TRAIN

The end of the line and as far west as you can ride a train in Tanzania. Trains go from Kigoma to Tabora (Tsh31,700/24,900/12,500 in 1st/2nd/economy class) at 5pm on Thursday and Sunday.

ⓘ Getting Around

The airport is about 5km east of the town centre. A taxi costs Tsh5000.

Dalla-dallas (Tsh400) park in front of the train station and run along the main roads to Bero bus stand, Kibirizi, Katonga and Ujiji. Taxis between the town centre and Bero bus stand or Kibirizi charge Tsh2000 to Tsh3000. Don't pay more than Tsh1000 for a motorcycle taxi anywhere within the city.

Gombe National Park

With an area of only 52 sq km, **Gombe National Park** (☑ Kigoma 028-280 4009; adult/child US$100/20, trekking fee US$20) is Tanzania's smallest national park, but its connection to Jane Goodall has given it world renown. Gombe's 100-plus chimps are well-habituated. Although it can be difficult, sweaty work traversing steep hills and valleys, if you head out early in the morning chimp sightings are nearly guaranteed.

🍴 Sleeping & Eating

Accommodation rarely fills up completely, but it's still best to book rooms in advance through the Gombe/Mahale Visitors Information Centre in Kigoma.

Tanapa Resthouse　　　　　GUESTHOUSE $
(☑ Kigoma 028-280 4009; r/camping US$20/30) Next to the visitor centre at Kasekela, this quite comfortable place has six simple rooms with electricity during morning and evening. Two overflow facilities have rooms of lesser quality and toilets at the back. The restaurant's prices are high (breakfast

---

ⓘ GOMBE NATIONAL PARK

Why Go Up-close encounters with chimpanzees.

When to Go The lodge is closed in March and April. June through October are the easiest (driest) months for chimpanzee tracking.

Practicalities The chimps can be a long walk from the two accommodation options. The only way here is by boat. All tourism activities are organised and paid for at Kasekela, on the beach near the centre of the park (this is where lake taxis drop you).

Budget Tips Excluding the high entry fees, it's perfectly possible to visit Gombe on a budget by taking one of the lake taxis to and from the park, staying in the park resthouse and self-catering.

WORTH A TRIP

LAKE TANGANYIKA

Lake Tanganyika is the world's longest (660km), second-deepest (over 1436m) and second-largest by volume freshwater lake. At somewhere between nine and 13 million years old, it's also one of the oldest. Thanks to its age and ecological isolation it's home to an exceptional number of endemic fish, including 98% of the 250-plus species of cichlids. Popular aquarium fish due to their bright colours, the cichlids make Tanganyika an outstanding snorkelling and diving destination.

Kigoma is the only proper town on the Tanzanian side, although small, rarely visited settlements line the scenic shoreline. If you have time to only explore one, the old mission station of **Kipili** makes an ideal destination, with its evocative hilltop ruins of an 1880s church (3km north of town) backed by wonderful lake views. Kipili is also the site of the universally praised **Lake Shore Lodge & Campsite** (☑ 0763 993166; www.lakeshoretz.com; camping US$14, banda s/d full board US$160/240, chalet s/d full board US$345/490; P ⚡), which offers chalets, cosy *bandas*, camping with spotless amenities, kayaking, quad biking, mountain biking, diving, village tours, island dinners and more. The lodge makes an ideal combination with Katavi and Mahale Mountains National Parks, and staff can take you to both using their own trucks and boats.

To reach Kipili from Sumbawanga, take a bus towards Kirando and get off at Katongoro (Tsh10,000, five hours). Walk the remaining 5km to Kipili or wait for a passing vehicle or ride on a motorbike (Tsh7000). Lake Shore Lodge will pick up its guests here for US$5. From Mpanda, head first to Namanyere (Tsh15,000, four hours), where you can catch a passing vehicle towards Kipili.

US$10, lunch US$15, dinner US$15) but you can bring your own food and use the kitchen for free.

ℹ️ Information

Currently, if you arrive late in the afternoon, park officials generously don't start the clock on your visit until the following morning, which means that for a two-night stay and one day of chimp tracking you'll only be charged one 24-hour entry (if you leave for Kigoma early in the morning). Children aged under 16 are not permitted to enter the forest, though they can stay at the resthouse. Visitors are limited to one hour with each group of chimps, but you are allowed to go and find another group after your hour is up for no extra cost.

All tourism activities are organised and paid for at Kasekela, on the beach near the centre of the park, and this is where lake taxis drop you.

ℹ️ Getting There & Away

Gombe is 16km north of Kigoma; the only way there is by boat.

At least one lake taxi to the park (Tsh4000, three hours) departs from Kibirizi around noon. Returning, it passes Kasekela as early as 7am.

You can also hire boats at Kibirizi; but don't believe the owners who tell you there are no lake taxis in an effort to get business. Hiring here requires hard bargaining, but the price will be a little cheaper than any of the charter options following (around US$250 return). You may have

to pay an advance for petrol, but don't pay the full amount until you've arrived back in Kigoma.

It's safer and more comfortable (in part because the boats will offer shade from the sun) to arrange a charter with one of the established companies. Chartering the park boat costs US$300 return plus US$20 for each night you spend at Gombe. Organise it through the Gombe/Mahale Visitors Information Centre in Kigoma. In Kigoma, Lake Tanganyika Hotel (US$450, US$50 per night overnight charge) and Mbali Mbali (US$655, no overnight charge for those not staying at its camp in Gombe; US$350 for camp guests) also have boats taking from 1½ to two hours.

With a chartered boat day trips are possible, but leave very early because late starts reduce your chances of meeting the chimps.

Mahale Mountains National Park

It's difficult to imagine a more idyllic combination: clear, blue waters and white-sand beaches backed by lushly forested mountains soaring straight out of Lake Tanganyika, plus some of the continent's most intriguing wildlife watching. Like Gombe, Mahale is most notable as a chimpanzee sanctuary, and there are about 900 of our primate relatives residing in and around the park, with leopard, blue duiker, black and white colobus, giant pangolin and many Rift Valley bird species not found elsewhere in Tanzania keeping them company. There are also hippos, crocs and otters in the lake, and lions, elephants, buffaloes and giraffes roaming the savannah of Mahale's difficult-to-reach eastern half.

Entry to **Mahale Mountains National Park** (☏0789 045090; www.mahalepark.org; ⊙6am-6pm) is at Bilenge park headquarters in the park's northwestern corner, about 10 minutes by boat south of the airstrip and 20 minutes north of Kasiha, site of the park *bandas* and guides' residences. Another park office, next to the airstrip, where fly-in guests can pay their entry fees, is open to coincide with flight arrivals on Monday and Thursday. As there's no phone service in the park, all advanced arrangements are done online via www.mahalepark.org.

There are no roads in Mahale; walking and boating along the shoreline are the only ways to get around. Children under seven years aren't permitted to enter the forest.

🛏 Sleeping

Mango Tree Bandas   BUNGALOW **$$**
(☏0789 045090; per person US$40) The lovely Mango Tree *bandas* are some of the better park-run *bandas* in Tanzania. They're set about 100m in from the shore and while they lack the lake views of the private camps, their position in the forest means the night sounds are wonderful.

Kungwe Beach Lodge   TENTED CAMP **$$$**
(☏0732 978879; www.mbalimbali.com; s/d all inclusive excl alcohol US$890/1430; ⊙mid-May–mid-Feb; ☏) This is a wonderfully low-key and enjoyable luxury camp with beautifully appointed safari tents (think big four-poster beds, weathered storage chests and piping-hot showers) hidden under beach-fringed trees. The centrepiece of the camp is the dhow-shaped dining area. The price includes daily chimp tracking and a boat safari.

ℹ Getting There & Away

AIR

Safari Airlink (www.flysal.com) and **Zantas Air** (☏0778 434343) fly to Mahale twice weekly, the former from Dar es Salaam and the latter from Arusha, assuming enough passengers. Zantas continues to Kigoma, but doesn't fly in the other direction. All flights stop at Katavi National Park en route. Expect to pay approximately US$930 one way from Dar, US$825 one way from Arusha and US$360 one way between Mahale and Katavi National Parks.

If you've booked with one of the lodges, a boat will meet your flight. Otherwise, arrange a boat in advance with park headquarters.

BOAT

Charter Boat

In Kigoma, Mbali Mbali (p165) charges US$2950 for a speedboat to Mahale (four to five hours).

Lake Taxi

Lake taxis head south from Ujili to Kalilani (Tsh7000), 2km north of park headquarters, most days of the week around 5pm to 6pm. The trip often takes more than a day. Generally they depart from Kalilani around noon. Park staff know what's up with the boats, so they can advise you on days and times.

One option to make the journey more bearable is take a Saratoga bus from Kigoma to Sigunga (Tsh7000, 11am, six to seven hours) and wait for the lake taxi there. Sigunga to Kalilani usually takes seven to eight hours. You could also have the park boat pick you up in Sigunga; it's two hours to headquarters. Sigunga has a basic guesthouse.

There are also a couple of weekly boats heading north from Kalema (Tsh20,000) or nearby Ikola each evening for an even choppier journey than the one from Kigoma. It can take anywhere from 12 to 36 hours depending on the winds. They head south from Kalilani about 3pm.

MV Liemba

It's hard to beat the satisfyingly relaxing journey to Mahale via ferry. The MV *Liemba* stops at Lagosa (also called Mugambo) to the north of the park (US$35/30/25 in 1st/2nd/economy class), about 10 hours from Kigoma. Under normal scheduling, it reaches Lagosa around 3am

---

ℹ MAHALE MOUNTAINS NATIONAL PARK

Why Go Up-close encounters with chimpanzees; stunning scenery with mountains rising up from the lakeshore.

When to Go Open year-round, but March to mid-May is too wet to enjoy it. June through October are the easiest (driest) months for hiking up the steep slopes.

Practicalities There are no roads to the park. Most visitors fly but various boats, including the historic MV *Liemba*, go from Kigoma, Kipili and other lakeshore towns.

Budget Tips Travel with the MV *Liemba* ferry, stay in the park *bandas* and self-cater for a budget visit to Mahale.

whether coming from the north (Thursday) or south (Sunday). With the frequent delays, southern arrivals present a good chance of passing the park during daylight, which makes for a very beautiful trip. It has often been out of service, though hopefully things will be better after the substantial overhaul it received in 2014. Services are every second week.

You can arrange in advance for a park boat (holding eight people with luggage) to meet the *Liemba*. It's one hour from the *Liemba* to the *bandas,* including stopping to register and pay at headquarters. The journey costs Tsh240,000. Chartering a fisherman's boat for the trip costs somewhat less. Lagosa has a basic guesthouse where you can wait for the *Liemba* after leaving the park.

Tanapa Boat

With a bit of luck you can travel for free on the park boat. Park staff travel to Kigoma several times a month and if space is available they'll take passengers. This is usually only possible when leaving the park since on the trip from Kigoma the boat will be carrying supplies. The Gombe/Mahale Visitors Information Centre in Kigoma knows when boats are travelling.

Mpanda

This small and somewhat scruffy town is a major transit point. Historically it was a significant trade hub and there are still many Arab businessmen living here.

The post office has reliable internet and the CRDB bank has an internationally linked ATM.

🛏 Sleeping & Eating

New Super City Hotel HOTEL $
(📞 0763 728903; d/tw Tsh15,000-18,000; 🅿) The hottest place in town has huge rooms with sofas, as well as some wear and tear, instant hot showers and an OK in-house restaurant. It's at the southern roundabout.

❶ Getting There & Away

BUS

Mpanda's bus station is east of the Sumbawanga road, near the southern roundabout, but most companies have ticket offices near the half-built Moravian church in the town centre, and their buses actually start there before going to the station.

Sumry serves Sumbawanga (Tsh15,000, five to six hours) via Ikuu near Katisunga Plain (Tsh3000, 45 minutes); NBS and Air Bus go to Tabora (Tsh20,000, eight hours) twice weekly; and Adventure goes daily to Kigoma (Tsh20,000, eight to 10 hours).

TRAIN

A branch of the Central Line connects Mpanda with Tabora (Tsh27,500/21,200/11,100 in 1st/2nd/economy class) via Kaliua at 4pm on Tuesday, Thursday and Sunday. If you're heading to Kigoma from Mpanda, you'll need to spend at least one night in Tabora. You can wait for the Kigoma connection at Kaliua, but as there are only simple guesthouses and little to do, most travellers wait at Tabora.

Katavi National Park

Katavi National Park (adult/child US$30/10; ☉6am-6pm), 35km southwest of Mpanda, is Tanzania's third-largest national park and one of its most unspoiled wilderness areas. The park's predominant feature is the 425 sq km Katisunga Plain. Small rivers and large swamps that last all year support huge populations of hippos and crocodiles, and Katavi has over 400 bird species. The park comes to life in the dry season, when the floodplains dry up and herds of buffaloes, elephants, lions, zebras, giraffes, elands, topis and many others gather at the remaining waters.

Walking safaris (short/long US$20/25 per group) with an armed ranger and **bush camping** (US$50 per person plus walking fee) are permitted. Payments for entry fees and all activities should be made at park headquarters, which are located 1km south of Sitalike, or at the Ikuu Ranger Post near the main airstrip.

🛏 Sleeping

🛏 In the Park

There are two **public campsites** (camping US$30), one at Ikuu near Katisunga Plain and the other 2km south of Sitalike. Both get a lot of wildlife walking through. Bring all food and drink with you.

Katavi Park Bandas BUNGALOWS $$
(katavi@tanzaniaparks.com; r per person US$30; 🅿) This is 2km south of the village and within park boundaries (so you need to pay park entry fees when staying here). The rooms are big, bright and surprisingly good. Zebras, giraffes and other animals are frequent visitors.

★**Katavi Wildlife Camp** TENTED CAMP $$$
(Foxes; 📞 0754 237422; www.kataviwildlifecamp. com; s/d all inclusive except drinks US$675/1150; ☉Jun-Feb; 🅿) 🐾 This comfortable, well-run

camp has a prime setting overlooking Kati-sunga making it the best place for in-camp wildlife watching. The six tents have large porches with hammocks and are down-to-earth comfortable without being over the top. The quality guides round out the experience. It's owned by Foxes African Safaris, who offer some excellent combination itineraries with southern parks. The price includes a wildlife drive.

Katuma Bush Lodge TENTED CAMP **$$$**
(☑ 0732 978879; www.mbalimbali.com; s/d all inclusive except drinks US$710/1070; ☺ mid-May–mid-Feb; P ☎ ⊛ ☲) With stunning views over the grasslands, the large safari tents here have four-poster beds, carved wooden showers and plenty of privacy. The defining feature is the relaxing lounge fronted by a deck with a small swimming pool. The price includes a wildlife drive.

Sitalike

Most backpackers stay at this little village on the northern edge of the park. There are a couple of small restaurants and groceries. Most places to stay have electricity only in the first few hours of the night.

Kitanewa Guesthouse GUESTHOUSE **$**
(☑ 0767 837132; s/d Tsh15,000/16,000; P) This fair-value spot by the bus-truck stop has adequate concrete-cube rooms with bucket showers and squat toilets. It only has electricity at night for the first few hours.

Riverside Camp BUNGALOWS, CAMPGROUND **$$**
(☑ 0767 754740; camping US$10, s/d US$30/60; P) Aimed at park visitors, hence the high prices. Its best feature is the resident pod of hippos, but the *bandas* are decent enough and the owner is a trustworthy guy who can rent out a jeep for a safari. It only has electricity in the first few hours of the night.

❶ Getting There & Away

AIR
Safari Airlink (p169) and Zantas Air (p169) fly twice a week to Ikuu Airstrip; the lodges will often let nonguests fly on their planes if space is available. All lodges provide free pick-up at Ikuu for their guests. If you aren't staying at a lodge, arrange a vehicle or a ranger for walking *before* you arrive.

BUS
Buses and trucks between Mpanda and Sumbawanga can pick you up and drop you off in

❶ KATAVI NATIONAL PARK

Why Go Outstanding dry season wildlife watching. Rugged and remote wilderness ambience.

When to Go August through October is best for seeing large herds of wildlife. February through May is very wet and most camps close.

Practicalities Drive in or bus from Mpanda or Sumbawanga; fly in from Ruaha National Park or Arusha.

Budget Tips Katavi is one of Tanzania's more budget-friendly parks. Take a bus to Sitalike, stay in budget accommodation there or camp in the park, and then do a walking or vehicle safari.

Sitalike or at park headquarters. Transport is fairly frequent in the mornings, but after lunch you may have to wait several hours for a vehicle to pass. Two dalla-dallas depart Sitalike for Mpanda (Tsh3000, 45 minutes) at dawn and return at noon and 4pm. If you're driving, the only petrol stations are in Mpanda and Sumbawanga.

Sumbawanga

While there's little reason to make the peppy and pleasant capital of the Rukwa region a destination in itself, anyone travelling through western Tanzania is likely to pass through, and most who do enjoy their time here. There are two ATMs on the main road and some internet cafes.

Bethlehem Tourism Information Centre (☑ 0784 704343; charlesnkuba450@hotmail.com; Mpanda Rd; ☺ 7am-10pm) can help with excursions in the surrounding area.

⌷ Sleeping & Eating

Libori Centre HOTEL **$**
(☑ 0757 494225; r Tsh15,000-25,000; P) This church-run place has rooms that are essentially clean and are very quiet and secure. Besides the addition of a chair, we couldn't see any discernible difference between the cheapest and most expensive rooms. A very basic breakfast is included. It's close to the bus station.

Holland Hotel HOTEL **$**
(☑ 0786 553753; r Tsh45,000; P) Unexpectedly swish for such a dusty little place, the Holland Hotel, which is close to the bus station, offers big, airy, bright rooms with desks and,

unfortunately, an awful lot of noise. The downstairs restaurant might not be the best place to eat in town, but it's certainly the nicest. Secure parking is available.

ℹ Getting There & Away

Numerous bus companies operate out of Sumbawanga and most ticket offices are located just outside the bus station. Most buses depart between 7am and 9.30am. Buses go to:

Mbeya (Tsh16,000 to Tsh17,000, seven hours) Via Tunduma.

Mpanda (Tsh15,000, five to six hours)

To get to Kasesya on the Zambian border there are two dalla-dallas daily (Tsh10,000, four to five hours).

SOUTHERN HIGHLANDS

Tanzania's Southern Highlands officially begin at Makambako Gap, about halfway between Iringa and Mbeya, and extend southwards into Malawi. Here, the term encompasses the entire region along the mountainous chain running between Morogoro in the east and Lake Nyasa and the Zambian border in the west.

The highlands are a major transit route for travellers to Malawi or Zambia. They are also wonderfully scenic and a delight to explore, with rolling hills, lively markets, jacaranda-lined streets, lovely lodges and plenty of wildlife.

Morogoro

POP 286,000

Morogoro would be a fairly scruffy town were it not for its verdant setting at the foot of the Uluguru Mountains, which brood over the landscape from the southeast. Hiking is one of the main attractions.

🛏 Sleeping

Princess Plaza Lodge & Restaurant   GUESTHOUSE $
(☑0754 319159; Mahenge St; d Tsh30,000; ❉ 🛜) Princess is a basic guesthouse with small no-frills rooms, all with hot water, air-con, fan and free wi-fi access. Some have interior windows only. There are no nets, but rooms are sprayed daily. Downstairs is an inexpensive local-style restaurant. It's one block in from the main road, and a five minute walk from the dalla-dalla stand in the town centre.

Amabilis Centre   HOSTEL $
(☑0716 880717, 0719 348959; amabilis. conferencecentre@yahoo.com; Old Dar es Salaam Rd; s Tsh20,000, s/tw without bathroom Tsh15,000/20,000; ℗) This church-run place on the northeastern edge of town offers small, spotless rooms in a multistorey building surrounded by small green gardens. All rooms have fan, net and hot water, and meals are available with advance order. Dalla-dallas heading towards Bigwa will drop you in front, or take a taxi from Msamvu bus stand (Tsh5000).

Hotel Oasis   HOTEL $$
(☑0754 377602, 023-261 4178; hoteloasistz@moro goro.net; Station St; s/d/tr from US$50/60/80; ℗❉🛜🏊) Oasis has acceptable albeit faded rooms that are redeemed by generally good service, a decent restaurant, convenient central location, small gardens and a sparkling, recently renovated swimming pool. All rooms come with fan, air-con, TV and fridge.

🍴 Eating

Pira's Supermarket   SUPERMARKET $
(Lumumba St; ⊙10am-6pm) For self-catering, try this well-stocked supermarket.

Dragonaire's   CHINESE, INTERNATIONAL $$
(☑0715 311311; meals from Tsh11,000; ⊙3-11pm Mon-Fri, noon-11pm Sat & Sun; ℗🛜🐾) Green grounds, a small children's play area, sports TV, pizzas on weekends and huge portions make this a popular choice. The rest of the menu covers Chinese dishes, seafood and beef, with some vegetarian choices; allow plenty of time for orders. Friday and Saturday are karaoke nights. It's 2.5km east of

---

DON'T MISS

CHILUNGA CULTURAL TOURISM PROGRAM

Chilunga Cultural Tourism (☑0754 477582, 023-261 3323; www.chilunga. or.tz; Rwegasore Rd) Organises day and overnight excursions around Morogoro, including village visits, hikes and Mikumi safaris. Its programs are a good introduction to local life. Prices run from US$25 per person per day for short excursions up to about US$75 per person per day for multiday hikes, including transport, guide, and village and forest fees.

Morogoro

town, signposted about 700m off the Old Dar es Salaam Rd.

Salon at Acropol INTERNATIONAL **$$**
(📱 0754 309410; Old Dar es Salaam Rd; meals from Tsh12,000; ⏰ 7am-8pm; 🅿 🛜 🍴) The Acropol has tasty soups, sandwiches, fish and meat platters, some vegetarian options, all-day breakfasts and good local coffee. Sit on the covered porch or in the dark, well-stocked bar overflowing with safari memorabilia and heavy, wooden furniture.

ℹ Information

Exim Bank (Lumumba St) ATM.
Internet Cafe (off Lumumba St; per hour Tsh2000; ⏰ 8am-10pm Sun-Fri, 7-10pm Sat) Ask for Pira's Supermarket; this tiny internet cafe is just around the corner.
NBC bank (Old Dar es Salaam Rd) ATM.

ℹ Getting There & Away

AIR
Due to increasing road congestion getting in and out of Dar es Salaam, the five weekly flights to/from Morogoro (one way US$100) with **Auric Air** (www.auricair.com; Old Dar es Salaam Rd) are an increasingly attractive alternative to the bus for travellers in a hurry.

BUS
The main bus station is 3km north of town on the main Dar es Salaam road, about 300m east of Msamvu roundabout (Tsh5000 in a taxi and Tsh400 in a dalla-dalla). No larger buses originate in Morogoro. Buses from Dar es Salaam going southwest towards Mikumi and Iringa begin passing Morogoro about 9am (Tsh6000 to Tsh7000, four hours Dar to Morogoro;

Tsh13,000 to Tsh15000, three to four hours Morogoro to Iringa). To Tanga, there's a direct bus daily (Tsh6000, five hours), departing by 8am.

The main dalla-dalla stand is in front of the market, where there is also a taxi rank.

TRAIN
Morogoro is on the Central Line. Service was suspended at the time of research. When functional, arrivals from Dar es Salaam are generally about 10pm.

Mikumi National Park

Mikumi (www.tanzaniaparks.com/mikumi.html; adult/child US$30/10) is Tanzania's fourth-largest national park. It's also the most accessible from Dar es Salaam. With almost guaranteed wildlife sightings, it makes an ideal safari destination for those without much time. Mikumi hosts buffaloes, wildebeests, giraffes, elephants, lions, zebras, leopards, crocodiles and more, and chances are high that you'll see a respectable

Southern Highlands

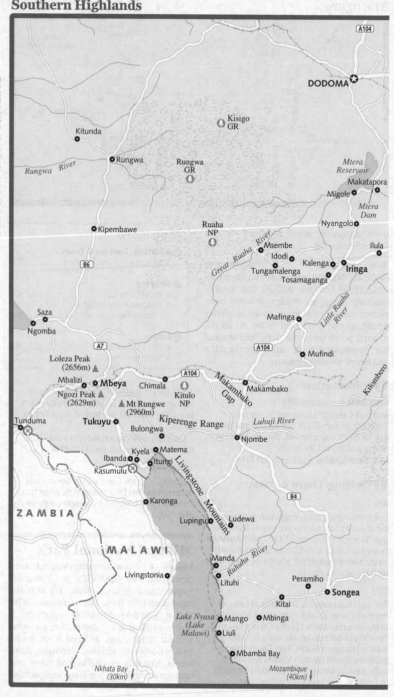

sampling of these within a short time of entering the park.

To the south, Mikumi is contiguous with Selous Game Reserve.

🛏 Sleeping & Eating

The park has four **campsites** (camping US$30). The two closest to the park headquarters have toilet facilities and one has a shower. There is a **special campsite** (camping US$50) near Choga Wale in the north of the park.

Mikumi Park Cottages & Resthouse
COTTAGES $$

(☑ 0767 536135, 0689 062334; mikumi@tanzaniaparks.com; s/d/tr US$50/75/90; P❄) About 3km from the gate, the park cottages and resthouse offer rooms in attached brick bungalows, all with bathroom, fan and air-con, and meals on order (Tsh10,000 per plate) at the nearby dining hall. The resthouse, which consists of two double rooms sharing an entrance, also has a kitchen (bring your own gas). Animals frequently wander just in front.

Mikumi Wildlife Camp
LODGE $$$

(Kikoboga; ☑ 0684 886306, 022-260 0252/3/4; www.mikumiwildlifecamp.com; s/d half board US$218/384; P❄) This camp, about 500m northeast of the park gate, has attractive stone cottages with shaded verandas and views over a grassy field frequented by grazing zebras and impalas. Given its proximity to the highway, it's not a wilderness experience, but the animals don't seem to mind and you'll probably see plenty from your porch. Vehicle rental is only possible with advance notice.

ⓘ Getting There & Around

BUS

All through-buses on the Dar es Salaam–Mbeya highway will drop you at the park gate. Pick-ups can also be arranged from here to continue your onward journey. While vehicle rental can sometimes be arranged privately with park staff, it's better to arrive with your own vehicle or hire one through a Mikumi town hotel.

CAR

The 145km road linking Mikumi's main gate with Kisaki village (21km west of Selous' Matambwe Gate) is now open except during the heavy rains, and makes a scenic 4WD alternative; allow about five hours between the two.

> ### ⓘ MIKUMI NATIONAL PARK
>
> **Why Go** Easy access from Dar es Salaam; rewarding year-round wildlife watching and birdwatching.
>
> **When to Go** Year-round.
>
> **Practicalities** Drive or bus from Dar es Salaam. Entry fees (valid for 24 hours, single entry only) are payable only with a Visa or MasterCard. Driving hours inside the park (off the main highway) are 6.30am to 6.30pm.
>
> **Budget Tips** Any bus along the highway will drop you at the gate. The park doesn't hire vehicles, but staff sometimes rent theirs. Arrange at the gate and be prepared to bargain. For sleeping, the park cottages are cheap and pleasant, with a dining room for meals. Post-safari: flag down an Iringa- or Dar-bound bus to continue your travels. More reliable (less risk of disappointment if vehicle negotiations don't work out with park staff): hire a safari vehicle through hotels listed under Mikumi town (about US$200 per five-person vehicle for a full-day safari). Bring your own lunch and drinks.

Mikumi

Mikumi is the last of the lowland towns along the Dar es Salaam–Mbeya highway before it starts its climb through the Ruaha River gorge up into the hills of the Southern Highlands, and it is of interest almost exclusively as a transit point for visits to Mikumi or Udzungwa Mountains National Parks.

🛏 Sleeping & Eating

Tan-Swiss Hotel & Restaurant   LODGE **$$**
(☑ 0787 191827, 0755 191827; www.tan-swiss.com; Main Rd; camping US$7, s/d/tr US$55/65/75, bungalow f US$90; P❋🕾🛋) This Swiss- and Tanzanian-run establishment has a walled-in camping area with hot-water showers, plus spacious grounds, comfortable rooms with private bathroom, and several double and family bungalows, some with small terraces. All are tidy, with fans and surrounding greenery. There's a tiny plunge pool and a good restaurant-bar, also selling takeaway sandwiches. Vehicle rental to Udzungwa/Mikumi costs US$145/220 per day.

Genesis Motel   GUESTHOUSE **$$**
(☑ 0653 692127, 0716 757707; udzungwamountainviewhotel@yahoo.com; camping US$5, r per person with/without air-con US$40/30; P❋) The functional Genesis, on the highway 2.5km east of the Ifakara junction, has small, closely spaced rooms (ask for a newer one), a restaurant and an attached snake park (admission US$5). One room has air-con. There's also a small, walled-in camping area with hot-water showers and nearby kitchen. Vehicle rental costs US$150/180 per day for

Udzungwa/Mikumi parks; advance notice is required.

ⓘ Getting There & Away

Mikumi's bus stand is at the western end of town on the main highway. For Udzungwa Mountains National Park, wait for one of the large Dar es Salaam to Ifakara buses, which begin passing Mikumi about 11am, going directly to Udzungwa's Mang'ula headquarters (Tsh6000, two hours) and on to Ifakara.

Going west, buses from Dar es Salaam begin passing Mikumi en route to Iringa (Tsh7000, three hours) from about 9.30am. Going east, there are large buses to Dar es Salaam (Tsh12,000 to Tsh13,000, 4½ hours) departing at 6.30am and 7.30am.

Iringa

POP 151,350

Perched at a cool 1600m on a cliff overlooking the valley of the Little Ruaha River, Iringa was initially built up by the Germans at the turn of the 20th century as a bastion against the local Hehe people. Now it's a district capital, an important agricultural centre and the gateway for visiting Ruaha National Park. It's also a likeable place, with its bluff-top setting, healthy climate and highland feel and is well worth a stop.

◉ Sights

Market Area   MARKET
Iringa's market is piled high with fruits and vegetables, plus other wares, including large-weave, locally made Iringa baskets. On its southern edge, in front of the police station, is a **monument** honouring Africans who fell during the Maji Maji uprising between

Iringa

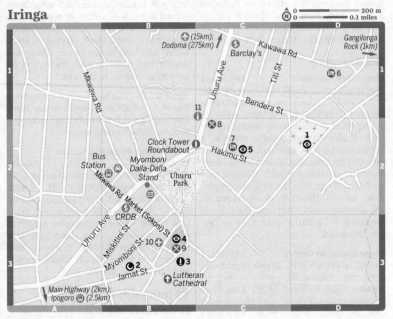

Iringa

⊚ Sights
1 Commonwealth War Graves
   Cemetery D2
2 Ismaili Mosque B3
3 Maji Maji Uprising Monument B3
4 Market Area B3
5 Neema Crafts C2

⊕ Activities, Courses & Tours
Warthog Adventures Tanzania ..... (see 11)

⊜ Sleeping
6 Iringa Lutheran Centre D1

7 Neema Umaki Guest House C2

⊗ Eating
8 Hasty Tasty Too C2
Neema Crafts Centre Cafe .... (see 5)
9 Ngow'o Supermarket B3

ⓘ Information
10 Greenzone Pharmacy B3
11 Iringa Info C1
Neema Crafts Centre Internet
   Cafe .... (see 5)

1905 and 1907. West along this same street is the main trading area, dominated by the German-built **Ismaili Mosque** with its distinctive clock tower.

Commonwealth War Graves
Cemetery   CEMETERY
At the southeastern edge of town is this cemetery, with graves of the deceased from both world wars.

Neema Crafts   CRAFT CENTRE
(☑ 0783760945; www.neemacrafts.com; Hakimu St; ⊙ 8.30am-6.30pm Mon-Sat) ✐ This vocational training centre for young deaf and

disabled people is operated by the Anglican church and sells beautiful crafts, handmade paper and cards, jewellery, quilts, clothing, batiks and more. Behind the craft shop is a weaving workshop, and adjoining is a popular **cafe**. Free tours of the workshops can be arranged. It's just southeast of the Clock Tower roundabout. Highly recommended.

⌖ Tours

Warthog Adventures Tanzania   TOUR
(☑ 0688 322888, 0718 467742, 026-270 1988; www.warthogadventures.com; Uhuru Ave) With well-maintained vehicles, this is a good

contact for arranging excursions to Ruaha National Park. Safaris cost US$300 per vehicle for the first day, then US$200 for each subsequent day. It's at Iringa Info.

🛏 Sleeping

Rivervalley Campsite CAMPGROUND $
(Riverside Campsite; ☑ 0782 507017, 026-270 1988; www.rivervalleycampsites.com; camping with own/ hired tent US$6/10, d tents/cottages US$40/60; P) Rivervalley has a lovely setting on the Little Ruaha River, expansive grounds, a large camping area, children's playground, twin-bedded tents, family cottages and tasty meals. It lies 13km northeast of Iringa; take an Ilula dalla-dalla to the signposted right-hand turn-off (Tsh1000), from where it's 1.5km further down a dirt lane. Taxis charge Tsh15,000 to Tsh20,000 from town or Ipogoro bus stand.

Iringa Lutheran Centre GUESTHOUSE $
(☑ 0755 517445, 026-270 0722; www.iringalutheran centre.com; Kawawa Rd; s/d/tr/ste incl full breakfast US$25/45/50/60; P🛜) This long-standing place has clean, quiet and pleasant twin and double-bedded rooms with bathrooms and hot water, and a restaurant. It's on the northeastern edge of town, about 700m southeast of the main road.

Neema Umaki Guest House GUESTHOUSE $
(☑ 0683 380492, 0786 431274; www. neemacrafts.com; Hakimu St; dm/s/d/f Tsh18,000/25,000/45,000/65,000; 🛜) 🖋 This centrally located guesthouse has an array of clean, comfortable rooms, all with nets and TV (fans coming soon), plus a three-bed dorm. It adjoins Neema Crafts Centre, but rooms are in a quieter section towards the back of the complex. Turn east off Uhuru Ave at the Clock Tower and go down about 100m.

🍴 Eating

Hasty Tasty Too TANZANIAN, INTERNATIONAL $
(☑ 026-270 2061; Uhuru Ave; meals from Tsh6000; ⏰ 7.30am-8pm Mon-Sat, 10am-2pm Sun; P) This long-standing Iringa classic has good breakfasts, yoghurt, shakes and reasonably priced main dishes, plus an agreeable mix of local and expat clientele. You can get toasted sandwiches packed to go and arrange food for Ruaha camping safaris.

Neema Crafts Centre Cafe CAFE $
(☑ 0683 380492; www.neemacrafts.com; Hakimu St; mains about Tsh6500; ⏰ 8am-6.30pm Mon-Fri; 🕾) 🖋 Located upstairs at Neema Crafts Centre, this cafe is justifiably popular, with local coffees and teas, homemade cookies, cakes, soups, and a small selection of sandwiches and light meals. In one corner is a small library where you can read up on development projects in the area.

Ngow'o Supermarket SUPERMARKET $
(Market St; ⏰ 8.30am-5.30pm Mon-Sat, 10am-2pm Sun) This well-stocked supermarket is a good bet for self-caterers.

Mama Iringa Pizzeria & Italian Restaurant ITALIAN $$
(☑ 0753 757007; mama.iringa@yahoo.com; Don Bosco Area; meals Tsh9000-15,000; ⏰ noon-2.30pm & 5-9pm Tue-Sun; P) Delicious Italian food – pizzas, gnocchi, lasagne and more, plus salads, served in the quiet courtyard of a former convent. It's about 3km from the town centre (Tsh5000 in a taxi). Take Mkwawa Rd to the Danish School junction and follow the signposts.

ℹ Information

Barclay's (Uhuru Ave) ATM.

CRDB bank (Uhuru Ave) ATM.

Greenzone Pharmacy (⏰ 8am-9pm) Opposite the market.

Iringa Info (☑ 0782 507017, 026-270 1988; infoiringa@gmail.com; Uhuru Ave; ⏰ 9am-5pm Mon-Fri, to 3pm Sat) A recommended first stop and a good place to get information on Ruaha safaris, reliable car rentals, town and village tours and excursions. It also has a cafe and a bookshop.

Neema Crafts Centre Internet Cafe (Hakimu St; per hour Tsh2000; ⏰ 8.30am-6.30pm Mon-Sat) Wi-fi only.

ℹ Getting There & Away

AIR
There are almost daily flights on Auric Air (p212) between Iringa and Dar es Salaam (one way US$160). Book at Iringa Info. Iringa's Nduli Airfield is about 12km out of town along the Dodoma Rd.

BUS
To catch any bus not originating in Iringa, you'll need to go to the main bus station at Ipogoro, 3km southeast of town below the escarpment where the Morogoro–Mbeya highway bypasses Iringa (Tsh5000 in a taxi to/from town, though initial quotes are usually much higher). This is also where you'll get dropped off if you're arriving on a bus continuing towards Morogoro or Mbeya. Dalla-dallas to Ipogoro (Tsh400) leave

from the Mashine Tatu (M/Tatu) area behind the town bus station, just off Uhuru Ave. The town bus station is the place to go for all buses originating in Iringa. These stop also at Ipogoro to pick up additional passengers.

To Dar es Salaam, JM Luxury goes daily, leaving from 7am onwards (Tsh20,000, seven to eight hours) from the town bus station; book in advance at the JM office behind the bus station.

To Mbeya, Chaula Express departs daily at 7am (Tsh12,000 to Tsh15,000, five hours). Otherwise, you can try to get a seat on one of the through-buses from Dar es Salaam that pass Iringa (Ipogoro bus station) from about 1pm.

To Njombe (Tsh8000 to Tsh9000, 3½ hours) and Songea (Tsh18,000, eight hours), Super Feo departs at 6am from the town bus station.

To Dodoma, Kimotco and several other lines depart daily from 6am (Tsh12,000, four hours), going via Nyangolo and Makatapora on a mostly tarmac, mostly good road.

❶ Getting Around

The main dalla-dalla stand ('Myomboni') is just down from the market and near the bus station. Taxi ranks are along the small road between the bus station and the market, and at the Ipogoro bus station. Fares from the town bus station to central hotels start at Tsh3000.

Ruaha National Park

Ruaha National Park (www.tanzaniaparks. com/ruaha.html; adult/child US$30/10), together with neighbouring conservation areas, forms the core of a wild and extended ecosystem covering about 40,000 sq km and providing home to one of Tanzania's largest elephant populations. In addition to the elephants, which are estimated to number about 12,000, the park (Tanzania's largest, with an area of approximately 22,000 sq km) hosts large herds of buffaloes, as well as greater and lesser kudus, Grant's gazelles, wild dogs, ostriches, cheetahs, roan and sable antelopes, and more than 400 different types of birds. Birdlife is especially prolific along the Great Ruaha River, which winds through the eastern side of the park, as are hippos and crocodiles.

🛏 Sleeping & Eating

🛏 Inside the Park

The park runs several **public campsites** (camping US$30) about 9km northwest of the Msembe park headquarters, with toilets and showers, and about five **special campsites** (camping US$50) with no facilities scattered in the bush well away from the Msembe area.

Ruaha Park Bandas & Cottages COTTAGES $$ (✆0756 144400; ruaha@tanzaniaparks.com; s/d bandas with shared bathroom US$30/60, s/d/f cottages US$50/100/100; ❒) Ruaha's 'old' park *bandas* are twin-bedded metal rondavels in a good setting on the river near park headquarters. Meals are available. Restoration work is underway; soon, all should have a private bathroom. About 3km beyond here are the 'new' tidy cement cottages (all with bathroom) on a rise overlooking the river in the distance. There's a dining hall on-site (meals Tsh6000).

Accommodation should be paid for at the entry gate with credit card.

---

❶ RUAHA NATIONAL PARK

Why Go Outstanding dry season wildlife watching, especially known for its elephants and hippos; excellent birdwatching; rugged scenery.

When to Go June through to November for wildlife; December through to April for birdwatching.

Practicalities Drive in from Iringa; fly in from Arusha or Dar es Salaam. Entry fees are per 24-hour period, single entry only, and payable only with Visa or MasterCard. The main gate (open 7am to 6pm) is about 8km inside the park boundary on its eastern side, near the park's Msembe headquarters. Driving is permitted within the park from 6am to 6.30pm.

Budget Tips Get a group of four or five, hire a vehicle in Iringa for an overnight safari and sleep at the old park *bandas*. Meals are available, but bring your own drinks. It's also possible to take the bus from Iringa to Tungamalenga, and arrange car hire there for a safari (about US$250 per day). Confirm in advance vehicle availability, and remember park fees are single entry only. Car hire from Iringa and sleeping inside the park usually works out at better value.

Mwagusi Safari Camp   TENTED CAMP $$$

(☑ UK +44 18226 15721; www.mwagusicamp.com; s/d all-inclusive US$660/1190; ⊙ Jun-Mar; P) This highly regarded 16-bed owner-managed camp is set in a prime location for wildlife viewing on the Mwagusi Sand River about 20km inside the park gate. The atmosphere is intimate and the guiding is top-notch. In addition to the superb surrounding wildlife, highlights are the spacious tented *bandas,* the rustic, natural feel and the romantic evening ambience.

Ruaha River Lodge   LODGE $$$

(☑ 0754 237422; www.tanzaniasafaris.info; s/d incl full board & wildlife drives US$405/650; P) This unpretentious, beautifully situated 28-room lodge was the first in the park and is the only place on the river. It's divided into two separate sections, each with its own dining area. The stone cottages directly overlook the river – elephants and hippos are frequently spotted here – and there's a tree-top-level bar-terrace with stunning riverine panoramas.

Mdonya Old River Camp   TENTED CAMP $$$

(☑ 022-260 1747; www.mdonya.com; per person incl full board & excursions US$390; ⊙ Jun-Mar; P) The relaxed Mdonya Old River Camp, about 1½ hours' drive from park headquarters, has 12 tents on the banks of the Mdonya Sand River, with elephants occasionally wandering through camp. It's a straightforward, unpretentious place with the necessary comforts tempered by a bush feel. If you take advantage of Coastal Travel's special fly-in offers, it offers good value for a Ruaha safari.

🏚 Outside the Park

There are several places just outside the park boundaries along the Tungamalenga village road (take the left fork at the junction when coming from Iringa). If staying here, remember that park entry fees are valid for a single entry only per 24-hour period.

Chogela Campsite   CAMPGROUND $

(☑ 0782 032025, 0757 151349; www.chogelasafari camp.wix.com/chogelasafaricamp; camping US$10, s/d safari tents US$30/60; P) Shaded grounds, a large cooking-dining area and hot-water showers make this a popular budget choice. There are also twin-bedded safari-style tents. Vehicle rental can be arranged (US$250 for a full-day safari, advance notice required),

as can meals. The camp is about 34km from the park gate along the Tungamalenga Road.

Ruaha Cultural Tourism Program

(☑ 0757 151349, 0752 142195; www.ruahacultural tours.com; half-/full-day tour US$20/40, per person full-board in Maasai village US$27) 🅿 also has a base here, for arranging nature walks, village tours and day or overnight visits to a nearby Maasai community.

Tungamalenga Lodge & Campsite   LODGE $

(☑ 026-278 2196, 0787859369; www.ruahatunga camp.com; Tungamalenga Rd; camping US$10, r per person with breakfast/full board US$40/65; P) This long-standing place, about 35km from the park gate and close to the bus stand, has a small garden for camping, basic but tidy rooms in double-storey bungalows and a restaurant. Village tours can be arranged. Vehicle rental is possible with advance arrangement only.

Tandala Tented Camp   TENTED CAMP $$$

(☑ 0755 680220, 0757183420; www.tandalacamp. com; s/d full board US$250/440; ⊙ Jun-Mar; P ≋) Lovely Tandala is just outside the park boundary, 12km from the gate. Its 11 raised tents are scattered around shaded grounds with a bush feel (elephants and other animals are frequent visitors). Staff can organise vehicle rental to Ruaha, and guided walks and night drives in park border areas. The swimming pool and low-key ambience make it a good family choice.

ℹ Getting There & Away

AIR

There is an airstrip at Msembe, near park headquarters.

Coastal Aviation (p212) flies from Dar es Salaam and Zanzibar to Ruaha via Selous Game Reserve (one way from Dar es Salaam US$350, from Zanzibar US$390) and between Ruaha and Arusha (US$330). Safari Airlink has similarly priced flights connecting Ruaha with Dar es Salaam, Selous and Arusha, and also with Katavi and Mikumi.

BUS

There's a daily bus between Iringa and Tungamalenga village (Tsh6000, five hours), departing Iringa's Mwangata bus stand (on the southwestern edge of town at the start of the Ruaha road) at 1pm. Look for the one marked 'Idodi-Tungamalenga'. Departures from Tungamalenga's village bus stand (along the Tungamalenga road, just before Tungamalenga Camp) are at 6am. From Tungamalenga, there's no onward transport to the park, other than rental vehicles

IRINGA TO MAKAMBAKO

From Iringa, the Tanzam highway continues southwest, past dense stands of pine, before reaching the junction town of Makambako. En route are some lovely possibilities for detours.

Kisolanza – The Old Farm House (☑ 0754 306144; www.kisolanza.com; camping US$7, s/d/tr/f cottages half-board from US$110/140/185/170, tw without bathroom US$40; ℗) This gracious 1930s farm homestead 50km southwest of Iringa is fringed by stands of pine and rolling hill country and recommended for its accommodation and its outstanding cuisine. There are two camping grounds (overlanders and private vehicles), twin-bedded rooms, cosy wooden chalets, family cottages with fireplace, and two luxury garden cottages. All are spotless, impeccably furnished and excellent value.

There's also a bar, a shop selling home-grown vegetables and other produce, and many beautiful walks in the area. Buses will drop you at the Kisolanza turn-off, from where it's a 1.5km walk in to the lodge. Advance bookings are advisable for accommodation, but there's always room for campers.

arranged in advance through the Tungamalenga road camps (prices start at US$250 per day). There's no vehicle rental once at Ruaha, except what you've arranged in advance with the lodges.

CAR
Ruaha is 115km from Iringa along an unsealed road. About 58km before the park, the road forks; both sides go to Ruaha and the distance is about the same each way, but it's best to take the more travelled Tungamalenga road (left fork). The closest petrol is in Iringa.

Makambako

Makambako (a stop on the Tazara railway line) is a windy highland town at the junction where the road from Songea and Njombe meets the Dar es Salaam–Mbeya highway.

Triple J Hotel (☑ 0767 310176, 026-273 0475; kaributriplejhotel@yahoo.com; Njombe Rd; s/d Tsh20,000/25,000; ℗) has small rooms and a restaurant with meals for about Tsh5000. It's 800m south of the main junction along the Njombe road, 700m north of the bus stand and signposted.

The bus stand is about 1.5km south of the main junction along the Njombe road. The first bus to Mbeya (Tsh8000 to Tsh9500, three hours) leaves at 6am, with another bus at 7am. The first buses (all smaller Coastals) to Njombe (Tsh3000, one hour) and Songea (Tsh12,000, five hours) depart about 6.30am, and there's a larger bus departing at 6.30am for Iringa (Tsh8000) and Dar es Salaam.

Njombe

Njombe, about 60km south of Makambako and 235km north of Songea, is a district capital, regional agricultural centre and home of the Bena people.

🛏 Sleeping & Eating

Hill Side Hotel HOTEL $
(Chani Motel; ☑ 0752 910068, 026-278 2357; chani hotel@yahoo.com; r Tsh30,000-50,000; ℗) This cosy place has modest twin- and double-bedded rooms, hot water (usually), small but lovely poinsettia-studded gardens, and a restaurant with TV and filling meals. There's currenty no signpost; turn off the main road onto the dirt lane next to the courthouse (Mahakamani); it's just downhill and diagonally opposite from the police station.

FM Hotel HOTEL $
(☑ 0786 513321; Songea Rd; s Tsh30,000-40,000, d Tsh50,000, ste Tsh70,000; ℗) This large, soulless multistory place bills as Njombe's sleekest option, with modern rooms boasting nets and TV. Some face the highway, with views over Njombe, others overlook an interior courtyard. There's a restaurant. It's on the main road 1km south of and diagonally opposite the bus stand.

Duka la Maziwa SELF-CATERING $
(Cefa Njombe Milk Factory; ☑ 026-278 2851; ⊙ 7am-6pm Mon-Sat, 10am-2pm Sun) Fresh milk, yoghurt and delicious Italian cheeses. It's just off the main road; turn in by the TFA building and go down about two blocks. The shop is to the left.

❶ Getting There & Away

The bus stand is on the west side of the main road, about 600m south of the large grey-water tank.

Buses go daily to Songea (Tsh9000 to Tsh12,000, four hours), Makambako (Tsh3000, one hour), Iringa (Tsh8000) and Mbeya (Tsh8000 to Tsh9000, four hours), with the first departures at 6.30am.

Mbeya

POP 385,280

The thriving town of Mbeya sprawls at about 1700m in the shadow of Loleza Peak (2656m), in a gap between the verdant Mbeya mountain range to the north and the Poroto mountains to the southeast. Today it's a major trade and transit junction between Tanzania, Zambia and Malawi. The surrounding area is lush, mountainous and scenic, with many nearby excursions.

⌲ Tours

Gazelle Safaris   TOUR, SAFARIS
(☑ 025-250 2482, 0784 666600; www.gazelle safaris.com; Jacaranda Rd) Arranges guides and transport for day tours around Mbeya, excursions to Kitulo National Park, car rental, and safaris further afield, especially in the southern circuit. It also does domestic and international flight bookings.

Sisi Kwa Sisi   TOUR
(Station Rd) Between the market and the bus station, this sometimes-on, sometimes-off budget operator can occasionally be useful for arranging a guide to local attractions. The unsignposted office is often unstaffed (whenever its owner is out leading an excursion), so send a text to the number he leaves on the door.

🛏 Sleeping

Karibuni Centre   GUESTHOUSE $
(☑ 0754 510174, 025-250 3035; www.mec -tanzania.ch/karibuni; camping Tsh5000, s/d Tsh20,000/32,000; 🅿) This quiet mission-run place is in a small, enclosed compound where you can also pitch a tent. Most rooms have bathrooms, and there's a restaurant. Karibuni is 3km southwest of the town centre. Take a taxi from the bus stand (Tsh4000).

If you are driving, go 1.2km west along the highway from the big town-airport junction at the entrance to Mbeya to the tiny signpost on Lehner St. Turn right, continue 300m to

the T-junction, turn right again. The compound is 200m up on the left.

Sombrero Hotel   HOTEL $
(☑ 0766 755227, 025-250 0663; Post St; s/tw/ste Tsh30,000/40,000/60,000) No-frills rooms in a convenient, central location, and a tiny restaurant downstairs. There are no screens in the windows, but most rooms have nets.

Mbeya Hotel   HOTEL $
(☑ 025-250 2224/2575; mbeyahotel@hotmail. com; Kaunda Ave; s/d/tr/ste Tsh50,000/70,000/ 90,000/100,000; 🅿✳❅🖭) The former East African Railways & Harbours Hotel has straightforward twins and doubles. The better ones (all doubles) are in an extension attached to the main building. More cramped rooms are in separate bungalows out back. There are also small gardens and a restaurant. It's opposite NBC bank.

New Millennium Inn   GUESTHOUSE $
(☑ 025-250 0599; Mbalizi Rd; r Tsh17,000-20,000) In a noisy but convenient location directly opposite the bus stand, with good-value 'newer' rooms upstairs and separate from the main building, and smaller, darker rooms near the reception. The more expensive rooms have beds big enough for two, but there's no same-gender sharing.

Utengule Coffee Lodge   LODGE $$
(☑ 0786 481902, 0753 020901; www.riftvalley-zanzibar.com; camping US$8.50, s US$85-140, d US$100-177, f US$165; 🅿❅🖭) This lovely lodge is set in expansive grounds on a working coffee plantation in the hills 20km west of Mbeya. Accommodation includes spacious standard rooms, two-storey balconied suites and a large family room. There are tennis courts and a **restaurant**. From Mbeya, follow the highway 12km west to Mbalizi junction. Turn right; continue 8.5km to the lodge entry on your right.

🍴 Eating

Azra Supermarket   SUPERMARKET $
(School St) Small but well stocked; just up from the Tanesco building.

Mbeya Hotel   INDIAN $$
(☑ 025-250 2224/2575; mbeyahotel@hotmail.com; Kaunda Ave; meals Tsh6000-10,000; ⊙7am-9pm; ☑) This popular hotel restaurant has a large menu featuring reasonably good Indian cuisine, including vegetarian selections, plus Chinese and continental fare. Meals tend to be on the heavy side (lots of extra oil), but

Mbeya

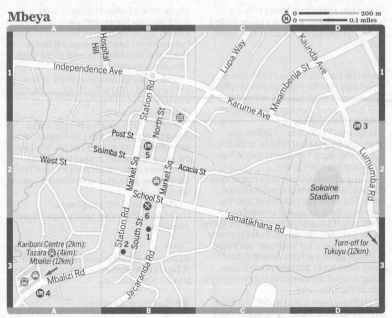

portions are large and it remains one of the better dining options in the town centre.

ℹ️ Information

DANGERS & ANNOYANCES

As a major transport junction, Mbeya attracts many transients, particularly in the area around the bus station. Watch your luggage, don't change money with anyone, only buy bus tickets in the bus company offices and avoid walking alone through the small valley behind the bus station. Also be very wary of anyone presenting themselves as a tourist guide and don't make tourist arrangements with anyone outside of an office. Bus ticketing scams abound, especially for cross-border connections. Ignore all touts, no matter how apparently legitimate, trying to sell you through-tickets to Malawi (especially) or Zambia. Pay the fare only to the border, and then arrange onward transport from there.

MEDICAL SERVICES

Babito Pharmacy (☎ 0754 376808, 025-250 0965; Station Rd; ⊗ 7.30am-6.30pm Mon-Fri, 8am-5pm Sat)

MONEY

CRDB bank (Karume Ave) ATM.
NBC bank (cnr Karume & Kaunda Aves) Changes cash; ATM.
Stanbic Bank (Karume Ave) ATM.

Mbeya

🎯 Activities, Courses & Tours
1 Gazelle Safaris	B3
2 Sisi Kwa Sisi	B3

🛏️ Sleeping
3 Mbeya Hotel	D2
4 New Millennium Inn	A3
5 Sombrero Hotel	B2

🍽️ Eating
6 Azra Supermarket	B2
Mbeya Hotel	(see 3)

TRAVEL AGENCIES

Juve Travel & Tours (☎ 0767 927627, 0655 656542; School St; ⊗ 8am-6pm Mon-Fri, 9am-2pm Sat) Fastjet agent; also does bookings for other airlines.

ℹ️ Getting There & Away

AIR

Flights on Auric Air, Air Tanzania, **Precision Air** (☎ 0686 310228; www.precisionairtz.com; School St; ⊗ 8am-5pm Mon-Fri, to 2pm Sat & Sun), Fastjet and Flightlink go daily between Mbeya's Songwe airport (22km from Mbeya near Mbalizi) and Dar es Salaam (one way Tsh55,000 to Tsh160,000), often for not much more than the cost of a bus fare, and much faster. Auric

Air also flies weekly from Mbeya to Ruaha (US$200). In Mbeya, all airlines can be booked through Gazelle Safaris (p182) or Juve Travel (p183).

BUS

Green Star Express, JM Luxury and other lines depart daily from the main bus station to Dar es Salaam from 6am (Tsh28,000 to Tsh44,000, 12 to 14 hours), going via Iringa (Tsh16,000) and Morogoro (Tsh30,000).

To Njombe (Tsh8000 to Tsh12,000, four hours) and Songea (Tsh17,000 to Tsh24,000, eight hours), Super Feo departs daily at 6am, with a later departure as well.

To Tukuyu (Tsh3000, one to 1½ hours), Kyela (Tsh5500, two to 2½ hours) and the Malawi border (Tsh5500, two to 2½ hours; take the Kyela bus), there are several smaller Coastal buses daily. It's also possible to get to the Malawi border via dalla-dalla, but you'll need to change vehicles in Tukuyu. For Itungi port, you'll need to change vehicles in Kyela. Note that there are no direct buses from Mbeya into Malawi, though touts at the Mbeya bus station may try to convince you otherwise.

To Matema, there is occasionally one direct bus daily via Kyela, departing Mbeya by about 1pm (Tsh9000 to Tsh10,000). Usually you'll need to take transport to Kyela, from there to Ipinda, and then Ipinda to Matema.

To Tunduma, on the Zambian border, there are daily minibuses (Tsh5000, two hours). Once

across, there's Zambian transport; we recommend doing the journey in this way. There is also a weekly bus between Dar es Salaam and Lusaka that sometimes takes passengers at Mbeya (Tsh35,000 from Mbeya to Lusaka), but ticketing scams are common.

To Sumbawanga, Sumry goes daily at 6am and 8am (Tsh13,000 to Tsh15,000, six hours), with some buses continuing on to Mpanda (Tsh29,000, 14 hours).

To Tabora, there are a few vehicles weekly during the dry season, going via Rungwa. Some, which you can pick up at Mbalizi junction, take the western route via Saza and Makongolosi, while others – catch them along the main Tanzam highway just east of central Mbeya – go via Chunya.

To Moshi (Tsh52,000) and Arusha (Tsh56,000, 18 gruelling hours), Sumry departs daily at 5am.

TRAIN

Book tickets at least several days in advance at **Tazara train station** (☉8am-noon & 2-5pm Mon-Fri, 10am-2pm Sat).

❶ Getting Around

Taxis park at the bus station and near Market Sq. Fares from the bus station to central hotels start at Tsh3000. The Tazara train station is 4km out of town on the Tanzania–Zambia highway (Tsh8000 in a taxi).

Around Mbeya

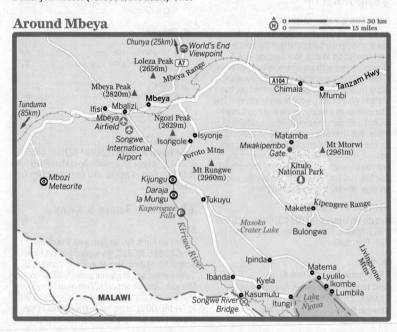

Tukuyu

The small, peppy town of Tukuyu is set in the heart of a beautiful area of hills and orchards near Lake Nyasa. There are many hikes and natural attractions nearby, but only the most basic tourist infrastructure. Destinations include the 2960m Mt Rungwe, Ngozi Peak and Crater Lake, and Daraja la Mungu (Bridge of God).

Activities

Hiking opportunities abound, with Rungwe Tea & Tours and Bongo Camping the main options for organising something. Afriroots (p204) also does tours here. Expect to pay Tsh20,000 to Tsh35,000 for most tours.

Tours

Rungwe Tea & Tours   HIKING
(✆0754 767389, 025-255 2489; rungweteatours@gmail.com) This is a one-man-show type of place where you can organise guides for hikes in the surrounding area. Prices start about Tsh15,000 per day including a guide and local community fee. It's in the Ujenzi area at the 'Umoja wa Wakulima Wadogo wa Chai Rungwe' building, behind the Landmark Hotel.

Sleeping & Eating

Landmark Hotel   HOTEL $
(✆0782 164160, 025-255 2400; camping US$5, s/d US$40/45; ℗) Spacious, good-value rooms, all with TV and hot water, a small lawn where it's sometimes permitted to pitch a tent, and a slow but good restaurant. The doubles have two large beds, and the singles have one bed that's big enough for two people. It's the large multistorey building at the main junction just up from NBC bank.

DM Motel   HOTEL $
(✆0764 061580, 025-255 2332; s/d/ste Tsh15,000/20,000/30,000, s without bathroom Tsh10,000; ℗) Clean rooms with a large bed (no same-gender sharing permitted) and meals on request. It's just off the main road at the turn-off into Tukuyu town, and signposted.

Bongo Camping   CAMPGROUND $
(✆0732 951763; www.bongocamping.com; camping with own/hired tent Tsh6000/8000; ℗) A backpacker-friendly place with a large, grassy area to pitch your tent, basic cooking facilities, hot-bucket showers, tents for hire and meals on order. It's at Kibisi village, 3.5km north of Tukuyu, and 800m off the main road (Tsh1000 in a taxi from Tukuyu bus stand). They also arrange **activities** (✆0732 951763; www.bongocamping.com).

ℹ Information

NBC bank in the town centre has an ATM.

ℹ Getting There & Away

Minibuses run several times daily between Tukuyu and both Mbeya (Tsh3000, one to 1½ hours along a scenic, tarmac road) and Kyela (Tsh2500, one hour).

Two roads connect Tukuyu with the northern end of Lake Nyasa. The main tarmac road heads southwest and splits at Ibanda, with the western fork going to Kasumulu (Songwe River Bridge) and into Malawi, and the eastern fork to Kyela and Itungi port. A secondary dirt road heads southeast from Tukuyu to Ipinda and then east towards Matema.

Lake Nyasa

Lake Nyasa (also known as Lake Malawi) is Africa's third-largest lake after Lake Victoria and Lake Tanganyika. It's more than 550km long, up to 75km wide and as deep as 700m in parts. It also has a high level of biodiversity, containing close to one-third of the world's known cichlid species. The Tanzanian side is rimmed to the east by the Livingstone Mountains, whose green, misty slopes form a stunning backdrop as they cascade down to the sandy shoreline.

Matema

This quiet lakeside settlement is the only spot on northern Lake Nyasa that has any sort of tourist infrastructure, and with its stunning beachside setting backed by the Livingstone Mountains, it makes an ideal spot to relax for a few days. There's nowhere in Matema to change money, so bring enough shillings with you.

Sleeping & Eating

Matema Lake Shore Resort   COTTAGES $
(✆0782 179444, 0754 487267; www.mec-tanzania.ch/matema; camping Tsh6000, d/tr/f Tsh50,000/50,000/60,000, d without bathroom Tsh25,000; ℗) This recommended Swiss-built place has several spacious, breezy, comfortable two-storey beachfront family chalets, some smaller, equally nice double and triple

cottages and a quad. All rooms front directly onto the lake – with lovely views – except the doubles sharing bathrooms. Breakfast is not included in room prices, but the restaurant serves tasty, reasonably priced meals.

★ **Blue Canoe Safari** CAMPGROUND, COTTAGES $
(☏ 0783 575451; www.bluecanoelodge.com; camping US$7, s/d bungalows US$70/90, bandas from US$20/35; P @) 🅿 This lovely beachfront place has camping with spotless amenity blocks, plus four 'luxury bungalows' with verandas overlooking the lake, polished wood floors and comfortable beds with spacious mosquito netting. Nearby are simple budget *bandas*. The bar is well-stocked and the cuisine delicious. Snorkelling and excursions can be arranged. It's 3.5km from Matema's main junction; pick-ups are possible with advance notice.

🛈 Getting There & Away

BOAT

Schedules are highly variable these days, but there is usually at least one boat weekly – either the MV *Iringa* or the MV *Songea* – which stops at Matema on its way from Itungi port down the eastern lake shore to Mbamba Bay. The boat stop for Matema is actually at Lyulilo village, about 25 minutes on foot from the main Matema junction. Just follow the main 'road' going southeast from the junction, paralleling the lake shore, and ask for the 'bandari'.

BUS

From Tukuyu, pick-ups to Ipinda leave around 8am most mornings from the roundabout by NBC bank (Tsh2500, two hours). Although drivers sometimes say they are going all the way to Matema, generally they go only as far as Ipinda. Once in Ipinda, pick-ups run sporadically to Matema (Tsh3000 to Tsh3500, 35km), departing around 2pm, which means you'll need to wait around in Ipinda for a while. Returning from Matema, departures are in the morning. Chances are better on weekends for finding a lift between Matema and Ipinda with a private vehicle. If you get stuck in Ipinda, there are several basic guesthouses.

Occasionally there is also a direct bus between Mbeya and Matema, departing Mbeya by about 1pm and Matema at 5am (Tsh9000, five hours). All transport in Matema departs from the main junction near the hospital.

CAR & MOTORCYCLE

From Kyela, the signposted turn-off to Ipinda and Matema is about 3km north of Kyela town centre. From here, it's about 14km to Ipinda, and another 25km to Matema along a readily passable but rough road. Allow one to 1½ hours for the 40km stretch. There's also a shorter, scenic, slightly less rough, route directly from Tukuyu to Ipinda.

Mbamba Bay

The relaxing outpost of Mbamba Bay is the southernmost Tanzanian port on Lake Nyasa. **St Benadetta Guest House** (r Tsh15,000) near the water has simple, clean rooms and meals. There's also the relaxing **Mbamba Bay Bio Camp** (☏ 0765 925255; info@bushkomba.de; d tent/banda Tsh30,000/70,000) 🅿, 5km north of town.

There's one direct vehicle daily from Songea (Tsh9000, five to six hours). Otherwise you will need to change vehicles at Mbinga.

Entering or leaving Tanzania via Mbamba Bay, you'll need to stop at the immigration office/police station near the boat landing to take care of passport formalities.

Songea

The sprawling town of Songea, just over 1000m in altitude, is capital of the surrounding Ruvuma region. The main tribal group here is the Ngoni. Songea takes its name from one of their greatest chiefs, who was killed following the Maji Maji rebellion and is buried about 1km from town near the Maji Maji museum.

⊙ Sights

Maji Maji Museum   MUSEUM
(admission Tsh10,000; ⊙ 8am-4pm) About 1km from the town centre, off the Njombe road, is this small museum commemorating the Maji Maji uprising. Behind it is Chief Songea's tomb. From town, take the first tarmac road to the right after passing CRDB bank and continue about 200m. The museum entrance is on the left with a pale-blue archway.

🛏 Sleeping & Eating

OK Hotels 92   GUESTHOUSE $
(d Tsh15,000-20,000) Small but decent rooms. From the bus stand, head uphill 400m past the market, take the second right (watch for the sign for the Lutheran church). After about 200m go right again, and look for the apricot-coloured house in a fenced compound to your left. Meals are available at Krista Park across the street.

Heritage Cottage
HOTEL $$

(☎0754 355306, 025-260 0888; www.heritage -cottage.com; Njombe Rd; s/d Tsh75,000/90,000; ☏✷) This good hotel has modern, clean rooms with TV (some with minifridge), a popular bar-restaurant, a large lawn area behind, and a playground for children. It's located 3km north of town along the Njombe Rd.

Seed Farm Villa
B&B $$

(☎0752 842086, 025-260 2500; www.seedfarm villa.com; s Tsh75,000-90,000, d Tsh85,000-105,000; ☏✷) This place has eight modern, quiet rooms with TV set in tranquil garden surroundings away from the town centre in the Seed Farm area. There's a sitting room with TV, and a restaurant (advance order necessary). Head out of town along the Tunduru Rd for 2.5km to the signposted turn-off, from where it's 200m further.

ℹ Information

CRDB bank (Njombe Rd) ATM.

Immigration (Uhamiaji; Tunduru Rd) At the beginning of the Tunduru Rd. Get your passport stamped here if you are travelling to/from Mozambique.

NBC bank Behind the market; ATM.

ℹ Getting There & Away

To Iringa (Tsh18,000, eight hours) and Dar es Salaam (Tsh40,000, 13 hours), Super Feo departs daily from 5am.

To Mbeya (Tsh18,000 to Tsh24,000, eight hours), Super Feo departs daily at 6am in each direction via Njombe (Tsh9000 to Tsh12,000, four hours). There are also departures to Njombe at 9.30am and 11am.

For Mbamba Bay, there's one direct vehicle departing daily by 7am (Tsh9000, five to six hours). Otherwise, get transport to Mbinga (Tsh4000, two hours) and from there on to Mbamba Bay (Tsh5000, three to four hours).

To Tunduru, there's a daily bus in the dry season departing by 7am (Tsh15,000, seven to eight hours). There's also one bus daily direct to Masasi (Tsh25,000, 13 hours), departing by 6am.

Transport to Mozambique departs from the Majengo C area, southwest of the bus stand and about 600m in from the main road; ask locals to point out the way through the back streets. If you're driving, head west 18km from Songea along the Mbinga road to the signposted turn-off, from where it's 120km further on an unpaved but decent road to the Mozambique border.

Tunduru

Tunduru, halfway between Masasi and Songea, is in the centre of an important gemstone-mining region. You're likely to need to spend the night here if travelling between Masasi and Songea.

Namwinyu Guest House (☎0655 447225, 0786 447225; Songea Rd; r Tsh30,000; ☏✷), at the western end of town on the main road, has clean, pleasant rooms and meals.

ℹ Getting There & Away

BUS

There's at least one bus daily between Tunduru and Masasi, departing by 6am (Tsh10,000, five hours) and a daily bus direct from Tunduru to Dar es Salaam (Tsh35,000). Between Tunduru and Songea, there's also daily transport in the dry season (Tsh15,000, seven to eight hours). In both directions from Tunduru, there is little en route, so bring food and water with you. Reserve a seat for onward travel when you arrive in Tunduru for rainy season travel, as vehicles fill up quickly.

CAR & MOTORCYCLE

The road from Tunduru in either direction is unpaved but easily passable in the dry season, although somewhat more challenging (especially between Tunduru and Songea) during the rains. Heading east, the sealed road currently starts about 55km before Masasi, and large sections in both directions from Tunduru are being prepared for paving.

SOUTHEASTERN TANZANIA

Time seems to have stood still in Tanzania's sparsely populated southeast. It lacks the development and bustle of the north and tourists numbers are a relative trickle. Yet, for adventurous travellers seeking to learn about traditional local life, for safari enthusiasts and for divers, the southeast makes an ideal destination. But, get here soon: the region's easy pace is already starting to show signs of strain from recent discoveries of offshore gas reserves.

Mafia

Stroll along sandy lanes through the coconut palms. Explore a coastline alternating between dense mangrove stands and

TANZANIA TUNDURU

white-sand beaches. Get to know traditional Swahili culture. If these appeal, you'll love Mafia.

◉ Sights & Activities

Chole Island
HISTORIC SITE

(day visit per person US$5) This is a good place to start exploring, especially around its crumbling but atmospheric ruins, dating from the 19th century. Also on Chole is what is probably East Africa's only **Fruit Bat Sanctuary** (Comoros lesser fruit bat). This is thanks to the efforts of a local women's group who bought the area where an important nesting tree is located.

Big Blu
DIVING

(☏ 0784 474108; www.bigblumafia.com/blog; Chole Bay) Next to Mafia Island Lodge, and under the direction of Moez, a veteran diver with long experience on Mafia. Offers diving, dive-certification courses, snorkelling, excursions around Mafia and reasonably priced accommodation.

Mafia Island Diving
DIVING

(☏ 0688 218569; www.mafiadiving.com; Mafia Island Lodge, Chole Bay) Offers snorkelling, diving, dive-certification courses and excursions.

Southeastern Tanzania

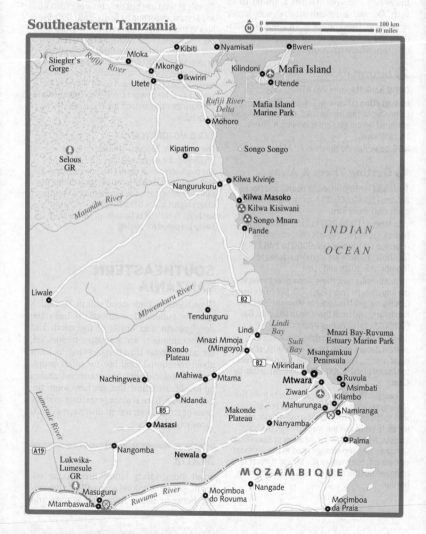

🛏 Sleeping & Eating

🛏 Kilindoni Area

Whale Shark Lodge   GUESTHOUSE **$**
(Sunset Camp; ☎ 0755 696067, 023-201 0201; car
pho2003@yahoo.co.uk; Kilindoni; s/d US$25/50;
@) This backpacker-friendly budget place,
in a quiet, clifftop setting overlooking a
prime whale-shark viewing area, is good value, with six simple, pleasant cottages with
fan, mosquito net and bathroom. There's
a large, lovely dining terrace with sunset
views and local-style meals (US$7) on order.
A short walk down the cliffside is a small
beach with high-tide swimming.

★**Butiama Beach**   LODGE **$$$**
(☎ 0784 474084; www.butiamabeach.com; s/d half
board US$180/300; @) This lovely 15-room
place is spread out in palm-tree-studded
grounds on a fine stretch of beach near
Kilindoni, about 2km south of the small
harbour. Accommodation is in spacious,
breezy, appealingly decorated cottages. It
has delicious Italian-style dining, sea kayaks
for exploring the birdlife in nearby creeks,
magnificent sunset views and a warm, classy
ambience. Very good value for money.

🛏 Utende & Chole Bay Area

For all Chole Bay accommodation (including
all budget hotels in Utende situated after
entering the park gate and all accommo-
dation on Chole Island), you'll need to pay
daily marine park entry fees, whether you go
diving or not. These fees are not included in
accommodation rates.

**Meremeta Guest House &
Apartment**   GUESTHOUSE **$**
(☎ 0787 345460, 0715 345460; www.meremeta
lodge.com; s/d/tr US$30/50/75) On the main
road about 800m before the marine-park en-
try gate, this tidy place has simple but clean
and pleasant budget rooms with fan, meals
(US$10 to US$15), and free coffee and tea.
It also offers bicycle rental and can help ar-
range excursions around the island. Look for
the pink building and local artwork display.

Big Blu   GUESTHOUSE **$**
(☎ 0784 474108; www.bigblumafia.com/blog;
Chole Bay; r per person US$45, s/d tent US$20/30;
⊙ Jul–mid-Apr; @) This friendly dive outfitter
on the beach at Chole Bay has several sim-
ple, good-value beachside rooms, plus a few
tents set back from the beach. It's primari-
ly for divers with Big Blu, although anyone
is welcome. Special dive-accommodation
packages are available. There's also a good
beachside restaurant serving sandwiches,
salads and other light meals.

Kinasi Lodge   LODGE **$$$**
(☎ 0777 424588; www.kinasilodge.com; Chole
Bay; s/d full board from US$200/360; @ ⊛)
🍴 A lovely, genteel choice, with 14 stone-
and-thatch cottages set on a long, green,
palm-shaded hillside sloping down to Chole
Bay. The Moroccan-influenced decor is at
its most attractive in the evening, when the
grounds are lit by small lanterns. There's an
open lounge area with satellite TV, a small
beach, a spa, a dive centre and a quiet, welcoming ambience.

Chole Mjini   TREEHOUSE **$$$**
(☎ 0787 712427, 0784 520799; www.cholemjini.
com; Chole island; s/d full board US$265/420;
⊙ Jun-Easter) 🍴 Chole Mjini is unique: an
upmarket bush adventure in synchrony
with the local community and environment.
Sleep in spacious, rustic and fantastic tree-
houses, eat fresh seafood, experience the
real darkness of an African night without
electricity, and take advantage of diving ex-
cursions, all while supporting Chole Mjini's
work with the local community.

Mafia ⓝ ⛰ 0 —— 20 km / 0 —— 10 miles

Map labels: INDIAN OCEAN, Nyororo, Ras Mkumbi, Nyamisati (30km), Bweni, Shungumbili, Mbarakuni, Kirongwe, Ras Mbisi, Mafia, Baleni, Kilindoni, Chole Bay, Bwejuu, Mange, Chole, Ras Kisimani, Utende, Kitoni, Kua, Juani, Mrima Reef, Mange Reef, Jibondo, Mafia Island Marine Park, Kitutia Reef, Boundary of Mafia Island Marine Park

MAFIA ISLAND MARINE PARK

Mafia Island Marine Park (adult/child US$20/10) – at around 822 sq km the largest marine protected area in the Indian Ocean – shelters a unique complex of estuarine, mangrove, coral reef and marine channel ecosystems. Diving and snorkelling here are highly rewarding; excursions are offered by Big Blu (p188) and Mafia Island Diving (p188). Both are based in the Chole Bay area, which is in the southeastern corner of Mafia island, and forms the heart of the marine park.

Entry fees (payable by everyone, whether you dive or not) are collected at a barrier gate across the main road about 1km before Utende (the closest village to Chole Bay), and can be paid in any major currency, cash only. Save your receipt, as it will be checked again when you leave. **Park headquarters** (☑ 023-240 2690; www.marineparktz.com) are also in Utende.

ℹ Information

Internet Café (Kilindoni; per hour Tsh3000; ⊙ 8am-6pm) At New Lizu Hotel.

National Microfinance Bank Just off the airport road, and near the main junction in Kilindoni; changes cash only (dollars, euros and pounds). There are no ATMs on Mafia.

ℹ Getting There & Away

AIR

Coastal Aviation (☑ 022-284 2700, 0767 404350, 0654 404350) flies daily between Mafia and Dar es Salaam (US$120), Zanzibar (US$160) and Kilwa Masoko (US$190, minimum five passengers), with connections also to Selous Game Reserve and Arusha. **Tropical Air** (☑ 024-223 2511; www.tropicalair.co.tz) has a similarly priced daily flight between Mafia and Dar es Salaam with connections to Zanzibar. Costs of a transfer from the airfield to Chole Bay cost US$15 to US$30 per person.

BOAT

There's at least one motorised boat daily in each direction between Mafia (Kilindoni port) and Nyamisati village on the mainland south of Dar es Salaam. **MV Baccara** (☑ 0686 649616; www.mafiarufijiexpress.com) (Tsh15,000, three to four hours) is the best, when it's running. In Kilindoni, the main ticketing office is next to the big mosque, with another office in the red-roofed building at the port; buy tickets the afternoon

before. In Nyamisati, buy tickets at the port. Smaller boats charge Tsh12,500 and take about four hours.

While a steady trickle of budget travellers reach Mafia this way, remember that there is no safety equipment on any of the boats. They are often overcrowded, there is little shade and the ride can be very choppy in the middle of the channel. Departure times for smaller boats depend on the weather and tides, but are usually at around 6am from Kilindoni; departure times from Nyamisati are irregular.

To reach Nyamisati, get a southbound dalla-dalla from 'Mbagala Rangi Tatu' (along the Kilwa road and reached via dalla-dalla from Dar es Salaam's Posta) to Nyamisati (Tsh6000, up to four hours). For evening arrivals on Mafia, unless you've made arrangements with the lodges for a pick-up, you will need to sleep in Kilindoni. Head straight up the hill from the port for about 300m to the town centre. If you get stuck overnight in Nyamisati, there's basic accommodation at the old Swedish mission.

ℹ Getting Around

Dalla-dallas connect Kilindoni with Utende (Tsh1500, 45 minutes), which has at least one vehicle daily in each direction.

It's easy to hire pick-ups or *bajajis* in Kilindoni to take you around the island. Bargain hard, and expect to pay from Tsh15,000 between Kilindoni and Utende for a vehicle (Tsh10,000 for a *bajaji*).

Between Utende and Chole Island local boats sail throughout the day from the beach in front of Mafia Island Lodge (Tsh400).

Selous Game Reserve

At the heart of southern Tanzania is the **Selous Game Reserve** (SW of Dar es Salaam; full US$30, admission by park entry fee; car tour from Dar es Salaam), a vast 48,000-sq-km wilderness area stretching over more than 5% of mainland Tanzania. It is Africa's largest wildlife reserve, and Tanzania's most extensive protected area, although the extended ecosystems of Ruaha National Park and the Serengeti come close. It's also home to large herds of elephants, plus Africa's largest lion population, buffaloes, crocodiles, hippos, wild dogs, many bird species and some of Tanzania's last remaining black rhinos. Bisecting it is the Rufiji River, which winds its way more than 250km from its source in the highlands through the Selous to the sea, and boasts one of the largest water-catchment areas in East Africa. En route, it cuts a path past woodlands and grasslands and stands of borassus palm, and provides the chance

Selous Game Reserve (Northern Section)

for some unparalleled water-based wildlife watching.

Boat safaris along the Rufiji are a highlight of a Selous safari, and are offered by most of the camps and lodges. Most also organise walking safaris, usually short (three-hour) hikes, or further afield, with the night spent at a fly camp.

🛏 Sleeping

🏕 Inside the Reserve

Special campsites (camping US$50) can be arranged in the area between Mtemere gate and Lake Manze (northeast of Lake Tagalala).

⭐**Selous Impala Camp**   TENTED CAMP **$$$**
(📲0753 115908, 0787 817591; www.adventure camps.co.tz; s/d full board plus excursions US$690/1200; 🕑 Jun-Mar; 🅿🐾) Impala Camp has eight well-spaced, nicely appointed tents in a prime setting on the river near Lake Mzizimia. Its restaurant overlooks the river and has an adjoining bar area on a deck jutting out towards the water, and the surrounding area is rich in wildlife.

Lake Manze Tented Camp   TENTED CAMP **$$$**
(📲0753 115908, 0787 817591; www.adventure camps.co.tz; s/d full board plus excursions

US$520/900; 🕑 Jun-Mar; 🅿) The rustic but comfortable Lake Manze is favourably situated, with 12 simple but pleasant tents in a good location along an arm of Lake Manze. The ambience is low-key with a bush feel, and the camp is recommended for those on

---

ℹ️ SELOUS GAME RESERVE

Why Go Rewarding wildlife watching against a backdrop of stunning riverine scenery; wonderful, small camps; excellent boat safaris and the chance for walking safaris.

When to Go June through December; many camps close from March through May, during the heavy rains.

Practicalities Fly or drive from Dar es Salaam; drive in from Morogoro or Mikumi. Both Mtemere and Matambwe gates are open from 6.30am to 6.30pm. **Reserve headquarters** (mtbutalii@gmail.com; Matambwe Gate) are at Matambwe on the Selous' northwestern edge.

Budget Tips Travel by bus from Dar es Salaam to Mloka village, and base yourself outside Selous' boundaries, paying park fees only when you enter the reserve.

SELOUS GAME RESERVE FEES

All fees are per 24-hour period and currently payable in US dollars cash only. At the time of writing, multiple entries within a 24-hour period are permitted, although this may soon change.

Admission US$50 per adult (US$30 per child aged five to 17 years of age)

Conservation fee US$25 per person for those staying at camps inside the Selous; US$15 per person for those staying at camps outside the Selous' boundaries.

Vehicle fee Tsh20,000 for Tanzania-registered vehicles

Camping at ordinary campsite US$30 per adult (US$20 per child)

Camping at special campsite US$50 per adult (US$30 per child)

Wildlife guard (mandatory in camping areas) US$25

Guide US$40 (US$25 for walking or boat safari guides)

tighter budgets, especially as part of Coastal Travels' (p61) flight-accommodation deals.

Rufiji River Camp TENTED CAMP $$$
(☑ 0784 237422; www.rufijirivercamp.com; s/d per person all inclusive US$465/730; P ☒) This long-standing, unpretentious camp is run by the Fox family, who own camps throughout southern Tanzania. It has a fine location on a wide bend in the Rufiji River about 1km inside Mtemere gate, tents with river views and a sunset terrace. Activities include boat safaris and overnight walking safaris. Overall good value for those on more limited budgets.

🛏 Outside the Reserve

Most lodges outside Mtemere gate arrange boat safaris on the Rufiji east of the reserve boundaries and walking tours outside the reserve, as well as wildlife drives inside Selous. Reserve fees are payable only for days you enter within the Selous' boundaries. It's 75km through the Selous between Mtemere and Matambwe gates. Spending a few days on each side, linked by a full-day's wildlife drive in between, is a rewarding option, although wildlife concentrations in the Matambwe area cannot compare with those deeper inside the reserve towards Mtemere.

Selous River Camp COTTAGES $$
(☑ 0784 237525; www.selousrivercamp.com; camping US$5, s/d tent full board US$105/155, s/d mud hut full board US$235/285; P) This friendly place is the closest camp to Mtemere gate. It has cosy, river-facing 'mud huts' with bathrooms, plus small standing tents surrounded by forest with cots and shared facilities. The bar-restaurant area is lovely, directly overlooking the river at a particularly scenic spot. Overall, it's a fine choice for budget travellers.

Selous Mbega Camp TENTED CAMP $$
(☑ 0784 624664, 0784 748888; www.selous-mbega-camp.com; s/d full board US$140/200, s/d backpackers' special full board US$95/140) This laid-back, family-friendly camp is located about 1km outside the eastern boundary of the Selous near Mtemere gate and just west of Mloka village. It has raised, no-frills tents set in the foliage directly overlooking the river, and reasonably priced boat safaris and vehicle safaris. Pick-ups and drop-offs to and from Mloka are free. It is very good budget value.

🛈 Getting There & Away

AIR
Coastal Aviation (p61), ZanAir (p77) and Safari Airlink (p212) have daily flights linking Selous Game Reserve with Dar es Salaam (one way US$185), Zanzibar (US$220), Mafia (via Dar; US$280) and Arusha (via Dar; US$525), with connections to other northern-circuit airstrips. Coastal also flies between Selous and Ruaha National Park (US$320). Flights into the Selous are generally suspended during the March to May wet season. All lodges provide airfield transfers.

BUS
There is a daily bus between Dar es Salaam's Temeke bus stand (Sudan Market area) and Mloka village, about 10km east of Mtemere gate (Tsh11,000, six to nine hours). Departures in both directions are at 5am. From Mloka, you'll need to arrange a pick-up in advance with one of the camps. Hitching within the Selous isn't permitted, and there are no vehicles to rent in Mloka.

If you are continuing from the Selous southwards, there's a daily dalla-dalla from Mloka to Kibiti, departing Mloka between 3am and 5am (three to four hours). Once at Kibiti, you'll need to flag down one of the passing buses coming from Dar es Salaam to take you to Nangurukuru junction (for Kilwa) or on to Lindi or Mtwara.

Coming from Morogoro, Tokyo Bus Line goes daily to/from Kisaki, departing in each direction between about 9am and 11am (Tsh9000, seven hours). From Kisaki, you'll need to arrange a pick-up in advance with the lodges to reach Matambwe gate, 21km further on.

CAR & MOTORCYCLE

You'll need a 4WD in the Selous. There's no vehicle rental at the reserve and motorcycles aren't permitted.

To get here via road, there are two options. The first: take the Dar es Salaam to Kibiti road, where you leave the tarmac and continue 100km further on a mostly decent dirt track to Mtemere gate (250km from Dar). Allow six hours from Dar es Salaam.

Alternatively, you can go from Dar es Salaam to Kisaki via Morogoro and then on to Matambwe via a scenic but rough route through the Uluguru Mountains. It's 141km from Morogoro to Kisaki, and 21km from Kisaki on to Matambwe gate. This route has improved considerably in recent times, but is still adventurous. In Morogoro, take the old Dar es Salaam road towards Bigwa. About 3km or 4km from the centre of town, past the Teachers' College Morogoro and before reaching Bigwa, you will come to a fork in the road, where you bear right. From here, the road becomes steep and scenic as it winds its way through the Uluguru Mountains onto a flat plain. Allow five to six hours for the stretch from Morogoro to Matambwe, depending on the season. If you are coming from Dar es Salaam and want to bypass Morogoro, take the unsignposted left-hand turn-off via Mikese, about 25km east of town on the main Dar es Salaam road that meets up with the Kisaki road at Msumbisi.

Coming from Dar es Salaam, the last petrol station is at Kibiti (about 100km northeast of Mtemere gate), although supplies aren't reliable. Otherwise try Ikwiriri; there is no fuel thereafter. Coming from the other direction, the last reliable petrol station is at Morogoro. Occasionally you may find diesel sold on the roadside at Matombo, 50km south of Morogoro, and at several other villages, although quality isn't reliable. If you plan to drive around the Selous, bring sufficient petrol supplies with you as there is none available at any of the lodges, nor anywhere close to the reserve.

TRAIN

All Tazara trains stop at Kisaki, which is about five to six hours from Dar es Salaam and the first stop for the express train. Ordinary trains also stop at Matambwe, near Selous headquarters, and at Kinyanguru and Fuga stations, although these latter two are seldom used these days. It works best to take the train from Dar es Salaam to Selous; be sure you have a pick-up confirmed in advance, as the train arrives after nightfall. Going the other way around be prepared for 20-hour-plus delays. For this reason, many lodges are unwilling to collect travellers coming from the Mbeya side. There are several basic, nonrecommendable local guesthouses in Kisaki, should you get stuck.

Kilwa Masoko

Kilwa Masoko (Kilwa of the Market) is a sleepy coastal town nestled amid dense coastal vegetation and several fine stretches of beach about halfway between Dar es Salaam and Mtwara. It's the springboard for visiting the ruins of the 15th-century Arab settlements at Kilwa Kisiwani and Songo Mnara.

◉ Sights & Activities

On the eastern edge of town is **Jimbizi Beach**, a short, pleasant stretch of sand. The best coastline is the long, idyllic palm-fringed open-ocean beach at **Masoko Pwani**, 5km northeast of town, and best reached by bicycle or *bajaji* (one way Tsh5000).

🛏 Sleeping

Kilwa Bandari Lodge   GUESTHOUSE **$**
(☑0713850745; s/d/twTsh39,000/49,000/49,000; meals Tsh7000; ℗) Six tidy, modern rooms with fan, mosquito net, window screens and Zanzibari-style beds make this one of the best budget bets in town. Local-style meals are available on order. It's about 1.5km south of the bus stand (Tsh1000 in a *bajaji*), along the main road and shortly before the port gates.

Kimbilio Lodge   LODGE **$$**
(☑0656 022166; www.kimbiliolodges.com; s/d/tr/q US$90/130/150/170; ℗) This pleasant place has a good beachside setting on the best section of Jimbizi Beach. Accommodation is in six, spacious, tastefully decorated rondavels with *makutis* directly on the sand. It's warmly recommended. There's good Italian cuisine and (with advance notice) diving. Snorkelling excursions and visits to the hippos and mangrove swamps can be arranged.

Kilwa Dreams   COTTAGES **$$**
(☑0784 585330; www.kilwadreams.com; Masoko Pwani; camping US$10, d/f bungalow US$70/95; meals Tsh25,000-35,000; ℗) This is an ideal spot for getting away from just about everything, with a handful of bright blue, spartan but well-tended bungalows with cold water and no electricity in an idyllic setting directly on the long, wonderful beach

Kilwa Masoko

Kilwa Masoko

⊙ Sights
1 Jimbizi Beach B2

🛏 Sleeping
2 Kilwa Bandari Lodge..............................A3
3 Kimbilio Lodge...B2

🚉 Transport
4 Buses to Dar es Salaam & Lindi A1
5 Coastal Aviation Booking Office A1
6 Transport to Kilwa Kivinje &
    Nangurukuru A1

Kivinje. It also rents bicycles. Prices for most excursions start at about US$25 per person for guide and transport (less with larger groups).

🛈 Getting There & Away

AIR
Coastal Aviation (p212) flies daily on demand between Dar es Salaam and Kilwa (one way US$250) and between Kilwa and Mafia (US$190, minimum two passengers). Book through its Dar es Salaam office, or in Kilwa through the **Coastal Aviation Booking Office** (Sudi Travel), north of the petrol station and just north of the transport stand. The airstrip is about 2km north of town along the main road.

BUS
To Nangurukuru (the junction with the Dar es Salaam–Mtwara road; Tsh2000, one hour) and Kilwa Kivinje (Tsh2000, 45 minutes), shared taxis depart several times daily from the transport stand on the main road just north of the market. The transport stand is also the place to hire taxis or *bajajis* for local excursions.

Between Kilwa and Dar es Salaam's Mbagala Rangi Tatu, there is at least one bus daily (stopping also in Kilwa Kivinje), departing in each direction by about 5.30am (Tsh12,000, four to five hours). Through Dar es Salaam–Mtwara buses will drop you at Nangurukuru, but charge the full Dar es Salaam–Mtwara fare.

To Lindi, there's at least one direct bus daily (Tsh7000, four hours), departing Kilwa about 6am. There are no direct connections to Mtwara.

at Masoko Pwani. There's also a beachside bar-restaurant. Take the airport turn-off and follow the signs along sandy tracks for about 4km to the beach. *Bajaji* charge Tsh5000 from town.

Kilwa Seaview Resort LODGE $$
(☎0784 613335, 023-201 3064; www.kilwa.net; Jimbizi Beach; camping US$10, s/d/tr/q half board US$100/130/160/190; 🅿🌊) This family-friendly place has spacious A-frame cottages perched along a rocky escarpment overlooking the eastern end of Jimbizi Beach. There's a restaurant built around a huge baobab tree with tasty meals, and the swimming beach is just a short walk away.

🛈 Information

The **National Microfinance Bank** (Main Rd) changes cash. There's no ATM.
District Commissioner's Office (Halmashauri ya Wilaya ya Kilwa; ⊙7.30am-3.30pm Mon-Fri) This is where you get permits to visit Kilwa Kisiwani and Songo Mnara. Ask for the 'Mambo ya Kale' (Antiquities) office.
Kilwa Islands Tour Guides Association (Main Rd) This small office provides information. It is where you need to go to get guides for visiting Kilwa Kisiwani, Songo Mnara and other local excursions, including to the caves near Kipatimo, the Mto Nyange hippo pools and Kilwa

Kilwa Kisiwani

Today **Kilwa Kisiwani** (Kilwa on the Island; adult/student Tsh27,000/13,000) is a quiet fishing village baking in the sun just offshore from Kilwa Masoko, but in its heyday it was the seat of sultans and centre of a vast trading network linking the old Shona kingdoms and the goldfields of Zimbabwe with Persia, India and China.

While these glory days are now well in the past, the ruins of the settlement are among the most significant groups of Swahili buildings on the East African coast and a Unesco World Heritage site.

◉ Sights

The ruins at Kilwa Kisiwani are in two groups. When approaching Kilwa Kisiwani, the first building you'll find is the Arabic **fort** *(gereza)*. It was built in the early 19th century by the Omani Arabs, on the site of a Portuguese fort dating from the early 16th century. To the southwest of the fort are the ruins of the beautiful **Great Mosque**, with its columns and graceful vaulted roofing, much of which has been impressively restored. In its day, this was the largest mosque on the East African coast. Further southwest and behind the Great Mosque is a smaller **mosque** dating from the early 15th century. To the west of the small mosque are the crumbling remains of the **Makutani**, a large, walled enclosure in the centre of which lived some of the sultans of Kilwa. It is estimated to date from the mid-18th century.

Almost 1.5km from the fort along the coast is **Husuni Kubwa**, once a massive complex of buildings covering almost a hectare and, together with nearby **Husuni Ndogo**, the oldest of Kilwa's ruins. Watch in particular for the octagonal bathing pool.

❶ Information

To visit the ruins, you will need to get a permit (per adult/student under 16 years Tsh27,000/13,000) from the District Commissioner's Office (p194) in Kilwa Masoko, diagonally opposite the post office. The permit is issued without fuss while you wait. To maximise your chances of finding the Antiquities Officer available, it's best to go in the morning. On weekends, telephone numbers of duty officers are posted on the door, and officials are gracious about issuing permits outside of working hours. You'll need to be accompanied by a guide to visit the island, arranged through the Kilwa Islands Tour Guides Association (p194).

There are no restaurants or hotels on the island.

❶ Getting There & Away

Local boats go from the port at Kilwa Masoko to Kilwa Kisiwani (Tsh200) whenever there are enough passengers – usually only in the early morning, about 7am. However, as you are required to go with a guide to the islands, you'll generally need to pay their prices. Guides from the Kilwa Islands Tour Guides Association (p194) charge US$25 per person for a guide including dhow transport (US$30 for a boat with motor, and less with larger groups). With a good wind, the trip in a sailing dhow takes about 20 minutes. Excursions arranged through the hotels cost about the same or more.

Mtwara

POP 108,300

Sprawling Mtwara is southeastern Tanzania's major town. While it lacks the historical appeal of nearby Mikindani and other places along the coast, it has decent infrastructure, easy access and a relaxed pace (somewhat less so in recent times, with the discovery of offshore natural gas reserves), and is a convenient entry/exit point for travelling between Tanzania and Mozambique.

Mtwara is loosely located between a business and banking area to the northwest, near Uhuru and Aga Khan Rds, and the market and bus stand about 1.5km away to the southeast. The main north–south street is Tanu Rd. In the far northwest on the sea, and 30 to 40 minutes on foot from the bus stand, is the Shangani quarter, with a small beach. In Mtwara's far southeastern corner, just past the market, are the lively areas of Majengo and Chikon'gola, and **St Paul's church**, with beautiful paintings inside.

🛏 Sleeping

Drive-In Garden & Cliff Bar　GUESTHOUSE **$**
(☑ 0784 503007; Shangani Rd; camping Tsh5000, r Tsh20,000) This friendly place allows campers to pitch their tent in the garden. There are also several simple, good-value rooms, plus a restaurant. Breakfast is not included in the price. It's just across the road from the beach, although for swimming you'll need to walk up to the main Shangani beach near Shangani junction.

VETA　HOSTEL **$**
(☑ 023-233 4094; Shangani; s/ste Tsh35,000/60,000; ⓟ❉🏊) This large compound has clean rooms, all with one large twin bed, fan, TV and views towards the water, plus a restaurant. It's in Shangani, about 200m back from the water (though there's no swimming beach here). From the T-junction in Shangani, go left and continue for about 2km. There's no public transport; *bajaji* charge around Tsh3000 from town.

Mtwara

0 ————————— 500 m
0 ————————— 0.25 miles

Indian Ocean

Shangani Beach

Msemo Hotel

Shangani Junction

SHANGANI

Drive-In Garden & Cliff Bar (700m); Naf Beach Hotel (1km); VETA (1.2km)

Shangani Rd

Dhow Port & Fish Market

Ferry

Msangamkuu Peninsula

Mtwara Bay

Port

Cathedral

Port Rd

Air Tanzania

Precision Air

Saba Saba Rd

Exim Bank

CRDB

Aga Khan St

CCM Building

Info Solutions

Monument

Uhuru Rd

LIGULA

Tanu Rd

NBC

Himo 2 Restaurant

Makonde Rd

Sokoine Rd

Jamhuri

CHIKON'GOLA

Sinani St

FL High Class Hotel

Mosque

Main Roundabout

Makonde Rd

Transport to Kilambo (for Mozambique)

Bus & Taxi Stand

Mtwara Lutheran Centre

Mikindani Rd

Zambia Rd

MAJENGO

St Paul's Church

(6km); Mikindani (11km)

Mtwara Lutheran Centre HOSTEL $
(📋 0686 049999, 0754 255576; Mikindani Rd; r Tsh10,000-30,000; 🅿) Clean-ish, no-frills rooms, some with private bathrooms and all with fans. Meals can be arranged with advance notice. It's on the southern edge of town, just off the main roundabout along the road heading to Mikindani (Tsh2000 with a *bajaji* from the bus stand). Arriving by bus, ask the driver to drop you at the roundabout.

FL High Class Hotel GUESTHOUSE $
(r Tsh50,000) This is a decent budget option near the bus stand. All rooms have a small double bed. Transport to Mozambique departs from next door. It's one block south of the bus stand.

Naf Beach Hotel HOTEL $$
(📋 0687 703042, 023-233 4706; www.nafbeach hotels.com; s/d from US$100/130; 🅿 ❄ 🛜) This hotel is probably Mtwara's closest to a Western-style business hotel. All rooms have one double bed, minifridge and satellite TV, some have sea views and there's a restaurant. It's just opposite the sea, but for swimming you'll need to go about 1.5km east to Shangani Beach. Visa and Mastercard are accepted. It's about 1.8km west of the Shangani junction.

✖ Eating

Himo 2 Restaurant TANZANIAN $
(Sokoine Rd; meals Tsh5000; ⊙ lunch & dinner) This popular local-style eatery serves chicken, *mishikaki* (marinated, grilled meat kebabs) and other standard local fare with rice, ugali (a staple made from maize or cassava flour, or both) or chips, as well as fruit juice. Coming from town, take the first right after NBC bank. Himo 2 is a few doors up to the left.

Msemo Hotel TANZANIAN, EUROPEAN $$
(Southern Cross Hotel; Shangani; meals Tsh12,000-20,000) This hotel restaurant, on a terrace overlooking the water, is popular for sundowners and has tasty meals.

ℹ Information

CRDB bank (Tanu Rd) ATM. Other CRDB ATMs are at St Augustine's University, next to the cathedral on Port Rd, and opposite the bus stand. Accepts Visa and MasterCard.

Exim Bank (Tanu Rd) ATM. This is also the best place to change cash. Accepts Visa and MasterCard.

Info Solutions (Uhuru Rd; per hour Tsh2000; ⊙ 8am-6pm Mon-Sat) On the side of the CCM building.

NBC bank (Uhuru Rd) ATM. Accepts Visa and MasterCard.

ℹ Getting There & Away

AIR

There are daily flights between Mtwara and Dar es Salaam (one way Tsh180,000 to Tsh230,000) with **Precision Air** (www.precisionairtz.com; Tanu Rd) and, less reliably **Air Tanzania** (📋 0713 506959, 0713 766230; www.airtanzania.co.tz; Tanu Rd) (four times weekly).

BUS

All long-distance buses depart between about 5am and noon from the main bus stand just off Sokoine Rd near the market.

To Masasi, there are roughly hourly departures between about 6am and 2pm (Tsh7500, five hours); once in Masasi you'll need to change vehicles for Tunduru and Songea.

To Kilwa Masoko, there's currently no direct bus. You'll need to go first to Lindi (Tsh4000, three hours) and get onward transport from there.

To Dar es Salaam, there are daily buses (Tsh26,000, eight hours to Temeke, another hour or two to Ubungo), departing in each direction from 6am. Book in advance. Most start and end in Dar at Temeke's Sudan Market area, where all the southbound bus lines also have booking offices.

To Mozambique, there are several pick-ups and at least one minivan daily to Mahurunga and the Tanzanian immigration post at Kilambo (Tsh5000), departing Mtwara between about 5am and 10am. Departures are from in front of Chilindima Guesthouse, one block south of the main transport stand.

The best places for updated information on the Kilambo river crossing are the Old Boma at Mikindani (p198) and Ten Degrees South Lodge (p198), both in Mikindani. Note that Mozambican visas are not issued at this border and there is no Mozambique consulate in Mtwara (the closest one is in Dar es Salaam).

ℹ Getting Around

Taxis to and from the airport (6km southeast of the main roundabout) cost Tsh10,000 (Tsh5000 in a *bajaji*). Town taxis are difficult to find. *Bajajis* wait at the bus stand and near the CCM building; the cost for a town trip is Tsh1000 to Tsh2000 (Tsh3000 from the town centre to Shangani).

There are a few dalla-dallas running along Tanu Rd to and from the bus stand, although none to Shangani.

Mikindani

Mikindani – set on a picturesque bay surrounded by coconut groves – is a quiet, charming Swahili town with a long history. Although easily visited as a day trip from Mtwara, many travellers prefer it to its larger neighbour as a base for exploring the surrounding area.

For David Livingstone fans, the famous explorer spent a few weeks in the area in 1866 before setting out on his last journey.

◉ Sights & Activities

Boma   HISTORIC BUILDING
The imposing German *boma,* built in 1895 as a fort and administrative centre, has been beautifully renovated as a hotel. Even if you're not staying here, it's worth taking a look and climbing the tower for views over the town.

Slave Market   HISTORIC BUILDING
Downhill from the *boma* is the old Slave Market building, which now houses several craft shops. Unfortunately, it was much less accurately restored than the *boma* and lost much of its architectural interest when its open arches were filled in. The original design is now preserved only on one of Tanzania's postage stamps.

Prison Ruins   RUINS
These ruins are opposite the jetty. Nearby is a large, hollow baobab tree that was once used to keep unruly prisoners in solitary confinement.

ECO2   DIVING
(☎0784 855833; www.eco2tz.com; Main Rd) This good outfit offers PADI instruction and diving in both Mikindani Bay and at Mnazi Bay-Ruvuma Estuary Marine Park.

🛏 Sleeping & Eating

Ten Degrees South Lodge   LODGE $
(ECO2; ☎0766 059380, 0684 059381; www.tendegreessouth.com; Mikindani; d without/with bathroom US$20/60) This good budget travellers' base has four refurbished rooms, all with large double beds and shared bathrooms, plus bay views and deck chairs up on the roof. Next door are a handful of newer, self-contained double-bedded rooms with hot-water showers. There's also an outdoor restaurant-bar with delicious wraps, pancakes, curries and other meals for about Tsh17,000.

★**Old Boma at Mikindani**   HISTORIC HOTEL $$
(☎0756 455978, 023-233 3875; www.mikindani.com; s US$77, r with/without balcony from US$188/120, ste US$223; P@🛜❄) ✈ This beautifully restored building is on a breezy hilltop overlooking the town and Mikindani Bay. It offers spacious, atmospheric, high-ceilinged doubles and the closest to top-end standards that you'll find in these parts. There's a sunset terrace overlooking the bay, a pool surrounded by bougainvillea bushes and lush gardens, and a restaurant.

ℹ Information

The closest banking facilities are in Mtwara.

The Old Boma at Mikindani has a tourist information office and an internet connection. Walking tours of towns and local excursions can be organised here and at Ten Degrees South Lodge.

ℹ Getting There & Away

Mikindani is 10km from Mtwara along a sealed road. Minibuses (Tsh400) run between the two towns throughout the day. Taxis from Mtwara charge from about Ts10,000.

Masasi

Masasi, a scruffy district centre and birthplace of former Tanzanian President Benjamin Mkapa, stretches itself out along the main road off the edge of the Makonde Plateau against a backdrop of granite hills. It's a potentially useful stop if you are travelling to/from Mozambique via the Unity Bridge. If you're cash-strapped there's an NBC bank with an ATM on the main road at the eastern end of town.

🛏 Sleeping & Eating

Holiday Hotel   MOTEL $
(Tunduru Rd; r Tsh35,000) Clean-ish, straightforward rooms with fan in a noisy but convenient location about 100m east of the bus stand.

Sechele Lodge   GUESTHOUSE $
(☎0784 534438; Newala Rd; r Tsh20,000-35,000; P) About 800m from the bus stand along the Newala road, this place has a handful of clean, decent rooms – some with bathrooms, others with a bathroom just outside – and is quieter than the more central guesthouses. Meals are available on order.

❶ Getting There & Away

The bus stand is at the western edge of Masasi at the intersection of the Tunduru, Nachingwea and Newala roads.

To Mtwara, buses go approximately hourly between 6am and 2pm daily (Tsh7500, five hours).

To Newala (Tsh5000, 1½ hours) transport leaves several times daily.

UNDERSTAND TANZANIA

History

Tanzania's history begins with the dawn of humankind. Hominid (human-like) footprints unearthed near Oldupai (Olduvai) Gorge, together with archaeological finds from Kenya and Ethiopia, show that our earliest ancestors were likely roaming the Tanzanian plains over three million years ago.

The Independence Struggle

The 1905 Maji Maji rebellion contains the earliest seeds of Tanzanian independence. During the following decades, the nationalist movement in Tanganyika – which is what mainland Tanzania was then known as – solidified. Farmers' cooperatives began to play an increasingly important political role, as did an up-and-coming group known as the Tanganyika Africa Association (TAA). Soon the TAA came to dominate Tanganyika's political scene, serving as the central channel for grassroots resentment against colonial policies.

In 1953 the TAA elected an eloquent young teacher named Julius Nyerere as its president. He quickly transformed the group into an effective political organisation. A new internal constitution was introduced on 7 July 1954 (now celebrated as Saba Saba Day) and the TAA became the Tanganyika African National Union (TANU), with the rallying cry of *'uhuru na umoja'* (freedom and unity).

Independence was the main item on TANU's agenda. In 1958 and 1959, TANU-supported candidates decisively won general legislative elections, and in 1959 Britain – which at the time held the reins in Tanganyika as governing 'caretaker' – agreed to the establishment of internal self-government. On 9 December 1961 Tanganyika became independent and on 9 December 1962 it was established as a republic, with Nyerere as president.

On the Zanzibar Archipelago, which had been a British protectorate ever since 1890, the predominant push for independence came from the radical Afro-Shirazi Party (ASP). Opposing the ASP were two minority parties, the Zanzibar and Pemba People's Party (ZPPP) and the sultanate-oriented Zanzibar Nationalist Party (ZNP). Both the ZPP and the ZNP parties were favoured by the British. As a result, at Zanzibari independence in December 1963, it was the two minority parties that formed the first government.

This new government did not last long. Within a month, a Ugandan immigrant named John Okello initiated a violent revolution against the ruling ZPPP–ZNP coalition, leading to the toppling of the government and the sultan, and the massacre or expulsion of most of the islands' Arab population. The sultan was replaced by an entity known as the Zanzibar Revolutionary Council, which comprised ASP members and was headed by Abeid Karume.

On 26 April 1964 Nyerere signed an act of union with Karume, thereby creating the United Republic of Tanganyika (renamed the United Republic of Tanzania the following October).

Formation of the union, which was resented by many Zanzibaris from the outset, was motivated in part by the then-prevailing spirit of pan-Africanism, and in part as a Cold War response to the ASP's socialist program.

Karume's government lasted until 1972, when he was assassinated and succeeded by Aboud Jumbe. Shortly thereafter, in an effort to subdue the ongoing unrest resulting from the merger of the islands with the mainland, Nyerere authorised formation of a one-party state and combined TANU and the ASP into a new party known as Chama Cha Mapinduzi (CCM; Party of the Revolution). This merger, which was ratified in a new union constitution on 27 April 1977, marked the beginning of the CCM's dominance of Tanzanian politics, which endures to this day.

The Great Socialist Experiment

Nyerere took the helm of a country that was economically foundering and politically fragile, its stability plagued in particular by the mainland's lack of control over the Zanzibar Archipelago. Education had also been neglected, and at independence there were only a handful of university graduates in the entire country.

THE MAJI MAJI REBELLION

The Maji Maji rebellion, which was the strongest local revolt against the colonial government in German East Africa, is considered to contain some of the earliest seeds of Tanzanian nationalism. It began around the turn of the 20th century when colonial administrators set about establishing enormous cotton plantations in the southeast and along the railway line running from Dar es Salaam towards Morogoro. These plantations required large numbers of workers, most of whom were recruited as forced labour and required to work under miserable salary and living conditions. Anger at this harsh treatment and long-simmering resentment of the colonial government combined to ignite a powerful rebellion. The first outbreak was in 1905 in the area around Kilwa, on the coast. Soon all of southern Tanzania was involved. In addition to deaths on the battlefield, thousands died of hunger brought about by the Germans' scorched-earth policy, in which fields and grain silos in many villages were set on fire. Fatalities were undoubtedly exacerbated by a widespread belief among the Africans that enemy bullets would turn to water before reaching them, and so their warriors would not be harmed – hence the name Maji Maji (*maji* means 'water' in Swahili).

By 1907, when the rebellion was finally suppressed, close to 100,000 people had lost their lives. The Ngoni put up the strongest resistance to the Germans. Following the end of the rebellion, they continued to wage guerrilla-style war until 1908, when the last shreds of their military-based society were destroyed. In order to quell Ngoni resistance once and for all, German troops hanged their leaders and beheaded their most famous chief, Songea.

Among the effects of the Maji Maji uprising were a temporary liberalisation of colonial rule and replacement of the military administration with a civilian government. More significantly, the uprising promoted development of a national identity among many tribal groups and intensified anti-colonial sentiment, kindling the movement for independence.

This inauspicious beginning eventually led to the Arusha Declaration of 1967, which committed Tanzania to a policy of socialism and self-reliance. The policy's cornerstone was the *ujamaa* (familyhood) village – an agricultural collective run along traditional African lines, with an emphasis on self-reliance. Basic goods and tools were to be held in common and shared among members, while each individual was obligated to work on the land.

Tanzania's experiment in socialism was acclaimed in the days following independence, and is credited with unifying the country and expanding education and health care. Economically, however, it was a failure. Per capita income plummeted, agricultural production stagnated and industry limped along at less than 50% of capacity. The decline was precipitated by a combination of factors, including steeply rising oil prices, the 1977 break-up of the East African Community (an economic and customs union between Tanzania, Kenya and Uganda), and sharp drops in the value of coffee and sisal exports.

Democracy

Nyerere was re-elected to a fifth term in 1980, amid continuing dissatisfaction with the great socialist experiment in the country. In 1985 he resigned from political office, handing over power to Zanzibari Ali Hassan Mwinyi. Mwinyi tried to distance himself from Nyerere and his policies, and instituted an economic recovery program. Yet the pace of change remained slow, and Mwinyi's presidency was unpopular. The collapse of European communism in the early 1990s, and pressure from Western donor nations, accelerated the move towards multiparty politics, and in 1992 the constitution was amended to legalise opposition parties.

Since then, four national elections have been held, generally proceeding relatively smoothly on the mainland, less so on the Zanzibar Archipelago, where tensions between the CCM and the opposition Civic United Front (CUF) are strong. In elections in 2010, Jakaya Mrisho Kikwete was elected president for a second term with 62% of the vote. His main opposition was candidate Willibrod Slaa of the Party for Democracy and Progress, who garnered 27% of the vote – the most decisive opposition showing to date in Tanzania's history. The next elections are scheduled for October 2015. As of this writing, the field of potential candidates is still wide open.

People

Tanzania is home to about 120 tribal groups, in addition to relatively small but economically significant numbers of Asians and Arabs, and a miniscule European community. Most tribes are very small; almost 100 of them combined account for only one-third of the total population. As a result, none has succeeded in dominating politically or culturally, although groups such as the Chagga and the Haya, who have a long tradition of education, are disproportionately well represented in government and business circles.

About 95% of Tanzanians are of Bantu origin. These include the Sukuma (who live around Mwanza and southern Lake Victoria, and constitute approximately 16% of the overall population), the Nyamwezi (around Tabora), the Makonde (Southeastern Tanzania), the Haya (around Bukoba) and the Chagga (around Mt Kilimanjaro). The Maasai and several smaller groups incorporating the Arusha and the Samburu (all in northern Tanzania) are of Nilo-Hamitic or Nilotic origin. The Iraqw, around Karatu and northwest of Lake Manyara, are Cushitic, as are the tiny northern-central tribes of Gorowa and Burungi. The Sandawe and, more distantly, the seminomadic Hadzabe (around Lake Eyasi), belong to the Khoisan ethno-linguistic family.

Tribal structures, however, range from weak to nonexistent – a legacy of Nyerere's abolishment of local chieftaincies following independence.

About 3% of Tanzania's total population live on the Zanzibar Archipelago, with about one-third of these on Pemba. Most African Zanzibaris belong to one of three groups: the Hadimu, the Tumbatu and the Pemba. Members of the non-African Zanzibari population are primarily Shirazi and consider themselves descendants of immigrants from Shiraz in Persia (Iran).

Religion

About 35% of Tanzanians are Muslim and between 35% and 40% are Christian. The remainder follow traditional religions. There are also small communities of Hindus, Sikhs and Ismailis. Muslims are traditionally found along the coast and in the inland towns that line the old caravan routes. The population of the Zanzibar Archipelago is almost exclusively Sunni Muslim, with tiny Christian and Hindu communities.

Music & Dance

The greatest influence on Tanzania's modern music scene has been the Congolese bands that began playing in Dar es Salaam in the early 1960s, and the late Remmy Ongala ('Dr Remmy'), who was born in the Democratic Republic of the Congo (DRC: formerly Zaïre), but gained his fame in Tanzania.

On Zanzibar, the music scene has long been dominated by *taarab*.

Visual Arts

Tanzania's Makonde, together with their Mozambican counterparts, are renowned throughout East Africa for their original and highly fanciful carvings. Although originally from the Southeast around the Makonde Plateau, commercial realities lured many Makonde north. Today the country's main carving centre is at Mwenge (p60) in Dar es Salaam, where blocks of hard African blackwood *(Dalbergia melanoxylon* or, in Swahili, *mpingo)* come to life under the hands of skilled artists.

ℹ CULTURAL TIPS

➡ Take time for greetings and pleasantries.

➡ Before entering someone's house, call out *hodi* (May I enter?), then wait for the inevitable *karibu* (welcome).

➡ Don't eat or pass things with the left hand.

➡ Respect authority: losing your patience is always counterproductive; deference and good humour will see you through most situations.

➡ Avoid criticising the government.

➡ Receive gifts with both hands, or with the right hand while touching the left hand to your right elbow.

➡ Always ask before photographing people.

TAARAB MUSIC

No visit to Zanzibar would be complete without spending an evening listening to the evocative strains of *taarab*, the archipelago's most famous musical export. A traditional *taarab* orchestra consists of several dozen musicians using both Western and traditional instruments, including the violin, the *kanun* (similar to a zither), the accordion, the *nay* (an Arabic flute) and drums, plus a singer. There's generally no written music, and songs – often with themes centred on love – are full of puns and double meanings.

Taarab-style music was played in Zanzibar as early as the 1820s at the sultan's palace, where it had been introduced from Arabia. However, it wasn't until the 1900s, when Sultan Seyyid Hamoud bin Muhammed encouraged formation of the first *taarab* clubs, that it became more formalised.

A good time to see *taarab* performances is during the **Festival of the Dhow Countries** (www.ziff.or.tz) in July.

Environment & National Parks

At over 943,000 sq km (almost four times the size of the UK), Tanzania is East Africa's largest country. It is bordered to the east by the Indian Ocean. To the west are the deep lakes of the Western Rift Valley with mountains rising up from their shores. Much of central Tanzania is an arid highland plateau averaging 900m to 1800m in altitude and nestled between the eastern and western branches of the Great Rift Valley.

Tanzania's mountain ranges are grouped into a sharply rising northeastern section (Eastern Arc), and an open, rolling central and southern section (the Southern Highlands or Southern Arc). A range of volcanoes, the Crater Highlands, rises from the side of the Great Rift Valley in northern Tanzania.

The largest river is the Rufiji, which drains the Southern Highlands en route to the coast. The Ruvuma River forms the border with Mozambique.

Wildlife

ANIMALS

Tanzania's fauna is notable for its sheer numbers and its variety, with 430 species and subspecies among the country's more than four million wild animals. These include zebras, elephants, wildebeests, buffaloes, hippos, giraffes, antelopes, dik-diks, gazelles, elands and kudus. Tanzania is known for its predators, with Serengeti National Park one of the best places for spotting lions, cheetahs and leopards. There are also hyenas and wild dogs and, in Gombe and Mahale Mountains National Parks, chimpanzees. Complementing this are over 1000 bird species of birds, including many endemics.

PLANTS

Small patches of tropical rainforest in Tanzania's Eastern Arc mountains provide home to a rich assortment of plants, many found nowhere else in the world. These include the Usambara or African violet *(Saintpaulia)* and *Impatiens*, which are sold as house plants in grocery stores throughout the West. Similar forest patches – remnants of the much larger tropical forest that once extended across the continent – are also found in the Udzungwas, Ulugurus and several other areas. South and west of the Eastern Arc range are stands of baobab.

Away from the mountain ranges, much of the country is covered by *miombo* ('moist' woodland), where the main vegetation is various types of *Brachystegia* tree. Much of the dry central plateau is covered with savannah, bushland and thickets, while grasslands cover the Serengeti Plain and other areas that lack good drainage.

National Parks & Reserves

Tanzania has 16 mainland national parks, 14 wildlife reserves, the Ngorongoro Conservation Area, three marine parks and several protected marine reserves.

NATIONAL PARKS

Tanzania's national parks are managed by the **Tanzania National Parks Authority** (Tanapa; www.tanzaniaparks.com; Dodoma Rd, Arusha).

Park entry fees, which are posted on the Tanapa website, range from US$30 to US$100 per adult per day, depending on the park. Other costs include guide fees of US$20 to US$25 per group for walking safaris, plus vehicle fees (US$40 per foreign-registered vehicle and Tsh20,000 for Tanzania-registered vehicles).

WILDLIFE RESERVES

Wildlife reserves are administered by the **Wildlife Division of the Ministry of Natural Resources & Tourism** (☏ 022-286 6064, 022-286 6376; scp@africaonline.co.tz; cnr Nyerere & Changombe Rds, Dar es Salaam). Selous is the only reserve with tourist infrastructure. Large areas of most others have been leased as hunting concessions, as has the southern Selous.

MARINE PARKS & RESERVES

Mafia Island Marine Park and the Dar es Salaam Marine Reserves (Mbudya, Bongoyo, Pangavini and Fungu Yasini Islands) and Tanzania's other marine protected areas are under the jurisdiction of the Ministry of Natural Resources & Tourism's **Marine Parks & Reserves Unit** (Map p58; www.marineparks. go.tz; Olympio St, Upanga, Dar es Salaam).

NGORONGORO CONSERVATION AREA

The Ngorongoro Conservation Area was established as a multiple-use area to protect wildlife and the pastoralist lifestyle of the Maasai, who had lost other large areas of their traditional territory with the formation of Serengeti National Park. It is administered by the **Ngorongoro Conservation Area Authority** (www.ngorongorocrater.org).

SURVIVAL GUIDE

❶ Directory A–Z

ACCOMMODATION

➡ Most upmarket hotels consider July, August and the Christmas and New Year holidays to be high season. A peak-season surcharge is sometimes levied on top of regular high-season rates from late December through early January.

➡ During the March to early June low season, it's often possible to negotiate significant discounts (up to 50%) on room rates.

➡ A residents' permit entitles you to discounts at some hotels and at national parks.

Camping

Carry a tent to save money and for flexibility off the beaten track. Note that camping in most national parks costs at least US$30 per person per night. All parks have campsites, designated as either 'public' ('ordinary') or 'special'. For most national park campsites, you'll need to bring everything in with you, including drinking water. Most parks also have simple huts or cottages (*bandas*), several have basic resthouses. Both the *bandas* and the resthouses have communal cooking facilities.

National Park Public Campsites These have toilets (usually pit latrines) and, sometimes, a water source.

National Park Special Campsites These are smaller, more remote and more expensive than public campsites, with no facilities. The idea is that the area remains as close to pristine as possible. Advance booking required; once you make a booking, the special campsite is reserved exclusively for your group.

Elsewhere There are campsites situated in or near most major towns, near many of the national parks and in some scenic locations along a few of the main highways (ie Dar es Salaam–Mbeya, and Tanga–Moshi).

Camping away from established sites is generally not advisable. In rural areas, seek permission first from the village head or elders before pitching your tent.

Camping is not permitted on Zanzibar.

Guesthouses

➡ In Tanzanian Swahili, *hotel* or *hoteli* refers to food and drink rather than accommodation. The better term if you're looking for somewhere to sleep is *nyumba ya kulala wageni* – or less formally, *pa kulala*.

➡ Water can be a problem during the dry season, and many of the cheapest places

---

NATIONAL PARK FEES

In theory, for all national parks and for Ngorongoro Conservation Area, entry fees and all other park fees must be paid electronically with a Visa card or MasterCard. However, if the park credit card machine is broken (a frequent occurrence), or not yet installed (as is the case in many parks outside the northern circuit), visitors are required to pay in US dollars cash. Some parks also accept Tanzanian shillings. It's also possible to pay using a 'smart card' available for purchase from CRDB and Exim banks. Until the kinks in the system are sorted out, our advice is to bring both a Visa or MasterCard and sufficient US dollars cash to cover payment of park entry fees, guide fees and park-run accommodation.

won't have running or hot water, though all will arrange a bucket if you ask.

Hotels & Lodges

➡ En suite rooms are widely referred to in Tanzania as 'self-contained' or 'self-containers' rooms.

➡ There's a good selection of midrange and top-end accommodation in major towns, as well as beautiful luxury lodges on safari and along the coast.

ACTIVITIES
Birdwatching

Birdwatching resources include the **Tanzania Bird Atlas** (www.tanzaniabirdatlas.com), the **Tanzania Hotspots page** (www.camacdonald. com/birding/africatanzania.htm) and **Tanzanian Birds & Butterflies** (www.tanzaniabirds.net).

Cycling

Tanzania bicycling contacts include the following:

Afriroots (www.afriroots.co.tz) Runs a Sunday-morning history walk (US$50 per person) around the centre of Dar es Salaam, exploring Dar's evolution from the Omani sultanate to key ANC and Frelimo hotspots in the struggle for independence. Also excellent is the 'behind-the-scenes' cycle tour ($40 per person) where you'll get to meet locals and hear their stories about living in the city. Proceeds from the tours benefit the communities you visit. Afriroots' community work extends beyond Dar to interesting hiking and cycling safaris.

International Bicycle Fund (www.ibike.org/ bikeafrica) Organises cycling tours in Tanzania and provides information.

Summits Africa (www.summits-africa.com; upper midrange & top end) Upmarket adventure safaris, including treks in the Ngorongoro Conservation Area and to Lake Natron with the option to climb Ol Doinyo Lengai, West Kilimanjaro walking safaris, multiday fully equipped bike safaris and combination bike–safari trips. Wayo Africa (p117) Upmarket rides around Arusha and in the Lake Manyara region.

Hiking & Trekking

Except in the western Usambaras around Lushoto (where there's an informal guide organisation and a network of guesthouses) and in the Crater Highlands (where most hiking is organised through operators), you'll need to organise things yourself when hiking in Tanzania. In most areas it's required or recommended to go with a guide, which, apart from adding to the cost, can feel constraining if you're used to just setting off on your own. When formalising your arrangements, be sure you and the guide agree on how much territory will be covered each day, as local expectations about suitable daily sections on standard routes are often unsatisfyingly short if you're an experienced hiker. A number of trekking operators (for Mt Kilimanjaro and Mt Meru treks), are located in Arusha, Moshi and Marangu; many safari operators also organise treks. All trekking requires local guides and (usually) porters.

Horse Riding

Riding safaris are possible in the West Kilimanjaro and Lake Natron areas. Contacts include **Equestrian Safaris** (www.safaririding.com) and **Makoa Farm** (☑ 0754 312896; www.makoa-farm.com; rates vary with packages; Ⓟ).

CUSTOMS REGULATIONS

Exporting seashells, coral, ivory and turtle shells is illegal. You can export a maximum of Tsh2000 without declaration. There's no limit on the importation of foreign currency; amounts over US$10,000 must be declared.

EMBASSIES & CONSULATES

Embassies and consulates in Dar es Salaam include the following:

Australian Consulate (www.embassy.gov.au) Contact the Canadian embassy.

British High Commission (Map p58; ☑ 022-229 0000; http://ukintanzania.fco.gov.uk; Umoja House, cnr Mirambo St & Garden Ave)

Burundian Embassy (Map p54; ☑ 022-212 7008; Lugalo St, Upanga) Just up from the Italian embassy, opposite the army compound and near Palm Beach Hotel. One-month single-entry visas cost US$90 plus one photo. The consulate in Kigoma also issues single- and multiple-entry visas.

Canadian High Commission (Map p58; ☑ 022-216 3300; www.canadainternational. gc.ca/tanzania-tanzanie/index.aspx; Umoja House, cnr Mirambo St & Garden Ave)

Democratic Republic of the Congo Embassy (formerly Zaïre) (Map p54; 435 Maliki Rd, Upanga) Visas are only issued to Tanzania residents. Any visa issued in Tanzania will not be honoured on entry in the DRC unless you have a Tanzania resident's permit.

French Embassy (Map p54; ☑ 022-219 8800; www.ambafrance-tz.org; 7 Ali Hassan Mwinyi Rd)

German Embassy (Map p58; ☑ 022-211 7409-15; www.daressalam.diplo.de; Umoja House, cnr Mirambo St & Garden Ave)

Indian High Commission (Map p54; ☑ 022-266 9040; www.hcindiatz.org; 82 Kinondoni Rd)

Irish Embassy (Map p54; ☑ 022-260 0629, 022-260 2355; www.embassyofireland.or.tz; 353 Toure Dr) Diagonally opposite Golden Tulip Hotel.

Italian Embassy (Map p54; ☑ 022-211 5935; www.ambdaressalaam.esteri.it; 316 Lugalo St, Upanga)

Kenyan High Commisssion (Map p54; ☑ 022-266 8285/6; www.kenyahighcomtz.org; cnr Ali Hassan Mwinyi Rd & Kaunda Dr, Oysterbay)

Malawian High Commission (Map p58; ☑ 022-277 4308, 022-277 4220; mmhcrdar@yahoo.co.uk; Rose Garden Rd, Mikocheni B) Many nationalities, including USA, UK and various European countries, do not require visas.

Mozambique High Commission (Map p58; ☑ 022-212 4673; 25 Garden Ave) One-month single-entry visas cost US$50 plus two photos, and are issued within five days (US$100 for 24-hour service).

Netherlands Embassy (Map p58; ☑ 022-211 0000; http://tanzania.nlembassy.org; Umoja House, cnr Mirambo St & Garden Ave)

Rwandan Embassy (Map p54; ☑ 0754 787835, 022-260 0500; www.tanzania.embassy.gov.rw; 32 Ali Hassan Mwinyi Rd) Three-month single-entry visas cost US$50 plus two photos, and are issued within four days. Citizens of the USA, Germany, South Africa, Canada and various other countries do not require visas.

Ugandan Embassy (Map p54; ☑ 022-266 7391; info@ughc.co.tz; 25 Msasani Rd) One-month single-entry visas cost US$50 plus two photos and are issued within 24 hours. Located opposite Oyster Bay Secondary School.

US Embassy (Map p54; ☑ 022-229 4000; http://tanzania.usembassy.gov; Old Bagamoyo & Kawawa Rds)

Zambian High Commission (Map p58; ☑ 022-212 5529; ground fl, Zambia House, cnr Ohio St & Sokoine Dr) One-month single-entry visas cost US$50 plus two photos, and are issued within two days.

GAY & LESBIAN TRAVELLERS

Homosexuality is officially illegal in Tanzania, including Zanzibar, incurring penalties of up to 14 years imprisonment. Prosecutions are rare, but public displays of affection, whether between people of the same or opposite sex, are frowned upon, and homosexuality is culturally taboo.

INTERNET ACCESS

If you will be in Tanzania for a while, consider buying a USB stick from one of the main mobile providers (US$25 to US$60), which you can then load with airtime (about Tsh10,000 for 1GB, valid for seven days) and plug into your laptop. Wireless access is easy to find in major cities.

LANGUAGE COURSES

Institute of Swahili & Foreign Languages (Map p68; ☑ 024-223 0724, 024-223 3337; www.suza.ac.tz; Vuga Rd; per hour/week US$10/200) Zanzibar is regarded as the home of Kiswahili, making this a great place to take some lessons. Experienced teachers and structured courses are offered by the institute along with homestay hook-ups (full board US$20 per person per night) and cultural excursions accompanied by a teacher.

KIU Ltd (☑ 0754 271263; www.swahilicourses.com) At various locations in Dar es Salaam, plus branches in Iringa and Zanzibar.

Makoko Language School (☑ 028-264 2518; swahilimusoma@juasun.net) This long-standing church-run school is in Makoko neighbourhood, on the outskirts of Musoma.

MS Training Centre for Development Cooperation (☑ 0754 651715, 027-254 1044; www.mstcdc.or.tz) About 15km outside Arusha, near Usa River.

Rivervalley Campsite (☑ 026-270 1988; www.rivervalleycampsites.com) Near Iringa.

University of Dar es Salaam (www.iks.udsm.ac.tz)

LEGAL MATTERS

Apart from traffic offences such as speeding and driving without a seatbelt (mandatory for driver and front-seat passengers), the main area to watch out for is drug use and possession. In Dar es Salaam, the typical scam is that you'll be approached by a couple of men who walk along with you, strike up a conversation and try to sell you drugs. Before you've had a chance to shake them loose, policemen (sometimes legitimate, sometimes not) suddenly appear and insist that you pay a huge fine for being involved in the purchase of illegal drugs. Protestations to the contrary are generally futile and there's often little you can do other than instantly hightailing it in the opposite direction if you smell this scam coming. If you are caught, insist on going to the nearest police station before paying anything and whittle the bribe down as far as you can. Initial demands may be as high as US$300, but savvy travellers should be able to get away with under US$50.

MAPS

Good country maps include those published by Nelles and Harms IC, both available in Tanzania and elsewhere, and both also including Rwanda and Burundi. Harms IC also publishes maps for Lake Manyara National Park, the Ngorongoro Conservation Area and Zanzibar. Hand-drawn 'MaCo' maps cover Zanzibar, Arusha and the northern parks.

MONEY

→ Tanzania's currency is the Tanzanian shilling (Tsh). There are bills of Tsh10,000, 5000, 1000 and 500, and coins of Tsh200, 100, 50, 20, 10, five and one shilling(s) (the latter three coins are rarely used).

→ Bill design has recently been changed for all amounts, with both the old and new styles currently accepted and in circulation.

→ Credit cards are not widely accepted. Where they are accepted, it's sometimes only with commissions. As a result, you will need to rely here rather heavily on cash and ATMs.

→ A Visa or MasterCard is essential for accessing money from ATMs.

→ Visa or MasterCard is required for paying entry fees at most national parks.

→ US dollar bills dated prior to 2006 are not accepted anywhere.

ATMs

ATMs are widespread in major towns, and all are open 24 hours. But they are often temporarily out of service or out of cash, so have back-up funds. All allow you to withdraw shillings with a Visa (most widely accepted) or MasterCard. Withdrawals are usually to a maximum of Tsh300,000 to Tsh400,000 per transaction (ATMs in small towns often have a limit of Tsh200,000 per transaction) with a daily limit of Tsh1.2 million.

Cash

US dollars, followed by euros, are the most convenient foreign currencies and get the best rates, although other major currencies are readily accepted in major centres. Bring a mix of large and small denominations, but note that US$50 and US$100 note bills get better rates of exchange than smaller denominations. Old-style (small head) US dollar bills and US dollar bills dated prior to 2006 are not accepted anywhere.

Credit Cards

Credit cards, mainly Visa, are essential for withdrawing money at ATMs. And, a Visa or MasterCard is required for paying park fees at many national parks. For payment, some upmarket hotels and tour operators accept credit cards, often with a commission averaging 5% to 10%, but confirm in advance.

Exchanging Money

→ Change cash at banks or foreign exchange (forex) bureaus in major towns and cities; rates and commissions vary, so shop around.

→ To reconvert Tanzanian shillings to hard currency, save at least some of your exchange receipts, although they are seldom checked. The easiest places to reconvert currency are at the airports in Dar es Salaam and Kilimanjaro, or try at forex bureaus in major towns.

→ For after-hours exchange and exchanging in small towns, as well as for reconverting back to dollars or euros, many Indian-owned businesses will change money, although often at bad rates.

→ In theory, it's required for foreigners to pay for accommodation, park fees, organised tours, upscale hotels and the Zanzibar ferries in US dollars, though (with the exception of some parks, where Visa card or US dollars are required) shillings are accepted almost everywhere at the going rate.

Taxes

Tanzania has an 18% value-added tax (VAT) that's usually included in quoted prices.

Tipping

On treks and safaris, it's common practice to tip drivers, guides, porters and other staff.

Travellers Cheques

Travellers cheques cannot be changed anywhere in Tanzania.

PUBLIC HOLIDAYS

New Year's Day 1 January
Zanzibar Revolution Day 12 January
Easter March/April – Good Friday, Holy Saturday and Easter Monday
Union Day 26 April
Labour Day 1 May
Saba Saba (Peasants' Day) 7 July
Nane Nane (Farmers' Day) 8 August
Independence Day 9 December
Christmas Day 25 December
Boxing Day 26 December

Islamic holidays are also celebrated as public holidays; see p626.

TELEPHONE

The major mobile companies are currently Vodacom, Airtel, Tigo and (on Zanzibar) Zantel. To reach a mobile telephone number from outside Tanzania, dial the country code, then the mobile phone code without the initial 0, and then the six-digit number. From within Tanzania, keep the initial 0 and don't use any other area code. Dialling from your own mobile is generally the cheapest way to call internationally.

Phone Codes

To make an international call, dial ☑ 000, followed by the country code, local area code (without the initial '0') and telephone number.

All landline telephone numbers are seven digits. Area codes (included with all numbers in listings) must be used whenever you dial long-distance.

TIME

Tanzania time is GMT/UTC plus three hours. There is no daylight saving.

TOURIST INFORMATION

The **Tanzania Tourist Board** (TTB; www. tanzaniatouristboard.com) is the official tourism entity.

VISAS

Almost everyone needs a visa, which costs US$50 for most nationalities (US$100 for citizens of the USA) for a single-entry visa valid for up to three months. Officially, visas must be obtained in advance by all travellers who come from a country with Tanzania diplomatic representation. One-month single-entry visas (but not multiple-entry visas) are also currently issued on arrival (no matter your provenance) at both Dar es Salaam and Kilimanjaro International Airports, at the Namanga border post between Tanzania and Kenya, and at the Tunduma border (between Tanzania and Zambia). In practice, visas are currently also readily issued at most other major land borders and ports (US dollars cash only, single entry only) with a minimum of hassle. Our advice: get your visa in advance if possible. If not possible, don't despair; it's well worth giving it a try at the border.

Visa Extensions

One month is the normal visa validity and three months the maximum. For extensions within the three-month limit, there are immigration offices in all major towns; the process is free and straightforward. Extensions after three months are difficult; you usually need to leave the country and apply for a new visa.

VOLUNTEERING

Volunteering opportunities are usually best arranged prior to arriving in Tanzania. Note that the Tanzanian government has recently changed the cost of volunteer (Class C) resident permits to US$200 for three months.

Help2kids (www.help2kids.org)

Indigenous Education Foundation of Tanzania (www.ieftz.org) Education work in Maasai areas of northern Tanzania.

Kigamboni Community Centre (www.kccdar. com) Teaching and other opportunities in a rural community on the outskirts of Dar es Salaam.

Trade Aid (www.tradeaiduk.org/volunteer. html) Skills training work in Mikindani village in southern Tanzania.

Ujamaa Hostel (www.ujamaahostel.com) Tutoring, skills training and health work in and around Arusha.

❶ Getting There & Away

ENTERING THE COUNTRY

➡ Visas are usually available at major points of entry, and must be paid for in US dollars cash.

➡ Yellow fever vaccination is required if you are arriving from an endemic area (which includes many of Tanzania's neighbours).

AIR
Airports

Julius Nyerere International Airport (DAR; ☑ 022-284 2402; www.taa.go.tz) Dar es Salaam; Tanzania's air hub.

Kilimanjaro International Airport (JRO; ☑ 027-255 4707, 027-255 4252; www. kilimanjaroairport.co.tz) Between Arusha and Moshi, and the best option for itineraries in Arusha and the northern safari circuit. (Note: not to be confused with the smaller Arusha airport (ARK), 8km west of Arusha, which handles domestic flights only.)

Kigoma airport (TKQ) Occasional regional flights.

Mtwara airport (MYW) Regional flights.

Mwanza airport (MWZ) Regional flights.

Songwe airport Near Mbeya; regional flights.

Zanzibar International Airport (ZNZ) International and regional flights.

Airlines

Regional carriers include the following (all servicing Dar es Salaam, except as noted):

Air Kenya (www.airkenya.com) Nairobi (Kenya) to Kilimanjaro International Airport (KIA).

Air Tanzania (p212) Bujumbura (Burundi) to Dar es Salaam.

Air Uganda (www.air-uganda.com) Entebbe (Uganda) to KIA and Dar es Salaam.

Fastjet (☑ 0685-680533; www.fastjet.com) Johannesburg (South Africa), Harare (Zimbabwe) and Lusaka (Zambia) to Dar es Salaam.

Kenya Airways (Map p58; ☑ 0786-390004, 0786-390005; www.kenya-airways.com; Upanga Rd) Nairobi (Kenya) to Dar es Salaam and KIA.

Precision Air (p212) Dar es Salaam to Entebbe (Uganda), Kigali (Rwanda), Nairobi (Kenya), Pemba (Mozambique), Lubumbashi (DRC) and Lusaka (Zambia).

ZanAir (p212) Mombasa to Arusha airport.

LAND

Buses cross Tanzania's borders with Kenya, Uganda, Rwanda, Burundi and Zambia.

➸ At the border, you'll need to disembark on each side to take care of visa formalities, then reboard and continue on. Visa fees aren't included in bus ticket prices for trans-border routes.

➸ For crossings with other countries, you'll need to take one vehicle to the border and board a different vehicle on the other side.

To enter Tanzania with your own vehicle you'll need:

➸ the vehicle's registration papers

➸ your driving licence

➸ temporary import permit (Tsh20,000 for one month, purchased at the border) or a *carnet de passage en douane*

➸ third-party insurance (Tsh50,000 for one year, purchased at the border or at the local insurance headquarters in the nearest large town)

➸ one-time fuel levy (Tsh5000)

Burundi

The main crossings are at Kobero Bridge between Ngara (Tanzania) and Muyinga (Burundi); and, at Manyovu (north of Kigoma).

Kobero Bridge From Mwanza, Zuberly and Nyehunge lines have buses daily at 5.30am to Ngara (Tsh17,000, seven to eight hours). Also, shared taxis run all day from Nyakanazi to Ngara (Tsh9500, two hours). Once in Ngara, there is onward transport to the Tanzanian border post at Kabanga.

Manyovu Hamza Transport and Burugo Travel (both with ticket offices at Kigoma's Bero bus stand) have direct service between Kigoma and Bujumbura (Burundi; Tsh15,000, seven hours) at 7am several times weekly. Otherwise, take a dalla-dalla from Kigoma to Manyovu (Tsh5000, one to two hours), walk through immigration and find onward transport. There's always something going to Mabanda (Burundi), where you can find minibuses to Bujumbura, three to four hours away.

Kenya

The main route to/from Kenya is the good sealed road connecting Arusha (Tanzania) and Nairobi (Kenya) via the Namanga border post (open 24 hours). There are also border crossings at Horohoro (Tanzania), north of Tanga; at Holili (Tanzania), east of Moshi; at Loitokitok (Kenya), northeast of Moshi; and, at Sirari (Tanzania), northeast of Musoma. With the exception of the Serengeti–Masai Mara crossing (which is currently closed), there is public transport across all Tanzania–Kenya border posts.

TRANSPORT IN TANZANIA

Tanzania has an extensive, albeit adventuresome, bus network and good domestic flight connections.

➸ Away from main routes (which are paved), expect lots of bumping and dust (or mud, during the rains).

➸ Distances and travel times are long. Don't try to squeeze too much in, and consider an internal flight or two.

➸ Trains are slow. Take them for glimpses into local life, rather than for efficiency.

➸ Never travel at night, especially on buses.

➸ Keep your luggage with you in the main part of the bus, and try to sit on the shadier side.

➸ Buy bus tickets the day before to minimise bus station chaos and dealings with touts on the morning of travel. Only buy your ticket from a proper office, not from a tout outside.

➸ Be prepared for hair-raising speeds.

Kisii Buses go daily from Mwanza to the Sirari–Isebania border post (Tsh10,000, four to five hours), where you can get Kenyan transport to Kisii. Also, several dalla-dallas go daily from Musoma to the border (Tsh6000, one hour).

Mombasa There are daily trips with **Modern Coast Express** (www.moderncoastexpress. com) between Dar es Salaam and Mombasa via Tanga, departing in the morning in each direction, and departing around noon from Tanga (Tsh15,000, four to five hours Tanga to Mombasa; Tsh25,000, 10 to 11 hours Dar to Mombasa). There's nowhere official to change money at the border. Touts here charge extortionate rates, and it's difficult to get rid of Kenyan shillings once in Tanga, so plan accordingly.

Nairobi Dar Express goes daily between Dar es Salaam and Nairobi (Tsh57,000, 14 to 15 hours), departing about 6am in each direction. You can also board in Arusha (Tsh23,000, five hours), if seats are available. Dar Express also has Nairobi-bound buses that begin in Arusha, leaving at 2pm.

Comfortable nine-seater minivans (Tsh7500, two hours) and decrepit, overcrowded full-sized vans (which stop frequently along the way) go between Arusha's central bus station (they park at the northernmost end) and the Namanga border frequently throughout the day from 6am. At Namanga, you'll have to walk a few hundred metres across the border and then catch one of the frequent *matatus* (Kenyan minibuses) or shared taxis to Nairobi (KSh500). From Nairobi, the *matatu* and share-taxi depots are on Ronald Ngala St, near the River Rd junction.

The most convenient and comfortable option between Moshi or Arusha and Nairobi are the shuttle buses. They depart daily from Arusha and Nairobi at 8am and 2pm (five hours) and from Moshi (seven hours) at 6am and 11am. The nonresident rate is US$25/30 one way from Arusha/Moshi, but with a little prodding it's usually possible to get the resident rate (Tsh25,000/30,000). Pick-ups and drop-offs are at their offices and centrally located hotels. Depending on the timing, they may pick you up or drop you off at Kilimanjaro International Airport. Confirm locations when booking.

Recommended companies:

Impala Shuttle (☏ 027-250 7197, 027-250 8451; Impala Hotel, Simeon Rd; per person US$25; ☉8am & 2pm) Leaves from the car park of the Impala Hotel.

Jamii Shuttle (off Simeon Rd; per person US$25; ☉8am & 2pm) Departs/arrives from just off Simeon Rd in Eastern Arusha.

Rainbow Shuttle (India St; per person US$25; ☉8am & 2pm) Booking office and departure point on India St.

Voi Raqib Coach's daily 8.30am bus from Moshi to Mombasa travels via Voi (Tsh16,000, four hours). Also, dalla-dallas go frequently between Moshi and the border town of Holili (Tsh2000, one hour). At the **border** (open 6am to 8pm) you'll need to hire a *piki-piki* (motorbike; Tsh1000) or bicycle to cross 3km of no-man's land before arriving at the Kenyan immigration post at Taveta. From Taveta, sporadic minibuses go to Voi along a rough road, where you can then find onward transport to Nairobi and Mombasa. If you're arriving/departing with a foreign-registered vehicle, the necessary paperwork is only done during working hours (8am to 1pm and 2pm to 5pm daily).

Malawi

The only crossing is at **Kasumulu** (Songwe River Bridge; ☉7am-7pm Tanzanian time, 6am-6pm Malawi time), southeast of Mbeya (Tanzania).

➡ From Mbeya there are daily minibuses and 30-seater buses (known as 'Coastals' or *thelathini*) to the border (Tsh5500, two hours). Once through the Tanzanian border post, there's a 300m walk to the Malawian side, and minibuses to Karonga. There's also one Malawian bus daily between the Malawi side of the border and Mzuzu (Malawi), departing the border by midafternoon and arriving by evening.

➡ Look for buses going to Kyela (these detour to the border) and verify that your vehicle is really going all the way to the border, as some that say they are actually stop at Tukuyu (40km north) or at Ibanda (7km before the border). Asking several passengers (rather than the minibus company touts) should get you the straight answer.

➡ Your chances of getting a direct vehicle are better in the larger *thelathini*, which depart from Mbeya two or three times daily and usually go where they say they are going.

➡ The border buses stop at the Kasumulu transport stand, about a seven-minute walk from the actual border; there's no real need for the bicycle taxis that will approach you.

➡ There are currently no cross-border vehicles from Mbeya into Malawi, although touts at Mbeya bus station may try to convince you otherwise. Going in both directions, plan on overnighting in Mbeya; buses from Mbeya to Dar es Salaam depart between 6am and 7am.

➡ If you get stuck at the Kasumulu border, there are basic bungalows, camping and meals at **MG Campsite Park** (☏ 0732 950054; malagcamp@yahoo.com; camping US$5, r US$10-20) and basic rooms (but no food) at **Lug Lodge** (☏ 0754 630531, 0758 913383; Main Road; r Tsh20,000-25,000).

Mozambique

The main vehicle crossing is via Unity Bridge over the Ruvuma at Negomano (Mozambique), reached via Masasi (Tanzania). There is also the Unity 2 bridge across the Ruvuma at Mtomoni village (Tanzania), 120km south of Songea. It's also possible to cross at Kilambo (south of Mtwara, Tanzania) via vehicle ferry. For those travelling along the coast by boat, there are immigration officials at Msimbati (Tanzania) and at Palma and Moçimboa da Praia (Mozambique). Mozambique visas are not issued anywhere along the Tanzania border, so arrange one in advance.

Buses depart daily from Mtwara between 5am and 10am to the Kilambo border post (Tsh5000, one hour) and on to the Ruvuma, which is crossed via dugout canoe and other small boats (Tsh5000 to Tsh10,000 depending on your negotiating skills; 10 minutes to one-hour-plus depending on water levels). There's also the **MV Kilambo** (per person/vehicle Tsh500/30,000) ferry, which is the best option when it's running. Once at the Mozambique side, there are usually two pick-ups daily to the Mozambique border post (4km further) and on to Moçimboa da Praia (US$13), with the last one departing by about noon. The Ruvuma crossing is notorious for pickpockets. Watch your belongings, especially when getting into and out of the boats, and keep up with the crowd when walking to/from the river bank.

Further west, one or two vehicles daily depart from Songea's Majengo C area by around 11am (Tsh12,000, three to four hours) to Mitomoni village and the Unity 2 bridge. Once across, you can get Mozambique transport on to Lichinga (Tsh25,000 to Tsh30,000, five hours). It's best to pay in stages, rather than paying the entire Tsh33,000 to Tsh40,000 Songea–Lichinga fare in Songea, as is sometimes requested. With an early departure, the entire Songea–Lichinga trip is very doable in one day via public transport.

The main vehicle crossing is via the Unity Bridge at Negomano, southwest of Kilambo, near the confluence of the Lugenda River. From Masasi, go about 35km southwest along the Tunduru road to Nangomba village, from where a 68km good-condition track leads southwest down to Masuguru village. The bridge is 10km further at Mtambaswala. On the other side, there is a decent 160km dirt road to Mueda. There are immigration facilities on both sides of the bridge (although you will need to get your Mozambique visa in advance). Entering Tanzania, take care of customs formalities for your vehicle in Mtwara.

The Unity 2 bridge south of Songea is another option. With a private vehicle the Songea to Lichinga stretch should not take more than about eight or nine hours.

At Kilambo, the MV *Kilambo* ferry operates most days around high tide (Tsh500/30,000 per person/vehicle). Inquire at ECO2 (p198) or

the Old Boma at Mikindani (p198) in Mikindani to confirm that the ferry is running.

Rwanda

The main crossing is at Rusumu Falls, southwest of Bukoba (Tanzania).

At the time of research, there were no direct buses to Kigali. From Mwanza, you will need to go in stages; reckon on about 12 to 14 hours and Tsh25,000 for the journey.

Uganda

The main post is at Mutukula (Tanzania), northwest of Bukoba, with good sealed roads on both sides. There's another crossing further west at Nkurungu (Tanzania), but the road is bad and sparsely travelled. From Arusha or Moshi, travel to Uganda is via Kenya.

Kampala Coach's air-con buses to Nairobi (Kenya) from both Dar es Salaam and Arusha continue to Kampala (Tsh105,000, 30 hours from Dar es Salaam to Kampala; Tsh66,000, 20 hours from Arusha to Kampala). The cost to Jinja is the same as Kampala.

Several companies (Friends Safari is best) leave Bukoba at 6am for Kampala (Tsh15,000 to Tsh17,000, six hours). Departures from Kampala are at 7am and usually again at 11am.

From Mwanza, there are currently no direct buses. You will need to travel in stages; allow about 16 to 18 hours for the journey.

Zambia

The main border crossing (open 7.30am to 6pm Tanzania time, 6.30am to 5pm Zambia time) is at Tunduma (Tanzania), southwest of Mbeya. There's also a crossing at Kasesya (Tanzania), between Sumbawanga (Tanzania) and Mbala (Zambia).

Car If driving from Zambia into Tanzania, note that vehicle insurance isn't available at the Kasesya border, but must be purchased 120km further on in Sumbawanga.

Minibus Travels several times daily between Mbeya and Tunduma (Tsh3000 to Tsh4000, two hours), where you walk across the border for Zambian transport to Lusaka (US$20, 18 hours). The Kasesya crossing is seldom travelled, and in the rainy season the road can be extremely bad. There's no direct transport; at least one truck daily goes to the border from each side (Tsh10,000, four to five hours from Sumbawanga to Kasesya). With luck you can make the full journey in a day, but since departures from both Sumbawanga and Mbala are in the afternoon, and departures from the borders are in the early morning, you're likely to need to sleep in one of the (rough) border villages.

Train The Tazara (p214) train line links Dar es Salaam with Kapiri Mposhi in Zambia twice weekly via Mbeya and Tunduma. 'Express' service departs Dar es Salaam at 3.50pm Tuesday

(Tsh104,000/84,600/72,600 in 1st/2nd/economy class, about 40 hours). Ordinary service departs Dar es Salaam at 1.50pm on Friday (Tsh86,500/70,600/60,500, about 48 hours). Delays of up to 24 hours on both express and ordinary are the rule. Departures from Mbeya to Zambia (Tsh58,000/46,000/40,200 in express 1st/2nd/economy class) are at 1.30pm Wednesday and 2.40pm Saturday. Students with ID get a 50% discount. From Kapiri Mposhi to Lusaka, you'll need to continue by bus. Departures from New Kapiri Mposhi are at 4pm Tuesday (express) and 2pm Friday (ordinary). Visas are available at the border in both directions.

SEA & LAKE

There's a US$5 port tax for travel on all boats and ferries from Tanzanian ports.

Burundi

Regular passenger ferry service between Kigoma (Tanzania) and Bujumbura (Burundi) is suspended. Inquire at the passenger port in Kigoma for an update. However, it's possible to travel on cargo ships between Kigoma's Ami port and Bujumbura (Tsh10,000, 18 hours), although expect to hear that ships are sailing 'tomorrow' for several days in a row. Lake taxis go once or twice weekly from Kibirizi (just north of Kigoma) to Bujumbura, but are not recommended as they take a full day and are occasionally robbed. However, you could use the afternoon lake taxis to Kagunga (the Tanzanian border post, where there's a simple guesthouse), cross the border in the morning, take a motorcycle taxi to Nyanza-Lac (Burundi) and then a minibus to Bujumbura.

Democratic Republic of the Congo (DRC; formerly Zaïre)

Cargo boats go roughly once weekly from Kigoma's Ami port to Kalemie (US$10, deck class only, seven hours) or Uvira. When running, the MV Liemba also sometimes travels to Kalemie during its off week. Inquire at Ami port, or check with the embassy of the DRC in Kigoma about sailing days and times. Bring food and drink with you, and something to spread on the deck for sleeping.

Kenya

Dhow Dhows sail sporadically between Pemba, Tanga and Mombasa (Tsh15,000 to Tsh20,000 between Tanga and Mombasa); the journey can be long and rough. Ask at the ports in Tanga, or in Mkoani or Wete on Pemba for information on sailings. In Kenya, ask at the port in Mombasa, or better, at Shimoni.

Ferry There's currently no passenger ferry service on Lake Victoria between Tanzania and Kenya, but cargo boats sail about twice weekly between Mwanza and Kisumu (occasionally stopping in Musoma). With luck, you may find a captain willing to take passengers, although most will not. Inquire at the Mwanza South port about sailings.

Malawi

There are currently no passenger ferries operating between Tanzania's Mbamba Bay and Malawi's Nkhata Bay. Cargo boats (Tsh10,000, six hours) accept passengers, but safety standards are minimal; departures are often in the middle of the night to take advantage of calmer waters. There are no fixed schedules; ask at Immigration for information on the next sailing.

Mozambique

Dhow Dhows between Mozambique and Tanzania (12 to 30 or more hours) are best arranged at Msimbati and Moçimboa da Praia (Mozambique).

Ferry There is currently no official ferry service between southwestern Tanzania and Mozambique. The main option is taking a cargo boat between Mbamba Bay and Nkhata Bay, and then the **MV Chambo** on its weekly run from Nkhata Bay on to Likoma Island (Malawi), Cóbuè (Mozambique) and Metangula (Mozambique); currently departures are from Nkhata Bay on Thursday and from Metangula on Wednesday. There are also small boats that sail along the eastern shore of Lake Nyasa between Tanzania and Mozambique. However, Lake Nyasa is notorious for its severe and sudden squalls, and going this way is risky and not recommended.

There's an immigration officer at Mbamba Bay, Mozambique immigration posts in Cóbuè and in Metangula, and Malawi immigration officers on Likoma Island and in Nkhata Bay. Get your Mozambique visa in advance.

Uganda

There's no passenger-ferry service, but it's relatively easy to arrange passage between Mwanza and Kampala's Port Bell on cargo ships (about 16 hours). Boats sail about three times weekly. On the Ugandan side, you'll need a letter of permission from the train station director (free). Ask for the managing director's office, on the 2nd floor of the building next to Kampala's train station. In Mwanza, a letter isn't required, but check in with the immigration officer at the South Port. Expect to pay about US$20, including port fees. Crew are often willing to rent out their cabins for a negotiable extra fee.

Zambia

The venerable **MV Liemba** (☏ 028-280 2811) has been plying the waters of Lake Tanganyika for the better part of a century on one of Africa's classic adventure journeys. It connects Kigoma with Mpulungu in Zambia every other week, with prices for 1st/2nd/economy class costing US$100/90/70 (payment must be in US dollars cash only). The trip takes at least 40 hours and stops en route at various lakeshore villages, including Lagosa (for Mahale Mountains National Park; US$35 for 1st class from Kigoma), Kalema (southwest of Mpanda; US$50), Kipili (US$70) and Kasanga (southwest of Sumbawanga; US$95). In theory, departures from Kigoma are on Wednesday at 4pm, reaching Mpulungu Friday morning. Departures from Mpulungu are (again, in theory) on Friday afternoon at about 2pm, arriving back in Kigoma on Sunday afternoon.

Delays are common and the *Liemba* has often been out of service, though hopefully things will be better after the substantial overhaul it received in 2014. Food, soda, beer and bottled water are sold on board, but it's a good idea to bring supplements. First class is surprisingly comfortable, with two clean bunks, a window and a fan. Second-class cabins (four bunks) are poorly ventilated and uncomfortable. There are seats for third (economy) class passengers, but it's more comfortable to find deck space for sleeping. Keep watch over your luggage. Booking (for inquiries ☑ 028-280 2811) early is advisable, but not always necessary, as 1st-class cabins are usually available.

There are docks at Kigoma, Kasanga and Mpulungu, but at all other stops you'll need to disembark in the middle of the lake, exiting from a door in the side of the boat into small boats that take you to shore. While it may sound adventurous, it can be rather nerve-wracking at night or if the lake is rough.

❶ Getting Around

AIR
Airlines in Tanzania

Auric Air (☑ 0783 233334; www.auricair.com) Bukoba, Mwanza, Zanzibar, Dar es Salaam and other towns, plus Katavi and Rubondo Island national parks.

Air Excel (☑ 027-254 8429; www.airexcel online.com) Arusha, Serengeti NP, Lake Manyara NP, Dar es Salaam, Zanzibar.

Air Tanzania (☑ 022-211 8411; www.air tanzania.co.tz) Dar es Salaam, Mwanza, Kigoma, Tabora, Mtwara, Kilimanjaro, Mbeya, plus Bujumbura (Burundi).

Coastal Aviation (☑ 022-284 2700; www.coastal.co.tz) Flights to many major towns and national parks, including Arusha, Dar es Salaam, Dodoma, Kilwa Masoko, Lake Manyara NP, Mafia, Mwanza, Pemba, Ruaha NP, Rubondo Island NP, Saadani NP, Selous GR, Serengeti NP, Tanga, Tarangire NP and Zanzibar.

Flightlink (☑ 0782 354448, 0782 354449; www.flightlinkaircharters.com) Flights connect-

ing Dar es Salaam with the Zanzibar Archipelago, Selous, Dodoma, Serengeti and Lake Manyara.

Precision Air (☑ 0787 888407, 022-216 8000; www.precisionairtz.com) Flies from Dar es Salaam to many major towns including Bukoba, Kilimanjaro, Mbeya, Mtwara, Mwanza and Zanzibar. Also Dar es Salaam to Entebbe (Uganda), Kigali (Rwanda), Nairobi (Kenya), Pemba (Mozambique), Lubumbashi (DRC) and Lusaka (Zambia).

Regional Air Services (☑ 027-250 4477, 027-250 2541; www.regionaltanzania.com) Arusha, Dar es Salaam, Kilimanjaro, Lake Manyara NP, Ndutu, Serengeti NP and Zanzibar.

Safari Airlink (☑ 0777 723274; www.safari aviation.info) Dar es Salaam, Arusha, Katavi NP, Mahale Mountains NP, Pangani, Ruaha NP, Selous GR and Zanzibar.

Tropical Air (☑ 0777 431431, 024-223 2511; www.tropicalair.co.tz) Zanzibar, Dar es Salaam, Mbeya, Pemba, Mafia and Arusha.

ZanAir (☑ 024-223 3670, 024-223 3678; www.zanair.com) Flights link Arusha, Dar es Salaam, Pemba, Saadani NP, Selous GR and Zanzibar. Also flies between Zanzibar, Mombasa (Kenya) and Arusha.

Zantas Air (☑ 0688 434343, 0713-409412; www.zantasair.com) Arusha, Katavi NP, Mahale Mountains NP, Kigoma, Lake Manyara NP and Serengeti NP.

BOAT
Dhow

Main routes connect Zanzibar and Pemba with Dar es Salaam, Tanga, Bagamoyo and Mombasa (Kenya); Kilwa Kivinje, Lindi, Mikindani and Msimbati with other coastal towns; and Mafia with the mainland. However, foreigners are officially prohibited on nonmotorised dhows, and on any dhows between Zanzibar and Dar es Salaam; captains are subject to fines if they're caught, and may be unwilling to take you. A better option is to arrange a charter with a coastal hotel, many of which have their own dhows.

Ferry

Ferries operate on Lake Victoria, Lake Tanganyika and Lake Nyasa, and between Dar es Salaam, Zanzibar and Pemba. There's a US$5 port tax per trip.

Lake Victoria The MV *Victoria* (p158) departs from Mwanza at 9pm on Tuesday, Thursday and Sunday (nine hours). Departures from Bukoba are at 9pm Monday, Wednesday and Friday. First class has two-bed cabins and 2nd-class sleeping has six-bed cabins. Second-class sitting isn't comfortable, so if you can't get a spot in 1st class or 2nd-class sleeping, the best bet is to buy a 3rd-class ticket. With luck, you may then be able to find a comfortable spot in the 1st-class lounge. First- and 2nd-class cabins fill up quickly in both directions, so book as soon as you know your plans. Food is available on board. Note that there's a risk of theft for all deck and seating passengers.

Lake Tanganyika The MV *Liemba* (p211) sails down Lake Tanganyika between Kigoma and Mpulungu (Zambia) via various Tanzanian towns.

Lake Nyasa In theory, the **MV Songea** (1st/economy class Tsh25,100/16,100) departs from Itungi port about noon on Thursday and makes its way down the coast via Matema, Lupingu, Manda, Lundu, Mango and Liuli to Mbamba Bay (18 to 24 hours). It continues to Nkhata Bay in Malawi, before turning around and doing the return trip, departing Mbamba Bay in theory on Saturday, and reaching Matema and Itungi port on Sunday. The smaller **MV Iringa** (1st/economy class Tsh22,000/15,000), which also services lakeside villages between Itungi and Manda (about halfway down the Tanzanian lake shore) was not operating at the time of research. When running, it usually alternates with the *Songea*. Schedules for both boats change frequently. For an update, ask in Kyela, or at one of the Matema hotels.

BUS

➔ On major long-distance routes, there's a choice of express and ordinary buses; price is usually a good indicator of which is which. Express buses make fewer stops, are less crowded and depart on schedule. Some have toilets and air-conditioning, and the nicest ones are called 'luxury' buses. On secondary routes, the only option is ordinary buses, which are often packed to overflowing, stop often and run to a less rigorous schedule (and often not to any recognisable schedule at all).

➔ For popular routes, book in advance. You can sometimes get a place by arriving at the bus station an hour prior to departure. Each bus line has its own booking office, at or near the bus station.

➔ Prices are basically fixed, although over-charging happens. Buy your tickets at the office and not from the touts, and don't believe anyone who tries to tell you there's a luggage fee, unless you are carrying an excessively large pack.

➔ For short stretches along main routes, express buses will drop you on request, though you'll often need to pay the full fare to the next major destination.

➔ On long routes (which should be avoided, if possible), expect to sleep either on the bus, pulled off to the side of the road, or at a grubby guesthouse.

CAR & MOTORCYCLE

Unless you have your own vehicle and are familiar with driving in East Africa, it's relatively unusual for travellers to tour mainland Tanzania by car. More common is to focus on a region and arrange local transport through a tour or safari operator. On Zanzibar, however, it's easy to hire a car or motorcycle for touring, and self-drive is permitted.

Driving Licence

On the mainland you'll need your home driving licence or (preferable) an International Driving Permit (IDP) along with your home licence. On Zanzibar you'll need an IDP plus your home licence, or a permit from Zanzibar, Kenya, Uganda or South Africa.

Fuel & Spare Parts

Petrol and diesel cost about Tsh2200 per litre. Tank up whenever you get the opportunity. It is common, including at major roadside filling stations, for petrol or diesel to be diluted with kerosene or water. Check with local residents or business owners before tanking up. It's also common for car parts to be switched in garages (substituting inferior versions for the originals). Staying with your car while it's being repaired helps minimise this problem.

Car Hire

In Dar es Salaam, daily rates for 2WD start at about US$70, excluding fuel, plus from US$30 for insurance and tax. Prices for 4WDs are US$100 to US$250 per day plus insurance (US$30 to US$40 per day), fuel and driver (US$20 to US$50 per day). There's also a 20% value added tax.

Outside the city, most companies require 4WD. Also, most will not permit self-drive outside of Dar es Salaam, and few offer unlimited kilometres. Charges per kilometre are around

---

PERILS OF THE ROAD

Road accidents are probably your biggest safety risk while travelling in Tanzania, with speeding buses being among the worst offenders. Road conditions are poor and driving standards leave much to be desired. Many vehicles have painted slogans such as *Mungu Atubariki* (God Bless Us) or 'In God we Trust' in the hope that a bit of extra help from above will see them safely through the day's runs.

To maximise your chances of a safe arrival, avoid night travel, and ask locals for recommendations of reputable companies. If you have a choice, it's usually better to go with a full-sized bus than a minibus or 30-seater bus.

US$0.50 to US$1. Clarify what the company's policy is in the event of a breakdown.

Elsewhere in Tanzania, you can hire 4WD vehicles in Arusha, Karatu, Mwanza, Mbeya, Zanzibar Town and other centres through travel agencies, tour operators and hotels. Except on Zanzibar, most come with a driver. Rates average US$100 to US$200 per day plus fuel, less on Zanzibar.

For motorcycle hire, try the Arusha-based **Dustbusters** (www.dustbusters-tz.com).

Road Conditions & Hazards

Around one-third of Tanzania's road network is sealed. Secondary roads range from good to impassable, depending on the season. For most trips outside major towns you'll need 4WD.

Road Rules

Unless otherwise posted, the speed limit is 80km/h; on some routes, including Dar es Salaam to Arusha, police have radar. Tanzania has a seat-belt law for drivers and front-seat passengers. The traffic-fine penalty is Tsh20,000.

Motorcycles aren't permitted in national parks except for the section of the Dar es Salaam–Mbeya highway passing through Mikumi National Park and on the road between Sumbawanga and Mpanda via Katavi National Park. In Saadani National Park, they're officially not permitted on the coastal road, but this often seems not to be enforced.

HITCHING

Hitching is generally slow going. It's prohibited inside national parks, and is usually fruitless around them. That said, in remote areas, hitching a lift with truck drivers may be your only option. Expect to pay about the same or a bit less than the bus fare for the same route, with a place in the cab costing about twice that for a place on top of the load.

MINIBUS & SHARED TAXI

For shorter trips away from the main routes, the choice is often between 30-seater buses ('Coastals' or *thelathini*) and dalla-dallas ('Hiace' minibuses). Both options come complete with chickens on the roof, bags of produce under the seats, no leg room and schedules only in the most general sense of the word. Dalla-dallas, especially, are invariably filled to overflowing. Shared taxis are rare, except in northern Tanzania near Arusha and several other locations. Like ordinary buses, dalla-dallas and shared taxis leave when full, and are the least safe transport option.

TRUCK

In remote areas, such as much of Western Tanzania, trucks operate as buses (for a roughly similar fare) with passengers sitting or standing in the back. Even on routes that have daily bus service, many people still use trucks.

LOCAL TRANSPORT
Dalla-Dalla

Local routes are serviced by dalla-dallas and, in rural areas, pick-up trucks or old 4WDs. Prices are fixed and cheap (Tsh100 to Tsh400 for town runs). The vehicles make many stops and are very crowded. Accidents are common, especially in minibuses. Many accidents occur when drivers race each other to an upcoming station to collect new passengers. Destinations are either posted on a board in the front window, or called out by the driver's assistant, who also collects fares.

Taxi

Taxis, which have white plates on the mainland and a '*gari la abiria*' (passenger vehicle) sign on Zanzibar, can be hired in all major towns. None have meters, so agree on the fare with the driver before getting in. Fares for short town trips start at Tsh2000. In major centres, many drivers have an 'official' price list, but rates shown (often calculated on the basis of Tsh1000 per 1km) are generally much higher than what is normally paid. Ask locals what the price should be and use this as a base for negotiations. For longer trips away from town, negotiate the fare based on distance, petrol costs and road conditions, plus a fair profit for the driver. Only use taxis from reliable hotels or established taxi stands. Avoid hailing taxis on the streets, and never get in a taxi that has a 'friend' of the driver or anyone else already in it.

TRAIN

There are two lines: **Tazara** (Tazara; www.tazarasite.com; cnr Nyerere & Nelson Mandela Rds, Dar es Salaam; 1st/2nd/economy class express btwn Dar es Salaam & Mbeya Tsh46,000/38,600/32,400), linking Dar es Salaam with Kapiri Mposhi in Zambia via Mbeya and Tunduma; and Tanzanian Railway Corporation's rundown **Central Line** (☑ 022-211 7833; cnr Railway St & Sokoine Dr, Dar es Salaam; 1st/2nd/economy class Dar es Salaam to Kigoma Tsh75,700/55,400/27,700), linking Dar es Salaam with Tabora and Kigoma. A Central Line branch also links Tabora with Mpanda. At the time of research, all Central Line service was suspended due to flooding damage in central Tanzania.

Tazara is considerably more comfortable and efficient, but on both lines, breakdowns and long delays (up to 24 hours or more) are common. If you want to try the train, consider shorter stretches, eg from Dar es Salaam into the Selous, or between Tabora and Kigoma. Food is available on both lines.

Classes

Tazara has four classes: 1st class (four-bed compartments); 2nd class (six-bed compartments); 2nd-class sitting ('super seater'); and, economy (3rd)-class (benches, usually very crowded). Men and women can only travel together in the sleeping sections by booking the entire compartment. At night, secure your window with a stick, and don't leave luggage unattended. Central Line, when operating, has 1st class (four-bed compartments), 2nd class (six-bed compartments) and economy.

Reservations

Tickets for 1st and 2nd class should be reserved at least several days in advance, although occasionally you'll be able to get a seat on the day of travel. Economy-class tickets can be bought on the spot.

Tazara runs two trains weekly between Dar es Salaam and Kapiri Mposhi in Zambia via Mbeya, departing Dar es Salaam at 3.50pm Tuesday (express) and 1.50pm Friday (ordinary). Express train fares between Dar es Salaam and Mbeya are Tsh46,000/38,600/32,400 in 1st/2nd/economy class (slightly less for ordinary trains). Departures from Mbeya are at 2.30pm Wednesday (express) and 3pm Saturday (ordinary). Linens are provided for sleeper cars.

When operational, Central Line trains depart Dar es Salaam for Kigoma at 5pm Tuesday and Friday (Tsh75,700/55,400/27,700 in 1st/2nd/economy class, approximately 40 hours). Departures from Kigoma are at 6pm Sunday and Thursday; departures from Mwanza are at 5pm Sunday and Thursday. Sleeper cars have mattresses only (no linens).

Trains between Tabora and Mpanda (economy class only, about 14 hours) depart from Tabora at 9pm Wednesday and Saturday and Mpanda at 1pm Thursday and Sunday.

Kenya

Best for Nature

➡ Masai Mara National Reserve (p251)

➡ Amboseli National Park (p298)

➡ Tsavo West National Park (p302)

➡ Mt Kenya National Park (p286)

➡ Kisite Marine National Park (p325)

Best for Culture

➡ Maasai Manyatta, Masai Mara National Reserve (p253)

➡ Lewa Wildlife Conservancy (p283)

➡ Loyangalani (p349)

➡ Il Ngwesi (p285)

➡ Nairobi nightlife (p233)

Why Go?

When you think of Africa, you're probably thinking of Kenya. It's the lone acacia silhouetted against a horizon stretching into eternity, the lush, palm-fringed coastline of the Indian Ocean, the Great Rift Valley. Peopling that landscape, adding depth and resonance to Kenya's age-old story, are some of Africa's best-known peoples, among them the Maasai, the Samburu, the Turkana, Swahili, the Kikuyu. Drawing near to these cultures could just be a highlight of your visit.

Then, of course, there's the wildlife. This is the land of the Masai Mara, of wildebeest and zebras migrating in their millions with the great predators of Africa following in their wake, of the red elephants of Tsavo, of the massed millions of pink flamingos stepping daintily through lake shallows. Africa is the last great wilderness where these creatures survive. And Kenya is the perfect place to answer Africa's call of the wild.

When to Go
Nairobi

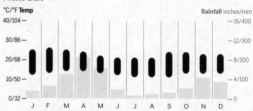

Jul–Oct The annual wildebeest migration arrives in the Masai Mara in all its epic glory.

Jan & Feb Hot, dry weather with high concentrations of wildlife in the major parks.

Nov–Mar Migratory birds present in their millions throughout the country.

NAIROBI

POP 3.36 MILLION / ELEV 1661M

Telling people that you like Nairobi is like voicing a guilty secret. Yes, Nairobi's reputation precedes it. And yes, it's a city where it pays to keep your wits about you. But there are many people who don't just like Nairobi but who actually wouldn't want to live anywhere else. For those who call it home, the city's muscular, cosmopolitan charms include a vibrant cultural life, fabulous places to eat and exciting nightlife. If you're just passing through, this melting pot of people and attractions includes the intriguing National Museum, an unlikely national park (black rhinos and all), an irresistible elephant orphanage, the ground zero for the Rothschild's giraffe, Karen Blixen's former home and so much more. Welcome to one of Africa's most dynamic cities, a place you'll almost certainly pass through, and one that you could learn to like if you give it half a chance.

⊙ Sights

◎ City Centre

★ National Museum   MUSEUM
(Map p220; ☑020-8164134; www.museums. or.ke; Museum Hill Rd; adult/child KSh1200/600, combined ticket with Snake Park KSh1500/1000; ⊙8.30am-5.30pm) Kenya's wonderful National Museum, housed in an imposing building amid lush, leafy grounds just outside the centre, has a good range of cultural and natural history exhibits. Aside from the exhibits, check out the life-sized fibreglass model of pachyderm celebrity, Ahmed, the massive elephant who became a symbol of Kenya at the height of the 1980s poaching crisis, and who was placed under 24-hour guard by Jomo Kenyatta; he's in the inner courtyard next to the shop.

Snake Park   ZOO
(Map p220; www.museums.or.ke; Museum Hill Rd; adult/child KSh1200/600, combined ticket with National Museum KSh1500/1000; ⊙8.30am-5.30pm) In the grounds of the National Museum, the zoo-like Snake Park has some impressive snake species, including the puff adder, black mamba, African rock python and the Gaboon viper (which rarely bares its 4cm-long fangs, the longest in the world). There are also local fish species, lizards, turtles and some sad-looking crocodiles.

Kenyatta Conference Centre   LOOKOUT
(Map p224; viewing platform adult/child KSh500/250; ⊙viewing platform 9am-6pm) Towering over City Square on City Hall Way, Nairobi's signature building was designed as a fusion of modern and traditional African styles, though the distinctive saucer tower looks a little dated next to some of the city's newer and flashier glass edifices. Take the lift up to the viewing platform and helipad on the roof for wonderful views over Nairobi.

Railway Museum   MUSEUM
(Map p220; Station Rd; adult/child KSh500/100; ⊙8am-5pm) The main collection here is housed in an old railway building and consists of relics from the East African Railway. There are train and ship models, photographs, tableware, and oddities from the history of the railway, such as the engine seat that allowed visiting dignitaries such as Theodore Roosevelt to take potshots at unsuspecting wildlife from the front of the

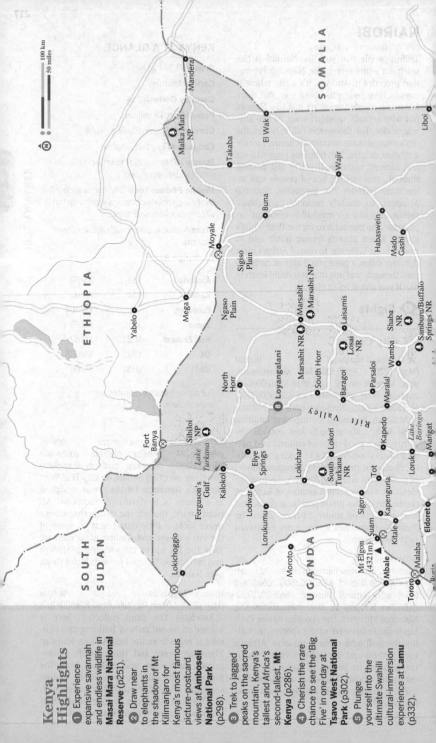

Kenya Highlights

1 Experience expansive savannah and endless wildlife in **Masai Mara National Reserve** (p251).

2 Draw near to elephants in the shadow of Mt Kilimanjaro for Kenya's most famous picture-postcard views at **Amboseli National Park** (p298).

3 Trek to jagged peaks on the sacred mountain, Kenya's tallest and Africa's second-tallest, **Mt Kenya** (p286).

4 Cherish the rare chance to see the 'Big Five' in one day at **Tsavo West National Park** (p302).

5 Plunge yourself into the ultimate Swahili cultural-immersion experience at **Lamu** (p332).

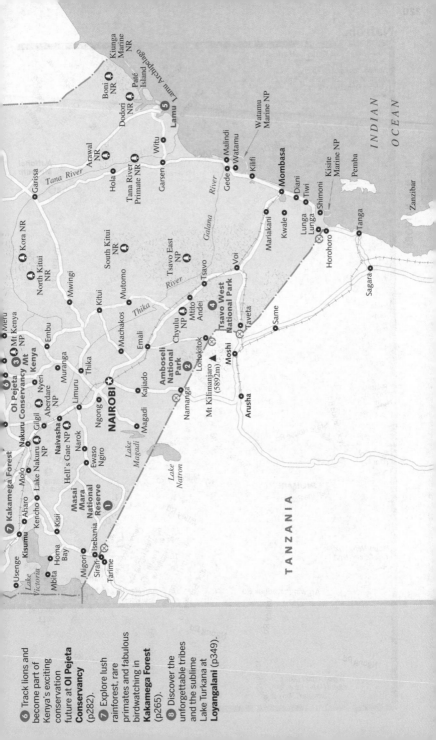

6 Track lions and become part of Kenya's exciting conservation future at **Ol Pejeta Conservancy** (p282).

7 Explore lush rainforest, rare primates and fabulous birdwatching in **Kakamega Forest** (p265).

8 Discover the unforgettable tribes and the sublime Lake Turkana at **Loyangalani** (p349).

Nairobi

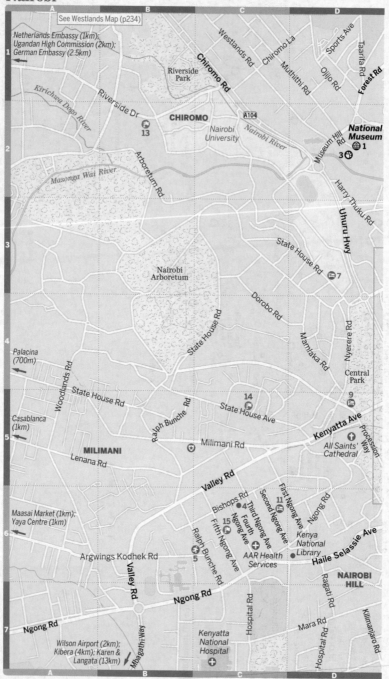

See Westlands Map (p234)

Netherlands Embassy (1km);
Ugandan High Commission (2km);
German Embassy (2.5km)

Chiromo Rd

Westlands Rd

Chiromo La

Muthithi Rd

Olijo Rd

Sports Ave

Taarita Rd

Forest Rd

Riverside Park

Riverside Dr

Kirichwa Dogo River

CHIROMO

A104

Nairobi University

Nairobi River

Museum Hill Rd

National Museum

3

1

Arboretum Rd

Masonga Wai River

Harry Thuku Rd

Uhuru Hwy

State House Rd

7

Nairobi Arboretum

Dorobo Rd

Nyerere Rd

Mamlaka Rd

State House Rd

Palacina (700m)

Woodlands Rd

State House Rd

Central Park

9

14

State House Ave

Casablanca (1km)

Ralph Bunche Rd

Milimani Rd

Kenyatta Ave

Procession Way

All Saints' Cathedral

MILIMANI

Lenana Rd

Valley Rd

Maasai Market (1km);
Yaya Centre (1km)

Bishops Rd

4

11

First Ngong Ave

Second Ngong Ave

Ngong Ave

Fourth Ngong Ave

15

Fifth Ngong Ave

Ralph Bunche Rd

5

Kenya National Library

AAR Health Services

Haile Selassie Ave

NAIROBI HILL

Ragati Rd

Argwings Kodhek Rd

Valley Rd

Ngong Rd

Hospital Rd

Mara Rd

Hospital Rd

Kilimanjaro Rd

Ngong Rd

Mbagathi Way

Wilson Airport (2km);
Kibera (4km); Karen &
Langata (13km)

Kenyatta National Hospital

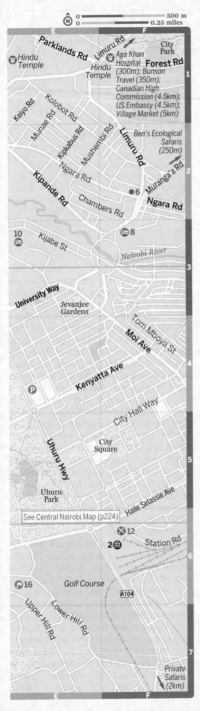

train. In the grounds are dozens of fading locomotives in various states of disrepair, dating from the steam days to independence. You can walk around the carriages at your leisure. At the back of the compound is the steam train used in the movie *Out of Africa*. It's a fascinating introduction to this important piece of colonial history.

The museum is reached by a long lane beside the train station.

◉ Nairobi National Park

★ **Nairobi National Park**   PARK
(Map p230; ☏ 020-2423423; www.kws.org/parks/parks_reserves/NANP.html; adult/child US$50/25) Welcome to Kenya's most accessible yet incongruous safari experience. Set on the city's southern outskirts, Nairobi National Park (at 117 sq km, it's one of Africa's smallest) has abundant wildlife which can, in places, be viewed against a backdrop of city skyscrapers and airliners coming in to land – it's the only national park on earth that borders a capital city. Remarkably, the animals seem utterly unperturbed by it all.

➡ **Wildlife**

Nairobi National Park has acquired the nickname 'Kifaru Ark', a testament to its success as a rhinoceros (*kifaru* in Kiswahili) sanctuary. The park is home to the world's densest concentration of black rhinoceros (over 50). But even proximity to Kenya's largest city couldn't prevent poachers from killing one of the park's rhinos in August 2013. It was the first such attack in six years.

Lions and hyenas are also commonly sighted within the park; park rangers at the entrance usually have updates on lion movements. You'll need a bit of patience and a lot of luck to spot the park's resident cheetahs and leopards. Other regularly spotted species include gazelle, warthog, zebra, giraffe, ostrich and buffalo.

The park's wetland areas also sustain approximately 400 bird species, which is more than in the whole of the UK.

➡ **Ivory Burning Monument**

Not far inside the park's main Langata Road gate, the **Ivory Burning Monument** marks the spot where, in 1989, Kenyan President Daniel arap Moi burnt 12 tons of ivory at a site near the main gate. This dramatic event improved Kenya's conservation image at a time when East African wildlife was being decimated by relentless poaching.

Nairobi

➡ **Getting There & Around**

Matatus 125 and 126 (KSh50, 30 to 45 minutes) pass by the main park entrance from the train station. You can also go by private vehicle. Nairobi tour companies offer half-day safaris (from US$75 per person).

Apart from the main entrance, which lies 7km from the CBD, there are other gates on Magadi Rd and the Athi River gate; the latter is handy if you're continuing on to Mombasa, Amboseli or the Tanzanian border. The roads in the park are passable with 2WDs, but travelling in a 4WD is never a bad idea, especially if the rains have been heavy.

Unless you already have your own vehicle, the cheapest way to see the park is on the park shuttle, a big KWS bus that leaves the main gate at 2pm on Sunday for a 2½-hour tour. You need to book in person at the main gate by 1.30pm. There was talk of this service being discontinued so ring ahead to avoid disappointment.

◎ Karen & Langata

★ **Giraffe Centre**   WILDLIFE RESERVE
(Map p230; ☏020-8070804; www.giraffecenter.org; Koitobos Rd; adult/child KSh1000/500; ⊙9am-5pm) This centre, which protects the highly endangered Rothschild's giraffe, combines serious conservation with enjoyable activities. You can observe, hand-feed or even kiss one of the giraffes from a raised wooden structure, which is quite an experience. You may also spot warthogs snuffling about in the mud, and there's an interesting self-guided forest walk through the adjacent **Gogo River Bird Sanctuary**.

★ **David Sheldrick
Wildlife Trust**   WILDLIFE RESERVE
(Map p230; ☏020-2301396; www.sheldrickwildlifetrust.org) Occupying a plot within Nairobi National Park, this nonprofit trust was established in 1977, shortly after the death of David Sheldrick, who served as the antipoaching warden of Tsavo National Park. Together with his wife Daphne, David pioneered techniques for raising orphaned black rhinos and elephants and reintroducing them back into the wild, and the trust retains close links with Tsavo for these and other projects. The centre is one of Nairobi's most popular attractions, and deservedly so.

After entering at 11am, visitors are escorted to a small viewing area centred on a muddy watering hole. A few moments later, much like a sports team marching out onto the field, the animal handlers come in alongside a dozen or so baby elephants. For the first part of the viewing, the handlers bottle-feed the baby elephants – a strangely heartwarming sight.

Once the little guys have drunk their fill, they romp around like big babies. The elephants seem to take joy in misbehaving in front of their masters, so don't be surprised if a few break rank and start rubbing up against your leg! The baby elephants also use this designated timeslot for their daily mud bath, which makes for some great photos; keep your guard up as they've been known to spray a tourist or two with a trunkful of mud.

While the elephants gambol around, the keepers talk about the individual orphans and their stories. Explanations are given about the the broader picture of the orphans project and some of the other projects the David Sheldrick Wildlife Trust is involved in. Visitors can also 'adopt' one of the elephants.

The Trust is also home to a number of orphaned rhinos, many of which, like the baby elephants, mingle with wild herds in Nairobi National Park during the day. One exception is Maxwell, a blind rhino who lives in a large stockade for his protection.

To get here by bus or matatu, take 125 or 126 from Moi Ave and ask to be dropped off at the KWS central workshop on Magadi Rd (KSh60, 50 minutes). It's about 1km from the workshop gate to the Sheldrick centre – it's signposted and KWS staff can give you directions. Be advised that at this point you'll be walking in the national park, which does contain predators, so stick to the paths. A taxi should cost between KSh1500 and KSh2000 from the city centre.

★ **Karen Blixen's House & Museum** HISTORIC BUILDING
(Map p230; www.museums.or.ke; Karen Rd; adult/child KSh1200/600; ⊙9.30am-6pm) If you loved *Out of Africa,* you'll love this place. This museum is the farmhouse where author Karen Blixen lived between 1914 and 1931. She left after a series of personal tragedies, but the lovely colonial house has been preserved as a museum. The museum is set in expansive gardens, and is an interesting place to wander around. That said, the movie was actually shot at a nearby location, so don't be surprised if things don't look entirely right!

Bomas of Kenya CULTURAL CENTRE
(Map p230; ☑020-8068400; www.bomasofkenya.co.ke; Langata Rd; adult/child KSh800/400; ⊙performances 2.30-4pm Mon-Fri, 3.30-5.15pm Sat & Sun, 'villages' 10am-6pm Sat & Sun) The talented resident artists at this cultural centre perform traditional dances and songs taken from the country's various tribal groups, including Arabic-influenced Swahili *taarab* music, Kalenjin warrior dances, Embu drumming and Kikuyu circumcision ceremonies. It's touristy, but still a spectacular afternoon out. The complex consists of a number of 'bomas' or villages, each constructed in the architectural style of Kenya's major ethnic groups.

KIBERA

Home to as many as one million residents, Kibera is the world's second-largest shanty town (after Soweto in Johannesburg, South Africa). Although it covers 2.5 sq km in area, it's home to somewhere between a quarter and a third of Nairobi's population, and has a density of an estimated 300,000 people per sq km. The neighbourhood was thrust into the Western imagination when it featured prominently in the Fernando Meirelles film *The Constant Gardener,* which is based on the book of the same name by John le Carré. The area is heavily polluted by open sewers, and lacks even the most basic infrastructure; residents of Kibera suffer from poor nutrition, violent crime and disease.

Orientation

Kibera is southwest of the CBD. The railway line heading to Kisumu intersects Kibera, though the shanty town doesn't actually have a station. However, the railway line does serve as the main thoroughfare through Kibera, and you'll find shops selling basic provisions along the tracks.

Visiting Kibera

A visit to Kibera is one way to look behind the headlines and touch on, albeit briefly, the daily struggles and triumphs of life in the town; there's nothing quite like the enjoyment of playing a bit of footy with street children aspiring to be the next Didier Drogba. Although you could visit on your own, security is an issue, and such visits aren't always appreciated by residents. The best way to visit is on a tour. Three companies we recommend are **Explore Kibera** (explorekibera.com; per person US$29; ⊙9am & 2pm daily), **Kibera Tours** (☑0721391630, 0723669218; kiberatours.com; per person KSh2500) and **KUFET** (☑0721751905; www.kiberaeverydayslumtours.com; per person US$25).

Getting There & Away

You can get to Kibera by taking bus 32 or matatu 32c from the Kencom building along Moi Ave. Be advised that this route is notorious for petty theft, so be extremely vigilant and pay attention to your surroundings.

Central Nairobi

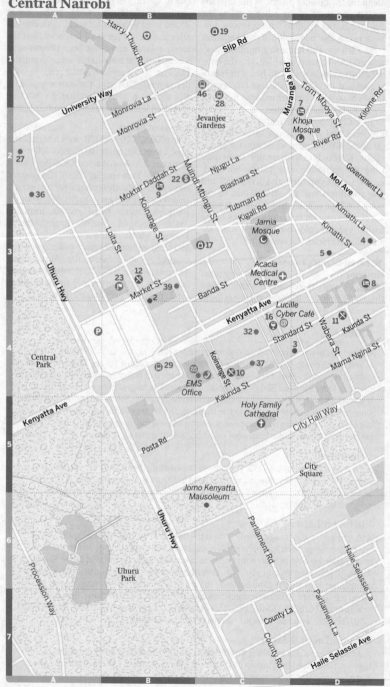

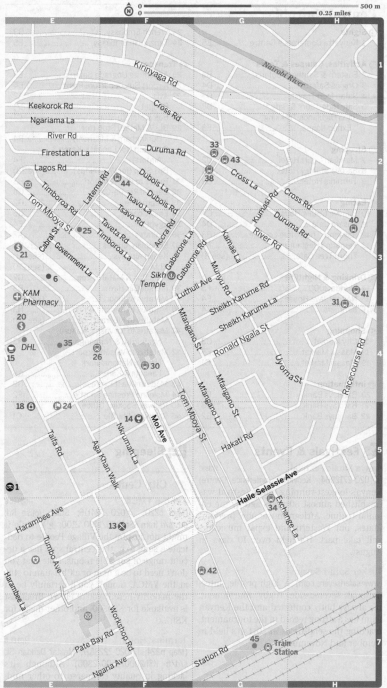

✦ Festivals & Events

Kenya Music Festival   MUSIC
(☏ 020-2712964; Kenyatta Conference Centre) Kenya's longest-running music festival was established almost 80 years ago by the colonial regime. African music now predominates, but Western and expat musicians still take part. It's held over 10 days in August.

Tusker Safari Sevens   RUGBY
(www.safarisevens.com) A high-profile, international seven-a-side rugby tournament. It's always hotly contested and the Kenyan team has a strong record in the tournament, reaching the semi-finals in 2011. It's held in October and November.

🛏 Sleeping

🛏 City Centre

Central YMCA   HOSTEL **$**
(Map p220; ☏ 020-2724116; State House Rd; dm/s/d from KSh1000/1400/2100; ⓟ) While it might not inspire the Village People to dedicate a song to it, this central spot has a decent range of passable rooms. Note that you don't need to be a man or a Christian to stay at the YMCA, though you'll certainly be in the majority here if you're either. Breakfast is available for KSh500, and other meals for KSh750.

Terminal Hotel   HOTEL **$**
(Map p224; ☏ 020-2228817; Moktar Daddah St; s/d/tr KSh2000/2500/2800) Although it's lacking in quality compared to other mid-

range offerings, the Terminal Hotel is preferable to the rock-bottom budget crash pads in the city centre. The emphasis here is on doing the basics well, with no overblown attempts at tourist frills, and the clean and adequate rooms speak for themselves.

★ **Kahama Hotel** HOTEL $$
(Map p220; ☎ 020-3742210; www.kahamahotels. co.ke; Murang'a Rd; s/d from US$50/60; P 🛜) Almost equidistant between the city centre and the National Museum, this place is a terrific choice. Its catchcry is 'economy with style' and it pretty much lives up to it, with pleasant rooms, comfy beds and free wifi. The only downside? The new highway passes by the front door – ask for a room at the back.

★ **Sarova Stanley Hotel** HOTEL $$
(Map p224; ☎ 020-2757000; www.sarovahotels. com/stanley; cnr Kimathi St & Kenyatta Ave; s/d from US$104/128; P ✳ 🛜 ⛱) A Nairobi classic. The original Stanley Hotel was established in 1902 – past guests include Ernest Hemingway, Clark Gable, Ava Gardner and Gregory Peck – and the hotel makes a cameo appearance in some of Hemingway's works. The latest version boasts large and luxurious rooms, and colonial decor prevails inside, with lashings of green leather, opulent chandeliers and old-fashioned fans. The real highlight (at least from our perspective!) is the Thorn Tree Café (p232), which inspired Lonely Planet's online community. Rates vary considerably with the seasons and availability, and are generally cheaper on weekends.

Meridian Court Hotel HOTEL $$
(Map p224; ☎ 020-2220006; www.meridian hotelkenya.com; Muranga'a Rd; s/d from KSh8650/9850; P @ 🛜 ⛱) The elaborate lobby here is rather more prepossessing than the rooms, but it's hardly worth complaining when you're essentially getting a suite for the price of a standard room. There's no great luxury involved and some of the furnishings have seen better days, but the pool, bar and restaurants make it terrific value in this price range. The superior rooms are rarely worth the extra.

Nairobi Serena Hotel HOTEL $$$
(Map p220; ☎ 020-2822000; www.serenahotels. com; Procession Way, Central Park; r from US$210; P ✳ @ 🛜 ⛱) Consolidating its reputation as one of the best top-flight chains in East Africa, this entry in the Serena canon has a fine sense of individuality, with its international-class facilities displaying a touch of safari style. Of

WORTH A TRIP

KIAMBETHU TEA FARM

Kiambethu Tea Farm (☎ 0733769976, 020-2012542; www.kiambethufarm.co.ke; guided tour & lunch per person KSh2600) A visit to the Kiambethu Tea Farm is a wonderful chance to get an insight into Kenya's tea plantations (Kenya is the world's largest exporter of black tea), as well as being an immensely enjoyable excursion from the city. The guided tour takes you through the history of Kenyan tea-growing, visits the lovely colonial-era farmhouse and can also encompass a nearby stand of primary forest.

Advance bookings are essential and some Nairobi tour companies can make the necessary arrangements, including transport. If you're coming in your own vehicle, print out the detailed directions from its website. The farm is around 25km northwest of central Nairobi.

KENYA NAIROBI

particular note is the onsite Maisha health spa. Opt for one of the amazing garden suites, where you can take advantage of your own private patio, complete with mini-pergola.

Norfolk Hotel HOTEL $$$
(Map p220; ☎ 020-2265000; www.fairmont.com/ norfolkhotel; Harry Thuku Rd; r from US$289; P ✳ 🛜 ⛱) Built in 1904 but overhauled many times since, Nairobi's oldest hotel was *the* place to stay during colonial days. The hotel remains the traditional starting point for elite safaris, and the Lord Delamere Terrace is still Nairobi's most famous meeting place. Thanks to the leafy grounds, it has an almost rustic feel, although the recently renovated rooms have lost a little of that classic Norfolk look.

🛏 Milimani & Nairobi Hill

★ **Wildebeest Eco Camp** TENTED CAMP $
(Map p230; ☎ 0734770733; wildebeestecocamp. com; 151 Mokoyeti Rd West, Langata; garden tent s/d from KSh4500/5500, deluxe garden tents s/d US$113/138) This fabulous place in Langata is arguably Nairobi's outstanding budget option. The atmosphere is relaxed yet switched on, and the accommodation is spotless and great value however much you're paying. The deluxe garden tents are as good as many exclusive such places out on safari – for a fraction of the price. A great Nairobi base.

Milimani Backpackers & Safari Centre BACKPACKERS $

(Map p230; ☏0722347616, 0718919020; www.milimanibackpackers.com; Karen St, St Helens Lane, off Langata Rd, Milimani; camping KSh700, dm KSh1000, cabins s/d KSh2200/2500; @☎) This terrific place is one of the friendliest accommodation options in town, and whether you camp out back, cosy up in the dorms or splurge on your own cabin, you'll end up huddled around the fire at night, swapping travel stories and dining on home-cooked meals (from KSh500) with fellow travellers. The friendly staff can also help you book a safari, organise onward travel or simply get your bearings.

Town Lodge HOTEL $$

(Map p220; ☏020-2881600; clhg.com; Second Ngong Ave, Milimani; s/d from KSh11,700/16,100; P@☎) The focus here is on affordable comfort for business travellers, with attractive if somewhat sterile rooms. It's one of the best-value midrange options in Nairobi – there's a small gym, excellent breakfasts and you can take advantage of the bars and restaurants at the Fairview next door.

Palacina BOUTIQUE HOTEL $$$

(Map p230; ☏020-2715517; www.palacina.com; Kitale Lane; ste 1-/2-person US$330/498, penthouse US$830, 1-/2-bedroom apt per month US$2995/4150; P☎☀) The fabulous collection of stylish suites – at what was one of the first genuine boutique hotels in Kenya – is perfect for well-heeled sophisticates who still like the personal touch. Intimate rooms are awash with calming tones, boldly accented by rich teak woods, lavish furniture and private Jacuzzis.

Nairobi National Park

★**Emakoko** LODGE $$$

(Map p230; ☏0787331632, 0771238218; www.emakoko.com; Uhuru Gardens; s/d US$525/860; P@☎☀) This stunning, artfully designed lodge inhabits a rise overlooking Nairobi National Park and the Mbagathi River. It's a wonderful way to begin or end your Kenyan safari by bypassing the hassles of Nairobi altogether, and the rooms and public areas are exquisite. Ask for one of the rooms that look out over the park.

Karen & Langata

Karen Camp CAMPGROUND $

(Map p230; ☏020-8833475, 0723314053; www.karencamp.com; Marula Lane, Karen; camping US$7, dm/s/d US$15/35/50, tw with shared bathroom US$40; P) You wouldn't expect to find a backpacker-friendly option out here in affluent Karen, which is why we like this friendly little spot so much. The quiet location and smart facilities are reason enough to make the trek out to the shady campsites, spick-and-span dorms and simple rooms (with mosquito nets).

Dea's Gardens GUESTHOUSE $$

(Map p230; ☏0733747443, 0734453761; www.deasgardens.com; Kwarara Road, off Ndege Rd; per person KSh7700) Following a similar formula to its sister property in Naivasha, Dea's Gardens Nairobi has simple yet light-filled and attractive rooms ranged across two floors of a large Karen home. The garden is green and lovely and Lisa is a gracious host.

Karen Blixen Cottages BOUTIQUE HOTEL $$$

(Map p230; ☏020-882138, 0733616206; www.karenblixencoffeegarden.com; 336 Karen Rd, Karen; s/d US$330/515; P☎☀) Located near Karen Blixen's House & Museum (p223), this gorgeous clutch of spacious cottages is centred on a formal garden, and adjacent to a small coffee plantation and a country restaurant. It's sophisticated, supremely comfortable and if you're keen on having an *Out of Africa* experience, then look no further.

KENYAN SAFARI COMPANIES

The following companies can organise safaris to Kenya's major safari destinations.

Abercrombie & Kent (Map p230; ☑ 020-6950000; www.abercrombiekent.com; Abercrombie & Kent House, Mombasa Rd, Nairobi; top end) Luxury travel company with excellent safaris to match.

Basecamp Explorer (☑ 0733333709; www.basecampkenya.com; Nairobi Head office, Gold Rock Bldg, off Mombasa Rd; top end) Scandinavian-owned ecotourism operator offering comprehensive and often luxurious camping itineraries with an environmentally sustainable focus.

Ben's Ecological Safaris (☑ 0722861072, 020-2431591; www.bensecologicalsafaris.com; 4th fl Aqua Plaza, Muranga'a Rd, Nairobi; midrange to top end) Birdwatching specialists but good for just about any natural history or cultural safaris across East Africa.

Bushbuck Adventures (☑ 0722356838, 020-7121505; www.bushbuckadventures.com; Peponi Rd, Westlands, Nairobi; top end) Small company specialising in personalised (including walking) safaris. It has a private, semipermanent camp in the Masai Mara.

Eastern & Southern Safaris (Map p224; ☑ 020-2242828; www.essafari.co.ke; 6th fl, Finance House, Loita St, Nairobi; midrange to top end) Classy and reliable outfit aiming at the midrange and upper end of the market, with standards to match. Does all the classic trips.

Eco-Resorts (☑ 0733618183; www.eco-resorts.com; top end) US-based company with a variety of activity-based volunteer and cultural packages and customised safaris around Kenya. A proportion of profits go to community and conservation projects.

Gametrackers (Map p230; ☑ 020-2002559; www.gametrackersafaris.com; Seminary Rd, off Magadi Rd, Karen, Nairobi; midrange to top end) Long-established and reliable company with a full range of camping and lodge safaris around Kenya; one of the best operators for Lake Turkana and the north.

IntoAfrica (☑ UK 0114-2555610; www.intoafrica.co.uk; 40 Huntingdon Cres, Sheffield, UK; midrange to top end) One of the most highly praised safari companies in East Africa, IntoAfrica specialises in 'fair-trade' trips providing insights into African life and directly supporting local communities. Combining culture *and* wildlife viewing is a speciality.

Origins Safaris (Map p224; ☑ 020-3312137; www.originsafaris.info; EcoBank Towers, Standard St, Nairobi; top end) A natural history and cultural focus, with everything from expert birdwatching to Samburu circumcision ceremonies, as well as other more mainstream safaris.

Pal-Davis Adventures (Map p220; ☑ 020-2522611, 0733919613; www.pal-davisadventures.com; 1st fl, Bhavesh Business Centre, Ngara Rd, Nairobi; midrange to top end) Small Kenyan company that gets excellent reports from travellers for their wide range of personalised safaris.

Pollman's Tours & Safaris (Map p230; ☑ 020-3337234; www.pollmans.com; Pollman's House, Mombasa Rd, Nairobi; midrange to top end) Kenyan-based operator that covers all the main national parks, with coastal and Tanzanian trips as well.

Private Safaris (Map p230; ☑ Mombasa 0722203780, Nairobi 020-3607000; www.private safaris.co.ke; 2nd fl, Mobil Plaza, Muthaiga, Nairobi; top end) Another safari agent offering trips that can be highly customised, Private can book trips all throughout sub-Saharan Africa.

Safari Icon Travel (Map p224; ☑ 0724112227, 020-2242818; www.safariicon.com; 4th fl, Nacico Chambers, cnr Kenyatta & Moi Aves; midrange) Well-regarded local company that covers a wide range of safari options in Kenya, Tanzania and Uganda.

Safe Ride Tours & Safaris (Map p224; ☑ 020-2101162; www.saferidesafaris.com; 2nd fl, Avenue House, Kenyatta Ave, Nairobi; budget) A relatively new budget operator recommended for camping excursions around the country.

Samburu Trails Trekking Safaris (☑ 020-2631594; www.samburutrails.com; budget to top end) Small British specialist outfit offering a range of foot excursions in some less-visited parts of the Rift Valley.

Nairobi National Park

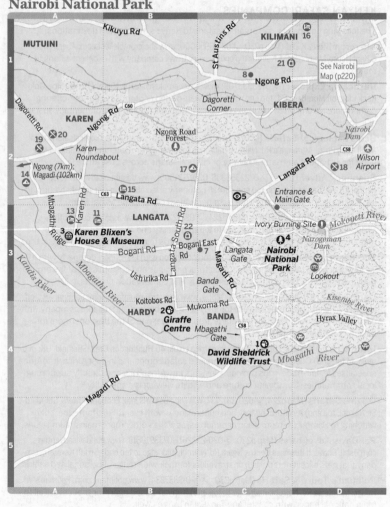

Giraffe Manor   HISTORIC HOTEL $$$
(Map p230; ☎020-8891078; www.thesafari
collection.com; Mukoma Rd, Karen; s/d full board
from US$772/1124; ℗) Built in 1932 in typical
English style, this elegant manor is situated on 56 hectares, much of which is given
over to the adjacent Giraffe Centre (p222).
As a result, you may find a Rothschild's giraffe peering through your bedroom window first thing in the morning. And yet,
the real appeal of the Giraffe Manor is that
you're treated as a personal guest of the
owners.

🍴 Eating

🍴 City Centre

⭐**Savanna: The Coffee Lounge**   CAFE $
(Map p220; Museum Hill Rd; snacks from KSh200,
mains KSh500-700; ⊗7am-8pm Mon-Sat, 9am-
6pm Sun) This classy little chain has outposts
across Nairobi, including a **branch** (Map
p224; Loita St; snacks from KSh200, mains KSh500-
700; ⊗7am-8pm Mon-Sat, 9am-6pm Sun) in the
town centre, but we particularly like the
tranquillity of this branch inside the grounds
of the National Museum. Decor is safari chic

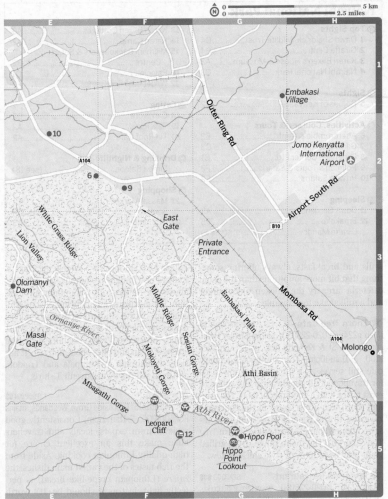

without being overdone, service is friendly and unobtrusive, and dishes include pies, wraps, samosas, sandwiches, burgers, pasta, soups and salads.

★ Beneve Coffee House CAFE $

(Map p224; ☑ 020-217959; cnr Standard & Koinange Sts; mains KSh150-350; ☺ 7am-4pm Mon-Fri) This small self-service cafe has locals queuing outside in the mornings waiting for it to open. Food ranges from African- and Indian-influenced stews to curries, fish and chips, samosas, pasties and a host of other choices, all at low, low prices.

Nyama Choma Stalls KENYAN $

(Map p220; Haile Selassie Ave; mains around KSh500) At these backstreet stalls near the Railway Museum, behind the Shell petrol station, foreigners are a rare sight, but you'll be warmly welcomed and encouraged to sample Kenyan dishes such as *matoke* (cooked mashed plantains) and wonderful barbecued meat.

Pasara Café INTERNATIONAL $

(Map p224; ground fl, Lonrho Bldg, Standard St; dishes KSh275-395; ☺ 7am-midnight Mon-Sat) At the forefront of Nairobi's burgeoning cafe culture, this stylish, modern bar-brasserie has a nifty selection of snacks, sandwiches,

Nairobi National Park

grills and breakfasts, always offering something that bit more ambitious than the usual cafeteria fare; try the chicken tikka burger and a milkshake for example.

★ **Thorn Tree Café** INTERNATIONAL $$
(Map p224; ☑020-228030; Sarova Stanley Hotel, cnr Kimathi St & Kenyatta Ave; mains KSh1000-2100; ⊙11am-10pm) The Stanley's legendary cafe still serves as a popular meeting place for travellers of all persuasions, and caters to most tastes with a good mix of food. The original thorn-tree noticeboard in the courtyard gave rise to the general expression, and inspired Lonely Planet's own online Thorn Tree Travel Forum. The menu ranges from grilled giant prawns to Kenyan-style chicken stew.

★ **Tamarind Restaurant** SEAFOOD $$$
(Map p224; ☑020-2251811; www.tamarind.co.ke; off Harambee Ave; mains KSh1100-2800; ⊙lunch & dinner Mon-Sat) Kenya's most prestigious restaurant chain runs Nairobi's best seafood restaurant, located in the monumental National Bank Building. The splendid menu offers all manner of exotic flavours, and the lavish dining room is laid out in a sumptuous modern Arabic-Moorish style. Starters range from Hibiscus-flamed seafood to an exquisite seafood platter.

✕ Westlands

Haandi Restaurant INDIAN $$
(Map p234; ☑020-4448294; The Mall Shopping Centre, Ring Rd, Westlands; mains KSh750-1700; ⊙noon-

2.30pm & 6.30-10.30pm; ❄) Widely regarded as Kenya's best Indian restaurant, Haandi rises above its nondescript shopping-mall location. The expansive menu includes wonderful Mughlai (North Indian) spreads, tandoori dishes and plenty of vegetarian curries. Most dishes are served with Haandi's signature stacks of naan and piles of basmati rice. It has sister restaurants in Kampala and London, and even sells its own souvenir T-shirts.

Abyssinia ETHIOPIAN $$
(☑0725151515; Brookside Grove, Westlands; mains KSh500-900; ⊙11am-11pm) Consistently good reviews from expats, locals and travellers alike make this an excellent choice for high-quality Ethiopian cooking. Aside from the rich tastes of the varied main dishes, the *injere* (Ethiopian crepe-like bread) is perfectly light, just as it should be. It's worth coming here just for the coffee ceremony.

✕ Karen & Langata

★ **Talisman** INTERNATIONAL $$
(Map p230; ☑0705999997; thetalismanrestaurant.com; 320 Ngong Rd, Karen; mains KSh1200-2200; ⊙8am-10pm Tue-Sat, 9am-10pm Sun) This classy cafe-bar-restaurant remains fashionable with the Karen in-crowd, and rivals any of Kenya's top eateries for imaginative international food. The comfortable lounge-like rooms mix modern African and European styles, the courtyard provides some welcome air, and specials such as pan-seared ostrich fillet perk up the palate no end.

Tin Roof Cafe
CAFE, INTERNATIONAL $$

(Map p230; ✆ 0706348215; www.facebook.com/TinRoofCafe; Dagoretti Rd, Karen; mains from Ksh500; ⏰ 8.30am-5.30pm; 🛜) This place has all the necessary ingredients to be a Nairobi favourite – a quiet garden setting in Karen, great coffee, the city's best salad bar and a commitment to healthy eating. Our only complaint? It doesn't open for dinner. Due to popular demand, it began to open on Sundays not long after our visit. Souk (p236), a fabulous shopping experience, is on the same property.

Carnivore
GRILLED MEATS $$$

(Map p230; ✆ 0733611608, 020-605933; www.tamarind.co.ke/carnivore/; off Langata Rd, Karen; buffet from KSh3000; ⏰ noon-3pm & 6.30-11pm; 🅿) Love it or hate it, Carnivore is hands down the most famous *nyama choma* (barbecued meat) in Kenya, an icon among tourists, expats and wealthier locals for the past 25 years. At the entrance is a huge barbecue pit laden with real swords of beef, pork, lamb, chicken and farmed game meats.

Carnivore was voted by UK magazine *Restaurant* as among the 50 best restaurants in the world in 2002 and 2003. This honour was largely in recognition of the fact that you could dine here on exotic game meats. In recent years, however, strict new laws mean that zebra, hartebeest, kudu and the like are now off the menu, and you have to be content with camel, ostrich and crocodile, in addition to more standard offerings. You also get soup, salads and sauces to go with the meats.

As long as the paper flag on your table is flying, waiters will keep bringing the meat, which is carved right at the table; if you're in need of a breather, you can tip the flag over temporarily. Note that dessert and coffee (but not other drinks) are included in the set price.

This meat-fest does have its critics – prices are high and the waiters, hats and all, can seem like the ringmasters of a circus with their enthusiastic bonhomie. But if you take it for what it is, you'll leave satisfied.

At lunchtime, you can get to Carnivore by matatu 126 from the city centre – the turn-off is signposted just past Wilson Airport, from where it's a 1km walk. At night, it's best to hire a taxi, which should run to about KSh800 each way depending on your bargaining skills.

At night you may wish to stay on for an all-night dance-athon at the adjacent Simba Saloon (p235).

WORTH A TRIP

NYAMA CHOMA AT THE RIFT

Olepolos Country Club
(✆ 0714032122; Corner Baridi, C58; meals from KSh750; ⏰ 10am-5.30pm Mon-Thu, 10am-8pm Fri, 9am-midnight Sat & Sun) If you've your own wheels and a taste for barbecued meat, take the road southwest out of Nairobi, past Kiserian on the road to Lake Magadi to Corner Baridi where this fine, simple little place serves up roasted meat and roast chicken. Wash it down with cold Tuskers as you look out over the Rift Valley, and we reckon you're somewhere close to heaven.

It's around 34km southwest of downtown Nairobi near the town of Kisamis. If you don't have your own wheels, take matatu 126 as far as Kiserian and then hire a taxi.

🍷 Drinking & Nightlife

Western cafe culture has hit Nairobi, seized upon enthusiastically by local expats and residents pining for a decent cup of Kenyan coffee. This is the best place in the country for *real* coffee.

There are plenty of cheap but very rough-and-ready bars around Latema Rd and River Rd, although these places aren't recommended for female travellers, and even male drinkers should watch themselves. You can also head to Westlands and Karen, where the drinking scene brings in a lot more expats. Be aware that, even in the 'burbs, foreign women without a man in tow will draw attention.

Nightclubs usually open from 9pm until 6am.

🍸 City Centre

⭐ **Nairobi Java House**
CAFE

(Map p224; ✆ 020-313565; www.nairobijavahouse.com; Mama Ngina St; coffee KSh150-350; ⏰ 6.30am-10pm Mon-Fri, 7am- 9pm Sat, 8am-8pm Sun) This fantastic coffeehouse is rapidly turning itself into a major brand, and you may see its logo on T-shirts as far afield as London and beyond. Aficionados say the coffee's some of the best in Kenya, and there are plenty of cakes and other sweet and savoury treats (even New York cheesecake).

Westlands

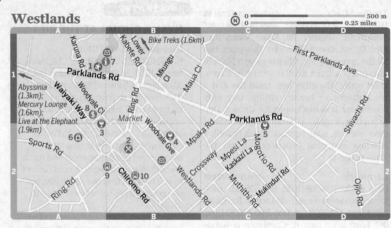

Westlands

★ **Simmers**   BAR
(Map p224; ☏ 020-217659; cnr Kenyatta Ave &
Muindi Mbingu St; admission free; ⊙ 8am-1am)
If you're tired of having your butt pinched
in darkened discos to the strains of limp
R&B, Simmers could be your place. The
atmosphere at this open-air bar-restaurant
is amazing, with enthusiastic crowds turning out to wind and grind the night away
to parades of bands playing anything from
Congolese rumba to Kenyan *benga* (contemporary dance).

★ **Lord Delamere Terrace & Bar**   BAR
(Map p220; www.fairmont.com/NorfolkHotel; Norfolk Hotel, Harry Thuku Rd; ⊙ 6.30am-10.30pm)
Once one of Africa's classic bars, the Lord
Delamere Terrace was the starting point
for so many epic colonial safaris, and the
scene of tall tales told by men such as Ernest
Hemingway and the Great White Hunters of
the early 20th century. Not much of the old
atmosphere remains, but come here as a pilgrimage to the Africa of old.

Florida 2000   CLUB
(Map p224; ☏ 0706577009; floridaclubskenya.com;
Moi Ave; men/women KSh300/200; ⊙ 9pm-6am)
This big dancing den, known by everyone as
F2, is near City Hall Way. It works to a fairly
uncomplicated formula of booze, beats and
tightly packed bodies. As is typical in Nairobi, every night is a little different: Thursday
is techno trance, Friday is rumba, Saturday
could be soul and so on.

Westlands

★ **Gypsy's Bar**   BAR
(Map p234; Woodvale Grove; ⊙ 11am-4am) This is
one of the most popular bars in Westlands,
pulling in a large, mixed crowd of Kenyans, expats and prostitutes. Snacks are available, and
there's decent Western and African music, with
parties taking over the pavement in summer.

K1 Klub House
BAR

(Map p234; ☎020-749870, 0714579265; www.klubhouse.co.ke; Parklands Rd; ⊙24hr) At the western end of Westlands, the Klub House is another old favourite. The spacious bar has plenty of pool tables and excellent DJs spinning reggae, dancehall, hip-hop and R&B until late. Watch for live bands on Saturday nights, Tuesday night is jazz, while Wednesday is Ladies' night.

Havana Bar
BAR

(Map p234; ☎020-4450653, 0723265941; www.havana.co.ke; Woodvale Grove, Westlands; ⊙noon-3am) Thursday nights at the Havana Bar are one of Nairobi's hottest tickets, drawing a broad cross-section of Nairobi night owls, prostitutes among them. Latin tunes that often stray into techno provide a varied soundtrack, and you can lubricate the night with anything from Kenyan coffee, South African wines and middle shelf international spirits to a rather fine mojito. Ask for the menu of Cuban cigars.

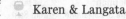

Karen & Langata

Simba Saloon
CLUB

(Map p230; ☎020-501706; www.tamarind.co.ke/simba-saloon; off Langata Rd; admission KSh250-400; ⊙5pm-late Wed-Sun; minibus 126, taxi) Next door to Carnivore out on the road to Karen, this large open-air bar and nightclub pulls in a huge crowd. There are video screens, several bars, a bonfire, and unashamedly Western music on the dance floor, although you might get the occasional African superstar playing live. It's usually crammed with wealthy Kenyans, expat teenagers, travellers and NGO workers, plus a fair sprinkling of prostitutes.

☆ Entertainment

For information on entertainment in Nairobi and for big music venues in the rest of the country, get hold of the *Saturday Nation*, the Saturday edition of Kenya's daily newspaper, which is sold by wandering vendors all over Nairobi and lists everything from cinema releases to live-music venues.

KENYA NAIROBI

NAIROBI SAFETY

First-time visitors to Nairobi are understandably daunted by 'Nairobbery's' unenviable reputation. Read the local newspapers and you'll quickly discover that carjacking, robbery and violence are daily occurrences.

The most likely annoyance for travellers is petty theft, which is most likely to occur at budget hotels and campsites. As a general rule, you should take advantage of your hotel's safe and never leave your valuables out in the open. While you're walking around town, don't bring anything with you that you wouldn't want to lose. As an extra safety precaution, it's best to only carry money in your wallet, and hide your credit cards and bank cards elsewhere.

In the event that you are mugged, never, ever resist – simply give up your valuables and, more often than not, your assailant will flee the scene rapidly. Remember that a petty thief and a violent aggressor are very different kinds of people, so don't give your assailant any reason to do something rash.

While it's important to understand the potential dangers and annoyances, you shouldn't let fear exile you to your hotel room – remember that the majority of foreign visitors in Nairobi never experience any kind of problem. Exude confidence, practise street smarts, don't wear anything too flashy and you should encounter nothing worse than a few persistent safari touts and the odd con artist.

Potential Trouble Spots

Nairobi's Central Business District (CBD), bounded by Kenyatta Ave, Moi Ave, Haile Selassie Ave and Uhuru Hwy, is quite relaxed and hassle-free by day. After sunset, mugging is a risk anywhere on the streets, and you should always take a taxi, even if you're only going a few blocks. This will also keep you safe from the attentions of Nairobi's street prostitutes, who flood into town in force after dark.

Other potential danger zones include the area around Latema and River Rds (east of Moi Ave), which is a hot spot for petty theft. This area is home to the city's bus terminals, so keep an eye on your bags and personal belongings at all times if passing through here.

★ **Live at the Elephant**   LIVE MUSIC

(📞 0721946710; Gate 3, Kanjata Rd; ⊙ from 8pm Fri) This could just be our favourite live music venue in town. It draws a trendy, up-market crowd with its fair share of Nairobi hipsters for the regular program of up-and-coming artists (mostly Kenyan with some from further afield in Africa). It's in the Lavington area. Check out the Facebook page (www.facebook.com/LiveAtTheElephant) to see what's coming up.

★ **Blankets & Wine**   LIVE MUSIC

(📞 0720801333, 0736801333; blanketsandwine.com; tickets KSh1500-2500; ⊙ 1st Sun of month) This monthly picnic-concert is one of the best-loved features on Nairobi's live music circuit. Musicians vary but the underlying principle is to support local and other East African acts, from singer-songwriter and acoustic to rock and roots. Families are welcome and the venue changes each month – next door to Simba Saloon (p235) is one of the popular locations.

🛍 Shopping

★ **Souk**   ARTS & CRAFTS

(Map p230; 📞 0706348215; www.souk-kenya.com; Dagoretti Rd; ⊙ 9.30am-5.30pm Mon-Sat) Some of Kenya's more creative artists, photographers, leatherworkers and other high-quality artisans have come together under one roof, and the result is some of Kenya's most discerning shopping experiences. It shares premises with the equally excellent Tin Roof Cafe (p233).

★ **Utamaduni**   HANDICRAFTS

(Map p230; www.utamaduni.com; Bogani East Rd, Karen; ⊙ 9am-6pm) Utamaduni is a large crafts emporium, with more than a dozen separate rooms selling all kinds of excellent African artworks and souvenirs. Prices start relatively high, but there's *none* of the hard sell you'd get in town. A portion of all proceeds goes to the Kenya Wildlife Foundation. There's an on-site restaurant and playground. It's close to the Giraffe Centre.

Spinners Web   HANDICRAFTS

(Map p234; 📞 020-2072629, 0731168996; www.spinnerswebkenya.com; Getathuru Gardens, off Peponi Rd, Spring Valley; ⊙ 9.30am-6.30pm Mon-Fri, 9.30am-5.30pm Sat & Sun) This place works with workshops and self-help groups around the country. It's a bit like a handicrafts version of Ikea,

with goods displayed the way they might look in a Western living room. There are some appealing items, including carpets, wall-hangings, ceramics, wooden bowls, baskets and clothing.

Maasai Market   MARKET

(Map p224; off Slip Road; ⊙ Tue) Busy, popular Maasai markets are held every Tuesday on the waste ground near Slip Rd in town. Souvenirs on offer include beaded jewellery, gourds, baskets and other Maasai crafts, but you'll have to bargain hard. The market is open from early morning to late afternoon. Other locations include Friday behind the Village Market shopping **complex** (Village Market, Limuru Rd; ⊙ Fri), **downtown** (Map p224; opposite Reinsurance Plaza, Taita Rd; ⊙ Sat) on Saturday, and on Sunday next to the **Yaya Centre** (Map p230; Argwings Kodhek; ⊙ Sun).

City Market   MARKET

(Map p224; Muindi Mbingu St; ⊙ 9am-5pm Mon-Fri, 9am-noon Sat) The city's main souvenir business is concentrated in this covered market, which has dozens of stalls selling wood carvings, drums, spears, shields, soapstone, Maasai jewellery and clothing. It's a hectic place and you'll have to bargain hard (and we mean *hard*), but there's plenty of good stuff on offer. It's an interesting place to wander around in its own right, though you generally need to be shopping to make the constant hassle worth the bother.

ℹ Information

EMERGENCY

Emergency services (📞 999) The national emergency number to call for fire, police and ambulance assistance. A word of warning, though – don't rely on prompt arrival.

Police (📞 020-240000) Phone for less-urgent police business.

St John's Ambulance (📞 2210000)

Tourist Helpline (📞 020-604767; ⊙ 24hr)

INTERNET ACCESS

Your hotel is probably your best bet. Otherwise, there are hundreds of internet cafes in downtown Nairobi, most of them tucked away in anonymous office buildings in the town centre and few of which seem designed to last the distance. Connection speed is decent assuming you're not streaming YouTube, though machine quality varies wildly. It can be difficult to find any internet cafes open in the downtown area on Sunday.

MEDICAL SERVICES

AAR Health Services (Map p220; ☎ 0731191070, 0725225225; www.aarhealth.com/aar_ke/; Williamson House, Fourth Ngong Ave; ⊙7.30am-8pm Mon-Fri, 8am-6pm Sat, 9am-5pm Sun) Probably the best of a number of private ambulance and emergency air-evacuation companies. It also runs private clinics at various locations around Nairobi, including in **Westlands** (Map p234).

Acacia Medical Centre (Map p224; ☎ 020-2212200; info@acaciamed.co.ke; ICEA Bldg, Kenyatta Ave; ⊙7am-7pm Mon-Fri, 7am-5pm Sat, 8am-5pm Sun) Privately run clinic in the city centre.

Aga Khan Hospital (☎ 020-3662020; Third Parklands Ave; ⊙24hr) A reliable hospital with 24-hour emergency services.

KAM Pharmacy (Map p224; ☎ 020-2227195; www.kampharmacy.com; Executive Tower, IPS Bldg, Kimathi St; ⊙8.30am-6pm Mon-Fri, 8.30am-2pm Sat) A one-stop shop for medical treatment, with a pharmacy, doctor's surgery and laboratory.

MONEY

Jomo Kenyatta International Airport has several exchange counters in the baggage reclaim area and a **Barclays Bank** (⊙24hr) with an ATM outside in the arrivals hall. There are Barclays branches with guarded ATMs throughout the city centre and further afield.

POST

Main Post Office (Map p224; ☎ 020-243434; Kenyatta Ave; ⊙8am-6pm Mon-Fri, 9am-noon Sat) The vast main post office is a well-organised edifice close to Uhuru Park. Around the back of the main building is the **EMS office** (Map p224; ⊙8am-8pm Mon-Fri, 9am-12.30pm Sat), for courier deliveries, and there's a Telkom Kenya office upstairs. Other post office locations are shown on the map.

TRAVEL AGENCIES

Bunson Travel (☎ 020-3685990; www.bunsontravel.com; 2nd fl, Park Place, Limuru Rd) A good upmarket operator (part of the Carlson Wagonlit stable) selling air tickets and upmarket safaris.

ⓘ Getting There & Away

AIR

Nairobi has two airports, Jomo Kenyatta International Airport (p369) and Wilson Airport (p369).

BUS

In Nairobi, most long-distance bus company offices are in the River Rd area, clustered around Accra Rd and the surrounding streets, although some also have offices on Monrovia St for their international services. You should always make your reservation up to 24 hours in advance and check (then double check) the departure point from where the bus leaves.

Dream Line (Map p224; ☎ 0731777799) A reliable company connecting Nairobi to Mombasa and Malindi.

Easy Coach (Map p224; ☎ 0726354301, 0738200301; www.easycoach.co.ke; Haile Selassie Ave, Nairobi) Long-standing company serving western Kenyan destinations as well as running some international buses to Uganda.

Modern Coast Express (Oxygen; Map p224; ☎ 0726778852, 0713202255; www.moderncoastexpress.com; cnr Cross Lane & Accra Rd) Safer, more reliable and slightly more expensive buses to Mombasa, Malindi and Kisumu, with Mombasa–Dar es-Salaam and Nairobi–Kampala services.

Riverside Shuttle (Map p224; ☎ 0722220176; www.riverside-shuttle.com; Monrovia St) Mostly international services to Arusha, Moshi and Kilimanjaro International Airport (Tanzania).

MATATU

Most matatus leave from the chaotic Latema, Accra, River and Cross Rds and fares are similar to the buses. Most companies are pretty much the same, although there are some that aim for higher standards than others. Mololine Prestige Shuttle, which operates along the Nairobi–Naivasha–Nakuru–Eldoret route, is one such company, with others set to follow their example on other routes.

BUSES FROM NAIROBI

TO	FARE (KSH)	DURATION (HR)	COMPANY
Eldoret	1250	7-8	Easy Coach
Kakamega	1450	7½	Easy Coach
Kisumu	1400	7	Easy Coach, Modern Coast (Oxygen)
Mombasa	500-1200	6-10	Dream Line, Modern Coast (Oxygen)
Malaba	1250	9-12	Easy Coach
Malindi	1100-1800	10-13	Dream Line, Modern Coast (Oxygen)

MAJOR MATATU ROUTES

TO	FARE (KSH)	DURATION (HR)	DEPARTURE POINT
Eldoret	800	6	Easy Coach Terminal
Kericho	750	3	Cross Rd
Kisumu	700-1000	4	Cross Rd
Meru	750	3	main bus & matatu area
Naivasha	350	1½	cnr River Rd & Ronald Ngala St
Nakuru	500	3	cnr River Rd & Ronald Ngala St
Namanga	500	2	cnr River Rd & Ronald Ngala St
Nanyuki	500	3	main bus & matatu area
Narok	500	3	Cross Rd
Nyahururu	500	3½	cnr River Rd & Ronald Ngala St
Nyeri	500	2½	Latema Rd

TRAIN

Until the new Nairobi-Mombasa railway line comes into existence a few (perhaps many) years from now, the existing railway is slow, old and unreliable but still something of an African epic. Do it because you love trains and aren't in a hurry, not for reasons of comfort or speed.

Scheduled departure times from Nairobi are at 6.30pm on Monday, Wednesday and Friday. All going well, you should arrive in Mombasa at 9.45am the following morning. Tickets cost US$75 per adult (child US$55) for 1st class (two-bed berths) and US$65 (child US$45) for 2nd class (four-bed berths) including bed and breakfast (you get dinner with 1st class). Book as far in advance as possible.

Railway Booking Office (Map p224; Station Rd; ⊙9am-noon & 2-6.30pm) Nairobi train station has a small booking office. You need to come in person to book tickets a few days in advance of your intended departure. On the day of departure, arrive early.

ⓘ Getting Around

TO/FROM JOMO KENYATTA INTERNATIONAL AIRPORT

Kenya's main international airport is 15km out of town, off the road to Mombasa. We recommend that you take a taxi (KSh1500 to KSh2000, but you'll need to bargain hard) to get to/from the airport, especially after dark.

A far cheaper way to get into town is by city bus 34 (KSh40), but a lot of travellers get robbed on the bus or when they get off. Always hold onto valuables and have small change ready for the fare. Buses run from 5.45am to 9.30pm weekdays, 6.20am to 9.30pm Saturdays and 7.15am to 9.30pm Sundays, though the last few evening services may not operate. Heading to the airport, the main departure point is along Moi Ave, right outside the Hotel Ambassadeur

Nairobi. Thereafter, buses travel west along Kenyatta Ave.

TO/FROM WILSON AIRPORT

To get to Wilson airport, the cheapest option is to take bus or matatu 15, 31, 34, 125 or 126 from Moi Ave (KSh35, 15 to 45 minutes depending on traffic). A taxi from the centre of town will cost at least KSh1000, depending on the driver. In the other direction, you'll have to bargain the driver down from KSh1500.

CAR

If you are driving, beware of wheel-clampers: parking in the centre is by permit only (KSH200), available from the parking attendants who roam the streets in bright yellow jackets.

MATATU

Nairobi's horde of matatus follow the same routes as buses and display the same route numbers. For Westlands, you can pick up 23 on Moi Ave or Latema Rd. Matatu 46 to the Yaya Centre stops in front of the main post office, and 125 and 126 to Langata leave from in front of the train station. As usual, you should keep an eye on your valuables while on all matatus.

TAXI

Taxis here are overpriced and under-maintained, but you've little choice, particularly at night. Taxis don't cruise for passengers, but you can find them parked on every other street corner in the city centre – at night they're outside restaurants, bars and nightclubs.

Fares around town are negotiable but end up pretty standard. Any journey within the downtown area costs KSh500, from downtown to Milimani Rd costs KSh600, and for longer journeys such as Westlands or the Yaya Centre, fares range from KSh750 to KS900. From the city centre to Karen and Langata is around KSh1200 one way.

SOUTHERN RIFT VALLEY

Africa's Great Rift Valley is one of the continent's grand epics. Here in Kenya, the battle of geological forces that almost rent Africa in two left the Rift Valley looking as if it were created by giants: the ribbon of soda lakes (inscribed on Unesco's World Heritage list in 2011) scars the valley like the footprints of a massive hippopotamus, and numerous dried-out volcanic cones stand to attention like amplified termite mounds.

The Rift Valley's dramatic landscapes are lent personality by some of central Kenya's

Southern Rift Valley

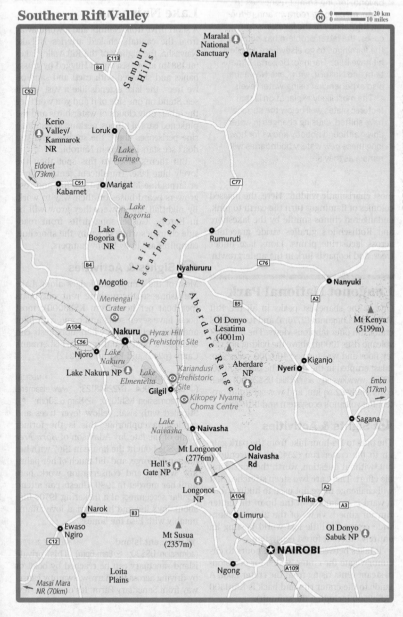

RIFT LAKES RISING

Whether alkaline or freshwater, Kenya's lakes have experienced an as-yet-unexplained rise in water levels. In some cases, these rises have been by metres, engulfing shorelines and beyond, forcing some businesses to close, maps to be redrawn and reducing the salinity of the lakes in some cases; the latter problem has caused the flamingos to go elsewhere. Hardest hit have been Baringo, Bogoria, Elmenteita and Nakuru, with Lake Naivasha also experiencing rising water levels.

The most likely explanation is that tectonic plates well below the surface have shifted, causing changes in water flows, although nobody knows for how long these new watery boundaries will remain as they are.

most charismatic wildlife. Here, the massed colonies of flamingos turn the earth to pink, endangered rhinos snuffle by the lakeshore and Rothschild's giraffes stride gracefully across lacustrine plains. Lions laze under trees, and leopards lurk in the undergrowth.

Longonot National Park

One of the shapeliest peaks in all the Rift Valley, Mt Longonot (2776m) and its serrated crater rim offer fabulous views. The dormant volcano rises 1000m above the baking hot valley floor and was formed 400,000 years ago; it last erupted in the 1860s. The park (☑ 050-50255; www.kws.org; adult/child US$20/10) itself covers only 52 sq km, and was set up to protect the volcano's ecosystem and little else.

◉ Sights & Activities

The one- to 1½-hour hike from the park gate up to the crater rim (2545m) is strenuous but, without question, worth the considerable effort. There are two steep stretches that will challenge those not used to hiking. Your reward is to emerge at the lip of the crater rim for superb views of the 2km- to 3km-wide crater – a little lost world hosting an entirely different forest ecosystem.

It takes between 1½ and 2½ hours to circumnavigate the crater; watch for occasional steam vents rising from the crater floor. A guide to the crater rim and back is KSh1500 (KSh2500 including the summit).

❶ Getting There & Away

Mt Longonot is 75km northwest of Nairobi on the Old Naivasha Rd. If you're without a vehicle, take a matatu from Naivasha to Longonot village, from where there's a path (ask locals) to the park's access road.

Lake Naivasha

A short drive from Nairobi and a world away from the capital's choked arteries is Lake Naivasha, the highest of the Rift Valley lakes (at 1884m above sea level.) Hugged by grassy banks and shingled with cacti and sand olive trees, the lake extends like a vast, sunlit sea. Stand on one side of it and you won't see the other; only clouds of water birds and the pinkened ears of hippos, peeking like submarine periscopes above the surface. And you don't see stars like this in Nairobi.

But there's more to this spot than the lovely blue lake. Translucent tents of flower farms line Moi South Lake Rd, and rose growers board buses on their way to work. By nightfall, the flowers they grow will be in Europe. Gospel song drifts from roadside churches while down by the shoreline, campfires are lit by happy campers.

◉ Sights & Activities

Most of the camps and lodges along Lake Naivasha's southern shore rent out boats (per boat per hour from KSh3000); most boats have seven seats and come with pilot and lifejackets. Places where nonguests can organise a boat rental include Fisherman's Camp (p242) and Elsamere (p242).

★ Elsamere   MUSEUM
(☑ 020-2050964, 0722648123; www.elsamere. com; admission KSh1050; ⊗ 8am-6.30pm; ℗) Stippled with sisal, yellow fever trees and candelabra euphorbia, this is the former home of the late Joy Adamson of Born Free fame. She bought the house in 1967 with her husband George, and did much of her painting, writing and conservation work here until her murder in 1980. Guests can attend regular screenings of a flickering 1970s film about Joy's life and her myriad love affairs, notably with Elsa the lioness.

★ Crescent Island   WILDLIFE RESERVE
(admission US$30; ⊗ 8am-6pm) This private island sanctuary can be reached by boat, or by driving across the narrow, swampy causeway from Sanctuary Farm. It's one of the few

Lake Naivasha

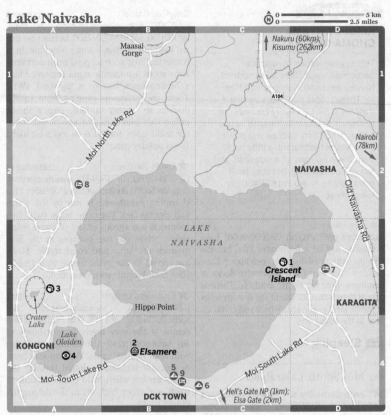

places in the Rift Valley where you can walk among giraffes, zebras, waterbucks, impalas and countless bird species. Lucky visitors might even spot a leopard. Island walks, led by a guide, last between 90 minutes and three hours. It's also a good spot for a picnic lunch.

Crater Lake Game Sanctuary WILDLIFE RESERVE
(per person US$25, plus car KSh200) Surrounding a beautiful volcanic crater lake fringed with acacias, this small sanctuary has many trails, including one for hikers along the steep but diminutive crater rim. The jade-green crater lake is held in high regard by the local Maasai, who believe its alkaline waters help soothe ailing cattle. As well as the impressive 150 bird species recorded here, giraffes, zebras and other plains wildlife are also regular residents on the more open plains surrounding the crater.

Lake Naivasha

DON'T MISS

KIKOPEY NYAMA CHOMA CENTRE

This agglomeration of roadside barbecued-meat stalls 31km north of Naivasha is famous throughout Kenya. These places don't survive long if their meat isn't perfectly cooked. The restaurants closest to the road hassle new arrivals to try to draw you in. We tried Acacia Restaurant, a little back from the main road on a side road, and found it outstanding, but they're all good. You'll pay around KSh400 per kilo of meat.

Lake Oloiden   LAKE

(boat safaris per 30/60min KSh2000/4000) Lake Naivasha may be a freshwater lake, but the alkaline waters of its near neighbour Lake Oloiden draw small but impressive flocks of flamingos. Boat safaris are available. The real appeal here is that it's one of the few stretches of public land in the area where you can walk near to the lakeshore.

🛏 Sleeping

🛏 Moi South Lake Road

⭐**Camp Carnelley's**   CAMPGROUND, BANDAS $
(☑ 050-50004, 0722260749; www.campcarnel leys.com; Moi South Lake Rd; camping Ksh600-800, r from KSh2500, bandas Ksh6000-12000, dm Ksh800; ℗) ✔ Right on the shoreline, this lovely, quiet spot has chic *bandas* (thatched huts), simple twin rooms with woolly blankets and camping pitches within earshot of the hippos. Head down to the wooden-beamed bar with its hip couches, roaring fireplace and creative menu. Boats are on standby for lake safaris.

Fisherman's Camp   CAMPGROUND, BANDAS $
(☑ 020-2139922, 0718880634, 0726870590; www. fishermanscamp.com; camping KSh600, tent hire KSh500, bandas per person KSh1000-2000; ℗) Scruffier and more sociable than its next-door neighbour Carnelley's, Fisherman's Camp attracts a young, backpacker crowd keen to eat and drink in the restaurant and hang out at the volleyball court. It's set in nice lake-shore gardens, shaded by dappled fever trees. The rooms are simple but comfortable (prices rise on weekends). Also plays host to the **Rift Valley Music Festival** each August.

Crayfish Camp   CAMPGROUND $
(☑ 0720226829; www.crayfishcamp.co.ke; camping KSh700, s/d KSh4750/7500, fantasy r per person KSh2200; ℗🐕📶🏊) Fancy sleeping in a converted boat with leopard-print curtains? How about a romantic night crammed into a broken-down bus or a toy-sized 4WD? There are 82 rooms ranging from vanilla doubles to fantasy options, plus a theme pub, a kids' play area and a restaurant serving milkshakes. Still, it does feel a bit like a 1980s holiday camp.

⭐**Dea's Gardens**   GUESTHOUSE $$
(☑ 0734453761, 0733747433; www.deasgardens. com; Moi South Lake Rd; half-board KSh9350) This charming guesthouse is run by the warm and elegant Dea. The main house (with two rooms) is a gorgeous chalet of Swiss inspiration, while the two cottages in the lush grounds are large and comfortable. Meals are served in the main house with Dea as your host. Warmly recommended.

⭐**Elsamere Lodge**   HOTEL $$
(☑ 050-2021055; www.elsamere.com; s/d KSh9500/15,000; ℗) ✔ The conservation centre at the very lovely former home of Joy Adamson (p240) also doubles as a lodge with high novelty value. You can stay here, in pleasant bungalows dotted through the pretty garden where wild colobus monkeys roam, and enjoy high tea in the Adamson's dining room.

Enashipai   HOTEL $$$
(☑ 051-2130000, 0713254035; www.enashipai. com; s/d US$350/485; ℗🐕📶🏊) By far the sleekest of the resorts along the lake shore, Enashipai comes from the Maasai name meaning 'state of happiness', and it's no misnomer. If you like your resorts polished and luxurious, with a private, gated-community feel, you're at the right place. Warm staff, a good restaurant and an ultra-chic spa make it easy to unwind here.

🛏 Moi North Lake Road

Olerai House   GUESTHOUSE $$$
(☑ 020-8048602; www.olerai.com; s/d full board US$495/800) Hidden under a blanket of tropical flowers, this beautiful house is like something from a fairy tale, where petals dust the beds and floors, zebras and vervet monkeys hang out with pet dogs, and the rooms are a delight. Perhaps best of all, the camp is owned by renowned elephant conservationists Iain and Oria Douglas-Hamilton – if

they're at home, there are few more fascinating hosts in Kenya.

Eating

★ Lazybones   RESTAURANT $$
(Camp Carnelley's, Moi South Lake Rd; mains from KSh450) Camp Carnelley's hip restaurant is popular with NGO workers and other Nairobians at weekends. Grab one of the gorgeous low-slung sofas, or pull up a chair around the roaring fireplace. Co-owner Chrisi's creative menu includes Indian fusion dishes, great salads, fresh fish and even breakfast smoothies. There's also a selection of wines, beers and spirits. Out back, you'll find a pool table.

★ Club House   RESTAURANT $$
(☑0722761940; Sanctuary Farm; lunch KSh2000, dinner KSh2500) Farm-to-table sustainable cuisine is more exciting when there are giraffes and hippos to spy on in the distance. The signature eatery at **Sanctuary Farm** (www. sanctuaryfarmkenya.com; s/d KSh15,000/20,000, camping KSh6000; P 🛜) 🍴 is relaxed but stylish, with tables strewn over a wooden verandah. Inside, there are framed black-and-white posters and Rift Valley wines. Expect dishes such as beetroot salad, red pepper chicken, home-baked focaccia and baklava with pineapple sorbet. Reservations only.

ℹ Getting There & Away

Frequent matatus (KSh100, one hour) run along Moi South Lake Rd between Naivasha town and Kongoni on the lake's western side, passing the turn-offs to Hell's Gate National Park and Fisherman's Camp (KSh70).

Bora Bora backpacker bus (☑0722504655; www.boraborabackperbus.com; tickets KSh1500) was in the process of launching at the time of research, offering easy shuttle runs from Nairobi to Lake Naivasha and beyond.

ℹ Getting Around

Most lodges and camps hire mountain bikes if you're heading for Hell's Gate National Park; costs start from KSh700 per day. Check the bikes carefully before paying.

Matatu hops around the lake shore cost upwards of 50KSh, depending on distance.

Hell's Gate National Park

Dry and dusty but infinitely peaceful, **Hell's Gate** (☑0726610508, 020-2379467; www.kws. org; adult/child US$30/20, bike hire KSh600, car entry KSh350, camping US$35; P) is that rare thing: an adventurous Kenyan park with large animals, safe to explore by bicycle or on foot. Large carnivores are very rare, so you can cycle to your heart's content past grazing zebras, giraffes, impalas and buffaloes, spot rock hyrax as they clamber up inclines and chase dust clouds as they swirl in the wind. And if the pedalling isn't enough exercise, you can hike the gorge or climb Fischer's Tower.

◉ Sights

Hell's Gate Gorge   CANYON
The gorge that runs through the heart of the park is a wide, deep valley hemmed in by sheer, rusty-hued rock walls. Marking its eastern entrance is Fischer's Tower, a 25m-high volcanic column named after Gustav Fischer, a German explorer who reached the gorge in 1882. Commissioned to find a route from Mombasa to Lake Victoria,

Hell's Gate National Park

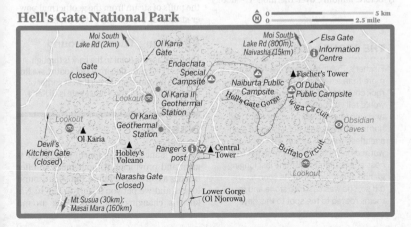

Fischer was stopped by territorial Maasai, who slaughtered almost his entire party.

All through this valley you'll come across zebras, the occasional giraffe, warthogs and various antelope species, while birds of prey circle overhead. Sadly, extensive geothermal excavation is now taking place close to the gorge, prompting complaints from visitors and concerns for the health of some animals. The road towards the gorge is now tarmacked, and you may spot industrial pipes.

Lower Gorge CANYON
(Ol Njorowa; guide per hr KSh500) Rising from the main gorge's southern end is the large **Central Tower**, an unusual volcanic plug. A picnic site and ranger's post are close by, from where a walk descends into the Lower Gorge (Ol Njorowa). In some places the riverbed is dry, in others you'll find yourself scrambling down a steep and slippery descent. Some steps have been cut into the rock, and some parts may be perilous. We recommend taking a guide.

🏃 Activities

If you intend to walk through the park, allow a full day and take plenty of supplies.

Cycling

Cycling is our favourite way to explore the park, and the main Hell's Gate Gorge is relatively flat; the distance from Elsa Gate to the Lower Gorge is around 7km. Bicycles are available at Lake Naivasha junction and at Elsa gate.

Elsa Gate Bike Hire BICYCLE RENTAL
(per day KSh600) Mountain bikes can be rented at Elsa gate, but test them out rigorously before handing over the money – dodgy

---

THE STONE LADY

Fischer's Tower may look like nothing more than a needle of rock, but if that rock could talk, which it once could, it would tell you how it was actually a pretty young Maasai woman, sent from her home village against her wishes to marry a fearless warrior. As she left she was warned not to turn back, but in her sadness she couldn't resist one last longing glance at her old home. As soon as she did so, she was cast into stone and remains rooted to the spot to this day.

---

brakes and gears are common problems, although rangers are on hand to assist.

Climbing

The sheer rock walls of Hell's Gate are just made for climbing and, thankfully, the park has two resident safety-conscious climbers.

Simon Kiane & James Maina ROCK CLIMBING
(☑ 0727039388, 0720909718) Simon and James work as climbing instructors and guides on weekends; they also have some basic equipment. They offer relatively easy 10- to 15-minute climbs of Fischer's Tower (US$10 to US$20) and more challenging routes on the gorge's sheer red walls (US$100). If they're not in their usual place at the base of Fischer's Tower, give them a call or check at the park gate before you enter.

🛏 Sleeping

Most visitors sleep at Lake Naivasha's many lodges and camps, but the park has a couple of gorgeous, if rudimentary, campgrounds.

Naiburta Public Campsite CAMPGROUND $
(camping US$35) 🍴 Naiburta, sitting on a gentle rise on the northern side of the Hell's Gate Gorge and commanding fine views west past Fischer's Tower, is the most scenic site in the area, and has basic toilets, an open *banda* for cooking and freshwater taps.

Ol Dubai Public Campsite CAMPGROUND $
(camping US$35) 🍴 Resting on Hell's Gate Gorge's southern side and accessible from the Buffalo Circuit track, Ol Dubai has basic toilets, a cooking *banda* and fresh water. It offers views west to the orange bluffs, and the puffs of steam from the geothermal power station at the far end of the park.

❶ Getting There & Around

The usual access point to the park is through the main Elsa gate, 1km from Moi South Lake Rd. With the two gates on the northwest corner of the park closed, the only other gate is Ol Karia.

Nakuru

POP 300,000

At first glance, Kenya's fourth largest city is grim and provincial, without much to offer besides a convenient refuel. But stick around longer and we bet you'll start to like it: Nakuru is changing fast, gentrifying around

Nakuru

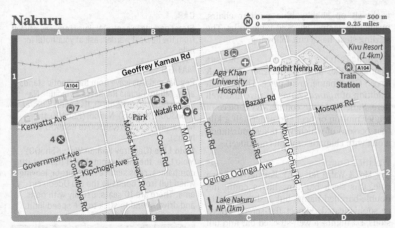

the edges and adopting some of the better aspects of Nairobi – minus the traffic, stress and crime.

◎ Sights

Menengai Crater VIEWPOINT
(adult/child KSh600/200, guides KSh1000; ⊙7am-5pm) With transport and 15 minutes to play with, you can be out of the grimy streets of Nakuru and standing on the rim of Menengai Crater, a 485m-high natural cauldron and local beauty spot. Outside of weekends, it's a peaceful place that affords striking views down below onto a cushion of lush vegetation. The crater was formed over one million years ago, and the last eruption was about 350 years ago.

🛏 Sleeping

Bontana Hotel HOTEL $$
(☑051-2210134; www.bontanahotel-nakuru.com; Tom Mboya Rd; s/d from US$120/180; P 🅿 ❄ 🛜 🏊) The statue of the buffalo seems to promise great things, but the lower rooms in this large hotel complex are a little dated. Still, you're away from the noise of traffic and there are the usual mod cons, including a reasonable restaurant and individual balconies. The better rooms are on the top floor.

★ Milimani Guest House GUESTHOUSE $$
(☑020-2441366, 0788619990; Maragoli Ave; s/d KSh4000/6000; P 🛜) Just outside of town at the foot of the crater, this well-run, stylish place looks like a modern country pile. Rooms wrap around a living room furnished with sofas and a fireplace, and breakfast is served in the pretty garden. The rooms are

Nakuru

◎ Activities, Courses & Tours
1 Pega Tours..B1

🛏 Sleeping
2 Bontana Hotel..................................A2
3 Merica Hotel....................................B1

🍴 Eating
4 Hygienic Butchery...........................A2
5 Planet Fries.....................................B1

🍷 Drinking & Nightlife
6 Whistles Guava...............................B1

🚌 Transport
7 Easy Coach.....................................A1
8 Molo Line..C1

bright and clean with hip touches, although noise carries at night.

Merica Hotel HOTEL $$
(☑051-2214232, 0706676557; www.mericagroup hotels.com; Kenyatta Ave; s/d US$120/185; ❄ 🛜 🏊) A longtime favourite with tour groups and business travellers, the Merica is starting to show its age. Nevertheless, it has good, well-equipped rooms housed in a whitewashed tower that wraps around a sunlit atrium. Very centrally located.

🍴 Eating & Drinking

Planet Fries CAFE $
(Watali Rd; mains from KSh500; ⊙breakfast, lunch & dinner) This quaint old diner does the usual chicken and *choma* plates, plus Indian variations. Outside on the pavement terrace,

you'll sit on shabby blue parlour chairs, pushed up against checked tablecloths. The sizzling steak has a cult following.

Hygienic Butchery KENYAN $

(Tom Mboya Rd; mains KSh180-250; ⊘lunch & dinner) Great name, great place. The Kenyan tradition of *nyama choma* is alive and well here. Sidle up to the counter, try a piece of tender mutton or beef and order half a kilo (per person) of whichever takes your fancy, along with chapatis or ugali (no sauce!).

Whistles Guava BAR

(cnr Moi & Watali Rds; ☎) Formerly Guava cafe, this sleek bar now has a confusing double-barrelled name, but inside it's rather sophisticated. Expect flat-screen televisions, DJ nights, a well-stocked bar and tall tables. There's wi-fi, too, and bar dishes to sate late-night hunger pangs.

ℹ Information

Changing cash in Nakuru is easy, with numerous banks and foreign exchange bureaus. Barclays Bank's ATMs are the most reliable.

Aga Khan University Hospital (Nakuru Medical Centre; Kenyatta Ave) Various lab services including malaria tests.

ℹ Getting There & Away

BUS

Easy Coach (Kenyatta Ave) Easy Coach is one of several bus companies offering services to Nairobi (KSh500, three hours), Eldoret (KSh650, 2¾ hours) and Kisumu (KSh750, 3½ hours).

CAR

Street parking in central Nakuru requires a ticket from the nearest warden; ask at your hotel for help.

MATATU

Regular matatus leave from the chaotic stands along Mburu Gichua Rd. Services include Naivasha (KSh150 to KSh200, 1¼ hours), Eldoret (KSh300, 2¾ hours), Nairobi (KSh400, three hours) and Kisumu (KSh500 to KSh600, 3½ hours).

Molo Line (Geoffrey Kamau Way; KSh500) Molo Line, the most reputable of the matatu companies, runs services to Nairobi, leaving when full from opposite the old Odeon cinema. There are 10 seats, usually with belts, and drivers tend to stick to the speed limit.

Lake Nakuru National Park

Just two hours' drive from Nairobi, Lake Nakuru (☎0726610508, 0726610509; www. kws.co.ke; adult/child $80/40; ⊘6.30am-6.30pm) is among Kenya's finest national parks. Flanked by rocky escarpments, pockets of forest and at least one waterfall, the park is pretty year-round. Rising water levels in 2014 forced the park's famous flamingos to flee, but water levels are prone to fluctuation and depending on the time of your visit, they may be back in residence. You can also expect to see both black and white rhinos; look past the hordes of horny baboons and you'll see hippos, or perhaps a lucky leopard or two. There are also

---

ℹ LAKE NAKURU NATIONAL PARK

Why Go

One of Kenya's best national parks is an easy drive from Nairobi. You have a chance of seeing rare tree-climbing lions as well as both black and white rhinos (plus flamingoes if they are in residence).

When to Go

Animal viewing is generally good year-round, but it's best to avoid the peak of the rainy season, from March to May.

Practicalities

Note that park tickets are valid for 24 hours exactly, so if you enter at 6.30am and plan to sleep in the park, you must leave by the same time the following day. Permits for longer stays are available.

Budget Tips

Stay outside the park and you'll pay far less for accommodation, and won't risk needing a permit for longer than 24 hours. Pega Tours (p249) offers cheap vehicle hire with guides for those without vehicles.

Lake Nakuru National Park

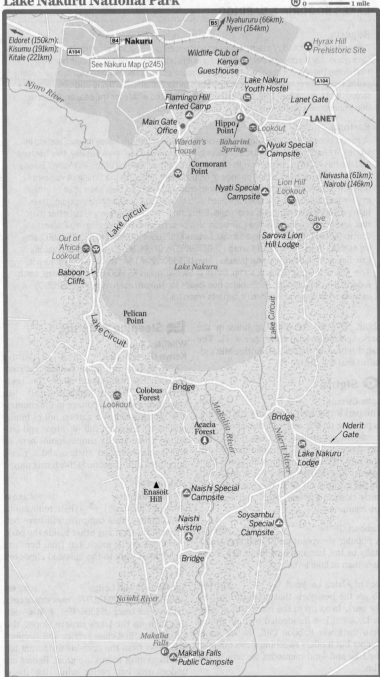

LAKES BOGORIA & BARINGO

Bogoria

Designated a wetland of international importance, Lake Bogoria is rather tempestuous. On a good day it appears sleek and pretty but is punctuated by hot springs bursting forth from the veneer of calm. There's even more going on beneath the surface: in recent years, rising water levels have sent the lake's famous flamingos flying and tempered the strength of the springs. Still, birdwatchers will be sated whatever the season: the rare and impressive greater kudu lurks in the undergrowth.

Baringo

Wild and beautiful, Lake Baringo is the most remote of the Rift Valley lakes. Steeped in stories, its harsh climate and rocky islets give it a faraway feel; on a hot day, this freshwater lake has more in common with northern Kenya than the rest of the Rift Valley. Baringo isn't fenced, so there's a high chance of hippos emerging, with the timing of vampires, from the shoreline. The murky waters hold crocodiles, too, so best keep your swimsuit in your bag. Up above, the skies are filled with over 460 species of bird including owls, nightjars and rare Hemprich's hornbills. Birdwatching in Kenya rarely gets better than this, and boat rides and village tours can also be arranged. For sleeping, try **Roberts Camp** (☑0717176656; Kampi ya Samaki; bandas Ksh2500-4500, tents Ksh2000-4000, camping Ksh500; ℗) ✆ or **Island Camp** (☑0735919878, 0728478638; www.islandcamp.com; Lake Baringo; full-board incl boat transfers from US$300; ☎☒) ✆. The latter's restaurant, **The Thirsty Goat** (Roberts' Camp, Kampi ya Samaki; mains KSh450-650; ☺breakfast, lunch & dinner), is outstanding. A 25-seater bus leaves for Nakuru each morning (KSh350) between 6.30am and 9.30am (it departs when full).

about 50 rare tree-climbing lions in the park, spotted several times per week. The usual zebras, buffaloes and Rothschild's giraffes seal the deal.

⊙ Sights

Lake Circuit
PARK

The park's relatively small size (180 sq km, depending on the reach of the lake) makes it easy to get around in a day. The forests anywhere in the park are good for leopards and rare tree-climbing lions imported from eastern Kenya. The park's black and white rhinos (around 60 altogether) tend to stick fairly close to the lake shore and sightings are common.

Baboon Cliffs
VIEWPOINT

A popular viewpoint and lunch spot, especially in the late morning when it's cooler here than at lake level.

Out of Africa Lookout
VIEWPOINT

To get the best view that takes in much of the park, head up to the rocky Out of Africa Lookout; less frequented by tour groups than the lower Baboon Cliff, the incline is steeper but it offers sweeping views out over the lake and fond memories for fans of the film.

🛏 Sleeping & Eating

Wildlife Club of Kenya Guesthouse
HOSTEL $

(☑020-267172; per person without bathroom KSh1250) For atmosphere alone, this beats anywhere in Nakuru hands down. It's like staying in a secluded cottage in the countryside, but instead of a garden full of bunny rabbits it's a garden full of rhinos and buffaloes! There are six simple rooms here, as well as an equipped kitchen and a nicely appointed dining room. Self-catering only.

Makalia Falls Public Campsite
CAMPGROUND $$

(camping US$30; ℗) ✆ When renovations are complete, this campsite will have better facilities than any other inside the park. That's not saying much, but from here you can at least walk to the falls and check out the view.

Sarova Lion Hill Lodge
LODGE $$$

(☑020-2315139, 0703327774; www.sarovahotels.com; s/d full board US$366/486; ℗☎☒) Sitting high up the lake's eastern slopes, this lodge offers first-class service and comfort. The views from the open-air restaurant-bar and from most rooms are great. Rooms are understated but pretty, while the flashy

Lake Baringo & Lake Bogoria National Reserve

Lake Nakuru Lodge LODGE $$$

(📞 0720404480, 020-2687056; www.lakenakuru lodge.com; s/d full board US$300/400; 🅿 @ 🛜 🏊)
The big draw here is the view, stretching outwards from the rustic wooden bar and pool into the park. It's a great dawn-to-dusk wildlife viewing spot. The lodge itself has pleasant, garden rooms with wall-to-ceiling balcony windows, and there's a decent buffet restaurant and helpful staff. Even if you're not staying here, this is *the* place for lunch.

ℹ Getting There & Away

The park is accessible in a 2WD. If you don't have your own wheels, **Pega Tours** (📞 0722776094, 0722743440; www.pegatours.co.ke; Utalii Arcade, Kenyatta Ave) in Nakuru is a good bet. Their daily hire rates include a pop top mini-bus and a knowledgeable driver/guide, from KSh2500 per person (based on four people).

MASAI MARA & WESTERN KENYA

For most people, the magic of western Kenya is summed up in two poetic words: Masai Mara. Few places on earth support such high concentrations of animals, and the Mara's wildebeest-spotted savannahs are undeniably the region's star attraction. Drama unfolds here on a daily basis, be it a stealthy trap co-ordinated by a pride of lions, the infectious panic of a thousand wildebeest crossing a river or the playful pounce of a cheetah kitten on its sibling. The Mara's appeal is greatly extended by the privately and community-owned conservancies and group ranches that surround the reserve.

But there is much more to western Kenya than these plains of herbivores and carnivores. The dense forests of Kakamega are buzzing with weird and wonderful creatures, the rain-soaked hills of Kericho and their verdant tea gardens bring new meaning to the word 'green', and amid the boat-speckled waters of Lake Victoria lie a smattering of seldom-visited islands crying out for exploration.

suites are large and absolutely stunning. It's certainly one of the friendlier top-end places, and on quiet days you may even get the residents' rate, which is less than half that quoted here.

Narok

POP 24,000

Three hours west of Nairobi, this ramshackle provincial town is civilisation's last stand before the vast savannahs of the Masai Mara and the region's largest town.

Western Kenya

N 0 ——— 50 km
0 ——— 25 miles

Marich Pass
Lomut
Cherangani Hills
Wei-wei River
B4
A104
Mt Elgon (Wagagai) (4321m)
Suam
Makutano
A1
Kapenguria
Tot
C52
Mbale
Kabichbich
Chesengoch
Endebess
Saiwa Swamp NP
Mt Elgon NP
Kitale
C45
Kapcherop
Tugen Hills
B4
Cherangani
B2
UGANDA
Kimilili
Turbo
Soy
Iten
Kerio Valley/ Lake Kamnarok NR
Tororo
Malaba
Webuye
A104
Kabarnet
Marigat
A109
Bungoma
A1
Eldoret
C51
Cheploch
B4
Busia
C37
Mumias
Kakamega
B53
B1
Butere
Khayega
Kakamega FR
Kapsabet
A104
B4
Siaya
Equator
Nakuru (5km)
Usengi
Bondo
KISUMU
Ahero
Londiani
Molo
LAKE VICTORIA
Ndere Island
Winam Gulf
B1
Mfangano Island
Rusinga Island
Luanda Kotieno
Kendu Bay
Sondu
Kericho
Mau Escarpment
Mbita
Homa Bay
C19
Takawiri Island
Ruma NP
Tabaka
Oyugis
Rod Kopany
Kisii
Sotik
Miranga
Mirogi
Rongo
B3
Bomet
Keroka
Karungu
Awendo
B3
Thimlich Ohinga
A1
Kilkoris
Ngorengore
Narok
Muhoro
Migori
Ewaso Ngiro
Maji Moto Group Ranch
Shirati
Suna
Mara North Conservancy
C13
Sirari
Isebania
Lolgorian
Olare-Orok Conservancy
Naboisho Conservancy
Olarro Conservancy
Talek
Bakitabu
Masai Mara NR
Siana Group Ranch and Conservancy
TANZANIA

It's a friendly and surprisingly hassle-free place but few travellers have reason to stop. Most people roll on in, browse the curio shops while their driver refuels, then roll on out again.

🛏 Sleeping & Eating

Chambai Hotel HOTEL $
(☎0722957609; s/d from KSh1500/2300; ℗)
Rooms in this town-centre place, near the matatu stand, are a little dark, but have inviting beds, balconies, small TVs and huge bathrooms.

ℹ Information

Barclays Bank (B3 Hwy) The only ATM around the Masai Mara is at Talek gate, so stock up on cash here – and take more than you think you'll need.

ℹ Getting There & Away

Narok Line matatus run between Narok and Nairobi (KSh500, three hours) from the Shell petrol station on the B6 Hwy. All other matatus leave from the main matatu stand just around the corner in the centre of town. Destinations include: Naivasha (KSh350, 2½ hours), Kisii (KSh500, three hours), Kericho (KSh500, 2½ hours) and Nakuru (KSh500, two hours).

Matatus and share taxis also leave from the matatu stand to Sekenani and Talek gates (matatu KSH500, taxi KSh700).

Several petrol stations pump the elixir of vehicular life – fill up, it's much cheaper here than in the reserve.

Masai Mara National Reserve

The world-renowned **Masai Mara National Reserve** (adult/child US$80/45, subsequent days if staying inside the reserve US$70/40; ⊙6am-7pm) – or the Mara, as locals refer to it – is the northern extension of Tanzania's equally famous Serengeti Plains and it's a huge expanse of tawny, sunburnt grasslands pocked with flat-topped acacia trees and heaving with animals big and small. Impressive at any time of year it's at its best between July and September when around a million migrating wildebeest and thousands of topis, zebras and others pour into the reserve from Tanzania in search of the fresh grass generated by the rains. It is, arguably, the most spectacular wildlife show on the planet and the one thing that no visitor to Kenya should even consider missing.

Reliable rains and plentiful vegetation underpin this extraordinary ecosystem. Wildebeest, zebras, impalas, elands, reedbucks, waterbucks, black rhinos, elephants, Masai giraffes and several species of gazelle all call the short-grass plains and acacia woodlands of the Mara home. This vast concentration of game accounts for high predator numbers including cheetahs, leopards, spotted hyenas, black-backed jackals, bat-eared foxes, caracals and some of the highest lion densities in the world.

◉ Sights

◉ Central Plains

The southeast area of the park, bordered by the Mara and Sand Rivers, is characterised by rolling grasslands and low, isolated hills. With the arrival of the migration, enormous herds of wildebeest and zebras as well as other plains game, all graze here. The **riverine forests** that border the Mara and Talek Rivers are great places to spot elephants, buffaloes and bushbucks. Leopards are sometimes seen near the Talek and Sand Rivers and around the Keekorok valleys.

◉ Rhino Ridge & Paradise Plains

Rhino Ridge is a good area to see black-backed jackals, as they are known to use the old termitaria here for den sites. **Lookout Hill** is worth a detour as it offers phenomenal views over the seasonal **Olpunyaia Swamp**. You may also get lucky and spot one of the few black rhinos that inhabit the reserve anywhere between Lookout Hill and Rhino Ridge and in the vicinity of Roan Hill.

For lions, the Marsh Pride near Musiara Swamp and the Ridge Pride near Rhino Ridge both starred in the BBC's *Big Cat Diary* and are fairly easy to find. Cheetahs on the other hand are far more elusive but are sometimes found hunting gazelles on the Paradise Plains.

◉ Mara River

Pods of hippos can be found in any of the major rivers, with the largest and most permanent concentrations occurring in the Mara River. The river is also home to huge Nile crocodiles, and is the scene where wildebeest make their fateful crossings during the migration. The New Mara Bridge in the south is the only all-weather crossing point and another great place to see hippos.

◉ The Mara Triangle

Unlike the rest of the park, which is under the control of the Narok County Council, the northwest sector of the reserve is managed by the nonprofit Mara Conservancy. The only way to reach this part of the park is from either the Olooloo gate or via the New Mara Bridge. Consequently, this area is less visited than elsewhere, despite having high game concentrations.

Masai Mara National Reserve

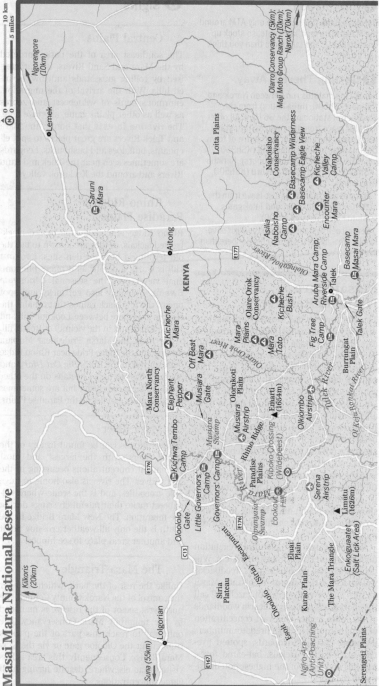

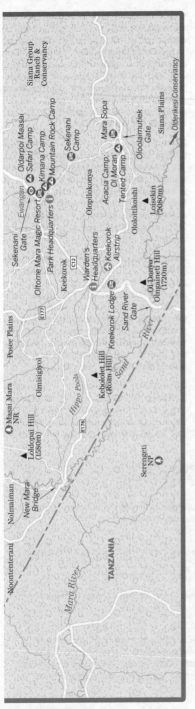

The **Olooolo Escarpment**, which forms the northwest boundary of the park, was once wooded but fire and elephant damage means that it is now mostly grasslands. Rock hyrax and klipspringer can be readily seen here.

🏃 Activities

Wildlife Drives

Whether you're bouncing over the plains in pursuit of elusive elephant silhouettes or parked next to a pride of lions and listening to their bellowed breaths, wildlife drives are the highlight of a trip to the Mara, although during the busy Christmas and migration seasons it can seem that there are as many minivans as animals.

If you're not here on an organised safari, all lodges organise game drives while self-driving is another possibility.

Guided Nature Walks

One of the best ways to experience the African bush is on foot; you'll learn all about the medicinal properties of various plants, see the tell-tale signs of passing animals and have some thrilling encounters with the local wildlife. Many lodges and camps can arrange a guided walk, although their rates vary.

As it is forbidden to walk within the reserve, guided walks (around US$20 per person) generally take place in the company of a Maasai *moran* (warrior) outside the park.

Balloon Safaris

Several companies operate dawn balloon safaris and there is no better way to start your day than soaring majestically over the rolling grasslands. Trips (flight per person US$450 to US$500) can be booked at most of the lodges or campsites. Flights include a 'champagne' (it's very rarely real champagne) breakfast, game drive and transport to and from the launch point.

Maasai Manyatta Visits

The Maasai are synonymous with the Masai Mara, and their slender frames, blood-red cloaks, ochre hairstyles and beaded jewellery make them instantly recognisable. Despite their reputation as fearsome warriors with somewhat lofty dispositions, some Maasai *manyattas* (villages) now welcome visitors (around US$20 per person).

🛏 Sleeping & Eating

Virtually all places to stay sell beds as part of a full-board deal.

Acacia Camp TENTED CAMP $
(☑ 0713751532; Oloolaimutiek gate; camping KSh600, tent per person US$22, full board per person US$80) Thatched roofs shelter closely spaced, spartan, semi-permanent tents in this quaint campground. There are numerous cooking areas, a bar and a campfire. The communal bathrooms are clean and hot water flows in the evening. The only downside for campers is the lack of shade.

★ Aruba Mara Camp TENTED CAMP $$
(☑ 0723997524; www.aruba-safaris.com; Talek gate; camping KSh700, safari tent without bathroom per person KSh3000, safari tent full board per person €85-115) 🖉 Set alongside a river filled with toothy crocs, this is arguably the Mara's best-value camp. There are nine wonderfully plush 'tents' with good self-contained bathrooms as well as several small but comfortable tents (meals not included) that share bathrooms. The nearby campsite is decent, with a kitchen area and reliable hot water in the shower block.

★ Ewangan HOMESTAY $$
(☑ 0721817757; www.maasaimaravillage.com; per person full board US$70, children free) 🖉 A traditional Maasai *manyatta* 2km north of Sekenani gate, offering a homestay with the Maasai. A number of families, and a whole load of cows and goats, live in the *manyatta* and during your stay you're likely to help

with daily chores such as milking the cows and goats and making jewellery. You'll also be encouraged to visit various Semadep projects.

Accommodation is basic – a hut with no electricity or running water – but it's all very cosy and the food is excellent. It's a particularly fun experience for children (we've stayed with a four year old and an 18 month old and they much preferred this to the fancy lodges and wildlife drives).

Kimana Camp TENTED CAMP $$
(☑ 0734599955; full board per person KSh5500; 🐾) This fairly large (34 tents), but otherwise tranquil, camp set in a shady patch of forest is unusually good value. Tents have three beds and hot-water bathrooms. There's also a pool, but it's normally as murky as the Mara River after a herd of wildebeest has crossed.

Mountain Rock Camp TENTED CAMP $$
(☑ 0722511252; www.mountainrockkenya.com; camping per tent KSh1000, safari tent full board per person KSh4500-5000) The simple safari tents here come in two categories, with the cheaper tents being a little darker and smaller than the pricier ones. All have private bathrooms, cloth wardrobes, firm beds and share the same pretty woodland glade around 3km from the Sekenani gate.

Oltome Mara Magic Resort TENTED CAMP $$
(☑ Nairobi 020-2498512; www.oltomemaramagic.com; tent s/d full board from US$75/150; Ⓟ) This small camp, which is something of a halfway house between the top-notch luxury

---

ℹ MASAI MARA NATIONAL RESERVE

Why Go
The 1510 sq km of open rolling grasslands that make up the Mara offer the quintessential African safari experience, with lion sightings virtually guaranteed.

When to Go
The Mara is superb at any time but is at its best during the annual wildebeest migration in July and August.

Practicalities
The Masai Mara's fame means that it can get very busy (and very pricey) during the annual migration.

Budget Tips
To share costs, join a group safari in Nairobi, scour the notice boards at Nairobi backpackers or go to www.lonelyplanet.com/thorntree in search of travel companions. Be aware that the much-peddled, three-day Nairobi–Mara safaris mean a large proportion of your time will be spent travelling to and from the Mara. It makes sense to add in at least one extra day.

TROUBLE IN EDEN

In many ways the Masai Mara National Reserve is the epitome of the African dream. Its golden, bleached savannah is covered with unparalleled densities of animals, great and small, and the vast majority of it is untouched by the destructive hand of man. Visitors can't help but be bowled over by its natural riches.

The reality, however, is that not everyone is happy with this wildlife haven. Many local Maasai living in the immediate vicinity of the reserve feel they gain nothing from its presence, despite the sacrifices and hardships they face because of it. The issues they raise are:

➡ Not being allowed to graze their cattle inside the reserve, which many of them consider to be 'their' land.

➡ Insufficient and poorly organised compensation when animals kill their cattle outside of the reserve.

➡ Neglected needs of the Maasai communities. Many communities don't have sufficient access to clean, safe water sources and education and health facilities. Many lodges and camps in and around the reserve advertise their community development projects, but many Maasai dispute that all of this money actually goes to such projects.

Ironically another problem the reserve faces comes from safari tourism itself. Sightings of big cats tend to attract large numbers of vehicles, and when the lion, cheetah or leopard eventually moves away, many guides (aware their clients want to see such animals up close) break park rules by following the animals off the designated tracks. Such constant attention has led some animals to change their patterns of behavior – for instance, cheetahs now frequently attempt to hunt under the midday sun, when most tourists are having lunch in their camp (unfortunately, it's also a time when the chance of a successful kill is radically reduced). Reports are now showing that many animals are spending less time in the reserve itself, choosing to roam in the surrounding conservancies where there are fewer safari vehicles (and, incidentally, where local communities also gain more from tourism).

camps and the nearby cheaper options, has 13 semi-permanent tents. They're tastefully furnished and feature stone floors, wooden verandahs and modern bathrooms. However, a few tears and mould on some of the tents mean the price is a little optimistic.

★ **Basecamp Masai Mara**   LODGE $$$
(☏0733333909;   www.basecampexplorer.com; tent s/d full board US$400/720; ☎) 🍃 'Eco' is a much-abused word in the tourism industry, but to see what an ecofriendly hotel really looks like, come to this upmarket lodge where everything is based around sustainabilty and recycling. If all this green scheming makes you think the accommodation might be rustic, fear not. Tents fall squarely into the luxury bracket with open-air showers and stylish furnishings.

★ **Mara Toto**   TENTED CAMP $$$
(☏Nairobi 020-6000457;   www.greatplainsconservation.com; s/d full board US$1343/1790; ☎) 🍃 A tiny camp that's so well hidden under the riverside trees it's impossible to see until you're pretty much in it. The five tents are the epitome of refined-safari style with leather armchairs, old travellers' trunks and brass bucket showers. As decadent as the camp is, this isn't a place for those scared of the bush. After dark the camp echoes to the sounds of lions roaring and hippos splashing around the river.

Fig Tree Camp   TENTED CAMP, LODGE $$$
(☏Nairobi 020-605328;   www.madahotels.com; s/d full board from US$435/580; ☎🖥) Vegetate on your tent's verandah, watching the Talek River gently flow past this sumptuous camp with a colonial-days feel. The gardens are about the most luxurious you'll ever see, and the bathrooms about the biggest and most inviting you'll find under canvas.

Kichwa Tembo Camp   TENTED CAMP $$$
(☏Nairobi 020-3688620;   www.andbeyond.com; s/d full board US$782/1030; 🖥) Just outside the northern boundary of the reserve, Kichwa has been recently renovated and has permanent tents with grass-mat floors, stone bathrooms and tasteful furnishings. Hop in a

hammock and take in spectacular savannah views. The camp has an excellent reputation for its food and is well positioned for the migration river-crossing points.

Mara Serena Safari Lodge LODGE $$$

(☑ 0732123333; www.serenahotels.com; s/d full board US$424/638; ☎☀) This large, resort-style lodge, which has a pool complex and even a gym, would be a better fit in a city rather than a supposed wilderness. Of all the park lodges, however, it has the best view. Built on a small hill, most rooms have commanding views over not one, but two, migration crossing points.

Oldarpoi Maasai Safari Camp TENTED CAMP $$$

(☑ 0721731927; www.oldarpoimaracamp.com; camping per person US$20, s/d full board US$140/260) Set on a hill of dry acacia woodland about 3km back from Sekenani gate, this Maasai-run place offers fairly hot and simple safari tents, but the welcome is equally warm and, with 40% of profits being ploughed into local community projects, staying here means your money goes into the pockets of locals.

ℹ Information

Although the main reserve (p251) is managed by the Narok County Council and the **Mara Triangle** (www.maratriangle.org) is managed by the Mara Conservancy, both charge the same, and an admission ticket brought at one is valid at the other. Keep hold of this ticket, as you will be asked to present it when travelling between the reserve's Narok and Transmara sections and on your eventual exit.

All vehicles seem to get charged KSh1000 at the gates instead of the KSh400 fee for vehicles with less than six seats – be insistent but polite and all will be well.

The only ATM in the area is a KCB one in Talek village (and note that KCB ATMs can be a little tempermental with foreign cards!) so come prepared with more cash than you think you'll need.

For more on the Masai Mara and surrounding conservancies see the independent website www.maasaimara.com.

ℹ Getting There & Away

AIR

Airkenya (☑ Nairobi 020-3916000; www.airkenya.com), **Mombasa Air Safari** (☑ Nairobi 0734400400; www.mombasaairsafari.com), **Safarilink** (☑ 020-600777; www.flysafarilink.com) and **Fly540** (☑ 0710540540; www.fly540.com), flying under the name of SAX, each have daily flights to any of the eight airstrips in and around the Masai Mara. Flights start at US$250 return.

MATATU, CAR & 4WD

Although it's possible to arrange wildlife drives independently, keep in mind that there are few savings in coming here without transport or pre-arranged game drives. That said, it is possible to access Talek and Sekenani gates from Narok by matatu (KSh500).

For those who drive, the first 52km west of Narok on the B3 and C12 are smooth enough, but after the bitumen runs out you'll find that there's just as much rattle as there is roll, and you'll soon come to dread this road. The C13, which connects Oloololo gate with Lolgorian out in the west, is very rough and rocky, and it's poorly signposted.

Petrol is available (although expensive) at Mara Sarova, Mara Serena and Keekorok Lodges, as well as in Talek village.

THE MASAI MARA CONSERVANCIES

Changing the face of conservation and tourism in Kenya are the private and community conservancies, many of which now border the Masai Mara National Reserve. Each conservancy operates in a slightly different manner but the general idea is to make tourism, conservation and the rights of local peoples work hand in hand with one another to the mutual benefit of all. Most conservancies involve the local Maasai landowners leasing their communal lands for an average of 15 years at a time to several high end lodges. The Maasai are still allowed to graze their cattle in the conservancies and receive a guaranteed fee from each camp. In addition all camps have to contribute to community development projects.

In return the wildlife is allowed to live in peace and the lodges can offer their clients a very exclusive kind of safari with minimal other visitors (tourists not staying in the conservancies are not allowed to enter them and go on safari) and the opportunity to partake in activities not allowed in the reserve itself such as walking safaris and bush breakfasts.

Entry fees to the conservancies are covered in the nightly cost of accommodation. There is no budget accommodation available in any of the conservancies.

THE LOITA HILLS

To the northeast of the Masai Mara National Reserve are the very little known, and spell-bindingly beautiful Loita Hills. When accessing them from the Mara area, the hills start out dry and unimpressive, but if you bounce along for enough hours (and we mean hours and hours – the roads here are some of the worst in Kenya) things start to change. The vegetation becomes greener and much more luxuriant, eventually becoming a virtual tangled jungle. The mountains also grow ever bigger, peaking at a respectable 2150m.

This is the most traditional corner of Maasai land and change, though it's coming, is way behind many other parts of the country. Despite the number of Maasai living here it's also an area of unexpected wildlife – colobus monkeys swing through the trees, turacos light the skies in colour and huge numbers of buffaloes, forest pigs and bushbucks move through the shadows. What makes this area so extraordinary is that it's not covered by any official protection, and yet the forests remain fairly untouched. The reason is that there are many places in the forests sacred to the Maasai and the elders tightly control the felling of trees and grazing of cattle. It's a brilliant example of how traditional cultures can thrive alongside wildlife without outside aid.

The best way to explore this area is on foot. And **Maasai Trails** (☑0718139359; www.maasaitrails.com), based out of the beautiful and low key **Jan's Camp** (☑0718139359; www.maasaitrails.com; s/d full board US$250/400) 🥾 , and about the only accommodation option in the hills bar a few basic boardings and lodgings in some villages, are the people to help you with this.

❶ Getting Around

If you do arrive by matatu, you can organise wildlife drives with most of the big lodges in and around the reserve itself and even some of the cheaper camps. Typically they charge around KSh12,000 to KSh15,000 for a full day's vehicle and driver hire, which can be split between as many of you as can be comfortably squeezed into the vehicle. There is no public transport within the park.

Maji Moto Group Ranch

Closer to Narok town than the reserve itself, Maji Moto (which translates as 'hot water', and true enough there are some hot springs here) is a blissfully tourist-free 600sq km group ranch. Its distance from the main Mara ecosystem, and the abundance of Maasai communities in the area, mean that wildlife numbers are far lower than in other conservancies, but this is a different type of conservancy and one where the emphasis is as much about enjoying and learning about Maasai culture as it is about the animals. If you want a totally different kind of 'safari' experience this could be the place.

★ **Maji Moto Eco-Camp**   TENTED CAMP **$$**
(☑716430722, 041-2006479; www.majimotocamp.com; per person full board US$80) 🥾 Set on a hillside among granite rocks contorted into fantastical plasticine shapes, Maji Moto is

around 60km north of the reserve proper. The camp is a fairly simple but beautifully conceived creation where guests sleep in large dome tents with mattresses on the floor. It's a brilliant camp for families, with warrior training, dances, village visits, bush walks, full-day safaris to the Mara and soaks in the hot springs all on offer. Multi-day walking safaris to the Masai Mara can be organised and your stay genuinely helps the locals.

Mara North Conservancy

Established in 2009, the 30,000-hectare **Mara North Conservancy** (www.maranorth.com), which abuts the northwestern edge of the Masai Mara National Reserve, is one of the better known, more popular and, in terms of local people and wildlife gaining, one of the most successful of the Mara area conservancies.

The countryside here is an absolute cliche of what East Africa is supposed to look like: the flat topped acacias, the long golden grass and animals everywhere. Leopard sightings are common, there are lots of very large lions as well as some cheetahs and masses of plains game. In fact during the migration the horizon can be utterly covered in the black dots of migrating wildebeest and seeing lions on a kill is very common.

★**Elephant Pepper**　　TENTED CAMP $$$
(☑0730127000; www.elephantpeppercamp.com; s/d full board US$952/1588; 🛜) 🍃 This intimate camp has eight tents that are luxurious without being over the top and food that is of a genuinely high standard. But what really makes Elephant Pepper stand out is its setting, under a dense thicket of trees with views over rolling grasslands that, at times, can be a seething mass of grunting, growling and trumpeting megafauna.

Saruni Mara　　TENTED CAMP $$$
(☑0735950903, Nairobi 020-2180497; www.saruni.com; Mara North; s/d full board US$910/1520; 🛜) 🍃 Way to the north of any of the other camps, and virtually on the border of the conservancy, this breathtaking camp has around a dozen tents dusted with antique furnishings and colonial bric-a-brac. Some even have open log fires inside! The setting, in animal-packed, forested hills, is very different to most other camps.

Naibosho Conservancy

Created in 2011, the Naboisho Conservancy is flourishing. There's plenty of wildlife here including cheetahs, elephants and a fair few lions, as well as all the plains game, and the landscape is a classic mix of open grasslands and light acacia woodlands.

Basecamp Wilderness　　TENTED CAMP $$$
(☑0733333909; www.basecampkenya.com; Naboisho; s/d full board US$400/720) 🍃 Of all the camps in the Mara conservancies, Wilderness is probably the most authentically 'safari'. There are five simple, very comfortable tents with hot bucket showers and good beds set in a hidden valley that's home to a resident leopard and other animals. Guests are encouraged to walk here from sister camp, **Basecamp Eagle View** (☑0733333909; www.basecampkenya.com; s/d full board US$530/980; 🛜) 🍃. If you want to get even closer to nature, 'fly camping' trips are offered out of here.

Olare-Orok Conservancy

Established in 2006 (as Olare Motorogi), this is now one of the longest established and most sucessful of the conservancies. It's also one with one of the highest concentrations of animals including loads of predators and the lowest density of tourists – just one tent for every 700 acres.

Mara Plains　　TENTED CAMP $$$
(www.greatplainsconservation.com; all-inclusive s/d US$1150/2300; 🛜) 🍃 This utterly captivating camp has a dozen tents – sorry, palaces – in which the beds and showers are carved from old wooden railway sleepers and quality rugs laze across the floors. The highlight for most, though, are the big, free-standing brass bathtubs overlooking a river of wallowing hippos.

Kicheche Bush　　TENTED CAMP $$$
(☑Nairobi 020-2493569; www.kicheche.com; s/d full board US$925/1580) 🍃 Run with the kind of casual efficiency that brings guests back again and again, Kicheche Bush has six well-spaced, enormous tents set within a light fringe of trees, beyond which stretches some of the most reliably impressive wildlife country-side in the whole Mara region.

Olderikesi Conservancy

In the far southeast of the Mara region, on the border of Tanzania and the famous Serengeti, the Olderikesi Conservancy covers around 8000 hectares. Though it's been in existence for many years, the conservancy's managers will openly say that it's only since 2011 that everything has clicked into place and the conservancy has started functioning as they hoped it would.

One of the most exclusive of the Mara conservancies, it's also one of the richest in wildlife including large numbers of lions.

Cottar's 1920s Camp　　TENTED CAMP $$$
(☑0733773378; www.cottars.com; s/d full board US$1184/1974; 🍴) One of the remotest camps in the greater Mara region, Cottar's, which is owned by a legendary safari family, induces a misty-eyed sense of longing from those lucky enough to have visited. As the name suggests, the enormous tents are dressed up like a well-to-do 1920s gentleman, with all manner of colonial and safari memorabilia.

Kisumu

POP 322,700

Set on the sloping shore of Lake Victoria's Winam Gulf, the town of Kisumu might be the third largest in Kenya, but its relaxed atmosphere is a world away from that of places like Nairobi and Mombasa. Once a busy port, Kisumu is now emerging from decades of decline.

Kisumu

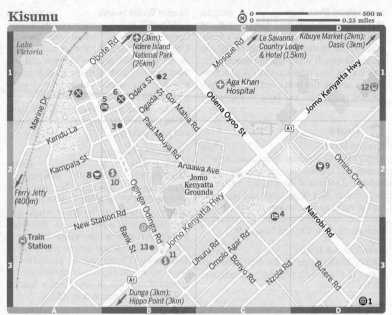

⊙ Sights & Activities

Kisumu Museum
MUSEUM
(Nairobi Rd; admission KSh500; ☺8am-6pm)
Southwest of the town centre, this museum
has three main sections. The first covers
western Kenya's three principal linguistic
groups: Luo, Bantu and Kalenjin. The second attraction is a traditional Luo homestead depicting the fictitious life of Onyango
as he undergoes the rite of passage to establish his own family compound. The last
section is a small aquarium displaying the
nearby lake's aquatic assets and a reptile
house holding examples of all the local
snakes you don't want to meet.

Ndere Island National Park
PARK
(www.kws.go.ke; adult/child US$25/15; ☺6am-
6pm) Gazetted as a national park in 1986, this
4.2-sq-km island has never seen tourism take
off. It is forested and very beautiful, housing
a variety of bird species, plus occassionally
sighted hippos, impalas (introduced) and
spotted crocodiles, a lesser-known cousin of
the larger Nile crocodiles.

There's nowhere to stay, and although
twice-daily matatus reach the shore just opposite the island, your only reliable option to
get to Ndere is with chartered boats. Expect
to pay around KSh15,000 to KSh17,000 for

a half-day trip. Chartered boat trips can be
arranged with any of the boat captains offering sightseeing trips from Hippo Point.

Hippo Point Boat Trips   BOAT TOUR

Hippo Point, sticking into Lake Victoria at Dunga, about 3km south of town, is a beautiful spot at which you're highly unlikely to see any hippos. It is, though, the launch point for pleasant boat rides around the lake. Prices vary among the boats, but expect to pay KSh500 per person, per hour in a group of five.

ⓖ Tours

Ibrahim Nandi   TOUR
(📲 0723083045; ibradingo@yahoo.com) A well-known and trusted tour guide to the many sights and sounds of the Kisumu region. He can arrange boat trips, birdwatching tours, nature walks and excursions to Ndere Island National Park. Ibrahim can be contacted through the New Victoria Hotel.

Zaira Tours & Travel   SAFARIS
(📲 0722788879; Ogada St) The best safari operator in town, with pop-top minivans and 4WDs.

🛏 Sleeping

Some of the cheaper Kisumu hotels are known for poor security, so consider using your own padlock to secure your room or deposit valuable items with reception. All rooms in Kisumu are equipped with fans.

★ New East View Hotel   HOTEL $
(📲 0711183017; Omolo Agar Rd; s KSh1700-2300, d KSh2300-2800; 🅿🛜) The town's stand-out cheapie is one of many family homes in the area that have been converted into hotels. Splashed in bright colours, it retains just enough furniture and decoration to give the rooms a homely, pre-loved feel and the welcome is, even for Kenya, unusually warm. Security is also tight.

LAKE VICTORIA

Spread over 68,000 sq km, yet never more than 80m deep, Lake Victoria, one of the key water sources of the White Nile, might well be East Africa's most important geographical feature, but is seen by surprisingly few visitors. This is a shame, as its humid shores hide some of the most beautiful and rewarding parts of western Kenya – from tranquil islands and untouched national parks like Ruma to lively cities such as Kisumu.

Sooper Guest House   BACKPACKERS $
(📲 0725281733; www.sooperguesthse.com; Oginga Odinga Rd; s/tw/d excl breakfast KSh1200/1500/1600; 🛜) Sooper has become the de facto backpackers in town and you have a good chance of meeting other travellers here. The rooms, which come in a dizzying array of styles, are immaculately well kept and have hot showers, though those facing the road are very noisy. Helpful staff and good security.

Le Savanna Country Lodge & Hotel   HOTEL $$
(📲 057-2021159, 0714995510; www.lesavanna countrylodge.com; Dewchurch Dr, Ondiek Hwy; s/d KSh5750/6750; 🅿🍽🛜) This delightfully calm place is where everyone who's anyone likes to stay when in town. The large, well-dressed rooms have good bathrooms, fast in-room wi-fi and no exterior noise or disturbance. There's also a reasonable in-house restaurant and a quiet garden bar. It's around 2km north of town and a KSh100 *boda-boda* (motorcycle taxi) ride.

🍴 Eating

If you want an authentic local fish fry, there are no better places than the dozens of smokey tin-shack restaurants sitting on the lake's shore at Railway Beach at the end of Oginga Odinga Rd. A midsized fish served with ugali or rice is sufficient for two people.

Green Garden Restaurant   INTERNATIONAL $
(Odera St; mains KSh380-500; ⊘8am-11pm) Surrounded by colourful murals and potted palms, the Green Garden is an oasis of culinary delight set in an Italian-themed courtyard. As you would expect, it's an expat hotspot and the word is that the tilapia (fish) in a spinach and coconut sauce is the way to go. Be prepared to wait a long time for your meal.

The Laughing Buddha   INTERNATIONAL $
(Swan Centre, Accra St; mains KSh350-500; ⊘10.30am-11pm Tue-Sun; 🍴) The Laughing Buddha has a limited menu (made even more so by the fact that half the items probably won't be available) of pastas, pizzas and chips – in dozens of different flavours – which will likely come as a surprise to anyone who grew up thinking chips were just chips! The streetside tables earn it big points.

Juiz Parlour CAFE $

(off Station Rd; juice from KSh70; ⏱7.30am-8pm) You name it and they'll stick it in a blender and pulverise the bejesus out of it. The pumpkin-and-beetroot juice looked foul so we shared a very special moment with a mango-and-pineapple combo instead.

🍷 Drinking & Nightlife

Kisumu's nightlife has a reputation for being even livelier than Nairobi's. Check flyers and ask locals who are plugged into the scene. Be careful when leaving as muggings and worse are not unheard of. Solo women should take a chaperone. The clubs are at their liveliest on Friday and Saturday nights, although folks don't get to bumping and grinding until after 10pm.

Oasis LIVE MUSIC

(Kondele, Jomo Kenyatta Hwy; entry KSh150-200) With live music most nights, this is the place to see Lingala music performed by Congolese bands. Be prepared for a fair bit of shaking and sweating.

Social Centre DANCE

(off Omino Cres; entry around KSh100) Tucked behind the main matatu stage, this club is big on *ohangla* (Luo traditional music) with the odd Kiswahili hip-hop tune thrown in for good measure.

ℹ Getting There & Away

At the time of writing there were neither train nor boat services from Kisumu, despite all the talk of services restarting.

AIR

Three airlines offer daily morning and afternoon flights to Nairobi (from KSh5500 one way, 50 minutes).

Fly540.com (www.fly540.com)

Jambo Jet (☑Nairobi 020 3274545; www.jambojet.com)

Kenya Airways (☑0711022090; www.kenya-airways.com; Alpha House, Oginga Odinga Rd)

BUS & MATATU

Buses, matatus and Peugeots (shared taxis) to numerous destinations within Kenya battle it out at the large bus and matatu station just north of the main market. Peugeots cost about 25% more than the matatu fares listed.

Easy Coach (www.emanamba.com; Jomo Kenyatta Hwy) offers the smartest buses out of town. It's booking office and departure point is in the carpark just behind (and accessed through) the Tusky's Shopping Centre. It has daily buses to Nairobi (KSh1400, seven hours, departures every couple of hours), Nakuru (KSh800, 4½ hours, departures every couple of hours), Narok (KSh800, five hours) and Kampala (KSh1500, seven hours, departures at 1.30pm and 10pm).

Matutu services from Kisumu include the following:

TO	FARE (KSH)	DURATION (HR)
Busia	300-370	2
Eldore	450-500	2½
Homa Bay	350-400	3
Isebania	700	4
Kakamega	200	1¾
Kericho	350	2
Kisii	350	2
Kitale	500	4
Nairobi	1000-1200	5½
Nakuru	800	3½

ℹ Getting Around

BODA-BODA & TUK-TUK

Both *boda-boda* (bicycle or motorbike taxis) and tuk-tuks (motorised minitaxis) have proliferated, and they are a great way to get around Kisumu. A trip to Hippo Point should be no more than KSh50/150 for a *boda-boda*/tuk-tuk.

MATATU

Matatus 7 and 9, which travel along Oginga Odinga Rd and Jomo Kenyatta Hwy, are handy to reach the main matatu station, main market and Kibuye Market – just wave and hop on anywhere you see one.

TAXI

A taxi around town costs between KSh100 and KSh200, while trips to Dunga range from KSh250 to KSh400, with heavy bargaining.

Homa Bay

POP 32,174

Homa Bay has a slow, tropical, almost Central African vibe, and the near total absence of other tourists means it's extraordinarily and genuinely friendly. There is little to do other than trudge up and down the dusty, music-filled streets or wander down to the lake edge to watch the marabou storks pick through the trash as they wait for the fishermen and their morning catch. The town makes a great base from which to visit Ruma National Park.

🛏 Sleeping & Eating

Twin Towers Hotel   HOTEL **$**
(📞0775612195; s/d from KSh2500/3000) The Twin Towers (slightly unfortunate name, that) is a solid choice if all you require is a comfy bed and a bathroom that doesn't require a biohazard suit to enter. It can suffer quite badly from street noise, though. The restaurant here offers decent, if unimaginative, mains for around KSh300. It's right in the town centre near the banks, mosque and park.

Homa Bay Tourist Hotel   HOTEL **$$**
(📞0727112615; s/d from KSh2850/4350; P 🛜) This lakeside 'resort' is the town's original hotel and though the rooms are rather faded they also have character and are a pleasure to sleep in. The expansive lawns, running down to the water's edge, are home to many a colourful songbird and there's an outdoor bar with live music on Saturdays (so avoid rooms at the front).

ℹ Information

Barclays Bank (Moi Hwy) With ATM.
KWS Warden's Office In the district commissioner's compound, it's the place for information on Ruma National Park.

ℹ Getting There & Away

The Easy Coach office is just down the hill from the bus station and in the Total petrol station compound. It has buses to Nairobi (KSh1000, nine hours) at 8.30am and 8pm. Several other companies and matatus (operating from the bus station) ply the routes to the following: Mbita (KSh250, 1½ hours), Kisii (KSh200, 1½ hours) and Kisumu (KSh300, three hours).

Ruma National Park

Bordered by the dramatic **Kanyamaa Escarpment**, and home to Kenya's only population of roans (one of Africa's rarest and largest antelope), is the seldom-visited, 120-sq-km **Ruma National Park** (📞0723097573; www.kws.go.ke; adult/child US$20/10, vehicle from KSh300; ⏱6am-6pm). Besides roan, other rarities like Bohor reedbuck, Jackson's hartebeest, the tiny oribi antelope and Kenya's largest concentration of the endangered Rothschild's giraffe can also be seen here. However, the most treasured residents are 28 (very hard to see) rhinos, both black and white, that have been translocated from other parks.

Birdlife is also prolific, with 145 different bird species present, including the migratory blue swallow that arrives between June and August.

The park is set up for those with vehicles; otherwise, contact the KWS rangers at the park gates who may be able to send a local with a pop-top minivan to collect you from Homa Bay.

🛏 Sleeping & Eating

There are two simple **campsites** (public/special camping US$20/30) near the main gate. The Nyati special campsite is the more scenic. In either case you need to be totally self-sufficient with food and water.

Oribi Guesthouse   COTTAGES **$$**
(📞0723097573; www.kws.go.ke; cottage excl breakfast KSh9000; P) This KWS-run guesthouse, near the park headquarters, is extortionate if there are only two of you, but quite good value for groups. It has dramatic views over the Lambwe Valley and is well equipped with solar power, hot showers and a fully functioning kitchen, but bring your own food.

ℹ Getting There & Away

With your own vehicle, head a couple of kilometres south from Homa Bay and turn right onto the Mbita road. After about 12km is the main access road, which is signed just as Kenya Wildlife Services (although coming from Homa Bay you might not see the sign as it faces the other way) and from there it's another 11km. The park's roads are in decent shape, but require a mega 4WD in the rainy season.

Kisii

POP 97,000

Let's cut straight to the chase. Kisii is a noisy, polluted and congested mess, and most people (quite sensibly) roll right on through without even stopping. However, it's an important transport point and there's a good chance you'll pass through at some point in your explorations of western Kenya.

🛏 Sleeping & Eating

St Vincent Guesthouse   GUESTHOUSE **$**
(📞0733650702; s/d/tw KSh1500/2000/2400; P) This Catholic-run guesthouse off the Moi Hwy isn't the place for a party, but it's hands down the best place to stay in Kisii. Rooms are very clean and cosy, it's quiet and security is good. No alcohol allowed.

Nile Restaurant, Fast Food & Guesthouse
HOTEL $

(☑0786706089; Hospital Rd; excl breakfast s & d KSh1000-1500, tw KSh2000) Clean, cheap rooms and a central location make the Nile the best deal in the town centre. The icing on the cake is that the 2nd-floor restaurant (mains KSh200 to KSh300) has a commanding view of the chaos below.

ℹ️ Getting There & Away

The congested matatu terminal in the centre of town is a chaos of loud, and often somewhat drunk, people trying to bundle you onto the nearest matatu whether or not you want to go where it's going. If you do manage to pick your own matatu you'll find regular departures to Homa Bay (KSh200, 1½ hours), Kisumu (KSh300, 2½ hours), Kericho (KSh500, two hours) and Isebania (KSh300, 1¾ hours) on the Tanzanian border.

Tabaka matatus (KSh100, 45 minutes) leave from Cemetery Rd. Returning, it is sometimes easier to catch a *boda-boda* (KSh70 to KSh100) to the 'Tabaka junction' and pick up a Kisii-bound matatu there.

Easy Coach has twice daily departures to Nairobi (KSh900, eight hours) at 10am and 9.30pm. They also have a bus to Narok (KSh550, four hours) at 1pm which is handy for the Mara.

Kericho
POP 150,000

Kericho is a haven of tranquillity. Its surrounds are blanketed by a thick patchwork of manicured tea plantations, each seemingly hemmed in by distant stands of evergreens, and even the town centre itself seems as orderly as the tea gardens. With a pleasant climate and a number of things to see and do, Kericho makes for a very calming couple of days.

◎ Sights & Activities

Tea Plantations

This is the centre of the most important tea gardens in all of Africa and the countryside surrounding town is one of interlocking pristine tea estates mixed with patches of forest. You might expect tea-plantation tours to be touted left, right and centre, but surprisingly they are fairly few and far between. If you just want to take a stroll in the fields, then the easiest plantations to get to are those behind the Tea Hotel.

If you want something more organised, **Mr Harman Kirui** (☑0721843980; kmtharman@

KISII SOAPSTONE

While the feted Kisii soapstone obviously comes from this area, it's not on sale here. Quarrying and carving go on in the Gusii village of **Tabaka**, 23km northwest of Kisii. Soapstone is relatively soft and pliable (as far as rocks go) and with simple hand tools and scraps of sandpaper the sculptors carve chess sets, bowls, animals and the unmistakable abstract figures of embracing couples. Each artisan specialises in one design before passing it on to someone else to be smoothed with wet sandpaper and polished with wax. Most pieces are destined for the curio shops of Nairobi and Mombasa and trade-aid shops around the world. As you would expect, prices are cheaper here than elsewhere. If you are undaunted by adding a few heavy rocks to your backpack, you can save a packet.

---

yahoo.com; per person KSh200) runs fun and informative tea estate and factory tours. Most tours involve walking around the fields and watching the picking in process (note that the pickers don't work on Sunday). If you want to actually see the process through to the end and visit a factory, you should book at least four days in advance through the Tea Hotel or by emailing Harman directly.

Gardens
Arboretum
GARDENS

(B4 Hwy; ⊘closed when raining) Eight kilometres east of town, this tropical park is popular with weekend picnickers and colobus, vervet and red-tailed monkeys (best seen in the early morning). The main attraction is the shade afforded by the tropical trees planted by estate owner Tom Grumbley in the 1940s. The nearby Chagaik Dam is responsible for the lovely lily-covered pond.

🛏️ Sleeping & Eating

Being a stronghold of the Kipsigis people, this is good place to try *kimyet* (maize-meal served with vegetables and beef) or *mursik* (soured milk). Naturally, tea is extremely popular and drunk from dawn to supper and every opportunity in between.

New Sunshine Hotel
HOTEL $

(☑052-2030037, 0725146601; Tengecha Rd; s/d/ tr KSh2000/2700/3000; 🛜) Without doubt,

Kericho

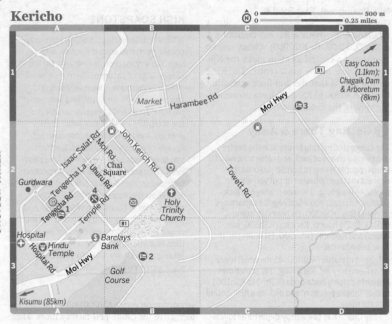

N
0 — 500 m
0 — 0.25 miles

Easy Coach
(1.1km);
Chagaik Dam
& Arboretum
(8km)

Market
Harambee Rd
Moi Hwy

KENYA KERICHO

Isaac Salat Rd
Moi Rd
John Kerich Rd
Chai Square
Uhuru Rd
Gurdwara
Tengecha La
Tengecha Rd
Temple Rd
Towett Rd

Holy Trinity Church

Hospital
Hindu Temple
Hospital Rd
Moi Hwy
Barclays Bank
Golf Course

Kisumu (85km)

Kericho

Sleeping
1 New Sunshine Hotel A2
2 Sunshine Upper Hill Hotel B3
3 Tea Hotel..D1

Eating
4 Litny's Restaurant A2

the best budget hotel in town (not that the competition is especially stiff). The rooms, while not large, are spotless and the showers are actually hot rather than lukewarm. The attached restaurant (meals KSh320 to KSh550) does a roaring trade.

Sunshine Upper Hill Hotel   HOTEL $$
(☎0721700358; www.sunshinehotel.co.ke; s KSh4000-5000, d KSh5000-6000; P🅟🛜) This large hotel block, consisting of modern new rooms overlooking the town park, is where biusness types settle in to do important stuff in Kericho. The rooms have comfortable beds, vast bathrooms and in-room wi-fi.

Tea Hotel   HOTEL $$
(☎0714510824; Moi Hwy; camping KSh700, s/d US$70/95; P🛜🅿) This grand property was built in the 1950s by the Brooke Bond company and still has a lot of (very faded) period charm.

The hotel's most notable features are the vast hallways and dining rooms full of mounted animal heads, and its beautiful gardens with their tea-bush backdrops. Many of the rooms, though, are literally falling to pieces.

Litny's Restaurant   KENYAN $
(Temple Rd; mains KSh250-400; ⊘5.30am-8pm) Along with New Sunshine Hotel, this is regarded as one of the better restaurants in town, though in truth the fried chicken and chips here was no different to the fried chicken and chips we ate elsewhere.

ⓘ Getting There & Away

Most buses and matatus operate from the main stand in the town's northwest corner, while those heading south and west (such as Kisii and Kisumu) leave from the Total petrol station on Moi Hwy.

Matatus to Kisumu (KSh300, 1½ hours) are frequent as are ones to Kisii (KSh300, two hours), Eldoret (KSh400 to KSh500, 3½ hours) and Nakuru (KSh300, two hours). The odd Peugeot also serves these destinations, but costs about 25% more.

Easy Coach offers the best buses, but its office and departure point is inconveniently located out of town opposite the Tea Hotel and inside the Libya Petrol Station. They have buses to Nairobi (KSh1100) throughout the day as well as frequent buses to Nakuru (KSh550) and Kisumu (KSh500).

Kakamega Forest

Not so long ago much of western Kenya was hidden under a dark veil of jungle and formed a part of the mighty Guineo–Congolian forest ecosystem. However, the British soon did their best to turn all that lovely virgin forest into tea estates. Now all that's left is this slab of tropical rainforest surrounding Kakamega.

Though seriously degraded, this forest is unique in Kenya and contains plants, animals and birds that occur nowhere else in the country. It's especially good for birders with turacos, which are like flying turkeys that have been given a box of face paints, being a favourite with everyone. Other stand out birds include flocks of African grey parrots and noisy hornbills that sound like helicopters when they fly overhead. If you prefer your animals furrier then Kakamega is home to several primates including graceful colobus monkeys, black-cheeked-white nosed monkeys and Sykes monkey.

◉ Sights & Activities

The best way, indeed the only real way, to appreciate the forest is to walk. While guides are not compulsory, they are well worth the extra expense. Not only do they prevent you from getting lost, but most are walking encyclopaedias and will reel off both the Latin and common name of almost any plant or insect you care to point out, along with any of its medicinal properties.

ANYONE FOR TEA?

Kenya is the world's third-largest tea exporter after India and Sri Lanka, with tea accounting for between 20% and 30% of the country's export income. It's unique in that its small landholders produce the bulk (60%) of the country's tea.

Tea-picking is a great source of employment around Kericho, with mature bushes picked every 17 days and the same worker continually picking the same patch. Good pickers collect their own body weight in tea each day!

Despite Kericho producing some of the planet's best black tea, you will have trouble finding a cup of the finest blends here – most of it's exported.

Kakamega Forest National Reserve PARK (www.kws.go.ke; adult/child US$25/15, vehicles KSh300) Rangers state that trails here vary in length from 1km to 7km. Of the longer walks, Isiukhu Trail, which connects Isecheno to the small Isiukhu Falls, is one of the most popular and takes a minimum of half a day. The 4km drive or walk to Buyangu Hill allows for uninterrupted views east to the Nandi Escarpment.

Guides, from a local association called **Kafkogoa** (☑ 0724143064), cost KSh2000 for up to three hours and can be arranged at the park gates.

ⓘ KAKAMEGA FOREST

Why Go
For a rare chance to see a unique rainforest ecosystem with over 330 species of birds, 400 species of butterfly and seven different primate species, one being the rare Kenya de Brazza's monkey. During darkness, hammer-headed fruit bats take to the air.

When to Go
The best viewing months are June, August and October, when many migrant bird species arrive. October also sees many wildflowers bloom, while December to March are the driest months.

Practicalities
As the northern section of the forest is managed by KWS and the southern section by the Forest Department, it is not possible to visit the whole park without paying both sets of admission charges. Both areas have their pros and cons.

Budget Tips
Entry fees to the southern Kakamega Forest Reserve are lower, and accommodation generally cheaper, than in the northern Kakamega Forest National Reserve so it makes sense for budget travellers to base themselves here.

Kakamega Forest Reserve PARK
(adult/child KSh600/150) Kakamega Forest Reserve is the more degraded area of the forest, yet it's the more popular area with tourists. The five-hour return hike to Lirhanda Hill for sunrise or sunset is highly recommended. An interesting short walk (2.6km) to a 35m-high watchtower affords views over the forest canopy and small grassland.

Next to the forest reserve office is the **Kakamega Rainforest Tour Guides** (☑0706158556; per person short/long walk KSh500/800) office, which supplies knowlegeable guides to the forest for a variety of walks, including recommended night walks (KSh1500 per person) and sunrise/sunset walks (KSh1000 per person).

🛏 Sleeping & Eating

🛏 Kakamega Forest National Reserve

If you're staying at either of the KWS-managed options, you will have to pay park entry fees for each night you're there.

Udo's Bandas & Campsite BANDA $
(☑Nairobi 020-2654658; www.kws.go.ke; camping adult/child US$20/15, bandas per person US$40) Named after Udo Savalli, a well-known or-nithologist, this lovely KWS site is tidy, well maintained and has seven simple thatched *bandas*. Nets are provided, but you will need your own sleeping bag and other supplies. There are long-drop toilets, bucket showers and a communal cooking and dining shelter.

New De Brazza's Campsite CAMPGROUND $
(☑0706486786; camping KSh1000, bandas per person KSh1250) Just before the park gates and hidden down a squiggle of squelchy, muddy lanes (ask for directions at the park gate), this simple campsite is as basic as basic gets. There's no electricity and the toilets are the kind where the long-drops aren't long enough. The setting though is top notch.

🛏 Kakamega Forest Reserve

Forest Rest House GUESTHOUSE $
(camping KSh650, r per person KSh500) The four rooms of this wooden house, perched on stilts 2m above the ground and with views straight onto a mass of jungle, might be very basic (no electricity, no bedding and cold-water baths that look like they'd crash through the floorboards if you used one), but they'll bring out the inner Tarzan in even the most obstinate city slicker.

★ Rondo Retreat GUESTHOUSE $$$
(☑0733299149, 056-2030268; www.rondoretreat.com; s/d full board KSh17,600/22,000; ℗) To arrive at Rondo Retreat is to be whisked back to 1922 and the height of British rule. Consisting of a series of wooden bungalows filled with a family's clutter, this gorgeous and eccentric place is a wonderful retreat

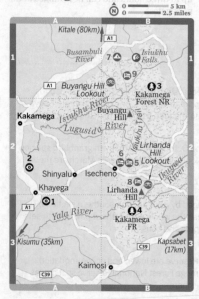

Kakamega Forest

🧭 0 ——— 5 km
0 ——— 2.5 miles

Kakamega Forest

WESTERN BULLFIGHTING

Bull fighting (between two bulls) is one of the more popular 'sports' in Western Kenya, and Khayega (6km south of Kakamega) has Saturday morning showdowns. They start early at 7am (the whole thing wraps up at around 8am), with a whole lot of horn blowing, drumming, chanting and stick waving.

The purpose-bred bulls are fed on molasses-spiked grass and, to help them preserve their energy, isolated from heifers, making them understandably tetchy. Then the bulls are fed secret concoctions guaranteed to make them even more aggressive.

When the bulls meet, they'll lock horns and fight until one submits and turns tail. Besides a bruised ego or two, no bulls are injured during the show of strength (cattle are valued too highly for owners to put them at risk). There are no safety barriers, so spectators should keep their distance and be prepared to run or climb a tree should a bull break away.

The winning bull (and all of the crowd) then race to the next venue, usually about 1km to 2km away, where they meet up with a similar winner and the whole performance is repeated.

Bull fighting is practised mostly by the Isukha and Idako peoples.

from modern Kenya. The gardens are absolutely stunning and worth visiting even if you're not staying.

ℹ Getting There & Away

KAKAMEGA FOREST NATIONAL RESERVE
Matatus heading north towards Kitale can drop you at the access road about 18km north of Kakamega town (KSh80). It is a well-signposted 2km walk from there to the park office and to Udo's.

KAKAMEGA FOREST RESERVE
Regular matatus link Kakamega with Shinyalu (KSh70), but few go on to Isecheno. Shinyalu is also accessed by a rare matatu service from Khayega. From Shinyalu you'll probably need to take a *boda-boda* for KSh100 to Isecheno.

Eldoret

POP 289,000

The Maasai originally referred to this area as *eldore* (stony river) after the nearby Sosiani River, but this proved too linguistically challenging for the South African Voortrekkers who settled here in 1910 and they named their settlement Eldoret instead.

In 2008 Eldoret achieved notoriety when 35 people (mostly Kikuyus) were burnt alive in a church on the outskirts of town. This incident was the largest single loss of life during the 2007 post-election violence.

Today, Eldoret is a thriving service town straddling the Kenya–Uganda highway but,

for the traveller, there is little to see, and even less to do.

◉ Sights

Doinyo Lessos Creameries
Cheese Factory   FOOD
(Kenyatta St; ⊗8am-6pm) The highlight of Eldoret is a visit to the Doinyo Lessos Creameries Cheese Factory to stock up on any one of 20 different varies of cheese. Enjoy.

⌨ Sleeping

White Highlands Inn   HOTEL $
(☑0734818955; Elgeyo St; s/d KSh2000/2500; 🅿) In a quiet corner on the edge of town, this place offers good value. Its spacious rooms were so spotless that we actually lay in the bathtub as opposed to just looking at it wistfully. The whole complex is a bit rambling, but retains a certain old-fashioned charm and has a popular bar and less-popular restaurant.

★ Boma Inn Eldoret   HOTEL $$$
(☑0719025000; www.bomahotels.com; Elgon View, off Elgon Rd; r from KSh12,650; 🅿🛜❄) 🍴 This new business-class hotel, 2km from the city centre, is hands down the best place to stay in Eldoret. The large rooms are smart, stylishly decorated and have comfortable beds, big desks to work at, piping-hot showers and there's a decent in-house restaurant as well as a pool and gym. All profits go to the Kenyan Red Cross.

Eldoret

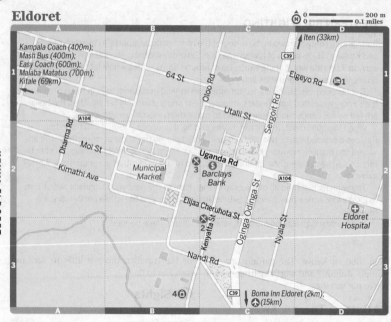

Eldoret

🛏 Sleeping
1 White Highlands Inn D1

🍴 Eating
2 Sunjeel Palace C3
3 Will's Pub & Restaurant B2

🛍 Shopping
4 Doinyo Lessos Creameries
   Cheese Factory B3

🍴 Eating

Will's Pub & Restaurant   INTERNATIONAL $
(Uganda Rd; mains KSh100-450; ⏰9am-midnight)
Looks and feels like an English pub, with
similarly heavyweight food – but it also produces a few African
dishes of the ugali and beef-stew ilk.
The big-screen TV makes it a great place for
a cold beer, and the low-key vibe makes it a
safe spot for solo female travellers.

⭐ **Sunjeel Palace**   INDIAN $$
(Kenyatta St; mains KSh450-600; ⏰11am-11pm;
📶) This formal, dark and spicy Indian restaurant
serves superb, real-deal curries. Portion
sizes are decent and if you mop up all

the gravy with a freshly baked butter naan,
you'll be as rotund as Ganesh himself.

ℹ Getting There & Away

AIR
Fly540 (📞 053-2030814; www.fly540.com;
Eldoret international airport) Frequent flights
between Eldoret and Nairobi, and less frequently
to Lodwar and Juba (South Sudan).

Jambo Jet (www.jambojet.com) This Kenya
Airways subsidary flies to Nairobi and Kisumu.

BUS
A string of bus companies line Uganda Rd west
of the Postbank.

Easy Coach (Uganda Rd) Buses to Nairobi
(KSh1250, 10am and 10pm) via Nakuru
(KSh700).

Kampala Coach (Uganda Rd) Noon and midnight
buses to Kampala (KSh2000, six hours).

Mash Bus (Uganda Rd) Direct bus to Mombasa
(KSh2000, 12 hours, 5pm).

MATATU
The main matatu stand is in the centre of town
by the municipal market although some local
matatus and more Kericho services leave from
Nandi Rd. Irregular matatus to Iten and Kabarnet
leave from Sergoit Rd. Further west on Uganda
Rd, matatus leave for Malaba on the Uganda
border.

Matutu services from Eldoret include the following:

TO	FARE (KSH)	DURATION (HR)
Iten	100	1
Kabarnet	350	2
Kakamega	350-400	2
Kericho	400	3
Kisumu	500	3
Kitale	250	1¼
Nairobi	800	6
Nakuru	300	2¾
Nyahururu	600	3½

Getting Around

A matatu to or from the international airport costs KSh80, and a taxi will cost around KSh1000 to KSh1500. *Boda-bodas* (especially the motorised variety) can be found on most street corners.

Kitale

POP 106,100

Agricultural Kitale is a small, friendly market town with a couple of interesting museums and a bustling market. If you're travelling further afield, it makes an ideal base for explorations of Mt Elgon and Saiwa Swamp National Parks. It also serves as the take-off point for a trip up to the western side of Lake Turkana.

Sights

Kitale Museum

MUSEUM

(A1 Hwy; adult/child KSh500/250; ⊙9.30am-6pm) Founded on the collection of butterflies, birds and ethnographic memorabilia left to the nation in 1967 by the late Lieutenant Colonel Stoneham, this museum has an interesting range of ethnographic displays of the Pokot, Akamba, Marakwet and Turkana peoples. There are also any number of stuffed dead things shot by various colonial types, including a hedgehog and a cheetah with a lopsided face.

Treasures of Africa Museum

MUSEUM

(A1 Hwy; admission KSh500; ⊙9am-12.30pm & 2-5pm Mon-Sat) This private museum is the personal collection of Mr Wilson, a former colonial officer in Uganda and quite a character. Based mainly on his experiences with the Karamojong people of northern Uganda, Mr Wilson's small museum illustrates his theory that a universal worldwide agricultural culture existed as far back as the last ice age.

Sleeping & Eating

Jehova Jireh Hotel

HOTEL $

(☑0716805512; s/d from KSh1500/2800) A solid choice that boasts spacious, quiet and clean rooms with exceptionally helpful management. It's not quite as God-fearing as it sounds. There's an excellent downstairs restaurant that serves food later than most.

Iroko Twigs Hotel

HOTEL $

(☑0773475884; Kenyatta St; s/d KSh3000/3500; ☎) If you can overlook a few missing bathroom tiles and a little wear and tear, this is far and away the smartest hotel in town. The rooms (doubles more than singles) are pleasingly decorated with polished wood and art and there are coffee- and tea-making facilities and even dressing gowns in the wardrobes. Cosy cafe downstairs.

Kitale

Top Sights
1 Kitale Museum B3

Sleeping
2 Iroko Twigs Hotel B3

Eating
3 Iroko Boulevard Restaurant A2

KENYA KITALE

Iroko Boulevard Restaurant   KENYAN $

(Askari Rd; mains KSh150-280; ☺ 6.30am-6.30pm)
It's got style, it's got glamour, it's got big-city
aspirations and it's totally unexpected in
Kitale. With cheap dishes and an old Mor-
ris car hanging from the ceiling, this is the
most popular place to eat in town. There are
two other places in town with very similar
names and menus – all are good.

ⓘ Getting There & Away

Matatus, buses and Peugeots are grouped by
destination, and spread in and around the main
bus and matatu park.

Regular matatus run to Endebess (KSh100, 45
minutes, change here for Mt Elgon National Park),
Kapenguria (KSh150, 45 minutes, change here
to continue north to Marich), Eldoret (KSh250,
1¼ hours), Kakamega (KSh250 to KSh300, 2½
hours) and Kisumu (KSh500, four hours).

Most bus companies have offices around the
bus station and serve Eldoret (KSh200, one
hour), Nakuru (KSh700, 3½ hours), Nairobi
(KSh900, seven hours) and Lodwar (KSh1500,
8½ hours) each day.

Easy Coach (Moi Ave) runs to Nairobi
(KSh1350; seven hours) at 8am and 8pm, The
same bus stops in Nakuru (KSh850, 3½ hours).

Saiwa Swamp National Park

North of Kitale, this small, rarely visited
Saiwa Swamp National Park (www.kws.
go.ke; adult/child US$25/15; ☺ 6am-6pm) is a
real treat. Originally set up to preserve the
habitat of Kenya's only population of sitatunga antelope, the 15.5-sq-km reserve is
also home to blue, vervet and de Brazza's
monkeys and some 370 species of birds.
The fluffy black-and-white colobus and the
impressive crowned crane are both present, and you may see the Cape clawless and
spot-throated otters (watch tower 4 is the
best place from which to look for these).

The park is only accessible on foot and
walking trails skirt the swamp, duckboards
go right across it, and there are some rickety
observation towers. Guides are not compulsory although your experience will be greatly enhanced by taking one.

🛏 Sleeping

Public Campsite   CAMPGROUND $

(www.kws.go.ke; camping US$20; P) A lovely site
with flush toilets, showers, two covered cooking *bandas* and colobus in the trees above.

Sitatunga Treetop House   HUT $

(www.kws.go.ke; tree house US$50; P) Perched
on stilts overlooking the Saiwa swamp, this
KWS tree house can sleep three in a double
and single bed. It has electricity, bedding
and mosquito nets. There are no cooking
facilities, but you can use those at the campsite next door.

Sirikwa Safaris   GUESTHOUSE $$

(Barnley's Guesthouse; ☎ 0723917953; www.sirikwa
safaris.com; camping KSh500, tents excl breakfast
s/d KSh1500/2500, s/d with shared bathroom excl
breakfast KSh4500/6000) Owned and run by
the family that started Saiwa, this beautiful
old farmhouse is 11km from the swamp. You
can chose between camping in the grounds,
sleeping in a well-appointed safari tent or,
best of all, opting for one of the two bedrooms full of *National Geographic* magazines, old ornaments and antique sinks.

ⓘ Getting There & Away

The park is 18km northeast of Kitale; take a
matatu towards Kapenguria (KSh130, 30 minutes) and get out at the second signposted turn-
off (KSh80, 15 minutes) from where it is a 5km
walk or KSh100 *moto-taxi* (motorcycle taxi) ride.

Mt Elgon National Park

Straddling the Ugandan border and peaking with Koitoboss (4187m), Kenya's second-highest peak, and Uganda's Wagagai
(4321m), the slopes of Mt Elgon are a sight
indeed – or at least they would be if they
weren't buried under a blanket of mist and
drizzle most of the time.

With rainforest at the base, the vegetation
changes as you ascend to bamboo jungle
and finally alpine moorland featuring the
giant groundsel and giant lobelia plants.

Common animals include buffaloes,
bushbucks (both of which are usually grazing on the airstrip near Cholim gate), olive
baboons, giant forest hogs and duikers. The
lower forests are the habitat of the black-
and-white colobus, and blue and de Brazza's
monkeys.

There are more than 240 species of birds
here, including red-fronted parrots, Ross's
turacos and casqued hornbills. On the peaks
you may even see a lammergeier dropping
bones from the thin air.

While there's plenty of interesting wildlife and plants here, the real reason people
visit **Mt Elgon National Park** (www.kws.go.ke;

Mt Elgon National Park

5 km
2.5 miles

Endebess (5km)

Koitoboss River

Chorlim Mt Elgon Lodge

Chorlim Gate

Chorlim Campsite

Nyati Campsite

Elephant National Park Platform Headquarters; Mt Elgon Guides & Porters Association

North Mt Elgon Forest Station

Masara Route

Masara

Kapkuro Bandas

Rongai

Rongai Campsite

Suam Saw Mill

Mbere River

Kimothon Forest Station

Chepnyalli Cave

Saito Campsite

Saito Dam

Mackingeny Cave

Endebess Bluff

Kitum Cave

Kassowai Gate (closed)

Kimothon Gate (closed)

Kantega River

Koitcut (3302m)

Park Route

Kassowai River

Kaberwonon River

Suam River

Trail head for 4WD vehicles

Mount Elgon NP

Chorlim-Koitoboss Route

KENYA

Chepkitale Forest Station (abandoned)

Suam Gorge

Koitoboss (4187m)

Cave

Austrian Hut (ruined)

Kimilili Route

Kibust River

Suam Hot Springs

Lower Elgon (4301m)

Sudek (4176m)

Sacred Lake (Lower Elgon Tarn)

Terim River

Mallkisi River

UGANDA

Round Top Hill (3890m)

Little Wagagai Peak (4298m)

Wagagai (4321m)

Mubiyi

Jackson's Summit

ⓘ MT ELGON NATIONAL PARK

Why Go
Some superb overnight treks along with some interesting half-day options to caves occasionally visited by salt-loving elephants.

When to Go
It's extremely wet most of the year; serious trekkers should visit between December and February when it is at its driest.

Practicalities
The easiest section of the park to visit is the area accessed via Chorlim gate, from where you can walk or drive to the caves and surrounding forest. Waterproof gear and warm clothing is essential; altitude may also be a problem for some people. KWS produce a 1:35,000 map (KSh450) of the park as well as a guidebook (KSh750), both of which are sold at Chorlim gate.

park entrance adult/child US$30/20, vehicles from KSh350; ⊙6am-6pm) is to stand atop the summit high above Kenya and Uganda. It is possible to walk unescorted, but due to the odd elephant and buffalo you will need to sign a waiver to do so.

Mt Elgon Guides & Porters Association (✆0733919347) is a cooperative of guides and porters based at the KWS headquarters. Their services (per day guide/porter KSh3000/1000) can be booked through KWS.

◉ Sights & Activities

Elkony Caves CAVE
Four main lava tubes (caves) are open to visitors: **Kitum, Chepnyalil, Mackingeny** and **Rongai**.

While rarely seen, elephants are known to 'mine' for salt from the walls of the caves. Kitum holds your best hope of glimpsing them, but sadly the number of these saline-loving creatures has declined over the years. Nonetheless, a torchlight inspection will soon reveal their handiwork in the form of tusking – the grooves made by their tusks during the digging process.

Koitoboss Trek HIKING
Allow at least four days for any round-trip hikes, and two or three days for any direct ascent of Koitoboss from the Chorlim gate. Once you reach the summit, there are a number of interesting options for the descent, including descending northwest into the crater to **Suam Hot Springs**.

Alternatively you could go east around the crater rim and descend the Masara Route, which leads to the small village of Masara on

the eastern slopes of the mountain (about 25km) and then returns to Endebess. Or you can head southwest around the rim of the crater (some very hard walking) to **Lower Elgon Tarn**, where you can camp before ascending **Lower Elgon Peak** (4301m).

If all this sounds too tiring, you'll be extremely pleased to know it's possible to get within 4km of the summit with a 4WD if you have decent weather.

⌣ Sleeping

If you're trekking, your only option is to camp. The fee is the same whether you drop tent in the official campsites (Chorlim, Nyati and Rongai) or on any old flat spot during your trek.

Kapkuro Bandas BANDA $
(www.kws.go.ke; per banda US$50) These decent stone *bandas* can sleep three people in two beds and have simple bathrooms and small, fully equipped kitchen areas.

Mt Elgon Lodge LODGE $$
(✆0722875768; s/d/tr US$40/65/100) A few hundred metres before the main gate, this very faded lodge is set in grassy grounds with views down to the lowlands. Rooms are plain but clean and meals are available.

ⓘ Getting There & Away

From Kitale, catch an Endebess-bound matatu (KSh100, 45 minutes), to the park junction from where it is a 15-minute motorbike taxi ride (KSh100 to KSh150) to the park gate. Be sure to grab your driver's phone number so you can contact him for a ride back to Endebess.

CENTRAL HIGHLANDS & LAIKIPIA

The Central Highlands are the green-girt, red-dirt spiritual heartland of Kenya's largest tribe, the Kikuyu. This is the land the Mau Mau fought for, the land the colonists coveted and the land whose natural, cyclical patterns define the lives of the country's largest rural population.

These highlands form one of the most evocative sections of Africa's Great Rift Valley. It is here that Mt Kenya, Africa's second-highest mountain, rises into the clouds – climbing it is one of the great most-satisfying rites of passage of African travel. In its shadow lie two of Kenya's most intriguing national parks: rhino- and lion-rich Meru National Park, and the Aberdare National Park, home to some of the oldest mountains on the continent.

And then there's Laikipia. Set against the backdrop of Mt Kenya, the **Laikipia Plateau** (www.laikipia.org) extends over 9500 sq km (roughly the size of Wales in Great Britain) of semi-arid plains, dramatic gouges and acacia thicket-covered hills. Conceived in 1992, this patchwork of privately owned ranches, wildlife conservancies and small-scale farms has become one of the most important areas for biodiversity in the country. It boasts wildlife densities second only to those found in the Masai Mara and is the last refuge of Kenya's African wild dogs. Indeed, these vast plains are home to some of Kenya's highest populations of endangered species including half of the country's black rhinos, half of the world's Grevy's zebras and one of the last viable lion populations in Kenya.

Central Highlands & Laikipia

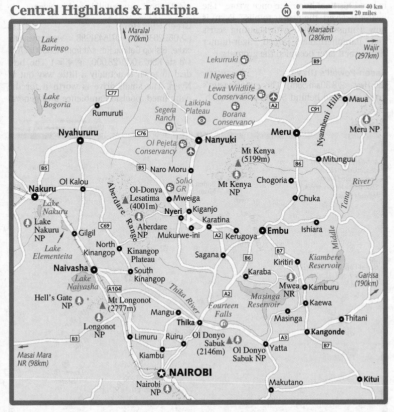

Nyeri

POP 125,357

Nyeri is a welcoming and bustling Kikuyu market town. It's as busy as the Central Highlands get, but unless you have a thing for chaotic open-air bazaars and the restless energy of Kikuyu and white Kenyans selling maize, bananas, arrowroot, coffee and macadamia nuts, there's no real reason to linger for longer than it takes to plot your onward journey. Boy Scouts might think otherwise.

⊙ Sights & Activities

Baden-Powell Museum MUSEUM
(admission KSh300; ⊘ opened on request) Lord Baden-Powell, the founder of the Boy Scout Association, spent his last three years at Paxtu cottage in the Outspan Hotel. The ultimate scoutmaster's retirement was somewhat poetic: to 'outspan' is to unhook your oxen at the end of a long journey. And he clearly loved his final home: he once wrote, 'The nearer to Nyeri, the nearer to bliss'. Paxtu is now a museum filled with scouting scarfs and paraphernalia. Famed tiger-hunter Jim Corbett later occupied the grounds.

Baden-Powell's Grave CEMETERY
(B5 Hwy; ⊘ 8.30am-5pm) The scoutmaster's grave is tucked behind **St Peter's Church**,

facing Mt Kenya and marked with the Scouts trail sign for 'I have gone home'. His more famous Westminster Abbey tomb is, in fact, empty.

☞ Tours

Bongo Asili Travel TOUR
(☑ 061-2030884, 0725556358; www.bongoasili travel.com; off Kanisa Rd; ⊘ 9am-5pm Mon-Sat) The only locally based tour operator, Bongo Asili can arrange safaris, book hotels throughout Kenya and coordinate airline ticketing.

⌸ Sleeping

**Nyama Choma Village
Accommodation** HOTEL $
(☑ 0788174384; Gakere Rd; r excl breakfast KSh1200) With its light-blue walls and blue-linoleum showers, Nyama Choma is as colourful as it is cheap. And, as you'd expect with a name like Nyama Choma (barbecued meat), meat-eaters will love this place.

Green Hills Hotel HOTEL $$
(☑ 061-2030604, 0716431988; www.greenhills. co.ke; Bishop Gatimu Rd; s/d from KSh500/7700, s/d ste KSh23,000/28,000; ▣ 🕱 ▣) The best deal in town is actually a little way out of Nyeri. The small drive is worth it for the palm-lined, poolside ambience and general

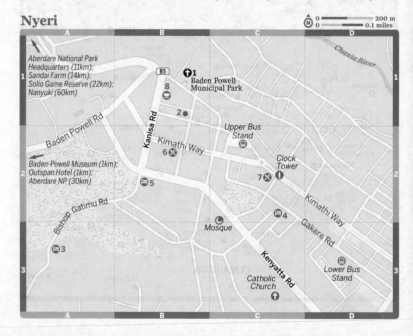

Nyeri

sense of serenity. A few questionable style choices notwithstanding, the rooms are nicely turned out and comfortable.

White Rhino Hotel HOTEL $$
(☏061-2030944, 0726967315; www.whiterhinohotel.com; Kanisa Rd; s/d/tw KSh6000/7000/7500; ▣@⊛) Since its remodelling in 2011, the hotel now boasts smart rooms that are polished to an inch of their lives, and swanky, tiled bathrooms. With three bars and two restaurants, this is the top hotel in the city centre.

Sandai Farm GUESTHOUSE $$$
(☏0721656699; www.africanfootprints.de; camping KSh500, s/d full board US$145/250, cottages from US$80; ▣@) Fourteen kilometres northwest of town (ask locals for directions), Sandai is run by the effervescent Petra Allmendinger, whose enthusiasm and warm welcome make this a great weekend escape from Nairobi's bustle or for those looking for something a little more personal than what's on offer elsewhere.

Outspan Hotel HOTEL $$$
(☏061-2032424, Nairobi 020-4452095; www.aberdaresafarihotels.com; s/d from US$179/276; ▣⊛☒) This atmospheric lodge was last decorated in the 1950s, when wood panelling was the height of interior design, and some of the plumbing seems to date from then as well... Nineteen of the 34 standard rooms have cosy fireplaces, and all have a whiff of history that won't necessarily be to everyone's taste.

Nyeri

✗ Eating & Drinking

Rayjo's Café KENYAN $
(Kimathi Way; meals KSh100-200; ⊙noon-9pm) This tiny canteen is usually packed with customers, including bus and matatu drivers, notoriously good judges of cheap places to eat.

Raybells INTERNATIONAL $
(Kimathi Way; mains KSh150-500; ⊙6am-8pm) Pretty much anything you want to eat (well, anything Kenyan or Western), from pizza to *nyama choma,* is available and cooked passably well here. You may want to avoid the fresh juice as it has tap water added to it.

Green Hills Hotel INTERNATIONAL $$
(Bishop Gatimu Rd; mains/buffet KSh750/800; ⊙7am-10pm) The full buffet here (when numbers permit) is an impressive piece of work, with some tasty mixed-grill options done up in a satisfyingly fancy fashion. Steaks are tender and come sizzling on a platter with a good mix of vegies.

Julie's Coffee Shop CAFE
(Kanisa Rd; snacks KSh50-150; ⊙7am-3pm; ⊛) The best place in town for genuine espresso coffee and free wi-fi.

❶ Getting There & Away

The Upper Bus Stand deals with sporadic buses and a plethora of matatus to destinations north and west of Nyeri including Nanyuki (KSh250, one hour), Nyahururu (KSh350, 1¼ hours) and Nakuru (KSh550, 2½ hours).

From the Lower Bus Stand matatus head in all directions south and east including Thika (KSh300, two hours) and Nairobi (KSh500, 2½ hours).

Aberdare National Park

While there's plenty of reason to wax rhapsodic over herds of wildlife thundering over an open African horizon, there's also something to be said for the soil-your-pants shock of seeing an elephant thunder out of bush that was, minutes before, just plants. And that's why people love **Aberdare National Park** (☏0774160327, Nairobi 020-2046271; www.kws.org; adult/child US$60/30; ⊙6am-6pm). Camera reflexes are tested as the abundant wildlife pops unexpectedly out of the shrubbery, including elephants, buffaloes, black rhinos, spotted hyenas, bongo antelope, bush pigs, black servals and rare black leopards.

Aberdare National Park

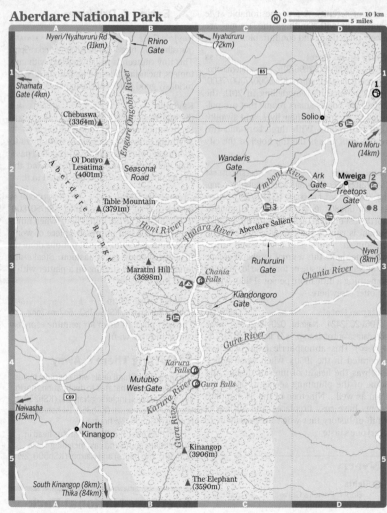

Aberdare National Park

◎ Sights
1 Solio Game Reserve D1

🛏 Sleeping
2 Aberdare Country Club D2
3 Ark C2
4 Public Campsite B3
5 Sapper Hut B4
6 Solio Game Reserve Lodge D2
7 Treetops D2

ℹ Information
8 Aberdare National Park
   Headquarters D2

The elephants are something of an anomaly. This is the highest-altitude resident elephant herd in Africa and it once migrated between the Aberdares and Mount Kenya, but human settlements and fences now block the route between these two upland habitats and the herd is effectively confined to the Aberdares.

The tallest regions of this range can claim some of Kenya's most dramatic up-country scenery, packed with 300m waterfalls, dense forests and serious trekking potential. The park has two major environments: an eastern hedge of thick rainforest and waterfall-studded hills known as the **Salient**, and the **Kinangop plateau**, an open tableland of coarse moors that huddles under cold mountain breezes.

A 400km-long electric fence completely encircles the park. Powered by solar panels, the fence is designed to reduce human–animal conflict by keeping would-be poachers and cattle on one side and marauding wildlife on the other.

Sights & Activities

To trek within the park requires advance permission from the warden at park headquarters, who may (depending on where you plan to walk) insist on providing an armed ranger to guide and protect you against inquisitive wildlife (KSh2000/4000 per half/full day).

The **Northern Moorland** and its four main peaks (all 3500m to 4000m) are excellent trekking spots; the tallest mountain in the park is Ol Donyo Lesatima (4000m), a popular bag for those on the East African mountain circuit. Between Honi Campsite and Elephant Ridge is the site of the hideout of Mau Mau leader Dedan Kimathi, who used these mountains as a base; many of his companions learned the ropes of jungle warfare fighting in Burma in WWII.

On the **Kinangop Plateau**, from the dirt track that connects the Ruhuruini and Mutubio West gates, it is possible to walk to the top of Karura Falls and watch Karura Stream slide over the rocky lip into the 272m abyss. Weather permitting, you may be able to make out the misty veil of Kenya's tallest cascade, the Gura Falls (305m), in the distance. Unfortunately there are no tracks to Gura Falls or the base of Karura Falls. You can, however, visit the far smaller Chania Falls further north.

Sleeping

Public Campsite   CAMPGROUND **$**
(☑ 0774160327; www.kws.go.ke; camping per adult/child US$20/15) Basic sites with minimal facilities – some have water.

Sapper Hut   BANDA **$**
(☑ 0774160327; www.kws.go.ke; bandas US$45) A simple *banda* with an open fire, two beds and a hot-water boiler, overlooking a lovely waterfall on the Upper Magura River. It's best to bring your own gear.

ℹ ABERDARE NATIONAL PARK

Why Go
Two interesting ecosystems to explore: a dense rainforest and high, Afro-alpine moorlands with great trekking possibilities and some spectacular waterfalls.

When to Go
The park receives plenty of rain year-round. The driest months are January to February and June to September.

Practicalities
During the rains, roads are impassable and the numbered navigation posts in the Salient are often difficult to follow. The most straightforward visit is to drive between the Ruhuruini and Mutubio West gates.

Budget Tips
Camp at public campsites or organise a day trip with other travellers from Nyeri.

Ark   HOTEL **$$$**
(☑ 0737799990; www.thearkkenya.com; s/d/tr US$180/305/434) The Ark dates from the 1960s, has large rooms and a lounge that overlooks a waterhole. Watch buffalo as you sip wine in a moulded chair lifted from *Austin Powers* and you'll have an idea of the ambience. An excellent walkway leads over a particularly dense stretch of the Salient, and from here and the waterhole lounge you can spot elephants, rhinos, buffaloes and hyenas. Sold as an overnight excursion from the **Aberdare Country Club** (☑ Nairobi 0737799990; www.aberdarecountryclub.com; s/d/tr full board US$195/260/370, day entry adult/child KSh500/300; P ☷) in Nyeri.

Treetops   HISTORIC HOTEL **$$$**
(☑ 061-2032425; www.aberdaresafarihotels.com; s/d US$229/352, s/d ste US$279/402; P @ ⟩) Treetops is sold as part of a package with the Outspan Hotel (p275) in Nyeri. Guests are given lunch at the Outspan, transported to Treetops, where they dine and sleep before being returned to the Outspan the following morning for breakfast. Rooms are small and the 2012 renovations have done wonders for this place with dark-wood floors, ochre feature walls and attractive prints. There's also excellent wildlife viewing.

RIGHT ROYAL CONNECTIONS

Trivia for royal-philes: Treetops isn't actually the spot where Princess Elizabeth became Queen Elizabeth II. Yes, Liz was sleeping in Treetops when George VI died in 1952, but in 1954 Mau Mau guerrillas blew the original lodge to twigs; three years later, a much larger rendition was built on the opposite side of the waterhole. 'Every time like the first time', goes the Treetops slogan, and we agree: sleeping here feels like travelling back to the day that the 25-year-old Elizabeth went to bed a princess and awoke a queen.

Fifty-eight years later, another young lady, this time a commoner, answered 'yes' to a question that will eventually see her crowned the Queen of the Commonwealth. On the verandah of a small log cabin, high on the flanks of Mt Kenya, Prince William asked Kate Middleton to be his wife. Under the guise of fishing on Lake Alice, William and Kate travelled to the remote Rutundu cabins where he popped the big question. And so it is, that while the fishing trip was a complete failure, Prince William still managed quite the catch.

ℹ️ Information

To enter the park through the Treetops or Ark gates, ask permission at **national park headquarters** (☑ 061-202379409; Mweiga; ⊙ 6am-6pm). Excellent 1:25,000 maps are available at the gates.

ℹ️ Getting There & Away

Access roads from the B5 Hwy to the Wanderis, Ark, Treetops and Ruhuruini gates are in decent shape. Keep in mind that it takes a few hours to get from the Salient to the moorlands and vice versa.

Nyahururu (Thomson's Falls)

POP 36,450 / ELEV 2360M

This unexpectedly attractive town leaps out of the northwest corner of the highlands and makes a decent base for exploring the western edge of the Aberdares. Thompson's Falls, its former namesake, are beautiful in their own right with great trekking potential, but they're largely off limits due a series of serious assaults in the area, with women a particular target.

◉ Sights & Activities

Thomson's Falls   WATERFALL
(adult/child KSh250/150) At the time of writing, the falls were not safe to visit. Set back in an evergreen river valley and studded with sharp rocks and screaming baboons, the white cataracts plummet over 72m. The dramatic sight of looking up at the falls as baboons pad over the surrounding cliffs is worth the drenching you get from the fall's spray.

🛏️ Sleeping & Eating

It's best to eat early in Nyahururu; for reasons we couldn't fathom, most eateries shut by 7pm.

Safari Lodge   HOTEL $
(☑ 065-2022334; Go Down Rd; s/d excl breakfast KSh750/1500; [P]) Clean toilets with *seats;* big, soft beds with couches in the rooms; a nice balcony; TV and a place to charge your phone – what did we do to deserve this luxury? Especially at this price, which makes Safari one of the best budget deals around.

Thomson's Falls Lodge   HOTEL $$
(☑ 065-2022006; www.thomsonsfallslodge. org; off B5 Hwy; camping KSh750, s/d/tr KSh5000/6000/9000; [P]) The undisputed nicest splurge in the area sits right above the falls and does a great job of instilling that good old 'I'm a colonial aristocrat on a hill-country holiday' vibe. Rooms are spacious but cosy, with parquetry floors, thanks in no small part to the log fireplaces.

Thomson's Falls Lodge   BUFFET $$
(☑ 2022006; breakfast/lunch/dinner buffet KSh550/1000/1250; ⊙ 7am-7pm) This is the best (and only) place in town to go for a fancy feast. There's a set buffet for each of the day's three meals, and while they're pricey for this area, you'll walk away well stuffed and satisfied. It's located off the B5 Hwy.

ℹ️ Getting There & Away

There are numerous matatus that run to Nakuru (KSh220, 1¼ hours) and Nyeri (KSh350, 1¾ hours) until late afternoon. Less plentiful are services to Naivasha (KSh400, two hours), Nanyuki (KSh420, three hours) and Nairobi (KSh500, 3½ hours). The occasional morning matatu reaches Maralal (KSh600, four hours).

Several early-morning buses also serve Nairobi (KSh450, three hours).

Nanyuki

POP 36,142

This small but bustling mountain town makes a living off sales, be it of treks to climbers, curios to soldiers of the British Army (which has a training facility nearby) or drinks to pilots of the Kenyan Air Force (this is the site of its main airbase). For all that mercantilism, it's laid back for a market town. Nanyuki also serves as a gateway to the Laikipia plateau, one of Africa's most important wildlife conservation sites.

⊙ Sights & Activities

Nanyuki is a popular base for launching expeditions to climb Mt Kenya's Sirimon or Burguret routes. One local group worth contacting for information and excellent trekking programs is Montana Trek & Information Centre (p289). There's also the possibility of camel safaris at Nanyuki River Camel Camp.

Mt Kenya Wildlife Conservancy
Animal Orphanage   ZOO
(☎062-2032406; www.animalorphanagekenya. org; Mount Kenya Safari Club; per person KSh1500; ⊙8am-12.30pm & 1.30-5.30pm) It may come off a little zoolike at first but this orphanage is one of the few places in the world to have successfully bred the rare mountain bongo. Its success is such that there are now plans to release some of the captive-bred ante-

lope into the Mt Kenya forests to bolster the current population of around 70. Children, and anyone who wants to have a baby monkey scramble over their head, will love this place.

Lily Pond Arts Centre   ART GALLERY
(☎0702006501; lilypondartscentre.com; off Nairobi–Nanyuki Rd; ⊙8am-7.30pm Sun-Thu, 8am-11pm Fri & Sat) This fascinating centre has many strings to its bow, among them some fascinating examples of contemporary African art. It's 3km south of town and signposted off the main highway.

🛏 Sleeping

Nanyuki River Camel Camp   HUT $
(☎0722-361642; www.fieldoutdoor.com; camping KSh1250, huts without bathroom half-/full board KSh5000) The most innovative sleep in town (well, 4km outside of it, off the C76 Hwy) is this ecocamp, set in a dry swab of scrub. The camp offers lodging in genuine Somali grass-and-camelskin huts imported from Mandera; they have been relocated to sit close to the Nanyuki River.

Kirimara Springs Hotel   HOTEL $
(☎0726370191; www.kirimarasspringshotel.com; Kenyatta Ave; s/d/tw KSh2300/3000/3500; 🅿🛜) While Kirimara isn't going to win any architecture awards, and its website's claim that the rooms are comfortable and luxuriously furnished is plainly absurd, the friendly staff and spacious and bright rooms were cleaner and cheaper than others in this price bracket. The rooms on

---

WORTH A TRIP

SOLIO GAME RESERVE

The family-run, private 19,000-acre **Solio Game Reserve** (☎061-2055271; B5 Hwy; admission US$70) and part of the larger Solio Ranch, is Kenya's oldest rhino sanctuary and an important breeding centre for black rhinos; many of the horned beasts you see wandering national parks were actually born here. The physical contours of the park, which run between clumps of yellow-fever acacia, wide skies and wild marsh, are lovely in and of themselves and in addition to rhinos you'll see oryxes, gazelles, hartebeests, giraffes, lions, hyenas and buffaloes. Self-drive safaris are permitted but you will need to be accompanied by a Solio guide (KSh750). Poaching is a particular problem here with a number of rhinos lost in the battle.

The reserve is 22km north of Nyeri.

Solio Game Reserve Lodge (☎Nairobi 020-5020888; thesafaricollection.com; s/d ste full board US$1015/1684; 🅿🛜) Built in 2010, this upmarket lodge forsakes the classic look of so much safari accommodation and goes instead for a refreshing contemporary look – slick curves, whitewashed walls and colourful prints. The suites are enormous and utterly gorgeous. Horse riding, mountain biking and helicopter trips are part of the mix.

Nanyuki

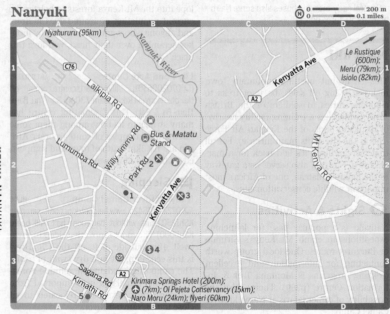

Nanyuki

🟢 Activities, Courses & Tours
1 Montana Trek & Information Centre	B2

⊗ Eating
2 Kungu Maitu Hotel & Butchery	B2
3 Walkers Kikwetu	B2

ℹ️ Information
4 Barclays Bank	B3
5 Boma Holidays	A3

the western side of the building catch less traffic noise, while those on the east get glimpses of Mt Kenya.

Kongoni Camp   BANDA $$
(☑ 0702868888, 062-2031225; www.kongoni camp.com; s US$56-95, d or rondavels US$100-175; 🅿️ @ 🛜) Founded by a friendly local-turned-Londoner-turned-local-again, Kongoni has five, concrete circular *bandas* as well as some newer rooms that are simple but designed with a touch of safari flair. It's one of the few genuinely midrange options around town and there's a barnlike restaurant-cum-bar.

Mount Kenya Safari Club   HOTEL $$$
(☑ Nairobi 020-2265555; www.fairmont.com; d from US$533; 🅿️ @ 🛜 🏊) For our money this is *the* top-end resort in the Central Highlands – it's the kind of place that makes you want to grow a moustache, kick back and smoke a pipe. The rooms have a luxurious, classic look to them and are decorated to a sumptuous standard, all with their own open fires and exquisite bathrooms. The whole shebang overlooks the Mt Kenya Wildlife Conservancy.

✗ Eating

★ **Kungu Maitu Hotel & Butchery** KENYAN $
(off Laikipia Rd; meals KSh200; ⊙ 8am-10pm) Friendly and utterly local, this simple place serves up Nanyuki's best barbecued meats. Choose your cuts of meat on the way, order a chapati or samosa to go with it and wait for it all to appear at your table. We found the toilets (upstairs) to be bearable only if you hold your breath and close your eyes – if you can wait, do so.

Walkers Kikwetu   BUFFET $
(Kenyatta Ave; mains KSh200-450; ⊙ 7am-11pm Mon-Sat) *Kikwetu* means 'ours' in Kikuyu and provides the inspiration behind the menu. Several African dishes from various

tribes are brought together and served buffet style (but charged according to the dishes you select). If you haven't tried *matoke* (cooked plantains), pilau (Swahili curried rice) or *mukimo* (mashed beans and vegetables), here's your chance.

★ **Lily Pond Arts Centre** CAFE **$$**
(☏0702006501, 0726734493; lilypondartscentre.com; off Nairobi–Nanyuki Rd; 2-/3-course menu KSh950/1150; ⏱8am-7.30pm Sun-Thu, 8am-11pm Fri & Sat) Fabulous home-cooked meals to be enjoyed while looking out over a lily pond right on the equator (you enter the restaurant from the southern hemisphere, but eat in the north...) makes for a winning combination here. You choose from a selection of dishes that might include soup or a Kenyan beef curry.

Cape Chestnut INTERNATIONAL **$$**
(☏0705250650; www.capechestnut.com; mains from KSh600; ⏱8.30am-6pm Sat-Thu, 8.30am-11.30pm Fri; 🌐) This coffee garden is a terrific place to come to eat, a little removed from the Nanyuki scrum. The food is excellent with dishes like rack of Timau lamb or rainbow trout with fresh greens, and the at-

mosphere is relaxed and popular with local expats. Friday night is tapas night. It's off Kenyatta Ave, 1km south of town.

Le Rustique INTERNATIONAL **$$**
(☏0721609601; www.lerustique.co.ke; off Kenyatta Ave; mains KSh1000-2200; ⏱noon-3pm & 6-11pm) This one-time Nairobi favourite has upped sticks and headed north to Nanyuki. The food, overseen to every last detail by owner Maike Potgeiter, is excellent with pizzas, crepes and an excellent wine list. But the atmosphere is as much of a drawcard, with an open fireplace for those cold Laikipia evenings or the quiet garden when things are warmer.

ℹ Information

Boma Holidays (☏Nairobi 020-2329683; www.bomaadventures.com; 2nd fl, Nakumart Centre, Kenyatta Ave) Travel agency that can arrange airline ticketing, car hire, airport transfers, hotel reservations and local safaris.

ℹ Getting There & Away

Nanyuki is well connected to all points north and south, as well as most major Rift Valley towns. Sample matatu fares include Nyeri (KSh250, one

WORTH A TRIP

LAIKIPIA CONSERVANCIES

Virtually all of Laikipia's lodges and camps (now numbering close to 50) fall squarely into the luxurious bracket and cater to the well-heeled who visit as part of prepackaged tours. The following list includes some of the options.

El Karama Eco Lodge (☏0720386616; www.laikipiasafaris.com; per person from US$370) One of few Laikipia places with modest prices (at least by Laikipia standards). The simple but pleasing *bandas* and cottages make use of natural materials such as stone and thatch. It's located on 14,000-acre El Karama Ranch, which is next to Segera Ranch. Watch out for African wild dogs and make sure you take a walking safari.

Loisaba Wilderness (s/d all inclusive US$594/990; 🏊) Refined accommodation (including four-poster beds under the stars) on a 61,000-acre ranch in northern Laikipia plus activities that range from walking safaris and wildlife drives to white-water rafting, horse riding and camel safaris; the latter two activities are not included in quoted rates.

Ol Malo (☏062-32715; www.olmalo.com; s/d all inclusive US$720/1220, plus US$80 conservation fee; 🏊) Posh rock and olive-wood cottages in a stunning setting close to the Ewaso Nyiro River make this a fine choice. The surrounding conservancy is quite small, but that's not how it feels from the swimming pool with views to the very distant horizon. The rooms have soaring thatched ceilings, stone-tiled floors and earth tones throughout. It's in northwestern Laikipia.

Sosian (☏0704909355; www.sosian.com; per person US$700; 🌐🏊) Horse riding, fishing and even cattle ranching make a nice change from the usual wildlife drives (they do these, too) on this 24,000-acre central Laikipia ranch which is home to lions, elephants, leopards and even African wild dogs. The lodge is centred around a colonial-era ranch house and accommodation is spacious and beautifully appointed.

hour), Isiolo (KSh280, 1½ hours), Meru (KSh250, 1½ hours), Nakuru (KSh650, three hours) and Nairobi (KSh500, three hours).

Airkenya (☑ Nairobi 020-3916000; www.air kenya.com; Nanyuki Airport; one way adult/ child US$173.50/131.40) Flies once or twice daily between Nairobi's Wilson Airport and Nanyuki.

Safarilink (☑ Nairobi 020-600777; www.fly safarilink.com; one way adult/child US$170/122) Flights at least daily between Wilson Airport in Nairobi and Nanyuki's airport.

Tropic Air (☑ Nairobi 020-2033032; www. tropicairkenya.com; Nanyuki Airport) Char ter-helicopter and light-aircraft services from Nanyuki's airport.

Ol Pejeta Conservancy

Ol Pejeta Conservancy (☑ 0752325379, 0707187141, Nairobi 020-2033244; www.olpejeta conservancy.org; adult/child/student US$90/45/23, vehicle from KSh400; ⊘ 7am-7pm) was once one of the largest cattle ranches in Kenya, but is now a 90,000-acre, privately owned wildlife reserve. It markets itself as the closest place to Nairobi where you can see the Big Five and possesses a full palette of African plains wild life, including a healthy population of rhinos.

It's the rhinos that form the centrepiece of what they do here – their (at last count) 102 black rhinos is the largest population in East Africa. A reminder of the challenges they face came when one of their rhinos was poached in March 2014, with another killed four months later.

ⓘ OL PEJETA CONSERVANCY

Why Go
East Africa's largest black-rhino sanctu ary; excellent wildlife-viewing and ac tivities; most accessible of the Laikipia conservancies.

When to Go
Year-round, although you'll need a 4WD from late March to late May.

Practicalities
Only the Serat and main Rongai gate (both in the conservancy's east) are open to visitors.

Budget Tips
Rent a matatu for the day with other travellers in Nanyuki; if staying over night, stay in one of the campsites.

Apart from its impressive conservation work, Ol Pejeta is, so far, the only one of the private conservancies open to the paying (but not necessarily staying) public – most other conservancies are accessible only for those who stay in one of their exclusive lodges.

◉ Sights & Activities

In addition to the following sights and activ ities, you can also arrange at the park gate or through your accommodation **guided bush walks, bird walks** and **night wildlife drives**; each costs US$40 per adult (US$20 per child).

★**Chimpanzee Sanctuary**   ZOO
(⊘ 10am-4.30pm) Home to 39 profoundly damaged chimpanzees rescued from captivi ty across Africa and further afield, Ol Pejeta's Chimp Sanctuary encompasses two large enclosures cut in two by the Ewaso Nyiro River. There's an elevated observation post and keepers are usually on hand to explain a little about each chimp's backstory; note the tiny replica cage in which one of the chimps was chained for years on end prior to being brought to the sanctuary.

Endangered Species Enclosure   ZOO
(adult/child US$40/20) This 700-acre drive through enclosure next to the Morani Infor mation Centre is home to three out of the world's last five remaining northern white rhinos, an ever-so-close-to-being-extinct sub species. The rhinos were brought here from the Dvur Kralove Zoo in the Czech Republic in 2009, but have not yet bred successfully. Also in the enclosure are the endangered Grevy's zebra and Jackson's hartebeest.

Morani Information Centre   MUSEUM
(⊘ 7am-6.30pm) FREE Part education or in terpretation centre, part museum, this three roomed structure is appealingly interactive and comes with the instructions to 'please touch' the leopard skin, antelope horns and other similar objects. You'll also find displays and information on Ol Pejeta's predator-proof *bomas* (cattle enclosures designed to keep predators out) and the history of the conserv ancy's rhino conservation work.

★**Lion Tracking**   WILDLIFE
(adult/child US$40/20) Easily our pick of the activities on offer, this nightly excursion trains you in the art of identifying individu al lions and takes you out to find lions using radio receivers. The data you gather forms

part of the conservancy's database on Ol Pejeta's estimated 65 to 70 resident lions.

Rift Valley Adventures CYCLING, ADVENTURE

(☏ 0707734776, 0712426999; www.riftvalleyadventures.com; cycling per person half/full day from US$70/120) This highly recommended operator runs cycling tours through Ol Pejeta, as well as other activities in the Mt Kenya area.

🛏 Sleeping & Eating

★ Ewaso Campsite CAMPGROUND $

(☏ 0707187141; info@olpejetaconservancy.org; camping adult/child KSh1000/500) Protected by dense foliage but with good river views, this is probably the pick of the sites in the park centre.

Ngobit Campsite CAMPGROUND $

(☏ 0707187141; info@olpejetaconservancy.org; camping adult/child KSh1000/500) Along the Ngobit River in the conservancy's far south, this is the quietest of Ol Pejeta's campsites.

★ Kicheche Laikipia TENTED CAMP $$$

(☏ Nairobi 020-2493569; www.kicheche.com; s/d all-inclusive US$800/1330; P) Close to the geographical centre of the park and overlooking a waterhole, this excellent tented camp has six stylishly furnished tents, an overall air of sophistication and impeccable service. It's Ol Pejeta's most exclusive accommodation.

Sweetwaters Serena Camp TENTED CAMP $$$

(☏ 0732123333; www.serenahotels.com; s/d full board from US$280/370; P@🛜🛝) The 39 large and beautifully appointed en-suite tents by the reliable Serena chain are high-end but with prices more accessible than other properties. The central location is a plus (handy for most of the conservancy) and a minus (things can get busy around here), depending on your perspective.

★ Morani's Restaurant CAFE $$

(☏ 0706160114; moranisrestaurant.com; mains KSh675-875; ⏱ 10.30am-6pm) Next to the Morani Information Centre, this terrific little cafe with outdoor tables serves up excellent dishes that range from the Morani burger made from prime Ol Pejeta beef to Kenyan beef stew or a Mediterranean wrap. Fresh juices, fine smoothies and Kenyan coffee round out an excellent package.

❶ Information

Pick up a copy of the *Ol Pejeta Conservancy* map (KSh700) from the entrance gate or download it for free from their website. Other useful (and free) resources include the *Mammal Checklist, Bird Checklist* and *Chimpanzee Factfile*.

❶ Getting There & Away

Ol Pejeta is 15km southwest of Nanyuki, which also has the nearest airport.

Segera Ranch

North of Ol Pejeta Conservancy, in southern Laikipia, this 50,000-acre ranch is a perfect example of how Laikipia works. It's a model cattle ranch, but wildlife is also prolific here, including the three big cats, elephants, buffaloes and endangered species such as Grevy's zebra (15 of them at last count), Patas monkey (a small troop lives along the ranch's eastern border) and the reticulated giraffe. The landscape here is classic Laikipia terrain – seemingly endless savannah country cut through with rocky river valleys and riverine woodland.

★ Segera Retreat LODGE

(segera.com; s/d all inclusive US$1940/2420; P❄🛜🛝) Wow! We can be difficult to impress, but this place left us speechless. Six villas and a couple of houses inhabit an oasis in the heart of the ranch, looking out onto the savannah, yet enclosed within their own natural compound that keeps dangerous animals out. The villas are utterly magnificent – spacious, luxurious in every way and steeped in safari tradition.

It's no coincidence that the villas capture perfectly that *Out of Africa* longing that caused a generation of would-be travellers to fall in love with the continent – one of the bar areas is strewn with original letters and personal effects from Karen Blixen, and the Retreat even has the plane that was used in the movie; flights can be arranged. The food, too, is memorable, and there's a wine list to match. There's a spa, hi-tech gym, sculpture garden and installations of African contemporary art fill the ranch's artfully converted stables.

Lewa Wildlife Conservancy

Although technically not a part of Laikipia, **Lewa Wildlife Conservancy** (LWC; ☏ 0722203562, 064-31405; www.lewa.org; conservation fee per adult/child per night US$105/53), a vast region of open savannah grasslands that falls away from the Mt Kenya highlands, is very much a part of Laikipia's story. It was at Lewa that the conservancy idea was pioneered and it remains a leader in all of the elements – serious wildlife protection wedded to innovative community engagement – that have come to define the private conservancies of Laikipia and elsewhere. And unlike in Kenya's national parks where off-road driving is prohibited, Lewa's guides delight in taking you to almost within touching distance of rhinos, elephants and other species.

◉ Sights & Activities

The following activities (with sample per-person prices) complement the day and night wildlife drives. Bookings are most easily made through your accommodation.

Excursions to Il Ngwesi US$40, half day

Flying Safari Price varies

Horse-riding safari US$55, one hour

Orphan Rhino Project US$15, 30 minutes (this is where the moving final scene in Sir David Attenborough's *Africa* series was filmed)

Quad bike/buggy safari Price varies

Tour of Lewa Wildlife Conservancy's HQ Free (US$10 if you visit the tracker dogs), one to two hours

Visit to local school US$50 donation

Walking Safari in Ndare Ndare Forest US$30 conservation fee, one to three hours

---

ⓘ LEWA WILDLIFE CONSERVANCY

Why Go
For some of the finest game-viewing in Kenya; almost guaranteed sightings of the Big Five; walking safaris and night safaris. No minibus circus.

When to Go
Year-round, but the dry season (June to March) is best.

Practicalities
Lewa is closed to casual visitors: you must be staying at one of the (very expensive) lodges in order to enter. Most visitors fly in from Nairobi but road access is easy from Isiolo or the Central Highlands.

Budget Tips
Not suitable for budget travellers.

🛏 Sleeping & Eating

★ Lewa Safari Camp
TENTED CAMP $$$
(☑ Nairobi 020-6003090; www.lewasafaricamp.com; s/d all inclusive US$708/1180; 🐾🗷) This impressive property lies in the northwest corner of the conservancy, about one hour's drive from the main Matunda gate. Its safari tents are large and have that whole chic-bush-living thing down to a tee; they're arrayed around a shallow valley and large wildlife is kept out so you can walk around freely (although they give you an escort at night). Service is impeccable.

Kifaru
LODGE $$$
(☑ Nairobi 020-2127844; kifaruhouse.com; per person US$1000; 🐾🗷) Luxury hilltop *bandas* with no expense spared, not to mention fine views over the plains and an air of exclusivity with no more than 12 guests in camp at any one time.

Lewa Wilderness
COTTAGES $$$
(☑ 0723273668; lewawilderness.com; r from US$1590; 🐾🗷) Nine cottages owned and run by the Craig family in Lewa's east. Rooms are classic safari in style and faultlessly luxurious.

ⓘ Getting There & Away

The turn-off to LWC is only 12km south of Isiolo and is well signposted on the A2 Hwy.

Airkenya (☑ Nairobi 020-3916000; www.airkenya.com; adult/child one way US$238/175.30) Up to twice daily flights between Lewa and Nairobi's Wilson Airport, sometimes via Nanyuki.

Safarilink (☑ Nairobi 020-6000777; flysafarilink.com; adult/child one way US$230/164) Up to three daily flights between Lewa and Wilson Airport in Nairobi.

Il Ngwesi

Abutting the northwestern side of Lewa Wildlife Conservancy, Il Ngwesi is another fine example of a private conservation project linking wildlife conservation and community development, albeit on a smaller scale. The Maasai of Il Ngwesi (the name Il Ngwesi translates as 'people of wildlife'), with help from the neighbouring LWC, have transformed this undeveloped land, previously used for subsistence pastoralism, into a prime wildlife conservation area hosting white and black rhinos, waterbucks, giraffes and other plains animals.

THE LEWA STORY

Like so many Laikipia properties that later became wildlife conservancies, Lewa Downs was an expansive cattle ranch. In 1983, the owners, the Craig family, along with pioneering rhino conservationist Anna Merz, set aside 5000 acres of Lewa as the Ngare Sergoi Rhino Sanctuary. They received their first rhino a year later, and the numbers grew to 16 in 1988. The Craigs doubled the sanctuary's size, and by 1994 the entire cattle ranch (along with the adjacent Ngare Ndare Forest Reserve) was enclosed within an electric fence to create a 62,000-acre rhino sanctuary. The Lewa Wildlife Conservancy in its current form was created in 1995.

True to its origins as a sanctuary to save Kenya's rhinos, Lewa's primary conservation focus continues to be rhinos. Lewa suffered not a single poaching event between 1983 and 2009 – the joke doing the rounds of the conservation community for much of this time was that Iewa was 'State House' (Kenya's presidential palace) for rhinos. Sadly, poaching has been on the rise ever since, with six of Lewa's rhinos killed in 2013, prompting a massive investment in anti-poaching operations.

At last count, Lewa was home to 66 black rhinos and 62 white rhinos (that's around 15% of the Kenyan total). And despite the poaching, the conservancy is close to its carrying capacity for rhinos. In 2014, the fence that separated Lewa from the 32,000-acre Borana Conservancy to the west was torn down, effectively increasing the size of the rhino sanctuary by 25%.

Rhinos aside, Lewa's conservation effort has been astounding and 20% of the world's Grevy's zebras call the reserve home.

Central to the Lewa model is a serious commitment to community development, fuelled by a recognition that local people are far more likely to protect wildlife if they have a stake (financial or otherwise) in its survival. LWC is a nonprofit organisation that invests around 70% of its annual US$2.5 million-plus budget into health care, education and various community projects for surrounding villages.

In 2013, Lewa Wildlife Conservancy was inscribed on Unesco's World Heritage List as an extension to the existing Mount Kenya National Park/Natural Forest site.

The south is quite steeply contoured in places, but the highest point (Sanga, at 1907m) lies on Il Ngwesi's western boundary. The northern lowlands mostly consist of light woodland. Just outside the eastern border of Il Ngwesi, Maasai, Turkana and Samburu villages line the trackside.

Il Ngwesi is north of Lewa and accessed off the main Isiolo to Nairobi Rd. Lewa Safari Camp organises half-day visits to Il Ngwesi from Lewa, which includes visits to a Maasai *manyatta* (village), nature walks and explanations of Maasai tradition.

Il Ngwesi Eco Lodge LODGE $$$
(☑ Nairobi 020-2033122; www.ilngwesi.com; s/d all inclusive US$485/830; ☒) ⬭ Il Ngwesi community supplements its herding income with tourist dollars gained from this award-winning ecolodge. The divine open-fronted thatched cottages here boast views over the dramatic escarpment, and at night the beds in some rooms can be pulled out onto the private 'terraces' allowing you to snooze under the Milky Way. Profits go straight to the Maasai community.

Borana

One of the longest-standing conservancies in the area, the 35,000-acre Borana cattle ranch, now the **Borana Conservancy** (www. borana.co.ke), has been owned by the Dyer family for three generations. The conservancy turned its focus onto wildlife and community projects in 1992. In 2013, rhinos from Lewa Wildlife Conservancy were translocated here, and the following year the fence between Borana and Lewa was torn down – Borana is now an integral part of one of Kenya's most important rhino sanctuaries. It's perfect rhino habitat and African wild dogs (as well as, at last count, 18 lions) are also a possibility here.

As is something of a Laikipia trademark, Borana ploughs its money into anti-poaching operations, community development and grasslands habitat management.

Borana Lodge LODGE $$$
(www.borana.com; s/d all inclusive US$855/1490; 🛜 🏊) On a hill and overlooking a waterhole, this appealing family-run lodge manages a perfect balance between rustic and luxury. The eight thatched cottages have stone floors and walls and look down to a waterhole where wildlife is common. The main building is wonderfully colonial from its fireplace to its stiff drinks.

Lekurruki Community Ranch

Ranged across almost 12,000 hectares north of Il Ngwesi and northwest of Lewa Wildlife Conservancy, this community ranch is the homeland of the Mukogodo Maasai. With a good mix of habitats – the Mukogodo Forest covers 74,000 acres and is often said to be one of the largest indigenous forests in East Africa, while the remainder of the ranch is made up of open savannah – the ranch has a rich variety of both flora and fauna. Of the latter, you'll find predators and buffaloes here, but elephants are the main drawcard with one herd almost 500-strong. More than 200 bird species and over 100 butterfly species have been recorded on the ranch.

Tassia Lodge LODGE $$$
(📱 0725972923; www.tassiasafaris.com; s/d all inclusive US$670/960; 🏊) The immensity of African landscapes and the intimacy of the community lodge experience are perfectly combined at Tassia Lodge, high on a rocky bluff on Lekurruki Community Ranch. Rooms are open sided and have an original handmade look with natural wood and stone used throughout. Views are splendid and activities include walking safaris and botanical walks.

Mt Kenya National Park

Africa's second-highest mountain is also one of its most beautiful. Here, mere minutes from the equator, glaciers carve out the throne of Ngai, the old high god of the Kikuyu. To this day the tribe keeps its doors open to the face of the sacred mountain, and some still come to its lower slopes to offer prayers and the foreskins of their young men – this was the traditional place for holding circumcision ceremonies. Besides being venerated by the Kikuyu, Mt Kenya and **Mt Kenya National Park** (📱 0722279502, Nairobi 020-3568763; www.kws.go.ke; adult/child day entry US$65/30, 4-/5-/6-day package adult US$255/315/380, child US$150/170/200) has the rare honour of being both a Unesco World Heritage Site and a Unesco Biosphere Reserve.

The highest peaks of Batian (5199m) and Nelion (5188m) can only be reached by mountaineers with technical skills, but Point Lenana (4985m), the third-highest peak, can be reached by trekkers and is the usual goal for most mortals. When the clouds part, the views are simply magnificent.

Environment

There are ecosystems on the slopes of Mt Kenya that cannot be found anywhere else in the country.

This extinct volcano hosts, at various elevations, upland forest, bamboo forest (2500m), high-altitude equatorial heath (3000m to 3500m) and lower alpine moorland (3400m to 3800m), which includes several species of bright everlasting flowers. Some truly surreal plant life grows in the Afro-alpine zone (above 3500m) and the upper alpine zone (3800m to 4500m), including hairy carpets of tussock grass, the brushlike giant lobelias, or rosette plants, and the sci-fi-worthy *Senecio Brassica*, or giant groundsel, which looks like a cross between an aloe, a cactus and a dwarf. At the summit it's all rock and ice.

Unfortunately, there's more rock than ice these days. Warmer weather has led to disappearing glaciers, and ice climbing in Mt Kenya is largely finished.

Trekking Mt Kenya

There are at least seven different routes up Mt Kenya. Of those, Naro Moru is the easiest and most popular, and Sirimon and Chogoria are excellent alternatives, as well as the exciting but demanding Summit Circuit, which circles Batian and Nelion, thus enabling you to mix and match ascending and descending routes. Other routes include the Timau Route and Burguret Route.

Safety

Many people ascend the mountain too quickly and suffer from headaches, nausea and other (sometimes more serious) effects of altitude sickness. By spending at least three nights on the ascent, you'll enjoy yourself more.

Unpredictable weather is another problem. The trek to Point Lenana isn't an easy hike and people die on the mountain every year.

Mt Kenya National Park

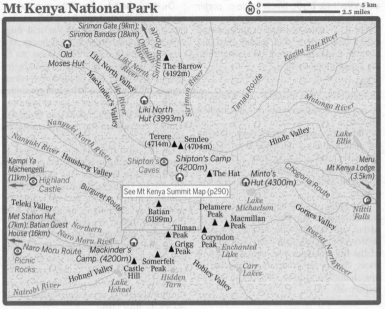

See Mt Kenya Summit Map (p290)

What to Bring

Consider the following to be a minimum checklist of necessary equipment. If you don't have your own equipment, items can be rented from some guiding associations. Prices vary, but expect to pay in the vicinity of KSh700/300/250/400 for a two-person tent/sleeping bag/pair of boots/stove per day.

➡ A good sleeping bag and a closed-cell foam mat or Therm-a-Rest, if you're camping (nightly temperatures near the summit often drop to below -10°C).

➡ A good set of warm clothes (wool or synthetics – never cotton, as it traps moisture).

➡ Waterproof clothing (breathable fabric like Gore-Tex is best) as it can rain heavily any time of year.

➡ A decent pair of boots and sandals or light shoes (for the evening when your boots get wet).

➡ Sunblock and sunglasses (at this altitude the sun can do some serious damage to your skin and eyes).

➡ A tent, stove, basic cooking equipment, utensils, a 3L water container (per person) and water-purifying tablets (if you don't

intend to stay in the huts along the way). Stove fuel in the form of petrol and kerosene (paraffin) is fairly easily found in towns.

➡ If you have a mobile phone, take it along; reception on the mountain's higher reaches is actually very good.

A few other things to remember:

➡ If a porter is carrying your backpack, always keep essential clothing (warm- and wet-weather gear) in your day pack because you may become separated for hours at a time.

➡ Don't sleep in clothes you've worn during the day because the sweat your clothes absorbed keeps them moist at night, reducing their heat-retention capabilities.

➡ Fires are prohibited in the open except in an emergency; in any case, there's no wood once you get beyond 3300m.

Guides, Cooks & Porters

Having a porter for your gear is like travelling in a chauffeured Mercedes instead of a matatu. A good guide will help set a sustainable pace and hopefully dispense interesting information about Mt Kenya and its flora, fauna and wildlife. With both on your team, your appreciation of this mountain will be enhanced a hundredfold. If you hire a guide or porter who can also cook, you won't regret it.

The KWS issues vouchers to all registered guides and porters, who should also hold identity cards; they won't be allowed into the park without them.

Costs

In addition to the following, park fees must be factored into the overall cost of climbing Mt Kenya.

The cost of guides varies depending on the qualifications of the guide, whatever the last party paid and your own negotiating skills. You should expect to pay a minimum of US$30/25/20 per day for a guide/cook/porter.

In addition to the actual cost of hiring guides, cooks and porters, tips are expected but these should only be paid for good service. For a good guide who has completed the full trek with you, plan on a tip of about US$50 per group. Cook and porter tips should be around US$30 and US$20 respectively.

🏃 Naro Moru Route

Although the least scenic, this is the most straightforward and popular route and is still spectacular.

Starting in Naro Moru town, the first part of the route takes you along a gravel road through farmlands for some 13km (all the junctions are signposted) to the start of the forest. Another 5km brings you to the park entry gate (2400m), from where it's 8km to the road head and the **Met Station Hut** (3000m), where you stay for the night and acclimatise.

On the second day, set off through the forest (at about 3200m) and Teleki Valley to the moorland around so-called **Vertical Bog**; expect the going here to be, well, boggy. At a ridge the route divides into two. You can either take the higher path, which gives better views but is often wet, or the lower, which crosses the Naro Moru River and continues gently up to **Mackinder's Camp** (4200m). This part of the trek should take about 4½ hours. Here you can stay in the dormitories or camp.

On the third day you can either rest at Mackinder's Camp to acclimatise or aim for **Point Lenana** (4895m). This stretch takes three to six hours, so it is common to leave around 2am to reach the summit in time for sunrise. From the bunk-house, continue past the ranger station to a fork. Keep right, and go across a swampy area, followed by a moraine, and then up a long scree slope – this is a long, hard slog. The KWS Austrian Hut (p293; 4790m) is three to four hours from Mackinder's and about one hour below the summit of Lenana, so it's a good place to rest before the final push.

The section of the trek from Austrian Hut up to Point Lenana takes you up a narrow rocky path that traverses the southwest ridge parallel to the Lewis Glacier, which has shrunk more than 100m since the 1960s. Be careful, as the shrinkage has created serious danger of slippage along the path. A final climb or scramble brings you up onto the peak. In good weather it's fairly straightforward, but in bad weather you shouldn't attempt the summit unless you're experienced in mountain conditions or have a guide.

ⓘ MT KENYA NATIONAL PARK

Why Go
Awe-inspiring views from Africa's second-highest mountain; unlike Mt Kilimanjaro, it's possible to take different routes up and down, with arguably better scenery.

When to Go
Climb during the driest months: mid-January to late February and late August to September.

Practicalities
Don't underestimate the difficulty of this trek. You'd be flirting with death by not taking a guide.

Budget Tips
Don't skimp on safety and time for acclimatisation; carry your own gear and cook your own meals; camp instead of staying in the huts.

ORGANISED TREKS

If you bargain hard, a package trek may end up costing only a little more than organising each logistical element of the trip separately. If you're keen to save money, think like a wildebeest and join a herd – the larger the group, the cheaper the per-person rate becomes. All prices listed here generally include guides, cooks and porters, park fees, meals and accommodation.

EWP (Executive Wilderness Programmes; ☑ UK 1550-721319; www.ewpnet.com/kenya; 3-day trip per person US$590-985) Employs knowledgeable local guides.

IntoAfrica (☑ Nairobi 0722511752, UK 0797-4975723; www.intoafrica.co.uk; 7-day trip per person US$1385-2630) An environmentally and culturally sensitive company offering both scheduled and exclusive seven-day trips ascending Sirimon route and descending Chogoria.

KG Mountain Expeditions (☑ 0733606338, Nairobi 020-2033874; www.kenyaexpeditions. com; 4-day treks per person around US$600) Run by a highly experienced mountaineer, KG offers all-inclusive scheduled treks.

Montana Trek & Information Centre (☑ 062-32731; www.montanatrekks.com; Lumumba Rd, Nanyuki; 4-day trip per person US$560-810) This community-based association in Nanyuki has friendly and knowledgeable guides. The centre is particularly useful for Sirimon trekkers.

Mountain Rock Safaris Resorts & Trekking Services (Bantu Mountain Lodge; ☑ Nairobi 020-242133; www.mountainrockkenya.com; Naro Moru) Runs the Bantu Mountain Lodge near Naro Moru. Its popular four-day Naro Moru–Sirimon crossover trek costs US$650 per person.

Mt Kenya Guides & Porters Safari Club (☑ 0723112483, Nairobi 020-3524393; www. mtkenyaguides.com; Naro Moru; per person per day from US$120) The most organised association of guides, cooks and porters in Naro Moru.

Mt Kenya Chogoria Guides & Porters Association (☑ 0733676970; anthonytreks@ yahoo.com; Chogoria; per person per day from US$120) A small association of guides, cooks and porters based in Chogoria's Transit Motel, specialising in the Chogoria route up the mountain.

Mountain View Tour Trekking Safaris (☑ 0722249439; mountainviewt@yahoo.com; Naro Moru; per person per day from US$120) An association of local guides working together who often approach independent travellers as they arrive in Naro Moru.

Naro Moru River Lodge (☑ 0708984005, 0708984002; www.naromoruriverlodge.com; Naro Moru; 4-day trip per person US$719-1497) Runs a range of all-inclusive trips and operates Met Station Hut (p293) and Mackinder's Camp (p293) on the Naro Moru route.

Rift Valley Adventures (☑ 0707734776, 0712426999; www.riftvalleyadventures.com) Based at Ol Pejeta Conservancy (p282) up on the Laikipia Plateau, this respected operator runs trekking and mountain-biking safaris on Mt Kenya, as well as climbing, canyoning and white-water rafting.

Sana Highlands Trekking Expeditions (Map p224; ☑ 0722243691, Nairobi 020-227820; www.sanatrekkingkenya.com; Contrust House, Moi Ave, Nairobi; 5-day trips per person from US$550) Sana Highlands Trekking Expeditions operates five-day, all-inclusive treks on the Sirimon, Naor Moru and Chogoria routes.

🏃 Sirimon Route

A popular alternative to Naro Moru, Sirimon has better scenery, greater flexibility and a gentler rate of ascent but takes a day longer. It's well worth considering combining it with the Chogoria route for a six- to seven-day traverse that really brings out the best of Mt Kenya.

The trek begins at the **Sirimon gate**, 23km from Nanyuki, from where it's about a 9km walk through forest to **Old Moses Hut** (3300m), where you spend the first night.

Mt Kenya Summit

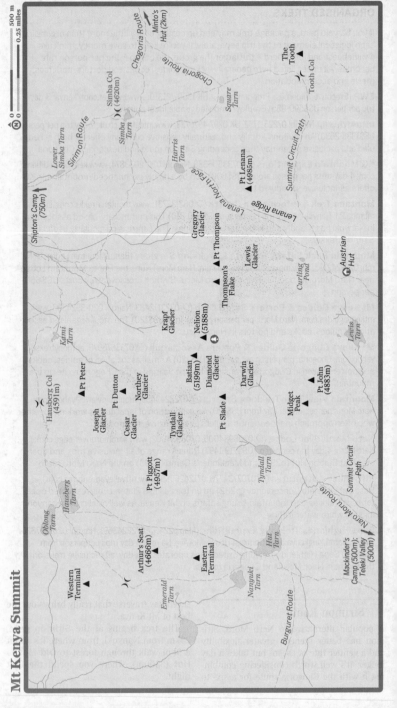

500 m
0.25 miles

Chogoria Route

Minto's Hut (2km)

The Tooth

Tooth Col

Square Tarn

Simba Col (4620m)

Simba Tarn

Lower Simba Tarn

Sirimon Route

Harris Tarn

Pt Lenana (4985m)

Summit Circuit Path

Shipton's Camp (750m)

Lewana North Face

Lenana Ridge

Gregory Glacier

Pt Thompson

Lewis Glacier

Curling Pond

Austrian Hut

Thompson's Flake

Krapf Glacier

Kami Tarn

Nelion (5188m)

Lewis Tarn

Batian (5199m)

Diamond Glacier

Darwin Glacier

Pt John (4883m)

Midget Peak

Hausberg Col (4591m)

Pt Peter

Pt Dutton

Northey Glacier

Joseph Glacier

Cesar Glacier

Tyndall Glacier

Pt Slade

Pt Piggott (4957m)

Hausberg Tarn

Tyndall Tarn

Summit Circuit Path

Naro Moru Route

Oblong Tarn

Arthur's Seat (4666m)

Eastern Terminal

Hut Tarn

Western Terminal

Emerald Tarn

Nanyuki Tarn

Mackinder's Camp (500m); Teleki Valley (500m)

Burguret Route

On the second day you could head straight through the moorland for Shipton's Camp, but it is worth taking an extra acclimatisation day via **Liki North Hut** (3993m), a tiny place on the floor of a classic glacial valley. The actual hut is in poor shape and meant for porters, but it's a good campsite with a toilet and stream nearby.

On the third day, head up the western side of Liki North Valley and over the ridge into Mackinder's Valley, joining the direct route about 1½ hours in. After crossing the Liki River, follow the path for another 30 minutes until you reach the bunk-house at **Shipton's Camp** (4200m), which is set in a fantastic location right below Batian and Nelion.

From Shipton's you can push straight for **Point Lenana** (4895m), a tough 3½- to five-hour slog via Harris Tarn and the tricky north-face approach, or take the Summit Circuit in either direction around the peaks to reach Austrian Hut (4790m), about one hour below the summit. The left-hand (east) route past Simba Col (4620m) is shorter but steeper, while the right-hand (west) option takes you on the Harris Tarn trail nearer the main peaks.

From Austrian Hut take the standard southwest traverse up to **Point Lenana**. If you're spending the night here, it's worth having a wander around to catch the views up to Batian and down the Lewis Glacier into the Teleki Valley.

🏃 Chogoria Route

This route crosses some of the most spectacular and varied scenery on Mt Kenya, and is often combined with the Sirimon route (usually as the descent). The main reason this route is more popular as a descent is the 29km bottom stage. While not overly steep, climbing up that distance is much harder than descending it.

The only disadvantage with this route is the long distance between Chogoria and the park gate. These days most people drive, although it's a beautiful walk through farmland, rainforest and bamboo to the park gate. Most people spend the first night here, either camping at the gate or staying nearby in **Meru Mt Kenya Lodge** (3000m).

On the second day, head up through the forest to the trailhead (camping is possible here). From here it's another 7km over rolling foothills to the Hall Tarns area and **Minto's Hut** (4300m). Like Liki North, this place is only intended for porters, but makes for a decent campsite. Don't use the tarns here to wash anything, as careless trekkers have already polluted them.

From here follow the trail alongside the stunning **Gorges Valley** (another possible descent for the adventurous) and scramble up steep ridges to meet the Summit Circuit. It is possible to go straight for the north face or southwest ridge of Point Lenana, but stopping at Austrian Hut or detouring to Shipton's Camp gives you more time to enjoy the scenery; see Sirimon and Naro Moru routes for details.

Allow at least five days for the Chogoria route, although a full week is better.

🏃 Summit Circuit

While everyone who summits Point Lenana gets a small taste of the spectacular Summit Circuit, few trekkers ever grab the beautiful beast by the horns and hike its entire length. The trail encircles the main peaks of Mt Kenya between the 4300m and 4800m contour lines and offers challenging terrain, fabulous views and a splendid opportunity to familiarise yourself with this complex mountain. It is also a fantastic way to acclimatise before bagging Point Lenana.

One of the many highlights along the route is a peek at Mt Kenya's southwest face, with the long, thin Diamond Couloir leading up to the **Gates of the Mists** between the summits of Batian and Nelion.

Depending on your level of fitness, this route can take between four and nine hours. Some fit souls can summit Point Lenana (from Austrian Hut or Shipton's Camp) and complete the Summit Circuit in the same day.

The trail can be deceptive at times, especially when fog rolls in, and some trekkers have become seriously lost between Tooth Col and Austrian Hut. It is imperative to take a guide.

🛏 Sleeping

As well as the sleeping options given for each route it is possible to camp anywhere on the mountain; the cost of camping is included in the four- to six-day park-fee packages payable at any gate. Most people camp near the huts or bunk-houses, as there are often toilets and water nearby.

Around Mt Kenya

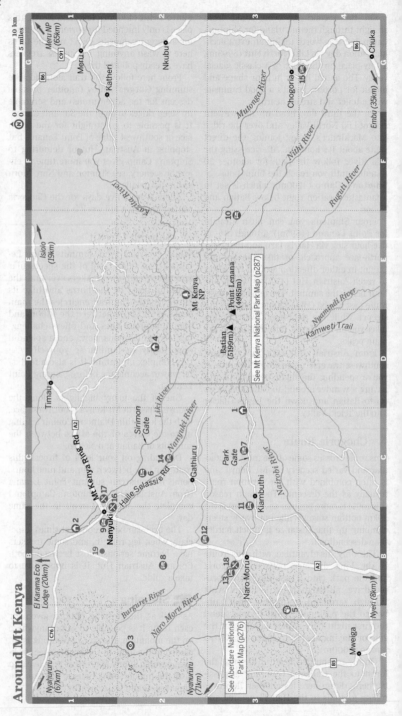

10 km
5 miles

Nyahururu
(67km)

Nyahururu
(71km)

See Aberdare National
Park Map (p276)

C76

B5

Mweiga

Nyeri (8km)

A2

Naro Moru River

Burguret River

El Karama Eco
Lodge (20km)

Nanyuki

Mt Kenya Ring Rd

Haile Selassie Rd

Timau

Isiolo
(19km)

A2

Naro Moru

13 18

5

3

8

12

11 Kiambuthi

Nairobi River

Park Gate

7

1

Gathiuru

6 14

16 17

9

2

19

Sirimon Gate

Likii River

Nanyuki River

Batian
(5199m)

Mt Kenya
NP

Point Lenana
(4985m)

See Mt Kenya National Park Map (p287)

Kazita River

Kamweti Trail

Nyamindi River

Ruguti River

Nithi River

Mutonga River

Chogoria

15

Meru NP
(65km)

Meru

Katheri

Nkubu

Chuka

B6

Embu (35km)

C91

B6

G

F

E

D

C

B

A

1   2   3   4

Around Mt Kenya

🛏 Naro Moru Route

There are three good bunk-houses along this route: **Met Station Hut** (dm US$23) is at 3000m, **Mackinder's Camp** (dm US$30) is at 4200m and **Austrian Hut** (dm KSh750) is at 4790m. Beds in Met Station and Mackinder's are harder to find, as they're booked through Naro Moru River Lodge. If you're denied beds, you can still climb this route if you camp and carry all the appropriate equipment.

Those needing more luxury can doss in lovely, KWS-run **Batian Guest House** (www. kws.go.ke; 8-bed banda US$180), which sleeps eight and is a kilometre from the Naro Moru gate.

🛏 Sirimon Route

Old Moses Hut (dm US$20) at 3300m and **Shipton's Camp** (dm US$20) at 4200m serve trekkers on this route. They're both booked through the Mountain Rock Lodge (p294).

Many trekkers acclimatise by camping at Liki North Hut. If you'd like a little more comfort, book into the excellent KWS **Sirimon Bandas** (two-bed banda US$80), which are located 9km from the Sirimon gate. Each *banda* sleeps four.

🛏 Chogoria Route

The only option besides camping on this route is **Meru Mt Kenya Lodge** (per person KSh2500), a group of comfortable cabins administered by **Meru South County Council** (☑ 0729390686; Chuka). Ask your guide to reserve these in advance, as during peak season they can be booked out.

✗ Eating

Increased altitude creates unique cooking conditions. The major consideration is that the boiling point of water is considerably reduced. At 4500m, for example, water boils at 85°C; this is too low to sufficiently cook rice or lentils (pasta is better) and you won't be able to brew a good cup of tea (instant coffee is the answer). Cooking times and fuel usage are considerably increased as a result, so plan accordingly.

Take plenty of citrus fruits and/or citrus drinks as well as chocolate, sweets or dried fruit to keep your blood-sugar level up.

To avoid severe headaches caused by dehydration or altitude sickness, drink at least 3L of fluid per day and bring rehydration sachets. Water-purification tablets, available at most chemists, aren't a bad idea either.

ⓘ Information

Mountain Club of Kenya (MCK; ☑ Nairobi 020-602330; www.mck.or.ke) Technical climbers and mountaineers should get a copy of the MCK *Guide to Mt Kenya & Kilimanjaro.* MCK also has reasonably up-to-date mountain information posted on its website.

Naro Moru

POP 9018

Naro Moru may be little more than a string of shops and houses, with a couple of very basic hotels and a market, but it's the most popular starting point for treks up Mt Kenya. There's a post office and internet, but no bank.

◉ Sights & Activities

In addition to gazing up at Mt Kenya (best before 6.30am, after which it is usually obscured by clouds) and starting the Naro Moru route up to its summit, there are a number of interesting day excursions. Some guide associations can organise **nature walks** on Mt Kenya and hikes to the **Mau Mau caves**, which are impressive from both a physical and historical perspective.

⌑ Sleeping & Eating

As a general rule, the basic hotels are in town, while the more tourist-oriented options are in the surrounding countryside, particularly on the bumpy road between Naro Moru and the park gates. Eating options in town are slim, but you won't starve if you like greasy chips and dining on goats who have lived long and eventful lives.

**Mt Kenya Guides &
Porters Safari Club**   BANDA $
(☑ Nairobi 020-3524393; www.mtkenyaguides. com; per person KSh2300) Principally in the business of supplying guides and porters, this association has branched out with a couple of excellent-value cottages with open fires. Meals can be arranged on request and, obviously, organising a trek here is a breeze.

★ Naro Moru River Lodge   LODGE $$
(☑ 0708984005; www.naromoruriverlodge.com; campsites/dm US$15/30, s full board US$117-173, d & tw full board US$162-218; ₱ ☏ ☏ ☏) A bit like a Swiss chalet, the River Lodge is a lovely collection of dark, cosy cottages and rooms embedded into a sloping hillside that overlooks the rushing Naro Moru River, 3km from town. All three classes of room are lovely, but the middle-of-the-road 'superior' option seems the best of the lot.

Bantu Mountain Lodge   HOTEL $$
(Mountain Rock Lodge; ☑ 0722858972, 0722511752; www.mountainrockkenya.com; camping US$8, s/tw from KSh3500/5000) Formerly the Mountain Rock Lodge, this is a major base for Mt Ken-
ya climbers and the operators of Old Moses Hut (p293) and Shipton's Camp (p293) on the mountain. There are three classes of rooms and like most hotels in this price bracket, the rooms are serviceable enough but in need of refurbishment. It's 9km north of Naro Moru, in woods that are occasionally frequented by elephants.

Colobus Cottages   COTTAGES $$
(☑ 0722840195, 0753951720; www.colobuscottages. wordpress.com; per person KSh3500) These cottages, some almost completely enveloped by trees, are more impressive from the outside, but the simple interiors are spacious, tidy, self-contained and exceptional value. There's a fireplace in each, a barbecue area and a communal treetop bar. It's 2km off the main highway; the turn-off is 6km north of Naro Moru.

★ Trout Tree Restaurant   FISH $$
(☑ 0726281704; www.trout-tree.com; Naro Moru-Nanyuki Hwy; mains KSh750-945) Inhabiting a marvellous fig tree overlooking the Burguret River, alongside colobus monkeys and tree hyrax, this place is one of the most original places to eat in Kenya's Central Highlands. It doesn't do much else, but we never get tired of the trout combinations – hot smoked trout and cucumber salad, trout chowder, trout curry, tandoori trout, whole grilled trout...char-grilled is best of all.

If you're lucky, you might be able to fish for your supper and have it cooked for you afterwards. Ask about Creaky Cottage, the fabulous riverside, self-contained house that sleeps six. It's 3km south of Nanyuki Airport and well-signposted off the main road.

❶ Getting There & Away

There are plenty of buses and matatus heading to Nanyuki (KSh70, 30 minutes), Nyeri (KSh170, 45 minutes) and Nairobi (KSh500, three hours) from either the northbound or southbound 'stages'.

Meru

POP 240,900

Meru is the largest municipality in the Central Highlands and the epicentre of Kenyan production of *miraa*, a mild, leafy stimulant more widely known outside of Kenya as khat. The town itself is like a shot of the stuff: a briefly invigorating, slightly confusing head rush but you'll wonder what the point of it all was when the first effects wear off.

Meru

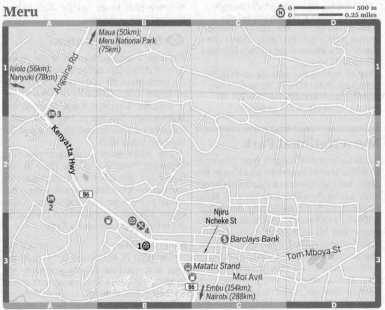

Maua (50km);
Meru National Park
(75km)

Isiolo (56km);
Nanyuki (78km)

Angaine Rd

Kenyatta Hwy

B6

Njiru
Ncheke St

Barclays Bank

Tom Mboya St

Matatu Stand

Moi Ave

B6

Embu (154km);
Nairobi (288km)

Sights

Meru National Museum MUSEUM
(☏ 0786559427; www.museums.or.ke; Kenyatta Hwy; adult/child KSh500/250; ⊙ 8.30am-5.30pm) There's a series of faded exhibits, desultory stuffed and mounted wildlife and a small but informative section concerning the clothing, weapons, and agricultural and initiation practices (including clitoridectomies) of the Meru people. Out back is a small menagerie of disheartened animals that have had the misfortune of ending up here.

Sleeping & Eating

Blue Towers Hotel HOTEL $
(☏ 064-30309; bluetowershotel@yahoo.com; Kenyatta Hwy; s/d excl breakfast KSh2200/2700; P) The architects here have done themselves proud, managing the tricky task of incorporating both a petrol station and a couple of castlelike towers into an otherwise unmemorable building. Not to be outdone on the peculiarity stakes, the rooms all have windows facing the hall. For all that, it's pretty good budget value.

★ Alba Hotel HOTEL $$
(☏ 0705556677; www.albahotels.co.ke; Milimani Rd; s/d Mon-Thu US$130/160, Fri-Sun US$100/120; P@☎❄) Easily Meru's best rooms, this

Meru

Sights
1 Meru National Museum B3

Sleeping
2 Alba Hotel A2
3 Blue Towers Hotel A1

Eating
4 Meru County Hotel B3

modern place has Western-style, Western-standard rooms with bright colours and modern furnishings. If you've only stayed here and in Nairobi, you might think this is the norm in Kenya – it's not.

Meru County Hotel KENYAN, INTERNATIONAL $
(Kenyatta Hwy; meals KSh350-800; ⊙ 8am-9pm) Thatched umbrellas hover over each table on this pretty *nyama choma* terrace. If you want to give the flaming flesh a rest, try the Western, Kenyan and Indian meals on offer.

Getting There & Away

All transport leaves from the area between the main mosque and the market at the eastern end of the town centre.

You'll find regular bus departures throughout the day from 6.45am onwards to Embu (KSh400, two hours), Thika (KSh400, 3½ hours) and Nairobi (KSh500, five hours). There's also at least one late-afternoon departure to Mombasa (KSh1600, 12 hours).

Regular matatus also serve Nairobi (KSh750, four hours), Thika (KSh650, 3½ hours), Embu (KSh450, two hours), Nanyuki (KSh350, 1½ hours) and Isiolo (KSh300, 1½ hours).

Meru National Park

Welcome to one of Kenya's most underrated parks. Marred by serious poaching in the 1980s and the subsequent murder of George Adamson (of *Born Free* fame) in 1989, **Meru National Park** (☏ 061-2303094, Nairobi 020-2310443; www.kws.org; adult/child US$75/40; ⊙6am-6pm) fell off the tourist map and has never quite managed to struggle back on. This is a pity because it has all the essential ingredients for a classic safari destination with some fine accommodation, excellent prospects for seeing lions and rhinos, and a landscape that incorporates Hemingway-esque green hills, arid, Tsavo-like savannah and fast-flowing streams bordered by riverine forests, baobab trees and doum palms. The advantage of being one of Kenya's best kept secrets is plain to see – you're likely to have much of it all to yourself.

⊙ Sights & Activities

Although a large park covering 870 sq km, most of the wildlife action is concentrated in the northern sector of the park. The triangle of largely open savannah between **Mururi Swamp**, **Leopard Rock Swamp** and **Mughwango Swamp** is easily the park's happiest hunting ground for lions and the herbivores they stalk.

The park's most significant waterway, **Rojewero River**, is a reliable place to view hippos and crocodiles. To the south you may want to check out **Elsa's Grave**, a stone memorial to the Adamson's star lioness. Access to the adjacent **Kora National Park** is via the bridge near **Adamson's Falls**.

Rhino Sanctuary NATIONAL PARK
(⊙6am-6pm) A signposted hard right not long after entering Murera gate takes you to Meru's 48-sq-km Rhino Sanctuary, one of the best places in Kenya to see wild rhinos. At last count, this fenced portion of the park was home to 24 black and 56 white rhinos, many of whom were reintroduced here from Lake Nakuru National Park after the disastrous poaching of the '80s.

Meru National Park

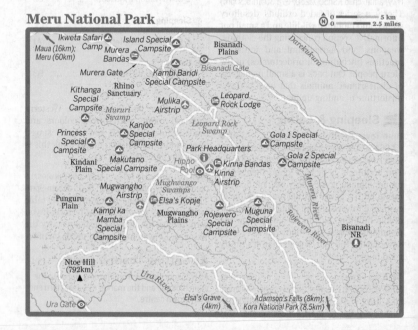

🛌 Sleeping & Eating

★ Ikweta Safari Camp   TENTED CAMP **$$**

(☑ 0705200050; www.ikwetasafaricamp.com; s/d full board US$100/165; P 🛜 ⛱) Opened in late 2011, this terrific place is outside the park, 2.5km from Murera gate on the road in from Meru, but you can be inside the park in minutes. The semi-luxurious tents (with wi-fi) are outrageously good value and put to shame many tented camps that charge so much more for so much less. The food here is another highlight and Susana and John are engaging hosts.

★ Elsa's Kopje   BANDA **$$$**

(☑ 0730127000; www.elsaskopje.com; s/d full board from US$648/1080; ⛱) Plenty of hotels claim to blend into their environment, but Elsa's did so in such a seamless manner that the bar on chic ecosuites was permanently raised. Carved from Mughwango Hill, these highly individualised 'three-walled' rooms open out onto views *The Lion King* animators would have killed for. Stone-hewn infinity pools plunge over the clifftops, while rock hyraxes play tag in your private garden.

Leopard Rock Lodge   LODGE **$$$**

(☑ Nairobi 0733333100, Nairobi 020-600031; www.leopardmico.com; per person full board US$240; ⛱) This beautiful unfenced lodge lets the wildlife right in; keep an eye on your possessions as the baboons and/or Sykes's monkeys will nick your stuff. Accommodation is in massive yet extremely comfortable *bandas*, the food is good and the location puts you right in the heart of the wildlife action.

🛈 Information

Entrance to Meru National Park also entitles you to enter the adjacent Kora National Park although visits into Kora must be prearranged with Meru's warden at the park headquarters.

The KWS *Meru National Park* map (KSh450), sold at the park gates, is essential if you want to find your way around. Even so you may want to hire a guide (six-hour/full-day tour KSh1500/3000).

🛈 Getting There & Away

J Kirimi Safaris (☑ 0721683700; safari@bestkenyasafari.com) John Kirimi of J Kirimi Safaris, a small safari operator, sometimes has a 4WD based in Maua (a small town 31km from the main gate). A full-day safari, including pick-up and drop-off at Meru town, costs around US$150.

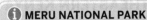

🛈 MERU NATIONAL PARK

Why Go

A pristine, seldom-visited park with rhinos and lions where you'll be guaranteed a 'congestion-free' experience.

When to Go

Because it falls within Mt Kenya's eastern rain shadow, the park is accessible year-round with a 4WD.

Practicalities

There is no public transport within the park but self-drive safaris are possible as park road junctions are numbered on the ground and labelled on park maps.

Budget Tips

Stay outside the park and try to join a larger group, perhaps from Ikweta Safari Camp.

Airkenya (☑ Nairobi 020-3916000; www.airkenya.com; adult/child one way US$252/186) Twice-daily flights connecting Meru to Nairobi's Wilson Airport.

Chogoria

POP 6264

This town shares its name with the most difficult route up Mt Kenya. It's a friendly enough place but, unless you're trekking, there's no reason to stop here.

If you haven't arranged your accommodation with one of the many touts offering Mt Kenya climbs, head to **Transit Motel** (☑ 064-22096, 0721973133; www.transitmotelchogoria.com; camping without/with own tent KSh500/300, s/d/tr KSh1400/2400/2800), 2km south of town. This is a large, friendly lodge with pleasant rooms (some with small balconies) and a decent restaurant (meals KSh650). Mt Kenya Chogoria Guides & Porters Association (p289) is also based here.

Chogoria is 3km off the main B6 drag. In all likelihood an express matatu will drop you at either the Kiriani (southern) junction or the Kirurumwe (northern) junction, from where you will have to catch a *boda-boda* to town. Sample fares include Meru (KSh220, one hour), Embu (KSh300, 1½ hours) and Nairobi (KSh500, four hours).

SOUTHEASTERN KENYA

Southern Kenya is one of the premier safari destinations in Africa. Here you find a triumvirate of epic wildlife parks – Amboseli, Tsavo West and Tsavo East – that are home to the Big Five and much more. In short, this is Kenya at its wildest and yet most accessible.

Amboseli National Park

Amboseli (☑0722992619, 0716493335, Nairobi 020-8029705; www.kws.org/parks/parks_reserves/AMNP; adult/child US$80/40; ☉6am-6pm) belongs in the elite of Kenya's national parks, and it's easy to see why. Its signature attraction is the sight of hundreds of big-tusked elephants set against the backdrop of Africa's best views of Mt Kilimanjaro (5895m). Africa's highest peak broods over the southern boundary of the park, and while cloud cover can render the mountain's massive bulk invisible for much of the day, you'll be rewarded with stunning vistas when the weather clears, usually at dawn and/or dusk. Apart from guaranteed elephant sightings, you'll also see wildebeest and zebras, and you've a reasonable chance of spotting lions and hyenas. The park is also home to over 370 bird species.

◉ Sights & Activities

Amboseli's permanent swamps of **Enkongo Narok**, **Olokenya** and **Longinye** create a marshy belt across the middle of the park and this is where you'll encounter the most wildlife. Elephants love to wallow around in the muddy waters and you've a good chance of seeing hippos around the edge. For really close-up elephant encounters, **Sinet Causeway**, which crosses Enkongo Narok near Observation Hill, is often good. Birdlife is especially rich in these swamps when the migrants arrive in November and stay until March.

Normatior (Observation Hill)   LOOKOUT
This pyramid-shaped hill is one of the only places in the park where you can get out and walk. The summit provides an ideal lookout from which to orientate yourself to the plains, swamps and roads below. The views from here are also pretty special, whether south to Kilimanjaro or east across the swamps. Wildlife is generally a fair way off, but the views here put them in their context.

Sinet Delta   LAKE
From Observation Hill, the northern route runs across the Sinet Delta, which is an excellent place for birdwatching. The vegetation is thicker the further south you go, providing fodder for giraffes and also framing some of the park's best Kilimanjaro views.

Kimana Gate   NATIONAL PARK
If you're taking the road that runs east across the park to the Kimana gate, watch for giraffes in the acacia woodlands; this is the best place inside the park for giraffe-spotting. Here you may also find gerenuks, an unusual breed of gazelle that 'browse' by standing on their hind legs and stretching their necks, as if yearning to be giraffes. There are numerous lodges and campsites just outside the gate, while the unpaved road continues on to Tsavo West National Park.

ⓘ AMBOSELI NATIONAL PARK

Why Go
To see big-tusked elephants, Africa's best Mt Kilimanjaro views, lions, wildebeest, zebras and rich birdlife.

When to Go
Year-round. The dry season (May to October and January to March) is best for spotting wildlife, while November to March is the best time to see migratory birds. Much of the wildlife moves beyond the park during and immediately after the rains.

Practicalities
Drive in from Nairobi or Mombasa; flying is also possible.

Budget Tips
Camp at a public campsite inside the park, or one of the private camps outside Kimana gate.

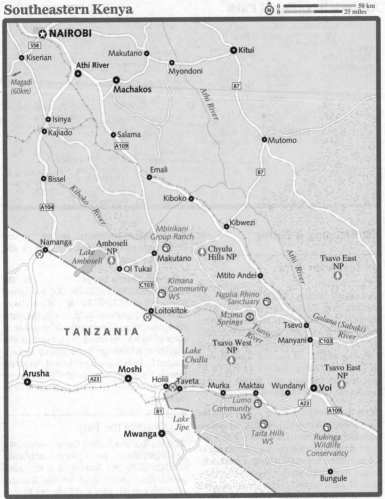

Elephant Research Camp WILDLIFE RESERVE (☎0714781699; www.elephanttrust.org; group of 10 or less US$800, group of more than 10 per person US$80; ☼by prior appointment 3.30pm Mon-Fri) The elephants of Amboseli are among the most studied in the world, thanks largely to the work of Dr Cynthia Moss, whose books include *The Amboseli Elephants* and *Elephant Memories*; she was also behind the famous documentary DVD *Echo of the Elephants*. The research camp remains in operation in the heart of the park, under the guidance of the **Amboseli Trust for Elephants** (www.elephanttrust.org).

Although the camp is not open for casual visits, it is possible, with prior arrangement, to attend a one-hour lecture at the camp, during which the researchers explain their work and other related issues of elephant conservation, with time for questions at the end. The visit doesn't come cheap. But this is one of the mother lodes for elephant research in Africa and a visit here is a rare opportunity to learn more about these soulful creatures. Bookings can be made via email.

Amboseli National Park

🛏 Sleeping & Eating

🛏 Inside the Park

KWS Campsite CAMPGROUND $
(www.kws.org; camping US$30) Just inside the southern boundary of the park, the KWS campsite has toilets, an unreliable water supply (bring your own) and a small bar selling warm beer and soft drinks. It's fenced off from the wildlife, so you can walk around safely at night, though *don't* keep food in your tent, as baboons visit during the day looking for an uninvited feed.

⭐**Ol Tukai Lodge** LODGE $$$
(📞045-622275, Nairobi 020-4445514; www.oltukai lodge.com; s/d full board US$350/450; 🅿@🛜🏊) Lying at the heart of Amboseli, on the edge of a dense acacia forest, Ol Tukai is a splendidly refined lodge with soaring *makuti* (thatched roofs of palm leaves) and tranquil gardens defined by towering trees. Accommodation is in wooden chalets, which are brought to life with vibrant zebra prints, while the split-level bar has a sweeping view of Kili and a pervading atmosphere of peace and luxury.

⭐**Tortilis Camp** TENTED CAMP $$$
(📞045-622195; www.tortilis.com; s/d full board US$522/870, family tent US$1740, private house US$2175; 🅿🛜) 🌿 This wonderfully conceived site is one of the most exclusive ecolodges in Kenya, commanding a superb elevated spot with perfect Kilimanjaro vistas. The luxurious canvas tents have recently been given a facelift; the family rooms have the biggest wow factor we found in southern Kenya. The lavish meals, which are based on North Italian traditional recipes, feature herbs and vegetables from the huge on-site organic garden.

Amboseli Serena Lodge LODGE $$$
(📞0735522361, Nairobi 020-2842000; www.serena hotels.com; s/d US$285/386; @🛜🏊) A classically elegant property in Amboseli, the Serena is comprised of fiery-red adobe cottages, some of which (rooms 68 to 75) overlook the wildlife-rich Enkongo Narok swamp and are fringed by lush tropical gardens of blooming flowers and manicured shrubs. There are no Kilimanjaro views from the lodge. Service is excellent.

🛏 Outside the Park

Oloirien Kimana Tented Camp CAMPGROUND $
(📞0720951500; per person tent/banda KSh2500/3000; 🅿) Just outside the park boundaries, 2.8km south of the Kimana gate, this camp is bare and dusty but friendly, with basic tents and simple *bandas* with cold showers. There's a kitchen for DIY cooking.

⭐**Tawi Lodge** LODGE $$$
(📞0722745552, Nairobi 020-2300943; www.tawi lodge.com; s/d full board US$530/820; 🅿🛜🏊) 🌿 Set on its own private 6000-acre conservancy close to Kimana gate and with its own airstrip, Tawi Lodge is our pick of the places southeast of the park. You've the choice of going into Amboseli or exploring Tawi's own wildlife-rich area, while the cottages are refined, beautifully furnished and most come with fine Kili views. There's even an onsite spa and night drives are possible.

Kibo Safari Camp TENTED CAMP **$$$**
(☑ 0721380539; www.kibosafaricamp.com; per person from US$160; P) Around 2km from Kimana gate, Kibo Safari Camp gives you the experience of a tented camp without asking the prohibitive fees of the lodges. The tents, and indeed the whole property, could do with an overhaul, but it's a good deal that enables you to be inside the park soon after sunrise.

ⓘ Getting There & Away

AIR

Airkenya (www.airkenya.com; one way from $175) Daily flights between Nairobi's Wilson Airport and Amboseli. You'll need to arrange with one of the lodges or a safari company for a vehicle to meet you at the airstrip, which is northwest of Ol Tukai.

CAR & 4WD

There are three main gates; approaches to the park from the west (Kitirua and Meshanani gates) are in poor condition, Iremito (northeast) or Kimana (southeast) gates are in better condition. The park is accessible in 2WD. Whichever route you take, allow around four hours from Nairobi.

Around Amboseli

Amboseli National Park occupies less than 5% of the broader Amboseli ecosystem's 8000 sq km, and surrounding the park itself are a series of group ranches inhabited almost exclusively by the Maasai and administered by Maasai elders. By one estimate, around 30,000 Maasai live in the Amboseli ecosystem, along with upwards of a million of their livestock.

The park effectively empties of wildlife during the rainy season when elephants, lions and all manner of species disperse out into the ecosystem, although there are healthy year-round wildlife populations.

It is on these group ranches that you'll find some of Kenya's most appealing and exclusive lodges.

★ Ol Donyo LODGE **$$$**
(☑ Nairobi 020-600457; www.greatplainsconservation.com; per person US$595-910; P 🛜 ⛲) 🍃 Welcome to what could just be our favourite place to stay in Kenya. Built into the foothills of Chyulu Hills at the remote eastern reaches of the 275,000-acre Mbirikani Group Ranch, Old Donyo is a temple to good taste grafted onto one of the loveliest corners of Africa.

The lodge is built entirely of local materials and employs advanced water recycling and solar-power systems. The rooms, each overlooking their own waterhole, are expansive and utterly gorgeous in both their scope and detail: private plunge pools, divinely comfortable four-poster beds with Kilimanjaro views, complete privacy and roof beds are merely the beginning of an overwhelming sensory experience that takes safari chic to a whole new level. The meals are world-class as well.

KENYA AMBOSELI NATIONAL PARK

LION GUARDIANS

Because lions are the easiest of the big cats to observe, few people realise that lions face an extremely uncertain future. A century ago, more than 200,000 lions roamed Africa. Now, fewer than 30,000 are thought to remain and lions have disappeared from 80% of their historical range, according to **Panthera** (www.panthera.org), the world's leading cat conservation NGO. In Kenya, lion numbers have reached critical levels: less than 2000 lions are thought to remain in the country. Fewer than 100 of these inhabit the Amboseli ecosystem and around half of these (many more in the rainy season) live outside park boundaries, sharing the land with the Maasai and their herds of livestock.

In Maasai culture, young male warriors (the *morran*) have traditionally killed lions and other wild animals to prove their bravery and as an initiation rite into manhood. But one organisation has come up with an innovative way of honouring Maasai tradition while protecting lions in the process. The **Lion Guardians** (www.lionguardians.org) has taken many of these young, traditional warriors and turned them into Lion Guardians, whose task is to protect the Maasai and the lions from each other. Each Lion Guardian, most of whom are former lion killers, patrols a territory, keeping track of the lions, and warning herders of lion locations and helping them to find lost livestock and even lost children. In areas where the Lion Guardians operate, lion killings (and livestock lost to lions) have fallen dramatically.

Day or night wildlife drives are, of course, possible, but so, too, are walking safaris out onto the plains or up onto the Chyulu Hills, horse-riding safaris and even running safaris for those eager not to let their exercise regimen slip.

★ **Campi ya Kanzi**   TENTED CAMP **$$$**
(☑ 045-622516; www.campiyakanzi.com; s/d US$950/1500, conservation fee per person US$100; P ☎) 🍃 Campi ya Kanzi is, quite simply, an outstanding place to stay. Set upon the slopes of the Chyulu Hills – these were Ernest Hemingway's 'Green Hills of Africa' and that sobriquet means so much more here than it does in Chyulu Hills National Park – accommodation here is in luxury tents scattered around an enormous ranch that is centred on a nostalgically decorated stone lodge.

Game drives (of both the day and night variety), walking safaris up into the Chyulu Hills, transcendental meditation sessions and visits to Maasai villages are all possible, but you'll also be tempted to simply nurse a drink as you gaze out across Maasailand towards Mt Kilimanjaro in all its glory.

Campi ya Kanzi was begun and continues to be overseen by Italians Luca and Antonella. While they bring so much personality to this place, Campi ya Kanzi is very much a Maasai concern. The camp's environmental credentials are also impeccable and the camp directly supports education, health care and environmental conservation in local communities, quite apart from employing dozens of local Maasai staff.

Tsavo West National Park

Welcome to the wilderness. **Tsavo West** (☑ 043-30049043-30049, 0724954745, Nairobi 020--600800; www.kws.org/parks/parks_reserves/TWNP; adult/child per day US$75/40; ⊙ 6am-6pm) is one of Kenya's larger national parks (9065 sq km), covering a huge variety of landscapes, from swamps, natural springs and rocky peaks to extinct volcanic cones, rolling plains and sharp outcrops dusted with greenery.

This is a park with a whiff of legend about it, first for its famous man-eating lions in the late 19th century and then for its devastating levels of poaching in the 1980s. Despite the latter, there's still plenty of wildlife here, although you'll have to work harder and be much more patient than in Amboseli or the Masai Mara to see them all. If possible, come here with some time to spare to make the most of it.

◉ Sights & Activities

Ngulia Rhino Sanctuary   WILDLIFE RESERVE
(⊙ 4-6pm) At the base of Ngulia Hills, this 90-sq-km area is surrounded by a 1m-high electric fence, and provides a measure of security for, at last count, 78 of the park's highly endangered black rhinos. There are driving tracks and waterholes within the enclosed area, but the rhinos are mainly nocturnal and the chances of seeing one are slim – black rhinos, apart from being understandably shy and more active at night, are browsers, not grazers and prefer to pass their time in thick undergrowth.

ⓘ TSAVO WEST NATIONAL PARK

Why Go
For the dramatic scenery, wilderness and good mix of predators (lion, leopard, cheetah and hyena), prey (lesser kudu, gazelle, impala) and other herbivores (elephant, rhino, zebra, oryx and giraffe).

When to Go
Year-round. The dry season (May to October and January to March) is best for spotting wildlife. November to March is the best time to see migratory birds.

Practicalities
Drive in from Mtito Andei or Tsavo gate along the Nairobi–Mombasa Rd. There is a campsite close to the park entrance and lodges throughout the park.

Budget Tips
Rent a matatu with other travellers in Mtito Andei; if staying in a lodge, June is much cheaper than July.

Rhino Valley
PARK

This is one of our favourite areas for wildlife watching, with plenty of antelope species keeping a careful eye out for the resident lions, leopards and cheetahs. You'll also see elephants, giraffes and, if you're lucky, black rhinos. Birdlife is also particularly diverse here. The signposted 'Rhino Valley Circuit' is a good place to start, while anywhere along the Mukui River's ponds and puddles is a place to watch and wait.

Ngulia Hills
MOUNTAIN

Rising more than 600m above the valley floor and to a height over 1800m above sea level, this jagged ridgeline ranks among the prettiest of all Tsavo landforms, providing a backdrop to Rhino Valley. The hills can be climbed with permission from the warden, while the peaks are also a recognised flyway for migrating birds heading south from late September through to November.

Mzima Springs
SPRING

Mzima Springs is an oasis of green in the west of the park and produces an incredible 250 million litres of fresh water a day. The springs, whose source rises in the Chyulu Hills, provides the bulk of Mombasa's fresh water. A walking trail leads along the shoreline. The drought in 2009 took a heavy toll on the springs' hippo population; the population is stable at around 20 individuals. There are also crocodiles and a wide variety of birdlife.

Chyulu Gate & the West
PARK

The plains, rocky outcrops and light woodland between Kilaguni Serena Lodge and the Chyulu gate are good for zebras and other herbivores, and sustains a healthy population of lions, leopards and spotted hyenas – the epic battle between rival hyena clans that we witnessed here on our last visit remains one of our favourite Tsavo memories. A leopard was also commonly seen early morning along the road close to the airstrip.

Chaimu Crater & Roaring Rocks
LOOKOUT

Just southeast of Kilaguni Serena Lodge, these two natural features offer stunning views of the Chyulu Hills and birds of prey circling high above the plains. The **Roaring Rocks** can be climbed in about 15 minutes; the name comes from the wind whistling up the escarpment and the persistent drone of cicadas. While there's little danger

---

POACHING IN TSAVO

As poaching reached epidemic proportions in Kenya in the 1980s, Tsavo was very much on the frontline – not surprising given the park's size and terrain. In a few short years, the elephant population dropped from 45,000 to just 5000, and rhinos were almost wiped out entirely; at the height of the crisis, an estimated 5000 elephants were being killed every year. Populations are slowly recovering, and, as of early 2011, there are close to 12,500 elephants in the two parks, but less than 100 rhinos, down from about 9000 in 1969.

Sadly, there has been a recent upsurge in poaching once again, with the northern half of Tsavo East (off-limits to travellers) of particular concern, as well as many areas bordering the two Tsavo parks; the area around Maktau gate at the southern edge of Tsavo West has been particularly hard hit.

---

when walking these trails, the KWS warns in its guidebook to the park that in **Chaimu Crater** 'be wary when exploring since the crater and lava may shelter snakes and large sleeping mammals'.

★Shetani Lava Flows
LOOKOUT, VOLCANO

About 4km west of the Chyulu gate of Tsavo West National Park, on the road to Amboseli, are the spectacular Shetani lava flows. 'Shetani' means 'devil' in Kiswahili: the flows were formed only a few hundred years ago and local peoples believed that it was the devil himself emerging from the earth. This vast expanse of folded black lava spreads for 50 sq km across the savannah at the foot of the Chyulu Hills, looking strangely as if Vesuvius dropped its comfort blanket here.

Tsavo River & the South
RIVER

Running west–east through the park, this lovely year-round river is green-shaded and surrounded for much of its path by doum palms. Along with Mzima Springs, the river provides aesthetic relief from the vast semi-arid habitats that dominate the park. The trees all along the river are known to shelter leopards.

Tsavo East & West National Parks

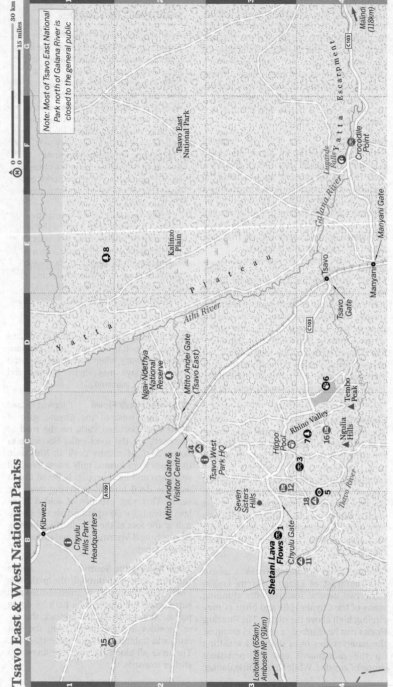

Note: Most of Tsavo East National Park north of Galana River is closed to the general public

Malindi (118km)

Yatta Escarpment

Crocodile Point

Lugards Falls

Galana River

Tsavo East National Park

Manyani Gate

Kalinzo Plain

Manyani

Tsavo

Ngai-Ndethya National Reserve

Tsavo Gate

Athi River

Yatta Plateau

Mtito Andei Gate (Tsavo East)

Temho Peak

Rhino Valley

Hippo Pool

Ngulia Hills

Tsavo West Park HQ

Mtito Andei Gate & Visitor Centre

Seven Sisters Hills

A109

Kibwezi

Chyulu Hills Park Headquarters

Shetani Lava Flows

Chyulu Gate

Loitokitok (65km); Amboseli NP (91km)

30 km
15 miles

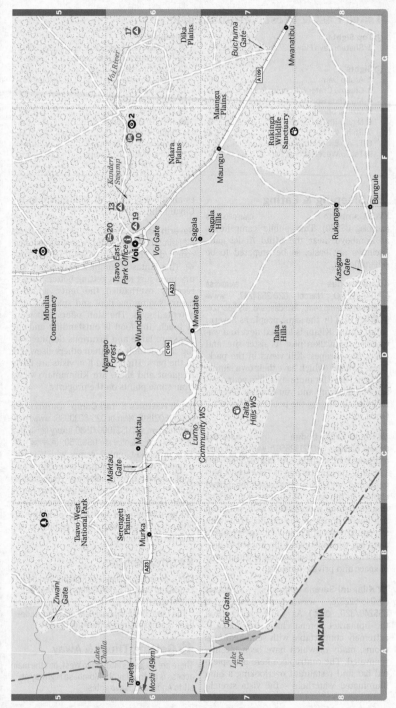

Tsavo East & West National Parks

🛏 Sleeping & Eating

KWS Campsite CAMPGROUND $
(camping US$20) This public campsite is at Komboyo, near the Mtito Andei gate. Facilities are basic, so be prepared to be self-sufficient.

Kitani Bandas BANDAS $$
(☑ 041-211000, Nairobi 020-2684247; www.severinsafaricamp.com; bandas s/d US$81/124; P 🛜 ☀) Run by the same people as Severin Safari Camp, Kitani is located next to a waterhole, about 2km past its sister site, and offers the cheapest Kili views in the park. These *bandas* (which have their own simple kitchens) have far more style than your average budget camp and you can use Severin's facilities (including the pool and free wi-fi). Great value.

★ Rhino Valley Lodge BANDAS $$$
(Ngulia Bandas; ☑ 0721328567; www.tsavolodges andcamps.com; bandas s/d US$150/200; P) This hillside camp is one of Tsavo's best bargains and one of the most reasonably priced choices in the parks of southern Kenya. The thatched stone cottages and tents perch on the lower slopes of the Ngulia Hills with sweeping views of Rhino Valley, overlooking a stream where leopards are known to hide out. The decor is designer rustic with plenty of space and private terraces.

★ Kilaguni Serena Lodge LODGE $$$
(☑ 045-622376; www.serenahotels.com; s/d US$240/320; @ ☀) As you'd expect from the upmarket Serena chain, this lodge is extremely comfortable with semi-luxurious rooms, many of which have been recently renovated. The centrepiece here is a splendid bar and restaurant overlooking a busy illuminated waterhole – the vista stretches all the way from Mt Kilimanjaro to the Chyulu Hills.

Severin Safari Camp TENTED CAMP $$$
(☑ Nairobi 020-2684247; www.severinsafaricamp.com; s/d full board from US$240/370; P 🛜 ☀) 🏊 This fantastic complex of thatched luxury tents just keeps getting better. They've recently overhauled the tents, added a luxury swimming pool and spa, and even a tented gym. The staff offers a personal touch, the food is outstanding and the tents are large and luxurious despite costing considerably less than others elsewhere in the park. Hippo and lion visits are fairly frequent and there are Kilimanjaro views from some points on the property.

Finch Hatton's Safari Camp TENTED CAMP $$$
(☑ 0716021818, Nairobi 020-8030936; www.finchhattons.com; s/d US$1000/1580, luxury family tent US$3360, presidential ste US$3750; P 🛜 ☀) 🏊 This upmarket tented camp, which is distinguished by its signature bone china and gold shower taps (guests are requested to dress for dinner), was named after Denys Finch Hatton, the playboy hunter and lover of Karen Blixen. He died at Tsavo, despite his obsession with maintaining civility in the middle of the bush.

ℹ Information

Fuel is generally available at Kilaguni Serena Lodge and Severin Safari Camp; fill up before entering park.

The *Tsavo West National Park* map and guidebook is available from Mtito Andei gate.

ℹ Getting There & Away

There are six gates into Tsavo West, but the main access is off the Nairobi-Mombasa Highway at Mtito Andei and Tsavo gates.

Tsavo East National Park

Kenya's largest national park, **Tsavo East National Park** (☎ 0775563672, 0722290009, Nairobi 020-6000800; www.kws.org/parks/parks_reserves/TENP; adult/child per day US$75/40; ⊙ 6am-6pm) has an undeniable wild and primordial charm and is a terrific wildlife-watching destination. Although one of Kenya's largest rivers flows through the middle of the park and the contrast between the permanent greenery of the river and the endless grasses and thorn trees that characterise much of the park is visually arresting, the landscape here lacks the drama of Tsavo West. Tsavo East is markedly flatter and drier than its sister park. The flipside is that spotting wildlife is generally easier thanks to the thinly spread foliage.

◉ Sights & Activities

Kanderi Swamp
RIVER

Around 10km from Voi Gate, the lovely area of green known as Kanderi Swamp is home to a resident pride of lions, and elephants also congregate near here; this is one of only two water sources in the park during the dry season. The landscape here has a lovely backdrop of distant hills. A number of vehicle tracks also follow the contours of the Voi River; keep an eye on the overhanging branches for leopards.

Aruba Dam
LAKE

Some 30km east of Voi Gate is the Aruba Dam, which spans the Voi River. It also attracts heavy concentrations of diverse wildlife; one the park's regularly spotted lion prides ranges around here. Away to the east and southeast, all the way down to the Buchuma Gate, the open grasslands provide the perfect habitat for cheetahs and sightings are more common here than anywhere else in southeastern Kenya.

Galana River
RIVER

Running through the heart of the park and marking the northernmost point in the park that most visitors are allowed to visit, the Galana River, which combines the waters of the Tsavo and Athi Rivers, cuts a green gash across the dusty plains. Surprisingly few visitors make it even this far and sightings of crocs, hippos, lesser kudus, waterbucks, dik-diks and, to a lesser extent, lions and leopards are relatively common.

Mudanda Rock
MOUNTAIN

Towering over a natural dam near the Manyani gate, this natural formation runs for over 1.5km. It attracts elephants in the dry season and is reminiscent of Australia's Uluru (Ayers Rock), albeit on a smaller scale. Leopards and elephants are among the wildlife to watch out for here.

⬚ Sleeping & Eating

⬚ Inside the Park

KWS Campsite
CAMPGROUND $

(camping US$20) Decent site with toilets, showers and a communal kitchen.

Voi Safari Lodge
LODGE $$$

(☎ Mombasa 041-471861041-471861; www.safari-hotels.com; s/d US$190/290; ☎ ⛱) Just 4km

---

ⓘ TSAVO EAST NATIONAL PARK

Why Go
Wilderness, red elephants and leopards, lions and cheetahs. The park also has close to 500 bird species.

When to Go
June to February. Wildlife concentrations are highest in the dry season (September to October and January to early March).

Practicalities
Drive in from Voi, Mandanyi or Tsavo gates along the Nairobi–Mombasa Rd. The Sala and Buchuma gates are good for Mombasa. There are a small number of lodges and camps throughout the park or close to Voi gate.

Budget Tips
Rent a matatu or organise a budget safari with other travellers in Voi or the coast; use public campsites.

from Voi gate, this is a long, low complex perched on the edge of an escarpment overlooking an incredible sweep of savannah. There's an attractive rock-cut swimming pool, as well as a natural waterhole that draws elephants, buffaloes and the occasional predator; a photographers' hide sits at the level of the waterhole. Rooms are attractive and many have superlative views.

Ashnil Aruba Lodge   LODGE $$$
(📞 Nairobi 020-4971008; www.ashnilhotels.com; s/d full board US$262/350; 🅿 @ 🕸) A stone's throw from the wildlife-rich Aruba Dam, this lodge has attractively decorated rooms decked out in safari prints. In the heart of the park, it's an ideal starting point for most Tsavo East safaris. Wildlife wanders around the property's perimeter at regular intervals.

Satao Camp   TENTED CAMP $$$
(📞 Mombasa 041-475074, Nairobi 020-2434600; www.sataocamp.com; s/d US$337/436; 🅿) Located on the banks of the Voi River, this luxury camp is run by the experienced safari operator Southern Cross Safaris. There are 20 canopied tents, all of which are perfectly spaced within sight of a waterhole that's known to draw lions, cheetahs and elephants on occasion.

🛏 Outside the Park

★ Tsavo Mashariki Camp   TENTED CAMP $$
(📞 0729179443; www.masharikicamp.com; s/d bed & breakfast from US$131/185) The closest camp to Voi gate just outside the park, this charming little Italian-run place has some fine tents made out of all-natural local materials; the family tent is brilliant and there are also two stone-built cottages. Best of all, the prices here put many other tented camps to shame. Highly recommended.

❶ Information

Fuel is available in Voi; fill up before entering park.

The *Tsavo East National Park* map and guidebook is available from Voi gate.

❶ Getting There & Away

A track through the park follows the Galana River from the Tsavo gate to the Sala gate; others fan out from Voi gate.

If travelling to/from Nairobi or Tsavo West, use the Voi, Tsavo and Manyani gates, to/from Mombasa use the Sala or Buchuma gates.

Voi
POP POP 17,152

Voi is a key service town at the intersection of the Nairobi–Mombasa road, the road to Moshi in Tanzania and the access road to the main Voi gate of Tsavo East National Park. While there is little reason to spend any more time here than is needed to get directions, fill up on petrol, change money and buy some snacks for the road, you'll inevitably pass through here at some point.

Frequent buses and matatus run to/from Mombasa (KSh200 to KSh500, three hours), and there are buses to Nairobi (KSh500 to KSh1200, six hours). There are at least daily matatus to Taveta (KSh450, two hours) on the Tanzanian border.

MOMBASA & THE SOUTH COAST

There's something in the air here. Thanks to the long interplay of Africa, India and Arabia, the coast feels different to the rest of Kenya. Its people, the Swahili, have created a distinctive Indian Ocean society – built on the scent of trade with distant shores – that lends real romance to the coast's sugar-white beaches and to a city the poets have embraced for as long as ivory has been traded for iron.

Mombasa
POP 939,000

Mombasa: city of salt and of spice, of dreams and of battles, of poetry, of seafaring stories and of wave upon wave of traders from faraway lands. 'It does not reveal the great secret it holds', wrote the classical Swahili poet Muyaka about his hometown. 'Even those who are well-informed do not comprehend it.'

Indeed, the city dubbed Kisiwa Cha Mvita in Swahili (the Island of War) has many faces. It is muttered chants echoing over the flagstones of a Jain temple, the ecstatic passion of the call to prayer, the teal break of a vanishing wave and the sight of a Zanzibar-bound dhow slipping over the horizon. It is row upon row of purveyors of herbal medicine, it is cows dozing outside hair-braiding salons, it is birds swooping low over great piles of smoking trash, and

The Coast

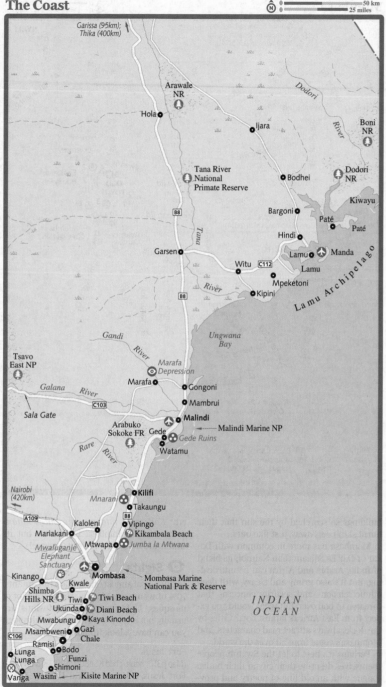

0 — 50 km
0 — 25 miles

Garissa (95km);
Thika (400km)

Arawale
NR

Hola

Ijara

Dodori River

Boni
NR

Dodori
NR

Tana River
National
Primate Reserve

Bodhei

Kiwayu

Bargoni

Paté
Paté

B8

Hindi

Garsen

Witu

C112

Lamu   Manda
Lamu

Mpeketoni

B8

Kipini

La mu Archipelago

Gandi

River

Ungwana
Bay

Tsavo
East NP

Marafa
Depression

Galana   River

Marafa

Gongoni

C103

Mambrui

Sala Gate

Arabuko
Sokoke FR   Gede

Malindi

Malindi Marine NP

Rare

River

Gede Ruins

Watamu

Nairobi
(420km)

Kilifi

Mnarani

Takaungu

A109

Kaloleni

Vipingo

B8

Mariakani

Kikambala Beach

Mwaluganje
Elephant
Sanctuary

Mtwapa

Jumba la Mtwana

Kinango

Mombasa

Mombasa Marine
National Park & Reserve

Kwale

Shimba
Hills NR   Tiwi

INDIAN
OCEAN

Tiwi Beach

Ukunda

Diani Beach

Mwabungu

Kaya Kinondo

Msambweni

Gazi

C106

Chale

Ramisi

Bodo

Lunga
Lunga

Funzi

Shimoni

Vanga   Wasini

Kisite Marine NP

Mombasa

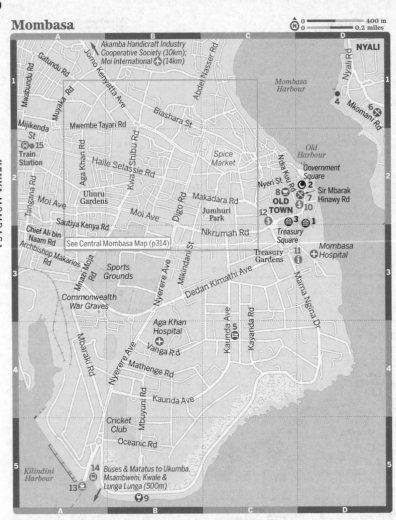

buildings so scorched by the sun that their burnt skin peels away, just like ours.

Mombasa has more in common with Dakar or Dar Es Salaam than Nairobi; its blend of India, Arabia and Africa can be intoxicating. But it's also grimy and sleazy, with deep ethnic tensions and security concerns that threaten to boil over. But what would you expect from East Africa's largest port? Cities by the docks always attract mad characters, and Mombasa's come from all over the world.

Perhaps it's best to let the Swahili people themselves describe their city in their native tongue with an old line of poetry and prov-erb: *Kongowea nda mvumo, maji maan-gavu. Male!* (Mombasa is famous, but its waters are dangerously deep. Beware!).

◉ Sights

In this city of almost one million inhabitants, 70% of whom are Muslim, there are a lot of mosques. Unfortunately, non-Muslims are usually not allowed to enter them, although you can have a look from the outside.

Fort Jesus   MUSEUM
(Map p310; adult/child KSh800/400; ⊙ 8am-6pm)
Fort Jesus, a Unesco World Heritage treas-

Mombasa

ure, is Mombasa's most-visited site. The metre-thick walls, frescoed interiors, traces of European graffiti, Arabic inscriptions and Swahili embellishment aren't just evocative, they're a record of the history of Mombasa and the coast writ in stone. The fort was built by the Portuguese in 1593 to serve as both symbol and headquarters of their permanent presence in this corner of the Indian Ocean.

It's ironic, then, that the construction of the fort marked the beginning of the end of local Portuguese hegemony. Between Portuguese sailors, Omani soldiers and Swahili rebellions, the fort changed hands at least nine times between 1631 and the early 1870s, when it finally fell under British control and was used as a jail.

The fort was the final project completed by Joao Batista Cairato, whose buildings can be found throughout Portugal's Eastern colonies, from Old Goa to Old Mombasa. The building is an opus of period military design – assuming the structure was well manned, it would have been impossible to approach its walls without falling under the cone of interlocking fields of fire.

These days the fort houses a **museum** built over the former barracks. The exhibits should give a good insight into Swahili life and culture but, like the rest of the complex, it's all poorly labelled and woefully displayed, which, considering it's the city's number-one tourist attraction, is fairly scandalous.

Elsewhere within the fort compound, the **Mazrui Hall**, where flowery spirals fade across a wall topped with wooden lintels left by the Omani Arabs, is worthy of note. In another room, Portuguese sailors scratched graffiti that illustrates the multicultural naval

ⓘ **TOURS & SAFARIS FROM MOMBASA**

A number of tour companies offer standard tours of the Old Town and Fort Jesus (per person from US$45), plus safaris to Shimba Hills National Reserve and Tsavo East and Tsavo West National Parks. Most safaris are expensive lodge-based affairs, but there are a few camping safaris to Tsavo East and West.

The most popular safari is an overnight tour to Tsavo, and though most people enjoy these, be warned that a typical two-day, one-night safari barely gives you time to get there and back, and that your animal-spotting time will be very limited. It's much better to add in at least one extra night.

We receive a constant stream of emails from travellers who feel that their promised safari has not lived up to expectations, but the following two companies have received positive feedback.

Natural World Tours & Safaris (Map p314; ☏041-2226715; www.naturaltoursandsafaris. com; Jeneby House, Moi Ave) The hard-sell prattled by the company 'representatives' on the street can quickly put you off, but otherwise it has a reputation for delivering what it promises.

Ketty Tours (Map p314; ☏041-2315178; www.kettysafari.com; Ketty Plaza, Moi Ave) Organised and reliable.

DON'T MISS

JUMBA LA MTWANA

These Swahili **ruins** (adult/child KSh500/100; ☉8am-6pm), just north of Mtwapa Creek, have as much archaeological grandeur as the more famous Gede Ruins. Jumba la Mtwana means 'Big House of Slaves' and locals believe the town was once an important slave port. Notice the Arabic inscription on the stela adjacent to the nearby graveyard: 'Every Soul Shall Taste Death'. Underneath is a small hole representing the opening all humans must pass through on the way to paradise.

In the dying evening light, your imagination will be able to run riot with thoughts of lost treasures, ghosts, pirates and abandoned cities. The remains of buildings, with their exposed foundations for mangrove beam poles, ablution tanks, floors caked with millipedes and swarms of safari ants, and the twisting arms of 600-year-old trees – leftover from what may have been a nearby *kaya* (sacred forest) – are quite magical.

Slaves may or may not have been traded here, but turtle shell, rhino horn and ambergris (sperm-whale intestinal secretions, used for perfume – mmm) all were. In return, Jumba received goods such as Chinese dishes, the fragments of which can be seen in the floors of some buildings today. While here, keep your eyes peeled for the upper-wall holes that mark where mangrove support beams were affixed, the **House of Many Doors**, which is believed to have been a guesthouse (no breakfast included), and dried-out, 40m-deep wells. You'd be remiss to miss the **Mosque by the Sea**, which overlooks a crystal-sharp vista of the Indian Ocean (and don't forget your swimmers for a splash in the empty waters here).

The custodian gives excellent tours for a small gratuity.

---

identity of the Indian Ocean, leaving walls covered with four-pointed European frigates, three-pointed Arabic dhows and the coir-sewn 'camels of the ocean': the elegant Swahili *mtepe* (traditional sailing vessel). Nearby, a pair of whale bones serves in the undignified role of children's see-saw. The **Omani house**, in the San Felipe bastion in the northwestern corner of the fort, was built in the late 18th century. It was closed at the time of research, but used to house a small exhibition of Omani jewellery and artefacts. The eastern wall includes an Omani audience hall and the Passage of the Arches, which leads under the pinkish-brown coral to a double-azure vista of sea floating under sky.

If you arrive early in the day, you may avoid group tours, but the same can't be said of extremely persistent guides, official and unofficial, who will swarm you the minute you approach the fort. Some of them can be quite useful and some can be duds. Unfortunately, you'll have to use your best judgement to suss out which is which. Official guides charge KSh500 for a tour of Fort Jesus or Old Town; unofficial guides charge whatever they can. If you don't want a tour, shake off your guide with a firm but polite 'no', otherwise they'll launch into their spiel and expect a tip at the end. Alternatively, you can buy the Fort Jesus guide booklet from the ticket desk and go it alone.

Old Law Courts
ART GALLERY
(Map p310; Nkrumah Rd; ☉8am-6pm) **FREE** Dating from 1902, the old law courts on Nkrumah Rd have been converted into an informal gallery, with regularly changing displays of local art, Kenyan crafts, school competition pieces and votive objects from various tribal groups.

Spice Market
MARKET
(Map p314; Langoni Rd; ☉to sunset) This market, which stretches along Nehru and Langoni Rds west of Old Town, is an evocative, sensory overload – expect lots of jostling, yelling, wheeling, dealing and, of course, the exotic scent of stall upon stall of cardamom, pepper, turmeric, curry powders and everything else that makes eating enjoyable.

Mandhry Mosque
MOSQUE
(Map p310; Sir Mbarak Hinawy Rd) Mandhry Mosque in Old Town is an excellent example of Swahili architecture, which combines the elegant flourishes of Arabic style with the comforting, geometric patterns of African design – note, for example, the gently rounded minaret.

Khonzi Mosque
MOSQUE
(Map p314; Digo Rd) One of the more modern Islamic buildings in Mombasa.

Holy Ghost Cathedral CHURCH

(Map p314; Nkrumah Rd) The Christian Holy Ghost Cathedral is a very European hunk of neo-Gothic buttressed architecture, with massive fans in the walls to cool its former colonial congregations.

Lord Shiva Temple TEMPLE

(Map p314; Mwinyi Ab Rd) Mombasa's large Hindu population doesn't lack for places of worship. The enormous Lord Shiva Temple is airy, open and set off by an interesting sculpture garden.

🏃 Activities

Tamarind Dhow BOAT TOUR

(Map p310; ✆041-4471747; www.tamarind.co.ke; lunch/dinner cruise per person US$50/75; ☺lunch/dinner cruise departs 1pm/6.30pm) This top-billing cruise is run by the posh Tamarind restaurant chain. It embarks from the jetty below Tamarind restaurant in Nyali and includes a harbour tour and fantastic meal. Prices include a complimentary cocktail and transport to and from your hotel, and the dhow itself is a beautiful piece of work.

Jahazi Marine BOAT TOUR

(✆01714967717; adult/child from €60/30) This big operator offers a range of dhow trips.

🛏 Sleeping

Many people choose to skip Mombasa and head straight for the beaches to the south and north, but we'd suggest spending at least one night in town. It's difficult to appreciate Mombasa's energy without waking up to the call to prayer and the honk of a *tuk-tuk*. All the places listed here have fans and mosquito nets as a minimum requirement.

★Berachah Guest House GUESTHOUSE $

(Map p314; ✆0725864704; Haile Selassie Rd; s/d KSh1000/1600) This popular central choice is located in the heart of Mombasa's best eat streets. It has variable but clean rooms in a range of unusual shapes. It's on the 2nd floor – on the stair landing, turn right into the hotel, not left into the evangelical church.

YWCA Mombasa HOSTEL $

(Map p310; ✆0412229856; cnr Kaunda & Kiambu Aves; r from KSh1600) If you're not already a member, you'll have to sign up (KSh300) to use this YWCA. It's primarily for women, but there is a men's floor as well. Rooms can also be split between mixed-sex couples or groups. There's a cheap restaurant that's popular with Kenyan students.

Tana Rest House GUESTHOUSE $

(Map p314; ✆041-490550; cnr Mwembe Tayari & Gatundu Rds; s/d KSh400/500) Probably the cheapest of Mombasa's safe guesthouses, this place isn't pretty on the outside (the name looks like it's been scrawled with a felt tip pen), but the rooms are clean and your purse will thank you. Perfectly fine for a night or two.

★Lotus Hotel HOTEL $$

(Map p314; ✆041-2313207; www.lotushotel mombasa.com; Cathedral Lane, off Nkrumah Rd; s/d KSh4300/5000) Close to the cathedral, this hotel is a reliable midrange bet. Both the hot water and air-conditioning were working when we took up residence, and the breakfasts set us up for the day. Plus, it's clean and slightly quieter than most other city-centre options.

INSECURITY IN MOMBASA

Although most of the sporadic attacks linked to the al-Qaeda affiliate al-Shabaab affected sections of Nairobi – the biggest being the one at Westgate Mall in September 2013 – Mombasa and the south coast has borne the brunt when it comes to a drop in tourism arrivals. Following two small-scale bomb blasts that killed four people at a bus station and a hotel in May 2014, several countries including the UK, USA and Australia issued warnings against travelling to Mombasa island and sections of the coast between Mtwapa Creek in the north to Tiwi in the south. Although this area did not include popular Diani Beach or Moi International Airport, British tour operators Thomson and First Choice pulled all guests out of the area as a precaution.

Although tourists are not typically targeted during periods of insecurity along the coast, robberies and violent attacks are more common during such periods, fuelled by anger, fear and the impact on unemployment levels. In the month following the bombings two foreign female tourists and a Ugandan guide were shot dead in separate incidents in the vicinity of Fort Jesus.

Central Mombasa

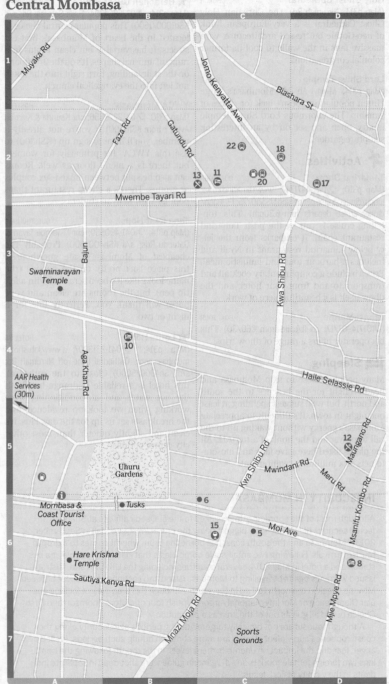

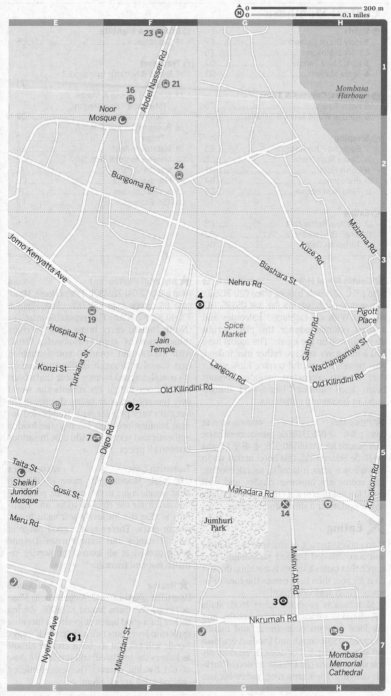

0 200 m
0 0.1 miles

Mombasa Harbour

23

16 · 21

Abdel Nasser Rd

Noor Mosque

24

Bungoma Rd

Mzizima Rd

Jomo Kenyatta Ave

Kuze Rd

Biashara St

Nehru Rd

4

Pigott Place

19

Hospital St

Spice Market

Samburu Rd

Jain Temple

Wachangamwe St

Konzi St

Turkana St

Langoni Rd

Old Kilindini Rd

Old Kilindini Rd

2

Digo Rd

Taita St

Sheikh Jundoni Mosque

Gusii St

Makadara Rd

7

Meru Rd

Kibokoni Rd

14

Jumhuri Park

3

Mwinvi Ab Rd

Nkrumah Rd

1

Nyerere Ave

Milkindani St

9

Mombasa Memorial Cathedral

Central Mombasa

★ Castle Royal Hotel   HISTORIC HOTEL $$
(Map p314; ☑ Nairobi booking office 020-315680; www.sentrim-hotels.net; Moi Ave; s/d US$95/130; ❄ @ 🖙) With old-fashioned balconies and a dated, colonial exterior, this place scrubs up pretty well on the inside. The rooms have had a makeover and are rather nice indeed, plus there's a beautiful terrace looking out over the city. Breakfast includes coconut beans and *mandazi* (semisweet doughnuts), or bacon and croissants.

★ Pride Inn   BUSINESS HOTEL $$
(Map p314; ☑ 041-2317895; www.prideinn.co.ke; Haile Selassie Rd; s/d US$80/105; ❄ @ 🖙) Right on Haile Selassie Rd, this hotel makes up in convenience what it lacks in soundproofing. The rooms are business quality and well cared for, but they're not fancy. A solid, mildly stylish option for a short Mombasa stay.

✗ Eating

If an endless parade of chicken, chips, meat and corn roasted beyond palatability, and starch that tastes like...well, nothing, doesn't do it for you, then here comes the coast. Flavours! Fresh seafood! Spice!

Mombasa is good for street food: stalls sell cassava, samosas, bhajis, kebabs and the local take on pizza (meat and onions wrapped in soft dough and fried). A few dish out stew and ugali. For dessert, vendors ply you with *haluwa* (an Omani version of Turkish delight), fried taro root, sweet baobab seeds and sugared doughnuts.

★ Shehnai Restaurant   INDIAN $
(Map p314; ☑ 041-2224801; Fatemi House, Maungano Rd; mains from KSh500; ◐ noon-2pm & 7.30-10.30pm Tue-Sun) This reputable *mughlai* (North Indian) curry house does delicious things such as *gosht palakwalla* (lamb with masala and spinach) and scrambled eggs tossed with green chillies and cumin. It's complemented by nice decor that's been copied from Indian restaurants the world over (pumped-in sitar music thrown in for free). It's very popular with well-heeled Indian families, probably because the food is authentic and very good. Add 25% in various taxes to all prices.

Tarboush Cafe   INTERNATIONAL $
(Map p314; Makadara Rd; mains KSh150-350) Most people come to this open-air, park-side restaurant for the chicken tikka, and rightfully so. Eat it with lovely soft naan bread, rice or chips. There's also a good range of Swahili staples and some curries. Despite being packed at all hours, the service remains fast and friendly.

★ Rozina   KENYAN $$
(Map p310; ☑ 041-2312642; Africa Hotel, Sir Mbarak Hinawy Rd; mains around KSh800) Rozina makes for a good lunch stop after a morning exploring Fort Jesus (it's a short walk away). Locals will tell you it's been around almost as long as the fort itself, and it retains a dose of old Swahili charm. The ginger-infused seafood grills are excellent.

⭐ **Hunter's Steak House** STEAKHOUSE $$
(Map p310; ☎041-4474759; Mkomani Rd, 'König-sallee', Nyali; mains KSh450-2000; ☺Wed-Mon)
Nyama choma this isn't. Instead you'll find thick sizzling steaks, served with serious comfort food such as garlic mushrooms, crunchy fries and husks of toasted bread. In fact, if you squint a little and stare at the decor you could almost be in the American Midwest. There's a nice range of beers, too.

⭐ **Singh Restaurant** INDIAN $$
(Map p314; ☎0733702145; Mwembe Tayari Rd; mains KSh350-850) Another great Indian restaurant steeped in Mombasa history: the owner first opened the doors in 1962 to serve arriving and departing railway passengers. The decor is plain, but your taste buds won't notice. Even things that don't sound great on paper, such as egg curry, are divine here. We rate the aubergine dishes highly.

🍷 Drinking & Nightlife

⭐ **Jahazi Coffee House** CAFE
(Map p310; ☎0720777313; Ndia Kuu Rd; ☺8am-8pm) With lashings of sexy Mombasa style, this lounge cafe is the perfect spot to chill out in arty surrounds. Did we mention that it has great coffee? The Swahili pot, if you're after something different, turns the grind into a ritual. You won't want to leave.

Casablanca BAR
(Map p314; Mnazi Moja Rd; ☺noon-late) Of all the gin joints, in all the towns...walking into this one isn't the worst thing you could do.

Classy but still cheeky, Casablanca is wildly popular. And yes, it's brimming with ladies of the night, but rumour has it that the late owner treated his resident girls so well, 300 of them turned up at his funeral.

New Florida Nightclub CLUB
(Map p310; Mama Ngina Dr; entry after 7.30pm KSh500; ☺6pm-6am) We know why this place was named after the Disney state. Like a theme park for grown-ups, there's all sorts to get into here: an outdoor pool, a 'crazy' blue bar, fluorescent palm trees and Vegas-style floor shows.

🛍 Shopping

Biashara St, west of its Digo Rd intersection (just north of the spice market), is Kenya's main centre for *kikoi* (brightly coloured woven sarongs for men) and *kangas* (printed wraps worn by women). *Kangas* come as a pair, one for the top half of the body and one for the bottom, and are marked with Swahili proverbs. You may need to bargain, but what you get is generally what you pay for; bank on about KSh500 for a pair of cheap *kangas* or a *kikoi*. *Kofia*, the handmade caps worn by Muslim men, are also crafted here; a really excellent one can run up to KSh2500.

Akamba Handicraft Industry
Cooperative Society HANDICRAFTS
(www.akambahandicraftcoop.com; Port Reitz Rd; ☺8am-5pm Mon-Fri, to noon Sun) This cooperative employs an incredible 10,000 people from the local area. It's also a nonprofit organisation and produces fine woodcarvings.

WORTH A TRIP

LUNATIC LINE: THE MOMBASA–NAIROBI RAILWAY

Few subjects divide our readers' letters more fiercely than the **train** (Map p310; ☎020-3596750, 0722106395, 0733681061; www.kenyatrainbooking.com; Mombasa Railway Station) from Nairobi to Mombasa. Once one of the most famous rail lines in Africa, the train is today, depending on whom you speak to, either a sociable way of avoiding the rutted highway and spotting wildlife from the clackety comfort of a sleeping car, or a ratty, tatty overrated waste of time. The truth lies somewhere in the middle. The train's state could be described as 'faded glory', occasionally bumping up to 'romantically dishevelled', or slipping into 'frustrating mediocrity'. The latter isn't helped by spotty scheduling and lax timetable enforcement. At the time of research, it wasn't uncommon for the Mombasa-Nairobi leg to take up to three days longer than planned. Still, if you're up for an adventure...

Currently the 'iron snake' departs Mombasa train station at 7pm on Tuesday, Thursday and Sunday, arriving in theory in Nairobi the next day somewhere between 9.30am and 1pm. Fares are US$75 for 1st class (two-bed berths) and US$65 for 2nd class (four-bed berths) including bed and breakfast (you get dinner with 1st class) – reserve as far in advance as possible.

Kwa Hola/Magongo matatus run right past the gates from the Kobil petrol station on Jomo Kenyatta Ave. Many coach tours from Mombasa also stop here.

ℹ Information

EMERGENCY

AAR Health Services (☏ 0731191067; www.aarhealth.com; Pereira Bldg, Machakos St, off Moi Ave; ☉ 24hr) Medical clinic.

MEDICAL SERVICES

Aga Khan Hospital (Map p310; ☏ 041-222771; www.agakhanhospitals.org; Vanga Rd)

Mombasa Hospital (Map p310; ☏ 041-2312191; www.mombasahospital.com; off Mama Ngina Dr)

TOURIST INFORMATION

Mombasa & Coast Tourist Office (Map p314; ☏ 041-2228722; Moi Ave; ☉ 8am-4.30pm) Provides information and can organise accommodation, tours, guides and transport.

ℹ Getting There & Away

AIR

Kenya Airways (☏ Mombasa 041-2125251, booking 020-3274747; www.kenya-airways.com; Nyali City Mall) Book online or in person at the ticket office in Nyali City Mall (next to Nakumatt). Nairobi–Mombasa return flights cost around KSh10,000.

Fly540 (☏ Mombasa 041-2319078, booking 0710540540; www.fly540.com; Moi International Airport) Flies between Nairobi and Mombasa at least five times daily (one way from KSh4200), as well as between Mombasa and Zanzibar. Malindi and Lamu flights go through Nairobi.

Air Kenya (☏ Nairobi 020-3916000; www.airkenya.com) Charter company unrelated to Kenya Airways. Flies between Nairobi and Diani Beach most days; from US$118.

BUS & MATATU

Most bus offices are on either Jomo Kenyatta Ave or Abdel Nasser Rd. Services to Malindi and Lamu leave from Abdel Nasser Rd, while buses to destinations in Tanzania leave from the junction of Jomo Kenyatta Ave and Mwembe Tayari Rd.

For buses and matatus to the beaches and towns south of Mombasa, you first need to get off the island via the Likoni ferry. Frequent matatus run from Nyerere Ave to the transport stand by the ferry terminal.

Nairobi

Dozens of daily departures in both directions.

Daytime services take at least six hours, and overnight trips eight to 10 hours, including a meal/smoking break about halfway. Fares vary from KSh500 to KSh3000, with Modern Coast the swishest (and most expensive) of the lot.

Most buses to Nairobi travel via Voi (KSh300 to KSh500), which is also served by frequent matatus from the Kobil petrol station on Jomo Kenyatta Ave (KSh200).

Coast (☏ 041-3433166; www.coastbus.com)
Mash (☏ 041-3432471)
Simba Coaches (Map p314; Abdel Nasser Rd)

DON'T MISS

MWALUGANJE ELEPHANT SANCTUARY

This **sanctuary** (☏ 040-41121; www.kws.org; adult/child US$15/2, vehicles KSh150-500; ☉ 6am-6pm) is a good example of community-based conservation with local people acting as stakeholders in the project. It was opened in October 1995 to create a corridor along an elephant migration route between Shimba Hills and Mwaluganje Forest Reserve, and comprises 2400 hectares of rugged, beautiful country along the valley of the Cha Shimba River.

Other than the 150 or so elephants, the big-ticket wildlife can be a little limited. However, you're likely to have the place to yourself, the scenery is almost a cliché of what East Africa should look like, and there's plenty of little stuff to see. All this makes Mwaluganje more suitable for those who've done a few safaris elsewhere and are after a wilder, more pristine experience. The drier country means that the wildlife in Mwaluganje differs slightly from that of wetter and greener Shimba Hills. This is especially noticeable when it comes to the birds, with many species found here that aren't to be seen anywhere else on the coast.

The main entrance to the sanctuary is about 13km northeast of Shimba Hills National Reserve, on the road to Kinango. A shorter route runs from Kwale to the Golini gate, passing the Mwaluganje ticket office. It's only 5km but the track is 4WD only. The roads inside the park are pretty rough and a 4WD is the way to go.

Heading North

There are numerous daily buses and matatus up the coast to Malindi, leaving from in front of the Noor Mosque on Abdel Nasser Rd. Buses take up to three hours (around KSh500), matatus about two hours (KSh350 rising to KSh600 during holidays and very busy periods).

Tawakal, Simba, Mombasa Raha and TSS Express have buses to Lamu, most leaving at around 7am (arrive 30 minutes early) from their offices on Abdel Nasser Rd. Buses take around seven hours to reach the Lamu ferry at Mokoke (KSh600 to KSh800) and travel via Malindi.

Heading South

Regular buses and matatus leave from the Likoni ferry terminal and travel along the southern coast.

For Tanzania, Simba and a handful of other companies have daily departures to Dar es Salaam (KSh1200 to KSh1600, eight hours) via Tanga from their offices on Jomo Kenyatta Ave, near the junction with Mwembe Tayari Rd. Dubious-looking buses to Moshi and Arusha leave from in front of the Mwembe Tayari Health Centre in the morning or evening.

ⓘ Getting Around

TO/FROM THE AIRPORT

There is currently no public transport to or from the airport. The taxi fare to central Mombasa is around KSh1200.

BOAT

The two Likoni ferries connect Mombasa island with the southern mainland. There's a crossing roughly every 20 minutes between 5am and 12.30am, less frequently outside these times. It's free for pedestrians, KSh75 per small car and KSh165 for a safari jeep. To get to the jetty from the centre of town, take a Likoni matatu from Digo Rd.

MATATU, TAXI & TUK-TUK

Matatus charge between KSh30 and KSh50 for short trips. Mombasa taxis are as expensive as those in Nairobi, and harder to find; a good place to look is in front of Express Travel on Nkrumah Rd. Assume it'll cost KSh250 to KSh400 from the train station to the city centre. There are also plenty of three-wheeled tuk-tuks about, which run to about KSh50 to KSh200 for a bit of open-air transit.

Shimba Hills National Reserve

Cool and grassy, this 320-sq-km **national reserve** (☏0704467855; www.kws.org; adult/child US$20/10; ⏱6am-6pm) makes an easy day trip from Diani Beach. Its lush hills are

ⓘ SHIMBA HILLS NATIONAL RESERVE

Why Go
It's an easy day trip from the coast, has good elephant-spotting, and is the only Kenyan home of the sable antelope.

When to Go
Year-round, but the dry season from November to March is best.

Practicalities
Diani Beach, 45 minutes away, is a popular base; numerous safari companies and hotels there offer safaris to Shimba Hills.

Budget Tips
Some of the package deals offered by Diani Beach hotels (starting at US$50 per person) represent the best value for a trip to Shimba Hills. If you prefer to go your own way, matatus run from the Likoni ferry to the town of Kwale, 3km from the gate of the reserve. From there you can walk to the main gate or board a matatu (KSh70). You may be able to link up with other travellers at the gate, but be prepared to wait around.

home to sable antelope, elephants, warthogs, baboons, buffaloes and masai giraffes, as well as 300 species of butterfly. The sable antelope have made a stunning recovery here after their numbers dropped to less than 120 in 1970.

In 2005, the elephant population reached an amazing 600 – far too many for this tiny space. Instead of culling the herds, Kenya Wildlife Service (KWS) organised an unprecedented US$3.2 million translocation operation to reduce the pressure on the habitat, capturing no fewer than 400 elephants and moving them to Tsavo East National Park.

There are over 150km of 4WD tracks that criss-cross the reserve.

⌂ Sleeping

There are four **public campsites** (per person US$15) within the reserve; included one located on the way to Sheldrick Falls. Most of the camps are large, with a capacity for around 50 tents, and all are basic with limited facilities. KWS also has two *bandas* available (US$25 per person), each fitted with twin beds.

Shimba Lodge LODGE $$
(📞 0722200952; www.aberdaresafarihotels.com; Kinango Rd; r from US$140) Staying here is quite an experience, although not one as luxurious as the price might suggest. The rooms are simple but clean and come with character; the highlight is the wildlife seen from the canopy tree platform, which looks out over a forest clearing. The restaurant is open until midnight and serves simple, hearty meals.

❶ Getting There & Away

You'll need a 4WD to enter the reserve. From Likoni, small lorry-buses to Kwale pass the main gate (KSh80).

Tiwi Beach

More sleepy, shaded and secluded than Diani Beach, Tiwi makes a lovely quiet, cottage-style escape by the ocean. The sand isn't that same peroxide shade, but the pretty beach is studded with skinny palms, and there are fewer hassles. Tiwi also has a beautiful coral reef, part of which teems with starfish of all shapes and colours. A stable, pool-like area between the shore and the coral is great for swimming.

⛏ Sleeping & Eating

Twiga Lodge HOTEL $
(📞 0721577614; twigakenya@gmail.com; camping KSh500, s/d KSh1500/2500, new wing s/d KSh3000/4800) Overlanders' favourite Twiga is great fun when there's a crowd staying, with the palpable sense of isolation alleviated by the sheer tropical exuberance of the place. The older rooms are set off from the beach – opt for one of the nicer, newer rooms if you can. The on-site restaurant is OK, but having a drink under thatch while stars spill over the sea is as perfect as moments come.

DON'T MISS

BEST BEACHES

Beaches, beaches everywhere, but which is the best? We think you'll never want to stop building sandcastles on the following beaches:

Tiwi Beach Sunny, sandy and empty.

Diani Beach Despite the tourist resorts and the crowds, Diani Beach is stunning.

Takaungu The very definition of a perfect beach.

⭐ **Sand Island Beach Cottages** COTTAGES $$
(📞 0722395005; www.sandislandbeach.com; cottages US$120-200) A favourite among worn-out Nairobians, Sand Island occupies a peaceful, blissful spot swathed in green and gold. Accommodation is in homely cottages nestled on the edge of the sand; each has its own style. The newest, Pweza cottage, features furniture made from salvaged Swahili doors. The cottages are self-catering, but you can hire your own cook for KSh1000 per day.

❶ Getting There & Away

To get to Tiwi, turn left off the main highway (A14) about 18km south of Mombasa (or right if you're coming from Diani), and follow the track until it terminates in a north–south T-junction.

Buses and matatus on the Likoni–Ukunda road can drop you at the start of either track down to Tiwi (KSh50). Although it's only 3.5km to the beach, both access roads are notorious for muggings so take a taxi or hang around for a lift.

Diani Beach

With a flawless stretch of white sand beach hugged by lush forest and kissed by surfable waves, it's no wonder Diani Beach is so popular. This resort town scores points with a diverse crowd: party people, families, honeymooners, backpackers and water sports enthusiasts.

But if that sounds like your typical resort town, think again. Diani has some of the best accommodation in Kenya, from budget tree houses to funky kitesurf lodges and intimate honeymoon spots. Most places are spread out along the beach road, hidden behind a swathe of forest.

When lazing in a hammock gets tiring, visit the coral mosques with archways that overlook the open ocean, venture into the sacred forests where guides hug trees that speak in their ancestors' voices, or choose to take in the monkey sanctuary – all are good ways of experiencing more of the coast than the considerable charms of sun and sand.

◉ Sights

Colobus Conservation Centre WILDLIFE RESERVE
(📞 0711479453; www.colobusconservation.org; Diani Beach Rd; tours adult/child KSh750/250;

IT'S A SAILOR'S LIFE

The salty breeze and the high seas, it's a sailor's life for you and me. There's no more romantic a way to explore the Kenyan coast than sailing by dhow (a traditional sailing boat that has been used here for centuries) past slivers of sand, offshore coral islands and reefs bubbling with colourful fish. Several companies offer dhow trips down the coast to Funzi and Wasini Islands. Pilli Pipa is probably the best known, but there are several other operators in Diani.

The **East African Whale Shark Trust** (☎0720293156; www.giantsharks.org; Aqualand) is an excellent conservation body monitoring populations of the world's largest fish – the harmless, plankton-feeding whale shark. In February and March (the busiest time for whale sharks) it occasionally opens survey and shark-tagging expeditions to paying guests. Trip costs vary depending on how much sponsorship money has been raised but averages US$150 per person, with a minimum of six people needed for a trip. Its offices are located in the Aqualand centre, about 4km south of Diani.

⊘8am-5pm Mon-Sat) Notice the monkeys clambering on rope ladders over the road? The ladders are the work of the Colobus Conservation Centre, which aims to protect the Angolan black-and-white colobus monkey, a once-common species now restricted to a few isolated pockets of forest south of Mombasa. It runs excellent tours of its headquarters, where you'll likely get to see a few orphaned or injured colobus and other monkeys undergoing the process of rehabilitation to the wild.

Kongo Mosque   MOSQUE

At the far northern end of the beach road (turn right at the three-way intersection where the sealed road ends) is the 16th-century Kongo Mosque – Diani's last surviving relic of the ancient Swahili civilisations that once controlled the coast, and one of a tiny handful of coral mosques still in use in Kenya.

🏃 Activities

★Pilli Pipa   WATER SPORTS

(☎0722205120, 0724442555; www.pillipipa.com; Colliers Centre, Diani Beach Rd; from KSh7500) The most reputable dive school in Diani, Pilli Pipa also offers dhow safaris, dolphin-spotting trips, whale watching, night dives and snorkelling trips to Wasini island.

Diani Marine   DIVING

(☎0707629061; www.dianimarine.com; Diani Marine Village) This highly regarded, German-run centre provides its own accommodation. Open-water diving courses cost €495, with single dives from €90.

Chui Adventure Centre   WATER SPORTS

(☎0708358095; www.chuiadventurecentre.com; Leopard Beach Resort & Spa) A reputable water sports outfit, also offering mountain biking, kitesurfing and diving or snorkelling trips to Wasini island.

Whaleshark Adventures   DIVING

(☎0726775047; Diani Beach Rd; dive courses from €399) The most budget friendly of all the dive outfits, this one specialises in viewing whale sharks housed inside its enormous seaquarium between Diani and Mombasa. The creatures are released every six months.

★H₂O Extreme   KITESURFING

(☎0721495876; www.h2o-extreme.com) The best-regarded kitesurfing outfit in Diani offers half-day beginner courses for €100. It has locations at Sands at Nomad, Kenyaways Kite Village and Forty Thieves Beach Bar.

🛏 Sleeping

Note that many of these places close for renovation between May and June, and most increase rates during the Christmas holidays up to mid-January.

★South Coast Backpackers BACKPACKERS $

(☎0715614038; www.dianibackpackers.com; off Diani Beach Rd; camping KSh600, dm KSh1200, s/d KSh2600/3600; 🅿🛜🏊) More stylish and security conscious than the average backpackers, South Coast has dorms and privates in a lovely house. Come to party at the 24-hour bar and pool, chill out in the lush garden, or catch up on sleep in the baobab dorm, where beds wrap around the trunk of a tree. There's a communal kitchen, great daily menu and lockers. Turn right after KFI supermarket.

Stilts Eco-Lodge   LODGE $

(☎0722523278; www.stiltsdianibeach.com; Diani Beach Rd; s/d KSh1800/2400; 🅿🛜) Tree-house heaven. Stilts has a handful of simple wooden tree houses, each in its own private cove in a swathe of coastal forest. A stilted lounge offers sofas, wi-fi, food and drinks, plus visits from the resident bush babies. Popular with backpackers and an eco-conscious crowd.

★ **Kenyaways Kite Village** BOUTIQUE HOTEL **$$**
(☎ calls 8am-4.30pm only 0728886821; www.thekenyaway.com; Diani Beach Rd; s/d US$64/151; 🛜🖥 🌿) This small, stylish kitesurfing lodge is our favourite place to stay in Diani. Rooms are simple but lovely, with driftwood bed frames, whitewashed walls and a sea breeze. Downstairs, there's an atmospheric bar/restaurant that attracts surfers, foodies and a chilled-out crowd. Throw in free wi-fi, cushion-strewn couches and lots of local info, and everyone's happy.

Flamboyant BOUTIQUE HOTEL **$$**
(☎ 0720843585, 0733411110; www.flamboyant.co; Diani Beach Rd; r from US$85; ❄@🛜🖥) This intimate boutique hotel has breathtaking beach views, subtly decorated rooms with some of the nicest bathrooms this side of the Indian Ocean and a fantastic pool complex.

★ **Water Lovers** HOTEL **$$$**
(☎ 0735790535; www.waterlovers.it; Diani Beach Rd; r €250-569; 🅿🛜🖥) Beautiful, peaceful and intimate, Water Lovers has eight rooms and one villa, all designed with aesthetics, sustainability and love in mind. The furniture is a mix of Swahili wood and Italian pottery, and the wonderful staff will cater for every need. As you might expect from Italian owners, there's a great private restaurant serving organic fare and homemade gelato.

✗ Eating

Rongai KENYAN **$**
(Palm Ave, Ukunda; mains KSh200; ☺ lunch & dinner) This rowdy joint is a popular place for *nyama choma* – if you've been missing your roast meat and boiled maize, Rongai's here for you.

Coast Dishes KENYAN **$**
(Palm Ave, Ukunda; mains KSh300; ☺ lunch & dinner) Want to give the overpriced tourist restaurants a miss? Want to eat where the locals eat? Coast Dishes ticks both of these boxes and, if you're sensible, you'll opt for a steaming great bowl of biryani, the house special.

Tiwi & Diani Beaches

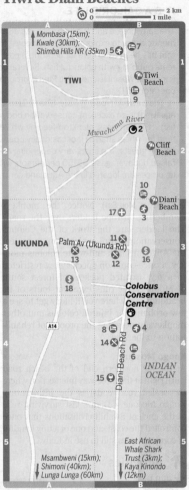

★ **Madafoos** KENYAN **$$**
(☎ 0714632801; www.thekenyaway.com; Diani Beach Rd) Fresh and funky, Madafoos sits right on the beach, in the same grounds as Kenyaways. Lounge on the sofas and order a plate of feta-coriander samosas, a chocolatey dessert, or a bowl of steaming pumpkin soup to replenish after a day in the ocean. Don't miss the cocktails, or the chance to ask owner Bruce how he came up with the name.

★ **Aniello's** ITALIAN **$$**
(☎ 0733740408; Colliers Centre; mains KSh400-1000; ☺ lunch & dinner; 🅿) Nurse a glass of red

Tiwi & Diani Beaches

and peruse the long list of good pizzas and pastas at this thoroughly authentic Italian restaurant. As you eat, the ageing patron will do the rounds, as cries of *'buonissimo'* erupt from nearby tables. It is indeed.

★**Sails** SEAFOOD $$$
(✆0717010670; www.villasdiani.com; Almanara Luxury Villas Resort, Diani Beach Rd; mains KSh850-3800; 🅿🛜🏊) By far the most stylish place to eat in Diani, Sails is gorgeous: a canopy of billowing white canvas separates the restaurant from the stars, while waiters serve up fine food, including fresh salads and seafood. After dark, fairy lights twinkle and the style set emerges. We've only ever heard good things.

🍸 Drinking & Nightlife

Be aware that there are many prostitutes and gigolos in Diani's bars.

Forty Thieves Beach Bar BAR
(✆0712294873; Diani Beach Rd; 🛜) Of all the phrases you'll hear in Diani, 'Meet you at Forty's?' is probably the most common, and the most welcome. A legendary boozer, it has movie nights, a pool table, live bands, there's a pub quiz at least once a week and it's open until the last guest leaves. It's a popular place to eat as well, dishing out comfort food (meals KSh700 to KSh1500) such as burgers and scampi. The Sunday roast is a big hit.

Shakatak CLUB
(Diani Beach Rd) The only full-on nightclub in Diani not attached to a hotel is Shakatak. It's quite hilariously seedy, but can be fun once

you know what to expect. Like most big Kenyan clubs, food is served at all hours.

ℹ Information

DANGERS & ANNOYANCES
Take taxis at night and try not to be on the beach by yourself after dark. Souvenir sellers are an everyday nuisance, sex tourism is pretty evident and beach boys are a hassle; you will hear a lot of, 'Hey, one love one love' Rasta-speak spouted by guys trying to sell you drugs or scam you into supporting fake charities for 'local schools'. Yes, very 'one love'.

EMERGENCY
Diani Beach Hospital (✆040-3300150, 0722569261; www.dianibeachhospital.com; Diani Beach Rd; ⊙24hr)

ℹ Getting There & Around

BUS & MATATU
Numerous matatus run south from the Likoni ferry in Mombasa directly to Ukunda (KSh100, 30 minutes), the junction for Diani, and onwards to Msambweni and Lunga Lunga. From the Diani junction in Ukunda, matatus run down to the beach all day for KSh50; check before boarding to see if it's a Reef service (heading north along the strip, then south) or a Neptune one (south beach only).

TAXI
Taxis hang around Ukunda junction and all the main shopping centres; most hotels and restaurants will also have a couple waiting at night. Fares should be between KSh150 and KSh800, depending on the distance. From Diani to Mombasa via the Likoni ferry, bank on one to two hours driving time, depending on traffic.

DON'T MISS

ENTERING THE SACRED FOREST

The *kaya* (sacred forests) of the Mijikenda are typically closed to visitors, with just a handful of exceptions: **Kaya Kinondo** (www.kaya-kinondo-kenya.com; admission KSh1500), near Diani Beach, is among them.

Visiting this small but sacred grove includes elements of nature walk, historical journey and cultural experience.

Before entering the Kaya Kinondo you have to remove headwear, promise not to kiss anyone inside the grove, wrap a black *kaniki* (sarong) around your waist and go with a guide; ours was Binti, who explained the significance of some of the 187 plant species inside.

They include the 'pimple tree', a known cure for acne, a palm believed to be 1050 years old, snatches of coral and the rather self-explanatory 'viagra tree'. Enormous liana swings (go on, try it) and strangling fig trees abound.

The Mijikenda (Nine Homesteads) are actually nine subtribes united, to a degree, by culture, history and language. Yet each of the tribes – Chonyi, Digo, Duruma, Giriama, Jibana, Kambe, Kauma, Rabai and Ribe – remains distinct and speaks its own dialect of the Mijikenda language. Still, there is a binding similarity between the Nine Homesteads, and between the modern Mijikenda and their ancestors: their shared veneration of the *kaya*.

This historical connection becomes concrete when you enter the woods and realise – and there's no other word that fits here – they simply feel *old*.

Many trees are 600 years old, which corresponds to the arrival of the first Mijikenda from Singwaya, their semi-legendary homeland in southern Somalia. Cutting vegetation within the *kaya* is strictly prohibited, to the degree that visitors may not even take a stray twig or leaf from the forest.

The preserved forests do not just facilitate dialogue with the ancestors; they provide a direct link to ecosystems that have been clear-felled out of existence elsewhere. A single *kaya* like Kinondo contains five possible endemic species within its 30 hectares. That's five endemic species – ie trees that only grow here – and 140 tree species classified as 'rare' within the space of a suburban residential block.

The main purpose of the *kaya* was to house the villages of the Mijikenda, which were located in a large central clearing. Entering the centre of a *kaya* required ritual knowledge to proceed through concentric circles of sacredness surrounding the node of the village; sacred talismans and spells were supposed to cause hallucinations that disoriented enemies who attacked the forest.

The *kaya* were largely abandoned in the 1940s, and conservative strains of Islam and Christianity have denigrated their value to the Mijikenda, but World Heritage status and a resurgence of interest in the forests will hopefully preserve them for future visitors. The *kaya* have lasted 600 years; with luck, the wind will speak through their branches for much longer.

Shimoni & Wasini Island

The final pearls in the tropical beach necklace that stretches south of Mombasa are the mainland village of Shimoni and the idyllic island of Wasini, located about 76km south of Likoni.

Wasini in particular is ripe with the ingredients required for a perfect backpacker beachside hideaway; it has that sit-under-a-mango-tree-and-do-nothing-all-day vibe, a coastline licked with pockets of white sand and the most gorgeous snorkelling reef on the coast. The island is a slowly decaying delight of coral houses and sticky alleyways.

There are no roads or running water, and the only electricity comes from generators. Long ago Lamu and Zanzibar must have felt a little like this.

Sights

Besides Wasini-based operators, Pilli Pipa (p321) and Chui Adventure Centre (p321) in Diani Beach also operate snorkelling and diving tours to Kisite Marine National Park.

Slave Caves   HISTORIC SITE
(admission KSh400; ⊙8.30-10.30am & 1.30-6pm) These caves, where slaves were supposedly kept before being loaded onto boats, are

the main attraction in Shimoni. A custodian takes you around the dank caverns to illustrate this little-discussed part of East African history. Actual evidence that slaves were kept here is a little thin, but as piles of empty votive rose water bottles indicate, the site definitely has significance for believing locals.

Kisite Marine National Park   PARK

(www.kws.org; adult/child US$20/10) Off the south coast of Wasini, this gorgeous marine park, which also incorporates the Mpunguti Marine National Reserve and the two tiny Penguti islands, is one of the best in Kenya. The park covers 28 sq km of pristine coral reefs and offers colourful diving and snorkelling. You have a reasonable chance of seeing dolphins and sea turtles. You can organise your own boat trip – the going rate is between KSh2000 and KSh3000 per person for a group.

Mkwiro Village   VILLAGE

Mkwiro is a small village on the unvisited eastern end of Wasini Island. There are few facilities here and there's not a lot to do, but the gorgeous hour-long walk from Wasini village, through woodlands, past tiny hamlets and along the edge of mangrove forests, is more than reason enough to visit. There are some wonderful, calm swimming spots around the village. Local children are sure to take you by the hand and show you the best swimming places.

Activities

Shimoni Reef   FISHING

(725643733; www.shimonireeflodge.com; trips per day from US$600) The Pemba Channel is famous for deep-sea fishing, and Shimoni Reef can arrange a variety of offshore fishing trips.

★ Charlie Claw's   WATER SPORTS

(0722205155/6; www.wasini.com) This highly regarded outfit, based on Wasini, offers diving and snorkelling trips to Kisite, as well as to Mako Koko reef a few kilometres west. Dhow sunset cruises are also on offer. Some of the day excursions include lunch at its eponymous restaurant on Wasini island.

Paradise Divers   WATER SPORTS

(0718778372; www.paradisediver.net) On the eastern side of Wasini, this dive outfit offers diving and snorkelling trips to the marine park, starting at €45 per day, as well as full PADI certification courses. It also has a small lodge at which you can stay.

Sleeping & Eating

Mpunguti Lodge   HOTEL $

(0722566623, 0710562494; r from KSh2500) The rooms here, which overlook the delicious turquoise ocean, are uncomplicated, with mosquito nets and small verandahs. Running water is collected in barrels. The food is excellent (ask for the seagrass starter, possibly the nicest thing we ate on the Kenyan coast) and it's a common lunch stop for boat trips. It's on the edge of Wasini village.

★ Paradise Lodge   LODGE $$

(0718778372; www.paradisediver.net; per person €44-85) This friendly little dive lodge on the eastern side of Wasini has a range of simple but colourful rooms, plus two furnished safari tents. Diving trips can also be arranged. You can sleep here independently, or as part of a diving tour.

Shimoni Reef Lodge   LODGE $$$

(0725643733; www.shimonireeflodge.com; s/d US$180/300; ☀) This waterfront fishing camp is a lovely place to while away a few days. It's also a good base for diving. The rooms, although spacious and colourful, aren't luxurious – they're best enjoyed after a day on the ocean wave.

Getting There & Around

Although most people come to Wasini on organised tours, you can cross the ocean by motorboat (from KSh2000 per passenger) or by simple wooden vessel with the islanders (KSh300). Head to Shimoni pier to assess your options.

There are matatus every hour or so between Likoni and Shimoni (KSh300, 1½ hours) until about 6pm. Matatus heading to the Tanzanian border from Ukunda (for Diani Beach) can also drop you at Shimoni.

LAMU & THE NORTH COAST

Kilifi

The town formerly known as 'God's waiting room' is now a dazzling highlight of any trip to the Kenyan coast. A passionate group of Kenyans and expats have transformed Kilifi from a sweet but soporific backwater into a stunning place renowned for its eco-projects and clean, green, joyful living.

Gorgeous beach houses stand atop the creek, yachts dance in the bay and warm

KILIFI'S BEST BEACHES

Kilifi Creek Beach is best reached by boat. If you're staying at Distant Relatives, trips leave regularly. Remote and magic, this is a lovely spot for a bit of wild camping.

Bofa Beach is all white sand, swaying palms and soft, pure water. The stuff that fantasies are made of.

Kitangani Beach was all but abandoned four years ago, when the owner of a landmark Italian restaurant went out for swim and never came back. Now its golden sands are popular for barbecues and as a training ground for a local acrobatic troupe. Beware of the tides.

waves wash fantasy beaches buttered with lashings of soft white sand. You'll find orange groves and hermit crabs, fresh oysters and pizza ovens, permaculture projects and sailing schools, beach barbecues and night swimming. And you might even spot a whale shark migration from windy Vuma Cliffs.

◉ Sights

Kilifi Creek   BEACH
This might be the only place where we wouldn't mind being up the creek without a paddle. It's just gorgeous, from the cliffs jutting up out of the water, to the hermit crabs scooting along the shoreline. Boat hire can easily be arranged, and there are lots of lovely spots for wild, romantic camping and impromptu campfires.

Mnarani   RUINS
(adult/child KSh500/250; ⊘ 7am-6pm) The partly excavated, atmospheric and deliciously peaceful ruins of the Swahili city of Mnarani are high on a bluff just west of the old ferry landing stage on the southern bank of Kilifi Creek. The site was occupied from the end of the 14th century to around the first half of the 17th century, when it was abandoned following sieges by Galla tribespeople from Somalia and the failure of the water supply.

Buccaneer Diving   DIVING
(☑ 0716430725; www.buccaneerdiving.com) The lovely Tim runs this excellent diving centre over at Mnarani Club, covering everything from the basics to instructor-level dives and wreck exploration. PADI open-water from US$550.

Three Degrees South   SAILING
(☑ 0714783915, 0714757763; www.3degreessouth. co.ke) This British Royal Yachting Association–affiliated sailing school is one of the best places to learn on the East African coast. Expect expert tuition for beginners and advanced sailors, serious attention to safety and a vast expanse of (beautiful) empty space.

🛏 Sleeping & Eating

★ Distant Relatives   LODGE, BACKPACKERS $
(☑ 0787535145, 0770885164; www.kilifiback packers.com; dm/r/bandas KSh1000/3000/4000, safari tents KSh1500; P 🛜 🐾 🏊) 🌿 If you need a reason to come to Kilifi, this is it. Both an ecolodge and a backpackers, this place gets it so right. The fantastic owners, staff and guests have created a living, breathing space that's a haven for everyone. Expect good cheer, good people and good conscience. We love the pizza oven and the amazing bamboo showers.

Takashack   COTTAGES $
(bruceryrie@yahoo.com; Takaungu beach; P) 🌿 On gorgeous Takaungu beach and off the electricity grid, this eclectic, relaxed house makes a great budget escape when split among friends. Catch the sunrise from the top floor, buy fresh fish every morning, jump in the ocean and, after dark, watch the house light up from the glow of amber hurricane lanterns. Email bookings only.

★ The Boatyard   SEAFOOD $$
(☑ 0721590502; mains from KSh600; ⊘ 7am-7pm) Jetties and boats, fresh crab and fries, old ropes and salty air...there's nothing better than a long, lazy meal at the Boatyard, especially when it involves fresh oysters (oyster night is Saturday). A boatman can pick you up from the other side of the creek for KSh300, or it's a 20-minute motorbike ride along tracks fringed by forest.

Distant Relatives Restaurant   INTERNATIONAL $$
(☑ 0787535145, 0770885164; www.kilifiback packers.com; mains KSh500-900) Even if you're not staying here, join your distant relatives for dinner at this great, laid-back eatery atop Kilifi Creek. We rate the bacon-and-avo sandwiches, the beetroot-and-hummus veggie bowls and the steaks. Friday is pizza night (there's a pizza oven) and Tuesday is burger night. The breakfast smoothies are the best we tried on the coast.

❶ Getting There & Away

All buses and matatus travelling between Mombasa (matatu KSh100 to KSh130, bus KSh100, up to 1½ hours) and Malindi (matatu/bus KSh150/100, 1¼ hours) stop at Kilifi.

Watamu

Like Malindi to its north, Watamu is something of a Janus; it has two faces, both completely different. The prettiest looks out over the ocean and is plastered with soft white sand and blessed by a soft breeze. The other looks out onto the main road, and is strewn with litter, stones, stores and tourist haunts. Whichever you choose, Watamu does make a good base for explorations between Malindi and Kilifi.

◉ Sights & Activities

Watamu Marine National Park   PARK
(adult/child US$15/10) The southern part of Malindi Marine National Reserve, this park includes some magnificent coral reefs, abundant fish life and sea turtles. To get here to snorkel and dive, you'll need a boat, which is easy enough to hire at the KWS office, where you pay the park fees, at the end of the coast road. Boat operators ask anywhere from KSh2500 to KSh4000 for two people for two hours; it's all negotiable.

Bio-Ken Snake Farm & Laboratory   ZOO
(☑ 042-2332303; www.bio-ken.com; adult/child KSh750/250; ◷ 10am-noon & 2-5pm) Don't be fooled by the wooden turquoise cages; this humble-looking place is one of the world's most renowned snake research centres. It specialises in antivenin research, and also acts as an emergency service for snake-bite victims throughout the region. Passionate guides lead excellent 45-minute tours (included in the price); they're highly recommended if you're heading into the bush and want to identify the most deadly serpents. Pricey snake safaris can also be organised.

Watamu Turtle Watch   WILDLIFE RESERVE
(www.watamuturtles.com; ◷ 2.30-4pm Mon, 9.30am-noon & 2.30-4pm Tue-Fri, 9.30am-noon Sat) ❂ All credit to the good guys: Watamu Turtle Watch provides a service protecting the marine turtles that come here to lay eggs on the beach. You can get up close and personal with various cutesy turtles at the trust's rehabilitation centre.

🛏 Sleeping

★ Mwamba Field Study Centre   GUESTHOUSE $
(☑ 042-2332023, Nairobi 020-2335865; www.arocha.org; Watamu Beach; r full board from US$25) ❂ This lovely guesthouse and eco-study centre has had a recent makeover. The rooms are bright and serene, with nice touches such as fresh flowers. Run by a Christian conservation society, there are plenty of opportunities to learn and volunteer. And it's only 50m from the beach; you'll hear the waves crashing as you drift off to sleep.

Turtle Bay Beach Club   RESORT $$$
(☑ 042-2332003, 042-2332226; www.turtle baykenya.com; d from KSh18,000; ❋@❋) ❂ With a silver ecotourism rating, this is easily one of Watamu's best top-end resorts. The hotel uses managed tree cover to reduce its environmental imprint, runs enough ecotourism ventures to fill a book (including birdwatching safaris and turtle protection programmes) and contributes to local charities.

🍴 Eating

Bistro Coffee Shop   CAFE $
(cakes from KSh150; ◷ 8am-5pm) Opening onto a little garden area (and also a car park), this pretty coffee shop has freshly baked cakes, gooey brownies, pastries and quiches, plus decent coffee.

★ Ocean Sports Restaurant   INTERNATIONAL $$
(☑ 0734195227; Ocean Sports Hotel; mains from KSh750; ℗ 🛜) This popular place is spread along a breeze-blown terrace and has some plusher seating inside. Expect sandwiches, burgers, great salads and finer dining such as seared tuna and other seafood creations. It's atmospheric at night, when the ocean rock formations glow under the moon. That's also when the music gets louder and the party starts.

❶ Getting There & Around

Watamu is about an hour's drive north of Kilifi and about 40 minutes' drive south of Malindi. Matatus run regularly between the three destinations. Heading north they depart from Watamu village; southbound vans leave from Gede ruins. Matatus to Malindi charge KSh100. Matatus to Kilifi charge KSh200.

DON'T MISS

MIDA CREEK

Mida Creek is a quiet and gentle place hugged by silver-tinged mudflats flowing with ghost crabs and long tides. It's a place where the creeping marriage of land and water is epitomised by a mangrove forest and the salty, fresh scent of wind over an estuary. Mida Creek saves its real appeal for evening, when the stars simply rain down on you.

The **Mida Creek Boardwalk** (adult/child KSh250/150, guides KSh500) takes you into the heart of the mangroves, while the **Mida Eco-Camp** (☑ 0729213042; www.midaecocamp. com; camping KSh500, huts per person KSh1400) is an excellent place to stay.

Any bus travelling between Mombasa and Malindi can drop you on the main road near Mida Creek from where it's a pleasant, leafy 20-minute walk to the camp.

Arabuko Sokoke Forest Reserve

This 420 sq-km tract of natural forest – the largest indigenous coastal forest remaining in East Africa – is most famous as the home of the golden-rumped elephant shrew. Yes, you read that right; it's a guinea-pig sized rodent with a long furry trunk and a monogamous streak, and the **Arabuko Sokoke Forest Reserve** (adult/child US$20/10; ⊘ 6am-6pm) is its only natural habitat.

Besides this marvellous creature, the forest is home to about 240 bird species, including the Amani sunbird, the Clarke's weaver and the Sokoko scoops owl – the smallest owl in Africa. More than 33 species of snake slither through the undergrowth and shy waterbucks hide behind mahogany trees.

From the visitors centre, nature trails and 4WD paths cut through the forest. There are more bird trails at Whistling Duck Pools, Kararacha Pools and Spinetail Way, located 16km further south. It's possible to spend the night in the forest, setting up camp on a tall tree platform (USD$10) with a spectacular view of the species below.

The forest is just off the main Malindi–Mombasa road. The main gate to the forest and visitors centre is about 1.5km west of the turn-off to Gede and Watamu, while the

Mida entrance is about 3km further south. All buses and matatus between Mombasa and Malindi can drop you at either entrance. From Watamu, matatus to Malindi can drop you at the main junction.

Arabuko Sokoke Visitor Centre   TOURIST INFORMATION
(www.kws.org; Malindi Rd; ⊘ 8am-4pm) The Arabuko Sokoke Visitor Centre is small but helpful; it's at Gede Forest Station, with displays on the various species found here. Three-hour guided tours leave from here (Ksh1500). Night walks can also be arranged in advance.

Gede Ruins

If you thought Kenya was all about nature, you're missing an important component of her charm: lost cities. The remains of medieval Swahili towns dot the coast, with perhaps the most impressive of the bunch being the **Gede Ruins** (adult/child KSh500/250; ⊘ 7am-6pm).

This series of coral palaces, mosques and townhouses lies quietly in the jungle's green grip, but excavation has unearthed many structures. Within Gede archaeologists found evidence of the modern nature of Swahili society: silver necklaces with Maria Teresa coins (from Europe) and Arabic calligraphy (from the Middle East), vermicelli makers from Asia, Persian sabres, Arab coffeepots, Indian lamps, Egyptian or Syrian cobalt glass, Spanish scissors and Ming porcelain.

Gede, which reached its peak in the 15th century, was inexplicably abandoned in the 17th or 18th century. Some theories point to disease and famine; others blame guerrilla attacks by Somalian Gallas and cannibalistic Zimba from near Malawi, or punitive expeditions from Mombasa. Or Gede ran out of water – at some stage the water table here dropped rapidly and the 40m wells dried up.

❶ Getting There & Away

The ruins lie off the main highway on the access road to Watamu. The easiest way here is via any matatu plying the main highway between Mombasa and Malindi. Get off at the village of Gede and follow the well-signposted dirt road from there – it's about a 10-minute walk. Gede is 16km southwest of Malindi or 105km northeast of Mombasa. Most people visit on a day trip from Malindi.

Malindi

With an Italian-sounding name, some of the best pizza in all of Africa and, well, plenty of Italian tourists, it would be easy to dismiss Malindi as just another European holiday resort. Until, that is, you wander through the alleys of the atmospheric old town, stop for fresh oysters beside the Indian Ocean and pause for Swahili cakes on Jamhuri St. Malindi, it turns out, is quite the charmer.

◉ Sights & Activities

National Museums of Kenya has smartly grouped the major cultural sites of Malindi under the one general ticket of the **Malindi Historic Circuit** (adult/child KSh500/250; ⊘8am-6pm).

House of Columns   HISTORIC BUILDING
(Mama Ngina Rd) The building itself is a good example of traditional Swahili architecture and contains great exhibits of all sorts of archaeological finds dug up around the coast.

Vasco da Gama Pillar   LANDMARK
More impressive for what it represents (the genesis of the Age of Exploration) than the edifice itself. Erected by da Gama as a navigational aid in 1498, the coral column is topped by a cross made of Lisbon stone, which almost certainly dates from the explorer's time.

There are good views from here down the coast and out over the ocean. To get here, turn off Mama Ngina Rd, by Scorpio Villas.

Portuguese Church   CHURCH
(Mama Ngina Rd) This church gets its name because Vasco da Gama is reputed to have erected it, and two of his crew are supposedly buried here. It's certainly true that St Francis Xavier visited on his way to India.

Malindi Marine National Park   PARK
(adult/child US$20/15, boats KSh3000; ⊘6am-6pm) The oldest marine park in Kenya covers 213 sq km of powder-blue fish, organ-pipe coral, green sea-turtles and beds of Thalassia seagrass. If you're extremely lucky, you may spot mako and whale sharks. Unfortunately, these reefs have suffered (and continue to suffer) extensive damage, evidenced by the piles of seashells on sale in Malindi. Note that monsoon-generated waves can reduce visibility from June to September.

🛏 Sleeping

Note that most of the top-end places close or scale down operations between April and June or July.

Dagama's Inn   INN $
(☑0701864446, 0722357591; Mama Ngina Rd; s/d without breakfast KSh1000/1200) This friendly little place is a real seaside travellers' inn – that's to say that seamen prop up the bar with mermaid stories, and drunken sailors

KENYA MALINDI

DON'T MISS

MARAFA

Away from the hedonistic delights of sun and sand one of the more intriguing sights along the north Kenyan coast is the **Marafa Depression**, also known as Hell's Kitchen or Nyari (the place broken by itself). It's an eroded sandstone gorge where jungle, red rock and cliffs upheave themselves into a single stunning Marscape.

About 30km northeast of Malindi, the Depression is currently managed as a local tourism concern by **Marafa village**. It costs KSh600 (that goes into village programs) to walk around the lip of the gorge, and KSh400 for a guide who can walk you into the sandstone heart of the ridges and tell Hell's Kitchen's story. Which goes like so: a rich family was so careless with their wealth that they bathed themselves in the valuable milk of their cattle. God became angry with this excess and sunk the family homestead into the earth. The white and red walls of the Depression mark the milk and blood of the family painted over the gorge walls. The more mundane explanation? The Depression is a chunk of sandstone geologically distinct from the surrounding rock and more susceptible to wind and rain erosion.

Most people visit here on organised tours, with a self-drive car or by taxi (KSh7000). Alternatively, there are one or two morning matatus from Mombasa Rd in Malindi to Marafa village (KSh150, three hours) and from there it's a 20-minute walk to Hell's Kitchen. There are two very basic places to stay if needed.

Malindi

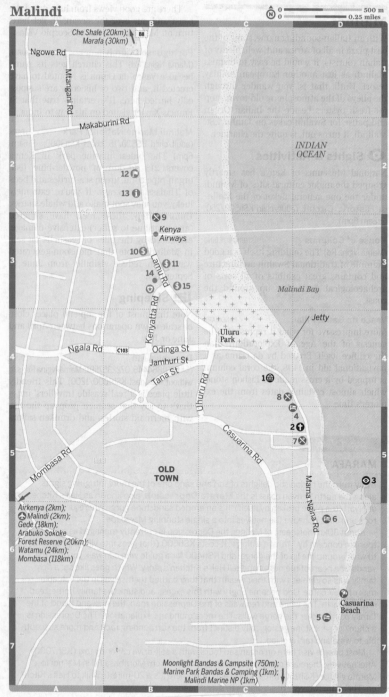

INDIAN
OCEAN

Che Shale (20km);
Marafa (30km)

B8

Ngowe Rd

Mtangani Rd

Makaburini Rd

Kenya
Airways

Lamu Rd

Kenyatta Rd

Ngala Rd   C103   Odinga St

Jamhuri St

Tana St

Uhuru Rd

Malindi Bay

Jetty

Uluru
Park

Casuarina Rd

Mombasa Rd

OLD
TOWN

Mama Ngina Rd

Airkenya (2km);
Malindi (2km);
Gede (18km);
Arabuko Sokoke
Forest Reserve (20km);
Watamu (24km);
Mombasa (118km)

Casuarina
Beach

Moonlight Bandas & Campsite (750m);
Marine Park Bandas & Camping (1km);
Malindi Marine NP (1km)

0   500 m
0   0.25 miles

Malindi

side selling deep-fried goodies, bhajis, dates and chapati.

★ Karen Blixen Restaurant & Coffee Shop
CAFE $$
(www.karenblixen.net; Lamu Rd; meals KSh500-1500; ℗☎) Everyone in Kenya, it seems, wants to be Karen Blixen these days. This place isn't sure if it's a shabby-chic Karen Blixen or a blinging Karen Blixen, so it's gone for both looks, with scruffy leather seats and blinding gold lampshades. The pizza is as good as the coffee, and the place acts as Malindi's expat epicentre.

Jahizi
SEAFOOD $$
(☎0720747180, 0720178982; Mama Ngina Rd) Another breeze-kissed Mama Ngina Rd hangout, this time with a hip slant on a fishing theme. Think big oysters, fish, juices, a long wine list and plenty of pizza. You could be in Sicily. Popular with everyone from waistcoated elderly gentlemen to stylish Malindians.

★ Baby Marrow
ITALIAN, SEAFOOD $$$
(☎0733542584; Mama Ngina Rd; mains KSh500-2000) Imagine an intimate honeymoon lodge restaurant, minus the lodge. That's what Baby Marrow is like. You can feast on smoked sailfish, pizza bianca, vodka sorbet or Sicilian ice cream (and plenty of other things) beneath the bamboo eaves. The jungle bar is a good spot for a digestif.

make eyes at the barmaid. The rooms are spacious but simple. If you can get hot water out of those rusty water-storage tanks, you're a better person than us.

★ Scorpio Villas
RESORT $$
(☎042-2120194; www.scorpio-villas.com; Mnarani Rd; s/d KSh4600/7200; ☒) Pretty and great value, Scorpio Villas is a winner. It's right by the ocean and within walking distance of some good restaurants. The 40-or-so rooms follow the hotel theme: gorgeous dark wood, white linen sofas and Swahili carvings. The bathrooms have huge monsoon showers. What's not to love?

Driftwood Beach Club
RESORT $$$
(☎042-2120155, 042-2130845; www.driftwoodclub.com; Mama Ngina Rd; r from KSh14,000; ❋☒) Somewhere between fancy pants and seaside chic, this place sees plenty of expat and Anglo-Kenyan traffic. The rooms are smart, but the hotel pulls off a relaxed vibe. The ambience is closer to palm-breezed serenity than the party atmosphere at similar hotels.

✗ Eating

With great seafood and strong Italian influences, there's a reason Malindi is known as Little Napoli. Street food heaven is Jamhuri St, where stalls line both sides of the road-

🍷 Drinking & Nightlife

Fermento Piano Bar
LOUNGE
(☎042-31780; Galana Centre, Lamu Rd; admission KSh200; ◷from 10pm Wed, Fri & Sat) Fermento, for 'your endless night'...or so the slogan goes. The dance floor was apparently once frequented by Naomi Campbell. It's young and trendy, so try to look so yourself.

ⓘ Information

DANGERS & ANNOYANCES
Being on the beach alone at night is asking for trouble, as is walking along any quiet beach back roads at night. Also, avoid the far northern end of the beach or any deserted patches of sand, as muggings are common. There are lots of guys selling drugs, so remember: everything from marijuana on up is illegal. Sales of drugs often turn into stings. There's also a lot of prostitution here.

TOURIST INFORMATION
Malindi Tourist Office (☎042-20689; Malindi Complex, Lamu Rd, Malindi; ◷8am-12.30pm & 2-4.30pm Mon-Fri)

TRAVEL AGENCIES

North Coast Travel Services (☏042-20370; Lamu Rd) Agent for Fly540.

ℹ️ Getting There & Away

AIR

Airkenya (☏042-30646; Malindi Airport) Daily afternoon/evening flights to Nairobi (US$100, two hours).

Kenya Airways (☏042-20237; Lamu Rd) Flies to Nairobi at least once a day (US$134).

BUS & MATATU

There are numerous daily buses and matatus to Mombasa (bus/matatu from KSh300/350, two hours). Bus company offices are found opposite the old market in the centre of Malindi.

All the main bus companies have daily departures to Nairobi at around 7am and/or 7pm (KSh500 to KSh3000, 10 to 12 hours), via Mombasa.

Matatus to Watamu (KSh100, one hour) leave from the not very new New Malindi Bus Station on the edge of town.

Usually at least six daily buses head to Lamu (from KSh800, four to five hours). Most leave around 9am.

ℹ️ Getting Around

You can rent bicycles from most hotels for around KSh500 per day. Cycling at night is not permitted. Tuk-tuks (minitaxis) are ubiquitous – a short hop through town should cost around KSh150 to KSh250. A taxi to the airport is at least KSh300 and a tuk-tuk is KSh150.

Lamu

Lamu town has that quality of immediately standing out as you approach it from the water (and let's face it – everything is better when approached from water). The shopfronts and mosques, faded under the relentless kiss of the salt wind, creep out from behind a forest of dhow masts. Then you take to the streets, or more accurately, the labyrinth: donkey-wide alleyways from which children grin; women whispering by in full-length *bui-bui* (black cover-all worn by some Islamic women outside the home); cats casually ruling the rooftops; blue smoke from meat grilling over open fires and the organic, biting scent of the cured wooden shutters on houses built of stone and coral. Many visitors call this town – the oldest living town in East Africa, a Unesco World Heritage site and arguably the most complete Swahili town in existence – the high-light of their trip to Kenya. Residents call it *Kiwa Ndeo* – The Vain Island – and, to be fair, there's plenty for them to be vain about.

👁️ Sights

Lamu is one of those places where the real attraction is just the overall feel of the place and there actually aren't all that many 'sights' to tick off.

Lamu Museum   MUSEUM
(Harambee Ave, Waterfront; adult/child KSh500/250; ⊙8am-6pm) The best museum in town is housed in a grand Swahili warehouse on the waterfront. This is as good a gateway as you'll get into Swahili culture and that of the archipelago in particular. Of note are the displays of traditional women's dress – those who consider the head-to-toe *bui-bui* restrictive might be interested to see the *shiraa*, a tent-like garment (complete with wooden frame to be held over the head) that was once the respectable dress of local ladies. There are also exhibits dedicated to artefacts from Swahili ruins, the bric-a-brac of local tribes and the nautical heritage of the coast (including the *mtepe*, a traditional coir-sewn boat meant to resemble the Prophet Mohammed's camel – hence the nickname, 'camels of the sea'). Guides are available to show you around.

Lamu Fort   FORTRESS
(Main Sq) This squat castle was built by the Sultan of Paté from 1810 and completed in 1823. From 1910 right up to 1984 it was used as a prison. It now houses the island's library, which holds one of the best collections of Swahili poetry and Lamu reference work in Kenya. Entrance is free with a ticket to the Lamu Museum.

Lamu Market   MARKET
(opposite Lamu Fort) Atmospheric and chaotic, this quintessential Lamu market is best visited early in the morning. Bargain for stinking fresh tuna and sailfish, wade through alleys teeming with stray cats, dogs and goats, and experience Lamu at its craziest. If you're sick of seafood, this is the place to find your five-a-day.

Swahili House   MUSEUM
(adult/child KSh500/250; ⊙8am-6pm) This preserved Swahili house, tucked away to the side of Yumbe House hotel, is beautiful, but the entry fee is very hard to justify, especially as half the hotels in Lamu are as well preserved as this small house.

DHOW TRIPS

More than the bustle of markets or the call to prayer, the pitch of, 'We take dhow trip, see mangroves, eat fish and coconut rice', is the unyielding chorus Lamu's voices offer up when you first arrive. That said, taking a dhow trip (and seeing the mangroves and eating fish and coconut rice) is almost obligatory and generally fun besides, although this depends to a large degree on your captain. There's a real joy to kicking it on the boards under the sunny sky, with the mangroves drifting by in island time while snacking on spiced fish.

Trips include dhow racing excursions (learning how to tack and race these amazingly agile vessels is quite something), sunset sails, adventures to Kipungani and Manda, deep-reef fishing and even three-day trips south along the coast to Kilifi (from US$100 per person).

Prices vary depending on where you want to go, who you go with and how long you go for. **Bwana Dolphin** (☑0726732746) is a recommended local captain. With bargaining you could pay around KSh2500 per person in a group of four or five people, on a half-day basis. Don't hand over any money until the day of departure, except perhaps a small advance for food. On long trips, it's best to organise your own drinks. A hat and sunscreen are essential.

German Post Office Museum MUSEUM
(Kenyatta Rd; adult/child KSh500/250; ⊘8am-6pm) In the late 1800s, before the British decided to nip German expansion into Tanganyika in the bud, the Germans regarded Lamu as an ideal base from which to exploit the interior. As part of their efforts, the German East Africa Company set up a post office, and the old building is now a museum exhibiting photographs and memorabilia from that fleeting period when Lamu had the chance of being spelt with an umlaut.

✹ Festivals & Events

Maulid Festival ISLAMIC
(www.lamu.org/maulid-celebration.html) The Maulid Festival celebrates the birth of the Prophet Mohammed. Its date shifts according to the Muslim calendar (December 2015). The festival has been celebrated on the island for over 100 years and much singing, dancing and general jollity takes place around this time. On the final day a procession heads down to the tomb of the man who started it all, Ali Habib Swaleh.

Lamu Cultural Festival CULTURAL
Exact dates for this colourful carnival vary each year, but it often falls in November. Expect donkey and dhow races, Swahili poets and island dancing.

🛏 Sleeping

The alleyways of Lamu are absolutely rammed with places to stay and competition means that prices are often lower than

in other parts of Kenya. There's always scope for price negotiation, especially if you plan to stay for over a day or two. Touts will invariably try and accompany you to get commission; the best way to avoid this is to book at least one night in advance, so you know what you'll be paying.

★**New Bahati Lodge** GUESTHOUSE $
(☑0726732746; www.lamuguesthouse.com; d/tr KSh1400/2500) This newly renovated budget house occupies prime position in Lamu's old town and pulls in plenty of budget travellers. The rooms are clean, fresh and spacious, but you'll probably spend most of your time in the loungey chill-out areas. The master bedroom at the top of the house has the best ocean view.

★**Baitul Noor House** BACKPACKERS $
(☑0725220271, 0723760296; www.lamuback packers.com; dm/s/d KSh1000/1500/2500) From the Arabic for 'house of light', this 16th-century townhouse is the stylish new backpackers on the block. The dorms are lovely and ecofriendly, featuring 7ft beds, homemade soaps and solar reading lamps. Don't miss the stylish roof terrace and the downstairs restaurant, which does lobster suppers for lemonade pockets. Helpful staff can arrange all manner of excursions.

Yumbe House BOUTIQUE HOTEL $
(☑0726732746; www.lamuguesthouse.com; s/d KSh2500/3200) This beautiful 17th-century house is made from coral, which is reason enough to stay here. Add spacious rooms

Lamu

0 _____ 100 m
0 _____ 0.05 miles

Lamu House (250m);
Uyoni Beach (500m)

10 ✕

11 ✕

Lamu
Medical
Clinic ✚

9 🏨

5 🏛

INDIAN
OCEAN

Lamu Museum 🏛 **1**

Catholic ✝
Church

Main
Jetty

Mokowe
(mainland) (5km)

Manda Island
(Airport) (1km)

Bohora 🕌
Mosque

13 🍴

@

Matondoni
(6km)

15 🔒

Kenyatta Rd

Harambee Ave

Kenya
Commercial
Bank 💲

Dhow
Moorings

7 🏨

6 🏨

8 🏨

3 🏰

Main
Square ●

Kipungani
(10km)

4 ◉

Shiaithna-
Asheri 🕌
Mosque

2 🏛

Tourist 🛈
Office ✉

14 🔒

16

Langoni
Nursing ✚
Home

King Fahd Lamu
District Hospital
(1.5km);
Shela (3km)

The AP's Canteen (300m);
Shela (Inland Track) (3.5km)

12 ✕

Lamu

decorated with pleasant Swahili accents, verandahs that are open to the stars and the breeze, and a ridiculously romantic top-floor suite. Top value for your shilling.

★**Subira House**   GUESTHOUSE **$$**
(☑ 0726916686; www.subirahouse.com; r KSh5000–8000) This beautiful house features graceful arches and twin gardens with wells. The Swedish owners certainly know a thing or two about style, as did the Sultan of Zanzibar when he built the house 200 years ago. As well as seven stylish bedrooms, there are galleries in which to relax and serious eco-credentials. We rate the restaurant highly.

★**Lamu House**   BOUTIQUE HOTEL **$$$**
(☑ 0708073164, 0708279905; www.lamuhouse.com; Harambee Ave; r US$230–490) In a town where every building wants to top the preservation stakes, Lamu House stands out. It looks like an old Swahili villa, but it feels like a stylish boutique hotel, blending the pale, breezy romance of the Greek islands into an African palace, with predictably awesome results. The excellent Moonlight restaurant

serves fine Swahili cuisine. A free boat service to Manda Island leaves from here every morning at 8am.

🍴 Eating

Lamu's fruit juices, which almost every restaurant sells, are worth drawing attention to. They're good. They're really, really good.

Many of Lamu's cheap places to eat close until after sunset during Ramadan.

★**Tehran**   KENYAN **$**
(Kenyatta Rd; mains from KSh100) This very atmospheric but basic place doesn't even have a sign, but it does serve dirt-cheap meals of fish, beans (the best is *maharagwe ya chumvi* – with coconut milk) and chapatis. It's consistently packed with locals and is pretty much open all the time.

Bustani Café   CAFE **$**
(meals KSh320–500) This pretty garden cafe has tables set about a lily-bedecked pond. The small menu includes lots of healthy salads and various snack foods. It also contains a decent bookshop and an evening-only internet cafe (KSh240 per hour).

Olympic Restaurant   AFRICAN **$**
(Harambee Ave; mains KSh450–900) The family that runs the Olympic makes you feel as if you've come home every time you enter, and their food, particularly the curries and biriyani, is excellent. There are few better ways to spend a Lamu night than with a cold mug of passionfruit juice and the noir-ish view of the docks you get here, at the ramshackle end of town.

★**Mwana Arafa Restaurant Gardens**   SEAFOOD **$$**
(Harambee Ave; meals KSh350–1200) Everyone loves Mwana Arafa. It has the perfect combination of garden seating and views over the dhows bobbing about under the moonlight. With barbecued giant prawns, grilled calamari, lobster or a seafood platter, we guess you'll be eating the fruits of the sea tonight.

🍷 Drinking & Nightlife

As a Muslim town, Lamu has few options for drinkers and local sensibilities should be respected. Full moon parties sometimes take place in season over on Manda Island.

Petley's Inn   BAR
(Harambee Ave) Right in front of the main jetty, Petley's seems to be the local watering hole for just about everyone. Expect almost

anything, from good fun and merriment to enough hassle to speed you through the doors.

Shopping

If you're into unusual fabrics, you can pick up bags made from the recycled cotton of dhow sails, often decorated with iconic Lamu images. Textile fans will also enjoy shopping for material sourced from Oman and Somalia. Head north along Kenyatta Rd from the direction of the fort and you'll find a scattering of places selling such wares, as well as some high-quality silversmiths. Perhaps the most charismatic among them is a chap called Slim, whose silversmith shop – with the original name of Slim Silversmith – sells beautiful rings created from ancient cuttings of coloured tiles.

Baraka Gallery ARTS & CRAFTS
(Kenyatta Rd) For upmarket Africana, Baraka Gallery has a fine selection, but stratospheric prices.

Black & White Gallery ARTS & CRAFTS
Spanish-run art shop with some beautiful tribal-inspired crafts and paintings.

Lamu Museum Shop BOOKS
(Harambee Ave) Specialists in Lamu and Swahili cultural books.

ℹ Information

DANGERS & ANNOYANCES

At the time of research, some governments were advising against travel to Lamu and the wider region.

When times are normal the biggest real issue are the beach boys. They'll come at you the minute you step off the boat, offering drugs, tours and hotel bookings (the last can be useful if you're disoriented).

Lamu has long been popular for its relaxed, tolerant atmosphere, but it does have somewhat conservative views as to what is acceptable behaviour. In 1999, a gay couple who planned a public wedding here had to be evacuated under police custody. Whatever your sexuality, it's best to keep public displays of affection to a minimum and respect local attitudes to modesty.

Female travellers should note that most Lamurians hold strong religious and cultural values, and may be deeply offended by revealing clothing. There have been some isolated incidents of rape, which locals say were sparked by tourists refusing to cover up. That may outrage some Western ears, but the fact remains that you risk getting into hot water if you walk around in small shorts and low-cut tops. There are miles of deserted beaches on which you can walk around butt naked if you choose, but we urge you to respect cultural norms in built-up areas.

INTERNET ACCESS

Cyberwings (across from Petley's Inn; per hr KSh40; ⊘ 8am-8pm)

SAFETY ON LAMU

In September 2011 an English couple staying on the island of Kiwayu, north of Lamu, were attacked by Somali pirates/militants. One person died and one was kidnapped and taken to Somalia. It was widely thought that this was a one-off attack and that Lamu itself was not at risk. However, despite a massive beefing up of security, just over two weeks later another attack occurred. This time a French woman was kidnapped from her home on Manda Island and taken to Somalia (where she later died from a diabetic incident).

Following a series of armed attacks in Mombasa in mid-2014, the coastal town of Mpeketoni (25km from Lamu Town) was hit by what was at the time believed to be Al-Shabaab militants claiming revenge for the presence of Kenyan troops in Somalia and the killing of Muslims. Further analysis suggested that these attacks were likely perpetrated by Somali and Oromo residents in an attempt to deflect blame onto Al-Shabaab (using the group's flag as a guise) and claim the area as their ancestral home after Kenya's first President, Jomo Kenyatta settled ethnic Kikuyus on their land after independence.

Many countries advised against travel to Lamu in the wake of these attacks, resulting in void travel insurance policies and a drop in tourism that devastated local communities. A curfew was in place on Lamu at the time of research and we urge you to check the latest on the security situation before travelling. At the time of going to print there had been no further attacks and independent travellers were starting to return to these otherwise blessed isles.

🏃 Town Walk
Lamu Town

START LAMU MAIN JETTY
FINISH SHIAITHNA-ASHERI MOSQUE
DISTANCE ABOUT 1KM
DURATION 45 MINUTES TO ONE HOUR

The best, indeed only, way to see Lamu town is on foot. Few experiences compare with exploring the far back streets, where you can wander amid wafts of cardamom and carbolic and watch the town's agile cats scaling the coral walls. There are so many wonderful Swahili houses that it's pointless for us to recommend specific examples – keep your eyes open wherever you go, and don't forget to look up.

Starting at the ❶ **main jetty**, head north past the ❷ **Lamu Museum** (p332) and along the waterfront until you reach the ❸ **door-carving workshops**.

From here head onto Kenyatta Rd, passing an original Swahili ❹ **well**, and into the alleys towards the ❺ **Swahili House Museum** (p332). Once you've had your fill of domestic insights, take any route back towards the main street.

Once you've hit the main square and the ❻ **fort** (p332), take a right to see the crumbled remains of the 14th-century ❼ **Pwani Mosque**, one of Lamu's oldest buildings – an Arabic inscription is still visible on the wall. From here you can head round and browse the covered ❽ **market**, then negotiate your way towards the bright Saudi-funded ❾ **Riyadha Mosque**, the centre of Lamu's religious scene.

Now you can take as long or as short a route as you like back to the waterfront. Stroll along the promenade, diverting for the ❿ **German Post Office Museum** (p333) if you haven't already seen it – the door is another amazing example of Swahili carving. If you're feeling the pace, take a rest and shoot the breeze on the ⓫ **baraza ya wazee** (old men's bench) outside the stucco minarets of the ⓬ **Shiaithna-Asheri Mosque**.

Carrying on up Harambee Ave will bring you back to the main jetty.

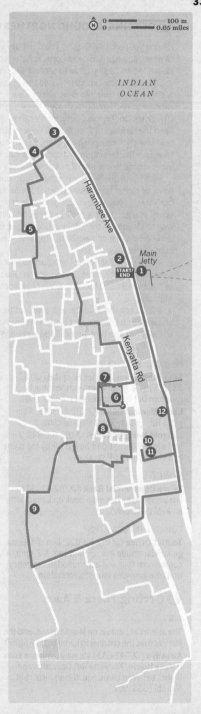

ⓘ GETTING AROUND NORTHERN KENYA

Having your own 4WD gives you flexibility but comes with its own challenges, thanks to wide-ranging road conditions. For starters, you'll need a large 4WD with high ground clearance and a skid plate to protect the undercarriage.

Do not underestimate how bad the roads are up here – on three recent research trips we have twice snapped drive shafts clean in two, replaced more springs and tyres than we care to remember, destroyed three suspension systems and shattered two radiators (thank you to the two Samburu *moran* with spears who, during our latest research trip, fixed the radiator at 2am somewhere south of Marsabit using a bar of soap and some tea leaves!). Unsurprisingly many car-rental companies will not allow their vehicles to be taken north of Samburu National Reserve. If you do come up here it's sensible to take an experienced driver and, if possible, travel in convoy with another 4WD.

Isiolo long marked the northern terminus of the tarmac road system, but the Chinese have, or rather had, been busy road building here. A pristine tarmac road runs about halfway up toward Marsabit before reverting to a rutted mess that will shake the guts out of you and your vehicle just beyond Laisamis. Eventually the road will extend all the way to Moyale on the Ethiopia border, but due to political in-fighting no work has been done on it since at least 2011. There were rumours in late 2014 that work was about to commence again.

There's regular public transport as far north as Kalokol and Lokichoggio on Turkana's west side, but it's more limited up the lake's east side, only reaching Baragoi via Maralal or North Horr via Marsabit. Buses run from Isiolo to Moyale on the Ethiopian border via Marsabit.

A few organised safaris and overland trucks now go to Lake Turkana's west, but most still stick to the lake's east side. Gametracker Safaris (p229) runs weekly overland safaris to Lake Turkana that generally depart on Wednesdays and Fridays from Nairobi.

MEDICAL SERVICES

King Fahd Lamu District Hospital (☏ 012-633075) This government-run hospital is rundown but has competent medical staff.

Lamu Medical Clinic (☏ 012-633438; Kenyatta Rd; ⊙ 8am-9pm) Medical clinic.

Langoni Nursing Home (☏ 012-633349; Kenyatta Rd; ⊙ 24hr) Don't be put off by the name; this clinic offers GP services.

MONEY

Kenya Commercial Bank (☏ 012-633327; Harambee Ave) The main bank on Lamu, with an ATM (Visa only).

TOURIST INFORMATION

Tourist Office (☏ 012-633132; lamu@tourism. go.ke; Harambee Ave; ⊙ 9am-1pm & 2-4pm) A commercial tour and accommodation agency that also provides tourist information.

ⓘ Getting There & Away

AIR

The airport at Lamu is on Manda Island, and the ferry across the channel to Lamu costs KSh150.

Airkenya (☏ 042-633445; www.airkenya.com; Baraka House, Kenyatta Rd) Daily afternoon flights between Lamu and Wilson Airport in Nairobi (US$195).

Fly540 (☏ 042-632054; www.fly540.com) Flies twice daily to Malindi (around US$45) and Nairobi (around US$170).

Safarilink (www.flysafarilink.com) Daily flights to Nairobi Wilson airport (around US$185).

BUS

There are booking offices for several bus companies on Kenyatta Rd on Lamu. The going rate for a trip to Mombasa (eight to nine hours) is KSh800 to KSh900; most buses leave between 7am and 8am, so you'll need to be at the jetty at 6.30am to catch the boat to the mainland. Book early and be on time. Buses deliberately leave on the dot in order to resell the seats of latecoming passengers further up the line. The most reliable companies are **Simba** (☏ 0707471110, 0707471111), **Tahmeed** (☏ 0724581015, 0724581004) and **Tawakal** (☏ 0705090122). Note that prices tend to increase by KSh100-200 during the high season.

At the time of research, armed guards were on every Lamu-bound bus from Mombasa. Matatus, as you'd imagine, have no such security assurances.

Coming from Mombasa to Lamu, buses will drop you at the mainland jetty at Mokowe. From there you can either catch the passenger ferry (KSh100, 30 to 40 minutes) or a speedboat (KSh150, 10 minutes travel).

❶ Getting Around

Ferries between the airstrip on Manda Island and Lamu cost KSh150 and leave about half an hour before the flights leave (yes, in case you're wondering, all the airline companies are aware of this and so that's sufficient time).

Between Lamu village and Shela there are plenty of motorised dhows throughout the day until around sunset; these cost about KSh150 per person and leave when full.

There are also regular ferries between Lamu and Paté Island.

Islands Around Lamu

The Lamu archipelago has plenty to offer outside Lamu itself. The easiest to get to is **Manda Island**, just across the channel, where most visitors go on dhow trips for snorkelling and to visit the Takwa ruins. The tiny **Manda Toto Island**, on the other side of Manda, has perhaps the best reefs on the coast.

Further northeast, **Paté Island** was the main power centre in the region before Lamu came to prominence, but is rarely visited now, preserving an uncomplicated traditional lifestyle as much by necessity as by choice. A regular motor launch shuttles between the towns of Mtangawanda, Siyu, Faza and Kizingitini.

NORTHERN KENYA

Calling all explorers! We dare you to challenge yourself against some of the most exciting wilderness in Africa. Step forward only if you're able to withstand appalling roads, searing heat, clouds of dust torn up by relentless winds, primitive food and accommodation, vast distances and more than a hint of danger.

The rewards include memories of vast shattered lava deserts, camel herders walking their animals to lost oases, fog-shrouded mountains full of mysterious creatures, prehistoric islands crawling with massive reptiles and jokes shared with traditionally dressed warriors. Additional perks include camel trekking through piles of peachy dunes, elephant encounters in scrubby acacia woodlands and the chance to walk barefoot along the fabled shores of a sea of jade.

Isiolo to Moyale

For most people this route means two things: the wildlife riches of the Samburu ecosystem or the road to the cultural riches of Ethiopia. But in between and beyond, this area has much more to offer. You can drink tea and track game with the Samburu

---

WARNING

The strong warrior traditions of northern Kenya's nomadic peoples have led to security problems plaguing the region for years. With an influx of cheap guns from conflict zones surrounding Kenya, minor conflicts stemming from grazing rights and cattle rustling (formerly settled by compensation rather than violence) have quickly escalated into ongoing gun battles that the authorities struggle to contain.

While travellers, who rarely witness any intertribal conflict, may consider the issue exaggerated, the scale of the problem is enormous and growing. Over the past decade hundreds of Kenyans are thought to have been killed and tens of thousands displaced by inter-tribal conflicts. Fortunately security on the main routes in the north, and anywhere a tourist is likely to be, is generally good. Fighting around Moyale has increased somewhat since 2011, and in 2012 there was serious inter-tribal fighting in Moyale itself that eventually saw the Ethiopian military get involved. There have also been times when access to the Samburu National Reserve (p342) has been restricted, and in 2011 a group of tourists were attacked on the Moyale to Isiolo road. In late 2014 convoys and armed guards were no longer used between Marich and Lodwar or between Isiolo and Moyale, on the Ethiopian border.

The remote northeastern region around Garsen, Wajir and Mandera is still unstable and you should avoid travelling there due to continuing conflicts. Likewise, a full-scale Kenyan military invasion of Somalia and renewed fighting in the region is a strong reason to stay well clear (the border is also closed).

Improvements or not, security in northern Kenya is a fluid entity. Travellers should seek local advice about the latest developments before visiting and never take unnecessary risks.

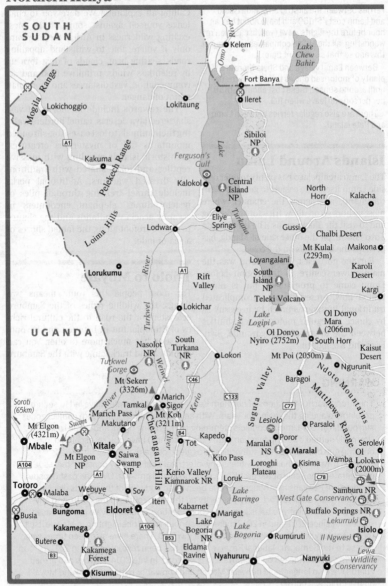

SOUTH SUDAN

Kelem

Lake Chew Bahir

Fort Banya
Ileret

Lokichoggio

Mogila Range

Lokitaung

A1

Sibiloi NP

Kakuma

Ferguson's Gulf

Peletkech Range

Lake

Kalokol

Central Island NP

North Horr

Kalacha

Loima Hills

Lodwar

Eliye Springs

Turkana

Gussi

Chalbi Desert

Mt Kulal (2293m)

Maikona

Lorukumu

A1

Rift Valley

Loyangalani

South Island NP

Karoli Desert

Teleki Volcano

Kargi

Turkwel

River

Lokichar

Lake Logipi

Ol Donyo Mara (2066m)

Ol Donyo Nyiro (2752m)

South Horr

UGANDA

Nasolot NR

South Turkana NR

Lokori

Mt Poi (2050m)

Kaisut Desert

Ngurunit

Tutkwel Gorge

Mt Sekerr (3326m)

Weiwei

River

Baragoi

Ndoto Mountains

Soroti (65km)

Tamkal

Marich

Sigor

Kerio

C46

C133

Suguta Valley

Lesiolo

C77

Parsaloi

Matthews Range

Mt Elgon (4321m)

Marich Pass

Makutano

Mt Koh (3211m)

B4

Kapedo

Poror

Serolevi

Mbale

Mt Elgon NP

Kitale

Saiwa Swamp NP

Tot

Kito Pass

Maralal NS

Maralal

Ol Lolokwe (2000m)

Wamba

Kerio Valley/ Kamnarok NR

Kisima

C78

Tororo

A1

Kabarnet

Loruk

Loroghi Plateau

Samburu NR

Malaba

Webuye

Soy

Iten

Lake Baringo

West Gate Conservancy

Buffalo Springs NR

Busia

Bungoma

Eldoret

Marigat

Lekurruki

Isiolo

Kakamega

Lake Bogoria NR

Rumuruti

Il Ngwesi

Butere

A104

B53

Eldama Ravine

Nyahururu

Nanyuki

Lewa Wildlife Conservancy

Kakamega Forest

B3

Kisumu

people, climb mist-shrouded volcanoes in the desert, blaze trails in untrammelled mountains and get so far off the beaten track you'll start to wonder whether you're still on the same planet.

Isiolo

Isiolo is where anticipation and excitement first start to send your heart a-flutter. This vital pit stop on the long road north is a true frontier town, a place on the edge, torn

One of the first things you'll undoubtedly notice is the large Somali population (descendants of WWI veterans who settled here) and the striking faces of Boran, Samburu and Turkana people walking the streets. It's this mix of people, cultures and religions that is the most interesting thing about Isiolo. Nowhere is this mixture better illustrated than in the hectic market.

🛏 Sleeping

★ Range Land Hotel   COTTAGES $

(☏0710114030; www.rangelandhotels.com; A2 Hwy; campsite per person KSh1000, s/d cottages KSh3000/4000; P🐾) About 4km south of town, this is a nice option for those with their own set of wheels. The sunny campground has bickering weaver birds and busy rock hyraxes in abundance, as well as neat-and-tidy stone bungalows with hot showers. Many people come to laze around in the gardens at the weekend, but during the week it's quiet.

Excellent meals are available and the house special is rabbit (KSh1200), a delicious rarity in Kenyan cuisine.

Moti Peal Hotel   HOTEL $

(☏064-52400; s/d KSh2500/3500; 🐾) This smart place markets itself as the 'Pearl of Isiolo'. This actually says more about the state of Isiolo than the quality of the hotel, but even so it's shockingly clean, well run and has friendly management.

🍴 Eating

There are numerous cheap eating establishments throughout the town, but in general the hotel restaurants tend to offer more variety as well as a more salubrious environment.

Northbound self-caterers should head to **101 Supermarket** (⊗8am-6pm Mon-Sat) and the daily market near the mosque to purchase food and drink, as there's very little available beyond here.

Bomen Hotel   KENYAN $$

(meals KSh400-650; ⊗7am-11pm) A rare place serving more than the local usuals, with fried tilapia, pepper steak, goulash and curries up for grabs.

ⓘ Information

Barclays Bank (A2 Hwy) With an ATM. Banks are scarce in the north, so plan ahead.
District Hospital (Hospital Rd; ⊗24hr)

between the cool, verdant highlands just to the south and the scorching badlands, home of nomads and explorers, to the north. On a more practical note it's also the last place with decent facilities until Maralal or Marsabit.

Isiolo

Samburu, Buffalo Springs & Shaba National Reserves

Blistered with termite skyscrapers, shot through with the muddy Ewaso Ngiro River and heaving with heavyweight animals, the three national reserves of **Samburu** (adult/child US$70/40, vehicle KSh1000), **Buffalo Springs** (adult/child US$70/40, vehicle KSh1000) and **Shaba** (adult/child US$70/40, vehicle KSh1000) are not as famous as some others, but they have a beauty that is unsurpassed, as well as a population of creatures that occur in no other major Kenyan park. These include the blue-legged Somali ostrich, super-stripy Grevy's zebras, unicornlike beisa oryxes, ravishing reticulated giraffes and the gerenuk – a gazelle that dearly wishes to be a giraffe. Despite comprising just 300 sq km, the variety of vegetation and landscapes here is amazing. Shaba, with its great rocky *kopjes* (isolated hills), natural springs and doum palms, is the most physically beautiful, as well as the least visited (but it often has a lot less wildlife than the other two reserves). Meanwhile the open savannahs, scrub desert and verdant river foliage in Samburu and Buffalo Springs virtually guarantee close encounters with elephants and all the others.

Sleeping & Eating

BUFFALO SPRINGS NATIONAL RESERVE

Samburu Simba Lodge LODGE $$$
(Nairobi 020-4444401; www.simbalodges.com; full board s/d US$495/575; @) It doesn't exactly blend harmoniously into the countryside, but this large lodge, with accommodation in big rooms scattered over several blocks, is ideal for those who prefer something other than canvas between them and the wildlife. It's one of the few options in Buffalo Springs.

Green Acres.com Cyber Cafe (per hr KSh180; 8am-8pm) The world eagerly awaits an email from you. Do it from here.

Kenya Commercial Bank (A2 Hwy) With an ATM.

❶ Getting There & Away

A couple of bus companies serve Nairobi with most buses leaving between 5.30am and 6.30am (KSh500, 4½ hours) from the main road through town and also stopping at the matatu and bus stand just south of the market. Evening buses operated by **Liban Buses** (0722244847; A2 Hwy) creep north to Marsabit (KSh700, five hours) at 4.30pm. **Moyale Star Buses** (A2 Hwy) head to Moyale (KSh1500, 10 hours) at 1.30pm via Marsabit (KSh700, five hours).

For Maralal take an early-morning matatu to Wamba (KSh330, 2½ hours), and then a Maralal-bound matatu (KSh500, 2½ hours) from there. Regular matatus leave from a chaotic stand around the market and also serve Archer's Post (KSh130 to KSh150, 25 minutes), Meru (KSh150, 1½ hours) and Nanyuki (KSh250, 1¾ hours).

SAMBURU NATIONAL RESERVE

Riverside Camp   TENTED CAMP $
(Edwards Camp; 📞 0721108032, 0721252737; per person KSh1500, per person full board KSh3500) On the northern bank of the Ewaso Ngiro River, the scrappy (and hot) dark canvas safari tents here might not climb as luxuriously high as some of the big-boy lodges but, let's face it, this is much more authentic Africa. Meals can be prepared on request. Vervet monkeys and baboons can be a menace, though. It's very close to the park headquarters.

Samburu Public Campsite   CAMPGROUND $
(camping US$30) The main public campsite is close to the park headquarters. It lacks even the most basic facilities and there are lots of baboons with light fingers. Arrange your stay through the park ticket office.

Elephant Watch Camp   TENTED CAMP $$$
(📞 0733639630, Nairobi 020-8048602; www.elephantwatchsafaris.com; s/d all inclusive US$800/1440, plus service charge per person US$25; ⊙ closed Apr–10 May & Nov–10 Dec) 🖉 Undoubtedly the most unique and memorable place to stay in Samburu. Massive thatched roofs cling to crooked acacia branches and tower over cosy, palatial, eight-sided tents and large, grass-mat-clad terraces. Natural materials dominate the exteriors, bright textiles the interiors, and the bathrooms are stunning.

Elephant Bedroom   TENTED CAMP $$$
(📞 Nairobi 020-4450035; www.atua-enkop.com; s/d all inclusive US$440/690; 🏊) Twelve absolutely superb riverfront tents that are so luxurious even budding princesses will feel a little overwhelmed by the surroundings. Exactly how luxurious are we talking? Well, when was the last time you saw a tent that came with a private plunge pool?

SHABA NATIONAL RESERVE

⭐ **Joy's Camp**   TENTED CAMP $$$
(📞 0730127000; www.joyscamp.com; s/d all inclusive from US$437/728; 🌐🏊) 🖉 Once the home of Joy Adamson, of *Born Free* fame, this is now an outrageously luxurious camp in Shaba's remotest corner. The accommodation is in 'tents', but these tents aren't like others – they come with underfloor lighting, lots of stained glass and giant, walk-in rain showers.

ℹ Information

Buffalo Springs, Shaba and Samburu entry tickets are interchangeable for all three parks, so you only pay once, but can visit all three in one day.

ℹ Getting There & Away

The vehicle-less can wrangle a 4WD and driver in Archer's Post for about US$100 per half-day.

Airkenya (www.airkenya.com) and **Safarilink** (www.flysafarilink.com) have frequent flights from Nairobi to Samburu, Kalama and Shaba.

The bridge between Samburu and Buffalo Springs has been collapsed for years, but Isiolo county's governor has promised it will be rebuilt soon. If it is still in pieces, and you want to visit both Samburu and Buffalo Springs, you'll need to make a long detour back to Archer's Post and the main A2 road, which can take up to three hours.

ℹ SAMBURU, BUFFALO SPRINGS & SHABA NATIONAL RESERVES

Why Go

To see some of Kenya's most unique creatures in a compelling and beautiful desert landscape. Samburu is also one of the best places in the country to see elephants. Crowds of visitors are nonexistent.

When to Go

There's little rain in these parts so it's possible to visit year-round, but between November and March animals congregate near the Ewaso Ngiro river.

Practicalities

Isiolo is the main gateway town. Conveniently, for the moment at least, Buffalo Springs, Shaba and Samburu entries are interchangeable, so you only pay once, even if you're visiting all three in one day. You must buy your ticket at the gate to the park in which you're staying. Petrol is available in Archer's Post.

Budget Tips

You can camp in any of the reserves (but you mostly need to be self-sufficient). However, you'll still need a vehicle to get around. These can be hired by the half-day in Archer's Post.

Samburu & Buffalo Springs National Reserves

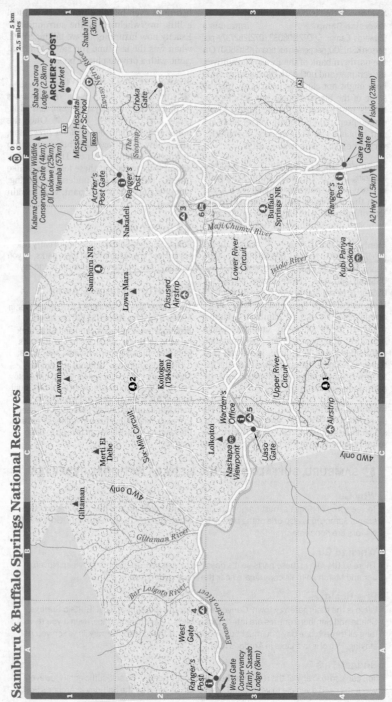

5 km
2.5 miles

Shaba NR (3km)

ARCHER'S POST
Market
Shaba Sarova Lodge (2.8km)
Mission Hospital
Church School
Kalama Community Wildlife Conservancy Gate (4km); Ol Lolokwe (25km); Wamba (57km)
A2
B20

Ewaso Ngiro River
Choka Gate
The Swamp
Archer's Post Gate
Ranger's Post
Nakadeli
Maji Chumvi River
Buffalo Springs NR
Ranger's Post
Gare Mara Gate
A2 Hwy (1.5km)
Isiolo (23km)
A2

Samburu NR
Lowa Mara
Disused Airstrip
Lower River Circuit
Isiolo River
Kubi Panya Lookout

Lowamara
Koitogor (1345m)
Upper River Circuit
Airstrip

4WD only
Six-Mile Circuit
Merti El Debe
Giltaman
Warden's Office
Lolkoitoi
Nashapa Viewpoint
Uaso Gate
4WD only

Giltaman River
Bôr Lolgoto River
Ewaso Ngiro River
West Gate
Ranger's Post
West Gate Conservancy (1km); Sasaab Lodge (8km)

Samburu & Buffalo Springs National Reserves

Marsabit

Marsabit is a long way from anywhere. The road from Isiolo is now smooth tarmac for about half the distance but, even so, for hour after scorching hour you'll pass a monotonous landscape of scrubby bush, where encounters with wildlife are common and elegant Samburu walk their herds of camels and goats. As the afternoon heats up, and your brain starts to cook, you'll find the world around you sliding in and out of focus, as mirages flicker on the horizon. Then, as evening comes, one final mirage appears: a massive wall of forested mountains providing an unlikely home to mammoth tusked elephants. But this is no mirage, this is Marsabit.

Sleeping & Eating

Water is a very scarce commodity in Marsabit and all the guesthouses have to truck it in. Use it sparingly.

Nomads Trail Hotel HOTEL $
(0726560846, Nairobi 020-8004454; A2 Hwy; s/d old rooms KSh1800/2700, new rooms KSh3000/4500; P奈) The rooms here are prim and proper and all have attached bathrooms that come with – wait for it – real hot water from a real shower! Upstairs are some newer rooms that, for Marsabit, are shockingly posh.

JeyJey Centre HOTEL $
(0728808801/2; A2 Hwy; camping KSh300, s/d/tw without bathroom KSh600/1000/1500, d KSh1200; P奈) This mud-brick castle bedecked in flowers is something of a travellers' centre and is always bursting with road-hardened souls. Basic rooms with mosquito nets surround a courtyard, and bathrooms (even shared ones) sport on-demand hot water. There's also an unattractive campground.

Jirime Hotel & Resort HOTEL $$
(0770834050; www.jirimehotel.com; A2 Hwy; camping KSh500, s/d KSh3000/5000; P奈) The smartest option in Marsabit is this new place, 2.5km north of town on the road to Moyale. It has little in the way of character but has big, tiled en-suite rooms, lots of peace and quiet, a decent in-house restaurant and pretty good wi-fi. Camping is also possible.

Five Steers Hotel KENYAN $
(A2 Hwy; meals KSh250-400; 8am-8pm) With a wooden fenced-off terrace, this place is the height of Marsabit style. The '½ Federation' meal (a bulging pile of rice, spaghetti, beef, vegetables and chapati) is filling and tasty. The owner is a good source of information on onward transport.

Information

Kenya Commercial Bank (off Post Office Rd) With ATM.
Medical Clinic (Post Office Rd; 8am-7pm Mon-Sat, noon-7pm Sun)

Getting There & Away

Although improved security means convoys and armed guards are no longer being used to Moyale or Isiolo, it's still wise to get the latest security and Ethiopian border information from locals and the police station before leaving town. As a rule, if buses and trucks travel in a convoy or take armed soldiers on board, you should too!

Moyale Raha Buses connect Marsabit to Moyale daily at 5.30pm (KSh800, six hours). The bus picks up passengers outside the Jey Jey Centre. Heading south both Moyale Raha and Liban Buses run buses to Isiolo (KSh700, six hours) at 6am (Liban Buses) and a flexible 11am (Moyale Raha Buses). Journey times will fall as the tarmac road grows. 'Buses' to North Horr via Kalacha leave at 5pm every other day and take at least 10 very hot, sandy hours to North Horr. Take note though that there's no reliable transport onward to the lake from North Horr.

Marsabit National Park

Within the larger national reserve, this small **park** (adult/child US$25/15; ☺ 6.30am-6pm), nestled on Mt Marsabit's upper slopes, is coated in thick forests and contains a wide variety of wildlife, including leopards, elephants (some with huge tusks) and buffaloes. The park forms a key point on an elephant migration route that extends as far as the slopes of Mt Kenya. The dense forest makes spotting wildlife very difficult, but fortunately help is at hand in the form of a couple of natural clearings with semi-permanent lakes where animal sightings are almost guaranteed.

In the increasingly common years when the rains fail, the park very quickly turns brown, parched and apparently lifeless. In more generous years the vegetation positively glows green, the lakes fill with water and animals seem to reappear from nowhere. At the time of research (2014) the park was looking the best we've seen it in years and visiting it was a real treat.

If you're without transport it's possible to walk to the Marsabit Lodge with an armed ranger (per person KSh1500; organise this through the park office the day before if possible). With luck you'll have some exciting encounters with buffaloes and elephants.

Marsabit National Park

🛏 Sleeping & Eating

Lake Paradise Special Campsite CAMPGROUND $
(camping adult US$35, plus set-up fee US$20) Although there's nothing except a dried-up lakebed and firewood, this picturesque site is the best place to camp in the park. Due to roaming buffaloes and elephants, a ranger must be present when you camp here.

Marsabit Lodge LODGE $$
(✆ Nairobi 020-2695468; www.marsabitlodge.com; s/tw KSh6500/8500) If you don't mind the rather faded rooms, this basic lodge has a deliciously peaceful setting overlooking the lake occupying Gof Sokorte Dika. Expect friendly service and a chef who, no doubt in pleasure at actually having something to do, puts together great meals. Electricity is by generator in the evening only.

Maralal to Turkana's Eastern Shore

Journeying to a sea of jade shouldn't be something that is easy to do and this route, the ultimate Kenyan adventure, is certainly not easy. But for the battering you'll take you'll be rewarded a thousand times over with memories of vibrant tribes, camel caravans running into a red sunset, mesmerising volcanic landscapes and, of course, the north's greatest jewel – the Jade Sea, Lake Turkana.

Maralal

Walking down Maralal's dusty streets, you can imagine Clint Eastwood emerging from a bar and proclaiming the town not big enough for the two of you. With its swinging cowboy doors and camels tied up outside colourful wooden shopfronts, it's impossible not to think that you've somehow been transported to the Wild West.

Maralal has gained an international reputation for its fantastically frenetic **International Camel Derby** and a visit over its duration is truly unforgettable. Less crazy, but almost as memorable, are the year-round camel safaris and treks that are offered here.

◉ Sights & Activities

Maralal National Sanctuary WILDLIFE RESERVE
FREE This sanctuary, home to zebras, impalas, hyenas and others, once completely surrounded the town. Today it only covers a small patch of land around what's left of the

Maralal

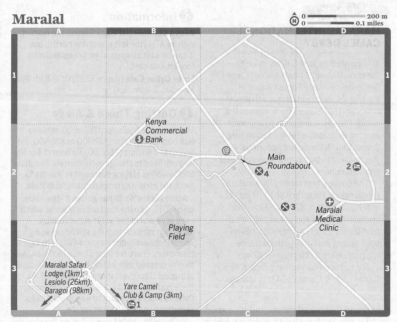

Maralal

🛏 Sleeping
1 Samburu Guest House B3
2 Sunbird Guest House D2

🍴 Eating
3 Coast Dishes C2
4 Pop Inn Hotel C2

Maralal Safari Lodge. With nowhere really to drive or walk on a safari, one of the only ways to take in the animals is with a cold beverage in hand at Maralal Safari Lodge's bar. You may need to bring your own beer, though, as this place may be on its last legs.

Loroghi Hills Circuit TREKKING
The Loroghi Hills Circuit, which takes in one of Kenya's most astounding vistas, Lesiolo, is a rewarding five-day (78km) trek. It's detailed in Lonely Planet's *Trekking in East Africa*. It should be posible to organise a guide through Yare Camel Club and Camp. Somewhat shorter walks are possible by just strolling aimlessly around the high country and down the paths linking *shambas* (small plots) that surround the town.

Yare Camel Club & Camp SAFARIS
(☎0729322500) Organises guides and camels for independent camel safaris in the region. Half-day camel hire is US$20, while an overnight trip with guides, camping equipment, food and cook costs US$120 per person.

🛏 Sleeping

Sunbird Guest House GUESTHOUSE $
(☎0720654567; s/d KSh1000/1200; 🅿) The single rooms are starting to look a little old and damp but, by and large, this very friend-

ly place has quiet, clean and comfortable rooms with nice linen, mosquito nets and hot water in the bathrooms. The courtyard has a sunny, garden vibe and there's a pleasant restaurant serving healthy fried stuff.

Samburu Guest House HOTEL $
(☎0725363471; www.samburuguesthouse.com; s/d KSh800/2000; 🅿🛜) Large, outrageously pink cube of a building on the edge of town with spacious rooms that take the cleanliness award for Maralal. The design of the building, though, is such that noise echoes through the rooms.

Yare Camel Club & Camp CAMPGROUND, CABINS $
(☎0729322500; camping KSh500, s/tw/tr US$23/38/55; 🅿@) This long-standing travellers' hangout, 3km south of town, has

DON'T MISS

MARALAL INTERNATIONAL CAMEL DERBY

Inaugurated by Yare Safaris in 1990, the annual Maralal International Camel Derby held in early August is one of the biggest events in Kenya, attracting riders and spectators from around the world. The races are open to anyone, and the extended after-parties at Yare Camel Club & Camp are notorious – you're likely to bump into some genuine characters here.

The derby's first race is for amateur camel riders. Pony up KSh1000 for your entry and another KSh3000 for your slobbering steed and get racing! It's a butt-jarring 11km journey. Don't even start feeling sorry for your backside – the professional riders cover 42km.

For further information contact Yare Camel Club & Camp (p347) in Maralal.

dreary and overpriced cabins, but it's a good spot for overlanders thanks to grassy lawns perfect for camping and a sociable bar.

 Eating

Unless you've got the ugali (a staple made from maize or cassava flour, or both) or *nyama choma* itch, few of your taste buds will be scratched here. That said, check out the restaurants of the Sunbird and Samburu Guest Houses. Stock up at the market or the Sunguia Supermarket if you're heading north.

Coast Dishes   KENYAN **$**
(mains KSh80-240) 'The neighbourhood will never be the same again,' the sign outside this place confidently reads. In fact the neighbourhood hasn't changed one jot in years, but even so this place, which is run by a couple from the sultry coast, does bring a flavour of other places to Maralal with coastal staples such as pilau, though made with goat rather than fish.

Pop Inn Hotel   KENYAN **$**
(meals KSh120-200; ⏱7am-8pm) This zebra-striped building has decent Kenyan staples, but its claim to have the 'best food south of the Sahara – and that's a fact' might not be a 'fact' at all – south of the roundabout seems more realistic.

ⓘ Information

Kenya Commercial Bank Behind the market, with an ATM (the last one going north), but it can be a bit stroppy when presented with foreign Visa cards.

Links Cyber Café (per hr KSh120; ⏱8am-8pm Mon-Sat, 2-8pm Sun)

ⓘ Getting There & Away

Matatus serve Nyahururu (KSh500, three to four hours), Rumuruti (KSh300 to KSh400, 2½ hours) and Wamba (KSh500, 3½ hours). For Nairobi you need to change in Nyahururu. Reaching Isiolo involves staying overnight in Wamba to catch the early-morning southbound matatu.

Access to the north has gotten a little easier since 2012, with the road out of Maralal, which used to be one of the worst in the country, being regraded (though it's still heavy going and self-drivers require a good 4WD with high clearance). There are buses too, which look like they're crossed with a tank, heading to Baragoi at around 11am every morning (KSh500). As there is still no regular transport north from there, it's more pleasant to wait in Maralal for something heading further north.

Waits for trucks to Loyangalani on the shore of Lake Turkana (KSh1000 to KSh1500, nine to 12 hours) might last from a few days to a week.

Baragoi

The long descent off the Loroghi Plateau towards Baragoi serves up some sweet vistas and for mile after gorgeous mile you'll literally see nothing but tree-studded grasslands alive with wildlife. Reaching Baragoi is a bit of an anticlimax though, as the dusty, diminutive town is clearly outdone by its surroundings.

The **Star Station Filling** sells pricey petrol and the bougainvillea-dressed **Morning Star Guest House** (s/d with shared bathroom KSh300/600) provides for a night's kip – though they don't supply the peg you'll need to place over your nose before entering the communal toilets.

Walking camel-train safaris (everything from bare bones to luxury) leave from the remote **Desert Rose lodge** (☑Nairobi 020-3864831; www.desertrosekenya.com; s/d all inclusive US$735/1250; ✈) just north of Baragoi.

ⓘ Getting There & Away

The dirt track from Maralal to Baragoi is very rocky in places, but massively better than it was in 2012. Even so, if there has been any rain it becomes treacherous. The drive takes a minimum of three hours.

Approaching the Lake

The road between Baragoi and South Horr, the next town along, is in reasonable shape and consists of compacted sand and bumpy rocky sections. Almost 23km north of South Horr, when the valley opens to the northern plains, you'll see massive Mt Kulal (2293m) in the distance and Devil's Hand, a large rock outcrop resembling a fist, to your immediate right. Just north is the eastern turn-off to Marsabit via Kargi, so if you're heading for Turkana keep left. If you get mixed up, just remember that Mt Kulal on your right is good and that Mt Kulal on your left is very, very bad (unless, of course, you're heading to Marsabit!).

Further north, the scrub desert scatters and you'll be greeted by vast volcanic armies of shimmering bowling-ball-sized boulders, cinder cones and reddish-purple hues – Mt Kulal's shattered lava fields. If this arresting and barren Martian landscape doesn't take your breath away, the first sight of the sparkling Jade Sea a few kilometres north certainly will.

As you descend to the lake, South Island stands proudly before you, while Teleki Volcano's geometrically perfect cone lurks on Turkana's southern shore. Before you jump in the water, remember that Turkana has the world's largest crocodile population.

Loyangalani

Standing in utter contrast to the dour desert shades surrounding it, tiny Loyangalani assaults all your senses in one crazy explosion of clashing colours, feather headdress-

LAKE TURKANA FESTIVAL

Held in mid-June, the Lake Turkana Festival is a jamboree of all that is colourful with the tribes of northern Kenya. Originally organised by the German embassy, it was taken on by the government in 2014 and word is was far less organised than in previous years... Even so, if you want to see people in their tribal best there's no better time to be in town.

es and blood-red robes. Overlooking Lake Turkana and surrounded by small ridges of pillow lava (evidence that this area used to be underwater), the sandy streets of this one-camel town are a meeting point of the great northern tribes: Turkana and Samburu, Gabbra and El Molo. It's one of the most exotic corners of Kenya and a fitting reward after the hard journey here.

◉ Sights & Activities

The El Molo tribe, which is one of Africa's smallest, lives on the lake shore just north of Loyangalani in the villages of Layeni and Komote. Although outwardly similar to the Turkana, the El Molo are linguistically linked to the Somali and Rendille people. Unfortunately, the last speaker of their traditional language died before the turn of the millennium. Visiting their villages is something of a circus and don't expect to see many people traditionally dressed.

South Island National Park PARK
(adult/child US$25/15) Designated a World Heritage site by Unesco in 1997, this

CAMEL SAFARIS IN NORTHERN KENYA

Days spent moving at the pace of a camel, and campfire nights under a star-spangled sky. A camel safari through the wild lands of northern Kenya will likely be the highlight of any trip to the country. One of the best-regarded camel safari operators is **Wild Frontiers** (☑ satellite phone 088216-43334103; www.wildfrontierskenya.com).

Safaris can be as tough or lazy as you want and while there's plenty of wildlife around, most of your animal sightings will, at best, be a fleeting glimpse of a fleeing animal. There will be lots of cultural interactions, though, as you pass by remote villages and herders with their livestock. The typical safari takes place in and around the magnificent Mathews and Ndoto mountains and lasts six nights, but much longer ones going all the way to Lake Turkana can be organised.

Wild Frontiers safaris help support the **Milgis Trust** (www.milgistrustkenya.com), which works with local communities to preserve the pastoral way of life and the wildlife of northern Kenya.

DON'T MISS

SIBILOI NATIONAL PARK

A Unesco World Heritage site and probably Kenya's most remote national park, **Sibiloi** (www.sibiloi.com; adult/child US$25/15) is located up the eastern shore of Lake Turkana and covers 1570 sq km. It was here that Dr Richard Leakey discovered the skull of a *Homo habilis* believed to be 2.5 million years old, and where others have unearthed evidence of *Homo erectus*. Despite the area's fascinating prehistory, fossil sites and wonderful arid ecosystem, the difficulties involved in getting this far north tend to discourage visitors, which is a real shame. It seems slightly ironic that the so-called 'Cradle of Mankind' is now almost entirely unpopulated.

The National Museums of Kenya (NMK) maintain a small museum and **Koobi Fora** (www.kfrp.com), a research base. It's usually possible to sleep in one of the base's **bandas** (per person KSh1000) or to pitch a tent in one of the **campsites** (camping per person KSh500).

Contact both the staff of the Loyangalani Desert Museum, the **KWS** (kws@kws.org) and **NMK** (www.museums.or.ke) before venturing in this direction.

In the dry season it's a tricky seven-hour drive north from Loyangalani to Sibiloi. You will need a guide from either KWS or the Loyangalani Desert Museum. Hiring a jeep in Loyangalani will work out at around KSh40,000 per day. It's also possible to hire a boat (KSh30,000 to KSh40,000 return with an overnight stop) from Fergusons Gulf on the western side of the lake.

39-sq-km purplish volcanic island is completely barren and uninhabited, apart from large populations of crocodiles, venomous snakes and feral goats. Spending the night at a **special campsite** (US$35) makes for an even eerier trip.

Mt Kulal   MOUNTAIN

Mt Kulal (2293m) dominates Lake Turkana's eastern horizon and its forested volcanic flanks offer some serious hiking possibilities. This fertile lost world in the middle of the desert is home to some unique creatures, including the Mt Kulal chameleon, a beautiful lizard first recorded in only 2003.

🛏 Sleeping & Eating

Let's face it: you came north for adventure, not comfort.

Malabo Resort   BANDA $

(☑ 0724705800;   resortmalabo@yahoo.com; camping KSh2000, huts from KSh2000, bandas KSh3000-4000; ℗) The newest, and best, place to stay in Loyangalani is a few hundred metres north of the village and has slight lake views. There's a range of decent *bandas* with arty wooden beds and attached bathrooms, or there are thatched huts based on a traditional Turkana design. The bar-restaurant area is a good place to hang out.

Cold Drink Hotel   KENYAN $

(meals KSh100-150; ⊙7am-8pm) Not just cold drinks but also, according to locals, the finest eating experience in all of Turkana country, which sadly might actually be true.

ℹ Getting There & Away

Trucks loaded with fish (and soon-to-be-smelly passengers) leave Loyangalani for Maralal (around KSh1000, nine to 12 hours) around once or twice a week at best. Trucks heading in any other direction are even rarer.

If you're travelling in your own vehicle, you have two options to reach Marsabit: continue northeast from Loyangalani across the dark stones of the Chalbi Desert towards North Horr, or head 67km south towards South Horr and take the eastern turn-off via Kargi. The 270km Chalbi route (10 to 12 hours) is hard in the dry season and impossible after rain. The 241km southern route (six to seven hours) via the Karoli Desert and Kargi is composed of compacted sands and is marginally less difficult in the rainy season.

Marich to Turkana's Western Shore

Despite boasting some of northern Kenya's greatest attributes, such as copious kilometres of Jade Sea shoreline, striking volcanic landscapes, ample wildlife and vivid Turkana tribes, this remote corner of the country sees relatively few visitors. With fairly reliable public transport this is definitely the easier side of the lake in which to grab a taste of the northern badlands.

Marich to Lodwar

The spectacular descent from Marich Pass through the lush, cultivated Cherangani Hills leads to arid surroundings, with sisal plants, cactus trees and acacias lining both the road and the chocolate-brown Morun River. Just north, the minuscule village of Marich marks your entrance into northern Kenya.

Activities

Mt Sekerr   TREKKING

Although the northern plains may beckon, it's worth heading into the hills for some eye-popping and leg-loving hiking action. Mt Sekerr (3326m) is a few kilometres northwest of Marich and can be climbed comfortably in a three-day round trip via the agricultural plots of the Pokot tribe, passing through forest and open moors.

Sleeping

Marich Pass Field Studies Centre   CAMPGROUND, BANDA $

(www.gg.rhul.ac.uk/MarichPass; camping KSh360, dm KSh420, s/tw KSh1450/1950, with shared bathroom KSh900/1240) Just north of Marich village, this is essentially a residential facility for visiting student groups, but it also makes a great base for independent travellers. The centre occupies a beautiful site alongside the misty Morun River and is surrounded by dense bush and woodland. Facilities include a secure campground as well as a tatty dorm and simple, comfortable *bandas*.

Getting There & Away

The road from Kitale via Makutano is the scenic A1 Hwy, which is often described as 'Kenya's most spectacular tarmac road'. The buses plying the A1 between Kitale and Lodwar can drop you anywhere along the route. You may be asked to pay the full fare to Lodwar (KSh1500), but a smile and some patient negotiating should reduce the cost.

Between Marich and Lokichar the A1 is a bumpy mess of corrugated dirt and lonely islands of tarmac. The first 40km north of Lokichar is better, but you'll still spend more time on the shoulder than on the road. The opposite is true for the remaining 60km to Lodwar, where patches outnumber potholes and driving is straightforward.

The security situation is in a constant state of flux in this area. In late 2014 convoys were not required, but in the recent past there have been numerous incidents of cattle rustling as well as tribal clashes. These problems have been most prevalent in the area between Marich and Lokichar.

Lodwar

Besides Lokichoggio near the South Sudan border, Lodwar is the only town of any size in the northwest. Volcanic hills skirted by traditional Turkana dwellings sit north of town and make for fine sunrise spots. If you're visiting Lake Turkana, you'll find it convenient to stay here for at least one night.

Sleeping

Nawoitorong Guest House   HOTEL $

(0704911947; camping KSh300, s/tw with shared bathroom KSh800/1500, cottages KSh1400-2000; P) Built entirely out of local materials and run by a local women's group, Nawoitorong is a solid budget option and the only one for campers. Thatched roofs alleviate the need for fans and all rooms have mosquito nets.

Ceamo Prestige Lodge   HOTEL $$

(0721555565; www.ceamolodge.com; s/d KSh6500/7500; P✳🛜) A short way out of town, this new place is also Lodwar's flashest place to stay, with large, cool, quiet, tiled rooms in a bungalow setting. It might be Lodwar's finest but it's still very overpriced.

Eating

Nawoitorong Guest House   KENYAN $

(meals KSh250-350; ⏲7am-8pm) Burgers and toasted sandwiches join local curries and various meaty fries on the menu. It offers

---

DID YOU KNOW?

➡ Lake Turkana, which is the world's largest permanent desert lake, has a shoreline that's longer than Kenya's entire Indian Ocean coast.

➡ The lake's water level was over 100m higher some 10,000 years ago and used to feed the mighty Nile. If the Gibe 3 Dam in Ethiopia is completed then the lake's waters may drop a further 10m.

➡ The first Europeans to reach the lake were Austrian explorers Teleki and von Höhnel in 1888. They proudly named it Lake Rudolf, after the Austrian Crown Prince at the time. It wasn't until the 1970s that the Kiswahili name Turkana was adopted.

CENTRAL ISLAND NATIONAL PARK

Bursting from the depths of Lake Turkana and home to thousands of living dinosaurs is the Jurassic world of Central Island Volcano, last seen belching molten sulphur and steam just over three decades ago. It is one of the most otherworldly places in Kenya. Quiet today, its stormy volcanic history is told by the numerous craters scarring its weathered facade. Several craters have coalesced to form two sizeable lakes, one of which is home to thousands of fish that occur nowhere else.

Both a **national park** (adult/child US$20/10) and Unesco World Heritage site, Central Island is an intriguing place to visit. Budding Crocodile Dundee types will love the 14,000 or so Nile crocodiles, some of which are massive in proportion, who flock here at certain times of year (May is the most crocodile-friendly month, but there are some crocs here year-round). The most northerly crater lake, which is saline, attracts blushing pink flocks of flamingos.

Camping (US$35) is possible and, unlike South Island National Park, there are trees to tie your tent to. But there's no water or any other facilities, so come prepared.

Hiring a boat from Ferguson's Gulf is the only option to get here. Organising one through KWS (who are comically disorganised) will set you back a hefty KSh18,000. Organising one through the locals down by the boat landing strip is likely to start at KSh15,000 and drop to KSh10,000. Don't ever think about being cheap and taking a sailboat. The 10km trip and sudden squalls that terrorise the lake's waters aren't to be taken lightly.

the most pleasant dining experience in the region, but give it time – lots of it – to prepare dinner!

Salama Hotel   KENYAN $
(meals KSh80-150; ⊘6am-9pm) The most popular place in the town centre. The culinary highlight of the Salama has to be its giant bowl of pilau (KSh100). There's always a crowd of people here waiting for buses to depart.

ⓘ Information

Kenya Commercial Bank Has an ATM and changes cash and travellers cheques.

ⓘ Getting There & Away

Fly540 (www.fly540.com) runs frequent flights from Nairobi to Lodwar and from Eldoret for around US$150.
Happy Safaris Buses operates along the route to Kitale (KSh1000, 8½ hours) with departures at 6am from close to the Salama Hotel. Erratic matatus serve Kalokol (KSh500, one hour). There's also a matatu to Eliye Springs (KSh300; 1½ hours).

Eliye Springs

Spring water percolates out of crumbling bluffs and oodles of palms bring a taste of the tropics to the remote sandy shores of Lake Turkana. Down on the slippery shore

children play in the lake's warm waters, while Central Island lurks magically on the distant horizon.

Eliye Springs is the best place to get a taste of the lake's western shore.

ⓘ Getting There & Away

The turn-off for Eliye Springs is signposted a short way along the Lodwar–Kalokol road. The gravel is easy to follow until it suddenly peters out and you're faced with a fork in the road – stay left.

If you don't have your own vehicle, you can usually arrange a car and driver in Lodwar for about KSh5000 including waiting time. There are also very occasional matatus for KSh300.

UNDERSTAND KENYA

History

The early history of Kenya, from prehistory to independence is covered in the History chapter (p552).

Mau Mau Rebellion

Kenya was Great Britain's East African heartland and the battle for independence was always going to be one of Africa's more bitter struggles for freedom.

Despite plenty of overt pressure on Kenya's colonial authorities, the real independence movement was underground. Tribal groups of Kikuyu, Maasai and Luo took secret oaths, which bound participants to kill Europeans and their African collaborators. The most famous of these movements was Mau Mau, formed in 1952 by disenchanted Kikuyu people, which aimed to drive the white settlers from Kenya forever.

The first blow was struck early with the killing of a white farmer's entire herd of cattle, followed a few weeks later by the massacre of 21 Kikuyu loyal to the colonial government. The Mau Mau rebellion had started. Within a month, Jomo Kenyatta and several other Kenyan African Movement (KAU) leaders were jailed on spurious evidence, charged with 'masterminding' the plot. The various Mau Mau sects came together under the umbrella of the Kenya Land Freedom Army, led by Dedan Kimathi, and staged frequent attacks against white farms and government outposts. By the time the rebels were defeated in 1956, the death toll stood at more than 13,500 Africans (guerrillas, civilians and troops) and just more than 100 Europeans.

Upon his release in 1959 Kenyatta resumed his campaign for independence. Soon even white Kenyans began to feel the winds of change, and in 1960 the British government officially announced their plan to transfer power to a democratically elected African government. Independence was scheduled for December 1963, accompanied by grants and loans of US$100 million to enable the Kenyan assembly to buy out European farmers in the highlands and restore the land to the tribes.

Independence

With independence scheduled for 1963, the political handover began in earnest in 1962, with the centralist Kenya African National Union (KANU) and the federalist Kenya African Democratic Union (KADU) forming a coalition government.

The run-up to independence was surprisingly smooth, although the redistribution of land wasn't a great success; Kenyans regarded it as too little, too late, while white farmers feared the trickle would become a flood. The immediate effect was to cause a significant decline in agricultural production, from which Kenya has never fully recovered.

The coalition government was abandoned after the first elections in May 1963

and Kikuyu leader, Jomo Kenyatta (formerly of the KANU), became Kenya's first president on 12 December, ruling until his death in 1978. Under Kenyatta's presidency, Kenya developed into one of Africa's most stable and prosperous nations.

While Kenyatta is still seen as one of the few success stories of Britain's withdrawal from empire, he wasn't without his faults. Biggest among these were his excessive bias in favour of his own tribe and escalating paranoia about dissent. Corruption soon became a problem at all levels of the power structure and the political arena contracted.

The 1980s

Kenyatta was succeeded in 1978 by his vice-president, Daniel arap Moi. A Kalenjin, Moi was regarded by establishment power brokers as a suitable frontman for their interests, as his tribe was relatively small and in thrall to the Kikuyu. Moi went on to become one of the most enduring 'Big Men' in Africa, ruling in virtual autocracy for nearly 25 years.

On assumption of power, Moi sought to consolidate his regime by marginalising those who had campaigned to stop him from succeeding Kenyatta. Lacking a capital base of his own, and faced with shrinking economic opportunities, Moi resorted to the politics of exclusion. He reconfigured the financial, legal, political and administrative institutions. For instance, a constitutional amendment in 1982 made Kenya a de jure one-party state, while another in 1986 removed the security of tenure for the attorney-general, comptroller, auditor general and High Court judges, making all these positions personally beholden to the president. These developments had the effect of transforming Kenya from an 'imperial state' under Kenyatta to a 'personal state' under Moi.

Winds of Change

By the late 1980s, most Kenyans had had enough. Following the widely contested 1988 elections, things came to a head on 7 July 1990 when the military and police raided an opposition demonstration in Nairobi, killing 20 and arresting politicians, human-rights activists and journalists. The rally, known thereafter as Saba Saba ('seven seven' in Swahili), was a pivotal event in the push for a multiparty Kenya. The resulting pressure led to a change in the constitution that allowed opposition parties to register for the first time.

Faced with a foreign debt of nearly US$9 billion and blanket suspension of foreign aid, Moi was pressured into holding flawed multiparty elections in early 1992. To make matters worse, about 2000 people were killed during tribal clashes in the Rift Valley. Moi was overwhelmingly re-elected.

The 1997 election, too, was accompanied by violence and rioting. European and North American tour companies cancelled their bookings and around 60,000 Kenyans lost their jobs. Moi was able to set himself up as peacemaker, calming the warring factions and gaining 50.4% of the seats for KANU. After the elections, KANU was forced to bow to mounting pressure and initiate some changes: some Draconian colonial laws were repealed, as well as the requirement for licences to hold political rallies.

But Kenya was about to enter a difficult period. On 7 August 1998, Islamic extremists bombed the US embassies in Nairobi and Dar es Salaam in Tanzania, killing more than 200 people and bringing al-Qaeda and Osama bin Laden to international attention for the first time. The effect on the Kenyan economy was devastating. It would take four years to rebuild the shattered tourism industry.

Democratic Kenya

Having been beaten twice in the 1992 and 1997 elections, 12 opposition groups united to form the National Alliance Rainbow Coalition (NARC). With Moi's presidency due to end in 2002, many feared that he would alter the constitution again to retain his position. This time, though, he announced his intention to retire.

Moi put his weight firmly behind Uhuru Kenyatta, the son of Jomo Kenyatta, as his successor, but the support garnered by NARC ensured a resounding victory for the party, with 62% of the vote. Mwai Kibaki was inaugurated as Kenya's third president on 30 December 2002.

When Kibaki assumed office in January 2003, donors were highly supportive of the new government. During its honeymoon period, the Kibaki administration won praise for a number of policy initiatives, especially a crackdown on corruption. In 2003–04, donors contributed billions of dollars to the fight against corruption, including support for the office of a newly appointed anticorruption 'czar', and the International Monetary Fund resumed lending in November 2003.

Corruption Continues

Despite initially positive signs, it became clear by mid-2004 that large-scale corruption was still a considerable problem in Kenya. Western diplomats alleged that corruption had cost the treasury US$1 billion since Kibaki took office. In February 2005, the British High Commissioner, Sir Edward Clay, denounced the 'massive looting' of state resources by senior government politicians, including sitting cabinet ministers. Within days, Kibaki's anticorruption 'czar', John Githongo, resigned and went into exile amid rumours of death threats related to his investigation of high-level politicians. With Githongo's release of a damning detailed dossier on corruption in the Kibaki regime in February 2006, Kibaki was forced to relieve three ministers of their cabinet positions.

But it hasn't all been bad news. The Kibaki government has succeeded in making primary and secondary education more accessible for ordinary Kenyans, while state control over the economy has been loosened.

Things Fall Apart

On 27 December 2007, Kenya held presidential, parliamentary and local elections. While the parliamentary and local government elections were largely considered credible, the presidential elections were marred by serious irregularities, reported by both Kenyan and international election monitors, and by independent nongovernmental observers. Nonetheless, the Electoral Commission declared Mwai Kibaki the winner, triggering a wave of violence across the country. The Rift Valley, Western Highlands, Nyanza Province and Mombasa – areas afflicted by years of political machination, previous election violence and large-scale displacement – exploded in ugly tribal confrontations. The violence left around 1300 people dead and over 600,000 people homeless. Fearing for the stability of the most stable linchpin of East Africa, former UN Secretary-General Kofi Annan and a panel of 'Eminent African Persons' flew to Kenya to mediate talks. A power-sharing agreement was finally signed on 28 February 2008 between President Kibaki and Raila Odinga, the leader of the ODM opposition. The coalition provided for the establishment of a prime ministerial position (to be filled by Raila Odinga) as well as a division of cabinet posts according to the parties' representation in parliament.

Rebuilding Confidence

Despite some difficult moments, the fragile coalition government has stood the test of time, thereby going some way towards reassuring Kenyans and the international community. The government has also begun the complex (and long-overdue) task of long-term reform. Arguably its most important success has been the 2010 constitution, which was passed in a referendum by 67% of Kenya's voters. Among the key elements of this new constitution are the devolution of powers to Kenya's regions, the introduction of a bill of rights and the separation of judicial, executive and legislative powers.

Kenya Today

It may seem a strange question to ask of a country that has proved to be one of Africa's most stable, but one of the hottest topics of conversation among ordinary Kenyans is this: can Kenya hold together? Kenyans were badly scarred by the post-election violence in 2007. So when Uhuru Kenyatta scraped over the line in the 2013 presidential elections amid allegations of electoral irregularities, the country, and the world, held their breaths. But somehow, a threshold was passed and the country held together – again. Had Kenya's political leaders grown in maturity sufficiently to recognise the dangers of escalating tensions? Or did they decide to bide their time for some future battle? At the time of writing, the answer remains unanswered.

But the fallout from the 2007 elections continues. In March 2011, the ICC indicted six prominent Kenyans, including presidential candidate Uhuru Kenyatta and former government minister William Ruto, for crimes against humanity allegedly committed during the violence that followed the disputed 2007 elections. Kenyan politicians soon began lining up to accuse the ICC and the Western governments who supported it of colonial attitudes and for interfering in Kenya's internal affairs. So successful was this argument that the ICC indictment of Kenyatta is widely credited with helping him to win the 2013 presidential election. In one of the more bizarre twists, Kenyatta's co-accused and former enemy at the 2007 elections, William Ruto, became Kenya's vice-president.

In October 2011, for the first time in its independent history, Kenya went to war. In response to attacks allegedly carried out by al-Shabaab, an al-Qaeda-affiliated Somali group, Kenya's military launched a large-scale invasion of Somalia, claiming that it was acting in self-defence; most Western governments agreed, and the mission later came under the banner of the African Union. Kenya has played a high price for its involvement in Somalia. The attack by al-Shabab operatives on the West Gate Shopping Mall on 21 September 2013 left 67 people dead and placed enormous strain on Kenya's relations with its large Somali population. Further attacks in the Nairobi suburb of Eastleigh in 2013, and on the area around Mpeketoni (close to Lamu) in June 2014 only heightened the sense of a nation under siege and unsure how to combat the threat. Quite apart from its impact upon Kenya's tourist industry, the episode served as a reminder that Kenya's future as a multicultural, multifaith state gets more complicated with each passing year.

Daily Life

Traditional cultures are what hold Kenya together. Respect for one's elders, firmly held religious beliefs, traditional gender roles and the tradition of *ujamaa* (familyhood) create a well-defined social structure with stiff moral mores at its core. Extended family provides a further layer of support, while historically, the majority of Kenyans were either farmers or cattle herders with family clans based in small interconnected villages. Even today, as traditional rural life gives way to a frenetic urban pace, this strong sense of community remains.

Kenya is home to over 40 tribal groups. Although most tribal groups have coexisted quite peacefully since independence, the ethnocentric bias of government and civil service appointments has led to escalating unrest and disaffection. During the hotly contested elections of 1992, 1997 and 2007, clashes between two major tribes, the Kikuyu and Luo, bolstered by allegiances with other smaller tribes like the Kalenjin, resulted in death and mass displacement.

Some analysts point out that election violence and ethnic tensions have more to do with economic inequality than with tribalism – they insist that there are only two tribes in Kenya: the rich and the poor.

Religion

As a result of intense missionary activity, the majority of Kenyans outside the coastal and eastern provinces are Christians (including some home-grown African Christian groups that do not owe any allegiance to the major Western groups). Hard-core evangelism has made some significant inroads and many TV-style groups from the US have a strong following.

In the country's east, the majority of Kenyans are Sunni Muslims. They make up about 11% of the population.

Arts

Music

With its diversity of indigenous languages and culture, Kenya has a rich and exciting music scene. Influences, most notably from the nearby Democratic Republic of Congo and Tanzania, have helped to diversify the sounds. More recently reggae and hip hop have permeated the pop scene.

The live-music scene in Nairobi is excellent – a variety of clubs cater for traditional and contemporary musical tastes, while the Blankets & Wine (p236) phenomenon has fast become a mainstay of the capital's live-music program. Beyond Nairobi, take what you can get.

Benga is the contemporary dance music of Kenya. It refers to the dominant style of Luo pop music, which originated in western Kenya, and spread throughout the country in the 1960s being taken up by Akamba and Kikuyu musicians. The music is characterised by clear electric guitar licks and a bounding bass rhythm. Contemporary Kikuyu music often borrows from benga.

Taarab, the music of the East African coast, originally only played at Swahili weddings and other special occasions, has been given a new lease of life by coastal pop singer Malika.

Popular bands today are heavily influenced by benga, *soukous* (African dance music) and also Western music, with lyrics generally in Kiswahili. These include bands such as Them Mushrooms (now reinvented as Uyoya) and Safari Sound. For upbeat dance tunes, Ogopa DJs, Nameless, Redsan and Deux Vultures are popular acts.

Literature

Ngũgĩ wa Thiong'o (b 1938), Kenya's best-known writer, is uncompromisingly radical, and his harrowing criticism of the neocolonialist politics of the Kenyan establishment landed him in jail for a year (described in his *Detained: A Prison Writer's Diary*), lost him his job at Nairobi University and forced him into exile. His works include *Petals of Blood, Matigari, The River Between, A Grain of Wheat, Devil on the Cross* and *Wizard of the Crow,* which was short-listed

---

KENYA PLAYLIST

➡ *Amigo* – Classic Swahili rumba from one of Kenya's most influential bands, Les Wanyika

➡ *Guitar Paradise of East Africa* – Ranges through Kenya's musical styles including the classic hit 'Shauri Yako'

➡ *Journey* – Jabali Afrika's stirring acoustic sounds complete with drums, congas, shakers and bells

➡ *Kenyan: The First Chapter* – Kenya's home-grown blend of African lyrics with R&B, house, reggae and dancehall genres

➡ *Mama Africa* – Suzanna Owiyo, the Tracy Chapman of Kenya, with acoustic Afropop

➡ *Nuting but de Stone* – Phenomenally popular compilation by band Hardstone combining African lyrics with American urban sounds and Caribbean *ragga*

➡ *Rumba is Rumba* – Infectious Congolese *soukous* (African dance music) with Swahili lyrics by Bilenge Musica du Zaire

➡ *Nairobi Beat: Kenyan Pop Music Today* – Regional sounds including Luo, Kikuyu, Kamba, Luhya, Swahili and Congolese

➡ *Virunga Volcano* – From Orchestre Virunga, with samba, sublime guitar licks, a bubbling bass and rich vocals

SWAHILI ARCHITECTURE

Swahili culture has produced one of the most distinctive architectures in Africa, if not the world. Once considered a stepchild of Arabic building styles, Swahili architecture, while owing some of its aesthetic to the Middle East, is more accurately a reflection of African design partly influenced by the Arab (and Persian, Indian and even Mediterranean) world.

One of the most important concepts of Swahili space is marking the line between the public and private while also occasionally blurring those borders. So, for example, you'll see Lamu stoops that exist both in the pubic arena of the street yet serve as a pathway into the private realm of the home. The use of stoops as a place for conversation further blends these inner and outer worlds. Inside the home, the emphasis is on creating an airy, natural interior that contrasts with the exterior constricting network of narrow streets. The use of open space also facilitates breezes that serve as natural air-conditioning.

You will find large courtyards, day beds placed on balconies and porches that all provide a sense of horizon within a town where the streets can only accommodate a single donkey. Other elements include: *dakas* (verandahs), which again sit in the transitional zone between the street and home and also provide open areas; *vidaka*, wall niches that either contain a small decorative curio or serve a decorative purpose in their own right; and *mambrui* (pillars), which are used extensively in Swahili mosques.

for the 2007 Commonwealth Writers' Prize. His latest works are memoirs: *Dreams in a Time of War* (2010) and *In the House of the Interpreter* (2012). All his works offer insightful portraits of Kenyan life and will give you an understanding of the daily concerns of modern Kenyans. Ngũgĩ has also written extensively in his native language, Gikuyu.

Another important Kenyan writer is Meja Mwangi (b 1948), who sticks more to social issues and urban dislocation but has a mischievous sense of humour, while Binyavanga Wainaina (b 1971) is one of Kenya's rising stars. Highly regarded female writers include Grace Ogot, Margaret Atieno Ogola, Marjorie Magoye and Hilary Ngweno.

To stay up to date with the contemporary scene, look out for *Kwani?* (kwani.org), Kenya's first literary journal, established by Wainaina in 2003. It hosts an annual literary festival that attracts a growing number of international names.

Environment

The Land

Kenya straddles the equator and covers an area of some 583,000 sq km, including around 13,600 sq km of Lake Victoria. It is bordered to the north by the arid bushlands of Ethiopia and Sudan, to the east by the Indian Ocean and the deserts of Somalia, to the west by Uganda and Lake Victoria, and to the south by Tanzania.

Kenya is dominated by the Rift Valley, a vast range of valleys that follows a 5500km-long crack in the earth's crust. The Rift's path through Kenya can be traced through Lake Turkana, the Cherangani Hills and Lakes Baringo, Bogoria, Nakuru, Elmenteita, Naivasha and Magadi. Within the Rift are numerous 'swells' (raised escarpments) and 'troughs' (deep valleys, often containing lakes), and there are some huge volcanoes, including Mt Kenya, Mt Elgon and Mt Kilimanjaro (across the border in Tanzania).

The African savannah covers an estimated two-thirds of the African land mass and owes its existence to the Rift Valley when volcanic lava and ash rained down upon the lands surrounding the Rift's volcanoes, covering the landscape in fertile but shallow soils. Grasses flourished as they needed little depth for their roots to grow. The perfectly adapted acacia aside, however, no other plants were able to colonise the savannah, their roots were starved of space and nourishment. In Kenya, the most famous sweeps of savannah are found in the country's west (particularly in the Masai Mara National Reserve) and south.

Along the coast of East Africa, warm currents in the Indian Ocean provide perfect conditions for coral growth, resulting in beautiful underwater coral reefs. In contrast, much of northern Kenya is extremely arid, with rainfall of less than 100mm a year. A number of contiguous deserts occupy the territory between Lake Turkana's eastern shore and the Ethiopian and Somali borders.

ECO TOURISM KENYA

Established in 1996, Eco Tourism Kenya (ecotourismkenya.org) is a private organisation set up to oversee the country's tourism industry and encourage sustainable practices. Part of that involves a helpful Eco-rating Certification scheme for Kenya's hotels, safari camps and other accommodation options.

Under the scheme, a bronze rating is awarded to businesses which 'demonstrate awareness of and commitment to environmental conservation, responsible resource use and socio-economic investment'.

The silver standard goes to those businesses who 'demonstrate innovation – progress towards achieving excellence in environmental conservation, responsible resource use and socio-economic investment'.

To attain the much-coveted gold rating, tourism concerns must 'demonstrate out-standing best practices, ie they have achieved superior and replicable levels of excellence in responsible resource use, environmental conservation and socio-economic investment'.

At the time of writing, just 13 places had received the gold certification, 54 had silver status and 30 were bronze-rated. To find out which properties made the cut, click on 'Eco-rated Facilities' under 'Directory Listings' on Eco Tourism Kenya's home page.

The main rivers in Kenya are the Athi/ Galana River, which empties into the Indian Ocean near Malindi, and the Tana River, which hits the coast midway between Malindi and Lamu. Aside from Lake Victoria, Kenya has numerous small volcanic lakes and mighty Lake Turkana, which straddles the Ethiopian border.

Wildlife

Kenya is home to all of the charismatic megafauna that draw so many visitors to Africa and the daily battle between predators and prey brings so much personality to the Kenyan wilds. The 'Big Five' – lion, buffalo, elephant, leopard and rhino – are relatively easy to spot in a number of places. The birdlife here is equally diverse – Kenya is home to over 1100 species with millions of migratory birds arriving or passing through the country from November to October.

ENDANGERED SPECIES

Many of Kenya's major predators and herbivores have become endangered because of the continuous destruction of their natural habitat and merciless poaching for ivory, skins, horn and bush meat.

The black rhino is probably Kenya's most endangered large mammal. It is also often described as Kenya's indigenous rhino – historically, the white rhino was not found in Kenya. Pursued by heavily armed gangs, the black rhino's numbers fell from an estimated 20,000 in the 1970s to barely 300 a decade later. Numbers are slowly recovering (rhinos are notoriously slow breeders), with an estimated 620 black rhinos surviving in the wild in Kenya, which represents around one-sixth of Africa's total (or close to 90% of the world population for the eastern subspecies of black rhino). **Rhino Ark** (☎ 020-2136010; www.rhinoark.org) is one organisation that raises funds to create rhino sanctuaries or to build fences around national parks, as they have done in Aberdare National Park, and donations are always appreciated. Your best chance of seeing the black rhino is at Ol Pejeta Conservancy, Lewa Wildlife Conservancy and Solio Game Reserve, as well as in the national parks of Nairobi, Tsavo West, Aberdare, Meru and Lake Nakuru.

While the elephant is not technically endangered, it is still the target of poachers, and a large number are killed every year, especially in the area around Tsavo East National Park. Elephant numbers in Kenya dropped to an estimated 5400 in 1988, but numbers have recovered to around 32,000. More than one-third of these inhabit Tsavo West and Tsavo East national parks.

Lions are also considered endangered in Kenya with fewer than 2000 thought to survive, although this is feared to be an overestimate. The only viable lion populations in the long-term are those in Laikipia, Meru National Park and Maasailand (which stretches across southern Kenya from the Masai Mara National Reserve to Tsavo East National Park).

Other endangered species include the hirola antelope (found in Tsavo East National Park), Grevy's zebra (found only in some Laikipia conservancies and the Samburu, Buffalo Springs and Shaba National Reserves) and the Rothschild's giraffe (which still roams Lake Nakuru and Ruma National Parks).

National Parks & Reserves

Kenya's national parks and reserves rate among the best in Africa. Around 10% of the country's land area is protected by law – that means, at least in theory, no human habitation, no grazing and no hunting within park boundaries. The parks range from the 15.5-sq-km Saiwa Swamp National Park to the massive, almost 21,000-sq-km Tsavo East and West National Parks. Together they embrace a wide range of habitats and ecosystems and contain an extraordinary repository of Africa's wildlife.

PARK & RESERVE ENTRY

Entry fees to national parks are controlled by the **KWS** (Kenya Wildlife Service; ☎020-6000800; www.kws.org; Nairobi National Park) and admission to parks in Kenya follows a 'safaricard' system for the payment of fees. There are two types of safaricards – permanent and temporary. For a full rundown on the system, visit www.kws.org/about/safaricard.

> **WHICH CURRENCY?**
>
> Note that Kenya Wildlife Service (KWS) now accepts euros and UK pounds, but you're still better off paying in Kenyan shillings or US dollars as KWS exchange rates are punitive.

To put it in the simplest terms, it's handy to know how the system operates, but if you turn up at any park gate with enough cash in your wallet, you will be fine.

Permanent safaricards are sold at a handful of park entrances (check the website for a full list). These can be charged with credit in advance and can be topped up at certain locations (usually the parks' main gates only, which can be inconvenient). Remaining credit is not refundable. Remember that not all parks accept safaricards, so check which ones will only accept cash before topping up unnecessarily.

In practice, it is difficult to see why you'd need a permanent safaricard. In those parks where safaricards are in use, you can actually purchase a temporary safaricard, which covers the duration of your stay and which you surrender upon leaving the park. In other words, whether you're paying to top up your permanent card or paying for a

KENYA ENVIRONMENT

PARK ENTRY FEES

KWS CATEGORY	PARK OR RESERVE	NONRESIDENT ADULT/CHILD (US$)	CAMPING NONRESIDENT ADULT/CHILD (US$)
N/A	Masai Mara	80/45	20/20
Premium	Amboseli, Lake Nakuru	80/40	30/25
Wilderness	Meru, Tsavo East & Tsavo West	75/40	20/15
Aberdare National Park	Aberdare	60/30	20/15
Urban Park	Nairobi National Park	50/25	20/15
Mountain Climbing (Day Trip)	Mt Kenya	55/25	20/15
Mountain Climbing (4-day package)	Mt Kenya	255/150	20/15
Scenic & Special Interest A	Hell's Gate, Mt Elgon, Ol Donyo Sabuk & Mt Longonot	30/20	20/15
Scenic & Special Interest B	Chyulu, Marsabit, Arabuko Sokoke, Kakamega, Shimba Hills & all other KWS parks	25/15	20/15
Marine Parks A	Kisite	25/15	n/a
Marine Parks B	Malindi, Watamu, Mombasa, Kiunga	20/15	n/a

PRIVATE VS PUBLIC CONSERVATION

Kenya Wildlife Service (KWS)

Conservation in Kenya has, for over two decades, been in the hands of the government-run **Kenya Wildlife Service** (www.kws.org) and few would dispute that they've done a pretty impressive job. In the dark years of the 1970s and '80s when poaching was rampant, a staggering number of Kenya's rhinos and elephants were slaughtered and many KWS officers were in league with poachers. It all changed after the famous palaeontologist Dr Richard Leakey cleaned up the organisation in the 1980s and '90s. A core part of his policy was arming KWS rangers with modern weapons and high-speed vehicles and allowing them to shoot poachers on sight, which seems to have dramatically reduced the problem. However, there have been several raids on elephant and rhino populations over the past decade and KWS rangers continue to lose their lives every year in battles with poachers.

Despite their excellent work in fighting poaching and maintaining Kenya's protected areas, the KWS is limited in what it can achieve. For a start, in times of shrinking government revenues, funding remains a major issue in how well the KWS can fulfil its mandate.

Just as importantly, much of Kenya's wildlife lives beyond national park and other publicly protected boundaries. In such an environment, the KWS has shown itself to be at times intransigent in handling incidents of human-wildlife conflict in the communities that surround national park areas. As a result, there is a widespread perception among some communities that the KWS is more interested in looking after wildlife than they are in protecting local people. In response, the KWS has in recent years been working hard to improve its community relations, particularly in and around Amboseli National Park.

Private Conservation

Serious private conservation began up on the Laikipia Plateau and surrounding areas, on large cattle ranches which had, in many cases, been owned by the same family of white settlers since colonial times. One of the first to turn its attention to conservation was Lewa Downs, now the Lewa Wildlife Conservancy (p283), which in 1983 set aside part of its land as a rhino sanctuary. Lewa remains a standard bearer for the conservancy model

---

temporary card, the process you'll encounter at park gates is almost identical.

At the time of writing the safaricard system was in use at Nairobi, Lake Nakuru, Aberdare, Amboseli and Tsavo national parks and at the Mombasa and Mailindi marine parks. The other parks still work on a cash-only system.

Environmental Issues

Kenya faces a daunting slew of environmental issues, among them deforestation, desertification, threats to endangered species and the impacts of tourism. In response, Kenya's private conservation community has taken matters into its own hands with, in many cases, exceptional results.

DEFORESTATION

Forest destruction continues on a large scale in parts of Kenya – today, less than 3% of the country's original forest cover remains. Land grabbing, charcoal burning, agricultural encroachment, the spiralling use of firewood and illegal logging, have all taken their toll over the years. However, millions of Kenyans (and the majority of hotels, lodges and restaurants) still rely on wood and charcoal for cooking fuel, so travellers to the country will almost certainly contribute to this deforestation, whether they like it or not.

The degazetting of protected forests is another contentious issue, sparking widespread protests and preservation campaigns. On the flipside, locals in forest areas can find themselves homeless if the government does enforce protection orders.

DESERTIFICATION

Northern and eastern Kenya are home to some of the most marginal lands in East Africa. Pastoralists have eked out a similarly marginal existence here for centuries, but recurring droughts have seriously de-

and there are now more than 40 such conservancies scattered across Laikipia and northern regions, with many more around the Masai Mara.

While wildlife conservation is a primary focus of nearly all conservancies – these places often have the resources to work more intensively on specific conservation issues than national parks and reserves can – community engagement and development are considered equally important. Most often this consists of funding local schools, health centres and other development projects. By giving local communities a stake in the protection of wildlife, so the argument goes, they are more likely to protect the wildlife in their midst.

Another important element of the conservancy model includes making tourism pay its way. In almost all of the conservancies, access to conservancy land is restricted to those staying at the exclusive and often extremely expensive lodges and tented camps. Most also charge a conservancy fee (usually around US$100 per day) which goes directly to local community projects and wildlife programs. All of this means a far more intimate safari experience as well as a much-reduced impact upon the land when compared with mass tourism.

Yet another advantage of visiting a private conservancy is that the range of activities on offer far exceeds what is possible in national parks. At the most basic level, this means off-road driving (to get you *really* close to the wildlife), night drives and walking safaris. Horseback safaris and visits to local communities are among the other possibilities, although you'll usually pay extra for these.

One exception to the overall rule, and it's a significant one, is Ol Pejeta Conservancy (p282). Although similar in terms of wildlife protection programs and community engagement, it has opened its doors to the public and receives tens of thousands of visitors every year. The experience of visiting Ol Pejeta is akin to visiting a national park but with a whole lot of really cool activities thrown in.

The private conservancies of the Laikipia plateau in particular have produced some startling results – without a single national park or reserve in the area, Laikipia has become a major safari destination, and is proving to be a particularly important area for viable populations of endangered black rhinos, Grevy's zebras, African wild dogs and lions. In fact, the black rhino may well have disappeared forever from Kenya were it not for the Laikipia conservancies.

graded the land, making it increasingly susceptible to creeping desertification and erosion. As a consequence, the UN estimates that the livelihoods of around 3.5 million herders may be under medium- to long-term threat.

SURVIVAL GUIDE

Directory A–Z

ACCOMMODATION

Kenya has a wide range of accommodation options, from basic hotels with cells overlooking city bus stands to luxury tented camps hidden away in remote corners of the country. There are also all kinds of campsites, budget tented camps, *bandas* (thatched-roof wood or stone huts) and cottages scattered around the parks and rural areas.

High-season prices usually run from June to October, from January until early March, and include Easter and Christmas. Low season usually covers the rest of the year, although some lodges and top-end hotels also have intermediate shoulder seasons.

On the coast, peak times tend to be July to August and December to March, and a range of lower rates can apply for the rest of the year.

Many places, particularly in national parks or other remote areas, offer full-board-only rates – prices may, therefore, seem higher than you'd expect, but less so once you factor in three meals a day. Some also offer what are called 'package rates' which include full-board accommodation but also things such as game drives, transfers and other extras.

Kenya operates on a dual pricing system – non-residents pay significantly more (often double or triple the price) than Kenyan (or other East African) residents. When things are quiet, you may be able to get the residents' rate if you ask, but don't count on it. Prices quoted in reviews are nonresident rates, unless otherwise stated.

We also quote prices in the currency preferred by the place in question (usually US$ or KSh), but in most cases you can pay in dollars, shillings, euros and (sometimes) other foreign currencies.

Bandas

These are Kenyan-style huts and cottages, usually with some kind of kitchen and bathroom, which offer excellent value. There are Kenya Wildlife Service (KWS) *bandas* at some national parks. Facilities range from basic dorms and squat toilets to kitchens and hot water provided by wood-burning stoves. In such places, you'll need to bring all your own food, drinking water, bedding and firewood.

Camping

There are many opportunities for camping in Kenya and, although gear can be hired in Nairobi and around Mt Kenya, it's worth considering bringing a tent with you. There are KWS campsites in just about every national park or reserve. These are usually very basic, with a toilet block with a couple of pit toilets, a water tap, perhaps public showers and very little else. They cost US$30/25 per adult/child in Amboseli and Lake Nakuru National Parks, begin at US$20 in Masai Mara National Reserve and US$20/15 in all other parks.

As well as these permanent campsites, KWS also runs so-called 'special' campsites in most national parks. These sites move every year and have even fewer facilities than the standard camps, but cost more because of their wilder locations and set-up costs. They cost US$50/25 per adult/child in Amboseli and Lake Nakuru, US$35/20 elsewhere; a reservation fee of KSh7500 per week is payable on top of the relevant camping fee.

All camping prices in reviews are per person unless otherwise specified.

Hostels

The only youth hostel affiliated with Hostelling International (HI) is in Nairobi. It has good basic facilities and is a pleasant enough place to stay, but there are plenty of other cheaper choices that are just as good. Other places that call themselves 'youth hostels' are not members of HI, and standards are variable.

Hotels & Guest Houses

Real bottom-end hotels (often known as 'board and lodgings' to distinguish them from *hotelis*, which are often only restaurants) are widely used as brothels, and tend to be very rundown; security at these places is virtually nonexistent.

Proper hotels and guesthouses come in many different shapes and sizes. As well as the top-end Western companies, there are a number of small Kenyan chains offering reliable standards across a handful of properties, and also plenty of private family-run establishments.

Self-catering options are common on the coast, where they're often the only midpriced alternative to the top-end resorts, but not so much in other parts of the country.

Terms you will come across in Kenya include 'self-contained', which just means a room with its own private bathroom, and 'all-inclusive', which generally means all meals, certain drinks and possibly some activities should be included. 'Full-board' accommodation includes three meals a day, while 'half board' generally means breakfast and dinner are included.

Safari Lodges

Hidden away inside or on the edges of national parks are some fantastic safari lodges. These are usually visited as part of organised safaris, and you'll pay much more if you just turn up and ask for a room. Some of the older places trade heavily on their more glorious past, but the best places feature five-star rooms, soaring *makuti*-roofed bars (with a thatched roof of palm leaves) and restaurants overlooking waterholes full of wildlife. Rates tend to fall significantly in the low season.

Tented Camps

As well as lodges, many parks contain some fantastic luxury tented camps. These places tend to occupy wonderfully remote settings, usually by rivers or other natural locations, and feature large, comfortable, semipermanent safari tents with beds, furniture, bathrooms (usually with hot running water) and often some kind of external roof thatch to keep the rain out; you sleep surrounded by the sounds of the African bush. Most of the camps are very upmarket and the tents are pretty much hotel rooms under canvas.

ACTIVITIES

Kenya has a long list of activities that are at once terrific ways to explore Kenya's varied terrain and fabulous experiences in their own right. These include the following:

PRICE RANGES

The order of accommodation listings is by budget and then author preference, and each place is accompanied by one of the following budget-category symbols (the price relates to a high-season double room with private bathroom and, unless stated otherwise, includes breakfast):

$ less than US$50

$$ US$50 to US$150

$$$ more than US$150

Ballooning Usually includes a 1½-hour flight, champagne breakfast and wildlife drive for around US$500 per person. In the Masai Mara only.

Cycling & Mountain-Biking Operators **Bike Treks** (☑ 020-2141757; www.angelfire.com/sk/ biketreks; Kabete Gardens, Westlands, Nairobi; midrange) and Rift Valley Adventures (p283) offer specialised cycling trips. Many places to stay (particularly campgrounds) can arrange bicycle hire for KSh600 to KSh1000 per day. Good places to go cycling include Masai Mara National Reserve, Ol Pejeta Conservancy and Hell's Gate National Park, although you can only do the first two as part of an organised group.

Diving & Snorkelling If you aren't certified to dive, almost every hotel and resort on the coast can arrange an open-water diving course. They're not much cheaper (if at all) than anywhere else in the world – a five-day PADI certification course starts at around US$470. Trips for certified divers including two dives go for around US$100. October to March is the best time, but during June, July and August it's often impossible to dive due to the poor visibility caused by heavy silt flow from some rivers. That said, some divers have taken the plunge in July and found visibility to be a very respectable 7m to 10m, although 4m is more common.

Trekking & Climbing Kenya has some of the best trekking trails in East Africa, ranging from strenuous mountain ascents to rolling hill country and forests. It is, of course, always worth checking out the prevalence of any wild animals you might encounter along the trail. In some instances, it may be advisable to take a local guide, either from the Kenyan Wildlife Service (KWS), if they operate in the area, or a local village guide.

Water Sports Conditions on Kenya's coast are ideal for windsurfing – the country's offshore reefs protect the waters, and the winds are usually reasonably strong and constant. Most resort hotels south and north of Mombasa have sailboards for hire. Diani Beach in particular is good for water sports.

White-Water Rafting The most exciting times for white-water rafting trips are late October to mid-January and early April to late July, when water levels are highest. The Athi/Galana River in particular has substantial rapids, chutes and waterfalls. The people to talk to are **Savage Wilderness Safaris** (Map p234; ☑ 020-7121590; www.savagewilderness.org; Sarit Centre, Westlands, Nairobi; midrange to top end).

CUSTOMS REGULATIONS

There are strict laws about taking wildlife products out of Kenya. The export of products made from elephant, rhino and sea turtle are prohibited. The collection of coral is also not allowed. Ostrich eggs will be confiscated unless you can prove you bought them from a certified ostrich

KENYA'S BEST TREKKING

Mountain Trekking
➡ Mt Kenya (5199m)
➡ Mt Elgon National Park (4187m)
➡ Mt Longonot (2776m)
➡ Cherangani Hills
➡ Loita Hills
➡ Aberdare
➡ Ndoto Mountains

Forest Trekking
➡ Kakamega Forest
➡ Arabuko Sokoke Forest Reserve

farm. Always check to see what permits are required, especially for the export of any plants, insects and shells.

You are allowed to take up to KSh100,000 out of the country.

Allowable quantities which you can bring into Kenya include the following:

Cigars 50
Cigarettes 200
Alcohol 1L
Perfume 250ml

EMBASSIES & CONSULATES

Australian High Commission (Map p220; ☑ 020-4277100; www.kenya.embassy.gov.au; ICIPE House, Riverside Dr, Nairobi)

Canadian High Commission (☑ 020-3663000; www.canadainternational.gc.ca/kenya/index.aspx; Limuru Rd, Gigiri, Nairobi)

Ethiopian Embassy (Map p220; ☑ 020-2732050; State House Ave, Nairobi)

French Embassy (Map p224; ☑ 020-2778000; www.ambafrance-ke.org; 15th fl, Barclays Plaza, Loita St, Nairobi)

German Embassy (☑ 020-4262100; www.nairobi.diplo.de; 113 Riverside Dr, Nairobi)

Netherlands Embassy (☑ 020-4288000; kenia.nlembassy.org; Riverside Lane, Nairobi)

South Sudan Embassy (Map p220; ☑ 020-2711384; 6th fl Bishops Gate House, 5th Ngong Ave, Nairobi)

Tanzanian Embassy (Map p224; ☑ 020-331057, 020-2311948; Reinsurance Plaza, Aga Khan Walk, Nairobi)

UK High Commission (Map p220; ☑ 020-2873000; www.gov.uk/government/world/kenya; Upper Hill Rd, Nairobi)

USA (☑ 020-3636000; http://nairobi.usembassy.gov; United Nations Ave, Nairobi)

PRACTICALITIES

➡ **Newspapers & Magazines** The *Daily Nation* (www.nation.co.ke), the *East African Standard* (www.standardmedia.co.ke), the *East African* (www.theeastafrican.co.ke) and the *New African* (newafricanmagazine.com).

➡ **TV** KBC and NTV, formerly KTN, are the main national TV stations. CNN, Sky and BBC networks are also widely available on satellite or cable (DSTV).

➡ **Radio** KBC Radio broadcasts across the country on various FM frequencies. BBC World Service is easily accessible.

➡ **Weights & Measures** Metric

➡ **Smoking** Banned in restaurants, bars and public areas, with fines for breaches.

GAY & LESBIAN TRAVELLERS

Negativity towards homosexuality is widespread in Kenya and recent events ensure that it's a brave gay or lesbian Kenyan who comes out of the closet.

In a 2007 poll, 96% of Kenyans surveyed stated that homosexuality should be rejected by society. Then, in early 2010, mob violence rocked a health centre where suspected homosexuals were targeted. In November 2010, Prime Minister Raila Odinga described homosexuality as 'unnatural' and called for gays and lesbians to be arrested, and when British PM David Cameron threatened in November 2011 to withdraw aid to some African countries if they did not improve their record on gay and lesbian rights, there was a vociferous public outcry in Kenya. In July 2014, 60 people were arrested for 'suspected homosexuality' in a Nairobi nightclub.

Underlying all of this is a penal code that states that homosexual (and attempted homosexual) behaviour is punishable by up to 14 years in prison.

Of course, people do live homosexual lifestyles covertly, particularly along the coast. There are very few prosecutions under the law, but it's certainly better to be extremely discreet – some local con artists do a good line in blackmail, picking up foreigners then threatening to expose them to the police.

Useful Resources

David Tours (www.davidtravel.com) Can arrange anything from balloon safaris to luxurious coastal hideaways, all with a gay focus.

Global Gayz (www.globalgayz.com) Links to country-by-country gay issues, including Kenya.

Purple Roofs (www.purpleroofs.com/africa/kenya) Lists a number of gay or gay-friendly tour companies in Kenya that may be able to help you plan your trip.

INTERNET ACCESS

Internet cafes Common in large and medium-sized Kenyan towns; connection speeds fluctuate wildly and prices range from KSh30 to KSh100 per hour.

Post offices Internet at almost every main post office in the country; prepaid cards with PIN are valid at any branch around Kenya.

Wireless Increasingly common in midrange and top-end hotels; often (but not always) available in upmarket safari lodges, less common in midrange places in remote areas.

Local networks Both Safari.com and Airtel have dongles/modems that you plug into your laptop, giving you wireless access anywhere that there's mobile coverage.

LANGUAGE COURSES

Taking a Swahili-language course (or any course) entitles you to a 'Pupil's Pass', which is an immigration permit allowing continuous stays of up to 12 months. You may have to battle with bureaucracy and the process may take months, but it can be worth it, especially as you will then have resident status in Kenya during your stay.

ACK Language & Orientation School (Map p220; ☑ 020-2721893; www.ackenya.org/institutions/language_school; Bishops Rd, Upper Hill, Nairobi) The Anglican Church runs full-time Swahili courses of varying levels lasting 14 weeks and taking up to five hours a day. Private tuition is available on a flexible part-time schedule.

Language Center Ltd (Map p230; ☑ 0721495774, 020-3870610; www.language-cntr.com/welcome.shtml; Ndemi Close, off Ngong Rd, Nairobi) A good Swahili centre offering a variety of study options ranging from private hourly lessons to daily group courses.

LEGAL MATTERS

All drugs except *miraa* (a leafy shoot chewed as a stimulant) are illegal in Kenya. Marijuana (commonly called *bhang*) is widely available but illegal; possession carries a penalty of up to 10 years in prison. Dealers are common on the beaches north and south of Mombasa and frequently set up travellers for sting operations for real or phoney cops to extort money.

African prisons are unbelievably harsh places – don't take the risk. Note that *miraa* is illegal in Tanzania, so if you do develop a taste for the stuff in Kenya you should leave it behind when heading south.

MAPS

The *Tourist Map of Kenya* gives good detail, as does the *Kenya Route Map;* both cost around KSh250. Otherwise, Marco Polo's *Shell Euro Karte Kenya (*1:1,000,000), Geocenter's *Kenya* (1:1,000,000) and IGN's *Carte Touristique: Kenya* (1:1,000,000) are useful overview maps that are widely available in Europe.

Most maps to Kenya's national parks might look a bit flimsy on detail (you won't get much in the way of topographical detail), but they include the numbered junctions in the national parks.

Macmillan publishes a series of maps to the wildlife parks that are not bad value at around KSh250 each (three are available in Europe: *Amboseli, Masai Mara* and *Tsavo East & West*). Tourist Maps also publishes a national park series for roughly the same price. The maps by the KWS are similar.

MONEY

The unit of currency is the Kenyan shilling (KSh), which is made up of 100 cents. Notes in circulation are KSh1000, 500, 200, 100, 50 and 20, and there are also coins of KSh40, 20, 10, five and one in circulation.

The most convenient way to bring your money is in a mixture of cash and a debit or credit card.

ATMs

Virtually all banks in Kenya now have ATMs at most branches, but their usefulness to travellers varies widely. Barclays Bank has easily the most reliable machines for international withdrawals, with a large network of ATMs covering most major Kenyan towns. They support MasterCard, Visa, Plus and Cirrus international networks.

Standard Chartered and Kenya Commercial Bank ATMs also accept Visa but not the other major providers, and are more likely to decline transactions. Whichever bank you use, the international data link still goes down occasionally, so don't rely on being able to withdraw money whenever you need it.

Cash

While most major currencies are accepted in Nairobi and Mombasa, once away from these two centres you'll run into problems with currencies other than US dollars, pounds sterling and euros.

Credit Cards

Credit cards are becoming increasingly popular, although the connections fail with tedious regularity. Visa and MasterCard are now widely accepted in midrange and top-end hotels, top-end restaurants and some shops.

Moneychangers

The best places to change money are foreign exchange or 'forex' bureaus, which can be found everywhere and usually don't charge commission. The rates for the main bureaus in Nairobi are published in the *Daily Nation* newspaper.

International Transfers

Postbank, a branch of the Kenyan Post Office, is the regional agent for Western Union, the global money-transfer company. Using its service is an easy way (if the phones are working) of receiving money in Kenya. Handily, the sender pays all the charges and there's a Postbank in most towns, often in the post office or close by.

Kenyans swear by M-Pesa, a quick-and-easy way of transferring money via mobile networks.

Tipping

Tipping is not common practice among Kenyans, but there's no harm in rounding up the bill by a few shillings if you're pleased with the service.

Hotel porters Tips expected in up-market hotels.

Restaurants A service charge of 10% is often added to the bill along with the 16% VAT and 2% catering levy.

Taxi drivers As fares are negotiated in advance, no need to tip unless they provide you with exceptional service.

Tour guides, safari drivers and cooks Will expect some kind of gratuity at the end of your tour or trip.

OPENING HOURS

Banks 9am-3pm Mon-Fri, 9am-11am Sat

Post Offices 8.30am-5pm Mon-Fri, 9am-noon Sat

Restaurants 11am-2pm & 5-9pm, some remain open between lunch and dinner

Shops 9am-3pm Mon-Fri, 9-11am Sat

Supermarkets 8.30am-8.30pm Mon-Fri, 10am-8pm Sat

ⓘ US DOLLAR TRICKS

➡ When getting US currency to take to Kenya, make sure you get US$100 bills manufactured in 2006 or later. Most banks and just about all businesses simply won't accept those that were printed earlier.

➡ If changing money at a forex bureau or other moneychanger, watch out for differing small-bill (US$10) and large-bill (US$100) rates; the larger bills usually get the better exchange rates.

POST

The Kenyan postal system is run by the government **Posta** (www.posta.co.ke). Letters sent from Kenya rarely go astray but can take up to two weeks to reach Australia or the USA. If sent by surface mail, parcels take three to six months to reach Europe, while airmail parcels take around a week.

Most things arrive eventually, although there is still a problem with theft within the system. Curios, clothes and textiles will be OK, but if your parcel contains anything of obvious value, send it by courier. Posta has its own courier service, EMS, which is considerably cheaper than the big international courier companies. The best place to send parcels from is the main post office in Nairobi.

PUBLIC HOLIDAYS

In addition to the following, Muslim festivals are significant events along the coast.

1 January New Year's Day
March/April Good Friday and Easter Monday
1 May Labour Day
1 June Madaraka Day
10 October Moi Day
20 October Kenyatta Day
12 December Independence Day
25 December Christmas Day
26 December Boxing Day

SAFE TRAVEL

While Kenya is a comparatively safe African destination, there are still plenty of pitfalls for the unwary or inexperienced traveller, from everyday irritations to more serious threats.

Banditry

The ongoing conflict in Somalia has had an effect on the stability and safety of northern and northeastern Kenya. AK-47s have been flowing into the country for many years, and the newspapers are filled with stories of hold-ups, shootouts, cattle rustling and general lawlessness. Bandits and poachers infiltrating from Somalia have made the northeast of the country particularly dangerous.

In the northwest, the main problem is armed tribal wars and cattle rustling across the South Sudanese border. There are Kenyan *shiftas* (bandits) too, of course, but cross-border problems seem to account for most of the trouble in the north of the country.

Despite all the headlines, tourists are rarely targeted, as much of the violence and robberies take place far from the main tourist routes. Security has also improved considerably in previously high-risk areas such as the Isiolo–Marsabit and Marsabit–Moyale routes. However, you should check the situation locally before taking these roads, or travelling between Garsen and Garissa or Thika.

The areas along the South Sudanese and Ethiopian borders are risky, so please enquire about the latest security situations if you're heading overland.

Crime

Even the staunchest Kenyan patriot will readily admit that one of the country's biggest problems is crime. It ranges from petty snatch theft and mugging to violent armed robbery, carjacking and, of course, white-collar crime and corruption. As a visitor you needn't feel paranoid, but you should always keep your wits about you, particularly at night.

Perhaps the best advice for when you're walking around cities and towns is not to carry anything valuable with you – that includes jewellery, watches, cameras, bumbags, daypacks and money. Most hotels provide a safe or secure place for valuables, although you should also be cautious of the security at some budget places.

While pickpocketing and bag-snatching are the most common crimes, armed muggings do occur in Nairobi and on the coast. Always take taxis after dark. Conversely, snatch-and-run crimes happen more in crowds. If you suddenly feel there are too many people around you, or think you are being followed, dive straight into a shop and ask for help.

Luggage is an obvious signal to criminals that you've just arrived. When arriving anywhere by bus, it's sensible to take a 'ship-to-shore' approach, getting a taxi directly from the bus station to your hotel. You'll have plenty of time to explore once you've safely stowed your belongings. Also, don't read a guidebook or look at maps on the street – it attracts unwanted attention.

In the event of a crime, you should report it to the police, but this can be a real procedure. You'll need to get a police report if you intend to make an insurance claim. In the event of a snatch theft, think twice before yelling 'Thief!' It's not unknown for people to administer summary justice on the spot, often with fatal results for the criminal.

Although crime is a fact of life in Kenya, it needn't spoil your trip. Above all, don't make the mistake of distrusting every Kenyan just because of a few bad apples – the honest souls you meet will far outnumber any crooks who cross your path.

Scams

At some point in Kenya you'll almost certainly come across people who play on the emotions and gullibility of foreigners. Nairobi is a particular hot spot, with 'friendly' approaches a daily, if not hourly, occurrence. People with tales about being refugees or having sick relatives can sound very convincing, but they all end up asking for cash. It's OK to talk to these people if they're not actively hassling you, but you should ignore any requests for money.

Be sceptical of strangers who claim to recognise you in the street, especially if they're vague about exactly where they know you from – it's unlikely that any ordinary person is going to be *this* excited by seeing you twice. Anyone who makes a big show of inviting you into the hospitality of their home also probably has ulterior motives. The usual trick is to bestow some kind of gift upon the delighted traveller, who is then emotionally blackmailed into reciprocating.

Tourists with cars also face potential rip-offs. Don't trust people who gesticulate wildly to indicate that your front wheels are wobbling; if you stop, you'll probably be relieved of your valuables. Another trick is to splash oil on your wheels, then tell you the wheel bearings, differential or something else has failed, and direct you to a nearby garage where their friends will 'fix' the problem – for a substantial fee, of course.

Terrorism

Terrorism is, unfortunately, something you have to consider when visiting Kenya, although the vast majority of the country is safe to visit. Remember that reports of an attack in, for example, Mombasa is likely to have very little impact upon the safety of visiting the Masai Mara or even Tsavo East National Park.

In September 2013 terrorists attacked the upscale Westgate Shopping Mall in Nairobi. In early 2014, a number of British tour operators withdrew all of their clients from and suspended tours to most coastal areas of Kenya. Other attacks have taken place – on commuter transport and markets in the Eastleigh suburb of Nairobi, and a series of attacks around Mpeketoni close to Lamu in mid-2014, for example – although these have primarily targeted locals rather than foreign tourists.

In recent years, there has been an upsurge in ethnic, political and religious tensions in Mombasa, and there have been a number of attacks on foreigners in and around Mombasa's old town, although at least one of these appeared to have been crime- rather than terrorism-related.

As of late 2014, most foreign government travel advisory services were warning against travel close to the Kenya–Somali border, as well as a number of areas along the coast, including Lamu and Tana River counties, some areas of Mombasa, and Eastleigh subrub of Nairobi. Check their websites for the latest warnings.

TELEPHONE

International call rates from Kenya are relatively expensive, though you can save serious cash by using VOIP programs like Skype. If you're calling internationally using a local SIM card, rates are likely to be cheaper (as little as KSh3 per minute) than from fixed-line phones.

Calls made through a hotel operator from your room will cost an extra 25% to 50%, so check before making a call.

Mobile Phones

More than two-thirds of all calls in Kenya are now made on mobile phones, and coverage is good in all but the furthest rural areas. Kenya uses the GSM 900 system, which is compatible with Europe and Australia but not with the North American GSM 1900 system. If you have a GSM phone, check with your service provider about using it in Kenya, and beware of high roaming charges. Remember that you will generally be charged for receiving calls abroad as well as for making them.

Alternatively, if your phone isn't locked into a network, you can pick up a prepaid starter pack from one of the Kenyan mobile-phone companies: **Safaricom** (www.safaricom.co.ke), **Airtel** (www.africa.airtel.com/kenya/) or **Orange** (orange.co.ke). A SIM card costs about KSh100, and you can then buy top-up scratchcards from shops and booths across the country. International calls can cost as little as KSh3 per minute.

You can easily buy a handset anywhere in Kenya, generally unlocked and with SIM card. Prices start at around KSh2500 for a very basic model.

Phone Codes

Kenya's regions have area codes which must be dialled, followed by the local number.

The international dialling code for Kenya is ☑ 254.

Phonecards

With Telkom Kenya phonecards, any phone can be used for prepaid calls – you just have to dial the access number (☑ 0844) and enter in the number and passcode on the card. There are booths selling the cards all over the country. Cards come in denominations of KSh200, KSh500, KSh1000 and KSh2000, and call charges are slightly more expensive than for standard lines.

TIME

Kenya time is GMT/UTC plus two hours. There is no daylight saving.

TOURIST INFORMATION

Local Tourist Offices Incredibly, there is still no tourist office in Nairobi. There are a handful of information offices elsewhere in the country, ranging from helpful private concerns to underfunded government offices.

Tourist Offices Abroad The Ministry of Tourism (www.tourism.go.ke) maintains a number of overseas offices, including in the UK, USA, Canada and Italy. Most only provide information by telephone, post or email. Visit the ministry website; click on 'Contact Us' for contact details around the world.

TRAVELLERS WITH DISABILITIES

Travelling in Kenya is not easy for physically disabled people, but it's not impossible. Very few tourism companies and facilities are geared up for travellers with disabilities, and those that are tend to be restricted to the expensive hotels and lodges. However, Kenyans are generally very accommodating and willing to offer whatever assistance they can. Visually or hearing-impaired travellers, though, will find it very hard to get by without an able-bodied companion.

In Nairobi, only the ex-London taxi cabs are spacious enough to accommodate a wheelchair, but many safari companies are accustomed to taking disabled people out on safari.

Many of the top-end beach resorts on the coast have facilities for the disabled, whether it's a few token ramps or fully equipped rooms with handrails and bathtubs.

Out on safari, other places may have varying degrees of disabled access, but in Amboseli National Park, Ol Tukai Lodge (p300) has two disabled-friendly cottages.

VISAS

Tourist visas can be obtained on arrival at international airports and at the country's land borders with Uganda and Tanzania. This applies to Europeans, Australians, New Zealanders, Americans and Canadians, although citizens from a few smaller Commonwealth countries are exempt. Visas cost US$50/€40/UK£30 and are valid for three months from the date of entry. Tourist visas can be extended for a further three-month period.

Under the East African partnership system, visiting Tanzania or Uganda and returning to Kenya does not invalidate a single-entry Kenyan visa, so there's no need to get a multiple-entry visa unless you plan to go further afield. Always check the latest entry requirements with embassies before travel. Applications for Kenyan visas are simple and straightforward in Tanzania and Uganda, and payment is accepted in local currency.

As of late 2014 Kenya is one of the countries covered by the new East Africa Tourist Visa, and for those also visiting Uganda and Rwanda on the same trip it is a cheaper alternative. The visa costs US$100, is valid for 90 days and is multiple entry – it is available upon arrival or from embassies abroad. If acquiring the visa before travel, your first port-of-call must be the country through which you applied for the visa.

Visas for Onward Travel

Since Nairobi is a common gateway city to East Africa and the city centre is easy to get around,

many travellers spend some time here picking up visas for other countries that they intend to visit. But be warned: although officially issuing visas again, the Ethiopian embassy in Nairobi was not issuing tourist visas for a number of years and the situation could change again. Call the embassy to check.

Most embassies will want you to pay visa fees in US dollars, and most open for visa applications from 9am to noon, with visa pick-ups around 3pm or 4pm. Again, contact the embassy in question to check the times as these change regularly in Nairobi.

VOLUNTEERING

There are quite a large number of volunteers in Kenya, and volunteering can be a great way to reduce the ecological footprint of your trip. As a general rule, volunteering works best for both the traveller and the organisation in question if you treat it as a genuine commitment rather than simply a fun extension of your trip. It's also preferable if you have a particular skill to bring to the experience, especially one that cannot be satisfied by local people.

Action for Children in Conflict (AfCiC; ☑ 01235539319; www.actionchildren.org; 2nd fl, Imara Plaza, Thika) A small, highly effective NGO working with Thika's children in poverty. AfCiC recruits skilled volunteers via its website for long-term placements.

Arabuko Sokoke Schools & Ecotourism Scheme (ASSETS, A Rocha Kenya; ☑ 042-2332023, 020-2335865; arocha.org/ke-en/work/communityconservation/assets) Programs (including Mida Ecocamp) near the Arabuko Sokoke Forest and Mida Creek. Also operates the Mwamba Field Study Centre at Watamu Beach.

Kenya Youth Voluntary Development Projects (Map p220; ☑ 0720453857; www.kvcdp.org; Nairobi International Youth Hostel, Ralph Bunche Rd, Nairobi) Excellent local organisation that runs a variety of three- to four-week projects, including road building, health education and clinic construction.

Volunteer Kenya (Inter-Community Development Involvement; www.volunteerkenya.org) Offers a number of longer community projects focusing on health issues such as AIDS awareness, agriculture and conservation in Western Kenya.

Watamu Turtle Watch (☑ 0713759627; watamuturtles.com) Helps protect the marine turtles that come to Watamu to lay eggs on the beach.

❶ Getting There & Away

Nairobi is a major African hub with numerous African and international airlines connecting Kenya to the world. By African standards, flights between Kenya and the rest of Africa or further afield are common and relatively cheap, and flying is by far the most convenient way to get to Kenya.

Kenya is also a popular and relatively easy waystation for those travelling overland between Southern Africa and Egypt. Finding your way here can be tricky – with several war zones in the vicinity – and such journeys should only be considered after serious planning and preparation. But they're certainly possible, and it's rarely Kenya that causes problems.

Flights, tours and rail tickets can be booked online at lonelyplanet.com/bookings.

ENTERING THE COUNTRY

Entering Kenya is generally pleasingly straightforward, particularly at the international airports. Visas are available on arrival at Mombasa and Nairobi international airports and Kenya's land borders with Uganda and Tanzania.

AIR

Airports

Kenya has three international airports; check out the website www.kenyaairports.co.ke for further information:

Jomo Kenyatta International Airport (NBO; Map p230; ☑ 0722205061, 020-822111; www. kaa.go.ke) Most international flights to and from Nairobi arrive at this airport, 15km southeast of the city. There are two international terminals and a smaller domestic terminal; you can walk easily between the terminals.

Moi International Airport (MBA; ☑ 020-3577058, 041-3433211) In Mombasa, 9km west of the centre, and Kenya's second-busiest international airport. Apart from flights to Zanzibar, this is mainly used by charter airlines and domestic flights.

Wilson Airport (WIL; Map p230; ☑ 0724255343, 0724256837; www.kaa.go.ke) Located 6km south of Nairobi's city centre on Langata Rd; with some flights between Nairobi and Kilimanjaro International Airport or Mwanza in Tanzania, as well as scheduled and charter domestic flights.

Airlines

The following airlines fly to/from Kenya. Kenya Airways is the main national carrier, and has a generally good safety record, with just one fatal incident since 1977.

African Express Airways (www.african express.co.ke)

Air Mauritius (☑ 020-822805; www.air mauritius.com)

Airkenya (☑ 020-3916000; www.airkenya. com)

British Airways (☑ 020-3277400; www. britishairways.com)

Brussels Airlines (☑ 020-4443070; www. brusselsairlines.com)

Daallo Airlines (☑ 020-317318; www.daallo. com)

Egypt Air (Map p224; ☑ 020-2226821; www. egyptair.com.eg)

Emirates (Map p224; ☑ 020-7602519; www. emirates.com)

Ethiopian Airlines (Map p224; ☑ 020-2296000; www.ethiopianairlines.com)

Kenya Airways (☑ 020-3274747; www.kenya-airways.com)

KLM (Map p224; ☑ 020-2958210; www.klm. com)

Precision Air (☑ 020-3274282; www.precision airtz.com)

Qatar Airways (☑ 020-2800000; www. qatarairways.com)

Rwandair (☑ 020-343870; www.rwandair.com)

Safarilink (☑ 020-6000777; flysafarilink.com)

South African Airways (☑ 020-2247342; www.flysaa.com)

Swiss International Airlines (☑ 020-2666967; www.swiss.com)

Thomson Airways (www.thomson.co.uk)

LAND

Ethiopia

With ongoing problems in Sudan and Somalia, Ethiopia offers the only viable overland route into Kenya from the north. The security situation around the main entry point at Moyale is changeable – the border is usually open, but security problems often force its closure. Some foreign governments were, at the time of writing, warning against travel to areas of Kenya bordering Ethiopia and even along the highway between Isiolo and Moyale, although we've travelled much of this route without problems. Even so, cattle- and goat-rustling are rife, triggering frequent cross-border tribal wars, so check the security situation carefully before attempting this crossing.

Although Ethiopian visas were being issued at the Ethiopian embassy in Nairobi at the time of research, that hasn't always been the case in recent years so check with your nearest Ethiopian embassy before setting out.

Public Transport There were no cross-border bus services at the time of writing. If you don't have your own transport from Moyale, there's a daily bus between Moyale and Marsabit (Ksh800), while lifts can be arranged with the trucks (KSh500).

From immigration on the Ethiopian side of town it's a 2km walk to the Ethiopian and Kenyan customs posts. A yellow-fever vaccination is required to cross either border at Moyale. Unless you fancy being vaccinated at the border, get your jabs in advance and keep the certificate with your passport. A cholera vaccination may also be required.

Car & Mortorcyle Those coming to Kenya with their own vehicle could also enter at Fort Banya, on the northeastern tip of Lake Turkana, but it's a risky route with few fuel stops. There's no border post; you must already possess a Kenyan visa and get it stamped on arrival in Nairobi. Immigration are quite used to this, but not having an Ethiopian exit stamp can be a problem if you want to re-enter Ethiopia.

Somalia

Don't even think about it.

South Sudan

Kenya's border with South Sudan is one of East Africa's more remote border crossings – check with the South Sudanese embassy in Nairobi to check whether it's open to foreign travellers. Most travellers travelling between the two countries fly from Nairobi to Juba.

There are no cross-border buses, although Simba Coaches has a bus from Eldoret to Juba (KSh4500, 24 hours) which travels via Kampala in Uganda.

Tanzania

The main land borders between Kenya and Tanzania are at Namanga, Oloitokitok, Taveta, Isebania and Lunga Lunga, and can be reached by public transport. There are no train services between the two countries.

Although all of the routes may be done in stages using a combination of buses and local matatus, there are six main routes to/from Tanzania:

➡ Mombasa–Arusha/Moshi

➡ Mombasa–Tanga/Dar es Salaam

➡ Nairobi–Arusha/Moshi (via Namanga)

➡ Nairobi–Dar es Salaam

➡ Nairobi–Moshi (via Oloitokitok)

➡ Nairobi–Mwanza

Bus companies include:

Easy Coach (☑ 020-3210711020-3210711; www.easycoach.co.ke)

Modern Coast Express (☑ 0737940000, 0705700888; www.modern.co.ke)

Riverside Shuttle (☑ 020-3229618; www.riverside-shuttle.com)

Uganda

The main border post for overland travellers is Malaba, with Busia an alternative if you're travelling via Kisumu.

Bus & Matatu Numerous bus companies run between Nairobi, Nakuru or Kisumu and Kampala. From the Kenyan side, we recommend Easy Coach and Modern Coast Express. If travelling from Nairobi or Nakuru, prices include a meal at the halfway point. Various other companies have cheaper, basic services, which depart from the Accra Rd area in Nairobi.

There are also regular matatus to Malaba from Cross Rd in Nairobi. Buses and matatus also run from Nairobi or Kisumu to Busia, from where there are regular connections to Kampala and Jinja.

The Ugandan and Kenyan border posts at Malaba are about 1km apart, so you can walk or take a *boda-boda* (bicycle taxi). Once you get across the border, there are frequent matatus until the late afternoon to Kampala, Jinja and Tororo.

SEA & LAKE

At the time of writing there were no international ferries operating on Lake Victoria, although there's been talk for years of a cross-lake ferry service between Kenya, Tanzania and Uganda. One company – **Earthwise Ferries** (www.earthwiseventures.com) – even has a website. If they actually end up with a boat, they could link Kisumu with Mwanza (Tanzania) and Kampala (Uganda).

ⓘ Getting Around

AIR

Airlines in Kenya

Including the national carrier, Kenya Airways, a handful of domestic operators of varying sizes run scheduled flights within Kenya. Destinations served are predominantly around the coast and the popular national parks, where the highest density of tourist activity takes place. Most operate small planes and many of the 'airports',

MAJOR KENYA–TANZANIA BUS ROUTES

FROM	TO	PRICE (US$)	DURATION (HR)	COMPANY
Mombasa	Tanga	8	4	Modern Coast Express
Mombasa	Dar es Salaam	11-15	5-8	Modern Coast Express
Nairobi	Moshi	40	7½	Riverside Shuttle
Nairobi	Arusha	35	5½	Riverside Shuttle
Nairobi	Kampala	28	10-12	Modern Coast Express
Nakuru	Kampala	24	11-12	Easy Coach

especially those in the parks, are dirt airstrips with very few if any facilities.

With all these airlines, be sure to book well in advance (this is essential during the tourist high season). You should also remember to reconfirm your return flights 72 hours before departure, especially those that connect with an international flight. Otherwise, you may find that your seat has been reallocated.

Airkenya (☑ 020-3916000; www.airkenya. com) Amboseli, Diani, Lamu, Masai Mara, Malindi, Meru, Nakuru, Mombasa, Nanyuki, Lewa and Samburu.

Fly540 (www.fly540.com) Eldoret, Kisumu, Lamu, Lodwar, Malindi and Mombasa.

Jambo Jet (☑ 020-3274545; www.jambojet. com) Subsidiary of Kenya Airways that flies to Nairobi, Mombasa, Kisumu and Eldoret.

Kenya Airways (Map p224; ☑ 020-3274747; www.kenya-airways.com) Kisumu, Malindi and Mombasa.

Mombasa Air Safari (☑ 0734400400; www. mombasaairsafari.com) Amboseli, Diani Beach, Kisumu, Lamu, Malindi, Masai Mara, Meru, Mombasa, Samburu and Tsavo West.

Safarilink (☑ 020-6000777; www.flysafarilink. com) Amboseli, Diani Beach, Kiwayu, Lamu, Lewa Downs, Loisaba, Masai Mara, Naivasha, Nanyuki, Samburu, Shaba and Tsavo West.

BOAT

The only ferry transport on Lake Victoria at the time of writing is across the Winam Gulf between Mbita Point (near Homa Bay) and Luanda Kotieno where matatus go to Kisumu. You might also find motorised canoes to Mfangano Island from Mbita Point.

Dhows (traditional Swahili sailing boats) are commonly used to get around the islands in the Lamu archipelago and the mangrove islands south of Mombasa. For the most part, these trips operate more like dhow safaris than public transport. Although some trips are luxurious, the trips out of Lamu are more basic. When night comes you simply bed down wherever there is space. Seafood is freshly caught and cooked on board on charcoal burners, or else barbecued on the beach on surrounding islands.

BUS

Kenya has an extensive network of long- and short-haul bus routes, with particularly good coverage of the areas around Nairobi, the coast and the western regions. Services thin out the further away from the capital you get, particularly in the north, and there are still plenty of places where you'll be reliant on matatus.

Buses are operated by a variety of private companies that offer varying levels of comfort, convenience and roadworthiness. They're considerably cheaper than taking the train or flying,

and as a rule services are frequent, fast and can be quite comfortable.

In general, if you travel during daylight hours, buses are a fairly safe way to get around – you'll certainly be safer in a bus than in a matatu. The best coaches are saved for long-haul and international routes and offer DVD movies, drinks, toilets and reclining airline-style seats; some of the newer ones even have wireless internet. On shorter local routes, however, you may find yourself on something resembling a battered school bus.

Whatever kind of conveyance you find yourself in, don't sit at the back (you'll be thrown around like a rag doll on Kenyan roads), or right at the front (you'll be the first to die in a head-on collision, plus you'll be able to see the oncoming traffic, which is usually best left to the driver or those with nerves of steel).

Busways (☑ 020-2227650) Western Kenya and the coast.

Coastline Safaris (Coast Bus; ☑ 0722206448; www.coastbus.com) Western and Southern Kenya, Mombasa.

Dream Line (☑ 0731777799) Nairobi, Mombasa and Malindi.

Easy Coach (☑ 020-3210711; www.easycoach. co.ke) Rift Valley and Western Kenya.

Modern Coast Express (☑ 0705700888; www. modern.co.ke) Nairobi, Mombasa, Malindi and Western Kenya.

Reservations

Most bus companies have offices or ticket agents at important stops along their routes, where you can book a seat. For short trips between towns reservations aren't generally necessary, but for popular longer routes, particularly the Nairobi–Kisumu, Nairobi–Mombasa and Mombasa–Lamu routes, buying your ticket at least a day in advance is highly recommended.

CAR & MOTORCYCLE
Automobile Associations

Automobile Association of Kenya (Map p234; ☑ 020-4449676; www.aakenya.co.ke; Sarit Centre, Westlands, Nairobi) Kenya's local automobile association.

Bribes

Although things have improved markedly in recent years, police will still stop you and most likely ask you for a small 'donation'. To prevent being taken advantage of, always ask for an official receipt – this goes a long way in stopping corruption. Also, always ask for their police number and check it against their ID card as there are plenty of con artists running about.

Driving Licence

An international driving licence is not necessary in Kenya, but can be useful. If you have a

British photo card licence, be sure to bring the counterfoil, as the date you passed your driving test (something car-hire companies may want to know) isn't printed on the card itself.

Fuel & Spare Parts

Fuel prices are generally lower outside the capital, but can creep up to frighteningly high prices in remote areas, where petrol stations are scarce, and you may end up buying dodgy supplies out of barrels from roadside vendors. Petrol, spare parts and repair shops are readily available at all border towns, though if you're coming from Ethiopia you should plan your supplies carefully, as stops are few and far between on the rough northern roads.

Car Hire

Hiring a vehicle to tour Kenya (or at least the national parks) is an expensive way of seeing the country, but it does give you freedom of movement and is sometimes the only way of getting to more remote parts of the country. However, unless you're sharing with a sufficient number of people, it's likely to cost more than you'd pay for an organised camping safari with all meals.

Starting rates for hire almost always sound very reasonable, but once you factor in mileage and the various types of insurance, you'll be lucky to pay less than US$50 per day for a saloon car, US$80 per day for a small 4WD or US$150 per day for a proper 4WD.

While hiring a 'chauffeur' may sound like a luxury, it can actually be a very good idea in Kenya for both financial and safety reasons. Most companies will provide a driver for anywhere between US$5 and US$40 per day – the big advantage of this is that the car is covered by the company's insurance, so you don't have to pay any of the various waivers and won't be liable for any excess in the case of an accident (though tyres, windows etc remain your responsibility).

Hiring a vehicle with unlimited kilometres is the best way to go. Rates are usually quoted without insurance, with the option of paying a daily rate (usually around KSh1500 to KSh3000) for insurance against collision damage and theft. It would be financial suicide to hire a car in Kenya without both kinds of insurance. Otherwise you'll be responsible for the full value of the vehicle if it's damaged or stolen.

Even if you have collision and theft insurance, you'll still be liable for an excess of anywhere between KSh5000 to KSh150,000 (depending on the company) if something happens to the vehicle; always check this before signing. You can usually reduce the excess to zero by paying another KSh1500 to KSh2500 per day for an excess loss waiver. Note that tyres, damaged windscreens and loss of the tool kit are always the hirer's responsibility.

As a final sting in the tail (unless you've been quoted an all-inclusive rate), you'll be charged 16% value added tax (VAT) on top of the total cost of hiring the vehicle. And a final warning: always return the vehicle with a full tank of petrol; if you don't, the company will charge you twice the going rate to fill up.

Unless you're just planning on travelling on the main routes between towns, you'll need a 4WD vehicle. Few of the car-hire companies will let you drive 2WD vehicles on dirt roads, including those in the national parks, and if you ignore this proscription and have an accident you'll be personally liable for any damage to the vehicle.

A minimum age of between 23 and 25 years usually applies for hirers. Some require you to have been driving for at least two years. You will also need acceptable ID such as a passport.

And if you plan to take the car across international borders, check whether the company allows this – many don't, and those that do charge for the privilege.

Car-hire companies include the following:

Adventure Upgrade Safaris (Map p224; ☑ 0722529228; www.adventureupgrade safaris.co.ke; Tom Mboya St, Nairobi) An excellent local company with a good range of vehicles and drivers.

Avis (Map p224; ☑ 020-2966500; www.avis. co.ke; College House, University Way, Nairobi) Also in Mombasa.

Budget (Map p224; ☑ 020-652144; www. budget.co.ke; College House, University Way, Nairobi)

Central Rent-a-Car (Map p224; ☑ 020-2222888; www.carhirekenya.com; ground fl, 680 Hotel, Kenyatta Ave, Nairobi) A recommended local company.

Market Car Hire (Map p224; ☑ 0722515053; www.marketcarhire.com; ground fl, Chester House, Koinange St, Nairobi) Local car-hire firm with a solid reputation.

Road Conditions

Road conditions vary widely in Kenya, from flat smooth highways to dirt tracks and steep rocky pathways. The roads in the north and east of the country are particularly poor. The main Mombasa–Nairobi–Malaba road (A104) is badly worn due to the constant flow of traffic, but has improved in recent years. The never-ending stream of trucks along this main route through the country will slow travel times considerably.

Roads in national parks are all made of *murram* (dirt) and many have eroded into bone-shaking corrugations through overuse by safari vehicles.

Road Hazards

The biggest hazard on Kenyan roads is simply the other vehicles on them, and driving defensively is essential. Ironically, the most dangerous roads in Kenya are probably the well-maintained ones, which allow drivers to go fast enough to do really serious damage in a crash. On the worse roads, potholes can be a problem.

On all roads, be very careful of pedestrians and cyclists – you don't want to contribute any more to the death toll on Kenya's roads. Animals are another major hazard in rural areas, be it monkeys, herds of goats and cattle or lone chickens with a death wish.

Certain routes have a reputation for banditry, particularly the Garsen–Garissa–Thika road, which is still essentially off limits to travellers. The roads from Isiolo to Marsabit and Moyale and from Malindi to Lamu have improved considerably security-wise in the last few years, but you're still advised to seek local advice before using any of these routes.

Road Rules

Driving practices here are some of the worst in the world and all are carried out at breakneck speed. Never drive at night unless you absolutely have to. Drunk driving is also very common.

Kenyans drive on the left – at least in theory. Kenyans habitually drive on the wrong side of the road whenever they see a pothole, an animal or simply a break in the traffic – flashing your lights at the vehicle hurtling towards you should be enough to persuade the driver to get back into their own lane.

Indicators, lights, horns and hand signals can mean anything from 'I'm about to overtake' to 'Hello *mzungu* (white person)!' or 'Let's play chicken with that elephant', and should never be taken at face value.

HITCHING

Hitchhiking is never entirely safe in any country, and we don't recommend it. Travellers who hitch should understand they are taking a small but potentially serious risk; it's safer to travel in pairs and let someone know where you are planning to go. Also beware of drunken drivers.

The traditional thumb signal will probably be understood, but locals use a palm-downwards wave to get cars to stop. Many Kenyan drivers expect a contribution towards petrol or some kind of gift from foreign passengers, so make it clear from the outset if you are expecting a free ride.

If you're hoping to hitch into the national parks, dream on! You'll get further asking around for travel companions in Nairobi or any of the gateway towns.

LOCAL TRANSPORT

Boda-boda

Boda-bodas (bicycle or motorcycle taxis) are common in areas where standard taxis are harder to find, and also operate in smaller towns and cities such as Nakuru or Kisumu. There's a particular proliferation on the coast, where the bicycle boys also double as touts, guides and drug dealers in tourist areas. A short ride should cost around KSh80 or so.

Matatu

Local matatus are the main means of getting around for local people, and any reasonably sized city or town will have plenty of services covering every major road and suburb. Fares start at around KSh20 and may reach KSh100 for longer routes in Nairobi.

For inter-city transport, apart from in the remote northern areas where you'll rely on occasional buses or paid lifts on trucks, you can almost always find a matatu going to the next town or further afield.

Matatus leave when full and the fares are fixed. It's unlikely you will be charged more than other passengers.

Despite a briefly successful government drive to regulate the matatu industry, matatus are once again notorious for dangerous driving, overcrowding and general shady business. Under no circumstances should you sit in the 'death seat' next to the matatu driver. Play it safe and sit in the middle seats away from the window.

Shared Taxi (Peugeot)

Shared Peugeot taxis are a good alternative to matatus. The vehicles are usually Peugeot 505 station wagons that take seven to nine passengers and leave when full.

Peugeots take less time to reach their destinations than matatus as they fill quicker and go from point to point without stopping, and so are slightly more expensive.

Taxi

Even the smallest Kenyan towns generally have at least one banged-up old taxi for easy access to outlying areas or even remoter villages, and you'll find cabs on virtually every corner in the larger cities, especially in Nairobi and Mombasa, where taking a taxi at night is virtually mandatory. Fares are invariably negotiable and start around KSh300 to KSh500 for short journeys.

Since few taxis in Kenya actually have functioning meters (or drivers who adhere to them), it's advisable that you agree on the fare prior to setting out.

Tuk-Tuk

They're an incongruous sight outside southeast Asia, but several Kenyan towns and cities have these distinctive motorised mini-taxis. The highest concentration is in Malindi, but they're also in Nairobi, Mombasa, Nakuru, Machakos and Diani Beach; Watamu has a handful of less-sophisticated motorised rickshaws. Fares are negotiable, but should be at least KSh100 less than the equivalent taxi rate.

TRAIN

The Uganda Railway was once the main trade artery in East Africa, but these days the network has dwindled to one functioning route between Nairobi and Mombasa.

Classes

There are three classes on Kenyan trains, but only 1st and 2nd class can be recommended.
➡ First class consists of two-berth compartments with a washbasin, wardrobe, drinking water and a drinks service.
➡ Second class consists of plainer, four-berth compartments with a washbasin and drinking water.
➡ Third class is seats only.

No compartment can be locked from the outside, so remember not to leave any valuables lying around if you leave it for any reason.

Always lock your compartment from the inside before you go to sleep.

Passengers in 1st class are treated to a meal typically consisting of stews, curries or roast chicken served with rice and vegetables. Tea and coffee is included; sodas (soft drinks), bottled water and alcoholic drinks are not. Cold beer is available at all times in the dining car and can be delivered to your compartment.

Reservations

There are booking offices at the train stations in Nairobi and Mombasa, and it's recommended that you show up in person rather than trying to call. You must book in advance for 1st and 2nd class, otherwise there'll probably be no berths available. Two to three days is usually sufficient, but remember that these services run just three times weekly in either direction. Note that compartment and berth numbers are posted up about 30 minutes prior to departure.

Uganda

Best for Nature

➜ Mountain gorillas (p437, p448)

➜ Tree-climbing lions (p436)

➜ Chimpanzees (p423)

➜ The 'Big Five' (p456, p459)

Best Sleeping

➜ Apoka Safari Lodge (p413)

➜ Wildwaters Lodge (p406)

➜ Kyaninga Lodge (p418)

➜ Byoona Amagara (p445)

➜ Red Chilli Hideaway (p382)

➜ Buhoma Community Rest Camp (p440)

Why Go?
Emerging from the shadows of its dark history, a new dawn of tourism has risen in Uganda, polishing a glint back into the 'pearl of Africa'. Travellers are streaming in to explore what is basically the best of everything the continent has to offer.

For a relatively small country, there's a lot that's big about the place. It's home to the tallest mountain range in Africa, the source that feeds the world's longest river and the continent's largest lake. And with half the remaining mountain gorillas residing here, as well as the Big Five to be ticked off, wildlife watching is huge.

While antigay sentiments have cast a shadow over an otherwise positive tourism picture, Uganda remains one of the safest destinations in Africa. Other than watching out for the odd hippo at your campsite, there's no more to worry about here than in most other countries.

When to Go
Kampala

Jan & Feb Perfect climate to head for the hills to climb the Rwenzoris or Mt Elgon.	**Jun–Sep** The best bet weatherwise: not too hot with minimal rainfall.	**Oct & Nov** Can be rainy, but fewer travellers means gorilla permits are much easier to obtain.

Uganda Highlights

1 Jaunt through the jungle to marvel at mountain gorillas in **Bwindi Impenetrable National Park** (p437).

2 Take on the wild waters of the **Nile River** (p401), some of the best white-water rafting in the world.

3 Check out the world's most powerful waterfall on a wildlife-watching bonanza of a boat ride up the Victoria Nile at **Murchison Falls** (p459).

4 Chill out at **Lake Bunyonyi** (p443), the most beautiful lake in Uganda.

5 Explore unvarnished Africa at its wild and colourful best in **Kidepo Valley National Park** (p412).

6 Tackle the ice-capped **Rwenzori Mountains** (p427), evocatively known as the 'Mountains of the Moon'.

7 Laze in a hammock on a powdery white-sand beach on the **Ssese Islands** (p455), in Lake Victoria.

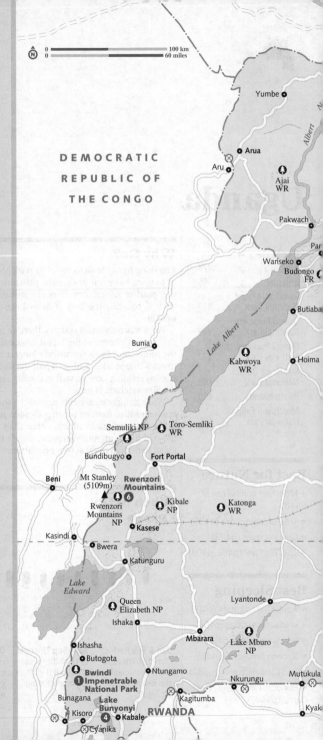

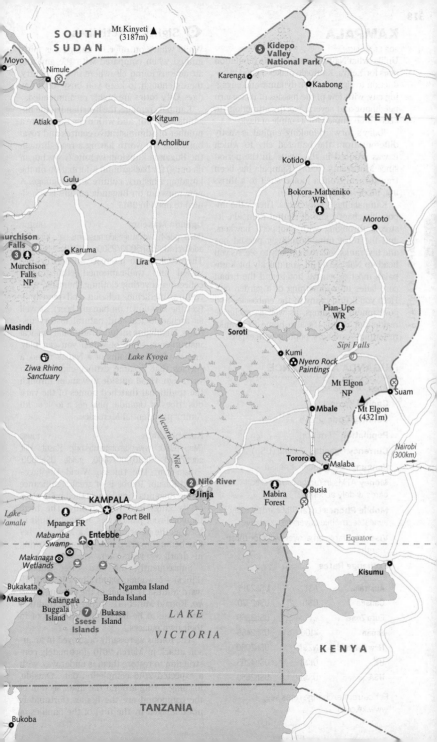

SOUTH SUDAN

Mt Kinyeti ▲
(3187m)

5 Kidepo Valley National Park

Moyo

Nimule

Karenga

Kaabong

KENYA

Atiak

Kitgum

Acholibur

Kotido

Gulu

Bokora-Matheniko
WR

Moroto

Murchison Falls **3**

Karuma

Murchison Falls NP

Lira

Masindi

Pian-Upe
WR

Ziwa Rhino Sanctuary

Lake Kyoga

Soroti

Kumi

Sipi Falls

Nyero Rock Paintings

Mt Elgon NP

Mt Elgon
(4321m)

Suam

Mbale

Victoria

Nile

Tororo

Malaba

*Nairobi
(300km)*

2 Nile River

Jinja

Mabira Forest

Busia

KAMPALA

Port Bell

*Lake
Jamala*

Mpanga FR

Entebbe

Equator

*Mabamba
Swamp*

*Makanaga
Wetlands*

Bukakata

Ngamba Island

Banda Island

Kisumu

Masaka

Kalangala

Buggala Island

7 Ssese Islands

Bukasa Island

LAKE VICTORIA

KENYA

Bukoba

TANZANIA

KAMPALA

POP 1.5 MILLION

Unlike what Nairobi's unfortunate reputation does for Kenya, Kampala makes a good introduction to Uganda. It's a dynamic and engaging city, with few of the hassles of its eastern neighbour and several worthy attractions to keep you occupied for a couple of days.

Today's forward-looking capital is vastly different from the battered city to which it was reduced in the 1980s. In the period since Museveni's victory, Kampala has been transformed from a looted shell to a thriving, modern place.

Kampala has several faces. There's the impossibly chaotic jam of central Kampala, its streets thronging with shoppers, hawkers, and the most mind-bogglingly packed bus and taxi ranks you're ever likely to see. As you head up Nakasero Hill, you quickly hit Kampala's most expensive hotels and the urban core fades into something of a garden city. Here you'll find many of the embassies and government buildings, as well as exclusive residential zones. It's also home to swanky restaurants and bars, popular with expats.

UGANDA AT A GLANCE

Area 241,038 sq km

Capital Kampala

Country Code ☑256

Population 37 million

Currency Ugandan Shilling (USh)

Languages Lugandan, English

Money ATMs in major towns, credit cards widely accepted

Mobile Phones Local SIM cards widely available; mobile coverage extensive

Visas Available on arrival; valid for three months

Exchange Rates

Australia	A$1	USh2315
Canada	C$1	USh2370
Euro Zone	€1	USh3360
Japan	¥100	USh2465
New Zealand	NZ$1	USh2080
UK	UK£1	USh4265
USA	US$1	USh2650

For current exchange rates see www.xe.com

◉ Sights & Activities

While what's on offer in Kampala is fairly limited when compared with the amazing attractions found elsewhere in the country, there's enough to keep you busy for a few days. **City tours** are highly recommended.

Kampala remains the heartland of the Buganda kingdom, and within the capital are a number of administrative centres and royal buildings. It's worth having a read through the Buganda kingdom website (www.buganda.or.ug) for background information on the kingdom's history, culture and language. A new museum on Buganda culture is scheduled to open in 2015.

Uganda Museum   MUSEUM

(Map p384; www.ugandamuseums.ug; Kira Rd; adult/child USh5000/2500; ⊗10am-5.30pm) There's plenty to interest you here with a varied and well-captioned ethnographic collection covering clothing, hunting, agriculture, medicine, religion and recreation (get the low-down on banana beer), as well as archaeological and natural history displays. Highlights include traditional musical instruments, some of which you can play, and the fossil remains of a Napak rhino, a species that became extinct eight million years ago. Head outside to wander through the traditional thatched homes of the various tribes of Uganda; plus get a look at Idi Amin's presidential Mercedes.

Kasubi Tombs   TOMBS

(Map p380; www.kasubitombs.org; Kasubi Hill; adult/child USh10,000/1000, guide USh5000; ⊗8am-6pm) The Unesco World Heritage–listed Kasubi Tombs is of great significance to the Buganda kingdom as the burial place of its kings and royal family. The huge thatched-roof palace was originally built in 1882 as the palace of Kabaka Mutesa I, before being converted into his tomb following his death two years later.

Subsequently, the next three *kabaka* (kings) – Mwanga; Daudi Chwa II; and Edward Mutesa II, father of the current *kabaka*, Ronald Mutebi II – broke with tradition and chose to be buried here instead of in their own palaces.

The tombs were sadly destroyed in an arson attack in March 2010; fortunately construction to restore them is under way, with a expected 2016 completion date. Outside, forming a ring around the main section of the compound are the homes (fortunately not damaged by the fire) of the families of the widows of former *kabaka*. Royal family members are buried amid the trees out the back, and the whole place has the distinct feel of a small rural village.

Kasubi Tombs is also the place to arrange a guide to the more low-key Buganda royal sights of **Wamala Tombs** (Map p380; admission incl guide USh10,000; ⊙8am-5pm), 11km north of Kasubi, and the less interesting **Tomb of Nnamasole Kanyange** (Map p380; admission incl guide USh10,000; ⊙10am-6pm), 4km from the Wamala Tombs.

Bulange Royal Building NOTABLE BUILDING
(Map p380; www.buganda.or.ug; Kabakanjagala Rd; admission incl guide USh10,000; ⊙8am-5pm) A great place to learn about the history and culture of the Buganda kingdom; guided tours take you inside the parliament building, providing interesting stories and details about the 56 different clans. Parliament is held twice a month on Monday mornings, though it is conducted in Lugandan. Buy your ticket at the adjacent **Buganda Tourism Centre** (Map p380; ☑0414-271166; ⊙7.30am-6pm Mon-Sat, 10am-5pm Sun) which also sells bark-cloth clothing and books on Bugandan culture.

Mengo Palace HISTORIC SITE
(Map p380; Lubiri Ring Rd, Twekobe; admission incl guide USh10,000; ⊙8am-5.30pm) Built in 1922 Mengo Palace is the former home of the king of Buganda, though it has remained empty since 1966 when Prime Minister Milton Obote ordered a dramatic attack to oust Kabaka Mutesa II (then president of Uganda). Led by the forces of Idi Amin, soldiers stormed the palace and, after several days of fighting, Mutesa was forced to flee and live in exile in the UK. The interior of the attractive palace remains off limits to tourists.

The building was duly converted to army barracks, while an adjacent site became a notorious underground prison and torture-execution chamber built by Idi Amin in the 1970s. Guides will lead you to this terrifying site, a dark concrete tunnel with numerous dark, damp cells, which were separated by an electrified passage of water to prevent escape. You'll see some original charcoal messages written by former prisoners on the walls: one reads 'Obote, you have killed me, but what about my children!' On the grounds are also the scrap-metal remains of Mutesa's Rolls Royce destroyed by Idi Amin.

Mengo Palace is at the end of a ceremonial drive leading from Bulange Royal Building.

National Mosque MOSQUE
(Map p384; Old Kampala Rd; admission incl tour USh10,000) One of Kampala's premier sights, the prominent National Mosque was begun by Idi Amin in 1972 and finished in 2007 by Colonel Gadaffi. The hour-long tour allows you to scale its soaring minaret for the best views of Kampala, and takes you within its gleaming interior. Free entry for Muslims.

Parliament House NOTABLE BUILDING
(Map p384; Parliament Ave; ⊙8.30am-4.30pm Mon-Fri) Open to the public, a visit to parliament is an interesting way to spend an hour or two. You can either tour the building, or see the government in action – parliament sits from 2.30pm Tuesday to Thursday and is conducted in English. You need to visit the public relations department (room 114) to arrange a visit, and make a written request to see question time. Usually you can arrange a visit on the spot. You'll need to bring an identification card and be decently dressed.

In the main lobby look out for the huge wooden cultural map of Uganda featuring the country's flora and fauna.

Uganda Martyrs' Shrine HISTORIC SITE
(Map p380; www.ugandamartyrsshrine.org.ug) Located in Namugongo, this shrine marks the spot where Kabaka Mwanga II ordered the execution of 14 Catholics who refused to denounce their faith, including church leader Charles Lwanga who was burnt alive on or around 3 June 1886 – which is now celebrated as Martyrs' Day. The shrine represents an African hut but looks more like something built by NASA than the Catholic church.

The shrine is just outside Kampala off Jinja Rd. To get here, you'll need to take a minibus from Kampala's Old Taxi Park.

Namirembe Cathedral CHURCH
(Map p380; Namirembe Hill) This huge domed Anglican cathedral, finished in 1919, has a distinct Mediterranean feel. In years past the congregation was called to worship by the beating of enormous drums, which can still be seen in a little hut located alongside the church.

Katereke Prison HISTORIC SITE
(Map p380; adult/child incl guide USh3000/1000; ⊙8am-5pm) Located on the outskirts of town, royal prisoners were starved in the prison ditch during the upheavals of 1888–89. Kabaka Kalema killed 30 of his brothers and sisters here in 1889 in his quest to keep control of the throne. It's not much more than a deep,

UGANDA KAMPALA

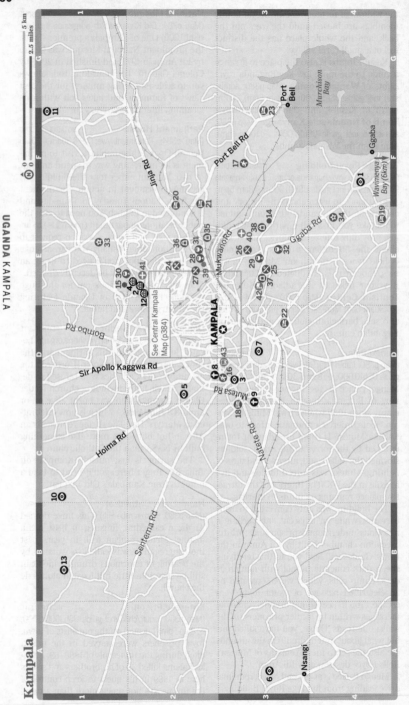

Kampala

UGANDA KAMPALA

circular trench, but it's an evocative site and is worth the trip if you have time. The unmarked turn-off is opposite the police post in Nsangi and the prison is 1.7km north. A *boda-boda* (motorcycle taxi) will cost USh3000.

Rubaga Cathedral CHURCH
(Map p380; Mutesa Rd) This twin-towered Roman Catholic cathedral has a memorial to the Uganda Martyrs, with 22 Catholic victims (later declared saints) enshrined in the stained-glass windows. They were among other Ugandan Christians burnt or hacked to death by Kabaka Mwanga II in 1885 and 1886 for refusing to renounce the 'white man's religion'.

Kampala Hindu Temple TEMPLE
(Map p384; Snay Bin Amir Rise; ⊙ 4-7.30pm) Right in the city centre, this temple has elaborate towers and a swastika-emblazoned gate. Peek inside to see the unexpected dome.

Skate Park SKATEBOARDING
(Map p380; ☎ 0752-397100; www.ugandaskateboard union.wordpress.com; Kitintale) Head to the outer

suburb of Kitintale to check out Kampala's home-grown skate scene, where skateboard pioneer Jack has set up East Africa's first skate park. Call ahead for directions. Kids skate all weekend and after 4pm on weekdays. Equipment donations are appreciated, and there are sometimes volunteer opportunities.

⭐ Festivals & Events

LaBa! Arts Festival ART
(www.labaartsfestival.wordpress.com) An open-air art space where artists sell their works alongside music and dance performances. Held in May or early June.

Royal Ascot Goat Races CULTURAL
(www.thegoatraces.com; ⊙ Sep) One of the biggest events on the *mzungu* (foreigner/white person) social calendar, goats really do race at this charity event, but that's largely beside the point. People come here to eat, drink and wear funny hats. However, its future remains unclear, as the event was not held in 2014.

Kampala City Festival CULTURAL

One of East Africa's biggest street parties is held each October with floats and performers celebrating Ugandan culture. Traditional and contemporary art, fashion and music are all showcased over multiple stages.

Kampala Contemporary Art Festival ART

(www.klaart.org) Held every even-numbered year in October, this month-long art festival exhibits contemporary Ugandan and East African artists, with a schedule of daily events.

🛏 Sleeping

Kampala has good accommodation on offer in all price brackets. The past few years have seen a number of quality new budget and midrange options open up, and there are some superb upmarket hotels at the upper end of the scale.

★ Red Chilli Hideaway BACKPACKERS $

(Map p380; ☑ 0312-202903; www.redchillihideaway.com; 13-23 Bukasa Hill View Rd, Butabika; camping per person US$7, dm US$10, s/d/tr US$30/40/45, s/d/tr without bathroom from US$25/30/35; @ 🛜 🏊) At its new location Red Chilli was given the golden opportunity to work from a blank canvas to create its dream hostel. Drawing upon all the needs of the modern backpacker, the end results are stunning: piping hot water, comfy beds, sparkling pool, beach volleyball, grassy lawn, pizzeria, multiple bars, tasty and cheap meals, free computers, wi-fi, TV lounge – it's all here. Its location on the outskirts of Kampala makes a nice escape, and there are free shuttles through the day to/from Oasis Mall (p391) in town.

Fat Cat Backpackers BACKPACKERS $

(Map p384; ☑ 0771-393892; www.fatcatkampala.com; 13 Bukoto St; dm US$15; 🛜) In a very cool 1950s art-deco building with prime location close to Kampala's best nightlife and restaurants, the British-Polish-owned Fat Cat is a top budget choice. The only downside is the absence of private rooms, but its dorms are spacious and beds are larger than normal. The rooftop terrace confirms its greatness, with panoramic views made for a sunset beer.

Ewaka Guesthouse & Backpackers BACKPACKERS $

(Map p380; ☑ 0712-930151; www.ewaka-kampala.com; 8/9 Salim Bey Rd, Ntinda; camping USh10,000, dm USh20,000, r per person USh40,000-50,000, r without bathroom USh25,000; 🛜) A friendly hostel hidden away in a suburban back-street, Ewaka has the cosy familiarity of staying at a mate's house. It's both social and laid-back, with clean rooms, a homely lounge, functional kitchen (handy as a market is up the road), plus a grassy yard with hammocks and an avocado tree.

To get here, go to New Market intersection from where it's a five minute walk east.

Backpackers Hostel BACKPACKERS $

(Map p380; ☑ 0772-430587; www.backpackers.co.ug; Natete Rd, Lunguja; camping USh14,000, dm USh25,000-30,000, r USh85,000, s/d without bathroom USh35,000/55,000; 🅿 @ 🛜) The first hostel to open its doors in Kampala, the Aussie-owned Backpackers is a relaxed escape from the bustle of the city – yet is only a short taxi ride out of the city centre. The facilities are generally good, but could do with some maintenance. The introduction of a boisterous nightclub hasn't worked in its favour. To get here take a Natete/Wakaliga taxi from the New Taxi Park.

This is also the place to get information on trekking in the Rwenzoris, as the Australian owner set up the world-class Rwenzori Trekking Services.

New City Annex Hotel HOTEL $

(Map p384; ☑ 0414-254132; ncahotel@gmail.com; 7 Dewinton Rd; r from USh60,000, s/d without bathroom from USh18,000/USh40,000) Regularly booked out with Peace Corp volunteers and budget travellers (reservations essential), the New City Annex certainly ain't fancy but it gets the job done with simple, functional rooms, and a handy city-centre location. It also has an excellent restaurant downstairs.

Aponye Hotel HOTEL $

(Map p384; ☑ 0414-349239; www.aponyehotel.com; 17 William St; s USh40,000, d USh45,000-60,000; 🅿 ❄ @ 🛜) A good find in this chaotic corner of the city, the scruffy (but comfy) hotel rooms have satellite TV, wi-fi, room service and some have air-con and balconies. There's also secure parking and a decent restaurant. Downsides are its chaotic downtown location, perpetually out-of-order lift and unreliable hot water.

Athina Club House GUESTHOUSE $$

(Map p384; ☑ 0414-341428; www.athinaclubhouse.com; 30 Windsor Cres; s/d US$50/65) The Cypriot-owned Athina has a wonderful sense of being stuck in a 1950s time warp, making it feel like you're staying at your grandma's house. Spacious rooms have lime green walls, retro fittings and floral curtains, large-sized poster beds, and bathrooms with reliable hot water. It has a great location in the well-heeled suburb of Kololo, perfect for nearby upmarket bars and restaurants.

Cassia Lodge
HOTEL $$

(Map p380; ☑0755-777002; www.cassialodge. com; Buziga Hill; s/d/tr from US$140/160/180; ❄@☎☀) This quiet spot boasts sweeping vistas of Lake Victoria and hills that seem to never end. The rooms, all facing the lake with balconies and patios for taking it all in, are simple but tasteful and feature minibars and wi-fi. There's a good stock of books on Uganda for sale. It's a long way from central Kampala, signposted 2.3km off Ggaba Rd.

Le Bougainviller
BOUTIQUE HOTEL $$

(Map p380; ☑0414-220966; www.bougainviller. com; Katazamiti Rd, Bugolobi; s/d from US$111/131; ❄@☎☀) A little slice of the Mediterranean in Africa, Le Bougainviller's 24 sleek rooms are split across two buildings. The nicest ones have plush four-poster beds and plasma TVs, and face a flower-filled garden, while the apartments feature contemporary lofts, kitchens and bathtubs. There's also a sauna. A French restaurant rounds out the experience.

Urban by City Blue
HOTEL $$

(Map p384; ☑0793-000001; www.citybluehotels. com/urban-by-cityblue-kampala-uganda; Akii Bua Rd; s/d from US$130/150, ste US$200; ❄@☎☀) A solid midrange choice, this affordable boutique-style hotel will suit those seeking some tranquillity within central Kampala. The modern, yet somewhat sterile rooms are centred on a sparkling pool and inviting lawn.

Fang Fang Hotel
HOTEL $$

(Map p384; ☑0414-235828; www.fangfang.co.ug; 9 Ssezibwa Rd; s/d from US$69/99; ❄@☎) Just beyond the city centre, this old-timer warrants consideration not only for its reasonable rates but surprisingly stylish rooms, most featuring bathtubs and pot plants. Discounts are available. There's a quality Chinese restaurant, not to be confused with its flagship, eponymous one in Colville St.

Makindye Country Club
HOTEL $$

(Map p380; ☑0414-510290; www.makindye countryclub.com; 59 Mobutu Rd, Makindye Hill; s/d from US$85/105, without bathroom US$70/85; ❄@☎☀) Formerly a members-only club

---

ⓘ BUDGET TIP: BRING YOUR OWN GEAR

Travellers on a tight budget should consider investing in a tent; not only handy for visiting national parks, but for lodges and backpackers across Uganda, most which offer cheap camping. In Kampala, department stores **Game** (Map p380; Lugogo Mall) and Nakumatt (p393; also in Entebbe) both sell inexpensive, portable tents (two-person from USh100,000) that should last for the duration of your trip, as well as other camping goods such as sleeping bags, chairs and ice coolers.

---

for US embassy staff, British owners have recently taken Makindye Country Club over and opened it for all. The eclectic mix of rooms, all with very '70s decor, are set over huge grounds with all kinds of recreational activities on offer: outdoor lap pool, clay tennis courts, gym, squash courts, Zumba classes, games room, TV lounge and a huge playground for kids. It's on the fringes of Kampala, just off the Entebbe Rd.

Fairway Hotel
HOTEL $$

(Map p384; ☑0414-257171; www.fairwayhotel. co.ug; 1 Kafu Rd; s/d US$105/120; ᴾ❄@☎☀) Overlooking a golf course, this older property has a few quirks and is fast approaching the classic category, but for central Kampala it offers good value – especially considering its convenient location, garden setting and facilities including pool, gym, and multiple restaurants and bars.

Speke Hotel
HOTEL $$

(Map p384; ☑0414-259221; www.spekehotel.com; Nile Ave; r incl full breakfast US$138; ❄@☎) One of Kampala's oldest hotels, this characterful, refurbished address adds creature comforts to age and grace. All rooms are rather simple, but have wooden floors and many have balconies. It's in a great central location and the terrace bar is a popular meeting place.

There's also a good Italian restaurant (Mammamia) but the heaving Rock Garden bar is right next door so take a room in the back.

★ Villa Kololo
BOUTIQUE HOTEL $$$

(Map p384; ☑0414-500533; www.villakololo. com/accommodations; 31 Acacia Ave, Kololo; s/d

Central Kampala

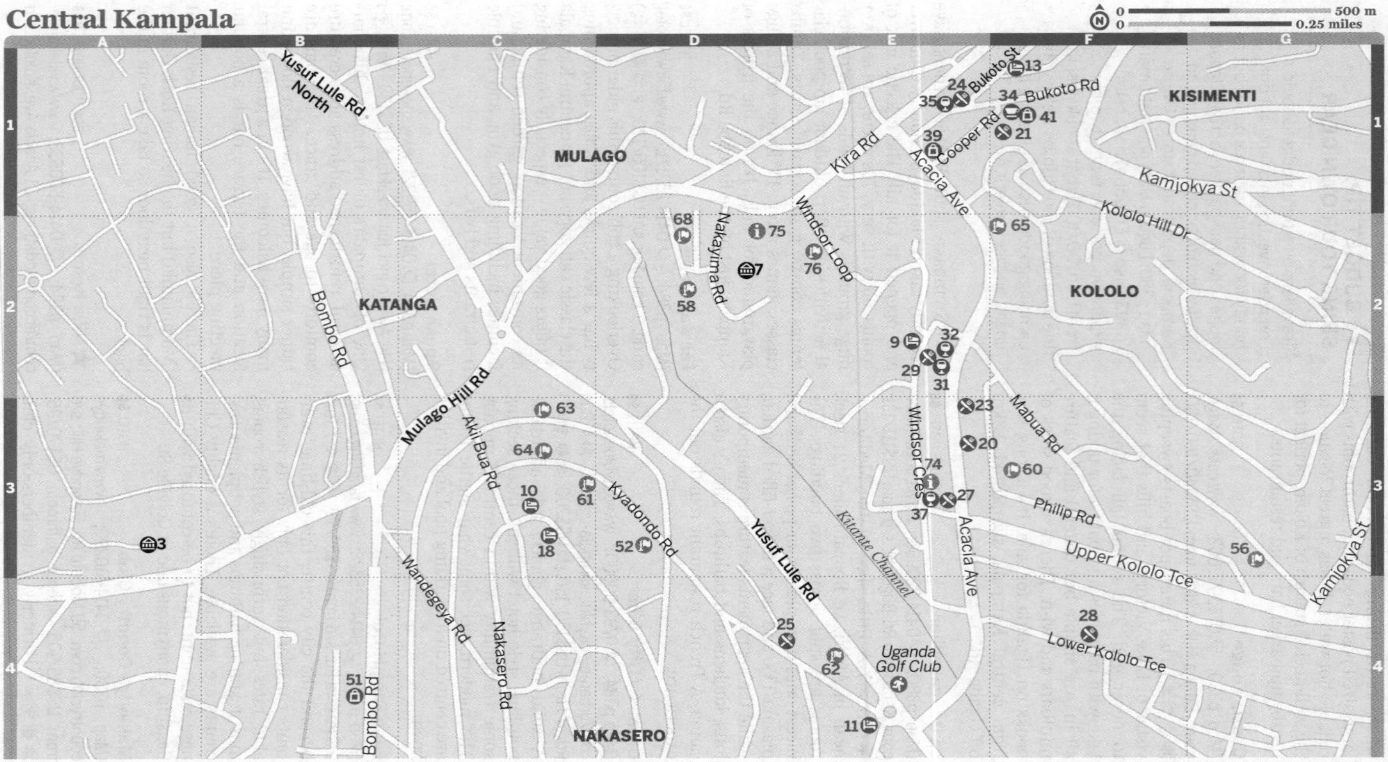
0 500 m
0 0.25 miles
KISIMENTI
KOLOLO
MULAGO
KATANGA
NAKASERO
Yusuf Lule Rd North
Yusuf Lule Rd
Bombo Rd
Mulago Hill Rd
Akii Bua Rd
Wandegeya Rd
Nakasero Rd
Kyadondo Rd
Kira Rd
Acacia Ave
Cooper Rd
Bukoto St
Bukoto Rd
Kamjokya St
Kololo Hill Dr
Windsor Loop
Nakayima Rd
Windsor Cres
Mabua Rd
Philip Rd
Upper Kololo Tce
Lower Kololo Tce
Kitante Channel
Uganda Golf Club

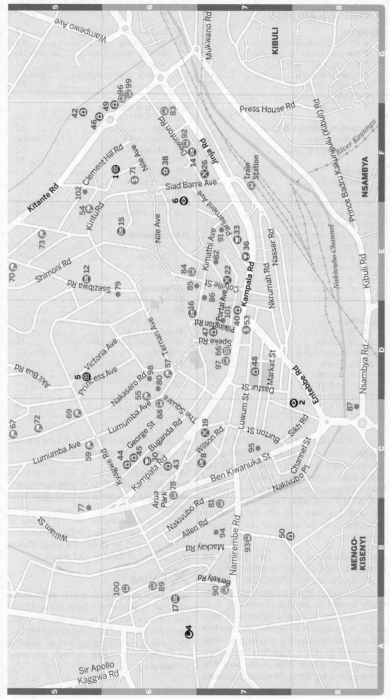

UGANDA KAMPALA

Central Kampala

from US$130/180, ste US$250; 🐱) With an excellent location in upmarket Kololo, this Italian-owned designer hotel has smart, well-priced rooms that balance tasteful North African decor and Rajasthani motifs with all the mod cons. The suite is a stand out with spa bath and antique furniture. Downstairs is the popular Mediterraneo restaurant.

Emin Pasha Hotel BOUTIQUE HOTEL $$$
(Map p384; ☎0414-236977; www.eminpasha.com; 27 Akii Bua Rd; s/d from US$250/270; 🅿 ✿ @ 🛜 🐱) Kampala's first boutique hotel is beautifully housed in an elegant property with rooms blending lodge atmosphere with luxury. The more expensive ones feature claw-foot bathtubs, while all have classic writing desks. Its manicured lawns boast bed lounges for relaxing with a book close to the pool. The well-regarded Fez Brasserie restaurant shares

the grounds, as does a wonderful spa if you're up for some more pampering.

Serena Hotel HOTEL $$$
(Map p384; ☎0414-309000; www.serenahotels.com; Kintu Rd; s/d from US$247/264; ✿ @ 🛜 🐱) Setting the standard in large, luxurious hotels, the stunning Serena is the result of a massive multimillion-dollar renovation of the former Nile Hotel. It's set in 17-acre grounds full of streams and ponds.

✗ Eating

Kampala is packed with quality restaurants, and the international population brings considerable variety to the dining scene. There are plenty of large supermarkets that are ideal for stocking up before heading up-country. For online delivery try www.hellofood.ug.

UGANDA KAMPALA

New City Annex Hotel

UGANDAN $

(Map p384; 7 Dewinton Rd; mains USh10,000-18,000; ☺6am-11pm; ⊘) This basic hotel restaurant is one of the best spots for Ugandan food, with excellent local flavours (including good vegetarian options) and healthy breakfasts, a rarity in Kampala. It regularly attracts members of parliament and Peace Corps volunteers.

Little Donkey

MEXICAN $

(Map p380; 4286 Henry Ford Close; mains from USh12,000; ☺noon-late) Though it's more Tex-Mex than your hipster street-food *taqueria* (taco restaurant), Little Donkey nevertheless brings decent Mexican food to Uganda. It's a great place to hang out, with picnic tables set up in the garden, and a menu of burritos, tacos and nachos to be washed down with icy, salt-rimmed margaritas. Proceeds go to assisting local students' education.

La Fontaine

INTERNATIONAL $

(Map p384; www.lafontaine-kampala.com; Bukoto St, Kisementi; mains USh8000-17,000; ☺10am-10pm; ☏) While you don't come here for fine dining or lightning-fast service, you do get cheap, tasty food in a laid-back, atmospheric environment. The fish dishes, such as grilled tilapia with garlic butter, are the pick.

Masala Chaat House

INDIAN $

(Map p384; ☑0414-236487; 3 Dewinton Rd; mains USh12,000-20,000; ☺9am-10pm; ⊘) A winning combination of authentic flavours (both south and north Indian) and affordable prices has kept this local institution going strong over the years. It offers plenty to keep both vegetarians and carnivores smiling for the night, and those familiar with south Indian cuisine will be pleased to see a selection of 15 dosas on the menu.

DON'T MISS

KAMPALA CITY TOURS

City tours are an excellent, engaging means of exploring Kampala while providing plenty of local perspective.

Kampala Walk Tour (☑0774-596222; www.kampalawalktour.com; 3/6hr tour US$20/30) Led by the charismatic Zulaika, these walking tours are a great way to get a feel for downtown Kampala, with plenty of insider knowledge and a good balance between the main sights and local spots. Tours depart from the main post office.

Walter's Boda-Boda Tours (☑0791-880106; www.walterstours.com; per person US$40) These unique, half-day city tours are taken sitting on the back of a *boda-boda* (motorcycle taxi) in a group travelling at a safe pace. Tours take in the main sights, and incorporate local experiences such as sampling Ugandan food and banana beer. It also runs tours further afield. Helmets are provided.

Uganda Bicycle (☑0787-016688; www.ugandabicycle.com; per person USh100,000; ⊗8am & 1pm) These popular bicycle tours explore less-visited areas on the outskirts of Kampala, including local villages. Tours depart daily, meeting at Cassia Lodge (p383) at 8am and 1pm, and last around five hours. It also offers nature cycling tours in Greater Kampala (USh130,000) and rents bikes (per day USh30,000).

Slum Tours (☑0392-859254; www.affcad.org; per person incl lunch US$25) While the nature of these tours is always contentious, a visit to one of Kampala's poorest districts in Bwaise-Kawempe is led by locals who grew up in the area, with 100% of funds going back into the community. The three- to four-hour tours shed brutal light on living conditions, giving participants a chance to meet residents and visit everyday sites such as water sources.

Coffee Safari (Map p384; ☑0772-505619; www.1000cupscoffee.com; per person US$100; ⊗7.30am Fri) You can trace your coffee from the cup to the farm on day tours run by 1000 Cups Coffee House. Book before noon on Thursday.

Antonio's UGANDAN $
(Map p384; Kampala Rd; mains USh8000-20,000; ⊗7am-10pm) A pretty good cafeteria-style greasy spoon serving Ugandan, Kenyan and Western favourites.

Crocodile Café & Bar CAFE $
(Map p384; ☑0414-254593; www.thecrocodilekampala.com; Cooper Rd; sandwiches & salads USh12,000-19,000, mains USh 18,000; ⊗9am-11pm Mon-Sat; 🛜) While there are fancier choices along this strip, we still love this Kampala classic for its scruffy-chic decor that exudes a certain Parisian literary vibe. Come for its menu of steaks, salads and sandwiches, or for a coffee or wine.

Tuhende Safari Lodge BARBECUE $
(Map p384; 8 Martin Rd, Old Kampala; mains USh7500-9900; ⊗4pm-midnight) Chargrilled steaks and fish are the speciality at this old-school, budget-traveller hangout. The vegetable stew is pretty good too. It also has good budget **rooms** (Map p384; ☑0772-468360; tuhendesafarilodge@yahoo.com; dm/r USh13,000/60,000) that are popular with NGO workers.

Mama Ashanti AFRICAN $$
(Map p384; www.mamaashanti.com; 20 Kyadondo Rd; mains USh16,000-40,000; ⊗9am-11pm Mon-Sat) Mama Ashanti specialises in delicious West African dishes such as *egusi* (minced spinach, pumpkin seed and groundnut) with pounded yam, or egg and goat stew. The spacious garden setting is a good place for a drink too.

Khana Khazana INDIAN $$
(Map p384; ☑0414-233049; 20 Acacia Ave; mains USh16,000-45,000; ⊗noon-3.30pm & 7-11pm Tue-Sun; 🚗) Regarded by many as the best Indian in town, classy Khazana is a great place to treat yourself. It features atmospheric Rajasthani-inspired decor, crisp white tablecloths and professional waiters serving a menu full of wonderful tandoori dishes and creamy north Indian curries. Home delivers, too.

Casablanca ETHIOPIAN $$
(Map p384; 26 Acacia Ave; mains from USh16,000; ⊗noon-late) Another big player in Kololo's fantastic multicultural food scene, Casablanca does tasty *injera* (flatbread) dishes in its outdoor candle-lit garden restaurant.

The perfect place to kick off proceedings for a night out on the town.

Prunes
CAFE $$

(Map p380; 8 Wampewo Ave; ⊘8am-10pm; 🛜) Kampala's best spot for brunch, laid-back Prunes is a popular expat hangout. It does great Ugandan coffee to go with comfort food of toasties, burgers and healthy salads such as beetroot, goats cheese, apple and nuts. Saturday mornings take on a different feel with its buzzy farmers market. The backyard and sandpit and Sunday art classes will keep the kids busy.

★ Mediterraneo
ITALIAN $$$

(Map p384; 📞0414-500533; www.villakololo.com; 31 Acacia Ave, Kololo; pizzas from USh25,000, mains from USh30,000; ⊘10am-10.30pm; 🛜) This classy, open-air Italian restaurant in atmospheric surrounds features wood decking in a tropical garden setting, lit at night with kerosene lamps. The Italian chef creates fantastic authentic dishes including thin-crust pizzas and handmade pastas such as pappardelle funghi with porcini imported from Italy. It also serves up steaks and gourmet mains such as grilled rock lobster. Reservations are recommended.

Tamarai
THAI $$$

(Map p384; 14 Lower Kololo Terrace; mains USh20,000-42,000; ⊘10am-10pm; 🛜) Kampala's premier Thai restaurant is a classy affair stylishly set in an immense open-air thatched hut. All your favourite Thai classics (plus a few Pan Asian dishes) are prepared authentically using fresh ingredients and fragrant herbs. Tea lovers will rejoice with 16 varieties to choose from.

Yujo Izakaya
JAPANESE $$$

(Map p384; Windsor Cres; sushi from USh18,000, mains USh24,000-50,000; ⊘noon-3pm & 6.30-11pm) In the process of shifting from its Japanese embassy location to Kololo, this popular eatery is known primarily for its sushi and sashimi selection, but also does tasty ramen and *okonomiyaki* (savoury pancake).

Fang Fang
CHINESE $$$

(Map p384; Colville St; mains from USh20,000; ⊘11am-midnight) Although there's much more competition these days, Fang Fang remains Kampala's best Chinese restaurant. The interior is lovely, typical of an upmarket Chinese restaurant anywhere, and there's a large, quiet outdoor terrace to enjoy a full selection of Chinese classics. Specialities include fried crispy prawns with ginger and garlic. There's also a more laid-back garden restaurant at its hotel.

Lawns
AFRICAN $$$

(Map p380; www.thelawns.co.ug; 34 Impala Ave; mains from USh34,000; ⊘noon-midnight; 🛜) The aptly named Lawns is a lovely garden restaurant where carnivores wanting something different can feast on anything from ostrich burgers and wildebeest steaks to crocodile in garlic wine sauce. If you're really into the idea, go the game-meat platter or the 1.5kg croc tail that feeds four. Less adventurous diners won't be disappointed with beef steaks. Thankfully the cute bunnies roaming the grounds aren't on the menu!

Fez Brasserie
INTERNATIONAL $$$

(Map p384; 27 Akii Bua Rd; mains USh30,000-38,000; ⊘12.30-3pm & 6.30-11pm; 📞) One of Kampala's most renowned restaurants, this gorgeous spot looking out over the leafy grounds of the Emin Pasha hotel has an ever-evolving fusion menu, which respects vegetarians, uniting flavours from five continents. Or just come for a drink on the comfy couches in the wine bar.

Le Chateau
BELGIAN $$$

(Map p380; Ggaba Rd; mains USh30,000-40,000; ⊘7am-11pm; 🛜) Popular for serious steaks, Le Chateau also features an extensive Belgian menu that includes Flemish stew, frogs' legs, snails and a selection of 11 Belgian beers all served under an enormous thatched roof.

While you're here, drop in to **Quality Hill** (Map p380; Ggaba Rd) next door for its superb La Patisserie bakery and Cellar wine shop to stock up on picnic supplies.

🍷 Drinking & Nightlife

Nightlife in Kampala is something to relish with a host of decent bars and clubs throughout the city. Caffeine lovers also have plenty of choice.

Be warned that pickpockets are prevalent, and it's not advisable to carry any valuables, especially phones. The presence of prostitutes is another tedious reality in many of Kampala's nightspots.

★ Yasigi Beer Garden
BREWERY

(Map p384; www.facebook.com/yasigibeergarden; 40 Windsor Cres, Kololo; ⊘11.30am-midnight Mon-Sat, from 2pm Sun; 🛜) Uganda's first microbrewery, Yasigi (named after the African goddess of beer) produces four beers onsite – an amber ale, wheat beer, pilsner and stout – to be enjoyed on picnic tables set up on its lawn. Fill up on wood-fired pizzas or pulled-goat sliders while you're here. During the day pop your head into the brewery to see the production side of things.

Bubbles O'Learys   PUB
(Map p384; ☑0312-263815; 19 Acacia Ave, Kololo; ⊙noon-late; ☎) A Kololo institution, Bubbles is the closest you'll find to a true pub in Kampala. Its bar and furnishings were shipped in from an old Irish boozer back on the Emerald Isle. It's a buzzing spot drawing a fun crowd of expats and locals, and has a great beer garden too.

Iguana   BAR
(Map p384; ☑0777-020658; 8 Bukoto St, Kisementi; ⊙5pm-late) Heaving with *wuzunga* and locals, divey Iguana is a contender for the most popular bar in town. Upstairs is a boozy affair, whether as a spot for after-work drinks or late evenings with DJs spinning anything from house, dance hall or old-school hip hop. Downstairs has a pool table and live reggae bands.

Big Mike's   BAR, CLUB
(Map p384; www.bigmikes.biz; 19 Acacia Ave, Kololo; ⊙5pm-late) Whether you're looking for a lively beer garden, swanky cocktail bar or pumping club, Big Mike's has it covered – all under the one roof! It's popular for good reason.

1000 Cups Coffee House   CAFE
(Map p384; ☑0775-667858; www.1000cupscoffee. com; 18 Buganda Rd; coffee from USh6500; ⊙8am-9pm Mon-Sat, 8am-7pm Sun) For espresso, aeropress or cold drip, caffeine aficionados will want to head here. There's a good range of single-origin beans from across East Africa – expect to pay a premium – and a menu of light bites, along with a selection of international newspapers and magazines.

Cayenne   BAR
(Map p380; www.cayennekampala.com; Kira Rd; ⊙noon-late Tue-Sun, from 4pm Mon; ☎) An attractive outdoor set-up with a sprawling tree, luxurious pool and popular restaurant, Cayenne is a top place to hit night or day. However the party only truly gets started late, when DJs, live music and multiple bars reach full swing. Dress is smart-casual (no shorts or flip flops), and there's a USh5000 cover charge after 11pm weekends.

Endiro   CAFE
(Map p384; www.endirocoffee.com; 23 Cooper Rd, Kisementi; ⊙7.30am-10pm; ☎) Full of diners plugged into their laptops, this smart, earthy cafe has free wi-fi to go with its strong Ugandan coffee, fresh juices and excellent breakfasts.

Rock Garden   BAR
(Map p384; Speke Hotel, Nile Ave) One of the definitive stops on the Kampala night shift, this cool place has a covered bar and a huge outdoor area. Be careful here; pickpocketing is often part of the experience.

Café Pap   CAFE
(Map p384; ☑0414-254570; www.cafepap.com; 13b Parliament Ave; coffee USh6000, mains USh16,000-35,000; ⊙7.30am-11pm Mon-Sat, 9.30am-11pm Sun; ☎) This busy cafe on Parliament Ave is a good spot for Uganda coffee, farmed on the slopes of Elgon, the Rwenzoris and the Virungas, as well as freshly squeezed juices and breakfasts. There's another branch in Garden City.

Deuces   BAR
(Map p380; Ggaba Rd; ⊙24hr) Taking over from Al's bar, one of Uganda's most famous bars (although notorious…), Deuces keeps the flag flying as the place in Kampala that never sleeps.

Mateo's   PUB
(Map p384; Parliament Ave) This sports bar is a relaxing spot in downtown Kampala for an evening tipple, unless a big football match is on or the DJ is spinning on weekend nights.

Boda Boda Bar   BAR
(Map p384; www.bodaboda.co.ug; Garden City; ⊙11am-late; ☎) This swish rooftop bar in Garden City mall has an attractive outdoor area that looks out to the greenery of the golf course.

Café Cheri   BAR
(Map p380; Muyenga Rd; ⊙24hr) An old timer along the notorious Kabalagala strip, this open-air shack is less raucous than others, but is still open around the clock.

Ange Noir   CLUB
(Map p380; ☑0414-230190; www.angenoir.net; 77a 1st St; ⊙Thu-Sun) The 'black angel' is in an industrial location and has long held Kampala's most popular dance floor.

Club Silk   CLUB
(Map p380; www.clubsilkuganda.com; 15/17 1st St; ⊙Thu-Sat) Popular with students, Club Silk has a pumping dance floor that goes until late.

☆ Entertainment

★ Ndere Centre
DANCE

(Map p380; ☎0414-597704; www.ndere.com; Kisaasi Rd; adult/child USh30,000/15,000) If you're interested in traditional dance and music, try to catch a dinner-theatre performance of the Ndere Troupe at Ndere Centre. They showcase dances from many of Uganda's tribal groups with high-energy shows taking place in a 700-seat amphitheatre on Sundays at 6pm, Wednesday at 7pm and Fridays afro-jazz from 7pm.

They also offer traditional drumming and dance classes. The troupe has a lovely base way out in Ntinda, which includes a restaurant-bar and guesthouse.

National Theatre
LIVE MUSIC

(Map p384; ☎0414-254567; www.uncc.co.ug; Siad Barre Ave) There's a quality program of music, film, dance and drama performances in the theatre itself, but most travellers come here for the popular, free nightly outdoor events. Grab a beer and a chair and catch an informal open-stage jam on Monday evenings, African drumming on Tuesdays or comedy night (USh10,000) at 8pm on Thursdays, where the merriment comes in a mix of English and Luganda. Check schedule online for events other nights.

PLOT54
LIVE MUSIC, ART

(Map p380; Ggaba Rd) Formerly the Happy Tilapia, this new venue has a calendar of events including indie cinema, live gigs (Afro electrica to hip hop) and art exhibitions, among other cultural happenings.

Century Cinemax
CINEMA

(Map p384; www.centurycinemax.co.ug; Acacia Ave, Acacia Mall) Modern, state-of-the-art cinema showing 3D blockbusters.

Cineplex
CINEMA

(Map p384; www.cineplexuganda.com; Garden City) Screens a mix of Hollywood and Bollywood fare. Also has another complex at nearby Oasis Mall.

🛍 Shopping

Kampala is a good place to do your craft shopping with items from all regions of the country plus neighbouring Kenya and Democratic Republic of the Congo (DRC). The airport also has a good bookstore and handicraft store, convenient for last-minute souvenirs.

If Kampala's taxi parks make you agoraphobic, then you'll definitely want to stay out of the markets. Kampala has a number of shiny, air-conditioned malls that offer all the usual chain stores and supplies. **Acacia** (Map p384; www.theacaciamall.com; Acacia Ave, Kisementi), **Oasis** (Map p384; Yusuf Lule Rd) and **Garden City** (Map p384; Yusuf Lule Rd) malls are the most useful for travellers.

Banana Boat
ARTS & CRAFTS

(Map p384; www.bananaboat.co.ug; Cooper Rd; ☺9am-7pm) 🍃 A sophisticated craft shop selling smart local items such as excellent batiks, and handmade stuff from all over Africa, including Congolese carvings. There's branches at **Garden City** (Map p384; www.bananaboat.co.ug; Kitante Rd; ☺9.30am-7pm Mon-Sat, 10am-4pm Sun), **Bugolobi Village Mall** (Map p380; Bugolobi) and an outlet with an emphasis on homes and interiors in **Lugogo Mall** (Map p380).

Uganda Crafts 2000
ARTS & CRAFTS

(Map p384; www.ugandacrafts2000ltd.org; Bombo Rd; ☺8am-6pm) A small fair-trade craft shop selling arty souvenirs and trinkets; 90% of the wares are Ugandan, made by widows and disadvantaged locals. It sells bark-cloth clothing (including custom-made orders) and excellent sustainable paper products.

Exposure Africa
ARTS & CRAFTS

(Map p384; www.sewacrafts.org/exposure-africa; 13 Buganda Rd; ☺7am-7pm) The largest of the city's craft 'villages', stocking woodcarvings, drums, sandals, batiks, basketry, beaded jewellery and '*mzungu*' T-shirts. Some items have price tags, but everything is negotiable.

Craft Africa
ARTS & CRAFTS

(Map p384; Buganda Rd) Making up one half of Kampala's main craft complex (along with Exposure Africa), this place has an excellent choice of Ugandan and Kenyan crafts and souvenirs.

Owino Market
MARKET

(Map p384) Sprawling around Nakivubo Stadium, Owino has everything from traditional medicines to televisions. It's most famous for its second-hand clothing, but you can also buy some material and let one of the army of tailors sew you something new. You're bound to spend a lot of time here: not only because it's so much fun, but also because once you're inside it's really difficult to find your way out.

Quality Hill ARTS & CRAFTS
(Map p380; Ggaba Rd) A guy with a great selection of Congolese carvings lays out his wares at this upmarket complex of patisseries and wine shops.

Def.i.ni.tion CLOTHING
(Map p384; www.definitionafrica.com; 1st fl, Acacia Mall, Acacia Ave; ☺9am-9pm) Cool local label selling hip, vibrant accessories, fabrics, designer T-shirts and clothing.

Bold CLOTHING
(Map p384; www.boldkla.com; 1st fl Acacia Mall, Acacia Ave; ☺9am-9pm) A team of local designers produce contemporary styles and accessories using African fabrics and designs.

Renzioni CLOTHING
(Map p380; www.renzioni.com; Tank Hill Rd) Set up by designer Okoronkwo Lawrence, Renzioni incorporates vibrant African prints into women's and men's clothing, shoes and accessories.

Gerald's Antiques ANTIQUES
(Map p384; Pilkington Rd) Gerald's has stamps and money from the past and present (including notes with Idi Amin's face), plus tribal artefacts that may or may not be old.

Aristoc BOOKS
(Map p384; 23 Kampala Rd; ☺8.30am-5.30pm Mon-Fri, 9am-4.30pm Sat) This is the best place for English-language publications, with a great selection of books on Uganda, as well

KAMPALA ART

With a number of decent galleries opening up over the years, Kampala is home to a healthy and dynamic contemporary-art scene. While it still lacks a major museum dedicated to art, many commercial galleries have monthly art shows, and a few have permanent exhibitions. **START** (www.startjournal.org) is an excellent online art journal that provides good info on Kampala's art scene.

Afriart Gallery (Map p380; ☎0414-375455; www.afriartgallery.org; 56 Kenneth Dale Dr; ☺9am-6pm Mon-Sat) Just off Kira Rd, this classy little gallery features works by serious local artists. Downstairs has changing monthly exhibits, while upstairs is a permanent collection, but everything is for sale. Just next door is **@The Hub** (Map p380; www.the-hubkampala.com; ☺8am-5pm Mon-Fri), a space for artists and freelancers, which features regular shows, film screenings and an outdoor cafe.

32° East Ugandan Arts Trust (Map p380; ☎0784-924513; www.ugandanartstrust.org; 2239 Ggaba Rd) A centre for Ugandan contemporary artists is in the process of setting up an exhibition space; keep an eye out for upcoming events on its website, including its biannual Kampala Contemporary Art Festival.

AKA Gallery at Tulifanya (Afrique Kontemporary Art Gallery; Map p384; www.tulifanya gallery.com; 28 Hannington Rd; ☺10am-5pm Tue-Fri, 10am-4pm Sat) Formerly known as Tulifanya, this well-established gallery has knowledgeable owners who can inform you about artists who matter. It features a notable Geoffrey Mukasa collection.

Makerere Art Gallery (Map p384; ☎0756-116751; www.makerereartgallery.wordpress.com; Makerere University; ☺9am-5pm Mon-Fri, 10am-4pm Sat, by appointment Sun) Small, but definitely worth a visit with fascinating monthly exhibitions; check website for events. There are also some cool sculptures on the grounds.

Umoja Art Gallery (Map p380; ☎0434-660484; www.umojaartgallery.com; 85 Kira Rd; ☺10am-6pm Mon-Sat, by appointment Sun) Small contemporary gallery featuring Ugandan paintings and abstract sculptures in monthly shows.

Karibu Art Gallery (Map p380; Kisasi Rd; ☺9am-6pm) Artist-run gallery and studio featuring emerging and established Ugandan abstract artists.

Nommo Gallery (Map p384; www.uncc.co.ug/nommo-gallery; Princess Ave; ☺8am-6pm Mon-Fri, 9am-4pm Sat & Sun) Established by the Ugandan Culture Centre in 1964, Nommo is a reliable spot for quality artwork.

Uganda Art Gallery (Map p380; 651 Willis Rd; ☺8am-7pm Mon-Fri, 9am-6pm Sat & Sun) Just down from Namirembe Cathedral, this small-scale gallery sells quality paintings by local artists at affordable prices.

ℹ TRAFFIC JAM NIGHTMARES

Traffic jams are a major headache in Kampala, so no matter where you're going in the city, plan ahead if you need to get there at an appointed time. Rush hours are particularly bad, usually from 7.30am to 9.30am, 1pm to 2.30pm and 4.30pm to 7.30pm; on Friday it seems to last all day.

It all comes to a head in central Kampala, where you get snared among the chaos of two taxi ranks, two bus parks and a bustling market, all within 1 sq km of each other. It's not uncommon for the last few kilometres crawl of your journey to take an hour, which can be demoralising after returning to town from a long ride. If your luggage is easy to reach, jump off and grab a *boda-boda* (motorcycle taxi) to clear the mess; if it's in the luggage storage compartment, you have no choice but to wait it out.

as novels. Stock up before a long road trip. There are branches at **Acacia Mall** (Map p384; Acacia Ave) and Garden City (p391).

Colour Chrome   PHOTOGRAPHY
(Map p384; ☎ 0441-230556; www.colour-chrome.com; 54 Kampala Rd; ⊗8am-7pm Mon-Sat) The best camera shop in Uganda stocks an impressive selection of film, including black and white and 400-speed slide film (for gorilla photos). Also at **Acacia Mall** (Map p384; Acacia Ave).

Nakasero Market   MARKET
(Map p384) The partially covered and hectic Nakasero Market near the junction of Kampala and Entebbe Rds is all about fresh food.

Nakumatt   SHOPPING CENTRE
(Map p384; www.nakumatt.net; Acacia Mall, Acacia Ave) Good all-round shopping centre, here you'll find anything from food supplies to camping equipment including tents. There's another at **Oasis Mall** (Map p384; Oasis Mall).

ℹ Information

DANGERS & ANNOYANCES
Kampala is a largely hassle-free city and is safe as far as Africa's capitals go. Take care in and around the taxi ranks, bus terminals and markets, as pickpockets operate. Bigger incidents can and sometimes do happen, like anywhere else in the world, so follow the ordinary big-city precautions. As elsewhere in Africa, thieves who are caught red-handed will often face a mob-justice beating, but the Kampala twist is that they'll also be stripped down to their 'Adam suits' before being sent off. Kampala is also notorious for traffic jams.

EMERGENCY
Police & Ambulance (☎ 999) You can also dial ☎ 112 from mobile phones.

INTERNET ACCESS
Wi-fi is common in hotels, restaurants, bars and cafes. Otherwise you can't walk far in Kampala without passing an internet cafe. Prices usually cost USh2000 to USh3000 per hour.

MEDICAL SERVICES
International Hospital Kampala (Map p380; ☎ 0312-200400, 0772-200400; St Barnabus Rd; ⊗24hr) For serious trauma.

The Surgery (Map p380; ☎ emergency 0752-756003, 0772-756003; www.thesurgery uganda.org; 42 Naggulu Dr, Naguru; ⊗8am-6pm Mon-Sat, emergency 24hr) A highly respected clinic run by Dr Dick Stockley, an expat British GP. Stocks self-test malaria kits.

MONEY
Stanbic Bank (Map p384; Crested Towers Bldg, 17 Hannington Rd) and **Barclays Bank** (Map p384; Kampala Rd) are the most useful banks in Kampala. Both accept international cards and have plenty of ATMs about town.

Most main bank branches and foreign exchange bureaus are along or near Kampala Rd.

POST
Main Post Office (Map p384; Kampala Rd; ⊗8am-6pm Mon-Fri, 9am-2pm Sat) Offers postal and telecom services. The reliable poste restante service is at counter 14.

TOURIST INFORMATION
Eye (www.theeye.co.ug) Free, bi-monthly magazine with all listings and reviews for Kampala and other tourist towns; available online and in hard copy.

Pearl Guide (www.thepearlguide.co.ug) Online and hard-copy magazine with good info on upcoming events, food reviews and features on Uganda.

Tourism Uganda (Map p384; ☎ 0414-342196; www.visituganda.com; 42 Windsor Cres; ⊗8.30am-5pm Mon-Fri, 9am-1pm Sat) More of a marketing office, this tourist office lacks any real useful info, but has a good website.

Visit Kampala (www.visitkampala.net) Good overview of things to see and do in Kampala, upcoming events and general tourist info.

ⓘ Getting There & Away

BUS

Destinations are posted in the front windows and buses generally follow the times they tell you, though the later it is in the day, the more likely there are to be delays. Buses leave early if they're full.

TO	FARE (USH)	DURATION (HR)
Arua	30,000	7
Fort Portal	20,000	5
Gulu	20,000	5
Hoima	15,000	5
Jinja	10,000	2
Kabale	30,000	8
Kasese	25,000	7
Kisoro	30,000	9
Kitgum	30,000	7
Kutunguru	25,000	8
Masaka	13,000	3
Masindi	15,000	4
Mbale	15,000	5
Soroti	20,000	7

Buganda Bus Park (Main Bus Park; Map p384; off Namirembe Rd) Kampala's main bus terminal has the most departures.

New Bus Park (Map p384; off Namirembe Rd) Buses to Kisoro, Kabale, Gulu and Kihihi.

Post Bus

The **Post Bus** (Map p384; ☎ 0414-255685; Speke Rd) is the most recommended means of public transport, having the best safety record and most experienced drivers. Buses depart around 7am to 8am from the Speke Rd side of the main post office. Information and day-before reservations are in the building behind the post office.

TO	FARE (USH)	DURATION (HR)
Kabale	25,000	8
Mbarara	15,000	5
Hoima	12,000	6½
Masindi	10,000	5
Gulu	25,000	6
Soroti	25,000	7
Tororo	10,000	4
Mbale	18,000	6

International Buses

Numerous bus companies offer direct daily links from Kampala to Kenya, Tanzania, Rwanda, South Sudan, the DRC and even Burundi.

MINIBUS TAXIS

Kampala has two main 'taxi' ranks for mini-buses, and both serve destinations around the country as well as within Kampala itself. Although packed, there's a degree of organisation. Buses to Entebbe leave from both parks.

Old Taxi Park (Map p384) The busier of the two taxi ranks serves towns in eastern Uganda.

New Taxi Park (Map p384) Services western and northern destinations.

ⓘ Getting Around

TO/FROM THE AIRPORT

The international airport is at Entebbe, 40km from Kampala. See Pineapple Express for its airport shuttle bus.

Minibus Taxis

Minibus taxis ply the route between Kampala (from either taxi rank) and Entebbe (USh2500, 45 minutes), from where you'll need another taxi from Entebbe's taxi rank (USh10,000) for the short trip to the airport.

Special-Hire Taxi

A special-hire taxi is obviously the least stressful option, and costs around USh60,000 to USh80,000. Try **CAB Transport** (☎ 0772-465378).

BODA-BODAS

Motorbike taxis are the fastest way to get around Kampala since they can weave in and out of the traffic jams. Though it comes with the catch of their horrendous safety record.

Drivers have imposed an unofficial minimum fare of USh1500 around the city centre and are pretty good about sticking to it. The fare from

---

ⓘ PINEAPPLE EXPRESS BUS SHUTTLE

While minibus taxis may be cheaper, they're also dangerous. A convenient, well-priced and safe alternative for travelling along the tourist routes of Entebbe–Kampala–Jinja is the **Pineapple Express** (Map p384; ☎ 0787-992277; www.entebbejinjashuttle.com; Nakumatt Oasis Mall; US$12) bus shuttle. It departs Oasis Mall at 10am for Entebbe (US$10, two hours), and 4.30pm for Jinja (US$12, 2½ hours); check website to confirm.

the centre out to the Uganda Wildlife Authority (UWA) office or museum is likely to be USh3000. *Boda-bodas* can also be hired by the hour or day, but prices will depend on how big a swath of the city you plan to tackle. If you go this route, buy them a newspaper to read while they wait and you'll have a new best friend.

MINIBUS TAXIS

The ubiquitous white and blue minibus taxis fan out from the city centre to virtually every point in Kampala. Many start in the taxi ranks (for most destinations you can use either rank), but it's quicker to flag one down on Kampala Rd as they don't need to navigate the nightmare tail-backs around the taxi ranks.

SPECIAL-HIRE TAXI

Most 'special-hire' taxis are unmarked to avoid licensing and taxes, but if you see a car with its door open or with the driver sitting behind the wheel while parked, it's probably a special-hire. It's best to grab the number of a recommended driver through your hotel or trusted contact.

A standard short-distance fare is around USh8000. You'll be looking at USh10,000 from the city centre to the UWA office or Kisimenti, and USh15,000 to the Kabalagala/Ggaba Rd area. Waiting time is around USh6000 per hour. Prices will be higher at night and during rush hour.

AROUND KAMPALA

There are some pretty nice places to visit around Kampala and, if you have the time, most can be reached by public transport.

Entebbe

POP 76,500

Entebbe is an attractive, verdant town that served as the capital city during the early years of the British protectorate, though it's the relaxed pace of life and natural attractions rather than any notable colonial relics that give the city its charm.

Unless you have reason to rush into Kampala, Entebbe makes a nice, chilled-out introduction to Uganda. It's also the ideal place to end your trip if you're stuck with one of the many early morning flights out of Uganda's only international airport.

⊙ Sights & Activities

There's enough to do here to spend a day or two sightseeing, especially for those interested in wildlife encounters, with day trips to

BODA-BODA SAFETY TIPS

While *boda-bodas* (motorcycle taxis) are perfect for getting through heavy traffic, they're are also notorious for their high rate of accidents. Most incidents occur as a result of reckless young drivers: the *New Vision* newspaper has reported that on average there are five deaths daily as a result of *boda-boda* accidents. If you decide to use their services, get a recommendation from your hotel for a reliable, safe driver. It's also *very* wise to find a driver with a helmet you can borrow, and insist they drive slowly. *Boda-bodas* are best avoided at night.

Ngamba Island Chimpanzee Sanctuary and Mabamba Swamp Wetlands an option, see p398 and p399.

Entebbe has several inviting beaches on the shores of Lake Victoria, most with white powdery sand. All are part of resorts comprising hotels, restaurants and bars. They get crowded on weekends, but are nearly empty on weekdays. The most central to town is **Imperial Resort Beach Hotel** (Mpigi Rd; weekend entry USh3000, swimming pool adult/child USh7000/4000) which has a bar/restaurant and swimming pool – handy given (like elsewhere in Lake Victoria), swimming in the lake is a no-no due to bilharzia.

Uganda Wildlife Education Centre ZOO (UWEC; ☑ 0414-320520; www.uwec.ug; 56/57 Lugard Ave; adult/child USh30,000/15,000; ◷ 8.30am-5.30pm) While it functions primarily as a zoo, this centre is actually a world-class animal refuge that has benefited from international assistance in recent years. Most of the animals on display were once injured or were recovered from poachers and traffickers. Star attractions include chimpanzees (a good alternative to pricey Ngamba Island), southern white rhinos, lions, leopards and shoebill storks. Keep an eye out for the baby elephant wandering about, too.

If you want to get closer to the animals, there's a variety of programs on offer that can range from behind the scenes tours (adult/child US$75/35) or zookeeper for the day (adult/child including lunch US$150/70) to long-term volunteering opportunities; book directly through UWEC

Entebbe

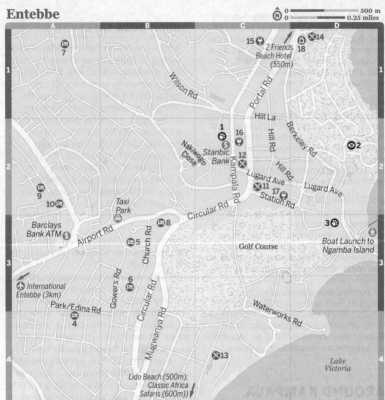

for discounts. There's decent lodging here, too.

Uganda Reptiles Village　　　　ZOO
(📞0782-349583; www.reptiles.ug; Bunono Village; adult/child US$8/5; ⏰9am-6.30pm) Get up close to some of the world's deadliest snakes, including cobras and vipers, as well as chameleons, crocs and lizards, all of which are rescued or injured. It's around 3km off the Entebbe–Kampala road, about a 20-minute drive from Entebbe.

Entebbe Botanical Gardens　　GARDENS
(admission　　　USh10,000,　　　camera/video USh2000/10,000; ⏰9am-7pm) Laid out in 1898, these expansive gardens are perfect for a leisurely stroll. The highlights are its pockets of thick rainforest, which locals claim some of the original *Tarzan* films were made in, and excellent birdwatching with 115 species (USh10,000 per guide). You'll see plenty of monkeys, including black and white colobus, and tree squirrels too.

🛌 Sleeping

Entebbe has a very good selection of accommodation options. Most places, except the cheapest, offer free airport transfers.

Entebbe Backpackers　　　BACKPACKERS $
(📞0414-320432; www.entebbebackpackers.com; 33/35 Church Rd; campsites per person with/without tent USh10,000/15,000, dm USh18,000, r USh60,000-80,000, s/d without bathroom USh20,000/25,000; 🌐) A popular, colourful, and straight-down-the-line backpackers without the whole party scene. The pricier rooms are spacious, while all are spotless. The helpful owners can suggest things to do around town and beyond. It's often full, so book ahead.

Uganda Wildlife Education Centre　BANDA $
(UWEC; 📞0414-320520; www.uwec.ug; 56-57 Lugard Ave; camping US$15, dm US$15, bandas US$40, apt US$50) Both a novel and well-priced arrangement that allows you to stay

Entebbe

on the premises of the wildlife centre and be privy to nightly lions' roars and hyenas' howls from nearby enclosures. The thatched brick *bandas* (thatched-roof huts) that back onto the giraffe enclosure are the most popular, but its hostel and apartments are also good choices. Rates include entry, plus your money helps fund the centre's rescue activities.

Shade Guesthouse GUESTHOUSE **$**
(☑0414-321715; Kiwafu Close; r without bathroom USh25,000-27,000) The pick of the bottom-end places around the taxi rank, with barebones but perfectly fine rooms that'll get you through the night.

★Airport Guesthouse GUESTHOUSE **$$**
(☑0414-370932; www.gorillatours.com; 17 Mugula Rd; s/d/tr US$70/80/112; @🛜) One of the best-value options in town, this guesthouse's newly renovated rooms maintain a great balance between style and homeliness. Rooms feature verandahs looking out to the peaceful garden full of birdlife and huge beds laden with pillows. The delicious three-course dinners (USh25,000) served on the lawn are worth hanging around for.

Boma B&B **$$**
(☑0772-467929; www.boma.co.ug; 20A Gowers Rd; s/d/tr US$142/165/212; @🛜🏊) One of Uganda's best B&Bs, this luxurious guesthouse has an intimate atmosphere thanks to lovely 1940s decor, a swimming pool and a landscaped, flower-filled yard. The food gets rave reviews. Mountain bikes are also available.

Karibu Guesthouse GUESTHOUSE **$$**
(☑0777-044984; www.karibuguesthouse.com; 84 Nsamizi Rd; s/d US$125/145; 🛜) Entebbe does boutique guesthouses superbly, and Karibu is no exception. It has peaceful gardens full of fruit trees and a boules pit, while its stylish rooms are decked in colourful African motif. The only stress here is choosing between garden patio or lake views.

2 Friends Beach Hotel HOTEL **$$**
(☑0772-236608; www.2friendshotel.com; 3 Nambi Rd; s/d from US$110-140; 🛜🏊) Mixing boutique motel with a Tiki island vibe, 2 Friends is one of the few places in Entebbe to utilise Lake Victoria's beaches, with its own private patch of beach, complete with bamboo bar! While you can't swim in the lake due to bilharzia, there's a small plunge pool across the road.

Papyrus Guesthouse GUESTHOUSE **$$**
(☑0787-778424; www.papyrusguesthouse.com; 2 Uringi Close; s/d/tr US$85/120/175; 🛜) Brought to you by the team who run the lovely Nkuringo Gorilla Campsite (p440) in Bwindi, Papyrus channels a rustic atmosphere with kerosene lamps on the patio and large rooms decorated with thoughtful touches.

Protea Hotel HOTEL **$$$**
(☑0414-323132; www.proteahotels.com; 36-40 Sebugwawo Dr; s/d US$235/275; ❄@🛜🏊) Plonked directly on Lake Victoria (and just across from the airport) this smart chain is the best of the upmarket hotels in Entebbe. Business-style rooms have all the mod cons for a comfortable stay, while its glassed-in lobby has terrific lake views. There's an attractive pool, private beach and small chip-and-putt golf course.

Lake Victoria Hotel   HOTEL $$$
(☑ 0312-310100;   www.laicohotels.com/
laico-lake-victoria; Circular Rd; s/d incl full breakfast
from US$165/230; ❉ @ ☎ ✿) This sprawling
hotel has the feel of a conference centre,
with well-appointed, business-style rooms.
Its worth upgrading for more space. Its mas-
sive swimming pool is the highlight here,
with a 9.2m diving board, sun lounges and
bar. Keep an eye out for the tortoises in the
garden.

✕ Eating

★ Anna's Corner   CAFE $$
(1 Station Rd; coffee USh5000, pizzas USh14,000-
20,000; ⊙ 8am-10pm; ☎) This Italian-run
garden cafe has the best coffee in town. Its
woodfired pizzas also hit the spot, while proceeds from home-baked cakes go to a local
orphanage. There's also a Congolese craft
store, Friday movie nights, Tuesday salsa lessons, coffee tasting and a farmers market on
the last Sunday of the month.

★ Faze 3   INTERNATIONAL $$
(Airport Rd; mains USh 14,000-30,000; ⊙ 7am-
midnight; ☎) Close to the airport, Faze 3 is
widely regarded as the best place to eat in
Entebbe. Its outdoor decking is a top spot
to catch lake breezes while feasting on anything from roast pork, tilapia tikka, chicken
schinztel burger or a good ol' meat pie.

Thammaphon Thai Restaurant   THAI $$
(Manyago Rd; mains from USh15,000; ⊙ 10am-
10pm Tue-Sun) Across from the Victoria
Shopping Mall, this relaxed garden shack
serves what is probably the best Thai in
Uganda, if not East Africa. Which makes
perfect sense given the owner-chef hails
from Bangkok.

Gately Inn Entebbe   INTERNATIONAL $$$
(www.gatelyinn.com/dining; 2 Portal Rd; mains from
USh21,000; ⊙ 6am-10pm; ☎) This open-air
restaurant surrounded by a wonderful African garden serves healthy salads, pita wraps
and meze plates, as well as not-so-healthy
peanut-butter smoothies and three-cheese
schnitzel. It has lovely rooms too, but traffic
noise is an issue.

🍷 Drinking & Nightlife

O's Bar   BAR
(9 Station Rd; ⊙ 5pm-late) Across from the golf
course this is the latest happening bar with
outdoor decking, indoor lounge and sports
on the TV.

Four Turkeys   PUB
(Kampala Rd; ⊙ 9am-4am) A local and NGO
hangout on the main strip with good pub
grub and cold beer.

Club Knight Riders   CLUB
(Kampala Rd; ⊙ 9pm-late Wed & Fri-Sun) The
place to kick on to once you're ready to hit
the dance floor.

🛍 Shopping

Victoria Mall   SHOPPING CENTRE
(Berkeley Rd; ⊙ 7am-10pm) Love it or loathe
it, mall culture has well and truly arrived in
Uganda, with this shiny new complex opening in 2013. As well as eateries and shops,
there's a Nakumatt supermarket that comes
in handy for groceries as well as camping
equipment.

ℹ Information

Exchange rates at the banks in town are better
than those at the airport, but worse than Kampala. Stanbic Bank and Barclays have ATMs.

ℹ Getting There & Away

BUS

The Pineapple Express (p394) shuttle runs
daily from the airport and guesthouses to Kampala (US$10, two hours) at 2.45pm.

Minibus taxis run between Entebbe and either
taxi rank in Kampala (USh2500, 1½ hours)
throughout the day. A special-hire from the
airport to Kampala will cost you anywhere from
USh60,000 to USh80,000.

FERRY

The ferry to Ssese Islands leaves from near
Entebbe.

ℹ Getting Around

Shared-car taxis run very infrequently to the airport (USh1500) from the taxi rank in Entebbe, so
most people use a special-hire taxi (USh15,000).

Ngamba Island Chimpanzee Sanctuary

**Ngamba Island Chimpanzee
Sanctuary**   WILDLIFE SANCTUARY
(☑ 0414-320662; www.ngambaisland.org; half-day
trip US$110; ⊙ departure 9am & 12.45pm) Lo-
cated 23km southeast of Entebbe in Lake
Victoria, Ngamba Island Chimpanzee Sanctuary, or 'Chimp Island', is home to over 40
orphaned or rescued chimpanzees who are
unable to return to the wild. Humans are

confined to one of the 40 hectares while the chimps wander freely through the rest, emerging from the forest twice a day for feeding at 11am and 2.30pm. This coincides with visitor arrival times to the island, with viewings of the chimps via a raised platform. The chimps return in the evening to sleep in their compound.

While it can't compare to the experience of seeing chimps in the wild, especially due to the large electrified fence that separates chimp from human, it still makes for a worthwhile excursion to observe the animals' remarkable behaviour. Guides here are informative, and there are individual profiles for each chimp, detailing both their distinct personalities and history. There are also big monitor lizards in residence as well as abundant birdlife.

The island is a project of the **Chimpanzee Sanctuary & Wildlife Conservation Trust** (CSWCT; ☎ 0414-320662; www.ngambaisland.org; Kampala Rd), which arranges bookings for day trips and accommodation.

Rates are based on a minimum group of four, with the price of a half-day trip costing US$110 per person, inclusive of entry, guide and boat transport. If you don't have a group of four people, you can share the boat with others; otherwise the cost rises to US$210 per person. Two trips depart from Entebbe per day; in the morning at 9am, returning at 12.45pm, or departing at 12.45pm and returning by 4.45pm.

The CSWCT also offer an overnight experience where you can spend two days on the island staying in a self-contained, solar-powered safari tent. Including full board, transport and entry, the cost of staying overnight is US$872 for singles, and US$1264 for doubles. Check the website for add-on activities.

Mabamba Swamp Wetlands & Around

Mabamba Swamp is one of the best places in Uganda to spot the highly sought-after shoebill in its natural habitat. Regularly featured on tourism brochures, these appealingly grotesque birds look like they've crawled straight out of the swamp (which they literally have), with out-of-proportion features and a massive dirty-yellow bill that resembles an old battered clog. Birdwatching is mostly via canoe, where you'll navigate waterways comprising lily pads and papyrus swamp. Among the 260 species in the region, other notable birds include the papyrus yellow warbler, pallid harrier and blue swallow.

While the swamp is 12km from Entebbe as the crow flies, it's a 40km (one hour) drive. To get here catch a minibus taxi to Kasanje, then a *boda-boda* to the Mabamba jetty. Otherwise a private car will cost around USh100,000 return.

Guides can be arranged from UWEC (p395) in Entebbe for around USh100,000 (per group of three) inclusive of boat hire.

Another good option for spotting shoebills is **Makanaga Wetlands**. Around a 60km drive from Entebbe, it's accessed via the Kampala–Masaka road, taking the road down from Kamengo trading centre.

Mpanga Forest Reserve

About 35km out of Kampala, the 453-hectare **Mpanga Forest Reserve** (☎ 0776-949226; admission USh5000) is a decent option if you want to escape the chaos of Kampala for a day or two. It's best known for its 181 species of butterfly, while red-tailed monkeys can be seen during the day and bushbabies during guided night walks (USh5000 per person). Most travellers visit on a day trip, but there's lodging at **Mpanga Ecotourism Site** (camping USh5000, dm/s/d USh8000/15,000/30,000). Take a Masaka minibus (USh4000, one hour) and get off at Mpanga, walking the last 800m.

The Equator

The equator crosses the Kampala–Masaka road 65km southwest of Kampala, with the expected monument that springs up in equator-hopping destinations. Two cement circles mark the spot. If you have a GPS you can get your photo taken on the real equator, about 30m to the south, but it's not nearly as photogenic.

Drop in to **Aidchild's Equation Cafe** (www.aidchild.org/aidchild-businesses; mains USh8000-16,000) 🍴 for a drink, coffee or a meal, and browse the artwork. All profits fund activities to assist HIV/AIDS orphans.

EASTERN UGANDA

Eastern Uganda, where the mighty Nile begins its epic journey north, is becoming a must experience on any East African sojourn thanks to an intoxicating blend of

Eastern Uganda

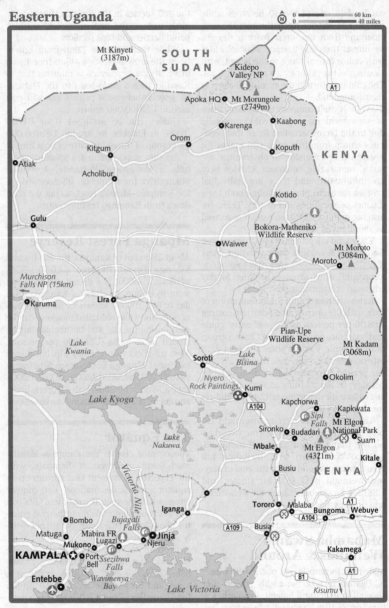

adrenaline adventures and superb scenery. White-water rafting on the Nile River undoubtedly leads the way as the biggest draw card, but trekking at Mt Elgon, and stunning Sipi Falls are also beautiful spots to soak up the scenery. If you're the adventurous sort, consider the overland assault through the heartland of the Karamojong, a tough tribe of cattle herders, where the seldom-visited route leads to Kidepo Valley National Park.

Jinja

POP 87,400

Famous as the historic source of the Nile River, Jinja has emerged as the adrenaline capital of East Africa. Here you can get your fix of white-water rafting, kayaking, quad biking, mountain biking, horseback riding and bungee jumping. The town itself is a buzzing little place with some wonderful, crumbling colonial architecture.

Coming from Kampala, the Owen Falls Dam forms a spectacular gateway to the town; but don't take pictures – people have been arrested for doing so, even though there are no signs informing people of this law.

◉ Sights

Source of the Nile River   RIVER
(admission per person/car/motorcycle USh10,000/2000/500; ⊙ admission charged 7am-7pm, open 24hr) The birthplace of the mighty Nile River (or one of them anyway...), here the water spills out of Lake Victoria on its journey to the Mediterranean flowing fast from the get-go. It's estimated no more than 5% of water here will end up in Egypt. There's a landmark identifying the source and a few restaurants and bars, which can make for a nice place for a sunset beer. Exploring the source by boat (per person USh20,000) is another popular option.

Despite being touted as one of Jinja's premier drawcards, on the Jinja side of the river there really isn't much to see. It's more pleasant across the river on the western bank with the **Source of the Nile Gardens** (admission USh10,000) and **Speke Monument** – a pillar commemorating where the British explorer first laid claim to the historic source of the Nile in 1858. In recent times the source has been traced anywhere from Rwanda to Burundi.

🏃 Activities

Those planning to do a few activities should look into the combos offered by the main adventure operators as they offer decent discounts.

White-Water Rafting

The source of the Nile is one of the most spectacular white-water rafting destinations in the world and for many visitors to Uganda a rafting trip is the highlight of their visit. Here you can expect long, rollicking strings of Grade IV and V rapids, with plenty of thrills and spills. Despite the intensity of some of the rapids, most people who venture here are first-time rafters; it's the perfect opportunity to get out of your comfort zone and try something different.

The three most reputable rafting companies are Nile River Explorers, Nalubale Rafting and Adrift, all equal in terms of professionalism and pricing, and each places an outstanding emphasis on safety (all rafting trips are accompanied by a fleet of rescue kayaks and a safety boat you can retreat to if you find things a bit too hairy for your liking).

They will also shuttle you out from Kampala for free, picking up punters from popular hostels and hotels, and bring you back again in the evening if you just want to make it a day trip. If you want to stick around, they'll give you a free night's accommodation in a dormitory. All also offer pick-ups from hotels in Jinja.

Besides the standard big water runs, there are also less extreme options for those who don't want to be flung into the raging water. Family float trips are offered, which bypass the big waves and are guaranteed to garner squeals of delight from young kids. A full-day family float with Nile River Explorers and Nalubale Rafting costs US$30 per person.

All the companies take on the Big Four – monster Grade V rapids, including Itanda (The Bad Place) – but there is always a safety boat on hand if you decide the rapids are just too big for you. All of them also include a host of incentives to lure you over, including meals and beers.

Nile River Explorers   RAFTING
(NRE; ☏ 0772-422373; www.raftafrica.com; half/full /2 day trips US$115/125/250) Long-established company set up by a South African. Accommodation is Explorers Backpackers in town or Explorers River Camp in Bujagali.

GANDHI IN UGANDA?

A surprising find at the source of the Nile is a shrine to Mahatma Gandhi. As per his wishes, on his death in 1948 his ashes were divided up to be scattered in several of the world's great rivers, including the Nile in Uganda. This bronze bust, donated by the Indian government, commemorates the act.

Jinja

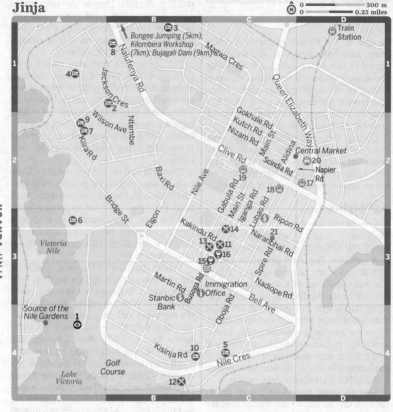

Adrift
RAFTING

(☎0312-237438; www.adrift.ug; half/full/2 day trips US$115/125/250) Rafting pioneer Adrift (originally established in Nepal) was set up by a Kiwi adventurer. It also operates bungee jumping and jet boating. Accommodation is at Nile High Camp.

Nalubale Rafting
RAFTING

(☎0782-638938; www.nalubalerafting.com; half/full/2 day trips US$115/125/250) British-run Nalubale has risen through the ranks to become one of the leading rafting companies. Free lodging is at Nalubale Teahouse or Nile River Camp.

Kayaking

An alternative to rafting is to go solo and kayak through the raging river, or take a more leisurely paddle on flat water. Jinja is mostly known among freestyle kayakers for its epic Nile Special wave.

Kayak the Nile
KAYAKING

(☎0772-880322; www.kayakthenile.com; white-water kayaking half/full day from US$85/115, tandem kayaking US$140, flat-water kayaking from US$75, SUP from US$75) Run by pro-kayaking husband-wife team (Sam and Emily), the main attraction here is white-water kayaking, which is suitable for beginners (solo or tandem) and advance freestyle kayakers. White-water SUP (stand-up paddle boarding) is another thrilling activity. However it's not all about taming rapids, with relaxing flat-water trips available on sit-on-top kayaks or SUPs. Multiday trips are available too. It's based at Nile River Explorers Campsite in Bujagali.

Boating

At Ripon Landing, next to Jinja Sailing Club, you'll find several guys hanging about the leisure centre offering trips on Lake Victoria; a half-hour ride to the source of the Nile and back costs USh20,000.

Jinja

Sights
1 Source of the Nile River A4

Activities, Courses & Tours
FABIO .... (see 13)
Nalubale Rafting .... (see 7)
Nile River Explorers .... (see 4)

Sleeping
2 2 Friends Guesthouse B1
3 Busoga Trust Guesthouse B1
4 Explorers Backpackers A1
5 Gately on Nile C4
6 Jinja Backpackers A3
7 Nalubale Teahouse A2
8 Safari Inn B1
9 Source of the Smile Guesthouse A2
10 Surjio's B4

Eating
11 Flavours C3
Gately on Nile .... (see 5)
12 Jinja Sailing Club B4
13 Leoz C3
14 Source Café C3

Drinking & Nightlife
15 Babez C3
Bourbon .... (see 6)
16 Spot 6 .... C3

Transport
17 Bus Station D2
18 Night-time Taxi Stage for
Bujagali C2
19 Night-time Taxi Stage for
Kampala C2
20 Taxi Park D2
21 Wemtec C3

Nile Cruises BOAT TOUR
(www.raftafrica.com/site/nile-cruises.html; lunch/sunset cruise incl drink & food US$30/45) Those who prefer to take in the river at a leisurely pace can set out on the Nile for a sunset booze cruise, or a lunchtime voyage.

African Queen CRUISE
(0776-237438; www.wild-uganda.com; per person 2hr cruise US$45, min 4 people) A classy way of exploring the Nile is to hop on board the *African Queen,* a restored 1920s steam riverboat allegedly used in the 1951 Hollywood blockbuster starring Humphrey Bogart and Katharine Hepburn. Rates include drinks and snacks.

Jet Boating BOATING
(www.adrift.ug/adventures/wild-nile-jet; adult/child US$75/50) Bringing a high-octane thrill to the Nile, Adrift's **Wild Nile Jet** is an exhilarating 90km/h speedboat trip over the rapids with plenty of thrills, 360-degree spins, jumps and near misses.

Other Activities

Bungee Jumping ADVENTURE SPORTS
(0772-286433; www.adrift.ug/adventures/nile-high-bungee; US$115) Nearer to Jinja, but more in tune with Bujagali's vibe, Uganda's only bungee jump is a 44m plunge to the Nile River from the Adrift rafting company's Nile High Camp. Night jumps are also available. Minimum age is 13 years.

Nile Horseback Safaris HORSE RIDING
(0774-101196; www.nilehorsebacksafaris.com; 1/2/3hr US$40/60/80) Exploring Jinja via horseback is a popular activity, taking you alongside the Nile River and through local villages, tea estates and sugar plantations. There are also sunset rides (US$60) and overnight safaris (from US$265). Riders need to wear long trousers, closed shoes and there's a 90kg weight limit. Trips depart at 10am and 2pm daily.

To get here, cross the bridge over Owen Falls dam and take a right at Kayunga Rd, from where it's 5km; a *boda-boda* from Jinja will cost around USh10,000 or, better yet, charter a water-taxi from Bujagali Dam.

Feather & Fin BIRDWATCHING, FISHING
(0772-900451; www.ffp.ug; birdwatching half/full day US$40/90, fishing half/full day US$50/110) Whether you're looking to land a Nile perch, or tick off a fishing eagle, kingfisher or stork, Feather & Fin can sort you out for a morning/full-day session of fishing and birdwatching. Longer trips are also available.

All Terrain Adventures ADVENTURE SPORTS
(0772-377185; www.atadventures.com; 1hr/half/full day US$49/119/195) Quad-biking along the beautiful banks of the Victoria Nile is a real blast. After a little spin on the practice circuit, it's time to explore the paths and trails criss-crossing the nearby countryside. There are several possible circuits, including a twilight safari that includes dinner in a village. It offers overnight trips too, and

THE ISIMBA DAM DEBATE

Following the completion of the Bujagali Dam, which resulted in several beloved rapids being lost and rafting companies relocating their launching point 10km down river, the impending Isimba Hydro Power Project looks set to deliver rafting companies another blow. While in the worst case scenario there will still be plenty of Grade V adrenaline and adventure, if the project goes ahead as planned the whole second section of rafting could be underwater (including the famed wave 'Nile Special' and Hairy Lemon Lodge), cutting a full day's rafting in half. The battle is still being fought to reduce the dam's size to lessen impact on both the environment and tourism. Follow Save Adventure Tourism in Uganda's Facebook page for updates.

kid-sized rides are also available. Located at Bujagali Falls.

Explorers Mountain Biking   MOUNTAIN BIKING
(☏ 0772-422373; www.raftafrica.com; from US$30) A range of guided rides are available around Jinja, including visits to villages between Bujagali Falls and Jinja, finishing off with a boat ride to the source of the Nile River. Further afield there's also hardcore trips through Mabira Forest Reserve (from US$45), as well as tailor-made trips. Mountain-bike hire is available from US$15 for a half day and US$25 for a full day.

Community Walks   WALKING TOUR
(http://raftafrica.com/site/other-activities/village-walk.html#main; per person US$7) A great opportunity to experience local culture, these three-hour walks visit places you wouldn't otherwise see, such as farms, rural villages and health clinics, and include stopovers to sample local food and village beers. Trips help fund projects in villages in the area.

FABIO   CYCLING, TOURS
(First African Bicycle Information Office; ☏ 0705-935030, 0434-121255; www.fabio.or.ug; 9 Main St; 24hr bike hire USh15,000, tours USh50,000) This NGO arranges bike tours around Jinja and Lake Victoria with a focus on discovering its rich history. It also rents out basic single-speed bikes and mountain bikes for those who prefer to go it alone.

🛏 Sleeping

Jinja has some wonderful guesthouses in its leafy suburbs away from the dusty city centre. And there's some good options further down-river or near Bujagali, around 5km from Jinja.

🛏 Jinja

Busoga Trust Guesthouse   GUESTHOUSE $
(www.busogatrust.co.uk/busogatrust/guesthouse; 18 Lubogo Lane; dm US$12, s/d from US$14/27; ☎) The perfect choice for those not into Jinja's backpacker scene, Busoga Trust has a chilled-out vibe with homely lounge, kitchen for self-caterers, fast wi-fi, a patio looking out to its garden, and spacious rooms. Proceeds go directly towards water sanitation projects in rural villages.

Explorers Backpackers   BACKPACKERS $
(☏ 0434-120236; www.raftafrica.com; 41 Wilson Ave; camping/dm/d US$5/7/25; @☎) Jinja's original crash pad is still the most popular budget choice in Jinja itself. Dorms are decent and there's one double room available. Overland trucks pop in now and then, but this is a much quieter spot than Bujagali.

Safari Inn   HOTEL $
(☏ 0434-122955; www.traveluganda.co.ug/safari-inn; 3 Nalufenya Rd; s/d USh51,000/60,000; ☒) Sure it's a bit scuffed around the edges, but this unpretentious hotel is easily one of the best budget deals in town; for its swimming pool, large lawn and big rooms.

Nalubale Teahouse   BACKPACKERS $
(☏ 0782-638938; www.nalubalerafting.com/rooms.html; 38 Kiira Rd; camping US$5, dm US$10) The base for Nalubale rafters (who stay for free), this lively backpacker hangout has clean dorms in a colonial house set in a leafy neighbourhood.

Jinja Backpackers   HOSTEL $
(☏ 0774-730659; www.jinjabackpackers.com; Bridge Close; camping US$5, dm US$10, r without bathroom US$40; ☎) This unassuming, relaxed backpackers is owned by a Kiwi–Aussie couple who've set up rooms in a large sheep-shearing-like shed with dorms and private rooms centred around a ping-pong table. It's conveniently set just back from Bourbon bar and the waterfront.

★ Gately on Nile   BOUTIQUE HOTEL $$
(☏ 0434-122400; www.gately-on-nile.com; 47 Nile Cres; s US$50-80, d US$70-105, house s/d US$130/150; @☎) The classiest guesthouse

in Jinja, Gately's stylish rooms are split between a lovely garden premises with a selection of thoughtfully decorated rooms, and loft apartments across the road looking on to Lake Victoria. The Mediterranean-style house is a great choice for honeymooners, families or larger groups. Its restaurant is one of the best in town.

Source of the Smile Guesthouse
GUESTHOUSE **$$**

(✆0783-842021; www.sourceofthesmile.com; 39 Kiira Rd; s US$77-87, d US$88-98; 🕾🗷) Mixing a relaxed vibe with a bohemian, arty design, flower garden and tiki pool this guesthouse is indeed likely to bring a smile to one's face. For a bit of character, opt for the poolside rooms; otherwise there's cheaper, more conventional rooms out back.

Surjio's
BOUTIQUE HOTEL **$$**

(✆0772-500400; www.surjios.com; 24 Kisinja Rd; s/d incl full breakfast US$80/125; 🕾🗷) Relaxed Surjio's is a top midrange choice with a pleasant garden set away from town near the edge of the Nile. Pricier rooms are spacious with polished blonde-wood floors, large beds and lovely bathrooms. Go for an upstairs room, which gets you a glimpse of the Nile. Staff are friendly, and it has a swimming pool and a popular woodfired pizzeria (from USh23,000).

2 Friends Guesthouse
GUESTHOUSE **$$**

(✆0783-160804; www.2friends.info; 5 Jackson Cres; s/d incl full breakfast from US$106/124; @🕾🗷) A relaxed guesthouse with smart rooms, a bamboo garden and good swimming pool.

🛏 Around Jinja

Nile River Explorers Campsite
BACKPACKERS **$**

(✆0772-422373; http://raftafrica.com/site/accommodation/explorers-river-camp.html; Bujagali; camping US$7, dm US$12, r with/without bathroom from US$50/30; @🕾) The most popular place to stay at Bujagali, this attractive camp is set on a grassy site with sensational river views. There's a good mix of budget rooms, often full with overland trucks and backpackers, but the pick of accommodation are the tented camps sloped along the terraced hill, which have superb outlooks – as do the showers!

The restaurant and its beer garden also have sensational views (definitely worth a visit, even if you're not staying here), and serve up tasty burgers and other favourites.

It's packed to the rafters come evening, and is one of Jinja's best places to party.

Nile River Camp
CAMPGROUND, BACKPACKERS **$**

(✆0776-900450; www.camponthenile.com; camping US$6, dm US$12, safari tent US$54; 🕾🗷) This laid-back site run by Nalubale Rafting has a scenic river location fringed with eucalyptus trees and an atmospheric thatched-roof restaurant-bar. There are hammocks strung about the place and the swimming pool is a huge drawcard.

★Haven
BANDA **$$**

(✆0702-905959; www.thehaven-uganda.com; camping US$15, lazy camping incl full board s/d US$75/130, bandas s/d incl full board from US$140/230; 🕾) ⚲ Located 15km from Jinja along Kayunga Rd (next to the starting point for white-water rafting), this wonderful lodge's main selling point is its sensational panoramic river location, enjoyed directly from its suave *bandas* and bungalows. It has numerous ecofriendly credentials, a safari-style restaurant and swimming pool with sun lounges.

The top-notch food is another draw, and nonguests can visit just for a meal (set menu breakfast US$12, lunch US$15, dinner US$18) but you must make a reservation. A *boda-boda* from Jinja will cost around USh10,000.

Nile Porch
LODGE **$$**

(✆0782-321541; www.nileporch.com; Bujagali; safari tent s/d US$113/136, cottages US$213; @🕾🗷) Bringing the safari lodge experience to Bujagali, the Nile Porch has luxurious tented camps that are all superbly set on a cliff above the river. There's a swimming pool, and family cottages (minus the views) which sleep six for those travelling in groups.

Hairy Lemon
BANDA **$$**

(✆0434-130349, 0772-828338; www.hairylemonuganda.com; incl full board camping US$30, dm from US$38, bandas s/d from US$69/118) Situated 15km downstream from the starting point for rafting, Hairy Lemon's isolated location on a small island makes it the perfect getaway retreat. More rustic than luxurious, dorms and *bandas* are basic and mostly share bathrooms. A short paddle away is Nile Special, a world-class wave for kayakers. It's essential to book ahead.

To get here, take a minibus from Jinja to Nazigo (USh4000, one hour) and then a *boda-boda* (USh4000) for the last 9km to the Hairy Lemon. A special-hire should be around USh60,000. There's a wheel hub here to bang on to alert the boat driver to come and pick you up. You need to arrive before 6pm.

Houseboat Safari HOUSEBOAT $$
(☑ 0772-422373; http://raftafrica.com/site/other-activities/houseboat-safaris; per person incl full board US$125) For something a bit different, spend a night cruising Lake Victoria in this houseboat equipped with double cabins, kitchen, top deck and lounge-bar area. Also available for day-trip rental (per person US$80).

★ **Wildwaters Lodge** LODGE $$$
(☑ 0772-237400; www.wild-uganda.com; s/d incl full board US$550/700; @ 🖥 🌊) One of Uganda's best luxury hotels, Wildwaters lives up to its name by overlooking a raging stretch of the Nile from its stunning island location. Accessed via a boardwalk, the private thatched-roof suites have canvas walls and palatial interiors with gleaming polished floorboards, poster beds and sofas. All open up to balconies with outdoor clawfoot baths overlooking unhindered Nile views.

The lovely restaurant, natural-style swimming pool and lounge deck are also perched right on the river. It's located on the west bank of the Nile along Kayunga Rd (turn off near the Nile Brewery), about 20km from Jinja, and is accessed by a five-minute boat trip. Day trippers are charged a US$15 entrance fee.

✗ Eating & Drinking

Due to its sizeable expat and NGO community, Jinja has some good eating options. Most travellers aren't here for the nightlife, though Main St offers a suitable strip for a bar crawl. **Spot 6** (Main St) and **Babez** (Main St), a few doors down from each other, are the liveliest.

★ **Flavours** CAFE $
(www.enjoyflavours.com; 12 Main St; coffee USh4500, sandwiches USh11,500; ⏲ 8.30am-11pm) Funky cafe that reminds *wazungu* of back home, with good coffee, baguettes and plenty of artwork on the walls. Also has a beer garden out back.

Source Café CAFE $
(www.source.co.ug; 20 Main St; mains from USh6000; ⏲ 8am-6.30pm Mon-Sat; 🖥) This church-affiliated cafe serves some of the best coffee in town, and has free wi-fi.

Leoz INDIAN $$
(☑ 0434-120298; 11 Main St; mains USh14,000-22,000; ⏲ 8.30am-10.30pm) This friendly laid-back Nepali-owned restaurant is the first word in authentic South Asian food, from Indian thalis to *dhaal bhaat* (lentil soup and rice), with some Ugandan dishes also available.

Black Lantern INTERNATIONAL $$
(www.nileporch.com; mains USh17,000-30,000; ⏲ 7.30am-9pm; 🖥) Bujagali's premier dining destination is set under an elegant traditional thatched-roof and has an extensive menu showcasing dishes from around the world. Spare ribs are a speciality, while tilapia grilled in banana leaves with salad is a tasty choice.

Gately on Nile INTERNATIONAL $$$
(www.gately-on-nile.com; 47 Nile Cres; mains USh19,000-27,000; ⏲ 7am-9.30pm; 🖥) The restaurant on the back porch of the popular boutique hotel of the same name exudes the atmosphere of a Balinese garden. The fusion menu shows plenty of international flair.

Jinja Sailing Club INTERNATIONAL $$$
(www.jinjasailingclub.com; Pier Rd; mains USh25,000-30,000; ⏲ 11am-11pm; 🖥) A long time coming, the Sailing Club has been completely rebuilt in modern resort style, but this is unimportant once you're sipping a drink on the lawn overlooking Lake Victoria. The menu features Indian, African and Western classics.

★ **Bourbon** BAR
(www.facebook.com/the-bourbon; Bridge Close; ⏲ 10am-2am) Right on the lakeside, Bourbon's open-air thatched bar and picnic tables set on the lawn are Jinja's liveliest spots for a drink. There are also DJs in the bar on the hill. Check the Facebook page for upcoming events.

🔒 Shopping

Kilombera Workshop HANDICRAFTS
(☑ 0793-439619; www.facebook.com/kilombera weaving; ⏲ 8.30am-5pm Mon-Fri, 9am-1pm Sat) The colourful cotton textiles (place mats, table runners, bedspreads) for sale around Jinja are made on hand-operated looms at this Nile-side workshop. Visitors are welcome to stop by and watch the process. There's a showroom here with items for sale. It's signposted 200m off the road, halfway between Jinja and Bujagali.

ℹ️ Information

You can get online at tons of places along Main St and wi-fi is available at many hotels and restaurants. Main St also has many banks with ATMs.

Immigration Office (Busoga Rd) The Immigration Office can arrange visa extensions, and is for a less hectic alternative to Kampala.

ℹ️ Getting There & Away

BUS

Most rafting companies offer complimentary transport to/from Kampala; even if you're not rafting it's worth checking to see if there's a spare seat available (USh10,000).

Pineapple Express (p394) shuttle makes a daily trip at 7.30am for Kampala/Entebbe.

The Post Bus is the best option for public transport. There are also frequent minibus taxis to Kampala (USh6000, two hours) and coaster buses to Kampala (USh5000), Mbale (USh10,000, two hours), Soroti (USh20,000, four hours) or Busia (USh10,000, two hours) on the Kenyan border. There's no need to travel to Nairobi in stages as you can book tickets on the big buses passing through from Kampala.

CAR

If you're driving yourself, the best route from Kampala is the longer but faster and almost completely truck-free road north through Kayunga.

ℹ️ Getting Around

The centre of Jinja is compact enough to wander about on foot. For getting elsewhere you'll want a boda-boda; a ride to Bujagali will cost about USh5000.

Mbale

POP 89,000

A bustling provincial city, you'll pass through Mbale if you're planning an assault on Mt Elgon or en route to Sipi Falls. Away from the dusty centre there are pockets of charm and it does have a scenic mountain backdrop, but there's no real reason to hang around here.

👁️ Sights

Moses Synagogue   SYNAGOGUE
(Nabugoye Hill) An unexpected find in this neck of the woods, the Jewish Abayudaya community in the outskirts of Mbale on Nabugoye Hill dates back to the early 20th century. The synagogue is a simple, yet appealing, rustic red-brick building (though

there are plans to redevelop it into a modern sleek design) with services in English and Hebrew held on Fridays from 6pm to 8pm, and Saturdays at 9am. There's also a guesthouse for those interested in staying.

Former military leader Semei Kakungulu founded the sect in 1913, fusing elements of Judaism and Christianity with a disbelief in Western medicine, leading to a falling out with British rulers. During the 20th century the group withstood widespread persecution, particularly under Idi Amin, who outlawed Judaism and destroyed synagogues.

A special-hire taxi from Mbale costs USh25,000; a boda-boda is USh3000.

🛏️ Sleeping & Eating

Casa Del Turista   BACKPACKERS $
(☑️0772-328085; 18 Nkokonjeru Tce; dm US$10, s/d US$16/25; 🛜) This friendly guesthouse is a relaxed place to hang out with fast wi-fi, spotless dorms and private beds. Its Eco Shamba cafe has quality food and top organic Mt Elgon coffee. Proceeds go to a local school.

New Mt Elgon View Hotel   HOTEL $
(☑️0772-445562; 5 Cathedral Ave; s/d USh45,000/70,000, without bathroom from USh15,000/30,000, annexe s/d/tr USh36,000/45,000/75,000) In a busy part of town, this budget hotel has the feel of an Indian guesthouse with good-value rooms and a fantastic rooftop hangout. Room 11 has splendid mountain views, but the spacious self-contained rooms in the annex across the street are the nicest. Downstairs is the excellent South Asian **Nurali's Café** (☑️0772-445562; 5 Cathedral Ave; mains USh9000-15,000; ⏱️8.30am-10.30pm). Note the 9am checkout time.

Landmark Inn   HOTEL $
(☑️0714-328333; Wanale Rd; r USh35,000) An old rundown mansion down a leafy residential street, Landmark has several massive rooms featuring high ceilings and spacious bathrooms. The downstairs restaurant serves some of the tastiest Indian food in Uganda. It's 200m from the Sports Club.

Mt Elgon Hotel   HOTEL $$
(☑️0454-433454; www.mountelgonhotel.com; 30 Masaba Rd; s US$80-150, d US$100-160; ❄️@🛜🏊) A colonial-era stalwart with modern flair, rooms here are spacious and are quite plush at the top of the price range. It's in a quiet area outside the city, surrounded by verdant grounds.

ⓘ Information

National Park Headquarters (☎0454-433170; www.ugandawildlife.org/national-parks/mt-elgon-national-park; 19 Masaba Rd; ⏰8am-5pm Mon-Fri, 8am-3pm Sat & Sun) Organise your Mt Elgon visit here, about 1km from the city centre.

ⓘ Getting There & Away

The Post Bus heads to/from Kampala daily via Jinja. There are frequent buses or minibuses to Kampala (USh15,000, four hours), Jinja (USh10,000, three hours), Kumi (USh7000, one hour), Soroti (USh10,000, three hours), Moroto (USh30,000, nine hours) and Kotido (USh40,000, 10 hours) from the main taxi rank off Manafa Rd. Behind it is the bus stand, with less-frequent transport to Jinja, Kampala, and Soroti. Prices are similar to minibus prices.

For Sipi Falls (USh7000, one hour), Kapchorwa (USh10,000, 1¼ hours) and Budadari (USh5000, 45 minutes), head to the Kumi Rd taxi rank northeast of town. Services are infrequent to these smaller places so it's best to travel in the morning.

Gateway (☎0414-234090; Cathedral Rd) has a bus to Nairobi (USh35,000, 12 hours).

Mt Elgon National Park

Trekking in **Mt Elgon National Park** (adult/child US$35/5, trekking per day incl fees & guide US$90) offers a good alternative to climbing Uganda's Rwenzori Mountains or Mt Kilimanjaro in Tanzania, with a milder climate, lower elevation and much more reasonable prices. The park encompasses the upper regions of Mt Elgon to the Kenyan border and this is said to be one of the largest surface areas of any extinct volcano in the world.

Elgon, whose name is derived from the Maasai name, Ol Doinyo Ilgoon ('Breast Mountain'), has five major peaks with the highest, Wagagai (4321m), rising on the Ugandan side. It's the second tallest mountain in Uganda (after Mt Stanley at 5109m) and the eighth tallest in Africa, though millions of years ago it was the continent's tallest. The mountain is peppered with cliffs, caves, gorges and waterfalls, and the views from the higher reaches stretch way across eastern Uganda's wide plains.

The lower slopes are covered in tropical montane forest with extensive stands of bamboo. Above 3000m the forest fades into heath and then Afro-alpine moorland, which blankets the caldera, a collapsed crater covering some 40 sq km. The moorland is studded with rare plant species, such as giant groundsel and endemic *Lobelia elgonensis,* and you'll often see duikers bounding through the long grass and endangered lammergeier vultures overhead. In September it's decorated with wildflowers. You'll probably see a few primates and lots of birds, including the rare Jackson's francolin, alpine chat and white-starred forest robin, but you'll be lucky to spot a leopard, hyena, buffalo, elephant or other big mammal.

Trekking Mt Elgon

Mt Elgon may be a relatively easy climb, but this is still a big, wild mountain. Rain, hail and thick mists aren't uncommon, even in the dry season, and night-time temperatures frequently drop below freezing. Pack adequate clothing and at least one day's extra food, just in case. Altitude sickness is rarely a problem, but heed the warning signs. It's also wise to check the latest security situation, as there are occasional incidents along the Kenyan border; an armed escort is provided.

While you can climb Mt Elgon year-round, the best time is from June to August or December to March. Seasons are unpredictable and it can rain at any time. You can get information and organise your trek at the **Mt Elgon National Park Headquarters** (☎0454-433170; 19 Masaba Rd; ⏰8am-5pm Mon-Fri, 8am-3pm Sat & Sun) in Mbale or at the visitor centres at each of the trailheads, all open in theory from 8am to 5pm weekdays, and 8am to 3pm weekends.

Even as the number of visitors on Mt Elgon staedily increases, tourism remains relatively underdeveloped and no more than 250 people reach the caldera in the busiest months. It's possible to hike for days without seeing another climber. The climb is nontechnical and relatively easy, as far as 4000-plus-metre ascents go.

If you're not up for the full climb there are also numerous options for day hikes.

Costs

Trekking on Mt Elgon costs US$90 per person per day, which covers park entry fees and a ranger-guide. Permits are issued at UWA offices at each trailhead. Guides are mandatory whether heading to the summit or just doing a day trip. Camping fees are USh15,000 more per night and porters, who are highly recommended, charge USh15,000 per day for carrying 18kg. Also factor in tips, which are highly appreciated.

Supplies

Rose's Last Chance (p410) in Budadari rents tents (USh10,000), trekking boots (USh10,000), sleeping bags (USh5000) and mats (USh5000) per night.

If you're not up for organising the trip independently, Sipi River Lodge (p411) offers well-organised and well-priced Mt Elgon tours.

There are several supermarkets in Mbale for stocking up on supplies. Porters can make campfires for cooking but, for environmental reasons, the park requests that you bring a campstove if you have one.

Trails

There are four routes up the mountain. Many people combine different routes going up and down for maximum variety. We've given the standard travel times for the various routes, but if you're up to the challenge these can all be shortened by a day or two. On the other hand, you may want to add an extra day to further explore the caldera or visit the Suam Gorge, or let the guides take you to waterfalls and caves. If summiting at Wagagai, it only takes an extra hour to hit Jackson's Summit (4165m) via Jackson's Pool, a little crater lake. You must use designated campsites, all of which have tent pads, latrines, rubbish pits and nearby water sources.

Climbers have the option of continuing their trek into Kenya. Park staff at the headquarters will take you to the immigration office in Mbale for the requisite paperwork and then hand you off to the Kenya Wildlife Service at the hot springs in the caldera. It's a two-day hike down the Kenyan side.

There are also many options for day hikes, with the most popular being a trio of short loops around the Forest Exploration Centre

at the start of the Sipi Trail. Rose's Last Chance offers day walks for USh30,000 (including lunch) or a two-day Budadari to Sipi Falls walk along the slopes of Mt Elgon, visiting villages and coffee plantations en route (USh300,000 per person inclusive of food, tents, guide, porter); no park permit required.

SASA TRAIL

The Sasa Trail is the original route to Wagagai, and still the busiest as it can easily be reached by public transport from Mbale. It's a three- to four-day round trip to the summit with a 1650m ascent on day one. From Budadari, which is considered the trailhead, a road leads 5km to Bumasola (you can take a car up this leg if you want) then it's a short walk to the forest. Almost as soon as you enter the forest, you reach Mudangi Cliffs, which are scaled via ladders, then it's 2½ hours of pure bamboo forest. The second day is an easier walk. On summit day, it's four hours from your campsite to Wagagai.

SIPI TRAIL

The Sipi Trail, which begins at the Forest Exploration Centre in Kapkwai, has become a popular return route as it allows you to chill out at Sipi Falls following your trip to the top. It's four to seven days round trip, though you can opt to descend via the Sasa Trail, an easier route. On the first day you can camp inside the huge Tutum Cave, which has a small waterfall over its entrance and once attracted elephants who dug salt out of the rock, much like some more famous caves on the Kenyan side still do.

PISWA TRAIL

Starting high, the Piswa Trail has a gentler ascent than the Sipi Trail. It's the best

---

ⓘ MT ELGON NATIONAL PARK

Why Go
Uganda's second-highest peak, Wagagai (4321m); trekking routes into Kenya or Sipi Falls.

When to Go
Year-round, but generally less rain from June to August and December to March. From September to October there are wildflowers.

Practicalities
Decent trekking equipment can be rented at Rose's Last Chance (p410) in Budadari. The park is best accessed via Mbale, a three-hour drive from Kampala.

Budget Tips
Rose's Last Chance can arrange a number of walks in the area that don't require paying for a park permit.

wildlife-watching route as it doesn't pass through bamboo stands, and it also offers the longest pass through the other-worldly moorland in the caldera. It's a six-day journey when returning by the Sasa Trail and seven days when coming back via the Sipi Trail. Piswa Trail is less used because it begins in the difficult to reach village of Kapkwata.

SUAM TRAIL

The rarely used Suam Trail is a five-day route starting at a higher elevation than the Sasa Trail and climbing through the Suam Gorge right along the Kenyan border.

🍴 Sleeping & Eating

★ **Rose's Last Chance**   GUESTHOUSE $
(☎0772-623206; www.roseslastchance.yolasite.com; camping USh15,000, dm USh20,000, s/d USh30,000/40,000) Located near the trailhead in Budadari, Rose's is a laid-back, comfortable, fun and friendly place that brings guests closer to the local scene. Testing local brews is a favourite activity and Rose sometimes brings in musicians and dancers at night. The dining room has good vibes and bedrooms are cosy and clean. It's located a few doors down from the UWA office.

Forest Exploration Centre   GUESTHOUSE $
(camping USh15,000, dm USh10,000, s/d USh40,000/55,000) This lovely spot run by UWA is right at the Sipi trailhead and has a little restaurant.

Wirr Community Campsite   CAMPGROUND $
(camping USh10,000) This campsite is just outside the park gate next to the Forest Education Centre, but the community seem to have given up on it. Sipi Falls is a better bet if you'd rather not pay the park fee on the first night.

Kapkwata Guesthouse   GUESTHOUSE $
(camping USh15,000, r USh35,000) This simple place serves the Piswa trailhead. Bring your own food.

Suam Guesthouse   GUESTHOUSE $
(camping USh15,000, r USh35,000) A budget UWA lodge (cold water only) at Suam trail where you'll need to bring your own food.

ℹ️ Getting There & Away

SASA TRAIL

There are regular minibuses from Mbale to Budadari (USh5000, one hour).

SIPI TRAIL

There's no regular transport to the Forest Exploration Centre, but minibuses between Mbale and Kapchorwa (USh10,500, 1½ hours) pass the signposted turn-off to Kapkwai and get off at Chuma, 6km up from Sipi, from where it's a 6km walk to the centre. A boda-boda from Sipi should cost USh10,000 to USh15,000 depending on how dry the road is; a fair special-hire price from Mbale to Kapkwai is around USh80,000. A more interesting way to get to the centre is to hire a guide at Sipi to walk you through the villages, about a 90-minute trip.

PISWA TRAIL

Getting to the Piswa trailhead in Kapkwata takes some effort. The excellent paved road ends at Kapchorwa. From here you'll have to take a minivan taxi to Kapkwata (USh10,000) for the often rough 33km trip that can take up to four hours. They run until around 3pm, so it's possible to make it from Mbale in a day.

SUAM TRAIL

From Mbale you could try for a minivan taxi to the Kenya border at Suam (USh35,000, five to six hours). Failing that there are minivans to Kapchorwa (USh10,000 1½ hours) from where you'll catch another to Suam (USh25,000, four hours). Otherwise there are trucks here from Kapkwata via a terrible road. You reach the border by early afternoon and should have little problem moving straight on to Kitale by matatu (minibus). There's basic lodging if you can't.

Sipi Falls

Sipi Falls, in the foothills of Mt Elgon, is a stunner – arguably the most beautiful waterfall in all of Uganda. There are three levels, and though the upper two are beautiful, it's the 95m main drop that attracts the crowds, and most of Sipi's lodging looks out over it. Not only are the falls spectacular, so too are the views of the wide plains disappearing into the distance below. It's well worth spending a night or two in this peaceful, pretty place.

🏃 Activities & Tours

Guides for activities are best organised through your hotel or the grassroots **Sipi Falls Tourism Guide Association** (☎0753-331078) based outside Sipi Falls Resort.

Rob's Rolling Rock   ABSEILING, ROCK CLIMBING
(☎0776-963078; www.rollingrocksipifalls.wordpress.com; abseiling/rock climbing US$50/40) Next to Lacam Lodge, this reliable local outfit's mainstay is a 100m abseil (US$50) alongside the main falls – providing the

undisputed best views in Sipi! It has also bolted in 14 rock-climbing routes (easy to intermediate), and there are plans to open accommodation and a bar on the property.

Walks to Sipi Falls

There are some excellent walks on a network of well-maintained local trails with beautiful scenery in every direction. The most popular walk is to the bottom of the falls, which during the rainy season is an awe-inspiring sight. It's a steep climb down through villages and crops, and a sweaty, exhausting climb back up. There's a cave behind the easy-to-reach second falls, that's really worth the climb. If it's a clear day you can literally see halfway across Uganda from the ridge at the top.

It's easy enough to ramble off on your own, but a guide is highly recommended as you'll cross much private property (without a guide you'll need to pay at several points) and will also be asked for money by children (either to be your guide or just because). Figure on about USh15,000 to get to the bottom of the main drop and USh25,000 for the four-hour, 8km walk to all three.

There are also village walks and the forest walking trails at Mt Elgon National Park's Forest Exploration Centre nearby, though you have to pay the national park fees to hike there.

Coffee Tours

A highlight of visiting Sipi is taking a coffee tour that walks you through the whole process: from picking the coffee berries, to shelling them, grinding them with a traditional mortar and pestle, roasting them on an open fire and – of course – finishing with a fine cup of strong arabica coffee (including a bag for you to take home). Tours cost USh25,000 per person and involve a village visit to one of the mudbrick houses that have a small coffee plantation plot.

Mountain Biking

Sipi River Lodge is in the process of developing a selection of mountain-biking routes ranging from hardcore technical rocky climbs to downhill sections; definitely one to keep your eye on. Bike hire is also on the cards.

🛏 Sleeping & Eating

Sipi has a good range of tasteful lodges. A word of warning: food can take a very long time to cook, so it's best to preorder.

Crow's Nest   GUESTHOUSE $
(☏ 0772-687924;   thecrowsnets@yahoo.com; camping USh10,000, dm USh20,000, cabins USh40,000-120,000) Set up by Peace Corps volunteers, Crow's Nest's log cabins are Scandinavian in style with private bathrooms and views of all three waterfalls from their terraces (go for cabin 2 or 3). Staff can arrange cultural walks (USh30,000) that cover everything from throwing spears to learning how to ward off evil spirits. Yes, someone really did make a mess of the email address: crowsnets, not nest!

Moses' Campsite   GUESTHOUSE $
(☏ 0752-208302; camping USh10,000, bandas per person USh20,000) Sipi's original backpacker, this small, laid-back operation has a good view of the falls from its wonderful rickety terrace and unhindered views of the plains below from a rocky cliff. The *bandas* are decent, the staff friendly and colobus monkeys often hang around here.

Sipi River Lodge   LODGE $$
(☏ 0751-796109; www.sipiriverlodge.com; incl full board dm US$60, banda s/d US$90/124, cottage d/q US$236/407) This attractive lodge has a tranquil setting among a garden full of flowers, with a flowing creek and Sipi's second waterfall as a memorable backdrop. Rooms range from charming country-style cottages, to bandas and 'dorms' (which you're unlikely to have to share) with wide, comfy beds.

Many of the ingredients on the menu come from the on-site vegetable garden. A nightly set menu (USh40,000 for drop-in diners) is served around an atmospheric dining room with a log fire and well-stocked bar. There are plenty of activities too, from Mt Elgon treks, mountain biking, fly fishing and coffee tours on its plantation.

Sipi Falls Resort   LODGE $$
(☏ 0753-153000; sipiresort@gmail.com; camping USh30,000, s/d/tr USh152,000/180,000/222,000) A very good all-round choice, Sipi Falls Resort's sublime waterfall views, good food, and affordable, character-filled *bandas* (with open-air private showers) ensure a memorable stay. The old house was used as a residence by the last British governor of Uganda, but the rooms in there are overpriced and lack atmosphere.

Lacam Lodge   LODGE $$
(☏ 0752-292554;   www.lacamlodge.co.uk; incl full board camping from USh65,000, dm from USh80,000, r without bathroom from

s/d USh90,000/120,000, bandas s/d/tr from USh130,000/220,000/300,000) This very attractive lodge is the closest to the big waterfall, and from the viewing area you can see the water crash on land. Accommodation here, from the three-bed dorms to the large *bandas,* is very stylish and comfortable, and the service is good. Rates include full board and fluctuate seasonally.

🛍 Shopping

Sipi Women's Craft Shop CRAFT
(⊙7am-7pm) Made by local women, proceeds from the quality crafts, clothes and accessories sold here go to the community. It also sells Sipi coffee and honey. It's on the outskirts of town as you approach from Mbale.

❶ Getting There & Away

Minibus taxis run between Mbale and Sipi Falls (USh10,000, one hour), but can take a long time to fill up.

For the return trip, most minibuses start at Kapchorwa and are often full when they pass through Sipi, so you may end up waiting a while. Ask at your lodge if they know when any minibuses will start the trip in Sipi.

To Mbale expect to pay around USh40,000 for a special hire or USh7000 for a *boda-boda.*

Nyero Rock Paintings

Of the many ancient rock-art sites scattered around eastern Uganda, this is one of the easiest to reach, and one of the few that's worth the effort to do so. The main site, known as **Nyero 2**, is a big white wall covered in groups of red circles, boats and some vaguely human and animal forms. Archaeologists have yet to unravel the significance of the designs, who painted them and even when they did so. If the caretaker is around, he'll charge USh5000 for an informative tour, otherwise local kids will show you around. **Nyero 1**, with a few more circles, lies just below the main site while **Nyero 3**, where you probably won't notice the modest painting unless someone shows you, is a few hundred metres north. The surrounding countryside is littered with bouldery peaks and cacti, giving it a Wild West feel.

The Nyero rock paintings are 9km west of Kumi, an easy day trip from Mbale (USh7000, one hour), Sipi or even Jinja. From Kumi the round trip (including waiting time) by special hire costs USh30,000 and by *boda-boda* around USh4000.

NORTHEASTERN UGANDA

Kidepo Valley National Park

Offering some of the most stunning scenery of any protected area in Uganda **Kidepo Valley National Park** (adult/child US$40/20) is hidden away in a lost valley in the extreme northeast of Uganda. The rolling, short-grass savannah of the 1442-sq-km national park is ringed by mountains and cut by rocky ridges.

Kidepo is most notable for harbouring a number of animals found nowhere else in Uganda, including cheetahs, bat-eared foxes, aardwolves, caracals, greater and lesser kudus. There are also large concentrations of elephants, zebras, buffaloes, bushbucks, giraffes, lions, jackals, leopards, hyenas and Nile crocodiles.

Amazingly, most of these animals, including even the occasional lion, are content to graze and lounge right near the park's accommodation, so you can see a whole lot without going very far: it's a safari from a lounge chair (or in Apoka Safari Lodge's case – from a bathtub!).

The bird checklist is fast approaching 500 species (second among the national parks only to the larger Queen Elizabeth National Park) and there are many 'Kidepo specials' – birds such as the ostrich, kori bustard, pygmy falcon, secretary bird, Karamoja apalis and Abyssinian ground hornbill – that are found in no other Ugandan national park.

🏃 Activities & Tours

Wildlife Drives
Kidepo is the only park in Uganda where UWA has a vehicle (day/night US$90/120) but it's not always available. For those with their own vehicles, there's an extensive network of tracks in the park, with Narus Valley being a top target for wildlife. Lions are often spotted lazing in rocky outcrops and climbing the branches of fig trees. Also popular are the borassus palm forest and Kanangorok hot springs by the Kidepo River near the South Sudan border; which is also the habitat of ostriches. With your own vehicle, night drives cost US$40 for guide and spotlight.

Nature Walks

A great option for wildlife viewing is to venture out on foot, accompanied by armed rangers.

Cultural Tours

UWA can organise visits (US$30) to Karamojong and Ik villages with hiking at Mt Morungole, both memorable experiences allowing you to interact with these northeastern tribal groups.

🛏 Sleeping & Eating

If you want to be in the thick of the action, the park maintains several isolated campsites (USh15,000) with latrines and water. You'll be accompanied by an armed guard who can arrange firewood for cooking.

Apoka Hostel   BANDA $
(📞 0392-899500; camping USh15,000, s/d USh60,000/70,000, without bathroom USh40,000/50,000) The best of UWA's park lodges, laid-back Apoka has basic *bandas* spread over its grassy site. There's plenty of wildlife about, so be sure to keep your distance and always carry a torch. You've got a good chance of hearing lions roaring at night. There's a small restaurant with a limited menu (meals USh8000) and cold beers to enjoy around the nightly campfire.

Buffalo Base   GUESTHOUSE $
(📞 0776-146548; www.buffalobase.com; Karenga; s/d USh30,000/45,000) Well outside the park in the small township of Karenga (8km from Kidepo's gate), this simple roadside guesthouse is a good option for those wanting to experience Karamoja culture by staying in a *manyata* (traditional Karamoja round hut). There are also basic rooms, and food is served in its pleasant little restaurant. Cultural performances can also be arranged.

★ Apoka Safari Lodge   LODGE $$$
(📞 0414-251182; www.wildplacesafrica.com; s/d incl full board & 2 activities US$530/740; 📶 🐾)
If you want something really special, you want Apoka Safari Lodge. Its large, private cottages with thatched-roofs and canvas walls all look out to wildlife grazing right on your doorstep. Each features an outdoor tub (watch animals graze while you have a bath), stone showers, perfect views and a writing desk that would suit Hemingway to a tee.

It has a lovely swimming pool (US$25 for nonguests) with a rocky bottom and sweeping savannah views, and meals are ocassionally available for nonguests (lunch US$30, dinner US$45), depending on how many guests are staying. Reception displays the skull of Kidepo's last rhino – shot by poachers in the early 1980s.

Nga'Moru Wilderness Camp   LODGE $$$
(📞 0754-500555; www.ngamoru.com; s/d incl full board US$160/240) This lovely, wild and peaceful spot just outside the edge of the park's border comprises luxury camping with bush showers and huge cottages with prime views. Lions occasionally hang out here. Owner Patrick is an excellent source of info for northern Uganda.

UGANDA KIDEPO VALLEY NATIONAL PARK

ℹ **KIDEPO VALLEY NATIONAL PARK**

Why Go

Stunning scenery; best variety of wildlife in Uganda including zebras, cheetahs and ostriches to go with lions, giraffes and elephants; the chance to visit a Karamojong village.

When to Go

November to January, when you might see some of the biggest buffalo herds in Africa. The rainy season (August to September) has long grass that impedes viewing, and it can also be problematic accessing the park on muddy roads. But you're sure to see lots of animals at any time.

Practicalities

Can be reached in a day from Kampala if you have your own car. Public transport takes a few days, with a night in Kitgum or Gulu; if approaching from the east you'll need to overnight in Moroto, Soroti or Kotdio.

Budget Tips

Apoka Hostel offers well-priced *bandas* at the park headquarters, as does Buffalo Base outside the park; consider getting a group together to chip in to hire a 4WD from Kampala.

JOURNEY THROUGH KARAMOJA

The far less-travelled route up to Kidepo National Park heads through the wilds of Karamojaland in the eastern reaches of Uganda, a two- or three-day journey that takes you though some of the most stunning scenery in the country. You'll pass by timeless plains peppered with tall jagged peaks and fields ablaze with sunflowers. You'll also encounter the Karamojong people – the highlight of the journey for most – pastoral herders recognisable by their traditional dress (similar to the Maasai). Males often sport dapper Dr Seuss–style top hats with a feather stuck in it, and brandish a cattle stick and a mini wooden stool (used as a seat, headrest and, in recent times, to steady their rifle for target practice!).

Until very recently Karamoja has had a deserved reputation as a dangerous destination. In the past the Karamojong have been known to ambush highway travellers: sometimes to steal food or money, sometimes for vengeance and sometimes just for fun. Safety has improved markedly since disarmament of the Karamojong people by the Ugandan military in 2011/12 when 40,000 AK-47s were confiscated. The main concern these days comes not from the Karamojong, but from the occasional skirmishes between armed Turkana people from Kenya who cross the border looking to steal cattle.

While an increasing number of tourists are travelling through these days (all without incident), it's still of paramount importance to check security warnings before setting out (national park staff will have the latest details) and again at every step of the way. Things can change very fast out here.

If coming from Kampala, the trip involves heading to **Kotido**, a small, gritty, dusty town with a large NGO presence. Be sure to stop by the Uganda Wildlife Authority (UWA) office, next to the central roundabout, where you can you can get onward travel advice. The smartest accommodation option is **Kotido Resort** (☑ 0783-933700; Lomukura St; s/d USh31,000/40,000), with quality rooms within a secure compound. Or try the more basic **Skyline Hotel** (☑ 0785-907625; s/d USh21,000/26,000), just down the road past the UWA office, with small but clean rooms and friendly staff.

Moroto is another likely stopover (particularly if heading south from Kidepo). It's 112km south of Kotido – around a three-hour drive (USh20,000). It's the biggest and most prosperous of Karamoja towns, with leafy streets and many NGOs. Keep an eye out to see if the Karamoja Museum is opened. The **Mt Moroto Hotel** (☑ 0392-897300; r USh75,000-140,000, cottage USh250,000; 🔊) is easily the best pick of accommodation with a spectacular setting at the foot of Mt Moroto. Gateway buses run from Kampala (USh14,000, eight hours) via Mbale.

The bus also stops in **Soroti** another major town that's an option to spend the night. The former government-run **Soroti Hotel** (☑ 0705-408000, 0772-301154; hotelsoroti01@gmail.com; r from USh70,000; 🔊) is a very good choice with large clean rooms, a bar and restaurant.

❶ Getting There & Away

There are two routes to reach Kidepo. The vast majority of visitors take the route through to Kitgum via Gulu, which is the shortest, easiest and safest route. Otherwise there's the more adventurous eastern route through spectacular scenery of Karamoja. Ideally one would combine the two routes into a northern loop of the country taking in Murchison National Park en route.

Undoubtedly your best bet is to rent a car, in which case you can make it in one day from Kampala to Kidepo if you get a very early start. Alternatively you could take a bus to Kitgum and negotiate a special hire from there.

Chartering a flight is another option (popular with high-end clients) as Kidepo has its own airstrip. Fly Uganda (p484) and Aerolink (p484) can arrange flights.

Otherwise Matoke Tours (p476) and **Buffalo Safari Camps** (☑ 0782-805639; www.buffalo safaricamps.com) are two reputable companies that specialise in affordable Kidepo safaris.

BUS

Getting to Kidepo Valley National Park by public transport is certainly possible, but you can't make it in one day. There are two possible routes, both are long and at times difficult journeys, but this is one place where travel is its own reward.

From Kampala, most opt for the bus to Kitgum (USh30,000, seven hours via Gulu) where you'll have to overnight. From Kitgum, your best bet is to jump on a truck heading to Karenga (USh20,000, three hours), the gateway town for the park. Trucks depart Kitgum from around 8am till 10am. From Karenga, you can arrange to be picked up by the UWA vehicle (for a pricey USh4000 per kilometre) for the 24km journey to the park's headquarters and lodging area. Make sure you pay for 24km, not 48km. Otherwise you can try your luck hitching a ride with other travellers heading into the park – try Fugly's, Bomah Hotel or the UWA office. A boda-boda is another option, which should cost around USh30,000 (including driver entry fees) into the park headquarters – though it can be a risky trip given the wildlife about.

The other route for getting to Kidepo from Kampala is via eastern Uganda through **Karamojaland**. Gateway has daily buses to Kotido (USh50,000, 15 hours), departing Kampala's New Bus Park in the early morning. From Kotido take a shared taxi (USh6500) or bus (USh15,000) for the 72km journey to Kaabong (two to three hours), a rough 'wild east' town. From there, jump on the less frequent trucks to Karenga (USh15,000, two to three hours), from where you can get a boda-boda into the park. Until recently the region has been volatile, so check the security situation before taking the eastern route.

Kitgum
POP 57,000

Those en route to Kidepo Valley National Park are likely to overnight in Kitgum, particularly those taking public transport. It suffered badly under the Lord's Resistance Army's (LRA's) reign of terror but it's a surprisingly bustling little town, with a sizeable NGO population.

🛏 Sleeping & Eating

Acholi Pride   GUESTHOUSE $
(☑ 0772-687793; Ogwok Rd; r with/without bathroom USh28,000/13,000) Next door to UWA, this is by far the best cheapie in town, with simple, clean and functional rooms.

Fugly's   GUESTHOUSE $$
(☑ 0785-551911; fuglys.limited@gmail.com; Church Cres; s/d USh80,000-160,000, without bathroom from USh50,000/100,000; ☒) South African–owned Fugly's is popular with NGOs and diplomats for its good range of rooms, plenty of lawn, small pool and barbecues in the evening. If it's full, try the similarly priced Bomah Hotel up the road.

ℹ Information

UWA (☑ 0777-328886; 4 Ogwok Rd; ⊙ 8am-5.30pm Mon-Sat) has an office here, and is a good source of information. There are several banks with ATMs, and an internet cafe across from Acholi Pride guesthouse.

ℹ Getting There & Away

The Post Bus heads to Kampala daily, as does Homeland (USh30,000, seven hours) at 8am, noon and 4pm.

Those without transport who are wanting to get to Kidepo can take a truck to Karenga (USh20,000, 3½ hours) departing from 'Little Village' opposte Stanbic around 8am to 10am. The other option is to ask around for a special hire, or enquire with UWA to see whether it has a car heading to the park (which is unlikely). Otherwise UWA can arrange a vehicle for USh750,000 for an overnight return trip.

Enquire with UWA about the state of the road and whether it's passable, particularly during rainy season.

Gulu
POP 150,000

Unless you're here volunteering or en route to Kidepo Valley National Park, there's no real reason to visit Gulu. It's the largest town in northern Uganda and one of the hardest hit during the LRA conflict. It's a town in transit and, in a sure sign of optimism, store shelves are full and people are arriving from elsewhere in the country hoping to cash in on the coming boom. There's no shortage of *wazunga* about with a lot of NGOs in town.

◎ Sights

Taks Centre   CULTURAL CENTRE
(☑ 0471-433906; www.takscentre.blogspot.co.uk; 3-5 Upper Churchill Dr) It's worth popping into this happening community arts centre to see what's on, whether it be an art exhibition or cultural perfomance, or just stopping by for a meal. There's also *banda* accommodation for USh50,000, including breakfast.

🛏 Sleeping

Happy Nest Hotel   HOTEL $
(☑ 0372-517584; 12 Coronation Rd; s/d USh35,000/45,000, r without bathroom USh30,000; @ 🛜) Great budget hotel with bright sunny rooms. Located a few blocks from the bus station.

Hotel Pearl Afrique
HOTEL **$**

(📞 0774-072277; pearlafrique@yahoo.com; Odongo Rd; s/d from USh55,000/67,000) A comfortable, good-value choice with spotless rooms, some with bathtubs. Pricier rooms are worth it, with tons more space. There's a restaurant and bar with live music on weekends.

Bomah Hotel
HOTEL **$$**

(📞 0779-945063; www.bomahhotels.com; 8 Eden Rd; s/d/ste from USh128,000/184,000/533,000; ✳@🛜🏊) In a leafy part of town, the colonial-style Bomah is Gulu's smartest option with sparkling rooms in a hotel block set over many levels. There's also an excellent gym overlooking the pool and a popular thatched-roof restaurant (mains USh18,000 to USh22,000).

✖ Eating & Drinking

★ Sankofa Cafe
CAFE **$**

(📞 0776-712198; Samuel Doe Rd; pizzas from 12,000; ⊙8am-10pm; 🛜) Recently relocated to a more relaxed part of town, this chilled-out, open-air eatery caters primarily to NGO workers with excellent woodfired pizzas, salads and fresh juices.

Coffee Hut
CAFE **$**

(Awich Rd; coffee USh4000, wraps USh8000; 🛜) Across from the bus terminal, this modern cafe is the place to go for excellent coffee, wi-fi, breakfast and tasty wraps.

Hotel Binen
AFRICAN **$**

(📞 0772-405038; Coronation Rd; mains from USh5000) A good place to try northern Ugandan food such as *malakwang* (a sour, leafy green vegetable) and *lapena* (pigeon peas).

BJz
PUB

(Eden Rd; ⊙6.30pm-late) Gulu's most popular drinking spot for locals and expats alike, with plenty of seating areas and live music on weekends.

ℹ Information

All major banks have branches here. There's a Uchumi supermarket for those heading to Kidepo.

ℹ Getting There & Away

To get here your best option is the Gulu–Kampala Post Bus, which continues through to Kitgum. Otherwise buses and minivans run between Kampala and Gulu (USh25,000, five hours) all day long from the bus terminal in town. Much of this road is new and in excellent shape.

Those heading to Kidepo can get a bus to Kitgum (USh12,000, three hours). Minibus taxis to Masindi (USh15,000, four hours) are infrequent, so it may be quicker to take a minibus to Kigumba (USh15,000, 2½ hours), and transfer to Masindi (USh7000, 1½ hours). There are also buses to Arua (USh 20,000, four hours).

Buses to Juba (USh60,000, 10 hours) in South Sudan also depart from here.

SOUTHWESTERN UGANDA

If Uganda is the 'pearl of Africa', then southwestern Uganda is the mother of pearl. Easily the most beautiful part of the country, it's a lush region of lakes, islands and mountains. And whether you're here for adventure or respite, the southwest has got you covered in spades.

There are world-class treks all along the western Rift Valley, whether it be taking in the three-nation vistas from atop the Virunga volcanoes or undergoing a weeklong slog though the otherworldly moorlands of the snowcapped Rwenzoris. After the mountains, head to the water for an all out R&R assault on Lake Bunyonyi or the Ssese Islands.

The southwest is Uganda's top wildlife-watching region and one of the world's best places to spot primates. There are, of course, the mountain gorillas, living *la vida* languorous on the steep slopes of Bwindi Impenetrable National Park and Mgahinga Gorilla National Park. Kibale National Park has what's often described as the greatest variety of primates on the planet, and this is just one of the places you can track a habituated troop of chimpanzees as they groove through the treetops. The famous tree-climbing lions steal the show at Queen Elizabeth National Park, but the area's largest and most diverse park is also full of other big wildlife and is one place certain to satisfy your safari urge.

Fort Portal
POP 46,300

The fort may be gone, but this city is definitely a portal to places that offer sublime scenery, abundant nature and genuine adventure. Explore the beautiful Crater Lakes, track the chimps in Kibale National Park or drop into Semuliki National Park with its hot springs and central African wildlife.

Fort Portal is the heartland of a verdant tea-growing area and an important commercial centre. Its pleasant cool climate and central location make it a very convenient base from which to explore the area, so many people end up staying here for a few days.

◉ Sights & Activities

Tooro Botanical Garden   GARDENS
(☑0752-500630; www.toorobotanicalgardens.org; entry incl tour USh10,000; ⊙8am-5pm) These homegrown botanical gardens have a lot of well-signed indigenous plants and trees, as well as an organic farming project that grows herbs, flowers, trees, natural dyes, vegetables and medicinal plants. Admission includes a tour through the extensive grounds. Morning and late afternoon birdwatching is a highlight. The entry is opposite the Mountains of the Moon Hotel.

Tooro Palace   PALACE
(guide USh5000, camera USh20,000) Looking down over the town from its highest hill, the palace is worth a visit purely for its 360-degree panoramic views. It's the residence of King Oyo, who ascended the throne in 1995 at the age of three! A guide will give you a quick history of the kingdom and explain the ceremonies that take place on the hill, but you can't go inside.

The circular structure was built in 1963, but fell into ruin after the abolition of the royal kingdoms by Idi Amin. It was restored in 2001 after Colonel Gadaffi met the king and donated the money for repairs.

Karambi Royal Tombs   TOMBS
(Kasese Rd; admission USh5000; ⊙8am-6pm) These royal tombs 4km south of town make for a peaceful excursion. While from outside it's not much to look at, if you can find the caretaker he'll let you in for a look at the tombs, which house drums, spears and other personal effects of several of the Toro kings who are buried here. The cemetery outside is the resting place for various other royal family members.

Mugusu Market   MARKET
(Kasese Rd) The Wednesday market, 11km south of Fort Portal, is the largest market in the west and attracts traders from all over, including many from the DRC selling fresh produce, clothing and bric-a-brac.

☞ Tours

Kabarole Tours   GUIDED TOURS
(☑0483-422183; www.kabaroletours.com; 1 Moledina St; ⊙8am-6pm Mon-Sat, 10am-4pm Sun) The best way to enjoy Fort Portal and its surrounds is to stop by the reputable Kabarole Tours – guides can take you anywhere in Uganda but focus on this little corner of the country. Popular day trips are the Crater Lakes, mountain-bike tours (guided or DIY), birdwatching, village walks, and treks in the foothills of the Rwenzoris. Check the website for other trips. Also has vehicle hire (sedan/4WD with driver US$70/120) and can arrange gorilla permits for both Uganda (US$30) and Rwanda (US$50).

⊨ Sleeping

The best accommodation is found in the scenic outskirts of Fort Portal at Boma or the nearby Crater Lakes, but there are a few decent options in the town itself.

⊫ Fort Portal

Y.E.S. Hostel   HOSTEL $
(Youth Encouragement Services; ☑0772-780350; www.yesugandahostel.weebly.com; Lower Kakiiza Rd; camping USh10,000, r USh20,000; ☏) ✐ Run by a charity that supports orphans, this simple and friendly hostel is exceptional value with a peaceful pastoral setting. Rooms are configured as dorms (four to six beds per room) but usually you'll get a room to yourself. There's a large kitchen (use is USh5000 per day), solar hot-water showers and wi-fi. It's 3km from the centre; a *boda-boda* costs USh2000.

Golf Course View Guesthouse   GUESTHOUSE $
(☑0772-485602; golfcourse71@gmail.com; Rwenzori Rd; camping USh10,000, s/d USh50,000/60,000, without bathroom USh30,000/40,000) Just outside of town, this well-priced, relaxed guesthouse has a faded colonial charm and spacious room with huge bathrooms. There's a restaurant, bar and kitchen that guests are free to use. On a clear day there are lovely views of the Rwenzoris.

Rwenzori Travellers Inn   HOTEL $
(☑0483-422075; www.travellersinn.com; 16 Kyebambe Rd; s/d USh52,000/64,000; @☏) This two-storey hotel on the main thoroughfare is still a popular budget choice, though it seems to be coasting on its reputation these days. There's a good restaurant, two bars, an internet cafe and craft shop.

Southwestern Uganda

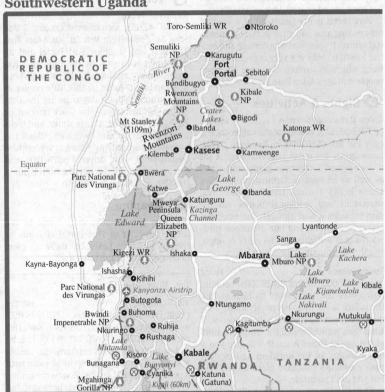

★ **Ruwenzori View**
Guesthouse GUESTHOUSE $$
(☎0483-422102; www.ruwenzoriview.com; Lower Kakiiza Rd; s/d USh125,000/180,000, without bathroom USh65,000/99,000; ⊛) A blissful little guesthouse run by a Dutch–Anglo couple, with a refreshingly rural and lovely homely atmosphere. The rooms with attached bathrooms have their own patios overlooking the superb garden and Rwenzori mountain backdrop. Rates include a hearty breakfast, while its social dinners (USh35,000) served around the family table are an institution (nonguests also welcome). Birdwatching tours take place here in the mornings.

Dutchess Guesthouse GUESTHOUSE $$
(☎0704-879474; www.dutchessuganda.com; 11 Mugusrusi Rd; s/d/tr US$60/70/90, s without bathroom US$25; @⊛) Above its fantastic restaurant, Dutchess offers excellent-value boutique rooms with plenty of flair, big beds,

couches and snazzy bathrooms. Wi-fi, powerboard adaptors and safes for laptops will please the flashpackers.

Mountains of the Moon Hotel HOTEL $$
(☎0775-557840; www.mountainsofthemoon.co.ug; Nyaika Ave; s/d from US$120/140; @⊛☒) With its classic country-club feel, this professionally run resort has comfortable rooms set among peaceful, well-maintained grounds. Guests have access to a pool, gym, sauna and business centre. It has a nice restaurant and lively bar too.

🛏 Around Fort Portal

★ **Kyaninga Lodge** LODGE $$$
(☎0772-999750; www.kyaningalodge.com; Lake Kyaninga; s/d incl full board US$260/390; ⊛☒) The stunning Kyaninga Lodge features eight epic thatched-roof, log cottages that soar high upon stilts. Adjoined by a wooden walking platform, they are a spectacular

including sandwiches, stews, pizza, *firinda* (mashed skinless beans) and lots of *moch-omo* (barbecued meat). There's also a good liquor list and a large African lunch buffet. Has excellent local coffee too.

Andrew & Brothers SUPERMARKET $
(Lugard Rd) For those needing to buy their own provisions, this is the best of several supermarkets in town.

★**Dutchess** INTERNATIONAL $$
(www.dutchessuganda.com/restaurant; 11 Mugus-rusi Rd; mains USh10,000-30,000; ☉7am-11pm; ☏) Easily Fort Portal's best place to eat (if not the entire country's), Dutchess has a creative menu featuring crocodile burgers, Flemish beef stew with Guiness and mash, and a selection of 46 excellent woodfired pizzas. They bake their own breads, make their own ice cream, stock European chees-es, fresh juices and Rwenzori coffee. Grab a chair indoors, or head out to the deck over-looking the garden.

The Forest BAR
(Rukidi III St; ☉1pm-late) The most popu-lar spot for a drink in Fort Portal, this Belgian-owned bar-club has outdoor seating and plenty of screens showing sports.

Gluepot Bar BAR
(Kaboyo Rd; ☉10am-late) In the centre of town, Gluepot bar has changed ownership yet continues as a lively upstairs drinking spot.

ℹ Information

Lugard Rd, Fort's main drag, has just about everything travellers may need including craft shops, internet cafes, post office and banks, in-cluding **Stanbic Bank** (Lugard Rd) and **Barclays Bank** (Bwamba Rd).

ℹ Getting There & Away

BUS

Kalita (☏0756-897920; www.kalita.co.ug) and **Link** (☏0312-108830) have regular buses to Kampala (USh20,000, four hours). Both also head to Kasese (USh5000, two hours), but only Kalita makes the journey to Kabale (USh35,000, eight hours), via Katunguru (USh9000, 1½ hours) in Queen Elizabeth Na-tional Park.

The easiest way to Hoima (USh25,000, six hours) is the coaster that goes at 7am every other day in front of the Bata shoe store.

sight – as are the views over Kyaninga Lake. The log cabins are spacious and private, with gleaming wooden floors and bath-rooms with classy touches, such as clawfoot baths and marble countertops.

The restaurant also has amazing views, both from the outdoor deck and in the cosy Nepali teahouse–like restaurant. It's popu-lar with nonguests for lunch (two-courses USh40,000, reservations required). There's a swimming pool and sundeck too (nonguests can use it for USh10,000).

Kyaninga Lodge is located 10km north-east of Fort Portal – either a long trek or USh5000 by *boda-boda*.

✕ Eating & Drinking

Gardens AFRICAN $
(☏0772-694482; Lugard Rd; mains from USh9000; ☉8am-11pm) This extremely popular restau-rant overlooking the busy junction has a quality menu of foreign and local dishes

Fort Portal

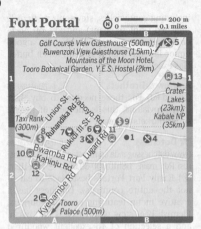

N 0 ——— 200 m
0 ——— 0.1 miles

Golf Course View Guesthouse (500m);
Ruwenzori View Guesthouse (1.5km);
Mountains of the Moon Hotel,
Tooro Botanical Garden, Y.E.S. Hostel (2km)

Crater
Lakes
(23km);
Kabale NP
(35km)

Taxi Rank
(300m)

Union St.
Ruhandika Rd
Kaboyo Rd
Rukidi III St.
Bwamba Rd
Kahinju Rd
Lugard Rd
Kyebambe Rd

Tooro
Palace (500m)

MINIBUS TAXI

There are regularish departures from the **Taxi Rank** (Malibo Rd) to Kampala (USh18,000, four hours), Ntoroko (USh15,000, 2½ hours) and Bundibugyo (USh10,000, 1½ hours).

Minibuses and shared-car taxis to Mbarara (USh20,000, 3½ hours), Kamwenge (for Kibale National Park; USh15,000, 1½ hours) and Rwaihamba (for Lake Nkuruba; USh5000, 45 minutes) leave from the intersection near where the main road crosses the river.

SPECIAL-HIRE TAXIS

Drivers hang around the vacant lot by the Continental Hotel and charge from USh100,000 per day if you aren't travelling too far. Kabarole Tours (p417) has cars with driver for US$70 per day.

Crater Lakes

The landscape south of Fort Portal is dotted with picturesque crater lakes (some over 400m deep), all of which are ringed with improbably steep hills. It's a great spot to settle in for a few days to explore the footpaths or cycle the seldom-used roads. Much of the land is cultivated, but there are still plenty of primates and birds at the lakeshores. Accommodation caters for all budgets and it's increasingly popular for visitors to stay at the lakes before continuing on to Kibale National Park.

Most lodges and guesthouses organise walks through the local villages or to other area attractions (which have entrance fees if you go without a guide), such as **Top of the World** (admission USh5000) viewpoint on the highest hill behind Lake Nyamirima where you can see up to five lakes (depending on the air clarity).

The common wisdom is that the lakes are bilharzia-free, but we wouldn't risk it. Also be aware that a lone hippo roams between Nyamirima, Nyinabulitwa, Nyabikere and, according to some, Nkuruba, so check with locals before plunging into the waters.

Lake Nkuruba

Probably the winner among the contenders for the title of most beautiful crater lake, Nkuruba is one of the few still surrounded by forest. Many monkeys, including black-and-white and red colobus, frolic here.

Minibuses and shared-car taxis from Fort Portal to Rwaihamba pass Lake Nkuruba (USh5000, 45 minutes). A special-hire will set you back about USh30,000, and a *boda-boda* around USh10,000.

🛏 Sleeping

Lake Nkuruba Nature Reserve Community Campsite   BANDAS $

(📞0773-266067; www.nkuruba.com; Lake Nkuruba; camping USh10,000, s/d without bathroom USh36,000/52,000, cottage USh72,000) Lake Nkuruba Nature Reserve Community Campsite is the best place to stay on the lake (not to be confused with the imitating lodge next door) with funds going towards community projects. The camp is set on a hill with nice views and easy access to the lake. The *bandas* are basic, but clean and comfortable. The cottage is down on the lakeshore for more privacy.

Meals are available (USh7000 to USh13,000), as are walks around the area (15,000 per person). There are plenty of birds here; keep your eye out for the great blue turaco. There are also black-and-white colobus monkeys, and it is possible to take night tours to spot bushbabies. Bicycles (USh15,000 per day) and motorcycles are available for exploring the area on your own.

Lake Nyinabulitwa

A beautiful and tranquil spot, the midsized 'Mother of Lakes' is set back a bit off the road to Kibale National Park.

🛏 Sleeping

Nyinabulitwa Country Resort LODGE $$
(☑ 0712-984929; www.nyinabulitwaresort.com; Lake Nyinabulitwa; camping US$15, s/d/tr from US$70/120/180) An intimate little place on the lake's south shore with five *bandas* and an excellent camping ground. With a beautiful garden setting, it's the perfect place to catch up on your journal. It runs boat trips (US$10 per person) around the lake and can deliver you to a treehouse for bird- and primate-watching. Alternatively, you can paddle around yourself for free.

It's 20km from Fort Portal, 1.5km off the main road just before Rweetera Trading Centre.

Lake Nyabikere

The 'Lake of Frogs' (you'll hear how it got its name at night!) lies just off the road to Kibale National Park, 12km northwest of Kanyanchu visitor centre or 21km from Fort Portal. A recommended footpath circles the lake.

🛏 Sleeping & Eating

CVK Lakeside Resort LODGE $
(☑ 0772-906549; www.cvklakeside.com; Lake Nyabikere; camping from USh15,000, s/d USh99,000/129,000; 🐾) The long-established CVK Lakeside Resort has wooden cabins overlooking the lake, but despite recent refurbishments it's well overpriced these days.

There's a restaurant and canoes for hire. It's just past Rweetera Trading Centre.

Chimpanzee Forest Guesthouse GUESTHOUSE $$
(☑ 0772-486415; www.chimpanzeeforestguesthouse.com; incl full board guesthouse s/d US$85/125, cottages US$100/160) Not actually on Lake Nyabikere, but near enough to snatch some views of it, is the wonderful Chimpanzee Forest Guesthouse. Set on manicured gardens overlooking tea plantations, there's a choice of *banda* cottages or rooms in the atmospheric 1950s colonial building with a fireplace and superb collection of antique books on Africa.

Food here is quality and they grow some of their own vegetables. Birdwatching and guided walks are also on the cards. The entrance is 300m south of the Kibale National Park office on the Fort Portal Rd.

Rweteera Safari Park & Tourist Camping LODGE $$
(☑ 0776-862153; www.rweteerasafaripark.com; Lake Nyabikere; camping per person US$10, tented camping s/d US$35/50) The new Rweteera Safari Park gets good feedback, with simple, comfortable tent camping by the lake. Any minibus (USh5000) heading south from Fort Portal can drop you right at the entrance.

Lake Nyinambuga

Emblazoned on Uganda's USh20,000 note, picturesque Lake Nyinambuga is a worthwhile stop with some excellent photo ops.

🛏 Sleeping

Ndali Lodge LODGE $$$
(☑ 0772-221309; www.ndalilodge.com; Lake Nyinambuga; s/d incl full board US$535/720; @🐾🌊) This luxurious, colonial-style lodge has a stunning location on a ridge above the lake. Its elegant (but well overpriced) cottages face west towards Mwamba and Rukwanzi lakes with the Rwenzori Mountains looming on the horizon. Day trippers should aim for a lunch stop here with homely toasted sandwiches served on a tranquil porch overlooking the lake.

Lake Kifuruka

Perhaps slighty less dazzling than the other crater lakes, Lake Kifuruka is beautiful nevertheless.

🛏 Sleeping

Lake Kifuruka Eco-Camp LODGE $

(✆ 0772-562513; www.ecolodge-uganda.com; Lake Kifuruka; camping USh10,000, bandas s/d USh40,000/70,000, s/d without bathroom USh20,000/40,000) Located 2km southwest of Rwaihamba this camp's log cabin *bandas* are basic but clean, and proceeds go to funding local schools. It's a good spot for those seeking a more authentic local experience and will suit those wanting to do a stint of volunteer teaching. The camp can also arrange village homestays.

Other activities include canoe hire (USh10,000 per three hours) and walks to visit all of the lakes (USh30,000 per person) or Mahoma Falls (entry USh15,000, guide USh10,000). Staff are friendly and meals are available from USh7000.

Lake Lyantonde

Just opposite Lake Kifuruka is pretty Lake Lyantonde.

🛏 Sleeping

Papaya Lake Lodge LODGE $$$

(✆ 0793-388277; www.papayalakelodge.com; Lake Lyantonde; s/d incl full board US$350/500; 🛜 ➰) An upmarket choice is the stunning new Papaya Lake Lodge with *banda* cottages all featuring balconies looking out to the water. It has arty touches throughout, and a memorable swimming pool perched high above everything, as well as a lakeside bar.

Lake Kasenda

Little Lake Kasenda isn't at the end of the road, but it sure feels like it.

🛏 Sleeping

Planet Ruigo Beach Resort GUESTHOUSE $

(✆ 0701-370674; camping USh10,000, s/d USh45,000/55,000, r without bathroom USh25,000) Planet Ruigo Beach Resort sits right down on the shore of Lake Kasenda looking up at the steep hills on the other side. Considering how few people come here it's rather surprising how well maintained the three self-contained *bandas* are. The 'treehouse' is secluded on the other side of the lake, and is great for those who want solitude.

Despite the name, there's no actual beach, but you can relax by the lake on its pleasant lawn. There's plenty of thick forest for walking and you can easily wander over to nearby lakes Mulusi and Murigamire. Birdwatching and forest walks can be arranged, but meals are a bit pricey.

Ruigo Beach is 35km south of Fort Portal and 11km south of Rwaihamba, from where a *boda-boda* will cost USh5000. You can drive here in about one hour: call to ask if the road is still in good enough shape for a car to make it. A special-hire taxi from Fort Portal should cost around USh80,000, but drivers are unlikely to know where it is.

Kihingami Wetlands Sanctuary

Kihingami Wetlands Sanctuary RESERVE

(✆ 0779-775790; ⊙ 8am-5pm) This ecotourism site, set up with the help of Fort Portal's Kabarole Tours (p417), preserves an attractive 13-sq-km valley that otherwise would have been gobbled up by the surrounding tea plantations. Despite its small size, a remarkable 384 bird species have been spotted here, including Jameson's wattle-eye and white-spotted flufftail. There's also a good chance of seeing red colobus monkeys and spotted-necked otters.

Local guides lead forest walks (USh20,000 per person) and birdwatching walks (USh20,000 per person), and for an extra USh5000 you can plant a tree. You can also tour a fair-trade tea factory (US$45 per group of 10 people) at 9am and 2pm.

Kihingami is 15km east of Fort Portal, just before the Sebitoli section of Kibale National Park. Take any minibus (USh2000, 30 minutes) heading east.

Amabeere Cave

Amabeere Cave CAVE

(admission incl guide USh25,000; ⊙ 8am-6pm) The water dripping from the roof of this small cave is milky white, hence the name Amabeere ('Breasts'). Most of the rock formations are broken, but it's fun to walk behind the waterfall covering it and past the wall of vines along the adjacent ridge.

It's 8km northwest of Fort Portal, signposted 1.5km off the Bundibugyo road; minibus taxis are USh3000 and take 30 minutes.

Kibale National Park

The 795-sq-km **Kibale National Park** (☑ 0483-425335; adult/child US$40/20) is a lush tropical rainforest, believed to have the highest density of primates in Africa. It's most famous for being one of the best places in the world to track wild chimpanzees, with five groups habituated to human contact. It's home to 13 primate species, with rare red colobus and L'Hoest's monkeys the other highlights.

Larger but rarely seen residents include bushbucks, sitatungas, buffaloes, leopards and quite a few forest elephants. There are also an incredible 250 species of butterfly that live here. While on the smaller side, Kibale also has a great bird list with 372 species, but keen birdwatchers may want to bypass it and spend their time in Bigodi Wetland Sanctuary or Kihingami Wetland where open-canopy and wetland species can be seen alongside most of the same forest species living in Kibale National Park.

The park visitor centre is at Kanyanchu, 35km southeast of Fort Portal.

🏃 Activities

Chimpanzee Tracking
With around a 90% chance of finding them on any particular day, Kibale National Park is undoubtedly the most popular place to track chimpanzees in Uganda. There's a morning (8am) and afternoon (2pm) departure, and while there are plenty of hills along the trails, the walking isn't difficult if you're in shape. Children aged 12 and under aren't permitted.

While you've a good chance of being issued a chimp permit at the park, it occasionally gets booked out during the holiday season, so reservations at the UWA office (p474) in Kampala are a good idea. Regular trackers get just one hour with the playful primates, but those on the **Chimpanzee Habituation Experience** (1/2/3 days US$220/440/660; ⊙ 6am-6pm Mar, Apr, May & Nov) can spend the whole day with them.

Note that chimpanzees are in the process of being habituated in the Sebitoli sector, 12km east of Fort Portal, with permits expected to be issued there from late 2015.

Nature Walks
You'll be very lucky to see chimps on a **nature walk** (excl park permit per person US$30) but as nearly 1500 dwell here, you never know your luck, and there's a good chance you'll hear some scamper off through the treetops. With frequent sightings of owls, civets and the 12cm-long Demidoff's dwarf galago, **night walks** (US$40) can be very rewarding.

🛏 Sleeping

You can easily visit Kibale while spending the night in Fort Portal or at the Crater Lakes.

★**Kibale Forest Camp** LODGE $
(☑ 0312-294894; www.naturelodges.biz/kibale-forest-camp; camping US$10, s/d lazy camping US$30/45, tented camping US$90/115) Nature Lodges succeeds in bringing luxury standards at affordable prices. The atmospheric camp is hidden away in the forest, offering tented camping with stone floors and porches, or ready-made lazy camping for the budget minded. There's also a safari-style restaurant in an attractive thatched *banda*. It's on the outskirts of Bigodi, 1km down a side road off the Kamwenge road.

Tinka's Homestay GUESTHOUSE $
(☑ 0772-468113; per person incl full board USh50,000) Tinka's has recently upgraded to a larger, more modern house, but it's still perfect for those seeking more of a homestay experience. It's located 6km from Kibale

---

ℹ KIBALE NATIONAL PARK

Why Go
The best place to track chimpanzees in the wild in Uganda; excellent birdwatching in nearby Bigodi Wetland Sanctuary.

When to Go
Year-round; for Chimpanzee Habituation Experience visit low season months of March, April, May and November.

Practicalities
Regular minibuses to Kamwenge from Fort Portal. Prebooking chimpanzee permits in Kampala is recommended.

Budget Tips
While US$150 for chimpanzee tracking may seem expensive, bear in mind these fees include your park permit, and offer a more affordable alternative to visiting the gorillas. Public transport and inexpensive accommodation are available.

BIGODI WETLAND SANCTUARY

Bigodi Wetland Sanctuary (☎0772-886865; www.bigodi-tourism.org; ☺7.30am-5pm)
Located 6km south of the Kibale National Park visitor centre at Kanyanchu (no park permit is required), Bigodi was established by a local development organisation to protect the 4-sq-km **Magombe Swamp** that's home to around 200 species of birds (highlights include papyrus gonolek, white-winged warbler and great blue turaco). It's also good for spotting butterflies and primates, with eight different species here, including grey-cheeked mangabey. Three-hour guided walks (USh40,000 per person, including binoculars and gumboots) depart on demand.

Other activities available include village walks (USh30,000 per person), Saturday-afternoon basket-weaving demonstrations, dance and drama performances, and fun interpretive meals (USh15,000 per person; book in advance) where your hosts share the stories behind the local food they serve you. Volunteer opportunities are also available. Any shared taxis (USh8000, 45 minutes) between Fort Portal and Kamwenge can drop you there.

HQ, right near the visitor centre of Bigodi Wetland Sanctuary, convenient if you're here to see birds as well as chimps.

★**Chimps' Nest** LODGE $$
(☎0774-669107; www.chimpsnest.com; r with shared bathroom US$25, s/d cottage US$90/120, treehouse US$150/190; @) This stunner of a lodge straddles Kibale Forest and Magombe Swamp. While its basic rooms are perfect for budget travellers, and the rustic cottages with outdoor showers are charming, take the treehouse if you can. It's perched up in the canopy among the birds and monkeys, with great 360-degree treetop views right from the bed. It's 4km down a rough road from Nkingo.

Primate Lodge LODGE $$
(☎0414-267153; www.ugandalodges.com/primate; Kanyanchu; camping without breakfast US$14, s/d treehouse US$49/64, safari tent US$113/128, cottage US$266/414; ☎) Inside the park next to the UWA headquarters, this deluxe lodge is perfectly located for those tracking chimps. The lovely cottages have stone floors and verandahs, while safari tents come with hardwood floors. Brave souls can take the rickety treehouse secluded in the forest 800m from the lodge, which overlooks an elephant wallow; if you're very lucky you might see one. Discounts available in low season.

Sebitoli

In the northern end of the park along Kampala Rd, this seldom visited part of the forest will change when the chimpanzees who live here are fully habituated, which is expected to occur in the next few years.

Sebitoli Forest Camp LODGE $
(☎0782-761512; camping USh15,000, s/d USh32,000/42,000) This UWA-run camp has a relaxing location surrounded by trees with black-and-white colobus monkeys. Rooms here are great value, with a canteen and friendly staff.

Jacaranda Hilltop Guesthouse GUESTHOUSE $
(☎0483-422183; Kasunga; s/d USh55,000/65,000) Immersed within the tea plantations, this atmospheric guesthouse is located inside a colonial building that was the former residence of the tea-estate manager. Its simple rooms have a relaxed rural feel. Bikes are available for hire (per day US$10), perfect for exploring the surrounding countryside. It's well placed on the fringes of Kibale for walks into the park; and chimpanzee tracking once they're habituated. It's 5km off Kampala Rd; any bus plying the Fort Portal route can drop you at the sign.

ⓘ Getting There & Away

Minibuses to Kamwenge from Fort Portal pass the park visitor centre (USh7000, one hour). For Sebitoli, take any minibus (USh2000, 30 minutes) heading east from Fort Portal.

Semuliki National Park

The Semliki Valley is a little corner of Congo poking into Uganda. The only tropical lowland rainforest in East Africa is a continuation of the huge Ituri Forest in the DRC and forms a link between the heights of East Africa and the vast, steaming jungles of central Africa. The **Semuliki National Park** (☎0382-276424; adult/child US$35/5) covers 220 sq km of the valley floor and harbours some intriguing wildlife, though sightings are difficult due to the thick vegetation. It's most famous for its primordial hot springs.

Birdwatchers come to look for over 440 birds, particularly the central African species, such as the Congo serpent eagle, residing at their eastern limits. At least 133 of the 144 Guinea–Congo forest species have been recorded here and nearly 50 species are found nowhere else in East Africa. There are nine primate species, including the De Brazza's monkey, and many mammals not found elsewhere in Uganda, such as Zenker's flying mice. Both the resident elephants and buffaloes are the forest variety, smaller than their savannah brethren.

◉ Sights & Activities

Hot Springs

Most people come here to see Semuliki's two boiling sulphur hot springs. Entry to the springs costs US$30 per person (excluding park entry), which includes a guided walk to them.

The **female hot spring** is where women from the Bamaga clan would make sacrifices to the gods before bathing naked in the natural springs. Its soupy atmosphere has a distinct prehistoric feel, and features a small burbling geyser. Your guide can demonstrate the water's temperatures by boiling an egg – available from the information centre for USh500 each; though with the stench of sulphur it's probably the last thing you feel like eating.

A half-hour's walk from the female spring, the **male hot spring** is where the men carried out their sacrificial rituals. It is accessed via a muddy forest trail with plenty of primates and birdlife along the way. It leads to a verdant clearing of swamp where a boardwalk passes through sweeping grass and squawking frogs to the hot spring located in a 12m pool.

Walking Trails

Walking options include the 11km **Kirimia Trail**, which is a full-day romp through the heart of the forest and the favoured destination of birdwatchers, and the somewhat shorter but hillier **Red Monkey Trail**. Both end at the Semliki River, which forms the border between Uganda and the DRC.

🛌 Sleeping

Bumaga Campsite CAMPGROUND $
(☎0772-367215; camping USh15,000, banda USh80,000-120,000) Bumaga is a pleasant grassy campsite on the edge of the forest with several *bandas,* and a campsite with showers and latrines. There's a lovely elevated dining area, but you may need to bring your own food. You'll need to arrange accommodation at the UWA office at the Sempaya gate. The campsite is located 2km past the gate.

Ntoroko Game Lodge LODGE $$$
(☎0756-000598; www.ntorokogamelodge.com; s/d US$202/304; @🐾) Sitting directly on the shores of Lake Albert these thatched-roof tented camps have wooden floors and patios overlooking the water. There's a good selection of activities including walks, community visits and biking, as well as trips into the park.

ℹ Getting There & Away

Semuliki National Park is just 52km from Fort Portal, but plan on taking two hours to reach it by car in the dry season.

There are regular minibuses and pick-ups between Fort Portal and Bundibugyo that pass the park (USh12,000, three hours). The last one heads to Fort Portal around 4pm, so if you leave early and hustle on the trails, you can see the hot

ℹ SEMULIKI NATIONAL PARK

Why Go
Sulphur hot springs, a feel for Congo tropical lowland rainforest, primate walks, birdwatching.

When to Go
Year-round.

Practicalities
Minibuses and pick-ups head from Fort Portal to Bundibugyo, near park headquarters. There's only basic accommodation here, so day trips are a popular way to see the park.

Budget Tips
Public transport, Uganda Wildlife Authority (UWA) campsites and canteen meals make Semuliki an affordable park to visit, but bear in mind visits to the hot springs costs an additional US$30 per person on top of park entry.

springs and hike the Red Monkey Trail as a day trip. You can also catch Kalita Transport's Kampala–Bundibugyo bus in Fort Portal departing at approximately 5pm for USh12,000; it returns to Fort Portal around 5am.

Toro-Semliki Wildlife Reserve

The **Toro-Semliki Wildlife Reserve** (☑0772-649880; adult/child US$35/5) is the oldest protected natural area in Uganda, having first been set aside in 1926. Once one of the best-stocked and most popular wildlife parks in East Africa, it suffered significant poaching during the civil war years and after the war with Tanzania.

Wildlife is recovering and you may encounter waterbucks, reedbucks, bushbucks, chimpanzees, pygmy hippos, buffaloes, leopards, elephants and hyenas. A number of lions have also recently returned to the reserve, most likely refugees from the conflict in the DRC.

🏃 Activities

Chimp Tracking

Likely the best wildlife experience in the park is the morning chimp tracking (which UWA prefers to call a primate walk; per person US$30). The hiking is more difficult than in Kibale and you're less likely to encounter chimps (around a 30% chance), but if you do, the thinner forest means your views are superior. These are rare 'dry-habitat chimps' that spend considerable time in the savannah and so walk upright more often than the others.

Wildlife Drives

With a line of mountains behind it, the savannah scenery from the main road is often superb, but the wildlife viewing along it isn't: Ugandan kob and baboons are the only sure things. Best to get a ranger (US$20) from the park headquarters to lead you down other tracks.

Nature Walks

Rangers lead nature walks (per person US$30) in various places around the park, including Nyaburogo Gorge behind the headquarters (which has lots of primates and butterflies), along the shore of Lake Albert and – via a steep climb to great views atop the mountains – on the southeastern edge of the park.

Boat Trips

A **Lake Albert boat trip** will likely reveal hippo and crocodiles, but it's mostly undertaken by birdwatchers for the near-guaranteed shoebill stork sightings. Semliki Safari Lodge charges US$180 for a half day on the water. You could also arrange the trip with fishers in Ntoroko village for about half the price, in a boat about half the size.

🛏 Sleeping & Eating

Ntoroko has some basic guesthouses but they are not recommended and attract some shady characters; if you try them, don't leave any valuables behind in your room.

UWA Camp　　　　　CAMPGROUND $
(☑0772-911499; camping USh15,000, banda without bathroom USh40,000) The small UWA campsite at Ntoroko is on the shores of Lake Albert, meaning you often have hippos joining you in the evening. There are three *bandas* without bathrooms and the canteen can cook you meals.

Semliki Safari Lodge　　　　LODGE $$$
(☑0414-251182; www.wildplacesafrica.com; s/d incl full board & activities US$455/700; 🗑🐾) One of the first luxury lodges in Uganda, here there are eight luxury tents set under thatched *bandas,* all with sumptuous Persian carpets and four-poster beds. While it's well overpriced for what you get, the prices include all food, alcohol and park activities.

ℹ Getting There & Away

AIR

Semliki Safari Lodge can arrange flights (one-way US$270, return US$450) from Entebbe airport.

CAR

From Fort Portal, head west toward Bundibugyo and then fork right at Karugutu, 27km from Fort Portal; the headquarters is 3km further on. A car can handle travel inside the reserve, but ask about conditions between Fort Portal and Karugutu as the road can be quite poor.

MINIBUS & TRUCK

Connecting Fort Portal to Ntoroko (USh12,000, three hours), minibuses and trucks can drop you at the park headquarters. You could also get one of the more frequent Bundibugyo-bound vehicles and get off at Karugutu (USh6000, 1½ hours), to continue on from there.

Kasese

POP 71,700

The long-closed Kilembe Copper Mines once brought great prosperity to this drab, dusty town, and the now-defunct train line from Kampala used to deposit a steady stream of visitors here. But these days Kasese seems to have passed its use-by date and the only reason travellers come here is to organise a trip to the Rwenzori Mountains.

Nearby Kilembe, 12km away in the foothills of the Rwenzoris, is an interesting town to walk through with old mining equipment and company housing.

🛏 Sleeping & Eating

There are some fairly well-stocked supermarkets for those heading up to the mountains, including **Titi's** (Rwenzori Rd), **ASWT** (Margarita St) and **City Top** (Rwenzori Rd).

White House Hotel   GUESTHOUSE $
(☑0782-536263; whitehse_hotel@yahoo.co.uk; 46 Henry Bwambale Rd; r USh40,000, s/d without bathroom USh21,000/35,000; @⊛) A mix of cleanliness and good prices makes White House one of Kasese's most popular budget options. The garden restaurant next door is the best in town for a feed and cold beer (mains from USh15,000).

Hotel Margherita   HOTEL $$
(☑0483-444015; www.hotel-margherita.com; s/d/ ste/apt from US$70/95/140/190; ℗⊛@⊛) Though it's the fanciest option around, Hotel Margherita's long silent corridors and faded '70s decor make you feel like you're stepping onto the set of *The Shining*. It has a delightful setting looking out towards the Rwenzoris, and some rooms feature amazing views. It's located 3km out of town on the road up to Kilembe. It has an excellent restaurant too.

❶ Information

Barclays (cnr Margherita St & Rwenzori Rd)
Stanbic Bank (Stanley St)

❶ Getting There & Away

The quickest connection to Kampala (USh20,000, five hours) is the Link or Kalita bus via Fort Portal (USh4000, one hour).

Getting to Queen Elizabeth National Park is straightforward. Catch any Mbarara-bound vehicle to Katunguru (USh4000, one hour).

Rwenzori Mountains National Park

The legendary, mist-covered Rwenzori Mountains are presumed to be the Mountains of the Moon, described in AD 350 by Ptolemy, who proclaimed them to be the source of the Nile River. Because of both its beauty and biodiversity, Unesco named **Rwenzori Mountains National Park** (www. ugandawildlife.org/explore-our-parks/parks-by-name-a-z/rwenzori-mountains-national-park; adult/child US$35/5) a World Heritage Site. It's the tallest mountain range in Africa and several of the peaks are permanently covered by ice and glaciers. The three highest peaks in the range are Margherita (5109m), Alexandria (5083m) and Albert (5087m), all on Mt Stanley, the third highest mountain in Africa.

The mountain range, which isn't volcanic, stretches about 110km by 50km wide and is a haven for an extraordinary number of rare plants and animals, and new examples of both are still being discovered. Two mammals are endemic to the range, the Rwenzori climbing mouse and the Rwenzori red duiker, as are 19 of the 241 known bird species. There's thick tropical rainforest on the lower slopes transitioning to the bizarre Afroalpine moorland on higher reaches.

Trekking the Rwenzoris

Back in Uganda's heyday, the Rwenzoris were as popular with travellers as Mt Kilimanjaro and Mt Kenya, but this is definitely a more demanding expedition. The Rwenzoris (known locally as the 'Rain Maker') have a well-deserved reputation for being very wet and muddy, with trails that are often slippery and steep. There are treks available to suit all levels and needs, from one-day jaunts in the forest to 10-day treks with technical climbs. The six-day treks are the most popular.

Two companies offer trekking in the Rwenzoris: the popular **Rwenzori Trekking Services** (RTS; ☑in Kampala 0774-114499, in Kilembe 0774-199022; www.rwenzoritrekking.com), which looks after the Kilembe Trail, and the long-established, community-owned **Rwenzori Mountaineering Services** (RMS; ☑in Kampala 0784 308425, in Kasese 0751-684363, Nyakalengija Office 0784-327754; www.rwenzori mountaineeringservices.com; Rwenzori Rd, Kasese) based in Kasese, which arranges treks from Nyakalengija. The Muhoma Nature Trail is

TREKKING ROUTES IN THE RWENZORIS

The peaks are accessed via two routes: the **Kilembe Trail** and the long-standing **Central Circuit** that starts from Nyakalengija village. For those short on time there's also the two- to three-day **Muhoma Nature Trail**, a 28km circuit set up by Uganda Wildlife Authority (UWA) in 2012, that's a shortened version of the Central Circuit.

All prices include guides, porters, accommodation and rescue fees. However they don't include park fees, which are an additional US$35 per day.

From Kilembe

Kilembe Trail is a hit among trekkers. Organised through Rwenzori Trekking Services (p427), this company has both lifted the standards and breathed new energy into trekking in the Rwenzoris. While treks to the main peaks are further away compared with the Nyakalengija route, it receives glowing reviews for its professional guides, quality equipment and safety measures, as well as comfortable mountain huts along the route.

For groups of one to two people, prices per person start at US$40 for one-day treks, US$190 for two days, US$330 for three days, US$470 for four days, US$610 for five days, US$790 for six days and US$1028 for nine-day treks to Margherita Peak. Prices include guides, porters, equipment, food and accommodation, but sleeping bags, waterproof items and bags are extra.

A range of tailor-made treks are offered, from technical climbs to leisurely strolls in the forested foothills. The most popular is the six-day trek to Weismann's Peak, which is at times steep and strenuous; there are no ropes or climbing equipment involved. During April to May and September to October, it's common to experience snowfalls.

TO WEISMANN'S PEAK: DAY 1

Starting from Rwenzori Trekkers Hostel in Kilembe, you'll pass scenic villages and coffee plantations en route to the trailhead. From here it's a relatively easy three-hour trek that takes you through untouched montane forest that's home to abundant birdlife. Continuing over several river crossings and ridge climbs, keep an eye and ear out for chimps, before you reach the bamboo forest that leads to the first overnight stop at Sine Camp (2596m).

DAY 2

Day 2 involves a four- to six-hour trek beginning in bamboo forest before hitting heather zones in a series of climbs and descents that lead through misty valleys looking out to Queen Elizabeth National Park, past moss-covered rocks, spongy grassy escarpments and giant heather trees draped in lichen. You'll spend the night at Mutinda Camp (3688m). The day also includes an acclimatisation hike up to magnificent Mutinda Lookout (3975m) for views of Weissman's Peak, often coverved in snow.

DAY 3

Prepare to get muddy as you trudge through boggy moorland, through Namusangi Valley with waterfalls and views of Mutinda Peak, and hit the alpine zone. It's a four- to six-hour trek ending at Bugata Camp (4062m) overlooking Lake Kopello and Weismann's Peak.

DAY 4

A five-hour trek through scenic Namusangi valley, with the reward of reaching the top of Weissman's Peak (sometimes requiring ropes in inclement weather). There's also the option of scaling Stella Peak (4620m) before returning to spend the night at Bugata Camp.

DAY 5

Your descent begins as you push down to Kiharo (3460m) or Samalira (3170m) past magnificent giant lobelia plants, giant groundsel, luxuriant grass and spongey moss for a memorable three- to four-hour trek.

DAY 6

The last day of the trek takes you down through rocky valleys with flowing streams, sections of bamboo and montane forest, arriving back at Kilembe midafternoon.

From Nyakalengija

The Central Circuit that starts from Nyakalengija village is arranged through Rwenzori Mountaineering Services (p427). Long-established RMS has received some negative feedback for using dodgy equipment and failing to maintain huts.

The standard six-day, five-night Central Circuit trek costs US$680 per person. It's US$780 if you want to summit Margherita Peak. Extra days cost US$120 and extra peaks are US$150. You can either arrange your own food or pay US$120 for RMS to buy it. Gas cookers can be hired for US$60, or you can hire a cook for US$20 per day. Prices do not include equipment, but they do have the following for hire at US$25 a pop: climbing boots, crampons, harnesses, ice-axes, ropes, rubber boots and sleeping bags.

The Central Trail loops back between the peaks of Mts Baker and Stanley.

DAY 1

Nyakalengija (1646m) to Nyabitaba Camp (2650m) is a fairly easy walk, taking about five hours. There are many primates and some forest elephants around.

DAY 2

The trail drops to cross the Bujuku River and then begins a long ascent on a rough, muddy path that eventually enters the amazing Afro-alpine zone just before arriving at John Mate Camp (3505m). At least seven hours, this section is the most difficult.

DAY 3

On this three- to five-hour trek you'll slog, often knee-deep, through Lower and Upper Bigo Bogs (there's a boardwalk on part of this path) before things dry out and you reach lovely Lake Bujuku, plopped between Mts Baker, Stanley and Speke. After more mud you reach Bujuku Camp (3962m), the base for climbing Mt Speke. There's usually time to check out the Irene Lakes or, if you want a more alpine experience, continue for three more difficult hours and sleep at Elena Camp (4541m), the primary starting point for ascending Mt Stanley.

DAY 4

The trail cuts through a profusion of giant groundsel before crossing Scott Elliot Pass (4372m), the highest point on the Central Circuit. There are great views of Margherita Peak and the Elena and Savoia glaciers. The circuit weaves though boulders at the foot of Mt Baker and passes the twin Kitandara lakes before reaching lakeside Kitandara Hut (4023m).

DAY 5

Begin with a long climb to Freshfield Pass (4282m) and then it's all downhill to the scenically set Guy Yeoman Hut (3505m). On the descent, you pass through a bog to the attractive Kabamba rock shelter and waterfall. It's at least five hours, but on this muddy, slippery stage it often takes longer.

DAY 6

The start of the trail descends very steeply and follows the Mubuku River down for five hours to Nyabitaba Hut. It's possible to spend the night here but by this point almost everyone is ready for a warm shower and a cold beer and continues the last two to three hours back to the bottom. Keep in mind that about an hour from Guy Yeoman Hut there's an unbridged river crossing, and when the river is high it can be dangerous. Your guides will surely want to get over it as fast as possible, but if you have any reservations about this, wait for the river level to fall.

UGANDA RWENZORI MOUNTAINS NATIONAL PARK

Rwenzori Mountains National Park

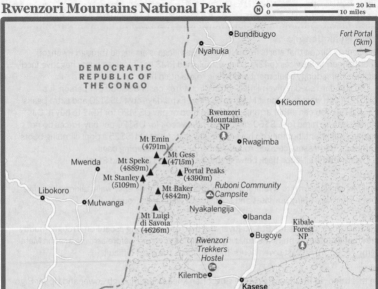

open to all, but Ruboni Community Campsite can assist with arranging guides, as can UWA.

The best times to trek are from late December to mid-March and from mid-June to mid-August, when there's *less* rain. Even at these times, the higher reaches are often enveloped in mist, though this generally clears for a short time each day. April and October are the wettest months.

Guides, who are compulsory, even if you've conquered the seven summits, are on perpetual standby so you can book in the morning and leave the same day.

Walking trails and huts are in pretty good shape, particularly on the Kilembe trail, where huts use polynum insulation to make life more comfortable. There are wooden pathways over the bogs and bridges over the larger rivers lessening the impact of walkers on the fragile environment.

Note trekkers should check their travel insurance policy carefully to ensure they're covered for adventure/mountaineering activities above 4000m.

Clothing & Equipment

The routes to the peaks on Mt Stanley require the use of ice-axes, ropes and crampons (depending on conditions you may have to rope in for Mts Baker and Speke), but you don't need mountaineering experience to reach the summits if your guide is experienced – the catch is that not all of them are. From all reports, the guides from Rwenzori Trekking Services (RTS) are the most reliable. No special equipment is required for a trek if you don't go onto the ice or snow (and if you do, this gear can be hired at the trailhead), but bring plenty of warm, waterproof clothing (temperatures often drop below zero). You'll also want a good sleeping bag. The most important item is a good, broken-in pair of trekking boots to get you over the slippery rock slabs, which can be quite treacherous at times. Rubber boots are also essential for the bogs – so ensure these are available. A small day pack is useful as your porters will travel at their own pace.

Before attempting a trek in the Rwenzoris get a copy of the *Guide to the Rwenzori* (2006) by Henry Osmaston, which covers routes, natural history and all other aspects of the mountains. A good companion to Osmaston's opus is *Rwenzori Map & Guide*, an excellent large-scale contour map by Andrew Wielochowski.

Safety

Be aware of the dangers of Acute Mountain Sickness (AMS, altitude sickness), in which symptoms can manifest above 3000m. In extreme cases it can be fatal. If exhibiting severe symptoms (headaches, hallucinations, and breathlessness) you'll need to descend immediately to the camp below. To reduce likelihood of AMS it's best to take the first day easy to acclimatise and not rush up. Drinking plenty of water is also essential.

🛏 Sleeping & Eating

Rwenzori Trekkers Hostel — HOSTEL $
(Rwenzori Backpackers; ☎0774-199022; www.backpackers.co.ug/rwenzoribackpack.html; Kyanjuki; camping USh15,000, dm USh25,000, s/d USh40,000/60,000; 🅿) Run by Rwenzori Trekking Services, this scenic and peaceful option is located in Kyanjuki just above Kilembe, 12km outside Kasese, a perfect starting point if you plan on tackling this side of the Rwenzori. Rooms are in restored miners' housing and are slightly run-down with peeling linoleum floors, but they're fine for the price.

The restaurant has a great trekking menu comprising T-bone steaks, Aussie meat pies, pizzas and a good vegetarian selection. They do some excellent work in the community, and also offer village walks and cultural performances.

Ruboni Community Campsite — HUT $
(☎0752-503445; www.rubonicamp.com; camping with/without tent US$5/15, r without bathroom per person US$20, banda per person US$25) This community-run place down the road from Nyakalengija is at the base of the hill just outside the park boundary, with an attractive setting and comfortable lodging. All profits go towards a health centre, tree-planting projects and more. It also offers guided walks into the hills outside the park, drumming lessons and traditional dance performances.

★Equator Snow Lodge — LODGE $$
(☎0414-258273; www.geolodges.com; s/d incl full board US$132/242) Conveniently located for the Central (and Mahoma) Trail, this luxury mountain lodge at the foot of the Rwenzoris has large cottages surrounded by plenty of forest and views from its porch. There's a heap of trekking opportunities in the immediate area, even if you're not keen on a hardcore mountaineering expedition. All up, excellent value.

ℹ Getting There & Away
Nyakalengija is 25km from Kasese, though minibuses only run as far as Ibanda (USh5000, one

ℹ RWENZORI MOUNTAINS NATIONAL PARK

Why Go
Trekking along Africa's tallest mountain range; ever-changing vegetation zones; snow-capped peaks.

When to Go
Year-round, but expect rain daily; late December to mid-March and mid-June to mid-August are less muddy.

Practicalities
Treks are booked at the park through Rwenzori Trekking Services (for the Kilembe Trail) and Rwenzori Mountaineering Services (for the Nyakalengija Trail). Kasese is best accessed either from Fort Portal or Queen Elizabeth National Park.

Budget Tips
You can only trek with a trekking company so keeping costs down is tricky, but packing your own equipment can save you money. Shorter treks require less of an outlay and still provide the Rwenzori experience; otherwise, hikes in Rwenzori's foothills don't require park permits.

hour). From here you can take a *boda-boda* to Nyakalengija (USh4000) or Ruboni Community Campsite (USh3500). Chartering a special-hire taxi from Kasese will set you back USh50,000.

For Kilembe (USh4000, 30 minutes), take one of the frequent shared-car taxis from near the Shell petrol station on Kilembe Rd. A special-hire taxi will cost around USh25,000 and *boda-boda* around USh7000.

Queen Elizabeth National Park

Covering 1978 sq km, scenic **Queen Elizabeth National Park** (☎0782-387805; www.queenelizabethnationalpark.com; adult/child US$40/20; ⏰6.30am-7pm, park gates 7am-7pm) is one of the most popular parks in Uganda. Few reserves in the world can boast such a high biodiversity rating. With landscape including savannah, bushland, wetlands and lush forests, the park is inhabited by 96 species of mammals, including healthy numbers of hippos, elephants, lions and leopards as well as chimps and hyenas. The remote

Queen Elizabeth National Park

Ishasha sector, in the far south of the park, is famous for its tree-climbing lions. There's also an amazing 611 bird species here; more than found in all of Great Britain.

Back in the 1970s, with its great herds of elephants, buffaloes, kob, waterbucks, hippos and topis, Queen Elizabeth was one of the premier safari parks in Africa. But during the troubled 1980s, Ugandan and Tanzanian troops (which occupied the country after Amin's demise) did their ivory-grabbing, trophy-hunting best. Thankfully, animal populations are recovering.

◉ Sights & Activities

Wildlife Drives

Most of the wildlife-viewing traffic is in the northeast of the park in Kasenyi, which offers the best chance to see lions, as well as elephants, waterbucks and kob. It's also one of the most scenic sections of any park in Uganda, particularly in the morning when the savannah landscape shines golden and is dotted with cactuslike candelabra trees. Night wildlife drives (per vehicle US$100, including guide) are also available.

There's also a small network of trails between Mweya Peninsula and Katunguru

Queen Elizabeth National Park

gate that usually reveal waterbucks and kob, elephants and, occasionally, leopards.

As well as being famous for its tree-climbing lions, Ishasha, in the south of the Queen Elizabeth National Park, is the only place to see topis and sitatungas.

You can get just about everywhere by car if it isn't raining, though having a 4WD is a good idea in Ishasha year-round. Taking a UWA ranger-guide (US$20) along for your drive is always a good idea, but more so in Ishasha than anywhere else because they know every fig tree in the area – the lions' preferred perches.

Kazinga Channel Boat Trip

Almost every visitor takes a two-hour launch trip (US$30) up the Kazinga Channel to see the thousands of hippos and pink-backed pelicans, plus plenty of crocodiles, buffaloes and fish eagles. With a little luck, it's also possible to catch sight of one of the elephant herds and – very occasionally – see a lion or a leopard. If numbers are low you may have to chip in to cover the boat's minimum costs. The boat docks below Mweya Safari Lodge, but you buy tickets at the UWA visitor centre (p437) next door. Trips departs at 9am, 11am, 3pm and 5pm.

Chimpanzee Tracking

In the eastern region of the park in the 100m-deep **Kyambura (Chambura) Gorge**, you can go chimpanzee tracking (per person US$50), with walks lasting from two to four hours and departing at 8am and 2pm. You've got a semireasonable chance of finding the habituated troop, but visits are often unfruitful; mornings are probably the best bet. The gorge is a beautiful scar of green cutting through the savannah, and from the viewing platform you can sometimes see primates, including chimps, frolicking in the treetops below.

Bookings can be made at the visitor centre (p437), or you can just show up and hope there are spots available. Children under 15 years aren't permitted.

ⓘ QUEEN ELIZABETH NATIONAL PARK

Why Go

Tree-climbing lions, elephants, leopards, scenic savannah landscapes, boat rides along Kazinga Channel.

When to Go

Year-round, but the dry seasons of December to March and May to August is best.

Practicalities

Park gates are open from 7am to 7pm. Katunguru is the main village in the park's centre, which is linked by buses from Kampala and Kasese. Cars for safari drives can be rented from here too.

Budget Tips

One of the most accessible parks by public transport; with some negotiation, safari vehicles can be arranged in Katunguru. Budget accommodation is available in most sectors of the park.

Nature Walks

Guided nature walks are available (US$30 per person), but aren't overly popular. Trips on the forest trails here are taken mostly by birdwatchers, though there are nine species of primate around. Down at Ishasha, hippo encounters are pretty likely on short walks along the river and, if you're there early in the morning, there's a chance of spotting a giant forest hog. You won't see much on a walk at Mweya that you can't see just hanging around on your own.

Wildlife Research Tours

A new initiative introduced by UWA involves a range of 'experiential tourism' activities to assure closer wildlife encounters. Most popular is **lion tracking** (using a combo of locator devices and radio collars; including vehicle US$150) in vehicles provided by UWA that head off track; it also yields good leopard sightings too. Other activities include mongoose tracking (US$30), and assisting with the hippo census and bird species counts.

Equator

Equator   LANDMARK

The equator crosses the northern sector of the park near Kasenyi and is marked with a circular monument on either side of the road, which is predictably popular with passerbys stopping for that quintessential holiday snap.

🛞 Tours

All tour operators can put together a short safari to Queen Elizabeth National Park. Kampala-based Great Lakes Safaris (p475) has three-day trips (from US$290 per person with six people) departing every Wednesday and Friday, while Red Chilli Hideaway (p476) has four-day safaris from US$400 per person.

Given there are numerous communities living within the park, there are plenty of worthwhile cultural tours in the area.

Salt Mine   CULTURAL TOUR

(☑ 0753-393450; US$10) The interesting village of **Katwe** on the north shore of Lake Edward, 4km west of Main gate (Kabatoro gate), is famous for its salt industry. Salt mining on the crater lake behind the village dates back to at least the 15th century, and today some 3000 people still use the same traditional methods. Women pull salt from evaporation ponds when it's dry enough (generally December to March and July to September) while men dig rock salt year-

round. Tours are booked at the Katwe Tourism Information Centre on the west side of the village, across from a defunct salt factory.

Leopard Village   CULTURAL TOUR

(☑ 0791-492245; www.uganda-carnivores.org/leopard-village; Muhokya) Visit Leopard Village, one of the communities within Queen Elizabeth National Park, to get insight into how locals coexist with wildlife, among other cultural activities.

Kikorongo Women Community   CULTURAL TOUR

(☑ 0757-548713; kikorongowomen@gmail.com) Visit Kikorongo Women Community for performances and craft demonstrations.

🛏 Sleeping & Eating

🛏 Mweya Peninsula & Around

The best variety of places to stay is on the Mweya Peninsula. A lot of wildlife roams through here, so you genuinely need to be careful at night, especially if you're walking to/from the Mweya campsite.

UWA Guesthouses & Cottages   LODGES, COTTAGES $

(Mweya; r USh80,000, s/d without bathroom USh20,000/40,000, cottages USh250,000-300,000) In an effort to provide more affordable accommodation in Queen Elizabeth National Park, UWA has acquired a range of properties along Mweya. The pick are the **Lower Cottages**, basic, comfortable-sized rooms in close proximity to the popular Tembo Canteen. Take care walking in the evening as plenty of wild animals graze here. The laid-back **Mweya Hostel** across from the information centre is also managed by UWA and is undergoing refurbishment. Self-caterers, families and groups can opt for one of the **cottages** equipped with fridge and cooking facilities, which can sleep six to eight people.

UWA Campgrounds   CAMPGROUND $

(camping USh15,000) Although the facilities are rustic, the setting is superb, making Mweya a great place to pitch a tent. The main Mweya Campsite 3 has little shade but is set away from the development on the peninsula and looks out over the channel. Much more isolated are Campsites 1 and 2, located 3.5km and 4.5km east of the visitor centre respectively. They have nothing but pit toilets and good channel views, especially Campsite 2.

Expect a lot of animal sightings and sounds; exercise extreme caution after dark. Book all camping at the visitor centre (p437) in Mweya before setting up your tent.

★**Mweya Safari Lodge** LODGE $$$
(☑ 0312-260260; www.mweyalodge.com; s/d incl full board from US$220/342; ✷ @ 🛜 🛋) Queen Elizabeth's iconic, classic safari lodge has a commanding location with excellent views over Lake Edward and the Kazinga Channel – full of hippos and buffaloes. Set in a resort-like complex, it offers everything from hotel-style rooms to luxury tents and plush cottages, most with views of the water. Come sunset, the terrace overlooking the water is the place to be with a cold drink.

Even if you're not staying here it's worth popping in for a meal (mains from USh20,000) or a G&T at the atmospheric bar with chesterfield couches, fireplace and hunting relics from yesteryear (including a giant set of tusks).

Tembo Canteen INTERNATIONAL $
(meals USh10,000-18,000; ⊘ 6.30am-11pm) A wonderful safari-style canteen, Tembo buzzes with campers, UWA staff, guides and drivers, all here for cheap, tasty food and cold beer. Head outdoors to its tables with epic lake views.

Simba Canteen SELF-CATERING
(⊘ 8am-noon & 5-8pm Tue-Sun) Selling basic groceries, Simba store is handy for campers, and doubles as a lively bar popular with hotel and UWA workers.

🛏 Katunguru & Around

Bush Lodge LODGE $
(☑ 0312-294894; www.naturelodges.biz/the-bush-lodge; lazy camping s/d US$30/40, s/d US$100/150) One of the park's most popular budget choices, this bush camp sits on the banks of Kazinga Channel where elephants and hippos often hang out. There's a choice between basic tents with beds (and power points), or pricier safari-tent rooms with outdoor stone bathrooms. At dinner, tables are brought around the campfire to provide some atmosphere.

Rwenzori Salaama Hotel & Lodging LODGE $
(☑ 0782-927350; s/d USh30,000/50,000, s without bathroom USh10,000) If you get stuck in Katunguru, this basic lodge has the cheapest and cleanest rooms and a decent attached restaurant.

🛏 Kichwamba Escarpment & Around

This ridgetop spot along the Kasese–Mbarara highway, outside the park's eastern boundary, has some of the best views in Uganda. It looks over the Maramagambo Forest and a wide sweep of savannah out to Lake Edward and the Rwenzori Mountains. It's a 15-minute drive to chimp tracking at Kyambura (Chambura) Gorge and 45 minutes to wildlife drives at Kasenyi. There are plenty of small-scale coffee plantations in the area.

Kingfisher Lodge Kichwamba LODGE $$
(☑ 0774-159579; www.kingfisher-uganda.net; s/d incl half board US$110/205; 🅿 @ 🛜 🛋) This little compound of whitewashed and thatched-roof towers is a tad dated but it's well-priced and has memorable Queen Elizabeth vistas. Rooms are smallish but nice and most come with their own porches.

★**Katara Lodge** LODGE $$$
(☑ 0773-011648; www.kataralodge.com; s/d incl full board US$236/354; @ 🛜 🛋) A lodge worth splashing out for, with five wood, thatch and canvas cottages made for taking in the stunning savannah views: the sides roll up, the beds roll out to the deck if you want to sleep under the stars and even the clawfoot tubs look out over the valley. Otherwise you can enjoy the outlooks from the luxurious pool and outdoor sun beds.

★**Kyambura Game Lodge** LODGE $$$
(☑ 0414-322789; www.kyamburalodge.com; Kyambura; s/d US$169/286; 🛜 🛋) One of Queen Elizabeth's best-value luxury lodges, Kyambura is a wonderful choice for those looking to slow things right down. Large rooms strike the perfect balance between deluxe and safari, with balconies made from scavenged wood and furnished with plush sofas looking over stunning savannah views. The swimming pool is lovely with hammocks and lounges on the deck – perfect for a sundowner.

The only downside is that you can see traffic passing through the park in the distance. Low-season rates offer healthy discounts.

Jacana Safari Lodge LODGE $$$
(☑ 0414-258273; www.geolodgesafrica.com; s/d incl full board US$210/330; 🛜 🛋) Jacana's large and luxurious cottages sit widely spaced in

ISHASHA TREE-CLIMBING LIONS

Somewhat off the beaten track in the far southern sector of the park, Ishasha is famous for its population of tree-climbing lions. It's one of the few places in Africa where lions are known to hang out in trees (you'll find them in Kidepo National Park too) and are often found lazing on the sprawling limbs of fig trees during the heat of the day. Generally the best time to spot them is outside the usual safari drive times (11am to 5pm, basically when they're not hunting). If it's wet, the lions generally won't climb.

Maramagambo forest and all look out over Lake Nyamusingiri. Relax at the pool, in the sauna or on the lake with a kayak, and then dine lakeside or on a pontoon boat. Its isolation comes at the cost of being a long way from the best wildlife-drive locales.

Kasenyi

A few new lodges have sprung up near Lake Bunyampaka, which, though a bit desolate, is perfect for those wanting to hear wild animals at night.

Kasenyi Wild Game Lodge   LODGE $$
(☏0392-847783; www.kasenyigamelodges.com; Kasenyi; s/d incl full board US$80/180) Given its location close to the prime wildlife-viewing area, these well-spaced thatched *bandas* are top value. All have porches looking out to the salt lake, a popular stop on safari drives.

Kasenyi Safari Camp   LODGE $$$
(☏0791-992038; www.kasenyisafaricamp.com; Kasenyi; cottages incl full board US$425; 🛜🖥) This luxury lodge, still undergoing construction, promises to be a gem. It's run by an enthusiastic American-Ugandan, with classic thatched tented-cottages spread out in a location good for wildlife encounters. A swimming pool is also on the cards.

Kikorongo

Simba Safari Camp   LODGE $
(☏0704-942646; www.ugandalodges.com/simba; Bwera Rd; camping US$8, dm US$26, s/d US$72/96; 🛜) Located just outside the northern sector of the park, Simba remains one of the best budget camps and is popular with many of the tour groups. Rooms are spotless with canopy beds and stone-floor showers. It has a social restaurant-bar and convenient location for wildlife drives in Kasenyi. To get here by public transport, take any bus from Kampala heading to Bwera and ask to be dropped off at Simba.

Ishasha

UWA Campsite & Bandas   CAMPGROUND $
(☏0752-680463; Ishasha; camping USh15,000, banda without bathroom USh40,000) A blissfully remote set-up with two basic *bandas* and a canteen serving local dishes (USh10,000). There are also two lovely campsites on the Ishasha River, which forms the border with the DRC. Be vigilant moving on foot at night as there's an abundance of wildlife present. The site shares a location with an army camp (being on the border and all), so most uniforms here aren't UWA officers.

★ **@The River**   LODGE $$
(☏0787-005888; www.attheriverishasha.com; incl full board camping US$35, tented camp without bathroom per person US$60, s/d US$95/190; 🖥) Providing a taste of what you get at the luxury camps, @The River offers up the same kind of atmosphere and set-up at very affordable rates. It has a laid-back camp atmosphere, with tasteful cottages, a plunge pool, riverside beach and open-air showers.

Ishasha Wilderness Camp   LODGE $$$
(☏0414-321479; www.ugandaexclusivecamps.com/ishasha-wilderness-camp; s/d incl full board US$475/720; 🌐) At these prices this tented camp is probably not as luxurious as it should be; rather, it's all about the location right on the Ntungwe River. It's one of the few lodges inside the park's boundaries. Rates drop during low season (April, May and November).

Enjojo Lodge   LODGE $$$
(☏0772-067070; www.facebook.com/Enjojolodge; 🖥) Currently under construction this Belgian resort is one to look out for. Its luxury tents and traditional *bandas* are surrounded by primeval palms, an attractive waterhole and swimming pool.

Kihihi

For affordable accommodation you can stay in Kihihi, 16km from Ishasha gate – but you'll miss out on the whole wildlife experience. Kihihi can make a handy base for those with a gorilla permit for Buhoma in Bwindi, 40km south. There's a Stanbic Bank with ATM.

Suba Motel GUESTHOUSE $
(☑ 0392-905978; www.subamotel.com; Kihihi; s/d US$25/35) A clean, cheap and straightforward hotel with rooms arranged around a courtyard, and a good little restaurant that makes a useful pit stop for those passing through.

Savannah Resort Hotel HOTEL $$
(☑ 0777-076086; www.savannahresorthotel.com; Kihihi; s/d/tr US$120/165/240; ☏ ☀) Located 4km outside Kihihi, a 30-minute drive from Ishasha, this pleasant hotel has a mix of comfortable rooms and *bandas* in a peaceful location surrounded by a golf course. It also has a good restaurant serving international and African dishes.

ℹ Information

Mweya Visitor Information Centre (Mweya Peninsula; ☉ 6.30am-6.30pm) This modern visitor information centre at Mweya has good displays on the park, as well as maps, books and info on activities and UWA's accommodation and campgrounds.

Queens Pavilion (☉ 8am-6pm; ☏) Near the equator monument, this stopover point has tourist info, a cafe with wi-fi and views over Lake George. It also sells maps and souvenirs.

ℹ Getting There & Away

CAR

The majority of people visit the park either as part of an organised tour or by renting their own car. If you're driving, take care of animals crossing the road along the high-speed tarmac section, particularly at night. Petrol is available at Mweya, but it's pricier than in towns.

Kazinga Channel Safari (☑ 0772-608614; www.kc-safari.webs.com) offers competitive prices for car hire from US$50 per day.

PUBLIC TRANSPORT

There are several direct buses to Katunguru (USh25,000, seven hours) from Kampala's main bus park including Kalita, Link and Poko which all go via Mbarara en route to Kasese (USh4000, one hour). Once in the park, you can either hitch or arrange a special-hire taxi for wildlife drives in Katunguru.

The road from Katunguru to the village of Ishasha cuts through the park and passes Ishasha gate. Although no park entry fees are needed to travel this road, you'll be fined US$150 if you're caught venturing off it and into the park. The Ishasha sector is 100km from Mweya down a pretty good road (due to oil exploration in the area) in the far south of the park.

From Ishasha, you can head south for Butogota and Bwindi Impenetrable National Park, reaching them in about two hours during the dry season.

Bwindi Impenetrable National Park

Home to almost half of the world's surviving mountain gorillas, the World Heritage-listed **Bwindi Impenetrable National Park** (☑ 0486-424121; adult/child US$40/25; ☉ park office 7.45am-5pm) is one of East Africa's most famous national parks. Set over 331 sq km of improbably steep mountain rainforest, the park is home to an estimated 360 gorillas: undoubtedly Uganda's biggest tourist drawcard.

The Impenetrable Forest, as it's also known, is one of Africa's most ancient habitats, since it thrived right through the last Ice Age (12,000 to 18,000 years ago) when most of Africa's other forests disappeared. In conjunction with the altitude span (1160m to 2607m) this antiquity has produced an incredible diversity of flora and fauna, even by normal rainforest standards. And we do mean rainforest; up to 2.5m of rain falls here annually.

It contains 120 species of mammal – more than any of Uganda's other national parks – though sightings are less common due to the dense forest. Lucky visitors might see forest elephants, 11 species of primate (including chimpanzees and L'Hoest's monkeys), duikers, bushbucks, African golden cats and the rare giant forest hog, as well as a host of bird and insect species. For birdwatchers it's one of the most exciting destinations in the country, with almost 360 species, including 23 of the 24 endemic to the Albertine Rift and several endangered species, such as the African green broadbill. With a good guide, sighting daily totals of over 150 species is possible. On the greener side of the aisle, Bwindi harbours eight endemic plants.

◉ Sights & Activities

Gorilla Tracking

A genuine once-in-a-lifetime experience, hanging out with mountain gorillas is one of the most thrilling wildlife encounters in the world, and Bwindi Impenetrable National Park is one of the best places to see them. There are theoretically 96 daily permits available to track gorillas in Bwindi. Permits cost US$600 (including park entry) and are booked through the UWA office (p474) in Kampala. Note you must be over 15 years of age to track the gorillas.

Trips leave from the park office nearest the group you'll be tracking at 8.30am daily, but you should report to park headquarters by 7.45am. For those who are based in Kisoro or Kabale and plan on leaving early in the morning, be mindful that during rainy season there are potential delays, such as landslides or being bogged.

Once you join a tracking group, the chances of finding the gorillas are almost guaranteed. But, as the terrain in Bwindi Impenetrable National Park is mountainous and heavily forested, if the gorillas are a fair distance away it can be quite a challenge to get close. The path is often steep and slippery, and it can take anywhere from 30 minutes to five hours to reach them, so you'll need to be in reasonable enough shape. If you think you're going to struggle it's strongly advised you hire a porter who can lend a hand getting up and down the hill. Walking sticks are also a very good idea and are provided by UWA.

ℹ BWINDI IMPENETRABLE NATIONAL PARK

Why Go
Tracking mountain gorillas, forest walks with Twa people, birdwatching.

When to Go
December to March and June to September have the least rain, but permits are easier to obtain at other times.

Practicalities
The rainy season often brings delays due to landslides, so be sure to leave enough time to get there; ideally it's best to stay close to the region in which you'll be tracking gorillas.

Budget Tips
During April, May and November gorilla permits are US$350. Budget accommodation is available; public transport is possible, but inconvenient and time-consuming.

Forest Walks

Even if you can't afford gorilla tracking, Bwindi is a rewarding park to visit just for a chance to explore the lush virgin rainforest. Several three- to four-hour nature walks penetrate the Impenetrable Forest around Buhoma. The walks begin at 9am and 2.15pm and cost US$10.

The **Waterfall Trail** includes, surprise, surprise, a 33m waterfall on the Munyaga River, but just as worthwhile is the magnificently rich forest it passes through. This is the best trail for spotting both orchids and primates. Weather permitting, the **Muzabijiro Loop Trail** and **Rushura Hill Trail** offer excellent views south to the Virunga volcanoes and the Western Rift Valley in the DRC. The latter, which is a more difficult climb, also serves up views of Lake Edward and, on an exceptionally clear day, the Rwenzoris.

A longer but much easier trek is along the **River Ivi Trail**, which follows the path of a planned-but-never-built road between Buhoma and Nkuringo. It's 14km through the forest and then another 6km uphill along a road to Nkuringo village; you might be able to hitch this last part.

☞ Tours

Batwa Experience   CULTURAL TOUR
(☎ 0392-888700; www.batwaexperience.com; 1/5hr US$30/80) The 'Batwa Experience' helps preserve the culture of the Twa (Batwa) people – who were displaced from their forest habitat when Bwindi became a national park – by allowing you to both meet the Twa and see how they lived in the forest. The five-hour tours include witnessing a mock hunting party with bow and arrows, stories from Twa legend, and song and dance – an intense and often emotional experience.

Full-day prices also include a traditional meal. All proceeds go to helping Twa communities in the region.

Bwindi Community Hospital   TOUR
(☎ 0392-880242; www.bwindihospital.com; Buhoma; donations appreciated; ⊙8am-6pm) For something a bit different, head to this well-run hospital for a behind-the-scenes look into the workings of a rural African hospital. You'll tour its various wards (while assuring patient privacy) and be eduated on health issues faced by locals. Donations are appreciated. Check online for volunteering options. It's around 7km from Buhoma's trailhead.

ⓘ BWINDI GORILLAS & PERMITS

Demand for gorilla permits exceeds supply for most of the year in Bwindi. During the 'low seasons' of April to May and October to November (the rainiest months), you may be able to confirm a space a week or two in advance of your trip. During the rest of the year it's not unheard of for permits to be booked up months in advance. If nothing is available that fits your schedule, check at the backpacker places in Kampala and Jinja, where the safari companies advertise excess permits they want to sell. It's no problem to buy these, even when someone else's name is on them. Cancellations and no-shows are rare, but you can get on the list at the park office: it's first-come, first-served. If you haven't prearranged a gorilla permit, this should be your number one priority upon arrival in Kampala.

At the time of research Uganda Wildlife Authority (UWA) were offering discount permits during the low season months of April, May and November for US$350 instead of the usual US$600.

Of the 28 gorilla groups living in Bwindi Impenetrable National Park, 12 have been habituated to be visited by tourists.

Buhoma

Nestled in the northwest corner of the park, Buhoma has three groups of gorillas: Rushegura (13 members), Mubare (11) and Habinyanza (17). As the first section of the park to open for gorilla tracking, Buhoma is by far the most developed in terms of tourist infrastructure, and with the most permits available it's also the most popular. Gorillas are probably the most accessible here too, sometimes as little as a 30-minute trek away.

Ruhija

In the northeast of the park, Ruhija has three groups: Bitukura (14 members), Oruzogo (14) and Kyaguriri (19). There's a good range of accommodation sprouting up here but otherwise it's also accessible from Kabale or Buhoma, a two-hour drive in either direction.

Nkuringo

While there's only one group in Nkuringo, a family of 11 that includes two silverbacks, it's regarded as one of the most entertaining and relaxed of the gorilla groups. Nkuringo is spectacularly set in the southwest of the park on a ridge opposite the wall of green that is Bwindi. From various spots you can spy Lake Edward, the Rwenzoris, all of the Virungas and even Nyiragongo Volcano by Goma, the DRC.

Rushaga

Located in the southeast of the park, Rushaga has 40 permits available for its five groups including Nshongi (family of eight gorillas, the most popular), Mishaya (eight gorillas), Kahungye (Bwindi's largest habituated group with 26 members), Busingye (nine gorillas) and Bweza (seven members). This lovely thick tract of forest is also home to elephants.

Buhoma Village Tourist Walk WALKING TOUR
(www.buhomacommunity.com; per person US$15; ⊙9am & 2pm) Offered by the Buhoma Community Rest Camp, these popular three- to four-hour walks head to the surrounding countryside to visit local healers, watch a Twa song-and-dance show, and witness the none-too-appetising production of banana wine and gin (the bananas are mashed by foot).

Ride 4 A Woman CYCLING TOUR
(☑0785-999112; www.ride4awoman.org; Buhoma; bicycle rental from US$25, tours from US$25) 🍃 This NGO runs guided mountain-bike tours through the forest or village and rents out bikes if you want to go exploring yourself. It also has a clothing and craft store near Buhoma Hospital, where it offers sewing classes from USh30,000. All proceeds go to helping women in the community.

Nyundo Community Eco-Trails WALKING TOUR
(☑0772-930304; www.pearlsofuganda.org; per person USh20,000) Based at Buhoma, this group offers a wide variety of village walks including several with a farming focus and others that visit caves and waterfalls. Traditional dances can also be arranged.

🛏 Sleeping & Eating

🛏 Buhoma

Given that there are only 24 gorilla permits per day available at Buhoma, there are a lot of lodges competing for your business.

★ Buhoma Community Rest Camp
LODGE $

(☎ 0772-384965; www.buhomacommunity.com; camping US$10, dm US$20, r with/without bathroom US$60/50) Next door to the park headquarters, this camp is Bwindi's most popular budget option with a stunning location looking directly out to the forest. *Bandas* and safari tents are spaced out on a hill heading down the valley, and the best are at the bottom, which puts you right at the jungle; gorillas sometimes pass by the clearing here.

Breakfast is US$10 and a set dinner and lunch is US$17. Some of the profits go towards funding community-development projects.

Gorilla Conservation Camp
BANDAS $

(☎ 0782-509151; www.ctph.org; Buhoma; camping US$10, s/d incl full board US$55/100; ☎) 🦋 A fantastic new budget camp set up by the community, here you get sweeping views of Bwindi from its bucolic hilltop location above Buhoma. Accommodation comprises raised self-contained safari tents with porches. All proceeds go to gorilla conservation and community projects.

Bwindi View Bandas
BACKPACKERS $

(☎ 0772-399224; www.gorilladestination.com; camping US$10, s/d US$50/80) Up on the ridge directly across from the park entrance, this friendly and affordable community-run lodge offers fairly generic-style rooms with slight glimpses of the forest.

Jungle View Lodge
GUESTHOUSE $

(☎ 0786-556140; s/d without bathroom USh40,000/60,000) Strictly for penny pinchers, this guesthouse has bare-bones rooms devoid of the atmosphere you'd hope for when visiting a national park.

Bwindi Lodge
LODGE $$$

(☎ 0414-346464; www.volcanoessafaris.com/lodges/bwindi-lodge; s/d incl full board & activities US$400/660; ☎) An ultraluxurious offering by Volcanoes hotel group, Bwindi Lodge has superb thatched, farm-style cottages that open up to thick jungle.

Sanctuary Gorilla Forest Camp
LODGE $$$

(www.sanctuaryretreats.com/uganda-camps-gorilla-forest; Buhoma; s/d incl full board US$600/1200; ☎) The most atmospheric of Bwindi's luxury lodges, this one is tucked within the park's boundaries. Its sumptuous safari tents have mahogany floorboards with private porches and are set on the forest's misty slopes. Its campfire on the lawn is tailor-made for gorilla debriefing.

Buhoma Lodge
LODGE $$$

(☎ 0414-321479; http://ugandaexclusivecamps.com/buhoma-lodge; s/d incl full board US$445/660) One of the few lodges inside the park, Buhoma Lodge is perfect for those wanting to make their 'gorilla experience' that bit more memorable. Spacious rooms are in stilted cottages where rustic touches are mixed with polished-wood floors and plenty of natural light. Each has a private porch with fantastic views of the dense forest, and a stone bathtub with seats.

🛏 Nkuringo

Once the domain of luxury clients, the good news for budget travellers is that several budget options have recently opened up in Nkuringo. It's a wonderfully scenic place, and it's worthing staying overnight to soak up the atmosphere before your trek.

Bwindi Backpackers
LODGE $

(☎ 0772-661854; www.bwindibackpackerslodge.com; camping US$15, dm US$20, s/d US$50/90, s/d without bathroom US$35/60; ☎) If there's one thing Nkuringo needed, it was affordable lodging. Thankfully Bwindi Backpackers stepped up with this lovely offering. Sure it has its imperfections, and rooms are basic, but all is forgiven with those full-frontal forest views! It's well located for both Nkuringo and Rushaga permit holders.

Albertine Gorilla Campsite
GUESTHOUSE $

(☎ 0782-644432; Nkuringo; camping US$7, r without bathroom USh40,000) Conveniently located at Nkuringo's UWA trailhead, this community-run guesthouse offers a great deal for budget travellers with basic, homely rooms. Also offers community walks and activities.

★ Nkuringo Gorilla Campsite
LODGE $$$

(☎ 0754-805580; www.gorillacamp.com; Nkuringo; incl full board lazy camping s/d US$82/143, s/d without bathroom US$200/250, cottages s/d US$300/418; ☎) A wonderful set-up with views looking out to the misty Virungas, the Nkuringo Gorilla Campsite is one of the best places to stay in Bwindi. Comfortable rooms and cottages mix safari-chic with boutique touches, while lazy camping provides a more cost-effective option. Little touches such as turn-over service and hot-water bottles go a long way.

The food is also good, served in the restaurant lit by paraffin lanterns with a bucket of glowing coals provided for warmth. It's a short walk from the trailhead.

Clouds Lodge `LODGE $$$`
(☎ 0414-251182; www.wildplacesafrica.com; s/d incl full board US$795/1220; @) No, those prices aren't a typo. Built as a project between the Uganda Safari Company, African Wildlife Foundation, International Gorilla Conservation Programme and the local community, this lodge offers a subtle sort of luxury, but if you can afford it, you'll enjoy it. The large stone cottages have big windows, original art and double-sided fireplaces, plus you get a butler during your stay. Rates include alcohol. Check the website for low-season discounts.

🛏 Rushaga

Rushaga is fast developing as one of Bwindi's finest places to stay with its affordable lodges surrounded by delightful nature. The rural township of Rubuguri also has an increasing number of budget lodges.

Nshongi Camp `BANDAS $`
(☎ 0774-231913; www.nshongicamp.altervista.org; Rushaga; camping US$5, banda incl full board s/d US$48/76) Right on the forest's edge, this delightful camp has simple mud-brick *bandas* scattered among its lovely garden. Friendly owner Silver is a local, and is very knowledgeable about the area. It's only a short walk up to the trailhead. There's no generator here, so be sure your camera batteries are fully charged.

Gorilla Valley Lodge `LODGE $$`
(☎ 0778-531524; www.naturelodges.biz/gorilla-valley-lodge; Rushaga; s/d US$95/106) Gorilla Valley delivers the complete Bwindi experience: spectacular forest views, atmospheric bar, and well-priced rooms with a rustic simplicity that one imagines would be to Dian Fossey's liking.

Nshongi Gorilla Resort `LODGE $$`
(☎ 0785-003091; www.nshongigorillaresort.com; Rubuguri; s/d incl full board US$70/140) Located in the small town of Rubugiri, this lodge has wonderful thatched cottages with attractive African decor. The rooms in the main building are much less appealing, however.

Gorilla Safari Lodge `LODGE $$$`
(☎ 0414-345742; www.gorillasafarilodge.com; Rushaga; s/d incl full board from US$230/360) Blending luxury with nature, this solar-powered lodge's cottages have great views, clawfoot baths and their own fireplaces. It's a five-minute walk from the trailhead. Discounts available.

🛏 Ruhija

Ruhija has a good mix of atmospheric, comfortable lodges and laid-back community camps, so there should no longer be the need for an early morning drive or day trip from Buhoma to visit these gorillas.

★ Ruhija Community Rest Camp `GUESTHOUSE $`
(☎ 0771-846635; camping US$10, r US$25-35, log cabin US$65) 🖋 Proving you don't need to spend a fortune for a view, this ultrarelaxed camp has the entire forest at its feet – best enjoyed from wicker chairs on your porch. The common area has a hostel vibe with fireplace, bar and board games. Proceeds go to water projects and a local orphanage. It also offers community walks.

Ruhija Gorilla Friends Resort & Campsite `GUESTHOUSE $`
(☎ 0754-323546; bitarihorobert@gmail.com; Ruhija; camping with/without tent US$10/15, s without bathroom US$20, tented r per person US$25, cottage s/d US$45/90) 🖋 One of Bwindi's best-value options for budget travellers, here you can pitch a tent, use one of theirs, go for a room or best of all – the tented rooms with great views. Proceeds go to the community.

Bakiga Lodge `LODGE $$`
(☎ 0774-518421; www.bakigalodge.com; Ruhija; s/d from US$100/160) 🖋 Run by an NGO that funds local water projects, Bakiga Lodge offers terrific value with its mix of stilted log cabins and safari tents looking out to the forested hills.

Gorilla Mist Camp `LODGE $$`
(☎ 0756-563577; www.gorillamistcamp.com; s/d incl full board US$130/250) A solid midrange lodge with views of hilly surrounds from its stilted thatched-roof cottages. Bathtubs and balconies add to its appeal.

❶ Getting There & Away

BUHOMA

Whether you have your own vehicle or not, getting to Buhoma can be complicated. A special-hire vehicle is the way to go, particularly if you can muster up a group to share the costs. The four-hour trip from Kabale to Buhoma costs around USh200,000 one way or USh300,000 return.

By public transport there are several options involving uncomfortable and often hair-raising truck journeys. If you're lucky you'll get a pick-up truck direct to Buhoma (USh15,000, four to six hours) from Kabale on Tuesday or Friday at around 10am. Otherwise you can try your luck with a truck from Kabale to Kihihi and disembark at Kanyantorogo (USh10,000, three hours). From here you'll need to get either another pick-up to Butogota (USh4000, 30 minutes) or wait for the bus from Kampala to pass (as early as 3pm, but usually later). Butogota is 17km northeast of Buhoma; for the last leg of the trip you have the option of catching the daily Green Bus at 8am, an infrequent pick-up to Buhoma (USh2000, one hour), or (most realistically) a special-hire taxi for USh60,000 or boda-boda for about USh20,000.

If you're heading to Buhoma from Kampala, there's a daily Bismarken bus to Butogota (USh25,000, 10 to 12 hours) departing Kampala's Buganda Bus Park around 6am; it departs in the other direction from Butogota at 3am.

If you're driving from Kabale to Buhoma, the best route is the long way through Kanungu (which can be done in a car if you're an experienced driver) rather than the rough road through Ruhija.

It's also possible to access Buhoma via walking through Bwindi Impenetrable National Park from Nkuringo, a lovely 12km stretch that takes five to seven hours.

If you're in a rush, charter flights can get you to the Kanyonza Airstrip, 19km from Buhoma.

If you're coming from Queen Elizabeth National Park, Buhoma is best accessed from Kihihi, which is around 30 minutes outside Ishasha; a special-hire taxi is the most realistic option, costing around USh100,000 for the 40km journey.

NKURINGO

There are occasional trucks (USh8000, four hours) from Kabale to Nkuringo but realistically you'll have to take a special-hire taxi (one-way USh180,000, return USh120,000, 2½ hours) or boda-boda (USh35,000).

From Kisoro a truck travels to Nkuringo (USh10,000, three hours) on Monday and Thursday. It leaves Nkuringo around 8am and returns about 3pm. A special-hire taxi from Kisoro (1½ hours) costs around USh100,000 one way or USh150,000 return. A boda-boda driver will charge you USh30,000, but it's a long, bottom-shaking ride. Be aware of the risks during rainy season when there can be lengthy delays due to the poor condition of the road.

The best way to travel from Nkuringo (you can also do it uphill from Kisoro) is to leave the road behind. **Nkuringo Walking Safaris** (☑ 0774-805580; www.nkuringowalkingsafaris.com; 2 people from US$70) will lead you on a 22km trek to Kisoro via Lake Mutanda (this can be shortened with some driving) and then a 2½-hour paddle in a dugout canoe.

You can also slip through the forest to/from Buhoma along the River Ivi Trail.

RUHIJA

Ruhija is about 50km (up to two hours) from Buhoma gate, and 52km from Kasese (a special-hire will cost about USh140,000 return). If you're chancing your luck with public transport, there are pick-up trucks that leave Kabale on Tuesday, Wednesday and Thursday, but there's no set departure time.

RUSHAGA

Located 54km from Kabale, Rushaga can be reached via a special-hire taxi (USh150,000, three hours), while a boda-boda is around USh30,000 one-way.

Otherwise it's 32km from Kisoro, which costs USh60,000 one way and USh90,000 return by special-hire taxi (one hour) or USh15,000 by boda-boda one way. Trucks (USh4500, two hours) depart in the afternoon on Monday and Thursday, and at 10am on Friday.

Kabale

POP 44,000

A dusty provincial town, Kabale is nothing to write home about. It's most of interest to travellers as a transport hub and gateway to both Lake Bunyonyi and Bwindi Impenetrable National Park.

◉ Sights & Activities

Home of Edirisa   MUSEUM
(☑ 0752-558222; www.edirisa.org; Muhumuza Rd; adult/child incl guide USh10,000/4000; ⊙9am-9pm) Inside the Home of Edirisa hostel, this simple and squashy (but very worthwhile) cultural museum houses a replica traditional homestead, built of sticks and papyrus, showing how the local Bakiga people lived a century ago.

Kabale

0 — 200 m
0 — 0.1 miles

Stanbic Bank

Post Bus/ Post Office

Rugabo Rd

Nyerere Ave

Garage St

Corryndon Rd

Sports Ground

Barclays Bank

Kisoro Rd

Kabale

◎ Sights
1 Home of Edirisa...................................A1

⬛ Sleeping
2 Engagi Guesthouse.............................A1
  Home of Edirisa............................(see 1)
3 White Horse Inn B2

🛏 Sleeping & Eating

Home of Edirisa · BACKPACKERS $

(☑ 0752-558222; www.edirisa.org; Muhumu-za Rd; dm USh15,000, s/d without bathroom USh20,000/30,000, d USh40,000; @🛜) With-in a very cool polka-dotted building, this chilled-out guesthouse has friendly staff and simple (but dark) rooms priced right for the budget traveller. All rooms have shared showers. The rooftop restaurant is *the* spot to hang out in Kabale. It also leads canoe-trekking trips on Lake Bunyonyi and runs a basic bush camp, the Heart, on Lake Bunyoni.

Engagi Guesthouse · BACKPACKERS $

(Kabale Backpackers; ☑ 0772-959667; www.engagiexperience.com/guesthouse.aspx; Muhu-muza Rd; camping USh9000, dm USh15,000, s/d USh25,000/35,000; @🛜) Your classic budget guesthouse, Engagi has a friendly vibe, good-value private rooms and a lively bar with pool table. Its Engagi Safaris books budget tours, which are excellent value, and rents mountain bikes.

White Horse Inn · HOTEL $$

(☑ 0772-459859; www.whitehorseinn kabale.com; Rwamafa Rd; s/d incl full breakfast USh102,000/145,000; @) Set on two grassy hectares on the outskirts of town, this fad-ed colonial hotel (built in 1937) has hosted many a visiting dignitary, including Jimmy Carter and Bill Gates. These days it's a relic of the glory days – but still a good option for those who like their accommodation to have some character.

❶ Information

Pick up a copy of the free *Gorilla Highlands* (www.gorillahighlands.com) pocket guide, which has information and history about the area including Bunyoni, Mgahinga and Bwindi. It's available online or from the Home of Edirisa; the ebook is also available online.

Stanbic and **Barclays** banks are on the main road.

❶ Getting There & Away

Home of Edirisa is a good source of information for onward travel, particularly public transport to Bwindi.

The Post Bus heads to Kabale to/from Kampa-la (USh25,000, eight hours) en route to Kisoro (USh10,000, two hours) at around 3pm from the post office. Other regular daily buses to Kampala – including Horizon, Bismarken and Jaguar – have similar prices and also contine to Kisoro.

There are buses to Fort Portal (USh30,000, eight hours) via Queen Elizabeth National Park and Kasese (USh25,000, seven hours).

Minibus taxis to the Rwandan border at Katuna (USh5000, 30 minutes) and on to Kigali are frequent. Jaguar buses also head to Kigale (USh20,000, four hours).

Lake Bunyonyi

Lake Bunyonyi (meaning 'place of many lit-tle birds') is undoubtedly the loveliest lake in Uganda. Its contorted shore encircles 29 islands, and the steep surrounding hillsides are intensively terraced, reminiscent of parts of Nepal. A magical place, especially with a morning mist rising off the placid waters, it has supplanted the Ssese Islands as *the* place for travellers to chill out on their way through Uganda.

◎ Sights & Activities

All guesthouses can arrange boat trips on the lake, either in motorboats or dugout canoes, which is still how most locals get about. This is one of the few places in Uganda where you

UGANDA LAKE BUNYONYI

can swim, with no crocodiles, hippos or bilharzia, so go ahead and jump in.

Akampeine Island
HISTORIC SITE

Translating to 'Punishment Island', this tiny island was so named because it was once the place where unmarried pregnant women were dumped to die. Their only rescue from drowning or starvation was if a man who was too poor to pay a bride-price came over to claim the banished woman as his wife. There's nothing to see here, with just one spindly tree in its centre.

Bwama & Njuyeera (Sharp's) Islands
HISTORIC SITE

Many boat drivers will take you to these islands, where British missionary Dr Leonard Sharp founded a leper colony and settled in 1921, but the story is more interesting than the sights. The colony on Bwama was shut down in the 1980s (there are two schools on the island now) and nearly all Njuyeera's history was stripped when it was converted into a (not recommended) hotel.

Kyahugye Island
WILDLIFE RESERVE

(www.bunyonyiecoresort.com; per person USh10,000) Run by Lake Bunyonyi Eco Resort, this 14-hectare island is worth a visit if you want to see to wildlife such as zebras, waterbucks, ipala and kob up close. All were brought here from Lake Mburo National Park.

Canoe Trekking

The best way to get intimate with Bunyonyi is by jumping in a canoe to paddle its peaceful waters. Excellent **tours** (☎0752-558558; www.canoetrekking.com; half-/1-/2-/3-day trek per person from US$35/50/125/185) are offered by the Home of Edirisa in Kabale, which range from five hours to its flagship three-day tour. The longer tours have the benefit of allowing you to get a very up-close look at local life with village homestays and visits to the Twa. Note prices are for groups of five.

Otherwise it's easy enough to grab a dugout canoe on your own for a leisurely paddle; but practise for a while before paddling off on an ambitious trip, as many travellers end up going round in circles, doing what's known locally as the *mzungu* corkscrew. Keep an eye out for otters, particularly along the shore during early morning and late afternoon.

Tours

All of the guesthouses at Lake Bunyonyi can set you up with village walks to see, among other things, local blacksmiths *(abahesi)* who

have replaced locally mined iron ore with scrap metal, but otherwise use traditional methods. But if you just want an easygoing amble along the lakeshore, it's straightforward enough to find your own way around.

Batwa Today
CULTURAL TOUR

(www.edirisa.org; from US$30) There are several Twa villages in the area, but Batwa Today is the most recommended, aiming to deliver a more authentic exchange. Trips head to Echuya Forest, the former home of local Twa, and while there's cultural performances, the experience is less contrived than those offered in Bwindi and Mgahinga. Rather than dwelling on the past, insights are offered from a more current context.

Arranged by the team from Home of Edirisa (p443), tours are led by Twa guides and sensitively balance preserving Twa culture and identity with improving living conditions, while minimising the human zoo element. Prices exclude transport, which can be arranged for US$15 for a taxi/*boda* combo, or US$60 per vehicle.

Sleeping & Eating

There's a good range of accommodation, both on the mainland and on several islands. All have restaurants and bars (order well in advance). Most feature crayfish on the menu, a local delicacy caught fresh from the lake, that resemble small prawns in size and taste.

Mainland

Kalebas Camp
GUESTHOUSE $

(☎0772-907892; camping per person US$5, s/d safari tents US$15/20, r from US$30) One of Bunyonyi's original lakeside lodges, Kalebas has a beautiful garden attracting plenty of birdlife. The stilted safari tents are the pick, and it's also well suited to camping. However, basic rooms are overpriced and lack atmosphere. It has a lovely restaurant with wonderful lake views.

Bunyonyi Overland Resort
BACKPACKERS $

(☎0772-409510; www.bunyonyioverland.com; camping with/without tent US$8/12, dm US$5, s/d from US$35/45, cottage s/d US$45/60; ☎) Overland's sprawling lakeside camp caters to all kinds with four-bed dorms, overlander campsites and comfortable, self-contained cottages (some with phones in them!). It's extremely popular, and its social bar is Bunyonyi's liveliest. It hires out mountain bikes (US$10) and canoes too.

TWA (BATWA) TOURS: TO GO OR NOT TO GO...

The Twa (Batwa) people have almost all been forced out of their ancestral forest homes, where they lived as nomadic hunters and gatherers, due to the clearing of forests for agriculture by neighbouring tribes or the creation of national parks. One of Africa's most ancient tribal groups, the Twa are now faced with a plight common to many indigenous peoples: they are a marginalised sector of the Ugandan community, often living in squalid conditions.

Many Ugandans view the Twa with disdain and will tell you they're lazy. But the Twa are uninterested in living in a modern agro-industrial society. Life in the forest was anything but easy, but this is the only life the older generation know, and even those who are making an effort to adopt farming have found it very hard to adapt to modern life.

In many of the places where the Twa now live, particularly near Lake Bunyonyi and Mgahinga, Bwindi and Semuliki national parks, guides will offer to take you to visit one of their villages. The visits invariably involve a song-and-dance demonstration, and once the music begins you can't help but notice that they project a genuine pride.

Most Twa today still rely on handouts, and so they're only too happy for a chance to cash in on their culture. (Your guide should be giving a good chunk of change to the village chairperson for the performance, and basketry is usually offered for sale.) In some ways it's this very commercialisation of their culture that ensures the survival of the Twa as a distinct tribal group within Uganda.

Despite this, visits can still end up taking on a 'human safari' feel, which can be unfortunate for everyone involved. The best way to visit the Twa is through initiatives in Lake Bunyonyi, and Bwindi and Mgahinga national parks. These allow you to explore the forest with Twa guides, receiving demonstrations on hunting and cultural performances. All money goes to helping local Twa communities and ultimately preserving their indigenous culture.

Crater Bay Cottage GUESTHOUSE $
(📞0486-426255; www.craterbaycottageslake bunyonyi.com; camping per person US$5, r without bathroom US$10, tented camping s/d US$20/25, cottages s/d US$50/70) A laid-back and inexpensive family-run resort, Crater Bay offers a choice of *banda* cottages or tented camping in its attractive grounds overlooking the lake. There are plenty of private areas to relax in the garden. For shoestringers, there are *very* basic rooms out back.

Arcadia Cottages LODGE $$
(📞0793-617741; www.arcadialodges.com/lake-bunyonyi.html; s/d US$120/190; 🛜) Wow! Built high on a hill, Arcadia has intoxicating views over the lake dotted with dozens of islands and a backdrop of the Virunga volcanoes in the distance. The lower row of cottages are the pick of the accommodation, boasting unhindered views, private porches and comfortable rooms, which could, however, do with a refurb. Even if you won't be sleeping here, stop by for a meal for the sweeping panoramic views. On chilly nights a brazier of hot coals is provided, which makes things nice and cosy. It sits 2km uphill off the main road to the lake.

Birdnest@Bunyoni Resort RESORT $$
(📞0754-252560; www.birdnestatbunyonyi.com; s/d incl full breakfast US$150/175; 🛜🏊) Resembling some sort of thatched palace, the Belgian-owned Birdnest is an impressive sight. It's the most upmarket choice in Bunyonyi, but remains excellent value. Open-plan rooms have vibrant decor with lovely private balconies looking out to the lake, while the outside terrace decking has a swimming pool with huge hammocks and free canoe hire. The restaurant has a quality European menu and a good wine list.

Lake View Coffee House CAFE $
(⏲6am-5pm; 🛜) Marking the starting point of Bunyonyi is this open-air cafe with decking looking out to the lake. Stop by for coffee, cold beer, crayfish and wi-fi.

🛏 Islands

Secure parking is available by the Rutinda landing for those driving here.

★Byoona Amagara LODGE $
(📞0752-652788; www.lakebunyonyi.net; Itambira Island; camping USh12,000, dm USh20,000-26,000, geodome per person USh43,000-58,000,

cabin per person USh48,000, cottage USh215,000; @) Byoona Amagara bills itself as a backpackers' paradise, and it's hard to disagree. There's a great choice of rooms, most built with natural materials and reasonably priced. The stars of the show are the open-faced geodome huts – birds and lizards can come in, but so do the unencumbered views – with comfortable beds, warm blankets, mosquito nets and thoughtfully positioned outdoor showers looking out to the lake.

The originality continues in the kitchen, which turns out tasty, creative dishes. There's even a cinema (USh2000) for hire. A dugout canoe from Rutinda is free until 6pm. Note private rooms have a two-person minimum during peak holiday periods, and a 25% single supplement at other times.

Bushara Island Camp   LODGE $

(☑ 0772-464585; www.busharaislandcamp.com; Bushara Island; camping US$6, safari tents s/d US$35/40, cottages s/d/tr US$35/40/58) One of Bunyonyi's best choices, this ultra-relaxed camp offers a wonderful selection of cottages and safari tents, all widely spaced through the eucalyptus forest. The 'treehouse' cottage (US$38) set on stilts is wonderfully rustic and features a great balcony. All have memorable outdoor showers. With top service (breakfast delivered to your door!), it's no surprise that there are many return visitors.

The thatched-roof restaurant serves excellent food and has a roaring fireplace. A motorboat transfer from Rutinda is free unless you're camping (per trip USh15,000). Other perks are free birdwatching tours and a fun rope swing into the lake. It's run by the Church of Uganda to raise funds for community development projects.

Lake Bunyonyi Eco Resort   LODGE $$

(☑ 0392-080344; www.bunyonyiecoresort.com; Kyahugye Island; camping USh15,000, s/d incl full board US$90/150) It's always nice to find somewhere that does things a bit differently, and this resort on Kyahugye Island certainly fits the bill, with its small population of zebras, kob, impala and bushbucks (and one monkey) imported from Lake Mburo to Lake Bunyonyi! Rooms are in private, wooden thatched cottages with lake views. Call ahead to arrange pick-ups from the pier to avoid the long climb up.

Nature's Prime Island   BUNGALOW $$

(☑ 0772-423215; www.naturesprimeisland.com; Akarwa Island; safari tents s/d from US$35/50, cab-

ins US$40/80) Occupying a lovely little wooded island right near Rutinda, Nature Prime mixes it up with Scandinavian-style rustic log cabins and safari tents set on raised platforms. Use of canoes is complimentary as is the boat transfer.

ⓘ Getting There & Away

Rutinda, where most of Bunyonyi's lodging and the main jetty are found, is situated 9km from Kabale. To get here take a special-hire taxi (USh20,000) or boda-boda (USh6000).

Kisoro

POP 12,700

While Kisoro – a gritty town with a frontier atmosphere – may not be much to look at, its verdant surrounds are undeniably beautiful. On a clear day the backdrop of the Virunga chain of volcanoes is stunning. Kisoro serves as a popular base for tourists, here primarily to access nearby Mgahinga Gorilla National Park to see mountain gorillas (if they're this side of the border, that is), track golden monkeys or climb volcanoes. It's also a convenient base for those with gorilla permits in the southern sector of Bwindi Impenetrable National Park or even Parc National des Virungas at Djomba, just over the border in the DRC. If you're en route to/from Rwanda it makes a pleasant place to spend the night.

Cold winds blow through town, so pack that jacket.

ⓒ Tours

There's not much to see and do in Kisoro itself, with Mgahinga Gorilla National Park and Lake Mutanda the real attractions, just outside of town. Kisoro's Monday and Thursday markets are large, colourful affairs, well worth some of your time.

United Organisation for Batwa
Development in Uganda   CULTURAL TOUR

(UOBDU; ☑ 0772-660810; 3 Bazanyamaso Rd; ⊙ 8am-5.30pm) If you're interested in visiting a Twa (Batwa) village, this organisation will ensure that your trip is culturally sensitive. If you have the chance, it's better to do the Batwa Trail in Mgahinga Gorilla National Park.

Mountain Gorilla Coffee Tours   TOUR

(☑ 0777-412288; www.mountaingorillacoffeetours. shutterfly.com; Main St; 1/2 people US$30/45) These excellent coffee tours, run by knowledgeable guides, take you through the whole process from bean to cup. It finishes with

Kisoro

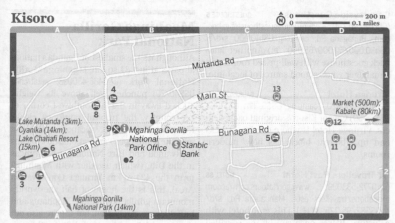

a cupping session to compare notes on aromas and tastes using different brewing and roasting techniques. A bag of coffee is included in the price. It also rents mountain bikes, and runs other tours, including canoeing Lake Mutanda and village homestays.

🛏 Sleeping & Eating

There's quality sleeping options at nearby Mgahinga Gorilla National Park and at Lake Mutanda.

Golden Monkey Guesthouse BACKPACKERS $
(☎0772-435148; www.goldenmonkeyguesthouse. com; dm US$10, r without bathroom US$15, s/d US$25/35; 🛜) Friendly and welcoming, Golden Monkey is popular with NGOs and return visitors. Well-maintained rooms are basic but good value, and it has the best menu in town. It also runs Virunga Adventure Tours, and can arrange trips across Uganda. If it's full, it has **Rafiki Guesthouse** up the road.

Sawasawa Guest House GUESTHOUSE $
(☎0785-642114; www.facebook.com/sawa sawaguesthouse; Bunagana Rd; s/d from USh30,000/50,000) Run by a friendly team, low-key Sawasawa makes an excellent budget choice with sparkling rooms and reliable hot water. The food is also good.

Mucha Bistro & Guesthouse GUESTHOUSE $
(☎0784-478605; www.hotel-mucha.com/ bistroandguesthouse; Kabale-Kisoro Rd; s/d USh35,000/45,000; 🛜) The idea of a designer guesthouse on this stretch of highway seems unlikely, but German-Bulgarian-owned Mucha pulls it off with affordable, clean and

Kisoro

comfortable rooms. Its smart bistro is also a winner. Its flagship lodge is in Lake Mutanda.

Lake Chahafi Resort LODGE $
(www.lakechahafiresort.com; Lake Chahafi; camping with/without tent US$8/12, dm US$20, s/d US$40/50) Located 15km outside Kisoro, on the road to the Rwanda border, these cottages are a great place to hide away by the lake. There are plenty of activities including biking, birdwatching and canoeing on the lake. The site has a remarkable history as the place of a WWI battle that saw British and Belgian troops up against the Germans in 1915; trenches can still be seen.

Countryside Guesthouse
GUESTHOUSE $

(☑0782-412741; countrysideguesthouse@yahoo.com; Bunagana Rd; camping USh10,000, s/d/tr USh30,000/50,000/65,000; ℗) Another laid-back guesthouse with well-priced rooms and a manager who's a good source of local info.

Virunga Hotel
BACKPACKERS $

(☑0782-360820; camping US$6, dm US$10, r US$25-50) One of Kisoro's original backpackers, Virunga Hotel is where overland trucks end up. Its rear block has new, modern rooms.

★ Travellers Rest Hotel
HOTEL $$

(☑0772-533029; www.gorillatours.com/accommodations/travellers-rest/; Mahuabura Rd; s/d/tr US$82/95/125; @🛜) This is a hotel with a history. It was once run by the so-called father of gorilla tourism, Walter Baumgärtel, and Dian Fossey called it her 'second home'. Through various thoughtful touches such as Congolese crafts, this otherwise simple place has become a lovely little oasis. The garden has lots of shade, and an atmospheric bar with fireplace.

It's also known for its set four-course dinners (USh38,000) which are worth the splurge; visitors need to prebook by 3.30pm.

Coffee Pot Café
CAFE $

(www.coffee-pot-cafe.com; Bunagana Rd; coffee USh5000, mains USh10,000-20,000; ⊙8.30am-9.30pm; 🛜) A smart German-owned cafe with decent coffee, burgers, BLTs and meatball dishes. It sells secondhand books and quality crafts next door.

❶ Information

There are several banks with ATMs. There's also a few internet places along the main road.

Mgahinga Gorilla National Park Office
(☑0414-680793; Main St; ⊙8am-5pm) The place to book your gorilla permits, it has information about everything in and around Kisoro.

❶ Getting There & Away

The Post Bus heads to Kampala (USh30,000, eight hours) via Kabale (USh10,000, 1½ hours) daily at 6am. Several bus companies (including Bismarken and Jaguar) also have departures during the morning, as do minibus taxis.

The Rwandan border south of Kisoro at Cyanika is now open 24 hours and it's a pretty simple, quick trip to Musanze (Ruhengeri). To the border a boda boda is around USh5000 and special-hire taxi is USh25,000.

Mgahinga Gorilla National Park

Although it's the smallest of Uganda's national parks at just 34 sq km, **Mgahinga Gorilla National Park** (☑0486-430098; adult/child US$40/20) punches well above its weight. Tucked away in the far southwest corner of the country, the tropical rainforest cloaks three dramatic extinct volcanoes and, along with the contiguous Parc National des Volcans in Rwanda and Parc National des Virungas in the DRC (which together with Mgahinga form the 434-sq-km Virunga Conservation Area), this is the home of half the world's mountain gorilla population. Elephants and buffaloes are rarely seen, but they're also out there, and 115 species of bird flutter through the forests, including the Rwenzori turaco and mountain black boo boo.

Gorilla tracking is still the main attraction here, but it's less popular than Bwindi Impenetrable National Park, due to the one habituated family having a tendency to duck across the mountains into Rwanda or the DRC. But there's much more on offer here than gorillas. Mgahinga also serves up some challenging but rewarding treks and an interesting cave, plus golden monkey tracking is almost as fun as hanging out with the big boys.

All activities are booked through UWA in Kisoro, or otherwise at the Mgahinga trailhead.

🏃 Activities

Gorilla Tracking

If you plan to come here specifically for gorillas, the first step is to check they're on this side of the border. When the gorillas are living on Ugandan soil, eight people can visit per day. The cost is US$600, including the entrance fee, a ranger-guide and armed guards. Due to the higher altitude, gorillas here have a fuzzier, luxuriant coat.

Trips depart from park headquarters at 8.30am, but check in at the park office in Kisoro the day before your trip to confirm your arrival.

Volcano Trekking

The park has three dormant volcanoes that can be climbed, which, though strenuous, require no mountaineering experience. Each volcano costs US$80 to climb, which includes park entry and a guide. The most popular climb is **Mt Sabyinyo** (3669m), which involves breathtaking walks along gorges and a few challenging ladder ascents with the reward of getting to the third and final peak where you'll be standing in Uganda, Rwanda and the DRC all at once. It's a 14km, eight-hour trek.

There's also the 12km, seven-hour trek to the crater lake at the summit of **Mt Muhavura** (4127m). It's the tallest of the volcanoes and almost too perfect to be true, with views reaching all the way to the Rwenzori Mountains. **Mt Gahinga** (3474m) is the least taxing of the climbs, an 8km, six-hour trek up to its swampy summit through bamboo zone. All treks lead you into the otherworldly Afro-alpine moorland, home of bizarre plants such as giant groundsel and lobelias.

Two less demanding treks (US$30 including guide), both about 10km long and great for birdwatchers, are the **Border Trail**, which starts at Sabyinyo but then cuts back south along the Congolese border, and the **Gorge Trail**, which heads to a small waterfall in a gorge halfway up Sabyinyo. You could combine these into one longer trek.

Golden-Monkey Trekking

While inevitably overshadowed by the gorillas, golden monkeys (a very rare subspecies of the rare blue monkey found only in this part of the world) are another top lure to Mgahinga. For US$90 (including park entry) you spend an hour with these beautiful creatures who live in large groups and are quite playful. Tracking starts at 8.30am, and the guides can find the habituated troop 85% of the time, though they are less easily spotted if it's raining.

If you're really into the idea, there are longer four-hour trips (US$100 excluding entry fees) which allow you to be involved with the habituation process.

MGAHINGA GORILLA PERMITS

Unlike permits for Bwindi, bookings for Mgahinga Gorilla National Park aren't taken at the UWA head office in Kampala. You must make your reservation by calling the park office in Kisoro no more than two weeks in advance. You pay at the park on the day of your tracking. Because of this system, tour operators rarely come here, making it a good place to get permits at the last minute. It is also possible to book permits in Kisoro for Rushaga at Bwindi Impenetrable National Park.

🗘 Tours

Batwa Trail   CULTURAL TOUR
(incl guide US$80) These forest tours are led by the local Twa (Batwa), who explain how they used to live in the forest before they were forcibly removed from Mgahinga when it was turned into a national park. The 3½-hour tours include tales from Twa legend, demonstrations of day-to-day practices such as hunting and fire lighting, and a visit to the 342m-long **Garama Cave**, a historic residing spot of the Twa, where you'll get a song-and-dance performance.

While it can feel a bit contrived, the tour provides a much better insight to the Twa people than the often depressing village visits.

MGAHINGA GORILLA NATIONAL PARK

Why Go
Mountain gorillas; golden monkeys; volcano trekking in the stunning Virungas; Batwa Trail.

When to Go
Year-round, but be sure to check the gorillas are here, as they sometimes hang out on the Rwandan side. The dry seasons (mid-December to February and June to October) are best for tracking primates.

Practicalities
Most travellers spend the night in Kisoro, a short drive from the park headquarters, but there are some good sleeping options in the park.

Budget Tips
Golden-monkey tracking offers a more affordable alternative to tracking the gorillas. Nearby Kisoro is a very backpacker-friendly town, but there's also affordable lodging at Mgahinga Gorilla National Park and Lake Mutanda.

LOCAL KNOWLEDGE

JOHN MUGISHA: UWA RANGER

John Mugisha was born in a village 1km from Mgahinga and has worked as a ranger/guide in both Bwindi and Mgahinga national parks for over a decade.

What do you like about Mgahinga? Well it's a tropical rainforest that's only 34 sq km, yet it has three volcanoes, the golden monkeys and mountain gorillas all in one!

Which volcano do you recommend to climb? My favourite volcano is Sabyinyo. In the local language Sabyinyo means 'old man's teeth' due to its jagged peaks. Up the top of the third peak not only will you be in three countries at once, but you can see all of the Virungas and other volcanoes in the DRC and Rwanda.

What about the golden monkeys? What is special about them is that here in Virunga are the only existing habituated groups in the world. So it's the only place where you can pause and view them in their natural habitat. It's a very rare species and is not found in any zoos. They have a beautiful golden colour and beautiful faces and are so playful and lovely.

What's the difference between seeing gorillas in Bwindi and Mgahinga? Mgahinga were the first gorillas to be habituated so they are very used to people. But the main difference is that in Mgahinga the gorillas are a bigger size, which people believe is because they eat bamboo here – which they don't in Bwindi.

Your most memorable experience? I very much like the gorillas. One day in Bwindi it rained so much while we were tracking the Nshongi group that the river became flooded, yet the gorillas wanted to cross. So we saw the silverback break a tree and carry it across and hold it down over the river so the others could cross safely. That was very nice. Another time when tracking gorillas in Mgahinga we unexpectedly encounted another (unhabituated) family who had crossed the border from the DRC. The DRC group started fighting them and tried to overpower them, so 'our' group came to us rangers for protection, nestling behind us! The other group feared us and luckily ran away!

🛏 Sleeping

Most people sleep in Kisoro, but there are two lovely choices just outside the park gate.

Amajambere Iwacu Community Campground　CAMPGROUND $

(📞 0782-306973, 0382-278464; www.mcdoa.org; camping with/without tent US$5/10, dm US$10, banda US$30) 🌿 Right at the park's gate, this friendly and extremely peaceful camp – set up and run by the local community – has a variety of rooms with nice verandahs for relaxing. It's a good choice for those seeking a local experience, and has volunteer opportunities (p482). Proceeds fund school projects in the area.

Mt Gahinga Lodge　LODGE $$$

(📞 0414-346464; www.volcanoessafaris.com; s/d incl full board US$236/285) Set within a rocky garden that blends in beautifully with the natural surrounds, this luxury lodge oozes charm. The homestead-style cottages have volcano views, plenty of space, sofas and even their own fireplaces. Rates include alcohol and a massage – both perfect after a day's trekking.

ℹ Getting There & Away

There's no scheduled transport along the rough 14km track between Kisoro and the park headquarters. You can try to hitch, although traffic is light so it's best to arrange a ride the night before.

Special-hire taxis (around USh60,000) or *boda-bodas* (USh10,000 return) are the most straightforward way of getting to the park, but be prepared for a long rough, slippery ride if it's wet.

Lake Mutanda

This scenic lake lies just north of Kisoro and stretches not far south of Bwindi, making it a relaxing base for your gorilla trip. It's a pretty spot, with a misty Virunga backdrop comprising a string of volcanoes and a lake ringed by papyrus swamp, and is a good alternative for those who find Lake Bunyonyi overdeveloped. There are also dugout canoes for hire if you fancy a paddle; you don't need to worry about hippos, crocodiles or bilharzia here.

It's easily accessible from Kisoro. The easiest, though not most direct, route is to head west to the hospital and then ask someone to show you which gap in the hills to cross. A *boda-boda* or special-hire taxi should cost USh5000 and USh20,000 respectively.

Lake Mutanda is also the starting point for eight-hour treks into Bwindi Impenetrable National Park with Nkuringo Walking Safaris (p442).

☐ Sleeping

Mutanda Eco-Community Centre   BUNGALOW **$**
(☎ 0772-435148; www.mcdoa.org/MECC.aspx; camping per tent US$6, dm US$10, cottage US$40) Run by the local community, the delightfully simple stilted cabins (number 4 and 5 have excellent lake views) and grassy campground all blend beautifully into the surrounds. Staff will cook local food from USh7000 and rent you a dugout canoe (per hour US$10). It even has a small beach.

Mucha   HOTEL **$$**
(☎ 0755-700362; www.hotel-mucha.com; Bwindi Rd; s/d US$110/165; ☎) While the idea of slick modern hotel rooms in such a pastoral setting is confounding, Mucha pulls it off. Choose between volcano views or creekside rooms. The European restaurant is a classy affair.

Mutanda Lake Resort   LODGE **$$$**
(☎ 0789-951943; www.mutandalakeresort.com; s/d incl full board US$155/220; ☎) In a superb location, plonked directly on the lake, this relaxed Dutch-owned resort has luxury tents raised on wooden platforms with lovely porches and polished wooden floorboards. It's within striking distance of gorillas at Nkuringo, Ruhaja and Mgahinga.

Chameleon Hill Lodge   LODGE **$$$**
(www.chameleonhill.com; s/d US$330/460; ☎) Finally a lodge in Uganda that's trying something original, hilltop Chameleon provides a memorable first impression with a series of multicoloured surrealist chimney-stack buildings. The flair doesn't stop there, with plenty of arty touches and colour in its comfortable chalets, all with porches and soaring lake panoramas.

Mbarara
POP 82,000

Mbarara is a large, gritty town that hosts many Ugandan business travellers. Unless you're an NGO or are wanting to break up your trip there's zero reason to stay here.

☐ Sleeping

Westland Hotel   HOTEL **$**
(☎ 0772-586769; Bananuka Dr; s/d USh25,000/45,000, without bathroom USh15,000/21,000) A construction project that just never ends, this labyrinth place offers passable budget rooms, but avoid ones on the bottom-end of the price scale.

Lake View Resort Hotel   HOTEL **$$**
(☎ 0772-367972; www.lakeviewresorthotel.co.ug; s/d from US$65/80; @ ☎ ☎) On the outskirts

---

WORTH A TRIP

HIGHWAY CULTURAL STOPS

Igongo Cultural Centre (www.igongo.co.ug; Mbarara-Masaka Rd; adult/child USh20,000/3000; ⊙7.30am-10pm) Located 12km from Mbarara on the road to Kampala, this new centre is worth a look. Set on the grounds of a former palace of the Ankole king, its quality museum explores the peoples of southwestern Uganda, particularly the Ankole, through artefacts, a cultural village replica and a heap of info. Also here is a restaurant serving traditional Ankole dishes, such as smoked Ankole cow milk and boiled meats.

There's a great bookshop with an interesting selection of Ugandan reading material, and newly opened resort-style accommodation. Directly across from the centre is **Biharwe Eclipse Monument** atop Biharwe Hill. It was built to commemorate a victory for Ankole kingdom 500 years ago, following an eclipse that saw the invading king retreat in fear (and never return), spooked as day plunged into sudden darkness.

Great Lakes Museum (www.greatlakesmuseum.co.ug; adult/child USh5000/4000; ⊙7.30am-8pm) Along the highway on approach to Kabale, keep an eye out for this museum. It has a varied collection of artefacts and masks, information on clans, and more quirky items such as displays on the evolution of phones and cameras. The cafe selling Ugandan coffee offers accommodation and mountain-bike hire.

of town off the road to Kasese, this modern hotel sits in front of a tiny lake and is easily the best option in town.

ℹ️ Getting There & Away

Departing from side-by-side parks, there are frequent buses and minibuses to Kampala (USh20,000, 4½ hours), Masaka (USh8000, 2½ hours) and Kabale (USh15,000, 3½ hours). For Kasese (USh13,000, three hours) and Queen Elizabeth National Park (Katunguru), jump on the daily Kalita bus at 11am. You can also catch the Kigali-bound buses that begin in Kampala.

Lake Mburo National Park

The 370-sq-km **Lake Mburo National Park** (☎ 0751-046904; adult/child US$40/20; ⊗ 7am-6.30pm) is an increasingly common stop on the safari circuit as it's the only place in southern Uganda to see zebras. It's also the only park in the country with impala, slender mongooses and giant bush rats, and is a great place to look for hyenas, leopards, topis and elands. Furthermore, it's rumoured giraffes will soon be introduced here. Lions are rarely sighted – it's thought there's only one left here. Some of the 325 species of bird include the martial eagle and red-faced barbet in the acacia-wooded savannah, and the papyrus yellow warbler and African finfoot in the wetlands.

Adjacent to the park are the ranches of the Bahima people, who herd the famed long-horned Ankole cattle, which are a common sight here (all too often inside as well as outside the park).

🏃 Activities

Launch Trip

The 1½-hour boat trips run by UWA are popular on Lake Mburo to get up close and personal with hippos, crocodiles and waterbirds. Trips cost US$15 per person and depart at 8am, 10am, noon, 2pm, 4pm and 5.30pm. If there's fewer than four people, prices rise to US$40 per person. Fishing permits (US$15) are also available, but you'll need to bring your own equipment.

Wildlife Drives

Animals are most abundant in the south during the dry season (as this is where the permanent water is) and in the northeast in the wet season. Guides cost US$20; night drives (US$30 per person) are also possible.

Wildlife Walks

Lake Mburo has some good nature walks (US$30 per person, particularly the guided early morning **hyena walk** at 6.30am. The other popular pedestrian destination is an observation blind overlooking a salt lick. Both walks take two hours. Birdwatchers should enquire about the Rubanga forest, which has a closed canopy in some places and you may find birds not yet recorded on the park's official list.

Horseback Safari

A novel way to explore the park is on horseback safari. Without the engine noise of a 4WD it's a peaceful way to get around to see wildlife and the park's lakes. Rides are booked through Mihingo Lodge and cost US$40 for one hour, US$100 for a half day and US$200 for a full day. Overnight and multiday trips can also be arranged.

ℹ️ LAKE MBURO NATIONAL PARK

Why Go
Most accessible park to Kampala; zebras, elands and impala; healthy population of hippos and crocodiles; hyena nature walk; horseback safari.

When to Go
Year-round.

Practicalities
It's a 3½-hour drive from Kampala. Reservations for boat trips are recommended from June to August and in December.

Budget Tips
If you don't have your own vehicle, a combination of bus and *boda-boda* (motorcycle taxi) can get you to the park headquarters, from where activities can be arranged. There's also camping and affordable *bandas* (thatched-roof huts).

📖 Sleeping & Eating

Rwonyo Rest Camp
BANDA, CAMPGROUND $

(camping USh15,000, banda s/d/f without bathroom USh35,000/40,000/60,000, safari tents without bathrooms s/d USh30,000/40,000) UWA's accommodation at the park headquarters has camping, simple *bandas* and safari tents on wooden platforms, all with shared bathroom facilities. Overall, it's a very nice set-up with a classic park feel. It sells beers and drinks, but the closest food is 1.25km away at the Lakeside Restaurant or upmarket Arcadia Cottages; UWA can arrange a *boda-boda* for USh10,000.

UWA Campsites
CAMPGROUND $

(camping per person USh15,000) There are three campsites, but most opt for the attractive Lakeside Camp 2, located 1.25km from the park headquarters. It has the scenic **Lakeside Restaurant** (mains USh15,000-20,000; ⊙7am-10pm), which is good if you can spare a long time to wait for your food. If you have your own vehicle, consider Kingfisher Campsite 3, which is more rustic. Be mindful of encounters with wildlife, particularly hippos.

Eagles Nest Lake Mburo
LODGE $$

(☑0312-294894, 0777-820071; www.naturelodges.biz; s/d US$60/70) Up the top of an impossibly steep hill outside the park, this new Dutch-owned lodge has memorable views out to Mburo's distant plains and lakes. Tented safari-style accommodation is simple, but fantastic value at these prices.

★ Mihingo Lodge
LODGE $$$

(☑0752-410509; www.mihingolodge.com; s/d incl full board from US$360/500; 🛜🏊) One of Uganda's best park lodges lies just outside Mburo's eastern border, with rustic tent-cottages spread along the ridge. All have amazing views, including some over a watering hole busy with zebras, impala and warthogs. Its luxurious pool also has views out to a salt lick. Another highlight of the lodge is its family of habituated bushbabies who are regular visitors at night. It also runs horseriding safaris.

Rwakobo Rock
LODGE $$$

(☑0755-211771; www.rwakoborock.com; s/d incl full board US$150/250; 🛜) ✍ It may officially be outside the park, but you'll feel well and truly immersed within, particularly with the soaring Mburo views from its namesake rock. *Bandas* are nestled away in the bush, while the thatched-roof restaurant has more

views and excellent meals. It has good eco credentials too. Check the website for activities on offer including bike safaris, cultural walks and wildlife drive/walk combos.

Kimbla-Mantana Lake Mburo Camp
LODGE $$$

(☑0392-967368; www.kimbla-mantana.com; s/d incl full board US$220/330) A classy camp offering luxury tents with commanding views of Lake Mburo (and sunsets behind the hills) available right from the hammocks on the big porches.

Arcadia Cottages
LODGE $$$

(☑0486-26231; www.arcadiacottages.net/mburo; s/d incl full board US$150/220) Near but not right on the lake, this camp features bright, attractive cottages that are a melange of concrete, canvas, wood and thatch. The small daily menu (USh20,000) always has something Italian on it; nonguests are welcome to dine here.

❶ Getting There & Away

There are two possible ways into the park from the main Masaka–Mbarara road.

CAR

If you're driving your own vehicle, it's better to use the Nshara gate, 13km after Lyantonde because you'll see much more wildlife on the drive in.

SPECIAL-HIRE TAXI, BODA-BODA & MINIBUS

If you're hoping to hitch in or arrange a special-hire taxi (USh60,000) or *boda-boda* (USh15,000), it's best to use the route from the Sanga gate, 27km after Lyantonde and 40km from Mbarara. Minibus taxis to Sanga cost USh6000 from Mbarara (45 minutes) and USh10,000 from Masaka (two hours). It's about a 25km drive to Rwonyo from either gate.

If you're really rushed, Lake Mburo can be done as a day trip from Kampala. It's about a 3½-hour drive each way. A bus to Kampala is USh17,000.

Masaka

POP 73,000

In 1979 Masaka was trashed by the Tanzanian army during the war that ousted Idi Amin. While the scars remain very visible, these days Masaka has turned the corner and is a suprisingly happening little town. For most travellers, it's a stop en route to the Ssese Islands or Tanzania, and an otherwise good place to break your journey for a meal or coffee.

Sights

Nabajjuzi Wetlands WETLANDS
(📞0414-540719; www.natureuganda.org) Just out of Masaka on the way to Mbarara, these Ramsar site–listed wetlands offer excellent opportunities to spy two of Uganda's most elusive animals: the shoebill stork and the sitatunga.

Weaver Bird ARTS CENTRE
(Camp Ndegeya; 📞0777-006726; www.weaverbirdartcommunity.org) This community arts centre in Ndegeya village, 7km from Masaka, has a cool outdoor sculpture park and holds art events throughout the year, including Fiestart in August. A *boda-boda* here costs USh3000.

Sleeping

Bandas BANDAS $
(📞0792-011010; www.banda.dk; 7 Kigamba Rd; dm US$12-20, s/d US$30/50; 🕸🏊) The Danish owners of Cafe Frikadellen run this peaceful, private guesthouse. It has a resort feel with smart, very affordable *bandas* arranged around a sparkling pool, and a restaurant with great views. It's within a large, unsigned compound.

Villa Katwe GUESTHOUSE $
(📞0791-000637; www.villakatwe.com; Somero Rd; camping US$12, dm US$14, s/d/tr US$40/60/81,

without bathroom US$25/40/48; 🕸) Run by Robin and Wycliffe, a fun young Dutch-Ugandan couple (who are a good source of travel info), this chilled-out guesthouse has a homely atmosphere with social kitchen table and lounge. There's also a backyard full of bunnies, and the Your Way Tours company.

Masaka Backpackers BACKPACKERS $
(📞0752-619389; www.masakabackpackers.webklik.nl/page/home; camping from USh10,000, dm USh16,000, s/d USh25,000/45,000; 🕸) This fun, friendly place 4.5km south of town has a rural feel and a helpful owner. It can arrange visits to the Nabajjuzi Wetlands and organise village tours. A *boda-boda* from Masaka costs around USh2000 and special-hire taxi is USh12,000.

Eating

Valley Cove UGANDAN $
(47 Hobat St; mains USh300-6000; ⊙7am-11pm) This popular eatery is a good spot to grab some local food.

Café Frikadellen DANISH, GREEK $$
(www.facebook.com/CafeFrikadellen; mains USh13,000-26,000; ⊙8am-10pm Mon-Fri, from 10am Sat, from noon Sun; 🕸) An expat fav, this Danish-owned eatery is best known for its Friday night all-you-can-eat barbecue (USh30,000) but also serves quality à-la-carte dishes from Greek to Danish, including a *frikadeller* (meatball) burger. Proceeds from its craft shop go to an orphanage.

Plot 99 CAFE $$
(www.plot99.ugogreen.eu; 99 Hill Rd, Kizungu; mains USh13,000-24,000; ⊙noon-10pm Mon, Wed & Thu, 10am-10pm Fri-Sun; 🕸) 🍴 This chilled-out Belgian-Dutch-owned coffeehouse serves everything from Belgian fries with mayo, fish croquettes, burgers and Greek salads. It has great coffee too, and proceeds go to a locally based charity, U Go Green (www.ugogreen.eu).

ⓘ Getting There & Away

Most minibuses pick up and drop off passengers at the Shell petrol station on Kampala Rd. Many buses, on the other hand, use the bypass rather than coming into town, so it's usually quickest to take a *boda-boda* (USh2000) to nearby Nyendo for eastbound services and Kyabakuza for westbound services. Service is frequent to Kampala (USh10,000, two hours) and Mbarara (USh10,000, 2½ hours), but less so to Kabale (USh20,000, five hours).

If you're crossing into Tanzania it's best to hop on the direct Friend Safaris bus from Kampala out at the junction.

Ssese Islands

If you're looking for a place to slow it right down, Ssese's lush archipelago of 84 islands along Lake Victoria's northwestern shore boasts some stunning white-sand beaches. The early 1990s saw their popularity peak, but the suspension of the ferry service largely removed them from the *mzungu* map until a ferry began running from Entebbe in 2006.

Early in the 20th century, sleeping sickness hit the islands (Ssese = Tsetse), which saw most of the original Bassese inhabitants flee. People slowly began to drift back about a decade and a half later, but it wasn't until the 1980s that serious settlement took place again. There are very few Bassese anymore and their Lussese language has all but died.

The lack of settlement left the islands largely unspoiled, though things have changed dramatically in the recent past. Massive scars of deforestation are visible on many of the islands, especially Buggala, and overfishing is an issue.

There's not much to do on Ssese other than grab a good book and relax. There are canoes for hire, but swimming is not advised due to the risks of bilharzia, and some outlaying islands have the occasional hippo and crocodile. Most guesthouses on the beach have nightly bonfires, which is a great way to relax with a few drinks after enjoying one of Ssese's famous sunsets.

Few people venture far beyond **Buggala Island** (the most accessible of the islands), but **Banda Island** is an old-school backpacker destination with a picturesque beach that's enjoying a resurgence (minus the noise pollution that's a blight on Buggala). Far flung **Bukasa**, the second largest of the Sseses is rarely visited, but has several spots worth exploring, including Musenyi Beach.

Sleeping & Eating

Almost all visitors limit themselves to Buggala or Banda islands, but Bukasa Island also has some basic sleeping options including **Agnes' Guesthouse**, near the pier, and **Father Christopher's Guesthouse**, a 30-minute walk further afield.

Buggala Island

Most of the Buggala Island lodging is centred on attractive Lutoboka Bay, right where the ferry drops you off, and most hotels will pick you up for free. All hotels have restaurants with decent food but expect a very long wait. Always ask for a discount if things look slow; you'll often get one.

Islands Club
GUESTHOUSE $
(☑ 0772-641376; www.sseseislandsclub.com; s/d USh70,000/130,000) One of the first lodgings on the island, the wooden bungalows here have a real beachy feel to them, which may have something to do with their location on a blinding stretch of white sand! The spiced, fried tilapia it serves is absolutely delicious and staff are friendly and helpful.

Ssese Islands Beach Hotel
HOTEL $
(☑ 0754-444684; www.sseseislandsbeachhotel.com; camping with/without tent USh26,000/31,000, s/d incl full breakfast from USh61,000/80,000; @) While motel-style rooms may not suit an island getaway, at least they're set right on the beach with great views from their private porches. It backs on to a basic golf course; a hit is inclusive in the rates.

Brovad Sands Lodge
RESORT $$
(☑ 0758-660020; www.sseseislandsresorthotel.com; s/d USh120,000/180,000; 🖥🛏) A stunning property comprising large, plush thatched cottages in a tropical garden with a soaring *banda* restaurant. This feels like a classic beach resort. Though it has its imperfections (for example some shoddy materials), all is forgiven when lazing in its pool or hanging out on the beach by the bonfire. Discounts available.

Banda Island

★ Banda Island Resort
GUESTHOUSE $
(☑ 0774-728747, 0772-222777; www.bandaisland.biz; Banda Island; incl full board camping USh80,000, dm & tented camping USh100,000, cottage USh120,000) Banda is exactly what an island escape should be: it has a picturesque beach and laid-back vibe, and days here feel like weeks. And if Banda is Gilligan's Island, its laid-back Aussie manager, Andrew, is the Professor; he's whipped the place into shape, namely by introducing running water but, more importantly, cold beer and hot showers! Accommodation is in comfortable rustic cottages, decent dorms or tented camps.

Food is a highlight, with the local catch being a major component in anything from fish samosas to sensational fish burritos. Guests can paddle around in canoes, learn to sail, pass the days with lazy games of outdoor backgammon, or perform some quality control on the hammocks. Hippos are common visitors come full moon.

ⓘ Information

The only full-on town is Kalangala on Buggala Island. There's a post office but no bank. The electricity supply on the island is erratic, though most lodges have generators.

ⓘ Getting There & Away

FROM NAKIWOGO

Visitors can get to Buggala Island on the MV *Kalangala* ferry from Nakiwogo near Entebbe. It departs the mainland at 2pm daily and leaves the island at 8am. The trip usually takes 3½ hours. First-class seating costs USh14,000 and second-class is USh10,000, but there's little difference between the two. Vehicles cost USh50,000. At weekends and on holidays the boat can be crowded, so show up early to claim a seat or you may have to stand on the deck.

FROM KASENYI

To get to Banda Island there are small wooden boats departing from Kasenyi, a gritty fishing village 7km off the Entebbe–Kampala road (the turn-off is 5km outside Entebbe), a 30-minute minibus ride (USh3000) from Kampala's Old Taxi Park.

Boats here to Banda Island (from USh20,000, 3¼ hours) leave daily, with a varied schedule that some days is direct and others stops via Kitobo Island. There's also a weekly boat on Fridays to Bukasa Island (USh15,000, four hours). Also note that schedules and prices are very fickle, so try to confirm things before heading out to the landing – Banda Island Resort (p455) is the definitive source of info here, and can also arrange lifejackets – which you should insist on wearing.

At Kasenyi, Mama Jane's restaurant is the place to hang out before your boat. Take note: there's no boat landing, so unless you opt to wade through bilharzia-infested waters, the only way onboard is to be carried! Male passengers ride piggyback on porter's shoulders, while females are carried cradle-style. It's all part of the fun.

FROM BUKAKATA

From the west, a free car ferry links Bukakata (36km east of Masaka) on the mainland with Luku on Buggala Island (50 minutes). The ferry sails either direction every few hours from early in the morning to late afternoon. There are no morning trips on Sunday. The schedule changes often, so call one of the resorts on Buggala Island to get the current times.

On Buggala Island, there are shared taxis that run from Kalangala to Luku (USh7000, one hour), while coming from the mainland there are taxis that run from Nyendo (3km east of Masaka) to Bukakata (USh5000, one hour). Taxis in both directions run to coincide with the car-ferry schedule, and neither is a fun trip as they're usually insanely overpacked with 15 passengers somehow squeezing into a five-seat car!

ⓘ Getting Around

On Buggala Island, Kalangala trading centre is 2km uphill from the pier; a *boda-boda* costs USh2000.

To get to the other islands is very pricey thanks to rising fuel costs, so island hopping is not really a popular activity. A special-hire boat from Buggala Island to Banda Island is US$70.

NORTHWESTERN UGANDA

For decades, the Lord's Resistance Army (LRA) and its war on civilians put most of northwestern Uganda effectively off limits. But now that the LRA has fled Uganda, this vast region is once again on the traveller's map. As before, Murchison Falls National Park remains the region's saving grace. The best all-round protected area in the country for wildlife and attractions, Murchison has large populations of lions, leopards, buffaloes, elephants, giraffes, hippos and chimpanzees, plus its namesake waterfall is world-class. Ziwa Rhino Sanctuary is also a popular stopover to see white rhinos.

Ziwa Rhino Sanctuary

The Big Five are back. Twenty years after poachers shot the nation's last wild rhino in Uganda, Rhino Fund Uganda opened this private 70-sq-km reserve (☑ 0772-713410; www.rhinofund.org; adult/child US$40/20; ⏱ 7.30am-5pm), 170km northwest of Kampala. There are now 15 southern white rhinos roaming the savannah and wetland, nine of which were born in the wild in Uganda. The long-term goal for these magnificent beasts is to reintroduce them in Murchison Falls and Kidepo Valley national parks.

Sadly, the situation is far more grim for the northern white rhino, which was indig-

Northwestern Uganda

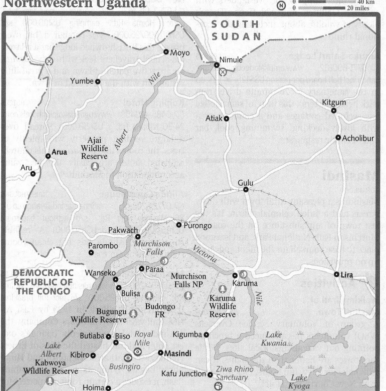

enous to Uganda. It is now so close to extinction there's little hope for its survival. There are only five confirmed members of the species left, all of them living in captivity.

A guide will lead you on an up-close encounter, either in your vehicle (a car is fine in the dry season, but you'll need a 4WD in the wet) or theirs (US$25). Once you reach the rhinos you finish your visit on foot. While tracking rhinos on foot sounds a bit foolhardy, the fact that they're in the company of armed antipoacher rangers 24 hours, means they're well and truly used to human presence.

Other animals living inside the 1.8m-tall electric fence include leopards, hippos (which you won't see), crocodiles, bushbucks and oribi.

It's also home to 350 species of bird, and birdwatching tours cost US$25, with highlights including the giant kingfisher, Ross's turaco and shoebill. The latter are best seen on early morning shoebill canoe trips (US$30 per person) to an adjoining swamp, where you've got a very good chance of spotting them.

There's occasionally volunteer opportunities, so enquire via the website.

All buses from Kampala heading to Gulu or Masindi pass nearby. Get off at little Nakitoma (USh13,000, three hours) and take a *boda-boda* 7km to the sanctuary gate for USh6000.

Sleeping & Eating

While most visit as a day trip en route to Murchison from Kampala, there are two good sleeping options in the park.

Ziwa Rhino Lodge   GUESTHOUSE $
(☏ 0775-521035; info@ziwarhino.com; camping per tent US$10, r with shared bathroom US$15, cottage US$40) Set around the camp headquarters, choose between the cottages or row of basic rooms with small porches. There's also a restaurant serving simple food and cold

drinks, plus camping for overlanders with cooking facilities and ablutions. There's plenty of wildlife about, including the occasional rhino.

Amuka Safari Lodge LODGE $$
(☑0771-600812; www.amukalodgeuganda.com; banda incl half board per person US$125; ⊠) Deep in the sanctuary (a 20-minute drive from park headquarters), this tasteful safari lodge has secluded cottages and a common area with lovely decking, swimming pool, bar and open-air restaurant.

Masindi

POP 43,000

Masindi is a pleasant rural town with dusty streets and a faded colonial charm. It's the last town of any substance on the road to Murchison Falls National Park, and is a good place to base yourself for the night and stock up on provisions.

🏃 Activities

**Walking Trail of
Masindi Town** WALKING TOUR
A group of Voluntary Service Overseas (VSO) volunteers has produced a brochure pointing out various historical sites. While the stories are better than the sights, it can still make for a few fun hours. Pick up a map from New Court View Hotel.

🛏 Sleeping & Eating

If you forget to pack anything in Kampala, there are some small supermarkets in Commercial St including **Lucky 7** (Commercial St) and **Wat General Agencies** (Commercial St).

New Court View Hotel BANDA $
(☑0752-446463; www.newcourtviewhotel.com; Hoima Rd; camping USh10,000, s/d USh80,000/95,000; 🐾) Though a bit overpriced, this British-owned lodge has a relaxed, old-school travellers feel with cosy *bandas*, an attractive patch of lawn and a great little restaurant with the best food in town.

Kolping Hotel HOTEL $
(☑0465-420458; www.ugandakolpinghotels.com; 24-30 Nthuha Rd; r USh50,000) Spread over a large, verdant property with plenty of trees, the rooms and *bandas* at this church-affiliated hotel are easily the best-value accommodation in Masindi.

Alinda Guesthouse GUESTHOUSE $
(☑0772-520382; alindamasindi@yahoo.co.uk; 86 Masindi Port Rd; s/d without bathroom USh15,000/30,000, d USh50,000) A reliable shoestringer, Alinda has big clean rooms right on the main road.

Masindi Hotel HOTEL $$
(☑0465-420023; www.masindihotel.com; Hoima Rd; camping USh25,000, s/d incl full breakfast US$95/115; @🐾) Built in 1923 by East Africa Railways and Harbours Company, the Masindi Hotel is reportedly Uganda's oldest hotel and has hosted the likes of Ernest Hemingway, Katharine Hepburn and Humphrey Bogart. While its rooms are nothing flash, it exudes a certain romance perfect for a pre-safari jaunt. The 'Hemingway' bar remains the best place for a drink.

Masindi map:

0 — 200 m
0 — 0.1 miles

Masindi Hotel (700m);
Murchison Falls National
Park (67km)

Kijunjubwa Rd
Masindi Port Rd
Nthuha Rd
Alinda Guesthouse (100m)
Market St
Tongue St
Nthuha Rd
Perse St
Commercial St
Market
Bikunya Rd

Travellers' Corner   AFRICAN, INTERNATIONAL $
(Masindi Port Rd; mains USh4000-7000; ⊙6.30am-11pm) This corner pub serves anything from tasty stews to fajitas in its rear courtyard sitting area.

ℹ Information

Stanbic Bank (Kijunjubwa Rd) and **Barclays** (Masindi Port Rd) have ATMs.

UWA Masindi Information Office (📞0465-420428; ⊙7am-12.30pm & 2-6.30pm Mon-Fri, to noon Sat) The UWA Masindi Information Office, down a dirt road north of the post office, has national park information.

ℹ Getting There & Away

The Post Bus stops in Masindi on its way to and from Kampala (USh10,000, five hours) en route to Hoima. Otherwise **Link** (📞0465-421073) has regular buses to Kampala (USh13,000, 3½ hours), which leave from the bus terminal on Masindi Port Rd between 7.30am and 4.30pm.

For Gulu you'll need to jump on a bus or taxi to Kafu Junction on the main highway and catch a northbound bus there. There are also departures to Butiaba (USh13,000, three hours), Bulisa (USh20,000, 2½ hours) and Wanseko (USh20,000, 2½ hours).

As a gateway town to Murchison Falls National Park, Masindi is a good place to arrange transport hire into the park. Two recommended companies for hiring a 4WD to take into the park are **Yebo Tours** (📞0772-637493; yebotours2002@yahoo.com; Masindi Port Rd; 4WD per day excl fuel US$100) and **Enyange** (📞0772-657403; 4WD per day excluding fuel US$80), opposite the taxi rank.

Hoima

POP 40,000

Hoima is the hub of the Bunyoro kingdom, the oldest in East Africa. For travellers it's a transport hub linking Murchison Falls and Fort Portal.

◉ Sights

Karuziika Palace   PALACE
(📞0782-128229; Main St) If you call his private secretary in advance you can visit the part-time home of the Bunyoro king to see the throne room, which is draped with leopard and lion skins.

Mparo Tombs   HISTORIC SITE
(admission USh10,000) Two kilometres down the Masindi road (4km out of Hoima) is the final resting place of the renowned Bunyoro king Omukama ('King') Chwa II Kabalega and his son. Kabalega was a thorn in the side of the British for much of his reign until he was exiled to the Seychelles in 1899. Inside are his spears, bowls, throne and other personal effects on display above the actual resting place.

🛏 Sleeping

African Village Guest Farm   BANDA $
(📞0772-335115; camping USh10,000, bandas s/d from USh30,000/60,000) Located on a small dairy farm, the *bandas* here have balconies, and Betty and her daughters are great hosts. It's a 10-minute drive outside Hoima; a *boda-boda* costs USh2000.

Nsamo Hotel   HOTEL $
(📞0754-134557; s/d USh35,000/40,000) Though ageing, with its convenient location in town Nsamo is a very good choice.

ℹ Getting There & Away

The Post Bus goes to Kampala via Masindi. Otherwise there are minibuses (USh14,000, three hours) and less-frequent buses (USh12,000, 2½ hours) to Kampala.

There are also minibuses to Masindi (USh10,000, two hours). For Fort Portal there's a coaster bus (USh25,000, six hours) that makes the run directly, but not every day. Otherwise it takes two minibuses to get to Fort Portal with a change in Kagadi. The total price is USh25,000 and it usually takes seven hours.

Minibuses also run to Butiaba (USh10,000, two hours) in the morning plus Bulisa (USh15,000, three hours) and Wanseko (USh15,000, 3¼ hours) all day long.

Murchison Falls National Park

Murchison Falls National Park is Uganda's largest **national park** (📞0392-881348; adult/child US$40/20; ⊙7am-7pm) and one of its very best; animals here are in plentiful supply and the raging Murchison Falls is a sight to behold. Sir Samuel Baker named Murchison Falls in honour of a president of the Royal Geographical Society, and the park was subsequently named after the falls. The Victoria Nile River flows through the park on its way to Lake Albert.

During the 1960s, Murchison (3893 sq km; 5081 sq km with the adjoining Bugungu and Karuma wildlife reserves) was one

Murchison Falls National Park

Murchison Falls National Park

of Africa's most famous parks; as many as 12 launches filled with eager tourists would buzz up the river to the falls each day. The park also had some of the largest concentrations of wildlife in Africa, including as many as 15,000 elephants. Unfortunately, poachers and troops wiped out practically all wildlife, except the more numerous (or less sought-after) herd species. While its rhino population was entirely killed off and remains absent from the park, other wildlife is recovering fast and you can find good numbers of elephants, Rothschild giraffes, lions, Ugandan kob (antelope), waterbucks, buffaloes, hippos and crocodiles these days. Sitatungas, leopards and spotted hyenas might also be seen. Birdlife consists of some 460 species, including quite a few shoebill storks.

Though wildlife is recovering, don't come to Murchison expecting a scene from the Serengeti. That said, even if there were no animals, the awesome power of Murchison Falls would make this park worth visiting.

In recent years, oil exploration within the park has caused concern in some quarters.

In 2010 phased drilling commenced, though at present the drilling is isolated to sections of the park away from wildlife drives. Developments over the next few years will be telling and are being watched carefully by conservationists around the world.

For more information on the park, pick up a copy of *Murchison Falls Conservation Area Guidebook* (2004) by Shaun Mann at the park office.

◉ Sights & Activities

Chimpanzee tracking in Budongo Forest Reserve (p464) is officially part of the park but is operated separately.

Top of the Falls   WATERFALL

Once described as the most spectacular thing to happen to the Nile along its 6700km length, the 50m-wide river is squeezed through a 6m gap in the rock and crashes through this narrow gorge with unbelievable power. The 45m waterfall was featured in the Katharine Hepburn and Humphrey Bogart film *The African Queen*. Murchison was even stronger back then, but in 1962 massive floods cut a second channel creating the smaller Uhuru Falls 200m to the north.

There's a beautiful **walking trail** from the top down to the river, and the upper stretch of this path offers views of Uhuru Falls, which a boat trip will not bring you close enough to to appreciate. A ranger (US$15 per person) is required on this walk. If you take the launch trip, the captain will let you off at the trailhead and a ranger will meet you there. The boat can then pick you up later if there's an afternoon launch. This is also a good way for campers to get to the campsite at the top of the falls before returning to Paraa the next morning. The hike takes about 45 minutes from the bottom.

Nile Boat Trip

The three-hour launch trip (US$30 per person) run by UWA from Paraa heads up to the base of the falls and is one of the highlights of the park for many visitors. There are abundant hippos, crocodiles and buffaloes; thousands of birds, including many fish eagles; and usually elephants along this 17km stretch of the Nile. In the rainy season even shoebills might make an appearance. The trip climaxes with fantastic frontal views of Murchison Falls, from around 500m from its base. Trips depart at 8am and 2pm. Cold drinks (including beers) are available, but no food. Bring sunscreen.

Wild Frontiers (www.wildfrontiers.co.ug; US$32; ⏲ 2.30pm daily, 8.30am Mon, Wed, Fri) also makes the journey in more comfortable boats and it also offers cheese-and-wine sunset cruises (US$75 per person). Another of its offerings is a longer Delta boat trip to the papyrus-filled delta where the Nile empties into Lake Albert (US$55 per person); shoebill sightings are common.

Wildlife Drives

Pretty much all wildlife watching on land happens in the Buligi area, on the point between the Albert and Victoria Niles. Just about all the park's resident species might be seen in the savannah on the Albert, Queen and Victoria tracks, and the chances of spotting lions and leopards are quite good. There's very little wildlife south of the river, and driving in from Masindi or Pakwach you'll probably only see baboons and warthogs.

You'll want to budget a minimum of four hours to get out there and back. Those with their own vehicle should definitely take a UWA ranger-guide (US$20) to boost their chances of sightings. Night drives (from 6pm to 10pm) are a new initiative enabling travellers to see nocturnal animals, and cost

---

ℹ MURCHISON FALLS NATIONAL PARK

Why Go

Excellent wildlife watching from boat or car; Rothschild giraffes; lions; sheer power and fury of Murchison Falls; chimpanzee tracking in Budongo Forest Reserve.

When to Go

Year-round, but February to April is best as grass is lower.

Practicalities

Public transport can be used to get to the fringes of the park, but you'll need a vehicle to get within; numerous hostels offer budget tours.

Budget Tips

Lodges outside the northern sections of the park are accessible via buses from Kampala, from where you can organise safari drives into the park. Otherwise sign up for an organised tour run by Red Chilli (p462) or Backpackers (p382), who both run well-priced three-day tours from Kampala.

THE MISADVENTURES OF HEMINGWAY IN UGANDA

Despite Ernest Hemingway's well-known love of Africa, having based several novels and short stories here, he certainly could be forgiven for not looking back fondly upon his time spent in Uganda. Having the misfortune of experiencing two plane crashes within a week, his time here was a total disaster.

As a Christmas present to his fourth wife, Mary Welsh, in 1954, Hemingway arranged a scenic flight from Nairobi to the Congo, which en route took in spectacular aerial views of the Nile around Lake Albert. While circling Murchison Falls at a low altitude, the small plane clipped a telegraph wire, causing the plane to crash into the dense forest. With relatively minor, yet painful, injuries including broken ribs and a dislocated shoulder, they emerged from the wreck to face a night stranded near the falls.

Anyone who's done the Murchison Falls launch trip can attest to its abundance of wild-life, and a night spent out in the open with crocodiles, hippos, elephants and leopards is far from ideal. Yet somehow they managed to survive the night, spent shooing off animals, and were fortuitously picked up by a passing boat en route to Butiaba the next day.

Undeterred by the shock of surviving a plane crash and in need of medical attention, Hemingway and Welsh decided to charter another flight to take them to Entebbe. But in a terrible stroke of bad luck, the plane crashed again! This time in a ball of flames upon take off. Injuries sustained this time were indeed far more serious, particularly for Hemingway who sustained a fractured skull while forcing his way out, as well as a ruptured liver, a collapsed intestine, several broken vertebrae, and a burnt scalp (among other injuries). It was widely reported in the international media that he'd died in the crash, and during time spent recovering in Nairobi, Hemingway was able to read over his obituaries.

The severity of his injuries prevented Hemingway from accepting his Nobel Prize for Literature 10 months later, and many believed he never physically or mentally recovered from the accidents. Hemingway wrote about the incident for *Look* magazine in 1954 in an article with the innocuous sounding title: 'The Christmas Gift'.

US$100 per vehicle. For self drivers staying across the river, take note of the Paraa ferry schedule to avoid missing the last boat back in the evening at 7pm (get there 10 minutes earlier). On the off-chance you haven't organised a vehicle, budget travellers sometimes have luck hanging out at the ferry and finding space in someone's vehicle.

Nature Walks

The 1.5km guided nature walk along the north bank of the Nile run by Paraa Safari Lodge (US$30 per person) is popular with birdwatchers, but you're not likely to see many other animals.

Sport Fishing

Murchison is one of the world's best places to fish for the gargantuan Nile perch. The normal catch ranges from 20kg to 60kg, but the record haul is 108kg. You can fish from the shore or get a boat, but be mindful of crocodiles and hippos. Catfish and tiger fish are other popular catches. Note that fishing here is strictly catch and release. Permits cost US$50 for one day, US$150 for four days. The best months are December to March and

June to October. For more information, check out www.fishingmurchison.com.

Wild Frontiers (p461) offer full-day fishing trips from US$115 per person (excluding permits).

🛏 Sleeping & Eating

Most of Murchison's lodges are located within the vicinity of the Paraa park headquarters, a convenient choice for wildlife drives and the falls. There are also more remote options in the far west, north and south sectors, providing a more peaceful experience.

🛏 Paraa

⭐ **Red Chilli Rest Camp**   BACKPACKERS $
(📞 0772-509150; www.redchillihideaway.com; camping US$7, d safari tents US$30, d banda with/without bathroom US$50/35, family banda US$85; ﹡) Close to Paraa, the popular Red Chilli team from Kampala offers the best budget option in Murchison. The *bandas* are great value, while well-priced safari tents get the job done. The restaurant-bar is set under a thatched roof with good nature views, and cheap, tasty Western dishes (from USh8500) as well as packed

breakfasts for safari drives. A swimming pool is being added. Book well in advance.

Hippos regularly graze here at night, so bring a torch and give them a very wide berth.

Paraa Safari Lodge LODGE $$$
(📞0772-788880; www.paraalodge.com; s/d/ste incl full board US$213/342/429; @🔒🛜🏊) On the northern bank of the river, this classic luxury lodge has a great location and views, as well as excellent facilities such as a swim-up bar. From across the river it looks rather like a POW camp, but up close it's lovely and the rooms are four-star standard. Go for an upstairs room for the best views.

Elsewhere in the Park

Top of the Falls Campsite CAMPGROUND
(per person USh15,000) On the river near the falls, this scenic and secluded camp has pit toilets and nothing else.

Chobe Safari Lodge LODGE $$$
(📞0312-259390; www.chobelodgeuganda. com; Chobe gate; s/d/ste incl full board from US$205/371/439; @🔒🏊) Isolated on the far eastern reaches of the park, renovations have returned Chobe – one of Murchison's original lodges from the 1950s – to its former splendour. Its gorgeous river location is teeming with honking hippos, enjoyed from its classy outdoor restaurant. The upstairs standard rooms are the best pick with great views, lovely decor and balconies. Its three-tiered swimming pool is another highlight.

The place has the feel of a celebrity hideaway, and even has its own airstrip – though it's more popular with grazing buffaloes.

Pakuba Safari Lodge LODGE $$$
(📞0414-253597; www.pakubasafarilodge.com; s/d incl full board US$177/236) Overlooking the Albert Nile, the Pakuba lodge was rebuilt on a site just up from the ruins of the old lodge formerly used by Idi Amin. Despite the wonderful location, it doesn't reach the expected level of luxury, with more motel-style rooms. A design flaw also means lake views aren't maximised.

Outside the Park

Buligi
Yebo Tours Safari Camp BANDA $
(📞0465-420029; camping per person US$5; bandas incl full board per person US$30) Yebo is a good budget option with basic mud-wall

bandas and a low-key, local atmosphere. It's 8km from Paraa.

Murchison River Lodge LODGE $$
(📞0714-000085; www.murchisonriverlodge.com; camping US$12, safari tents s/d US$130/200, without bathroom US$75/130, cottage s/d US$175/260; 🛜🏊) While firmly in the luxury lodge category, Murchison River opens its doors to all budgets, whether you're here to pitch a tent, do some lazy camping or live it up in its lavish double -story thatched cottages. The safari-style open-air restaurant has superb views of the Victoria Nile, with common sightings of elephants in the distance. Except for basic camping, prices are full board. However, campers can use the pool, making it a popular choice.

Nile Safari Lodge LODGE $$$
(📞0414-258273; www.geolodgesafrica.com; camping US$10, s/d incl full board US$236/354; 🏊) For those who want views from their rooms, Nile Safari is the pick of the lot, with each of its stilted cottages featuring superb Victoria Nile outlooks from private balconies. However, at these prices the accommodations are a bit dated, though the outdoor showers are an experience. For campers, the grassy Shoebill site (US$30 for tent hire) is a good spot by the river, though you'll need to pay extra to use the pool.

Bakers Lodge LODGE $$$
(📞0414-321479; www.wildfrontiers.com) Still under construction, Wild Frontiers' new luxurious thatched *bandas* look stunning with a wonderful location on the Victoria Nile. With its fleet of boats, it'll be a good spot for fishing enthusiasts.

Pakwach
To the northwest of the park a bunch of quality, affordable lodges have opened up around 5km from the Tangi gate.

Heritage Safari Lodge LODGE $$
(📞0792-212618; www.heritagesafarilodge.com; Tangi gate, Pakwach; lazy camping US$20, s/d US$90/120; 🛜) This Ugandan-owned lodge has wonderful *bandas* built using traditional methods and decked out with comfortable interiors. All look over the Albert Nile, and elephants are regular visitors.

Bwana Tembo Safari Camp LODGE $$
(📞0791-217028; www.bwanatembosafaricamp. com; Bwana Tembo Rd; s/d incl full board from US$115/200; 🛜) Set on a grassy plot of land, this relaxed, Italian-owned camp has a mix

of tented camping and cottages. Its home-made pastas and Italian meat dishes get rave reviews. It offers safari vehicles with driver for US$100 for a half day, and US$180 for full-day trips.

Fort Murchison　　　　　　LODGE **$$**
(✆0312-294894; www.naturelodges.biz/fort-murchison; Pakwach; tented camping s/d US$35/60, s/d US$125/150) The newest (and most ambitious) venture by Dutch-owned Nature Lodges takes the form of an Islamic fort, with an appropriately commanding location overlooking the Albert Nile. Rooms have plenty of character and style (go for an upstairs room for the best views).

If you're looking for a more classic safari-style accommodation, there's tented camping set up on an expansive campsite. The rooftop bar is another perk.

Wankwar Gate

Murchison Safari Lodge　　　BACKPACKERS **$**
(✆0776-799899; incl full breakfast camping USh20,000, dm USh40,000, banda without bathroom USh80,000) This bush camp in the northern sector, 7km from Wankwar gate (and 10km from Purongo town), has basic *bandas* and dorms in a peaceful spot but lacks atmosphere. Most people who stay here are on a safari with Backpackers Hostel in Kampala.

❶ Getting There & Away

BUGUNGU & KICHUMBANYOBO GATES

The park headquarters at Paraa is on the southern bank of the Victoria Nile. From Masindi you can take the direct route through the Kichumbanyobo gate or the longer, but more scenic, route west to Lake Albert and then enter the park via the western Bugungu gate. For those with their own vehicle, consider entering via one route and leaving by the other. Both routes go through Budongo Forest Reserve, a recommended stopover.

The cheapest way into Murchison Falls National Park is to get to Bulisa or Wanseko, the latter an interesting fishing village where the Nile empties into Lake Albert. Minibuses run to these neighbouring towns daily from Hoima and Masindi for USh15,000. You can go as far as Bulisa, from where you can get a *boda-boda* to take you to Paraa for around USh40,000. *Boda-boda* drivers are required to pay park admission of USh15,000 but often don't, so negotiate a fee without the admission costs and you might get lucky. Alternatively, continue the 6km to Wanseko and then negotiate with the minibus driver to continue to Paraa as a special-hire (perhaps as low as USh80,000).

NORTHERN GATES

With security now restored to northern Uganda, the northern gates – Chobe (near Karuma Falls on the Gulu road), Tangi (reached from Pakwach) and Wankwar (from Purongo) – are now viable options again.

The northern section of the park is surprisingly accessible from Kampala by public transport, with **KK Traveller** (✆0718-204665; www.kkcoaches.co.ug; Arua Park) and Gaaga bus making the trip to Pakwach (USh30,000 six hours) via Purongo (for Wankwar gate, USh25,000) and Karuma (for Chobe gate). Buses depart from Arua Park at 1pm.

❶ Getting Around

BOAT

A vehicle ferry crosses the river at Paraa. The crossings take five minutes and ferries are scheduled approximately every hour between 7am and 7pm. The ferry holds eight vehicles, but will make as many crossings as necessary to get everyone over. The one-way fare is USh5000 for passengers and USh20,000 for cars. Unscheduled crossings cost USh100,000. Ferry fees are payable at a small booth near the landing.

CAR

Tracks within the park are generally well maintained, and though a 4WD is highly recommended, cars should have little trouble getting around. However, some tracks, especially in the Buligi area (where most wildlife drives are done), can be treacherous during the wet season.

Fuel is available on the northern side of the Victoria Nile River at Paraa, but it costs about 10% more than in Masindi.

Budongo Forest Reserve

The **Budongo Forest Reserve** is a large (825 sq km) tract of virgin tropical forest on the southern fringes of Murchison Falls National Park. Its main attractions are chimpanzees and birds (366 species), but the huge mahogany trees are also worth a look. It's a great add-on to your Murchison Falls National Park visit. As it's actually part of the park, you'll need to pay entry fees (per adult US$40, child US$20).

Kaniyo Pabidi

Kaniyo Pabidi Tourist Site in Budongo Forest Reserve is on the main park road, 29km north of Masindi and inside the southern boundary of Murchison Falls National Park. It's regarded as one of the more reliable places to track chimpanzees in Uganda with an estimated 70% chance of finding them. You have to pay the park entry fee on top of the activity fees. This was the first place in Uganda to employ a female ranger, and Sauda still works here.

Kaniyo Pabidi isn't served by public transport, but it's possible to arrange a charter from Masindi for about USh60,000 or take a *boda-boda* for about USh15,000 (more if the guards make the driver pay admission fees).

🏃 Activities

Activities in the reserve are organised through Budongo Eco Lodge and while they can be booked at the lodge itself, it's safer to prebook permits through Great Lake Safaris (p475), the current concession holders. Low season runs from March until mid-June.

Chimpanzee Tracking

Chimpanzee-tracking trips take place daily and you have a good chance of finding the chimps, though it's not guarenteed. The walking is easy as the terrain is level, and walks last from two to four hours.

Treks cost US$75 during low season, and US$85 during high season, excluding national park entry fees. Once you find the chimps, you get to spend an hour with them; two lucky visitors (October through June only) are allowed to spend a whole day for US$150 per person. Trekkers must be over 15 years old.

Forest Walks

These worthwhile forest walks pass through East Africa's last remaining mahogany forest. The largest specimens are 60m tall and 300 years old. Black-and-white colobus monkeys and duikers are commonly seen. Guided walks cost US$15 for 2½ hours and US$20 for four hours.

Birdwatching Walks

Those here for birdwatching usually seek Puvel's Illadopsis, which isn't known anywhere else in East Africa. Other highly sought species are the rufous-sided broadbill and white-naped pigeon. Guided walks cost US$20 for a half day and US$35 for a full day.

🛏 Sleeping

Boomu Women's Group   GUESTHOUSE $
(☎ 0772-448950; www.boomuwomensgroup. org; camping per person USh10,000, bandas per person without bathroom USh45,000) 🍴 Just outside the Kichumbanyobo gate, the simple thatched *bandas* here are run by local women and offer an insight in to how rural Ugandans live. The money helps raise funds for a local preschool. There's a fascinating cooking tour (USh20,000 per person) among other activities. A *boda-boda* from Masindi costs USh10,000.

Budongo Eco Lodge   LODGE $$
(☎ 0414-267153; www.ugandalodges.com/ budongo; dm/s/d/tr US$26/81/134/156; 🔊) With excellent prices for a national park lodge, the attractive cabins here are surrounded by forest and have hot water, solar power and eco-toilets. It serves good food too, and sell greeting cards made from materials obtained from animal snares removed from the forest, with proceeds funding further removal.

Busingiro

Busingiro Tourist Site, also within Budongo and 40km west of Masindi on the Bulisa Rd, is for the birdwatchers. It's a great place to add the yellow-footed flycatcher and African pitta to your spotting list. There used to be chimp tracking here too, but when the chimps lost their fear of humans they started raiding local farms, forcing an end to the program. The chimps are still here though, so you may get lucky and meet them.

The **Royal Mile** (guided walks half/full day US$20/35) is regarded by many as having the best **birdwatching** in the whole country, both because there are some rare species and because sightings are so easy. The bird list exceeds 350 species, including several types of flycatcher, sunbird, kingfisher, hornbill and eagle. At dusk it's possible to view bat hawks.

Busingiro is on the route used by minibuses heading for Bulisa from Masindi. The trip costs USh8000 and can take about an hour. You'll need your own vehicle to get to the Royal Mile. The first turn-off is 25km from Masindi, marked by the Nyabyeya Forestry College signpost, and there's another, also with a college sign, closer to Busingiro.

UNDERSTAND UGANDA

History

Independence

Unlike Kenya and, to a lesser extent, Tanzania, Uganda never experienced a large influx of European colonisers and the associated expropriation of land. Instead, farmers were encouraged to grow cash crops for export through their own cooperative groups. Consequently, Ugandan nationalist organisations sprouted much later than those in neighbouring countries, and, when they did, it happened along tribal lines. So exclusive were some of these that when Ugandan independence was discussed, the Baganda people considered secession.

By the mid-1950s, however, Lango school teacher Dr Milton Obote managed to put together a loose coalition headed by the Uganda People's Congress (UPC), which led Uganda to independence in 1962 with the promise that the Buganda kingdom would have autonomy. The *kabaka* (king), Edward Mutesa II, became the president of the new nation, and Milton Obote became Uganda's first prime minister.

It wasn't a very favourable time for Uganda to come to grips with independence. Civil wars were raging in neighbouring Sudan, the DRC and Rwanda, and refugees streamed into Uganda, adding to its problems. Also, it soon became obvious that Obote had no intention of sharing power with the *kabaka*. A confrontation loomed.

Obote moved in 1966, arresting several cabinet ministers and ordering his army chief of staff, Idi Amin, to storm the *kabaka*'s palace in Kampala. The raid resulted in the flight of the *kabaka* and his exile in London, where he died in 1969. Following this coup, Obote proclaimed himself president, and the Buganda monarchy was abolished, along with those of the Bunyoro, Ankole, Toro and Busoga kingdoms. Meanwhile, Idi Amin's star was on the rise.

The Amin Years

Under Milton Obote's watch, events began to spiral out of control. Obote ordered his attorney general, Godfrey Binaisa, to rewrite the constitution to consolidate virtually all powers in the presidency and then moved to nationalise foreign assets.

In 1969 a scandal broke out over US$5 million in funds and weapons allocated to the Ministry of Defence that couldn't be accounted for. An explanation was demanded of Amin. When it wasn't forthcoming, his deputy, Colonel Okoya, and some junior officers demanded his resignation. Shortly afterwards Okoya and his wife were shot dead in their Gulu home, and rumours began to circulate about Amin's imminent arrest. It never came. Instead, when Obote left for Singapore in January 1971 to attend the Commonwealth Heads of Government Meeting (CHOGM), Amin staged a coup. Uganda's former colonial masters, the British, who had probably suffered most under Obote's nationalisation program, were among the first to recognise the new regime. Obote went into exile in Tanzania.

So began Uganda's first reign of terror. All political activities were quickly suspended and the army was empowered to shoot on sight anyone suspected of opposition to the regime. Over the next eight years an estimated 300,000 Ugandans lost their lives, often in such brutal ways as being bludgeoned to death with sledgehammers and iron bars. Among those who suffered most were the Acholi and Lango people, who were decimated in waves of massacres; whole villages were wiped out. Next Amin turned on the professional classes. University professors, doctors, cabinet ministers, lawyers, businesspeople and even military officers who might have posed a threat to Amin were dragged from their offices and shot or simply never seen again.

Also targeted was the 70,000-strong Asian community. In 1972 they were given 90 days to leave the country. Amin and his cronies grabbed the billion-dollar booty the evictees were forced to leave behind squandering it on 'new toys for the boys' and personal excess. Amin then turned on the British, nationalising US$500 million worth of investments in tea plantations and other industries without compensation.

Meanwhile the economy collapsed, industrial activity ground to a halt, hospitals and rural health clinics closed, roads cracked and became riddled with potholes, cities became garbage dumps and utilities fell apart. The prolific wildlife was machine-gunned by soldiers for meat, ivory and skins, and the tourism industry evaporated. The stream of refugees across the border became a flood.

Faced with chaos and an inflation rate that hit 1000%, Amin was forced to delegate more and more powers to the provincial governors, who became virtual warlords in their areas. Towards the end of the Amin era, the treasury was so bereft of funds it was unable to pay the soldiers. One of the few supporters of Amin at the end of the 1970s was Colonel Gadaffi, who bailed out the Ugandan economy in the name of Islamic brotherhood (Amin had conveniently become a Muslim by this stage) and began an intensive drive to equip the Ugandan forces with sophisticated weapons.

The rot had spread too far, however, and was beyond the point where a few million dollars in Libyan largesse could help. Faced with a restless army beset with intertribal fighting, Amin looked for a diversion. He chose a war with Tanzania, ostensibly to teach that country a lesson for supporting anti-Amin dissidents. It was his last major act of recklessness, and in it lay his downfall.

War with Tanzania

On 30 October 1978 the Ugandan army rolled across northwestern Tanzania virtually unopposed and annexed more than 1200 sq km of territory. Meanwhile, the airforce bombed the Lake Victoria ports of Bukoba and Musoma.

Tanzanian President Julius Nyerere ordered a full-scale counterattack, but it took months to mobilise his ill-equipped and poorly trained forces. By early 1979 he had managed to scrape together a 50,000-strong people's militia, composed mainly of illiterate youngsters from the bush. This militia joined with the many exiled Ugandan liberation groups – united only in their determination to rid Uganda of Amin. The two armies met. East Africa's supposedly best-equipped and best-trained army threw down its weapons and fled, and the Tanzanians pushed on into the heart of Uganda. Kampala fell without a fight, and by April 1979 organised resistance had effectively ceased.

Amin fled the country and eventually ended up in Saudi Arabia where he died in 2003, never having faced justice.

Post-Amin Chaos

The Tanzanian action was criticised, somewhat half-heartedly, by the Organisation for African Unity (OAU, now called the African Union), but most African countries breathed a sigh of relief to see Amin finally brought to heel. All the same, Tanzania was forced to foot the entire bill for the war, estimated at US$500 million, a crushing blow for an already desperately poor country.

The rejoicing in Uganda was short-lived. The Tanzanian soldiers, who remained in the country, supposedly to assist with reconstruction and to maintain law and order, turned on the Ugandans when their pay did not arrive. They took what they wanted from shops at gunpoint, hijacked trucks arriving

IDI AMIN: BUTCHER OF UGANDA

Regarded as one of Africa's most notorious and ruthless dictators, the name Idi Amin continues to be synonymous with Uganda despite it being nearly four decades since he was ousted as president. Following his defeat in the Uganda–Tanzania war in 1979, Amin fled the country never to return, heading to Libya and Iraq before living in exile in Saudi Arabia, where he died from kidney failure in 2003, aged 78. He never faced justice for the atrocities he committed, with an estimated 300,000 losing their lives under his rule. President from 1971 to 1979, Amin will be remembered not only for executions, human-rights violations and ethnic persecution, but for corruption and the transformation of the once prosperous Ugandan economy into financial ruin.

Amin was a highly charismatic leader who had the ability to charm everyone he met. Physically imposing at 1.91m, with a broad build, Amin was a champion boxer who held Uganda's light heavyweight boxing championship from 1951 to 1960. To many Africans, Amin was (and, for many, remains) highly respected for his fierce nationalism and courage to stand up to colonial powers.

On the flipside, he was also known for his wild mood swings and paranoia. Henry Kyemba, one of Amin's most trusted ministers at the time, states in his autobiography State of Blood that Amin dabbled with cannibalism and blood rituals. Persistent rumours from exiled Ugandans also suggest that he kept the heads of his most prized enemies in a freezer, which he would take out on occasion to lecture them on their evil ways.

OPERATION ENTEBBE: 1976 HOSTAGE RESCUE

The site of one of the most well-known hostage-rescue missions, Uganda's international airport in Entebbe was where a hijacked Air France flight landed on 27 June 1976. Carrying 248 passengers, the flight from Tel Aviv en route to Paris was hijacked by Palestinian and German terrorists and diverted to Libya, before eventually being given permission to land in Entebbe by Idi Amin, a pro-Palestine supporter. Demanding the release of 53 Palestine Liberation Organization (PLO) prisoners in return for the release of the hostages, terrorists held passengers in the main hall of the airport building (now the old terminal building, and a popular site for Israeli tourists) for over a week. Eventually all non-Jewish passengers were released, leaving around 105 hostages onboard.

In what's considered one of the most daring and dramatic hostage operations to ever take place, the covert operation comprised an Israeli taskforce of around 100 commandos touching down in Entebbe at 11pm in a C-130 Hercules cargo plane. Several Mercedes rolled off the plane to give the appearance of being part of Idi Amin's entourage, from where Israeli commandos emerged to storm the terminal. Within 30 minutes, seven terrorists and around 40 Ugandan soldiers were killed, while three Israeli hostages also died in the crossfire. The freed hostages were loaded on to the plane while Ugandan soldiers fired away, resulting in one Israeli soldier being killed: the brother of Israeli prime minister, Benjamin Netanyahu. In the meantime more than half of Uganda's air force planes were destroyed by the Israelis to prevent retaliatory air strikes upon Israel. In response Amin ordered the killing of 75-year-old Dora Bloch, a British-Jewish hostage who remained in Kampala recovering in hospital following the ordeal.

from Kenya with international relief aid and slaughtered more wildlife.

Once again, the country slid into chaos and gangs of armed bandits roamed the cities, killing and looting. Food supplies ran out and hospitals could no longer function. Nevertheless, thousands of exiled Ugandans began to answer the call to return home and help with reconstruction.

Yusuf Lule, a modest and unambitious man, was installed as president with Nyerere's blessing. But when he began speaking out against Nyerere, he was replaced by Godfrey Binaisa, sparking riots supporting Lule in Kampala. Meanwhile, Obote bided his time in Dar es Salaam.

Binaisa quickly came under pressure to set a date for a general election and a return to civilian rule. Obote eventually returned from exile to an enthusiastic welcome in many parts of the country and swept to power in what is widely regarded as a rigged vote.

It was 1981 and the honeymoon with Obote proved short. Like Amin, Obote favoured certain tribes. Large numbers of civil servants and army and police commanders belonging to the tribes of the south were replaced with Obote supporters belonging to the tribes of the north. The State Research Bureau, a euphemism for the secret police, was re-established and the prisons began to

fill once more. Obote was on course to complete the destruction that Amin had begun. More and more reports of atrocities and killings leaked out of the country. Mass graves unrelated to the Amin era were unearthed. The press was muzzled and Western journalists were expelled. It appeared that Obote was once again attempting to achieve absolute power. Intertribal tension was on the rise, and in mid-1985 Obote was overthrown in a coup staged by the army under the command of Tito Okello.

The NRA Takeover

Okello was not the only opponent of Obote. Shortly after Obote became president for the second time, a guerrilla army opposed to his tribally biased government was formed in western Uganda under the leadership of Yoweri Museveni.

A group of 27 soon swelled to a guerrilla force of about 20,000, many of them orphaned teenagers. In the early days few gave the guerrillas, known as the National Resistance Army (NRA), much of a chance, but the NRA had a very different ethos to the armies of Amin and Obote. New recruits were indoctrinated in the bush by political commissars and taught they had to be servants of the people, not oppressors. Discipline was tough. Anyone who got badly out of line was executed. Museveni was determined that the army would never again disgrace Uganda. A central thrust of the NRA was to win the hearts and minds of the people, who learnt to identify with the persecuted Baganda in the infamous Luwero Triangle, where people suffered more than most under Obote's iron fist.

By the time Obote was ousted and Okello had taken over, the NRA controlled a large slice of western Uganda and was a power to be reckoned with. Museveni wanted a clean sweep of the administration, the army and the police. He wanted corruption stamped out and those who had been involved in atrocities during the Amin and Obote regimes brought to trial.

The fighting continued in earnest, and by January 1986 it was obvious that Okello's days were numbered. The surrender of 1600 government soldiers holed up in their barracks in the southern town of Mbarara brought the NRA to the outskirts of Kampala itself. With the morale of the government troops low, the NRA launched an all-out offensive to take the capital. Okello's troops fled, almost without a fight, though not before looting whatever remained and carting it away in commandeered buses. It was a typical parting gesture, as was the gratuitous shooting-up of many Kampala high-rise offices.

During the following weeks, Okello's rabble were pursued and finally pushed north over the border into Sudan. The long nightmare was finally over.

Rebuilding

Despite Museveni's Marxist leanings, he proved to be a pragmatist after taking control. He appointed several arch-conservatives to his cabinet and made an effort to reassure the country's large Catholic community.

In the late 1980s, peace agreements were negotiated with most of the guerrilla factions who had fought for Okello or Obote and were still active in the north and northeast. Under an amnesty offered to the rebels, as many as 40,000 had surrendered by 1988, and many were given jobs in the NRA. In the northwest of the country, almost 300,000 Ugandans returned home from Sudan.

With peace came optimism: services were restored, factories that had lain idle for years were again productive, agriculture was back online, the main roads were resurfaced, and the national parks' infrastructure was restored and revitalised.

The 1990s

The stability and rebuilding that came with President Museveni's coming to power in 1986 was followed in the 1990s with economic prosperity and unprecedented growth. For much of the decade Uganda was the fastest-growing economy in Africa, becoming a favourite among investors. One of the keys to its success was the bold decision to invite back the Asians who, as in Kenya, had held a virtual monopoly on business and commerce. Not surprisingly, they were very hesitant about returning, but assurances were given and kept, and property was returned.

The darkness didn't end for northern Uganda, however, due to the Lord's Resistance Army (LRA), the last remaining rebel group founded during the time of the NRA rebellion. Its leader, Joseph Kony, grew increasingly delusional and paranoid and shifted his focus from attacking soldiers to attacking civilians in an attempt to found a government based on the Biblical Ten Commandments.

His vicious tactics included torture, mutilation (slicing off lips, noses and ears), rape and abducting children to use as soldiers and sex slaves. Eventually over one million northerners fled their homes to Internally Displaced Persons (IDP) camps and tens of thousands of children became 'night commuters', walking from their villages each evening to sleep in schools and churches or on the streets of large and (sometimes) safer towns. In their half-hearted fight against the LRA, government forces reportedly committed their own atrocities too.

In 1993, a new draft constitution was adopted by the National Resistance Council (NRC). One surprising recommendation in the draft was that the country should adopt a system of 'no-party' politics. Given the potential for intertribal rivalry within a pluralist system, it was a sensible policy. Under the draft constitution, a Constituent Assembly was formed, and, in 1994, elections for the assembly showed overwhelming support for the government. Also, in 1993, the monarchies were restored, but with no actual political power.

Democratic 'no-party' elections were called for May 1996. The main candidates were President Museveni and Paul Ssemogerere, who had resigned as foreign minister in order to campaign. Museveni won a resounding victory, capturing almost 75% of the vote. The only area where Ssemogerere had any real support was in the anti–National Resistance Movement (NRM) north.

Museveni's election carried with it great hope for the future, as many believed Uganda's success story could only continue with a genuine endorsement at the ballot box. But Museveni's period as a democratically elected leader has been far less comfortable than his leadership period prior to the elections. At home, one corruption scandal after another has blighted the administration, though Museveni has so far stayed clean. Museveni's focus seemed to drift from the homefront and he played a heavy hand with events in the DRC and Rwanda. Despite this, Museveni remained popular for the stability he brought to the lives of average Ugandans and he was re-elected in 2001.

Into the New Millennium

Eventually Museveni shifted his position on political parties, and in July 2005 a referendum was held that overwhelmingly endorsed the change. This political shift was of much less concern to the average Ugandan than the other that occurred the same month; parliament approving a constitutional amendment scrapping presidential term limits. Museveni himself had put the two-term limit in place, but had regrets as the end of his tenure drew closer. It was alleged that MPs were bullied and bribed into voting for the change. International criticism was strong and even many Ugandans who back Museveni remain angry at his move. The 'Big Man' school of African politics is better known to Ugandans than most, and plenty of people are worried he is setting himself up to be president for life. Some even draw unflattering comparisons with Robert Mugabe. Museveni convincingly won his fourth election in 2011 with 68.4% of the vote.

By early in the 2000s the LRA's campaign of terror had ebbed, though certainly not ceased. In 2002 the LRA lost its Sudanese support and the Ugandan military launched Operation Iron Fist, attacking the LRA's bases across the northern border. The mission failed and an angered Kony not only increased attacks in Uganda but expanded his targets to areas such as Soroti that had not previously been affected. In the years that followed there were various ceasefires and nominal peace talks, but little progress was made until 2005, when the LRA fled to Garamba National Park in the DRC. The following year the Juba Peace Talks commenced and, though things progressed slowly, they showed genuine promise. Museveni guaranteed Kony amnesty (a move supported in Uganda as practical) and a legitimate ceasefire began in September. After on-again, off-again talks a peace deal was reached in February 2008, though Kony then broke his promise to sign it and the LRA began abducting more child soldiers and even attacked a Sudanese army base. Although the LRA hasn't threatened Uganda since 2007, most northern Ugandans remain too terrified to return to their homes.

Uganda Today

Leading into the 2016 presidential elections Museveni has announced he will be running again. Though his popularity wanes, no credible opposition has arisen. A new potential candidate emerged in Amama Mbabazi, the former prime minister who was sensationally sacked by Museveni in September 2014. Even if Mbabazi does run, it's considered unlikely he will challenge Museveni.

Addressing the nation in his 52nd anniversary of Independence Day speech, Museveni drew attention to the fact that since the disarmament of the Karamojong in 2012, it was the first time Uganda has been at peace for 114 years. A rare moment of positivity for a nation beseiged by confict and violence.

Though there's been no further incident since the horrific bombings in Kampala in 2010 that left 74 dead, threats of terrorism remain a concern. The ongoing involvement of Ugandan troops in peace-keeping missions in Somalia have put the nation firmly in the targets of the Al-Shadab militia group. In light of the Nairobi attacks in 2013, Kampala remains on high alert with thorough security checks at malls, bars and restaurants now an everyday part of life.

Tensions have also bubbled to the surface with ethnic clashes involving kingdom disputes. An incident in Kasese and Bundibugyo regions in July 2014 saw 100 killed in ethnic uprisings; though these remain an isolated incident.

Uganda's controversial antigay bill also keeps the country in the international media spotlight for all the wrong reasons. The 'miniskirt law' is another worrying sign of Draconian measures, in which under the vague 'antipornography' bill, women would effectively be banned from wearing skirts above the knees. The bill was misinterpreted by many, which led to ugly scenes with vigilantes taking to the streets to harass and abuse women wearing short skirts. Fortunately it's an aspect of the bill that since seems to have been relaxed, with no further incident.

Meanwhile efforts continue to find and bring Kony to justice. In March 2014 the US deployed special operation troops and military aircraft to tackle the LRA in the Central African Republic (where Kony is believed to be hiding), the DRC and Sudan, to go with the 5000 African Union troops already on the ground. President Obama has also announced US$5 million reward for Kony's capture. The much publicised documentary *Kony 2012*, a slick campaign produced by Gulu-based Invisible Children, succeeded in bringing the atrocities of the LRA to the attention of a worldwide audience when it went viral as a YouTube sensation – but didn't suceed in its objective to get its man.

Culture

The National Psyche

Despite the years of terror and bloodshed, Ugandans are a remarkably positive and spirited people, and no one comes away from the country without a measure of admiration and affection for them. Most Ugandans are keen debaters, discussing politics and personality in equal measure. They are opinionated and eloquent during disagreements, yet unfailingly polite and engagingly warm.

Ugandans will often greet strangers on public transport or while walking in rural areas. The greeting comes not just with a simple 'hello' but also with an enquiry into how you and your family are doing – and the interest is genuine. In fact, you risk offending someone (though Ugandans would likely never show it) if you don't at least ask 'How are you?' before asking for information or beginning a conversation.

Many Ugandans fear a fractured future. The country has had a remarkable run since 1986 when Museveni saved the nation, but nationalism has never taken hold. Tribe comes first. In fact, many Baganda still desire independence. This tribal divide has always manifested itself in politics, but the re-emergence of political parties is exacer-

bating the problem. Recently, even opposition to a vital land reform bill fell largely along tribal not economic lines.

There is also a serious north–south divide, and it doesn't appear to be closing with the advent of peace. Without Joseph Kony around to blame any more, northerners seem to be turning their resentment for the lack of prosperity and education opportunities towards the south; and not without some justification. During the war, many military officers used their power to swipe land, and today many of the new businesses in the north are owned and new jobs taken by carpetbaggers. Even most of the students in the vast new Gulu University, opened in 2002, come from the south.

Daily Life

Life in Uganda has been one long series of upheavals for the older generations, while the younger generations have benefited from the newfound stability. Society has changed completely in urban areas in the past couple of decades, but in the countryside it's often business as usual.

Uganda has been heavily affected by HIV/AIDS. One of the first countries to be struck by an outbreak of epidemic proportions, Uganda acted swiftly in promoting AIDS awareness and safe sex. This was very effective in radically reducing infection rates throughout the country, and Uganda went from experiencing an infection rate of around 25% in the late 1980s to one that dropped as low as 4% in 2003.

But things have changed. Due in large part to pressure from the country's growing evangelical Christian population, led on this issue by Museveni's outspoken wife (though the president himself has taken her lead), Uganda has reversed its policy on promoting condoms and made abstinence the focus of fighting the disease. The result is that the infection rate has since risen to 7.2%.

Education has been a real priority in Uganda and President Museveni has been keen to promote free primary education for all. It's a noble goal, but Uganda lacks the resources to realise it, and one-third of the population is illiterate. While more pupils are attending class, often the classes are hopelessly overcrowded and many teachers lack experience.

Agriculture remains the single most important component of the Ugandan economy, and it employs 75% of the workforce.

The main export crops include coffee, sugar, cotton, tea and fish. Crops grown for local consumption include maize, millet, rice, cassava, potatoes and beans.

Population

Uganda's population is estimated at 37 million, and its annual growth rate of 3.6% is one of the world's highest. The environmental impacts resulting from this population boom, such as deforestation and erosion, will only get worse with time. The median age is 15, with a life expectancy of 59 years.

Uganda is made up of a complex and diverse range of tribes. Lake Kyoga forms the northern boundary for the Bantu-speaking peoples, who dominate much of east, central and southern Africa and, in Uganda, include the Baganda (17%), Banyankole (9.5%), Basoga (8.4%) and Bagisu (4.6%). In the north are the Lango (6%) near Lake Kyoga and the Acholi (4.7%), who speak Nilotic languages. To the east are the Iteso (6.4%) and Karamojong (2%), who are related to the Maasai, and also speak Nilotic languages. Small numbers of Twa (Batwa) people live in the forests of the southwest. Non-Africans, including a sizeable community of Asians, compose about 1% of the population.

Sport

The most popular sport in Uganda, as throughout most of Africa, is football (soccer) and it's possible to watch occasional international games at the Nelson Mandela Stadium on the outskirts of Kampala. There's also a domestic league (October to July), but few people follow it.

Cricket is also growing in popularity (tests are held at Lugogo Cricket Ground), while boxing has lost much of its popularity in recent years, though past world champions include John 'The Beast' Mugabi and Kassim 'The Dream' Ouma, a former child soldier.

Religion

Eighty-five percent of the population is Christian, split evenly between Catholics and Protestants, including a growing number of born-agains. Muslims, mostly northerners, compose about 12% of the population. The Abayudaya are a small but devout group of native Jewish Ugandans living around Mbale.

Arts

Cinema

Hollywood put Uganda on the movie map with a big-screen version of *The Last King of Scotland* (2006) starring Forest Whitaker as the 'Big Daddy'. While not set in Uganda, much of the Hollywood classic *The African Queen* starring Humphrey Bogart and Katharine Hepburn was shot near Murchison Falls.

The conflict in the north has spawned many harrowing documentaries including *Invisible Children* (2006), *The Other Side of the Country* (2007) and *Uganda Rising* (2006). In a different vein is the Oscar-nominated *War/Dance* (2006), an inspiring tale of northern refugee schoolchildren competing in Uganda's National Primary and Secondary School Music and Dance Competition. *God Loves Uganda* (2013) is a documentary that delves into the controversial antigay bill and the involvement of US evangelists.

Books

LITERATURE

Most of the interesting reading coming out of Uganda revolves around the country's darkest hours. Aristoc (p392) in Kampala stocks a good selection of local writers.

Giles Foden's *The Last King of Scotland* (1998) chronicles the fictional account of Idi Amin's personal doctor as he slowly finds himself becoming confidant to the dictator. This best-selling novel weaves gruesome historical fact into its *Heart of Darkness*–esque tale.

The highly regarded and somewhat autobiographical *Abyssinian Chronicles* (2001) is the best-known work by Moses Isegawa. It tells the story of a young Ugandan coming of age during the turbulent years of Idi Amin and offers some fascinating insights into life in Uganda.

Waiting (2007), the fourth novel by Goretti Kyomuhendo, one of Uganda's pioneering female writers (and founder of Femrite: the Ugandan Women Writers' Association and publishing house), was published in the United States. It looks in on a rural family's daily life (and daily fear) as they await the expected arrival of marauding soldiers during the fall of Idi Amin. Femwrite titles include *A Woman's Voice* (1998) and *Words from a Granary* (2001), two collections of short stories.

Song of Lawino (1989) is a highly regarded poem (originally written in Acholi) by Okot p'Bitek about how colonialism led to a loss of culture.

Fong & the Indians (1968) by Paul Theroux is set in a fictional East African country that bears a remarkable likeness to Uganda, where he taught English for four years in the 1960s. It's set in precivil war days, and is at times both funny and bizarre as it details the life of a Chinese immigrant and his dealings with the Asians who control commerce in the country.

NONFICTION

Keen birdwatchers will be best served by *The Birds of East Africa* (2006) by Terry Stevenson and John Fanshawe, with *The Bird Atlas of Uganda* (2005) making a good secondary resource. Also available is *Butterflies of Uganda* (2004) by Nancy Carder et al.

The Uganda Wildlife Authority has published informative books on the natural history of some of the most popular national parks. They can be bought at the UWA office (p474) in Kampala, and occasionally at the parks themselves, although you may have to request them. Andrew Roberts' *Uganda's Great Rift Valley* (2006) is an entertaining study of the natural and human history of western Uganda.

Uganda: From the Pages of Drum (1994) is a lively compilation of articles that originally appeared in the now-defunct *Drum* magazine. These chronicle the rise of Idi Amin and the atrocities he committed, as well as President Museveni's bush war and his coming to power. It forms a powerful record of what the country experienced.

Ugandan Society Observed (2008) is another recommended collection of essays, these by expat Kevin O'Connor, that originally appeared in the *Daily Monitor* newspaper.

The Man with the Key has Gone! (1993) by Dr Ian Clarke is an autobiographical account of the time spent in Uganda's Luwero Triangle district by a British doctor and his family. It's a lively read and the title refers to a problem travellers may encounter in provincial Uganda.

Widely available in Uganda, Henry Kyemba's *State of Blood* (1977) is an inside story of the horrors committed by Idi Amin, with insight only one of his former ministers could provide.

Aboke Girls (2001) by Els de Temmerman is a heart-wrenching account of female child soldiers and an Italian nun's attempt to rescue them during LRA's decade-long reign of terror in northern Uganda.

Music & Dance

Kampala is the best place to experience live music and several local bands play at nightclubs each weekend. Try to catch the Afrigo Band and Maurice Kirya, plus the weeknightly events at the National Theatre.

To listen to Ugandan music, from hip hop to northern-style thumb piano playing, log on to www.musicuganda.com.

The most famous dancers in the country are the Ndere Troupe (p391). Made up from a kaleidoscope of Ugandan tribes, they perform traditional dances from all regions of the country.

Handicrafts

Uganda's most distinctive craft is bark-cloth, made by pounding the bark of a fig tree. Originally used for clothing and in burial and other ceremonies, these days it's turned into a multitude of items for sale to tourists including hats, bags, wall hangings, pillows and picture frames.

Ugandans also produce some really good raffia and banana-stem basketry, particularly the Toro of the west, who have the most intricate designs and still use natural dyes. Traditional products are easy to find, but the old methods have also been adopted to make new items such as table mats and handbags for sale to tourists.

Baganda drum-makers are well known: the best place to buy is at Mpambire, along the Masaka road. Uganda also has interesting pottery, though all the soapstone carving comes from Kenya and almost all of the interesting woodwork is Congolese.

Environment

Uganda suffers the same environmental problems as the rest of the region: poaching, deforestation and overpopulation.

Currently the biggest threat to Uganda's national parks and other protected areas comes from the oil industry. Significant oil finds in the Kabwoya Wildlife Reserve on Lake Albert have spurred invasive searches for more black gold in the Ishasha sector of Queen Elizabeth National Park and the delta area at Murchison Falls National Park. Providing the drilling companies explore and extract responsibly, then there is hope for a sustainable marriage of interests; but conservationists are sceptical.

The Land

Uganda has an area of 241,038 sq km, small by African standards, but similar in size to Britain. Lake Victoria and the Victoria Nile River, which cuts through the heart of the country, combine to create one of the most fecund areas in Africa. Most of Uganda is a blizzard of greens, a lush landscape of rolling hills blanketed with fertile fields, where almost anything will grow if you stick it in the soil. The climate is drier in the north and some of the lands of the far northeast are semidesert.

The tropical heat is tempered by the altitude, which averages more than 1000m in much of the country and is even higher in the cooler southwest. The highest peak is Mt Stanley (5109m) in the Rwenzori Mountains on the border with the DRC.

Wildlife

Uganda can't compete with Kenya or Tanzania for density of wildlife, but with 500 species of mammal it has amazing diversity. You have a good chance of spotting all the classic African animals including lions, elephants, giraffes, leopards, hippos, zebras, hyenas, and up north, cheetahs and ostriches. Furthermore, with the opening of the Ziwa Rhino Sanctuary, the Big Five are all here again.

It's main attraction however are mountain gorillas. Uganda is home to more than half the world's mountain gorillas, and viewing them in their natural environment is one of Uganda's highlights. On top of this, Uganda has a good number of chimpanzees and there are several places where you can track them. With well over 1000 species recorded inside its small borders, Uganda is one of the best birdwatching destinations in the world.

GORILLA TRACKING

Gorilla tracking is one of the major draws for travellers in Uganda. These gentle giants live in two national parks: Bwindi Impenetrable and Mgahinga Gorilla.

CHIMPANZEE TRACKING

Chimpanzee tracking is a very popular activity in Uganda, with Kibale National Park, Budongo Forest Reserve in Murchison Falls National Park, Kyambura Gorge in Queen Elizabeth National Park and Toro-Semliki the main areas.

BIRDWATCHING

Uganda is one of the world's best birdwatching destinations, a twitcher's fantasy offering 1041 species; that's almost half the total found in all of Africa. Even non-birdwatchers will be enthralled by the diversity of beauty among Uganda's birdlife.

A good starting point is **Uganda Birding** (www.birding-uganda.com), an excellent online resource with all there is to know – from birdwatching hotspots, recommended tour operators, to info on the birds themselves. **Bird Uganda** (www.birduganda.com) also has plenty of good info. The country's top guides are members of the **Uganda Bird Guides Club** (www.ugandabirdguides.org).

National Parks & Reserves

Uganda has an excellent collection of national parks and reserves. Twenty percent of your admission fees benefit local communities for things such as construction of schools and health clinics, so you earn a warm fuzzy for every park you visit.

The **Uganda Wildlife Authority** (UWA; Map p384; ☑ 0414-355000; www.ugandawildlife.org; 7 Kira Rd; ⊙8am-5pm Mon-Fri, 9am-1pm Sat) administers all Uganda's protected areas. It's the place to make bookings to see the gorillas in Bwindi Impenetrable National Park, and should be the first port of call for those needing to book permits. It's also the place to reserve accommodation in the parks. Some other activities, such as chimpanzee tracking, the launch trips in Murchison Falls and Queen Elizabeth national parks can also be reserved here, though activities such as nature walks are arranged at the parks. Payments are accepted in shillings, US dollars, euros and pounds in cash or Amex travellers cheques (1% commission). While credit cards aren't accepted, a new cashless 'smart-card' system was introduced to allow one to load up entry fees in Kampala before heading off to the main national parks.

Most national parks charge US$35 to US$40 (US$5 to US$20 for children aged five to 15) and admission is valid for 24 hours. Other charges, which can add up quite fast, include vehicle entry (USh10,000/20,000/30,000 per motorcycle/car/4WD) for locally registered vehicles.

PRIMATE HABITUATION

When it comes to tracking mountain gorillas in the wild, one common question is how it's possible to safely get mere metres from these beautiful, yet intimidating beasts that can weigh in excess of 200kg and have the strength to rip your arms out of their sockets? The simple answer lies in whether the gorilla group is habituated or not. Habituation is the process by which a group of primates (or other animals) are slowly exposed to human presence to the point where they regard us neutrally. While habituated and non-habituated gorillas are both considered wild, the latter are *truly* wild in the sense that they're unaccustomed to human presence, so they're either likely to flee into the forest or be downright dangerous and aggressive. Thankfully neither of these are the case when tracking gorillas in Bwindi – even though you might get the odd mock charge from a grumpy silverback.

The process of habituating gorillas is a long and patient affair that takes around two to three years. It's even longer for chimpanzees – normally around seven years before they're fully habituated. It involves spending time with a group every day and eventually winning over their trust, which is done by mimicking their behaviour: pretending to eat the same food as they do at the same time, grunting and even beating one's chest when they do. With gorillas, the first few weeks are fraught with danger for the human habitué, with repeated charges commonplace.

Habituation took place well before someone had the bright idea of charging tourists US$600 a pop to see the gorillas. It's a vital process for research that allows primatologists to observe the behavioural patterns of gorillas, chimps, golden monkeys, baboons etc. Some hold the view that the process of habituation is unethical: subjecting the creatures to our presence each day interferes with nature by changing their behavioural patterns. One example of things going wrong occurred in Busingiro on the edge of Murchison Falls National Park, where chimp tracking had to be abandoned when chimps lost their fear of humans and started raiding local farms. It also puts primates at risk of contagious ailments and disease while making them more susceptible to attacks from poachers or nonhabituated 'wild' groups. But, pure and simple, had there not been habituation of gorillas (and the tourist trade to go with it), there's every chance the species would've been wiped out by poachers decades ago.

If you're coming in with a foreign registered vehicle, the prices are very expensive (US$30/50/150 per motorcycle/car/4WD). Nature walks cost US$30 per person and rangers for wildlife-watching drives are US$20. Most prices are lower for Ugandan residents and much lower again for Ugandan citizens. For the most up-to-date prices, check the UWA website.

If you're pressed for time, or money is no issue, you can charter flights to most of the parks.

SAFARI OPERATORS

By far the most convenient way to visit the parks is on an organised safari, with a good range of options that cover most budgets.

Amagara Tours　　　　　SAFARIS
(☑0752-197826; www.amagaratours.com; Kabale; budget) Based out of Engagi Guesthouse (p443) in Kabale, which also manages the wonderful Byoona Amagara on Lake

Bunyonyi, this budget-focused company has great packages for all the national parks in the southwest, and a great option for the gorillas too.

Bird Uganda Safaris　　　　SAFARIS
(☑0777-912938; www.birduganda.com; Kampala; midrange) Herbert Byaruhanga, one of Uganda's pioneering birdwatchers, leads most of the trips himself but also enlists local guides at all of the sites to ensure top spotting. Gorilla tracking and other wildlife encounters can be added to the mix.

Classic Africa Safaris　　　　SAFARIS
(☑0414-320121, in the US 304-724-8235; www.classicuganda.com; midrange to top end) One of the best luxury companies in Uganda, Classic offers excellent service both in trip planning and in the parks. Top end.

Great Lakes Safaris　　　　SAFARIS
(☑0414-267153; www.safari-uganda.com; budget to top end) One of the better all-round sa-

UGANDA ENVIRONMENT

fari companies in Uganda, it offers a wide variety of safaris and cultural encounters at prices for every pocket.

Gorilla Tours
SAFARIS

(📞 0414-200221; www.gorillatours.com; 21/22 Quality Shopping Mall, Kampala; midrange) Gorillas are the speciality, but this company has itineraries covering all the major parks of southwest Uganda. The trips offer very good value, and it manages some of the country's best midrange hotels.

Kombi Nation Tours
SAFARIS

(Map p384; www.kombitours.com; 13 Bukoto St, Kampala; budget to midrange) Though style may outweigh practicality, the opportunity to get around Uganda in a vintage '70s VW Kombi (complete with all original parts) makes this one of the coolest tour companies in the country. It offers both tailor-made trips and scheduled tours, and also has Land Cruisers for 4WD accessible parts of the country.

Matoke Tours
SAFARIS

(Map p380; 📞 0312-202907; www.matoketours. com; 1 Senfuka Rd, Kampala; midrange) The Dutch-run Matoke team stands out for excellent and enthusiastic service for a midrange clientele, with trips ranging from classic safaris to more intrepid overland journeys to Kidepo Valley National Park and Karamojaland.

Red Chilli Hideaway
SAFARIS

(📞 0312-202903; www.redchillihideaway.com; budget to midrange) An excellent choice for budget safaris to Murchison Falls and Queen Elizabeth national parks. Also very affordable car-hire rates too.

Road Trip Uganda
SELF-DRIVE TOURS

(Map p380; 📞 0773-363012; www.roadtripuganda. com; Grace Musoke Rd, Kampala; budget to midrange) Popular with a younger generation of traveller, this Dutch-owned company fills in a much needed market by providing an affordable option for self-drive (or guided) tours in fully equipped RAV4s. They offer a good selection prebooked self-drive routes, which include accommodation bookings and detailed itineraries. Full camping equipment is available for an extra US$5 per day.

Food & Drink

Local food is much the same as elsewhere in the region, except in Uganda *ugali* (a food staple usually made from maize flour or, rarely, cassava) is called *posho,* and is far less popular than *matoke* (cooked plantains). Rice, cassava and potatoes are also common starches and vegetarians travelling beyond the main tourist destinations will end up eating any of these with beans quite often, although Western, Indian and Chinese food is available at most hotels frequented by tourists. Kampala, Jinja and Entebbe (as well as the top hotels in many provincial towns) offer other international flavours such as Italian, Greek, Japanese and Mexican. One uniquely Ugandan food is the *rolex,* a chapati rolled around an omelette. Grasshoppers are very popular during April and November and are sold by many street vendors.

Like all East Africans, Ugandans love their beer. Uganda Breweries and Nile Breweries are the two main local brewers, and they produce some drinkable lagers such as Nile, Club and Bell.

Waragi is the local millet-based alcohol and is relatively safe, although it can knock you around and give you a horrible hangover. It's similar to gin and goes down well with a splash of tonic. In its undistilled form it's known as *kasezi bong* and would probably send you blind if you drank enough of it.

Imported wines are quite expensive and not common beyond the tourist trail. Imported spirits are relatively cheaper, although, like wine, availability is somewhat restricted.

SURVIVAL GUIDE

❶ Directory A–Z

ACCOMMODATION

In 2014 an 18% Value Added Tax (VAT) was introduced to accommodation rates outside Kampala, which is mostly included in quoted prices.

Camping

Almost every popular destination in Uganda offers camping, so it's worth carrying a tent if you're on a budget. In provincial towns many upmarket hotels allow camping on their grounds, and include the use of swimming pools and other facilities in their rates.

Hotels

Hotels range from fleapit to five-star, and even in many smaller towns there's plenty of choice. You can count on even very small towns having at least one basic (and perhaps clean) lodge.

PRACTICALITIES

Weights & Measures Uganda uses the metric system.

Electricity 240V, 50 cycles; British three-pin plugs are used.

Magazines & Newspapers Local newspapers include the government-owned daily the *New Vision* and the more independent *Daily Monitor.* International magazines, such as *Time* and the *Economist,* are readily available in Kampala, as is the local equivalent the *Whisper* (www.whisper.co.ug).

TV The state-run UBC and the private WBS are the main stations available on broadcast TV, but most hotels and bars have satellite TV for international news and sport.

Radio BBC World Service broadcasts on 101.3MHz and the phenomenally popular Capital FM can be found at 91.3MHz.

Outside the capital, the cheapest single rooms are available from around USh20,000, while doubles are around USh35,000. Singles rooms with bathroom usually start at USh30,000, while doubles start from USh45,000; for another USh5000 to USh10,000 breakfast will be included. Modern, comfortable rooms with satellite TV (although often only the same channel that's turned on in the restaurant/bar) can be found from USh50,000 for a single, and USh70,000 for a double. Even most budget places, except at the very bottom of the price range, have hot water and attached restaurants. Top-end hotels and lodges start at around US$200 and can go much higher.

National Parks & Reserves

The main national parks have a wide range of accommodation available, including luxury lodges and tented camps with outlandish prices. Always ask for discounts at these top-end places. The less-popular parks have simple campsites and basic *bandas* (thatched-roof huts).

Camping in national parks costs USh15,000 per person per night, and tents are sometimes available for hire (the quality is usually low) for an additional USh10,000. *Bandas* are also common in the budget lodgings, starting from around USh20,000 for singles and USh30,000 for doubles with shared facilities.

ACTIVITIES

By far the most popular activity involves wildlife viewing, whether tracking mountain gorillas or on safari in one of Uganda's many national parks. But Uganda has always had a strong attraction for the dedicated trekking fraternity, mainly for the opportunities presented by the Rwenzori Mountains and Mt Elgon. It's also possible to walk up the three volcanoes at Mgahinga Gorilla National Park.

White-water rafting is another big attraction, with the Nile River offering world-class Grade V rapids near Jinja.

CHILDREN

Although there are some risks and challenges when travelling Uganda with kids, with some great national parks and lots of water-based activities, Uganda can be a lot of fun for children. On the city side of things, Kampala isn't exactly bursting with activities for young people, but Entebbe and Jinja have plenty on offer.

EMBASSIES & CONSULATES IN UGANDA

Embassies and consulates are located in Kampala. Most close for an hour during lunch, and many close earlier on Fridays.

Australian Consulate (Map p384; ☎ 0312-515865; 40 Kyadondo Rd, Nakasero; ◷9am-12.30pm & 2-5pm Mon-Fri) Opposite the Nakasero Primary School.

Belgium Embassy (Map p384; ☎ 0414-349559; www.diplomatie.be/kampala; Lumumba Ave, Rwenzori House; ◷8.30am-1pm & 2-4pm Mon-Thu, 8.30am-1pm Fri)

Burundi Embassy (Map p384; ☎ 0414-235850; 12a York Tce; ◷visas 10am-1pm Mon-Thu) A one-month visa costs US$90, requires two passport photos and takes two days to process. It's also issued at land borders and the airport.

Canadian Embassy (Map p384; ☎ 0414-258141; canada.consulate@utlonline.co.ug; 14 Parliament Ave; ◷2-5pm Tue & Thu)

Danish Embassy (Map p384; ☎ 0312-263211; www.uganda.um.dk; 3 Lumumba Ave; ◷8am-4pm Mon-Thu, to 2pm Fri)

UGANDA DIRECTORY A–Z

SET YOUR BUDGET

Budget hotel double room US$30

Meal at decent restaurant US$7 to US$15

Litre of petrol US$1.50

Tracking mountain gorillas US$600

DRC Embassy (Map p384; ☎ 0414-250099;
20 Philip Rd, Kololo; ⏱ 9am-4pm Mon-Fri)
One-month single-entry visa costs US$115,
requiring two passport photos and 48 hours to
process; expect to wait. Otherwise try your luck
for a seven-day visa at the border for US$50.

Dutch Embassy (Map p384; ☎ 0414-346000;
www.uganda.nlembassy.org; Lumumba Ave,
Rwenzori Courts; ⏱ 10am-noon Mon-Thu, by
appointment)

Ethiopian Embassy (Map p384; ☎ 0414-
348340; ethiokam@utlonline.co.org; 3c
Nakayima Rd; ⏱ 8.30am-12.30pm & 2-5.30pm
Mon-Fri)

French Embassy (Map p384; ☎ 0414-304500;
www.ambafrance-ug.org; 16 Lumumba Ave;
⏱ 9am-5pm Mon-Thu, to 1pm Fri)

German Embassy (Map p384; ☎ 0414-501111;
www.kampala.diplo.de; 15 Philip Rd, Kololo;
⏱ 8am-2pm Mon & Fri, 8am-5pm Tue-Thu)

Indian Embassy (Map p384; ☎ 0414-344631;
11 Kyadondo Rd; ⏱ 9.30am-12.30pm Mon-Fri)

Irish Embassy (Map p384; ☎ 0417-713000;
www.embassyofireland.ug; 25 Yusuf Lule Rd,
Nakasero; ⏱ 10am-noon & 2-4pm Mon-Fri)

Italian Embassy (Map p384; ☎ 0312-188000;
www.ambkampala.esteri.it; 11 Lourdel Rd,
Nakasero; ⏱ 10am-1pm Tue-Thu)

Japanese Embassy (Map p384; ☎ 0414-
349542; www.ug.emb-japan.go.jp; 8 Kyadondo
Rd; ⏱ 8.30am-12.30pm & 1.30-5.15pm Mon-Fri)

Kenyan High Commission (Map p384;
☎ 0414-258235; kampala@mfa.go.ke; 8a Acacia Ave; ⏱ 9am-12.30pm & 2-4pm Mon-Fri)

Nigerian High Commission (Map p384;
☎ 0414-233691; 33 Nakasero Rd; ⏱ 9am-
12.30pm & 2-5pm Mon-Thu, to 1pm Fri)

Rwandan Embassy (Map p384; ☎ 0414-
344045; www.uganda.embassy.gov.rw; 2
Nakayima Rd, Kamwokya; ⏱ 9am-12.30pm
Mon-Fri) For nationalities that require them,
visas cost US$30, require one passport photo
and will take around 72 hours to process.
They're also available on arrival at the airport
and at borders, but depending on your na-
tionality you'll need to apply online at www.
migration.gov.rw.

South African High Commission (Map p384;
☎ 0417-702100; 15A Nakasero Rd; ⏱ 9am-
noon)

South Sudan Embassy (Map p384; ☎ 0414-
271625; 2 Ssezibwa Rd; ⏱ 9am-noon Thu)
Single-entry visas cost US$100 and you'll need
two passport photos. It takes three days to
process. Visas weren't available at the border
at the time of research.

Sudan Embassy (Map p384; ☎ 0414-230001;
21 Nakasero Rd; ⏱ 8.30am-4pm Mon-Thu, to
1pm Fri) A single-entry visa costs USh125,000
and you need two passport photos. Visas take
24 hours to process.

Tanzanian High Commission (Map p384;
☎ 0414-256272; 6 Kagera Rd; ⏱ 9am-12.30pm
& 2-5pm Mon-Thu, to 1pm Fri) Visas are valid
for three months, require two passport photos
and take 24 hours to issue. Costs vary according to your country of origin. Single-entry visas
are also available on entry.

UK Embassy (Map p384; ☎ 0312-312000;
http://ukinuganda.fco.gov.uk; Windsor Loop,
Kamwokya; ⏱ 8.30am-1pm & 2-5pm Mon-Thu,
8.30am-1pm Fri)

US Embassy (Map p380; ☎ 0414-259791;
http://kampala.usembassy.gov; Ggaba Rd,
Nsambya; ⏱ 8-11.45am Mon-Wed, 8-10.45am
Fri)

GAY & LESBIAN TRAVELLERS

As in other East African nations, homosexuality
is illegal in Uganda and in theory can result in a
sentence of up to 14 years in prison. In recent
years, the government has attempted to introduce stricter penalties (including anything from
life in prison to the death penalty for certain
acts). The gay community here remains very
much underground. For safe travel, gay, lesbian,
bisexual or transgender tourists are advised to
likewise keep things discrete.

INTERNET ACCESS

Wi-fi is common in most towns, but less likely (or
very slow) in national parks and remote regions.
Internet cafes, charging around USh2000 per
hour, are ubiquitous in all towns.

Laptop users can easily get online by purchas-
ing a wireless USB internet/dongle for around
US$30, with the best networks being MTN and
Orange, which have reliable access for most
parts of the country (but not in the remote
parks).

LANGUAGE COURSES

The **City Language Centre** (CLC; ☎ 0772-
501679; www.clckampala.com; off Entebbe Rd,
Bunamwaya) offers private lessons in Luganda,
Luo and Swahili. It's located 6km south of Kampala and you can catch a Zana-bound taxi from
the Old Taxi Park.

MAPS

The Uganda maps by ITMB (1:800,000) and
Nelles (1:700,000) will get you where you need
to go. Only the latter is available in Uganda.

Being both beautiful and useful, Uganda
Maps national park maps, available at Aristoc
bookstore (p392), UWA, safari lodges and tour
companies, are a great buy if you're headed to
any of the national parks.

The best available map of Kampala is the *Kampala A-Z* street atlas, but Macmillan's *Kampala
Traveller's Map* (1:8500) is good enough for
most visitors. Both are available in bookshops
and hotels around Kampala.

THE ANTIGAY BILL

Since the controversial antigay bill that proposed the death penalty for homosexual behaviour was first drafted in 2009, Uganda has predictably come under fire from the international community. US President Barack Obama described it as 'odious', as the US and several European governments cut foreign aid in protest, while the World Bank postponed its US$90 million loan. Though all references to the death penalty have since been removed, it's a piece of legislation that continues to rear its ugly head.

In February 2014 the Uganda Anti-Homosexuality Act was officially passed by parliament and signed off by President Museveni. The law made provisions for a life prison sentence to be applied to those convicted of 'aggravated homosexuality', a term that incorporated homosexuals convicted of rape, sex with a minor or knowingly spreading HIV, as well as 'serial offenders' – a clause that remains vague. Furthermore, under the legislation, anyone who failed to report homosexual behaviour could be imprisoned for up to three years.

In August 2014, Uganda's constitutional court found the Anti-Homosexuality Act to be illegal and it was overturned. Not to be deterred, the government is planning to introduce new, further-reaching legislation, incorporating prison sentences for those seen to be 'promoting' homosexuality.

Though homosexuality has officially been illegal in Uganda since the British introduced these laws in the 19th century, it is rarely, if ever, policed. The influence of visiting US evangelists has been widely reported, with many suggesting their preaching played a hand in whipping up antigay sentiment and influenced the anti-homosexuality bill. The documentary *God Loves Uganda* (2013) provides an interesting analysis on the subject.

In October 2010 there was an escalation of violence when the short-lived tabloid newspaper *Rolling Stone* (not to be confused with the music magazine) ran a front cover story publishing the names and addresses of 100 gay Ugandans, leading to several attacks. This included the death of David Kato in February 2011, a notable gay activist, who was widely believed to be the victim of a hate crime.

So what does all this mean for gay, lesbian, bisexual and transgender travellers to Uganda, and is it safe to travel there? There's no doubt Ugandan culture is generally homophobic, so (as in other East African nations) discretion is vital. If travellers follow the lead of the local and expat gay community, who remain very much underground, there shouldn't be any threat. Keep in mind that displays of public affection – whether couples are heterosexual, gay or lesbian – are largely considered socially taboo.

MONEY

The Ugandan shilling (USh) is a relatively stable currency that floats freely on international markets. Most tour operators and upscale hotels quote in US dollars (a few in euros) but you can always pay with shillings.

Notes in circulation are USh1000, USh5000, USh10,000, USh20,000 and USh50,000, and commonly used coins are USh50, USh100, USh200 and USh500.

ATMs

The biggest banks (Barclays, Stanbic, Centenary, Crane, Orient and Standard Chartered) have ATMs that accept international cards. Even many remote small towns will have at least one of these banks, though try not to let your cash run out as the system sometimes goes down and machines sometimes run out of cash. You'll also notice tents and benches outside ATMs, which tells you how long the lines can get.

Cash

The Ugandan shilling trades at whatever it's worth against other major currencies, and there's usually little fluctuation from day to day. US dollars are the most useful hard currency, especially in small towns, though euros and pounds sterling are also widely accepted.

If you're using US dollars, try to avoid bills printed before 2006, as often they're not accepted (due to a higher risk of them being counterfeit notes). If exchanging US dollars, small denominations *always* get a much lower rate than US$50 and US$100 notes.

The best exchange rates by far are offered in Kampala. Forex bureaus offer slightly better rates than banks plus much faster service and longer hours; but they're rare outside Kampala.

Note that UWA offers fair exchange rates for park fees and accepts dollars, pounds and euros and either cash or travellers cheques.

CASH AT THE AIRPORT

There are no banks, ATMs or forex bureaus before immigration, but, if you're in a pinch, an officer will hold your passport while you go get money from the ATM just beyond airport customs.

Credit Cards

Very few places other than top-end hotels and tour companies accept cards for payment, and there's usually a surcharge of 5% to 8%. Visa is the most widely accepted card, but MasterCard is increasingly accepted.

Tipping & Bargaining

Tipping isn't expected in Uganda but, as wages are very low by Western standards, it will always be appreciated. The size of a given tip is up to the individual, but as a guideline USh1000 to USh1500 is enough in ordinary restaurants, while USh5000 to USh10,000 is reasonable for ranger-guides in national parks.

You'll usually need to bargain with *boda-boda* and special-hire drivers, though there are still many honest drivers out there.

OPENING HOURS

Government offices and businesses in Uganda are generally open between 8.30am and 5pm, often with a short break for lunch sometime between noon and 2pm. Most shops and banks don't break for lunch, but most banks close at 3pm. Few banks are open on Saturday, but more and more shops are adding weekend hours, usually closing about 1pm.

Local restaurant hours are 7am to 9pm or 10pm, while international-type restaurants are likely to be open 11.30am to 2.30pm and 5.30pm to 10.30pm.

POST

Sending a postcard costs USh2000 to Europe and USh2500 to the US or Australia. Kampala's post office is slow but reliable; there's a chance things will go missing at provincial branches.

PUBLIC HOLIDAYS

New Year's Day 1 January
Liberation Day 26 January
International Women's Day 8 March
Easter (Good Friday, Holy Saturday and Easter Monday) March/April
Labour Day 1 May
Martyrs' Day 3 June
Heroes' Day 9 June
Independence Day 9 October
Christmas Day 25 December
Boxing Day 26 December

Banks and government offices also close on the major Muslim holidays.

SAFE TRAVEL

Despite a disarmament program, banditry still occurs in the Karamojong area of the far northeast (though not within Kidepo Valley National Park), and the border areas in the far northwest have their own problems. Various rebel groups hang out in the far eastern DRC and they occasionally slip across the porous border to make havoc and, even with additional Ugandan troops in the area, the chances of this happening again cannot be completely discounted. Finally, there are smugglers and Kenyan rebels on and around Mt Elgon, though the risk to visitors is small.

TELEPHONE

The country code for Uganda is 🖉 256. To make an international call from Uganda, dial 🖉 000 or, on a mobile, the + button. If you're calling Uganda from outside the country, drop the 🖉 0 at the start of the phone number.

In case of emergency, dial 🖉 999 from a landline or 🖉 112 from a mobile phone.

Landline telephone connections, both domestic and international, are pretty good, although not always so reliable in the provincial areas. Mobile (cell) phones are very popular as the service is better than landlines, though it's not 100% reliable. All mobile numbers start with 🖉 07. Mobile-phone companies sell SIM cards for USh2000 and then you buy airtime vouchers for topping up credit from street vendors. Simple phones are available for USh45,000 in all sizeable towns and also at the airport. MTN and Orange currently have the best coverage across the country.

VISAS

Most non-African passport holders visiting Uganda require visas, including Americans, Australians, Canadians and almost all Europeans. Single-entry tourist visas valid for up to 90 days cost US$50. Be sure to ask for a 90-day visa, or you'll probably be given 30 or 60 days. It's easiest just to rock up at the airport or border and arrange one there; no photos needed. A yellow fever certificate is required if arriving from an affected area, but is rarely requested. Multiple-entry visas aren't available on arrival, but it is possible for embassies abroad to issue them (US$100 for six months). Students should also enquire about student visas, which (if applicable) are US$20; bring your card.

Uganda is one of the countries covered by the new East Africa Tourist Visa, and for those also visiting Kenya and Rwanda on the same trip it is a cheaper alternative. The visa costs US$100, is valid for 90 days and is multiple entry – it is available upon arrival or from embassies abroad. If acquiring the visa before travel, your first port-of-call must be the country through which you applied for the visa.

Kampala is a good place for picking up visas to other countries as there are rarely queues at the various embassies.

Visa Extensions

In Kampala, the **Immigration Office** (Map p380; ☑ 0414-595945; Jinja Rd; ☺ 9am-1pm & 2-5pm) is just east of the centre. Regardless of how many days you were given on your original tourist visa, you can apply for a free two-month extension. Submit a letter explaining the reason for your request, stating where you're staying and detailing when and how you'll be leaving the country. Attach a copy of your passport and plane ticket, if you have one. It takes seven days to process, but extensions are much quicker at immigration offices outside the capital, and these exist in most large towns, including Jinja and Fort Portal.

VOLUNTEERING

Uganda has more volunteering opportunities than many African countries, thanks to a number of good grassroots organisations. The Uganda Community Tourism Association and Pearls of Uganda are in touch with many communities around the country and can connect you to a variety of projects, including tree-planting and teaching. Many volunteering roles involve an expenditure/ donation on top of living costs.

Kampala

Sanyu Babies Home (Map p380; ☑ 0414-274032; www.sanyubabies.com; Mengo) Receives and raises abandoned babies, many of whom have been left to die in ditches or latrines. Has a craft shop and a hostel popular with those volunteering here.

Entebbe

Uganda Wildlife Education Centre (UWEC; ☑ 0414-320520; www.uwec.ug; 56/57 Lugard Ave, Entebbe) Assist rescued and injured animals at Uganda Wildlife Education Centre in Entebbe, with month-long stints involving animal keeping and rehabilitation, and staying in a local homestay.

Jinja

Soft Power Education (☑ 0774-162541; www. softpowereducation.com) Has a number of projects to upgrade schools and improve education in the areas around Jinja and around Murchison Falls National Park. Volunteering opportunities extend from one day to long-term roles.

Soft Power Health (☑ 0782-690127; www. softpowerhealth.com) Offers volunteering positions in its Malaria Education and Family Planning Outreach programmes. No medical training is necessary.

Fort Portal

Y.E.S. Hostel (www.caroladamsministry.com/ yes_hostel.html) Long-term voluntary work with orphaned children.

Mpora Rural Family (☑ 0776-555732; www. ugandahomestay.com) This orphanage and school offers a number of short- and long-term volunteering opportunities including teaching, farming and eco-tourism initiatives. Also runs accommodation (☑ 0752-555732; www.uganda homestay.com; camping incl full board €10, banda without bathroom per person €20) on its rural property 15km from Fort Portal.

Gulu

Thrive-Gulu (www.thrivegulu.org) Does a range of work involving rehabilitating those who suffered during the LRA, including child soldiers. Occasionally looking for skilled volunteers.

UGANDA DIRECTORY A–Z

COMMUNITY PROJECTS

A visit to Uganda proves definitively that travel can have a positive impact. Nearby all of the national parks and in many towns frequented by travellers, there are a variety of community-run programs where a significant portion of the profits goes towards schools, health clinics and other projects that benefit local residents. The community-run Bigodi Wetland Sanctuary (p424), for example, is the main reason Bigodi is one of the few villages in Uganda where nearly everyone lives above the poverty line.

Many of these projects are set up and supported by the **Uganda Community Tourism Association** (UCOTA; ☑ 0414-501866; www.ucota.or.ug) and **Pearls of Uganda** (www.pearlsofuganda.org). Both offer a range of initiatives that provide memorable cultural experiences, from creative cooking tours offered by Boomu Women's Group (p465) to mock hunting parties with the Twa (Batwa) people in the forest. They also run the nearly ubiquitous village walks, as well as dance groups, which are often worth checking out.

There are also some superb accommodations commited to benefitting the local community, such as Ruboni Community Campsite (p431). Not all are small-scale. The residents of Nkuringo village are part owners of Clouds Lodge (p441) at Bwindi Impenetrable National Park, which charges a whopping US$1220 for a double per night.

St Jude Children's Home (☎0782-896897; www.stjudechildrenshome.com) Orphanage welcoming volunteers to work with children teaching, or running games or sports, from one-week stints to long-term. Accommodation inclusive.

Lake Bunyonyi

Loving Hearts Uganda (☎0700-933151; www.lovingheartsuganda.com) Short- and long-term volunteering opportunities for backpackers in varied roles such as teaching, farming, building, crafts and media.

Kisoro

Mgahinga Community Development Organisation (www.mcdoa.org/VolunteerProgramme.aspx) A community initiative based around Mgahinga National Park and Kisoro provides a range of opportunities including teaching, farming, animal conservation and beekeeping.

Mbale

Foundation for Development of Needy Communities (FDNC; ☎0772-494285; www.fdncuganda.or.ug) Runs a host of community-development programs in the area.

Uganda Charity Trust Fund (UCTF; ☎0782-469402; www.uctf.org) A charity specialising in youth development offers varied roles for skilled volunteers including teaching and coaching disadvantaged kids.

ⓘ Getting There & Away

AIR

Located about 40km south of the capital, **Entebbe International Airport** (EBB) is the only aerial gateway to Uganda.

Uganda is well linked to its East African neighbours with daily flights to Kenya, Tanzania, Rwanda, Burundi and Sudan.

Air Uganda's operations had been suspended at the time of research and its future remained in doubt.

Airlines in Uganda

Air Uganda (Map p384; ☎0414-258262; www.air-uganda.com; Parliament Ave) Grounded from mid-2014; if services resume it flies to East African capital cities, as well as Mombasa and Zanzibar.

British Airways (Map p384; ☎0414-257414; www.britishairways.com; Centre Court, Plot 4 Ternan Ave, Nakasero, Kampala)

Brussels Airlines (Map p384; ☎0414-234201; www.brusselsairlines.com; 1 Lumumba Ave, Rwenzori House, Kampala)

Emirates (Map p384; ☎0414-770444; www.emirates.com; Kimathi Ave, Kampala)

Ethiopian Airlines (Map p384; ☎0414-345577; www.flyethiopian.com; Kimathi Ave, Kampala)

Kenya Airways (Map p384; ☎0312-360000; www.kenya-airways.com; Parliament Ave, Kampala) Flies to most East Africa cities via Nairobi.

KLM (Map p384; ☎0414-338000; www.klm.com; 4 Parliament Rd, Jubilee Insurance Building, Kampala) Direct flights to Amsterdam.

Qatar Airways (Map p384; ☎in Entebbe 0417-800900; www.qatarairways.com; 1st fl, Rwenzori Towers, Nakasero Rd, Kampala)

RwandAir (Map p384; ☎0414-344851; www.rwandair.com; Lumumba Ave, Garden City, Kampala) Direct flights to both Kigali and Juba.

South African Airways (Map p384; ☎0414-345772; www.flysaa.com; 1 Pilkington Rd, Kampala)

Turkish Airlines (Map p384; ☎0414-253433; www.turkishairlines.com; 3rd fl, 15a Clement Hill Rd, Ruth Towers, Kampala)

LAND

Uganda shares land border crossings with Kenya, Rwanda, Tanzania, South Sudan and the DRC. Direct bus services connect the major cities in each country, and local transport from towns nearer the border is available for those wanting to break their journey along the way.

Kenya

The busiest border crossing is at Busia on the direct route to Nairobi through Kisumu. Frequent minibuses link Jinja to Busia (USh10,000, 2½ hours), and then again between Busia and Kisumu or Nairobi. The border crossing is straightforward, though there are a number of shady moneychangers: check everything twice.

The other busy border crossing to Kenya is through Malaba, a bit north of Busia and just east of Tororo. Finding onward transport from here to Nairobi is less frequent than at Busia.

To visit Mt Elgon National Park or Sipi Falls, the Suam border crossing, beyond which lies the Kenyan city of Kitale, may be convenient, but this is a pretty rough route. Trekkers in either the Ugandan or Kenyan national parks on Mt Elgon also have the option of walking over the border.

Most travellers avoid local transport altogether and opt for the direct buses running between Kampala and Nairobi, which range from luxurious to basic. You can also pick up these buses (or get dropped off on your way into Uganda) in Jinja. The journey takes about 12 to 13 hours.

Easy Coach (Map p384; ☎0757-727273; www.easycoach.co.ke; Dewinton Rd, Kampala) Reputable company with modern buses. Daily departures to Nairobi (USh73,000) at 6.30am, 2pm and 7pm.

Queens Coach (Map p384; ☎0773-002010; www.queenscoach.com; Oasis Mall, Kampala) Comfortable bus servicing Nairobi (USh70,000) departing 8pm.

Mash (Map p384; ☑ 0793-234312; www. masheastafrica.com; 7 Dewinton Rd, Kampala) Twice daily departures to Nairobi (USh70,000) at 5pm and 10pm.

For information on crossing the border from Kenya into Uganda, see p370.

Rwanda

There are two main border crossing points between Uganda and Rwanda: between Kabale and Kigali via Katuna (Gatuna on the Rwandan side), and between Kisoro and Musanze (Ruhengeri) via Cyanika. The Kagitumba border isn't very practical for most people, but there is public transport on both sides.

The busiest crossing by far is at Katuna/ Gatuna, and it can take over an hour to get through immigration stations on both sides. From Kabale there are lots of shared-car taxis to the border, and a few minibuses each morning (except Sunday) direct to Kigali. You can also wait at the main junction in the morning for the Kigali-bound buses from Kampala to pass through and hope they have free seats. On the Rwandan side there are minibuses travelling to Kigali (RFr1500, two hours) throughout the day.

From Kisoro to Cyanika there's no public transport, so you'll need to get a special-hire (USh25,000 to USh35,000) or a *boda-boda* (USh7000). Transport on the Rwandan side to Musanze (Ruhengeri) is frequent and the road in good condition; altogether it only takes about 1½ hours to travel between Kisoro and Musanze (Ruhengeri). The border is open 24 hours.

There's also the option of taking a direct bus between Kampala and Kigali (USh35,000 to USh40,000), a seven- to nine-hour journey including a slow border crossing.

Horizon (Map p384; ☑ 0772-504565; 2 Berkely Rd, Kampala) Daily 8pm bus to Kigali from Monday to Saturday.

Jaguar Executive Coaches (Map p380; ☑ 0782-417512; Namirembe Rd, Kampala) Reliable company with daily services to Kigali at 7am, 9am, 8pm and 9pm. Also has a 'VIP' option with more comfortable seats.

Simba (Namayiba Terminal) (Map p384; Rashid Khamis Rd, Kampala) Daily buses to Kigali (USh40,000, 11 hours) at 2am.

For information on travelling into Uganda from Rwanda, see p534.

South Sudan

With the advent of peace in northern Uganda and South Sudan, tenuous as it may be, travel has picked up dramatically. The principal, and shortest, route from Kampala to Juba is the 15-hour (much longer if it rains) trip via Gulu, crossing at Nimule.

Although the border to South Sudan is open (you'll need to arrange your visa in Kampala, and not the border), travel by land between South Sudan and Sudan is nearly impossible due to civil war, so Juba is effectively a dead-end.

Kampala Coach (☑ 0772-384906; Namayuba Bus Terminal, Old Kampala; USh50,000-60,000; ☺ departs 11pm) Heads to Juba each evening at 11pm.

Bakulu Coaches (Map p384; ☑ 0772-381274; Arua Park; USh50,000-60,000) Daily departure to Juba, though has had recent safety issues.

Tanzania

The most commonly used direct route between Uganda and Tanzania is on the west side of Lake Victoria between Bukoba and Kampala, via Masaka; the border crossing is at Mutukula. Road conditions are good and the journey takes about six hours by bus from Kampala (you can also catch these buses in Masaka).

There's another border crossing located at Nkurungu, west of Mutukula, but the road is bad and little transport passes this way.

The journey to Dar es Salaam takes a day and a half via Nairobi.

Friends Safari (Map p384; ☑ 0788-425952; Rashid Khamis Rd, Kampala) Recommended bus departs at 11am for Bukoba (USh35,000, seven hours) and Mwanza (USh65,000, 12 hours) at 6am.

Falcon (Map p384; ☑ 0781-338066; 4 Lumumba Ave, Kampala) Departs for Dar-es-Salaam (USh140,000, 28 hours) on Wednesday, Friday and Sunday at 6am.

For information on getting to Uganda from Tanzania, see p210.

Democratic Republic of the Congo (DRC)

The main border crossings into the DRC are at Bunagana (8km from Kisoro) and Arua, however due to civil instability it would be very unwise to visit the DRC. Check, check and check again in Kampala and Kisoro about the current security situation before risking a crossing.

LAKE

The 'passenger' service on Lake Victoria to Mwanza (Tanzania) is more one for adventure travellers, via the MV *Umoja* cargo ferry that departs from Kampala's Port Bell. Typically these sail two or three days a week. Check the schedule at the Marine Services offices on the 2nd floor of the train station in downtown Kampala. Enter through the eastern gate. Pay your USh5000 port fee in the office in the green shipping container and then USh40,000 directly to the captain. The trip takes 16 to 17 hours and it's usually possible to make a deal with one of the crew for their bunk.

ⓘ Getting Around

AIR

Several airlines operate charter flights, which get you to the national parks in comfort, but cost a fortune. Eagle Air has scheduled flights to Arua and Yei, South Sudan most days of the week, but is likely to be of little interest for tourists.

Eagle Air (Map p384; ☑ 0414-344292; www.eagleair-ug.com; 11 Portal Ave, Kampala)

Fly Uganda (☑ 0772-712557; www.flyuganda.com)

Aerolink (☑ 0776-882205; www.aerolinkuganda.com)

BOAT

Boat travel in Uganda is limited to reaching the Ssese Islands, either by ferry from Port Bell, Nakiwogo (right by Entebbe), Bukakata (east of Masaka) or small fishing boats operating from Kasenyi (also near Entebbe).

BUS

Standard buses and sometimes half-sized 'coasters' connect major towns on a daily basis. The longer your journey is, the more likely it will be on a bus rather than a minibus. Bus fares are usually a little less than minibus fares and buses stop far less frequently, which saves time. Buses generally leave Kampala at fixed departure times; however, returning from provincial destinations, they usually leave when full. There are many reckless drivers, but buses are safer than minibuses. Night travel is simply best avoided.

The safest buses to travel with are the post buses run by the Ugandan Postal Service (UPS). Post buses run daily (except Sunday) from Kampala to Kasese (via Mbarara), Kabale (via Masaka and Mbarara), Soroti (via Mbale) and Hoima (via Masindi).

Minibus Taxis

Uganda is the land of shared minibuses (called taxis, or occasionally *matatus*), and there's never any shortage of these blue-and-white minivans. Except for long distances, these are the most common vehicles between towns. There are official fares (you can check at the taxi rank offices if you want) but in reality the conductor charges whatever they think they can get, and not just for a *mzungu* but for locals as well. Ask fellow passengers the right price.

Minibuses leave when full and 'full' means exactly that! As soon as you're a fair distance away from towns, where police spot-checks are less likely, more passengers will be crammed in. As is clearly painted on their doors, minibuses are licensed to carry 14 passengers, but travelling with less than 18 is rare, and the number often well exceeds 20. For all but the shortest journeys, you're better off taking a bus as they stop less frequently and are safer due to their size.

Many minibus and bus drivers drive much too fast to leave any leeway for emergencies. Crash stories are regular features in the newspapers. Most crashes are head-on, so sit at the back for maximum safety.

Way out of the way places use shared-car taxis rather than minibuses, and these are similarly insanely overloaded with passengers. If the roads are exceptionally bad, then the only choice is to sit with bags of maize and charcoal, empty jerry cans and other cargo in the backs of trucks.

CAR & MOTORCYCLE

There's a pretty good system of sealed roads between most major population centres. Keep your wits about you when driving; cyclists, cows and large potholes often appear from nowhere.

The quality of *murram* (dirt) roads varies depending on whether it's the wet or dry season. In the dry, *murram* roads are very dusty and you'll end up choking behind trucks and minibuses while everything along the road gets covered in a fine layer of orange-brown dust. In the wet season, a number of the *murran* roads become muddy mires, almost carrot soup, and may be passable only in a 4WD vehicle. If you're travelling around Uganda in the wet seasons, always ask about the latest road conditions before setting off on a journey.

As with other transport, avoid travelling at night due to higher risks of accidents and banditry. Take care in the national parks where there's a US$500 fine for hitting animals and US$150 for off-track driving.

Road signs are rare in Uganda so it's possible to get hopelessly lost. Don't hesitate to ask for directions frequently along the way.

Driving Licence

If you have an International Driving Permit, you should bring it, although you really only need your local driving licence from home.

Fuel & Spare Parts

In Kampala petrol costs about USh3700 per litre while diesel is about USh3540 per litre. Prices rise as you move out into provincial areas. Like everywhere in the world, petrol prices are highly volatile.

Filling and repair stations are found even in some small towns, but don't let the tank run too low or you may end up paying around USh5000 per litre to fuel up from a jerry can in some really remote place.

Hire

Due to high taxes and bad roads, car-hire prices tend to be expensive compared with other parts of the country. Add fuel costs and there will be some real shock at the total price if you're considering driving around the country. Also remember that if you're going to national parks, you'll have to pay the driver's fees as well as your own.

The big international operators are **Europcar** (Map p384; ☎ 0414-237211; www.europcar.com; Nsambya Rd, Kampala), and **Hertz** (Map p384; ☎ 0772-450460; www.hertz.com; Colville St, Kampala), each with offices in downtown Kampala and at the airport in Entebbe.

In virtually all instances it's better to deal with one of the local companies, though shop around. Quoted prices for a small car with driver can range from US$50 to US$150. The highest prices are just rip-offs by companies who hope *wazungu* don't know any better, but with the others, the difference is in the details. Always ask about the number of free kilometres (and the price for exceeding them) and driver costs for food and lodging. Try negotiating with special-hire drivers, but generally speaking they aren't as reliable. Red Chilli backpackers (p382) offers very good rates for car hire.

Alpha Car Rentals (Map p384; ☎ 0772-411232; www.alpharentals.co.ug; 3/5 Bombo Rd, EMKA House, Kampala) A car with driver costs USh80,000 for the day around Kampala, while a 4WD with driver is US$100 (his food and lodging inclusive) if you head upcountry, or US$70 for self-drive. It also has RAV4s from US$50 per day. All prices are exclusive of fuel, but have unlimited mileage.

Road Trip Uganda (☎ 0773-363012; www.roadtripuganda.com) Popular company hiring self-drive fully equipped RAV4s from US$50 per day. Also offers a car with driver.

Wemtec (☎ 0772-221113; wemtec@source.co.ug; 14 Spire Rd, Jinja) Well-known company based in Jinja but delivers country-wide. Hires a variety of 4WDs with driver from around USh200,000. Prices all-inclusive (minus fuel), with no limits on mileage.

HITCHING

Without your own transport, hitching is virtually obligatory in some situations, such as getting into national parks. Most of the lifts will be on delivery trucks, usually on top of the load at the back, which can be a very pleasant way to travel, though sun protection is a must. There's virtually always a charge for these rides.

LOCAL TRANSPORT

Kampala has a local minibus network, as well as special-hire taxis for private trips. Elsewhere you'll have to rely solely on two-wheel taxis, known as *boda-bodas* as they originally shuttled people between border posts: from 'boda to boda'. Most are now motorcycles, but you get the occasional bicycle in the smaller towns. Never hesitate to tell a driver to slow down if you feel uncomfortable with his driving skills, or lack thereof. Outside Kampala, there are few trips within any town that should cost more than USh3000.

Rwanda

Includes ➜

Best for Nature

➜ Volcanoes National Park (p501)

➜ Nyungwe Forest National Park (p516)

➜ Akagera National Park (p523)

Best for Culture

➜ National Museum of Rwanda (p513)

➜ Iby'Iwacu Cultural Village (p506)

➜ Rukari Ancient History Museum (p515)

Why Go?

Mention Rwanda to anyone with a small measure of geo-political conscience, and that person will no doubt recall images of the horrific genocide that brutalised this tiny country in 1994. But since those dark days a miraculous transformation has been wrought and today the country is one of tribal unity, political stability and a promising future.

Tourism is once again a key contributor to the economy and the industry's brightest star is the chance to track rare mountain gorillas through bamboo forests in the shadow of the Virunga volcanoes. These conical mountains are shrouded in equatorial jungles and helped earn Rwanda the well-deserved moniker of 'Le Pays des Mille Collines' (Land of a Thousand Hills).

So, while Rwanda's scars may run deep, now is the time to help the country look to its future and embrace its new-found optimism.

When to Go
Kigali

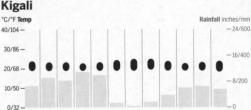

Dry seasons
Rains ease during the long dry (mid-May to Sep) and short dry (mid-Dec to mid-Mar).

Jun & Jul
Baby gorillas are named during the Kwita Izina ceremony.

The long rains Although often wet from mid-March to mid-May, travel is still possible.

Rwanda Highlights

❶ Hike the forested slopes of the Virungas for a close encounter with mountain gorillas and golden monkeys in **Volcanoes National Park** (p501).

❷ Hack your way through steamy rainforests in search of colobus monkeys and chimpanzees in the **Nyungwe Forest National Park** (p516).

❸ Watch an Intore dance performance at the **National Museum of Rwanda** (p513), the finest museum in the country, in Huye (Butare).

❹ Confront the horrors of the genocide at the haunting **Kigali Memorial Centre** (p489) on the outskirts of the capital.

❺ Kick back with a locally brewed Bralirwa on the sandy shores of Lake Kivu at **Gisenyi** (p508) or the equally beautiful **Kibuye** (p521) further south.

❻ Take a Rwandan-style safari in the up-and-coming **Akagera National Park** (p523).

KIGALI

POP 1.13 MILLION

Spanning several ridges and valleys, Kigali, with its lush hillsides, flowering trees, winding boulevards and bustling streets, is arguably one of the most attractive capital cities in Africa, as well as one of the cleanest and safest.

It wasn't always like this. Kigali exists as a testament to the peace and order that has defined Rwanda's trajectory for more than two decades, though it bore the brunt of the genocide in 1994. When the Rwandan Patriotic Front (RPF) finally captured Kigali after 100 days of systematic slaughter, dead and decaying bodies littered the streets and dogs

RWANDA AT A GLANCE

Area
26,338 sq km

Capital
Kigali

Country Code
☑250

Population
12.3 million

Currency
Rwandan franc (RFr)

Languages
Kinyarwanda, English, French

Money
Most banks in larger towns have international ATMs.

Mobile Phones
Local SIM cards widely available and phone coverage excellent.

Visas
Needed by most visitors. Available to some nationalities upon arrival. Others must apply in advance.

Exchange Rates

Australia	A$1	RFr529
Canada	C$1	RFr547
Euro Zone	€1	RFr781
Japan	¥100	RFr574
New Zealand	NZ$1	RFr507
UK	UK£1	RFr1052
USA	US$1	RFr690

For current exchange rates see www.xe.com

were shot en masse as they had developed a taste for human flesh.

In recent years, a massive amount of rehabilitation work has restored the city to its former graces, while increasing waves of foreign investment have sparked a number of ambitious building projects. Indeed, the rebirth of the capital has seen a surprising measure of cosmopolitanism take hold; there's plenty of good places to eat, some lively night-time action, interesting and well-presented museums and a general buzz on the streets that leaves many a visitor picturing a very bright future for the city.

History

Kigali was founded in 1907 by German colonisers, but did not become the capital until Rwandan independence in 1962. Although Rwandan power was traditionally centred in Huye (Butare), Kigali was chosen because of its central location. Walking Kigali's streets today, it is hard to imagine the horrors that unfolded here during those 100 days of madness in 1994. Roadblocks, manned by Interahamwe militia, were set up at strategic points throughout the city and tens of thousands of Rwandans were bludgeoned or hacked to death. People swarmed to the churches in search of sanctuary, but the killers followed them there and showed a complete lack of mercy or compassion.

While all of this horror took place for days and nights on end, the UN Assistance Mission for Rwanda (UNAMIR) stood by and watched, held back by the bureaucrats and politicians who failed to grasp the magnitude of what was unfolding and dithered over whether to get involved or not. In its defence, UNAMIR was bound by a restrictive mandate that prevented it from taking preliminary action, though it has been argued that the tragedy is that more deliberate action could have saved untold lives.

After 10 Belgian peacekeepers were murdered at the start of the genocide, the Belgian government withdrew its contingent, leaving UNAMIR to fend for itself with a minimal mandate and no muscle. There was little the 250 troops that remained could do but watch, and rescue or protect the few that they could.

Even more unbelievable is the fact that a contingent of the RPF was holed up in the parliamentary compound throughout this period, a legacy of the Arusha 'peace' process. Like the UNAMIR troops, there was little they could do to stop such widespread killing, though they did mount some spectacular rescue missions from churches and civic buildings around the city.

When the RPF finally swept the *génocidaires* from power in early July 1994, Kigali was wrecked; much of the city's buildings were destroyed, and what little of the population remained alive were traumatised. As the Kigali Memorial Centre so aptly puts it, Rwanda was dead.

Remarkably, there are few visible signs of this carnage today. Kigali is now a dynamic and forward-looking city, the local economy is booming, investment is a buzzword, and buildings are springing up like mushrooms. In fact, so complete is the rebirth of the city that many first-time visitors spend their first few days walking around in a state of wonder that so much appears to have been achieved in so short a space of time.

○ Sights

★ Kigali Memorial Centre   MEMORIAL
(www.kigaligenocidememorial.org;   ⊘ 8am-5pm, last entry 4pm, closed public holidays) FREE In the span of 100 days, an estimated one million Tutsis and moderate Hutus were systematically butchered by the Interahamwe and army. This memorial honours the estimated 250,000 people buried here in mass graves and tries to explain how it was that the world watched as the genocide unfolded.

This is an intensely powerful and moving memorial for which you should dedicate at least half a day.

The informative audio tour (US$15) includes background on the divisive colonial experience in Rwanda and as the visit progresses, the exhibits become steadily more powerful, as you are confronted with the crimes that took place here and moving video testimony from survivors. If you have remained dispassionate until this point, you'll find that it will all catch up with you at the section that remembers the children who fell victim to the killers' machetes. Life-sized photos are accompanied by intimate details about their favourite toys, their last words and the manner in which they were killed.

The memorial concludes with sections on the search for justice through the international tribunal in Arusha as well as the local *gacaca* courts (traditional tribunals headed by village elders).

Upstairs is a moving section dedicated to informing visitors about other genocides that have taken place around the world and helps set Rwanda's nightmare in a historical context.

After you've absorbed the museum displays take a rose (by donation) to leave on one of the vast concrete slabs outside that cover the mass graves. There's also a wall of names, a rose garden and a pleasant **cafe** serving good coffee, lunch buffets (RFr3000), snacks and juices that is an ideal place to reflect and gather yourself before facing the outside world again.

The Kigali Memorial Centre is located in the northern Kisozi district of the capital, which is a short *moto-taxi* (motorcycle taxi) ride from the centre (RFr500 to RFr600).

Camp Kigali Memorial   MEMORIAL
(Rue de l'Hopital; ⊘ 8am-5pm) FREE The 10 stone columns you find here mark the spot where 10 Belgian UN peacekeepers were murdered on the first day of the genocide. Originally deployed to protect the home of moderate prime minister Agatha Uwilingimana, the soldiers were captured, disarmed and brought here by the Presidential Guard before being killed.

RWANDA KIGALI

DON'T MISS

NYAMATA & NTARAMA GENOCIDE MEMORIALS

During the genocide, victims fled to churches seeking refuge, only to find that some of the clergy was providing information to the Interahamwe. As a result of this lack of compassion, some of the most horrific massacres took place inside the sanctums of churches throughout Rwanda.

Both of these memorials can be visited on a day trip from Kigali. Sotra Tours (p496) runs buses every half-hour to Nyamata (RFr700, 45 minutes) from Kigali; the memorial is a 1km walk from the Nyamata bus station. Ntarama can easily be reached from Nyamata by *moto-taxi* (RFr1500). To return to Kigali, head back to the main road and catch a passing bus.

Nyamata Church (Nyamata; ⊘ 8am-4.30pm Mon-Thu, 9am-4pm Fri-Sun) Nyamata church, about 30km south of Kigali, is a deeply disturbing genocide memorial where some 50,000 people died. Today the skulls and bones of the many victims are on display. While the visual remains of the deceased are a visceral sight, their inclusion here is to provide firm evidence to would-be genocide deniers.

Ntarama Church (Ntarama; ⊘ 8am-4.30pm Mon-Thu, 9am-4pm Fri-Sun) Ntarama church, about 25km south of Kigali, has not been touched since the genocide ended and the bodies were removed. Today, there are many bits of clothing scraps still on the floor.

Kigali

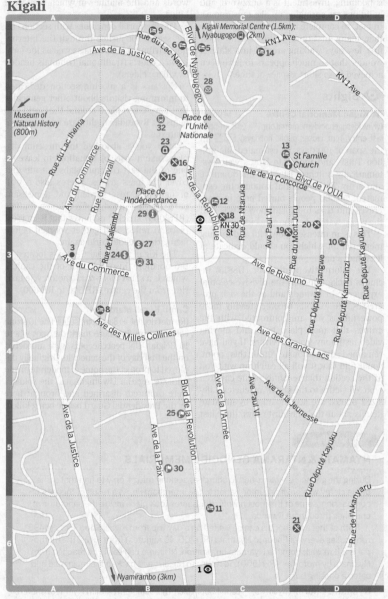

Each stone column represents one of the soldiers and the horizontal cuts in it represent the soldier's age.

The bullet-sprayed building in which the soldiers died now houses a small exhibition on the genocide.

Inema Art Center   GALLERY

(☎0788653683; www.inemaartcenter.com; Kacyiru) FREE Opened in 2012, the privately run Inema Art Center is a collective of 10 resident artists as well as invited others. It's quickly established itself as the foremost modern art gal-

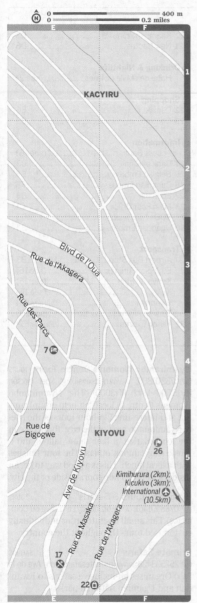

Museum of Natural History   MUSEUM
(www.museum.gov.rw; off Ave de la Justice; adult/child/student incl guide RFr6000/3000/3000; ⊙8am-6pm) This small museum houses a few simple exhibits on Rwanda's geology, fauna and flora. More interesting is the fact that this was the 1907 residence of explorer Richard Kandt and is reputed to be the first building in Kigali. The view from the garden is sensational, and looking over the urban sprawl, it's hard to imagine that it all started with this rather modest home. Few *moto* drivers have heard of the museum. Ask for Richard Kandt's house instead.

State House Museum   MUSEUM
(www.museum.gov.rw; Kanombe; adult/child/student incl guide RFr6000/3000/3000; ⊙8am-6pm) This former presidential palace on the eastern outskirts of the city is slowly being restored. It has few exhibits, but it's interesting to explore, with 'secret' rooms and an odd presidential nightclub. Wreckage from Juvenal Habyarimana's presidential plane can still be seen where it was shot down – just over his garden wall. The perpetrators were never caught, but this act proved to be a rallying call for Hutu extremists and helped trigger the genocide. The museum is a short way east of the airport. To get here, catch a Kanombe-bound minibus to the military hospital, from where it's a short walk.

Hotel des Mille Collines   NOTABLE BUILDING
(Hotel Rwanda; ☑0788192530; www.millecollines.net; Ave de la République) The inspiration for the film *Hotel Rwanda,* this luxury hotel was owned by the Belgian airline Sabena in 1994. At the time of the genocide, the hotel's European managers were evacuated, and control of the Mille Collines was given to Paul Rusesabagina.

As the situation in Kigali reached its boiling point, Paul allowed fleeing Tutsis and moderate Hutus to take refuge in the hotel, bribing the Interahamwe with money and alcohol in exchange for food and water.

Paul, his family and a few lucky survivors were eventually evacuated in a UN convoy as the Interahamwe seized the hotel. Today, Paul lives in Brussels, is an outspoken humanitarian and has been involved in a public feud with Rwandan president Paul Kagame.

Nyanza Genocide Memorial   MEMORIAL
(Kicukiro; ⊙8am-5pm Mon-Fri) FREE Located in Kicukiro, a suburb southeast of the city centre towards the airport, this memorial has little to see other than the tiled tops of

lery in Kigali. As well as paintings, sculptures and contemporary takes in traditional crafts there are dance and music performances and courses. Much of the art is for sale (and can be shipped internationally), but if you're not buying you're welcome just to admire.

Kigali

four mass graves believed to contain the remains of the 5000 Tutsis who took refuge in the Ecole Technique Officielle (ETO) grounds and numerous unmarked wooden crosses.

Following the assassination of 10 Belgian soldiers at Camp Kigali and the subsequent withdrawal of Belgian troops, the Tutsis here were left unprotected and ultimately taken to Nyanza and massacred. If arriving by *moto-taxi* (RFr1000 from town), tell the driver you're heading to *'urwibutso rwa Nyanza ya Kicukiro'*.

Tours

RDB City Tour
TOURS
(Rwanda Development Board; 🗹 252576514; www.rwandatourism.com; per person by bus/car US$20/40; ☺ departs 8am or 2pm) Requiring a minimum of two people, this three-hour tour includes the Kigali Memorial Centre (p489), as well as a few other prominent buildings around town. It's not amazing value given the memorial currently has no entry charge, but the guides are very knowledgeable and can give a local's perspective on the capital.

Tours leave from the RDB office on the ground floor of the Grand Pension Plaza.

Nyamirambo Women's Centre Tours
TOURS
(🗹 0782111860; www.nwc-kigali.org; per person RFr15,000, lunch RFr3000) The Nyamirambo Women's Centre (a local self-help group) runs fun and interesting 2½-hour tours of the lively Nyamirambo area of the city. Tours take in the local market, a hair salon, tailors and a music shop among others. The tour finishes with a local lunch. This is a good way to get an insider's view of a non-touristy side of the city.

Bizidanny Tours & Safaris
TOURS
(🗹 0788501461; www.bizidanny.com; Ave du Commerce) This small operator runs individually customised tours throughout the country.

Primate Safaris
SAFARIS
(🗹 252503428; www.primatesafaris.info; Ave de la Paix) Organises all-inclusive safaris to Rwandan and Ugandan national parks.

Volcanoes Safaris
TOURS
(🗹 252502452; www.volcanoessafaris.com; Hotel des Mille Collines, Ave de la République) Probably the most professional operator in Rwanda, Volcanoes Safaris runs customised trips and owns the exclusive Virunga Lodge (p500) in Volcanoes National Park.

🛏 Sleeping

In the years since the genocide, Kigali has played host to legions of international aid workers, diplomats, bureaucrats, travellers and investors, and the city now has an array of good accommodation to suit all pockets.

🏙 City Centre

Hôtel Isimbi
HOTEL **$**

(📞0786090557; hotelisimbi@hotmail.com; Rue de Kalisimbi; s/d US$40/45; 🛜) The most central of all the budget hotels, Isimbi is a good option for those who don't fancy walking up and down Kigali's endless hills. While the functional rooms here are somewhat lacking in atmosphere, they constitute a real bargain by Kigali standards. If given a choice, opt for any room other than those that face the noisy street.

Procure d'Accueil Religieux
HOTEL **$**

(📞0252576334; off Blvd de l'OUA; s/d without bathroom RFr9000/12,000; 🅿) This small church-run lodging can be found tucked behind the St Famille Church next to the Gemera petrol station, in the heart of town. The rooms are very simple, but it's secure, quiet and fairly clean and as cheap as you'll get in central Kigali.

Auberge La Caverne
HOTEL **$**

(📞0785656343; aubecav@yahoo.fr; Blvd de Nyabugogo; s US$20-24, d/tw US$30/40) This little hotel has just 15 basic but clean rooms of varying sizes and shapes arranged around a nondescript courtyard. The unifying factor between all is that they're rather grotty but quiet – thanks to their position away from the road.

Iris Guest House
GUESTHOUSE **$$**

(📞0728501181; www.irisguesthouse-rw.com; Rue Député Kamuzinzi; s/d/tw US$75/93/100; 🅿🛜) Very deservedly, this is one of the more popular midrange guesthouses in Kigali. It's well run and has bright, airy and charmingly old-fashioned rooms and a pleasingly leafy little garden. Its popularity means it's well worth booking ahead. It's in an upscale neighbourhood a short *moto* ride or walk from the city centre.

Motel Le Garni du Centre
BOUTIQUE HOTEL **$$**

(📞252572654; www.garnirwanda.com; Ave de la République; s/d US$145/180; 🅿❄🛜🏊) This intimate and atmospheric little *auberge* (inn) was the first boutique hotel in Kigali, and it's still about the best. Le Garni du Centre boasts individually decorated rooms with clean lines and African art, arranged around an inviting swimming pool and gorgeous flower garden. The tariffs get cheaper with every night you stay. It can organise safaris to Akagera National Park from US$210 per person (minimum two people) for a day trip.

Step Town Motel
GUESTHOUSE **$$**

(📞0785005662; www.step-town.com; KN 1 Ave, Kiyovu; s/d US$50/55; 🅿🛜) Not far from the city centre, and down a quiet dusty lane (and a very steep hill!), this place, with its prim white rooms splashed in blue, is one of Kigali's better-value offerings. As well as decent rooms, there's a garden terrace with views and a small bar-restaurant.

Impala Hotel
HOTEL **$$**

(📞250500226; Rue du Lac Nasho; s/d US$70/90; 🅿🛜) We like this place. It's smart and has its own unique sense of decoration, which includes theatre-red curtains and, mounted on one wall, a row of what we can only guess are alien heads. Aliens or not, the beds have good mattresses on them and the management cares.

Dream Apple Hotel
HOTEL **$$**

(📞0782793753; dreamapple333@yahoo.com; Blvd de Nyabugogo; d incl breakfast US$40-60; 🅿🛜) Despite the slightly odd name, the Dream Apple is a solid choice with massive rooms, garish bedspreads and a whole load of cleanliness. The choice rooms are the quieter ones at the back of the complex. A chilled restaurant and bar are next to the reception area.

Hotel Gorillas
HOTEL **$$**

(📞252501717; www.gorillashotels.com; Rue des Parcs, Kiyovu; s/d from US$90/120; 🅿@🛜) A slick little hotel in the upmarket Kiyovu area of the city, this place has won over a lot of customers thanks to its spacious rooms and friendly staff. The highlight of the property is Le Dos Argenté (mains RFr4200 to RFr7000), an open-air bistro serving an eclectic offering of Rwandan and Continental classics.

Hotel des Mille Collines
HISTORIC HOTEL **$$$**

(📞0788192530; www.millecollines.net; Ave de la République; s/d from US$230/250; 🅿❄🛜🏊) Welcome to the real Hotel Rwanda. While a colonial South African hotel was used in the movie, the real deal is more of a cement-and-glass construction. The foyer and pool area are spacious and elegant, and although the rooms aren't wildly exciting, they are better value than most top-end places in the city centre. Use of the hotel swimming pool costs a small fee for nonguests; it's a popular place to relax at weekends. There's also a poolside bar, a tennis court and a business centre.

Kigali Serena Hotel　　　LUXURY HOTEL **$$$**
(☑ 252597100; www.serenahotels.com; Blvd de la Revolution; r from US$400; P❀🔊🏊) The capital's first and only five-star hotel, the Kigali Serena is as swish as you would expect and has a grand and stately style. As inviting as the rooms and restaurants are, we think the real selling point is the hotel's impressive pool complex.

🏠 Outer Suburbs

★Discover Rwanda Youth Hostel　HOSTEL **$**
(☑ 0782265679; www.discoverrwanda.hostel.com; Kacyiru; 4/6/8 bed dm US$19/16/15, tw without bathroom US$23, d US$50; P@🔊) Easily the most popular backpackers' in Kigali, this hostel offers a very sociable atmosphere, lots of fun events (live music, barbecues and acrobatic nights) and a certain amount of disorganisation. Accommodation is either in dorms with four to eight beds and shared bathrooms or private en-suite rooms.

It's a five-minute *moto* ride from the city centre (RFr400 to RFr500).

★Garr Hotel　　　GUESTHOUSE **$$**
(☑ 0783831292; www.garrhotel.com; KG 9 Ave, Nyarutarama; s/d/tw/ste US$95/110/120/160; P🔊🏊) Head and shoulders above much of the competition, this homely guesthouse has large and rather classically styled rooms with wood furnishings and quality beds. It's in a smart part of town (but it's a long way from the city centre), and there are a number of excellent places to eat within walking distance. The swimming pool is another nice touch.

ℹ AN UPHILL BATTLE

In Kigali it's a sorry child indeed who's given a bicycle as a gift. The city sprawls over several hills, and two points that appear relatively close on a map may be separated by a valley in reality. Our tip: unless you have the inclination of a goat and the thighs of a mountain gorilla, jump on the back of a *moto-taxi* (motorcycle taxi) and whiz to your destination in breezy comfort – just hang on tight during gear changes.

Eating

The dining scene in Kigali is increasingly sophisticated. There's some great local food available, and despite Rwanda's current dislike of all things French, it doesn't seem keen to let go of the Francophone love of food and food culture. All this means that eating in Kigali is generally far more rewarding than eating in any of the Anglophone East African countries.

★Chez John　　　RWANDAN **$**
(Rue de Masaka; buffet RFr3500; ⊙noon-11pm) A popular local haunt, Chez John serves up authentic, country-style Rwandan standards – namely meat and maize – in upmarket surrounds. The lunch buffet is extremely popular and offers a great opportunity to try a number of local dishes in one sitting. If you don't like them here, it's going to be a long trip around the rest of Rwanda.

Meze Fresh　　　MEXICAN **$**
(Kacyiru; mains RFr3400; ⊙11am-11pm Tue-Sat, noon-8pm Sun) A fun Tex-Mex place serving huge crispy tortilla and burritos stuffed with beef or chicken and a range of sides. It's hardly authentic Mexican but it's tasty, cheap, filling and a cool place to hang out over a few drinks.

Blues Café　　　AMERICAN **$**
(Ave de la Paix; light meals RFr3500-4000; ⊙7am-8pm) This American-style diner is great if you're in the heart of town and just want something fast and fatty. Our cheeseburger had slabs of cheese on it so thick, forget clogging the arteries, it could have dammed the Nile. Salads, sandwiches, soups and spaghetti were also on the menu.

Bourbon Coffee Shop　　　AMERICAN **$**
(Union Trade Centre, Ave de la Paix; mains RFr3500-5400; ⊙7am-8pm; 🔊) Head to this popular Western-style coffee shop where locals and expats queue for oversized coffees, sandwiches, burgers and light meals.

★Zen　　　CHINESE **$$**
(☑ 0733503503; www.zenkigali.com; Nyarutarama; mains RFr5000-8000; ⊙noon-3pm & 6-11.30pm) With tinkling fountains and covered courtyard dining, this sublime restaurant offers Kigali's best Chinese meals as well as Rwanda's first sushi dishes. This is where the well-to-do of Kigali come when they want to impress. It's a long way out of the city centre in a swanky neighbourhood.

⭐ **Khana Khazana** INDIAN $$

(☎0788499600; www.khanakhazana.rw; Rue Député Kajangwe, Kiyovu; mains RFr4500-6000; ☺noon-3.30pm & 6-10.30pm) Statues of a rotund Ganesh and a blissed-out Shiva dot what many a local claim is the best Indian restaurant in Kigali. The menu has a long list of all the Indian classics prepared with panache and the waitstaff are dressed in imitation traditional Indian dress.

New Cactus FRENCH $$

(☎0788678798; Rue Député Kayuku; mains RFr6500; ☺noon-2pm & 6-10.30pm; 🛜) This Mexican-style hacienda is set on a ridge where you can soak up the sparkling lights of Kigali by night or get a bird's-eye appreciation of the city during the day. It boasts a broad menu of French favourites and, for something a little different, some delicious Congolese dishes full of spices and flavours.

Chez Robert RWANDAN $$

(KN 30 St; lunch buffet RFr6999, mains RFr4500-6000; ☺7am-late) This upmarket restaurant, which lives in a large, converted house with a shady terrace, offers the finest dining experience in the city centre. Lots of smoothly turned-out business types roll in at lunch time for the monster-sized buffet, which mixes Rwandan tastes with old-fashioned European dishes.

Heaven Restaurant & Bar EUROPEAN $$$

(☎0788486581; Rue du Mont Juru 7; mains RFr5000-9000; ☺5-10.30pm Mon-Fri, 10am-2pm & 5-10.30pm Sat & Sun) A highlight of the Kigali restaurant scene, Heaven has a relaxed, open-air deck bistro with a wide-ranging menu drawing from a variety of international influences. Saturday night is 'open-mike' night when anyone who fancies themselves as a budding Mick Jagger can take to the stage and ruin their fellow diners' evening!

🍷 Drinking & Nightlife

The good folk of Kigali take their drinking and partying pretty seriously, and there are a number of decent bars around town, some of which turn into clubs as the night wears on.

Hotel des Mille Collines BAR

(Ave de la République) The swimming pool bar at the Hotel des Mille Collines serves as the city's most popular daytime bar at weekends, with expats coming here to relax by the water and partake of the Sunday brunch. The Thursday happy hour (6pm to 7.30pm) is also extraordinarily popular with every-body who is anybody (although those bodies who are nobodies are just as welcome).

Planet Club CLUB

(Kigali Business Centre, Ave du Lac Muhazi; admission RFr2000-2500; ☺6pm-late) This trendy nightclub is often called KBC by locals due to its location in the Kigali Business Centre, well out of the city centre. Drinks are pricey, but from about 11pm onwards on a Friday and Saturday the place is jumping.

🛍 Shopping

Rwanda produces some attractive handicrafts. Look for finely woven *nyiramabuno* (basketry), *iayansi* (flasks once used to store milk), batiks, drums and the striking symmetrical paintings called *imigongo*.

Sellers claim many items are 'antiques' and price their goods accordingly; the reality is most are 'antiques' made last week and you should bargain prices down to something more sensible.

Caplaki ARTS & CRAFTS

(Ave de Kiyovu; ☺8am-6pm) This association of 38 stalls has banded together to market itself as Caplaki, although each stall is an independent business. As you would expect, there is a great selection of Rwandan handicrafts on sale, but you'll also find lots of carvings and masks from the DRC, banana-fibre products from Uganda, and items from Kenya.

Cootrac ARTS & CRAFTS

(Ave de la Paix; ☺8am-7pm) An association of 22 stalls selling handicrafts from Rwanda and the greater region can be found in this old warehouse close to the centre of the city.

ℹ️ Information

EMERGENCY

Police (☎112) A 24-hour emergency number, but don't rely on anyone answering!
SAMU Ambulance Service (☎912)

INTERNET ACCESS

Internet access is widespread and very cheap in Kigali. All but the cheapest hotels offer free wi-fi as do many of the more upmarket coffee shops and restaurants. The Rwandan government is halfway through implementing a plan to provide free wi-fi in all public spaces across the city (and eventually across the country).

MAPS

Eye Magazine A free tri-monthly magazine with several maps and a directory of businesses within the service industry.

MEDICAL SERVICES

Some embassies also have medical attachés who offer services through private practices.

Adventist Dental Clinic (☏ 0788777720, 252582431; Blvd de l'Umuganda, Kacyiru) About 3.5km from the centre of town in Kacyiru district, this place is run by an international dentist based in Kigali. If you can't find it, ask for the nearby Umubano Hotel.

King Faisal Hospital (☏ 252588888; www.kfh. rw) This South African–operated hospital is the best in Kigali.

MONEY

Euros and US dollars can be changed at any of the numerous banks in town or at any of the foreign-exchange bureaus near the Bank of Kigali. Most exchange bureaus give better rates than the banks, although the one at the airport is an exception.There are ATMs at virtually every bank, but Bank of Kigali machines seem to be the least temperamental when it comes to accepting foreign Visa cards (trying to use MasterCard or American Express is a good way of making the ATM close itself down!).

Access Bank (2fl, Union Trade Centre, Ave de la Paix) Over-the-counter cash advances on MasterCard.

Bank of Kigali (Ave du Commerce) Has an ATM (Visa only), over-the-counter cash advances on MasterCard, and Western Union services.

Ecobank (Ave de la Paix) Besides the ATM (Visa only) here, there's also a machine at the airport.

POST

Main Post Office (off Blvd de Nyabugogo; ⊙7am-5pm Mon-Fri, 7am-1pm Sat)

TOURIST INFORMATION

RDB (Rwanda Development Board; ☏ 252576514; www.rwandatourism.com; ground fl, Grand Pension Plaza; ⊙7am-5pm Mon-Fri, 8am-noon Sat & Sun) RDB, the national tourism office, has friendly staff who help promote tourism to the increasing stream of foreign visitors. Independent travellers can make reservations to track the gorillas and golden monkeys at Volcanoes National Park as well as chimps at Nyungwe Forest National Park and various other activities. The office couldn't be more central.

ⓘ Getting There & Away

AIR

International airlines fly in and out of Gregoire Kayibanda International Airport.

RwandAir (☏ 0788177000; www.rwandair.com; Union Trade Centre, Ave de la Paix) Has domestic flights to Kamembe (from US$150 one-way).

BUS

Several bus companies operate services to major towns, which are less crowded and safer than local minibuses. The Nyabugogo bus terminal, about 2km north of the city centre, is a bustling place. The terminal is unusually well organised, with each bus company having a separate office and, in general, destinations and fares listed on the wall of each office. There are also surprisingly few touts in the station, and those that there are tend to be quite helpful. The station is easily reached by minibuses heading down Blvd de Nyabugogo. Buses usually depart from the office you bought your ticket at. Most bus services dry up around mid-afternoon.

Capital Half-hourly departures for Kibuye (RFr2600, 2½ hours) via Gitarama (RFr900, one hour).

Horizon Express To Nyanza (RFr1700, 1¾ hours) and Huye (Butare; RFr2500, 2½ hours) every half-hour. Horizon operate some of the better buses.

Impala Runs buses west to Kibuye (RFr2600, 2½ hours) and Cyangugu (RFr5200, six hours) roughly every 1½ hours from 5.30am to 3pm.

International Heads to the town of Gatuna, on the border with Uganda, every half-hour (RFr3500, 2½ hours).

Kigali Safaris To Musanze (Ruhengeri; RFr1700, two hours) every half-hour until 6.30pm.

Omega Hourly to Cyangugu (RFr5000, six hours).

Onatracom Express Public-owned bus company with large, old and uncomfortable 45-seat buses running to Musanze (Ruhengeri; RFr1700, two hours) and Gisenyi (RFr3000, three hours), plus Huye (Butare; RFr2600, 2½ hours) and Cyangugu (RFr6000, six hours). Seeing as the prices are generally the same as the private bus companies or even more expensive, it's better to go private when you can.

Select Express Buses to the Rwanda–Tanzania border crossing of Rusumo (RFr3000, three hours) every half-hour.

Sotra Tours To Nymata (RFr600, 45 minutes), Rusumo (RFr3000, three hours, every half-hour) and Huye (Butare; RFr2500, 2½ hours, every half-hour).

Stella To Kayonza (RFr1400, 1½ hours) every half-hour.

Virunga Express Good buses to Musanze (Ruhengeri; RFr1700, two hours) and Gisenyi (RFr3000, three hours) every half-hour.

Volcano Express Reliable operator for Huye (Butare; RFr2500, 2½ hours) and Nyanza (RFr1700, 1¾ hours) every half-hour.

MINIBUS

Local minibuses depart from the Nyabugogo bus terminal for towns all around Rwanda, including Huye (Butare; RFr2500, two hours), Katuna (RFr1500, 1½ hours), Kibuye (RFr3000, two hours), Musanze (Ruhengeri; RFr1700, two hours) and Gisenyi (RFr3000, four hours). These minibuses leave when full throughout the day, except at weekends when they tend to dry up after 3pm. Accepted practice for foreigners is to turn up, wander around for bit, eventually tell someone where you're going and then be directed to the appropriate minibus.

ⓘ Getting Around

TO/FROM THE AIRPORT

Gregoire Kayibanda International Airport is at Kanombe, 10km east of the city centre. A taxi/moto-taxi costs RFr10,000/1500, but a KBS, International or Sotra Tours bus is cheaper (RFr250) and can be caught from outside the airport gates. In town you can catch one opposite the Bank of Kigali.

MINIBUS

Minibuses cruise the streets looking for passengers. All advertise their destination in the front window and run to districts throughout the city. They charge a set price of RFr200.

MOTO-TAXI

These small Japanese trail bikes can be a swift way to get around Kigali, although it can be quite scary as the drivers really hit the throttle. Short hops are just RFr300 to RFr500, while trips out to the suburbs cost RFr700 to RFr1000.

TAXI

Taxis are not metered but a fare within the city centre costs, on average, RFr3000 to RFr4000, double that out to the suburbs or later at night.

NORTHWESTERN RWANDA

A formidable natural border between Rwanda, Uganda and the Democratic Republic of the Congo (DRC; formerly Zaïre), the Virunga volcanoes are where Rwanda really earns its nickname as the 'Land of a Thousand Hills'. Home to the mighty mountain gorillas, the Rwandan Virungas are protected by Volcanoes National Park, the undisputed highlight of the country. The region is also home to the tranquil town of Gisenyi on the sandy shores of Lake Kivu, Rwanda's top spot for a 'beach' holiday.

Musanze (Ruhengeri)

POP 115,000

For most travellers, Musanze (Ruhengeri) is the preferred staging post on their way to the magnificent Volcanoes National Park, one of the best places in East Africa to track the mountain gorilla. Since permit holders are required to check in at the park headquarters in nearby Kinigi at 7am on the day of tracking, staying in Musanze is a much safer option than leaving from Kigali at the crack of dawn.

Musanze is a pleasant enough town to explore on foot, and it's situated near a number of interesting natural sights, with the massive Virunga volcanoes looming to the north and west.

◎ Sights & Activities

The outskirts of Musanze are home to **Lake Ruhondo** and **Lake Burera**, two large lakes dotted with small villages and accessed via a network of undeveloped dirt roads. The scenery here is breathtaking as the shores of the lakes are heavily terraced and cultivated with crops, and the Virunga volcanoes loom ominously in the distance.

While Ruhondo and Burera are not officially set up for tourism, you can easily have a DIY adventure here, especially if you have your own transport and are able to arrange a lake trip with a local fisherman.

Musanze Cave   CAVE

(admission US$50) These huge caves, 2km from the town centre along the road to Gisenyi (and also accessible from the road to Kinigi), were created when different lava flows joined to create the Albertine Rift Valley. Bat roosts are a significant feature of the caves, as are huge roof collapses that create vast arrays of coloured light shafts.

Unfortunately, few people visit the cave due to the high entry price and the fact that you can't currently buy the entry ticket from the RDB office in Musanze. Instead you have to go all the way to the RDB office just beyond Kinigi (an arrangement that might change in the near future).

☞ Tours

Most tour operators who visit Muzanse and Volcanoes National Park are based in Kigali.

Amahoro Tours   TOURS

(☏0788655223; www.amahoro-tours.com) A small, locally run operator that can help

Musanze (Ruhengeri)

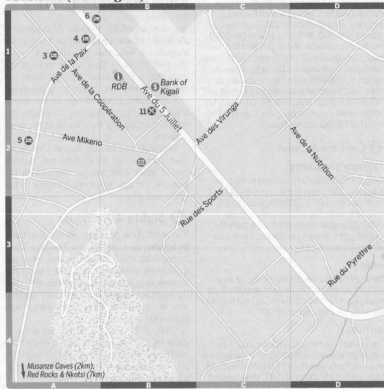

arrange gorilla-tracking permits, cultural activities and homestays in the surrounding area at reasonable prices. The office is unsigned and down a small dirt alleyway next to the brick 'COODAF' building, behind the bus station. It's signed as Greenhill Camping Site (though there's actually no campsite here).

🛏 Sleeping

As the main jumping-off point for Volcanoes National Park, there are a number of decent accommodation options in Musanze.

🛏 Town Centre

Hotel Muhabura HOTEL **$**
(🕿 0788364774; www.muhaburahotel.com; Ave du 5 Juillet; s/d from RFr30,000/35,000; 🅿 🛜) Long-time favourite Muhabura was once the town's leading hotel, and although it has been superseded by a whole slew of

midrange options, it straddles the niche between midrange and budget options nicely and retains a pleasant old-fashioned feel.

Ste Anne Hotel HOTEL **$**
(🕿 0785450505; www.sainteannehotel.com; off Ave du 5 Juillet; s/d/tw RFr25,000/30,000/40,000; 🅿) These rooms may be a step down in quality from other budget options, but they're a good choice if you want to save some money without scraping the bottom of the barrel. You still get satellite TV and a clean bathroom; it's all just a little tired. Prices are negotiable if you don't take the breakfast.

Amahoro Guesthouse GUESTHOUSE **$**
(🕿 0788655223; www.amahoro-guesthouse.com; dm US$25, s/d US$30/50; 🅿) A little difficult to find as it doesn't have a sign, Amahoro Guesthouse is tucked behind a green gate in a house with a green roof. The rooms are painted in bright, noisy primary colours, and there's

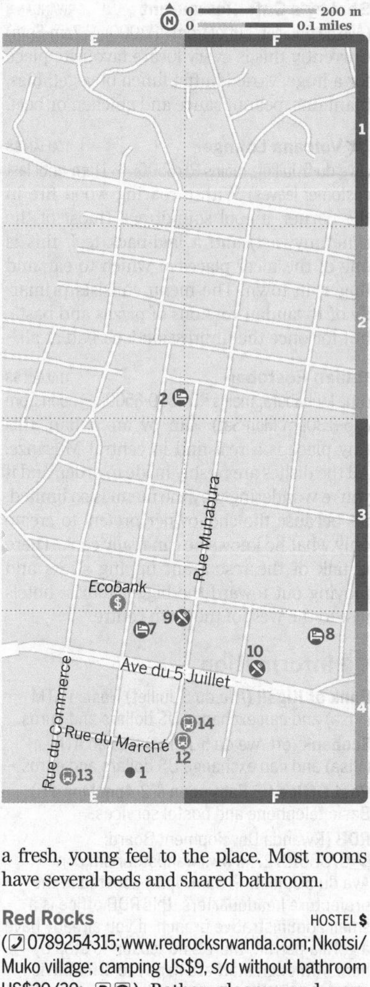

Musanze (Ruhengeri)

Activities, Courses & Tours
1 Amahoro Tours E4

Sleeping
2 Amahoro Guesthouse E2
3 Garden House A1
4 Gorillas Volcanoes Hotel A1
5 Home Inn A2
6 Hotel Muhabura A1
7 New Silver Hotel E4
8 Ste Anne Hotel F4

Eating
9 Italian Restobar E4
10 Shakey's Cafe-Restaurant F4
11 Volcana Lounge B2

Transport
12 Baby Coach E4
13 Bus Station E4
14 Horizon F4
Jaguar Coaches ..... (see 13)
Kigali Safaris ..... (see 13)
Virunga Express ..... (see 13)

a fresh, young feel to the place. Most rooms have several beds and shared bathroom.

Red Rocks HOSTEL $
(☎0789254315; www.redrocksrwanda.com; Nkotsi/Muko village; camping US$9, s/d without bathroom US$20/30; P ☎) Rather gloomy and very basic rooms that on their own wouldn't be worth mentioning. However, this place wins big points for its relaxed vibe and easy social scene. It also organises an array of interesting cultural activities (p500). It's 7km south of town on the road to Gitarama (Muhanga) and a RFr3000/600 taxi/*moto* ride.

New Silver Hotel HOTEL $
(☎0783565900; s/d/tw RFr15,000/20,000/30,000; ☎) A reasonable-value local hotel with big rooms – even the singles are unusually well proportioned – that are well maintained. Try to snag one overlooking the neighbouring garden restaurant rather than the busy, noisy road.

★ **Garden House** GUESTHOUSE $$
(☎0788405760, 0788427200; emgardner1@yahoo.co.u; Rue de la Coopération 53; s/d RFr35,000/45,000; P ☎) This English-Rwandan-run guesthouse in a beautifully converted villa has five cute, artistically decorated whitewashed rooms with double glass doors giving views of the large, leafy gardens. The hosts are helpful, the dogs friendly and the breakfast of homemade breads, jams and local honey, is as good as you'll get anywhere in Rwanda. There's no sign board: just look for the big double gates.

Home Inn HOTEL $$
(☎0784141000; www.homeinnhotel.com; Ave de la Paix; d/tw/apt US$70/90/110; P ☎) Painted an alarming shade of apricot, the Home Inn has fresh and bright rooms with 'gorgeously' garish bedspreads. The tiled bathrooms are spotless and each room has its own balcony that catches a refreshing breeze. Peaceful location.

Gorillas Volcanoes Hotel HOTEL $$
(☎252546700; www.gorillashotels.com; Ave de la Paix; s/d US$90/110; P ☎ ≋) Part of the Gorilla group and one of the smartest hotels in Musanze town, this establishment caters mostly to package tours. Facilities include a restaurant-cum-bar, a massage/sauna room and a swimming pool. Some rooms catch a bit of road noise.

DON'T MISS

CULTURAL ACTIVITIES

Nkotsi Village (also known as Muko) is a small village 7km southwest of Musanze. It's home to the Red Rocks (p499) campsite and hostel, which, through the Hands of Hope organisation and Amahoro Tours (p497), organises a lively and interesting package of cultural activities open to all. These range from basket-weaving demonstrations (free) to learning how to brew (and yeah, OK; drink) banana beer (US$25). Other activities include village walks (US$10), bee-keeping (US$30) and learning about traditional medicine (US$30).

It's best to arrange all activities in advance through either Red Rocks or Amahoro Tours.

Lakes Ruhondo & Burera

Virunga Lodge   LODGE $$$
(☑252502452; www.volcanoessafaris.com; s/d full board US$840/1400; ℙ🛜) One of the most stunningly situated camps in the region, the Virunga Lodge, nestled on a ridge above Lake Burera, offers incredible views across to the Virunga volcanoes, and is one of the finest lodges in Rwanda. Accommodation is in stone chalets decorated with local crafts and hardwood furnishings, though this place is definitely more about eco-atmosphere than opulent luxury.

Eating & Drinking

Musanze is one of the few towns outside Kigali that has independent restaurants that might tempt you away from your hotel restaurant at night. There are also a number of cheap 'local' restaurants that serve brilliant value, very tasty buffets at lunchtime. Of the hotel restaurants, our favourite is the one found at Hotel Muhabura. It has a nice atmosphere, though its food (steaks, brochettes, pasta and salad) is only marginally better than the food served elsewhere.

An interesting alternative and a memorable night out are the 'storytelling' meals organised by Amahoro Tours (p497). The idea is to bring together inquisitive tourists and community members who can exchange ideas and questions over the course of a local meal. The cost is US$30 per person, excluding the actual cost of the meal.

Shakey's Cafe-Restaurant   RWANDAN $
(Ave de 5 Juillet; buffet from RFr1000; ⊗7am-8pm) Currently this is every local's favourite place for a huge, varied buffet lunch of vegetables, plantains, peanut sauce and chicken or beef.

★**Volcana Lounge**   ITALIAN $$
(Ave du 5 Juillet; mains RFr6500; ⊗11am-until last customer leaves) With a roaring wood fire in the corner, a cool soundtrack (most of the time anyway!) and a laid-back feel, this is one of the nicer places at which to eat, and linger, in town. The menu consists primarily of Rwandan versions of pizzas and pasta, but for once the impression isn't bad at all.

Italian Restobar   ITALIAN $$
(Rue Muhabura; mains RFr4500-6500; ⊗noon-3pm & 6-8.30pm Mon-Sat) Run by an Italian, this tiny place is a real find in central Musanze. All the dishes are freshly made to order, and if you're wondering why the menu is so limited, it's because the chef-owner prefers to create only what he knows he can really cook. There is talk of the restaurant upping sticks and moving out toward the bigger tourist hotels just to the west of the town centre.

ℹ Information

Bank of Kigali (Ave du 5 Juillet) Has an ATM (Visa) and can exchange US dollars and euros.
Ecobank (off Ave du 5 Juillet) Has an ATM (Visa) and can exchange US dollars and euros.
Post Office (⊗8am-noon & 2-4pm Mon-Fri) Basic telephone and postal services.
RDB (Rwanda Development Board; ☑0788519727; www.rwandatourism.com; Ave du 5 Juillet; ⊗8am-5pm) Located in the prefecture headquarters, this RDB office is a small administrative branch. If you already have a gorilla permit, there's no reason to stop by here. Although staff are happy to offer advice about any RDB-organised activity, they couldn't issue permits or tickets at the time of research. They will, however, phone the Kigali or Kinigi office to see if gorilla permits or others are available. There is talk of this office being able to issue tickets and permits shortly.

ℹ Getting There & Away

Numerous bus companies offer scheduled hourly services between Musanze and Kigali (RFr1700, two hours) and between Musanze and Gisenyi (RFr1100, 1½ hours). The three most reliable are **Kigali Safaris** (Rue du Commerce), **Horizon** (Rue Muhabura) and **Virunga Express** (Rue du Commerce). The town's best station is home to most bus offices and sits at the end of Rue du Commerce.

Minibuses also travel these routes for much the same price, but they stop frequently to let passengers on and off, fill up with petrol and buy bananas.

Virunga Express (and an armada of minibuses) also travels to Cyanika (RFr400, 45 minutes), on the Rwanda–Uganda border. Several companies go direct to Kampala.

Baby Coach (Rue Muhabura) Buses to Kampala at 8am, 9am and 3pm (RFr8000, 11 hours).

Horizon (Rue Muhabura) A 3pm bus to Kampala (US$20, 11 hours).

Jaguar Coaches (Rue du Commerce) A 4.30pm service to Kampala (RFr12,000, 11 hours).

ⓘ Getting Around

There are few taxis in Musanze, but plenty of bicycle taxis and *moto-taxis* for those needing a rest. A typical fare from the town centre to the Hotel Muhabura is around RFr300 on a *moto-taxi*.

Volcanoes National Park

Volcanoes National Park, which runs along the border with the DRC and Uganda, is home to the Rwandan section of the Virungas. Comprising five volcanoes – Karisimbi (the highest at 4507m), Bisoke (Visoke), Sabinyo, Gahinga (Mgahinga) and Muhabura (Muhavura) – the Virungas are utterly spell-

binding and few would argue that this is not one of the most exciting national parks in Africa. We probably needn't remind you, but of all the extraordinary sights and attractions around the Virungas the one that really draws people here are the mountain gorillas, which were first studied in depth by primatologist George Schaller, and later thrust into the international spotlight during the life of Dian Fossey.

While most tourists to the park are understandably driven by the desire to have a face-to-face encounter with real gorillas in the mist, there is good reason to stay in the area once you've finished tracking: the gorillas share the park with rare golden monkeys, a troop of which has also been habituated to human contact. The Virungas, which tower over Rwanda, Uganda and the DRC, also present a variety of rewarding climbing and trekking options. To get the most from the Virungas give yourself as much time as you possibly can. This is absolutely a park that rewards those who linger.

History

Belgian colonists, who intended to protect the mountain gorillas on Karisimbi, Bisoke and Mikeno in Rwanda and the Belgian Congo from poachers, first gazetted the Virungas as a national park in 1925. This

Volcanoes National Park

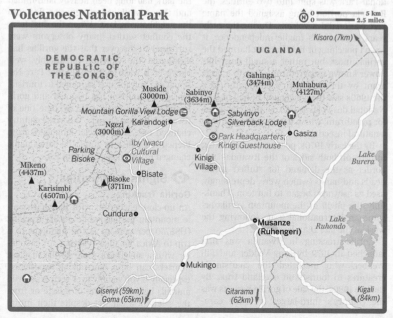

① VOLCANOES NATIONAL PARK

Why Go
Five bamboo- and rainforest-covered volcanoes that are sanctuaries to rare mountain gorillas and endangered golden monkeys.

When to Go
The long dry season from June to September is the ideal time to track mountain gorillas as it is, well...drier.

Practicalities
Reservations for gorilla tracking are sold out months in advance in high season, so make your booking as early as possible. Access to the park is via Musanze (Ruhengeri), although all trekkers need to report to the park headquarters in Kinigi (12km north of Musanze) at 7am on the day of their trek. The park does not provide transport to the trailheads.

Budget Tips
Put simply, there's no cheap way to go and see the mountain gorillas. You can, however, have other equally memorable and much more adventurous experiences in the park for a more reasonable budget. Try trekking up some of the volcanoes and, to keep costs lower, stay in a guesthouse near Kinigi village and take a *moto-taxi* to trailheads.

small conservation triangle was the first protected area to be created on the continent of Africa. Four years later, the borders were extended further to form Parc National Albert (Albert National Park), a massive area that encompassed more than 8000 sq km.

Following the independence of the Congo in 1960 and Rwanda in 1962, Albert National Park was split into two entities, the Rwanda portion being assigned the name Parc National des Volcans. During the early years of Rwanda's fragile independence, it wasn't poaching or fighting that harmed the gorillas most, but rather a small daisy-like flower known as pyrethrum. Due to a large grant by the European Community (EC), the 1960s saw the conversion of half of Parc National des Volcans into commercial farms for pyrethrum, which can be processed into a natural insecticide.

By the early 1970s, poachers were making inroads on both sides of the Rwanda–DRC border as the demand for stuffed gorilla heads and hands (which were, depressingly, used as ashtrays) began to burgeon. Thankfully, the plight of the mountain gorilla became an international issue following the work of the late Dian Fossey.

Gorilla tracking in Rwanda was first launched in 1979 by Amy Vedder and Bill Webber, who marketed the charismatic creatures to tourists on overland trips. By the late 1980s, the sale of gorilla permits was the country's third-largest revenue earn-

er, which was enough to convince ordinary Rwandans that these great apes were indeed a valuable natural resource worth protecting.

In 1991, Rwanda was plunged into civil war, and Parc National des Volcans became a battlefield. By the time the perpetrators of the genocide swept across Rwanda in 1994, the park had long been heavily land-mined and then abandoned as refugees fled into the neighbouring DRC. When the dust from the conflict settled, many observers were surprised to discover that the gorillas had weathered the violence remarkably well. However, it wasn't until 1999 that Parc National des Volcans was reopened to tourism. Since then tourism has boomed and gorilla tracking has once again become one of Rwanda's biggest earners. When the country changed one of its official languages from French to English in 2008, the park's name changed to Volcanoes National Park.

⊙ Sights & Activities

Gorilla Tracking
An up-close encounter with the charismatic mountain gorillas while gorilla tracking (US$750 per person) is the highlight of a trip to Africa for many visitors. An encounter with a silverback male gorilla at close quarters can be a hair-raising experience, especially if you've only ever seen large wild animals behind the bars of a cage or from the safety of a car. Yet despite their intim-

idating size, gorillas are remarkably non-aggressive animals, entirely vegetarian and usually quite safe to be around.

GORILLA FAMILIES

There are 10 habituated gorilla groups (excluding those groups set aside solely for research purposes, which tourists are not allowed to visit) in Volcanoes National Park, including the Susa group, which has around 28 members and a set of twins born in 2011. Although nearly everyone who shows up at the park headquarters is probably hoping to track the Susa group, the rangers usually select only the most able-bodied and all-round fit visitors. Even though the Susa group is the largest in the park, it's also the hardest to reach – you need to trek for three to four hours up the slopes of Karisimbi at an altitude of more than 3000m.

The Sabinyo group (eight members) is a good choice for anyone who doesn't want a strenuous tracking experience, as it can usually be found in less than 30 minutes. The Agashya (23 members) and Amahura (18 members) groups are also popular with visitors, although no matter which group you end up tracking, you're most likely going to have a memorable experience.

THE TREK

How hard is the trek to reach the gorillas? This is a question every other visitor seems to ask. It's a difficult question to answer, as it depends on which group of gorillas you go and see – some journeys are just a short stroll but others a half-day slog. You will most likely spend several hours scrambling through dense vegetation up steep, muddy hillsides, sometimes to altitudes of more than 3000m. At this altitude you will certainly be a little breathless, but someone of good fitness who does a reasonable amount of walking is unlikely to find the walk all that tough. If you're not used to walking though it might be a very different story and you should request a group closer to the trailheads. At higher altitudes, you'll also have to contend with the thick overgrowth of stinging nettles, which can easily penetrate light clothing. As if fiery skin rashes weren't enough of a deterrent, it also rains a lot in this area and can get very cold. Oh, and when people say it gets muddy what they mean is it can get MUDDY. Children (and Lonely Planet authors) would have the time of their lives rolling about in this stuff.

THE ENCOUNTER

Visits to the gorillas are restricted to one hour, and flash photography is banned. While you are visiting the gorillas, do not eat, drink, smoke or go to the bathroom in their presence. If you have any potential airborne illness, do not go tracking as gorillas are extremely susceptible to human diseases.

In theory, visitors are requested to remain more than 5m from the gorillas at all times, though in practice the guides (and the gorillas) tend to flout this rule. Although no tourists have ever been harmed by the gorillas, you should give them the respect and wide berth you would any wild animal.

RESERVATIONS

The hefty US$750 fee includes park entry, compulsory guides and guards. The number of people allowed to visit each of the groups is limited to a maximum of eight people per day, limiting the total number of daily permits to

---

KWITA IZINA: THE GORILLA NAMING CEREMONY

In traditional Rwandan culture, the birth of a child is a momentous event that is celebrated with a tremendous amount of fanfare. The birth is marked by the presentation of the new infant to the general public, who then proceed to suggest round after round of possible names. After careful consideration, the proud parents select one for their newborn, and celebrate the naming with copious amounts of dining, drinking and dancing.

Gorillas in Rwanda are often awarded the same level of respect and admiration as humans, which is why it's fitting they should be named in a similar manner. Since 2005, the annual Kwita Izina (Gorilla Naming Ceremony; late June–early July) has been a countrywide event that is increasingly drawing a larger share of the spotlight. From local community events in Musanze (Ruhengeri) to gala balls in Kigali and Gisenyi, Kwita Izina is well on its way to becoming a global brand.

The event has even attracted a number of celebrities and conservationists, which is testament to the growing appeal of the event and the future potential for Rwandan tourism. For more information on Kwita Izina, check out the official website: www.kwitizina.org.

THE LIFE OF DIAN FOSSEY

'When you realise the value of all life, you dwell less on what is past and concentrate more on the preservation of the future.'
Dr Dian Fossey, zoologist (1932–85)

Dian Fossey was an American zoologist who spent the better part of her life at a remote camp high up on the slopes of the Virungas studying the mountain gorillas. Without her tenacious efforts to have poaching stamped out, and the work of committed locals since her violent murder, there possibly wouldn't be any of the great apes remaining in Rwanda.

Although trained in occupational therapy, in 1963 Fossey took out a loan and travelled to Tanzania where she met Dr Louis and Mary Leakey. At the time, she learned about the pioneering work of Jane Goodall with chimpanzees and George Schaller's groundbreaking studies on gorillas.

By 1966 Fossey had secured the funding and support of the Leakey family, and began conducting field research of her own. However, political unrest caused her to abandon her efforts the following year at Kabara (in the Democratic Republic of the Congo), and establish the Karisoke Research Center, a remote camp on Bisoke in the more politically stable Rwandan Virungas.

Fossey was catapulted to international stardom when her photograph was snapped by Bob Campbell in 1970 and splashed across the cover of *National Geographic*. Seizing her newfound celebrity status, Fossey embarked on a massive publicity campaign aimed at saving the mountain gorillas from impending extinction.

Tragically, Fossey was murdered on 26 December 1985. Her skull was split open by a *panga,* a type of machete used by local poachers to cut the heads and hands off gorillas. This bloody crime scene caused the media to speculate that poachers, who were angered by her conservationist stance, murdered her.

While this may have been the case, a good measure of mystery still surrounds Fossey's murder and despite the 1986 conviction of a former student, many people believe the murderer's true identity was never credibly established and her former student was merely a convenient scapegoat.

Following her death, Fossey was buried in the Virungas next to her favourite gorilla, Digit, who had previously been killed by poachers. Throughout her life Dian Fossey was a proponent of 'active conservation', the belief that endangered species are best protected through rigorous anti-poaching measures and habitat protection. As a result, she strongly opposed the promotion of tourism in the Virunga range, though the Dian Fossey Gorilla Fund International has changed its position on the issue since her untimely death.

Today, Fossey is best known for her book *Gorillas in the Mist,* which is both a description of her scientific research and an insightful memoir detailing her time in Rwanda.

Parts of her life story were later adapted in the film *Gorillas in the Mist: The Story of Dian Fossey,* starring Sigourney Weaver. The movie was criticised for several fictitious scenes in which Fossey aggressively harasses local poachers, as well as its stylised portrayal of her affair with photographer Bob Campbell.

an absolute maximum of 80. Children under 15 are not allowed to visit the gorillas.

Bookings for gorilla permits can be made through the RDB tourist office (p496) in Kigali or a Rwandan tour company. Those visiting on a tour package will have everything arranged for them, while independent travellers can secure permits if they make reservations early on. Frustratingly, it's not always easy to deal with the RDB by phone or email from overseas, so it's sometimes easier to book a permit through a Rwandan tour operator (although you will of course have to pay a small surcharge if doing it this way).

With demand often exceeding supply, you'll need to book well in advance if you want to be assured of a spot, especially during the peak seasons of December–January and July–August. Bookings made direct through RDB are secured with a US$100 deposit (via bank transfer), and full payment must be made upon your arrival in Kigali.

Independent travellers who have only decided to visit the gorillas in Rwanda once in the East Africa region can turn up at the RDB office in Kigali and try to secure a booking at the earliest available date. During the high season waits of several days to more than a week are not uncommon.

You'll need to present yourself at 7am on the day that your permit is valid at the park headquarters 3km from Kinigi. It's worth emphasising that if you are late, your designated slot will be forfeited, and your money will not be refunded.

CLOTHING & EQUIPMENT

You need to be prepared for a potentially long, wet and cold trek through rainforest. A pair of hiking shoes is a must, as is warm and waterproof clothing. The stinging nettles at higher elevations can really put a damper on the experience, so consider wearing trousers and long-sleeve shirts with a bit of thickness.

Despite the high altitudes and potentially cold temperatures, you also need to be prepared for the strong sun. Floppy hats, bandanas, sunglasses and lots of sunscreen are a good idea, as are plenty of cold water and hydrating fluids. Sugary snacks are also good for a quick energy boost.

When you check in at the park headquarters, you may be asked for identification by the park rangers. To avoid any potential hassles, carry your passport with you at all times in addition to your gorilla-tracking permit.

Porters (US$10) are available for the trek, though they're not absolutely necessary unless you're carrying a lot of gear. The guides, guards, drivers and any porters will expect a tip – the amount is up to you, and ultimately depends on the quality of the service. However, keep in mind that the locals know you're paying US$750 for the privilege of gorilla tracking, so try not to be too stingy.

Golden Monkey Tracking

Golden monkey tracking (US$100 per person) is a relative newcomer on the wildlife scene of East Africa, but is rapidly rising in popularity. More like chimp-viewing than a gorilla encounter, these beautiful and active monkeys bound about the branches of bigger trees. If you're looking for a reason to spend an extra day in the park, don't miss the chance to track these rare animals.

Golden monkeys, which are a subspecies of the wider-spread blue monkey, are endemic to the Albertine Rift Valley and are distinguished by their gold body colouration, which contrasts sharply with black patches on their extremities. Classified as an endangered species, golden monkeys can only be seen in the Virungas, as deforestation and population growth in the Great Lakes region has greatly affected their home range.

Permits to track the golden monkeys are easy to get hold of – simply enquire at the RDB office in Kigali or Musanze, or at the park headquarters in Kinigi. As with the gorillas, your time with the monkeys is limited to one hour. But unlike the gorillas, children are allowed to take part (permit price is the same as for adults).

Trekking the Volcanoes

Dian Fossey once declared: 'In the heart of Central Africa, so high up that you shiver more than you sweat, are great, old volcanoes towering up almost 15,000ft, and nearly covered with rich, green rainforest – the Virungas.'

Indeed, these stunning volcanoes serve as an evocative backdrop for a guided climb or trek. As you make your way along the ascents, you'll pass through some remarkable changes of vegetation, ranging from thick forests of bamboo and giant lobelia or hagenia to alpine meadows. And there's further rewards in store: if the weather is favourable, you can enjoy spectacular views over the mountain chain.

There are several possibilities for climbing up to the summits of one or more of the volcanoes in the park, with treks ranging in length from several hours to two days. A guide is compulsory and is included in your trekking fee; additional porters are optional (US$20 per day). Note that it is forbidden to cut down trees or otherwise damage vegetation in the park, and you are only allowed to make fires in the designated camping areas.

One of the best parts of climbing and trekking the volcanoes is that you will be awarded ample opportunities to view wildlife (sans gorillas and golden monkeys, of course). The most common herbivores in the park are bushbucks and black-fronted duikers; buffaloes, bush pigs and giant forest hogs are infrequently spotted. Also, be sure to inspect the hollows of trees for hyraxes, genets, dormice, squirrels and forest pouched rats. The richest birdwatching zone is in the hagenia forests, where you can expect to see turaco, francolins, sunbirds, waxbills, crimson-wings and various hawks and buzzards.

DON'T MISS

CULTURE IN THE MOUNTAINS

Iby'Iwacu Cultural Village
(✆0788374545, 0788451289; www.
rwandaecotours.com; per person US$20;
🚼) Yes, it might be a bit fake, but while
most of the focus of Volcanoes National
Park falls squarely onto the animals,
this 'cultural village' puts the spotlight
back onto the people. And, despite
the stage-managed atmosphere, it's a
fun experience all round. Visitors get
to experience Rwandan village life by
grinding seeds, firing bows and arrows,
taking part in a traditional *intore* dance
and even partaking in the marriage of a
King to his Queen.

Children will love it, adults will learn
from it, and the money goes straight
to the local communities. It's a brilliant
complement to a morning with the
gorillas. The village is located close to
the parking for the Sabyinyo gorilla
group. Call at least an hour ahead of
your intended visit. You can also stay the
night here.

KARISIMBI

Climbing Karisimbi (4507m), the highest
summit in the Virungas, takes two long
and taxing days. The track follows the
saddle between Bisoke and Karisimbi, and
then ascends the northwestern flank of the
latter. Some five hours after beginning the
trek, there is a metal shelter under which
you can pitch your tent. The rocky and
sometimes snow-covered summit is a further two to four hours walk through alpine
vegetation.

To do this trek, take plenty of warm clothing, your own food, a sturdy tent (these can
be rented from the park office for US$20)
and a very good sleeping bag. It gets very
cold, especially at the metal shelter, which
is on a bleak shoulder of the mountain at
3660m. The wind whips through here, frequently with fog, so there is little warmth
from the sun.

The two-day climb up Karisimbi costs
US$400 for a solo climber or US$300 per
person for groups of two or more, including
park fees and a guide.

BISOKE

The most popular hike is the return trip
up Bisoke (3711m), which takes six to seven
hours from the parking lot at Bisoke. The
ascent takes you up the steep southwestern
flanks of the volcano to the summit, where
you can see the crater lake. The descent follows a track on the northwestern side, from
where there are magnificent views. This
climb costs US$75 per person, including
park fees and a guide.

DIAN FOSSEY'S GRAVE

A popular trek is to the site of the former
Karisoke Research Center, where Dian Fossey is buried alongside many of her primate
subjects, including the famous Digit. From
the park headquarters it's about a 30-minute
drive to the trailhead, followed by a two- to
three-hour hike to the ruins of the camp.
This excursion costs US$75 per person, in-
cluding park fees and a guide (though you
are responsible for your own transport to/
from the trailhead).

NGEZI

The return walk to Ngezi (about 3000m)
takes three to four hours from the parking
lot at Bisoke. This is one of the easiest of the
treks, and at the right time of the day it is
possible to see a variety of animals coming
down from the hills to drink at streams and
springs. This trek is slightly cheaper than the
others at US$55 per person including a guide.

GAHINGA & MUHABURA

Climbing Gahinga (3474m; in Uganda)
and Muhabura (4127m) is a two-day trip
from Gasiza (US$200 per person including
guide). The summit of the first volcano is
reached after a climb of about four hours
along a track that passes through a swampy
saddle between the two mountains. The trip
to the summit of Muhabura takes about four
hours from the saddle. It is also possible to
climb these volcanoes separately. The trekking fee is US$100 for Muhabura and US$75
for Gahinga, including a guide.

🛏 Sleeping & Eating

There are a number of places to stay on the
edge of the park, although you will still need
your own transport to get to park trailheads
and the like.

Kinigi Guesthouse   HOTEL **$**
(✆0788533606; kinigi2020@yahoo.fr; s/d from
RFr20,000/25,000; 🅿🛜) 🍃 This locally run
guesthouse, located within walking distance
of the park headquarters, is a good bet. Accommodation is in a small clutch of wooden

bungalows that are set in lush gardens with views of the towering Virungas.

All profits from the lodge are ploughed back into the Association de Solidarité des Femmes Rwandaises, which assists vulnerable Rwandan women of all backgrounds and ages.

La Paillotte Gorilla Place   HOTEL $
(☑ 0783398944; www.lapaillottegorillaplace.com; r RFr15,000-25,000; ⓟ) Right in Kinigi village, not far from the market and bus stand, this small hotel offers exceptional value for money. Rooms come in two categories, with the pricier ones having stone floors with bamboo matting, good bathrooms, pot plants and desks. Cheaper rooms lack the arty touches but are polished white and very comfortable. The attached restaurant with its wood burner for frigid nights is a relaxed place to eat.

★ Iby'Iwacu Cultural Village   HUT $$
(☑ 0788451289,   0788374545;   www.rwanda ecotour.com; per adult/child half board US$75/60) 🍴 This recreation of a traditional village is one of the most novel places to stay in Rwanda. Although its main purpose is to provide a 'cultural experience', you can also stay the night, and that's when things get interesting. Guests sleep in one of the cosy huts and are entertained long into the evening by local villagers. All up, it's a great way of forming fast friends with locals and learning a bit about their lives – and if you have children with you, this is likely to be *the* highlight of their Rwandan adventure. You should reserve in advance.

★ Sabyinyo Silverback Lodge   LODGE $$$
(www.governorscamp.com;   s/d   full   board US$1038/1686; ⓟ📶) 🍴 With space for a maximum of only 20 people, this is a place where guests are treated as friends of the management, which results in a highly personalised level of service. Accommodation is in Venetian plaster cottages with Rwandese-style terracotta-tile roofs, spacious sitting areas, individual fireplaces, stylish en suite bathrooms and sheltered verandahs.

The Sabyinyo Silverback Lodge is a joint partnership between the Sabyinyo Community Lodge Association (SACOLA) and the exclusive Governors' Camp. SACOLA gets US$70 per bed per night in addition to a percentage of all profits. To date, these revenues have been used to implement several community projects, including the erection of a 74km fence to protect local crops from hungry buffalo.

Mountain Gorilla View Lodge   LODGE $$$
(☑ 0788305708; www.3bhotels.com; s/d full board from US$240/300; ⓟ📶) These 30 rock cottages set in lush, grassy grounds and with impressive views down the volcano range are more functional than comfortable. A cultural show featuring traditional dancers is held here at 4.30pm every evening during the high season.

ℹ️ Information
Volcanoes National Park Headquarters (RDB; ☑ 0788771633; ⊙ 6am-4pm) You are required to register at this office, 3km east of the village of Kinigi, at 7am on the day of your scheduled gorilla tracking. If you are late, your designated slot will be forfeited. This is also the place to arrange permits for golden-monkey tracking, as well as climbs and treks in the Virunga volcanoes.

ℹ️ Getting There & Away
The main access point for Volcanoes National Park is the nearby town of Musanze (Ruhengeri).

The park headquarters is located near the village of Kinigi, approximately 12km north of Musanze. The condition of this road has been greatly improved over recent years and Virunga District Service runs buses every 30 minutes between Musanze and Kinigi (first departure 6am, RFr350, 35 minutes). From Kinigi it's a further 3km to the park headquarters (RFr700 to RFr1000 by *moto-taxi*).

It's also necessary to arrange transport from the park headquarters to the point where you start climbing up to where the gorillas are situated. Some solo travellers opt to hitch a ride with other tourists going to see the same gorilla group as them, although this may be seen as freeloading and even if you offer to contribute your share towards the vehicle there's always the chance you'll be refused, which would mean you not being able to get to the trek start point and therefore wasting the money you spent on the gorilla permit – false economy all round!

If you want the assurance of your own wheels and the peace of mind of knowing that you'll meet the critical 7am meeting time, the best option is to join a group in Musanze. Ask around at Amahoro Tours (p497) or Hotel Muhabura (p498). The cost of hiring a vehicle and driver is US$80 at either of these places.

Gisenyi

POP 113,000

Landlocked Rwanda may be a long way from the ocean, but that doesn't mean you can't have a beach holiday here. On the contrary, if you take another look at the map, you'll quickly realise that Rwanda's border with the DRC runs along the entire length of Lake Kivu. One of the Great Lakes in the Albertine Rift Valley, Lake Kivu has a maximum depth of nearly 500m and is one of the 20 deepest and most voluminous lakes in the world.

Of course, most travellers in Gisenyi are perfectly content to stick to the shores, especially since they're surprisingly sandy and fringed with all manner of tropical vegetation. While much of the Lake Kivu frontage is lined with landscaped villas and private clubs, the town itself projects a languid air of some forgotten upcountry backwater. But this is precisely the low-key charm that lures an eclectic mix of rich Rwandans, expat escapees and independent travellers.

Gisenyi is roughly divided into upper and lower towns, with most tourist services clustered around the lower end along the shores of Lake Kivu.

History

The first European to visit Lake Kivu was the German count Adolf von Götzen in 1894, although it was the early accounts of the Duke of Mecklenburg that are credited with fixing the lake in the European imagination. In 1907 the Duke declared that Kivu was 'the most beautiful of all the Central African lakes, framed by banks which fall back steeply from the rugged masses of rock and at the rear the stately summits of eight Virunga volcanoes'.

Of course, the lake's history stretches back eons before the age of European colonisation. A shallow lake was most likely formed here approximately two million years ago by the very same tectonic activity that wrenched open the Albertine Rift Valley. However, the lake in its present shape formed about 20,000 years ago when lava flows from the Virungas created a natural dam, separating Kivu from Lake Edward and substantially increasing its water levels.

◉ Sights

Rubona Peninsula   LANDSCAPE

Roughly 4km south of town, along a lovely lakeshore road, is the Rubona Peninsula. The peninsula is Lake Kivu at its finest. Hills

Gisenyi

N 0 ————— 200 m
   0 ————— 0.1 miles

Nyakabongo (2km)
Ave de l'Umuganda
(2km); Goma (5km)
Ave de la Révolution
Rue de l'Industrie
Ave du Marché
Rue de l'Hospital
Rue de Ruhengeri
Ave de l'Indépendance
Ave de la Coopération
Rue de Ruhengeri
Ave de la Production
Pfunda Tea Factory (5km)
Lake Kivu
Rubona Peninsula; Paradis Malahide (4km)

Gisenyi

⊙ **Sights**
  1 Public Beach...B2

🛏 **Sleeping**
  2 Auberge de Gisenyi B1
  3 Centre d'Accueil de l'Église
      Presbytérienne.................................B1
  4 Gorillas Lake Kivu Hotel......................A2
  5 Lake Kivu Serena Hotel.......................B2
  6 Stipp Hotel...A1

✖ **Eating**
  Stipp Hotel..................................(see 6)

🍸 **Drinking & Nightlife**
  7 New Tam-Tam Bikini Bar &
      Restaurant.......................................B3

🛍 **Shopping**
  African Work Art
      Exposition ....(see 11)

ℹ **Information**
  8 Bank of Kigali.......................................B1
  9 Cyber Café la Confiance B1
  10 Ecobank B1
  11 RDB...B2

THE CONGO NILE TRAIL

It's possible to walk from Gisenyi at the northern end of Lake Kivu to Cyangugu at the lake's southern extremity. It's a 10-day hike of 227km in a country renowned for its hills, so you'd have to be extremely fit to tackle the trail in its entirety without prior training. It is possible to walk a portion of the trail: the Gisenyi to Kibuye section can be covered in four days if you're prepared to walk from 7am to 5pm each day, averaging 18km a day. A more popular way of covering the route in its entirety is by bike. This takes five days.

You'll need to carry a tent and food for breakfast and lunch, but it's possible to get local families to cook for you in the evenings. There are dedicated campsites along the route. Trekkers should contact the RDB (p511) for the latest information; maps can be downloaded from its website. For help with the practicalities of the walk, including the renting of camping equipment and bikes, get in touch with **Rwandan Adventures** (☑ 0786571414; www.rwandan-adventures.com). This Gisenyi-based tour company specialises in walking and cycling tours along the Congo Nile Trail, and as well as kitting out those who want to go fully independent, it can organise fully guided tours. In addition to the Congo Nile Trail it organises much shorter walking and cycling tours.

rise steeply from the lake foreshore and are a patchwork of garden plots and small homesteads. The shore itself is often rocky, although there are enough sandy spots and places suitable for swimming. It's a very popular weekend destination.

Rubona is also home to some natural **hot springs**, which are reported by locals to cure a variety of ailments and are great for boiling potatoes. You'll have to ask around if you want to find them, but it's certainly worth the effort.

Public Beach BEACH

The strip of sand beneath the main town is a justifiably popular place to take a dip. That said, some travellers imagining Caribbean sands are disappointed to discover the waters are grey-green and the sand coarse and yellowish. There is, however, plenty of it, and after days on the road Lake Kivu represents a welcome opportunity to throw down a beach towel or do as the locals do and spread a picnic blanket under one of the many shade trees.

For those with money to burn, there are a variety of water sports and boat trips available at the upmarket hotels.

Pfunda Tea Factory FACTORY

(admission US$10; ⊙ 7am-4pm Mon-Fri, 7am-noon Sat) During the rainy season, at the height of production, the Pfunda Tea Factory processes 60 tonnes of tea from the surrounding plantations daily. Guided tours follow the tea production from arrival of the green leaf through to the withering, cutting, drying and sorting stages, before it is packaged for shipment to Mombasa (Kenya). The fac-

tory is about 5km from town and most easily reached by *moto-taxi* (RFr500 for locals but you'll most likely pay double that).

🛏 Sleeping

Centre d'Accueil de l'Église
Presbytérienne HOTEL $

(☑ 0785730113, 0784957945; Ave du Maré; dm RFr2500, camping RFr5000, s/d/tr RFr5000/10,000/10,000; P) This church-run hotel has the cheapest beds in town – dorms come with varying numbers of beds, while the double rooms are spick and span with en suite facilities. Basic meals are served in a small restaurant, and there's a craft shop selling banana-leaf cards and stuffed toys to raise money for local women's groups.

Auberge de Gisenyi HOTEL $

(☑ 0783663537; Ave de l'Umuganda; s/d/tw excl breakfast RFr8000/10,000/12,000) The rooms here face onto a busy local restaurant, which means it can be a little noisy early in the evening, but otherwise the rooms are reasonable enough. Showers are cold but buckets of hot water are provided for those who ask nicely.

Paradis Malahide HOTEL $$

(☑ 0788756204; www.paradisemalahide.com; Rubona Peninsula; r from US$75; P 🛜) Located along the shores of the Rubona Peninsula just south of Gisenyi, this lodge continues to get wonderful reviews from loyal guests. Accommodation is in stone bungalows scattered around a small bar and restaurant, but the highlight of the property is clearly the stunning lakeside location.

LIMNIC ERUPTIONS

Lake Kivu is one of only three known 'exploding lakes' (the other two are Lakes Nyos and Monoun in Cameroon), which experience violent lake overturns dubbed 'limnic eruptions'. This rare type of natural disaster results when carbon dioxide (CO_2) suddenly erupts from deep lake water, suffocating wildlife, livestock and humans, and causing violent tsunamis.

To date, only two limnic eruptions have been observed; on both occasions the consequences were deadly. In 1984, 37 people were asphyxiated following a limnic eruption at Lake Monoun. Two years later, an even deadlier eruption occurred at neighbouring Lake Nyos, releasing over 80 million cu metres of CO_2 and killing between 1700 and 1800 people.

A major limnic eruption has never been recorded at Kivu, though the deep-water lake contains massive amounts of dissolved CO_2 as well as methane. In fact, sample sediments taken by Professor Robert Hecky from the University of Michigan indicate that living creatures in the lake tend to go extinct approximately every thousand years or so.

While not as catastrophic as a full-scale eruption, in the absence of a strong wind, toxic gases can also collect on the surface of the water, and quite a few people have been asphyxiated as a result.

If an eruption does occur, the exploding underwater methane is likely to push a huge cloud of CO_2 above the surface of the lake, as well as triggering a series of tsunamis along the shoreline. Since CO_2 is denser than air, it sinks quickly to the ground, pushing breathable air up into the sky. At this point, there is little you can really do to survive, and it's only a matter of time before you succumb to CO_2 poisoning, suffocation, drowning or a dastardly combination of all three. To make matters worse, the last thing you will probably smell will be the warm vapour of the combusting methane, which is somewhat reminiscent of a giant, earthy fart.

To reach Paradis Malahide, follow the road towards Rubona and turn right onto the lakeshore road just before you reach the brewery; the lodge will be on your left.

Stipp Hotel   BOUTIQUE HOTEL **$$**
(☑ 252540450; www.stipphotelrwanda.com; Ave de la Révolution; s/d from US$100/120; P ❄ 🐱 🏊)
Preferring intimacy to opulence, the Stipp is home to a small assortment of individually decorated rooms, striking an ideal blend of colonial elegance and modern convenience. Whether you're soaking in the enormous bathtubs, strolling around the lush garden or dining in one of the town's best restaurants, you're sure to have a relaxing stay here.

Gorillas Lake Kivu Hotel   HOTEL **$$**
(☑ 0788200522; www.gorillashotels.com; Ave de l'Independance; s/d from US$80/100; P 🐱 🏊)
Part of the successful Gorilla chain, this hotel has more of a resort feel than its sisters elsewhere in Rwanda, largely thanks to the big, phallic-shaped (!) swimming pool (nonguests RFr4000). The rooms themselves are plain and sturdy and good value for those after something approaching luxury.

Lake Kivu Serena Hotel   HOTEL **$$$**
(☑ 0788200430; www.serenahotels.com; Ave de la Coopération; s/d from US$200/260; P ❄ 🐱 🏊)
The Lake Kivu Serena brims with refined luxury from the grand colonial dining rooms to the manicured grounds. The Serena has a stunner of a swimming pool (nonguests RFr5000), a slice of prime beachfront real estate and the best rooms in the area.

🍴 Eating & Drinking

There are several simple restaurants on the main road in the upper part of town serving cheap meals and buffet lunches for around RFr2000, although the price varies depending on how much meat you take. One of the best is the small courtyard restaurant in the Auberge de Gisenyi (p509).

If you like something more upmarket with a little more ambience, then head to one of the bigger hotels down by the lake.

Paradis Malahide   EUROPEAN **$$**
(Rubona Peninsula; mains RFr5000-7000; ⏰ 7am-9pm) Out on the Rubona Peninsula, the Paradis Malahide is *the* place to unwind and soak up the views. The outdoor seating and open-air restaurant make the most of the

lush hibiscus- and bougainvillea-filled gardens. Service can be slow, but the steak is worth the wait.

Stipp Hotel
FRENCH $$

(Ave de la Révolution; mains RFr4000-7000; ⊘6am-10pm) Currently the Stipp Hotel has the best restaurant in town and draws a large crowd most nights. The menu, which makes the most of the locally grown vegetables and fruit, is a classic mixture of Rwandan and Western dishes presented with a little extra flair.

New Tam-Tam Bikini
Bar & Restaurant
BEER GARDEN

(Ave de la Production; mains RFr1500-6000; ⊘11am-11pm) While we don't know who came up with the name, we can vouch for the great beachfront location. This is a *very* popular spot for a beer and gets busy on the weekends when the drinking crowd rolls in from Kigali. Give your beachside beer a friendly accompaniment in the form of a plate of brochettes and chips.

🛍 Shopping

African Work Art Exposition
ARTS & CRAFTS

(Ave de la Indépendance; ⊘8am-6pm Mon-Sat) This small curio store has a varied and colourful collection of handicrafts from the DRC, Uganda and Rwanda, including lots of Congolese masks and other wooden items.

ⓘ Information

Bank of Kigali (Ave de l'Umuganda) With ATM that accepts foreign Visa cards.

Cyber Café la Confiance (Ave du Maré; 1hr RFr400; ⊘8am-10pm) This cybercafe is hidden away up on the 1st floor of a small shopping centre.

Ecobank (Rue de Ruhengeri) Currency exchange, Western Union and an ATM (Visa only).

RDB (Rwanda Development Board; www.rwandatourism.com; Ave de l'Indépendance; ⊘7am-5pm Mon-Fri, 8am-noon Sat & Sun) This office can direct you to the hotel that is currently offering boat trips, and book national-park activities.

ⓘ Getting There & Away

It's a beautiful journey from Musanze (Ruhengeri) through rural farms and villages and there are panoramic views of Lake Kivu as the road descends into Gisenyi. All bus ticket offices are at the bus station 2km west of the town centre towards the DRC border.

Virunga Express, Kigali Coach and others operate buses between Gisenyi and Kigali (RFr3000, 3½ hours) via Musanze (Ruhengeri; RFr1100, 1½ hours). Departures are half-hourly from 7am until 4pm.

There is a daily service between Gisenyi and Kibuye (RFr3000, six hours) with Ontracom, departing sometime between 5.30am and 6.30am.

Local minibuses for outlying villages gather at the main bus station on Ave du Marché. Follow the sounds of honking horns and racing engines.

Horizon Express has a 3.30pm bus to Kampala (US$15 to US$20, 14 hours). Jaguar and Baby Coach also operate along this route. Prices are normally quoted in dollars for this route, but tickets are payable in francs.

ⓘ Getting Around

If you need wheels, *moto-taxis* swarm everywhere. From town to the bus station should cost around RFr300. It's a RFr800 blast out to the Rubona Peninsula.

SOUTHWESTERN RWANDA

The endless mountains and valleys don't stop as you head south towards the border with Burundi. While the gorillas in Volcanoes National Park tend to garner almost everybody's attention, southwestern Rwanda is home to East Africa's largest montane forest, Nyungwe Forest National Park, one of the most primate-rich areas in the world. The region is also home to the historic colonial and intellectual centre of Huye (Butare), which plays hosts to one of East Africa's best ethnographic museums.

Huye (Butare)

POP 107,000

Huye (Butare) is one of the most distinguished towns in Rwanda, having served as the country's most prominent intellectual centre since the colonial era. Home to the National University of Rwanda, the National Institute of Scientific Research and the excellent National Museum of Rwanda, Huye may be a step down in size after the capital, but it's certainly no lightweight on the Rwandan stage.

Historically speaking, Huye has always played a prominent role in regional affairs. During the era of Belgian occupation, the town was the colonial administrative

Huye (Butare)

National
Museum of
Rwanda

Centre d'Accueil
Matar Boni Consili
(350m)

Stadium

Rue de Kigali

Ave du Commerce
Market
Rue Rwamamba
Rue de la
Prefecture
Ave de la Cathédral
Ave de l'Université
Inzozi Nzira
(200m)
National University of
Rwanda, Arboretum
de Ruhande (800m)

0   200 m
0   0.1 miles

headquarters of the northern half of Ruanda-Urundi. While Huye may have lost a bit of ground to Kigali after independence, today it still manages to maintain its political relevance, especially since it's ruled by legions of Rwanda's academic elite.

While Huye isn't a tourist destination in the traditional sense, it's nevertheless an interesting stopover and the heavy concentration of liberal college students roaming the streets makes for an interesting atmosphere.

History

The tradition of Butare as an academic centre dates back to 1900 when it hosted the first Catholic mission in present-day Rwanda. As prominent intellectuals and religious figures were drawn to the area, Butare grew in favour among the Belgian occupiers. Following the death of Queen Astrid, the Swedish wife of King Leopold III, the town was renamed Astrida in 1935.

After independence in 1962, the town's name was changed back to Butare as it launched a strong bid to serve as the capital of Rwanda. Although Kigali was eventually chosen, due to its central location, Butare was selected to host the country's first university, which opened its doors to students in 1963.

In the early days of the 1994 genocide, Tutsis and moderate Hutus fled to Butare in the hope that its intellectual tradition would reign over the ensuing madness. For a short while, the Tutsi prefect of Butare, Jean Baptiste-Habyarimana, managed to maintain peace and order in the town.

Sadly, however, Habyarimana was quickly murdered by the Interahamwe and replaced by Colonel Tharchisse Muvunyi. Under his tenure, Butare was the site of horrific massacres that claimed the lives of nearly a quarter of a million people. Although Muvunyi fled to Britain after the genocide, he was eventually arrested and convicted.

In 2006, the name of the town was changed from Butare to Huye following an administrative reorganisation of Rwanda's 12 former provinces.

⊙ Sights & Activities

★ National Museum of Rwanda   MUSEUM

(www.museum.gov.rw; Rue de Kigali; adult/child RFr6000/3000; ☺8am-6pm, last Sat of month from 11am) This outstanding museum was given to the city as a gift from Belgium in 1989 to commemorate 25 years of independence. While the building itself is certainly one of the most beautiful structures in the city, the museum wins top marks for having one of the best ethnological and archaeological collections in the entire region. The seven exhibition halls contain some very interesting items and everything is unusually well lit and presented.

The first hall contains the museum shop. The second hall has geological displays including a large relief map that depicts the topography of Rwanda as something akin to a crumpled piece of paper. The middle halls exhibit items used in agriculture, hunting, animal husbandry, weaving, pottery and woodwork. The *kagondo* hut forms the centrepiece of an exhibit on housing and living compounds in precolonial times. The final halls feature traditional clothing – including an *isinde* (wicker raincoat), pounded bark garments and goat-skin capes – and information on Rwandan prehistory, including an interesting section on divination. There is also a side hall used to house temporary exhibitions.

The museum is also the venue where the Intore dancers and drummers perform. Ask at reception about arranging a performance. The museum is about 1km north of the centre, past the minibus stand. You can either walk or jump on a *boda-boda* (motorcycle taxi) for around RFr300.

National University of Rwanda   GARDENS

(off Ave de l'Universite) Rwanda's finest institution of learning suffered terribly during the 1994 genocide, though today it's turned towards the future with hope and optimism. Strolling through its campus is a pleasant diversion, especially if you find yourself at the **Arboretum de Ruhande**. Started by the Belgians in 1934, this attractive and peaceful arboretum is a great place to learn about African flora while indulging in a bit of leafy shade.

Cathedral   CHURCH

(off Ave de la Cathédral) Huye is home to Rwanda's largest cathedral, which was constructed in the 1930s to commemorate the life of Queen Astrid. The red-brick building is still used for religious worship, so stop by if you happen to hear the sounds of gospel.

🛏 Sleeping

Hotel Faucon   HOTEL $

(☏0788890877; Rue de Kigali; s/d RFr15,000/30,000; 🅿) At one point in time (quite a long way back), this was the place to stay in town, although standards have slipped over the decades. However, the great news for budget travellers is that it offers cavernous rooms and apartments at low prices. The bar out front is the place in Huye to catch all the English Premier League matches and other big games.

Hôtel des Beaux-Arts   HOTEL $

(☏0788460877; Ave du Commerce; s/d/tw RFr5000/8000/7500) Set a little way back from Ave du Commerce, this hotel has quite a bit of character for a cheapie. The hotel is attractively decorated with local products and the skulls of various East African megafauna and there's a pleasant courtyard to unwind in.

Hotel Ineza   HOTEL $

(☏0784266968; off Rue de Kigali; r RFr5000-6000) The rooms at this quiet place aren't very big but they're bright and clean, so if you're a solo traveller and after something cheap, look no further. Double rooms here have only three-quarter-sized double beds that might struggle to fit two *mzungu*-sized bodies. There's no name board for the hotel, just a sign reading '*Chambre à Louer*'.

Hotel Ibis   HOTEL $$

(☏0738323000; campionibis@hotmail.com; Rue de Kigali; s RFr12,000-27,000, d RFr19,000-35,000, apt RFr30,000-38,000; 🅿🛜) The stock choice for travellers passing through Huye, the Ibis is a classic hotel with smart, midlevel rooms that are large and quiet with a certain old-fashioned charm. The price system is a little bewildering – ask to see a few rooms before committing.

Centre d'Accueil Matar Boni Consilii   HOTEL $$

(☏0788283903; www.mbcrwanda.com; incl breakfast s RFr25,000-40,000, d RFr45,000, ste RFr75,000; 🅿🛜) This church-run place, 500m northeast of the town centre, is the smartest place in Huye, although the cheapest singles are a bit pokey. Its location, in a quiet residential area, means that the nights are so quiet that instead of the normal racket of car horns and motorbike engines all you're likely to hear is the gentle whirr of cicadas.

RWANDA HUYE (BUTARE)

✗ Eating & Drinking

Like many towns in Rwanda, Huye is another place where most visitors tend to eat at the hotel they stay in. For something more traditional there are a number of local eateries offering brochettes and lunch buffets for around RFr2000 per person. As usual, they involve mounds of carbs and a dollop of protein.

Inzozi Nziza ICE CREAM $
(Ave de l'Université; ice cream from RFr600, lunch specials RFr1000; ⊘9am-5pm) Three words: cookies, coffee and ice cream. Need we say more? It's 200m south of the town centre.

Hotel Ibis Restaurant INTERNATIONAL $$
(Rue de Kigali; meals RFr4000-8000; ⊘6am-11pm) This hotel restaurant, with its open-air terrace and pleasantly faded dining room, is the most popular place in town for locals and tourists alike. The menu is something of a culinary tour of the world and includes a selection of meats, fish, pizzas, pastas and a wholesome range of salads.

The Chinese Restaurant CHINESE $$
(Rue Rwamamba; mains RFr1500-5500; ⊘9.30am-10.30pm) The name might not be wildly imaginative, but at least you know what you're getting here: in other words all the usual Chinese menu suspects, including spring rolls and beef in black bean sauce, but there are also a few local dishes for good measure.

Meals are large, and one main with a side of rice or noodles is enough for two.

C&C Café Connexion CAFE
(Ave de l'Université; coffee from RFr3000; ⊘10am-6pm) This industrial space turned coffee shop, which uses only the finest beans, is dominated by a massive coffee-bean roaster and grinder. It is *the* place in town for a caffeine rush.

☆ Entertainment

Traditional Rwandan Dance Troupe DANCE
(National Museum of Rwanda; 1-5 people RFr50,000, 6-10 people RFr60,000) There is a traditional Rwandan dance troupe based in Huye, and its show is spectacular. The Intore dance originated in Burundi and involves elaborate costumes and superb drumming routines. Performances can be organised through the National Museum, and the larger the group, the cheaper it will be per person. Photographers will need to pay an additional RFr2000. Note that prices substantially increase on weekends and during the evening.

🛍 Shopping

La Copabu Expo Vente ARTS & CRAFTS
(Ave de l'Université; ⊘7am-7pm) Large handicraft shop selling local products, postcards and other souvenir-worthy items. Opening hours are a little flexible.

ℹ Information

Bank of Kigali (Rue de Kigali) Western Union and cash advances on Visa card.

Peace Cyber Cafe (Rue de Kigali; per hour RFr600; ⊘8am-9pm) One of several internet cafes in town.

Post Office (Rue de Kigali) The main city post office.

ℹ Getting There & Away

There are several bus companies found on Rue de Kigali that operate between Huye and Kigali (RFr2500, 2½ hours); some of these also have services to Nyamagabe (RFr500, 30 minutes), Nyanza (RFr600, 45 minutes) and Cyangugu (RFr4000, four hours). Volcano Express runs comfortable, reliable buses to Bujumbura (Burundi; RFr6000, four hours).

The local **minibus stand** is just a patch of dirt about 1km north of the town centre, by the stadium. Arriving buses often drop passengers here first before continuing to the centre of town.

The road from Huye to Kamembe (for Cyangugu) passes through the Nyungwe Forest National Park and some spectacular virgin rainforest.

Horizon (cnr Rue de la Prefecture & Rue de Kigali) Frequent departures for Kigali (RFr2500), Nyanza (RFr600) and Nyamagabe (RFr500).

Sotra Tours (Rue de Kigali) Half-hourly departures for Kigali via Gitarama, and six buses a day to Cyangugu.

Volcano Express (Rue de Kigali) Operating the best buses in and out of Huye with hourly buses to Kigali (RFr2500) and Nyanza (RFr600).

Around Huye (Butare)

Murambi Genocide Memorial MEMORIAL
(⊘8am-4pm, closed public holidays) FREE
Nyamagabe (formerly called Gikongoro) and the satellite town of Murambi was the site of one of the most unforgettable horrors of the genocide. Refugees flocked to Murambi, the location of a half-built technical college, after being told that they would be safe there. It was merely a ploy though and on 21 April the army and Interahamwe moved in and, depending on who's doing the counting, between 27,000 and 40,000 people were murdered here.

This is by far the most graphic of the many genocide memorials in Rwanda, as hundreds of bodies have been exhumed and preserved with powdered lime, and appear as they did when the killers struck.

A visit starts with well-presented museum-style information panels (many of which seem to lay the blame for it all on the French) and short films. You then walk through rooms with larger-than-life photographs of some of the victims (and some glass tombs which one day will contain some of the remains of victims) and accounts from some of the few who survived.

Heading outside, you pass by some mass graves and then over to what were once planned to be classrooms. Many of these contain wooden racks filled with hundreds of preserved bodies. Wandering through these rooms the scene becomes more and more macabre, with many of the displayed corpses – men, women and children – still contorted in the manner in which they died. The last rooms are perhaps the most moving of all. These contain the toddlers and babies and, just as with the adults, you can sometimes get a good guess as to their final moments: some, presumably calling for their mothers, are still holding their arms out; another covers his or her eyes in what might be a vain attempt to hide from the killers. Many others have fractures in their skulls from the machetes.

As you can imagine from this description, Murambi can be overwhelming, and not everyone can stomach it. It is, however, another poignant reminder to us all of what came to pass here, and why it must never be allowed to happen again.

Nyamagabe is 28km west of Huye, and there are regular Horizon buses running between the two (RFr600, 30 minutes). The memorial is 2km beyond the town at Murambi. *Moto-taxis* can run you there for RFr500 if you don't fancy the walk.

Nyanza (Nyabisindu)

POP 55,000

In the 2006 provincial reshuffle, Nyanza – and not, as everyone assumed, Huye (Butare) – ended up as the capital of the South Province. The most plausible explanation lies in the town's past. In 1899, Mwami Musinga Yuhi V established Rwanda's first permanent royal capital here. Until then, the royals had divided their time between 50 or so homes scattered throughout their kingdom.

Today his traditional palace (well, actually a very good replica of it) and the first home built by his son and successor Mutara III Rudahigwa have been restored and form the Rukari Ancient History Museum.

After visiting Belgium and seeing the stately homes there, Mutara concluded his own home wasn't up to scratch and had a second, and altogether grander, palace built on nearby Rwesero Hill, which today is the Rwesero Art Museum.

Most people visit the Nyanza museums as a day trip from either Kigali or Huye.

◉ Sights

Rukari Ancient History Museum   MUSEUM
(www.museum.gov.rw;   adult/child/student RFr6000/3000/3000;   ☉8am-6pm) Situated on a hill 2km from town, this fascinating museum is less about ancient history and more about royal residences. The displays centre on a replica king's '**palace**'. Inclusive in the ticket price is a guided tour that helps explain some of the architectural idiosyncrasies inside the royal compound, including why the royal beer brewer's hut had an entrance without a lip, and why the woman who looked after the king's milk was never able to marry.

Behind the royal compound are the *inyambo* (sacred cows) with their super-sized horns. In some, the span between horn tip and horn tip exceeds 2.5m. Despite their fearsome appearance they seem to like nothing better than having lullabies sung to them!

Crowning the hill itself is the **royal residence of King Mutara III Rudahigwa** (☉8am-6pm), built by Belgium in 1931. This colonial-style home served as the royal palace until he died. Unfortunately most of the furniture and gifts he received from visiting dignitaries were stolen during the genocide, but it's still an interesting home to wander through, with its peculiarities including three sitting rooms, the best of which was reserved for receiving white people. Mutara was the first *mwami* (king) to convert to Catholicism and in the beginning was so enthralled by the Belgian rulers that he once thanked 'Christ-the-King to have given Rwanda the divine light of Belgian colonial administration along with its science of good government'. He may have jumped to the wrong conclusion on that one.

Keep hold of your ticket, as admission to this museum gains you entry to the Rwesero Art Museum.

Rwesero Art Museum
MUSEUM

(www.museum.gov.rw; adult/child/student RFr6000/3000/3000; ⊗8am-6pm) Rwanda's most prestigious art museum is housed inside what was meant to be King Mutara III Rudahigwa's new palace (he died before the building was completed in somewhat mysterious circumstances after a routine vaccination went wrong). Today it houses mostly contemporary paintings and stylistic sculptures on themes dealing with the genocide, unity and brotherhood. Keep hold of your ticket, as admission to this museum entitles you to enter the Rukari Ancient History Museum.

🍴 Sleeping & Eating

Boomerang Hotel
HOTEL $

(☑0788526617; s/d/tw RFr10,000/12,000/15,000; ℗) On the slopes of Rwesero Hill, this popular local hotel and restaurant has presentable rooms and friendly staff. The hot water for the showers comes by the bucket.

Dayenu Hotel
HOTEL $$

(☑0788559220; s/d/tw RFr20,000/30,000/ 30,000; ℗🤖🏊) This multistorey hotel in the centre of town has rooms with frilly bedspreads – we thought we looked ever so good wrapped up in the pink bedsheets. As well as the bedspreads, it also has a bar and even a swimming pool, which probably isn't what you'd have expected to find in dusty Nyanza.

ℹ️ Getting There & Around

Any of the minibuses or buses that ply the main road between Kigali and Huye (Butare) can drop you at the turn-off for Nyanza. From here you can catch a *moto-taxi* to town (5km, RFr400 to RFr600). Better still, catch a Volcano Express or Horizon bus directly to Nyanza from either Kigali (RFr1700, 1¾ hours) or Huye (RFr600, 45 minutes).

The Rukari Ancient History and Rwesero Art Museums are a further 2km from town and can be reached on foot or by *moto-taxi* (RFr400).

Nyungwe Forest National Park

Quite simply, Nyungwe Forest National Park is Rwanda's most important area of biodiversity and has been rated the highest priority for forest conservation in Africa. While Nyungwe is the newest of Rwanda's parks to receive national-park status, its protected area covers one of the oldest rainforests in Africa.

Despite its huge biodiversity Nyungwe is little known outside of East Africa and remains overlooked by many tourists. A shame given the range of activities available here.

Nyungwe's strongest drawcard is the chance to track chimpanzees, which have been habituated over the years to human visits. Hiking through equatorial rainforest in search of our closest genetic cousin is an unparalleled experience that more than a few people rate above tracking the mountain gorillas. However, of the four big-name chimpanzee parks in East Africa (in addition to Nyungwe these are Kibale National Park in Uganda, and Mahale Mountains and Gombe Stream National Parks in Tanzania), the apes of Nyungwe are far and away the most timid.

While chimps tend to garner most of the spotlight in Nyungwe, sightings of habituated troops of other monkeys – Angolan colobus (troops of which number up to 400), Dent's monkey (a local race of blue monkey) and grey-cheeked mangabeys (often seen with Dent's monkeys) – are virtually guaranteed on guided walks.

Other monkey possibilities include l'Hoest's and diademed monkeys, which sometimes associate with colobus and blue monkeys. Olive baboons and vervet monkeys loiter near the park's eastern edge, while owl-faced monkeys and possibly golden monkeys live in the extensive bamboo stands in the southeastern part of the reserve. Nocturnal prosimian attractions include needle-clawed and greater galagos as well as the potto.

In addition to primates, you also have a fairly good chance of spotting some other mammals, particularly in and around Kamiranzovu Marsh. Marsh mongooses and Congo clawless otters stick to the water's edge, while giant forest hogs, bush pigs and duikers are sometimes startled along the trails. Rainforest squirrels are also commonly spotted, and include giant forest, montane sun and Boehm's bush squirrels.

Nocturnal mammals are a bit tricky to spot, but you do have a chance of running across jackals, civets and genets.

But for many, though, the real highlight of Nyungwe turns out to be the simple pleasure of hiking for hours along well-maintained trails over the the lush, green valleys of the rainforest and passing through enormous stands of hardwoods, up to waterfalls and through large marshes.

History

Part of the Albertine Rift Valley, Nyungwe is virgin equatorial rainforest that survived the last ice age. As a result, it's one of the oldest green expanses on the African continent, and is something of a 'Lost World' for rare and endangered species. It also spans several altitudinal bands, which facilitates its largely unparalleled biodiversity of both flora and fauna.

One of the largest protected montane rainforests in Africa, Nyungwe covers 970 sq km, and extends across the border to Parc National de la Kibira in Burundi. It also serves as a watershed for Africa's two largest rivers, the Nile and the Congo, and contains several springs that are believed to feed the headwaters of the Albertine Nile.

As stunning as Nyungwe is in its present manifestation, it is sadly nothing but a poor shadow of its former grandeur. Today, the outskirts of Nyungwe are heavily cultivated with rolling tea plantations and lush banana plantations. Beautiful though they may be, agriculture to feed the burgeoning masses of the Great Lakes region is largely to blame for the past deforestation.

In the past 100 years, the rainforests of the Albertine Rift Valley have been felled with little regard for the biodiversity they harboured. While Nyungwe received official protection under the Belgian colonial government as early as 1933, it lost 15% of its original size in the 1960s and 1970s to encroaching farms.

Fortunately, the Peace Corps, the World Conservation Society and the Rwandan government targeted Nyungwe for increased conservation in the 1980s. The original project aims were to promote tourism in an ecologically sound way, while also studying the forest and educating local people about its value.

Although tourism in the region was brought to a standstill by the tragic events of the 1990s, Nyungwe Forest is once again firmly on the tourist map. Having received official national-park status in 2004 and a great deal of support from the World Conservation Society, Nyungwe Forest National Park is now setting its sights on becoming one of East Africa's leading ecotourism destinations.

ℹ NYUNGWE FOREST NATIONAL PARK

Why Go

Nyungwe Forest National Park enjoys some of the richest forest biodiversity in all of Africa, with no less than 1000 plant species, 13 species of primates, 75 species of other mammals, at least 275 species of birds and an astounding 120 species of butterflies. The park's star activities are tracking chimpanzees and the world's largest troop of colobus monkey (around 400). Both species have been habituated to humans.

When to Go

Nyungwe can be visited year-round and the chimps often descend from the higher elevations (and are therefore easier to find) during the wet season. No matter when you visit, expect rain and plenty of it. Nyungwe receives more than 2m of rainfall annually.

Practicalities

Trails can get extremely wet and muddy, so make sure you have good hiking shoes, waterproof trousers, a solid raincoat and perhaps even a floppy hat or bandana. All activities begin at the Uwinka Reception Centre or at the Gisakura Booking Office (but some then require a vehicle to reach the trailheads).

While public transport does pass by the park, your ability to move around the park will be greatly restricted without access to a private vehicle. This is especially true if you want to see the chimps.

Budget Tips

By showing a little resourcefulness it's possible for budget travellers to visit Nyungwe and enjoy most of the activities. There's cheap accommodation available near both park offices and some walking trails begin close by.

◉ Sights & Activities

Prices for activities tend to fall the more times you do them. If, for example, you track chimpanzees once then you pay US$90, but if you do it for two or three days in a row you only pay US$110 in total. However, it does have to be the same activity, which means few people take advantage of this.

Chimpanzee Tracking

They may pale in size when compared to the hulking masses that are the mountain gorillas, but there is no denying the affinity that we humans have for chimpanzees. Sharing an estimated 94% of our genetic material, chimps display an incredible range of human-like behaviours ranging from tool use to waging war.

Chimps are highly sociable creatures, and one of the few primates to form complex communities ranging upwards of 100 individuals. During the day these communities break down into smaller units that forage for food, a behaviour that has been dubbed 'fission-fusion' by anthropologists. Since they cover a greater daily distance than the relatively docile gorilla, chimpanzee tracking (US$90 per person) is a much more uncertain enterprise.

Chimpanzee habituation in Nyungwe is still very much a work in progress, and although you will almost certainly encounter them, it might not be all that close up. This is especially so because Nyungwe's chimps seem to spend longer periods of time high in the treetops than many other East African chimps.

Much like gorilla tracking, you need to be prepared for lengthy hikes that can take up to several hours. However, the vegetation on the forest floor is much less dense than in the Virunga mountains where the gorillas live, so the walk is generally a little less tiring. In the rainy season you have a good chance of successfully tracking the chimps on the coloured trails, though in the dry season they have a tendency to head for higher elevations.

Although there are groups of chimps throughout Nyungwe, the habituated group that most people are taken to is actually located in the Cyamudongo Forest, a very small, isolated 'island' of forest surrounded by tea estates a little over an hour's drive from the park office at Gisakura. This group consists of about 30 individuals. At certain times, though, visitors might be taken to

see a second habituated group, the Uwinka group, which is the largest with around 65 individuals. They are usually found within 12km of the Uwinka Reception Centre. Whichever group you end up visiting, having a car is something of a necessity for chimp tracking, as you'll need to arrange transport for you and your guide to the trailhead.

Visits are limited to one hour.

Colobus Monkey Tracking

A subspecies of the widespread black-and-white colobus, the Angolan colobus is an arboreal Old World monkey that is distinguished by its black fur and long, silky white locks of hair. Weighing 10kg to 20kg, and possessing a dexterous tail that can reach lengths of 75cm, Angolan colobus are perfectly suited to a life up in the canopy.

Colobi are distributed throughout the rainforests of equatorial Africa, though they reach epic numbers in Nyungwe Forest National Park. While they may not be as a charismatic as chimps, colobus are extremely social primates that form enormous group sizes – one of the two semi-habituated troops in Nyungwe numbers no less than 400 individuals.

As you might imagine, finding yourself in the presence of literally hundreds of primates bounding through the treetops can be a mesmerising experience. Curious animals by nature, colobi in Nyungwe seem to almost revel in their playful interactions with human visitors.

Troops of Angolan colobus maintain fairly regimented territories, which is good news for those planning a colobus track (US$70 per person), as the semi-habituated group in Nyungwe tends to stick to the coloured trails. While watching wildlife is never a certainty, generally speaking, the rangers can find the colobus monkey troop in an hour or so.

There is a smaller, and often more accessible, troop of around 70 individuals near the Gisakura Tea Plantation. Be sure to ask which troop you'll be tracking when you make your reservation. This second troop is less worthwhile to visit as the walk is only about two to five minutes from the Gisakura park office and it feels like a lot of money to pay to stand in a tea field looking at monkeys you could almost see without leaving the park office!

Trekking Nyungwe Forest

In addition to tracking primates, Nyungwe Forest National Park has a number of walking trails that begin at either the Uwinka Reception Centre (p520) or the Gisakura Booking Office (p520).

It's not possible to walk in the park without a guide, and one is included when you pay your trek fees. To trek on trails that are 5km or less costs US$40 per person per day, and to walk on any of the 5km to 10km trails costs US$50 per person per day. Rates for subsequent days decrease thereafter.

Walks begin at set times; the first departures are around 9am, with further departures around 11am and 2pm.

COLOURED TRAILS

This system of colour-coded trails was constructed in the late 1980s in an attempt to open up Nyungwe to tourists. While tourism in the national park remains relatively low-key, these seven trails are nevertheless reasonably well maintained. Hikers can choose trails ranging from the 2km-long **Buhoro Trail**, a proverbial walk in the woods, right up to the 10km-long **Imbaraga Trail**, which winds steeply up forested slopes.

In 2010 a further effort was made to draw tourists south with the construction of a 160m-long and at times 60m-high **canopy walkway** (per person US$60). You won't encounter any wildlife while on the suspension bridge, but you'll certainly appreciate the jungle anew from this unique monkey's-eye perspective. The canopy walkway is located on the **Igishigishigi Trail**.

Although you need to specifically request to engage in either chimpanzee or colobus tracking, in theory you could run across either primate while hiking the coloured trails. Even if you don't come across these two star billings, you're likely to spot some of Nyungwe's other 11 primates, as well as a whole slew of birdlife, and possibly even the odd mammal or two.

All coloured trails originate from the Uwinka Reception Centre.

WATERFALL TRAIL

While not as popular as the coloured trails, the **Waterfall Trail** (per person US$50) is a stunner of a hike and one of the highlights of Nyungwe. It's one of the few treks that start from the Gisakura side of the park and takes three to five hours to complete depending on your fitness level. The trail winds up and down steep hillsides through primeval-looking rainforest where the trees are festooned in vines and mosses and the air is heavy and damp. The highlight (quite obviously) is a remote waterfall, where you can take a shallow dip and refresh your body after the hot and humid hike.

KAMIRANZOVU TRAIL

If you have your own wheels, the **Kamiranzovu Trail** (per person US$40) starts somewhere between Uwinka and Gisakura, and runs for about 4km to Kamiranzovu Swamp. Sadly, the last elephant was shot here in 1999, though the swamplands are still your best bet for spotting other large mammals. Even if you don't come across any other fauna, this trail is particularly famous for its rare species of orchids.

Birdwatching

Nyungwe has something of a legendary status among birdwatchers in East Africa, and is by far the country's top spot for birdwatching with some 275-plus species, which include no less than 25 Albertine Rift Valley endemics. However, the dense forest cover means actually getting a good view of a bird (or any other animal for that matter) can often be frustratingly hard, which means that only serious birdwatchers are likely to get feathered into excitement by many of the park's birds.

For those people, the dirt Rangiro road, which starts 1.5km east of Uwinka, and the Imbaraga, Umugote and Kamiranzovu Trails are all highly recommended for birdwatching. The paved road through the park permits viewing at all levels of the forest: expect mountain buzzards and cinnamon-chested bee-eaters perched along here, plus numerous sunbirds, wagtails and flocks of waxbills. Other commonly sighted birds include francolins, turacos, African crowned eagles, hornbills and even Congo bay owls.

There are four specialist birdwatching guides based in Nyungwe who need to be booked in advance for specalist birdwatching (US$70 per person) trips – email the Uwinka Reception Centre (p520). There are more than 25 endemics in the park, including Rwenzori turacos as well as other large forest specialities such as African crowned eagles and various hornbills. Depending on what you hope to see, the guide will choose a trail that maximises your chances of spotting your quarry.

If you're unsure of what to ask for, opt for the dirt Rangiro road. Thanks to the frequent changes in elevation along this route you have increased chances of spotting a good number of Nyungwe's fine feathered friends.

🛏 Sleeping & Eating

There are two main bases for Nyungwe. Both have park offices and both have at least some form of accommodation, but it's the Gisakura area that receives the most visitors on account of having the most varied accommodation.

🛏 Uwinka

Uwinka Campsite   CAMPGROUND $
(camping per person from US$30) The campsite at RDB's reception centre is currently the only option at Uwinka. There are several choice spots, many with impressive views overlooking the forest and one under a shelter with a tin roof that's a godsend in the likely event of rain. There's also a small canteen with basic meals, clean toilets and a simple shower block (the rangers will bring you a bucket of hot water).

Although there are no kitchen facilities, one of the rangers will light a campfire that you can cook on if you wish. You no longer need to be as self-sufficient as you once did to stay here; tents (RFr10,000) can be hired and the staff can usually rustle up an extremely thin sleeping mat and sleeping bag for those who haven't brought their own. There is little point in staying here unless you also plan to do an activity, as campers who visit but do not sign up for any activity are charged US$50 per person per night as opposed to the standard US$30 per night.

🛏 Gisakura

Gisakura Guest House   GUESTHOUSE $
(☑ 0788675051; www.gisakuraguesthouse.com; s/d with shared bathroom RFr23,600/35,400; 🅿) This guesthouse offers accommodation in simple but functional rooms that share communal showers and toilets and are set in a beautiful garden. The staff is very friendly and helpful, but it's hard not to think that it's overpriced. It's near the RDB booking office and often known locally as the Resthouse.

Cafe-Resto Bar Keza   GUESTHOUSE $
(☑ 0783396666; r excl breakfast RFr20,000) The cheapest, and perhaps the best value, rooms around. This small hotel in the centre of Gisakura has tidy rooms with all but one having an attached hot-water bathroom. The establishment also doubles as the bar of choice for locals.

★ Nyungwe Forest Lodge   LODGE $$$
(☑ 0786657270; www.nyungweforestlodge.com; d full board US$320-590; 🅿🛜🏊) Located in the heart of a tea plantation with a stunning jungle backdrop, it is very easy to while away days here as you lounge in the heated infinity pool or sip cocktails on the terrace. The rooms are as impressive as the views. All have woodburners, flat-screen satellite TVs, lounging areas and classy decorations.

The food is unusually good, and there's even an afternoon tea-tasting ceremony.

Nyungwe Top View Hotel   LODGE $$$
(☑ 0788772087; s/d US$130/200; 🅿🛜) High on a hill above Gisakura, this place has large and finely decorated cottages with excellent bathrooms and a tiny lounge area with fireplace (staff will light the fire for you on cold nights – which means most nights). The dining and reception area is disappointingly characterless.

ⓘ Information

Nyungwe Forest National Park is sliced in two by the Huye–Cyangugu road. Visitors can access the park through either the Uwinka Reception Centre or the Gisakura Booking Office, both of which lie along this road. For information online, see www.nyungwepark.com and www.rwanda-tourism.com.

Uwinka Reception Centre (☑ tourist warden for bookings 0788436763; kambogoi@yahoo.fr) The park headquarters is a little over halfway to Cyangugu from Huye (Butare). It got a revamp in 2010, and there is now a small but informative display on the ecology of the park, a new toilet block and an outdoor terrace area. From here you can get a good overview of the trails, arrange guides, book activities and pay fees.

Gisakura Booking Office (☑ 0788841079) This booking office can be found in Gisakura (near the Gisakura Guest House), where you can also pay fees and organise chimpanzee tracking. This is the one most frequently used by park visitors.

ⓘ Getting There & Around

Nyungwe Forest National Park lies between Huye (Butare) and Cyangugu. Impala Express and Omega Car Express buses travel between Huye (RFr4000, two hours, 90km) and Kamembe (for Cyangugu; one hour, 55km) throughout the day. Any one of these buses can drop you at either Uwinka Reception Centre or Gisakura, but in both cases they charge the full RFr4000 fare.

The trouble is that having arrived, your ability to move around the park is severely limited if you don't have a car. If you're sticking to the coloured trails and don't have your own transport, consider camping at Uwinka where most of the walks begin (although there are some that go from close to Gisakura, plus there's a small group of habituated colobus within easy walking distance of Gisakura).

Leaving is more problematic as many of the passing buses are full and you may have to wait some time before one will stop. The rangers on duty at either of the booking centres will normally phone one of the bus companies on your behalf and secure a seat. Once the ranger has made the booking he'll hold your fare because in the past some travellers have gone on to find lifts with other tourists and then refused to pay for the empty seat being held for them.

Cyangugu

POP 69,000

Clinging to the southern tip of Lake Kivu, and looking across to Bukavu in the DRC, Cyangugu is an attractively situated town on the lake's shore.

The town has two distinct settlements. **Kamembe**, a few kilometres above the lake, is the main town and an important location for the processing of tea and cotton. This is the commercial heart of Cyangugu and you'll need to come here to change money and catch onward transport. Most of the better hotels are down below in Cyangugu proper, which is far prettier, far quieter and right next to the DRC border.

🛏 Sleeping & Eating

All the hotels mentioned here have attached restaurants that are as good as the food is going to get in this town. There are lots of cheap and noisy hotels in Kamembe, including the **Ten to Ten Paradise Hotel**. Always one of the better places to stay in town, it was undergoing major renovations at the time of research and when it reopens you'd hope it will be even better.

🛏 Kamembe

La Petite Colline Guest House   GUESTHOUSE **$**
(✐0788412210; r RFfr10,000-15,000; P) With a restaurant and reception area full of African statues, bows and arrows and calabashes, this place, whose publicity says it's for 'backparkers', will probably appeal to backpackers as well. Rooms come in two classes with more expensive ones having loads of space and views to the Congo. Cheaper ones have

views of absolutely nothing at all. La Petite Colline Guest House serves simple local meals.

🛏 Cyangugu

Hotel des Chutes   HOTEL **$**
(✐0784343191; r RFfr25,000-50,000; P 🛜) Hotel des Chutes offers well-equipped rooms with spacious balconies that boast fine views across the narrow strip of water to Bukavu. There's also a smart terrace restaurant that enjoys the same DRC views and the shade of a jacaranda tree. Understandably, this pretty setting is popular with locals.

Hotel du Lac   HOTEL **$**
(✐0784914508; r RFfr10,000-45,000; P 🛜 🍴) So close to the border it's almost in the DRC, this local landmark has a good mix of rooms, even though some of them have aged less than gracefully over the years. Cheaper rooms have cold showers only and breakfast isn't included. The Hotel du Lac has a restaurant overlooking the river that serves a mix of local and international dishes.

ℹ Information

You'll find all the banks and most other essential services (including internet cafes) in Kamembe.

Moneychangers near the border in Cyangugu will change Rwandan francs to DRC francs, although US dollars are the currency of choice for all but the smallest of purchases in the DRC.

ℹ Getting There & Around

Minibuses/*moto-taxis* for the short hop between Cyangugu and Kamembe cost RFr300/500.

Impala Express and Omega Car Express have several daily departures between them to Kigali (RFr5000, six hours) via Uwinka (RFr4000, two hours) and Huye (Butare; RFr4000, four hours). Onatracom has a 6am bus to Kibuye (RFr3000, seven hours).

Cyangugu is literally a stone's throw away from the DRC, and providing you have all your paperwork in place, you can walk across the bridge and into the Congo. It's also possible to reach Bujumbura (Burundi) from here.

The bus station is in Kamembe.

Kibuye

POP 50,000

Although it has a stunning location, spread across a series of tongues jutting into Lake Kivu, Kibuye has not caught on as a tourist destination for sun and sand in the same way that Gisenyi has, but for our money – and there are plenty who will disagree – this is the better of the two. True, on this part of the lake good beaches are a lot less common but the steep hills that fall into the deep green waters and the indented shoreline with a smattering of islands nearby make it extremely picturesque. It's also, even by Rwandan standards, a very clean and green little town where nothing much seems to happen in a hurry.

One of the best ways to get accustomed to the town is to follow the ring road around the shores of the lake. There are some amazing views to be had along the way, and you're likely to find a few sandy patches where you can pause to take a cooling dip.

History

During the 100 days of madness in 1994, Kibuye witnessed some of the most horrific and despicable mass killings in all of Rwanda. Prior to the outbreak of the genocide, more than 20% of the local population was Tutsi; in 1994 the Interahamwe killed an estimated nine out of every 10 Tutsi. While these scars still run deep, today the residents of Kibuye are working together as a community to embrace the prospect of future tourism. A couple of memorials to the slain victims ensure that the past is not forgotten, while the frames of new buildings are signs of a brighter future.

◉ Sights

At the time of research, a new **museum**, next to the Hotel Golf Eden Rock down on the lake shore, was nearing completion. Said to be the first of its kind in Africa, the museum will focus on the environment, renewable energy and the impact of environmental degradation on Rwanda and Africa more generally. If the contents are anywhere near as impressive as the purpose-built building housing it then it will be an unmissable attraction.

Iglesia St Pierre   CHURCH, MEMORIAL
While a good number of memorials in Rwanda are stark reminders of the past atrocities, the genocide memorial church of St Pierre is a beautiful, calm and evocative testament to the strength of the human spirit. The interior is adorned with colourful mosaics and vivid stained-glass windows while outside a rock memorial displays a few skulls from some of the 11,000 people who were killed by a drunken mob here. There are no set opening hours or entry fee, but someone is normally available to open up.

Hill of Resistance   MEMORIAL
The uphill road from Kibuye leads to the small village of **Bisesero**, which is home to stunning scenery and a stirring genocide memorial.

During the early days of the genocide, more than 50,000 Tutsis fled here in the hope of evading the Interahamwe. For more than a month, these brave individuals were able to fend off their aggressors with little more than basic farming implements.

On 13 May, a reinforced regiment of soldiers and militia descended on Bisesero, slaughtering more than half of the refugees. By the time the French arrived on the scene in June, there were less than 1300 Tutsis remaining.

🏃 Activities

Not surprisingly, most activities in Kibuye revolve around Lake Kivu. Most guests are content to simply sun themselves for days on end, occasionally taking breaks to go **swimming**.

Boat Trips

Every visitor to Kibuye seems to head out onto the wide blue yonder for a boat trip around the lake. The most popular excursion is a half-day tour (boat holding 12 people around RFr50,000) taking in six of the gorgeous forested islands and islets sitting offshore of Kibuye, including the Chapeau de Napeleo, which is home to thousands of birds.

Boats for charter can be found at the water's edge beneath Hotel Centre Béthanie and Hotel Golf Eden Rock. Rates aren't fixed and will depend on how far you wish to venture and for how long you wish to go.

🛏 Sleeping & Eating

Backpackers rejoice! Rooms here are a lot more affordable than those in Gisenyi, making this an ideal spot to chill for a few days. Just bear in mind that Kibuye is a leading conference venue and it pays to ring ahead.

There are some local eateries in town, but the best food can be found at the hotels.

★**Hotel Centre Béthanie**   GUESTHOUSE $
(📞252568235, 0784957945; s RFr20,000-35,000, d RFr28,000-45,000; P 🛜) This popular guesthouse occupies a charming location on a wooded peninsula jutting into the lake. The older rooms are in red-brick blocks and are small but cosy. There are also some bright, modern, tiled rooms in a new block. Which-

ever you choose, all are kept spick and span and many have amazing views to the islands.

Hôme St Jean GUESTHOUSE $
(📞0784725107; excl breakfast dm RFr2500, s/tw with shared bathroom RFr5000/8000, s/d RFr10,000/15,000; 🅿️🛜) Sitting on its own hillside with stunning 270-degree views across Lake Kivu, this church-run pad has some of the cheapest, and best, digs in town. The double beds in the self-contained rooms are smaller than your average double bed so better suited to solo travellers. It's very well managed and a relaxing place to stay.

★Cormoran Lodge LODGE $$
(📞0728601515; www.cormoranlodge.com; s/d from US$135/180; 🅿️🛜) Three kilometres out of town along a very rough road, this stunner of a lodge melds rock, lake and wood into a memorable place to stay. The rooms, which are spaced throughout landscaped grounds tumbling to the lake shore, are like little treehouses on stilts and are built entirely out of logs and beach pebbles. There's a small manmade beach ideal for children. Good value.

ℹ️ Information

There is a post office, a Bank of Kigali (with ATM) and an internet cafe in the centre of town.

ℹ️ Getting There & Away

The road linking Kibuye with Kigali is endlessly winding but in excellent shape, making Kibuye very accessible from the capital. Impala Express and Capital Express run the most comfortable buses to Kigali (RFr2500, 2½ hours) via Gitarama (RFr2000, 1½ hours). Bus services start around 6am and continue hourly until 5.30pm. A bus goes to Cyangugu (RFr3000, five hours) at 6am. It's a spectacular ride, but the road was still under construction at the time of research.

An 8am (and occasional 2pm) bus leaves for Gisenyi (RFr3000, five hours) every morning. This is one of the most spectacular roads in the country.

The bus station is right in the centre of town – a long, sweaty walk from the lakeside hotels.

At the time of writing, there were no regularly scheduled ferry services in operation on Lake Kivu. However, it is sometimes possible to arrange a boat trip to Gisenyi or Cyangugu if there's enough demand.

ℹ️ Getting Around

Moto-taxis wait for arriving buses in the centre of town. It's a RFr400 hop from here to Hotel Centre Béthanie or Hôme St Jean.

EASTERN RWANDA

While much of Rwanda is characterised by equatorial rainforest, rolling hills and mountains and richly cultivated farmland, eastern Rwanda is something else entirely. Contiguous with the dry and flat savannah lands of Tanzania, this region is more reminiscent of the classic images of East African landscapes. While sights are scarce in this part of the country, Akagera National Park is one of Rwanda's highlights, especially if you're looking to get your safari fix.

Akagera National Park

Created in 1934 to protect the lands surrounding the Kagera River, **Akagera National Park** (www.african-parks.org; adult/child 1 day US$30/20, vehicle from US$10; ⏲6am-6pm) once protected nearly 10% of Rwanda and was considered to be one of the finest wildlife reserves in the whole of Africa. However, due to the massive numbers of refugees who returned to Rwanda in the late 1990s, over half of the park was de-gazetted and resettled with new villages. Increased human presence took an incredible toll on the national park. Human encroachment facilitated poaching and environmental degradation, and Akagera's wildlife was very nearly decimated.

For more than a decade, Akagera was something of a vegetarian safari. However, the Rwandan government alongside **African Parks** (www.african-parks.org) has recently implemented strict conservation laws (which are certainly complementary to their increased push for tourism in Rwanda) aimed at protecting Akagera. Furthermore, the once decrepit Akagera Game Lodge has been rehabilitated and a brand new luxury tented camp established (and there's talk of another, even more exclusive one, being constructed in the remote, little visited and wildlife-filled north of the park).

There are three distinct environments in the park: standard savannah as seen in much of the region; an immense swampy area along the border with Tanzania that contains six lakes and numerous islands, some of which are covered with forest; and a chain of low mountains on the flanks of the park with variable vegetation, ranging from short grasses on the summits to wooded savannah and dense thickets of forest.

Truth be told, Akagera is still a shadow of its former self, and you will be extremely disappointed if you come here expecting concentrations of wildlife on a par with Kenya and Tanzania. Carnivores in Akagera are limited to very rarely seen leopards and hyenas as well as genets, servals and jackals, but it's likely that lions will be reintroduced very shortly. Of the other large 'trophy' animals there are an estimated 90 elephants in the park, which are quite commonly seen. Buffalo are also present in reasonably healthy numbers, and there are masses of hippos in the lakes. Antelope and other plains wildlife are well represented, though herds tend to be small and the animals rather skittish. Common safari staples include impala, topi, zebra and waterbuck, as well as the majestic but rare roan antelope and the diminutive Oribi. Maasai giraffe, never native to the park, have been introduced and are faring well. Park authorities are also hoping to reintroduce black rhinos in the near future. Like the giraffe these were never native to the park but were present prior to the genocide following a previous reintroduction.

Of the primates olive baboons and vervet monkeys are very common. The blue monkey, which was thought to have been extinct in Akagera, was recently rediscovered. Needless to say it's not easy to find.

Even if you don't come across too many animals, you probably won't come across too many other wildlife-viewing drivers either. Indeed, the tourist trail has yet to fully incorporate Akagera, which means you can soak up the park's splendid nature in relative peace and isolation.

◉ Sights & Activities

For all the activities listed here bar the wildlife drives in your own vehicle, you should book in advance through the park office.

Lake Ihema Boat Trips

Park authorities can arrange **boat trips** (1hr tour per person US$30, sunset tour per person US$40; ⊙ departures 7.30am, 9am, 3.30pm & 5pm) on Lake Ihema to see the hippo pods and some of the huge Nile crocodiles that are otherwise difficult to observe. This is also the best way to view the park's abundant waterbirds, including breeding colonies of noisy and smelly cormorants and openbill storks. For our money this is the single nicest way of exploring the park. It's important to make a reservation through the park office at least an hour or so in advance.

Behind the Scenes Tour

One of the most innovative, and interesting, activities offered is a 'behind the scenes tour' (US$20 per person), which requires a minimum of four people. You will get to meet and talk to rangers, anti-poaching patrols and community-projects managers. It's a fascinating insight into the often very political world of modern wildlife conservation in East Africa and the day-to-day running of a protected zone. This is one of the only places in East Africa where such a unique insight is available to the general public. It's organised through the park office, and you need to give at least a day or so notice.

Wildlife Drives

For a classic wildlife drive, most people hire a 4WD safari jeep in Kigali, but this is very expensive (around US$370 per day including fuel from most reputable agencies). If you do this, ranger guides are provided by the park authorities at no extra charge, although a tip is expected. One long but worthwhile safari option is to enter the park at the main gate, pick up your guide and spend the day making your way to the park's northern Nyungwe gate (wildlife populations are much higher in the north). Once there, you could drop off your guide (with a *moto-taxi* fare to get him back to park headquarters) before returning to Kigali.

The other option is to rent one of the park's safari jeeps for US$175 for a half-day and US$275 for a full day. You should arrange this in advance through the park office.

Night Drives

As dusk comes and all the daylight wildlife heads off to bed somewhere, a whole new cast of rarely seen characters emerges from the gloom. A night drive gives you the opportunity to see some of these creatures. The safari (US$40 per person), which starts at 5.30pm, lasts around two hours and requires a minimum of two participants.

Birdwatching

Akagera lies on the great Nile Valley bird migration route, which means that you could potentially spot nearly 500 species of birds, including several endemics, more than 40 different kinds of raptors and, in wetland areas, the much sought-after shoebill. It's Rwanda's best birdwatching destination outside of Nyungwe Forest National Park. The many kilometres of waterside habitat support African eagles, kingfishers, herons,

ℹ AKAGERA NATIONAL PARK

Why Go
While wildlife populations are still recovering, Akagera's strongest drawcard is its unique ecology: a mix of woodland habitats, swampy wetlands and jagged mountains.

When to Go
The best time to visit is during the dry season (mid-May to September). November and April are the wettest months.

Practicalities
Tsetse flies and mosquitoes can be bad enough to seriously detract from your safari enjoyment, so bring a good insect repellent.

While in theory it is possible to reach the park by public transport, you really do need a private vehicle in order to move around the park. Akagera can also be visited as a day trip from Kigali.

Budget Tips
Due to the necessity of hiring your own vehicle, Akagera is a tough park to explore on a budget. Costs can be reduced by camping and just going on a boat safari. However, you'd still need some kind of transport to both the campsite and the lake shore, though a normal saloon car should be suitable. Per day costs for both adults and children decrease for stays of two or three days.

ibises, storks, egrets, crakes, rails, cormorants, darts and pelicans. Seasonal visitors include large flocks of ducks, bee-eaters and terns, and the woodland areas are particularly good places for barbets, shrikes, orioles and weavers. Birdwatching guides cost US$70, including park entry fee.

🛏 Sleeping

Lake Shakani Campsite　　　CAMPGROUND **$**
(camping US$30) The basic campsite at Lake Shakani, a few kilometres north of the park headquarters, offers firewood and a basic toilet and shower. If you don't partake of any of the park activities, the per person rate is raised to US$50 per night. Book through the park office.

Lake Ihema Campsite　　　CAMPGROUND **$**
(camping US$30) This campsite is on the shores of Lake Ihema, at the park headquarters. Facilities are minimal, although firewood is provided and there's a basic toilet and shower. If you don't take part in any of the park activities, the per person rate is raised to US$50 per night. Book through the park office.

Akagera Game Lodge　　　HOTEL **$$**
(☑ 252567805, 0785201206; www.akageralodge.com; s/d/ste US$80/100/150, cottage from US$300; P🖥☀) Recently revamped, this motel-like place has large and comfortable rooms with views over the hills to the hippo-filled lake below for a very good price. The restaurant is kind of soulless (day trippers should take note that this is the only restaurant in the park open to nonguests), but there's a decent pool and a kids' playpark.

★Ruzizi Tented Camp　　　TENTED CAMP **$$$**
(☑ 0787113300; www.ruzizilodge.com; half board s/d/child/under 5yr US$210/300/60/free; P🖥) 🍃 Hidden under a tangle of dense riverine trees on the shore of Lake Ihema, this relaxing and refined tented camp is managed by African Parks, with all profits being returned to conservation projects. True, it's not as ornate as some top-end camps elsewhere in East Africa, but you can't fault the price.

Sitting on the raised decks outside each tent watching the birds and hippos go about their daily lakeside lives will be a highlight of Akagera for many.

ℹ Information

Park Office (☑ 0782166015, 0786182871; ◷ 6am-6pm) The very helpful park office is where you need to book most activities. It also houses an interesting display on the park.

ℹ Getting There & Away

Akagera is really only accessible for those with their own transport. Safari and tour companies in Kigali can arrange a vehicle, or you can negotiate with private taxis around Kigali, although taxis are far from ideal for a safari.

UNDERSTAND RWANDA

History

Decolonisation & Independence

Rwanda and neighbouring Burundi were colonised by Germany and later Belgium, both of whom played on ethnic differences to divide and conquer the population. Power was concentrated in the hands of the minority Tutsi, with the Tutsi *mwami* (king) playing the central role in political and legislative decision-making.

In 1956, Mwami Rudahigwa called for independence from Belgium, which influenced Rwanda's colonial occupiers to switch allegiance to the Hutu majority. The Tutsis favoured fast-track independence, while the Hutus wanted the introduction of democracy followed later by independence.

After the death of Rudahigwa in 1959, tribal tensions flared as the 'Hutu Revolution' resulted in the deaths of an estimated 20,000 to 100,000 Tutsis. Another 150,000 Tutsis were driven from the country and forced to resettle as refugees in Uganda, Kenya and Tanzania.

Following independence in 1962, the Hutu majority came to power under Prime Minister Gregoire Kayibanda, who introduced quotas for Tutsis that limited their opportunities for education and work. In the fresh round of bloodshed that followed, thousands more Tutsis were killed, and tens of thousands fled across the borders.

Intertribal tensions erupted once again in 1972 when tens of thousands of Hutu were massacred in Burundi by the Tutsi-dominated government in reprisal for a coup attempt. The slaughter reignited old hatreds in Rwanda, which prompted Major General Juvenal Habyarimana to oust Kayibanda in 1973.

During the early years of his regime, Habyarimana made progress towards healing tribal divisions, and the country enjoyed relative economic prosperity. However, events unfolding in Uganda in the 1980s were to have a profound impact on the future of Rwanda.

In 1986, Yoweri Museveni became president of Uganda after his National Resistance Army (NRA) fought a brutal bush war to remove General Tito Okello from power. One of Museveni's key lieutenants was the current Rwandan president Paul Kagame, who capitalised on the victory by joining together with other exiled Tutsis to form the Rwandan Patriotic Front (RPF).

The Civil War Erupts

On 1 October 1990, 5000 well-armed soldiers of the RPF invaded Rwanda. All hell broke loose. Two days later at Habyarimana's request, France, Belgium and the DRC flew in troops to help the Rwandan army repel the invasion.

With foreign support assured, the Rwandan army went on a rampage against the Tutsis, as well as any Hutu suspected of having collaborated with the RPF. Thousands of people were shot or hacked to death, and countless others indiscriminately arrested, herded into football stadiums or police stations and left there without food or water for days.

Many died. Congolese Hutu troops joined in the carnage. Once again thousands of Tutsi refugees fled to Uganda. However, the initial setback for the RPF was only temporary as President Museveni was keen to see the repatriation of the now 250,000 Tutsi refugees living in western Uganda.

While he fervently denied such allegations, Museveni allegedly helped to reorganise and re-equip the RPF. In 1991, Kagame's forces invaded Rwanda for a second time, and by 1993 were garrisoned only 25km outside of Kigali.

With Habyarimana backed into a corner, the warring parties were brought to the negotiating table in Arusha, Tanzania. Negotiations stalled, hostilities were renewed, and French troops were flown in to protect foreign nationals in Kigali, though they were accused by the RPF of assisting the Rwandan army. A report released in 2008 by the Rwandan government accused the French government of committing war crimes, though all allegations were fervently denied by the French.

Meanwhile, with morale in the Rwandan army fading fast, the RPF launched an all-out offensive on the capital. Once again backed into a corner, Habyarimana invited the RPF to attend a conference of regional presidents. Power-sharing was on the agenda.

Tragically, on 6 April 1994, the airplane carrying Habyarimana and Cyprien Ntaryamira, the president of Burundi, was shot down by a surface-to-air missile while on approach to Kigali airport. It will probably never be known who fired the missile, though most observers believe it was Hutu extremists who had been espousing ethnic cleansing over the airwaves of Radio Télévision Libre des Mille Collines.

Regardless of who was responsible, the event unleashed one of the 20th century's worst explosions of bloodletting.

The Genocide

In the 100 days that followed, extremists among Habyarimana's Hutu political and military supporters embarked on a well-planned 'final solution' to the Tutsi 'problem'. One of the principal architects of the genocide was the cabinet chief of the Ministry of Defence, Colonel Theoneste Bagosora, who had been in charge of training the Interahamwe ('those who stand together') militia for more than a year.

One of Bagosora's first acts was to direct the army to kill the 'moderate' Hutu prime minister, Agathe Uwilingiyimana, as well as 10 Belgian UN peacekeepers. The killing of the UN peacekeepers prompted Belgium to withdraw all of its troops – precisely what Bagosora had calculated – which paved the way for the genocide to begin in earnest.

Rwandan army and Interahamwe death squads ranged at will over the countryside, killing, looting and burning, and roadblocks were set up in every town and city to prevent Tutsis from escaping. Every day, thousands of Tutsi and any Hutu suspected of sympathising with them or their plight were butchered on the spot. The streets of Kigali were littered with dismembered corpses, and the stench of rotting flesh was everywhere.

Those who attempted to take refuge in religious missions or churches often did so in vain. In some cases, it was the nuns and priests themselves who betrayed the fugitives to the death squads. Any mission that refused the death squads access was simply blown apart.

Perhaps the most shocking part of the tragedy was the willingness with which ordinary Hutu – men, women and even children as young as 10 years old – joined in the carnage. The perpetrators of the massacre were caught up in a tide of blind hatred, fear and mob mentality, which was inspired, controlled and promoted under the direction of their political and military leaders.

The UN Assistance Mission for Rwanda (UNAMIR) was in Rwanda throughout the genocide, but was powerless to prevent the killing due to an ineffective mandate. Although UN Force Commander Lieutenant General Romeo Dallaire had been warning senior UN staff and diplomats about the coming bloodshed, his warnings went unheeded.

The international community left Rwanda to face its fate. While the RPF eventually succeeded in pushing the Rwandan army and the Interahamwe into the DRC and Burundi, around a million people were killed, while another two million were huddled in refugee camps across the borders.

UNAMIR was finally reinforced and given a more open mandate in July, but it was in the words of Dallaire, 'too much, too late'. The genocide was already over – the RPF had taken control of Kigali.

The Aftermath

Of course, that is far from the end of the story. Within a year of the RPF victory, a legal commission was set up in Arusha, Tanzania, to try those accused of involvement in the genocide. However, many of the main perpetrators – the Interahamwe and former senior army officers – fled into exile beyond the reach of the RPF.

Some went to Kenya, where they enjoyed the protection of President Moi, who long refused to hand them over. Others – including Colonel Theoneste Bagosora, the principle architect of the genocide, and Ferdinand Nahimana, the director of the notorious Radio Télévision Libre des Mille Collines, which actively encouraged Hutus to butcher Tutsis – fled to Cameroon where they enjoyed the protection of that country's security boss, John Fochive. However, when Fochive was sacked by the newly elected president of Cameroon, Paul Biya, the Rwandan exiles were arrested.

Of greater importance were the activities of the Interahamwe and former army personnel in the refugee camps of the DRC and Tanzania. Determined to continue their fight against the RPF, they spread fear among the refugees that if they returned to Rwanda, they would be killed. When Rwanda began to demand the repatriation of the refugees, the grip of the Interahamwe on the camps was so complete that few dared move.

What was of most concern to the RPF was that the Interahamwe was using the refugee camps as staging posts for raids into Rwanda, with the complicity of the Congolese army. By 1996, Rwanda was openly warning the DRC that if these raids did not stop, the consequences would be dire.

RWANDA HISTORY

The raids continued, and the RPF held true to its threat by mounting a lightning strike two-day campaign into the DRC, targeting one of the main refugee camps north of Goma. The Interahamwe fled deep into the jungles of the Congo, which allowed hundreds of thousands of refugees to return home to Rwanda.

Events changed in October 1996 when a guerrilla movement known as the Alliance of Democratic Forces for the Liberation of Congo-Zaïre, led by Laurent Kabila, emerged with the secret support of Rwanda and Uganda. The rebels, ably supported by Rwandan and Ugandan regulars, swept through the eastern DRC, and by December were in control of every town and city in the region.

The Congolese army, alongside the Interahamwe and former Rwandan army personnel, retreated west in disarray towards Kisangani, looting and pillaging as they went. However, the grip the Interahamwe had on the refugee camps was finally broken, which allowed the remaining refugees to stream back into Rwanda, not only from the DRC, but also from Tanzania.

Faced with a huge refugee resettlement task, the government began to build new villages throughout the country. Huge tracts of Akagera National Park were de-gazetted as a national park and given over to this 'villagisation' program, along with much of the northwest region, which had previously hosted some of the most intense battles of the civil war.

The Healing Begins

Rwanda has done a remarkable job healing its wounds, and has achieved an astonishing level of safety and security in a remarkably short space of time – albeit with considerable help from a guilty international community that ignored the country in its darkest hour. Visiting Kigali today, it is hard to believe the horror that swept across this land in 1994.

On the international front, however, things have been rather less remarkable. In 1998, Rwanda and Uganda joined forces to oust their former ally Laurent Kabila who was by now president of the DRC. What ensued was Africa's first great war, sucking in as many as nine neighbours at its height, and costing an estimated three to five million deaths, mostly from disease and starvation.

Rwanda and Uganda soon fell out, squabbling over the rich resources that were there for the plunder in the DRC. Rwanda backed the Rally for Congolese Democracy, Uganda the Movement for the Liberation of the Congo, and the two countries fought out a brutal and prolonged proxy war.

Peace treaties were signed in 2002, and foreign forces were withdrawn from the DRC, though if and when an international inquiry is launched, Rwanda may find itself facing accusations of war crimes. Rwanda's motives for entering the fray were to wipe out remnants of the Interahamwe militia and former soldiers responsible for the genocide, but somewhere along the line, elements in the army may have lost sight of the mission. A leaked 2010 report by the UN high commissioner for human rights has even accused the current Rwandan administration of commiting genocide against Hutus in the DRC. And in 2012 a rebel milita in the DRC, the M23, took over large tracts of eastern DRC, including the Congolese side of the Virungas and even, briefly, Goma. Both Rwanda and Uganda have been accused of supporting and equipping the M23 rebels.

Back on the domestic front, Paul Kagame assumed the presidency in 2000, and was overwhelmingly endorsed at the ballot box in presidential elections in 2003 and 2010 that saw him take 93% of the vote.

An Optimistic Future

Looking at the bigger picture, Rwanda remains the home of two tribes, the Hutu and the Tutsi. The Hutu presently outnumber the Tutsi by more than four to one, and while the RPF government is one of national unity with a number of Hutu representatives, it's viewed in some quarters as a Tutsi government ruling over a predominantly Hutu population.

However, the RPF government has done an impressive job of promoting reconciliation and restoring trust between the two communities. This is no small achievement after the horrors that were inflicted on the Tutsi community during the genocide of 1994, especially since it would have been all too easy for the RPF to embark on a campaign of revenge and reprisal.

On the contrary, Kagame and his government are attempting to build a society with a place for everyone, regardless of tribe. There are no more Tutsis, no more Hutus, only Rwandans. Idealistic perhaps, but it is realistically the best hope for the future. Rghtly or wrongly Paul Kagame has plenty of detrac-

THE SLOW HAND OF JUSTICE

Following a slow and shaky start, the **International Criminal Tribunal for Rwanda** (ICTR; www.ictr.org) has managed to net most of the major suspects wanted for involvement in the 1994 genocide.

The tribunal was established in Arusha, Tanzania, in 1995, but was initially impeded in its quest for justice by the willingness of several African countries to protect suspects. Countries such as Cameroon, the Democratic Republic of the Congo (DRC; formerly Zaïre) and Kenya long harboured Kigali's most wanted, frustrating the Rwandan authorities in their attempts to seek justice. However, due to changes in their attitude or government, many of the former ministers (including the former prime minister, Jean Kambanda) of the interim cabinet that presided over the country during the genocide have now been arrested.

While the architects of the tragedy are tried at the ICTR, Rwanda's judicial system suddenly found itself facing a backlog that would take a century to clear. With too many cases (in excess of 120,000) and too few jails to humanely detain such a large percentage of the population, an age-old solution was revived.

Across the country thousands of *gacaca* courts were set up and hundreds of thousands of judges appointed. Modelled on traditional hearings that were headed by village elders, these tribunals are empowered to identify and categorise suspects. Category 1 suspects who are thought to have organised, encouraged or instigated the genocide are remanded for processing in the formal judicial system. The *gacaca* court tries category 2 and 3 suspects, those accused of murder, bodily injury or causing property damage. Each court must contain a minimum of 15 community-elected judges and be witnessed by 100 citizens. It is hoped that these small courts will not only find the guilty but provide closure for the families of their victims and help relieve the burden the larger courts face.

tors, but on the surface at least it's hard not to see Rwanda today as anything other than buzzing with potential for the future.

Culture

The National Psyche

Tribal conflict has torn Rwanda apart during much of the independence period, culminating in the horrific genocide that unfolded in 1994. With that said, there are basically two schools of thought when it comes to looking at Rwandan identity.

The colonial approach of the Belgians was to divide and rule, issuing ID cards that divvied up the population along strict tribal lines. They tapped the Tutsis as leaders to help control the Hutu majority, building on the foundations of precolonial society in which the Tutsi were considered more dominant. Later, as independence approached, they switched sides, pitting Hutu against Tutsi in a new conflict, which simmered on and off until the 1990s when it exploded onto the world stage.

In the new Rwanda, the opposite is true. Tribal identities have been systematically eliminated, and everyone is now treated as a Rwandan. The new government is at pains to present a singular identity, and blames the Belgians for categorising the country along tribal lines that set the stage for the savagery that followed. Rwanda was a peaceful place beforehand: Hutu and Tutsi lived side by side for generations, and intermarriage was common – or so the story goes.

The truth, as is often the case, is probably somewhere in between. Rwanda was no oasis before the colonial powers arrived. However, Tutsis probably had a better time of it than Hutus, something that the Belgians were able to exploit as they sought control.

But it is true to say that there was no history of major bloodshed between the two peoples before 1959, and the foundations of the violence were laid by the Belgian insistence on ethnic identity and their cynical political manipulation of it. The leaders of the genocide merely took this policy to its extreme, first promoting tribal differences, and then playing on them to manipulate a malleable population.

Paul Kagame is trying to leave the past behind, and create a new Rwanda for Rwandans. Forget the past? No. But do learn from it, and move on to create a new spirit of national unity.

All this, of course, will take time, maybe a generation or more, but what has been achieved in just over a decade is astonishing. Rwandans are taking pride in their country once more, investment is on the boil, and people are optimistic about their future.

Daily Life

Urban Rwanda is a very sophisticated place. People start the day early before breaking off for a long lunch. Late dinners inevitably lead into drinking and socialising that sometimes doesn't wind down until the early morning.

In rural areas people work long hours from dawn until dusk, but also take a break during the hottest part of the day. However, it is a hard life for women in the countryside, who seem burdened with the lion's share of the work, while many menfolk sit around drinking and conversing.

Faith is an important rock in the lives of many Rwandan people, with Christianity firmly rooted as the dominant religion. Churches from different denominations in Rwanda were tainted by their association with the genocide in 1994, though that doesn't seem to have dampened people's devotion to the faith.

Like many countries in Africa, Rwanda actively promotes universal primary education. Despite suffering terribly during the genocide, the education system continues to improve and the literacy rate, according to Unicef, now stands at around 65.9%, up from 58% in 1991.

Economy

Rwanda's economy was decimated during the genocide – production ground to a halt, and foreign investors pulled out altogether. However, the current government has done

LEAVE YOUR PLASTIC BAGS AT HOME

In an effort to preserve the natural beauty of Rwanda, the government enforces a strict ban on plastic bags throughout the country. Police at borders may even search you and confiscate any plastic bags they find.

a commendable job of stimulating the economy, which is now fairly stable and boasts steady growth and low inflation. Foreign investors are once again doing business in Kigali, and there are building projects springing up all over the capital. Tourism too has rebounded and is again the country's leading foreign-exchange earner.

The agricultural sector is the principle employer and a major export earner, contributing around 33% of Rwanda's GDP. Coffee is by far the largest export, accounting for about 60% of export income, while tea and pyrethrum (a natural insecticide) are also important crops. However, the vast majority of farmers live subsistence lives, growing plantain, sweet potato, beans, cassava, sorghum and maize.

Population

The population exceeded 12.3 million in 2011, which gives Rwanda one of the highest population densities of any country in Africa. While tribal identities are very much a taboo subject in Rwanda, the population is believed to be about 84% Hutu, 15% Tutsi and 1% Twa. The Twa is a Central Africa indigenous group that has suffered from discrimination over the generations, though is slowly gaining a political and cultural foothold.

Religion

About 65% of the population are Christians of various sects (Catholicism is predominant), a further 25% follow tribal religions, often with a dash of Christianity, and the remaining 10% are Muslim.

Arts

Rwanda's most famous dancers are the Intore troupe – their warrior-like displays are accompanied by a trance-like drumbeat similar to that of the famous Tambourinaires in Burundi.

Environment

The Land

In the 'Land of a Thousand Hills', it is hardly surprising to find that endless mountains stretch into the infinite horizon. Rwanda's 26,338 sq km of land is one of the most densely populated places on earth, and almost every

A NEW LANGUAGE

In 2008, teachers woke to a shock. A curt government decree required that public school teachers throughout Rwanda were to instruct their students in English – a tongue that few spoke with proficiency. Prior to this, early grades had been taught in Kinyarwanda and senior classes in French. From 2011 all classes at primary (from fourth grade onwards), secondary and university levels have been conducted in English.

Officially, the reason cited for dropping French as the national language was based on economics. English is the international language of commerce, and since Rwanda is surrounded by anglophone neighbours, a switch to English is hoped to attract foreign investment and open up future opportunities for generations to come.

Others feel the abrupt move reflects a cooling of the close relations Rwanda once had with France. Leading up to the genocide, Rwanda's Hutu-supremacist leader Juvenal Habyarimana received aid and arms from the French. (An error of judgement not easily forgotten by the Uganda-bred English-speaking rebels led by current president Paul Kagame.)

So while the French are out, the English are in and not just linguistically. On 29 November 2009, Rwanda, although it lacks any British colonial ties, joined the Commonwealth.

available piece of land is under cultivation (except the national parks). Since most of the country is mountainous, this involves a good deal of terracing. Coffee and tea plantations take up considerable areas of land.

Environmental Issues

Soil erosion, resulting from the overuse of land, is the most serious problem confronting Rwanda today. The terracing system in the country is fairly anarchic, and unlike much of Southeast Asia, the lack of coordinated water management has wiped out much of the topsoil on the slopes. This is potentially catastrophic for a country with too many people in too small a space, as it points to a food-scarcity problem in the future.

Food & Drink

In the rural areas of Rwanda, food is very similar to that in other East African countries. Popular meats include tilapia (Nile perch), goat, chicken and beef brochettes (kebabs), though the bulk of most meals are centred on ugali (maize meal), *matoke* (cooked plantains) and 'Irish' potatoes. In the cities, however, Rwanda's French roots are evident in the *plat du jour* (plate of the day), which is usually excellently prepared and presented Continental-inspired cuisine.

Drinking tap water is not recommended in Rwanda, though bottled water is cheap and widely available. Soft drinks (sodas) and the local beers, Primus (720mL) and Mulzig (330mL and 660mL), are available every-

where, as is the local firewater, *konyagi*. A pleasant, nonalcoholic alternative is the purplish juice from the tree tomato (tamarillo), which is a sweet and tasty concoction that somewhat defies explanation!

SURVIVAL GUIDE

ⓘ Directory A–Z

ACCOMMODATION

Generally, the price and quality of budget accommodation in Rwanda is on a par with Kenya and Uganda and better value than Tanzania. Cheap hotels are often noisy though – largely due to the fact that most have attached bars. However, they are essentially clean, if characterised by missing toilet seats and lukewarm (if not completely cold) showers. Mission- and church-run hostels are quieter and cleaner than most other forms of budget accommodation, as they seem to attract an exceptionally conscientious type of manager who takes the old adage 'cleanliness is next to godliness' fairly seriously. Top-end hotels and ecolodges are found mostly found in Kigali, Gisenyi and near the national parks.

INTERNET ACCESS

Internet access is widely available in all towns and cities. It generally costs between RFr500 and RFr1000 per hour and speeds are pretty reasonable. All midrange and top-end hotels bar a few remote ecolodges have free wi-fi available (often in room but sometimes just around the reception area), and even an increasing number of budget hotels and restaurants offer wi-fi.

If you're travelling with a laptop or tablet computer and require mobile internet access, it's

PRACTICALITIES

➡ Rwanda uses the metric system (distances are in kilometres).

➡ Electricity in Rwanda is 240V, 50Hz, and plugs are mainly two-pin.

➡ The English-language *New Times* is published several times a week, plus the Ugandan *New Vision* and *Monitor* are also available as is the *East African* – a region-wide paper.

➡ Radio Rwanda is the government-run station, broadcasting in Kinyarwanda, French, Swahili and English.

➡ TV Rwandaise (TVR) is the state-owned broadcaster.

cheap and easy to pick up an internet modem dongle from any of the main mobile-phone providers (MTN offers the best network coverage).

MAPS

It's difficult to get hold of decent maps of Rwanda before arriving in the country. The best map currently is *Rwanda & Burundi – International Travel Map* by **ITMB Publishing** (www.itmb.ca) at a scale of 1:300,000.

MONEY

The unit of currency is the Rwandan franc (RFr). It is divided into 100 centimes. Notes come in RFr100, RFr500, RFr1000, RFr5000 and RFr10,000 denominations. Coins come in RFr10, RFr20 and RFr50.

ATMs

Banks in all towns and cities have ATMs, but not all work with foreign Visa cards (despite the Visa signs most proudly boast). The notable exceptions are the Bank of Kigali, I&M Bank and Ecobank. Unfortunately, the only things ATMs were giving out with MasterCards were headaches.

Cash

Banks throughout the country can exchange US dollars or euros, although they can be very slow to do so. Most people use the foreign-exchange bureaus in Kigali instead and this is quite safe.

Rwanda, like other African countries, is very particular on which notes it will or will not accept. Anything older than 2006 or deemed too dirty, crinkled or tatty will be meet with scorn, and your pleas to have it changed, with indifference.

Credit Cards

Credit cards are increasingly accepted at midrange and top-end tourist hotels and restaurants, and the RDB office in Kigali also accepts them, as do some national park offices (though lines are sometimes down at these). It is possible to make cash withdrawals against credit cards at some banks in the capital (both Visa and MasterCard), though you can expect to pay a hefty commission (around 3.5%) and lose a lot of time waiting for the privilege.

Tipping

Tipping is common in the cities these days due to the large international presence. Rwandan salaries are low and a tip of about 10% will be appreciated.

Travellers Cheques

Despite what your travel agent may have told you, travellers cheques are not accepted in Rwanda.

POST

Postal rates for postcards going overseas are around RFr275 to Europe and Africa, RFr450 to everywhere else.

PUBLIC HOLIDAYS

New Year's Day 1 January
Democracy Day 8 January
Easter (Good Friday, Holy Saturday and Easter Monday) March/April
Labour Day 1 May
Ascension Thursday May
Whit Monday May
National Day 1 July
Peace & National Unity Day 5 July
Harvest Festival 1 August
Assumption 15 August
Culture Day 8 September
Kamarampaka Day 25 September
Armed Forces Day 26 October
All Saints' Day 1 November
Christmas Day 25 December

SAFE TRAVEL

Mention Rwanda to most people and they think of it as a highly dangerous place. However, the reality today is very different, and stability has returned to all parts of the country.

Urban Rwanda is undoubtedly one of the safer places to be in this region, and Kigali is a genuine contender for the safest capital in Africa. However, like in any big city the world over, take care at night.

Never take photographs of anything connected with the government or the military (post offices, banks, bridges, border crossings, barracks, prisons and dams) – cameras can and will be confiscated.

TELEPHONE

The main operators in Rwanda are MTN, Tigo and Airtel.

There are currently no area codes in Rwanda. The international country code is 📞250. Mobile numbers begin with either 📞078 or 📞072.

Most people and businesses use mobile phones rather than landlines to stay in touch, and it's cheap, fast and painless to get a Rwandan SIM card for your (unlocked) phone. Top-up cards start from as little as RFr100. Mobile phone calls cost about RFr1 per second, although rates vary depending on when you call.

TIME

If you're crossing borders, be advised that Rwanda (and Burundi) is one hour behind the rest of East Africa.

TOURIST INFORMATION

The Rwanda Development Board (RDB) runs the state tourist board. Currently it has three tourist offices: one in Kigali, one in Musanze (Ruhengeri) and another in Gisenyi. While they have only limited amounts of promotional information, staff are – for East Africa – unusually well trained, knowledgable and helpful.

VISAS

Visa rules changed in late 2014. Before that date visas were not required for nationals of Germany, South Africa, Sweden, UK, USA, DRC and other East African countries as well as one or two others. After October 2014 everyone except nationals of East African countries and the DRC required visas. For Germans, Israelis, South Africans, Swedes, Brits and Americans visas are now available on arrival for US$30. Everyone else needs to apply for a visa in their country of residence at a Rwandan embassy or high commission. These visas (called class T2) cost US$50, are valid for 90 days and are good for multiple entries within that time.

If Rwanda isn't represented in your country then you need to register online at **Rwanda Immigration** (www.migration.gov.rw) before you travel. The website is a little confusing, but once you've submitted the online form you'll receive your letter of entitlement within three days. Present this letter at the border along with the US$30 fee to obtain a single-entry, 30-day visa (called a V1 visa). Multiple entry V1 visas are US$60. It is no longer possible to obtain a visa on arrival without first obtaining the aforementioned letter of entitlement.

Points to note: firstly, due to the changing nature of Rwandan tourist visas double-check the above information carefully before travelling. Secondly, although the online form asks you to attach a letter of invitation this is not a compulsory prerequisite and it's fine to skip this section. Thirdly, if things go awry you'll have a devil of a time trying to make contact with Rwanda Immigration.

Rwanda is one of the countries covered by the new East Africa Tourist Visa, and for those also visiting Kenya and Uganda on the same trip it is a cheaper alternative. The visa costs US$100, is valid for 90 days and is multiple entry – it is available upon arrival or from embassies abroad. If acquiring the visa before travel, your first port of call must be the country through which you applied for the visa.

Visa Extensions

If you've arrived on a T2 visa and need to extend it, you must do so at **Rwanda Immigration** (Ministère de l'Intérieur; 📞0788152222; www.migration.gov.rw; Blvd de l'Umuganda; ⊙ application submission 7-11.30am Mon-Wed & Fri, visa collection 1-4.30pm Mon-Wed & Fri, 1-3.30pm Thu) in Kigali's Kacyiru district, about 7km northeast of the city centre near the American Embassy. Bring the appropriate form (available online), a passport-sized photo, your passport, a letter of introduction or a letter addressed to the Director of Immigration explaining why you require a visa, and RFr30,000. Extensions take five days to issue. V1 visas cannot be extended.

🛈 Getting There & Away

AIR

Gregoire Kayibanda International Airport is located at Kanombe, 10km east of Kigali's city centre.

Airlines

Ethiopian Airlines (📞252570440; www.flyethiopian.com; Union Trade Centre, Ave de la Paix, Kigali) To Addis Ababa (Ethiopia) and good connections to elsewhere in Africa.

Kenya Airways (📞280306850; www.kenya-airways.com; Union Trade Centre, Ave de la Paix, Kigali) Connects Kigali with Bujumbura (Burundi) and Nairobi (Kenya).

KLM (📞252577972; www.klm.com; Union Trade Centre, Ave de la Paix, Kigali) KLM bookings are handled by Kenya Airways.

RwandAir (📞252575757; www.rwandair.com; Union Trade Centre, Ave de la Paix, Kigali) Rwanda's national airline has flights to Accra (Ghana) Libreville (Gabon), Brazzaville (Republic of Congo), Kampala (Uganda), Nairobi (Kenya), Mombasa (Kenya), Johannesburg (South Africa), Bujumbura (Burundi), Douala (Cameroon), Dubai (United Arab Emirates), Addis Ababa (Ethiopia), Dar es Salaam (Tanzania), Kilimanjaro (Tanzania), Lagos (Nigeria), Juba (South Sudan) and Brussels (Belgium).

INTERNATIONAL BUSES

All international bus services listed depart from the Nyabugogo bus terminal in Kigali.

International Heads to the Uganda border town of Gatuna every half-hour (RFr3500, 2½ hours).

Jaguar Executive Coaches Operates buses to Kampala (RFr8000, nine hours) at 6am, 8am, 11.30am, 5.30pm, 7pm and 8pm.

Kampala Coach Has a 6pm bus to Kampala (RFr10,000, eight hours), and there is also a 6pm bus to Nairobi (RFr27,000, 24 hours) via Nakuru (RFr23,000, 20 hours) or Eldoret (RFr20,000, 16½ hours).

Select Express Buses to the Rwanda–Tanzania border crossing of Rusumo (RFr3000, three hours) every half-hour.

Taqwa For the ultimate in long bus rides, this company sends buses to Dar es Salaam (Tanzania; RFr35,000, 27 hours) at 4.30am. The bus stops for four hours in the middle of the night near Dodoma.

Volcano Express Hourly buses to Bujumbura (RFr6000, six hours) between 6am and 2pm.

Yahoo Express Operates buses to Bujumbura (Burundi; RFr6000, six hours) at 7am and noon.

Turkish Airlines (📞 0280444851; www.turkishairlines.com; 4th fl, Grand Pension Plaza, Kigali) Connects to Istanbul and beyond.

LAND

Rwanda shares land borders with Burundi, the DRC, Tanzania and Uganda.

Burundi

The main border crossing between Rwanda and Burundi is via Huye (Butare) and Kayanza, on the Kigali–Bujumbura road, which is sealed all the way. The border post is called Kayanza Haut and Burundian transit visas are available on arrival.

There is also a direct road between Cyangugu and Bujumbura. There are no direct buses between the two, although you can catch a bus from Cyangugu to Rugombo (RFr1500, one hour), from where a minibus can take you to Bujumbura (you may have to change in Cibitoke).

Tanzania

Only one bus company, Taqwa operates cross-border buses to Tanzania and this goes all the way to Dar es Salaam (although you can change buses for Arusha). But doing it, as most people do, in stages is no great hassle, with a number of companies sending frequent buses to the border, after which you can get another bus to the tiny Tanzanian town of Benako (marked as Kasulo on some maps), about 20km south-east of the frontier. From here get a bus to the pleasant little town of Biharamulo, where you'll probably have to overnight. The following day catch a bus to Mwanza or Bukoba.

The DRC

There are two crossings between Rwanda and the DRC, both on the shores of Lake Kivu. To the north is the crossing between Gisenyi and Goma. The southern border is between Cyangugu and Bukavu. Providing the DRC remains politically stable and you have prearranged visas, the crossings are relatively straightforward.

Uganda

There are two main crossing points for foreigners: between Kigali and Kabale via Gatuna/Katuna (called Gatuna on the Rwandan side, Katuna on the Ugandan side), and between Musanze (Ruhengeri) and Kisoro via Cyanika.

There are direct buses between Kigali/Musanze and Gisenyi and Kampala. Buses also run between Kigali and the border at Gatuna (RFr3500, 1½ hours) throughout the day. Plenty of shared taxis (USh4000) and special-hire taxis (USh20,000 for the whole car) travel back and forth between Katuna and Kabale.

From Musanze (Ruhengeri) to Kisoro via Cyanika the road is in excellent shape on the Rwandan side and in rather poor condition on the Ugandan side. Minibuses link either side of the border with Musanze (RFr400, 25km).

ℹ Getting Around

AIR

RwandAir (p496) operate domestic flights between Kigali and Kamembe (Cyangugu).

BUS & MINIBUS

Rwanda has efficient and reliable public transport. Privately run buses cover the entire country, and with scheduled departure times you won't find yourself waiting for hours while the driver scouts for more passengers. Tickets are bought in advance from a ticket office, which is usually the point of departure.

You will also find plenty of well-maintained, modern minibuses serving all the main routes. Head to the bus stand in any town between dawn and about 3pm and it is quite easy to find one heading to Kigali and nearby towns. Destinations are displayed in the front window and the fares are fixed (you can ask other passengers to be sure). However, anyone who gets stuck somewhere late in the afternoon is going to have to pay top price for the privilege of getting out. Minibuses leave when full. Neither buses nor minibuses are supposed to charge extra for baggage.

CAR & MOTORCYCLE

Cars are suitable for most of the country's main roads, but those planning to explore Akagera National Park might be better off with a 4WD.

Car hire isn't well established in Rwanda, but most travel agents and tour operators in Kigali can organise something.

Jean-Paul Birasa (✆ 0788517440; birasajean paul@yahoo.fr) If you just need a car and driver,

Kigali-based Jean-Paul Birasa can organise no-frills car and jeep rental (the jeeps are small 4WDs such as a RAV4, which is fine for anywhere in Rwanda) with drivers for considerably lower prices than any of the big travel agencies.

LOCAL TRANSPORT
Taxi

Taxis are only really necessary in Kigali. It's also possible to find the odd taxi in most other major towns.

Moto-Taxi

Most towns are compact enough to walk around, but otherwise a *moto-taxi* is a good bet. It's just a motorcycle, but the driver can usually sling a pack across the petrol tank. They're generally fast but safe, and there's usually a helmet for the passenger.

Tours

Most of the country's tour operators are based in Kigali, and while they specialise in multiday excursions and gorilla tracking – the mainstay of Rwanda's tourism – they can arrange any number of day trips on request.

For an extensive list of operators, visit the website of the **Rwanda Tours and Travel Association** (www.rttarwanda.org).

Burundi

Best for Nature

➜ Parc National de la Rusizi (p543)

➜ Parc National de la Kibira (p543)

➜ Chutes de la Karera (p544)

➜ Source du Nil (p544)

Best for Culture

➜ Les Tambourinaires drummers (p539)

➜ Bujumbura Central Market (p538)

➜ Musée National de Gitega (p544)

Why Go?

Tiny Burundi is an incongruous mix of soaring mountains, languid lakeside communities and a tragic past blighted by ethnic conflict.

When civil war broke out in 1993, the economy was shattered and the tourist industry succumbed to a quick death. Since then, many of the upcountry attractions have been off limits, including the southernmost source of the Nile and the ancient forest of Parc National de la Kibira.

Now the word is out that the war is over, Burundi has begun receiving a trickle of travellers and the country is safer than it has been for years. The steamy capital, Bujumbura, has a lovely location on the shores of Lake Tanganyika, and just outside the city are some of the finest inland beaches on the continent. Burundians also have an irrepressible *joie de vivre*, and their smiles are as infectious as a rhythm laid down by a Les Tambourinaires drummer.

When to Go
Bujumbura

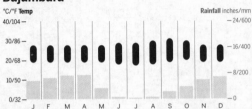

Year-round
Altitude affects regional temperature. Bujumbura is warmer than elsewhere.

Oct–May Mild rainy season with a brief dry spell in December and January.

Jun & Aug Locals flock to Lake Tanganyika beaches during the 'long dry' season.

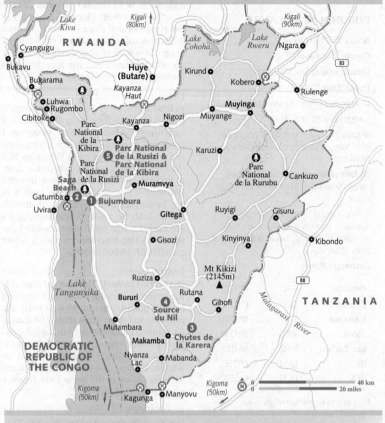

Burundi Highlights

Dine out in style and dance into the wee hours of the morning in Burundi's surprisingly vibrant capital **Bujumbura** (p537).

Down a cold one under the shade of a palm tree on **Saga Beach** (p538),

one of Africa's finest inland beaches.

Take a cold shower under one of four waterfalls at the **Chutes de la Karera** (p544).

Travel to Burundi's very own pyramid, a memorial marking a small

stream in Kasumo, at the southernmost **Source du Nil** (p544).

Be among the first to rediscover the wildlife of the **Parc National de la Rusizi** (p543) and remote **Parc National de la Kibira** (p543).

BUJUMBURA

Largely frozen in time thanks to more than a decade of conflict, there has been very little development in Burundi's capital, Bujumbura. The steamy little city retains much of its grandiose colonial town planning, with wide boulevards and imposing public buildings. The peace and relative stability of the last few years mean that change is coming, but for the moment Buju (as it's commonly

known) retains an obviously different feel to any other East African capital. This is most obviously manifest in the city's distinctly French outlook on life.

Perhaps it's thanks to this French influence that Bujumbura has earned a freewheelin' reputation for its dining, drinking and dancing scene; despite its village-like size this is one of the best places to eat out in East Africa. While the security situation is greatly

BURUNDI AT A GLANCE

Area 27,835 km sq

Capital Bujumbura

Country code ☑257

Population 10.4 million

Currency Burundian franc (BFr)

Languages Kirundi, French

Money Some ATMs in Bujumbura accept foreign Visa cards. Elsewhere you'll need cash.

Mobile phones Local SIM cards are widely available; reception is generally good.

Visas Needed by most nationalities. Available on arrival for plane arrivals; overland travellers should obtain a visa prior to arrival.

Exchange Rates

Australia	A$1	Bfr1225
Canada	C$1	Bfr1248
Euro Zone	€1	Bfr1781
Japan	¥100	Bfr1339
New Zealand	NZ$1	Bfr1135
UK	UK£1	Bfr2360
USA	US$1	Bfr1570

For current exchange rates see www.xe.com

improved, Buju isn't exactly the safest city in the region. Pick-pocketing is very common (keep a sharp eye on those street kids!), so keep your wits about you; especially once the sun goes down. Violent crime is much rarer.

◉ Sights & Activities

The so-called sights of Bujumbura aren't really up to much. The biggest drawcards are the beaches and the general feel of the place.

★**Saga Beach**   BEACH

Bujumbura's Lake Tanganyika beaches are some of the best urban beaches of any land-locked country in Africa. The sand, though not exactly pristine white and clean, is still an inviting place to drop a towel, the swimming is safe and the water warm.

The stretch of beach that lies about 5km northwest of the capital is the most beautiful and used to be known as **Plage des Cocoti-ers** (Coconut Beach). However, a number of resorts are located along the road and most locals now call it **Saga Plage** (pronounced Sagga), in honour of what was once the most popular restaurant and bar here. It's at its liveliest best at the weekend.

La Pierre de Livingstone et Stanley   HISTORIC SITE

FREE This large rock allegedly marks the spot where the infamous 'Dr Livingstone, I presume?' encounter between Livingstone and Stanley took place on 25 November 1871 (Ujiji in Tanzania has a much better claim to being the location of this event, though). Wherever it was, this is as good a place as any to do your own re-enactment, though it'll probably be a solo performance as it's not too likely that you'll meet another tourist here. A taxi from the city costs a rather excitable BFr40,000 one-way.

Central Market   MARKET

(Ave de l'Enseignement) This covered market is the largest in Burundi and is an interesting place to poke around in, with its maze-like corridors and closet-sized stalls. The market is organised into sections, from the colourful fresh produce stores to shops selling nothing but secondhand clothing donated by Western nations. The tiny fish, which smell so badly when fresh, are a local delicacy when dried (*mukeke*).

Musée Vivant   ZOO

(Ave du 13 Octobre; adult/child BFr5000/2000; ⊘7am-6pm) This small zoo won't win the approval of animal rights activists. In fact, it probably won't win approval from many people at all. Currently it houses a chimp, a leopard, several crocodiles, various snakes and some antelopes in cramped, dirty and exposed cages. The guinea pigs for sale at the reception are food for the carnivores, and if you buy one, you'll get a graphic demonstration of the food chain in action. There's also a 'cultural exhibit' which consists of a mildly interesting reconstructed traditional Burundian hut and living compound.

★Institut Français Burundi   CULTURAL CENTRE

(☑22222351; www.ifburundi.org; Chaussée Prince Rwagasore, 9) As is pretty much standard with French cultural institutes the world over, this one hosts a diverse and exciting array of cultural events which take in everything from art-house films to exhibitions and food related events (it's French, after all). The website lists upcoming events, or you can pick up a brochure from the more upmarket hotels and restaurants. You don't need to be French to attend.

👉 Tours

Augustine Tours TOURS
(Burundi Access; ☑ 022278000, 078283273; www.augustinetours.com; Blvd Patrice Lumumba, Excellence House Bldg) Augustin Ndikuriyo at Augustine Tours is passionate about promoting Burundi to the world and has a wealth of local knowledge that he happily shares. He can take care of everything from airport transfers to day trips to every corner of the country.

🛏 Sleeping

Budget hotels in Bujumbura are no bargain but there are some good deals in the mid-range category.

🛏 Town Centre

★Hôtel de l'Amitié HOTEL $
(☑ 22226195; www.hoteldelamitie.bi; Rue de l'Amitié; r US$25-40; P🛜) One of the best budget places in town, particularly for couples, as all rooms contain either twin or large double beds (although only one breakfast is included in the quoted rates). The wi-fi and cheap(ish) laundry service are added bonuses, and thanks to a generator you'll still have power when the electricity cuts out.

Hotel Amahoro HOTEL $
(☑ 22247550; www.hotelamahoro.com; Rue de l'Industrie; s US$55-100, d & tw US$60-105; P❄🛜) Filling the gap between a budget and mid-range hotel, the Amahoro has established a name for itself as a comfortable, centrally located place to stay with a good range of amenities. More expensive rooms include air-con, but all have satellite TVs, fridges and hot water in the bathroom.

Shammah Hotel HOTEL $
(☑ 22275760; shammahhotel2006@yahoo.fr; Blvd de l'Uprona; s/d US$45/55; P❄🛜) This well-run enterprise has spotless rooms with satellite TVs, small balconies and reliable hot water. Its central location and helpful staff are other major drawcards.

★Hotel le Chandelier HOTEL $$
(☑ 022276804; www.hotel-lechandelier.com; Ave de la JRR; s/d from US$110/130; P❄🛜) This fine hotel, which offers a huge amount of comfort and excellent service, is the stand-out choice in this price range. The enormous rooms have classic dark wood furnishings, excellent modern bathrooms and good sound insulation, as well as a breakfast worthy of kings. Prices are very negotiable at quiet times.

Hotel Dolce Vita Resort HOTEL $$
(☑ 078333000, 022258569; Kigobe; s/d US$70/100; P❄🛜🏊) A five-minute taxi ride from the city centre (BFr4000) and almost next door to the new, fortress-like US embassy, this pretty little guesthouse, with shocking pink bougainvillea flowers surrounding a small pool, has modern, comfortable rooms and helpful staff.

Hotel Botanika BOUTIQUE HOTEL $$
(☑ 22226792; www.hotelbotanika.com; Blvd de l'Uprona; r US$90; ❄🛜) There's an easy tropical charm to Bujumbura's first, and only real, boutique hotel. The seven-room Botanika

---

LES TAMBOURINAIRES DRUMMERS

Les Tambourinaires du Burundi are the country's most famous troupe and have performed in cities such as Berlin and New York. The troupe's recitals are a high-adrenaline mix of drumming and dancing that drowns the audience in waves of sound and movement. Unfortunately, without a national theatre or any other such venue, you'll have to be content with a smaller beachside performance or an impromptu practice session.

From around 4.30pm on Sundays, drummers run through a series of routines at Saga Beach Resort on Saga Beach. There is no charge, but tips are appreciated and you'll be charged (BFr5000) if you take photos.

Occasionally you will also find Les Tambourinaires drummers practising at the Office National du Tourisme (p543; usually between 3pm and 4pm on Fridays) or sometimes at the Musée Vivant, but once they notice a tourist snooping around, they'll only continue playing for a cash incentive.

Bujumbura

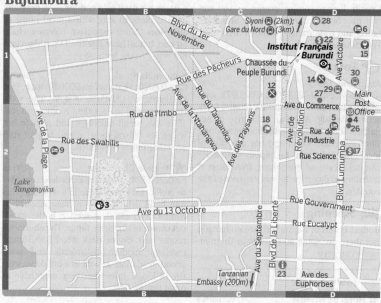

Map labels:

Blvd du 1er Novembre
Rue des Pêcheurs
Rue du Tanganika
Rue de la Ntahangwa
Ave de la Ntahangwa
Ave de la Plage
Rue de l'Imbo
Rue des Swahilis
Lake Tanganyika
Ave des Paysans
Ave du 13 Octobre
Ave du 3 Septembre
Blvd de la Liberté
Siyoni (2km); Gare du Nord (3km)
Chaussée du Peuple Burundi
Institut Français Burundi
Ave Victoire
Ave du Commerce
Ave de Révolution
Rue de l'Industrie
Rue Science
Blvd Lumumba
Rue Gouvernment
Rue Eucalypt
Main Post Office
Ave des Euphorbes
Tanzanian Embassy (200m)

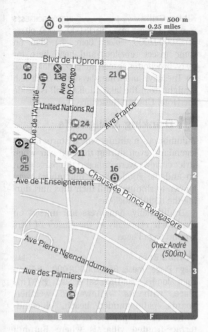

Eating

Despite its diminutive size Bujumbura has some great places to eat. The beachside drinking places also do meals of the brochettes (kebabs) and chips type, if you need some food to go with that beer. On the other hand if you're looking for a cheap, no-frills buffet (usually lunch only) you'll find no shortage of them around town. Most serve identical fare for identical prices. Expect a big helping of carbohydrates in the form of cassava, potatoes, rice and beans and some meat or fish in a tasty stew-like sauce.

★ **Le Café Gourmand** BAKERY $
(Ave de France; cakes around BFr3500; ⊙7am-9pm Mon-Fri & Sun, 10.30am-9pm Sat) This might well be the most authentically French patisserie we've ever encountered in eastern Africa. The delicate little strawberry and lemon tarts are miniature works of art and the croissants have just the right amount of flaky crispness to them. It also serves great coffee as well as salads and crêpes (after 10.30am only).

Tropicana Net Cafe AMERICAN $
(Chaussée Prince Rwagasore; mains BFr5000-9000; ⊙6.30am-11pm) This trendy internet cafe does decent light meals (toasted sandwiches, burgers and steaks), salads and soups in air-conditioned, classic Starbucks-esque comfort.

★ **Le Jardin Gourmand** FRENCH, INTERNATIONAL $$
(☑079671257; Place de l'Independence, Galerie Alexander; mains BFr8500-16,000; ⊙7am-5pm Mon-Fri, 10.30am-5pm Sat) This tucked-away courtyard restaurant is a mainstay of the French expat scene. The menu ranges far

is a charming retreat from the rigours of life in Burundi. The only drawback is that on Friday and Saturday nights the noise produced by the neighbouring bars would wake the dead. The breakfast here is top-notch.

Hôtel Ubuntu Residence HOTEL $$
(☑22244064; www.ubunturesidence.com; Ave de la Plage; apt from US$100; P❋☎☀❀) Perfect for those staying a while, all the apartments here have small kitchens, and larger ones also have balconies. Most rooms face the garden, which has some resident crowned cranes and the excellent Kibiko Grill restaurant. For some reason this place also appeals to mosquitoes.

🛏 Lake Tanganyika

Hotel Club du Lac Tanganyika HOTEL $$$
(☑22250220; www.hotelclubdulac.com; r US$140-160, ste US$200-500; P❋☎☀❀) With a prime lakeside setting, the Hotel Club du Lac Tanganyika is the only four-star hotel in Bujumbura (and by extension, Burundi) with a huge swimming pool (nonguests BFr6000), two restaurants and numerous other facilities. Some rooms need a little sprucing up to be truly four-star material but, by and large, the hotel creates an excellent, resort-style ambience.

BURUNDI BUJUMBURA

> ### ⓘ SAFE TRAVEL IN BUJUMBURA
>
> It is generally safe to wander about on foot during the day, though the streets empty at night – it is imperative to use a taxi or private vehicle once the sun goes down. Street crime is fairly common in Bujumbura, and foreigners are especially vulnerable given their perceived wealth. It's best to leave your camera behind any time you go out as locals often don't care to be photographed and *les petits bandits* have sticky fingers.

from Burundi (and France) and takes in curries, brochettes, pasta, steaks, salads and what some say are the nation's best burgers. It's French-run and at times feels like a little France (albeit a hot, sticky one with banana plants). The open-plan kitchen is a nice touch and the owner likes to busy herself checking her customers are all contented.

L'Hacienda FRENCH, INTERNATIONAL **$$**
(☑ 22256643; Blvd de l'Uprona; mains BFr14,000-17,000; ☺ 7am-11pm Mon-Sat) Funky art and garden fountains make this new Belgian-run restaurant a rising star among Buju's elite. The food is a mixture of French classics with tropical tints such as yam and manioc chips accompanying traditional French steak. If you're not hungry, it's a nice place to come for a drink.

Botanika FRENCH **$$$**
(☑ 22226792; Blvd de l'Uprona; mains BFr16,000; ☺ 7am-10pm; ☎) Located in the Hotel Botanika, this excellent restaurant offers delightful dining under the bougainvillea-coloured courtyard trestles. The food is a fusion of modern French and Moroccan with African accents and includes delights such as rabbit glazed in honey, and lamb tajines. Understandably popular with the French expat community.

Chez André FRENCH **$$$**
(Chaussée Prince Rwagasore; mains BFr14,00-17,000; ☺ 7am-11pm Mon-Sat; ℗) Housed in a huge villa on the eastern extreme of Chaussée Prince Rwagasore, this French-inspired institution is one of the best restaurants in the city, with a white-tablecloth atmosphere and old-fashioned French cuisine.

> ### ⓘ SATURDAY COMMUNITY WORK
>
> From 8am to 11am every Saturday the country comes to a grinding halt. The reason? *Ibikorwa rusangi* – a time for obligatory community work. During these hours the populace is required to lend a hand on community projects for the greater good of their country. Shops, taxis, buses and restaurants are closed and instead rubbish is gathered, grass cut and drains dug. One of the few exceptions is the international buses, which have special dispensation to operate.

Kibiko Grill INTERNATIONAL **$$$**
(Ave de la Plage; mains BFr18,000-21,000, pizzas BFr15,000-17,000; ☺ 7am-10pm; ☎) Slap on some insect repellent and head here for tasty brochettes, excellent pizza (half-price on Tuesdays and Thursdays) and fresh fish straight from the lake. Kibiko Grill is inside the Hôtel Ubuntu Residence.

🍷 Drinking & Nightlife

Bujumbura's nightlife, which starts late, is legendary; even during the civil war when strict curfews were imposed the party went on and the good folk of Bujumbura were known to shimmy until their hips hurt during the nightly 'lock-ins'.

Traditionally, hangovers are nursed on the beach, especially at the cluster of bars around Saga Plage.

★ Bora Bora BAR
(Saga Plage; meals BFr10,000-18,000; ☺ 11am-11pm Mon-Fri, 9am-11pm Sat & Sun; ☎) This place, with its whitewashed weatherboards, palm-studded beach, blue-and-white nautical-inspired decor and a huge terrace-fronted villa, is where Burundi tries (quite succesfully) to be Ibiza. The big draw is the free pool and the chilled Caribbean vibe. On Saturday and Sunday nights the laid-back reggae and Cuban jazz give way to a mix of African and Western house and pop.

Havana Club BAR
(Balneo Lounge Bar; Blvd de l'Uprona; meals BFr9000-15,000) Out the front is the trendy Balneo Lounge Bar with comfy leather chairs, mood lighting and private nooks. The Havana Club itself is out back and is one of the city's most popular nightspots, drawing a mixed crowd of locals and internationals. The party starts late (at around 11pm) and goes until sunrise.

🛍 Shopping

La Legumiere HANDICRAFTS
(Chaussée Prince Rwagasore) If you're looking for souvenirs you could try this small shop, which stocks masks, spears, woven baskets and wooden carvings.

ⓘ Information

EMERGENCY
The official emergency number for police is ☑ 17, though it's unlikely anyone will answer should you call. It's best to make contact with your em-

NATIONAL PARKS

Burundi isn't known for its wildlife viewing but the country has a trio of national parks that, after years of civil war and strife inflicted closure, have recently become more accessible to tourists. In all of the parks, tourist facilities remain basic and animals rather skittish and nervous around people, but for a fun and off-beat safari Burundi offers potential.

Parc National de la Rusizi This is the most accessible, and popular, national park, as Bujumbura is just 15km away. It's a wetland environment, and provides a habitat for hippos, sitatungas (aquatic antelopes) and a wide variety of birds. Tour companies and some top-end hotels in Bujumbura can organise half- or full-day safaris. These generally include a 1½-hour boat ride along the park's river channels. The Hotel Club du Lac Tanganyika (p541) is probably the easiest hotel to go through. It charges US$100 for one person and US$20 for each extra person.

Parc National de la Kibira The largest rainforest in Burundi is contiguous with Nyungwe Forest National Park in Rwanda, and is believed to still be home to hundreds of colobus monkeys. There are also a number of chimpanzees present (although they're very hard to see). Access to the park is via the northern town of Kayanza (which has several places to stay of reasonable standard), but the park itself is fairly uncharted and you would do well to organise a visit through a tour agency.

Parc National de la Ruvubu In the east of the country, Parc National de la Ruvubu is the largest and least visited national park in Burundi, although the recent creation of some camping areas in the park might lead to higher visitor numbers. It certainly has potential as a great park with its grasslands and riverine forests providing a home to waterbuck, buffalo, leopard and lots of hippos as well as over 400 bird species.

bassy in the event of an emergency. If your country doesn't have an embassy in Burundi, then the French or Belgian embassies are your best bets.
Police (☏222223777) Direct line to the police, but don't expect much help from them.

INTERNET ACCESS
Bujumbura has a healthy sprinkling of internet cafes and provided there isn't a power outage, you'll have no trouble getting a good connection. Many cafes offer free wi-fi as do pretty much all but the absolute cheapest, grottiest hotels.
Tropicana Net Cafe (Chaussée Prince Rwagasore; per hr BFr3000; ☉6.30am-11pm) The swankiest internet cafe in town – it's a cafe, too.

MEDICAL SERVICES
In the event of a medical emergency, it is best to get out of Burundi to somewhere with first-class medical facilities, such as Nairobi in Kenya.

MONEY
Banque du Crédit de Bujumbura (Rue Science) Offers credit-card cash advances.
CRDB (Chaussée Prince Rwagasore) The ATM at this central bank is probably the best behaved when it comes to accepting foreign Visa cards.
Interbank Burundi (Blvd de l'Uprona) Has several branches around town and represents Western Union if you need an urgent transfer.

POST
Main Post Office (cnr Blvd Lumumba & Ave du Commerce; ☉8am-noon & 2-4pm Mon-Fri, 8-11am Sat)

TOURIST INFORMATION
Office National du Tourisme (☏22222023; www.burundi-tourism.com; Ave des Euphorbes; ☉7.30am-noon & 2-4pm Mon-Fri) Not many tourists in Burundi equals not much information in the tourist office.

☷ Getting There & Away
International buses and minibuses leave from the Siyoni bus station at the Buyenzi Market, which is 2km north of the city centre, while those bound for Gitega leave from the Gare du Nord bus station, which is 3km north of the city centre.

☷ Getting Around
Taxi fares range from BFr1000 for short hops in the centre to BFr6000 out to the beaches and BFr5000 to the bus stations. A taxi to the airport costs BFr12,000. *Moto-taxis* (motorcycle taxis) are banned from the city centre and environs and so are of little use to most tourists.

Minibuses to Gatumba can drop you off at Saga Beach (BFr350). These, along with minibuses to all places around Bujumbura (including Siyoni and Gare du Nord bus stations where the long-distance buses leave from), can be caught at the Central Ville bus station at Bujumbura's Central Market.

AROUND BUJUMBURA

As Burundi is so small, it is feasible to visit these sights during the day and return to Bujumbura before nightfall. However, most towns have some form of basic accommodation so if you want to prolong your enjoyment of the stunning Burundian countryside then it's perfectly possible, and safe, to overnight close to any of these attractions.

Source du Nil

Source du Nil SPRING
(Source of the Nile; admission BFr5000) It is not quite as obvious and impressive as Jinja in Uganda, but this insignificant-looking little spring at Kasumo, 115km southeast of Bujumbura, may well be the southernmost Source du Nil. In a nice touch, a stone pyramid marks the site, but unless you have your own transport it is almost impossible to reach. If you fancy a swim there are some **hot springs** a further 10km south.

Gitega

Gitega is the second-largest town in Burundi, which makes it more a village than a town. It's a worthy day trip from Bujumbura and there are a selection of reasonable places to stay.

Minibuses (BFr5000) and shared taxis (BFr7000) from Bujumbura's Gare du Nord bus station make the run to Gitega throughout the day (two hours). Once in Gitega, the museum is a short walk or BFr500 bicycle-taxi hop out of town.

◉ Sights

Musée National de Gitega MUSEUM
The Musée National de Gitega, although unlikely to enthral you, is the best museum Burundi has to offer. The one-room hall has a dusty collection of traditional household items including cow-horn snuffboxes, bark clothing, medicinal instruments and jewellery. There are also some interesting photos including our favourite, an 1896 shot of Bujumbura when the capital was little more than a few tents and a tree.

Chutes de la Karera

Chutes de la Karera WATERFALL
(admission incl guide BFr5000, vehicle BFr1000) The Chutes de la Karera is the collective name for the four beautiful waterfalls near Rutana. The prettiest is the cascade **Nyakai I** where you park your car. Upstream from this is the smallest of the four falls, **Nyakai II**, an ideal spot for an impromptu shower. This watercourse is joined by that of **Mwaro Falls** before creating the namesake and tallest waterfall in the area, **Karera Falls**.

As you would expect, the falls are at their best during the wet season (especially from October to January). The falls are 64km south of Gitega, but as there's no public transport, you'll have to charter a vehicle in Bujumbura to get here.

UNDERSTAND BURUNDI

History

A Fragile Independence

Burundi, like Rwanda, was colonised first by Germany and then later by Belgium, and like its northern neighbour, the Europeans played on ethnic differences to divide and conquer the population. Power was traditionally concentrated in the hands of the minority Tutsi, though Hutus began to challenge the concentration of power following independence in 1962.

In the 1964 elections, Tutsi leader Mwami Mwambutsa refused to appoint a Hutu prime minister, even though Hutu candidates attracted the majority of votes. Hutu frustration soon boiled over, and Hutu military officers and political figures staged an attempted coup. Although it failed, Mwambutsa was exiled to Switzerland, and replaced by a Tutsi military junta.

A wholesale purge of Hutu from the army and bureaucracy followed, and in 1972 another large-scale Hutu revolt resulted in more than 1000 Tutsi being killed. The Tutsi military junta responded with the selective genocide of elite Hutu; after just three months, 200,000 Hutu had been killed and another 100,000 had fled into neighbouring countries.

In 1976, Jean-Baptiste Bagaza came to power in a bloodless coup, and three years later he formed the Union pour le Progrès

National (Uprona). His so-called democratisation program was largely considered to be a failure, and in 1987 his cousin Major Pierre Buyoya toppled him in another coup.

The new regime attempted to address the causes of intertribal tensions by gradually bringing Hutu representatives back into positions of power. However, there was a renewed outbreak of intertribal violence in northern Burundi during the summer of 1988; thousands were massacred and many more fled into neighbouring Rwanda.

A Bloody Civil War

Buyoya finally bowed to international pressure, and multiparty elections were held in June 1993. These brought a Hutu-dominated government to power, led by Melchior Ndadaye, himself a Hutu. However, a dissident army faction, led by a Tutsi, Colonel Sylvestre Ningaba, staged yet another coup in late October the same year, and assassinated president Ndadaye. The coup eventually failed, though thousands were massacred in intertribal fighting, and almost half a million refugees fled across the border into Rwanda.

In April 1994, Cyprien Ntaryamira, the new Hutu president, was killed in the same plane crash that killed Rwanda's president Juvenal Habyarimana and ignited the subsequent genocide over there. In Burundi, Sylvestre Ntibantunganya was immediately appointed interim president, though both Hutu militias and the Tutsi-dominated army went on the offensive. No war was actually declared, but at least 100,000 people were killed in clashes between mid-1994 and mid-1996.

In July 1996 former president Major Pierre Buyoya again carried out a successful coup, and took over as the country's president with the support of the army. However, intertribal fighting continued between Hutu rebels and the Tutsi-dominated government and Tutsi militia. Hundreds of thousands of political opponents, mostly Hutus, were herded into 'regroupment camps', and bombings, murders and other horrific activities continued throughout the country.

A Fragile Peace

At the end of 2002, the Forces for the Defence of Democracy (FDD), the largest rebel group, signed a peace deal. In April 2003, prominent Hutu Domitien Ndayizeye succeeded Buyoya as president, and a road-map to elections was hammered out.

In 2004, the UN began operations in Burundi, sending more than 5000 troops to enforce the peace. Parliamentary elections were successfully held in 2005, and the former rebels, the FDD, emerged victorious. Pierre Nkurunziza, leader of the FDD, was sworn in as president in August. The 2010 elections were marred by violence and allegations of fraud and corruption. Despite international observers recognising the local elections as mainly free and fair, a growing mistrust between the incumbent's commitments to democracy saw all opposition withdraw their candidacy and Nkurunziza was re-elected unopposed.

Although there have been periods of tension and occasional violence the peace has, by and large, held, and development has started in Bujumbura and in many rural areas. Burundi remains politically very fragile and continues to sit near the bottom of most development and quality of life indexes, but it does appear that the country has turned a leaf and has a brighter future.

Culture

Like Rwanda to the north, Burundi has been torn apart by tribal animosities, and the conflict between Hutus and Tutsis has claimed hundreds of thousands of lives since independence. The Belgians masterminded the art of divide and rule, using the minority Tutsis to control the majority Hutus. Generations of intermarriage and cooperation went out the window, as the population was forced into choosing sides. The pattern continued into independence as the minority Tutsis clung to power to protect their privileges, and marginalised the Hutu majority. Only with the advent of peaceful elections does it look like this cycle may come to an end.

Economy

According to both the International Monetary Fund (IMF) and World Bank, Burundi is one of the four poorest countries in the world. Civil wars, corruption, landlocked geography, poor education, AIDS and a lack of economic freedom have all but economically crippled the country and today it is largely dependent on foreign aid.

Burundi's largest industry is agriculture and its largest source of revenue is coffee.

Environment

Taking up a mere 27,835 sq km, most of the country is made up of mountains that vanish into the horizon. Like its neighbour Rwanda this is a very densely populated country and most areas that can be farmed are being farmed. There are three national parks worthy of the name and surprisingly healthy animal populations within them.

SURVIVAL GUIDE

 Directory A–Z

ACCOMMODATION

The choice of accommodation is reasonable in Bujumbura. In other towns you can usually rely on finding one or two reasonably basic but clean guesthouses or hotels for a fair price.

EMBASSIES & CONSULATES

Foreign embassies in Bujumbura include the following:

Belgian Embassy (☑ 22226176; www.diplo-matie.be/bujumbura; Blvd de la Liberté)

DRC Embassy (☑ 22226916; Ave du RD Congo)

French Embassy (☑ 22203000; www.amba-france-bi.org; 60 Blvd de l'Uprona)

Rwandan Embassy (☑ 22228755; www.burundi.embassy.gov.rw; Ave du RD Congo)

Tanzanian Embassy (☑ 22248636; Ave de Gihungwe, Kabondo)

US Embassy (☑ 22207000; http://burundi.usembassy.gov; Ave des Etats-Unis)

MONEY

The unit of currency is the Burundi franc (BFr).

Many midrange and top-end hotels quote prices in US dollars but payment in local currency is always accepted; some of them accept credit cards but don't rely on this.

A few ATMs in Bujumbura accept foreign Visa cards (and occasionally MasterCard) but when travelling outside of the city take all the cash you might need with you. There are plenty of currency exchange bureaus (forex bureaus) around the Central Market and along Chaussée Prince Rwagasore. Travellers cheques are next to useless.

OPENING HOURS

Businesses tend to close for a couple of hours at lunch, from approximately noon to 2pm. Most eateries are open from 7am to about 9pm.

PUBLIC HOLIDAYS

Unity Day 5 February

Labour Day 1 May

Independence Day 1 July

Assumption 15 August

Victory of Uprona Day 18 September

Anniversary of Rwagasore's Assassination 13 October

Anniversary of Ndadaye's Assassination 21 October

All Saints' Day 1 November

SAFE TRAVEL

At long last Burundi's civil war has ended, and though the country is still somewhat unpredictable safety-wise, travelling here is far safer and easier than it was just a couple of years ago. You should, however, always check the latest safety warnings on your government's travel advice website before venturing here.

Unfortunately street crime is reasonably common in Bujumbura, and foreigners are an especially easy target, so be particularly aware of your surroundings, especially once the sun goes down. Most crime is of the non-violent pick-pocketing type.

TELEPHONE

There are no telephone area codes within the country. The country code for Burundi is ☑ 257.

VISAS

One-month tourist visas from the Burundian embassies in most neighbouring countries cost US$90, except for the consulate in Kigoma (Tanzania), which charges US$40 for a two-week visa. Visas are available on arrival at the international airport in Bujumbura. For those arriving overland who haven't obtained a visa from an embassy elsewhere, your only option is to get a three-day transit visa (US$40) at the border and have it extended in Bujumbura.

Visa extensions are fairly straightforward although at first glance it seems all hell is breaking loose when you spot the disorderly queues at the **Bureau de l'immigration** (near Police de l'Air et Frontières, Ngagara; ☉ 7.30am-noon & 2-4pm Mon-Fri). Besides your passport, you need a photocopy of your passport ID page and the page containing your border-entry stamp, a passport-sized photo and US$20. If you apply for a visa extension in the morning, you can collect your passport that afternoon or the following day.

ⓘ Getting There & Away

AIR

Bujumbura International Airport is located about 12km north of the city centre. Thanks to the protracted war, very few international airlines still serve Burundi, and Air Burundi itself, the national airline, has suspended operations and now functions only as a travel agency.

Kenya Airways (☎ 22223542; www.kenya
-airways.com; Blvd Lumumba, Bujumbura) Hub:
Nairobi.

RwandAir (www.rwandair.com; Ave du Commerce, Bujumbura) Hub: Kigali.

LAND

Burundi shares land borders with the DRC,
Rwanda and Tanzania.

DRC

The main crossing between Burundi and the
DRC is at Gatumba on the road between Bujumbura and Uvira (the DRC), about 15km west of
the capital. There's very little onward transport
to Bukavu (the DRC). It would be wiser to stay
on the Burundi side of the border and travel to
Cyangugu in Rwanda and cross to Bukavu from
there. Whichever way you do it, be sure to check
the security situation in the DRC first.

Rwanda

The main crossing point is between Kayanza
(Burundi) and Huye (also known as Butare, in
Rwanda) on the main road linking Bujumbura
and Kigali. The quickest option for travel between Bujumbura and Kigali is to use one of
the scheduled bus services listed following (six
hours, BFr13,000), which pass through Huye
(four hours, BFr13,000). Buses depart hourly
from 6am to 1pm from the Siyoni bus station,
although some have booking offices in the centre
of town.

Horizon Coaches (Siyoni bus station) Has
frequent services to Kigali.

Volcano Express (booking office Chaussée
Prince Rwagasore) The best, and most frequent, service to Rwanda. It has a booking
office in town but buses depart from the Siyoni
bus station.

Yahoo Car Express (booking office Chaussée
Prince Rwagasore) A couple of buses a day to
Rwanda (Kigali and Huye).

Tanzania

For Kobero, the trip is done in stages via Ngara
(Tanzania). There are daily buses between
Mwanza (Tanzania) and Ngara, from where there
is onward transport to the border. From Kigoma
(Tanzania), take a bus to Nyakanazi (Tanzania)
and get onward transport to Ngara from there.

For the Manyovu crossing, there is a daily bus
operated by Hamza Transport between Kigoma
and Bujumbura at 7am. The journey takes eight
hours and costs Tsh8000. Cargo boats sail
around three times a week between Kigoma and
Bujumbura and it might be possible to negotiate
a lift. The trip takes around 18 hours.

ⓘ Getting Around

AIR

There are no internal domestic flights in
Burundi.

MINIBUS & SHARED TAXI

Travelling around the countryside is not as
dangerous as it once was, though things change
quickly (for better or for worse) in this part of
the world.

As in Rwanda, most major roads in Burundi are
sealed. Public transport mostly consists of modern Japanese minibuses, which are cheaper than
shared taxis and not overcrowded. Destinations
are displayed in the front window, and minibuses
depart when full. You can usually find a minibus
or shared taxi heading in your direction any day
between early morning and early afternoon at
the *gare routière* (bus station) in any town.

Understand
East Africa

East Africa Today

All East African countries have been independent for over 50 years. In what state do we find them? A collection of stable countries that offers hope to the rest of the continent? Or a region perpetually on the brink of crisis? Which state will triumph remains the region's burning question. Beyond that, the spectre of terrorism remains in Kenya, Uganda and Burundi due to their involvement in an African Union force trying to bring peace to Somalia.

Best on Film

Out of Africa (1985) Caused a generation to dream of East Africa.
People of the Forest – The Chimps of Gombe (1988) Documentary following a chimpanzee family.
Echo of the Elephants (1993) Elephants of Amboseli National Park.
Hotel Rwanda (2004) and **Shooting Dogs in Rwanda** (2005) Two powerful stories from the Rwandan genocide.
Last King of Scotland (2006) Uganda under Idi Amin.
The Great Rift (2010) BBC natural history documentary about the Rift Valley.

Best in Print

Out of Africa (Karen Blixen; Isak Dinesen, pseud; 1937) The definitive account of colonial Kenya.
The Tree Where Man Was Born (Peter Matthiessen; 1972) Lyrical account of East Africa's people, wildlife and landscapes.
We Wish to Inform You That Tomorrow We Will Be Killed with Our Families (Philip Gourevitch; 1998) Searing study of Rwanda's 1994 genocide.
No Man's Land (George Monbiot; 1994) The modern struggle of the region's nomadic tribes.
Petals of Blood (Ngũgĩ wa Thiong'o; 1977) Perhaps East Africa's finest novel.

Ethnic & Political Tensions

If there's one thing that could darken East Africa's future, it's ethnic tension and the role it plays in politics. In so many parts of East Africa – Tanzania is a notable exception – the first question on locals' minds upon meeting a fellow countryman or countrywoman is this: from which tribe do you come? The question lay at the heart of what happened in Burundi in 1993, in Rwanda in 1994 and in Kenya in 2007.

For all the progress since Kenya erupted into violence after the 2007 elections – in this regard, the 2010 constitution was a huge step forward – the politics of ethnicity and its inextricable link to political patronage continue to hold the country back. In Burundi and Rwanda, ethnic identity remains the great subtext to everything that happens in both countries. Even in Uganda, a sense of grievance simmers below the surface. Perhaps everyone should take a leaf out of Tanzania's playbook – despite having more than 120 tribal groups, ethnic conflict is extremely rare. Indeed, that most identify themselves as Tanzanian first and only later by their ethnic group is one of the region's most enduring nation-building success stories.

Environmental Struggles

East Africa stands on the frontline of some of the most urgent environmental issues of our time – deforestation, land degradation and threats to endangered species are three serious issues among many. At one level, Kenya's private and community sectors are leading the way in finding solutions. Building on the country's impressive public portfolio of national parks and other protected areas while at the same time recognising their limitations, private and community landowners are building revolutionary partnerships between wildlife conservation, community development and tourism. It's one of the most exciting advances to take hold in the area in a generation and has already begun to spread beyond into Laikipia and the northern Kenyan heartland.

But it's not all good news. South of the border, in Tanzania, the national government has two of northern Tanzania's most important attractions in its sights. At remote Lake Natron, the government continues to seek investment in a soda ash mine that, conservationists argue, could threaten one of the Rift Valley's most significant flamingo breeding grounds. Just as worryingly, the government has announced plans to appeal against a decision by a regional East African court that forbade the government from building a road across the Serengeti. Both promise to be bitter battles.

Hope for the Future

When you look around East Africa today, there is much to admire. Yes, politics here is a robust business and a sense of crisis seems never far away. But by any measure East Africa is one of the more stable and increasingly prosperous corners of Africa. Rwanda has, in less than a generation, built a new nation. Next door, Burundi has a long way to go but the peace that currently prevails is progress indeed. Uganda, like Rwanda, has forged a confident personality in the decades following brutal civil war and, also like Rwanda, it has taken a strong leader to do it – where both countries go after Messrs Museveni and Kagame leave the stage is one of the region's more interesting questions. For all its ethnic tensions, Kenya, too, has pulled back from the brink after the violence of 2007 – it doesn't work perfectly but which country does? And then there's Tanzania, that beacon of stability.

Zoom in a little closer and you'll also come across many encouraging stories, especially at the village and community level. It is here where investment in education and health, successful microlending schemes, income from cultural tourism programs and other ventures, combined with East Africans' renowned resilience, ingenuity and humour, are turning prospects for the future from bleak to bright.

POPULATION: **150.3 MILLION**

AREA: **1,816,753 SQ KM**

HIGHEST POINT: **MT KILIMANJARO (5896M)**

HIGHEST GDP PER CAPITA: **KENYA (US$1800)**

LOWEST GDP PER CAPITA: **BURUNDI (US$600)**

belief systems
(% of population)

64 Christian

18 Muslim

16 Indigenous Beliefs

2 Other/None

if East Africa were 100 people

80 would live in a rural area
20 would live in an urban area

population per sq km

TANZANIA KENYA UGANDA

≈ 45 people

History

East Africa has one of the longest documented human histories of any region in the world. Home to some of humankind's earliest ancestors, it later became one of the great crossroads of the world, a constant ebb and flow of peoples drawn by trade and migration, by exploration and exploitation. In more recent times, the region was profoundly marked by the struggles against colonialism and for independence, struggles which continue to shape the region's story to this day.

The Dawn of Humankind

'...Two days' beyond, there lies the...last market-town of the continent of Azania, which is called Rhapta... in which there is ivory in great quantity, and tortoise-shell...'
(Periplus of the Erythraean Sea)

Ancient hominid (human-like) skulls and footprints, some over three million years old, have been found at various sites in East Africa, including at Oldupai Gorge in Tanzania and Lake Turkana in Kenya. Although similarly ancient traces have also been found elsewhere on the continent, the East African section of the Great Rift Valley is popularly considered the 'cradle of humanity'.

By about one million years ago, these early ancestors had come to resemble modern humans, and had spread well beyond East Africa, including as far as Europe and Asia. Roughly 100,000 years ago, and possibly earlier, Homo sapiens – modern man – had arrived on the scene.

The earliest evidence of modern-day East Africans dates to around 10,000 years ago, when much of the region was home to Khoisan-speaking hunter-gatherer communities. On the western fringes of East Africa, including parts of the area that is now Rwanda and Burundi, there were also small populations of various so-called Pygmy groups.

The Great Migrations

Beginning between 3000 and 5000 years ago, a series of migrations began that were to indelibly shape the face of East Africa. Cushitic- and Nilotic-speaking peoples from the north and Bantu speakers from the west converged on the Khoisan and other peoples already in the area, creating over the centuries the rich tribal mosaic that is East Africa today.

The first to arrive were Cushitic-speaking farmers and cattle herders who made their way to the region from present-day Ethiopia, and settled

TIMELINE	c 25 million BC	c 3.7 million BC	c 100 BC
	Tectonic plates collide and East African plains buckle. Formation of the Great Rift Valley begins, as do changes that result ultimately in formation of Kilimanjaro and other volcanoes.	Fossils found at Lake Turkana (Kenya) and at Laetoli (Tanzania) show that hominid (human-like) creatures wandered the East African plains over three million years ago.	The first Bantu speakers arrive in the region, part of a series of great population migrations that continue to shape the face of modern-day East Africa.

both inland and along the coast. They moved mostly in small family groups, and brought with them traditions that are still practised by their descendents, including the Iraqw around Tanzania's Lake Manyara and the Gabbra and Rendille in northern Kenya.

The next major influx began around 1000 BC when Bantu-speaking peoples from West Africa's Niger Delta area began moving eastwards, arriving in East Africa around the 1st century BC. Thanks to their advanced agricultural skills and knowledge of ironworking and steel production – which gave them a great advantage in cultivating land and establishing settlements – these Bantu speakers were able to absorb many of the Cushitic and Khoisan speakers who were already in the region, as well as the Pygmy populations around the Great Lakes. Soon, they became East Africa's most populous ethnolinguistic family – a status which they continue to hold today.

A final wave of migration began somewhat later when smaller groups of Nilotic peoples began to arrive in East Africa from what is now South Sudan. This influx continued through to the 18th century, with the main movements taking place in the 15th and 16th centuries. Most of these Nilotic peoples – whose descendants include the present-day Maasai and Turkana – were pastoralists, and many settled in the less fertile areas of southern Kenya and northern Tanzania where their large herds would have sufficient grazing space.

Today the population diversity resulting from these migrations is one of the most fascinating aspects of travel in East Africa.

Monsoon Winds

As these migrations were taking place in the interior, coastal areas were being shaped by far different influences. Azania, as the East African coast was known to the ancient Greeks, was an important trading post as early as 400 BC, and had likely been inhabited even before then by small groups of Cushitic peoples, and by Bantu speakers. The *Periplus of the Erythraean Sea,* a navigator's guide written in the 1st century AD, mentions Raphta as the southernmost trading port. Although its location remains a mystery, it is believed to have been somewhere along the Kenyan or Tanzanian coast, possibly on the mainland opposite Manda or Paté Islands (north of Lamu), or further south near the Pangani or Rufiji estuaries.

Trade seems to have grown steadily throughout the early part of the first millennium. Permanent settlements were established as traders, first from the Mediterranean and later from Arabia and Persia, came ashore on the winds of the monsoon and began to intermix with the indigenous peoples, gradually giving rise to Swahili language and culture. The traders from Arabia also brought Islam, which by the 11th century had become entrenched.

Swahili Ruins

Kilwa Kisiwani (Tanzania)

Kaole Ruins (Tanzania)

Gede Ruins (Kenya)

Jumba la Mtwana (Kenya)

Takwa Ruins (Kenya)

Mnarani (Kenya)

Historical Unesco World Heritage Sites

Mijikenda Kaya (Kenya)

Kasubi Tombs (Uganda)

Lamu Old Town (Kenya)

Fort Jesus (Kenya)

Kondoa Rock-Art Sites (Tanzania)

Kilwa Kisiwani & Songo Mnara (Tanzania)

Stone Town (Zanzibar, Tanzania)

Kasubi Tombs (Uganda)

c 750–1200 AD	1331	15th Century	c 1400–1700
Monsoon winds push Arab trading ships to the East African coast and Swahili civilisation is born. Settlements are established at Lamu, Gede, Kilwa and elsewhere along the coast.	Moroccan traveller Ibn Battuta visits Kilwa (Tanzania) and finds a flourishing town of 10,000 to 20,000 residents, with a grand palace, mosque, inn and slave market.	The king of Malindi sends the Chinese emperor a giraffe. Vasco da Gama reaches East Africa en route to the Orient, stopping at Mombasa and Malindi before continuing to India.	In several waves, small bands of nomadic cattle herders migrate south from the Sudan into the Rift Valley – ancestors of the Maasai who today live in Kenya and Tanzania.

Between the 13th and 15th centuries these coastal settlements – including those at Shanga (on Paté Island), Gede, Lamu and Mombasa (all in present-day Kenya) and on the Zanzibar Archipelago and at Kilwa Kisiwani (both in Tanzania) – flourished, with trade in ivory, gold and other goods extending as far away as India and China.

Europeans & Arabs

The first European to reach East Africa was the intrepid Portuguese explorer Vasco da Gama, who arrived in 1498, en route to the Orient. Within three decades, the Portuguese had disrupted the old trading networks and subdued the entire coast, building forts at various places, including Kilwa and Mombasa. Portuguese control lasted until the early 18th century, when they were displaced by Arabs from Oman.

As the Omani Arabs solidified their foothold, they began to turn their sights westwards, developing powerful trade routes that stretched inland as far as Lake Tanganyika and Central Africa. Commerce grew at such a pace that in the 1840s, the Sultan of Oman moved his capital from Muscat to Zanzibar Island.

The slave trade also grew rapidly during this period, driven in part by demand from European plantation holders on the Indian Ocean islands of Réunion and Mauritius. Soon slave traders, including the notorious Tippu Tip, had established stations at Tabora (Tanzania) and other inland towns. By the mid-19th century, the Zanzibar Archipelago had become the largest slave entrepôt along the East African coast, with up to 50,000 slaves, abducted from as far away as Lake Tanganyika, passing through Zanzibar's market each year.

Colonial Control

In addition to reports of the horrors of the still-ongoing regional slave trade, tales of the attractions of East Africa also made their way back to Europe, and Western interests were piqued. In 1890 Germany and Great Britain signed an agreement defining 'spheres of influence' for themselves, which formally established a British protectorate over the Zanzibar Archipelago. Most of what is now mainland Tanzania, as well as Rwanda and Burundi, came under German control as German East Africa (later Tanganyika), while the British took Kenya and Uganda.

The 19th century was also the era of various European explorers, including Gustav Fischer (a German whose party was virtually annihilated by the Maasai at Hell's Gate on Lake Naivasha in 1882), Joseph Thomson (a Scot who reached Lake Victoria via the Rift Valley lakes and the Aberdare Highlands in 1883) and Count Teleki von Szek (an Austrian who explored the Lake Turkana region and Mt Kenya in 1887). Anglican bishop James Hannington set out in 1885 to establish a diocese in Ugan-

> Portuguese influence is still seen in East Africa's architecture, customs and language. The origin of the Swahili word *gereza* (jail), from Portuguese *igreja* (church), dates to the days when Portuguese forts contained both in the same compound.

1593	1850–70	1890	1899
The Portuguese construct the coral Fort Jesus in Mombasa. Accounts from the garrison at Mombasa record the first evidence of maize production in Africa.	Zanzibar's slave market becomes the largest in East Africa. According to some estimates, up to 50,000 slaves passed through its gates each year.	Britain and Germany create 'spheres of influence'. Zanzibar becomes a British 'protectorate'. After WWI the German area of Rwanda-Urundi (later to be Rwanda and Burundi) comes under Belgian control.	Nairobi is founded in an area of rivers, plains and swamps traditionally known by the Maasai as *uaso nairobi* (cold water). Residents had to carry guns to defend against wild animals.

SWAHILI

The word Swahili ('of the coast', from the Arabic word *sāhil*) refers both to the Swahili language, as well as to the Islamic culture of the peoples inhabiting the East African coast from Mogadishu (Somalia) in the north down to Mozambique in the south. Both language and culture are a rich mixture of Bantu, Arabic, Persian and Asian influences.

Although Swahili culture began to develop in the early part of the first millennium AD, it was not until the 18th century, with the ascendancy of the Omani Arabs on Zanzibar, that it came into its own. Swahili's role as a lingua franca was solidified as it spread throughout East and Central Africa along the great trade caravan routes. European missionaries and explorers soon adopted the language as their main means of communicating with locals. In the second half of the 19th century, missionaries, notably the German Johann Ludwig Krapf, also began applying the Roman alphabet. Prior to this, Swahili had been written exclusively in Arabic script.

da, but was killed when he reached the Nile. Other explorers included Burton and Speke, who were sent to Lake Tanganyika in 1858 by the Royal Geographical Society, and the famous Henry Morton Stanley and David Livingstone.

By the turn of the 20th century, Europeans had firmly established a presence in East Africa. Both the British and German colonial administrations were busy building railways and roads to open their colonies to commerce, establishing hospitals and schools, and encouraging the influx of Christian missionaries. Kenya's fertile and climatically favourable highlands proved eminently suitable for European farmers to colonise. In Tanganyika, by contrast, large areas were unable to support agriculture and were plagued by the tsetse fly, which made cattle grazing and dairy farming impossible.

Zamani: A Survey of East African History, edited by renowned Kenyan historian BA Ogot with JA Kieran, is a classic introduction to the region's precolonial and colonial history from an African perspective.

Independence

As the European presence in Africa solidified, discontent with colonial rule grew and demands for independence became more insistent. In the 1950s and early 1960s, the various nationalist movements coalesced and gained force across East Africa, culminating in the granting of independence to Tanzania (1961), Uganda, Rwanda and Burundi (all in 1962), and Kenya (1963). In Kenya, the path to independence was violent and protracted, with some of the underlying issues reflected in the country's current political difficulties; in Tanzania and Uganda the immediate pre-independence years were relatively peaceful, while in Rwanda and Burundi, long-existing tribal rivalries were a major issue – the effects of which are still being felt today.

1905–07	1952	1961–63	1978–79
In the Matumbi Hills near Kilwa (Tanzania), the mystic Kinjikitile stirs African labourers to rise up against their German overlords in what became known as the Maji Maji rebellion.	The Mau Mau rebellion begins as a protest against colonial land-grabbing in Kikuyu lands. By the time it was suppressed, thousands of Kikuyu had been killed or put into detention camps.	Following a period of increasing discontent with colonial rule, the countries of East Africa gain independence, with Tanganyika (now Tanzania) leading the way in December 1961.	Ugandan dictator Idi Amin invades Tanzania, burning villages along the Kagera River believed to harbour Ugandan rebels. Tanzania's army marches to Kampala to topple Amin and restore Milton Obote to power.

THE SLAVE TRADE

Slavery has been practised in Africa throughout recorded history, but its greatest expansion in East Africa came with the rise of Islam, which prohibits the enslavement of Muslims. Demands of European plantation holders on Réunion and Mauritius were another catalyst, particularly during the late 18th century.

Initially, slaves were taken from coastal regions and shipped to Arabia, Persia and the Indian Ocean islands. Kilwa Kisiwani, off Tanzania's southern coast, was a major export gateway. As demand increased, traders made their way inland, and during the 18th and 19th centuries, slaves were being brought from as far away as Malawi and the Congo. By the 19th century, with the rise of the Omani Arabs, Zanzibar had eclipsed Kilwa Kisiwani as East Africa's major slave-trading depot. According to some estimates, by the 1860s from 10,000 to as many as 50,000 slaves were passing through Zanzibar's market each year. Overall, close to 600,000 slaves were sold through Zanzibar between 1830 and 1873, when a treaty with Britain paved the way for the trade's ultimate halt in the region in the early 20th century.

As well as the human horrors, the slave trade caused major social upheavals. In the south of present-day Tanzania, it fanned up inter-clan warfare as ruthless entrepreneurs raided neighbouring tribes for slaves. In other areas, it promoted increased social stratification and altered settlement patterns. Some tribes began to build fortified settlements encircled by trenches, while others concentrated their populations in towns as self-defence. Another major societal change was the gradual shift in the nature of chieftaincy from a position based on religion to one resting on military power or wealth.

The slave trade also served as an impetus for European missionary activity in East Africa, prompting the establishment of the first mission stations and missionary penetration of the interior. A tireless campaigner against the horrors of slavery was Scottish missionary-explorer David Livingstone (1813–74), whose efforts, combined with the attention attracted by his funeral, were an important influence in mobilising British initiatives to halt human trafficking in the region. For more on the British campaign to end slavery, read Adam Hochschild's *Bury the Chains*.

By the time slavery was abolished, between eight and 20 million Africans had been sold into slavery.

Kenya

In Kenya, the European influx increased rapidly during the first half of the 20th century, so that by the 1950s there were about 80,000 settlers in the country. Much of the land that was expropriated for their farms came from the homelands of the Kikuyu people. The Kikuyu responded by forming an opposition political association in 1920, and by instigating the Mau Mau rebellion in the 1950s, which marked a major turning point in Kenyan politics and ultimately led the way to independence.

1984	1994	7 August 1998	2004
Kenya reports its first AIDS case. Within a decade, an estimated 800,000 people are infected with HIV with more than five million now living with HIV/AIDS in East Africa.	The presidents of Rwanda and Burundi are killed when their plane is shot down during landing, unleashing the Rwandan genocide, leaving more than one million dead in its wake.	Within minutes of each another, Al-Qaeda truck bombs explode at the American embassies in Nairobi and Dar es Salaam, killing and injuring dozens.	Uganda's aggressive anti-AIDS campaign begins to show results, as adult prevalence rates fall to about 6%, down from about 18% around a decade earlier.

Tanganyika (Tanzania)

In Tanganyika, the unpopular German administration continued until the end of WWI, when the League of Nations mandated the area to the British, and Rwanda and Burundi to the Belgians. British rule was equally unpopular, with the Brits neglecting development of Tanganyika in favour of the more lucrative and fertile options available in Kenya and Uganda. Political consciousness soon began to coalesce in the form of farmers' unions and cooperatives through which popular demands were expressed. By the mid-20th century, there were over 400 such cooperatives, which soon joined to form the Tanganyika Africa Association (TAA), a lobbying group for the nationalist cause based in Dar es Salaam.

Uganda

In Uganda, the British tended to favour the recruitment of the powerful Buganda people for the civil service. Members of other tribes, unable to acquire responsible jobs in the colonial administration or to make inroads into the Buganda-dominated commercial sector, were forced to seek other ways of joining the mainstream. The Acholi and Lango, for example, chose the army and became the tribal majority in the military. As resentment grew, the seeds were planted for the intertribal conflicts that were to tear Uganda apart following independence.

Rwanda & Burundi

In Rwanda and Burundi, the period of colonial rule was characterised by increasing power and privilege of the Tutsi. The Belgians' administrators found it convenient to rule indirectly through Tutsi chiefs and their princes, and the Tutsi had a monopoly on the missionary-run educational system. As a result, long-existing tensions between the Tutsi and Hutu were exacerbated, igniting the spark that was later to explode in the 1993 Burundi and 1994 Rwanda genocides.

Modern Historical Sites

Kigali Memorial Centre (Kigali, Rwanda)

National Museum (Dar es Salaam, Tanzania)

National Museum (Nairobi, Kenya)

Uganda Museum (Kampala, Uganda)

Mwalimu Julius K Nyerere Museum (Butiama, Tanzania)

HISTORY INDEPENDENCE

Dec 2007–Jan 2008	**2011**	**21 September 2013**	**2014**
Kenya is wracked by post-election violence as hundreds are killed and thousands displaced from their homes in the Rift Valley and central areas.	After attacks blamed on Somalia's al-Shabab militia, Kenya invades Somalia to try and drive the Islamists from power. The African Union, including soldiers from Uganda and Burundi, later take over the mission.	Somalia's militant al-Shabab group attacks Nairobi's upmarket West Gate Shopping Mall. The siege lasts for days and ends with 67 people dead, including the attackers.	East Africa's regional court rules against the Tanzanian government's attempts to build a road across Serengeti National Park. Tanzania later launches an appeal against the ruling.

Life in East Africa

Traditional cultures hold East Africa together (and sometimes tear it apart). Feeding into these traditions are all manner of affiliations, and respect for one's elders, firmly held religious beliefs, traditional gender roles, *ujamaa* (familyhood) and even national identity all play their part in helping East Africans make sense of their worlds. Watching how these traditions equip East Africans to deal with the assault of modernity is one of the more interesting elements of travelling in the region.

Daily Life & Customs

Hospitality

Former Kenyan president Jomo Kenyatta once argued that female genital mutilation (FGM) was such an integral part of initiation rites and Kikuyu identity that its abolition would destroy the tribal system.

It's a wild place, the East African bush, and hospitality counts because it has to. You never know if you'll soon be the one on the asking end – whether for a cup of water, a meal or a roof over your head for the night – and strangers are traditionally welcomed as family. In a region where it is commonplace for a 10km walk to get you to the nearest water source, the nearest medical clinic or the nearest primary school, time takes on an altogether different dimension. Daily rhythms are determined by the sun and the seasons, and arriving is the most important thing, not when or how. *Nitafika* (I will arrive). *Safiri salama* (Travel in peace). *Umefika* (You have arrived). *Karibu* (Welcome). Additional words are not necessary.

Support Networks

No monthly social security cheques arrive in the mail in East Africa, so community life is essential – for support in times of sickness and for the ageing, as well as in ensuring a proper upbringing for the young people. Mourning is a community affair, as is celebrating. It would be unheard of not to attend the funeral of your mother's second cousin once removed, just as it would be equally unheard of to miss celebrating the wedding of your father's stepbrother's neighbour. Salaried jobs are scarce, and if you're one of the lucky few to have found one, it's expected that you'll share your good fortune with the extended family. Throughout East African society, 'I' and 'me' are very much out, while 'our' and 'we' are in and always have been.

Extended family has traditionally provided a critical layer of support for East Africans. In recent decades, extended family has become increasingly important as parents migrate to cities for lucrative work, leaving their children to be cared for by grandparents, aunts and uncles. This fluid system has also enabled many to deal with the devastation wrought by the HIV/AIDS epidemic.

In all aspects of daily life, emphasis is on the necessary. If you do attend that funeral, forget bringing flowers; a bag of rice, or money, would be a more appropriate way of showing your solidarity with the bereaved.

Social Hierarchies

At all levels of society, invisible social hierarchies lend life a sense of order. Age-based groups play a central role among many tribes, and the elderly and those in positions of authority are respected. Men rule the roost in the working world and, at least symbolically, in the family as well. Although women arguably form the backbone of the economy throughout the region – with most juggling child-rearing plus work on the family farm or in an office – they are frequently marginalised when it comes to education and politics. Some positive contrasts to this situation are found in Kenya, which is notable for its abundance of non-government organisations, many headed by women, and in Uganda, where women play prominent roles in educational and literary circles.

Ways of Belonging

With the exception of Tanzania, where local chieftaincies were abolished following independence, tribal identity and structures are strong. In fact, stay long enough and you'll quickly see the differences from country to country. Tanzanians, for example, almost always identify themselves as Tanzanian first, with other layers of identity (tribe, region etc) a distant second. The result is, on the surface at least, a remarkably harmonious society.

In Kenya, on the other hand, the situation is reversed and while most are proud to be Kenyan, national identity is only one (perhaps even subordinate) way among many in which Kenyans understand their world. Family ties, the pull of religion and gender roles are all prominent issues in the public domain and in the daily lives of ordinary people. Perhaps even above all of these, the tribe remains an important aspect of a Kenyan's identity: upon meeting a fellow Kenyan, the first question on anyone's mind is, 'What tribe do you come from?'

The importance of tribe (or the political manipulation of tribal affiliations) has had disastrous consequences, as seen in the Burundian genocide in 1993, the Rwandan genocide in 1994 and in the 2007 post-election violence in Kenya. All three countries have since sought to overcome these divisions. Both Burundi and Rwanda have undergone significant programs of nation-building in which, for the most part, national identity is promoted as more important than tribal identity. In Kenya the 2010 constitution recognises the rights of ethnic minorities and even calls for the cabinet to 'reflect the regional and ethnic diversity of the people of Kenya'.

Multicultural Melting Pot

Almost since the dawn of humankind, outsiders have been arriving in East Africa and have been assimilated into its seething, simmering and endlessly fascinating cultural melting pot. From the Bantu-, Nilotic- and Cushitic-speaking groups that made their way to the region during the early migrations, to Arab and Asian traders, and to colonial-era Europeans,

> Negotiations of bride price still play a major role in marriages in the region. Although cash is becoming an increasingly common replacement, cattle are still coveted in many areas.

HIV/AIDS IN EAST AFRICA

Together with malaria, AIDS is the leading cause of death in sub-Saharan Africa, and East Africa is no exception. According to the World Health Organisation (WHO), in a ranking of countries with the most inhabitants living with HIV/AIDS, Kenya ranked fourth in the world (1.65 million people), Uganda was sixth (almost 1.55 million) and Tanzania came in seventh (1.47 million). By another measure, 7.2% of Ugandans, 6.1% of Kenyans and 5.1% of Tanzanians have HIV/AIDS. In Uganda alone, there are nearly one million AIDS orphans under 17 years of age.

Encouragingly, AIDS awareness has improved in the region; East African governments now discuss the situation openly, and you'll notice AIDS-related billboards in Dar es Salaam, Nairobi, Kampala and elsewhere. Yet at the grassroots level in many areas, the stigma remains and, especially away from urban centres, real discussion remains limited. AIDS-related deaths are often kept quiet, with tuberculosis used euphemistically as a socially acceptable catch-all diagnosis. In one study in Kenya, over half of the women surveyed who had acquired HIV hadn't told their partners because they feared being beaten or abandoned.

a long stream of migrants have left their footprints. Today the region's modern face reflects this rich fusion of influences, with 300-plus tribal groups, as well as small but economically significant pockets of Asians, Arabs and Europeans all rubbing shoulders.

Kenya's first permanent settlers from the Indian subcontinent were indentured workers, brought here from Gujarat and the Punjab by the British to build the Uganda Railway. After the railway was finished, the British allowed many workers to stay and start up businesses, and hundreds of *dukas* (small shops) were set up across the country. After WWII, the Indian community came to control large sectors of the East African economy. However, few gave their active support to the black nationalist movements in the run-up to independence, despite being urged to do so by India's prime minister, and many were hesitant to accept local citizenship after independence. This earned the widespread distrust of the African community and the African response reached a lowpoint with the anti-Asian pogroms that swept Uganda during the reign of Idi Amin.

> In Swahili-speaking areas of East Africa, it's common for a woman to drop her own name, and become known as *Mama* followed by the name of her oldest son (or daughter, if she has no sons).

Sports

Despite football-crazy fans, East African countries remain the great underachievers of African football. No East African team has ever won the African Cup of Nations and nor has any of the five countries ever qualified for the World Cup Finals. As of late 2014, Uganda was the highest-ranked East African team (84th out of 208 in the FIFA World Rankings), followed by Rwanda (95th), Tanzania (110th), Kenya (116th) and Burundi (128th).

On the international sports stage, Kenya's athletes have won gold medals in long-distance running events at every Olympics since 1968, save for 1976 and 1980 when Kenya did not participate.

The East African Safari Rally (www.eastafricansafarirally.com), which has been held annually since 1953, passes through Kenya, Uganda and

---

FEMALE GENITAL MUTILATION

Female genital mutilation (FGM), often euphemistically referred to as female circumcision, is the partial or total removal of the female external genitalia. FGM is usually carried out for reasons of cultural or gender identity, and it is entrenched in tribal life in some areas. Yet among the very real risks of the procedure are infection, shock and haemorrhage, as well as lifelong complications and pain with menstruation, urination, intercourse and childbirth. For women who have had infibulation – in which all or part of the external genitalia are removed, and the vaginal opening then narrowed and stitched together – unassisted childbirth is impossible, and many women and children die as a consequence.

Since the mid-1990s there have been major efforts to reduce the incidence of the practice, with slow but real progress. In both Kenya and Tanzania, FGM has been declared illegal with prison sentences for violators, although the number of prosecutions is miniscule and the practice continues in many areas. An estimated 27% of Kenyan women (including 98% in Northeastern Province, near Somalia, but just 1% in Western Province) have undergone FGM: it is particularly prevalent among the Kisii and Maasai. In Tanzania, the figures are estimated at around 15% and the practice is particularly common in the north.

In Uganda, FGM was finally banned by the government in 2009, with penalties of 10 years' imprisonment for violators (or life, if the girl dies), although enforcement remains a concern. The main area where FGM is still practised is in northeastern Uganda, near the border with Kenya, with the national prevalence rate at around 5%.

Several nongovernmental women's organisations, in Kenya in particular, have taken a leading role in bringing FGM to the forefront of media discussion. There is also a growing movement towards alternative rites that offer the chance to maintain traditions while minimising the health complications, such as the practice of *ntanira na mugambo* (circumcision through words).

Tanzania along public roadways, and attracts an international collection of drivers with their vintage (pre-1971) automobiles.

The epic Tour d'Afrique (www.tourdafrique.com) bicycle race passes through East Africa (Kenya and Tanzania) en route between Cairo (Egypt) and Cape Town (South Africa).

Bao

It's not exactly sport, but *bao* (also known as *kombe, mweso* and various other names) is one of East Africa's favourite pastimes. It's especially popular on the Zanzibar Archipelago and elsewhere along the coast, where you'll see men in their *kanzu* (white robe-like outer garment) and *kofia* (hat) huddled around a board watching two opponents play. The rules vary somewhat from place to place, but the game always involves trying to capture the pebbles or seeds of your opponent, which are set out on a board with rows of small hollows. Anything can substitute for a board, from finely carved wood to a flattened area of sand on the beach.

Religion

Christianity and Islam dominate spiritual life in East Africa, but there are also a sizeable number of adherents of traditional religions, as well as small communities of Hindus, Sikhs and Jains.

Christians are in the majority in Rwanda (88.9% of the population), Burundi (86%), Uganda (83.9%) and Kenya (82.1%). In Tanzania, the country is split fairly evenly between Muslims (35%), those adhering to traditional religions (35%) and Christians (30%); 99% of Zanzibar's population is Muslim.

Christianity

The first Christian missionaries reached East Africa in the mid-19th century. Since then the region has been the site of extensive missionary activity, and today most of the major denominations are represented, including both Catholics and Protestants. In many areas, mission stations have been the major, and in some cases the only, channels for health care and education, with missions still sometimes providing the only schools and medical facilities in remote areas.

In addition to the main denominations, there is also an increasing number of home-grown African sects, especially in Kenya. Factors that are often cited for their growth include cultural resurgence, an ongoing struggle against neo-colonialism and the alienation felt by many jobseekers who migrate to urban centres far from their homes.

Church services throughout East Africa are invariably very colourful and packed to overflowing. Even if you can't understand the language, it's worth going to listen to the unaccompanied choral singing, which East Africans do with such beauty and harmony.

Islam

In 1984 archaeologists discovered a mosque's foundations in Lamu, Kenya, along with coins dating to AD 830, suggesting that Islam had a foothold on the East African coast as early as the 9th century, barely 100 years after the death of the Prophet Mohamed. It should be hardly surprising that Islam took hold so quickly in East Africa, given the region's trading connections with southern Arabia.

Further evidence suggests an Islamic presence in Zanzibar from at least the 11th century, while the famous traveller Ibn Batuta found that by the early 14th century, Islam was the dominant religion all along the East African coast as far as South Africa. These days, Islam here – in typical East African fashion – has developed in a considerably less dogmatic form than in other parts of the world.

Life Expectancy

Burundi –
59.55 years

Kenya –
63.52 years

Rwanda –
59.26 years

Tanzania –
61.24 years

Uganda –
54.46 years

The Tanzanian town of Mto wa Mbu, close to Lake Manyara National Park, is famous for being the only place in the country (perhaps aside from major cities) where all of Tanzania's 120 tribal groups are present.

CONDUCT IN EAST AFRICA

East Africa comfortably mixes a generally conservative outlook on life with a great deal of tolerance and openness towards foreigners. Following are a few tips to smooth the way.

➡ While most East Africans are likely to be too polite to tell you so directly, they'll be privately shaking their head about travellers not wearing enough clothing or sporting tatty clothes. Especially along the Muslim coast, cover up your shoulders and legs, and avoid plunging necklines and skin-tight fits.

➡ Pleasantries count. Even if you're just asking for directions, take time to greet the other person. Handshake etiquette is also worth learning, and best picked up by observation. In many areas, East Africans often continue holding hands for several minutes after meeting, or even throughout an entire conversation.

➡ Don't eat or pass things with the left hand.

➡ Respect authority; losing your patience or undermining an official's authority will get you nowhere, while deference and a good-natured demeanour will benefit most situations.

➡ Avoid criticising the government of your host country as well as offending locals with public nudity, open anger and public displays of affection (between people of the same or opposite sex).

➡ When visiting a rural area, seek out the chief or local elders to announce your presence, and ask permission before setting up a tent or wandering through a village – it will rarely be refused.

➡ Receive gifts with both hands, or with the right hand while touching the left hand to your right elbow. Giving a gift? Don't be surprised if the appreciation isn't expressed verbally.

Most East African Muslims are Sunnis, with a small minority of Shiites, primarily among the Asian community. The most influential of the various Shiite sects represented are the Ismailis, followers of the Aga Khan.

The five pillars of Islam that guide Muslims in their daily lives:

Haj (pilgrimage) It is the duty of every Muslim who is fit and can afford it to make the pilgrimage to Mecca at least once.

Sala (prayer; sometimes written *salat*) This is the obligation of prayer, done five times daily when muezzins call the faithful to pray, facing Mecca and ideally in a mosque.

Sawm (fasting) Ramadan commemorates the revelation of the Quran to Mohammed and is the month when Muslims fast from dawn to dusk.

Shahada (the profession of faith) 'There is no God but Allah, and Mohammed is his Prophet' is the fundamental tenet of Islam.

Zakat (alms) Giving to the poor is an essential part of Islamic social teaching.

Traditional Religions

The natural and spiritual worlds are part of the same continuum in East Africa, and mountain peaks, lakes, forests, certain trees and other natural features are viewed by many as dwellings of the supreme being or of the ancestors.

Most local traditional beliefs acknowledge the existence of a supreme deity. Many also hold that communication with this deity is possible through the intercession of the ancestors. The ancestors are thus accordingly honoured, and viewed as playing a strong role in protecting the tribe and family. Maintaining proper relations is essential for general wellbeing. However, among the Maasai, the Kikuyu and several other tribes, there is no tradition of ancestor worship, with the supreme deity (known as Ngai or Enkai) the sole focus of devotion.

Traditional medicine in East Africa is closely intertwined with traditional religion, with practitioners using divining implements, prayers, chanting and dance to facilitate communication with the spirit world.

Tribal Cultures

East Africa has a rich mosaic of tribal cultures, with over 300 different groups in an area roughly one-quarter of the size of Australia. Their traditions are expressed through splendid ceremonial attire, pulsating dance rhythms, refined artistry and highly organised community structures, and experiencing these will likely be a highlight of your travels.

Akamba

The Akamba, who live east of Nairobi towards Tsavo National Park, first migrated here from the south about 200 years ago in search of food. Because their own low-altitude land was poor, they were forced to barter for food stocks from the neighbouring Maasai and Kikuyu peoples. Soon, they acquired a reputation as savvy traders, with business dealings (including in ivory, beer, honey, iron weapons and ornaments) extending from the coast inland to Lake Victoria and north to Lake Turkana. Renowned also for their martial prowess, many Akamba were drafted into Britain's WWI army, and today they are still well represented among Kenyan defence and law enforcement brigades.

In the 1930s, the British colonial administration settled large numbers of white farmers in traditional Akamba lands and tried to limit the number of cattle the Akamba could own by confiscating them. In protest, the Akamba formed the Ukamba Members Association, which marched en masse to Nairobi and squatted peacefully at Kariokor Market until their cattle were returned. Large numbers of Akamba were subsequently dispossessed to make way for Tsavo National Park.

All Akamba go through initiation rites at about the age of 12, and have the same age-based groups common to many of the region's peoples. Young parents are known as 'junior elders' (*mwanake* for men, *mwiitu* for women) and are responsible for the maintenance and upkeep of the village. They later become 'medium elders' *(nthele),* and then 'full elders' *(atumia ma kivalo),* with responsibility for death ceremonies and administering the law. The last stage of a person's life is that of 'senior elder' *(atumia ma kisuka),* with responsibility for holy places.

Baganda

Uganda's largest tribal group, the Baganda, comprise almost 20% of the population and are the source of the country's name ('Land of the Baganda'; their kingdom is known as Buganda). Although today the Baganda are spread throughout the country, their traditional lands are in the areas north and northwest of Lake Victoria, including Kampala. Due to significant missionary activity most Baganda are Christian, although animist traditions persist.

The Baganda, together with the neighbouring Haya, have a historical reputation as one of East Africa's most highly organised tribes. Their traditional political system was based around the absolute power of the *kabaka* (king), who ruled through district chiefs. This system reached its zenith during the 19th century, when the Baganda came to dominate various neighbouring groups, including the Nilotic Iteso (who now comprise

> Swahili's role as a lingua franca was solidified as it spread throughout East and Central Africa along the great trade caravan routes. Today it is spoken in more countries and by more people than any other language in sub-Saharan Africa.

THE SWAHILI

The East African coast is home to the Swahili ('People of the Coast'), descendants of Bantu-Arab traders who share a common language and traditions. Although generally not regarded as a single tribal group, the Swahili have for centuries had their own distinct societal structures, and consider themselves to be a single civilisation.

Swahili culture first began to take on a defined form around the 11th century, with the rise of Islam. Today most Swahili are adherents of Islam, although it's generally a more liberal version than that practised in the Middle East. Thanks to this Islamic identity, the Swahili have traditionally considered themselves to be historically and morally distinct from peoples in the interior, with links eastwards towards the rest of the Islamic world.

Swahili festivals follow the Islamic calendar. The year begins with Eid al-Fitr, a celebration of feasting and almsgiving to mark the end of Ramadan fasting. The old Persian new year's purification ritual of Nauroz or Mwaka was also traditionally celebrated, with the parading of a bull counter clockwise through town followed by its slaughter and several days of dancing and feasting. In many areas, Nauroz has now become merged with Eid al-Fitr and is no longer celebrated. The festival of *maulidi* (celebrating the birth of the Prophet) is another Swahili festival, marked by decorated mosques and colourful street processions.

The World of the Swahili by John Middleton is a good place to start for anyone wanting to learn more about Swahili life and culture.

about 8% of Uganda's population). Baganda influence was solidified during the colonial era, with the British favouring their recruitment to the civil service. During the chaotic Obote/Amin years of the late 1960s and early 1970s, the Bagandan monarchy was abolished; it was restored in 1993, although it has no political power.

El-Molo

The Cushitic-speaking El-Molo are a small tribe, numbering less than 4000. Historically the El-Molo were one of the region's more distinct groups, but in recent times they have been forced to adapt or relinquish many of their old customs in order to survive, and intermarriage with other tribes is common.

The El-Molo, whose ancestral home is on two small islands in the middle of Kenya's Lake Turkana, traditionally subsisted on fish, supplemented by the occasional crocodile, turtle, hippopotamus or bird. Over the years an ill-balanced diet and the effects of too much fluoride began to take their toll. The El-Molo became increasingly susceptible to disease and, thus weakened, to attacks from stronger tribes. Their numbers plummeted.

Today the El-Molo face an uncertain future. While some continue to eke out a living from the lake, others have turned to cattle herding or work in the tourism industry. Commercial fishing supplements their traditional subsistence and larger, more permanent settlements in Loyangalani, on Lake Turkana's southeastern shores, have replaced the El-Molo's traditional dome-shaped island homes.

Hadzabe

The area close to Lake Eyasi in Tanzania is home to the Hadzabe (also known as Hadzapi, Hadza or Tindiga) people who are believed to have lived here for nearly 10,000 years. The Hadzabe are often said to be the last true hunter-gatherers in East Africa and of the around 1000 who remain, between one-quarter and one-third still live according to traditional ways.

Traditional Hadzabe live a subsistence existence, usually in bands or camps of 20 to 30 people with no tribal or hierarchical structures. Families engage in communal child-rearing, and food and all other resources are shared throughout the camp. Camps are often moved, sometimes due to illness, death or the need to resolve conflicts, while camps may even relocate to the site of a large kill, such as a giraffe; one enduring characteristic of Hadzabe society is that their possessions are so few, each person may carry everything they own on their backs when they travel.

The Hadzabe language is characterised by clicks and may be distantly related to that of southern Africa's San, although it shows only a few connections to Sandawe, the other click language spoken in Tanzania, and genetic studies have shown no close link between the Hadzabe and any other East African peoples.

Haya

The Haya, who live west of Lake Victoria around Bukoba, have both Bantu and Nilotic roots, and are one of the largest tribes in Tanzania. They have a rich history, and in the precolonial era boasted one of the most highly developed early societies on the continent.

At the heart of traditional Haya society were eight different states or kingdoms, each headed by a powerful and often despotic *mukama* (ruler), who ruled in part by divine right. Order was maintained through a system of chiefs and officials, assisted by an age group–based army. With the rise of European influence in the region, this era of Haya history came to an end. The various groups began to splinter, and many chiefs were replaced by persons considered more malleable and sympathetic to colonial interests.

Resentment of these propped-up leaders was strong, spurring the Haya to regroup and form the Bukoba Bahaya Union in 1924, which soon developed into the more influential and broad-based African Association. Together with similar groups established elsewhere in Tanzania, it constituted one of the country's earliest political movements and was an important force in the drive towards independence.

Academic studies of the Hadzabe abound, but there is no finer treatment of the group than in the final chapter of Peter Matthiessen's *The Tree Where Man Was Born*.

Hutu & Tutsi

The Hutu and the Tutsi are related peoples of Bantu origin who live in Burundi, Rwanda, eastern regions of the Democratic Republic of Congo and Uganda. The Hutus are the majority ethnic group in both Burundi (where 85% of the population is Hutu, 14% Tutsi) and Rwanda (84% and 15% respectively).

Almost every aspect of shared Hutu-Tutsi history is disputed and ethnic conflicts between the two groups were a recurring theme throughout much of the 20th century. The Belgian colonial authorities favoured the Tutsi as the ruling elite. After independence, the battle for political power between the Hutu and Tutsi caused great instability in both Burundi and Rwanda. In 1993, an estimated 500,000 Burundians died in a little-reported genocide, followed a year later by the Rwandan genocide in which more than 800,000 people were killed.

Both Hutu and Tutsi speak the same Bantu language (Kinyarwanda in Rwanda, Kirundi in Burundi) and some scholars argue that the difference between the two groups is one of caste rather than any ethnic distinction. Intermarriage between the two groups was traditionally common. Both Hutu and Tutsi are predominantly Christian, although many maintain traditional beliefs in which the spirits of ancestors play an important role.

FOREST DWELLERS

The clash between traditional and Western ways of life in East Africa is particularly apparent among the region's hunter-gatherer and forest-dwelling peoples. These include the Twa, who live in the western forests of Rwanda and Burundi, where they comprise less than 1% of the overall population, and the Hadzabe (or Hadza), in north-central Tanzania around Lake Eyasi. Typically, these communities are among the most marginalised peoples in East African society.

For the Twa and the Hadzabe, the loss of land and forest is the loss of their only resource base. With the rise of commercial logging, the ongoing clearing of forests in favour of agricultural land, and the establishment them of parks and conservation areas, the forest resources and wildlife on which they depend have dramatically decreased. Additional pressures come from hunting and poaching, and from nomadic pastoralists (many of whom have also been evicted from their own traditional areas) seeking grazing lands for their cattle.

Although some Hadzabe have turned to tourism and craft-making for subsistence, the benefits of these are sporadic. Some now only hunt for the benefit of tourists, and others have given up their traditional lifestyle completely. In Rwanda, the Twa have begun mobilising to gain increased political influence and greater access to health care and education.

Kalenjin

The Kalenjin are one of Kenya's largest groups. Together with the Kikuyu, Luo, Luyha and Kamba, they account for about 70% of the country's population. Although often viewed as a single ethnic entity, the term 'Kalenjin' was actually coined in the 1950s to refer to a loose collection of several different Nilotic groups, including the Kipsigis, Nandi, Marakwet, Pokot and Tugen (former Kenyan president Daniel arap Moi's people). These groups speak different dialects of the same language (Nandi), but otherwise have distinct traditions and lifestyles. Due to the influence of arap Moi, the Kalenjin have amassed considerable political power in Kenya. They are also known for their female herbalist doctors, and for their many world-class runners.

The Kalenjin have age-set groups into which a man is initiated after circumcision. Administration of the law is carried out at the *kok* (an informal court led by the clan's elders).

The traditional homeland of the various Kalenjin peoples is along the western edge of the central Rift Valley area, including Kericho, Eldoret, Kitale, Baringo and the land surrounding Mt Elgon. Originally pastoralists, Kalenjin today are known primarily as farmers. An exception to this are the cattle-loving Kipsigi, whose cattle rustling continues to cause friction between them and neighbouring tribes.

The Nandi, who are the second largest of the Kalenjin communities, and comprise about one-third of all Kalenjin, settled in the Nandi Hills between the 16th and 17th centuries, where they prospered after learning agricultural techniques from the Luo and Luyha. They had a formidable military reputation and, in the late 19th century, managed to delay construction of the Uganda railway for more than a decade until Koitalel, their chief, was killed.

Karamojong

The marginalised Karamojong, at home in Karamoja, in northeastern Uganda, are one of East Africa's most insulated, beleaguered and colourful tribes. As with the Samburu, Maasai and other Nilotic pastoralist peoples, life for the Karamojong centres around cattle, which are kept at night in the centre of the family living compound and graze by day on the surrounding plains. Cattle are the main measure of wealth, ownership is a mark of adulthood, and cattle raiding and warfare are central parts of the culture. When cattle are grazed in dry-season camps away from the family homestead, the Karamojong warriors tending them live on blood from live cattle, milk and sometimes meat. In times of scarcity, protection of the herd is considered so important that milk is reserved for calves and children.

The Karamojong have long been subjected to often heavy-handed government pressure to abandon their pastoralist lifestyle; their plight has been exacerbated by periodic famines, as well as the loss of their traditional dry-season grazing areas with the formation of Kidepo Valley National Park in the 1960s. While current Ugandan president Yoweri Museveni has permitted the Karamojong to keep arms to protect themselves against raids from other groups, including the Turkana in neighbouring Kenya, government expeditions targeted at halting cattle raiding continue. These raids and expeditions, combined with easy access to weapons from neighbouring South Sudan and a breakdown of law and order, have made the Karamoja area off-limits to outsiders in recent years.

Kikuyu

The Kikuyu, who comprise about 22% of Kenya's population and are the country's largest tribal group, have their heartland surrounding Mt Kenya. They are Bantu peoples who are believed to have migrated into the area from the east and northeast from around the 16th century onwards, and have undergone several periods of intermarriage and splintering. According to Kikuyu oral traditions, there are nine original *mwaki* (clans), each tracing its origins back to male and female progenitors known as Kikuyu and Mumbi. The administration of these clans, each of which is made up of many family groups *(nyumba)*, was originally overseen by a council of elders, with great significance placed on the roles of the witch doctor, medicine man and blacksmith.

Initiation rites consist of ritual circumcision for boys and female genital mutilation for girls, though the latter is becoming less common. The practice was a source of particular conflict between the Kikuyu and Western missionaries during the late 19th and early 20th centuries. The issue eventually became linked with the independence struggle, and the establishment of independent Kikuyu schools.

The Kikuyu are also known for the opposition association they formed in the 1920s to protest European seizure of large areas of their lands, and for their subsequent instigation of the Mau Mau rebellion in the 1950s. Due to the influence of Jomo Kenyatta, Kenya's first president, the Kikuyu today are disproportionately represented in business and government (President Mwai Kibaki is a Kikuyu). This has proved to be a source of ongoing friction with other groups.

The Kikuyu god, Ngai, is believed to reside on Mt Kenya, and many Kikuyu homes are still oriented to face the sacred peak. Some Kikuyu still come to its lower slopes to offer prayers and the foreskins of their young men – this was the traditional place for holding circumcision ceremonies.

Luo

The Luo live on the northeastern shores of Lake Victoria. They began their migration to the area from Sudan around the 15th century. Although their numbers are relatively small in Tanzania, in Kenya they comprise about 12% of the population and are the country's third-largest tribal group.

During the independence struggle, many of Kenya's leading politicians and trade unionists were Luo and they continue to form the backbone of the Kenyan political opposition.

The Luo have had an important influence on the East African musical scene. They are notable especially for their contribution to the highly popular benga style, which has since been adopted by musicians from many other tribes.

The Luo were originally cattle herders, but the devastating effects of rinderpest in the 1890s forced them to adopt fishing and subsistence agriculture, which are now the main sources of livelihood for most Luo today. Luo family groups consist of the man, his wife or wives, and their sons and daughters-in-law. The family unit is part of a larger grouping of families or *dhoot* (clan), several of which make up *ogandi* (a group of geographically related people), each led by a *ruoth* (chief). Traditional Luo living compounds are enclosed by fences, and include separate huts for the man and for each wife and son. The Luo consider age, wealth and respect as converging, with the result that elders control family resources and represent the family to the outside world.

Instead of circumcision, the Luo traditionally extracted four to six teeth at initiation. It's still common to see Luo elders with several pegs missing.

Maasai

The Maasai are pastoral nomads who have actively resisted change, and many still follow the same lifestyle the Maasai have had for centuries. Their traditional culture centres on their cattle, which along with their land, are considered sacred. Cows provide many of their needs: milk, blood and meat for their diet, and hides and skins for clothing, although sheep and goats also play an important dietary role, especially during the dry season.

Maasai society is patriarchal and highly decentralised. Maasai boys pass through a number of transitions during their life, the first of which is marked by the circumcision rite. Successive stages include junior warriors, senior warriors, junior elders and senior elders; each level is distinguished by its own unique rights, responsibilities and dress. Junior elders, for example, are expected to marry and settle down, somewhere between ages 30 and 40. Senior elders assume the responsibility of making wise and moderate decisions for the community. The most important group is that of the newly initiated warriors, *moran*, who are charged with defending the cattle herds.

The Maasai's artistic traditions are most vividly seen in their striking body decoration and beaded ornaments. Women are famous for their magnificent beaded plate-like necklaces, while men typically wear the red-checked *shuka* (blanket) and carry a distinctive balled club.

Maasai women play a markedly subservient role and have no inheritance rights. Polygamy is widespread and marriages are arranged by the elders, without consulting the bride or her mother. Since most women are significantly younger than men at the time of marriage, they often become widows; remarriage is rare.

The Samburu, who live directly north of Mt Kenya, are closely related to the Maasai linguistically and culturally.

Makonde

The Makonde are famed throughout East Africa and beyond for their highly refined ebony woodcarvings. The tribe has its origins in northern Mozambique, where many Makonde still live; although in recent years a subtle split has begun to develop between the group's Tanzanian and Mozambican branches. Today, most Tanzanian Makonde live in southeastern Tanzania on the Makonde plateau, although many members of the carving community have since migrated to Dar es Salaam.

AGE-BASED GROUPS

Age-based groups (in which all youths of the same age belong to a group, and pass through the various stages of life and their associated rituals together) continue to play an important role in tribal life throughout much of East Africa. Each group has its own leader and community responsibilities, and definition of the age-based groups is often highly refined. Among the Sukuma, for example, who live in the area south of Lake Victoria, each age-based group traditionally had its own system for counting from one to 10, with the system understood by others within the group, but not by members of other groups. Among the Maasai, who have one of the most highly stratified age-group systems in the region, males are organised into age groups and further into sub-groups, with inter-group rivalries and relationships one of the defining features of daily life.

LAND PRESSURES

During the colonial era in Kenya, it was largely Maasai land that was taken for European colonisation through two controversial treaties. The creation of Serengeti National Park in Tanzania and the continuing colonial annexation of Maasai territory put many of the traditional grazing lands and waterholes of the Maasai off-limits. During subsequent years, as populations of both the Maasai and their cattle increased, pressure for land became intense and conflict with the authorities was constant. Government-sponsored resettlement programs have met with only limited success, as Maasai traditions scorn agriculture and land ownership.

One consequence of this competition for land is that many Maasai ceremonial traditions can no longer be fulfilled. Part of the ceremony where a man becomes a *moran* (warrior) involves a group of young men around the age of 14 going out and building a small livestock camp after their circumcision ceremony. They then live alone there for up to eight years before returning to the village to marry. Today, while the tradition and will survive, land is often unavailable.

The Makonde are matrilineal. Although customs are gradually changing, children and inheritances normally belong to the woman, and it's still common for husbands to move to the villages of their wives after marriage. Makonde settlements are widely scattered (possibly a remnant of the days when the Makonde sought to evade slave raids), and there is no tradition of a unified political system. Despite this, a healthy sense of tribal identity has managed to survive. Makonde villages are typically governed by a hereditary chief and a council of elders. The Makonde traditionally practised body scarring, and many elders still sport facial markings and (for women) wooden lip plugs.

Because of their remote location, the Makonde have succeeded in remaining largely insulated from colonial and postcolonial influences. They are known in particular for their steady resistance to Islam. Today, most Makonde follow traditional religions, with the complex spirit world given its fullest expression in their carvings.

Pare

The Bantu-speaking Pare inhabit the Pare mountains in northeastern Tanzania, where they migrated several centuries ago from the Taita Hills area of southern Kenya.

The Pare are one of Tanzania's most educated groups. Despite their small numbers, they have been highly influential in shaping Tanzania's recent history. In the 1940s they formed the Wapare Union, which played an important role in the independence drive.

The Pare are also known for their rich oral traditions, and for their elaborate rituals centring on the dead. Near most villages are sacred areas in which the skulls of tribal chiefs are kept. When people die, they are believed to inhabit a netherworld between the land of the living and the spirit world. If they are allowed to remain in this state, ill fate will befall their descendants. As a result, rituals allowing the deceased to pass peacefully into the world of the ancestors hold great significance. Traditional Pare beliefs hold that when an adult male dies, others in his lineage will die as well until the cause of his death has been found and 'appeased.' Many of the possible reasons for death have to do with disturbances in moral relations within the lineage or in the village, or with sorcery.

Among the Pare, a deceased male's ghost influences male descendants for as long as the ghost's name is remembered. Daughters, too, are dependent on their father's goodwill. However, since property and status are transmitted through the male line, a father's ghost only has influence over his daughter's descendants until her death.

Sukuma & Nyamwezi

The Sukuma, Bantu speakers from southern Lake Victoria, comprise almost 15% of Tanzania's total population, although it is only relatively recently that they have come to view themselves as a single entity. They are closely related to the Nyamwezi, Tanzania's second-largest tribal group around Tabora.

The Sukuma are renowned for their drumming and for their dancing. Lively meetings between their two competing dance societies, the Bagika and the Bagulu, are a focal point of tribal life.

The Sukuma are also known for their highly structured form of village organisation in which each settlement is subdivided into chiefdoms ruled by a *ntemi* (chief) in collaboration with a council of elders. Divisions of land and labour are made by village committees consisting of similarly aged members from each family in the village. These age-based groups perform numerous roles, ranging from assisting with the building of new houses to farming and other community-oriented work. As a result of this system, which gives most families at least a representational role in many village activities, Sukuma often view houses and land as communal property.

Among the most famous Sukuma dances are the *banungule* (hyena dance) and the *bazwilili bayeye* (snake and porcupine dance). Before beginning, dancers are treated with traditional medicaments as protection from injury. It's not unheard of for the animals, too, to be given a spot of something to calm their tempers.

Turkana

The colourful Turkana are a Nilotic people who live in the harsh desert country of northwestern Kenya where they migrated from South Sudan and northeastern Uganda. Although the Turkana only emerged as a distinct tribal group during the early to mid-19th century, they are notable today for their strong sense of tribal identification. The Turkana are closely related linguistically and culturally to Uganda's Karamojong.

Like the Samburu and the Maasai (with whom they are also linguistically linked), the Turkana are primarily cattle herders, although in recent years increasing numbers have turned to fishing and subsistence farming. Personal relationships based on the exchange of cattle, and built up by each herd owner during the course of a lifetime, are of critical importance in Turkana society and function as a social security net during times of need.

The Turkana are famous for their striking appearance and traditional garb. Turkana men cover part of their hair with mud, which is then painted blue and decorated with ostrich and other feathers. Despite the intense heat of the Turkana lands, the main garment is a woollen blanket, often with garish checks. Turkana accessories include a stool carved out of a single piece of wood, a wooden fighting staff and a wrist knife. Tattooing is another hallmark of Turkana life. Witch doctors and prophets are held in high regard, and scars on the lower stomach are usually a sign of a witch doctor's attempt to cast out an undesirable spirit. Traditionally, Turkana men were tattooed on the shoulder and upper arm for killing an enemy – the right shoulder for killing a man, the left for a woman.

In addition to personal adornment, other important forms of artistic expression include finely crafted carvings and refined a cappella singing. Ceremonies play a less significant role among the Turkana than among many of their neighbours, and they do not practice circumcision or female genital mutilation.

Environment

The story of East Africa's natural environment is one of fragile abundance. It is the tale of a continent's extraordinary natural beauty and diversity, of all that we imagine Africa to be – from the Great Rift Valley to horizonless savannah, spectacular lakes and deep, deep forests. Inhabiting these epic landforms are some of the last great herds of wildlife left on the planet. But these landforms and wild herds are under threat, making the urgency to see them that much greater.

The Land

Straddling the equator, edged to the east by the Indian Ocean and to the west by a chain of Rift Valley lakes, East Africa is as diverse geographically and environmentally as it is culturally.

Great Rift Valley

The Great Rift Valley is one of Africa's defining landforms and this great gouge in the planet cuts a swathe through the heart of East Africa. It was formed between eight and 30 million years ago, when the tectonic plates that comprise the African and Eurasian landmasses collided and then diverged again. As the plates moved apart, massive tablets of the earth's crust collapsed between them, resulting over the millennia in the escarpments, ravines, flatlands and lakes that mark much of East Africa today.

The Rift Valley is part of the Afro-Arabian rift system that stretches 5500km from the salty shores of the Dead Sea to the palm trees of Mozambique. The East African section of the Rift Valley consists of two branches formed where the main rift system divides north of Kenya's Lake Turkana. The western branch, or Western Rift Valley, makes its way past Lake Albert in Uganda through Rwanda and Burundi down to Lake Tanganyika, after which it meanders southeast to Lake Nyasa. Seismic and volcanic disturbances still occur throughout the western branch. The eastern branch, known as the Eastern or Gregory Rift, runs south from Lake Turkana past Lake Natron and Lake Manyara in Tanzania before joining again with the Western Rift in northern Malawi.

The forces that created the Rift Valley also gave rise to Africa's highest mountains, among them Mt Kilimanjaro, Mt Kenya, Uganda's Rwenzori Mountains and the Virunga range in the Democratic Republic of the Congo (DRC; formerly Zaïre). Most began as volcanoes and most are now extinct, but no fewer than 30 remain active, among them the DRC's Nyiragongo volcano. Other places where the escarpments of the Rift Valley are particularly impressive include Kenya's Rift Valley Province, the Nkuruman Escarpment east of Kenya's Masai Mara National Reserve, and the terrain around Ngorongoro Conservation Area and Lake Manyara National Park in Tanzania.

Savannah

The African savannah – broad rolling grasslands dotted with lone acacia trees – is a quintessentially African landscape, so much so that it covers an estimated two-thirds of the African land mass.

Peter Matthiessen's classic The Tree Where Man Was Born is an evocative and beautifully written 1960s picture of East Africa's physical, environmental and cultural make-up. His Sand Rivers (1981), a timeless account of a foot safari through Tanzania's Selous Game Reserve, is less known but just as brilliant.

Savannah is often located in a broad swathe surrounding tropical rainforest. The term itself refers to a grasslands ecosystem. While trees may be (and usually are) present, such trees do not, under the strict definition of the term, form a closed canopy.

The East African savannah was formed during the Rift's great upheavals, when volcanic lava and ash rained down upon the lands surrounding the Rift's volcanoes, covering the landscape in fertile but shallow soils. Grasses, the most successful of plant forms, flourished as they needed little depth for their roots to grow. The perfectly adapted acacia aside, however, no other plants were able to colonise the savannah: their roots were starved of space and nourishment.

Thus created, savannah flourishes in areas where there are long wet seasons alternating with long dry seasons, creating ideal conditions for the growth of dense, nutritious grasses. Shaped by fire – which both devastates and regenerates – and by grazing animals, savannah is a dynamic habitat in constant flux with its adjacent woodlands.

In East Africa, the most famous sweeps of savannah are found in Tanzania's Serengeti National Park and Kenya's Masai Mara National Reserve.

Forest Cover

Tanzania: 36.8%

Kenya: 6.1%

Uganda: 14.1%

Rwanda: 18.4%

Burundi: 6.6%

Forests

East Africa's forests border the great rainforest systems of central Africa which once formed part of the mighty Guineo–Congolian forest ecosystem. The most intact stands of rainforest are found in places such as the Rwenzori Mountains National Park in southwestern Uganda and the DRC's Virunga range, although important blocks of rainforest still exist in Rwanda and Burundi; in the latter two countries, the pressure on forests from soaring populations is particularly acute. Kenya has few forests, although the Kakamega Forest shows what most of Western Kenya must have once looked like, while the Arabuko Sokoke Forest Reserve is the largest surviving tract of coastal forest in East Africa. There are also small patches of tropical rainforest in Tanzania's Eastern Arc mountains, such as the Usambara Mountains.

Lakes

Mangroves

Wasini Island, Kenya

Mida Creek, Kenya

Zanzibar Archipelago, Tanzania

Pemba, Tanzania

Tanga, Tanzania

Mafia Island Marine Park, Tanzania

Lake Victoria, which is shared between Uganda, Tanzania and Kenya, is Africa's largest freshwater lake (and the second-largest by area in the world after the USA's Lake Superior). Its surface covers an area of over 68,000 sq km. Water levels fluctuate widely, depending largely on the rains, with depths never more than 80m and more often lower than 10m. More than 90% of the lake falls within Tanzanian or Ugandan territory. Lake Victoria is also considered one of the sources of the Nile.

Lake Tanganyika is the world's longest freshwater lake and is estimated to have the second-largest volume of freshwater in the world (after Lake Baikal in Siberia), with 45% belonging to the DRC and 41% to Tanzania.

Lake Nyasa (also known as Lake Malawi), Africa's third-largest and second-deepest freshwater lake, is the Rift Valley's southernmost lake. Its waters reportedly contain more fish species than any other freshwater lake on earth.

Besides providing fertile soil, the volcanic deposits of the Rift Valley have created alkaline waters in most Rift Valley lakes. Its largest is a sea of jade, otherwise known by the more boring name of Lake Turkana, which straddles the Ethiopian border in the north; Lake Turkana is the world's third-largest salt lake. Other important alkaline lakes include Bogoria, Nakuru, Elmenteita and Natron. These shallow soda lakes, formed by the valley's lack of decent drainage, experience high evaporation rates, which further concentrates the alkalinity. The strangely soapy and smelly waters are the perfect environment for the growth of microscopic blue-green algae, which in turn feed lesser flamingos, tiny crustaceans (food for greater flamingos) and insect larvae (food for soda-resistant fish). In 2011, Kenya's Rift Valley lake system (primarily Lakes Nakuru, Elmenteita and Bogoria) was inscribed on Unesco's list of World Heritage Sites.

Wildlife

East Africa is arguably the premier wildlife-watching destination on earth. The wildlife that most visitors come to see ranges from the 'Big Five' (lion, buffalo, elephant, leopard and rhino) to some of the last great herds of zebras, hippos, giraffes, wildebeest and antelopes left on earth, plus major populations of primates. Each of these animals are not only impressive to watch, they are also essential linchpins in a beautifully complex natural web where each species has its own niche in any given ecosystem.

In addition to the large animals, other players include over 60,000 insect species, several dozen types of reptiles and amphibians, many snake species and abundant marine life, both in the Indian Ocean and inland water systems. Completing the picture are close to 1500 different types of birds, including many rare ones – Tanzania, Kenya and Uganda are each home to more than 1000 species.

Many of East Africa's most important species have become endangered over the past few decades as a result of poisoning, the ongoing destruction of their natural habitat, and merciless poaching for ivory, skins, horn and bush meat.

Elephants

In the 1970s and 1980s, the numbers of African elephants plummeted from an estimated 1.3 million to around 500,000 thanks to widespread poaching. In Kenya, elephant numbers fell from 45,000 in 1976 to just 5400 in 1988. The slaughter ended only in 1989 when the trade in ivory was banned under the Convention for International Trade in Endangered Species (Cites). When the ban was established, world raw ivory prices plummeted by 90%, and the market for poaching and smuggling was radically reduced. The same year, Kenyan president Daniel arap Moi dramatically burned 12 tons of ivory in Nairobi National Park as a symbol of Kenya's resolve in the battle against poachers.

But poaching is once again on the rise. Africa has lost more than 30,000 elephants a year since 2010 and in 2014, for the first time in decades, a critical threshold was crossed when more elephants were killed on the continent than were born. Adding to the problem is that elephant numbers have yet to recover from previous decades when poaching was rampant – in Tanzania's Selous Game Reserve, for example, there were more than 110,000 elephants in the late 1970s, but the latest survey found just 13,500.

Amboseli Trust for Elephants (ATE; www.elephanttrust.org) and **Save the Elephants** (www.savetheelephants.org) are invaluable resources of information about East Africa's elephants.

East African governments remain on the frontline in the war against poaching, but other organisations are also active, such as the **Big Life Foundation** (www.biglife.org).

Black Rhinoceros

These inoffensive vegetarians are armed with impressive horns that have made them the target of both white hunters and poachers; rhino numbers plummeted to the brink of extinction during the 20th century and the illegal trade in rhino horns is still driven by their use in traditional medicines in Asian countries and the demand for dagger handles in Yemen.

ENVIRONMENT WILDLIFE

Few visitors to East Africa know that the term 'Big Five' was coined by white hunters for those five species deemed most dangerous to hunt.

Black Rhino Hot Spots

Ol Pejeta Conservancy, Kenya

Lewa Wildlife Conservancy, Kenya

Lake Nakuru National Park, Kenya

Ngorongoro Conservation Area, Tanzania

Selous Game Reserve, Tanzania

Tsavo West National Park, Kenya

Nairobi National Park, Kenya

Despite having turned the situation around from the desperate lows of the 1980s, wildlife authorities in East Africa are battling a recent upsurge in rhino poaching. It was in 2009 that the crisis began again; in the following year Kenya's Lewa Wildlife Conservancy lost its first rhinos to poaching in almost three decades. In the years since, all of the major rhino sanctuaries – Nairobi National Park, Solio Game Reserve, Lewa Wildlife Conservancy, Ol Pejeta Conservancy, and Ngulia Rhino Sanctuary in Tsavo West National Park – have lost rhinos. Most worrying of all is that each of these have extremely high security and sophisticated anti-poaching programs.

There are two species of rhino – black and white – both of which are predominantly found in savannah regions. The black rhino is probably East Africa's most endangered large mammal: its population plummeted by over 97% between 1960 and 1992, with the low point reached in 1995 when just 2410 were thought to remain in the wild. By 2014, numbers were thought to have rebounded to 5055. Kenya has East Africa's largest share, with an estimated 650 black rhinos surviving in the wild.

Lions

Because lions are the easiest of the big cats to observe, few people realise that they face an extremely uncertain future. No one quite knows how many lions there once were, but there were probably more than a million when colonial explorers arrived in East Africa in the 19th century. Now, fewer than 30,000 are thought to remain and lions have disappeared from 80% of their historical range, according to **Panthera** (www.panthera. org), the leading cat conservation NGO, based in New York. More than half of the continent's total population resides in Tanzania, while in Kenya lion numbers have reached critical levels: fewer than 2000 lions are thought to remain in the country.

Across their range, numbers are falling alarmingly, thanks primarily to human encroachment and habitat loss. The poisoning of lions, either in retaliation for lions killing livestock or encroaching onto farming lands, has also reached dangerous levels, to the extent that some lion conservationists predict that the lion could become regionally extinct in Kenya within 20 years.

Lion Guardians (www.lionguardians.org) and **Living With Lions** (www. livingwithlions.org) are Kenyan organisations fighting to protect lions and are important sources of information. **Wildlife Direct** (www.wildlifedirect. org) is another useful source of information, particularly on the threats posed by poisoning.

Mountain Gorillas

Gorillas are the largest of the great apes and share 97% of their biological make-up with humans. Gorillas used to inhabit a swathe of land that cut right across central Africa, but the last remaining eastern mountain gorillas number somewhere between 680 and just over 700, divided between two 300-plus populations in the forests of Uganda's Bwindi Impenetrable National Park and on the slopes of the Virunga volcanoes, encompassing Uganda's Mgahinga Gorilla National Park, Rwanda's Volcanoes National Park and the DRC's Parc National des Virungas.

Mountain gorilla numbers have held firm over the past 15 years or so despite the widely publicised execution-style killings of seven gorillas in the DRC's Parc National des Virungas in 2007, ongoing threats from instability in the DRC, poaching, mining exploration, the Ebola and Marburg viruses and the trade in bush meat. The **IUCN Redlist of Threatened Species** (www.iucnredlist.org) lists the eastern mountain gorilla as endangered.

There is no finer resource on Africa's wild cats than *Cats of Africa* by L Hunter. It is an authoritative but highly readable book covering their behaviour, conservation and ecology, with superb photos by G Hinde. The author is the president of Panthera (www.panthera. org), the leading cat conservation NGO.

CATTLE-FREE NATIONAL PARKS?

Nothing seems to disappoint visitors to Kenya's national parks more than the sight of herders shepherding their livestock to water sources within park boundaries. In the words of former Kenya Wildlife Service head Dr Richard Leakey: 'People don't pay a lot of money to see cattle'. The issue is, however, a complicated one.

On the one hand, what you are seeing is far from a natural African environment. For thousands of years people, and their herds of cattle, lived happily (and sustainably) alongside the wildlife, and their actions helped to shape the landscapes of East Africa. But with the advent of conservation and national parks, many of Kenya's tribal peoples, particularly pastoralists such as the Maasai and Samburu, found themselves and their cattle excluded from their ancestral lands or waterholes of last resort, often with little or no compensation or alternative incomes provided (although, of course, some do now make a living through tourism and conservation).

Having been pushed onto marginal lands, with rapidly growing populations and with limited access to alternative water sources in times of drought, many have been forced to forgo their traditional livelihoods and have taken to leading sedentary lifestyles. Those that continue as herders have little choice but to overgraze their lands. Such policies of exclusion tend to reinforce the perception among local peoples that wildlife belongs to the government and brings few benefits to local communities. This position is passionately argued in the excellent (if slightly dated) book *No Man's Land* (2003) by George Monbiot.

At the same time, tourism is a major (and much needed) source of revenue for Kenya and most visitors to Kenya want to experience a natural wilderness – on the surface at least, the national parks and reserves appear to provide this Edenesque slice of Africa. It also remains questionable whether allowing herders and their livestock to graze within park boundaries would alleviate the pressures on overexploited land and traditional cultures, or would instead simply lead to the degradation of Kenya's last remaining areas of relatively pristine wilderness.

Things get even more complicated when talking about private and community conservancies. Many Laikipia and Mara conservancies – Ol Pejeta Conservancy (p282) and Segera Ranch (p283) are two prominent examples – consider livestock to be an important part of habitat management, arguing that well-maintained livestock herds can help reduce tick infestations for wildlife. Carefully controlled grazing can also, they argue, actually assist in the regeneration of grassland ecosystems.

Grevy's Zebras

Kenya (along with neighbouring Ethiopia) is home to the last surviving wild populations of Grevy's zebra. In the 1970s, approximately 15,000 Grevy's zebras were thought to survive in the wild. Just 2600 are estimated to remain and less than 1% of the Grevy zebra's historical range lies within protected areas. Distinguished from other zebra species by having narrow stripes and bellies free from stripes, the Grevy's zebra is found in the Lewa Wildlife Conservancy, Ol Pejeta Conservanc, Segera Ranch and Samburu National Reserve.

Rothschild Giraffes

The most endangered of the nine giraffe subspecies, the Rothschild giraffe has recently been hauled back from the brink of extinction. At the forefront of the fight to save the Rothschild giraffe (which, unlike other subspecies, has distinctive white 'stockings' with no orange-and-black markings below the knee) is the Giraffe Centre (p222) in Nairobi. Rothschild giraffes are making a comeback with populations having been reintroduced into the wild at Lake Nakuru National Park and Ruma National Park (both in Kenya). There's also a small population in Uganda's Murchison Falls National Park.

African Wild Dogs

The **IUCN Redlist of Threatened Species** (www.iucnredlist.org) lists the African wild dog as endangered, with no more than 6600 left on the continent (of which just 1400 are mature individuals). Most range across southern Africa, but southern Tanzania does have East Africa's most important regional populations. Your best chance of seeing the species is in Selous Game Reserve, but they're also found in Ruaha National Park. Kenya's only significant population is found on the Laikipia Plateau.

Environmental Issues

East Africa is confronting some pressing environmental issues including deforestation, desertification, poaching, threats to endangered species and the impacts of tourism.

Deforestation

More than half of Africa's forests have been destroyed over the last century, and forest destruction continues on a large scale in parts of East Africa where forest areas today represent only a fraction of the region's original forest cover. On the Zanzibar Archipelago, for example, only about 5% of the dense tropical forest that once blanketed the islands still remains. In sections of the long Eastern Arc chain, which sweeps from southern Kenya down towards central Tanzania, forest depletion has caused such serious erosion that entire villages have had to be shifted to lower areas. In densely populated Rwanda and Burundi, many previously forested areas have been completely cleared to make way for agriculture.

Native hardwood such as ebony and mahogany is often used to make the popular carved wooden statue souvenirs sold in East Africa. Though this industry supports thousands of local families who may otherwise be without an income, it also consumes an estimated 80,000 trees annually. The WWF and Unesco campaigned to promote the use of common, faster-growing trees, and many handicraft cooperatives now use wood taken from forests managed by the Forest Stewardship Council. If you buy a carving, ask if the wood is sourced from managed forests.

Eastern Arc Mountains Information Source (www.easternarc.org) is an information clearing house for the many environmental and community-based projects being undertaken in the Eastern Arc range in Kenya and Tanzania.

Tourism

Unregulated tourism and development pose serious threats to East Africa's ecosystems. In northern and eastern Zanzibar, for example, new hotels are being built at a rapid rate, without sufficient provision for waste disposal and maintenance of environmental equilibrium. Inappropriate visitor use is another aspect of the issue; prime examples are the tyre tracks criss-crossing off-road areas of Kenya's Masai Mara National Reserve, the litter found along some popular trekking routes on Mt Kilimanjaro, and the often rampant use of firewood by visitors and tour operators alike.

One positive development has been the rise of community-based conservation as tour operators, funding organisations and others recognise that East Africa's protected areas are unlikely to succeed in the long term unless local people obtain real benefits.

Among the most impressive projects are the private conservancies that have become a feature of conservation tourism in the Laikipia and Masai Mara regions of Kenya.

WAYNE LYNCH / GETTY IMAGES ©

Wildebeest, Masai Mara National
Reserve (p251), Kenya

Wildlife & Habitat

Think of East Africa and the word 'safari' comes to mind, but travel west from the big wildlife parks of Tanzania and Kenya and you cross through a world of gorgeous lakes and rivers, before ascending into a mystical realm of snowy, cloud-draped peaks that straddle Africa's continental divide. Many parts of the verdant western region remain relatively unknown and are seldom visited, providing welcome respite from overbooked safaris and lodges to the east. But no matter where you travel, East Africa – home to a dazzling number and variety of animals – is sure to amaze.

– David Lukas

Big Cats

The three big cats – leopards, lions and cheetahs – provide the high point for so many memorable Kenyan safaris. The presence of these apex predators, even the mere suggestion that they may be nearby, is enough to draw the savannah taut with attention. It's the lion's gravitas, roaring at night, stalking at sunset. It's the elusive leopard that remains hidden while in plain view. And it's the cheetah in a fluid blur of hunting perfection.

Leopard

Weight 30-60kg (female), 40-90kg (male); length 170-300cm More common than you realise, the leopard relies on expert camouflage techniques to stay hidden. During the day you might only spot one reclining in a tree after it twitches its tail, but at night there is no mistaking their bone-chilling groans. Best seen in Masai Mara NR, Serengeti NP.

1. Leopard 2. Cheetah 3. Female lions

Cheetah

Weight 40-60kg; length 200-220cm The cheetah is a world-class sprinter. Although it reaches speeds of 112km/h, the cheetah runs out of steam after 300m and must cool down for 30 minutes before hunting again. This speed comes at another cost – the cheetah is so well adapted for running that it lacks the strength and teeth to defend its food or cubs from attack by other large predators. Best seen in Masai Mara NR, Serengeti NP, Tsavo East NP, Amboseli NP.

Lion

Weight 120-150kg (female), 150-225kg (male); length 210-275cm (female), 240-350cm (male) Those lions sprawled out lazily in the shade are actually Africa's most feared predators. Equipped with teeth that tear effortlessly through bone and tendon, they can take down an animal as large as a bull giraffe. Each group of adults (a pride) is based around generations of females that do the majority of the hunting; swaggering males typically fight among themselves and eat what the females catch. Best seen in Masai Mara NR, Serengeti NP, Selous GR, Ruaha NP.

ARIADNE VAN ZANDBERGEN / GETTY IMAGES ©

Wildcat **2.** Caracal **3.** Serval

Small Cats

While big cats get the lion's share of attention from tourists, East Africa's small cats are equally interesting though much harder to spot. You won't find these cats chasing down gazelles or wildebeest, instead look for them slinking around in search of rodents or making incredible leaps to snatch birds out of the air.

Wildcat

Weight 3-6.5kg; length 65-100cm Readily found on the outskirts of villages, or wherever there are abundant mice and rats, the wildcat looks like a common tabby and is in fact the direct ancestor of the domesticated housecat. The wildcat is best identified by its unmarked rufous ears and longish legs. Widely distributed but rarely seen.

Serval

Weight 6-18kg; length 90-130cm Twice as large as a housecat, with towering legs and large ears, the beautifully spotted serval is highly adapted for walking in tall grass and making prodigious leaps to catch rodents and birds. This elegant cat is often observed hunting in the daytime. Best seen in Masai Mara NR, Serengeti NP, Aberdare NP (black servals).

Caracal

Weight 8-19kg; length 80-120cm The caracal is a gorgeous tawny cat with long, pointy ears. This African version of the northern lynx has jacked-up hind legs like a feline dragster. These beanpole kickers enable this slender cat to make vertical leaps of 3m and swat birds out of the air. Widespread in East Africa's parks, although difficult to spot.

Ground Primates

East Africa is the evolutionary cradle of primate diversity, giving rise to over 30 species of monkeys, apes and prosimians (the 'primitive' ancestors of modern primates), all of which have dextrous hands and feet.

Vervet Monkey

Weight 4-8kg; length 90-140cm Each troop of vervets is composed of females who defend home ranges passed down from generation to generation, and males who fight each other for bragging rights and access to females. Check out the extraordinary blue and scarlet colours of their sexual organs when they're aroused. Widespread throughout East Africa.

Chimpanzee

Weight 25-40kg; length 60-90cm Travelling to the forests of western East Africa to see chimpanzees may take you off the beaten path, but it's hard to deny the allure of these human-like primates, with deep intelligence and emotion lurking behind their familiar deep-set eyes. Researchers at Gombe and Mahale Mountains NPs are making startling discoveries about chimp behaviour. Best seen in Kabale Forest NP, Mahale Mountains NP, Gombe Stream NP, Nyungwe Forest NP.

1. Vervet monkey 2. Chimpanzee 3. Mountain gorillas

Mountain Gorilla

Weight 70-115kg (female), 160-210kg (male); length 140-185cm Gorilla-viewing is a big draw in Uganda and Rwanda, so expect some effort or expense getting a coveted slot on a tour into gorilla habitat. Seems like a hassle? Just wait until you're face-to-face with a massive silverback male on his home turf and nothing else will matter! Best seen in Volcanoes NP, Bwindi Impenetrable NP, Mgahinga NP.

Olive Baboon

Weight 11-30kg (female), 22-50kg (male); length 95-180cm Although the formidable olive baboon has 5cm-long fangs and can kill a leopard, its best defence may be its ability to run up trees and shower intruders with liquid excrement. Widespread throughout East Africa.

ARIADNE VAN ZANDBERGEN / GETTY IMAGES ©

Greater galago 2. Black-and-white colobus 3. Blue monkey

Arboreal Primates

Forest primates are a diverse group that live entirely in trees. These agile, long-limbed primates generally stay in the upper canopy where they search for leaves and arboreal fruits. It might take the expert eyes of a professional guide to help you find some of these species.

Greater Galago

Weight 550-2000g; length 55-100cm A cat-sized nocturnal creature with a dog-like face, the greater galago belongs to a group of prosimians that have changed very little in 60 million years. Best known for its frequent bawling cries (hence the common name 'bushbaby'), the galago would be rarely seen except that it readily visits feeding stations at many popular safari lodges. Living in a world of darkness, galagos communicate with each other through scent and sound. Widespread throughout East Africa, including Nyungwe Forest NP, Rwanda Jozani Forest, Zanzibar.

Black-and-White Colobus

Weight 10-23kg; length 115-165cm The black-and-white colobus is one of East Africa's most popular primates due to the flowing white bonnets of hair across its black body. Like all colobus, this agile primate has a hook-shaped hand so it can swing through the trees with the greatest of ease. When two troops run into each other expect to see a real show. Best seen in Kakamega Forest, Lake Nakuru NP, Arusha NP, Nyungwe Forest NP.

Blue Monkey

Weight 4-12kg; length 100-170cm These long-tailed monkeys are widespread primates that have adapted to many forested habitats throughout sub-Saharan Africa, including some of the forested parks in Tanzania where they are among the easiest monkeys to spot. The versatile primates live in large social groups that spend their entire lives among trees. Best seen in Rwenzori Mountains National Park, Volcanoes NP, Lake Manyara NP.

Cud-Chewing Mammals

Africa is arguably most famous for its astounding variety of ungulates – hoofed mammals that include everything from buffaloes to giraffes. In this large family, the cud-chewing antelope are particularly numerous, with 40 different species in East Africa alone.

Wildebeest

Weight 140-290kg; length 230-340cm Few animals evoke the spirit of the African plain like the wildebeest. Over one million gather in vast, constantly moving herds on the Serengeti. Best seen in Masai Mara NR, Serengeti NP.

Thomson's Gazelle

Weight 15-35kg; length 95-150cm Lanky and exceptionally alert, the long-legged Thomson's gazelle is built for speed. The 400,000 living on the Serengeti Plains migrate with wildebeest and zebras. Widespread throughout southern Kenya and northern Tanzania.

African Buffalo

Weight 250-850kg; length 220-420cm Imagine a big cow with curling horns, and you have the African buffalo. Fortunately, they're usually docile – an angry or injured buffalo is an extremely dangerous animal. Widespread from central Kenya to southern Tanzania.

Gerenuk

Weight 30-50kg; length 160-200cm The gerenuk is one of the strangest creatures you'll ever see – a tall slender gazelle with a giraffe-like neck that stands on its hind legs to reach 2m-high branches. Best seen in Samburu NR, Amboseli NP.

Uganda Kob

Weight 60-120kg; length 170-200cm Kob gather in great numbers on the flood plains of Uganda, where males fight and show off their curved horns in front of gathered females.

2

1. Wildebeest 2. Thomson's gazelles 3. African buffaloes
4. Gerenuk

4

1. Black rhinos 2. Plains zebras 3. African elephants 4. Giraffe

IGNACIO PALACIOS / GETTY IMAGES ©

Hoofed Mammals

The continent has a surprising diversity of hoofed animals that have been at home here for millions of years. Those that don't chew cuds can be seen over a much broader range of habitats than the cud-chewing antelope. Without human intervention, Africa would be ruled by elephants, zebras, hippos and warthogs.

Black Rhinoceros

Weight 700-1400kg; length 350-450cm Pity the black rhinoceros for having a horn that is worth more than gold. Once widespread and abundant on open plains south of the Sahara, the slow-moving rhino has been poached to the brink of extinction. Best seen in Ol Pejeta Conservancy, Lake Nakuru NP, Nairobi NP, Meru NP, Ngorongoro Crater.

Plains Zebra

Weight 175-320kg; length 260-300cm Scientists first thought the stripes, each distinct as a human fingerprint, were to confuse predators by making it difficult to distinguish the outline of individual zebras in a herd. However, new studies suggest stripes help combat disease carrying horseflies. Widespread throughout southern and central Kenya.

African Elephant

Weight 2200-3500kg (female), 4000-6300kg (male); height 2.4-3.4m (female), 3-4m (male) Bull elephants are commonly referred to as 'the king of beasts,' but elephant society is actually ruled by a lineage of elder females who lead each group along traditional migration routes between watering holes. Best seen in Amboseli NP, Tarangire NP, Serengeti NP, Tsavo East NP, Samburu NR.

Giraffe

Weight 450-1200kg (female), 1800-2000kg (male); height 3.5-5.2m The 5m-tall giraffe does such a good job reaching up to grab mouthfuls of leaves on high branches that stretching down to get a drink of water is difficult. Masai giraffes are widespread in Tanzania and southern Kenya, while Rothschild's giraffes and reticulated giraffes best seen in Lake Nakuru NP and Samburu NR respectively.

More Hoofed Mammals

This sampling of miscellaneous hoofed animals highlights the astonishing diversity in this major group of African wildlife. Every visitor wants to see elephants and giraffes, but don't pass up a chance to watch hyraxes or warthogs.

Rock Hyrax

Weight 1.8-5.5kg; length 40-60cm It doesn't seem like it, but those funny tailless squirrels you see lounging around on rocks are an ancient cousin to the elephant. You won't see some of the features that rock hyraxes share with their larger kin, but look for tusks when one yawns. Easily spotted in many Kenyan and Tanzanian parks.

Warthog

Weight 45-75kg (female), 60-150kg (male); length 140-200cm Despite their fearsome appearance and sinister tusks, only the largest male warthogs are safe from lions, cheetahs and hyenas. To protect themselves when attacked, most warthogs run for burrows, then back in while slashing wildly with their tusks. Widespread throughout East Africa.

1. Rock hyrax 2. Warthog 3. Hippos

Hippopotamus

Weight 510-3200kg; length 320-400cm The hippopotamus is one strange creature. Designed like a big grey floating beanbag with tiny legs, the 3000kg hippo spends all its time in or very near water, chowing down on aquatic plants. Placid? No way! Hippos display a tremendous ferocity and strength when provoked. Best seen in Masai Mara NR, Serengeti NP, Tsavo West NP.

Banded mongoose 2. Spotted hyena 3. Golden jackal

Carnivores

It is a sign of Africa's ecological richness that the continent supports a remarkable variety of predators. When it comes to predators, expect the unexpected and you'll return home with a lifetime of memories!

Banded Mongoose

Weight 1.5-2kg; length 45-75cm Bounding across the savannah on their morning foraging excursions, family groups search for delicious snacks like toads, scorpions and slugs. Easily spotted in many East African parks.

Spotted Hyena

Weight 40-90kg; length 125-215cm Living in groups that are ruled by females (who grow penis-like sexual organs), hyenas use bone-crushing jaws to disembowel terrified prey on the run. Widespread and easily seen throughout many East African parks.

Golden Jackal

Weight 6-15kg; length 85-130cm Through a combination of sheer fierceness and bluff, the trim little jackal manages to fill its belly while holding hungry vultures and hyenas at bay. Best seen in Masai Mara NR, Ngorongoro Crater.

Hunting Dog

Weight 20-35kg; length 100-150cm Organised in complex hierarchies maintained by rules of conduct, these social canids are incredibly efficient hunters, running in packs of 20 to 60 to chase down antelope and other animals. Sadly, these beautiful dogs are now highly endangered. Best seen in Laikipia, Selous GR, Ruaha NP.

Honey Badger (Ratel)

Weight 7-16kg; length 75-100cm Some Africans say they would rather face a lion than a honey badger, and even lions relinquish their kill when a badger shows up. It finds its favourite food by following honey guide birds to bee hives. It's also known as a 'ratel'. Best seen in Mikumi NP.

1. White-backed vulture 2. African fish eagle 3. Bateleur
4. Secretary bird

Birds of Prey

East Africa has nearly 100 species of hawks, eagles, vultures and owls. More than 40 species have been spotted within a single park, making these some of the best places in the world to see an incredible variety of birds of prey.

White-Backed Vulture

Length 80cm Mingling around carcasses with lions, hyenas and jackals, vultures use their sheer numbers to compete for scraps of flesh and bone. Best seen in Masai Mara NR, Serengeti NP.

African Fish Eagle

Length 75cm This replica of the American bald eagle presents an imposing appearance but is most familiar for its loud, ringing vocalisations that have become known as 'the voice of Africa.' Best seen in Amboseli NP, Lake Baringo, Saadani NP.

Bateleur

Length 60cm French for 'tightrope-walker,' bateleur refers to this bird's distinctive low-flying aerial acrobatics. At close hand, look for its bold colour pattern and scarlet face. Widespread throughout East Africa.

Secretary Bird

Length 100cm With the body of an eagle and the legs of a crane, the secretary bird stands at 1.3m tall and walks up to 20km a day in search of vipers, cobras and other snakes, which it kills with lightning speed and agility. This idiosyncratic, grey-bodied raptor is commonly seen striding across the savannah. Best seen in Amboseli NP, Kidepo Valley NP, Mkomazi NP.

Augur Buzzard

Length 55cm Perhaps the most common raptor in the region, the augur buzzard occupies a wide range of wild and cultivated habitats. They hunt by floating motionlessly in the air then swooping down quickly to catch unwary critters. Widespread in western regions of East Africa.

1. Lilac-breasted roller 2. Lesser flamingos 3. Ostriches 4. Shoebill

IGNACIO PALACIOS / GETTY IMAGES ©

Other Birds

Birdwatchers from all over the world visit East Africa in search of the region's 1400 species of birds.

Lilac-Breasted Roller

Length 40cm Nearly everyone on safari gets to know the gorgeously coloured lilac-breasted roller. The roller gets its name from its tendency to 'roll' from side to side in flight as a way of showing off its iridescent blues, purples and greens. Commonly seen throughout East Africa.

Lesser Flamingo

Length 100cm Coloured deep rose-pink and gathering by the hundreds of thousands on shimmering salt lakes, the lesser flamingo creates one of Africa's most dramatic wildlife spectacles when they fly in formation or perform synchronised courtship. Best seen in Lake Natron, Lake Magadi and (depending on the year) Lake Nakuru NP and Lake Bogoria NR.

Ostrich

Length 200-270cm Standing at 270cm and weighing upwards of 130kg, these ancient flightless birds escape predators by running away at 70km/h or lying flat on the ground to resemble a pile of dirt. Widespread throughout Kenya, Uganda and northern Tanzania. Blue-legged Somali Ostrich commonly seen in Laikipia and Samburu NR.

Shoebill

Length 124cm The reclusive shoebill is one of the most highly sought-after birds in East Africa. Looking somewhat like a stout-bodied stork with an ugly old clog stuck on its face, the shoebill baffles scientists because it has no clear relative in the bird world. Best seen in Akagera NP, Mabamba Swamp.

Grey-Crowned Crane

Length 100cm Uganda's national bird is extremely elegant. Topped with a frilly yellow bonnet, this blue-grey crane dances wildly and shows off its red throat pouch during the breeding season. Best seen from central Kenya down into Tanzania, especially Amboseli NP.

Habitats

Nearly all the wildlife in East Africa occupies a specific type of habitat, and you will hear rangers and fellow travellers refer to these habitats repeatedly as they describe where to search for animals. If this is your first time in East Africa some of these habitats and their seasonal rhythms take some getting used to, but your wildlife-viewing experiences will be greatly enhanced if you learn how to recognise them and the animals you might expect to find in each one.

Savannah

Savannah is *the* classic East African landscape – broad rolling grasslands dotted with lone acacia trees. The openness and vastness of this landscape makes it a perfect home for large herds of grazing animals, and fast-sprinting predators like cheetahs. Shaped by fire and grazing animals, savannah is a dynamic habitat in constant flux with its adjacent woodlands. One of the best places in the world for exploring African savannah is found at Serengeti National Park.

High Mountains

High mountains are such a rare habitat in East Africa that the massive extinct volcanoes of Mts Kilimanjaro, Kenya and Elgon, and the remarkable highlands of the Rwenzori Mountains, stand out dramatically in the landscape. These isolated peaks are islands of montane forest, ethereal bogs, giant heathers, and moorlands perched high above the surrounding lowlands. The few animals that survive here are uniquely adapted to these bizarre landscapes.

Woodland

Tanzania is the only place in East Africa where you'll find dry woodlands, locally known as *miombo*. This important habitat provides homes for many birds, small mammals and insects. Here the trees form a continuous canopy that offers shelter from predators and harsh sunlight, and is a fantastic place to search for wildlife. In places where fingers of woodland mingle with savannah, animals such as leopards and antelope often gather to find shade and places to rest during the day. During the dry season, fires and elephants can wreak havoc on these woodlands, fragmenting large tracts of forest habitat into patches. Ruaha National Park in Tanzania is a great place to explore a wide diversity of mixed savannah and *miombo* habitats.

Semiarid Desert

Much of eastern and northern Kenya and parts of northeastern Tanzania see so little rainfall that shrubs and hardy grasses, rather than trees, are the dominant vegetation. This is not the classic landscape that many visitors come to see, and it doesn't seem like a great place for wildlife, but the patient observer will be richly rewarded. While it's true that the lack of water restricts larger animals such as zebras, gazelles and antelope to waterholes, this habitat explodes with plant and animal life whenever it rains. Tsavo East National Park in Kenya is a massive and gorgeous region of semiarid wilderness.

1. Mt Kenya (p286), Kenya's highest peak 2. Serengeti National Park (p135), Tanzania

White rhinos, Lake Nakuru (p246), Ker

National Parks & Reserves

East Africa's national parks and reserves rank among the best in Africa and some of the parks – Serengeti, Masai Mara and Mt Kilimanjaro to name just three – are the stuff of travellers' lore. Although some of the parks are under siege, and as much as 75% of the region's wildlife lives outside the protected areas, the region's national parks have, almost single-handedly, ensured that East Africa endures as one of the last remaining repositories of charismatic megafauna left on the planet.

History

The idea of setting aside land to protect nature began during colonial times, and in many cases this meant forcibly evicting the local peoples from their traditional lands. Enforcement of any vague notions of conservation that lay behind the reserves was often lax, and local anger was fuelled by the fact that many parks were set aside as hunting reserves for white hunters with anything but conservation on their minds. Many of these hunters, having pushed some species to the brink of extinction, later became conservationists and by the middle of the 20th century, the push was on to establish the national parks and reserves that we see today.

Africa's oldest national park is Parc National des Virungas in the Democratic Republic of the Congo (DRC); it was set aside by the Belgian colonial authorities in 1925. It was more than 20 years later, in 1946, that Nairobi National Park became East Africa's first such officially protected area.

> **Protected Areas of Country**
>
> Tanzania: 38.4%
>
> Kenya: 12.7%
>
> Uganda: 26.3%
>
> Rwanda: 7.6%
>
> Burundi: 5.6%

Visiting National Parks & Reserves

Tanzania

With more than one-third of Tanzanian territory locked away as a national park, wildlife reserve or marine park, Tanzania has the widest selection of protected areas to choose from.

Park entry fees range from US$30 to US$100 per adult per day (US$10 to US$20 per child per day), depending on the park, with Serengeti, Kilimanjaro, Mahale Mountains and Gombe parks the most expensive.

Except at some of the less-visited parks, where credit-card machines are planned, all park fees must be paid electronically with a Visa card or MasterCard. It's also possible to pay using a 'smart card' available for purchase from CRDB and Exim banks. Just in case, always bring both Visa or MasterCard as well as US dollars in cash or the equivalent in Tanzanian shillings (the latter to cover cases where the card machines are non-existent or not working).

Kenya

Kenya has 22 national parks, plus numerous marine parks and national reserves. Entry to some marine parks starts at US$20 per adult (US$15 per child) per 24 hours, while mainland parks start at US$25 (US$15 per child) and reach as much as US$80 (US$45 per child) for the Masai Mara National Reserve. Vehicles cost extra, with US$10 per day the norm.

Major National Parks & Reserves of East Africa

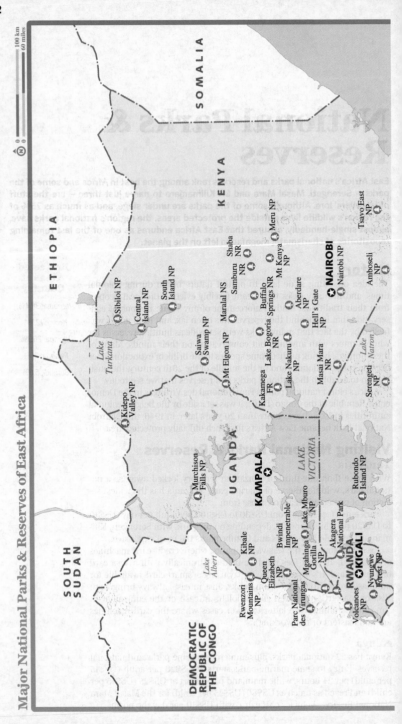

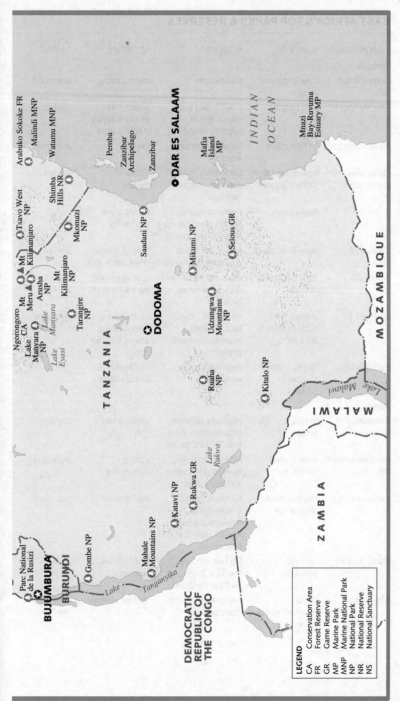

LEGEND

CA	Conservation Area
FR	Forest Reserve
GR	Game Reserve
MP	Marine Park
MNP	Marine National Park
NP	National Park
NR	National Reserve
NS	National Sanctuary

INDIAN OCEAN

DAR ES SALAAM

DODOMA

TANZANIA

MOZAMBIQUE

MALAWI

ZAMBIA

DEMOCRATIC REPUBLIC OF THE CONGO

BURUNDI

BUJUMBURA

Arabuko Sokoke FR
Malindi MNP
Watamu MNP
Pemba
Zanzibar Archipelago
Zanzibar
Mnazi Bay-Ruvuma Estuary MP
Mafia Island MP
Shimba Hills NR
Tsavo West NP
Mkomazi NP
Saadani NP
Mikumi NP
Selous GR
Mt Kilimanjaro
Ngorongoro CA
Mt Meru
Arusha NP
Mt Kilimanjaro NP
Lake Manyara NP
Lake Manyara
Tarangire NP
Lake Eyasi
Udzungwa Mountains NP
Kitulo NP
Ruaha NP
Lake Malawi
Lake Rukwa
Rukwa GR
Katavi NP
Mahale Mountains NP
Lake Tanganyika
Gombe NP
Parc National de la Rusizi

EAST AFRICA'S TOP PARKS & RESERVES

PARK/RESERVE	HABITATS	WILDLIFE	ACTIVITIES	BEST TIME TO VISIT
Tanzania				
Gombe Stream NP	Lake Tanganyika, forest	chimpanzees	chimp tracking	year-round
Lake Manyara NP	Lake Manyara	tree-climbing lions, hippos, hyenas, leopards, elephants	wildlife drives, walking & cycling in nearby areas	Jun-Feb
Mt Kilimanjaro NP	Mt Kilimanjaro	buffaloes, elephants, leopardS	trekking	year-round
Ngorongoro Conservation Area	Ngorongoro Crater, Crater Highlands	black rhinos, lions, elephants, zebras, flamingos	wildlife drives, trekking	Jun-Feb
Ruaha NP	Ruaha River	elephants, hippos, giraffes, cheetahs, more than 400 bird species	wildlife drives, short walks	Jul-Oct
Saadani NP	Wami River, beach	hippos, crocodiles, elephants, lions, giraffes	boating, wildlife drives, beach walks	Jun-Feb
Selous GR	Rufiji River, lakes, woodland	elephants, hippos, wild dogs, black rhinos, birds	boat safaris, walking, wildlife drives	Jun-Oct, Jan-Feb
Serengeti NP	plains & grasslands, Grumeti & Mara rivers	wildebeest, zebras, lions, cheetahs, leopards, elephants, giraffes	wildlife drives, balloon safaris, walking in border areas	year-round
Tarangire NP	Tarangire River, woodland, baobabs	elephants, zebras, wildebeest	wildlife drives, limited walking	Jun-Oct
Kenya				
Amboseli NP	dry plains, scrub forest	elephants, buffaloes, lions, antelope, more than 370 bird species	wildlife drives	Jun-Oct
Kakamega Forest NR	virgin tropical rainforest	red-tailed monkeys, flying squirrels, about 330 bird species	walking, birdwatching	year-round
Lake Nakuru NP	hilly grassland, alkaline lake	flamingos, black & white rhinos, tree-climbing lions, leopard, more than 400 bird species	wildlife drives	year-round
Masai Mara NR	savannah, grassland	Big Five, antelope, cheetahs, hyenas, wildebeest migration	wildlife drives, ballooning	Jul-Oct
Mt Kenya NP	rainforest, moorland, glacial mountain	elephants, buffaloes, mountain flora	trekking, climbing	Jan-Feb, Aug-Sep

PARK/RESERVE	HABITATS	WILDLIFE	ACTIVITIES	BEST TIME TO VISIT
Nairobi NP	open plains with urban backdrop	black rhinos, lions, leopards, cheetahs, giraffes, more than 400 bird species	wildlife drives	year-round
Tsavo West & East NPs	plains, ancient volcanic cones	Big Five, cheetahs, giraffes, hippos, crocodiles, around 500 bird species	rock climbing, wildlife drives	year-round
Uganda				
Bwindi Impenetrable NP	primeval tropical forest	eastern mountain gorillas	gorilla tracking, birdwatching	May-Sep
Kibale NP	lush forest	highest density of primates in Africa, including chimpanzee, red colobus & L'Hoest's monkey	chimp tracking, forest elephant viewing	May-Aug
Mgahinga Gorilla NP	volcanoes	eastern mountain gorillas, golden monkeys, elephants	gorilla tracking, visiting Twa (Batwa) villages, birdwatching	Jun-Sep
Murchison Falls NP	thundering falls, the Victoria Nile	elephants, hippos, crocodiles, lions, leopards, hyenas, Rothschild giraffes, Ugandan kob, more than 460 bird species	launch trip, wildlife drives, birdwatching	year-round
Queen Elizabeth NP	lakes, gorges, savannah	hippos, elephants, lions, leopards, chimpanzees, 611 recorded bird species	launch trip, chimp tracking, birdwatching	year-round
Rwenzori Mountains NP	Africa's highest mountain range	blue monkeys, chimpanzees, Rwenzori red duiker, 241 recorded bird species	trekking	Jun-Aug
Rwanda				
Volcanoes NP	towering volcanoes	eastern mountain gorillas, golden monkeys	gorilla & golden monkey tracking, volcano climbing	May-Sep
Nyungwe Forest NP	one of Africa's oldest rainforests, waterfalls	chimpanzees, Angolan colobus monkeys, about 275 bird species	chimp & colobus monkey tracking	May-Sep
Parc National des Virungas (DRC)	volcanoes, dense rainforest	eastern mountain gorillas, chimpanzees, forest elephants, okapis	gorilla & chimp tracking, volcano climbing	May-Sep

606

NATIONAL PARKS & RESERVES THE CONSERVANCY MODEL

TOP KENYAN CONSERVANCIES

In theory you pay your park entry fees with cash or a credit card. We strongly recommend that you pay in US dollars or Kenyan shillings, as KWS exchange rates are punitive. When it comes to credit cards, you'll often find the connection to be down so always carry enough cash with you to cover all the necessary fees.

Uganda

More than one-quarter of Uganda is protected in some form, with a particularly rich concentration of protected areas in the country's southwest. Most national parks charge US$40 per adult (US$20 per child) per 24 hours, with additional charges for vehicles, nature walks and ranger-guides; 20% of park fees go directly to local communities. Payments can be made in Ugandan shillings, dollars, euros and pounds in cash or travellers cheques (1% commission). And remember that if you're here to track gorillas, the US$600 permit fee includes park entry fees.

Rwanda

Rwanda has three national parks worthy of the name and entry fees depend on the reason for your visit. A permit to track the gorillas in Volcanoes National Park costs US$750, which includes park entry fees. Tracking chimpanzees (US$90) or golden monkeys (US$100) is considerably cheaper. Payments are usually made in cash, and preferably in US dollars.

Burundi

Burundi has three national parks, although visitor facilities are basic to non-existent and visitors are just as rare. Each of the parks is best visited as part of an organised safari arranged in Bujumbura. As always in Burundi, check the security situation before setting out.

The Conservancy Model

In Kenya, and increasingly in Tanzania, some of the most important conservation work is being done (and some of the most rewarding conservation tourism experiences are to be found) on private or community land.

Private Conservancies

The conservancy idea took hold on the large cattle ranches on Kenya's Laikipia Plateau and surrounding areas. One of the first to turn its attention to conservation was Lewa Downs, now the Lewa Wildlife Conservancy, which in 1983 set aside part of its land as a rhino sanctuary. There are now more than 40 such conservancies scattered across Laikipia and northern regions, with more around the Masai Mara.

The conservancy model differs from government-run national parks and reserves in a number of important ways:

➡ Nearly all conservancies focus on both wildlife conservation *and* community engagement and development; the conservancy entrance fees directly fund local community projects and wildlife programs. By giving local communities a stake in the protection of wildlife, so the argument goes, they are more likely to protect the wildlife in their midst.

➡ Access to conservancy land is, in most cases, restricted to those staying at the exclusive lodges and tented camps; Kenya's Ol Pejeta Conservancy is a notable exception. The result is a far more intimate wildlife-watching experience.

➡ Most private conservancies offer far more activities (including walking, horseback safaris and off-road driving) than national parks.

Tanzania has two private conservancies: **Manyara Ranch Conservancy** (www.manyararanch.com), between Lake Manyara and Tarangire National Parks, and the **Kilimanjaro Conservancy** (☑0754 333550, 027-250 2713; www.thekiliconservancy.org), in the West Kilimanjaro region.

Community-Run Conservancies

Community conservancies are an extension of the private conservancy model. Rather than being owned by wealthy landowners or families, community conservancies are owned by entire communities and administered by community representatives. With financial and logistical support from outside sources, these communities have in many cases built ecolodges whose income now provides much-needed funds for their education, health and humanitarian projects.

Northern Kenya appears to provide particularly fertile ground for the community conservancy model, but there are also some excellent examples around Amboseli National Park and in the Masai Mara region.

The Arts

East Africa's artistic traditions are lesser known than those emerging from elsewhere on the continent, but that means there are some real discoveries to be made. Outstanding literary and Swahili architectural traditions, in particular, give expression and voice to the region's fascinating local cultures, while Makonde woodcarving is one of the more refined in Africa. East Africans are also gaining plaudits in the world of cinema, while local musicians have perfected the art of adapting better-known musical traditions into something irresistibly East African.

Rwanda has a small but notable film festival (www.rwanda filmfestival.net), spearheaded by Rwandan filmmaker Eric Kabera. It takes place in July and is centred in Kigali, with screenings also in villages outside the capital.

Swahili-Style Architecture

East Africa is one of the continent's architectural treasures, particularly for its colonial-era buildings and religious architecture, including both churches and mosques. The real highlights, however, are the old town areas of Zanzibar and Lamu (both Unesco World Heritage Sites) and of Mombasa, all of which display mesmerising combinations of Indian, Arabic, European and African characteristics in their buildings and street layouts.

In Lamu, Pate and elsewhere along the coast, Swahili architecture predominates. At the simplest level, Swahili dwellings are plain rectangular mud-and-thatch constructions, set in clusters and divided by small, sandy paths. More elaborate stone houses are traditionally constructed of coral and wood along a north–south axis, with flat roofs and a small open courtyard in the centre, which serves as the main source of light.

The various quarters or neighbourhoods in Swahili towns are symbolically anchored by a central mosque, usually referred to as the *msikiti wa Ijumaa* (Friday mosque). In a sharp break with Islamic architectural customs elsewhere, traditional Swahili mosques don't have minarets; the muezzin gives the call to prayer from inside the mosque, generally with the help of a loudspeaker.

Cinema

East Africa's long languishing and traditionally under-funded film industry received a major boost with the opening of the **Zanzibar International Film Festival** (ZIFF; www.ziff.or.tz), also known as the Festival of the Dhow Countries. The festival, which has been held annually on Zanzibar Island since 1998, continues to be one of the region's premier cultural events. It serves as a venue for artists from the Indian Ocean basin and beyond, and has had several local prize winners, including two winners of the prestigious Golden Dhow Award. The first came in 1998 with *Maangamizi: The Ancient One,* shot in Tanzania and co-directed by Tanzanian Martin M'hando. M'hando is also known for his film, *Mama Tumaini* (Women of Hope). More recently, Kenya's Bob Nyanja won the coveted prize in 2011 for *The Rugged Priest*, in which an American Catholic priest battles the powers-that-be among the Maasai amid ethnic conflict in Kenya's Rift Valley.

Other regional winners of prizes at the Zanzibar festival have included *Makaburi Yatasema* (Only the Stones are Talking), a film about AIDS directed by Chande Omar Omar, and *Fimbo ya Baba* (Father's Stick), a 2006 Chande Omar Omar production also focusing on AIDS. In 2005 Tanzania's Beatrix Mugishawe won acclaim (and two prizes) for *Tumaini*, which focuses on AIDS orphans.

Rwandan Eric Kabera is known worldwide for *Keepers of Memory*, as well as *100 Days* (produced together with Nick Hughes) and *Through My Eyes*, both sobering documentaries on the Rwandan genocide and its aftermath, and both also ZIFF award winners.

In 2013, Kenyan actress Lupita Nyong'o became the first East African to win an Oscar. She was awarded Best Supporting Actress for her role in *12 Years a Slave.*

East African Literature

East Africa's first-known Swahili manuscript is an epic poem dating from 1728 and written in Arabic script. However, it wasn't until the second half of the 20th century – once Swahili had become established as a regional language – that Swahili prose began to develop. One of the best-known authors from this period was Tanzanian poet and writer Shaaban Robert (1909–62), who spearheaded development of a modern Swahili prose style. Among his works are the autobiographical *Maisha yangu* (My Life), and several collections of folk tales.

Arguably the region's most celebrated writer is Ngũgĩ wa Thiong'o (1938–). His harrowing criticism of the Kenyan establishment's neo-colonialist politics landed him in jail for a year (described in *Detained: A Prison Writer's Diary*), lost him his job at Nairobi University and forced him into exile. His works include *Petals of Blood, Matigari, The River Between, A Grain of Wheat, Devil on the Cross* and *Wizard of the Crow*. His latest works are memoirs: *Dreams in a Time of War* (2010) and *In the House of the Interpreter* (2012). He has also written extensively in his native language, Gikuyu.

Other important regional writers include Binyavanga Wainaina (1971–; Kenya), Okot p'Bitek (1931–82; Uganda), Moses Isegawa (1963–; Uganda) and Abdulrazak Gurnah (1948–).

There is also a rich but often overlooked body of English-language literature written by East African women, particularly in Uganda. Watch out for Mary Karooro Okurut, whose *A Woman's Voice: An Anthology of Short Stories by Ugandan Women* provides a good overview of the work of some of Uganda's female writers.

Another name to look for is that of the internationally recognised Kenyan writer Grace Ogot, known in particular for *The Promised Land*. Born in Nyanza Province, she sets many of her stories against the scenic background of Lake Victoria, and offers an insight into Luo culture in precolonial Kenya. Also from Kenya, Margaret Atieno Ogola was the author of the celebrated novel *The River and the Source* and its sequel, *I Swear by Apollo*, which follow the lives of four generations of Kenyan women in a rapidly evolving country.

Ngoma: Music & Dance

Congolese Roots

The single greatest influence on the modern East African music scene has been the Congolese bands that began playing in Dar es Salaam and Nairobi in the early 1960s, and brought the styles of rumba and soukous into the East African context. Among the best known is Orchestre Super Matimila, which was propelled to fame by the late Congolese-born Remmy Ongala ('Dr Remmy'). Many of Ongala's songs (most are in Swahili) are commentaries on contemporary themes such as AIDS, poverty and hunger. Another of the Congolese bands is Samba Mapangala's Orchestra

For information about East African music, see www.east africanmusic. com, which provides a broad overview of the region's music; for kanga sayings, see www.glcom. com/hassan/ kanga.html and www.mwambao. com/methali. htm, both of which provide a sampling of what is being said around you.

MAKONDE WOODCARVINGS

Tanzania's Makonde people are renowned for their woodcarvings. Among their most common carving styles are those with *ujamaa* motifs, and those known as *shetani*, which embody images from the spirit world. *Ujamaa* carvings are designed as a totem pole or 'tree of life' containing interlaced human and animal figures around a common ancestor. Each generation is connected to those that preceded it, and gives support to those that follow. Tree of life carvings often reach several metres in height, and are almost always made from a single piece of wood. *Shetani* carvings are much more abstract, and even grotesque, with the emphasis on challenging viewers to new interpretations while giving the carver's imagination free reign. Although Makonde carvings have inspired other East African woodcarvers, particularly among the Akamba people of southern Kenya, true Makonde carvings remain the finest examples of the genre.

Virunga. Mapangala, a Congolese vocalist, first gained a footing in Uganda in the mid-1970s with a group known as Les Kinois before moving to Nairobi and forming Orchestra Virunga.

As Swahili lyrics replaced the original vocals, a distinct East African rumba style was born. Its proponents include Simba Wanyika (together with offshoot Les Wanyika), which had its roots in Tanzania but gained fame in the nightclubs of Nairobi.

Benga

In the 1970s Kenyan benga music rose to prominence on the regional music scene. It originated among the Luo of western Kenya and is characterised by its clear electric guitar licks and bounding bass rhythms. Its ethnic roots were maintained, however, with the guitar taking the place of the traditional *nyatiti* (folk lyre), and the bass guitar replacing the drum, which originally was played by the *nyatiti* player with a toe ring. One of the best-known proponents of benga has been DO Misiani, whose group Shirati Jazz has been popular since the 1960s.

Dance

For links on art in Africa, including many on East Africa, see the listings on Columbia University's African Studies page (www.library.columbia.edu/locations/global/africa).

Throughout East Africa, dance plays a vital role in community life, although masked dance is not as common as it is in West Africa. A wide variety of drums and rhythms are used depending on the occasion, with many dances serving as expressions of thanks and praise, or as a means of communicating with the ancestors or telling a story. East Africa's most famous dance group is the globally acclaimed Les Tambourinaires du Burundi (p539).

Kanga, Kikoi & Handicrafts

Women throughout East Africa wear brightly coloured lengths of printed cotton cloth, typically with Swahili sayings printed along the edge, known as *kanga* in Kenya, Tanzania and parts of Uganda. Many of the sayings are social commentary or messages – often indirectly worded, or containing puns and double meanings – that are communicated by the woman wearing the *kanga*. Others are simply a local form of advertising, such as those bearing the logo of political parties.

In coastal areas, you'll also see the *kikoi*, which is made of a thicker textured cotton, usually featuring striped or plaid patterns, and traditionally worn by men. Also common are batik-print cottons depicting everyday scenes, animal motifs or geometrical patterns.

Jewellery, especially beaded jewellery, is particularly beautiful among the Maasai and the Turkana. It is worn in ceremonies as well as in everyday life, and often indicates the wearer's wealth and marital status.

Basketry and woven items – all of which have highly functional roles in local society – also make lovely souvenirs.

Visual Arts

East Africa is renowned for its exceptional figurative art, especially that crafted by Tanzania's Makonde, who are acclaimed throughout the region for their skill at bringing blocks of hard African blackwood (*Dalbergia melanoxylon* or, in Swahili, *mpingo*) to life in often highly fanciful depictions.

In comparison with woodcarving, painting has a much lower profile in East Africa. One of the more popular styles is Tanzania's Tingatinga painting, which takes its name from the self-taught artist Edward Saidi Tingatinga, who began the style in the 1960s. Tingatinga paintings are traditionally composed in a square format, and feature brightly coloured animal motifs set against a monochrome background.

A Taste of East Africa

East Africa's culinary tradition has generally emphasised feeding the masses as efficiently as possible, with little room for flair or innovation. Most meals centre around ugali, a thick, dough-like mass made from maize and/or cassava flour. While traditional fare may be bland but filling, there are some treats to be found. Many memorable eating experiences in the region are likely to revolve around dining alfresco in a safari camp, surrounded by the sights and sounds of the African bush.

The Street-Food Scene

Urojo is a filling, delicious soup with *kachori* (spicy potatoes), mango, limes, coconut, cassava chips, salad and sometimes *pili-pili* (hot pepper). Originally from Zanzibar, it's widely available along the coast.

Whether for the taste or simply the ambience, the street-food scene is one of the region's highlights. Throughout East Africa vendors hawk grilled maize, or deep-fried yams seasoned with a squeeze of lemon juice and a dash of chilli powder. Along the coast *pweza* (octopus) kebabs sizzle over the coals, and women squat near large, piping-hot pots of sweet *uji* (millet porridge). Other East African streetside favourites include *sambusas* (deep-fried pastry triangles stuffed with spiced mince meat) – but be sure they haven't been sitting around too long – *maandazi* (semi-sweet doughnut-like products) and *chipsi mayai* (a puffy omelette with chips mixed in). *Nyama choma* (seasoned barbecued meat) is found throughout the region and is especially popular in Kenya.

Ugali & Other Staples

One of the most common staples in East Africa is ugali (a thick, filling dough-like mass made from maize or cassava flour, or both); it's known as *posho* in Uganda. Around Lake Victoria, the staple is just as likely to be *matoke* (cooked plantains), while along the coast rice with coconut milk is the norm. Whatever the staple, it's always accompanied by a sauce, usually with a piece of meat – often a rather tough piece of meat – floating around in it.

Vegetarian Cuisine

While there isn't much in East Africa that is specifically billed as 'vegetarian', you can find cooked rice and beans almost everywhere. The main challenges are keeping dietary variety and getting enough protein. In larger towns, Indian restaurants are wonderful for vegetarian meals. Elsewhere, Indian shop owners may have suggestions, while fresh yoghurt, peanuts and cashews, and fresh fruits and vegetables are all wide-

WE DARE YOU

If you're lucky (!) and game (more to the point), you may be able to try various cattle-derived products beloved of the pastoral tribes of Kenya, Tanzania and elsewhere. Samburu, Pokot, Maasai and Karamojong warriors all have a taste for cattle blood. The blood is taken straight from the jugular, which does no permanent damage to the cattle. *Mursik* is made from milk fermented with grass ash, and is served in smoked gourds. It tastes and smells pungent, but it contains compounds that reduce cholesterol, enabling the warriors to live quite healthily on a diet of red meat, milk and blood.

DINING EAST AFRICAN STYLE

If you're invited to join in a meal, the first step is hand washing. Your hostess will bring around a bowl and water jug; hold your hands over the bowl while she pours water over them. Sometimes soap is provided, and a towel for drying off.

At the centre of the meal will be ugali or some other similar staple. Take some with the right hand from the communal pot (your left hand is used for wiping – and we don't mean your mouth!), roll it into a small ball with the fingers, making an indentation with your thumb, and dip it into the accompanying sauce. Don't soak the ugali too long (to avoid it breaking up in the sauce), and keep your hand lower than your elbow (except when actually eating) so the sauce doesn't drip down your forearm. Eating with your hand is a bit of an art and may seem awkward at first, but after a few tries it will start to feel more natural.

The underlying element in all meal invitations is solidarity between the hosts and the guests. If you receive an invitation to eat but aren't hungry, it's OK to explain that you have just eaten. However, still share a few bites of the meal in order to demonstrate your solidarity with the hosts, and to express your appreciation.

Don't be worried if you can't finish what's on your plate; this shows that you have been satisfied. But try to avoid being the one who takes the last handful from the communal bowl, as your hosts may think that they haven't provided enough.

Except for fruit, desserts are rarely served; meals conclude with another round of hand washing.

ly available. Most tour operators are willing to cater to special dietary requests, such as vegetarian, kosher or halal, with advance notice.

Drinks

Water & Juice

Tap water is best avoided; also be wary of ice and fruit juices that may have been diluted with unpurified water. Bottled water is widely available, except in remote areas, where it's worth carrying a filter or purification tablets.

Sodas (soft drinks) are found almost everywhere. Freshly squeezed juices, especially pineapple, sugar cane and orange, are a treat, although check whether they have been mixed with safe water. Also refreshing, and never a worry hygienically, is the juice of the *dafu* (green) coconut. Western-style supermarkets sell imported fruit juices.

Coffee & Tea

Although East Africa exports high-quality coffee and tea, what's usually available locally is far inferior, and instant coffee is the norm. The situation is changing in major cities and tourist areas, albeit slowly. Both tea and coffee are generally drunk with lots of milk and sugar. On the coast, sip a smooth spiced tea *(masala chai)* or sample a coffee sold by vendors strolling the streets carrying a freshly brewed pot in one hand, cups and spoons in the other.

Beer & Wine

Among the most common beers are the locally brewed Tusker, Primus and Kilimanjaro, and South Africa's Castle Lager, which is also produced locally. Many locals prefer their beer warm, especially in Kenya, so getting a cold beer can be a task. Good-quality South African wines are readily available in major cities.

Locally produced home brews (fermented mixtures made with bananas or millet and sugar) are widely available. However, avoid anything distilled; in addition to being illegal, it's also often lethal.

Especially along the coast, coffee vendors carry around a stack of coffee cups and a piping-hot kettle on a long handle with coals fastened underneath. They let you know they're coming by clacking together their metal coffee cups.

Dining Out

Hotelis & Night Markets

For dining local-style, find a local eatery, known as *hoteli* in Swahili-speaking areas. The day's menu, rarely costing more than US$1, is usually written on a chalkboard. Rivalling *hoteli* for local atmosphere are the bustling night markets, where vendors set up grills along the roadside and sell *nyama choma* (seasoned barbecue meat) and other street food.

Portuguese explorers in the colonial era introduced maize, cassava, potatoes and chillies from South America, all of which are now staples of the East African diet.

Restaurants

For Western-style meals, cities and main towns will have an array of restaurants, most moderately priced compared with their European counterparts. Every capital city has at least one Chinese restaurant. In many parts of East Africa, especially along the coast, around Lake Victoria and in Uganda, there's also usually a selection of Indian cuisine, found both at inexpensive eateries serving Indian snacks, as well as in pricier restaurants.

Self-Catering

Supermarkets in main towns sell imported products, such as canned meat, fish and cheese.

Local Customs & Traditions

Typical East African style is to eat with the right hand from communal dishes in the centre of the table. It is not customary to share drinks. Children generally eat separately.

Avoid handling or eating food with the left hand; in many areas, it's even considered impolite to give someone something with the left hand.

European-style restaurant dining, while readily available in major cities, is not an entrenched part of local culture. More common are meal-centred gatherings at home to celebrate special occasions.

Lunch is served between noon and 2.30pm, and dinner from about 6.30pm or 7pm to 10pm. The smaller the town, the earlier its dining establishments are likely to close; after about 7pm in rural areas it can be hard to find alternatives to street food. During Ramadan, many restaurants in coastal areas close completely during daylight fasting hours.

Food & Drink Glossary

bia	beer
biryani	rice dish, sometimes in a casserole form, often served with chicken or meat
chai	tea
chai ya asubuhi	breakfast
chakula cha jioni	dinner
chakula cha mchana	lunch
chakula kutoka bahari	seafood
chapati	Indian-style bread
chenye viungo	spicy
chipsi mayai	puffy omelette with chips mixed in
chumvi	salt
githeri	mix of beans and corn
irio	mashed greens, potato and boiled corn or beans (also called *kienyeji*)
jusi	juice
kaa	crab
kahawa	coffee

karanga	peanut
kiazi	potato
kienyeji	mashed greens, potato and boiled corn or beans (also called *irio*)
kiti moto	fried or roasted pork bits, sold by the kilo, served with salad and fried plantain
kuku	chicken
kumbwe	snack
maji	water
maji ya machungwa	orange juice
maji ya madini	mineral water
mandazi	semisweet doughnut served warm, with lashings of milk and brown sugar
masala chai	tea with cardamom and cinnamon
matoke	mashed green plantains
maziwa	milk
mboga	vegetable
mchuzi	sauce, sometimes with bits of beef and vegetables
mgahawa	restaurant
mishikaki	marinated grilled meat kebabs, usually beef
mkate mayai	literally 'bread eggs'; a wheat dough pancake, filled with minced meat and egg and fried on a hotplate
mkate wa kumimina	sesame-seed bread, found along the coast
mtindi	cultured milk, usually sold in small bags and delicious on a hot day
mukimo	sweet potatoes, corn, beans and plantains
mwanakondoo	lamb
nyama	meat
nyama choma	seasoned barbecued meat
nyama mbuzi	mutton
nyama ng'ombe	beef
nyama nguruwe	pork
nyama ya ndama	veal
pilau	rice dish, often served with chicken, meat or seafood, sometimes cooked in broth (a coastal speciality)
pilipili	pepper
posho	Ugandan version of ugali
samak	fish
sambusas	deep-fried pastry triangles stuffed with spiced mince meat; similar to Indian samosas
sukari	sugar
sukuma wiki	braised or stewed spinach
tambi	pasta
ugali	thick, dough-like mass made from maize and cassava flour, or both
uji	thin, sweet porridge made from bean, millet or other flour
vitambua	small rice cakes resembling tiny, thick pancakes
wali	cooked rice
wali na kuku/samaki/ nyama/maharagwe	cooked white rice with chicken/fish/meat/beans

baraza — peanut
kiazi — potato
kikwayu — mashed green peas and boiled corn or beans (also 'Iro')
Kiti moto — load of roasted pork unit, sold by the kilo, served with salad and fried plantain
kuku — chicken
kumbawa — jack
mali — crab
maji ya machungwa — orange juice
maji ya madini — mineral water
mandazi — semisweet doughnut served warm with lashings of milk and brown sugar
mas'ala chai — tea with cardamom and cinnamon
matoke — mashed green plantains
maziwa — milk
mboga — vegetable
mchuzi — sauce, sometimes with bits of beef into vegetables
mseehawa — rostin' sth(?)
mishikaki — marinated grilled meat kebabs, usually beef
mkate mayai — literally 'bread eggs' – a wheat dough pancake, filled with minced meat and egg and fried on a hotplate
mkate wa kumimba — sesame seed bread, found along the coast
mtindi — cultured milk, usually sold in small bags and delicious on a hot day
mufino — sweet potato, corn, beans, and plantains
mwana/samaki — lamb
nyama — meat
nyama choma — seasoned barbecued meat
nyama mbuzi — mutton
nyama ng'ombe — beef
nyama nguruwe — pork
nyama ya mbuli — veal
pilau — rice dish often served with chicken, meat or seafood, sometimes coconut in broth (a coastal speciality)
pilipili — pepper
posho — lighter version of ugali
samak — fish
sambusa — deep fried pastry triangles stuffed with spiced mincemeat, similar to Indian samosas
sukari — sugar
sukuma wiki — braised or stewed spinach
tambi — pasta
ugali — thick dough-like mass made from maize and cassava flour, or both
uji — thin sweet porridge made from beans, millet, or other flour
vitumbua — small rice cakes resembling fluffy thick pancakes
wali — cooked rice
wali na kuku/samaki, nyama (mbuzi/ngwe) — coconut water rice with chicken/fish/meat, beans

Survival Guide

Safe Travel

It's difficult to generalise about safety in East Africa. While there are significant risks in some areas, most places are extremely safe. The list of potential dangers may sound daunting, but most visitors to the region never experience any difficulties. The best approach is to stay alert and informed about the risks, and enjoy your trip without being paranoid.

Common Dangers

Banditry

Banditry tends to occur in quite localised areas – northeastern Kenya, northeastern Uganda and rural Burundi are common trouble-spots, but these areas are well known and easily avoided, and even these are safer than they used to be. Always check the international travel advisories and make enquiries locally – with expats, police and local guides – before setting out.

Crime

Petty theft is a risk throughout East Africa, primarily in capital cities and tourist areas. The risks are especially high in crowded settings (markets, public transport, and bus and train stations) or in isolated areas (dark streets or deserted beaches). Muggings and violent crime are less frequent but nonetheless do occur. By following a few simple precautions, you'll minimise the risks:

➡ Avoid isolated areas, including beaches, at any time of day, especially at night.

➡ In cities, especially Nairobi (Kenya), be alert for hustlers who will try any ploy to get you into a back alley and away from the watching eyes of onlookers.

➡ Don't tempt people by flaunting your wealth. Avoid external money pouches, dangling backpacks and camera bags, and leave jewellery, fancy watches, electronics and the like at home or in the hotel safe.

➡ When out walking, keep a small amount of cash separate from your other money and handy, so that you don't pull out large wads of bills for making purchases.

➡ Try not to look lost, even if you are. Walk purposefully and confidently, and don't refer to a guidebook or a map while on the street.

➡ Take particular care when arriving for the first time at a bus station, particularly in places such as Nairobi and Arusha (Tanzania). Try to spot the taxi area before disembarking, and make a beeline for it.

➡ Store valuables in a hotel safe, if there's a reliable one, ideally inside a lockable pouch.

➡ Keep the windows up in vehicles when stopped in traffic, and keep your bags out of sight.

➡ On buses and trains, never accept food or drink from fellow passengers. Also avoid travelling at night.

Terrorism

Terrorism is, unfortunately, something you have to consider when visiting East Africa, although the vast majority of the region is safe to visit. Remember that reports of an attack in, for example, Mombasa (Kenya), is likely to have very little impact upon the safety of visiting Rwanda.

Kenya has come under major terrorist attack on at least three occasions: in August 1998 the US embassy in Nairobi was bombed; in November 2002 the Paradise Hotel, north of Mombasa, was car-bombed at the same time as a rocket attack on an Israeli jet; and in September 2013 terrorists attacked the upscale Westgate Shopping Mall in Nairobi. In early 2014, a number of British tour operators withdrew all of their clients from and suspended tours to most coastal areas of Kenya.

Other, smaller attacks have taken place in and around Mombasa; on commuter transport and in markets in the Eastleigh suburb of Nairobi; and around Mpeketoni close to Lamu – although these have primarily targeted locals rather than foreign tourists.

Kenya has been targeted particularly because its forces invaded Somalia in 2011 in an attempt to rid the country of Islamist militants. Since then, both Uganda and Burundi have contributed soldiers to an African Union (AU) force inside Somalia which has increased their own threat levels – in 2010, a terrorist bombing claimed 74 lives in Kampala (Uganda), while Burundi remains on alert after a number of threats were directed at the country as a result of its participation in the Somali mission.

Terrorism is rare in Tanzania, although the US embassy in Dar es Salaam was attacked by suicide bombers in 1998. In Rwanda, there have been several isolated grenade attacks since 2011.

Road Accidents

Perhaps the most widespread threat to your safety comes from travelling on the region's roads. Road conditions vary, but driving standards are almost universally poor and high speeds are common.

To minimise the risk, consider the following:

➡ Never travel at night.

➡ Choose a full-sized bus over a minibus.

➡ If travelling in a matatu (usually a minivan), never take the seat next to the driver.

Scams

The region's thieves have invented numerous ways to separate you from your money. Most are deceptively simple, and equally simple to avoid.

➡ Be sceptical of anyone who approaches you on the street saying 'Remember me?' or claiming to be collecting donations for school fees. Your money has a better chance of reaching those most in need when channelled through registered charities or churches.

➡ You're walking along a busy city street, and suddenly find your way blocked by someone. Before you know it, his buddy has come up behind you and relieved you of your wallet, and they both disappear into the crowds.

➡ Someone strikes up a conversation and tries to sell you marijuana (*bangi* or *ganja*). Before can shake them loose, police officers (sometimes legitimate, sometimes not) appear insisting you pay a huge fine for being involved in the purchase of illegal drugs. Insist on going to the nearest police station before paying anything.

➡ A smooth-talker befriends you and his friend just happens to have a taxi. When you get in, you're joined by his buddies, who then force you to turn over your ATM card and PIN, and ride with them to various ATMs around the city until your account is emptied. Only take taxis from established ranks, and avoid getting into taxis with a 'friend' of the driver or someone else already in it.

By Country

Tanzania Although you should take all the usual precautions, Tanzania is one of the safest countries in the region. Muggings and petty thefts do occur, especially in Dar es Salaam and Zanzibar, while touts can be a particular annoyance in Arusha, Mbeya and Zanzibar.

Kenya Nairobi is notorious for muggings and more serious crime, but the situation has improved and the greatest dangers are relatively easy to avoid. Crime can be a problem in Mombasa and other coastal areas, especially beach resorts. Northern Kenya has an ongoing problem with banditry. The problem is particularly acute close to the Somali border. Terrorism is also an issue that you need to consider.

Uganda Generally safe for foreign travellers and Kampala is one of the region's safer large cities. The main threats come from bandits in the Karamojong area of far northeastern Uganda and the border areas of the country's far northwest.

Rwanda Few visitors to Rwanda experience any problems, although you should take the usual safety precautions. You should also always check the prevailing security situation close to Rwanda's borders with Burundi and the DRC.

Burundi The security situation for visitors to Burundi has improved recently, although the country remains subject to political instability and violence. Bujumbura has a reputation for street crime, while some rural areas remain off-limits; the road from Bujumbura north to the Rwandan border is considered fairly safe.

Directory A–Z

Accommodation

Accommodation ranges from no-frills rooms with communal bucket bath to some of Africa's most luxurious safari lodges.

Except for low-budget local guesthouses (where you get a room only), prices listed include private bathroom and continental breakfast (coffee or tea, bread, jam and sometimes an egg).

Many lodges and luxury camps around the parks quote all-inclusive prices, which means accommodation and full board plus excursions such as wildlife drives, short guided walks or boat safaris. Park entry fees are generally excluded.

Camping prices are per person, except as noted.

Camping

➜ There are campsites in most national parks and in or near many major towns. In some rural tourist areas, local villagers maintain camping grounds. Facilities range from none at all to full service, with hot showers and cooking areas.

➜ In Kenyan and Tanzanian parks there are both public campsites (usually very basic, with a toilet block with a couple of pit toilets, a water tap and perhaps public showers) and special campsites (have even fewer facilities than the standard camps, but cost more because of their wilder locations and set-up costs). Public campsites can cost up to US$30/20 per adult/child and special campsites start at US$50/25.

➜ Except for the national parks, prices average US$5 to US$10 per person per night.

➜ Camping away from established sites is not advisable; in rural areas, ask the village head or elders before pitching your tent. Camping is not recommended in Rwanda and Burundi, where camping options in any case range from limited to non-existent.

➜ In coastal areas, bungalows or *bandas* (simple wooden or thatched huts, often with only a mattress and mosquito net) offer an alternative to camping.

Hostels, Guesthouses & Budget Hotels

➜ True hostels are rare, but mission hostels and guesthouses are scattered throughout the region. While intended primarily for missionaries and aid-organisation staff, they're generally happy to accommodate travellers if space is available. Most are clean, safe and good value.

➜ In budget guesthouses and hotels, you generally get what you pay for, though there's the occasional good deal. The cheapest ones (every town will have one) are poorly ventilated cement-block rooms with sometimes clean sheets, shared toilets, cold showers or a bucket bath, mosquito net, sometimes a fan and often only a token lock on the door. Rates for this type of place average from US$5 per room per night. A few dollars more will get you a somewhat more comfortable room, often with a bathroom (although not always with running or hot water).

➜ Many budget places double as brothels, and at many of the cheapest ones solo women travellers are likely to feel uncomfortable. For peace and quiet, guesthouses without bars are the best choice.

➜ Backpackers and dormitory-style places aren't as common as in southern Africa, but there are a few,

---

BOOK YOUR STAY ONLINE

For more accommodation reviews by Lonely Planet authors, check out www.lonelyplanet.com/hotels. You'll find independent reviews, as well as recommendations on the best places to stay. Best of all, you can book online.

with prices slightly higher than you'd pay for a room in a basic local guesthouse.

Hotels, Lodges & Luxury Safari Camps

➡ Larger towns will have one or several midrange hotels, most with private bathrooms, hot water and a fan or an air-conditioner. Facilities range from faded to good value, and prices range from US$50 to US$200 per person.

➡ Major tourist areas also have a good selection of top-end accommodation, with prices ranging from about US$200 upwards per person per night. On the safari circuits, top-end prices are generally all-inclusive or sold on a full-board basis.

➡ National parks often have 'permanent tented camps' or 'luxury tented camps'. These offer comfortable beds in canvas tents, usually with a private toilet, screened windows and most of the comforts of a hotel room, but with a wilderness feel.

➡ 'Mobile' or 'fly' camps are temporary camps set up for several nights, or for one season, and used for walking safaris or a more intimate bush experience away from the main tented camp.

Activities

Diving & Snorkelling

If you want to learn to dive, or to refresh your skills, East Africa is a rewarding if somewhat pricey place to do this.

WHEN TO GO

There are distinct seasons for diving in East Africa. October (or September) to March is the best time. From June to August it's often impossible to dive, especially in Kenya, due to the poor visibility caused by the heavy silt flow from some rivers. That said, some divers have taken the plunge in July and found visibility to be a very respectable 7m to 10m, although 4m is more common.

DIVE OPERATORS & SAFETY

When choosing a dive operator, quality rather than cost should be the priority. Consider the operator's experience and qualifications; the knowledge and competence of staff; and the condition of equipment and frequency of maintenance. Assess whether the overall attitude is serious and professional, and ask about safety precautions: radios, oxygen, boat reliability and back-up engines, emergency evacuation procedures, first-aid kits, safety flares and life jackets. On longer dives, do you get an energising meal, or just tea and biscuits?

There are decompression chambers in Matemwe on Zanzibar's east coast; in Mombasa in Kenya (although this is an army facility, and not always available to the general public); and in Johannesburg (South Africa). Also check the **Divers Alert Net-**

work Southern Africa (DAN; www.dansa.org) website; it's highly recommended to take out insurance coverage with DAN (their coverage includes Kenya and Tanzania).

Be sure to allow a sufficient surface interval between the conclusion of your final dive and any onward flights. The Professional Association of Dive Instructors (PADI) recommends at least 12 hours, or more if you have been doing daily multiple dives for several days. Another consideration is insurance, which you should arrange before coming to East Africa. Many policies exclude diving, so you'll likely need to pay a bit extra, but it's well worth it in comparison with the bills you will need to foot should something go wrong.

Hiking & Trekking

Almost all hikes and climbs in the region require local guides, and some require a full range of clothing, from lightweight for the semitropical conditions at lower altitudes to full winter gear for the high summits. Waterproof clothing and equipment is important at any altitude and season.

The best time to trek is from June to February – avoid the March to May rainy season.

Electricity

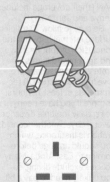

220-250V/50Hz

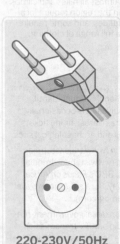

220-230V/50Hz

Gay & Lesbian Travellers

Officially, male homosexuality is illegal in Uganda, Tanzania and Kenya. While prosecutions rarely occur, discretion is advised as gay sexual relationships are culturally taboo, and public displays of affection, whether between people of the same or opposite sex, are frowned upon. In Uganda and Kenya in particular, anti-gay public discourse has become increasingly common in recent times.

Initial contacts include **Purple Roofs** (www.purpleroofs.com/africa/kenya), which lists gay or gay-friendly tour companies in the region.

Insurance

Worldwide travel insurance is available at www.lonelyplanet.com/travel-insurance. You can buy, extend and claim online anytime, even if you're already on the road.

➜ Shop around before choosing a policy, as those designed for short package tours in Europe may not be suitable for East Africa.

➜ Read the fine print: some policies specifically exclude 'dangerous activities', which can mean scuba diving, motorcycling and even trekking. A locally acquired motorcycle licence isn't valid under some policies.

➜ Most policies valid in East Africa require you to pay on the spot and claim later, so keep all documentation.

➜ Most importantly, check that the policy covers an

emergency flight home or at least medical evacuation to Western-standard health facilities, and understand in advance the procedures you need to follow in an emergency.

➜ Before heading to East Africa, consider taking out a membership with one of the following, both of which operate 24-hour air ambulance services and offer emergency medical evacuation within East Africa:

African Medical & Research Foundation (☎020-6993000; www.amref.org) A one-month Gold membership costs US$24 and covers two air ambulance evacuations and 24-hour medical treatment in all five East African countries.

First Air Responder (www.firstairresponder.com) A two-week/one-month membership costs US$20/35 and entitles you to emergency evacuation within Tanzania and Kenya as well as local ground support in the vicinity of Dar es Salaam, Arusha and several other Tanzanian cities.

Internet Access

➜ There are internet cafes in all capitals and major towns. In rural areas, connections remain spotty.

➜ Prices average US$1 per hour; truly fast connections are rare.

➜ Many hotels and cafes have wireless access points. Connections are possible at some but not all safari camps.

➜ If you'll be in East Africa for a while, consider buying a

EATING PRICE RANGES

Price ranges used in individual listings reflect the cost of a main dish:

$ less than US$6

$$ US$6 to US$12

$$$ more than US$12

RESPONSIBLE TREKKING

The huge number of visitors in some of East Africa's wilderness areas are beginning to take their toll. Mt Kilimanjaro is a prime example, although there are many others. Following are some tips for helping to preserve the region's delicate ecosystems and beauty:

➡ Carry out all your rubbish, and make an effort to carry out rubbish left by others. Sanitary napkins, tampons, condoms and toilet paper should be carried out despite the inconvenience. They burn and decompose poorly.

➡ Minimise waste by taking minimal packaging and no more food than you will need. Take reusable containers or stuff sacks.

➡ Contamination of water sources by human faeces can lead to the transmission of all sorts of nasties. Where there is a toilet, use it. Where there is none (as is the case in many of the region's trekking areas), bury your waste. Dig a small hole 15cm (6in) deep and at least 100m (320ft) from any watercourse. Cover the waste with soil and a rock. In snow, dig down to the soil. Also ensure that these guidelines are applied to a portable toilet tent if one is being used by a large trekking party.

➡ Don't use detergents or toothpaste in or near watercourses, even if they are biodegradable. For personal washing, use biodegradable soap (best purchased at home) and a water container at least 50m (160ft) away from the watercourse. Disperse the waste water widely to allow the soil to filter it fully. Wash cooking utensils 50m (160ft) from watercourses using a scourer, sand or snow instead of detergent.

➡ Hillsides and mountain slopes, especially at high altitudes, are prone to erosion. Stick to existing trails, and avoid short cuts. If a well-used trail passes through a mud patch, walk through the mud so as not to increase the size of the patch. Avoid removing the plant life that keeps topsoils in place.

➡ Don't depend on open fires for cooking. The cutting of wood for fires in popular trekking areas such as Kilimanjaro can cause rapid deforestation. Cook on a light-weight kerosene, alcohol or Shellite (white gas) stove and avoid those powered by disposable butane gas canisters.

➡ If you are trekking with a guide and porters, supply stoves for the whole team. In cold conditions, ensure that all members are outfitted with enough clothing so that fires are not a necessity for warmth. If you patronise local accommodation, try to select places that don't use wood fires to heat water or cook food.

➡ Ensure that you fully extinguish a fire after use. Spread the embers and flood them with water.

USB stick or dongle from one of the main mobile providers (US$20 to US$80), which you can then load with credit and plug into your laptop.

Legal Matters

Apart from traffic offences such as speeding and driving without a seatbelt (mandatory in many areas for driver and front-seat passengers), the main area to watch out for is drug use and possession. Marijuana (*bangi* or *ganja*) is widely available in places such as Nairobi, Dar es Salaam and Zanzibar, and is frequently offered to tourists, invariably part of a set-up involving the police or fake police. If you're caught, expect to pay a large bribe to avoid arrest or imprisonment.

If you're arrested for whatever reason, you can request to call your embassy, but the help they can give you will be limited.

If you get robbed, most insurance companies require a police report before they'll reimburse you. You can get these at the nearest police station, though it's usually a time-consuming process.

Maps

Recommended maps include the following:

➡ Nelles *Tanzania, Rwanda, Burundi*

➡ Nelles *Kenya*

➡ Nelles *Uganda*

➡ Bartholomew's *Kenya & Tanzania*

➡ Hallwag *Kenya & Tanzania* (also includes Uganda, Rwanda and Burundi)

➡ Michelin *Africa: Central & South* (covers most of the region on a smaller scale)

RESPONSIBLE DIVING & SNORKELLING

Wherever you dive, consider the following tips, and help preserve the ecology and beauty of the reefs:

➡ Never use anchors on a reef, and take care not to ground boats on coral.

➡ Avoid touching or standing on living marine organisms or dragging equipment across a reef. Polyps can be damaged by even the gentlest contact. If you must hold on to a reef, only touch exposed rock or dead coral.

➡ Be conscious of your fins. Even without contact, the surge from fin strokes near a reef can damage delicate organisms. Take care not to kick up clouds of sand, which can smother organisms.

➡ Practise and maintain proper buoyancy control. Major damage can be done by divers descending too fast and colliding with a reef.

➡ Take great care in underwater caves. Spend as little time within them as possible, as your air bubbles may be caught within the roof and thereby leave organisms high and dry. Take turns inspecting the interior of a small cave.

➡ Resist the temptation to collect or buy corals or shells – which you'll frequently be offered by vendors on the beaches – or to loot marine archaeological sites (mainly shipwrecks).

➡ Ensure that you take home all your rubbish and any litter you may find as well. Plastics in particular are a serious threat to marine life.

➡ Do not feed fish.

➡ Minimise your disturbance of marine animals, and never ride on the backs of turtles or attempt to touch dolphins.

Money

Bring a mix of US dollars or euros in cash (large and small denominations); a credit card (Visa and Master-Card are most widely accepted) for withdrawing money from ATMs; and some travellers cheques as an emergency standby (although note that these are generally changeable in major cities only, and with very high commissions).

ATMs

There are ATMs in all capital cities and most major towns (except for Burundi, where they are found almost exclusively in Bujumbura, and to a lesser extent Rwanda). They take Visa, MasterCard or both (Visa only in Rwanda). Some banks in Kenya, Tanzania and Uganda also have machines linked to the Plus and Cirrus networks. However, despite their growing

use, ATMs are out of order or out of cash with enough frequency that you should always have some sort of back-up funds. There are few ATMs away from major routes.

Bargaining

Bargaining is expected by vendors in tourist areas, except in a limited number of fixed-price shops. However, away from tourist areas and for nontourist items, the price quoted will often be the 'real' price, so don't automatically assume that the quote you've been given is too high.

Where bargaining is appropriate, if you pay the first price asked, you'll probably be considered naive and you'll also be doing fellow travellers a disservice by creating the impression that all foreigners are willing to pay any named price. Paying consistently above the curve can contribute to goods being priced out of the reach of locals.

While there are no set rules for bargaining, it should be conducted in a friendly and spirited manner; losing your temper or becoming aggressive or frustrated will be counterproductive. In any transaction, the vendor's aim is to identify the highest price you will pay, while your aim is to find the lowest price at which the vendor will sell. Before starting, shop around to get a feel for the 'value' of the item you want, and ask others what they paid. Once you start negotiating, if things seem like a waste of time, politely take your leave. Sometimes sellers will call you back if they think their stubbornness is counterproductive. Few will pass up a sale, however thin the profit. If the vendor won't come down to a price you feel is fair, it means that they aren't making a profit, or that too many high-rolling foreigners have passed through already.

Black Market

Except possibly in Burundi, there is essentially no black market for foreign currency. Nevertheless, you'll still get shady characters sidling up beside you in Nairobi, Dar es Salaam and major tourist areas, trying to get you to change money and promising enticing rates. It's invariably a set-up; changing on the street should be avoided.

Cash

US dollars, followed by euros, are the most convenient foreign currencies and get the best rates. Other major currencies are readily accepted in major cities, but often not elsewhere, or at less favourable rates. You'll get higher rates for larger denomination bills (US$50 and US$100 notes), but carry a supply of smaller denomination notes as well, as change can be difficult to find.

Throughout the region, the only US dollar notes that are accepted for exchange are those from 2006 or newer.

Credit Cards

Visa and MasterCard can be used for some top-end hotels and a few tour operators, especially in major towns and in Kenya. However, they're best viewed as a stand-by unless you've confirmed things in advance with the establishment. In Rwanda and Burundi you'll need to rely almost exclusively on cash, although a few banks in major cities give cash advances against a credit card with a high commission. Some places, especially in Tanzania, attach a commission of about 5% to 10% to credit card payments.

Exchanging Money

You can change cash with a minimum of hassle at banks or foreign exchange (forex) bureaus in major towns and cities; rates and commissions vary, so it pays to shop around. In addition to regular banking hours, most forex bureaus are also open on Saturday mornings. Outside banking hours and away from an ATM, ask shop owners if they can help you out, rather than changing with someone on the street (which should always be avoided). It's better to say something like 'The banks are closed; do you know someone who could help me out?' rather than directly asking if they will change money.

Tipping

Tipping generally isn't practised in small, local establishments. But in major towns, upmarket places and anywhere frequented by tourists, tips are expected. If a service charge hasn't been included, either round out the bill or calculate about 10%. Tips are expected by guides, drivers and others with whom you have spent a number of days – count on US$10 to US$15 per day per group, more if you've been travelling alone for a number of days. Some safari camps keep a box for tips that are later shared among all staff.

Travellers Cheques

Throughout the region, travellers cheques can be changed either not at all (as in Rwanda, Burundi and Tanzania) or only in major cities, with high commissions and with great difficulty. They should not be relied upon. Where they can be changed, rates are lower than for cash. American Express and Thomas Cook are the most widely recognised; get your cheques in US dollars or euros. Bring a range of denominations because some banks charge a per-cheque levy. Carry the *original* purchase receipt with you (and separately from the cheques), as many banks and forex bureaus will ask to see it.

If your cheques are stolen, getting replacements while still in the region is generally not possible.

Opening Hours

Banks 8.30am to 3pm or 4pm Monday to Friday, sometimes also 9am to noon Saturday

Bars/drinking establishments 5pm onwards

Tourist information 9am to 5pm Monday to Saturday

Western-style restaurants lunch noon to 2.30pm, dinner 6.30pm to 10pm

Local restaurants 7.30am to 8pm Monday to Saturday

Shops 8.30am to 5.30pm Monday to Friday, 8.30am to 1pm Saturday

Many shops and offices close for one to two hours between noon and 2pm and, especially in coastal areas, on Friday afternoons for mosque services. Supermarkets in major cities are often open on Saturday afternoon and Sunday for a few hours around midday.

Photography

Equipment

Nairobi has the best selection of camera equipment, followed by Dar es Salaam and Kampala, though it's best to bring what you'll need, including extra memory cards, with you.

Many internet cafes and speciality shops can help with transferring digital images to storage devices. It's a good idea to carry a USB converter for memory cards if you want to burn your photos onto CDs or DVDs, as many internet cafes don't have card reader slots.

Whatever equipment you carry, be sure to keep it well protected against dust. Lonely Planet's *Travel Photography: A Guide to Taking Better Pictures* by Richard l'Anson is full of helpful tips for taking photographs while on the road.

Photographing People

Always ask permission before photographing people, and always respect their wishes. In many tourist areas, locals will ask for a fee before allowing you to photograph them, which is fair enough, though rates can be high. If you promise to give someone a photo, follow through with it, as your promise will be taken seriously.

Restrictions

Avoid taking pictures of anything connected with the government or the military, including army barracks, land or people anywhere close to army barracks, government offices, post offices, banks, ports, train stations, airports, bridges and dams.

Some locals may object if you take pictures of their place of worship (this includes natural features with traditional religious significance), so always ask first.

Public Holidays

In Tanzania, parts of Kenya and Uganda, major Islamic holidays are also celebrated as public holidays. The dates depend on the moon and fall about 11 days earlier each year. The most important ones include the following:

Eid al-Fitr The end of Ramadan, and East Africa's most important Islamic celebration; celebrated as a two-day holiday in many areas.

Eid al-Kebir (Eid al-Haji) Commemorates the moment when Abraham was about to sacrifice his son in obedience to God's command, only to have God intercede at the last moment and substitute a ram. It coincides with the end of the pilgrimage (hajj) to Mecca.

Eid al-Moulid (Maulidi) The birthday of the Prophet Mohammed.

Ramadan The annual 30-day fast when adherents do not eat or drink from sunrise to sunset. Although Ramadan is not a public holiday, restaurants are often closed during this time in the coastal areas.

Telephone

Country Codes

Burundi	257
Kenya	254
Rwanda	250
Tanzania	255
Uganda	256

Mobile Phones

The mobile network reaches most areas of the region. Most companies sell prepaid starter packages for about US$2, and top-up cards are on sale at shops everywhere. Although several mobile companies have a presence throughout the region (meaning you can keep the same SIM card in different countries), it's cheaper to buy a local SIM card when you cross the border – roaming costs remain high across the region although agreements between governments are increasingly lowering costs.

Local SIM cards can be used in European and Australian phones. Other phones must be set to roaming.

Phone Codes

Throughout the region, except in Rwanda and Burundi, area codes must be used whenever you dial long-distance. Codes are included in all listings.

Time

Time in Kenya, Uganda and Tanzania is GMT/UTC plus three hours year-round; in Rwanda and Burundi it's GMT/UTC plus two hours.

Toilets

Toilets vary from standard long drops to full-flush luxury conveniences. Most midrange and top-end hotels sport flushable sit-down types, although at the lower end of the price range, toilet seats are a rare commodity. Budget guesthouses often have squat toilets, sometimes equipped with a flush mechanism, otherwise with a bucket and scoop.

Toilets with running water are a rarity outside major hotels. If you see a bucket with water nearby, use it for flushing. Paper (you'll invariably need to supply your own) should be deposited in

MAJOR ISLAMIC HOLIDAYS

HOLIDAY	2015	2016	2017
Ramadan begins	18 Jun	7 Jun	28 May
Eid al-Fitr (end of Ramadan)	17 Jul	6 Jul	26 Jun
Tabaski	24 Sep	13 Sep	2 Sep
Maulidi (Prophet Mohammed's birthday)	2 Jan	22 Dec (2015)	11 Dec (2016)
New Year begins	28 Oct (1436)	17 Oct (1437)	6 Oct (1438)
Eid al-Adha (Feast of Sacrifice)	26 Sep	15 Sep	4 Sep

the can that's usually in the corner.

A number of the upmarket bush camps have 'dry' toilets – just a fancy version of the long drop toilet with a Western-style seat perched on the top.

Travellers with Disabilities

While there are few facilities specifically for people with disabilities, East Africans are generally quite accommodating, and willing to offer whatever assistance they can as long as they understand what you need. In general, Kenya and northern Tanzania are probably the easiest destinations, and safari companies in these areas often have experience taking disabled people on safari. Some considerations:

➡ While some newer lodges have wheelchair-accessible rooms, few hotels have lifts, many have narrow stairwells and there are generally no grips or rails in bathrooms.

➡ Many park lodges and camps are built on ground level. However, access paths, in an attempt to maintain a natural environment, are sometimes rough or rocky, and rooms or tents raised. It's best to enquire about access before booking.

➡ As far as we know, there are no Braille signboards at any parks or museums, nor any facilities for deaf travellers.

➡ In most places, taxis are small sedans. Minibuses are widely available in Kenya, Tanzania and Uganda, and can be chartered for transport and customised safaris. Large or wide-door vehicles can also be arranged through car-hire agencies in major cities, and often with safari operators as well.

Accessible Journeys (www. disabilitytravel.com) Offers a handful of Kenyan and Tanzanian safari tours.

SWAHILI TIME

In Swahili-speaking areas, locals use the Swahili system of telling time, in which the first hour is *saa moja (asubuhi)*, corresponding with 7am. Counting begins again with *saa moja (jioni)*, the first hour in the evening, corresponding with 7pm. Although most will switch to the international clock when speaking English with foreigners, confusion sometimes occurs, so ask people to confirm whether they are using *saa za kizungu* (international time) or *saa za kiswahili* (Swahili time). Signboards with opening hours are often posted in Swahili time.

Access-Able Travel Source (www.access-able. com) US information portal with a small number of listings for Kenya and Tanzania.

Society for Accessible Travel and Hospitality (SATH; ☎212-447 7284; www. sath.org; USA) A good resource which gives advice on how to travel with a wheelchair, kidney disease, sight impairment or deafness. The website has a section called 'African Safaris'.

Visas

➡ It's best to arrange visas in advance, although at the time of writing all countries in the region except Rwanda were issuing visas at the airport. Kenya, Tanzania and Uganda also issue visas at most land borders. Although not rigorously enforced,

officially visitors to Tanzania should have a visa before arrival. Regulations change frequently so call the relevant embassy for an update.

➡ Once in East Africa, a single-entry visa for Kenya, Tanzania or Uganda allows you to visit either of the other two countries (assuming you've met their visa requirements and have been issued a visa) and then return to the original country without having to apply for second visa for the original country. Thus, if you're in Tanzania on a single-entry visa, you can go to Kenya (assuming you also have a Kenyan visa), and then return to Tanzania without needing a new Tanzanian visa. This doesn't apply to Rwanda and Burundi, so if you will be including visits to these or other African

---

ON TIME IN EAST AFRICA

While the discussion of time makes everything sound quite official and precise, when all is said and done, time is a very different concept in East Africa than in many parts of the West. Buses that are going 'now' rarely leave until they're full, regardless of how much engine revving takes place in the meantime. Agreed-upon times for appointments are treated as approximate concepts. Getting upset when things don't go like clockwork is generally counterproductive. The best way to get things done efficiently is to stay relaxed, treat the person you're dealing with as a person, enquire how their family is going or how their children are doing at school, and take the time to listen to the answer. Then, sit back, wait and be patient.

EAST AFRICA TOURIST VISA

In early 2014, the governments of Kenya, Uganda and Rwanda announced the creation of a new East Africa Tourist Visa (EATV). Under the scheme, tourists are entitled to a 90-day, multiple-entry visa that covers travel in and out of these three countries for a single fee of US$100. Neither Burundi nor Tanzania are yet part of the EATV, but in November 2014 Tanzania announced its intention to join. The visas are available upon arrival at airports and most land crossings. Applications can also be made prior to travelling to the region, either at an embassy or consulate for one of the three countries in your home country or online. Although requirements vary from embassy to embassy, most applications require a single passport photo and a letter to the embassy outlining your travel plans.

With the visa duly in your passport, your first port of call must be the country through which you applied for the visa, whereafter there are no restrictions on travelling in or out of the three countries. No visa extensions are possible.

Apart from convenience, the East African Tourist Visa could save you money, with individual visas for most (but not all) nationalities costing US$50 for Kenya, US$50 for Uganda and US$30 for Rwanda.

For more information and links to online application forms, visit www.visiteastafrica.org/visa.

countries in your regional itinerary, it saves money to get a multiple-entry visa at the outset. Note that visas issued at airports and land borders are usually for single entry only.

➡ At most borders and at airport immigration, visa fees must be paid in US dollars cash, although other major currencies are sometimes accepted (including at Nairobi's Jomo Kenyatta International Airport).

➡ Ensure that your passport has plenty of blank pages for entry and exit stamps, and is valid for at least six months after the conclusion of your planned travels.

➡ Carry extra passport-sized photos for visa applications.

➡ Proof of an onward ticket or sufficient funds is rarely required if you apply for a visa at land borders. It's occasionally requested at airports in the region, but generally only if you give immigration officials reason to doubt that you'll leave.

Volunteering

There are various opportunities for volunteering, generally teaching, or in environmental or health work; these are almost always best arranged prior to arriving in East Africa.

Camps International (www.campsinternational.com) Community-focused budget and/or gap-year itineraries in Tanzania and Kenya.

Coordinating Committee for International Voluntary Service (www.ccivs.org) A range of community options in the region.

Earthwatch (www.earthwatch.org) Volunteering trips with an environmental focus.

Frontier (www.frontier.ac.uk) Options in Kenya, Tanzania and Uganda.

Global Volunteer Network (www.globalvolunteernetwork.org) Rwanda and Uganda.

Idealist.org (www.idealist.org) Hundreds of options in the region.

International Volunteer HQ (www.volunteerhq.org) Uganda, Kenya and Tanzania.

International Volunteer Programs Association (www.volunteerinternational.org) Possibilities in all East African countries.

i-to-i (www.i-to-i.com) Kenya and Tanzania.

Peace Corps (www.peacecorps.gov) Two-year placements for US citizens.

Voluntary Service Overseas (VSO; www.vso.org.uk) One of the UK's biggest agencies for volunteering.

Volunteer Abroad (www.goabroad.com/volunteer-abroad) Possibilities in all East African countries.

Volunteers for Peace (www.vfp.org) Kenya, Uganda, Tanzania and Rwanda.

Working Abroad (www.workingabroad.com) Work with sea turtles in Watamu, Kenya.

Worldwide Experience (www.worldwideexperience.com) Focus on wildlife and conservation.

Women Travellers

East Africa (especially Kenya, Tanzania and Uganda) is a relatively easy region to travel in, either solo or with other women, especially when compared with parts of North Africa, South America and certain Western countries. In Rwanda and Burundi, verbal hassles, hisses and the like tend to be more common than elsewhere in the region, although things rarely go further than this. Otherwise, you're unlikely to encounter any more specifically gender-related problems than you would elsewhere in the world and, more often than not, you'll meet only warmth, hospitality and sisterly regard.

To avoid unwanted attention, consider the following:

➡ Dressing modestly is the single most successful strategy for minimising unwanted attention. Wear trousers or a long skirt, and a conservative top with sleeves. Tucking your hair under a cap or scarf, or tying it back, also helps.

➡ Use common sense, trust your instincts and take the usual precautions when out and about. Try to avoid walking alone at night. Avoid isolated areas at all times, and be particularly cautious on beaches, many of which can become isolated very quickly. Hassling tends to be worse in tourist areas along the Kenyan coast than elsewhere in the region.

➡ If you find yourself with an unwanted suitor, explain that your husband (whether real or fictitious) or a large group of friends will be arriving imminently at that very place. The easiest response to the question of why you aren't married is to explain that you are still young ('bado kijana' in Swahili), which, whether you are or not, will at least have some humour value. As for why your family isn't with you, you can always explain that you will be meeting them later.

➡ Seek out local women, as this can enrich your trip tremendously. Good places to try include tourist offices, government departments or even your hotel, where at least some of the staff are likely to be formally educated young to middle-aged women. In rural areas, starting points include women teachers at a local school, or staff at a health centre.

➡ In mixed-race situations in some areas of the region – specifically if you're a black woman with a white male – some East Africans may assume that you're a prostitute. Taking taxis if you go out at night and ignoring any comments may help minimise problems here.

➡ Arrange tour and trekking guides through a reputable hotel or travel agency. Avoid freelance guides who approach you on the street.

➡ Ignore hissing and catcalls; don't worry about being rude, and don't feel the need to explain yourself.

➡ A limited selection of tampons is available at pharmacies or large supermarkets in major towns throughout the region. Elsewhere, the choice is usually limited to pads. Ladies will likely come to appreciate the benefits of Western-style consumer testing when using local sanitary products.

Work

➡ The most likely areas for employment are the safari industry, tourism, scuba diving and teaching. For safari-, diving- and tourism-related positions, competition is stiff and the best way to land something is to get to know someone already working in the business. Also check safari operator and lodge websites, some of which advertise vacant positions.

➡ Work and residency permits generally must be arranged through the employer or sponsoring organisation; residency permits normally should be applied for before arriving in the region. Be prepared for lots of bureaucracy.

➡ Most teaching positions are voluntary, and best arranged through voluntary agencies or mission organisations at home. Also start your search from home for international staff positions with aid agencies. There are numerous opportunities, especially in Kenya, Uganda and Burundi. However, most organisations require applicants to go through their head office.

Transport

GETTING THERE & AWAY

Flights and tours can be booked online at www.lonely planet.com/bookings.

Lake

The main lake ferry connections to/from East Africa are between Malawi and Tanzania on Lake Nyasa, and between Zambia and Tanzania on Lake Tanganyika.

Land

Several possibilities for combining East Africa travels with overland travel elsewhere in Africa are outlined here. For more on driving your own vehicle to the region, check out the *Adventure Motorcycling Handbook* by Chris Scott et al (useful especially if you're combining the Sahara and West Africa with East Africa) and *Africa by Road* by Bob Swain and Paula Snyder.

North & West Africa

For information on trans-Saharan routes, see Lonely Planet's *West Africa*, and check the website of **Chris Scott** (www.sahara-overland. com). Once through West Africa, most travellers fly from Douala (Cameroon) over the Central African Republic and the Democratic Republic of the Congo (DRC) via Addis Ababa (Ethiopia) to any of the East African capitals, from where you can continue overland.

Northeast Africa

The Nile route through northeast Africa goes from Egypt into Sudan (via Lake Nasser, and then on to Khartoum). From Khartoum, it's straightforward to make your way to Ethiopia, and then into Kenya. Note, however, that going in the other direction, obtaining Ethiopian visas in Kenya can be problematic.

There are regular flights between Juba (South Sudan) and Entebbe (Uganda) and even a bus service between the two countries. For all travel involving routings in Sudan and South Sudan, get an update on the security situation before setting your plans.

Southern Africa

The main gateways between southern and East Africa are Zambia and Malawi, both of which are readily reached from elsewhere in southern Africa. Once in Zambia, head to Kapiri Mposhi where you can get the Tanzania–Zambia Railway (Tazara) northeast to Mbeya (Tanzania). From Mbeya, continue by road or rail towards Dar es Salaam (Tanzania), and then by road towards Kenya's Mombasa and Nairobi. Another route from Zambia goes to Mpulungu on the Zambian shore of Lake Tanganyika, from where you can travel by steamer to Kigoma. From Kigoma (Tanzania), head by rail east to Dar es Salaam or northeast by road towards Lake Victoria, Uganda and western Kenya.

CLIMATE CHANGE & TRAVEL

Every form of transport that relies on carbon-based fuel generates CO_2, the main cause of human-induced climate change. Modern travel is dependent on aeroplanes, which might use less fuel per kilometre per person than most cars but travel much greater distances. The altitude at which aircraft emit gases (including CO_2) and particles also contributes to their climate change impact. Many websites offer 'carbon calculators' that allow people to estimate the carbon emissions generated by their journey and, for those who wish to do so, to offset the impact of the greenhouse gases emitted with contributions to portfolios of climate-friendly initiatives throughout the world. Lonely Planet offsets the carbon footprint of all staff and author travel.

From Malawi, after entering East Africa at Songwe River Bridge (at the Tanzanian border), head by bus to Mbeya and continue as outlined above.

For Burundi, options include following the route outlined earlier from Mpulungu to Kigoma, from where you can continue by boat or overland to Bujumbura, travel through Burundi, Rwanda and Uganda, and on into Kenya or Tanzania.

Tours

Organised tours can be low-budget affairs, where you travel in an 'overland truck' with 15 to 30 other people and some drivers/leaders, carrying tents and other equipment, buying food along the way, and cooking and eating as a group. At the other end of the spectrum are individually tailored tours, ranging in price from reasonable to very expensive.

The following is a small sampling of tour companies operating in East Africa. For more information on safaris, see p30.

Australia & New Zealand

African Wildlife Safaris (www.africanwildlifesafaris.com.au) Customised itineraries in Kenya, Uganda, Rwanda and Tanzania.

Classic Safari Company (www.classicsafaricompany.com.au) Upmarket customised itineraries in Kenya, Rwanda, Tanzania and Uganda, including gorilla-tracking.

Peregrine Travel (www.peregrineadventures.com) Everything from overland truck tours to upscale wildlife safaris and family safaris.

South Africa

Africa Travel Co (www.africatravelco.com) Overland tours combining eastern and southern Africa.

Wild Frontiers (www.wildfrontiers.com) A range of itineraries in Tanzania and Uganda.

UK

Abercrombie & Kent (www.abercrombiekent.co.uk) Customised luxury tours and safaris.

Africa-in-Focus (www.africa-in-focus.com) East and southern Africa overland tours and safaris.

African Initiatives (www.african-initiatives.org.uk) Fair-traded safaris in northern Tanzania.

Baobab Travel (www.baobabtravel.com) A culturally responsible operator with itineraries in Kenya and Tanzania.

Dragoman (www.dragoman.com) East Africa overland tours.

Expert Africa (www.expertafrica.com) A long-standing, experienced operator with a wide selection of itineraries in Tanzania, Kenya and Rwanda.

Nature Trek (www.naturetrek.co.uk) Respected company with a long-standing focus on wildlife and tours in Kenya, Rwanda, Tanzania and Uganda.

Responsible Travel.com (www.responsibletravel.com) Matches you up with ecologically and culturally responsible tour operators to plan an itinerary.

Safari Drive (www.safaridrive.com) Self-drive safaris, primarily in northern Tanzania and Kenya.

Tribes Travel (www.tribes.co.uk) Fair-traded safaris and treks in Tanzania, Kenya, Uganda and Rwanda, including gorilla tracking.

USA & Canada

Abercrombie & Kent (www.abercrombiekent.com) Customised luxury tours and safaris.

Africa Adventure Company (www.africa-adventure.com) Upscale specialist safaris in Kenya, Tanzania, Uganda and Rwanda.

African Horizons (www.africanhorizons.com) A small operator offering various packages throughout East Africa.

Deeper Africa (www.deeperafrica.com) Socially responsible, upmarket safaris in Kenya and Tanzania, and gorilla tracking in Uganda and Rwanda.

Eco-Resorts (www.eco-resorts.com) Socially responsible itineraries in Kenya, Tanzania and Rwanda.

Explorateur Voyages (www.explorateur.qc.ca) Itineraries in Kenya, Tanzania, Uganda and Rwanda.

Good Earth (www.goodearthtours.com) Itineraries in Tanzania, Kenya and Uganda, with detours also to Rwanda.

International Expeditions (www.ietravel.com) Naturalist-oriented safaris in Kenya, Tanzania and Uganda.

Mountain Madness (www.mountainmadness.com) Upmarket treks on Mt Kilimanjaro, Mt Kenya, Mt Meru and the Rwenzoris.

Thomson Family Adventures (www.familyadventures.com) Family-friendly northern Tanzania safaris and Kilimanjaro treks.

Other

Access2Tanzania (www.access2tanzania.com) Customised, community-focused itineraries.

Basecamp Explorer (www.basecampkenya.com) Scandinavian-owned ecotourism operator offering comprehensive and often luxurious camping itineraries with an environmentally sustainable focus.

Hoopoe Safaris (www.hoopoe.com) Community-integrated luxury camping and lodge safaris in Tanzania.

Into Africa (www.intoafrica.co.uk) Specialises in 'fair-trade' trips providing insights into African life and directly supporting local communities.

GETTING AROUND

Air

Flying between Kenya, Tanzania, Uganda, Rwanda and Burundi is a relatively simple proposition – **Kenya Airways** (www.kenya-airways.com) has the largest regional network.

While air service within East Africa is relatively reliable, cancellations and delays should still be expected at any time. Always reconfirm your ticket, and allow cushion time between regional and intercontinental flights.

Bicycle

Cycling can be an enjoyable, adventurous way to explore East Africa. When planning your trip, consider the following:

➔ Main sealed roads aren't good for cycling, as there's usually no shoulder and traffic moves dangerously fast.

➔ Distances are very long, often with nothing in between. Consider picking a base, and doing exploratory trips from there.

➔ Cycling is best well away from urban areas, in the early morning and late afternoon hours, and in the cooler, dry season between June and August.

➔ When calculating daily distances, plan on taking a break from the midday heat, and don't count on covering as much territory each day as you might in a northern European climate.

➔ Mountain bikes are best for flexibility and local terrain, and should be brought from home. While single-speed bicycles (and occasionally mountain bikes) can be rented in many towns (ask hotel staff or enquire at the local bicycle repair stand), they're only suitable for short rides.

➔ Other planning considerations include water (carry at least 4L), rampaging motorists (a small rear-view mirror is a worthwhile investment), sleeping (bring a tent) and punctures (thorn trees are a problem in some areas).

➔ Bring sufficient spares (including several spare inner tubes, a spare tyre and plenty of tube patches), and be proficient at repairs.

➔ Bicycles can be transported on minibuses and buses (though for express or luxury buses, you may need to make advance arrangements with the driver to stow your bike in the hold). There's also no problem or additional cost to bring your bicycle on any of the region's lake or coastal ferries. Cycling isn't permitted in national parks or wildlife reserves.

➔ As elsewhere in the world, don't leave your bike unattended unless it's locked, and secure all

DHOW TRAVEL

With their billowing sails and graceful forms, dhows (ancient Arabic sailing vessels) have become a symbol of East Africa for adventure travellers. Yet, despite their romantic reputation, the realities can be quite different. Before undertaking a longer journey, test things out with a short sunset or afternoon sail. Coastal hotels are good contacts for arranging reliable dhow travel. If you decide to give a local dhow a try, keep the following tips in mind:

➔ Be prepared for rough conditions. There are no facilities on board, except possibly a toilet hanging off the stern. Sailings are wind and tide dependent, and departures are often predawn.

➔ Journeys often take much longer than anticipated; bring extra water and sufficient food.

➔ Sun block, a hat and a covering are essential, as is waterproofing for your luggage and a rain jacket.

➔ Boats capsize and people are killed each year. Avoid overloaded boats and don't set sail in bad weather.

➔ Travel with the winds, which blow from south to north from approximately July to September and north to south from approximately November to late February.

Note that what Westerners refer to as dhows are called either *jahazi* or *mashua* by most Swahili speakers. *Jahazi* are large, lateen-sailed boats. *Mashua* are smaller, and often with proportionately wider hulls and a motor. The *dau* has a sloped stem and stern. On lakes and inland waterways, the *mtumbwi* (dugout canoe) is in common use. Coastal areas, especially Zanzibar's east-coast beaches, are good places to see *ngalawa* (outrigger canoes).

removable pieces. Taking your bike into a hotel room is generally no problem (and is a good idea).

➡ A recommended contact is the US-based **International Bicycle Fund** (www.ibike. org/bikeafrica), a socially conscious, low-budget organisation that arranges tours in East Africa and provides information.

Boat

➡ On the Tanzanian section of Lake Victoria, there are passenger boats connecting Mwanza with Bukoba, Ukerewe Island and various lakeside villages. In the Kenyan section of the lake, small boats connect the mainland around Mbita Point with the Mfangano, Rusinga and Takawiri Islands. In Uganda, small boats connect mainland villages with the Ssese Islands; there are also regular cargo boats from Kampala to Mwanza that accept passengers.

➡ On Lake Tanganyika, a passenger ferry connects Kigoma (Tanzania) with Mpulungu (Zambia).

➡ On Lake Nyasa, the main route is between Mbamba Bay and Itungi (both in Tanzania), via numerous lakeside villages. There's also a boat between Mbamba Bay and Nkhata Bay (Malawi).

➡ The main coastal routes are between Dar es Salaam, Zanzibar and Pemba, and the short run between the coast and the Lamu archipelago (Kenya).

Bus

Buses are the most useful type of public transport. They're usually faster than trains or trucks, and safer and more comfortable than minibuses. In Kenya and Tanzania, you sometimes have the choice of going by 'luxury' or 'ordinary' bus. Luxury buses are more com-

BUS SAFETY

Public transport is a fine (and often the only) choice for getting around East Africa, but be savvy when using local buses and minibuses.

➡ Never accept food and drink from fellow passengers, even if it appears to be sealed.

➡ Avoid night travel, especially on long-distance routes such as Nairobi–Kampala.

➡ Be especially wary of pick-pockets on minibuses, and when boarding.

➡ At bus stations, keep your luggage compact and your valuables well-concealed.

➡ Road safety is a major issue. Get advice locally about the best (safest) bus lines, and stick to established lines.

fortable and more expensive, although not always quicker than ordinary buses. Some also have the dubious advantage of a video system, usually playing bad movies at full volume for the entire trip. Uganda has mostly ordinary buses, although there are luxury buses on some cross-border routes. There are a few full-size buses in Rwanda and Burundi, although, especially in Burundi, minibuses are the rule.

Car & Motorcycle

Touring East Africa by car or motorcycle is quite feasible, although vehicle rental rates can be expensive.

Throughout East Africa, main roads are sealed and in reasonable states of repair. In rural areas, they range from decent to terrible, especially in the wet season when many secondary routes become impassable. Trips in remote areas require 4WD; motorcycles generally aren't permitted in national parks.

Whether you drive your own or a rental vehicle, expect stops at checkpoints where police and border officials will ask to see your driving licence, insurance paperwork and vehicle papers.

Bring Your Own Vehicle

➡ To bring your own vehicle into East Africa, you'll need to arrange a *carnet de passage*. This document allows you to take a vehicle duty-free into a country where duties would normally be payable. It guarantees that if a vehicle is taken into a country but not exported, the organisation that issued the *carnet* will accept responsibility for payment of import duties (generally between 100% and 150% of the new value of the vehicle). The *carnet* should also specify any expensive spare parts that you'll be carrying.

➡ To get a *carnet*, contact your national motoring organisation at home, which will give you an indemnity form for completion by either a bank or an insurance company. Once you have deposited a bond with a bank or paid an insurance premium, the motoring organisation will issue the *carnet*. The cost of the *carnet* itself is minimal; allow at least a week to complete the process.

➡ For longer trips, in addition to a *carnet* and mechanical knowledge, bring along a good collection of spares.

TRAVEL TIP

Use only reliable hotel taxis, or those from established ranks, and avoid freelancers (known in Swahili-speaking areas as 'taxi bubu'). Also avoid taking matatus, dalla-dallas, boda-bodas and their kind after dark.

Driving Licence

If you're taking your own vehicle or considering hiring one in East Africa, arrange an International Driving Permit (IDP) before leaving home. They're available at minimal cost through your national motoring organisation.

Fuel & Spare Parts

➤ Fuel costs in the region average US$1.75 per litre of petrol or diesel. Filling and repair stations are readily available in major towns but scarce elsewhere. In many areas, diesel is easier to find than petrol.

➤ Top your tank up at every opportunity and carry basic spares. For travel in remote areas and in national parks, also carry jerry cans with extra fuel.

➤ Petrol sold on the roadside is unreliable, as it's often diluted with water or kerosene. Diluting is also a common problem at established petrol stations in much of the region, so ask around locally before filling up.

Hire

Car, 4WD and motorcycle hire is expensive throughout East Africa, averaging US$100 to US$200 per day for a 4WD. Few agencies offer unlimited kilometres, and many require that you take a chauffeur (which is a good idea anyway). For self-drive rentals, you'll need a driving licence and often also an IDP. If you'll be crossing any borders, you'll need to arrange the necessary paperwork with the hire agency in advance.

Insurance

Throughout the region, liability insurance must generally be bought at the border upon entry. While cost and quality vary, in many cases you may find that you're effectively travelling uninsured, as there's often no way to collect on the insurance. With vehicle rentals, even if you're covered from other sources, it's recommended to take the full coverage offered by hire companies.

Road Rules

➤ Drive on the left: Tanzania, Kenya and Uganda.

➤ Drive on the right: Rwanda and Burundi.

➤ Roundabouts: traffic already in the roundabout has the right of way.

Road Conditions & Hazards

➤ Nighttime road travel isn't recommended anywhere; if you must drive at night, be alert for stopped vehicles in the roadway without lights or hazard warnings.

➤ If you're not used to driving in Africa, watch for pedestrians, children and animals, as well as for oncoming vehicles on the wrong side of the road. Especially in rural areas, remember that many people have never driven themselves and are not aware of necessary braking distances and similar concepts; moderate your speed accordingly.

➤ Tree branches on the road are the local version of flares or hazard lights and mean there's a stopped vehicle, crater-sized pothole or similar calamity ahead.

➤ Passing (including on curves or other areas with poor visibility) is common practice and a frequent cause of accidents.

Hitching

As in other parts of the world, hitching is never entirely safe, and we don't recommend it. Those travellers who decide to hitch should understand that they are taking a potentially serious risk. If you do hitch, you'll be safer doing so in pairs and letting someone know of your plans.

Hitching may be your only option in remote areas, although it's rare that you'll get a free ride unless you're lucky enough to be offered a lift by resident expats, well-off locals or aid workers; even then, at least offer to make a contribution for petrol on longer journeys, or to pick up a meal tab. To flag down a vehicle, hold out your hand at about waist level and wave it up and down, with the palm to the ground; the common Western gesture of holding out your thumb isn't used.

A word of warning about taking lifts in private cars: smuggling across borders is common practice, and if whatever is being smuggled is found, you may be arrested even though you knew nothing about it. Most travellers manage to convince police that they were merely hitching a ride (passport stamps are a good indication of this), but the convincing can take a long time.

Local Transport

Minibus

➤ Most East Africans rely heavily on minibuses for transport. They're called matatus in Kenya, dalla-dallas in Tanzania, and taxis or matatus in Uganda.

➤ Except in Rwanda and Burundi, minibuses are invariably packed to the bursting point, and this – combined with excessive speed, poor maintenance and driver recklessness – means that they're not the safest way of getting around. In fact, they can be downright dangerous, and newspaper reports of matatu and dalla-dalla crashes are a regular feature of life here. In Rwanda and Burundi, travelling in minibuses is generally safer.

➡ If you have a large backpack, think twice about boarding, especially at rush hour, when it will make the already crowded conditions even more uncomfortable for others.

Taxi

In Kenya, northern Tanzania and Uganda, shared taxis operate on some routes. These officially take between five and nine passengers, depending on size, leave when full and are usually faster, though more expensive, than bus travel. They're marginally more comfortable than minibuses but have their share of accidents too. Private taxis for hire are found in all major towns.

Motorcycle taxis (*boda-boda* in Kenya, Tanzania and Uganda, *moto-taxi* in Rwanda, Burundi and the DRC) are also widely available, at a

fraction of the cost of standard vehicle taxis.

Truck

➡ In remote areas, trucks may be the only form of transport, and they're invariably the cheapest. For most regular runs there will be a 'fare', which is more or less fixed and is what the locals pay. It's usually equivalent to, or a bit less than, the bus fare for the same route. For a place in the cab, expect to pay about twice what it costs to travel on top of the load.

➡ Many truck lifts are arranged the night before departure at the 'truck park' – a compound or dust patch that you'll find in most towns. Ask around for a truck that's going your way, and be prepared to wait, especially on remote routes where there may be trucks leaving only once or twice a week. For longer trips, ask what to do about food and drink, and bring plenty of snacks and extra drinking water – enough for yourself and to share.

Train

➡ The main passenger lines are the Nairobi–Mombasa route (Kenya), the Tazara 'express' line from Dar es Salaam to Mbeya (Tanzania),

and the meandering Central line connecting Dar es Salaam with Kigoma (Tanzania).

➡ First class costs about double what the bus would cost but is well worth it for the additional comfort. Second class is reasonably comfortable, but the savings over first class are marginal. Economy-class travel is cheap, crowded and uncomfortable. There are no assigned seats, and for long trips you'll probably wind up sitting and sleeping on the floor. Reservations for first class are best made as early as possible, although sometimes you'll get lucky and be able to book a cabin on the day of travel.

➡ In all classes, keep an eye on your luggage, especially at stops. In first and second class, make sure the window is jammed shut at night to avoid the possibility of someone entering when the train stops (there's usually a piece of wood provided for this), and keep your cabin door shut.

➡ Food and drink (mainly soft drinks) are available on trains and from station vendors, but bring extra food and water. Have plenty of small change handy.

Health

If you stay up to date with your vaccinations and take basic preventive measures, you'd be unlucky to succumb to most of the health hazards covered here. The exception is malaria, which is a real risk throughout much of East Africa.

BEFORE YOU GO

Predeparture planning will save you trouble later.

➡ Get a check-up from your dentist and doctor if you have any regular medication or chronic illness (eg high blood pressure or asthma).

➡ Organise spare contact lenses and glasses (and take your prescription with you).

➡ Get a first-aid and medical kit together and arrange necessary vaccinations. Get an International Certificate of Vaccination ('yellow booklet') listing vaccinations you have received.

➡ Carry medications in their original (labelled) containers. If carrying syringes or needles, have a physician's letter documenting their medical necessity.

Insurance

Check whether your insurance plan will make payments directly to providers or reimburse you later for overseas health expenditures. Most doctors in East Africa expect cash payment.

Ensure that your travel insurance will cover any emergency transport required to get you at least as far as Nairobi (Kenya), or, preferably, home, by air and with a medical attendant if necessary. Consider temporary membership with the following:

African Medical & Research Foundation (AMREF; ☎254-20-600 2299, 254-722-314239, 254-733-639088, Nairobi emergency lines 254-20-315454/5; www.amref. org) Air evacuation in medical emergencies for most of East Africa.

First Air Responder (www. firstairresponder.com) Emergency air evacuation in Tanzania and Kenya.

IN EAST AFRICA

Availability & Cost of Health Care

Good, Western-style medical care is available in Nairobi (which is the main medical hub for the region and the main regional destination for medical evacuations), and to a lesser extent in Dar es Salaam (Tanzania). Elsewhere, reasonable to good care is available in larger towns, and in some mission stations, though availability is patchy off the beaten track. Private or mission-run clinics and hospitals are generally better equipped than government ones. If you fall ill in an unfamiliar area, ask staff at top-end hotels or resident expatriates where the best nearby medical facilities are; in an emergency, contact your embassy. Most towns have at least one clinic where you can get an inexpensive malaria

---

RECOMMENDED VACCINATIONS

The **World Health Organization** (www.who.int) recommends that all travellers be covered for diphtheria, tetanus, measles, mumps, rubella and polio, as well as for hepatitis B, regardless of their destination.

According to the **Centers for Disease Control & Prevention** (www.cdc.gov), the following vaccinations are recommended for East Africa: hepatitis A, hepatitis B, meningococcal meningitis, rabies and typhoid, and boosters for tetanus, diphtheria, polio and measles. It is also advisable to be vaccinated against yellow fever.

Yellow fever is required for all visitors to Rwanda, and recommended for elsewhere in the region.

test and, if necessary, treatment. With dental treatment, there is often an increased risk of hepatitis B and HIV transmission via poorly sterilised equipment.

Most drugs can be purchased over the counter in East Africa, without a prescription. However, there are often problems with ineffectiveness (eg if the drugs are counterfeit, or if they have been improperly stored). Most drugs are available in capital cities, but almost none in remote villages. Bring all drugs for chronic diseases from home.

There can be a high risk of contracting HIV from infected blood if you receive a blood transfusion. To minimise this risk, seek out treatment in reputable clinics. The **BloodCare Foundation** (www.bloodcare.org. uk) is a useful source of safe, screened blood, which can be transported to any part of the world within 24 hours.

Infectious Diseases

Bilharzia (Schistosomiasis)

This disease is spread by flukes (minute worms) that are carried by a species of freshwater snail. Don't paddle or swim in any freshwater lakes or slow-running rivers anywhere in East Africa unless you have reliable confirmation that they are bilharzia-free. A blood test can detect antibodies if you might have been exposed, and treatment is possible in specialist travel clinics. If not treated the infection can cause kidney failure or permanent bowel damage.

Cholera

Cholera is spread via contaminated drinking water. The main symptom is profuse watery diarrhoea, which causes debilitation if fluids are not replaced quickly. An oral cholera vaccine is available but is not particularly effective. Pay close attention to good drinking water and avoid potentially contaminated food. Treatment is by fluid replacement (orally or via a drip), but sometimes antibiotics are needed. Self-treatment is not advised.

Dengue Fever

Mini-epidemics of this mosquito-borne disease crop up with some regularity in Tanzania, notably in Dar es Salaam. Symptoms include high fever, severe headache and body ache. Some people develop a rash and experience diarrhoea. There is no vaccine, only prevention. The dengue-carrying *Aedes aegypti* mosquito is active at day and night, so use DEET-mosquito repellent periodically throughout the day. See a doctor to be diagnosed and monitored (dengue testing is available in Dar es Salaam). There is no specific treatment, just rest and paracetamol; do not take aspirin as it increases the likelihood of haemorrhaging. Severe dengue is a potentially fatal complication.

Diphtheria

Found throughout East Africa, diphtheria is spread through close respiratory contact. Vaccination is recommended for those likely to be in close contact with locals in infected areas and is more important for long stays than for short-term trips.

Filariasis

Tiny worms migrating in the lymphatic system cause filariasis. The bite from an infected mosquito spreads the infection. Symptoms include localised itching and swelling of the legs and/or genitalia. Treatment is available.

Hepatitis A

Hepatitis A is spread through contaminated food (particularly shellfish) and water. It causes jaundice, and although rarely fatal, it can cause prolonged lethargy and delayed recovery. If you've had hepatitis A, don't drink alcohol for up to six months afterwards; once you've recovered, there won't be long-term problems. Early symptoms include dark urine and a yellow colour to the whites of the eyes, sometimes with fever and abdominal pain. Hepatitis A vaccine (Avaxim, VAQTA, Havrix) gives protection for up to a year; a booster after a year gives 10-year protection. Hepatitis A and typhoid vaccines can also be given as a single-dose vaccine (hepatyrix or viatim).

Hepatitis B

Hepatitis B is spread through infected blood, contaminated needles and sexual intercourse. It can also be spread from an infected mother to the baby during childbirth. It affects the liver, causing jaundice and occasionally liver failure. Most people recover completely, but some might be chronic carriers of the virus, which could lead eventually to cirrhosis or liver cancer. Those visiting high-risk areas for long periods or those with increased social or occupational risk should be immunised.

HIV

Human immunodeficiency virus (HIV), the virus that causes acquired immune deficiency syndrome (AIDS), is an enormous problem throughout East Africa. It's spread through infected blood and blood products, by sexual intercourse with an infected partner and from an infected mother to her baby during childbirth and breastfeeding. It can be spread through 'blood to blood' contact, such as with contaminated instruments during medical, dental, acupuncture and other body-piercing procedures, and through sharing used intravenous needles. If you think you might have been infected with HIV, a blood test is necessary.

Malaria

Malaria is endemic throughout East Africa (except at altitudes higher than 2000m, where risk of transmission is low). The disease is caused by a parasite in the bloodstream spread via the bite of the female *Anopheles* mosquito. There are several types of malaria, with falciparum malaria the most dangerous type and the predominant form in the region. Infection rates vary with climate and season. Rates are higher during the rainy season, but the risk exists year-round. It is extremely important to take preventive measures, even just for short visits.

There is no vaccination against malaria (yet). However, several different drugs are used for prevention with new ones in the pipeline. Up-to-date advice from a travel-health clinic is essential. The pattern of drug-resistant malaria changes rapidly, so what was advised several years ago might no longer be current.

SYMPTOMS

Malaria's early stages include headaches, fevers, generalised aches and pains, and malaise, which could be mistaken for flu. Other symptoms can include abdominal pain, diarrhoea and a cough. Anyone who develops a fever while in East Africa or within two weeks after departure should assume malarial infection until blood tests prove negative, even if you have been taking antimalarial medication. If not treated, the next stage could develop within 24 hours, particularly if falciparum malaria is the parasite: jaundice, then reduced consciousness and coma (also known as cerebral malaria) followed by death. Treatment in hospital is essential; the death rate might still be as high as 10% even in the best intensive-care facilities.

SIDE EFFECTS & RISKS

Many travellers are under the impression that malaria is a mild illness, that treatment is always easy and successful and that taking antimalarial drugs causes more illness through side effects than actually getting malaria. Unfortunately, this is not true. Side effects of the medication depend on the drug taken. Doxycycline can cause heartburn and indigestion; mefloquine (Lariam) can cause anxiety attacks, insomnia and nightmares and (rarely) severe psychiatric disorders; chloroquine can cause nausea and hair loss; and proguanil can cause mouth ulcers. These side effects are not universal and can be minimised by taking medication correctly, eg with food. Also, some people should not take a particular antimalarial drug – for example, people with epilepsy should avoid mefloquine, and doxycycline should not be taken by pregnant women or children younger than 12.

If you decide against taking antimalarial drugs, you must understand the risks and be obsessive about avoiding mosquito bites. Use nets and insect repellent, and report any fever or flu-like symptoms to a doctor as soon as possible. Malaria in pregnancy frequently results in miscarriage or premature labour and the risks to both mother and foetus during pregnancy are considerable. Travel in East Africa when pregnant should be carefully considered.

STAND-BY TREATMENT

Carrying emergency stand-by treatment is essential for travel in remote areas. Seek your doctor's advice as to recommended medicines and dosages. However, this should be viewed as emergency treatment only and not as routine self-medication, and should only be used if you will be far from medical facilities and have been advised about the symptoms of malaria and how to use the medication. If you resort to emergency self-treatment, seek medical advice as soon as possible to confirm whether the treatment has been successful. In particular, you want to avoid contracting cerebral malaria, which can be fatal within 24 hours. Self-diagnostic kits, which can identify malaria in the blood from a finger prick, are available in the West and are worth buying.

ANTIMALARIAL A TO D

A Awareness of the risk. No medication is totally effective, but protection of up to 95% is achievable with most drugs, as long as other measures have been taken.

B Bites: avoid at all costs. Sleep in a screened room, use mosquito spray or coils and sleep under a permethrin-impregnated net at night. Cover up at night with long trousers and long sleeves, preferably with permethrin-treated clothing. Apply repellent to all areas of exposed skin in the evenings.

C Chemical prevention (ie antimalarial drugs) is usually needed in malarial areas. Expert advice is needed as resistance patterns change and new drugs are in development. Most antimalarial drugs need to be started at least a week in advance and continued for four weeks after the last exposure to malaria.

D Diagnosis. If you have a fever or flu-like illness within a year of travel to a malarial area, malaria is a possibility; immediate medical attention is necessary.

Meningococcal Meningitis

Meningococcal infection is spread through close respiratory contact and is most likely contracted in crowded situations. Infection is uncommon in travellers. Vaccination is particularly recommended for long stays and is especially important towards the end of the dry season. Symptoms include fever, severe headache, neck stiffness and a red rash. Immediate medical treatment is necessary.

The ACWY vaccine is recommended for all travellers in sub-Saharan Africa. This vaccine is different from the meningococcal meningitis C vaccine given to children and adolescents in some countries; it is safe to be given both types of vaccine.

Rabies

Rabies is spread by receiving the bites or licks of an infected animal on broken skin. It is always fatal once the clinical symptoms start (which might be months after an infected bite), so postbite vaccination should be given as soon as possible. Postbite vaccination (whether or not you've been vaccinated before the bite) prevents the virus from spreading to the central nervous system. Animal handlers should be vaccinated, as should those travelling to remote areas where a reliable source of postbite vaccine is not available. Three preventive injections are needed over a month. If you haven't been vaccinated you will need a course of five injections starting 24 hours or as soon as possible after being exposed. If you have been vaccinated, you will need fewer postbite injections, and have more time to seek medical help.

Rift Valley Fever

This fever is spread occasionally via mosquito bites. The symptoms are of a fever and flu-like illness; and the good news is it's rarely fatal.

Trypanosomiasis (Sleeping Sickness)

Spread via the bite of the tsetse fly. It causes headache, fever and eventually coma. If you have these symptoms and have negative malaria tests, have yourself evaluated by a reputable clinic, where you should also be able to obtain treatment.

Tuberculosis (TB)

TB is spread through close respiratory contact and occasionally through infected milk or milk products. The BCG vaccine is recommended for those likely to be mixing closely with the local population, although it only provides moderate protection. It's more important for long stays than for short-term visits. Inoculation with the BCG vaccine is not available in all countries, but it is given routinely to many children in developing nations. It is a live vaccine and should not be given to pregnant women or immuno-compromised individuals.

TB can be asymptomatic, only being picked up on a routine chest X-ray. Alternatively, it can cause a cough, weight loss or fever, months or even years after exposure.

Typhoid

This is spread through food or water contaminated by infected human faeces. The first symptom is usually a fever or a pink rash on the abdomen. Sometimes septicaemia (blood poisoning) can occur. A typhoid vaccine (typhim Vi, typherix) will give protection for three years. In some countries, the oral vaccine Vivotif is also available. Antibiotics are usually given as treatment, and death is rare unless septicaemia occurs.

Yellow Fever

Tanzania, Kenya, Uganda and Burundi no longer officially require you to carry a certificate of yellow fever vaccination unless you're arriving from an infected area (which includes from anywhere in East Africa). However, it's still sometimes asked for at some borders, and is a requirement in some neighbouring countries, including Rwanda. The vaccine is recommended for most visitors to Africa by the **Centers for Disease Control & Prevention** (www.cdc.gov). Also, there is always the possibility that a traveller without a legally required, up-to-date certificate will be vaccinated and detained in isolation at the port of arrival for up to 10 days, or possibly even repatriated.

Yellow fever is spread by infected mosquitoes. Symptoms range from a flu-like illness to severe hepatitis (liver inflammation), jaundice and death. The yellow fever vaccination must be given at a designated clinic and is valid for 10 years. It is a live vaccine and must not be given to immunocompromised or pregnant travellers.

Traveller's Diarrhoea

Diarrhoea is the most common travel-related illness. Sometimes dietary changes, such as increased spices or oils, are the cause. To help prevent diarrhoea: avoid tap water unless you're sure it's safe to drink; only eat fresh fruits or vegetables if cooked or peeled; and be wary of dairy products that might contain unpasteurised milk. Although freshly cooked food can often be a safe option, plates or serving utensils might be dirty, so be selective when eating food from street vendors (make sure that cooked food is piping hot all the way through). If you develop diarrhoea, be sure to drink plenty of fluids, preferably lots of an oral rehydration solution containing water, and some salt and sugar. A few loose stools don't require treatment, but if you start having more than four or five stools a day, you should start taking an antibiotic (usually a quinoline drug, such as ciprofloxacin or norfloxacin) and an anti-diarrhoeal agent (such as loperamide) if you are not within easy reach of a toilet. If diarrhoea is bloody, persists for more than 72 hours or is accompanied by fever, shaking chills or severe abdominal pain, you should seek medical attention.

Amoebic Dysentery

Contracted by consuming contaminated food and water, amoebic dysentery causes blood and mucus in the faeces. It can be relatively mild and tends to come on gradually, but seek medical advice if you think you have the illness, as it won't clear up without treatment (which is with specific antibiotics).

Giardiasis

This, like amoebic dysentery, is also caused by ingesting contaminated food or water. The illness usually appears a week or more after you have been exposed to the offending parasite. Giardiasis might cause only a short-lived bout of typical traveller's diarrhoea, but it can also cause persistent diarrhoea. Ideally, seek medical advice if you suspect you have giardiasis, but if you're in a remote area you could start a course of antibiotics, with medical follow-up when feasible.

Environmental Hazards

Altitude Sickness

The lack of oxygen at high altitudes (over 2500m) affects most people to some extent. Symptoms of Acute Mountain Sickness (AMS) usually develop in the first 24 hours at altitude but may be delayed up to three weeks. Mild symptoms are headache, lethargy, dizziness, difficulty sleeping and loss of appetite. Severe symptoms are breathlessness, a dry, irritated cough (followed by the production of pink, frothy sputum), severe headache, lack of coordination, confusion, vomiting, irrational behaviour, drowsiness and unconsciousness. There's no rule as to what is too high: AMS can be fatal at 3000m, but 3500m to 4500m is the usual range when it can cause problems. *Symptoms should never be ignored;* trekkers die every year on East Africa's mountains, notably Mt Kilimanjaro.

Treat mild symptoms by resting at the same altitude until you have recovered, usually a day or two. Paracetamol or aspirin can be taken for headaches. If symptoms persist or grow worse, however, immediate descent is necessary; even 500m can help. Drug treatments should never be used to avoid descent or to enable further ascent. Diamox (acetazolamide) reduces the headache of AMS and helps the body acclimatise to the lack of oxygen. It is only available on prescription.

Suggestions for preventing acute mountain sickness:

➡ Ascend slowly. On Mt Kilimanjaro, this means choosing one of the longer routes (eg Machame) that allow for a more gradual ascent. On Mt Kenya, it means spending at least three nights on the ascent.

➡ Sleep at a lower altitude than the greatest height reached during the day if possible ('climb high, sleep low').

➡ Drink extra fluids. Monitor hydration by ensuring that urine is clear and plentiful.

➡ Eat light, high-carbohydrate meals for more energy.

➡ Avoid alcohol, sedatives and tobacco.

Heat Exhaustion

This condition occurs following heavy sweating and excessive fluid loss with inadequate replacement of fluids and salt, and is particularly common in hot climates when taking unaccustomed exercise before full acclimatisation. Symptoms include headache, dizziness and tiredness. Dehydration is already happening by the time you feel thirsty – aim to drink sufficient water to produce pale, diluted urine. Self-treatment requires fluid replacement with water and/or fruit juice, and cooling by cold water and fans. Treatment of the salt-loss component consists of consuming salty fluids, as in soup, and adding a little more table salt to foods than usual.

Insect Bites & Stings

Mosquitoes might not always carry malaria or dengue fever, but they (and other insects) can cause irritation and infected bites. To avoid these, take the same precautions as you would for avoiding malaria. Use DEET-based insect repellents. Excellent clothing treatments are also

TSETSE FLIES

Tsetse flies can be unwelcome safari companions in some areas, delivering painful, swelling bites. To minimise the nuisance, wear thick, long-sleeved shirts and trousers in khaki or other drab shades, and avoid bright, contrasting and very dark clothing. The flies are also attracted by heat (eg the heat of a running car motor), so if you're idling, keep the windows rolled up.

available, and mosquitoes that land on the treated clothing will die.

Bee and wasp stings cause real problems only to those who have a severe allergy to the stings (anaphylaxis). If you are one of these people, carry an 'epipen' – an adrenaline (epinephrine) injection, which you can give yourself. This could save your life.

Scorpions are frequently found in arid or dry climates. They can cause a painful sting that is sometimes life threatening. If stung by a scorpion, seek immediate medical assistance.

Bed bugs are often found in hostels and cheap hotels. They lead to very itchy, lumpy bites. Spraying the mattress with crawling insect killer after changing bedding will get rid of them.

Scabies is also frequently found in cheap accommodation. These tiny mites live in the skin, particularly between the fingers. They cause an intensely itchy rash. The itch is easily treated with malathion and permethrin lotion from a pharmacy; other members of the household also need treatment to avoid spreading scabies, even if they do not show any symptoms.

Snake Bites

Avoid getting bitten! Do not walk barefoot, or stick your hand into holes or cracks. However, 50% of those bitten by venomous snakes are not actually injected with poison (envenomed). If you are bitten by a snake, do not panic. Immobilise the bitten limb with a splint (such as a stick) and apply a bandage over the site, with firm pressure, similar to bandaging a sprain. Do not apply a tourniquet, or cut or suck the bite. Get medical help as soon as possible so antivenom can be given if needed. Try to note the snake's appearance to help in treatment.

Water

Don't drink tap water unless it has been boiled, filtered or chemically disinfected (such as with iodine tablets). Never drink from streams, rivers and lakes. Also avoid drinking from pumps and wells; some do bring pure water to the surface, but the presence of animals can contaminate supplies. With bottled water, check that the bottles are properly sealed, and haven't just been refilled with ordinary tap water.

Language

SWAHILI

Swahili, the national language of Tanzania and Kenya, is also one of the most widely spoken African languages and the key language of communication in the East African region. Although the number of speakers of Swahili throughout East Africa is estimated to be well over 50 million, it's the mother tongue of only about 5 million people, and is predominantly used as a second language or a lingua franca by speakers of other African languages. Swahili belongs to the Bantu group of languages from the Niger-Congo family and can be traced back to the first millenium AD. It's hardly surprising that in an area as vast as East Africa many different dialects of Swahili can be found, but you'll be understood if you stick to the standard coastal form, as used in this book.

Most sounds in Swahili have equivalents in English. In our coloured pronunciation guides, ay should be read as in 'say', oh as the 'o' in 'role', dh as the 'th' in 'this' and th as in 'thing'. Note also that the sound ng can be found at the start of words in Swahili, and that Swahili speakers make only a slight distinction between r and l – instead of the hard 'r', try pronouncing a light 'd'. The stressed syllables are indicated with italics.

Basics

Jambo is a pidgin Swahili word, used to greet tourists who are presumed not to understand the language. If people assume you can speak a little Swahili, they might use the following greetings:

WANT MORE?

For in-depth language information and handy phrases, check out Lonely Planet's *Swahili Phrasebook* or *Africa Phrasebook*. You'll find them at **shop. lonelyplanet.com**.

Hello. (general)	Habari?	ha·ba·ree
Hello. (respectful)	Shikamoo.	shee·ka·moh
Goodbye.	Tutaonana.	too·ta·oh·na·na
Good ...	Habari za ...?	ha·ba·ree za ...
morning	asubuhi	a·soo·boo·hee
afternoon	mchana	m·cha·na
evening	jioni	jee·oh·nee
Yes.	Ndiyo.	n·dee·yoh
No.	Hapana.	ha·pa·na
Please.	Tafadhali.	ta·fa·dha·lee
Thank you (very much).	Asante (sana).	a·san·tay (sa·na)
You're welcome.	Karibu.	ka·ree·boo
Excuse me.	Samahani.	sa·ma·ha·nee
Sorry.	Pole.	poh·lay

How are you?
Habari?   ha·ba·ree

I'm fine.
Nzuri./Salama./Safi.   n·zoo·ree/sa·la·ma/sa·fee

If things are just OK, add *tu* too (only) after any of the above replies. If things are really good, add *sana* sa·na (very) or *kabisa* ka·bee·-sa (totally) instead of *tu*.

What's your name?
Jina lako nani?   jee·na la·koh na·nee

My name is ...
Jina langu ni ...   jee·na lan·goo nee ...

Do you speak English?
Unasema   oo·na·say·ma
Kiingereza?   kee·een·gay·ray·za

I don't understand.
Sielewi.   see·ay·lay·wee

Accommodation

Where's a ...?	... iko wapi?	... ee·koh wa·pee
campsite	Uwanja wa kambi	oo·wan·ja wa kam·bee
guesthouse	Gesti	gay·stee
hotel	Hoteli	hoh·tay·lee
youth hostel	Hosteli ya vijana	hoh·stay·lee ya vee·ja·na
Do you have a ... room?	Kuna chumba kwa ...?	koo·na choom·ba kwa ...
double (one bed)	watu wawili, kitanda kimoja	wa·too wa·wee·lee kee·tan·da kee·moh·ja
single	mtu mmoja	m·too m·moh·ja
twin (two beds)	watu wawili, vitanda viwili	wa·too wa·wee·lee vee·tan·da vee·wee·lee
How much is it per ...?	Ni bei gani kwa ...?	nee bay ga·ne kwa ...
day	siku	see·koo
person	mtu	m·too
bathroom	bafuni	ba·foo·nee
key	ufunguo	oo·foon·goo·oh
toilet	choo	choh
window	dirisha	dee·ree·sha

Directions

Where's the ...?
... iko wapi?   ... ee·koh wa·pee

What's the address?
Anwani ni nini?   an·wa·nee nee nee·nee

How do I get there?
Nifikaje?   nee·fee·ka·jay

How far is it?
Ni umbali gani?   nee oom·ba·lee ga·nee

Can you show me (on the map)?
Unaweza   oo·na·way·za
kunionyesha   koo·nee·oh·nyay·sha
(katika ramani)?   (ka·tee·ka ra·ma·nee)

It's ...	Iko ...	ee·koh ...
behind ...	nyuma ya ...	nyoo·ma ya ...
in front of ...	mbele ya ...	m·bay·lay ya ...
near ...	karibu na ...	ka·ree·boo na ...
next to ...	jirani ya ...	jee·ra·nee ya ...
on the corner	pembeni	paym·bay·nee
opposite ...	ng'ambo ya ...	ng·am·boh ya ...
straight ahead	moja kwa moja	moh·ja kwa moh·ja

Turn ...	Geuza ...	gay·oo·za ...
at the corner	kwenye kona	kway·nyay koh·na
at the traffic lights	kwenye taa za barabarani	kway·nyay ta za ba·ra·ba·ra·nee
left	kushoto	koo·shoh·toh
right	kulia	koo·lee·a

Eating & Drinking

I'd like to reserve a table for ...	Nataka kuhifadhi meza kwa ...	na·ta·ka koo·hee·fa·dhee may·za kwa ...
(two) people	watu (wawili)	wa·too (wa·wee·lee)
(eight) o'clock	saa (mbili)	sa (m·bee·lee)

I'd like the menu.
Naomba menyu.   na·ohm·ba may·nyoo

What would you recommend?
Chakula gani ni   cha·koo·la ga·nee nee
kizuri?   kee·zoo·ree

Do you have vegetarian food?
Mna chakula   m·na cha·koo·la
bila nyama?   bee·la nya·ma

I'll have that.
Nataka hicho.   na·ta·ka hee·choh

Cheers!
Heri! — hay·ree

That was delicious!
Chakula kitamu sana! — cha·koo·la kee·ta·moo sa·na

Please bring the bill.
Lete bili. — lay·tay bee·lee

I don't eat ...	Sili ...	see·lee ...
butter	siagi	see·a·gee
eggs	mayai	ma·ya·ee
red meat	nyama	nya·ma

beer	bia	bee·a
bottle	chupa	choo·pa
breakfast	chai ya asubuhi	cha·ee ya a·soo·boo·hee
coffee	kahawa	ka·ha·wa
cold	baridi	ba·ree·dee
dinner	chakula cha jioni	cha·koo·la cha jee·oh·nee
fish	samaki	sa·ma·kee
fork	uma	oo·ma
fruit	tunda	toon·da
glass	glesi	glay·see
hot	joto	joh·toh
juice	jusi	joo·see
knife	kisu	kee·soo
lunch	chakula cha mchana	cha·koo·la cha m·cha·na
market	soko	soh·koh
meat	nyama	nya·ma
plate	sahani	sa·ha·nee
restaurant	mgahawa	m·ga·ha·wa
spoon	kijiko	kee·jee·koh
tea	chai	cha·ee
vegetable	mboga	m·boh·ga
water	maji	ma·jee
wine	mvinyo	m·vee·nyoh

SIGNS

Mahali Pa Kuingia	Entrance
Mahali Pa Kutoka	Exit
Imefunguliwa	Open
Imefungwa	Closed
Maelezo	Information
Ni Marufuku	Prohibited
Choo/Msalani	Toilets
Wanaume	Men
Wanawake	Women

Emergencies

Help!	Saidia!	sa·ee·dee·a
Go away!	Toka!	toh·ka

I'm lost.
Nimejipotea. — nee·may·jee·poh·tay·a

Call the police.
Waite polisi. — wa·ee·tay poh·lee·see

Call a doctor.
Mwite daktari. — m·wee·tay dak·ta·ree

I'm sick.
Mimi ni mgonjwa. — mee·mee nee m·gohn·jwa

It hurts here.
Inauma hapa. — ee·na·oo·ma ha·pa

I'm allergic to (antibiotics).
Nina mzio wa (viuavijasumu). — nee·na m·zee·oh wa (vee·oo·a·vee·ja·soo·moo)

Where's the toilet?
Choo kiko wapi? — choh kee·koh wa·pee

Shopping & Services

I'd like to buy ...
Nataka kununua ... — na·ta·ka koo·noo·noo·a ...

I'm just looking.
Naangalia tu. — na·an·ga·lee·a too

Can I look at it?
Naomba nione. — na·ohm·ba nee·oh·nay

I don't like it.
Sipendi. — see·payn·dee

How much is it?
Ni bei gani? — ni bay ga·nee

That's too expensive.
Ni ghali mno. — nee ga·lee m·noh

Please lower the price.
Punguza bei. — poon·goo·za bay

ATM	mashine ya kutolea pesa	ma·shee·nay ya koo·toh·lay·a pay·sa
post office	posta	poh·sta
public phone	simu ya mtaani	see·moo ya m·ta·nee
tourist office	ofisi ya watalii	o·fee·see ya wa·ta·lee

Time, Dates & Numbers

The Swahili time system starts six hours later than the international one – it begins at sunrise (about 6am year-round). So, *saa mbili* sa m·bee·lee (lit: clocks two) means '2 o'clock Swahili time' and '8 o'clock European time'.

QUESTION WORDS

What?	Nini?	nee·nee
When?	Wakati?	wa·ka·tee
Where?	Wapi?	wa·pee
Who?	Nani?	na·nee

What time is it?
Ni saa ngapi?   nee sa n·ga·pee

It's (10) o'clock.
Ni saa (nne).   nee sa (n·nay)

Half past (10).
Ni saa (nne) na nusu.   nee sa (n·nay) na noo·soo

morning	asubuhi	a·soo·boo·hee
afternoon	mchana	m·cha·na
evening	jioni	jee·oh·nee
yesterday	jana	ja·na
today	leo	lay·oh
tomorrow	kesho	kay·shoh

Monday	Jumatatu	joo·ma·ta·too
Tuesday	Jumanne	joo·ma·n·nay
Wednesday	Jumatano	joo·ma·ta·noh
Thursday	Alhamisi	al·ha·mee·see
Friday	Ijumaa	ee·joo·ma
Saturday	Jumamosi	joo·ma·moh·see
Sunday	Jumapili	joo·ma·pee·lee

1	moja	moh·ja
2	mbili	m·bee·lee
3	tatu	ta·too
4	nne	n·nay
5	tano	ta·noh
6	sita	see·ta
7	saba	sa·ba
8	nane	na·nay
9	tisa	tee·sa
10	kumi	koo·mee
20	ishirini	ee·shee·ree·nee
30	thelathini	thay·la·thee·nee
40	arobaini	a·roh·ba·ee·nee
50	hamsini	ham·see·nee
60	sitini	see·tee·nee
70	sabini	sa·bee·nee
80	themanini	thay·ma·nee·nee
90	tisini	tee·see·nee
100	mia moja	mee·a moh·ja
1000	elfu	ayl·foo

Transport

Which ...	... ipi	... ee·pee
goes to (Mbeya)?	huenda (Mbeya)?	hoo·ayn·da (m·bay·a)
bus	Basi	ba·see
ferry	Kivuko	kee·voo·koh
minibus	Daladala (Tan) Matatu (Ken)	da·la·da·la/ ma·ta·too
train	Treni	tray·nee

When's the ... bus?	Basi ... itaondoka lini?	ba·see ... ee·ta·ohn·doh·ka lee·nee
first	ya kwanza	ya kwan·za
last	ya mwisho	ya mwee·shoh
next	ijayo	ee·ja·yoh

A ... ticket to (Iringa).	Tiketi moja ya ... kwenda (Iringa).	tee·kay·tee moh·ja ya ... kwayn·da (ee·reen·ga)
1st-class	daraja la kwanza	da·ra·ja la kwan·za
2nd-class	daraja la pili	da·ra·ja la pee·lee
one-way	kwenda tu	kwayn·da too
return	kwenda na kurudi	kwayn·da na koo·roo·dee

What time does it get to (Kisuma)?
Itafika (Kisumu)   ee·ta·fee·ka (kee·soo·moo)
saa ngapi?   sa n·ga·pee

Does it stop at (Tanga)?
Linasimama (Tanga)?   lee·na·see·ma·ma (tan·ga)

I'd like to get off at (Bagamoyo).
Nataka kushusha   na·ta·ka koo·shoo·sha
(Bagamoyo).   (ba·ga·moh·yoh)

I'd like to hire a ...	Nataka kukodi ...	na·ta·ka koo·koh·dee ...
4WD	forbaifor	fohr·ba·ee·fohr
bicycle	baisikeli	ba·ee·see·kay·lee
car	gari	ga·ree
motorbike	pikipiki	pee·kee·pee·kee

regular	kawaida	ka·wa·ee·da
unleaded	isiyo na risasi	ee·see·yoh na ree·sa·see

Is this the road to (Embu)?
Hii ni barabara   hee nee ba·ra·ba·ra
kwenda (Embu)?   kwayn·da (aym·boo)

Where's a petrol station?
Kituo cha mafuta   kee·too·oh cha ma·foo·ta
kiko wapi?   kee·ko wa·pee

(How long) Can I park here?
Naweza kuegesha — na·way·za koo·ay·gay·sha
hapa (kwa muda gani)? — ha·pa (kwa moo·da ga·ni)

I need a mechanic.
Nahitaji fundi. — na·hee·ta·jee foon·dee

I have a flat tyre.
Nina pancha. — nee·na pan·cha

I've run out of petrol.
Mafuta yamekwisha. — ma·foo·ta ya·may·kwee·sha

FRENCH

French is the official language in Burundi (along with Kirundi) and Rwanda (along with the English and the national language, Kinyarwanda).

French has nasal vowels (represented in our pronunciation guides by o or u followed by an almost inaudible nasal consonant sound m, n or ng). Note also the 'funny' u (ew in our guides) and the deep-in-the-throat r. The last syllable in a word is lightly stressed.

Hello.	*Bonjour.*	bon·zhoor
Goodbye.	*Au revoir.*	o·rer·vwa
Excuse me.	*Excusez-moi.*	ek·skew·zay·mwa
Sorry.	*Pardon.*	par·don
Yes./No.	*Oui./Non.*	wee/non
Please.	*S'il vous plaît.*	seel voo play
Thank you.	*Merci.*	mair·see
You're welcome.	*De rien.*	der ree·en

How are you?
Comment allez-vous? — ko·mon ta·lay·voo

Fine, and you?
Bien, merci. Et vous? — byun mair·see ay voo

What's your name?
Comment vous appelez-vous? — ko·mon voo·za·play voo

My name is ...
Je m'appelle ... — zher ma·pel ...

Do you speak English?
Parlez-vous anglais? — par·lay·voo ong·glay

I don't understand.
Je ne comprends pas. — zher ner kom·pron pa

What time is it?
Quelle heure est-il? — kel er ay til

How much is it?
C'est combien? — say kom·byun

Where are the toilets?
Où sont les toilettes? — oo son lay twa·let

Can you show me (on the map)?
Pouvez-vous m'indiquer (sur la carte)? — poo·vay·voo mun·dee·kay (sewr la kart)

I'm lost.
Je suis perdu/perdue. — zhe swee·pair·dew (m/f)

Help!
Au secours! — o skoor

Leave me alone!
Fichez-moi la paix! — fee·shay·mwa la pay

Call a doctor.
Appelez un médecin. — a·play un mayd·sun

Call the police.
Appelez la police. — a·play la po·lees

I'm ill.
Je suis malade. — zher swee ma·lad

What's the local speciality?
Quelle est la spécialité locale? — kel ay la spay·sya·lee·tay lo·kal

Cheers!
Santé! — son·tay

a ... room	*une chambre ...*	ewn shom·brer ...
single	*à un lit*	a un lee
double	*avec un grand lit*	a·vek un gron lee

a ... ticket	*un billet ...*	un bee·yay ...
one-way	*simple*	sum·pler
return	*aller et retour*	a·lay ay rer·toor

1	*un*	un
2	*deux*	der
3	*trois*	trwa
4	*quatre*	ka·trer
5	*cinq*	sungk
6	*six*	sees
7	*sept*	set
8	*huit*	weet
9	*neuf*	nerf
10	*dix*	dees
20	*vingt*	vung
30	*trente*	tront
40	*quarante*	ka·ront
50	*cinquante*	sung·kont
60	*soixante*	swa·sont
70	*soixante-dix*	swa·son·dees
80	*quatre-vingts*	ka·trer·vung
90	*quatre-vingt-dix*	ka·trer·vung·dees
100	*cent*	son
1000	*mille*	meel

GLOSSARY

The following is a list of words and acronyms from Burundi (B), Kenya (K), Rwanda (R), Tanzania (T) and Uganda (U) that appear in this book. For a glossary of food and drink terms, see p614.

askari – security guard, watchman

ASP (T) – Afro-Shirazi Party on Zanzibar Archipelago

banda – thatched-roof hut with wooden or earthen walls; simple wooden and stone-built accommodation

bangi – marijuana; also ganja

bao – a board game widely played in East Africa

baraza – the stone seats seen along the outside walls of houses in the Stone Towns of Zanzibar and Lamu, used for chatting and relaxing

Big Five, the – the five archetypal large African mammals: lion, buffalo, elephant, leopard and rhino

boda-boda (U) – bicycle taxi

boma – a living compound; in colonial times, a government administrative office

bui-bui – black cover-all garment worn by some Islamic women outside the home

CCM (T) – Chama Cha Mapinduzi (Party of the Revolution); Tanzania's governing political party

chai – tea; bribe

Cites – Convention on International Trade in Endangered Species

dalla-dalla (T) – minibus

dhow – traditional Arabic sailing vessel, common along the coast

duka – small shop or kiosk

fly camp – a camp away from the main tented camps or lodges, for the purpose of enjoying a more authentic bush experience

forex – foreign exchange bureau

gacaca (R) – traditional tribunal headed by village elders

gof – volcanic crater

injera – unleavened bread

Interahamwe (R) – Hutu militia

kabaka (U) – king

kanga – printed cotton wraparound, incorporating a Swahili proverb, worn by Tanzanian women

karibu – Swahili for welcome

kikoi – printed cotton wraparound traditionally worn by men in coastal areas

KWS (K) – Kenya Wildlife Service

makuti – palm thatching

manyatta (K) – Maasai or Samburu livestock camp often surrounded by a circle of thorn bushes

matatu (K) – minibus

Maulid – birth of the prophet Mohammed and Muslim feast day, celebrated in many areas of East Africa

mihrab – prayer niche in a mosque showing the direction of Mecca

moran (K) – Maasai or Samburu warrior

mpingo – African blackwood

mwami (B; R) – king

mzungu – white person, foreigner (plural wazungu)

NCA (T) – Ngorongoro Conservation Area

Ngai – Kikuyu god

ngoma – dance and drumming

NRA (U) – National Resistance Army

NRM (U) – National Resistance Movement

nyatiti – traditional folk lyre

panga – machete, carried by many people in the east African countryside

papasi (T) – literally 'tick'; used on the Zanzibar Archipelago to refer to street touts

RMS (U) – Rwenzori Mountaineering Services

RPF (R) – Rwandan Patriotic Front

shamba – small farm or plot of land

shetani – literally, demon or something supernatural; in art, a style of carving embodying images from the spirit world

shuka – tie-dyed sarong

soukous – see *lingala*

taarab (T) – Zanzibari music combining African, Arabic and Indian influences

Tanapa (T) – Tanzania National Parks Authority

TANU (T) – Tanganyika African National Union

taxi-motor – motorcycle taxi

tilapia – Nile perch

TTB (T) – Tanzania Tourist Board

Ucota – Uganda Community Tourism Association

uhuru – freedom or independence

ujamaa (T) – familyhood, togetherness

Unguja (T) – Swahili name for Zanzibar Island

UWA (U) – Uganda Wildlife Authority

ZNP – Zanzibar Nationalist Party

ZPPP – Zanzibar & Pemba People's Party

Behind the Scenes

SEND US YOUR FEEDBACK

We love to hear from travellers – your comments keep us on our toes and help make our books better. Our well-travelled team reads every word on what you loved or loathed about this book. Although we cannot reply individually to postal submissions, we always guarantee that your feedback goes straight to the appropriate authors, in time for the next edition. Each person who sends us information is thanked in the next edition – the most useful submissions are rewarded with a selection of digital PDF chapters.

Visit **lonelyplanet.com/contact** to submit your updates and suggestions or to ask for help. Our award-winning website also features inspirational travel stories, news and discussions.

Note: We may edit, reproduce and incorporate your comments in Lonely Planet products such as guidebooks, websites and digital products, so let us know if you don't want your comments reproduced or your name acknowledged. For a copy of our privacy policy visit lonelyplanet.com/privacy.

OUR READERS

Many thanks to the travellers who used the last edition and wrote to us with helpful hints, useful advice and interesting anecdotes: Emily Brackstone, Ed Carlisle, David Carr, Paymon Daneshpay, Carlotta Fabian, Mick Groucott, Anne Gunn, Yael & Gil Hartman, Fredrik Janson, Colin Kenning, Rikke Palm, Emilia Pawłowska, Kelly Pickerill, Jim Pincini, Nina Plumbe, Derek Rosen, David Ryder, Cornelius Schröder, Anfrew Seitz, Maddy Smith, Elgin Tay, Rachel Wheeler

AUTHOR THANKS

Anthony Ham

Heartfelt thanks to Matt Phillips, Mary Fitzpatrick and Peter Ndirangu, three wise companions of the Africa road of long-standing. Thanks also to Stuart Butler, Kate Thomas, Luke Hunter, Philipp Henschel, Thomas Temple, George Muriuki, Leela Hazzah, Stephanie Dolrenry, Kamunu Saitoti, Eric ole Kesoi, Richard Bonham, Rosie Kempson, Alex Walters, Nadia Walford, Lucy Cameron (Lewa Safari Camp), Wanjiku Kinuthia (Lewa Wildlife Conservancy), Annick Mitchell (Ol Pejeta), Daryll Pleasants (Ol Pejeta), Luca Belpietro (Campi y Kanzi), Jens Kozany (Segera Retreat), Tamsin Corcoran (Mbulia Conservancy), Katito Sayialel (Am-

boseli), Dr Cynthia Moss (Amboseli), Sandy Evans, (Manyara Ranch Conservancy), Ingela Jansson (Ngorongoro Lion Project), Daniel Rosengren and Craig Packer (Serengeti Lion project). To Marina, Carlota and Valentina – next time with you.

Stuart Butler

First and foremost I must thank my wife, Heather, and children Jake and Grace for once again putting up with my absence for too long while I worked on this book. It is ever appreciated. In Rwanda and Burundi I would like to thank Sarah Hall at Akagera National Park and Daniel Niyonsaba at Nyungwe Forest National Park. At the RDB office in Kigali huge thanks to Isaac Niyoyita and Norbert. At Volcanoes National Park big thanks to Prosper Uwingeli and the fine folk of the Iby'Iwacu Cultural Village for the good times. Finally thank you to Jean-Paul Birasa and, for great driving and company, Damas.

Mary Fitzpatrick

My gratitude goes in particular to Matt Phillips and Anthony Ham for their insights, wise perspectives, patience and assistance with this project, and with many others. Thank you also to the inimitable J4 in Dar es Salaam, to the outstanding Mtemere entry gate rangers at Selous Game Reserve and – most of all – to Rick, Christopher, Dominic and Gabriel for the companionship, love and humour on this and all our journeys.

Trent Holden

Thanks first up to Matt Phillips for giving me
the amazing opportunity to work again on
Uganda – seriously a dream gig. Anne-Marie
Weeden, for taking the time and effort to help
out with incredibly useful tips, contacts and
hilarious anecdotes. The guys from UWA for
their assistance, info and efforts in maintaining the parks, as well as John Mugisha
in Mgahinga for letting me interview him.
Plus Benson, Hassan and Noor for getting
me around in one piece. Lance Goettsch for
his help in Masaka, and to all those I met on
the road and shared a beer with along the
journey. But as always my biggest thanks
goes to my beautiful girlfriend Kate, and my
family and friends whom all I miss back home
in Melbourne.

ACKNOWLEDGMENTS

Finlayson BL & McMahon TA (2007) 'Updated
World Map of the Köppen-Geiger Climate
Classification', Hydrology and Earth System
Sciences, 11, 1633–44.

Cover photograph: Bull elephant, Ngorongoro
Crater, Tanzania; Nigel Pavitt/AWL

THIS BOOK

This 10th edition of Lonely
Planet's *East Africa* guidebook
was researched and written by
Anthony Ham, Stuart Butler,
Mary Fitzpatrick and Trent
Holden. The previous edition
was written by Mary Fitz-
patrick, Anthony Ham, Trent
Holden and Dean Starnes. This
guidebook was produced by
the following:

Destination Editor
Matt Phillips
Product Editors
Briohny Hooper,
Martine Power
Senior Cartographer
Corey Hutchison
Book Designer
Wibowo Rusli
Assisting Editors
Melanie Dankel, Kate Evans,
Samantha Forge, Andi Jones,
Jodie Martire, Kate Mathews,
Lauren O'Connell, Kristin Odijk,

Gabrielle Stefanos, Simon
Williamson
Assisting Cartographers
Julie Dodkins, David Kemp,
James Leversha
Cover Researcher
Naomi Parker
Thanks to Sasha Baskett,
Elin Berglund, Kate Chapman,
Ryan Evans, Larissa Frost,
Clara Monitto, Katie O'Connell,
Samantha Tyson, Diana Saeng-
kham, Dianne Schallmeiner,
Ellie Simpson, Luna Soo, Tony
Wheeler, Amanda Williamson

Index

NOTES

Map Legend

Sights

- Beach
- Bird Sanctuary
- Buddhist
- Castle/Palace
- Christian
- Confucian
- Hindu
- Islamic
- Jain
- Jewish
- Monument
- Museum/Gallery/Historic Building
- Ruin
- Shinto
- Sikh
- Taoist
- Winery/Vineyard
- Zoo/Wildlife Sanctuary
- Other Sight

Activities, Courses & Tours

- Bodysurfing
- Diving
- Canoeing/Kayaking
- Course/Tour
- Sento Hot Baths/Onsen
- Skiing
- Snorkelling
- Surfing
- Swimming/Pool
- Walking
- Windsurfing
- Other Activity

Sleeping

- Sleeping
- Camping

Eating

- Eating

Drinking & Nightlife

- Drinking & Nightlife
- Cafe

Entertainment

- Entertainment

Shopping

- Shopping

Information

- Bank
- Embassy/Consulate
- Hospital/Medical
- Internet
- Police
- Post Office
- Telephone
- Toilet
- Tourist Information
- Other Information

Geographic

- Beach
- Hut/Shelter
- Lighthouse
- Lookout
- Mountain/Volcano
- Oasis
- Park
- Pass
- Picnic Area
- Waterfall

Population

- Capital (National)
- Capital (State/Province)
- City/Large Town
- Town/Village

Transport

- Airport
- Border crossing
- Bus
- Cable car/Funicular
- Cycling
- Ferry
- Metro station
- Monorail
- Parking
- Petrol station
- Subway station
- Taxi
- Train station/Railway
- Tram
- Underground station
- Other Transport

Routes

- Tollway
- Freeway
- Primary
- Secondary
- Tertiary
- Lane
- Unsealed road
- Road under construction
- Plaza/Mall
- Steps
- Tunnel
- Pedestrian overpass
- Walking Tour
- Walking Tour detour
- Path/Walking Trail

Boundaries

- International
- State/Province
- Disputed
- Regional/Suburb
- Marine Park
- Cliff
- Wall

Hydrography

- River, Creek
- Intermittent River
- Canal
- Water
- Dry/Salt/Intermittent Lake
- Reef

Areas

- Airport/Runway
- Beach/Desert
- Cemetery (Christian)
- Cemetery (Other)
- Glacier
- Mudflat
- Park/Forest
- Sight (Building)
- Sportsground
- Swamp/Mangrove

Note: Not all symbols displayed above appear on the maps in this book